Cytochrome Systems

**Molecular Biology
and Bioenergetics**

Cytochrome Systems

Molecular Biology and Bioenergetics

Edited by

S. Papa
University of Bari
Bari, Italy

B. Chance
University of Pennsylvania
Philadelphia, Pennsylvania

and

L. Ernster
University of Stockholm
Stockholm, Sweden

Plenum Press • **New York and London**

Library of Congress Cataloging in Publication Data

UNESCO International Workshop on Cytochrome Systems: Molecular Biology and
  Bioenergetics (1987: Bari, Italy)
  Cytochrome systems.

  "Proceedings of the UNESCO International Workshop on Cytochrome Systems:
Molecular Biology and Bioenergetics, which was IUB Symposium No. 159, held
April 14–18, 1987, in Bari, Italy"—Verso t.p.
  Includes bibliographical references and index.
  1. Cytochrome—Congresses. I. Papa, S. II. Chance, Britton. III. Ernster, L. IV.
Title.
QP671.C85U54   1987   574.19'218   87-25766
ISBN-13: 978-1-4612-9078-0   e-ISBN-13: 978-1-4613-1941-2
DOI: 10.1007/ 978-1-4613-1941-2

The Symposium was generously supported by the following organizations:

   UNESCO European Expert Committee on Biomaterials
   International Union of Biochemistry, Committee on Symposia
   International Union of Pure and Applied Biophysics
   Consiglio Nazionale delle Ricerche
   Università di Bari
   Regione Puglia
   Calabrese Veicoli Industriali S.p.A., Bari
   Sigma Chemical Company

Proceedings of the UNESCO International Workshop on Cytochrome Systems:
Molecular Biology and Bioenergetics, which was IUB Symposium No. 159, held
April 14–18, 1987, in Bari, Italy

© 1987 Plenum Press, New York
Softcover reprint of the hardcover 1st edition 1987
A Division of Plenum Publishing Corporation
233 Spring Street, New York, N.Y. 10013

This volume is based on the proceedings of an International Symposium on "Cytochrome Systems: Molecular Biology and Bioenergetics" that was held at Selva di Fasano near Bari, Italy, between April 7 and 11,1987. It contains papers covering the subjects discussed at the Symposium, contributed both by participants of the meeting and by some invited speakers who were not able to attend.

The aim of the Symposium was to bring together experts in various research strategies currently being applied to the study of cytochrome systems, including molecular genetics, protein chemistry, enzymology of electron transfer and protonmotive activity in energy-transducing biological membranes. Because of the high degree of complexity of cytochrome systems and the increasing sophistication in recent years of the different experimental approaches, there has been a growing specialization - sometimes even a tendency to "over-specialization" - among scientists working in this field. This in itself seemed to justify a meeting where representatives of various disciplines could exchange their results and discuss their conclusions. In addition, and perhaps even more importantly, it was felt that meetings of this kind provide an opportunity for a "cross-fertilization" of approaches and ideas among representatives of various fields of science. The present meeting proved to be an ample illustration of the success of such an interaction.

Most cytochrome systems - and especially those involved in bioenergetics, which were the main subjects of this Symposium - are highly complex membrane proteins, consisting of several species of polypeptide subunits. The understanding of their reaction mechanisms in electron transfer and proton translocation is critically dependent on knowledge of their structure and membrane topology. Genetic approaches, including cloning, DNA-sequencing and, in the case of eukaryotic cells, information concerning the coordination between nuclear and organellar gene expression, vectorial processing and assembly, have already made fundamental contributions to the elucidation of these problems. Recent spectacular progress in unraveling the three-dimensional structure of cytochrome-containing membrane proteins have implied a further, most important breakthrough toward the understanding of the mechanism of biological electron transfer and associated proton translocation at the molecular and submolecular levels. Much of this progress, as well as a number of still unanswered and sometimes controversial questions, are highlighted in the papers presented in this volume.

The present Symposium, similar to a Symposium on "H^+-ATPase (ATP Synthase):Structure, Function and Biogenesis" (S.Papa et al. eds., Adriatica Editrice, Bari, 1984) held here 3 years ago, was structured in such a way that each session was introduced by a chairman, who gave a brief survey of the topic concerned and who was in charge of organizing the following presentations and of leading the discussion after each presentation as well as a general discussion at the end of the session. As chairmen of the sessions served R.B.Gennis, G.Attardi, W.Neupert, C.Saccone, E.Margoliash, L. Ernester and S.Papa. The Symposium was concluded by a plenary session devoted to the memory of Albert L. Lehninger, with an introduction by E.Quagliariello, lectures by E.C.Slater, B.Chance, P.Slonimski and A.Tzagoloff and concluding remarks by L. Ernster.

The Symposium was generously supported by UNESCO for which we thank Professor J. Jaz, Head of the Scientific Cooperation Bureau of the European and North American Region of UNESCO, for his personal interest and support.
We are also grateful to the Symposium Committee of the International Union of Biochemistry and to the International Union of Pure and Applied Biophysics for their sponsorship and for travel fellowships. Economic support from the Italian Research Council, the University of Bari, Regione Puglia and Comune di Fasano is also gratefully acknowledged.
Finally we wish to express our warm thanks to Drs. M.Lorusso, D.Boffoli, N.Capitanio, D.Gatti and T.Cocco of the Department of Biochemistry, Faculty of Medicine and Surgery, University of Bari and to Mrs.C.Concilio Del Pesce and M.De Biase, for wholehearted assistance in the organization of the Symposium and the editing for this volume and to the Staff of Plenum Publishing Company for their kind cooperation.

S.Papa
B.Chance
L.Ernster

CONTENTS

II. BIOSYNTHESIS

II. BIOSYNTHESIS: Short Report

III. PROTEIN STRUCTURE

III. PROTEIN STRUCTURE: Short Reports

IV. REACTION DOMAINS AND OXIDO-REDUCTION MECHANISMS

IX. PROTON-MOTIVE ACTIVITY: Short Report

APPENDIX

INTRODUCTION*

*Introductory lecture given by E.C.Slater at the Plenary
Session devoted to the memory of Albert Lehninger.

CYTOCHROME SYSTEMS: FROM DISCOVERY TO PRESENT DEVELOPMENTS

INTRODUCTION

E.C. Slater

Department of Biochemistry
University of Southampton
Southampton, U.K.

PREFACE

On March 21, at Magdalene College, Cambridge, where David Keilin was a Fellow, former students, colleagues and friends remembered his birth precisely 100 years earlier. It is appropriate, then, that in this Introductory Lecture to the Plenary Session at the first Bari Symposium exclusively devoted to cytochrome, we play homage to its discoverer. Although it is now 23 years since Keilin died, former students remain under the influence of his inspiring example and remain conscious of the great debt that they owe him. How often do we still think when confronted by a scientific problem : "how would Keilin have tackled it?" - or, when struggling to express oneself when writing up one's work, "how would Keilin have put it?" For those of us who had the enormous good fortune to work under his guidance at the Molteno Institute in Cambridge - and I was lucky enough to do so for nine years - Keilin is our scientific father.

HISTORY OF DISCOVERY OF CYTOCHROME

Where does one begin an historical account?

The problem is well put by Keilin[1] himself in the Introduction to his book "The history of cell respiration and cytochrome": "The study of the history of a subject shows how arbitrary and difficult it is to fix the date of its beginning, simply because we may be specially interested in only one aspect of it. However important a particular discovery may appear to us, it is only one of the links in the chain of achievements in the development of the whole subject. It would, for instance, be somewhat arbitrary to fix the year which marks the beginning of the study of the chemistry of haemoglobin. Was it in 1838, when Lecanu isolated haematin (then named "haematosin') and studied its composition; was it 1840, when Hünefeld observed crystals in an almost dry blood film but did not know what they were; or was it 1847 when Reichert obtained crystals of guinea-pig haemoglobin, being well aware that he was dealing with the first case of a crystalline 'albumin'? (Although Reichert carefully investigated its properties and demonstrated it to several distinguished men of the time, he considered the colouring matter of the crystals to be an impurity. The nature of the blood crystals was first recognized by Funke, who prepared crystalline haemoglobin from horse blood in 1851 and who, in 1853, wrote of 'the peculiar crystallization of the albuminous contents of red blood-corpuscles in combination with their colouring matter'.) Does the chemistry of haemoglobin begin in 1857 when Teichmann obtained for the first time crystals of haemin free from protein, or a few years later when Nencki, Piloty, Küster, Willstätter, Hans Fischer and several others unravelled the structure of its porphyrin nucleus, or was it when the haematin nucleus was synthesized?"

However that might be, for me the history of cytochrome begins in 1925 with the appearance of Keilin's[2] paper entitled " On Cytochrome, a Respiratory Pigment, Common to Animals, Yeast, and Higher Plants". Its pre-history is described in the opening sentence of this paper: "Under the names myohaematin and histohaematin MacMunn (1884-1886) described a respiratory pigment, which he found in muscles and other tissues of representatives of almost all orders of the animal kingdom."

In fact, when Keilin unexpectedly saw the absorption bands of cytochrome, he was completely unaware of MacMunn's[3] work. Soon after the latter was published, it was strongly criticised by Hoppe-Seyler[4] and, as Keilin[1] put it at the close of the introduction to his paper: "Hoppe-Seyler's note ended the discussion and MacMunn's new respiratory pigment was completely forgotten. The term myohaematin still made occasional appearances in the literature, but authors mentioning it have seldom seen the pigment or even read MacMunn's original papers; those who have seen the pigment have misunderstood its properties, and have not failed to show that they were aware of Hoppe-Seyler's criticisms, with which they were in full agreement." If Warburg had accepted the existence of this respiratory pigment, he would certainly have incorporated it into his theory that intracellular respiration is brought about by a respiratory enzyme containing all the iron in the cell. The nature of the iron compound was not specified at that time. As I recall Keilin telling me : "When I was ready to write up the work, Joseph Barcroft told me that he seemed to remember an Irishman who had published something similar a long time ago". Although perhaps you might think that 1925 and 1890 equally belong to ancient scientific history, there is, in fact, a gap of 35 years, larger than that separating today from the discovery of the genetic code.

Already in his first paper on cytochrome, Keilin established the most important features of what became known as the respiratory chain. Particularly remarkable was the resolution, of the four-banded spectrum as being derived from three separate compounds, cytochromes $\underline{a}$, $\underline{b}$ and $\underline{c}$. Fourteen years later, he showed together with Hartree[5] that band a is derived from two components, $\underline{a}$ and $\underline{a_3}$, and 16 years further on, 30 years after the discovery of cytochrome, again together with Hartree[6], he ressurrected Okunuki's discovery[7] of cytochrome $\underline{c_1}$. In this latter work, Keilin used for the first time a spectrophotometer - all his previous discoveries were made with his unaided eye and a spectroscope. The discovery that the band b is also derived from two different haem groups, as we now know bound to the same polypeptide, required the further refinements of spectrophotometry introduced by Britton Chance[8].

Even more important than his resolution of the spectrum was Keilin's demonstration in this first paper that the cytochromes are reduced by metabolites in the cell and oxidized in a cyanide-sensitive reaction. Two consecutive sentences in the Summary are of particular significance:
"8. Under natural conditions in the living animal cytochrome is in the oxidized or in only partly reduced form.
9. The condition of cytochrome as seen spectroscopically in the living organism denotes only the state of equilibrium between the rate of its oxidation and reduction at that particular time."

He also observed cytochrome in the non-coloured portions of various plants and made a brief reference to its presence in aerobic bacteria, such as <u>Bacillus subtilis</u>, but most of the section dealing with bacteria was removed from the paper, because the editor found it too long, with a promise of a future paper in a footnote. However, Keilin was not one of the world's fastest paper-writers and, before he got around to it, Tamiya[9] published in 1928 a detailed study of cytochrome in bacteria, the first of many important contributions to cytochrome by the Japanese school. It was Robin Hill[10], one of Keilin's associates, who discovered the chloroplast cytochromes.

Now, we give the name cytochrome to any haemoprotein whose function is in electron transfer. Cytochromes are involved, not only in intracellular respiration, that is in the reduction of oxygen to water, but also in the reduction of of highly oxidized inorganic compounds such as nitrate and sulphate, in the oxidation of water in photosynthesis, in the desaturation of hydrocarbons and, quantitatively also most important, in the oxygenation of a large number of different compounds. This talk will, however, be restricted to the cytochromes involved in the main energy-yielding electron-transfer reactions.

4

CYTOCHROME OXIDASE

Although, in his first paper on cytochrome, Keilin reported that the oxidation of cytochrome is sensitive to cyanide, he did not discuss the nature of the cytochrome-oxidizing system. Indeed, there is no reference to Warburg, whose theory that cell respiration is brought about by an iron-containing enzyme, atmungsferment, was based on the inhibitory effect of cyanide. It is important to note, in this connection, that Warburg's[11] demonstration of the photo-sensitive inhibition of respiration by CO, which led him to conclude that atmungsferment is a *haem*-containing protein, was not made until 1926, a year after Keilin had proved the role as electron carriers of the three haemoprotein components of cytochrome. Keilin was, however, aware of the extensive literature on what was then called indophenol oxidase, the enzyme catalysing the oxidation of a mixture of alpha-naphthol and dimethyl-p-phenylenediamine to the dyestuff indophenol. As long ago as 1912, Battelli and Stern[12] had shown that the enzyme is sensitive to cyanide.

The month of May, 1927, is an important one in the history of bioenergetics. On May 7, Keilin[13] published a letter to *Nature*, in which, after referring to Warburg's experiments on the light-sensitive inhibition of respiration by CO, he showed that indophenol oxidase is likewise inhibited by CO and that this inhibition is also reversed by light. Keilin concluded that "Warburg's respiratory ferment is a polyphenol or indophenol oxidase system". Five days later, on May 12, Warburg delivered a lecture to the Royal Society in London, in which he suggested that the respiratory enzyme is a pigment probably related to haemoglobin. A short account[14] of this lecture was published on June 30. Still in this same month of May, on the 27th or 28th, Keilin gave a lecture to the Société de Biologie in France on cytochrome, the preprint[15] of which contains the conclusion that cytochrome is oxidized by indophenol oxidase, but the experiments on inhibition by CO, which were probably carried out between preparing the precirculated paper and May 7, are not included.

The stage was now set for one of those controversies which adorn the field of bioenergetics. The problem was that Keilin had demonstrated that three haemoproteins are involved in intracellular respiration, but none appeared to qualify for the cyanide- and CO-sensitive oxygen-activating enzyme. On the basis, however, of the known properties of haemoglobin, Warburg had good reason to believe that the oxygen-reacting enzyme is also a haemoprotein. It was not until 1938 that Keilin and Hartree[16] showed that one of the components of cytochrome - c - is required, in addition to the cyanide- and CO-sensitive oxidase, for the indophenol oxidase reaction. Dimethyl-p-phenylenediamine reduces cytochrome c, which was present in all preparations of indophenol oxidase, and the cytochrome c is in turn oxidized by the oxidase. Other reducing agents, notably cysteine, can also be oxidized, but only if cytochrome c is added to the enzyme preparation. (I shall return later to this point). Since the function of the cyanide- and CO-sensitive component of the system is to catalyse the oxidation of cytochrome c, Keilin and Hartree named it cytochrome oxidase.

In the following year, Keilin and Hartree[5] showed that band a of cytochrome is derived not only from component a but from a second component, a_3, and that cytochrome a_3 reacts with cyanide, CO and oxygen in a manner to be expected if it is identical with Warburg's atmungsferment. The few reservations that Keilin had with this identification were removed by Chance[17], who was able to show the identity of the photochemical action spectrum of respiration with both the light absorption spectrum of the CO compound of cytochrome a_3 and the photochemical action spectrum of dissociation of this compound.

However, this was not the end of the story. Only a year before their identification of cytochrome a_3, Keilin and Hartree[18] had expressed doubts that cytochrome oxidase is a haemoprotein and they brought forward reasons for thinking that it might be a copper-protein. Although this possiblity became redundant after the 1939 paper, it was revived by Wainio[19] on the basis of the presence of copper in purified preparations of the enzyme. In fact, most of this copper is an impurity, that can be removed without affecting the activity of the enzyme, but some remains bound[20] and, moreover, has a different EPR spectrum[21].

In retrospect, everyone (except Hoppe-Seyler) has turned out to be mainly right, which is a satisfactory conclusion to a controversy. We can now make the following identifications:

atmungsferment = cytochrome a_3

indophenol oxidase = cytochrome c + cytochrome c oxidase

cytochrome c oxidase contains two haems a (cytochrome aa_3) and two (or three[22]) copper atoms.

In their 1939 paper, Keilin and Hartree[5] expressed their views on the relationship between components a and a_3 in the following words : "the invariable coexistence and proportionality of these two compounds, the identity of their haem nuclei, a certain similarity in their absorption spectra and in the properties of their proteins suggest that they must be intimately connected if not interconvertible." The possibility of interconvertibility in the sense that the differences in reactivity towards inhibitors and in redox potential of the second haem are induced by the binding of inhibitors to or reduction of one of the two haems, respectively, was indeed canvassed in many studies in the 1970s. More recent structural studies have confirmed the intimate connection between the two haems in the sense that they are both bound to the same polypeptide in the multi-subunit cytochrome c oxidase, but have not supported the interconvertibility. In the folded protein, one haem is bound sufficiently close to a copper atom, probably in the same polypeptide, to allow the formation of an -O-O- bridge between the two metal atoms[22]. The EPR-visible copper is bound to a second polypeptide. It has been suggested[23] that the recently postulated third copper atom is bound to the same polypeptide as the two haems and the first copper.

CYTOCHROME, CYTOCHROMES AND CYTOCHROME SYSTEMS

Although Keilin knew already in 1925 that there are number of different cytochromes and, indeed, in 1930[24] extracted cytochrome c in soluble form free from the other cytochromes, in his earlier papers he liked to think of cytochrome as a single entity. In his later papers, he wrote cytochrome c, but components b, a and a_3. In his book, Keilin[1] wrote : "Although I was able to show that cytochrome is composed of three distinct haemochromogens, the term 'cytochrome' was, and often still is, used in the singular. This was done in order to indicate that the components of cytochrome are not a haphazard mixture of physiologically independent compounds, but are intimately linked and interdependent in their oxidation-reduction activity and form part of the normal respiratory mechanism of the cell." In a footnote, he added : "This was later referred to as the cytochrome system or respiratory chain."

Keilin and Hartree[25] were kind enough in 1949 to give me the credit of providing "reasoned arguments in favour of an oxido-reduction catalyst linking b and c." We now know that the BAL-labile factor[26] that they were referring to is identical[27] with the later discovered Rieske iron-sulphur protein[28] and that the earlier discovered[7] cytochrome c_1 and two species of protein-bound ubisemiquinone[29] are also involved in this region of the respiratory chain. Moreover, cytochrome b is not concerned directly in electron transfer to cytochrome c of c_1, but the two-haem cytochrome b functions as a shunt between the two species of ubisemiquinone[30]. Thus, the respiratory chain is now no longer seen as an exclusive domain of the cytochromes, with nicotinamide and flavin nucleotides involved at the substrate end, as it was in Keilin's day, and a simple linear chain has also had to be abandoned.

Accessibility of Components of Cytochrome

Keilin and Hartree's[31] 1940 paper, entitled "Succinic dehydrogenase - cytochrome system of cells", concluded that : "The succinic dehydrogenase-cytochrome system even in the cell-free colloidal preparations behaves as a true respiratory system of the cell, showing a high catalytic activity and being affected by all inhibitors in the same way and to the same degree as the normal respiration of intact cells. The efficiency of the system depends, however, not only on the integrity of the components, but also on that of the colloidal structure which supports them and assures their mutual accessibility". This statement was also quoted in their 1949 paper[25]. In the remainder of this lecture,

6

I would like to explore further Keilin's concept of mutual accessibility of components of the system.

Keilin did not concern himself with the cytological origin of these "cell-free colloidal preparations", and the word "mitochondria" does not appear in any of his papers until a review article in 1953[32]. In 1946, Albert Claude[33] showed that cytochrome oxidase is located in liver mitochondria, and shortly afterwards Lehninger and Kennedy[34] showed that the enzymes responsible for the oxidation of fatty acids and pyruvate are also in the mitochondria. In 1952-3, Palade[35] and Sjöstrand[36] showed that these contain two membrane systems - an outer envelope and a heavily folded inner membrane. Significantly, the amount of internal membranes could be correlated with the respiratory activity of the tissue, being particularly rich in heart muscle[36]. Also in 1953, we[37] showed, predictably on the basis of the just cited work, that the Keilin and Hartree preparation is formed by mechanical rupture into small particles of the large membrane vesicle obtained when mitochondria are suspended in a highly hypotonic medium.

At this time, we were puzzled by the behaviour of cytochrome c in these particles. When extracted from tissues and purified to homogeneity, cytochrome c behaves like a soluble protein that can be precipitated only at very high salt concentrations. However, although during the preparation of the particles, the heart muscle is exhaustively washed with water, the particles contain much cytochrome c and catalyse the rapid oxidation of succinate without any addition of the purified cytochrome, and the oxidation rate is normally stimulated only by about 30% by added cytochrome c. On the other hand, the oxidation of ascorbate, like cysteine used in the earlier experiments by Keilin and Hartree[16] a substrate for the cytochrome c - cytochrome oxidase system, requires added cytochrome c in amounts far exceeding that present in the particles. Clearly, succinate can deliver its electrons to cytochrome c in the particles, but ascorbate cannot, or, in other words, the endogenous cytochrome c in the particles is accessible to electrons derived from succinate but not to electrons derived from ascorbate. To make it more puzzling, another reductant of cytochrome c - $\underline{p}$-phenylenediamine - can be oxidized quite rapidly in the absence of cytochrome c, but its oxidation rate is more than doubled by added cytochrome c. The rate of oxidation extrapolated to infinite cytochrome c concentration is the same with ascorbate and $\underline{p}$-phenylenediamine. Typical values are given in Table 1.

Mitchell's[41] concept of the sidedness of the membrane, i.e. that cytochrome c is accessible only to one side of the membrane and succinate dehydrogenase only to the other, and, in particular, Lee and Ernster's[42] proposal that submitochondrial particles have the the opposite orientation from intact mitochondria have provided a partial explanation. We can now easily explain why succinate is rapidly oxidized by succinate in the absence of added cytochrome c, since the endogenous cytochrome c is bound to the inner face of the membrane and, even if dissociated by high salt concentration, will remain within the particle. We could explain the stimulation by added cytochrome c by assuming that about one quarter of the particles have the same orientation as mitochondria. At the high salt concentration used in these experiments, cytochrome c in such particles would be extracted and be diluted in the suspending medium. Indeed, we have to assume that cytochrome c oxidase is, at least in some of the particles, accessible to cytochrome c from outside, as in intact mitochondria; otherwise, Keilin would never have discovered cytochrome oxidase!

However, we still have problems in explaining the data quantitatively. In the first place, it is not immediately clear why the stimulation by cytochrome c is greater with $\underline{p}$-phenylenediamine than with succinate. More important, the turnover number for the cytochrome c oxidase, calculated on the basis of the total concentration of oxidase in the preparation from the activity at infinite cytochrome c concentration, is about the same as that of isolated oxidase[40] (238 s^{-1} at $25°$). This strongly suggests that all the oxidase is accessible to external cytochrome c in this preparation.

Two possible explanations of this result might be considered. First, the relatively high K_m for cytochrome c found in these experiments[38] indicates that it is essentially the low-affinity site that was being measured. It is conceivable that this is accessible to the opposite side of the membrane from the high-affinity site, with which cytochrome c normally reacts. However, so far as I am aware, it is generally believed that the low-affinity site is close to the high-affinity site[43].

Table 1. Respiratory activity of Keilin and Hartree heart-muscle preparation

$TN\ (s^{-1})^{a}$ at 38°		
Substrate	Added cytochrome c	
	−	+
Succinate	45	62
p-Phenylenediamine	64	317
Ascorbate	0	317^{b}

[a] Activities measured in 0.13 M phosphate with succinate and 0.065 M phosphate with other substrates. Data taken from Slater[38,39]
[b] 218 at 25° (van Buuren et al.[40])

The second explanation is that the components of the respiratory chain are "scrambled" in sub-mitochondrial particles, as suggested by Schatz and colleagues[44]. Even though ETP_H particles are completely inverted with respect to the ATP synthase, the rate of oxidation of externally added cytochrome c is about the same as that catalysed by internal cytochrome c. Oxidation of external cytochrome c could be inhibited by an antibody to cytochrome c oxidase. It is not coupled to oxidative phosphorylation or to proton translocation. Earlier, Chance and co-workers[45] had found that 40% of the cytochrome c in their particles is accessible to ferricyanide or cytochrome c peroxidase and that NADH reduces the cytochromes biphasically[46]. They suggested that the particles contain adjacent coupled and uncoupled respiratory assemblies, inhibited by and resistant to oligomycin, respectively, with slow cross connections between the two assemblies. In agreement with these earlier data, Scholes and Hinkle[47] have recently reported that 40% of cytochrome c and c_1 in ETP_H are reduced by ascorbate, which does not traverse the membrane.

Although the evidence of some sort of "scrambling" is quite strong, I find it difficult to picture the physical process that brings about the scrambling or what "scrambled" particles would look like and I am left with no satisfactory explanation for a well-established phenomenon. In any case, it would appear that independent measurements of the sidedness are desirable in any experiments with sub-mitochondrial particles.

Oxidative phosphorylation in cytochrome system. Early work on oxidative phosphorylation was carried out before anything was known about the structure of the mitochondria. Al Lehninger and I did not even know that they contained two membranes, let alone anything about the selective permeability of the outer and inner membranes. After Al Lehninger[48] had demonstrated phosphorylation coupled with the oxidation of NADH by the respiratory chain, the next step was to localize the phosphorylation steps within the chain. Uninhibited by any knowledge that cytochrome c does not penetrate intact mitochondria, I was able to obtain good yields of phosphorylation with added ferricytochrome c as electron acceptor and 2-oxoglutarate as substrate[49]. In this respect, I was fortunate in my mitochondrial preparation, since presumably those mitochondria in the preparation that were capable of oxidizing 2-oxoglutarate were sufficiently damaged to allow cytochrome c to reach the inner membrane. However, I was misled by the fact the preparation of heart mitochondria that I used must have contained the same sort of "scrambled" membranes discussed above, since I found very little phosphorylation with ferrocytochrome c as electron donor. This did not worry me, since, with 2-oxoglutarate as substrate, I had found a P:2e ratio with ferricytochrome c as acceptor approaching that with oxygen. I concluded, then, that oxidative phosphorylation occurs only between substrate and cytochrome c and not between cytochrome c and oxygen. This was incorrect, as Lehninger[50] showed with liver mitochondria, osmotically shocked to make the outer membrane permeable to the cytochrome c. Using this treatment, I[51] was able to show phosphorylation in the cytochrome oxidase reaction with my preparation, although the P:O ratio was never better than 0.35. Apparently, the "scrambled" membranes oxidize ferrocytochrome c more rapidly than swollen mitochondria do, and the reverse is the case with 2-oxoglutarate. In those days we were so much in the dark about the structure of mitochondria or even of biological membranes in general that perhaps we can be excused some stumblings.

How do the components bound in some way or other to the mitochondrial membrane interact with one another in order to catalyse rapid and specific electron transfer? Two extreme positions may be considered - (i) that all members of the respiratory chain are freely diffusible in the membrane and can collide with other members (ii) the components of the chain are built into a rigid structure, a sort of macromolecule, that came to be referred to as a respiratory assembly[52]. Chance and Williams[53], who, in their classical review in 1956, were, sofar as I can recall, the first to give serious consideration to this problem, favoured an arrangement in assemblies in which adjacent members of respiratory chain have sufficient thermal vibration and rotation to cause juxtaposition of their haems with those of their neighbours to account for rapid electron transfer. They recognized the possibility of electron transfer between respiratory assemblies, but assumed that collisions of members of the same assembly are more probable than with other assemblies. Indeed, I[52] had already clearly shown that all the cytochrome c, a and a_3 in the particles is accessible to electrons from succinate even when more than 90% of the component acting between cytochromes b and c, now known to be the Rieske iron-sulphur protein, is irreversibly destroyed by BAL treatment. Thus, the idea of a completely rigid macromolecule was untenable. Nevertheless, the idea of some sort of macromolecule or respiratory assembly dominated thinking for a long time. Lehninger[52] suggested that such respiratory assemblies (minimum weight 1.35×10^6 Daltons) are arranged at regularly spaced intervals, and even Green[55], whose isolation of specific respiratory proteins (called by him Complexes) that catalyse specific segments of the respiratory chain was so important for the future development of our knowledge of the system, thought, at one time, that the four complexes come together in a super-complex that he called the "elementary particle".

The present-day view is somewhere between the two extremes mentioned above. Hackenbrock[56] has presented a convincing random-collision model (Fig. 1) in which it is envisaged that the large multi-subunit proteins (Green's Complexes) and ubiquinone diffuse independently and laterally in the membrane and cytochrome c diffuses primarily in three dimensions in the inter-membrane space.

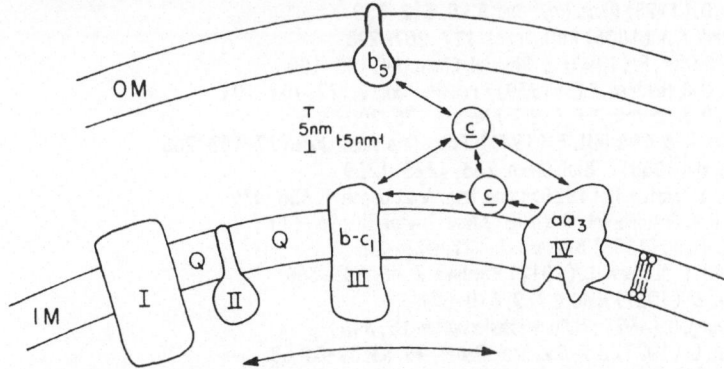

Fig. 1. Hackenbrock's[56] random-collision model (to scale) of mitochondrial electron transfer. O.M., outer membrane; I.M., inner membrane; I, NADH : Q oxidoreductase; II, succinate : Q oxidoreductase; III, QH_2 : cytochrome c oxidoreductase; IV, cytochrome c oxidase. Reproduced, with permission, from Hackenbrock et al.[56].

Collision between the components occurs randomly. Electron transfer follows collision between suitable reaction partners, for example between ferrocytochrome c and oxidized cytochrome c oxidase, because, to use Keilin's terminology, in the collision complex the electron on ferrocytochrome c is accessible to an electron-accepting site, probably the copper atom in subunit II of cytochrome c oxidase. Electron transfer does not take place in the collision complex between, for example, reduced NADH:Q oxidoreductase and ferricytochrome c, despite the favourable ΔG, since the electron in NADH dehydrogenase is not accessible to the iron atom in the cytochrome c. Electrons enter and leave the iron atom of cytochrome c by the same pathway. A specific domain on the cytochrome c molecule presumably interacts, probably electostatically, with a domain on the reductase, oxidase and cytochrome b_5 (in the outer membrane), that gives access to the electron-donating or -accepting metal atom in these molecules. Such a domain is apparently lacking on the NADH-Q oxidoreductase.

I do not think that Keilin would have been too unhappy with this picture, even if it had been presented to him in 1940. Succinate dehydrogenase, cytochrome b, cytochrome c and cytochrome aa_3 are parts of separate proteins and the close relationship between cytochromes a and a_3 is retained. The difference that he envisaged between **cytochrome** c and **components** b,a and a_3 are still present. Q has been added and additional electron acceptors have been found to be present in the large membrane-spanning subunits - FMN and several Fe-S clusters in NADH : Q oxidoreductase; FADH, two or three Fe-S clusters and another cytochrome b in succinate : Q oxidoreductase; in QH_2 : cytochrome c oxidoreductase, cytochrome c_1 has been added, the additional electron carrier postulated in 1948[26] has been found to be a high-potential Fe-S cluster, cytochrome b has been shown to contain two haems and there are two specific ubisemiquinone-binding sites; cytochrome c oxidase contains copper as well as haem.

According to this model, all cytochrome c molecules are equally accessible to all molecules of cytochrome reductase and oxidase, just as if all the molecules were dissolved in a homogeneous solution. However, the Rieske Fe-S subunit in a reductase molecule is not accessible to a cytochrome c_1 subunit in another reductase molecule, only to that in the same molecule. Thus, the concept of a single molecule is correct for the large proteins, containing several different electron carriers, but not for the respiratory chain as a whole. This is what I meant when I wrote above that the present-day view is somewhere between the two extremes of a homogeneous dispersion and a super-molecule.

REFERENCES

1. Keilin, D. (1966) The History of Cell Respiration and Cytochrome, University Press, Cambridge
2. Keilin, D. (1925) Proc. Roy. Soc. B 98, 312-339
3. MacMunn, C.A. (1886) Phil. Trans. 177, 267-298
4. Hoppe-Seyler, F. (1890) Z. Physiol. Chem. 14, 106-108
5. Keilin, D. & Hartree, E.F. (1939) Proc.Roy. Soc. B 127, 167-191
6. Keilin, D. & Hartree, E.F. (1955) Nature 176, 200-206
7. Okunuki, K. & Yakushiji, E. (1941) Proc. Imp. Acad. Japan 17, 163-265
8. Chance, B. (1958) J. Biol. Chem. 233, 1223-1229
9. Yaoi, H. & Tamiya, H. (1928) Proc. Imp. Acad. Japan 4, 436-439
10. Hill, R. & Scarisbrick, R. (1951) New Phytol. 50, 98-111
11. Warburg, O. (1926) Biochem. Z. 177, 471-486
12. Battelli, F. & Stern, L. (1912) Biochem. Z. 46, 343-366
13. Keilin, D. (1927) Nature 119, 670-671
14. Warburg, O. (1927) Naturwissenschaften 15, 346
15. Keilin, D. (1927) C. R. Soc. Biol. Paris, 96, S.P.39-S.P.68
16. Keilin, D. & Hartree, E.F. (1938) Proc. Roy. Soc. B 125, 171-186
17. Chance, B. (1952) J. Biol. Chem. 202, 397-406
18. Keilin, D & Hartree, E.F. (1938) Nature 141, 870-871
19. Eichel. B., Wainio, W.W., Person, P. & Cooperstein, S.J. (1950) J. Biol. Chem. 183, 89-103
20. Takemori, S., Sekuzu, I. & Okunuki, K. (1960) Biochim. Biophys. Acta 38, 158-160
21. Beinert, H., Griffiths, D.E., Wharton, D.C. & Sands, R.H. (1962) J. Biol. Chem. 237, 2337-2346

22. Steffens, G.C.M., Biewald, R. & Buse, G. (1986) EBEC Short Rep. 4, 191

23. Chance, B., Naqui, A. & Powers, L. (1985) in Achievements and Perspectives of Mitochondrial Research, Vol. 1, Bioenergetics (Quagliariello, E.,Slater, E.C., Palmieri, F., Saccone,C. & Kroon, A.M., eds) pp 45-59, Elsevier, Amsterdam

24. Keilin, D. (1930) Proc. Roy. Soc. B 106, 418-444

25. Keilin, D. & Hartree, E.F. (1949) Biochem. J. 44, 205-218

26. Slater, E.C. (1948) Nature 161, 405-406

27. Slater, E.C. & de Vries, S. (1980) Nature 288, 717-718

28. Rieske, J.S., Hansen, R.E. & Zaugg, W.S. (1964) J. Biol. Chem. 239, 3017-3022

29. de Vries, S., Albracht, S.P.J., Berden, J.A. & Slater, E.C.(1981) J. Biol. Chem. 256, 11996-11998

30. Mitchell, P. (1975) FEBS Lett. 56, 1-6

31. Keilin, D. & Hartree, E.F. (1940) Proc. Roy. Soc. B 129, 277-306

32. Keilin, D. & Slater, E.C. (1953) Brit. Med. Bull. 9, 89-97

33. Hogeboom, G.H., Claude, A. & Hotchkiss, R.D. (1946) J. Biol. Chem. 165, 615-629

34. Lehninger, A.L. & Kennedy, E.P. (1948) J. Biol. Chem.172, 753-771.

35. Palade, G.E. (1952) Anat. Rec. 114, 427

36. Sjöstrand, F.S. (1952) Nature, 171, 30-31

37. Cleland, K.W. & Slater, E.C. (1953) Biochem. J. 53, 547-566

38. Slater, E.C. (1949) Biochem. J. 44, 305-318

39. Slater, E.C. (1949) Biochem. J. 45, 1-8

40. van Buuren, J.H., van Gelder, B.F. & Eggelte, T.A. (1971) Biochim. Biophys. Acta 234, 468-480

41. Mitchell, P. (1966) Biol. Rev. 41, 445-502

42. Lee, C.P. & Ernster, L. (1966) in Symp. on Regulation of Metabolic Processes in Mitochondria (Tager, J.M., Papa, S., Quagliariello, E. & Slater, E.C., eds.) pp 218-236, Elsevier, Amsterdam

43. Wilms, J., Veerman, E.C.I., König, B.W., Dekker, H.L. & van Gelder, B.F. (1981) Biochim. Biophys. Acta 635, 13-24

44. Eytan, G.D., Carroll, R.C., Schatz, G. & Racker, E. (1975) J. Biol. Chem. 250, 8598-8603

45. Chance, B., Erecinska, M. & Lee, C.P. (1970) Proc. Nat. Acad. Sci. U.S. 66, 928-935

46. Lee, C.P., Ernster, L. & Chance, B. (1969) Eur. J. Biochem. 8, 153-163

47. Scholes, T.A. & Hinkle, P.C. (1984) Biochemistry 23, 3341-3345

48. Friedkin, M. & Lehninger, A.L. (1948) J. Biol. Chem. 174, 757-758

49. Slater, E.C. (1950) Nature 166, 982-983

50. Nielsen, S.O & Lehninger, A.L. (1954) J. Amer. Chem. Soc. 76, 3860

51. Slater, E.C. (1954) Nature 174, 1143

52. Lehninger, A.L. (1965) The Mitochondrion, Benjamin, New York

53. Chance, B. & Williams, G.R. (1956) Adv. Enzymol. 17, 65-134

54. Slater, E.C. (1949) Biochem. J. 45, 14-30

55. Green, D.E., Wharton, D.C., Tzagoloff, A., Rieske, J.S. & Brierley, G.P. (1965) in Oxidases and Related Redox Systems (King, T.E., Mason, H.S. & Morrison, M.,eds.), Vol. 2, pp. 1032-1076, Wiley, New York

56. Hackenbrock, C.R., Chazotte, B. & Gupte, S.S. (1986) J. Bioenerg. Biomembranes 18, 331-368

I. GENETICS

GENETICS OF E. COLI CYTOCHROMES WHICH ARE COMPONENTS OF THE AEROBIC RESPIRATORY CHAIN

Robert B. Gennis

Departments of Biochemistry and Chemistry
University of Illinois
Urbana, Illinois 61801

INTRODUCTION

The cytochromes of E. coli have been studied for many years, but it has only been recently that the methods of genetics and molecular biology have been effectively directed at these systems (see 1). The impact has been substantial and it is the purpose of this paper to briefly review the current status of this field with an emphasis on some current problems being examined using molecular biology.

Table I: Membrane-Bound Cytochromes of Aerobically Grown E. coli

		Cytochrome Component(s)	Genetics	Comments	References
(1)	Cytochrome d Complex	cyt. d cyt. b_{558} cyt. b_{595}	cyd (min 16.5)	cloned, sequenced	7,14-18 22,24,28
(2)	Cytochrome o Complex	cyt. b_{555} cyt. b_{562}	cyo (min 10.2)	cloned, sequencing in progress	8-10 20,21
(3)	Succinate dehydrogenase	cyt. b_{556}	sdh (min 16.7)	cloned, sequenced, purified as isolated subunit	12,13
(4)	Cytochrome b_{561}	cyt. b_{561}	cybB (near min 16)	cloned, sequenced, unknown function, a very minor component	2,3

Table I lists the cytochromes which have been identified in the cytoplasmic membrane of E. coli grown under aerobic conditions. Each of these four cytochromes or complexes has been purified and biochemically

characterized. Only one, cytochrome b_{561}, which is a very minor component, is presently without a known function (2,3). Together, these
account for all the cytochromes which have been previously defined on
the basis of spectroscopic and electrochemical studies of intact membranes from aerobically grown cells (e.g., 4). Since the aerobic respiratory system of E. coli does not require soluble components, analogous
to mitochondrial cytochrome c, these membrane-bound cytochromes represent all the cytochromes known to be involved in the bioenergetics of
aerobically grown cells.

During the past several years the combination of biochemical and
genetic studies have greatly clarified the structure and function of the
aerobic respiratory chain of E. coli. The current scheme is remarkably
simple (see 5,6). There are two classes of enzymes which comprise the
system:

(1) Dehydrogenases: Enzymes responsible for the two-electron
oxidation of organic substrates. Presumably,
these all reduce ubiquinone-8 within the
bilayer. Examples are succinate dehydrogenase, NADH dehydrogenase, and D-lactate
dehydrogenase.

(2) Quinol Oxidases: Enzymes which oxidize ubiquinol-8 and reduce
molecular oxygen to water. There are two
such enzymes in E. coli, the cytochrome o
complex and the cytochrome d complex.

Presumably, ubiquinone in the cytoplasmic membrane functions as a
mobile pool, capable of diffusing between the two classes of enzymes,
completing the oxidation-reduction circuit.

Coupling sites are known to exist at each of the two terminal
oxidases (7-10). In each case, it appears that one proton appears in
the periplasmic space per electron passing through the enzyme. There
may also be a proton translocation site associated with the NADH dehydrogenase, but this is not certain (see 11).

All of the cytochromes in the cytoplasmic membrane have now been
biochemically and genetically characterized. Cytochrome b_{556} was initially isolated as a single subunit (12) and its function remained a
mystery until it was shown that the amino acid sequence at the N-terminus coincides with that of the sdhC gene (13). Therefore, it is clear
that this cytochrome is one of the "anchor" subunits of the succinate
dehydrogenase complex. Presumably, the cytochrome component is involved
in electron transfer to ubiquinone. The role of cytochrome b_{561} is
still not known, but possibly this minor component plays a similar role
in facilitating ubiquinone reduction.

All the remaining cytochromes in the cytoplasmic membrane are
components of the two terminal oxidases.

(1) The Cytochrome d Complex (14-17) is a two-subunit enzyme which
contains four heme prosthetic groups. Subunit I (mol. wt.
58,000) contains cytochrome b_{558}, whose prosthetic group is
protoheme IX. Subunit II (mol. wt. 43,000) is required for
binding of the other three hemes in the complex: one protoheme IX, responsible for cytochrome b_{595} (previously called
cytochrome a_1); and two d-type hemes (chlorins), corresponding
to the two cytochrome d components of the enzyme. Evidence
strongly suggests that subunit I (i.e., cytochrome b_{558})

(18,19) is directly involved in the oxidation of ubiquinol.

(2) The Cytochrome o Complex (9,10,20) is a three- or four-subunit enzyme which contains two protoheme IX groups, cytochrome b_{562} and cytochrome b_{555}, as well as two copper ions per complex. Nothing is known about the stoichiometry of the subunits or their functions within the complex.

GENETIC STUDIES ON THE TWO OXIDASES

It is typical of prokaryotes that they have multiple terminal oxidases, resulting in "branched" respiratory chains (see 5). The reason for the existence of the two oxidases in E. coli is not known, but under a variety of growth conditions tested, the cytochrome o and cytochrome d complexes appear to be redundant (21,22). The two oxidases are under different genetic regulation, and this is one aspect of interest in genetic studies. The cytochrome o complex predominates when the cells are grown with high oxygen levels, whereas, the cytochrome d complex is induced by low oxygen tension in the growth medium (see 5,6). This corresponds to a cell density attained when the cells reach the mid-exponential phase of batch growth. Possibly, the selective advantage of having the alternative oxidase (cyt.d) relates either to its lower K_m for O_2 (0.024 µM compared to 0.2 µM for cytochrome o) (23), or to lower sensitivity to respiratory inhibitors, such as azide (24).

Whatever the phylogenetic advantage of maintaining two oxidases, their functional redundancy has made traditional genetic approaches more complicated. A mutant lacking either of the two enzymes can still grow aerobically on non-fermentable substrates such as succinate or D,L-lactate, so a simple screen for "aerobic-minus" colonies is not sufficient to locate oxidase-deficient strains (21,22)). This problem was solved by determining that under appropriate conditions the dye TMPD is preferentially oxidized by cells containing the cytochrome d complex (22). Mutants lacking this activity do not turn blue on "TMPD plates." In this way, mutations in the structural gene encoding the cytochrome d complex were first isolated (22). The simultaneous loss of cytochromes b_{558}, b_{595} (a_1) and d in the membranes of these cyd mutants confirmed that all these spectroscopically defined components are, in fact, part of a single complex (4).

Strains lacking the cytochrome d complex (i.e., cyd) grow normally under aerobic growth conditions (22), though they are more sensitive to cyanide and azide in the growth medium (24). Subsequent mutagenesis of these cyd strains did result in mutants unable to grow aerobically on non-fermentable substrates (21). Some of these were characterized and shown to be lacking the cytochrome o complex due to mutations in another genetic locus, cyo (21). A screening protocol was devised so that mutations resulting in the loss of either heme or ubiquinone were not obtained (21). These would also be expected to be unable to grow aerobically on non-fermentable substrates. The protocol takes advantage of the fact that E. coli is a facultative anaerobe, and can utilize nitrate as a terminal electron acceptor in place of oxygen. The electron transfer chain to nitrate requires both ubiquinone and heme, so by requiring the mutants to be able to grow on glycerol-nitrate plates anaerobically, we can be certain that the strains are not defective in heme or ubiquinone biosynthesis.

Figure 1 shows the genetic map positions of a number of genes related to the aerobic respiratory chain . Most of these are required for heme (hem) or ubiquinone (ubi) biosynthesis. It is clear that these genes are not clustered. However, it is noteworthy that the genes encoding the cytochrome-containing enzymes, while not genetically linked, are in the same general area of the chromosome

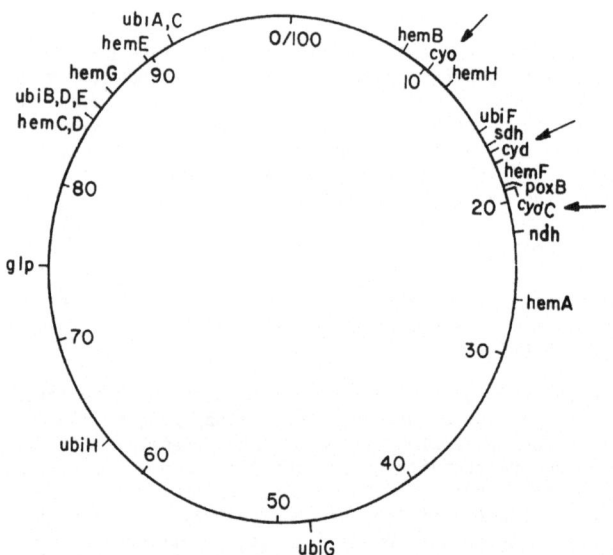

Figure 1. E. coli genetic linkage map showing genes involved in the aerobic electron transfer system. The three arrows indicate genetic loci specifically related to the terminal oxidases.

The latest gene to be characterized is cydC, which is required for the functional expression of the cytochrome d complex (25). The cydC locus is not genetically linked to the operon encoding the two subunits of the enzyme (cydAB). However, mutations in cydC result in much lower levels of the polypeptides in the membrane, and the complete absence of the spectroscopic features associated with the cytochrome d component of the complex. Possibly cydC encodes an enzyme required for the bio-synthesis of the unique heme d prosthetic group utilized by this enzyme. Alternatively, this gene may be involved in regulation of expression of cydAB.

18

CLONING AND MOLECULAR BIOLOGY

Both of the operons encoding the terminal oxidase complexes have been cloned onto multicopy plasmids (26,27). In both cases, the enzymes, properly assembled in the membrane, are overexpressed by 5-10-fold over the best which can be obtained with wild-type strains. Clearly, the biosynthesis of the heme prosthetic groups keeps up with the overexpressed polypeptides. Electron microscopy of bacteria overexpressing the cytochrome d complex shows no morphological abnormalities, such as internal membrane tubules or vesicles (Swafford and Gennis, unpublished). Strains which overproduce these enzymes have been especially useful for large scale biochemical purification of the two oxidases.

It is noteworthy, both aesthetically and scientifically, that strains which overproduce these cytochromes are colored. The cytochrome d complex is dark green due to the presence of the heme d prosthetic group. Cells which contain an abundance of this enzyme are consequently green, and this is even evident in colonies on agar plates containing minimal medium. Strains which overproduce the cytochrome o complex are red, due to the b-cytochrome component of this enzyme. These features are useful for the rapid assessment of mutants.

The complete sequence of a 4 kb DNA fragment encoding both subunits of the cytochrome d complex has been determined (Lin, Newton, Georgiou, Green and Gennis, unpublished). Two open reading frames were shown to correspond to the genes for subunits I and II of the complex. These appear to be under the control of a single promotor, adjacent to the gene for subunit I. The DNA sequence has also revealed the existence of a third open reading frame immediately downstream of the gene for subunit II and apparently part of the cyd operon. The protein encoded by this gene is not necessary for expression of the functional oxidase and its function is currently under investigation.

The deduced amino acid sequences of the two subunits of the cytochrome d complex suggest that both proteins contain multiple transmembrane α-helices. This is indicated by hydropathy profiles using several different algorithms. Experimental work has identified one large region within subunit I which is accessible to proteolysis on the periplasmic side (Lorence and Gennis, unpublished). Further studies are required to accurately determine the topography of the two subunits with respect to the lipid bilayer. This is of particular importance since one goal is to locate the active sites for quinol oxidation and for the reduction of oxygen to water.

One experimental approach to obtain information concerning the active centers is to identify residues required for heme binding. It is likely that histidines function as axial ligands. Fortunately, there are only ten His residues in the complex, six in subunit I and four in subunit II. These are currently being changed to other residues by site-directed mutagenesis. The complete set has not yet been altered. However, it has been determined, for example, that three of the six His residues within subunit I can be mutated without altering either the spectrum or the enzymatic activity of the enzyme (Fang and Gennis, unpublished). It is clear that this approach will be fruitful in determining the heme binding sites, and could be useful in determining the mechanism of the enzyme.

Earlier studies have already shown that subunit I contains the cytochrome b_{558} component of the enzyme. This was done first by analyzing chromosomal mutants lacking subunit II (28), and later by cloning and selectively overproducing subunit I, which was then purified and biochemically characterized (19). It is important to note that the identification of particular subunits directly involved in heme-binding, let alone the specific residues serving as axial ligands, is often very difficult to do biochemically. This is one opportunity which results from being able to manipulate the genes encoding multi-subunit cytochrome systems.

DNA sequencing of the cyo locus is in progress (Au, Chepuri, Cross and Gennis, unpublished). The entire enzyme is encoded on a 5.5-kb DNA fragment. So far, two complete open reading frames have been located. Each encodes what appears to be a very hydrophobic protein which would be expected to cross the bilayer several times. In addition, a third open reading frame has been located. Further studies will be needed in order to determine the correspondence between these genes and the polypeptides determined by SDS-PAGE to be components of the purified enzyme. By selectively mutating and by cloning individual subunits, it is hoped that the role of each subunit can be determined.

CONCLUSION

This brief paper is intended only as a short status report on the use of genetics to study the cytochromes which are critical components of the aerobic respiratory chain of E. coli. The two terminal oxidases are of particular importance because they are directly involved in coupling electron transfer to the generation of a proton motive force. Identifying, cloning and sequencing the genes encoding these enzymes, although a prodigious task in itself, is only the preamble to serious structure-function studies. In order to fully exploit the capabilities of current methodologies, it is necessary to set up the system for easy genetic manipulation, so that interesting mutants can not only be generated, but can be rapidly evaluated both in vivo and in vitro and also conveniently mapped and sequenced to precisely determine the nature of each genetic alteration. In addition, gene fusion methods are useful for exploring membrane protein topography as well as aspects of genetic regulation and membrane assembly, and these methods can be most easily utilized with the cloned genes.

Our laboratory is currently engaged in such projects and it is hoped that in the near future they will provide valuable insights into how these cytochrome systems function in energy transduction in E. coli.

REFERENCES

1. R. B. Gennis, The Cytochromes of Escherichia coli, FEMS Microbiol. Rev., submitted (1987).

2. H. Murakami, K. Kita, and Y. Anraku, Purification and Properties of a Diheme Cytochrome b_{561} of the Escherichia coli Respiratory Chain, J. Biol. Chem., 261:548-551 (1986).

3. H. Murakami, K. Kita, and Y. Anraku, Cloning of cybB, the gene for cytochrome b_{561} of Escherichia coli K12, Mol. Gen. Gent., 198:1-6 (1984).

4. R. L. Lorence, G. N. Green, and R. B. Gennis, Potentiometric Analysis of the Cytochromes of E. coli Utilizing a Mutant Strain Lacking the Cytochrome d Terminal Oxidase Complex, J. Bacteriol., 157:115-121 (1984).

5. Y. Anraku, and R. B. Gennis, The Aerobic Respiratory Chain of
    Escherichia coli, Trends in Biochem. Sci., in press (1987).

6. W. J. Ingledew, and R. K. Poole, The Respiratory Chains of Escheri-
    chia coli, Microbiol. Rev., 48:222-271 (1984).

7. M. J. Miller, and R. B. Gennis, The Cytochrome d Complex is a
    Coupling Site in the Aerobic Respiratory Chain of Escherichia
    coli, J. Biol. Chem., 260:14003-14008 (1983).

8. K. Carter, and R. B. Gennis, Reconstitution of the Ubiquinone-
    dependent Pyruvate Oxidase System of Escherichia coli with the
    Cytochrome o Terminal Oxidase, J. Biol. Chem., 260:10986-10990
    (1985).

9. K. Matsushita, L. Patel, and H. R. Kaback, Cytochrome o Type Oxi-
    dase from Escherichia coli. Characterization of the Enzyme and
    Mechanism of Electrochemical Proton Gradient Generation, Bio-
    chem., 23:4703-4714 (1984).

10. K. Matsushita, L. Patel, R. B. Gennis, and H. R. Kaback, Recon-
    stitution of Active Transport in Proteoliposomes Containing
    Cytochrome o Oxidase and lac Carrier Protein Purified from E.
    coli, Proc. Natl. Acad. Sci., USA, 80:4889-1893 (1983).

11. K. Matsushita, and H. R. Kaback, D-Lactate Oxidation and Generation
    of the Proton Electrochemical Gradient in Membrane Vesicles from
    Escherichia coli GR19N and on Proteoliposomes Reconstituted with
    Purified D-Lactate Dehydrogenase and Cytochrome o Oxidase,
    Biochem., 25:2321-2327 (1986).

12. K. Kita, I. Yamato, and Y. Anraku, Purification and Properties of
    Cytochrome b_{556} in the Respiratory Chain of Aerobically Grown
    Escherichia coli K12, J. Biol. Chem., 253:8910-8915 (1978).

13. H. Murakami, K. Kita, H. Oya, and Y. Anraku, The Escherichia coli
    cytochrome b_{556} gene, cybA, is assignable as sdhC in the suc-
    cinate dehydrogenase gene cluster, FEMS Microb. Lett., 30:307-
    311 (1985).

14. M. J. Miller, and R. B. Gennis, Purification and Characterization
    of the Cytochrome d Terminal Oxidase Complex from Escherichia
    coli, J. Biol. Chem., 248:9159-9165 (1983).

15. J. G. Koland, M. J. Miller, and R. B. Gennis, Potentiometric Analy-
    sis of the Purified Cytochrome d Terminal Oxidase Complex From
    E. coli, Biochemistry, 23:1051-1056 (1984).

16. R. M. Lorence, J. G. Koland, and R. B. Gennis, Coulometric and
    Spectroscopic Analysis of the Purified Cytochrome d Complex of
    Escherichia coli: Evidence for the Identification of Cytochrome
    a_1 as Cytochrome b_{595}, Biochem., 25:2314-2321 (1986).

17. K. Kita, K. Konishi, and Y. Anraku, Terminal Oxidase of Escherichia
    coli Aerobic Respiratory Chain II, J. Biol. Chem., 259:3375-3381
    (1984).

18. R. G. Kranz, and R. B. Gennis, Characterization of the Cytochrome d
    Terminal Oxidase Complex of Escherichia coli Using Polyclonal
    and Monoclonal Antibodies, J. Biol. Chem., 259:7998-8003
    (1984).

19. G. N. Green, R. M. Lorence, and R. B. Gennis, The Specific Over-production and Purification of the Cytochrome b_{558} Component of the Cytochrome d Complex from Escherichia coli, Biochem., 25:2309-2314 (1986).

20. K. Kita, K. Konishi, and Y. Anraku, Terminal Oxidases of Escherichia coli Aerobic Respiratory Chain I, J. Biol. Chem., 259:3368-3374 (1984).

21. D. C.-T. Au, R. M. Lorence, and R. B. Gennis, Isolation and Characterization of E. coli Mutant Lacking the Cytochrome o Terminal Oxidase, J. Bacteriol., 161:123-127 (1985).

22. G. N. Green, and R. B. Gennis, Isolation and Characterization of mutant Lacking Cytochrome d, a Component of the E. coli Respiratory System, J. Bacteriol., 154:1269-1275 (1983).

23. C. W. Rice, and Hempfling, Oxygen-Limited Continuous Culture and Respiratory Energy Conservation in Escherichia coli, J. Bacteriol., 134:115-124 (1978).

24. G. N. Green, J. E. Kranz, and R. B. Gennis, Cloning the cyd locus Coding for the Cytochrome d Complex of E. coli, Gene, 32:99-106 (1984).

25. C. D. Georgiou, H. Fang, and R. B. Gennis, Identification of the cydC locus Required for the Expression of the Functional Form of the Cytochrome d Terminal Oxidase Complex in Escherichia coli, J. Bacteriol., in press (1987).

26. D. C.-T. Au, and R. B. Gennis, Cloning of the cyo Locus Encoding the Cytochrome o Terminal Oxidase Complex of Escherichia coli, J. Bacteriol., in press (1987).

27. G. N. Green, R. G. Kranz, R. M. Lorence, and R. B. Gennis, Identification of Subunit I as the Cytochrome b_{558} Component of the Cytochrome d Terminal Oxidase Complex of Escherichia colil, J. Biol. Chem., 259, 7994-7997 (1984).

MOLECULAR GENETIC APPROACHES TO STUDYING THE STRUCTURE AND FUNCTION OF THE CYTOCHROME c_2 AND THE CYTOCHROME bc_1 COMPLEX FROM *RHODOBACTER CAPSULATUS*

Fevzi Daldal

Cold Spring Harbor Laboratory
P. O. Box 100
Cold Spring Harbor, N. Y.   11724

INTRODUCTION

According to the chemiosmotic theory of Mitchell, generation of the transmembrane proton gradient is the result of electron flow through a series of membrane-bound electron carriers[1]. These multisubunit complexes, which can be isolated as distinct, functional entities, are interconnected via small electron carriers, like quinones and cytochrome c. The ubiquinol:cytochrome c oxidoreductase (or the cytochrome bc_1 complex), is one of the most common example of these complexes. It is responsible for the transfer of electrons from ubiquinol to cytochrome c, a central step in respiratory and photosynthetic energy transduction pathways, while in doing so it translocates protons across the impermeable membrane. The proton gradient and the membrane potential thus established are then used for cellular functions like ATP production and transport. Cytochrome bc_1 complexes are present in many prokaryotes, including photosynthetic bacteria, and in mitochondria of eukaryotes. A similar structure, the cytochrome b_6/f complex, also exists in chloroplasts of plants. Although the subunit compositions of these complexes vary according to their origin, the essential redox-active components, cytochromes b and c_1, Rieske Fe-S protein and ubiquinone, are always conserved[2].

Photosynthetic bacteria of the genus *Rhodobacter* provide an excellent experimental system for studying the cytochrome bc_1 complex by multidisciplinary approaches including genetic, biochemical and biophysical techniques. In these bacteria, the photochemical reaction center generates upon illumination both the reductant and oxidant of the cytochrome bc_1 complex. Thus, secondary electron transfer reactions within the cytochrome bc_1 complex can be studied during a single turnover initiated by a brief flash of light which oxidizes the reaction center[3]. Furthermore, these organisms have various modes of growth that allow mutants with a defective cytochrome bc_1 complex to grow via other pathways. Among the purple sulfur bacteria, *Rhodobacter capsulatus* (formerly called *Rhodopseudomonas capsulata*) is particularly suitable for molecular genetic approaches because of the availability of a number of sophisticated genetic techniques[4].

During the past several years, structural and mechanistic aspects of the cytochrome bc_1 complex have been investigated by biophysical and biochemical approaches[5]. These studies have defined the structural components and their thermodynamic and spectroscopic characteristics, and models have been proposed to describe the chemical reactions and the functional sites involved[6,7]. However, bioenergetic reactions catalyzed by the cytochrome bc_1 complex are not simple, and are far from being well understood. In the past, genetic approaches have been helpful for unraveling the mechanistic intricacy of complex biological structures. In photosynthetic bacteria a molecular genetic approach to understanding the mechanism of the cytochrome bc_1 complex has only recently been initiated[8,9]. In this chapter current molecular genetic studies of the structure and function of cytochrome c_2 and cytochrome bc_1 complex from *R. capsulatus* are described.

CYTOCHROME c_2

Until recently, it has been generally accepted that the membrane-bound photochemical reaction center and cytochrome bc_1 complex do not interact directly with each other for electron transfer during photosynthesis. Rather, two mobile electron carriers, ubiquinone and cytochrome c_2, were thought to assume this role at the reducing and the oxidizing ends of the reaction center, respectively[3,5]. Furthermore, cytochrome c_2 is also involved in aerobic growth where it was thought to carry electrons from the cytochrome bc_1 complex to the terminal oxidase known as cytochrome b_{410}[10] (Fig. 1). Therefore, in *R. capsulatus*, the presence of cytochrome c_2 was considered obligatory for photosynthesis and for cytochrome oxidase$_{410}$-dependent respiration. These conclusions were partly based on spectroscopic analyses of non photosynthetic mutants, such as MT113, lacking c_2[11]. However, recent studies using MT113 revealed that this strain lacks not only cytochrome c_2 but most of the other known c-type cytochromes, including cytochrome c_1, and it does not contain a functional bc_1 complex[12]. These findings, precluding any possible correlation between the absence of c_2 and the impairment of photosynthetic growth, indicated that the role of c_2 in photosynthesis and respiration needed to be reexamined.

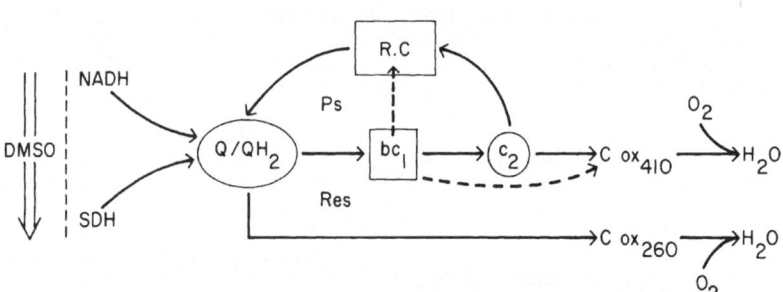

Fig. 1   Electron pathways during various modes of growth of *R. capsulatus*.
Ps, Photosynthesis; Res, Respiration; DMSO, anaerobic, dark growth in the presence of DMSO, NADH and SDH, respiratory dehydrogenases; Q/QH_2, quinone pool; R.C, Reaction center; bc_1, cytochrome bc_1 complex; c_2, cytochrome c_2; C ox$_{410}$ (cytochrome oxidase) and C ox$_{260}$ (quinol oxidase), respiratory terminal oxidases. Dotted arrows indicate the newly discovered electron pathways.

The correct determination of the interactions between cytochrome c_2 and the components of the photosynthetic and respiratory machinery requires simple mutants lacking only this cytochrome. Thus, a c_2^- mutant was sought by a reverse genetic approach that required the cloning of the structural gene for cytochrome c_2 (cycA). cycA was isolated using synthetic mixed oligonucleotide probes derived from the known amino acid sequence of cytochrome c_2, and its nucleotide sequence was determined[13]. This revealed the presence of a 21 amino acid long signal sequence at the beginning of the gene, in agreement with the known periplasmic location of c_2[14]. An insertion-deletion allele of cycA was constructed in vitro by replacing the heme-binding domain of c_2 with an insert encoding resistance to kanamycin. This allele was then introduced, via homologous recombination, into the chromosome of an otherwise wild type strain, yielding a mutant strain (MT-G4/S4, Table I) defective solely in cycA. The absence of cytochrome c_2 in this mutant was proven by various genetic, immunological and spectroscopic analyses[13].

Somewhat unexpectedly, c_2^- mutants grew by photosynthesis at near wild-type rates, especially when high light intensity was provided[13]. This demonstrated that cytochrome c_2 was not indispensable for photosynthetic growth of R. capsulatus, and raised an interesting question about the nature of the electron donor to the reaction center. Through spectroscopic studies no alternative soluble electron carrier serving in stead of c_2 was found, but rather substantial spectral, kinetic and thermodynamic data were obtained indicating that during photosynthesis a c-type cytochrome, most likely c_1 of the cytochrome bc_1 complex, was the electron donor to about 20% of the oxidized reaction centers[15]. This electron donation was rapid (t1/2<100 us), and the donor had a redox mid-point potential of 345 mV. Moreover, it appeared that in wild type cells, an additional 20% of the reaction centers rapidly receive an electron from c_2, probably associated with this complex. Another 30-40% of the reaction centers accept an electron more slowly, perhaps reflecting a requirement for the diffusion of c_2 from the cytochrome bc_1 complexes to the reaction centers which are spacially distant[15]. Apparently, at least in chromatophores, the remaining 20% of the reaction centers seem completely disconnected from the cytochrome bc_1 complexes. These data also suggested that the former attribution of the different "phases" of the carotenoid bandshift to different components of the cyclic photosynthesis may need to be reinterpreted in the case of R. capsulatus[15].

To test whether another c-type cytochrome(s), distinct from c_1 was also involved in the above mentioned electron transfer, a strain lacking both of the cytochromes c_2 and c_1 was constructed. Analysis of this double mutant revealed the presence of two previously undetected c-type cytochromes, one presumably periplasmic and the other located in the membrane. Although both of these cytochromes had high redox mid-point potentials (316 and 312 mV, respectively) neither of them was photooxidizable[16]. This conclusively indicated that the cytochromes c_1 and c_2 are the only physiological electron donors to the photochemical reaction center of R. capsulatus, and that other membrane-bound or soluble c-type cytochromes are not participants in light-induced electron transfer between the reaction center and the cytochrome bc_1 complex[16]. Moreover, the direct electron transfer by cytochrome c_1 to the reaction center strongly suggests that a fraction of these two membrane-bound complexes may be present in close vicinity of each other to assure direct interaction. The existance of a photochemical reaction center/cytochrome bc_1 oxidoreductase "supercomplex" in the membranes of R. capsulatus might then be an interesting possibility.

Earlier, Prince and his colleagues have studied the effect of the antibodies raised against cytochrome c_2 from Rhodobacter sphaeroides and

R. capsulatus on c-type cytochrome oxidation by the reaction center in partially permeabilized chromatophores[14]. They have found that, using homologous anti-c_2 antibodies, c-type cytochrome photooxidation could be completely inhibited in *R. sphaeroides*, but only partly (approximately 50%) in *R. capsulatus*. It was then recently suggested that cytochrome c_1 oxidation by the reaction center may obligatorily involve cytochrome c_2 in *R. sphaeroides*, but not in *R. capsulatus*[15]. This was further strengthened by the very recent finding that a c_2^- mutant of *R. sphaeroides* was, in contrast to that of *R. capsulatus*, deficient in photosynthesis[17]. This difference is intriguing considering that the two species are closely related. To find out whether the c_2-independent electron pathway discovered in *R. capsulatus* is a structural property of its cytochrome bc_1 complex the corresponding structural genes of this bacterium were deleted and replaced by those from *R. sphaeroides*. The heterologous merodiploids obtained were able to grow photosynthetically indicating that the bc_1 genes from *R. sphaeroides* were expressed, and that their products assembled correctly in *R. capsulatus*. More interestingly, the *R. sphaeroides* bc_1 complex was also able to support the photosynthetic growth of a bc_1^- mutant of *R. capsulatus* even in the absence of cytochrome c_2. This latter finding indicates that the direct, c_2-independent electron pathway from the cytochrome bc_1 complex to the reaction center can also be assumed by a bc_1 complex derived from *R. sphaeroides*. Therefore, the ability to perform this direct electron flow may be related to components other than the ubiquinol:cytochrome c_2 oxidoreductase, such as the reaction center and the light-harvesting complexes surrounding it. In this respect it is noteworthy that the light-harvesting I antenna complexes appear to play very different roles in the assembly of the photochemical reaction center to the membranes of these two species[18]. Furthermore, interestingly, the light harvesting II antenna complexes also have different subunit compositions in *R. capsulatus* and in *R. sphaeroides*[19].

A c_2^- mutant is proficient in respiration and it grows at a rate identical to that of a wild-type strain[13]. However, the respiratory pathway of R. capsulatus is branched and while one branch involves cytochrome bc_1 complex and cytochrome c_2, the other, called the "alternate pathway", is independent of c_2[20,21] (Fig. 1). Thus, the role of c_2 in respiration can only be assessed in the absence of this second respiratory branch. In a mutant defective in quinol oxidase (formerly called cytochrome oxidase$_{260}$), the terminal oxidase of the "alternate pathway", respiration proceeds only via the cytochrome bc_1 complex, cytochrome c_2 and cytochrome oxidase$_{410}$[22]. It was recently shown that the introduction of a c_2 deletion-insertion allele into this mutant does not abolish the respiratory growth[23]. Moreover, the aerobic dark growth in this mutant (M6G-G4/S4, Table I) remains sensitive to myxothiazol, a potent inhibitor of the bc_1 complex. These results conclusively indicate that, in *R. capsulatus*, a c_2-independent electron pathway between the cytochrome bc_1 complex and the terminal oxidase$_{410}$ must be present. Hopefully, further studies of this mutant will indicate whether the electron donor to cytochrome oxidase$_{410}$ is, as in photosynthesis, the cytochrome c_1 of the bc_1 complex. However, it is also plausible that other electron carrier(s), distinct from c_2 and c_1, may be involved in electron shuttling under respiratory growth conditions[24].

CYTOCHROME bc_1 COMPLEX

A thorough genetic analysis of the role and the mechanism of the cytochrome bc_1 complex requires the isolation of the structural genes of its components. For this purpose a non photosynthetic mutant of *R. capsulatus*, R126, originally isolated by Marrs[25], and later found defective in the quinol oxidation (Q_z) site of this complex by Robertson and his colleagues[26], was used. From a gene library, a plasmid which complemented this mutant for photosynthetic growth was isolated[27]. The location of the structural genes for the Rieske Fe-S protein (*pet*A), cytochrome *b* (*pet*B) and cytochrome c_1 (*pet*C) on this plasmid was determined using synthetic, mixed oligonucleotides probes that recognized highly conserved amino acid sequences of the corresponding proteins available from other organisms. In the 5' to 3' direction, petA, petB and petC were found located very close to each other spanning two adjacent EcoRI fragments of approximately 4 kb[27] (Fig. 2). The close proximity of these genes, their identical orientation, and the polarity of the insertion mutations located in *pet*A on *pet*B and *pet*C suggested that they may constitute an operon (*pet*). Indeed, mapping of the corresponding RNA transcript from a very closely related strain indicated that these genes are expressed as an operon[9]. The nucleotide sequence of the entire *pet* operon was determined, establishing the primary structure of the three subunits of the cytochrome bc_1 complex[28].

According to these sequence data the Rieske Fe-S protein has 191 amino acid residues and a molecular weight of approximately 20 kDa. It shows considerable overall homology to corresponding proteins from *Neurospora crassa* and *Saccharomyces cereviciae*, especially at its COOH-terminal region where several cysteines thought to be the ligands for the 2Fe-2S cluster are located. The hydropathy profile for this protein is compatible with the current thinking that the Rieske Fe-S protein is located almost entirely in the periplasm, with the exception of an NH_2-terminal membrane-spanning helix anchoring it to the membrane. It may be folded in such a way that the Fe-S cluster positioned in an hydrophobic pocket is not too far from the membrane/aqueous interface at the periplasmic side of the membrane[28].

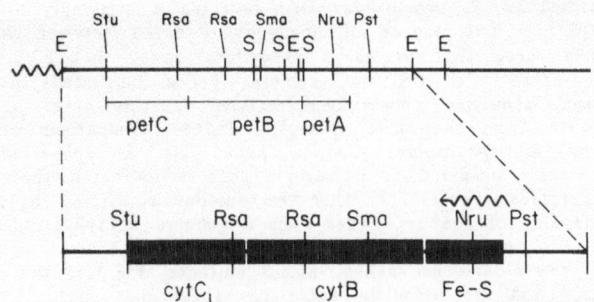

Fig. 2   *pet* operon containing (5' to 3' direction), *pet*A (Rieske Fe-S protein), *pet*B (Cytochrome *b*) and *pet*C (Cytochrome c_1), the structural genes for subunits of the cytochrome bc_1 complex. Arrow indicates the direction of the transcription; E, *Eco*RI, S, *sal*I restriction enzyme sites.

The 437 amino acid long cytochrome *b* protein, of a calculated molecular weight of approximately 50 kDa, shows strong homology to cytochrome *b* proteins from various other sources, and has a characteristic hydropathy profile with 9 membrane spanning regions[28]. The four histidine residues postulated to coordinate the two heme groups on each side of the membrane[29], are also conserved in *R. capsulatus*. It has been recently suggested that proline residues play some role in the function of transport proteins since they are found in membrane-spanning regions of these proteins more frequently than those not involved in transport[30]. Several such proline residues conserved among all available cytochrome *b* sequences can be noticed, but how they are involved in the translocation of protons is not yet clear.

Cytochrome c_1 of *R. capsulatus* consists of 279 amino acid residues with a molecular weight of approximately 31 kDa[28]. It most likely contains a signal sequence of 21 residues, and its c-type heme binding sequence, Cys-X-Y-Cys-His, is located close to the NH_2-terminal portion of the protein. The hydropathy profile of this protein indicates the presence of an other hydrophobic region located at the COOH-terminal end in addition to the signal sequence. Most likely, in a manner comparable to its analogs from mitochondria or chloroplasts, this region anchors cytochrome c_1 to the membrane while leaving the majority of the protein, including the heme containing portion, exposed to the periplasm. The degree of homology of cytochrome c_1 to its counterpart of mitochondrial sources is not very high and it is even lower to those of chloroplast origin. Previously, two regions of the beefheart cytochrome c_1 containing several acidic residues have been proposed as being the cytochromes c_1/c interaction sites[31]. The corresponding regions in *R. capsulatus* cytochrome c_1 also contain a high proportion of acidic residues and are good candidates for site of interaction with cytochrome c_2. Whether or not these regions are also involved in its direct interaction with the photochemical reaction center is not known.

The structural genes, named *fbc*, corresponding to another bacterial cytochrome bc_1 complex have also been isolated and sequenced by Gabellini and her colleagues[8,9]. A comparison of the nucleotide sequences of the *pet* genes (from *R. capsulatus* strain SB1003) with the *fbc* operon (from a strain described as *R. sphaeroides* GA) revealed a strikingly high homology of over 90%[28]. The degree of homology observed between various other proteins from these two species is in general lower that 80%. The high homology observed with the bc_1 complex genes suggested that either a highly unusual sequence conservation existed in this case, or that both sequences were from the same species. Indeed, comparison of the strain described as *R. sphaeroides* GA to *bone fide R. sphaeroides* and *R. capsulatus* strains obtained from various sources indicated that it was not an *R. sphaeroides* species[32]. This was further confirmed by cloning and partial sequencing of the bc_1 genes from a genuine *R. sphaeroides* strain.

Using the cloned *pet* genes various mutants affecting the bc_1 complex were obtained and are listed in Table I. These bc_1^- mutants, in contrast to c_2^- mutants, were unable to grow photosynthetically, demonstrating that each of the three components of the complex is essential for photosynthesis[27]. However, the absence of a functional bc_1 complex does not abolish respiration because of the presence of a bc_1-independent, "alternate" respiratory pathway[22] (Fig. 1). The availability of several bc_1^- mutants affecting various components of this complex in concert with monoclonal and polyclonal antibodies will be very useful for studies aimed at the understanding of the biogenesis and the assembly of the bc_1 complex.

Although the prosthetic groups (Fe-S cluster, *c* heme and the two spectrally distinct *b* hemes) of the cytochrome bc_1 complex can be assigned with some confidence to their binding sites on their respective apoproteins it is currently difficult to identify the quinone processing sites. Null bc_1^- mutants have been very useful in defining essential components required for various modes of growth of *R. capsulatus*. However, they are of less use for elucidating the structure of the functional sites because they often yield strains totally devoid of the bc_1 complex. Mutants able to assemble a functionally perturbed or inactivated complex, like R126 (Table I), will be essential for this purpose. A general technique, called "interposon tagging", which consists of introducing a silent insertion into the close proximity of the gene studied, was devised to isolate and quickly map this type of mutation. This silent insertion, or the 'tagging interposon', providing a selectable genetic marker linked to the region to be studied, can then be used for mapping and cloning. Among a collection of spontaneous mutations those localized in the bc_1 cluster may be found without difficulty using this powerful tool. With this approach the *aer*126 mutation of R126 affecting the quinol oxidation site was shown to be located in the *pet* cluster, most likely in the cytochrome *b* gene.

Table I.   R. capsulatus mutants affecting various electron transfer components involved in photosynthesis and in repiration.

Strain	Mutated Gene	Defective Component	Relevant Properties
MT1131	wild type	none	$Ps^+,Res^+,DMSO^+,Nadi^+$
MT-G4/S4	$\Delta(cycA::kan)$	$cytc_2^-$	$Ps^+,Res^+,DMSO^+,Nadi^+$
MT-RK2	*petA::kan*	$Rieske^-$ (bc_1^-)	$Ps^-,Res^+,DMSO^+,Nadi^+$
MT-CB1	*petB::kan*	$cytb^-$ (bc_1^-)	$Ps^-,Res^+,DMSO^+,Nadi^+$
MT-CC1	*petC::kan*	$cytc_1^-$ (bc_1^-)	$Ps^-,Res^+,DMSO^+,Nadi^+$
MT-CBC1	$\Delta(petB,C::spe)$	$cytb^-,cytc_1^-$ (bc_1^-)	$Ps^-,Res^+,DMSO^+,Nadi^+$
MT-GS18	$\Delta(petB,C::spe)$, $\Delta(cycA::kan)$	$cytb^-,cytc_1^-,cytc_2^-$ (bc_1^-,c_2^-)	$Ps^-,Res^+,DMSO^+,Nadi^+$
M6G*	*qox*	$Q.ox_{260}^-$	$Ps^+,Res^+,DMSO^+,Nadi^+$
M7G*	*cox*	$C.ox_{410}^-$	$Ps^+,Res^+,DMSO^+,Nadi^-$
M6G-G4/S4	$qox,\Delta(cycA::kan)$	$Q.ox_{260}^-,cytc_2^-$	$Ps^+,Res^+,DMSO^+,Nadi^+$
M7G-G4/S4	$cox,\Delta(cycA::kan)$	$C.0x_{410}^-,cytc_2^-$	$Ps^+,Res^+,DMSO^+,Nadi^+$
M7G-GS18	$cox,\Delta(petB,C::spe)$	$C.ox_{410}^-,bc_1^-$	$Ps^-,Res^+,DMSO^+,Nadi^-$
R126*	*aer*126	bc_1^-	$Ps^-,Res^+,DMSO^+,Nadi^+$
MT113*	?	all $c-cyt^-$	$Ps^-,Res^+,DMSO^-,Nadi^-$
Y142*	*rxc*	$R.C.^-$	$Ps^-,Res^+,DMSO^+,Nadi^+$

*These strains have been originally isolated by B. L. Marrs and generously provided to us; the other mutants listed were obtained in this laboratory.

Nadi, ability to catalyze the a-naphthol + dimethyl-p-phenylenediamine + O_2 indophenol blue + H_2O reaction; Ps, photosynthetic growth; Res, Respiratory growth; DMSO, anaerobic dark growth in the presence of DMSO; $Q.ox_{260}$ (also previously called $C.ox_{260}$) quinol oxidase; $C.ox_{410}$, cytochrome oxidase; bc_1, cytochrome bc_1 complex; R.C., photochemical reaction center.

Another class of mutations very useful for analyzing the structure of the functional sites of the bc_1 complex are those conferring resistance to inhibitors of the bc_1 complex[33]. At least three distinct classes of such inhibitors have been studied in vitro[34]. Myxothiazol, strobilurin (mucidin), and oudemensin were shown to interfere with electron transfer between the ubiquinol and the Rieske Fe-S protein at the quinol oxidation site; antimycin, funiculosin and HQNO affect the cytochrome b/ubiquinone step at the quinone reduction site, and finally, a third class of inhibitors like stigmatellin, UHDBT and UHNQ act on the electron flow from the Rieske Fe-S protein to the cytochrome c_1. Several spontaneous mutants resistant to mxyothiazol, mucidin and stigmatellin under photosynthetic growth conditions were obtained, and many of them mapped using the above described genetic tool. All of the myxothiazol-, but only some of the stigmatellin-resistant mutants mapped so far were found linked to the pet cluster[33]. The analysis of mucidin-resistant mutants are currently underway. Interestingly, some of the myxothiazol-resistant mutants were also resistant to stigmatellin or to stigmatellin and to mucidin (Table II). Whether the cross-resistances observed are indications of the overlaps between the binding sites of these inhibitors is an important point which remains to be seen. Several of these inhibitor resistant mutations have now been cloned using the "interposon-tagging" technique, and the determination of their molecular nature is in progress. It is expected that some of these mutations will affect the functional sites indirectly through unspecific conformational changes inflicted to the complex or its subunits, but hopefully others will directly modify the essential constituents of these sites. In the absence of a three dimensional structure with atomic resolution the ability to distinguish between these two broad classes of mutations will constitute an exciting challenge to workers in this field.

Table II.   Some R. capsulatus mutants resistant to inhibitors of the cytochrome bc_1 complex.

Strain	Genotype	Inhibitor Resistance Phenotype
MT1131	wild type	Mxt^S, Stg^S, Muc^S
MXT101	mxt101	$\underline{Mxt^R}, Stg^S, Muc^R$
MXT102	mxt102	$\underline{Mxt^R}, Stg^R, Muc^S$
MXT103	mxt103	$\underline{Mxt^R}, Stg^S, Muc^S$
MXT110	mxt110	$\underline{Mxt^R}, Stg^R, Muc^R$
MUC1	muc1	$Mxt^R, Stg^S, \underline{Muc^R}$
MUC2	muc2	$Mxt^R, Stg^S, \underline{Muc^R}$
STG1	stg1	$Mxt^S, \underline{Stg^R}, Muc^S$
STG10	stg10	$Mxt^R, \underline{Stg^R}, Muc^S$

underlined phenotype indicates the initial selection, the others were scored later.

Interestingly, photosynthetic growth of *R. capsulatus* is readily sensitive to myxothiazol, mucidin and stigmatellin, all inhibitors of the oxidizing branch of the electron pathway in the bc_1 complex, but it appears naturally resistant to even high concentrations of antimycin, funiculosin and HQNO, inhibitors of the quinone reducing site. The latter inhibitors are very potent when assayed using chromatophores, and are also effective[35] on resting cells, collapsing the membrane potential at least partly[35]. It may well be possible that an "antimycin insensitive" pathway still allows the cytochrome bc_1 complex to function partially even when the quinone reductase site is completely inhibited by antimycin, assuring the photosynthetic growth of *R. capsulatus*. If correct, this attractive hypothesis may obviously have some implications on the Q cycle model.

CONCLUSIONS

The isolation of a mutant defective only on cytochrome c_2 revealed the presence of a c_2-independent electron pathway between the reaction center and the bc_1 complex. In this pathway, the donor during photosynthesis being the cytochrome c_1 possibly these two complexes interact directly to some extend. Further comparisons of *R. sphaeroides* with R. capsulatus will undoubtedly help to better elucidate the direct interplay between some of the membrane-bound energy transducing complexes. Moreover, the ability to exchange *in vivo* the bc_1 complexes between various organisms will hopefully initiate new approaches directed to the understanding of their global structural and functional properties.

The availability of clones containing the structural gene for cytochrome c_2, expressed and overproduced in *R. capsulatus*, along with deletion strains devoid of it, now fulfills one of the major genetic requirements for in vitro mutagenesis. This approach will allow the critical testing of the physical binding and subsequent electron transfer between the water soluble cytochrome c_2 and its known natural membrane-bound counterparts involved in respiration and photosynthesis. Furthermore, since c_2 is expendable for either respiration or photosynthesis in *R. capsulatus*, production of large amounts of mutant cytochrome c_2 required for kinetic studies in vitro should be without difficulty. Also, c_2 mutations potentially lethal in other purple bacteria should not present any problem in this species. The recent crystallization of *R. capsulatus* c_2, along with the possibility to test in vitro the electron flow using artificial electron acceptors make this small molecule an attractive model system[36].

The establishment of the complete primary structure of the bc_1 complex and the availability of bc_1^- mutants make this complex from *R. capsulatus* one of the most advanced model systems among the ubiquinol;cytochrome c oxidoreductases. In the future, elucidation of the molecular nature of mutations yielding altered bc_1 complexes, and correlation of these structural modifications with the perturbations of the enzymatic activity will hopefully contribute to define the structural elements of the functional sites. The discrimination between the mutations affecting the catalytic sites directly from those perturbing them at distance through indirect conformational changes will constitute, especially in the absence of a three-dimentional structure, an exciting challenge which will require multidisciplinary approaches. It may be confidently expected that future combinations of biophysical and genetic studies of the cytochrome bc_1 complex from *R. capsulatus* will lead to a better understanding of the relationship between the structure and function of all bc_1-type complexes involved in the transfer of protons and electrons.

ACKNOWLEDGMENTS

This work was supported by grant 1RO1 GM38237 from National Institutes of Health. The work described here has been a group effort. I acknowledge, in particular, my colleagues Edgar Davidson, Susan Rook and Beverly Naiman, and my collaborators Roger Prince and Dan Robertson.

REFERENCES
1. P. Mitchell, Chemiosmotic coupling in oxidative and photosynthetic phosphorylation, Biol. Rev. 41:445-502 (1966).

2. R. C. Prince, Light-driven electron and proton transfer in the cytochrome bc_1 complex, in "Encyclopedia of Plant Physiology, New Series, Photosynthesis III," L.A. Staehelin and C.J. Arntzen, eds., p.539 Springer-Verlag, Heidelberg (1986).

3. P. L. Dutton, Energy transduction in anoxygenic photosynthesis, in "Encyclopedia of Plant Physiology, New Series, Photosynthesis III," L.A. Staehelin and C.J. Arntzen, eds. p.197 Springer-Verlag, Heidelberg (1986).

4. D. C. Youvan and B.L. Marrs, Molecular genetics and light reactions of photosynthesis, Cell 39:1-3.

5. A. R. Crofts, The Mechanism of the ubiquinol cytochrome c oxidoreductase of mitochondria in "The enzymes of Biological Membranes", A.N. Martonosi, ed., p.347 Plenum Press, New York (1984).

6. A. R. Crofts, S.W. Reinhardt, K.R. Jones and M. Snozzi, The role of the quinone pool in the cyclic electron transfer, Biochem. Biophys. Acta 723:202 (1983).

7. M. Wikstrom and M. Saraste, in "Bioenergetics" L. Ernester, ed. p.49 Elsevier, Amsterdam and New York (1984).

8. N. Gabellini, U. Harnish, J.E.G. McCarthy, G. Hauska and W. Sebald, Cloning and expression of the fbc operon encoding the Fe-S protein, cytochrome b and cytochrome c_1 from Rhodopseudonomas sphaeroides bc_1 complex, EMBO J. 4:549 (1985).

9. N. Gabellini and W. Sebald, Nucleotide sequence and transcription of the fbc operon from Rhodopseudomonas sphaeroides Evaluation of the deduced amino acid sequences of the FeS protein, cytochrome b and cytochrome c_1, Eur. J. Biochem. 154:569 (1986).

10. A. Baccarini-Melandri, O.T.G. Jones and G.A. Hauska, Cytochrome c_2, an electron carrier shared by the respiratory and photosynthetic transport chain of Rhodopseudomonas capsulata, FEBS Lett. 86:151 (1978).

11. D. Zannoni, R.C. Prince, P.L. Dutton and B.L. Marrs, Isolation and characterization of a cytochrome c_2-deficient mutant of Rhodopseudomonas capsulata, FEBS Lett. 113:289 (1980).

12. E. Davidson, R.C. Prince, F. Daldal, G. Hauska and B.L. Marrs, Rhodobacter capsulatus MT113, a single mutation results in the absence of the cytochrome bc_1 complex, Biochem. Biophys. Acta 890:292 (1987).

13. F. Daldal, S. Cheng, J. Applebaum, E. Davidson and R.C. Prince, Cytochrome c_2 is not essential for photosynthetic growth of Rhodopseudomonas capsulata, Proc. Natl. Acad. Sci. USA 83:2012 (1986).

14. R. C. Prince, A. Baccarini-Melandri, G.A. Hauska, B.A. Melandri and A.R. Crofts, Assymetry of an energy transducing membrane: The location of cytochrome c_2 in Rhodopseudomonas sphaeroides and Rhodopseudomonas capsulata, Biochem. Biophys. Acta 387:212 (1975).

15. R. C. Prince, E. Davidson, C.E. Haith and F. Daldal, Photosynthetic electron transfer in the absence of cytochrome c_2 in Rhodopseudomonas capsulata: cytochrome c_2 is not essential for electron flow from the cytochrome bc_1 complex to the photochemical reaction center, Biochemistry 25:5208 (1986).

16. R. C. Prince and F. Daldal, Physiological electron donors to the photochemical reaction center of Rhodobacter capsulatus, (Biochem. Biophys. Acta. to be submitted) (1987).

17. T. J. Donohue, A.G. McEwan and S. Kaplan, Cloning DNA sequence and expression of the Rhodobacter sphaeroides cytochrome c_2 gene, J. Bacteriol. 168:962 (1986).

18. W. J. Jackson, R.C. Prince, G.J. Stewart and B.L. Marrs, Energetic and topographic properties of a Rhodopseudomonas capsulata mutant deficient in the B870 complex, Biochemistry 25:8440 (1986).

19. G. Drews, Structure and functional organization of high-harvesting complexes and photochemical reaction centers in membrane of phototrophic bacteria, *Microbiol. Rev.* 49:59 (1985).

20. R. F. Lamonica and B.L. Marrs, The branched respiratory system of photosynthetically grown *Rhodopseudomonas capsulata*, *Biochem. Biophys. Acta* 423:431 (1976).

21. D. Zannoni, B.A. Melandri and A. Baccarini-Melandri, Composition and function of the branched oxidase system in wild type and respiration deficient mutants of *Rhodopseudomas capsulata*, *Biochem. Biophys. Acta* 423:413 (1976).

22. B. Marrs and H. Gest, Genetic mutations affecting the respiratory electron-transport system of the photosynthetic bacterium *Rhodopseudomonas capsulata*, *J. Bacteriol.* 114:1045 (1973).

23. F. Daldal, Role of the cytochrome c_2 in respiratory growth of *Rhodobacter capsulatus*, (*J. Bacteriol.*, to be submitted) (1987).

24. H. Hudig and G. Drews, Characterization of a new membrane-bound cytochrome *c* of *Rhodopseudomona capsulata*, *FEBS Lett.* 152:251 (1983).

25. D. Zannoni and B.L. Marrs, Redox chain and energy transduction in chromatophores from *Rhodopseudomonas capsulata* cells grown anaerobically in the dark on glucose and dimethylsulfoxide, *Biochem. Biophys. Acta* 637:96 (1981).

26. D. E. Robertson, E. Davidson, R.C. Prince, W.H. vandenBerg, B.L. Marrs and P.L. Dutton, Discrete catalytic sites for quinones in the ubiquinol cytochrome c_2 oxidoreductase of *Rhodopseudomonas capsulata*, *J. Biol. Chem.* 261:584 (1986).

27. F. Daldal, E. Davidson and S. Cheng, Isolation of the structural genes for the Rieske Fe-S protein, cytochrome *b* and cytochrome c_1, all components of the ubiquinol: cytochrome c_2 oxidoreductase complex of *Rhodopseudomonas capsulata*, *J. Mol. Biol.* 194 (in the press) (1987).

28. E. Davidson and F. Daldal, Primary structure of the bc_1 complex of *Rhodopseudomonas capsulata* Nucleotide sequence of the *pet* operon encoding the Rieske, cytochrome *b* and cytochrome c_1 apoproteins, *J. Mol. Biol.* 194 (in the press) (1987).

29. W. R. Widger, W.A. Cramer, R.G. Herrmann and A. Trebst, Sequence homology and structural similarity between cytochrome *b* of mitochondrial complex III and the chloroplast b_6/f complex: Position of the cytochrome *b* hemes in the membranes, *Proc. Natl. Acad. Sci.* U.S.A. 81:674 (1984).

30. C. J. Brandl and C. M. Deber, Hypothesis about the function of membrane-buried proline residues in transport proteins, *Proc. Natl. Acad. Sci.* U.S.A 83:917 (1986).

31. J. Stonehuerner, P. O'Brien, L. Geren, F. Millet, J. Steidl, L.Yu and C. Yu, Identification of the binding site on cytochrome c_1 for cytochrome *c*, *J. Biol. Chem.* 259:5392 (1985).

32. E. Davidson and F. Daldal, *fbc* operon encoding the Rieske FeS protein, cytochrome *b* and cytochrome c_1 Apoproteins, previously described from *Rhodopseudomonas sphaeroides* is from *Rhodopseudomonas capsulata*, *J. Mol. Biol.* 194 (in the press) (1987).

33. F. Daldal, E. Davidson, S. Cheng, B. Naiman and S. Rook, Genetic Analysis of the structure and function of the ubiquinol cytochrome c_2 oxidoreductase of *Rhodopseudomonas capsulata*, in "Current Communications in Molecular Biology, Microbial Energy Transduction", D. C. Youvan and F. Daldal, eds, p.113, Cold Spring Harbor Laboratory Press, New York (1986).

34. G. von Jagow and T.A. Link, Use of specific inhibitors on the mitochondrial bc_1 complex, *Methods Enzymol* 126:253 (1986).

35. J. F. Myatt, N.P.J. Cotton and J.B. Jackson, Protonmotive activity

of the bc_1 complex in chromatophores of *Rhodobacter capsulatus* in the presence of myxothiazol and antimycin A, Biochem. Biophys. Acta 890:251 (1987).

36. H. Holden, T.E. Meyer, M.A. Cusanovich, F. Daldal and I. Rayment, Crystallization and preliminary analysis of crystals of cytochrome c_2 from *Rhodopseudomonas capsulata*, J. Mol. Biol. (in the press) (1987).

STRUCTURAL HOMOLOGIES IN THE CYTOCHROME B/C₁ COMPLEX FROM RHODOBACTER

Nadia A. Gabellini

Max-Planck-Institut für Biochemie
8330 Martinsried bei München
FRG

INTRODUCTION

The purple photosynthetic bacteria carry out anoxygenic photosynthesis. This process provides the energy for the synthesis of ATP and for the fixation of nitrogen and CO_2 (Pfennig 1978).
These organisms possess only one photosystem which is part of their cyclic photosynthetic electron transport chain. The photochemical reaction center contains a special dimer of bacteriochlorophyll that undergoes photooxidation; the electrons are delivered to the primary acceptor quinone molecule $(Q)_A$ and to the secondary electron acceptor $(Q)_B$ (Okamura et. al 1982). The electrons are then transferred to a freely diffusable pool of quinone molecules. During photosynthesis the separation of charges in the reaction center induces membrane potential. The oxidized bacteriochlorophyll dimer is reduced, in turn, by a water - soluble cytochrome c_2. The photochemical reaction center is functionally coupled to the membrane bound enzyme: ubiquinol - cytochrome c reductase (b/c_1 complex). This enzyme is composed of four redox centers. The cytochrome b polypeptide carries two hemes with a redox midpoint potential at pH 7 (Em_7) of +50 mV (b_H) and -90 mV (b_L). The heme c of cytochrome c_1 and the Fe2-S2 center of the Rieske FeS protein compose the high potential arm of the oxidoreductase ($Em_7 \sim 300$ mV) that reduces the cytochrome c_2. The oxidation of ubiquinol occurs on the positive side of the membrane through a concerted reaction involving the heme b_L and the FeS center (Crofts et al. 1983). The electrons follows a branched pathway. The FeS protein reduces cytochrome c_1 on the positive side of the membrane, which in turn reduces cytochrome c_2. The second electron from heme b_L is transferred to the heme b_H located near the opposite side of the membrane, negatively charged. The heme b_H forms the catalytic site for the reduction of the quinone. As a result of this branched electron flow, there is a vectorial transport and accumulation of protons on the outer - positive side of the membrane.
The electron transport through the b/c_1 complex establishes an electrochemical potential that drives the synthesis of ATP. The characteristic proton translocating activity of the b/c_1 complex, which occurs with a stoichiometry of $2H^+/e^-$, is best explained by the Q - cycle mechanism (Mitchell 1976).

In the presence of oxygen and in the dark, the purple photosynthetic bacteria of the genera Rhodobacter are capable of aerobic respiration.

Most probably these organisms developed a respiratory chain by connecting the energy transducing segment of the photosynthetic electron tranport chain to terminal oxidases able to reduce oxygen. Among the mechanisms devoted to energy transduction, the electrogenic oxidation of quinol seems to be one of the most ancient and conserved. The plastoquinol oxidase site of the b_6/f complex part of the photosynthetic electron tranport chain of cyanobacteria and chloroplasts, is homologous with the quinol oxidase site of the b/c_1 complex of purple photosynthetic bacteria and mitochondria. The ubiquity of such an enzyme in the electron transport systems of procaryotes like purple photosynthetic bacteria, cyanobacteria and green sulfur bacteria, provides further evidences that the prokaryotic lines descend from a common ancestor (Fox et al. 1980)

ORGANIZATION OF THE GENES FOR THE CYTOCHROME b/c_1 COMPLEX IN PURPLE PHOTOSYNTHETIC BACTERIA

The first identification of the prokaryotic genes for the cytochrome b/c_1 complex was achieved by means of cross-hybridization with part of the nuclear gene for the FeS protein of N.crassa (Gabellini et al. 1985). Restriction fragments (5 - 9 Kb) of genomic DNA from a green derivative of the genera Rhodobacter were screened by means of colony filter hybridization. The DNA probe, encoded the highly conserved region of the Rieske FeS protein from N.crassa , that binds the Fe2-S2 center. The positive plasmids were expressed in a cell free system, by means of immunoabsorbtion with specific antibodies directed against each subunit of the b/c_1 complex of Rhodobacter, it was found that the plasmid drived the synthesis of all three polypeptides: FeS protein, cytochrome b and cytochrome c_1. This finding indicated that the three subunits were clustered in the prokaryotic genome and suggested that they could be part of an operon. This was confirmed by the identification of one polycistronic mRNA that covers the total length of the three genes.

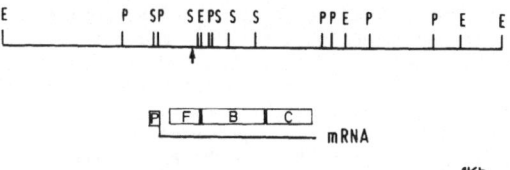

Fig.1. The genes for the cytochrome b/c_1 complex of purple photosynthetic bacteria are organized into one operon. The genes are transcribed as one polycistronic mRNA from one promoter (P) located approximately 240 bp upstream the start codon of gene F, for the FeS protein. A detailed restriction map of the cloned 10 Kb region of chromosomal DNA from Rhodobacter capsulatus, including the three fbc genes was obtained for the restriction endonucleases EcoRI (E), PstI (P) and SalI (S). The position of the sequence hybridizing with the DNA from N.crassa is indicated by an arrow.

The operon was named fbc to recall the prosthetic groups bound to the encoded polypeptides: Fe, heme b and heme c, and also in accordance with the order in wich the genes are transcribed: fbcF for the FeS protein, fbcB for the cytochrome b and fbcC for the cytochrome c_1. As shown in Fig.1 the fbc genes are transcribed from one promoter located upstream the gene F (Gabellini and Sebald 1986). The genes are constitutively expressed in R̲h̲o̲d̲o̲b̲a̲c̲t̲e̲r̲ since the b/c_1 complex is used for both respiratory and photosynthetic metabolisms. The organization of the f̲b̲c̲ genes into one operon, could be advantageous in purple photosynthetic bacteria, for the coordinate expression of the genes under different metabolic conditions.

The f̲b̲c̲ operon was isolated from a green derivative of R̲h̲o̲d̲o̲b̲a̲c̲t̲e̲r̲ thought to be R̲.̲s̲p̲h̲a̲e̲r̲o̲i̲d̲e̲s̲, Ga. The DNA sequence of the f̲b̲c̲ operon (Gabellini and Sebald 1986) was found to be very similar to that of R̲.̲c̲a̲p̲s̲u̲l̲a̲t̲u̲s̲ SB1003 (Davidson and Daldal 1987) suggesting that the two sequences could be derived from the same species. Further characterization of the strain GA (Gabellini) indicated that this is more similar to R̲.̲c̲a̲p̲s̲u̲l̲a̲t̲u̲s̲ than to R̲.̲s̲p̲h̲a̲e̲r̲o̲i̲d̲e̲s̲ (Davidson and Daldal 1987), and that most probably is a green derivative of R̲.̲c̲a̲p̲s̲u̲l̲a̲t̲u̲s̲ Kb1 (Gabellini 1987). Therefore the sequence of the f̲b̲c̲ operon, originally reported as being from R̲.̲s̲p̲h̲a̲e̲r̲o̲i̲d̲e̲s̲ is now attributed to R̲.̲c̲a̲p̲s̲u̲l̲a̲t̲u̲s̲.

The strain GA was also used for the first isolation of a prokaryotic b/c_1 complex (Gabellini et al.1982). Besides the three redox polypeptides the isolated oxidoreductase showed one additional polypeptide, whose relative molecular mass was about 10 KDa. Recently it has been demonstrated that this polypeptide is a contaminating light harvesting protein (Gabellini 1987).

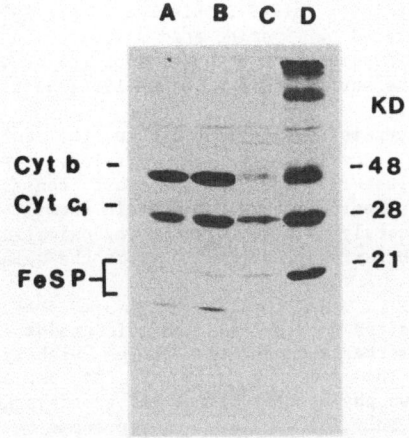

Fig.2. The b/c_1 complex of purple photosynthetic bacteria as R̲.̲c̲a̲p̲s̲u̲l̲a̲t̲u̲s̲ is composed of three subunits. The molecular mass of the three polypeptides: cytochrome b, cytochrome c_1, and FeS protein as deduced from the amino acid sequence is given in Kilo Daltons (KD). The FeS protein migrates as a doublet in lanes A and B, (4 µg and 8 µg of b/c_1 complex were respectively applied after incubation in solubilization buffer at room temperature). The FeS protein runs as a single band if the preparation is incubated shortly at 65°C in solubilization buffer, as shown in lane C and D (2 and 12 µg of b/c_1 were applied respectively). At high temperature the cytochrome b forms irreversible aggregates.

A purer preparation was obtained by octyl glucoside solubilization, omitting the addition of cholate. The preparation shown in Fig.2 is composed of three polypeptides: cytochrome b (48 KDa), cytochrome c_1 (28 KDa) and FeS protein (21 KDa). This preparation catalyses the anti-mycin-sensitive reduction of cytochrome c, indicating that the three polypeptides encoded by the f̲b̲c̲ operon compose the whole catalytic structure of the prokaryotic b/c_1 complex.

During evolution, the structure of the b/c_1 complex became more elaborate, the mitochondria that most probably arose from purple photosynthetic bacteria are provided of a b/c_1 complex that besides the three redox polypeptides, includes 6 to 8 additional subunits.

SEQUENCE HOMOLOGY AND TOPOLOGY OF THE b/c_1 COMPLEX SUBUNITS

The elucidation of the primary structure of the b/c_1 subunits derived from the DNA sequence of the fbc operon, has revealed that the structure of all three polypeptides is highly conserved between Rhodobacter and mitochondria (Gabellini and Sebald 1986), see Fig.3. The topology of the three subunits of the b/c_1 complex in relation to the membrane, as deduced from the hydropathy profiles of the amino acid sequence, is in agreements with the functional location of the three subunits. The cytochrome b is the most hydrophobic polypeptide of the oxidoreductase. The hydrophobic sequences of cytochrome b most probably form nine transmembrane segments in α-helical conformation, which are connected by hydrophilic loops. The cytochrome c_1 is bound to the membrane only through one hydrophobic sequence near the C-terminus. The FeS protein has a short hydrophobic "anchor" near the N-terminus. The two hemes of cytochrome b are coordinately bound between membrane spanning segment II and V by two pairs of conserved histidines (his-97, his-111, his-198, his-212). The histidines are separated by 13 amino acid residues in each helix. This spatial arrangement provides for a location of the hemes near the opposite sides of the membrane surface (Widger et al.1984; Saraste 1984).

The Fe2-S2 center is covalently bound to the sulfur atom of four conserved cysteines (cys-133, cys-138, cys-153, cys-155). The region including the FeS cluster is one of the most conserved parts of the oxidoreductase. This region of the FeS protein forms, together with the cytochrome b_L, the catalytic site (Q_z) for the oxidation of ubiquinol. The part of cytochrome b carrying the heme b forms the quinol reductase site (Q_c).

The catalytic sites for the electrogenic redox reaction with the quinone are most remarkably conserved between prokaryotes, mitochondria and chloroplasts. The reducing site of the oxidoreductase is not homologous in the two phylogenetic lines of photosynthetic bacteria and cyanobacteria. Thus only the topology of cytochrome c_1 and cytochrome f are conserved. The cytochrome c_1 of Rhodobacter is homologous to that of mitochondria. The heme is covalently bound two the sulfur atoms of two cysteine residues (cys-55, cys-58) located near the N-terminus. A histidine also found in this region (his-59) binds the heme iron. An additional bond with the heme iron is established through the sulfur atom of a conserved methionine residue (met-205). The topology of the heme ligands suggests that the membrane - bound cytochrome c_1 and the water-soluble cytochrome c are folded in a similar way (Dickerson and Timkovich 1975). The cytochrome c_1 of Rhodobacter is synthesized as a larger precursor. The N-terminal sequence of the mature subunit starts from the asn-22 of the DNA deduced sequence (Gabellini and Sebald 1986). The pre-apo-cytochrome c_1, includes a hydrophobic pre-sequence that leads the secretion of the polypeptide to the outer side of the cytoplasmic membrane. The three subunits of the b/c_1 complex from Rhodobacter are larger then the homologous subunits of mitochondria. The functional role of the additional sequences in the prokaryotic subunits could be analogous to that of the numerous small subunits of the mitochondrial oxidoreductase. Each of the three polypeptides encoded by the fbc operon include additional sequences carrying a number of charged residue, that could be involved in the interaction between subunits.

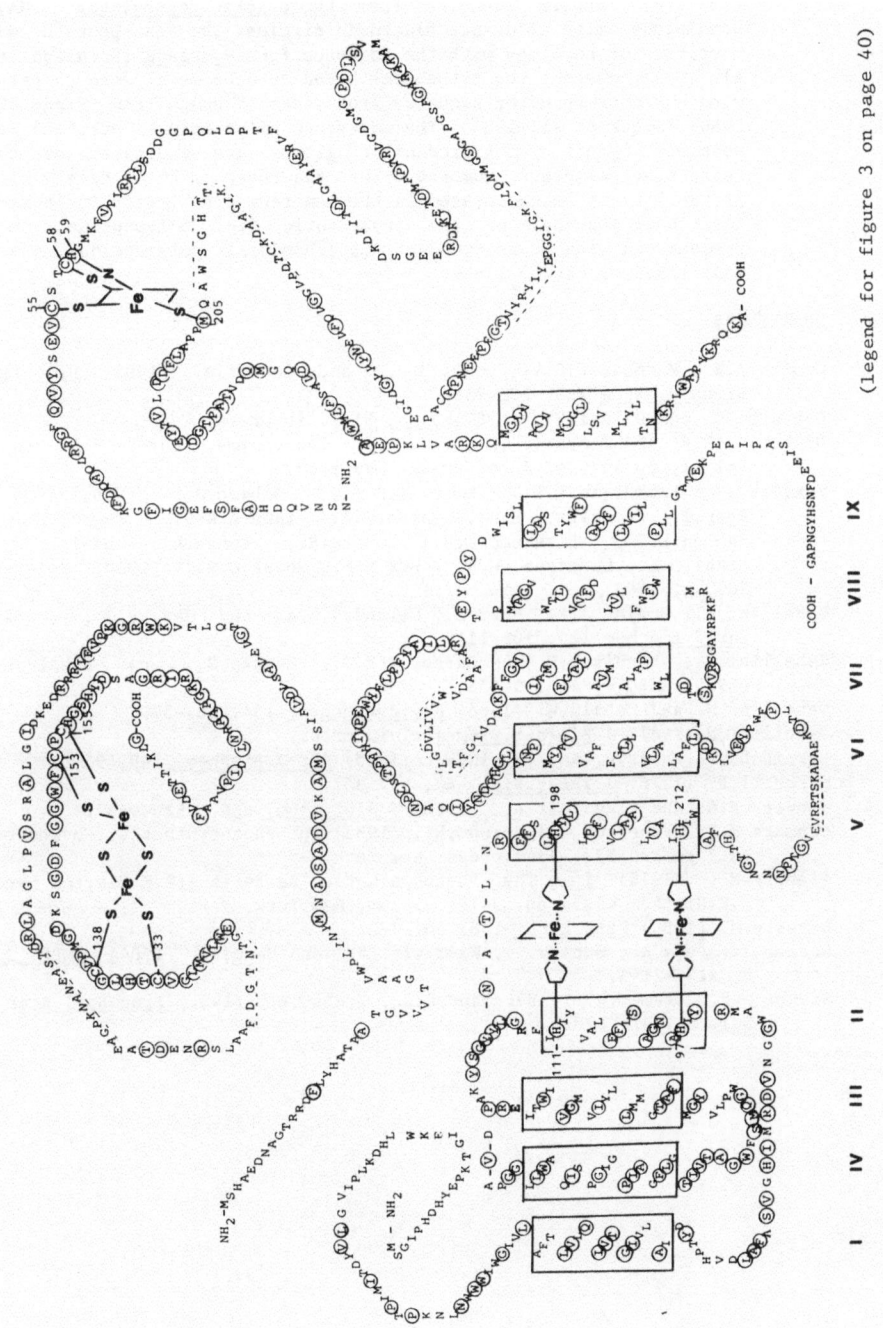

(legend for figure 3 on page 40)

39

Fig.3. Amino acid sequence, homology, topology and chromophore ligands of the b/c_1 complex subunits from <u>Rhodobacter capsulatus</u> (GA). Homologous amino acids are placed in circles. The FeS protein was compared for homology with the sequence from <u>N.crassa</u> (Harnisch et al. 1985), whereas the cytochrome b and cytochrome c_1 were compared with the corresponding sequence from yeast (Nobrega and Tzagoloff 1980; Sadler et al. 1984). The conserved amino acid identified as possible ligands of the prosthetic groups are indicated by the respective sequence numbers. The sequences that have high probability of being located in the membrane are placed in boxes. Additional sequences of the prokaryotic b/c_1 polypeptides, not present in the correspondent mitochondrial polypeptides, are underlined by broken lines.

REFERENCES

Crofts,A.R., Meinhardt,S.V., Jones,K.R., and Snozzi,M. (1983) <u>Biochim. Biophis. Acta</u> 723, 202-218.

Davidson,E. and Daldal,F., (1987) <u>J.Mol.Biol.</u> in press.

Dickerson,R.E. and Timkovich,R., (1975) <u>in</u>: The enzyme, (Boyer P.D. ed.) Vol 11, pp 397-547 Acad. Press, New York.

Fox,G.E., Stackebrandt,E., Hespell,R.B., Gibson,J., Maniloff,J., Dyer,T.A., Wolfe, R.S., Balch,W.E., Tanner,R.S., Magrum,L.J., Zablen,L.B., Blankemore,R., Gupta,R., Bonen,L., Lewis,B.J., Stahl,D.A., Luehrsen, K.R., Chen,K.N., Woese,C.R., (1980) <u>Science</u> 209, 457-463.

Gabellini,N., Bowyer,J.R., Hurt,E., Melandri,B.A. and Hauska,G., (1982) <u>Eur.J.Biochem</u> 126, 105-111.

Gabellini,N., Harnisch,U., McCarthy,J.E.G., Hauska,G., and Sebald,W. (1985) <u>EMBO J.</u> 4, 549-553.

Gabellini,N. and Sebald,W. (1986) <u>Eur.J.Biochem.</u> 154, 569-579.

Gabellini,N.(1987) <u>J.Bioener.Biomembr.</u> in press.

Harnisch,U., Weiss,H. and Sebald,W., (1985) <u>Eur.J.Biochem.</u> 149, 95-99.

Mitchell,P. (1976) <u>J.Theor.Biol.</u> 62, 327-367.

Nobrega,F.G. and Tzagoloff,A., (1980) <u>J.Biol.Chem.</u> 255, 9828-9837.

Okamura,M.Y., Feher,G. and Nelson,N., (1982) <u>in</u>: Photosynthesis (Govindjee ed.) pp 195-272, Acad.press. New York.

Pfennig,N., (1978) <u>in</u>: The Photosynthetic Bacteria (R.K.Clayton and W.R.Sistrom eds.). pp. 3-18, Plenum, New York.

Saraste,M. (1984) <u>FEBS Lett.</u> 166, 367-372.

Sadler,I., Suda,K., Schatz,G., Kaudewitz,F., and Haid,A., (1984) <u>EMBO J.</u> 3, 2137-2143.

Widger,W.R., Cramer,W.A., Herrmann,R.G., Trebst,A., (1984) <u>Proc.Natl.Acad. Sci.</u> 81, 674-678.

GENES AND SEQUENCES FOR SUBUNITS OF RESPIRATORY

COMPLEXES IN Paracoccus denitrificans

Bernd Ludwig, Barbara Kurowski,
Gunnar Panskus, and Peter Steinrücke

Institute of Biochemistry, Medical University
D 2400 Lübeck, West Germany

INTRODUCTION

The bacterium Paracoccus denitrificans has long been discussed in context of the evolutionary origin of mitochondria (1) based on a number of features suggesting its ancestral role in organelle formation. Recent studies indeed show surprising homology in molecular terms of respiratory chain components, notably its cytochrome oxidase and bc_1 complex, with the challenging fact that their subunit structure is much simpler than that of the corresponding mitochondrial complexes.

Cytochrome c oxidase from Paracoccus has been isolated as a two-subunit enzyme (for a review, see (2)) which is active in electron transport and proton translocation; recently, the gene for a third subunit has been identified (3). All three subunits were suggested to be homologous to the 3 largest, mitochondrially coded oxidase subunits of the mitochondrial enzyme. Similar considerations apply to the Paracoccus bc_1 complex. Only three subunits make up the complex: cytochrome c_1, cytochrome b, and a subunit presumed to bind the FeS center (4,5).

Here, we describe the cloning and sequencing of the genes for cytochrome c_1 and oxidase subunit II of Paracoccus and evaluation of the DNA deduced amino acid sequences.

METHODS

Two different Paracoccus gene libraries were constructed as detailed elsewhwere (6,7): one in the inducible expression vector pUC 8 (8) used to isolate the oxidase subunit II gene, the other in pBR 322 yielding the gene for cytochrome c_1. They were identified by an immunological screening procedure (6) using antibodies specific for the gene product of interest. DNA was sequenced according to the didesoxy nucleotide chain termination technique (9).

RESULTS AND DISCUSSION

Subunit II of the Paracoccus cytochrome c oxidase

The gene coding for subunit II of Paracoccus oxidase is isolated by screening for expression of the polypeptide in E.coli. An analysis of the size of the product after separation of a total host cell lysate by SDS polyacrylamide gel electrophoresis using specific antibodies for detection reveals three differently migrating bands; the fastest, faint component is identical in size to authentic subunit II (Fig. 1; see also below).

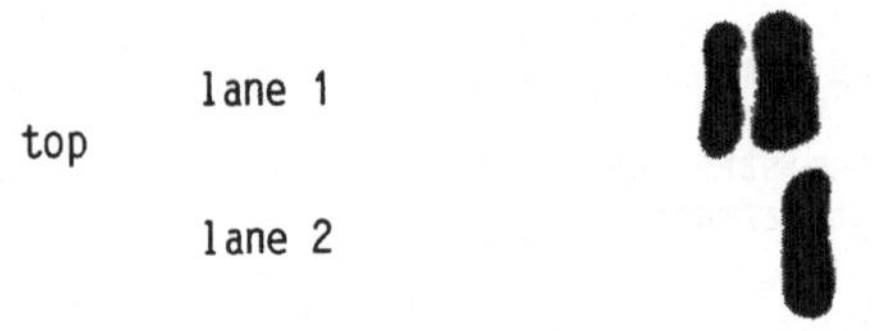

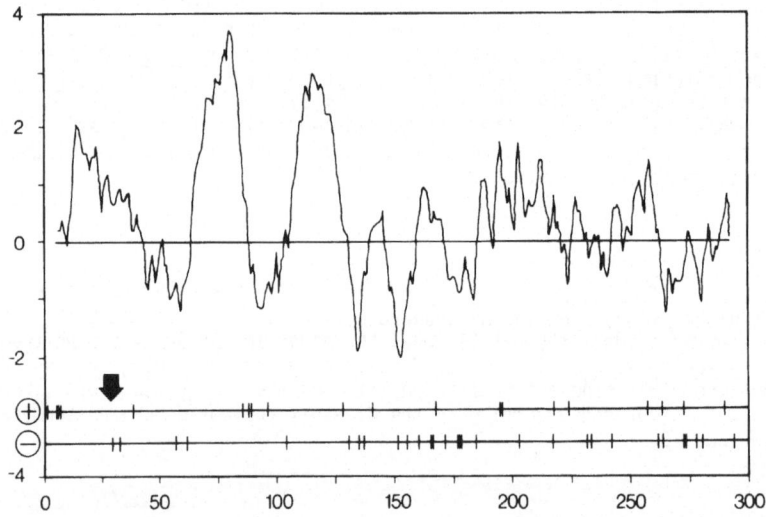

lane 1

top

lane 2

Fig. 1 : The gene for subunit II of the Paracoccus oxidase is
expressed in E.coli.
A total lysate (lane 1) of a recombinant cell harbouring the
subunit II gene was separated on a 12% SDS gel along with a
standard of authentic oxidase (lane 2); bands were detected
by specific antibody and (125)I-protein A .

Fig. 2 : Hydropathy profile of subunit II of Paracoccus oxidase.
Values for windows of 11 residues each were calculated
according to (10). Positive ordinate: hydrophobic character;
+/- : charge distribution; ↓ : signal sequence cleavage

The hydropathy plot of the DNA-derived polypeptide sequence is shown in Fig. 2. Two hydrophobic stretches of 22 and 23 residues (pos. 65-86, and 107-129) in the first half of the molecule strongly resemble the membrane topology seen for the mitochondrial subunit II where these two regions were found (11) to traverse the lipid bilayer as α-helices, with most of the remaining mass of the polypeptide exposed on the outside (for a review, see (12)).

Several other structural details are conserved in the bacterial subunit as well (see Fig. 3 and ref. (6)): 4 conserved residues (2 histidines and two cysteines; pos. 147,244,248,252) are presumed ligands to copper A. A cluster of aromatic residues (pos. 149-155) has been linked to electron transport functions of the subunit, 3 acidic residues (pos. 158, 206, 246) with the binding of cytochrome c; other acidic amino acids conserved in all mitochondrial sequences are not seen in Paracoccus, possibly the consequence of a different cytochrome c acting as electron donor to oxidase (see (13)).

Comparison of the DNA deduced amino acid sequence with that obtained from peptide sequencing (6) clearly shows that the Paracoccus subunit II is the product of N- as well as C-terminal modifications. The primary translation product comprises additional 28 amino acids at the N-terminus which show features characteristic of signal sequences (14). An empirically developed prediction for cleavage sites (14) is exactly confirmed by a mass spectroscopic analysis (6): it shows that the blocked mature polypeptide starts with a pyro-glutamate residue (formed from the glutamine) at pos. 29. On the C-terminus, 17 amino acid residues are removed from the primary translation product to yield the mature form as isolated.

So at least three different forms of the polypeptide have to be taken into account: the primary translation product (M_r = 32 473), an N-terminally processed form (29 715), and the polypeptide with both N- and C-terminus modified (27 999). Fig. 1 indeed shows 3 different bands expressed in E.coli which may represent these 3 forms mentioned.

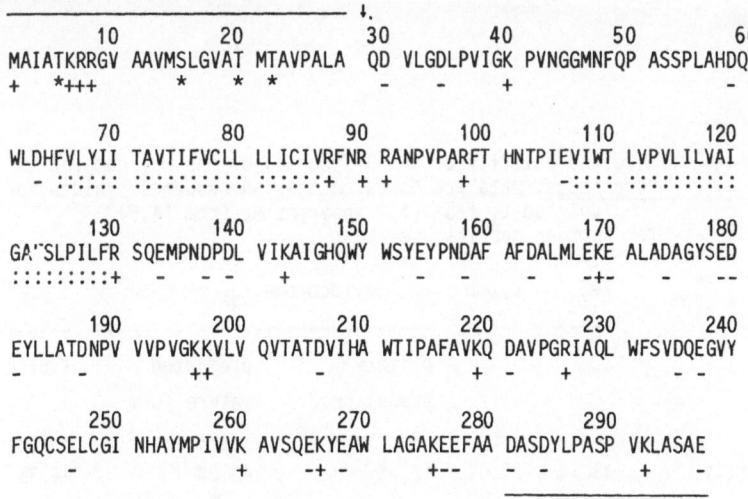

```
                                            ↓.
          10        20        30        40        50        60
     MAIATKRRGV AAVMSLGVAT MTAVPALA  QD VLGDLPVIGK PVNGGMNFQP ASSPLAHDQQ
     +  *+++      *    *   *          -     -     +                  -

          70        80        90       100       110       120
     WLDHFVLYII TAVTIFVCLL LLICIVRFNR RANPVPARFT HNTPIEVIWT LVPVLILVAI
      - :::::: :::::::::: ::::::+ + +     +         -:::: ::::::::::::

         130       140       150       160       170       180
     GA*SLPILFR SQEMPNDPDL VIKAIGHQWY WSYEYPNDAF AFDALMLEKE ALADAGYSED
     :::::::::+  -    - -   +        -  -        - -+-  -    --

         190       200       210       220       230       240
     EYLLATDNPV VVPVGKKVLV QVTATDVIHA WTIPAFAVKQ DAVPGRIAQL WFSVDQEGVY
      -      -       ++     -          + -    +       - -

         250       260       270       280       290
     FGQCSELCGI NHAYMPIVVK AVSQEKYEAW LAGAKEEFAA DASDYLPASP VKLASAE
       -             +     -+ -      +--   - -           +    -
```

Fig. 3 : Paracoccus oxidase subunit II amino acid sequence
         Arrow denotes signal sequence cleavage site; first
         residue in mature sequence is a pyro-glutamate.
         +/- : charged residues; ::: hydrophobic stretches
         * : hydroxylated amino acids within the presequence;
         solid lines: N- and C-terminal extensions

Cytochrome c_1

The cytochrome c_1 gene is part of the bc_1 operon (7) in Paracoccus. Based on DNA sequence, size and polarity of the 3 subunits, the FeS subunit, and cytochromes b and c_1, are given in Table I. Even though the apparent M_r of the cytochrome c_1 determined from gels represent an over-estimation, this bacterial polypeptide still is considerably larger than the mitochondrial c_1 (for a review on the mitochondrial bc_1, see (15)). The amino acid sequence of the Paracoccus c_1 (Fig. 4) may be divided into three regions:

1. appr. residue no. 220 to the end: a region of homology to other cytochromes c_1. As detailed in (7), there is excellent homology to the c_1 of Rhodobacter (16), but, except for the heme binding domain, rather poor analogy with the mitochondrial sequences, which again may be due to different electron acceptors present in Paracoccus. Within this region, a single hydrophobic domain near the C-terminus is evident (Fig.5), which may act as a membrane anchor, while most of the molecule is exposed on the outer surface of the membrane.

2. Amino acid position 46-197 (Fig. 4) represents a unique sequence of extremely monotonous character not found in any other cytochrome c_1. It consists of 40% alanine, 14% proline, 38% negatively charged residues (almost all glutamates), and does not contain any positive charge at all. Certain repeats within this sequence are obvious, such as a 14mer (pos. 141 and 174: APA EEA AAE EAP AE) and an 11-fold repeat of the trimer PAA. The highly acidic nature of this region directs attention to very acidic sequence regions of some of the smaller subunits found in the mitochondrial bc_1 complex (17,18); however, while the overall amino acid composition is analogous, no clear positional homology with any of the available sequences is obtained in a computer search. The structural and, moreover, functional role of this 150 amino acid long segment remains unresolved so far.

Table I : Size and polarity of the 3 subunits of the bc_1 complex in Paracoccus. Data are based on the DNA sequence, values for the isolated c_1 from (4), apparent M_r from (4,5); for further details, see text.

	FeS	cyt b	cytochrome c_1		
			primary transl.prod.	predicted mature form	isol.c_1
polarity	43.7%	27.0%	42.2%	43.2%	44.3%
no. of residues	190	440	450	426	
M_r from sequence	20302	50122	46879	44654	
app. M_r from SDS gels	20000	39000			60-68000

```
        10        20        30        40        50        60
MTLRNASLTAVAALTVALAGGAVAQDASTAPGTTAPAGSSYHTNEAAPAAADTAPAAEAA
 +                -              +  -        -      -

        70        80        90       100       110       120
DEPAAEEAEAGEAEVTEEPAATETPAEEPAADEPAATEEPDAEAEPAAEEAQATTEEAPA
--    --  --    --   --   --      --  -  - -   --      --

       130       140       150       160       170       180
EEPAAEEPAAEEPAEEPAADAPAEEAAAEEAPAEPEAAAEEPAAEEPEATEEEAPAEEAA
--    --   --  --   -   --     --   -  -   --   --  -  ---  --

       190       200       210       220       230       240
AEEAPAEEVVEDEAAADHGDAAAQEAGDSHAAAHIEDISFSFEGPFGKFDQHQLQRGLQV
--    --   ---   -+ -    - -+  + --     -     + - +  +

       250       260       270       280       290       300
YTEVCSACHGLRYVPLRTLADEGGPQLPEDQVRAYAANFDITDPETEEDRPRVPTDHFPT
 -     + +    +   --      -- +        -  - - ---+ +   -+

       310       320       330       340       350       360
VSGEGMGPDLSLMAKARAGFHGPYGTGLSQLFNGIGGPEYIHAVLTGYDGEEKEEAGAVL
 -     -    + +  +                   - +      - --+--

       370       380       390       400       410       420
YHNAAFAGNWIQMAAPLSDDQVTYEDGTPATVDQMATDVAAFLMWTAEPKMMDRKQVGFV
 +               --    --      -      -       - +  -++

       430       440       450
SVIFLIVLAALLYLTNKKLWQPIKHPRKPE
              ++       ++ ++ -
```

Fig. 4 : DNA deduced amino acid sequence of the <u>Paracoccus</u>
cytochrome <u>c</u>₁.

Table II : Signal sequence cleavage sites on <u>Paracoccus</u>
polypeptides facing the periplasmic space.
(pE : pyro-glutamate residue)

...AGGAVA ↓ QDASTAP...   cytochrome <u>c</u>₁ (hypothetical)

...AVPALA ↓ pEDVLGDL...   subunit II of oxidase (confirmed)

            pEDGDAAK...   cytochrome <u>c</u> (confirmed, (19))

...TAPATA ↓ NDSLVEL...   methanol-DH (confirmed; N.Harms,

                                           personal commun.)

45

3. The cytochrome c_1 sequence suggests the presence of an N-terminal extension as well. The hypothetical cleavage site according to general predictions (14) is arranged with sequences of other <u>Paracoccus</u> polypeptides with their N-termini facing to or exposed in the <u>periplasmic space</u> (Table II): this suggests a pattern of sequence requirements for recognition by a presumed signal peptidase.

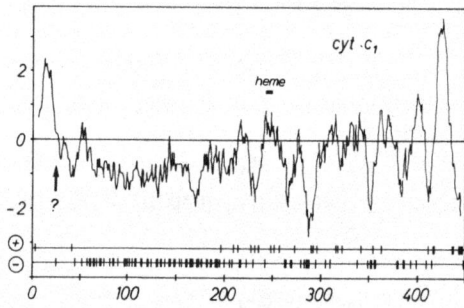

Fig. 5 : Hydropathy plot for the <u>Paracoccus</u> cytochrome c_1.
heme: site of covalent heme attachment; arrow: presumed
signal peptide processing site.

CONCLUDING REMARKS

With the availability of the genes and sequences for subunits of respiratory chain complexes of <u>Paracoccus</u>, we are not only able to confirm the previously assumed structural homology of these bacterial polypeptides with corresponding mitochondrial ones; due to their functional analogy paired with a quite simple subunit structure of the bacterial complexes, we should also be able to apply techniques of site-directed mutagenesis to learn more about structure/function relations in electron transport.

REFERENCES

1. P. John and F.R. Whatley, Paracoccus denitrificans and the evolutionary origin of the mitochondrion, Nature 254:495 (1975)
2. B. Ludwig, Cytochrome c oxidase in prokaryotes, FEMS Microbiol.Rev. 46:41-56 (1987)
3. M. Saraste, M. Raitio, T. Jalli, and A. Perämaa, A gene in Paracoccus for subunit III of cytochrome oxidase, FEBS L. 206:154 (1986)
4. B. Ludwig, K. Suda, and N. Cerletti, Cytochrome c_1 from Paracoccus denitrificans, Eur.J.Biochem. 137:597 (1983)
5. X. Yang and B.L. Trumpower, Purification of a three-subunit ubiquinol-cytochrome c oxidoreductase complex from Paracoccus denitrificans, J.Biol.Chem. 261:12282 (1986)
6. P. Steinrücke, G.C.M. Steffens, G. Panskus, G. Buse, and B. Ludwig, Subunit II of cytochrome c oxidase from Paracoccus denitrificans: DNA sequence, gene expression, and the protein, Eur.J.Biochem. (subm.)
7. B. Kurowski and B. Ludwig, The genes for the Paracoccus denitrificans bc_1 complex - Nucleotide sequence and homologies between bacterial and mitochondrial subunits, J.Biol.Chem. (subm.)
8. J. Vieira and J. Messing, The pUC plasmids, a M13mp7-derived system for insertion mutagenesis and sequencing with synthetic universal primers, Gene 19:259 (1982)
9. F. Sanger, S. Nicklen, and A.R. Coulson, DNA sequencing with chain-terminating inhibitors, Proc.Natl.Acad.Sci.USA 74:5463 (1977)
10. J. Kyte and R.F. Doolittle, A simple method for displaying the hydro-pathic character of a protein, J.Mol.Biol. 157:105 (1982)
11. R. Bisson, G.C.M. Steffens, and G. Buse, Localization of lipid binding domains on subunit II of beef heart cytochrome c oxidase, J.Biol.Chem. 257:6716 (1982)
12. M. Wikström, M. Saraste, and T. Penttilä, Relationships between struc-ture and function in cytochrome oxidase, in: "The enzymes of biological membranes", 2. edition, A.N. Martonosi, ed., Plenum Press, New York (1985)
13. E.A. Berry and B.L. Trumpower, Isolation of ubiquinol oxidase from Paracoccus denitrificans and resolution into cytochrome bc_1 and cytochrome caa_3 complexes, J.Biol.Chem. 260:2458 (1985)
14. G. von Heijne, Signal sequences - The limits of variation, J.Mol.Biol. 184:99 (1985)
15. Y. Hatefi, The mitochondrial electron transport and oxidative phospho-rylation system, Ann.Rev.Biochem. 543:1015 (1985)
16. N. Gabellini and W. Sebald, Nucleotide sequence and transcription of the fbc operon from Rhodopseudomonas sphaeroides, Eur.J.Biochem. 154:569 (1986)
17. S. Wakabayashi, H. Takeda, H. Matsubara, C.H. Kim, and T.E. King, Identity of the heme-not-containing protein in bovine heart cytochrome c_1 preparation with the protein mediating c_1-c complex formation - A protein with high glutamic acid content, J.Biochem. 91:2077 (1982)
18. A.P.G.M. van Loon, R.J. de Groot, M. de Haan, A. Dekker, and L.A. Grivell, The DNA sequence of the nuclear gene coding for the 17-kd subunit VI of the yeast ubiquinol-cytochrome c reductase: a protein with an extremely high content of acidic amino acids, EMBO J. 3:1039 (1984)
19. R.P. Ambler, T.E. Meyer, M.D. Kamen, S.A. Schichman, and L. Sawyer, A reassessment of the structure of Paracoccus cytochrome c_{550}, J.Mol.Biol. 147:351 (1981)

ORGANIZATION AND EXPRESSION OF NUCLEAR

GENES FOR YEAST CYTOCHROME c OXIDASE

Richard M. Wright, John D. Trawick, Cynthia E. Trueblood,
Thomas E. Patterson, and Robert O. Poyton

Department of Molecular, Cellular, and Developmental
Biology, University of Colorado, Boulder, Colorado, 80309

INTRODUCTION

In eukaryotes the assembly and function of holocytochrome c oxidase requires the protein products of both nuclear and mitochondrial genes[1]. Some of these genes provide protein subunits of the holoenzyme itself while others are required specifically for the biosynthesis or assembly of these subunits into a functional oligomer[2]. In the budding yeast Saccharomyces cerevisiae, three mitochondrial genes (COX1, COX2, and COX3) and six nuclear genes (COX4, COX5a, or COX5b, COX6, COX7, COX8, and COX9) encode the subunit polypeptides of the complex. COX5a and COX5b encode interchangeable isologs of subunit V, designated V_a and V_b[3-5]. All other subunits are specified by unique genes present in single copy on their respective genomes. Considering that nine structural genes in two different cellular compartments specify the subunit polypeptides of cytochrome c oxidase, the synthesis and assembly of the holoenzyme poses many interesting questions. Is the expression of this set of genes coordinated? If so, at what level (transcription, transcript processing, translation, or assembly) is their expression regulated? What is the nature of the intracellular effectors (metabolites, trans-acting proteins, etc.) that serve to modulate the level of each subunit and determine the overall level of holocytochrome c oxidase activity in cells? Are COX5a and COX5b expressed differentially and if so, do their protein products, V_a and V_b, confer different properties on the holoenzyme?

We are following two approaches to address these questions: one makes use of mutants[2,7,8] generated by the techniques of classical genetics; the other makes use of cloned genes[3-6,9-11] and reverse genetics. Although these studies are in their early phase, they have already yielded a number of interesting and, in some cases, surprising results. In this paper we will summarize some of these findings.

AT LEAST 38 NUCLEAR GENES ARE REQUIRED SPECIFICALLY FOR CYTOCHROME c OXIDASE BIOGENESIS IN YEAST

It has been clear for some time that only three mitochondrial genes - COX1, COX2, and COX3 - are specifically required for the biogenesis of yeast cytochrome c oxidase[12]. Through the use of a new screening method[7] and gene cloning techniques[3,4,9-11], we have begun to identify and characterize nuclear genes that are also specifically required for the biogenesis of yeast cytochrome c oxidase. These combined approaches have identified at least 38 nuclear genes (i.e., complementation groups) that are required. From Table 1, it is clear that these genes represent 3 different classes. Seven of them are structural genes for the nuclear-coded subunits. These will be discussed in more detail below. Seventeen genes are regulatory and encode *trans*-acting factors that are required for the specific expression of each COX gene encoded by mitochondrial DNA. Eight of these specifically affect the expression of COX1 only, three specifically affect the expression of COX2 only, three specifically affect the expression of COX3 only, and three specifically affect the expression of COX1 and COB, the mitochondrial gene encoding cytochrome b. Some of these *trans*-acting nuclear genes affect transcription, some transcript processing, and some translation[8]. The existence of these genes provides clear evidence that each of the mitochondrial COX genes can be regulated independently and that this regulation can be affected at any of the major steps in gene expression.

Table 1. Currently Identified Nuclear Genes (Complementation Groups) Required Specifically For The Biogenesis Of Yeast Cytochrome c Oxidase.

Complementation Group	Gene	Gene Product Or Phenotype	Ref.
I. Subunit structural genes.			
18	COX4	Subunit IV	2,22,31
19	COX5a	Subunit Va	4-6
35	COX5b	Subunit Vb	4-6
36	COX6	Subunit VI	9,23
-	COX7	Subunit VII	-
37	COX8	Subunit VIII	11
20	COX9	Subunit VIIa	10
II. *Trans*-acting genes that affect expression of COX genes encoded on mitochondrial DNA.			
1-8	NN[a]	Lack Subunit I	2,8
9-11	NN	Lack Subunit I and cytochrome b	2,8
12	PET111 }		2,29
13,14	NN }	Lack Subunit II	2,8
15	PET494 }		25
16	PET122 }	Lack Subunit III	2,8,26,27
17	PET54 }		28
III. Genes That May Affect Holoenzyme Assembly.			
21-34	NN	Have normal levels of subunits but no functional holoenzyme	2

Complementation groups 35-37 were constructed as null mutations of COX5b, COX6, and COX8 respectively by reverse genetics.

[a]NN - Not named; genes corresponding to complementations groups 1-11,13,14, and 21-34 have not been named yet.

The third class of genes (Table 1) contains 14 members[2]. These genes do not specify subunits of the holoenzyme or regulatory factors required for their synthesis but are, nevertheless, essential for the assembly of a functional holoenzyme. As yet, neither the products of these genes nor their mode of action have been identified. They may be required for a late step in heme synthesis that only affects heme $\underline{a}$ production, or for the synthesis of cardiolipin, a component of holocytochrome $\underline{c}$ oxidase. Alternatively, the products of these genes may affect the assembly of cytochrome $\underline{c}$ oxidase indirectly, by altering the lipid composition of the inner mitochondrial membrane (see ref.2 for discussion).

The large number of nuclear genes required specifically for cytochrome $\underline{c}$ oxidase biogenesis is surprising. Yet, it is clear (from the finding that many of the complementation groups identified by classical genetic techniques are represented by only one mutant[2] and from our failure to isolate mutants in the structural genes COX6, COX7, and COX8 by classical genetic techniques) that additional nuclear genes required for the biogenesis of cytochrome $\underline{c}$ oxidase exist. One class of genes that we are especially interested in finding are those that encode *trans*-acting factors required for the regulation and/or expression of the nuclear COX structural genes. As a prelude to searching for this class of genes, we have studied the organization and transcription of the nuclear COX genes.

ORGANIZATION AND TRANSCRIPTION OF NUCLEAR COX SUBUNIT STRUCTURAL GENES

As summarized in Table 2, COX4, COX5a, COX5b, COX6, COX8, and COX9 exist in single copy in the haploid yeast genome, are unlinked, and are present on different chromosomes. The transcription units for each gene have been characterized in detail recently (Fig.1). Like transcripts from many yeast nuclear genes, the 5' ends of these mRNAs exhibit microheterogeneity (indicated in parentheses in Fig.1). Based on the patterns of transcripts shown in Fig.1, it is possible to recognize three

Table 2. Saccharomyces Cerevisiae Nuclear Structural Genes For Subunits Of Cytochrome $\underline{c}$ Oxidase

Gene	Subunit	Copy No.[a]	Tentative Chromosome Assignment[b]
COX4	IV	1	VII or XV
COX5a	Va	1	XIV
COX5b	Vb	1	IX
COX6	VI	1	V or VIII
COX8	VIII	1	XIII or XVI
COX9	VIIa	1	IV

[a] Copy number has been established in 2 ways: the demonstration of a unique chromosomal location, by genomic Southern blot analysis (c.f., ref.9), and the demonstration that a null mutation within the gene produces a respiration-modified phenotype (c.f., ref.10).

b The localization of each gene to a chromosome or set of chromosomes has been determined by orthogonal-field alteration gel electrophoresis[13] and by establishing genetic linkage to known chromosomal markers (in the case of COX5a and COX5b).

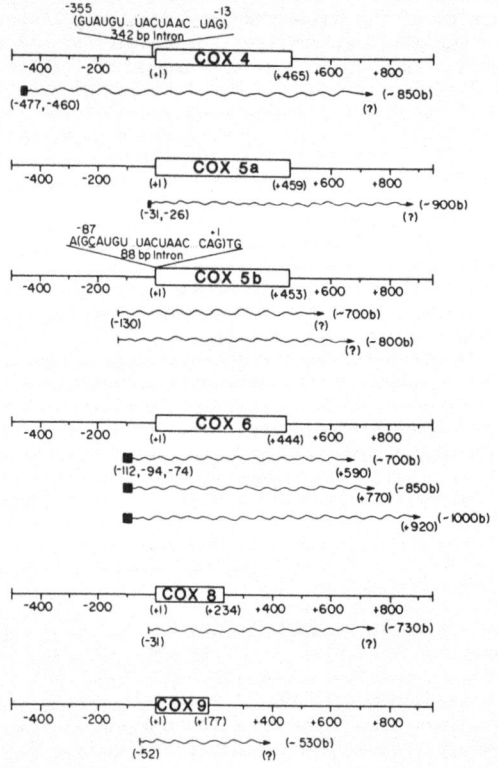

Figure 1. Transcripts from the nuclear COX genes in S. cerevisiae. The
coding region of each gene is boxed. The introns in COX4 and
COX5b are designated above each gene. Transcripts are given
below each gene as wavy lines. All numbers indicate distance,
in nucleotides, from the A of the ATG initiation codon. COX4,
refs.14,22; COX5a and COX5b, ref.5; COX6, ref.23; COX8, ref.24;
COX9, ref.10.

types of genes: 1) simple genes (COX5a, COX8, and COX9) that produce one
major transcript; 2) complex genes (COX5b, COX6) that produce multiple
transcripts; and 3) split genes (COX4 and COX5b) that contain introns. At
present, it is not clear why some of these genes are simple while others
are more complex, nor is it clear if the added complexity is important for
expression. In principle, the presence of introns and multiple 3' ends
could afford cells the opportunity to control the expression of these genes
at levels (i.e., intron removal, transcript termination) other than the
initiation of transcription.

EXPRESSION OF NUCLEAR COX SUBUNIT STRUCTURAL GENES

To determine if these genes are coordinately expressed, we have begun
to quantitate their transcript levels in cells grown under conditions that
are known to alter intracellular cytochrome c oxidase activity levels. So
far, we have studied the effects of glucose repression and heme depri-

vation. To assess the relative magnitudes of each effect we have relied on Northern blot hybridization followed by quantitation of counts in each hybrid and their normalization to the transcripts from the actin gene, a gene whose expression is presumed to be constitutive[15]. Heme deprivation leads to a 3 to 5 fold decrease in the expression of all genes except COX5b. Transcription of COX5b is increased substantially in the absence of heme (see below). Glucose affects the expression of these genes differentially. Under the conditions used in our studies, glucose does not appear to affect the transcript levels of COX4 or COX5b. However, it does repress the transcript levels of COX5a (about 1.5 fold) and COX6 (about 4.5 fold). In contrast, glucose stimulates the expression of COX8 (about 1.5 fold) and COX9 (3 fold).

These observations are somewhat surprising because they imply that transcription of the nuclear COX structural genes does not respond uniformly to glucose repression and heme deprivation. Moreover, they suggest that transcription of these genes may not be coordinated. Of course, the expression of these genes may be coordinated at some level (e.g., transcript processing, translation, holoenzyme assembly) other than transcription. It is also possible that common *trans*-acting factors govern their expression but act on them differentially[16,30]. Clearly, further study is required to identify how expression of these genes is regulated and to identify the factors involved.

COX5a AND COX5b ARE EXPRESSED DIFFERENTIALLY

COX5a and COX5b encode isologs of subunit V that are divergent in sequence but interchangeable as subunits of holocytochrome c oxidase[4,5]. To further analyze the differential expression of these genes, we have made use of gene fusions[5] to the lacZ gene from E. coli. So far, we have found that: 1) when yeast are grown aerobically on glucose, the expression of COX5a is substantially higher (25 to 55 fold) than COX5b, and 2) when yeast are grown aerobically in the absence of heme, COX5b expression is increased and COX5a expression is decreased[17]. When cells are shifted to anaerobic conditions COX5b expression also increases whereas COX5a expression decreases[18]. Since heme synthesis requires oxygen, it is possible that both anaerobiosis and heme deprivation affect the expression of COX5a and COX5b through heme availability. The differential expression of COX5a and COX5b could be advantageous if their products, V_a and V_b, confer functional differences on cytochrome c oxidase (e.g., altered Km for O_2 binding).

Although these findings clearly suggest that COX5a and COX5b are differentially transcribed, they do not preclude the possibility that other steps in gene expression (i.e., RNA processing and/or translational initiation) lead to the differential regulation of COX5a and COX5b expression. In this regard, it is interesting that the COX5b transcript has two features that the COX5a transcript lacks. COX5b mRNA contains an 88 base pair intron (Fig.2) that may be inefficiently removed due to an unusual 5' splice junction: GCAUGU rather than the consensus junction, GUAUGU[4]. The 5' end of the V_b mRNA also contains a short open reading frame 30 nucleotides upstream of the V_b initiation codon[5,6]. If ribosomes initiate at the first AUG and fall off at the stop codon, initiation at the second AUG may be inefficient. The significance of these differences is currently under study.

DISSECTION OF THE COX6 PROMOTER

As a prelude to identifying regulatory circuits and *trans*-acting factors that affect the expression of nuclear COX genes, we have begun to

COX5a mRNA

```
       -30                                      +1
  5' AACACAAGAUCAACUAAGAACGCAUCUACAAUG,UUA,CGU...
```

COX5b mRNA

```
                                -87                        +1
                               GCAUGU ... UACUAAC ... CAG
                                                88bp intron
       -129
  5' AAACUUUCACAAUG,GAA,UAACGCCACAUAUUCAUUGUAAAGAUG,UUG,CGU...
```

Figure 2. 5' nucleotide sequences of COX5a and COX5b mRNA. Whereas COX5a
         mRNA contains no introns COX5b mRNA contains an 88 bp intron
         that disrupts its initiation codon. In addition it contains a 2
         codon upstream open reading frame (in bold face).

dissect the promoter of COX6, through deletion mutagenesis. This analysis
has been confined to DNA sequences between the initiation codon (position
+1) and -600bp upstream of it, because a plasmid carrying the COX6 coding
sequence and this 5' flanking region is capable of normal expression. By
constructing Bal31 deletions in this region and assaying them, in a COX6-
lacZ fusion[6], for expression under repressing (glucose) and de-repressing
(galactose) conditions and under conditions of heme deprivation we have
been able to identify two domains that are important for COX6
transcription. One domain lies between -91 and -135bp. Deletion of this
region shows a loss of activity under all conditions assayed. Since two of
the three 5' - termini of COX6 mRNA (i.e., positions - 112, and -94, see
Fig.2) map in this region, it is likely to be required for transcriptional
initiation of COX6. The second domain is centered at -275bp and extends
from -259 to -323. Constructs that delete this region also show a dramatic
loss of activity. Shorter deletions within the region lead to only partial
loss of activity and to altered ratios of expression in the presence and
absence of heme or under repressing and derepressing conditions.

     Recently, several yeast promoters have been shown to have two types
of domains; those required absolutely for transcription and those required
for regulation of transcription[19-21]. The former include TATA boxes and
transcriptional start sites, like the COX6 domain that lies between -91 and
-135bp. The latter have been termed upstream activators (UAS) or
enhancers. These are frequently located between -250 and -300bp upstream
from the initiation codon, and work in both orientations. Moreover, the
distance between them and the transcription start sites can be varied
without effect[19]. To determine if the second domain (-259 to -323bp) for
COX6 satisfies these criteria, we constructed plasmids in which the
distance between it and the initiation codon has been reduced and in which
the second domain has been inverted. Both types of gene constructs are
subject to glucose-repression and respond to heme deprivation. Thus, it
appears likely that the second domain identified for COX6 is an upstream
activator (UAS). The sequence of this UAS is shown in Figure 3. Attempts
to further refine this domain are making use of shorter deletions within it
and computer similarity searches with UAS sequences from other yeast genes.
Thus far, the latter have failed to reveal any sequences that exhibit
significant homology with other well-characterized UAS sequences. Notable
is the absence of any sequences that exhibit homology with the UAS1 or UAS2
sequences that are important for the regulation of CYC1[30], the structural
gene for yeast iso-1-cytochrome c. Also of note is the absence of striking

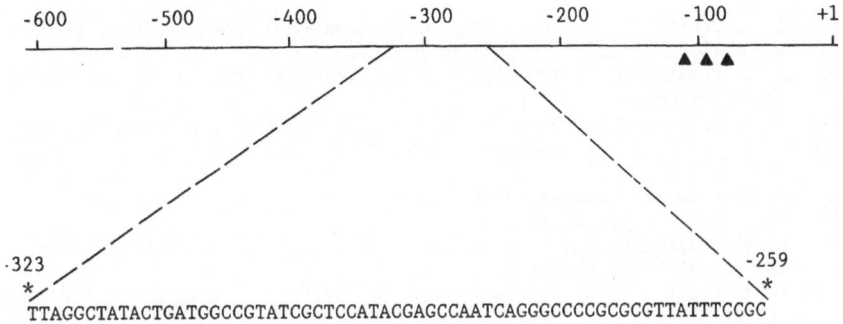

Figure 3. Location and sequence of a *UAS* region from the COX6 gene of
        Saccharomyces *cerevisiae*. The numbers indicate distance, in
        nucleotides, from the A of the ATG initiation codon. The major
        5′ termini of the COX6 mRNAs are indicated by triangles.

homology between the COX6 *UAS* and the 5′ flanking regions of the other
nuclear-coded yeast COX genes.

CONCLUSIONS

      From the results summarized here, the following conclusions can be
reached. 1) Each of the subunits, except V, of yeast cytochrome c oxidase
are encoded by single copy genes. 2) Two genes, COX5a and COX5b, encode
subunit V isologs, V_a and V_b. 3) COX5a and COX5b are expressed at
different levels and are effected differently by glucose repression and
heme deprivation. 4) Glucose repression and heme deprivation do not affect
the transcription of all of the nuclear COX genes in yeast uniformly. 5)
The COX6 promoter contains a *UAS* which has glucose repression and heme
deprivation-responsive elements but which does not exhibit any obvious
homology with *UAS1* or *UAS2* of CYC1. 6) The expression of the three
mitochondrial genes COX1, COX2, and COX3 may be regulated independently of
one another, by the *trans*-acting products of a number of nuclear genes. At
present, it is not clear if, or how many, nuclear genes specify *trans*-
acting factors that specifically affect the expression of the nuclear COX
genes. Also unclear is whether the expression of these genes is regulated
at some level other than transcription and to what extent their expression
is coordinated with the expression of the mitochondrial COX genes.

ACKNOWLEDGEMENTS

      This work was supported by grants GM 29838 and GM 30228 from the
National Institutes of Health.

REFERENCES

1. R. O. Poyton, G. Bellus, and A. C. Kerner, in: "Membranes and
      Transport," A. Martonosi, ed., Vol.1, pp.237-247, Plenum Publishing
      Corp., N.Y. (1982).
2. J. E. McEwen, C. Ko, B. Kloeckener-Gruissem, and R. O. Poyton, J. Biol.
      Chem. 261:11872-11879 (1986).
3. J. E. McEwen, M. G. Cumsky, C. Ko, S. D. Power, and R. O. Poyton, J.
      Cell Biochem. 24:229-242 (1984).

4. M. G. Cumsky, C. Ko, C. E. Trueblood, and R. O. Poyton, Proc. Natl. Acad. Sci. U.S.A. 82:2235-2239 (1985).
5. M. G. Cumsky, C. E. Trueblood, C. Ko, and R. O. Poyton, Mol. Cell. Biol., submitted (1987).
6. C. E. Trueblood and R. O. Poyton, Mol. Cell. Biol., submitted (1987).
7. J. E. McEwen, V. C. Cameron, and R. O. Poyton, J. Bacteriol. 161:831-835 (1985).
8. B. Kloeckener-Gruissem, J. E. McEwen, and R. O. Poyton, Current Genetics, in press (1987).
9. R. M. Wright, C. Ko, M. G. Cumsky, and R. O. Poyton, J. Biol. Chem. 259:15401-15407 (1984).
10. R. M. Wright, L. K. Dircks, and R. O. Poyton, J. Biol. Chem. 261:17183-17191 (1986).
11. T. E. Patterson and R. O. Poyton, J. Biol. Chem. 261:17192-17197 (1986).
12. A. Tzagoloff and A. M. Myers, Ann. Rev. Biochem. 55:248-285 (1986).
13. G. F. Carle and M. V. Olson, Proc. Natl. Acad. Sci. U.S.A. 82:3756-3760 (1985).
14. J. C. Schneider and L. Guarente, Nucleic Acids Res. 15, in press (1987).
15. E. Skekely and D. L. Montgomery, Mol. Cell. Biol. 4:939-946 (1984).
16. J. Verdiere and E. Petrochilo, Mol. Gen. Genet. 175:209-216 (1979).
17. C. E. Trueblood and R. O. Poyton, in preparation.
18. M. G. Cumsky, unpublished observations.
19. K. Struhl, in: "From Gene To Protein: Steps Dictating The Maximal Level Of Gene Expression," W. Reznikoff and L. Gold, eds., pp.35-78, Butterworths Publ. Co., Boston (1986).
20. K. Struhl, Mol. Cell. Biol. 6:3847-3853 (1986).
21. J. E. Ogden, C. Stanway, Kim Sunyoung, J. Mellor, A. J. Kingsman, and S. M. Kingsman, Mol. Cell. Biol. 6:4335-4343 (1986).
22. J. E. McEwen, unpublished.
23. R. M. Wright and R. O. Poyton, in preparation.
24. T. E. Patterson and R. O. Poyton, in preparation.
25. E. Ebner, T. L. Mason, and G. Schatz, J. Biol. Chem. 248:5369-5378 (1973).
26. B. Kloeckener-Gruissem, Ph.D. Dissertation, University of Colorado (1985).
27. B. Kloeckener-Gruissem, J. E. McEwen, and R. O. Poyton, Embo. J., submitted (1987).
28. M. C. Costanzo, E. C. Seaver, and T. D. Fox, EMBO. J. 5:3637-3641 (1986).
29. C. G. Poutre and T. D. Fox, Genetics 115:637-647 (1987).
30. K. Pfeifer, T. Prezant and L. Guarente, Cell 49:19-27 (1987).
31. W. Dowhan, C. R. Bibus, and G. Schatz, EMBO J. 4:129-184 (1985).

THE cDNA AND A STRUCTURAL GENE FOR RAT LIVER CYTOCHROME C OXIDASE

SUBUNIT VIc

Guntram Suske, Christel Enders, Thomas Mengel
and Bernhard Kadenbach

Biochemie, FB der Philipps-Universität
Hans-Meerwein-Strasse, D-3550 Marburg

INTRODUCTION

In mammalian tissues cytochrome c oxidase is composed of thirteen
different subunits (Kadenbach and Merle, 1981; Kadenbach et al., 1983;
Mariottini et al., 1986). The three largest subunits, which are responsible
for the catalytic functions, are products of the mitochondrial genome
(Anderson et al., 1981; Anderson et al., 1982), whereas the ten smaller
subunits are encoded by nuclear DNA and synthesized in the cytosol (Kadenbach and Merle, 1981; Wikström et al., 1981). The functions of these small
subunits still remain unknown, although regulatory functions were proposed
(Kadenbach and Merle, 1981; Kadenbach, 1986). For yeast it was shown, that
subunits IV and VIIa (yeast nomenclature) are essential for proper assembly
of the holoenzyme (Dowhan et al., 1985; Wright et al., 1986).

The genes for mitochondrial-encoded subunits I-III have been characterized and sequenced from many species (for review see Wikström et al., 1985)
but only for subunit IV and VIc (Kadenbach nomenclature) cloning of cDNA
sequences are reported from mammalian sources (Lomax et al., 1984; Parimoo
et al., 1984). In this paper we report the synthesis, cloning and sequence
analysis of cytochrome c oxidase subunit VIc cDNA and its use for Northern
blots, Southern blots and isolation of structural genes.

MATERIALS AND METHODS

Cloning of double-stranded cytochrome c oxidase subunit VIc cDNA

Double stranded cDNA to poly A^+ RNA from rat H35 hepatoma cells was
synthesized according to standard procedures (Gubler and Hoffman, 1983).
After addition of Eco R I linkers the cDNA was ligated to Eco R I-cleaved
and alkaline phosphatase-treated λ gt 11 DNA, packed into phage and amplified on E. coli Y 1088. Recombinant λ gt 11 phages were plated on a lawn
of E. coli Y 1090 to a density of 10 000 plaques per 90 mm plate and
screened with an antiserum to cytochrome c oxidase holoenzyme according
to Young and Davis (1983). The screening procedure with the monospecific
antiserum to subunit VIc was identical but we used only plaques which gave
already positive signals with the anti holoenzyme serum.

DNA sequence analysis

For nucleotide sequence analysis we subcloned the relevant DNA fragments into pUC8. The procedure for labelling 3' and 5' ends was as described (Maxam and Gilbert, 1980). The Maxam and Gilbert method was used throughout (Maxam and Gilbert, 1977).

Northern blot analysis

Whole RNA from various tissues of the rat was isolated according to Chirgwin et al. (1979). Poly A^+ RNA was obtained after passing through an oligo d(T) cellulose column. RNA was separated on a 1.5 % agarose gel containing 2.2 M formaldehyde and blotted to nitrocellulose filters according to standard procedures (Maniatis et al., 1982). Prehybridization and hybridization were carried out in 5 SSC, 5 Denhardt's solution, 25 mM sodium phosphate, pH 6.4, 0.1 % SDS, 250 μg/ml sonicated herring sperm DNA, 25 μg/ml poly A, 50 % formamide at 37°C overnight, using the nick translated cDNA insert ($1-2 \cdot 10^8$ cpm/μg).

Analysis of subunit VIc gene sequences in genomic DNA and recombinant phages

High molecular DNA (HMW DNA) was isolated and purified from cell lines and tissues according to standard procedures (Maniatis et al., 1982). HMW DNA and phage DNA were restricted and separated on 0.8 % agarose gels. After blotting to nitrocellulose filters prehybridization and hybridization was carried out as described above with the exception that in addition 10 % dextran sulfate in the hybridization solution was used for the analysis of HMW DNA.

Screening of the rat EMBL 3 library

The rat EMBL 3 gene library was screened by the in situ plaque-hybridization technique (Maniatis et al., 1982). Approximately 10^6 phage plaques were screened with the purified and nicktranslated cDNA insert (spec. act. $5 \cdot 10^7$ cpm/μg). Positive plaques were replated 3 times.

RESULTS AND DISCUSSION

Cloning of a cytochrome c oxidase subunit VIc cDNA probe

A first screening of 80 000 plaques with an antiserum to the holoenzyme and (^{125}J) protein A yielded 15 positive clones which gave reproducible signals. In order to identify a specific clone coding for subunit VIc, we used a subunit VIc-specific antiserum (Kuhn-Nentwig and Kadenbach, 1985) in an additional experiment. Four out of the fifteen clones showed signals with the antiserum to subunit VIc.

Fig. 1 shows the DNA sequence of the largest cDNA clone together with the deduced amino acid sequence. A comparison with the amino acid sequence of subunit VIc from bovine heart cytochrome oxidase (Erdweg and Buse, 1985) confirms that we have indeed cloned cDNA's coding for subunit VIc. This clone contains 292 bp including codons for 76 amino acids in an open reading frame starting with a methionine codon. The protein should therefore have 3 additional amino acids at the NH2-terminal end compared to the corresponding mature bovine heart protein which starts with a serine (Erdweg and Buse, 1985). A stop codon in phase eighteen nucleotides upstream of the first ATG codon indicates that subunit VIc is not synthesized as a larger precursor with an additional cleavable signal sequence at the NH2-terminal end. The nucleotide sequence overlaps with a previously published

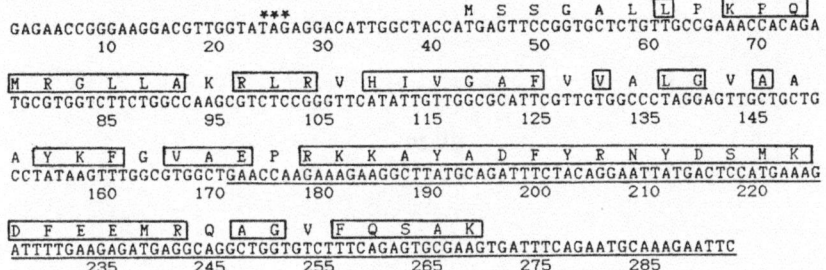

```
                        ***                            M  S  S  G  A  L [L] P [K  P  Q]
GAGAACCGGGAAGGACGTTGGTATAGAGGACATTGGCTACCATGAGTTCCGGTGCTCTGTTGCCGAAACCACAGA
      10        20        30        40        50        60        70

[M  R  G  L  L  A] K [R  L  R] V [H  I  V  G  A  F] V [V  A] L [G  V] A  A
TGCGTGGTCTTCTGGCCAAGCGTCTCCGGGTTCATATTGTTGGCGCATTCGTTGTGGCCCTAGGAGTTGCTGCTG
      85        95       105       115       125       135       145

A [Y  K  F] G [V  A  E] P [R  K  K  A  Y  A  D  F  Y  R  N  Y  D  S  M  K]
CCTATAAGTTTGGCGTGGCTGAACCAAGAAAGAAGGCTTATGCAGATTTCTACAGGAATTATGACTCCATGAAAG
      160       170       180       190       200       210       220

[D  F  E  E  M  R] Q [A  G] V [F  Q  S  A  K]
ATTTTGAAGAGATGAGGCAGGCTGGTGTCTTTCAGAGTGCGAAGTGATTTCAGAATGCAAAGAATTC
      235       245       255       265       275       285
```

Fig. 1. Nucleotide sequence of the subcloned cDNA insert coding for subunit VIc. The corresponding amino acid sequence is shown starting with a methionine. Amino acids which are identical to the bovine heart subunit VIc (Erdweg and Buse, 1985) are boxed. The nucleotide sequence which is identical to a previously published rat liver cDNA (Parimoo et al., 1984) is underlined. The stop codon in the reading frame preceeding the first ATG codon is marked by asterisks.

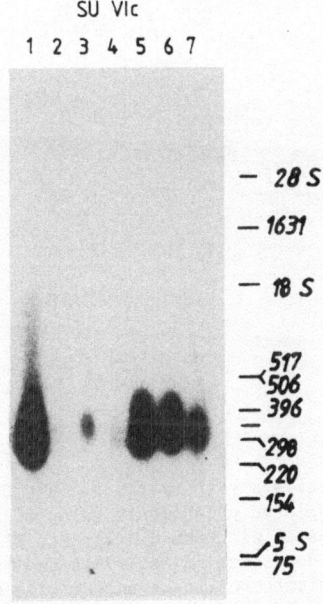

SU VIc

1 2 3 4 5 6 7

— 28 S
— 1631
— 18 S
⟨ 517
⟨ 506
— 396
⟨ 298
⟨ 220
— 154
⟨ 5 S
⟨ 75

Fig. 2. Northern blot analysis with whole RNA and poly A⁺ RNA from different tissues.

15 µg whole RNA from H 35 cells (1), rat liver (2), heart (3), kidney (4) and 3 µg of poly A⁺ RNA from liver (5), heart (6) and muscle (7) were separated on a 1.5 % agarose gel containing 2.2 M formaldehyde and analysed as described in Materials and Methods. The numbers on the right indicate the positions of nucleotide weight markers (pBR 322 DNA fragments obtained after Hinf I digestion and 28 S, 18 S, 5 S markers).

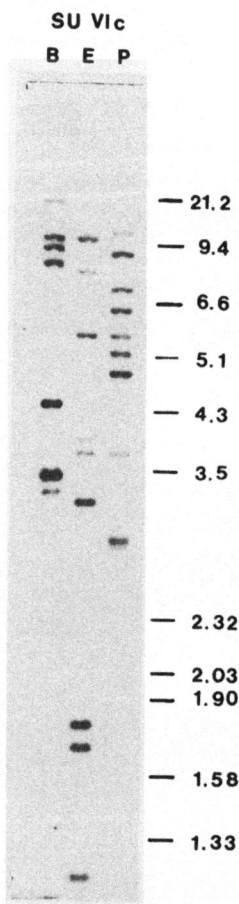

Fig. 3. Southern blot analysis with restricted HMW DNA from H 35 cells
and the nicktranslated cDNA insert as hybridization probe. 10 µg
HMW DNA was digested with Bam HI (B), Eco RI (E) and Pst I (P)
and analysed as described in Materials and Methods. The numbers
on the right indicate the positions of molecular weight markers
(λ DNA fragments obtained after Hind III and Hind III/Eco RI
digestion).

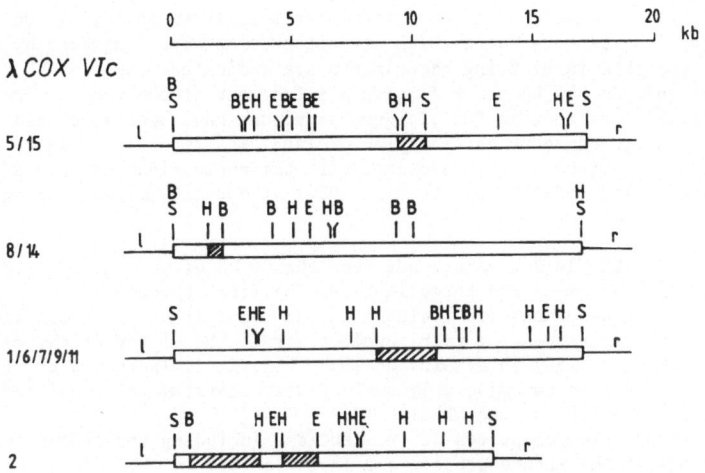

Fig. 4. Structure of recombinant phages that contain COX VIc sequences,
1 = left arm, r = right arm of the phage.
Abbreviations for restriction sites are: Bam H I (B), Eco R I (E),
Sal I (S), Hind III (H).
The hatched regions denote the presence of COX VIc coding sequences.
The 20 kb scale on the top is the reference scale in kilobases.

rat liver cDNA sequence (Parimoo et al., 1984) of subunit VIc which starts
171 bp downstream of the 5' end of our clone (see fig. 1) and extends 97 bp
to the 3' end. The comparison with this rat liver cDNA clone demonstrates
that the Eco R I site at the 3' end of our clone is an internal Eco R I
site and not an Eco R I linker sequence.

Northern blot analysis

To determine the size of the mRNA coding for subunit VIc we performed
Northern blot analysis with RNA from various tissues (fig. 2). The size
for the subunit VIc mRNA revealed to be 400 to 450 nucleotides. No significant size differences can be seen between RNA's from different tissues
(see fig. 2).

Southern blot analysis

To determine the number of genes in the rat genome coding for subunit
VIc of cytochrome c oxidase, Southern blot analysis was performed using the
nicktranslated cDNA insert as hybridization probe. Fig. 3 demonstrates that
the cDNA clone hybridizes with at least 8 restriction fragments of high
molecular weight DNA, indicating a multigene family.

Isolation and structural analysis of a cytochrome c oxidase
subunit VIc gene (COX VIc 2)

For the isolation of COX VIc genes a rat EMBL 3 gene library was
screened with the described cDNA. Out of $6 \cdot 10^5$ plaques tested, sixteen
independent phage clones were found after three plaque purification steps.
DNA was prepared from ten clones and further analysed.

A partial restriction map of the inserts is shown in fig. 4. Only four different inserts were found which did not overlap. The fragments hybridizing to the cDNA in blotting experiments are indicated. The 1.65 kb Eco R I fragment and the 3.5 kb Eco R I - Bam H I fragment of the lamda clone 2 (see fig. 4) that contain COX VIc gene sequences have been subcloned in pUC8 and their sequences partially determined. The results are shown in fig. 5. A comparison of this sequence with the nucleotide sequence of the cDNA (fig. 1 and ref. Parimoo et al., 1984) allows the following conclusions to be made.

(1) The COX VIc 2 gene extends more than 5 kb of genomic DNA and is composed of four exons and three introns. The first three exons and several kb 5' flanking sequences are included in the recombinant phage COX VIc 2. A fourth exon corresponding to 97 nucleotides at the 3' end of the mRNA (Parimoo et al., 1984) is missing on lamda COX VIc 2. Therefore the first and the fourth exon comprise only nucleotides referring to the 5' and 3' nontranslated region of the mRNA.
(2) The second exon comprises 130 nucleotides including the codons for 39 amino acids of the mature protein and 13 nucleotides of the 5' nontranslated region of the mRNA. There is a single nucleotide substitution (marked by an asterisk in fig. 5) compared to the cDNA which however does not change the amino acid sequence.
(3) The third exon comprises 129 nucleotides and encodes 37 amino acids of subunit VIc and 18 nucleotides of the nontranslated region at the 3' end of the mRNA.
(4) The 5' end of the first exon which corresponds to the cap site of the mRNA must be determined by S1 analysis or (and) primer extension experiments. Nevertheless several canonical "TATA" motifs are found in the region upstream of the first exon.
(5) The lengths of the first and the second introns are 843 bp and 3.2 kb, respectively. The length of the third intron is not known but is at least 500 bp. The exon-intron transitions agree with the canonical sequence 5' ex/GT...intron...AG/3' ex that has been found in most other eukaryotic spliced genes (Mount, 1982).

Taken all together the COX VIc 2 gene contains the typical features of a functional gene, so we conclude that this gene is expressed at least in rat liver.

Fig. 5. Sequence strategy and partial nucleotide sequence of the COX VIc 2 gene and its 5' flanking region.
A: Restriction map of the 5.2 kb region of rat DNA containing most of the COX VIc 2 gene. Only sites relevant to the sequence analysis are shown. The hatched boxes represent the first three exons of the COX VIc 2 gene.
B: Partial nucleotide sequence of the COX VIc 2 gene and its putative 5' flanking region. The sequence starts at the first Eco R I site shown at the left in A. The sequences which are homologous to the cDNA are underlined.
The single nucleotide change compared to the cDNA is marked by an asterisk. The region of the gene expressed into protein is shown by the corresponding amino acid sequence. Putative regulatory "TATA" sequences preceding the 1. exon are boxed. The exon-intron transitions are overlined.

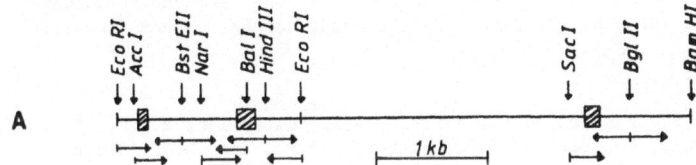

A

EcoRI / AccI BstEII / NarI BalI / HindIII EcoRI SacI BglII BamHI

1kb

B

```
GAATTCCTCAACATTGGGCAAGATTAATATTTGTAATTTATTTAAGGAATCTTTGTAGGTAGTCAGAACTCGTTT

TCAAGGTTCCACTTAGAAGAAAACCATAGTCCAGCTAATATAGGTTTCAGTTGTGACCAACTGGATGCGCGTTTG

TATACTTTTGAACTCCTTAGGCCACCGTCGCCGATTCCTCCATCGGCTCCTGCGCATGCGTGCTGCTAGGAGGCT

CTCCGTTTCTCCGAGAACCGGCAAGGACGTTGGTATAGAGCCTGAGAATGGTGGAGAGAGAGAGAGGAGATCCT

GGGGTTTGACAACTGTGGTTTTCGGCTTCTCGTGGGGCGGCGAACTAGGATTTGTTCCATGTCCCAGCCTAGTGG

AGCCGCGGGCCTGCCTTCCTCGTGGCCGCGCTTGTCCCCTCCGGGTCCTCAGGAGGCTGCGGGCTTGGTGGGCCT

GAGAGCTCGGGCGGCCCCGCTGTTTACCCGAGTGCGCTATCGGGGCCTTGGAGGAGCTCTGCGGAGCCTCTGGGC

CTCGCTGATGGCCGGCCGGGCCCGTTACCCGTTGTGTTTTGCTGCGGCTAGGGTGACCTTGATTGGGTCGTTGTA

CTTGTGGGGCCTGGTGCTCCACTTGGATAAGGGCTGCGATCTTGGAGGGGACGGAGGCACCCAGGGGCCCTGGTG

GTCGGCCTAGTGTGGAAGTAGAGCTGGGAAGCTGGAGGGTCCCCGACATGTCTGTCGCGCCTGCTCCACCGGCCC

TCGGGGCGCCTGCTGGGCCCCAGTTCCGCAGTCTCAGTGACCTGAGTTCTTACCGAAGACTTTTCTTAAGGGTAA

ATTCTGAAAAGGCTACAGCTAGGTCGCATCTGCCTTTCTGTAGATGGGGTATGACACTACTGTCGTAGTTTTTGC

GCATCGGTTGTGCCAGTTACCGCCTTGTTGGGGGTAATGGAACTATATAGGAGCGAAGCGGAACCGGCAAAGATA

AAGCTGCCCAAGTCACCGAAACCTTGCAGAAGTCAGTCCGCAGTTACTAAAATACGATGTGCACGTAGAGTTCAT
```
```
                                                                         M
TCAATCACTTACCCCATTCTCAGGCTTTTTTGTTTGTTTGTTTGTTTTACTTGCAAAGGACATTGGCTACCATGA
 S  S  G  A  L  L  P  K  P  Q  M  R  G  L  L  A  K  R  L  R  V  H  I  V  G
GTTCCGGTGCTCTGTTGCCGAAACCACAGATGCGTGGTCTTCTGGCCAAGCGTCTGCGGGTTCATATTGTTGGCG
                                                                       *
 A  F  V  V  A  L  G  V  A  A  A  Y  K
CATTCGTTGTGGCCCTAGGAGTTGCTGCTGCCTATAAGGTATGTGCTTGCTTGTGTGTGCTTTAGGTTACAAGGT

TTAAACCTAGTTTAAGAGCTTTTTAAAAAAGAAACTCCCATCTCTTAAGATATTCCCCTCTTTAAGCTTGGCCGTG

GGCCCCGTGTAGTTGACCCTATCTACAAATGGAGCTGTGTTTGCTATATCAAAGAACCAGGCCGAGTGGTTTAAAT

GCAGAAATTTGCTTTCTTACAGGGCTGTTTTTGAGATAGGTCTTACTATATAACCCTGCCTAGGCAAGGCTGGCC

AGGAGCTCATGTGATTTGCCTGCCTCTACCCCACAATGCTGGGATCAAAAGATGTGCACCACCATACTCCCAGTT

TTTAAGATCAAGGTTAATGCCTTCTGAATCTTTTCTTTTTTGCCTTCTTCCTTACATGGCCTTCTGTTACTGAAT

TC ........2.4 kb intron sequences .....................................

CCCACCCCCCCGTCTAGGAAATAGAGGGCTCAGTGAAGACAGAGCACAAGGATGCTCTTATTTTGTTCGTAAGTA
                                                          F  G  V  A  E  P  R  K
TTTCAAATAATCTGAAAAGTAAGTTCTATAATGGGCTATGTTACCTTTCAGTTTGGCGTGGCTGAACCAAGAAAG
 K  A  Y  A  D  F  Y  R  N  Y  D  S  M  K  D  F  E  E  M  R  Q  A  G  V  F
AAGGCTTATGCAGATTTCTACAGGAATTATGACTCCATGAAAGATTTTGAAGAGATGAGGCAGGCTGGTGTCTTT
 Q  S  A  K
CAGAGTGCGAAGTGATTTCAGAATGCAAAGTAATACAGTCTCTTGAAGTTATGCCTAAGAAATGCTTAACCAGT

GAGGTACAAAGTATCTTAATGTACAATTCGTAAGAACATGCTCCTTCTAGGAAGGAGCCCCATGCTGCCTTCTGAC

TGACAGTTAGTGCTTACTTCTTATGAATTGGTTCTCCCTTTTTCTTATTCTATGGGAGTATTGTACATGAATGCA

CGCCAGAGGGTGTCTTTGGAGTTGCTTTTCTTCCCACCCATTATATGGAACGGGTTTGCAGATCTAGGCAGAGAG

TGCTTTACCTGTTGGTCTTCGCTGGCCCTTTGTCAGTTTGTGACTGGCTTCAGTTAGTACACTGTTTGACATTTT

AGAAATCCCCTCCTTTATTAAGGCTGAAAATACTCCAATGTAGTTTCTGAGAATTGAATCTGGAGTATTGTGCAT

ACTTGGCAAACATTCTACCATTGACTACATCTTTGTTCTATATACATACATATGCACATATACATACATATCATA

TGTATACACACGGCACGGTTT
```

Acknowledgements: This work was supported by the Deutsche Forschungsgemeinschaft (DFG, Ka 192/17-2) and the Fonds der Chemischen Industrie.

REFERENCES

Anderson, S., Bankier, A.T., Barrell, B.G., de Bruijn, M.H.L., Coulson,A.R. Drouin, J., Eperon, I.C., Nierlich, D.P., Roe, B.A., Sanger, F., Schreier, P.H., Smith, A.J.H., Staden, R., and Young, I.G., 1981, Sequence and organisation of the human mitochondrial genome, Nature 290:457.

Anderson, S., de Bruijn, M.H.L., Coulson, A.R., Eperon, I.C., Sanger, F., and Young, I.G., 1982, Complete sequence of Bovine Mitochondrial DNA, J. Mol. Biol. 156:683.

Chirgwin, J.M., Przybyla, A.E., MacDonald, R.J., and Rutter, W.J., 1979, Isolation of Biologically Active Ribonucleic Acid from Sources Enriched in Ribonuclease, Biochemistry 18:5294.

Dowhan, W., Bibus, C.R., and Schatz, G., 1985, The cytoplasmically-made subunit IV is necessary for assembly of cytochrome c oxidase in yeast, EMBO J. 4:179.

Erdweg, M., Buse, G., 1985, Studies on cytochrome c oxidase, XI The Amino-acid sequence of Bovine heart Polypeptide VIc, Biol. Chem. Hoppe-Seyler 366:257.

Gubler, U., and Hoffman, B.J., 1983, A single and very efficient method for generating cDNA libraries, Gene 25:263.

Kadenbach, B., 1986, Mini Review. Regulation of respiration and ATP-synthesis in higher organisms: Hypothesis, J. Bioenerg. Biomembr. 18:39.

Kadenbach, B., and Merle, P., 1981, On the function of multiple subunits of cytochrome c oxidase from higher eucaryotes, FEBS Lett., 135:1.

Kadenbach, B., Jarausch, J., Hartmann, R., and Merle, P., 1983, Separation of mammalian cytochrome c oxidase into 13 polypeptides by a sodium dodecyl sulfate-gel electrophoretic procedure, Anal. Biochem., 129:517.

Kuhn-Nentwig, L., and Kadenbach, B., 1985, Orientation of rat liver cytochrome c oxidase subunits investigated with subunit-specific anti-sera, Eur. J. Biochem., 153:101.

Lomax, M.I., Bachmann, N.J., Nasoff, M.S., Caruthers, M.H., and Grossman, L.I., 1984, Isolation and characterisation of a cDNA for bovine cytochrome c oxidase subunit IV, Proc. Natl. Acad. Sci. USA 81:6295.

Maniatis, T., Fritsch, E.F., Sambrock, J., 1982, Molecular Cloning, A Laboratory Manual, Cold Spring Harbor Laboratory, New York.

Maxam, A.M., and Gilbert, W., 1980, Sequencing End-Labeled DNA with Base-Specific Chemical Cleavages, in: Methods Enzymol. 65:499.

Maxam, A.M., and Gilbert, W., 1977, A new method for sequencing DNA, Proc. Natl. Acad. Sci. USA, 74:560.

Mariottini, P., Chomyn, A., Doolittle, R.F., and Attardi, G., 1986, Antibodies against the COOH-terminal Undecapeptide of Subunit II, but not those against the NH2-terminal Decapeptide, Immunoprecipitate the Whole Human Cytochrome c Oxidase, J. Biol. Chem., 259:6564.

Mount, S.M., 1982, A catalogue of splice junction sequences, Nucleic Acids Res., 10:459.

Parimoo, S., Seelan, R.S., Desai, S., Buse, G., and Padmanaban, G., 1984, Construction of a cDNA clone for a nuclear-coded subunit of cytochrome c oxidase from rat liver, Biochem. Biophys. Res. Comm., 118:902.

Wikström, M., Krab, K., and Saraste, M., 1981, Cytochrome oxidase - A Synthesis, Academic Press, London.

Wikström, M., Saraste, M., and Pentillä, T., 1985, Relationships between Structure and Function in Cytochrome oxidase, in: The Enzymes of Biological Membranes, A. N. Martonosi, ed., 4:111, Plenum Publishing Corporation, New York.

Wright, R.M., Dircks, L.K., and Poyton, R.D., 1986, Characterisation of COX 9, the nuclear gene encoding the yeast mitochondrial protein cytochrome c oxidase subunit VIIa, J. Biol. Chem. 261:17183.

Young, R.A., and Davis, R.W., 1983, Yeast RNA Polymerase II Genes: Isolation with antibody probes, Science, 222:778.

GENETICS OF YEAST COENZYME QH_2-CYTOCHROME C REDUCTASE

Mary Crivellone, Alexandra Gampel, Ivor Muroff, Mian Wu, and Alexander Tzagoloff

Department of Biological Sciences
Columbia University
New York, N. Y. 10027

INTRODUCTION

It is now a generally accepted dictum that the maintenance of respiratory functional mitochondria depends not only on the expression of genes residing in mitochondrial DNA but also on a much vaster pool of genetic information provided by the nucleus. Respiratory defective mutants of yeast with lesions in nuclear DNA were first described by Sherman and Slonimski (1) and were named pet mutants. Such strains were shown in some instances to lack specific respiratory carriers such as cytochromes a, a_3, b, or c (2-4). More recently, a number of laboratories have amassed more comprehensive collections of pet mutants that have served as useful aids in probing questions related to mitochondrial metabolism, RNA processing, and synthesis of multisubunit enzymes with functions in electron transport and oxidative phosphorylation (5-7).

One such collection obtained in our laboratory is composed of several thousand independent non-conditional pet isolates which based on genetic crosses have been assigned to approximately 200 complementation groups. These strains, selected for their inability to utilize a non-fermentable carbon source (glycerol), describe a number of phenotypic classes, one of which is characterized by a deficiency in the respiratory complex coenzyme QH_2-cytochrome c reductase. In this article we report the properties of this class of mutants and where possible identify the gene products responsible for the phenotype.

Due to the complexity of the genetic system being analyzed, it is not possible to apply statistical methods to estimate the total number of complementation groups needed to saturate all PET genes (8). Our experience in working with the current collection, however, suggests that it is representative of most of the genes needed for respiratory competency in this organism. Thus, mutants in products predicted to affect respiration have generally been found, even when the gene has a small target size. The coenzyme QH_2-cytochrome c reductase mutants described here are therefore likely to define a nearly complete set of nuclear genes having direct roles in the synthesis of this enzyme.

STRUCTURE AND GENETIC ORIGIN OF COENZYME QH_2-CYTOCHROME C REDUCTASE

Coenzyme QH_2-cytochrome c reductase is an important member of bacterial and mitochondrial respiratory chains. Purified preparations of this complex from mammalian and fungal sources consist of at least eight distinct polypeptides (9-11). Three of the subunits have obligatory functions in electron transport; cytochrome b, cytochrome c_1, and a non-heme iron protein. The other five subunits (core 1, core 2, 17 kDa, 14 kDa, and 11 kDa) have no recognizable prosthetic groups and their functions remain largely unknown. This group of proteins will be referred to as the non-catalytic subunits. In contrast, the bacterial enzyme purified from P. denitrificans has been shown to be composed of only three subunits whose spectroscopic properties are similar to the three catalytic components of the mitochondrial complex (12). Although cytochrome b and the non-heme iron protein from both sources are nearly identical in size, the bacterial cytochrome c_1 is some 30 kDa larger than the mitochondrial protein (Table I). Even if it is assumed that bacterial cytochrome c_1 is fused to one or more of the non-catalytic subunits, the size increment is not sufficient to account for all the compositional differences between the two enzymes.

Table 1. Subunit Compositions of Yeast and Bacterial
Coenzyme QH_2-cytochrome c Reductases

S. cerevisiae[a]	P. denitrificans[b]
cytochrome b (44 kDa)	cytochrome b (39 kDa)
cytochrome c_1 (30 kDa)	cytochrome c_1 (62 kDa)
non-heme iron (20 kDa)	non-heme iron (19 kDa)
core 1 (44 kDa)	
core 2 (40 kDa)	
17 kDa	
14 kDa	
11 kDa	

[a] ref. 10; [b] ref. 12

In all higher and lower eukaryotes studied to date, cytochrome b is the only mitochondrially encoded constituent of coenzyme QH_2-cytochrome c reductase. The remaining seven subunits are products of nuclear DNA. All the yeast genes have been cloned and the sequences of the proteins derived from the genes (13-16).

STRUCTURE OF THE YEAST CYTOCHROME B GENE AND PROCESSING OF THE TRANSCRIPT

The structure and expression of the yeast mitochondrial cytochrome b gene has been extensively studied (17-20) and as a consequence a great deal of information has been obtained about the sequence of events leading to the synthesis of the active protein. Two structurally different forms of the gene have been described, each occuring in laboratory stocks of S. cerevisiae. The more simple form commonly referred to as the "short" gene is depicted in Fig. 1. It is organized in

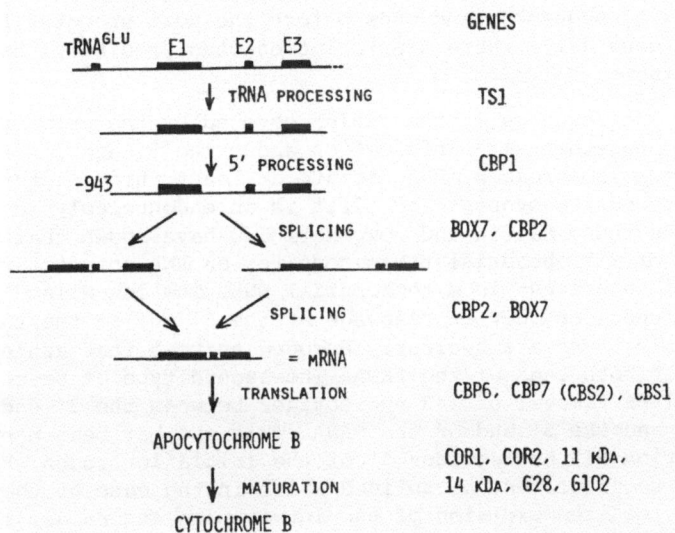

Fig. 1. Mitochondrial and nuclear genes involved in synthesis of cyto-chrome b. The three exons (E1, E2, E3) of the short gene are drawn as solid bars. TS1 is a mitochondrial locus that codes for a 9S RNA required for 5' processing of tRNAs. BOX7 refers to the maturase encoded by the reading frame in the first intron. The other genes are located in nuclear DNA. CPB1 and CBP2 function in 5' processing and splicing of the second intervening sequence, respectively. CBP6, CBP7 or CBS2, and CBS1 are needed for trans-lation of the mRNA. Mutations in the 44 kDa (COR1), 40 kDa (COR 2), 14 kDa, and 11 kDa subunits prevent maturation of apocyto-chrome b. This phenotype is also seen in mutants of complementa-tion groups G28 and G102.

three exons and two introns. The first intron has a reading frame contiguous with the coding sequence of the upstream exon. The single reading frame made up of both exon and intron sequences has been shown to code for a maturase essential for processing of the first IVS in the pre-mRNA (19). A more com-plex variant ("long" gene) found in other strains of yeast has three additional introns all located within the region corres-ponding to the first exon of the short gene (18). Since the parental strain of yeast (D273-10B) used to isolate the pet mutants harbors a short gene, our discussion here will concentrate on those genetic elements that control expression of this particular variant. There is evidence, however, that additional gene products are required for processing of the pre-mRNA transcribed from the long gene (5, 18-20).

Most of the genetic information of the yeast mitochondrial genome is transcribed on polycistronic RNAs that undergo multiple processing steps to yield the mature mRNAs, tRNAs, and rRNAs. This is also true of the cytochrome b gene. As shown in Fig. 1, the promoter used to transcribe this region is located 5' to the glutamyl tRNA gene which lies some 1.1 kb upstream of the cytochrome b initiation codon. The primary transcript therefore contains both the tRNA and the cytochrome b coding sequences and ends before the next promoter for the olil gene (21); where transcription ends precisely, however, is not known.

The sequence of the region covered by the primary transcript together with information about the 5' and 3' ends of the mature cytochrome b mRNA dictate at least three different kinds of processing events. The first is an endonucleolytic excision of the tRNA. Martin and coworkers (22) have shown that maturation of mitochondrial tRNAs requires an RNA cofactor whose gene (TS1) is present in mitochondrial DNA. The low-molecular weight RNA functions only in cleavage at the 5' end of the tRNA. Presumably there are nuclearly encoded enzymes that achieve cleavage at both ends of the tRNA. The second type of processing involves removal of 143 nucleotides between the 3' end of the tRNA and the 5' end of the mRNA. This end has been mapped to a position 943 nucleotides 5' of the initiation codon. Finally, the precursor must be spliced which in the case of the short gene requires excision of two intervening sequences. There may be still another step leading to cleavage at the 3' end of the pre-mRNA, although this is likely to be catalyzed by a general 3' processing enzyme.

NUCLEAR MUTANTS DEFECTIVE IN PROCESSING OF THE CYTOCHROME B PRE-mRNA

The coenzyme QH_2-cytochrome c reductase deficiency of pet mutants of two complementation groups (G36, G60) has been correlated with their failure to correctly process the cytochrome b pre-mRNA. Northern hybridization analysis of mitochondrial RNA of G60 mutants indicate an almost complete absence of cytochrome b transcripts. This phenotype is induced by mutations in a nuclear gene (CBP1) whose product probably cleaves the pre-mRNA at the -943 site and confers stability on the mRNA (23). The mutational block can be alleviated by a rearrangement in mitochondrial DNA (ρ^- genome) in which the normal untranslated leader is deleted and the gene is fused to the leader of the downstream olil gene (23). The ρ^- suppressor overrides cbp1 mutations by permitting synthesis of a new mRNA with a stable olil leader.

The other class of processing defective mutants (G36) lacks

cytochrome b mRNA and accumulates a longer transcript that has been shown to be a splicing intermediate with an intact terminal IVS. This nuclear gene (CBP2) codes for a protein with an accessory function in excision of the terminal IVS from the pre-mRNA (24). Again, the respiratory deficiency of cbp2 mutants can be suppressed by a mutation in mitochondrial DNA causing a precise loss of the last intron from the gene (25).

Even though mutations in CBP2 block in vivo splicing of the IVS, this is not true when splicing is assayed in vitro under the conditions of Cech and coworkers (26). Both the native precursor and an SP6 generated substrate containing the entire 5' exon (E2), the intervening sequence (IVS) and part of the 3' exon (E3) self-splice efficiently in the absence of added protein factors (Fig. 2). Analysis of the linear IVS and of the E2-E3 ligation products has confirmed that the autocatalytic reaction is accurate with splice sites matching those of the cytochrome b mRNA (27). As seen in Fig. 2, a substrate with an intron mutation previously found to prevent in vivo processing also blocks excision of the IVS in vitro. This suggests that the basic chemistry by which excision of the IVS takes place in vivo and in vitro is probably identical. In vivo, however, this reaction is strictly dependent on the product of the CBP2 gene. Whether the CBP2 protein stabilizes a splicing-competent secondary structure in the RNA or has some other function is not clear at present.

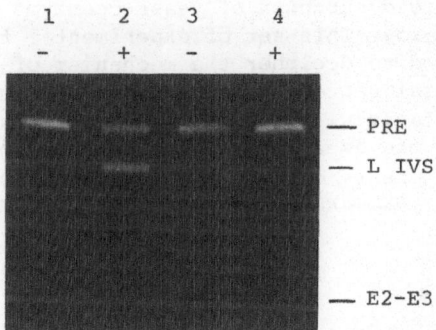

Fig. 2. Self-splicing of the cytochrome b terminal IVS. A 928 bp region of yeast mitochondrial DNA spanning the entire last intron and flanking exon sequences of the cytochrome b gene was cloned in pSP65. The identical regions were cloned from wild type yeast (D273-10B) and from the mit⁻ mutant M6-200 with an intron mutation blocking in vivo processing of the IVS (28). The RNA substrates transcribed from the two constructs were assayed in the absence (-) or presence (+) of 0.2mM GTP and all the other components shown to be necessary for self-splicing of the Tetrahymena rRNA IVS (26). Lanes 1, 2: wild type substrate; lanes 3, 4: mutant substrate. The migrations of the substrates (PRE), of the excised linear IVS (L IVS) and of the ligated exons (E2-E3) are marked in the margin.

MUTATIONS AFFECTING TRANSLATION OF CYTOCHROME B mRNA

Nuclear genes are important not only for processing of

the cytochrome b pre-mRNA but also play a role in facilitating translation of the mRNA. One such gene (CBP6) codes for a low-molecular weight protein which stimulates synthesis of the apoprotein (29). Mutants in this gene have wild-type concentrations of cytochrome b mRNA but are impaired in their ability to synthesize the protein. A similar but not identical phenotype is seen in strains of complementation group G162. These pet mutants are defective in processing the first intervening sequence. The phenotype can be explained either by a translational defect preventing expression of the maturase encoded in the first intron or by a direct requirement of the protein in RNA splicing. The responsible gene (CBP7) is probably identical to CBS2 whose product has been proposed by Rödel et al (30) to enhance translation of the maturase encoded by the cytochrome b pre-mRNA. These authors have described yet another gene (CBS1) with a similar role (30). It appears therefore that at least three different nuclear gene products promote translation of either the pre-mRNA or of the fully processed mRNA. A similar situation exists in the case of mitochondrial mRNAs coding for subunits of cytochrome oxidase whose translation is also contingent on specific PET products (31,32).

PHENOTYPES OF MUTANTS IN THE STRUCTURAL SUBUNITS OF COENZYME QH₂-CYTOCHROME C REDUCTASE

In the past few years combined efforts in several laboratories have led to the isolation and description of all the nuclearly encoded subunits of yeast coenzyme QH_2-cytochrome c reductase (13-15). This set of experimental tools is currently being exploited to decipher the mechanism of assembly of the complex. Several approaches have been used in our studies to screen for mutants with lesions in various subunits of the complex. With the exception of the 17 kDa subunit, mutants in the other components of the complex have been identified. These data are summarized in Table 2. The structural gene

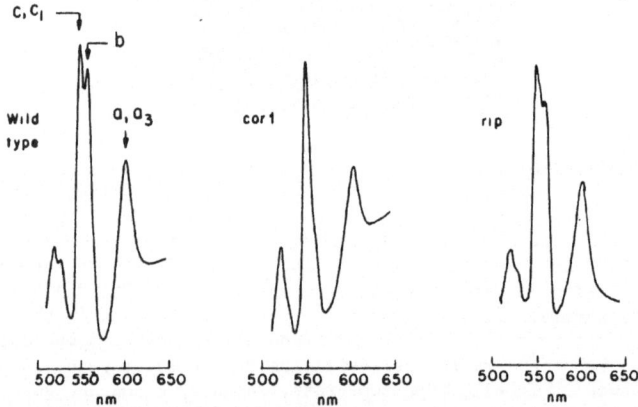

Fig. 3. Absorption spectra of mitochondria from wild type, a core 1 (cor1), and a non-heme iron (rip) mutant. Spectra were recorded at room temperature. The positions of α-absorption bands of cytochromes a, a_3, b, c_1, and c are marked.

mutants fall into two distinct spectral types illustrated in Fig. 3. Mutants with lesions in the non-catalytic subunits exhibit a deficiency in the absorption bands of cytochrome $\underline{b}$. The second type exemplified by cytochrome $\underline{c_1}$ and non-heme iron mutants have reduced but spectrally detectable amounts of cytochrome $\underline{b}$.

Table 2

Phenotypes of Coenzyme QH_2-cytochrome $\underline{c}$ Reductase Mutants

Group	Gene	Product	Phenotype	
			Cyt. b mRNA	Hemoprotein
G60	CBP1	5' processing	-	-
G36	CBP2	RNA splicing	-	-
G154	CBP6	trans. of mRNA	+	-
G162	CBP7	trans. of pre-mRNA	+/-	-
G7	COR1	44 kDa core 1	+	-
G144	COR2	40 kDa core 2	+	-
G67		14 kDa subunit	+	-
G153		11 kDa subunit	+	-
G101	CYT1	cytochrome c_1	+	+/-
G12	RIP	non-heme iron	+	+
G28		39 kDa protein	+	-
G102		20 kDa protein	+	-

Mutations in the structural subunits of the complex exert different effects on the levels of immunologically detectable apocytochrome $\underline{b}$ (Fig. 4). Except for non-heme iron mutants which have wild type amounts of the apoprotein, all the other mutants show variable but substantial decreases of apocytochrome $\underline{b}$. Whether this is due to proteolytic degradation or lowered rates of synthesis has not been determined. The former explanation seems more likely since the apoprotein appears to be synthesized normally in mutants pulse-labeled $\underline{in\ vivo}$ in the presence of cycloheximide. The nuclear mutants as well as a mitochondrial mutant in cytochrome $\underline{b}$ also display uniformly reduced levels of the non-heme iron protein.

Because the decrease in the non-heme iron protein is so uniform in the strains examined, we favor the idea that this is the result of proteolytic breakdown rather than an effect on the synthetic rate. The latter possibility, however, cannot be excluded. The other four subunits probed with antibodies (core 1, core 2, non-heme iron protein, cytochrome c_1) are present at concentrations comparable to those seen in the wild type strain (Fig. 4). These results are qualitatively similar to what has been reported by Schoppink et al (33) who also have noted reductions of the non-heme iron protein and of cytochrome $\underline{b}$ in strains with mutations in COR2, the 14 kDa, and the 11 kDa subunit genes. The observed reduction of cytochrome $\underline{b}$ and of the non-heme iron protein in strains carrying mutations in the non-catalytic subunits suggests that this set of proteins interacts with the two catalytic components to form a core structure which in the case of apocytochrome $\underline{b}$ is necessary either for heme attachment and/or protection against proteolysis.

MUTATION

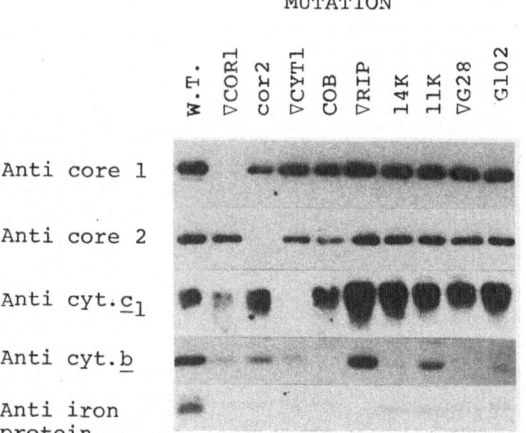

Fig. 4. Western blot analysis of mitochondria from wild type and from different coenzyme QH_2-cytochrome $\underline{c}$ reductase mutants. Total mitochondrial proteins (40 µg) were separated electrophoretically on 12% polyacrylamide gels, transferred to nitrocellulose sheets, and reacted with antibodies against core 1, core 2, cytochrome $\underline{b}$, cytochrome $\underline{c}_1$, and the non-heme iron protein. Antibody-antigen complexes were visualized autoradiographically following a second reaction with ^{125}I-protein A. The strains examined had mutations in core 1 (∇COR1), core 2 (cor2), non-heme iron protein (∇RIP), cytochrome $\underline{b}$ (COB), cytochrome $\underline{c}_1$ (∇CYT1), the 14 kDa subunit (14K), the 11 kDa subunit (11K), and the genes of two other cytochrome $\underline{b}$ deficient complementation groups (G28 and G102).

MUTATIONS IN NON-STRUCTURAL MEMBRANE PROTEINS

In addition to the mutants described in the previous sections, two other complementation groups (G28, G102) were found to be comprised of cytochrome $\underline{b}$ deficient mutants. The phenotype of these strains is very similar to that seen in mutants with lesions in the non-catalytic subunits of the complex. They lack spectrally measurable cytochrome $\underline{b}$ and have virtually no apocytochrome $\underline{b}$ when analyzed by Western blotting (see Fig. 4). In vivo labeling of mitochondrial translation products, however, indicates that mutants of both complementation groups are capable of synthesizing the apoprotein. The similarity in phenotype extends to the other subunits as well. While there is no significant difference in the mitochondrial content of the two core proteins and of cytochrome $\underline{c}_1$, both groups of mutants have highly reduced concentrations of the non-heme iron protein.

The nuclear genes defined by complementation groups G28 and G102 have been cloned and their sequences determined. The derived proteins sequences are not homologous to any proteins in the current banks. Although both proteins are tightly associated with the membrane, they do not appear to be subunits of yeast coenzyme QH_2-cytochrome c reductase. Antibodies against the G28 and G102 proteins react with membrane components of sizes predicted by the gene sequences but do not recognize any components of purified coenzyme QH_2-cytochrome c reductase. The phenotype of G28 and G102 mutants implies that the products encoded by these genes are also essential for the assembly of the complex, even though they are not integral constituents of the enzyme.

COENZYME QH_2-CYTOCHROME C REDUCTASE MUTANTS WITH WILD TYPE SPECTRAL PROPERTIES

The last groups of mutants we wish to mention have a normal cytochrome spectrum but do not catalyze the oxidation of coenzyme QH_2. Several complementation groups with this phenotype have been found. Not all strains in the collection have been assayed for this activity and therefore the actual number of groups with this phenotype may be larger. Even though the mutants have not been studied, it is not surprising that the synthesis of a functional complex may depend on proteins other than those already described. For example, the formation of the iron-sulfur prosthetic group in the non-heme iron component could be an enzyme catalyzed process. The catalytic efficiency of the complex could also be affected by still unrecognized regulatory or structural elements in the membrane. Whatever their functions, it is clear that the genetic contribution of nuclear DNA is even more extensive than indicated by mutants with gross aberrations in the properties of the enzyme.

CONCLUDING COMMENTS

The utility of yeast pet mutants for investigations of mitochondrial biogenesis is only now beginning to be exploited. The coenzyme QH_2-cytochrome c reductase defective strains reported here shed light on several aspects of the assembly of this inner membrane enzyme. First, they show the synthesis of cytochrome b to be dependent on an unexpectedly large number of nuclear gene products acting at the levels of processing of the pre-mRNA, translation of the mRNA (or pre-mRNA), and maturation of the apoprotein to form the mature cytochrome. Two such genes have been found to code for protein factors essential for translation of the intron-encoded maturase as well as of the apocytochrome b. At present it is difficult to conceive why yeast maintain such a diverse array of enzymes and factors to manufacture a single mitochondrial protein. Implicit in these findings, however, is the notion that RNA processing enzymes or translational factors may have auxiliary functions among which could be modulating the expression of select regions of mitochondrial DNA. Physiological conditions such as carbon source or availability of oxygen are known to affect the respiratory potential of this organism by repressing transcription of nuclear genes coding for components of the respiratory chain. The synthesis of specific mitochondrial proteins such as cytochrome $\underline{b}$ could be subject to regulation by the same metabolic signals if transcription of the genes for RNA processing or the translational factors is also under the control of the same circuit.

The phenotypes of mutants with lesions in the structural genes of the coenzyme QH_2-cytochrome $\underline{c}$ reductase complex reveal that the synthesis of cytochrome $\underline{b}$ is coupled to the presence in the membrane of the non-catalytic subunits. Mutations in the two core proteins and in the 14 and 11 kDa subunits cause loss of enzyme activity and of spectrally and immunologically detectable cytochrome $\underline{b}$. These observations point to the importance of this set of proteins for maturation of apocytochrome $\underline{b}$. This effect is most likely due to a higher rate of turnover of the protein and suggests that the apoprotein is physically associated with one or more of the non-catalytic subunits in a stable core structure. The formation of this core assembly may be a sin qua non for attachement of heme and probably also shields the protein from proteolytic destruction. Lastly, studies of pet mutants have enabled us to identify other nuclear genes that affect the synthesis of an enzymatically active complex. Mutants in two of the newly identified genes express the same phenotype seen in mutants of the non-catalytic subunits. Studies of their roles should further expand our understanding of how this membrane enzyme is assembled.

ACKNOWLEDGMENT

This research was supported by Research Grant HL22174 from the National Institutes of Health, United States Public Health Service.

REFERENCES

1. Sherman, F. and Slonimski, P.P. (1964) Biochim. Biophys. Acta 90, 1-12.

2. Ebner, E. and Schatz, G. (1973) J. Biol. Chem. 248, 5379-5384.

3. Tzagoloff, A., Akai, A. and Needleman, R.B. (1975) J. Biol. Chem. 250, 8228-8235.

4. Kovac, L. (1974) Biochim. Biophys. Acta 346, 101-135.

5. Pillar, T., Lang, B.F., Steinberger, I., Vogt, B., and Kaudewitz, F. (1983) J. Biol. Chem. 258, 7954-7959.

6. Michaelis, G., Mannhaupt, G., Pratje, E., Fischer, E., Naggert, J., and Schweizer, E. (1982) in Mitochondrial Genes (P.P. Slonimski, P. Borst and G. Attardi, eds) Cold Spring Harbor Laboratory, Cold Spring Harbor, pp. 311-321.

7. Dieckmann, C.L., Bonitz, G.S., Hill, J., Homison, G., McGraw, P. Pape, L., Thalenfeld, B.E. and Tzagoloff, A. in Mitochondrial Genes (P.P. Slonimski, P. Borst, A. Attardi, eds) Cold Spring Harbor Laboratory, Cold Spring

Harbor, N.Y., pp. 213-223.

8. Myers, A.M., Pape, L.K. and Tzagoloff, A. (1985) EMBO J. 4, 2087-2092.

9. Marres, C.A.M. and Slater, E.C. (1977) Biochim. Biophys. Acta 462, 531-548.

10. Katan, M.B., Pool,L., and Groot, G.S.P. (1976) Eur. J. Biochem. 65, 95-105.

11. Sidhu, A. and Beattie, D.S. (1982) J. Biol. Chem. 257, 7879-7886.

12. Yang, X. and Trumpower, B.L. (1986) J. Biol. Chem. 261, 12282-12289.

13. Tzagoloff, A., Wu, M. and Crivellone, M. (1986) J. Biol. Chem. 261, 17163-17169.

14. Sadler, I., Suda, K., Schatz, G., Kaudewitz, F. and Haid, A. (1984) EMBO J. 3, 2137-2143.

15. Beckmann, J., Ljungdahl, P. and Trumpower, B.L. (1985) Fed. Proc. 45, 1873.

16. Van Loon, A.P.G.M., de Groot, R.J., Van Eyk, E., Van der Horst, G.T.J. and Grivell, L.A. (1982) Gene 20, 323-337.

17. Nobrega, F.C. and Tzagoloff, A. (1980) J. Biol. Chem. 255, 9828-9837.

18. Lazowska, J., Jacq, C. and Slonimski, P.P. (1980) Cell, 22, 333-348.

19. Dhwahle, S., Hanson, D.K., Alexander, N.J., Perlman, P.S. and Mahler, H.R. (1981) Proc. Natl. Acad. Sci. U.S.A. 78, 1778-1782.

20. Bechmann, H., Haid, A., Schweyen, R.J., Mathews, S. and Kaudewitz, F. (1981) J. Biol. Chem. 256, 3525-3531.

21. Christianson, T., Edwards, J.C., Mueller, D.M. and Rabinowitz, M. (1983) Proc. Natl. Acad. Sci. U.S.A. 80, 5564-5568.

22. Miller, D.L. and Martin, N.C. (1983) Cell 34, 911-917.

23. Dieckmann, C.L., Homison, G. and Tzagoloff, A. (1984) J. Biol. Chem. 259, 4732-4738.

24. McGraw, P. and Tzagoloff, A. (1983) J. Biol. Chem. 258, 9459-9468.

25. Hill, J., McGraw, P. and Tzagoloff, A. (1985) J. Biol. Chem. 260, 3235-3238.

26. Cech, T.R., Zaug, A.J. and Grabowski, P. (1981) Cell 27, 487-496.

27. Gampel, A. and Tzagoloff, A. (1987) submitted for publication.

28. Haldi, M.L. (1985) Ph.D. Dissertation, Ohio State University, Ohio.

29. Dieckmann, C.L. and Tzagoloff, A. (1985) J. Biol. Chem. 260, 1513-1520.

30. Rodel, G. (1986) Curr. Genet. 11, 41-45.

31. Muller, P.P., Reif, M.K., Zonghou, S., Sengstag, C., Mason, T.L. and Fox, T.D. (1984) J. Mol. Biol. 175, 431-452.

32. Costanzo, M.C., Poutre, C.G., Strick, C.A. and Fox, T.D. In Achievements and Perspectives of Mitochondrial Research (E. Quagliariello et al, eds) Elsevier, Amsterdam, pp. 355-360.

33. Schoppink,P.J., Grivell, L.A. and Berden, J.A. (1987) in Membrane Biochemistry and Bioenergetics, in press.

SEQUENCE ANALYSIS OF

MAMMALIAN CYTOCHROME b MUTANTS

Neil Howell and Karin Gilbert

Division of Research
Department of Radiation Therapy
The University of Texas Medical Branch
Galveston, Texas 77550

INTRODUCTION

A series of mouse cell mutants with increased resistance to inhibitors of electron transport through the protonmotive cytochrome b of Complex III (ubiquinol - cytochrome c oxidoreductase) have been isolated in this laboratory (Howell et al., 1983a; Howell et al., 1983b; Howell and Nalty, submitted for publication). Biochemical and somatic cell genetic analyses indicated that these resistance phenotypes were determined by mutations within the mitochondrial gene encoding the apocytochrome b.

We are using these mitochondrial mutants to derive structural information on the inhibitor binding domains of the cytochrome b protein. In addition, there is preliminary biochemical evidence that at least some of the mutations have pleiotropic effects on electron transport and energy transduction, thus indicating that these mutations will be useful for mechanistic studies.

The sequence alteration of one of these cytochrome b mutations has recently been reported elsewhere (Howell et al., 1987). The molecular basis of inhibitor resistance in two additional cytochrome b mutants is reported here.

EXPERIMENTAL PROCEDURES

Mitochondrial DNA (mtDNA) was purified from mouse cell lines using the digitonin-based procedure (Howell and Nalty, 1986) and digested to completion with XhoI and BglII. These restriction endonucleases cleave the 16.3 kb mouse mtDNA at sites 13,551 and 15,329, respectively (all nucleotide coordinates are from Bibb et al., 1981), yielding 1.8 kb and 14.5 kb fragments. The smaller fragment completely spans the 1,143 bp gene encoding the cytochrome b apoprotein, nucleotides 14,139 - 15,282. The two mtDNA fragments were separated by slab gel electrophoresis in 0.5% "Sea Plaque" agarose (FMC Corp.) and the 1.8 kb fragment forced-cloned into SalI/BamHl-cleaved pUC 18 using the in-gel ligation procedure of Crouse et al. (1983).

Positive transformants carrying recombinant plasmids with the inserted

1.8 kb mtDNA fragment were grown on a large scale and the plasmid DNA purified by CsCl-ethidium bromide dye-buoyant density equilbrium centrifugation. For each mutant, the plasmid DNA from three independent transformants was pooled and digested to completion with AatII and Sau3A. Among the cleavage products were the 581, 297, and 533 bp Sau3A fragments spanning the cytochrome b gene (see Figure 1 of Howell et al., 1987). These fragments were separated by slab gel electrophoresis in 4% "NuSieve" agarose (FMC Corp.) and purified by electroelution and ethanol precipitation. The purified fragments were then cloned into BamHl-cleaved Messing M13 mp18/19 sequencing vectors (Messing, 1980).

Nucleotide sequencing was carried out using the dideoxy chain termination procedure (Sanger et al., 1977) and the S35/gradient gel modification (Biggin et al., 1983). DNA sequences were stored and compared to the wild type sequence using the MUTANT string-searching program and a DEC VAX 11/780 computer (Howell and Howell, manuscript in preparation).

At least two independent clones of each cytochrome b gene fragment were sequenced for both orientations of insertion. For each mutant, the entire cytochrome b gene was sequenced and no sequence changes other than those reported below were found. For both the ANT-R and MYX-R4 mutations, it was possible to confirm the nucleotide alteration by sequencing both the coding and non-coding strands.

RESULTS

The LA9 ANT-R1 and MYX-R4 mitochondrial cytochrome b mutants were selected for resistance to the inhibitors antimycin A and myxothiazol, respectively (Howell et al., 1983a; 1983b). The patterns of resistance to other cytochrome b inhibitors are summarized in Table 1. While the ANT-R1 mutant is highly resistant to antimycin (and funiculosin; Howell et al., 1983a), it is fully sensitive to HQNO, another inhibitor of electron transport through the $b562$ heme group, and to myxothiazol and stigmatellin, inhibitors of the $b566$ heme group (von Jagow and Link, 1986). For comparison, it should be noted that the HQN-R11 mutation causes low levels of resistance to all $b562$ inhibitors (Howell et al, 1983b). In contrast, the MYX-R4 mutation results in high levels of resistance to myxothiazol (and mucidin; Howell et al, 1983b) but not to stigmatellin or to $b562$ inhibitors.

Table 1. INHIBITOR RESISTANCE OF LA9 CYTOCHROME b MUTANTS

CELL LINE[a]	ANTIMYCIN	HQNO	MYXOTHIAZOL	STIGMATELLIN
LA9	1.0	1.0	1.0	1.0
LA9 HQN-R11	19	17	1.7	1.6
LA9 ANT-R1	1,300	3.5	2.3	2.4
LA9 MYX-R4	4.4	3.6	22,800	5.0

a) The results are expressed as relative levels of inhibitor resistance and are based upon the I_{50} values obtained from assays of mitochondrial

succinate - cytochrome c oxidoreductase (Howell et al., 1983a; 1983b; Howell and Nalty, submitted for publication).

DNA sequence analysis of the LA9 ANT-R1 mitochondrial cytochrome b gene revealed that there was a G:T transversion on the coding strand at nucleotide position 14,251. This results in a GGA-to-GTA codon change and causes a valine for glycine replacement at amino acid position #38.

80

Sequence analysis of the MYX-R4 mutant demonstrated that the cytochrome b gene contained a G:C transversion on the coding strand at nucleotide position 14,563. This transversion changes a GGT codon to GCT and results in the substitution of an alanine residue for glycine at amino acid position #142. These results are summarized in Table 2.

Table 2. MUTATIONS IN THE MOUSE CYTOCHROME b GENE

MUTANT	BASE CHANGE	NUCLEOTIDE POSITION	AMINO ACID POSITION	AMINO ACID CHANGE
LA9 HQN-R11	G - A	14,830	231	GLY - ASP
LA9 ANT-R1	G - T	14,251	38	GLY - VAL
LA9 MYX-R4	G - C	14,563	142	GLY - ALA

DISCUSSION

Models for the Folding of the Cytochrome b Protein

We have now determined the molecular basis for inhibitor resistance in three independent mouse cytochrome b mutants (Table 2). The location of these mutations within the cytochrome b protein provides some important clues as to the sites of inhibitor binding or interaction and to the possible folding of the protein.

Widger et al. (1984) and Saraste (1984) independently derived a model for the folding of cytochrome b based upon the predicted amino acid sequences of several evolutionarily divergent cytochrome b proteins. The basic features of this model are that the protein folds into nine hydrophobic transmembrane domains with two pairs of invariant histidine residues forming the ligation sites of the b562 and b566 heme groups. The proximity of the altered gly231 in the LA9 HQN-R11 mutant to one of these invariant histidine residues has been discussed elsewhere (Howell et al., 1987).

However, when we locate the ANT-R1 and MYX-R4 mutations within the cytochrome b protein folded according to the Widger-Saraste model, serious inconsistencies appear. Thus, the altered gly38 of the former lies within the N-terminal portion of hydrophobic domain I (cf. Figure 3 of Howell et al., 1987), placing the ANT-R1 and HQN-R11 mutations on opposite sides of the membrane and proximate to different heme groups. This is inconsistent since both mutations increase resistance to inhibitors of the b562 heme group. Secondly, according to this model, the altered gly142 of the MYX-R4 mutation would be located within the small hydrophilic loop connecting transmembrane domains III and IV. This position places the MYX-R4 and HQN-R11 mutations on the same side of the membrane, both in reasonable proximity to the same heme group. This is inconsistent because the mutations increase resistance to inhibitors that derange different reaction centers and heme groups (von Jagow and Link, 1986).

There are two general explanations for these apparent inconsistencies. In the first, the basic predictions of the Widger-Saraste model would be correct but hypotheses about the mechanisms of inhibition of cytochrome b electron transport would be incomplete. For example, the ANT-R1 and MYX-R4 mutations may increase resistance through an indirect mechanism such as interaction with the small Complex III accessory proteins. There have been several reports that antimycin does have such mechanism of binding (e.g., Ho et al., 1985; van Keulen et al., 1985).

The second explanation, and the one that we feel is more compatible with the available experimental evidence, is that the Widger-Saraste model requires modification. More direct tests for the presence of transmembrane hydrophobic domains in other proteins have shown that models of this type can be inaccurate (e.g., Sayre et al., 1986). More importantly, Crofts (personal communication) has recently proposed a simple modification of the Widger-Saraste model which resolves the apparent discrepancies noted above. Crofts has hypothesized that the assignment of transmembrane domain IV is incorrect and that this stretch of amino acids lies outside the membrane. In Figure 1, we present a simple model for the folding of the cytochrome b protein which incorporates this modification. We have also assumed that since the cytochrome b protein is synthesized

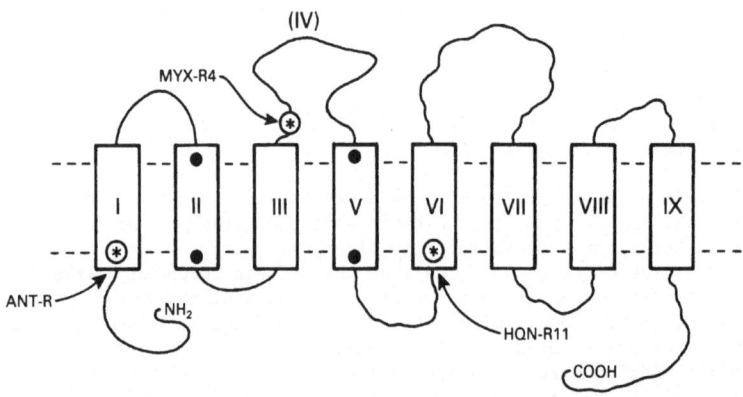

Figure 1. A Model for the Folding of Cytochrome b. The four invariant histidines postulated to ligate the two heme groups are denoted by the filled circles. The locations of the mutations are shown by open circles with asterisks.

within the mitochondrion, it will integrate into the membrane in the opposite orientation of that implied in the Widger-Saraste model. That is, insertion will be from the inner side of the membrane rather than the outer. The orientation of the protein model of Figure 1 is also more compatible with the biochemical studies which indicate that the antimycin sensitive, high potential b562 heme group is on the inner side of the mitochondrial membrane (Mitchell, 1976; Berry and Trumpower, 1985; Rich, 1986). With this new model, the ANT-R1 and HQN-R11 mutations are now proximal to the same heme group and the MYX-R4 mutation is proximal to the opposing heme center. Further biochemical and genetic studies will be important to confirm this model.

82

Structure and Evolution of Antimycin and Myxothiazol Domains

More than a dozen genes encoding mitochondrial cytochrome $\underline{b}$ or chloroplast cytochrome $\underline{b}6$ have now been sequenced. Comparison of the sequences surrounding the amino acid residues altered in the ANT-R1 and MYX-R4 mutations has revealed several interesting features of these regions of the cytochrome protein. The sequences surrounding the gly38 residue - mutated to a valine residue in the ANT-R1 mutation - are summarized in Table 3. The first important feature is that gly38 itself is highly conserved, being replaced among the mitochondrial cytochrome $\underline{b}$ molecules only by alanine in Aspergillus and Rhodobacter. It is also conserved in the trypanosomal cytochrome $\underline{b}$ which shows extensive divergence from the other mitochondrial cytochrome $\underline{b}$ proteins. In marked contrast, the chloroplast $\underline{b}6$ proteins all contain a leucine at the position equivalent to gly38.

Table 3. EVOLUTION OF THE MITOCHONDRIAL CYTOCHROME $\underline{b}$ ANTIMYCIN DOMAIN

	30	40	REFERENCE
MOUSE[a]	W-W-N-F-G-S-L-L G V-C-L-M-V-Q		b
HUMAN	W-W-N-F-G-S-L-L-G-A-C-L-I-L-Q		b
BOVINE	W-W-N-F-G-S-L-L-G-I-C-L-I-L-Q		b
XENOPUS	L-W-N-F-G-S-L-L-G-V-C-L-I-A-Q		c
DROSOPHILA	W-W-N-F-G-S-L-L-G-L-C-L-I-I-Q		d
YEAST	W-W-N-M-G-S-L-L-G-L-C-L-V-I-Q		b
ASPERGILLUS	L-W-N-F-G-S-L-L-A-L-C-L-G-I-Q		b
MAIZE	W-W-G-F-G-C-L-A-G-I-C-L-V-I-Q		e
WHEAT	W-W-G-F-G-S-L-A-G-I-C-L-V-I-Q		f
RHODOBACTER	W-W-I-W-G-S-L-L-A-F-T-L-V-L-Q		g
T. BRUCEI	I-Y-G-V-G-F-S-L-G-F-F-I-A-L-Q		h
SPINACH b6	F-Y-C-L-G-G-I-T-L-T-C-F-L-V-Q		b
TOBACCO b6	F-Y-C-L-G-G-I-T-L-T-C-F-L-V-Q		i
LIVERWORT b6	F-Y-C-L-G-G-I-T-L-T-C-F-L-V-Q		j

a) All sequences are aligned relative to the mouse sequence. The under-lined sequence lies within transmembrane hydrophobic domain I; b) Widger et al. (1984); c) Roe et al. (1985); d) Clary and Wolstenholme (1985); e) Dawson et al. (1984); f) Boer et al. (1985); g) Gabellini and Sebald (1986); h) Benne et al. (1983); i) M. Sugiura, personal communication; j) K. Ohyama, personal communication.

There are additional conserved features of the cytochrome $\underline{b}$ proteins that are apparent from the data in Table 3. Firstly, there is generally a pair of aromatic amino acids at positions 30 and 31. Secondly, there is an invariant glycine at position 34 in all cytochrome $\underline{b}$ and $\underline{b}6$ molecules; this is predicted to be the first residue of hydrophobic domain I. There is also an invariant glutamine at position 44. There is a conserved serine at position 35 and a conserved cysteine at position 40; when these are replaced, it is by amino acids which have hydroxyl or sulfhydryl moieties. Finally, there are conserved leucine residues at positions 36, 37, and 41 of the hydrophobic domain.

The suggestion that this region of the cytochrome $\underline{b}$ protein constitutes at least part of the antimycin domain is supported by the following data. Firstly, Colson has found that a diuron resistant yeast mutant, which is antimycin cross-resistant, has an altered amino acid at position 32 (Rago et al., 1986). More importantly, Colson has recently sequenced an antimycin resistant yeast mutant and found that it also has a valine replacement of gly38 (personal communication). Secondly, the occurrence of leucine residues at position 38 in the cytochrome b6 proteins is significant because chloroplast electron transport is about 1000-times less antimycin sensitive than that of mitochondria (Hauska et al., 1983). Other features of the mitochondrial protein such as the conserved leucines and the serine at position 35 are also lacking in the chloroplast cytochrome.

Based upon this comparative sequence data, and the mutational analyses, we suggest that antimycin binds to a pocket or crevice in cytochrome b which is formed by the amino acid side chains in this region of hydrophobic domain I. The conformation of this binding region would be particularly sensitive to alterations of the gly38 residue and replacement with larger side chains would cause sufficient distortion to eliminate or severly reduce inhibitor binding. The conformation of the inhibitor binding domain is likely to be determined principally by the hydrophobic amino acid residues including the conserved leucines. However, the conservation of the ser35 and cys40 residues suggests they may be important also in inhibitor binding or, alternatively, in maintaining the conformation of the domain. Mutational analysis of the binding of quinone-type herbicides to the chloroplast D1 protein of photosystem II has indicated that increased resistance often results from replacement of a conserved serine residue; other amino acids which are mutated include valine, phenylalanine and alanine (Erickson et al., 1985; Johanning-meir et al., 1987). Further analysis of antimycin resistant mutants from other organisms will be helpful in confirming and refining these predictions.

The limited studies that have been done on the structural features of the antimycin molecule are also compatible with this working model. The antimycins are characterized by a 3-formamidosalicylic acid moiety linked through an amide bond to an acyl- and alkyl-substituted nine-member dilactone ring (Rieske, 1980). Analogue studies have established that it is the formamido and phenolic hydroxyl groups of the salicyclic acid portion which are required for inhibition with the dilactone ring portion probably involved in the specificity of binding (Rieske, 1980).

Table 4. EVOLUTION OF THE MITOCHONDRIAL CYTOCHROME b MYXOTHIAZOL DOMAIN

	140	150
MOUSE[a]	G-Q-M-S-F-W-[G]-A-T-V-I-T-N-L-L
HUMAN	G-Q-M-S-F-W-G-A-T-V-I-T-N-L-L
BOVINE	G-Q-M-S-F-W-G-A-T-V-I-T-N-L-L
XENOPUS	G-G-M-S-F-W-G-A-T-V-I-T-N-L-L
DROSOPHILA	G-Q-M-S-F-W-G-A-T-V-I-T-N-L-L
YEAST	G-Q-M-S-H-W-G-A-T-V-I-T-N-L-F
ASPERGILLUS	G-Q-M-S-L-W-G-A-T-V-I-T-N-L-M
MAIZE	G-Q-M-S-F-W-G-A-T-V-I-T-S-L-A
WHEAT	G-Q-M-S-F-W-G-A-T-V-I-T-S-L-A
RHODOBACTER	G-Q-M-S-F-W-G-A-T-V-I-T-G-L-F
T. BRUCEI	T-M-M-S-Y-W-G-L-T-V-F-S-N-I-I
SPINACH b6	D-Q-I-G-Y-W-A-V-K-I-V-T-G-V-P
TOBACCO b6	D-Q-I-G-Y-W-A-V-K-I-V-T-G-V-P
LIVERWORT b6	D-Q-I-G-Y-W-A-V-K-I-V-T-G-V-P

a) Glycine 142 is enclosed by a box. The underlined sequence lies within domain IV. References for the sequences are given in Table 3.

The finding that the ANT-R1 mutant retains normal sensitivity to HQNO indicates that this $\underline{b}$562 inhibitor has a different mechanism of binding or interaction with the cytochrome protein (Howell et al., 1983a).

The comparative amino acid sequence data for the putative myxothiazol domain is presented in Table 4. In this case, the conservation of the region is even more striking than for the antimycin domain: the gly142 which is mutated in the MYX-R4 mutant is invariant in all mitochondrial cytochrome $\underline{b}$ proteins. However, it is replaced by alanine (the same change as seen for the mutant) in the chloroplast $\underline{b}$6 proteins, a fact which is compatible with the decreased sensitivity of chloroplast electron transport to myxothiazol (Hauska et al., 1983). The trypanosome sequence shows significant divergence from the consensus mitochondrial sequence and it will be interesting to determine antimycin and myxothiazol inhibition curves for this class of organisms: we would predict significant differences from those obtained from mammals or fungi.

In contrast to the antimycin domain, the myxothiazol domain apparently lies within a domain of the protein which is not transmembrane (Figure 1). Like the antimycin domain, there are both highly conserved aromatic and hydrophobic residues as well as hydroxyl residues in the gly142 region. Thus, both domains are probably amphiphilic rather than purely hydrophobic in character.

While myxothiazol is known to alter the properties of the $\underline{b}$566 heme group, it also increases the mid-point potential of the Rieske non-heme iron protein (von Jagow et al., 1984). From the location of the gly142 residue, it is tempting to speculate that domain IV of the cytochrome $\underline{b}$ protein interacts with the non-heme iron protein. However, the sites of interaction between these two redox centers are likely to be extensive since we have begun sequencing the cytochrome $\underline{b}$ gene from a stigmatellin resistant mutant. Stigmatellin also binds to cytochrome $\underline{b}$ but has an even greater effect on the mid-point potential of the non-heme iron protein than myxothiazol (von Jagow and Link, 1986). This mutation does not map within the region of the gene encoding this amphiphilic region.

In conclusion, analyses of cytochrome $\underline{b}$ mutants with increased inhibitor resistance - when coupled to biochemical analyses - provide a useful experimental approach to elucidating the structure-function relationships of key redox proteins such as the protonmotive cytochrome $\underline{b}$. The potential of genetic analysis for understanding bioenergetic processes, however, is just beginning to be actualized.

ACKNOWLEDGEMENTS

This research was funded by grant GM33683 from The National Institutes of Health.

REFERENCES

Benne, R., De Vries, B. F., van den Burg, J., and Klaver, B., 1983, Nucl. Acids Res., 11:6925.

Berry, E. A., and Trumpower, B. L., 1985, in: "Coenzyme Q. Biochemistry, Bioenergetics and Clinical Applications,"G. Lenaz, ed., John Wiley and Sons, New York, p. 365.

Bibb, M. J., Van Etten, R. A., Wright, C. T., Walberg, M. W., and Clayton, D. A., 1981, Cell, 26:167.

Biggin, M. D., Gibson, J. J., and Hong, G. F., 1983, Proc. Natl. Acad. Sci. USA, 80:3963.

Boer, P. H., McIntosh, J. E., Gray, M. W., and Bonen, L., 1985, Nucl. Acids Res., 13:2281.

Clary, D. O., and Wolstenholme, D. R., 1985, J. Mol. Evol., 22:252.

Crouse, G. F., Frischauf, A., and Lehrach, H., 1983, Meth. Enzymol., 101:78.

Dawson, A. J., Jones, V. P., and Leaver, C. J., 1984, EMBO J., 3:2107.

Di Rago, J.-P., Perea, X., and Colson, A.-M., 1986, FEBS Letters, 208:208.

Erickson, J. M., Rahire, M., Rochaix, J.-D., and Mets, L., 1985, Science, 228:204.

Gabellini, N., and Sebald, W., 1986, Eur. J. Biochem., 154:569.

Hauska, G., Hurt, E., Gabellini, N., and Lackau, W., 1983, Biochim. Biophys. Acta, 726:97.

Ho., S. H. K., Das Gupta, U., and Rieske, J. S., 1985, J. Bioenerget., 17:269.

Howell, N., Huang, P., Kelliher, K., and Ryan, M. L., 1983a, Somatic Cell Genet., 9:143.

Howell, N., Bantel, A., and Huang, P., 1983b, Somatic Cell Genet., 9:721.

Howell, N., Nalty, M. S., and Appel, J., 1986, Plasmid, 16:77.

Howell, N., Appel, J., Cook, J. P., Howell, B., and Hauswirth, W. W., 1987, J. Biol. Chem., 262:2411.

Johanningmeir, U., Bodner, U., and Wildner, G. F., 1987, FEBS Letters, 211:221.

Messing, J., 1983, Meth. Enzymol., 101:20.

Mitchell, P., 1976, J. Theoret. Biol., 62:327.

Rich, P. R., 1986, J. Bioenerget., 18:145.

Rieske, J. S., 1980, Pharmacol. Ther., 11:415.

Roe, B. A., Ma, D.-P., Wilson, R. K., and Wong, J. F.-H., 1985, J. Biol. Chem., 260:9759.

Sanger, F., Nicklen, S., and Coulson, A. R., 1977, Proc. Natl. Acad. Sci. USA, 74:5463.

Saraste, M., 1984, FEBS Letters, 166:367.

Sayre, R. T., Anderson, B., and Bogorad, L., 1986, Cell, 47:601.

Van Keulen, M. A., and Berden, J. A., 1985, Biochim. Biophys. Acta, 808:32

Von Jagow, G., Ljungdahl, P. O., Graf, P., Ohnishi, T., and Trumpower, B. L., 1984, J. Biol. Chem., 259:6318.

Von Jagow, G., and Link, T. A., 1986, Meth. Enzymol., 126:253.

Widger, W. R., Cramer, W. A., Herrmann, R. G., and Trebst, A., 1984, Proc. Natl. Acad. Sci. USA, 81:674.

PLANT MITOCHONDRIAL GENES, CYTOCHROME C OXIDASE AND CYTOPLASMIC MALE

STERILITY

Malcolm J. Hawkesford and Christopher J. Leaver

Department of Botany, University of Edinburgh
Edinburgh EH9 3JH, Scotland

SUMMARY

In the mitochondrial genome of cytoplasmic male sterile plants multiple
recombination events have created unique chimaeric genes. These may be
expressed as variant polypeptides, in one specific case as a modified
form of cytochrome c oxidase subunit 1 polypeptide, and in another as a
novel polypeptide apparently associated with this same subunit. Models
for the molecular basis of cytoplasmic male sterility are discussed in
relation to function and biogenesis of cytochrome c oxidase.

INTRODUCTION: PLANT MITOCHONDRIA

    Plant mitochondria are distinguished in the multiple and changing
roles they must fulfil during plant growth and development (see 1).
Energy metabolism within plant cells is dependent on a complex coordination
of both chloroplast and mitochondrial function. These organelles must
satisfy a constantly changing demand for cellular energy if growth and
differentiation are to be sustained in the variable external environment
experienced by the plant during its life cycle.

    In addition to fulfilling a role in the provision of ATP via oxidative
phosphorylation, a primary function in non-green cells, mitochondria play
vital roles in the cycling of carbon skeletons to produce biosynthetic
precursors, particularly in dividing cells, a role facilitated by an
enzyme unique to plant mitochondria -NAD-linked malic enzyme. In the
photosynthetic tissue of C3 plants mitochondria have an essential role,
together with chloroplasts and peroxisomes, in photorespiration - the
oxidative decarboxylation of glycine by glycine decarboxylase. In C4
plants another level of complexity of mitochondrial function is introduced
with the occurence of dimorphic photosynthetic cells, each with functionally
distinct mitochondria. These functions may be limitated by coupled oxidative phosphorylation but may be moderated by a specific uncoupled electron
transfer pathway associated with the cyanide insensitive oxidase. Whilst
progress has been made in our understanding of the metabolism of the plant
mitochondrion and its regulation, information on the molecular biology,
biogenesis and turnover of the component enzymes is lacking.

    Analysis of the regulation of plant mitochondrial biogenesis will

involve a detailed investigation of the biosynthesis of both the matrix
enzymes and the inner membrane enzyme complexes. Fundamental studies on
these enzymes, both those common to all mitochondria and those unique to
plant mitochondria, have been initiated. Of particular interest is the
cytochrome c oxidase complex, especially in view of recent findings that
the products of specific mitochondrial mutations causing cytoplasmic male
sterility, may be associated with this complex. In this report we summarise
data on the isolation and characterisation of mitochondrial genes and polypeptides for plant cytochrome c oxidase including specific variant gene
products apparently associated with the CMS phenotype.

THE PLANT MITOCHONDRIAL GENOME

The higher plant mitochondrial genome is much larger and more variable
in size than its animal (16-17Kb) and yeast (ca. 70Kb) counterparts. The
size varies between ca. 218Kb in various Brassica sp, 430Kb in Triticum
sp, 570Kb in Zea mays and up to 2400Kb in muskmelon.[2] The genome can be
represented as a covalently closed, circular molecule containing a number
of repeated sequences. Recombinations between some of these repeated
sequences can generate sub-genomic circular molecules, creating a multi-
partite genome. The number and relative frequency of recombination between
the different pairs of repeated DNA sequences, and the efficiency of
different replication origins, apparently determines the genome organisation
in vivo.[3]

The large and variable size of the plant mitochondrial genome cannot
be explained as due to the presence of repetitive DNA, which constitutes
less than 10% of the genome.[2] It is also unlikely that plant mtDNA contains
proportionally many more genes than other mitochondrial DNAs as the genes
identified so far in higher plants, are with one or two exceptions, similar
to those described for other organisms. In higher plants the genome is
known to encode the three largest hydrophobic polypeptides of the cytochrome c oxidase complex, cox I,[4] II,[5] and III,[6] in common with all other
mitochondrial genomes characterised to date. In addition the genome encodes
three mitochondrial specific ribosomal RNA genes (26S, 18S and 5S) and a
number of transfer RNA genes (at least 20), together with other genes encoding integral components of the energy transducing complexes of the inner
mitochondrial membrane. These include genes encoding the apocytochrome b
polypeptide (cob)[7] of the bc_1 complex, the alpha-subunit of the F_1-ATPase
complex (atpA)[8] and subunits 6[9] and 9[10] of the F_0-ATPase (atp6 and 9).
Recently a gene has been identified in Cucumis showing high homology to the
animal mitochondria urf1 gene which has been shown to encode one of the
complex I NADH dehydrogenase subunits.[11] It is likely that, in common
with animal mitochondria, higher plant mtDNA will be shown to encode
additional components of complex I.

The sequences of genes isolated from Z. mays show high homology with
the corresponding genes in other organisms at the predicted amino acid
level, particularly in regions of the polypeptide which have functional
importance, for example at the haem binding sites. The sequence data has
also revealed several major differences in gene structure and codon usage,
compared to mitochondria from other organisms. In contrast to a number of
fungal systems where the coxI and cob genes contain multiple intervening
sequences (introns), the homologous genes in those plants examined to date
do not. However in contrast to other organisms a single, centrally located
intron is found in the coxII[5] gene of several monocotyledonous plants, as
well as in artichoke and sunflower, although not in a number of other
dicotyledons (Pisum, Oenothera). In higher plants the UGA codon acts as
a terminator codon as specified by the universal code, whereas in other
mitochondrial systems UGA specifies tryptophan. The one codon assignment

which is apparently unique to higher plants is CGG, which specifies
arginine in the universal code, and functions as a tryptophan codon in
plants.[5] The availability of specific gene probes has also allowed them
to be mapped on the circular linkage map of mtDNA from Z. mays constructed
by Lonsdale and his colleagues.[12]

MITOCHONDRIAL GENE EXPRESSION

Analysis of the transcriptional patterns of Z. mays mitochondrial
protein-coding genes reveals in most cases a complex situation suggesting
extensive processing of the primary transcripts and/or multiple initiation
or termination sites.[13] We have characterised a sequence 5' to the coxI
gene as being a putative plant mitochondrial promoter sequence.[4] Several
other putative mitochondrial promoter sequences have now been characterised
(Brennicke and Hauswirth, personal communications) and in common with the
putative coxI promoter provide a consensus sequence which shows homology
with the corresponding nonanucleotide sequence described in yeast mitochondrial DNA. In collaboration with Axel Brennicke we have also identified
a sequence motif which acts as a transcript terminator.[14]

In contrast to the large and complex RNA transcript patterns the
number of polypeptides which can be identified as mitochondrial translation
products is relatively small. Isolated intact, coupled mitochondria in the
presence of an oxidisable substrate (or alternatively an ATP generating-
system) will incorporate radioactively labelled amino acids into protein.
The labelled mitochondrial proteins can be resolved by either one or two-
dimensional IEF/SDS gel electrophoresis. There are between ca. 15 and 30
polypeptides ranging in estimated molecular weight from 8000-58000 daltons
and with the exception of the two highest molecular weight species the
major translation products fractionate with the inner membrane. While the
number and range of translation products synthesised by mitochondria of
different species remains very similar, there are marked and reproducible
quantitative differences depending upon the developmental state of the
tissue from which the mitochondria are isolated.

Immunoprecipitation and protein immunoblot analysis with antibodies
raised against yeast, animal and plant mitochondrial polypeptides, coupled
with the partial purifications of specific enzyme complexes has enabled the
identification of a number of mitochondrial translation products. These
include the alpha-subunit[15] and subunit 9 (DCCD-binding protein)[16] of the
F_1F_0-ATPase, cytochrome c oxidase subunits I and II, apocytochrome b of the
bc_1 complex and a ribosomal protein.[17] The higher resolution afforded by
two dimensional electrophoresis suggests that in excess of 30 polypeptides
are synthesised in mitochondria, although it is possible that certain
labelled polypeptides are products of premature termination, charge modification or proteolytic cleavage.

CYTOPLASMIC MALE STERILITY

Due to the inability of higher plants to survive without functional
mitochondria it has proved impossible to apply the elegant techniques of
genetic and molecular analysis which have produced our current understanding
of the structure, organisation and expression of the yeast mitochondrial
genome. However one class of non-lethal mutations which are known to have
their origins in the plant mitochondrial genome have been identified because
of their dramatic and significant effect on the plant phenotype. These

mutations result in the failure of the mature plant to produce functional pollen, thus giving rise to a male sterile phenotype which is cytoplasmically inherited. Cytoplasmic male sterility (CMS) is a trait common to many species and is of considerable economic importance in the production of F_1 hybrid seed. The best characterised system at the molecular level is in Zea mays L where three different cytoplasms (CMS-T,C and S) giving rise to the male sterile phenotype have been identified on the basis of distinct nuclear genes which restore fertility (Rf genes). The three types of CMS can also be distinguished from each other and from the fertile (N) cytoplasm on the basis of the restriction endonuclease digestion pattern of their mitochondrial DNAs and the synthesis of characteristic additional or variant mitochondrial translation products.[17]

The work of Dewey and Levings[18] on CMS in Z. mays has led to the hypothesis that many of the rearrangements found in the mitochondrial genomes of the different Z. mays cytoplasms is due to the fixation of the product of rare or unique aberrant recombination events which have become stabilised and amplified. In the case of the CMS-T mitochondrial genome at least seven recombination events have generated a chimaeric DNA sequence homologous to portions of the flanking and/or coding regions of the 26S rRNA gene, the ATPase subunit 6 gene and the chloroplast tRNA-arg gene. Sequence analysis of the unique DNA fragment has revealed that it contains two transcriptional units, one of which contains a unique open reading frame (ORF) with the capacity to encode a polypeptide with a predicted molecular weight of 12,961 daltons. The molecular weight of the polypeptide encoded by the CMS-T specific ORF corresponds to the 13000 dalton variant polypeptide which we have previously shown is characteristically synthesised by mitochondria isolated from CMS-T plants.[17] Transcription of the CMS-T specific ORF is modified in the presence of nuclear restorer genes and this is correlated with a reduction in the synthesis and abundance of the 13000 dalton polypeptide by isolated mitochondria.[18]

Electron microscopy of early stages of pollen development and studies using DABS labelling have demonstrated mitochondrial breakdown and respiratory chain dysfunction. However analysis of respiratory functions of mitochondria isolated from CMS lines has failed to demonstrate any metabolic inadequacy of the isolated mitochondria and indeed performance and yield of these plants is comparable to the normal fertile lines. However a major exception is the sensitivity of the Z. mays male sterile line to the toxin (a polyketone – polyalcohol) produced by the fungal pathogen Helminthosporium maydis race T, which was responsible for the 1970 Southern Corn Leaf Blight in the USA. This toxin is effective at very low concentrations (5 ng cm^{-3}) in isolated mitochondria and is quite specific to the T mitochondria. The primary action is to depolarise the membrane and uncouple oxidative phos-phorylation and this leads to multiple secondary effects (see 17 for review).

The CMS phenotype is also extensively used in the production of hybrid Sorghum bicolor and while examining the polypeptides synthesised by mito-chondria from lines containing the 9E cytoplasm we noted the presence of a variant polypeptide.[20] This characteristic polypeptide had an apparent molecular weight of 42000 daltons as estimated by SDS-polyacrylamide gel electrophoresis and replaces the normal 38000 dalton polypeptide synthesised by mitochondria from other Sorghum cytoplasms. Yet again we have no direct evidence that the presence of the variant polypeptide has any effect on the activity of seedling mitochondria, however activity at other developmental stages has yet to be investigated.

Thus while some progress has been made on the identification of variant mitochondrial polypeptides and in our understanding of the molecular events underlying their synthesis, we still have to establish a causal relationship with the CMS phenotype.

CYTOCHROME C OXIDASE AND CYTOPLASMIC MALE STERILITY

Little detailed information on plant cytochrome c oxidase is available. There are only a few reports of the partial purification and characterisation of the protein complex, and the exact complexity of the enzyme compared to the yeast or mammalian enzyme is not known. We are currently undertaking a study of the polypeptide composition of Zea mays cytochrome c oxidase which involves a purification using a classical cytochrome c affinity procedure. In contrast our knowledge of the plant mitochondrial genes for the three largest polypeptides is well documented and they have all been isolated, sequenced and characterised.[4,5,6] This is not however the case for the nuclear genes, none of which have been identified to date.

One of our reasons for concentrating on the cytochrome c oxidase complex is that by the use of yeast antibodies against individual cytochrome c oxidase subunits we have shown that the variant 42000 dalton polypeptide characteristic of S. bicolor 9E is in fact subunit I which replaces the usual 38000 dalton subunit found in all other Sorghum cytoplasms (as estimated by the gel system employed). Using a gene probe containing part of the Z. mays coxI gene, the genes for coxI in both the milo (fertile) and the sterile 9E lines of S. bicolor were isolated and sequenced.[21] The normal milo coxI gene encodes a 530 amino acid polypeptide (58,483 daltons) which is of a similar size to the Z. mays coxI gene with which it shares 98% sequence homology. In contrast, the coxI gene in the 9E Sorghum encodes a 631 amino acid protein (70,358 daltons). The increased size of the coxI gene in 9E is due to a 3'-extension of the ORF resulting in the addition of 101 amino acids to the carboxyl terminus of the protein. The two Sorghum coxI genes are identical from position -100 bp 5' to the presumptive AUG codon, to position +1579 bp within the coxI ORF (Fig. 1). Directly repeated DNA sequences are located at both the 5' and 3' points of divergence. An 8 bp direct repeat is found within the homologous region, 3 bp from the 5' divergence point (Fig. 1B). A 10 bp direct repeat is found within the coxI ORF at the 3' point of divergence. This repeat is actually part of a 26 bp direct repeat in 9E cytoplasm, since the 16 bp that follow the 10 bp are repeated in the non-homologous region (Fig. 1C). Additional fragments of Milo and 9E mtDNA have been identified that hybridize weakly to the unique 5' and 3' coxI sequences. By characterizing these mtDNA fragments, we may be able to model the events that led to the relocation of the 9E coxI ORF. Since the coxI gene is situated in a single genomic location in 9E mtDNA, we predict that the 9E coxI gene resulted from novel mtDNA rearrangements that were subsequently propagated. Such events may underlie the variation in mitochondrial genome organisation observed within plant species.

Our observation of rearrangement within and adjacent to a mitochondrial gene is paralleled in other organisms. In S. cerevisiae, recombination within the mitochondrial gene for cytochrome c oxidase subunit III has been observed.[22] In this case, a larger form of the protein, with an amino-terminal extension, was generated by recombination with another mitochondrial ORF.

COI is a very hydrophobic protein that may have up to 12 trans-membranous segments with the carboxyl terminus of the protein located on the matrix side of the inner mitochondrial membrane. Analysis of the hydrophobicity of the 101 amino acid 3' extension of the 9E coxI ORF reveals two additional hydrophobic domains, followed by a hydrophilic region.

In order to extend our understanding of the molecular events which lead to the generation and expression of variant mitochondrial proteins we have continued our investigation of the 13000 dalton polypeptide synthesised

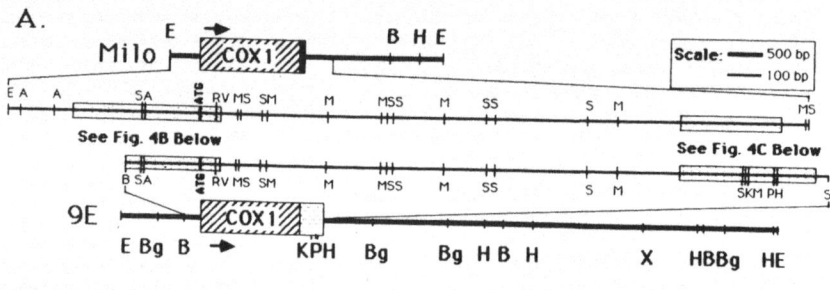

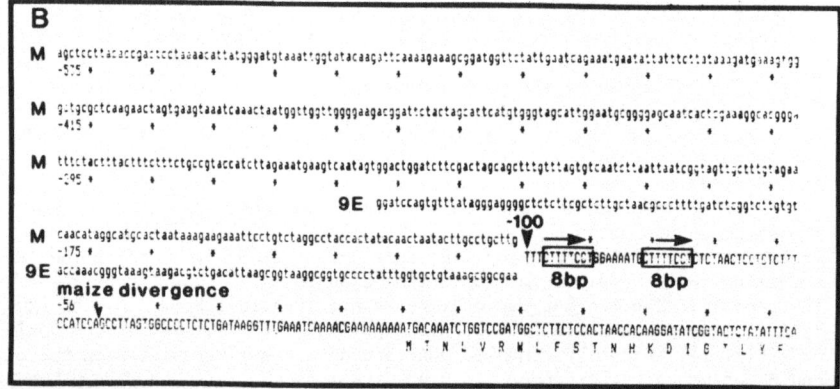

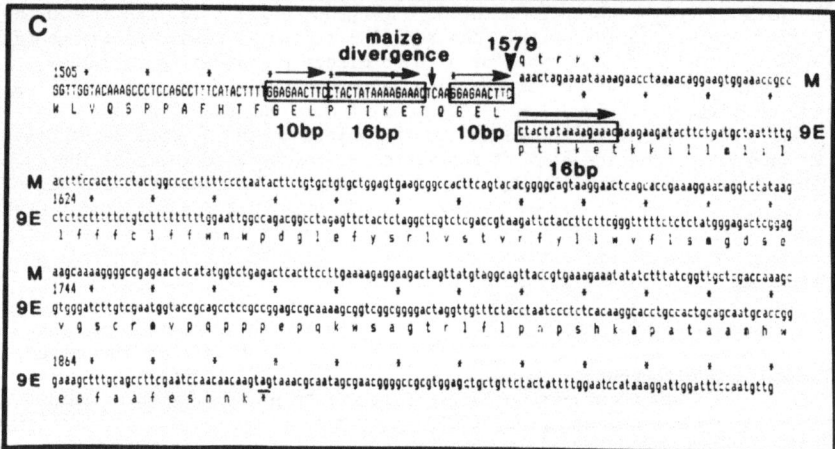

Fig. 1. Location, Sequence, and Rearrangement of the coxl Gene in Milo and
9E MtDNA

(A) Restriction map of the Milo 4.3 kb (pSM4.3) and 9E 10.4 kb (pS9E10.4)
EcoR1 fragments, location of coxI, and restriction map of the region
sequenced (E, EcoR1; B, BamH1; H, Hindlll; Bg, Bgl11; X, Xhol; P,Pst1; S,
Sau3A; M, Msp1; A, Alu1; K, Kpn1). There are no sites for Sal1 within the
10.4 kb fragment, or for Sal1, Pst1, or Xhol within the 4.3 kb fragment.
(B and C). Selected DNA and amino acid sequence of coxI from Milo (M) and

92

9E mtDNA. Numbering of the nucleotide sequence begins at the A of the putative initiator methionine codon. The entire coxI gene sequence of Milo and 9E is not shown here because the ORF encoding col of sorghum is virtually identical with the corresponding gene of maize. The 5' (-49 bp) and 3' (+1566 bp) points of divergence between sorghum and maize are indicated. The 5' (-100 bp) and 3' (+1579 bp) points of divergence between Milo and 9E are indicated. An 8 bp repeated DNA sequence at the 5' divergence point, a 10 bp repeated sequence in Milo and a 10 bp + 16 bp repeated sequence in 9E at the 3' divergence point are boxed. Reprinted with permission from 21.

---

by mitochondria from the T male sterile line of Z. mays. We have shown that an antibody raised against a synthetic oligopeptide corresponding to part of the carboxyl terminus of the polypeptide predicted by the T specific ORF (kindly provided by Lonsdale and Rottman) will immunoprecipitate the 13000 dalton polypeptide synthesised by mitochondria from CMS-T plants. We are also attempting to determine the specific location of this polypeptide within the mitochondrial inner membrane (Hawkesford, Liddell and Leaver, in preparation). Antibodies to representative subunits of a number of inner membrane complexes have been used to immunoprecipitate the native complexes from Triton X-100 solubilised membranes isolated from mitochondria labelled with ^{35}S-methionine or a variety of protein labelling reagents. In both cases only a yeast antibody to cytochrome c oxidase subunit I specifically co-immunoprecipitated the cytochrome c oxidase subunit I and the 13000 dalton variant polypeptide, however the other subunits of the cytochrome c oxidase complex were notably absent. It is therefore possible that there is a specific association of the variant polypeptide with subunit I of cytochrome c oxidase, although not necessarily with the mature complex.

MODELS FOR THE MOLECULAR, BIOCHEMICAL AND PHYSIOLOGICAL BASIS OF CYTOPLASMIC MALE STERILITY

The data reviewed above suggests that the mitochondrial genotypes characteristic of each form of CMS probably arose by aberrant intra- and/ or inter-molecular recombination events leading to the generation of chimaeric mtDNA sequences. Such rearrangements can generate new or extended open reading frames, which, providing they are downstream of a suitable promoter and translational control sequences, may be expressed as variant polypeptides. The variant polypeptide(s) may contain completely novel amino acid sequences and/or blocks of amino acid sequence homologous to normal polypeptide(s) encoded by the DNA sequences from which they were derived. These domains may endow the variant polypeptide with some of the structural and/or enzymic properties of the progenitor protein(s), which may target it to the inner mitochondrial membrane where it could compete with related native polypeptides and become associated with specific enzyme complexes, e.g. of the electron transport chain. However no evidence has been obtained linking a functional impairment of the energy coupling apparatus with the presence of a variant mitochondrial polypeptide and no investigations of mitochondrial biogenesis or function during pollen development in male sterile lines have been carried out.

Thus it is still likely that during microsporogenesis, a developmental stage associated with increased rates of respiration and mitochondrial biogenesis, impairment of mitochondrial oxidative phosphorylation may prevent further cellular development and lead to pollen abortion. An alternative model suggests that the CMS mutation acts at the level of biogenesis of mitochondria rather than directly on function. The presence of additional or of modified polypeptides may impose constraints on the biosynthesis and assembly of the multimeric respiratory complexes of the inner membrane (e.g. cytochrome c oxidase). The variant polypeptides may cause steric hinderence during assembly, perhaps in a competitive manner and impair optimal biogenesis of new mitochondrial components. These models imply that mitochondrial biogenesis and function does not limit cellular development during all other stages of the plant life cycle. For example, during critical stages of plant development, such as seed germination, which is heavily dependent upon mitochondrial function and where hydration of pre-existing mitochondria is initially of major importance rather than the biosynthesis of additional mitochondria.

If either of the proposed models is correct then cytoplasmic male sterile mutations may prove to be a useful tool to probe and elucidate the process of biosynthesis of the plant cytochrome c oxidase complex.

Acknowledgements: This work was supported by research grants from the SERC and AFRC to C.J.L.

REFERENCES
1. R. Douce, "Mitochondria in Higher Plants"., Academic Press, Orlando (1985).
2. B.L. Ward, R.Anderson and A. J. Bendich. The size of the mitochondrial genome is large and variable in a family of plants (Cucurbitaceae). Cell 25:793 (1981).
3. D. M. Lonsdale, T. P. Hodge and C. M.-R. Fauron, The physical map and organisation of the mitochondrial genome from the fertile cytoplasm of maize, Nucleic Acids Res. 12:9249 (1984).
4. P. G. Isaac, V. P. Jones and C. J. Leaver, The maize cytochrome c oxidase subunit I gene: sequence, expression and rearrangement in cytoplasmic male sterile plants, EMBO J. 4:1617 (1985).
5. T. D. Fox and C. J. Leaver, The Zea mays mitochondrial gene coding cytochrome oxidase subunit II has an intervening sequence and does not contain TGA codons, Cell 26:315 (1981).
6. R. Hiesel, W. Schobel, W. Schuster and A. Brennicke, The cytochrome oxidase subunit I and subunit III genes in Oenothera mitochondria are transcribed from identical promoter sequences, EMBO J. 6:29 (1987).
7. A. J. Dawson, V. P. Jones and C. J. Leaver, The apocytochrome b gene in maize mitochondria does not contain introns and is preceded by a potential ribosome binding site, EMBO J. 3:2107 (1984).
8. P. G. Isaac, A. Brennicke, S. M. Dunbar and C. J. Leaver, The mito-chondrial genome of fertile maize (Zea mays L.) contains two copies of the gene encoding the alpha-subunit of the F_1-ATPase, Curr. Genet. 10:321 (1985).
9. R. E. Dewey, C. S. Levings III and D. H. Timothy, Nucleotide sequence of ATPase subunit 6 gene of maize mitochondria, Plant Physiol. 79:914 (1985).
10. R. E. Dewey, A. M. Schuster, C. S. Levings and D. H. Timothy, Nucleotide sequence of F_0-ATPase proteolipid (subunit 9) gene of maize mitochondria, Proc. Natl. Acad. Sci. USA 82:1015 (1985).
11. D. B. Stern, A. G. Band and W. F. Thompson, The watermelon mito-chondrial URF-1 gene: evidence for a complex structure, Curr. Genet. 10:857 (1986).
12. A. J. Dawson, T. P. Hodge, P. G. Isaac, C. J. Leaver and D. M. Lonsdale, Location of the genes for cytochrome oxidase subunits I and II, apocytochrome b, alpha-subunit of the F_1-ATPase and the ribo-somal RNA genes on the mitochondrial genome of maize (Zea mays L.), Curr. Genet. 10:561 (1986).
13. A. J. Dawson, V. P. Jones and C. J. Leaver, Identification and char-acterisation of higher plant mitochondrial genes. Methods in Enz. 118:400 (1986).

14. W. Schuster, R. Hiesel, P. G. Isaac, A. Brennicke and C. J. Leaver, Transcript termini of messenger RNAs in higher plant mitochondria, Nucleic Acids Res. 14:5943 (1986).

15. E. Hack and C. J. Leaver, The alpha-subunit of the maize F_1-ATPase is synthesised in the mitochondrion, EMBO J. 2:1783 (1983).

16. E. Hack and C. J. Leaver, Synthesis of a dicyclohexylcarbodiimide-binding proteolipid by cucumber (Cucumissativus L.) mitochondria, Curr. Genet. 8:537 (1984).

17. C. J. Leaver and M. W. Gray, Mitochondrial genome organization and expression in higher plants, Ann. Rev. Plant Physiol. 33:373 (1982).

18. R. E. Dewey, C. S. Levings and D. H. Timothy, Novel recombinations in the maize mitochondrial genome produce a unique transcriptional unit in the Texas male sterile cytoplasm, Cell 44:437 (1986).

19. B. G. Forde and C. J. Leaver, Nuclear and cytoplasmic genes controlling synthesis of variant mitochondrial polypeptides in male-sterile maize, Proc. Natl. Acad. Sci. 77:418 (1980).

20. L. K. Dixon and C. J. Leaver, Mitochondrial gene expression and cytoplasmic male sterility in sorghum, Plant Mol. Biol. 1:89 (1982).

21. J. Bailey-Serres, D. K. Hanson, T. D. Fox and C. J. Leaver, Mitochondrial genome rearrangement leads to extension and relocation of the cytochrome c oxidase subunit I gene in Sorghum, Cell 47:567 (1986).

22. P. P. Mueller, M. K. Reif, S. Zonghou, C. Sengstag, T. L. Mason and T. D. Fox, A nuclear mutation that post-transcriptionally blocks accumulation of a yeast mitochondrial gene product can be suppressed by mitochondrial gene rearrangement. J. Mol. Biol. 175:431 (1984).

A MUTATION AFFECTING LARIAT FORMATION, BUT NOT SPLICING OF A YEAST MITOCHONDRIAL GROUP II INTRON

R. van der Veen, J.H.J.M. Kwakman and L.A. Grivell

Section for Molecular Biology
Laboratory of Biochemistry
Kruislaan 318
1098SM, Amsterdam, The Netherlands

INTRODUCTION

The fifth intron in the yeast mitochondrial gene for subunit I of cytochrome c oxidase is of the group II type. This intron (aI5), along with three other introns in yeast mtDNA, possesses the potential to form a secondary structure that is distinct from that formed by group I introns and it lacks the set of consensus sequences, which is characteristic of this latter group (Michel and Dujon, 1983). Precursor RNA containing this intron is capable of self-splicing in vitro and this reaction differs in two important respects from that catalyzed by introns of the group I type (Van der Veen et al., 1986; Peebles et al., 1986a). First, activity is not dependent on the presence of a guanosine nucleotide. Second, splicing leads to the formation of branched circular intron molecules, which like the lariats formed during splicing of nuclear precursor RNAs, arise from the ligation of the 5'-terminus of the intron to an internal adenosine via a 2'-5' phosphodiester bond.

Despite these differences, similar models for the catalytic mechanism have been proposed for introns of both groups, based on the theme of trans-esterification. As suggested by Van der Veen et al. (1986) and shown in Fig. 1a, lariat formation could trigger splicing if the initial step in the reaction is a nucleophilic attack of the 2'-OH group of the branchpoint adenosine on the 5'-intron/exon junction. The resulting free 5'-exon could then in its turn initiate an attack on the 3'-intron/exon junction, with transesterification leading to exon-exon ligation and lariat release. Although this scheme is supported by all experimental observations made so far, the sequences responsible for the specificity and efficiency of catalysis have yet to be identified.

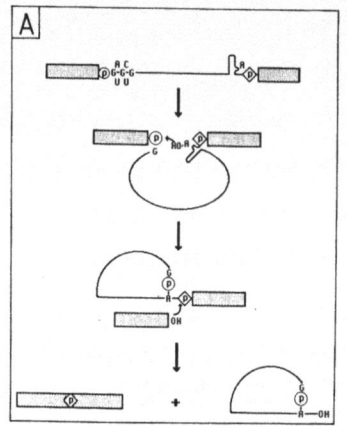

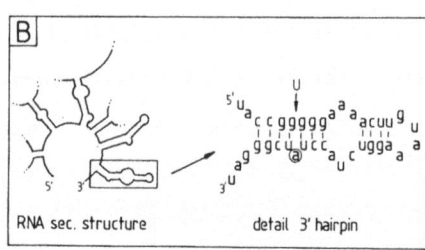

RNA sec. structure   detail 3' hairpin

Fig. 1. Self-splicing of group II introns
   A. Reaction scheme based on a transesterification theme. In the first
   step   nucleophilic attack of the 2-OH group of the branchpoint
   adenosine on the 5'-exon/intron junction results in lariat formation
   and release of the 5'-exon. In the second step, the released 5'exon
   attacks the 3'-intron/exon junction, freeing the intron and leading to
   exon-exon ligation. B. Schematic representation of the secondary
   structure of intron aI5, as proposed by Michel and Dujon (1983). The
   3'-terminal conserved hairpin has been enlarged in order to show the
   branchpoint adenosine (encircled) and the position of the T addition
   in mutant T_{856} .

One of the most characteristic features of all group II introns is the
presence of a stable hairpin close to the 3'-end (Grivell et al., 1983). This hairpin
contains the branchpoint adenosine, an unpaired residue embedded in a short
consensus sequence (Van der Veen et al., 1986), that shows some resemblance to
that determined for the branchpoint environment in the introns of nuclear pre-
mRNAs. The importance of sequences surrounding the branchpoint nucleotide
has been illustrated by the finding that a single base deletion in this region
results in splicing-deficiency (Schmelzer et al., 1982, Schmelzer and
Schweyen,1986) and that insertions which restore the architecture of the
hairpin also restore activity. However, the limited number of changes studied
permits few conclusions as to the molecular interactions involved. We have
begun a mutagenic study in order to clarify this point, concentrating initially on
the branchpoint itself.   This report deals with a single mutant in intron aI5,
whose phenotype has important implications for our understanding of the
reaction   mechanism.

RESULTS

The branchpoint adenosine is present in a single base bulge in a hairpin formed by the 3'-terminus of all group II introns so far characterized. As shown in Fig. 1b, mutant T_{856} contains an insertion of a single T residue at a site in the hairpin directly opposite the branchpoint nucleotide. The mutation should therefore result in the formation of a perfect hairpin at this point. To investigate the ability of the mutant to carry out splicing in vitro, artificial precursor RNA was generated by in vitro transcription of mutant

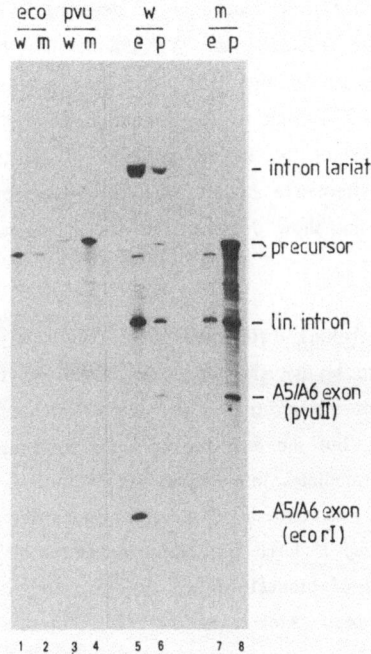

Fig. 2. Self-splicing of mutant T_{856} in the virtual absence of lariat formation Run-off transcripts of wild type intron al5 (pSP64/6) and mutant T_{856} (pS/al5+T856) were generated by in vitro transcription of DNA templates truncated with either EcoRI or PvuII. Products were analyzed by electrophoresis through 4% polyacrylamide-8M urea gels either before (lanes 1 to 4) or after incubation (lanes 5 to 8) for 60 min at 45°C in 100 mM Tris-HCl, 70 mM MgCl$_2$, 200 mM(NH$_4$)$_2$SO$_4$.

template DNA, making use of different truncation sites to facilitate identification of RNAs containing 3'-exon sequences. Incubation under the conditions normally employed for the splicing of group II introns (Van der Veen et al., 1986) failed to elicit any activity (data not shown). However, as shown in Fig. 2, incubation in the presence of an increased concentration of Mg^{2+} and NH_4^+ ions led to the disappearance of the precursor species with somewhat slower kinetics than those displayed by the wild type precursor RNA, and resulted in the appearance of bands corresponding in length to the linear form of the excised intron and the ligated exons. The identity of both species was subsequently confirmed by reverse transcription (data not shown). A lariat form of the intron, which is abundantly present in incubations with wild type RNA, is conspicuously absent and can in fact only be detected in trace amounts after extended exposure of the autoradiogram. We assume that this lack of lariat reflects lack of formation. The alternative, that the mutation results in the use of an alternative branch site leading to the formation of a highly unstable lariat, is neither supported by examination of the products of shorter incubations nor is it to be expected, since alternative branch sites in lariats formed during splicing of nuclear pre-mRNAs do not show decreased stability (Jacquier et al., 1986a).

DISCUSSION

One of the most striking differences in splicing catalyzed by group I and group II introns in vitro is that the latter are capable of the formation of lariats as bone fide products of the reaction. Some lariat formation is also observed during group I splicing, but the structure of these molecules is such that they are unlikely to be intermediates in splicing and they most probably arise in side reactions undergone by an extremely reactive precursor molecule (Arnberg et al., 1986). In vitro, group II lariat formation appears to be an efficient process as judged from the amount of product formed. In vivo, the linear form of the excised introns is not seen (Arnberg et al. 1980), but this may merely reflect differences in stability between linear and lariat forms.

Mechanistically, group II lariat formation might be expected to present problems. Phosphodiester bond formation in the absence of an added energy source is energetically impossible unless it can be coupled via transesterification to the cleavage of a second bond. However, such cleavage may not be easy to achieve, since as pointed out by Cech and Bass (1986), internal 2'-OH groups in RNA are relatively poor nucleophiles. The ability of the branchpoint adenosine to promote efficient lariat formation in vitro must therefore be due to a combination of factors, including stressing of the 5'exon/intron junction by intron folding, activation of the 2'-OH by a neighbouring proton-abstracting group and exclusion of water or OH⁻ from the active site.

100

The distances and geometry required to generate such interactions are obviously critical, since results presented above show that trapping of the branchpoint adenosine in a base pair in mutant T_{856} reduces lariat formation to an extremely low level. Release of the 5'-exon is presumably the result of site-specific hydrolysis, catalyzed by OH^- instead of the 2'-OH group of the branchpoint adenosine. OH^--mediated cleavage has also been reported to occur under certain extreme incubation conditions which lead also to loss of exon-exon ligation (Peebles et al., 1986b) and during the trans-splicing reactions studied by Jacquier and Rosbash (1986b). In the latter case, the authors have speculated that binding of an exon analogue in *trans* may distort intron folding sufficiently to permit access of OH^- ions to the active site. Mutant T_{856} provides proof that OH^--catalyzed exon cleavage can occur in what appears to be a normal *cis*-splicing reaction.

The fact that efficient exon-exon ligation can be induced to occur in the virtual absence of lariat formation raises the question why group II introns should have maintained this step as part of their splicing mechanism. One explanation is that the same active region of the intron is involved in both 5'-exon cleavage and in the subsequent attack of the released exon on its 3'-partner. For the success of this second step, exclusion of OH^- ions is essential . Folding of the active centre may thus create an environment such that not only is water excluded, but that the nucleophilicity of the branchpoint adenosine is raised above the critical level necessary for attack on the 5'-splice junction. In vivo, exclusion of water may additionally be achieved by electrostatic shielding by protein, since it may be impossible to achieve the configuration required for the uncoupled reaction under the ionic conditions prevailing in mitochondria. It may be significant in this respect that in many other RNAs, unpaired adenosine residues are often involved in protein binding (Peattie et al., 1981). An alternative explanation has a basis in the probable differences in catalytic rate in vitro and in vivo: lariat formation may stabilize an intron configuration that promotes attack of the 5'-exon on its 3'-counterpart and differences in efficiency between linear and branched forms may not be evident at the lower rates of catalysis operative in vitro.

ACKNOWLEDGEMENTS

We thank Dr. R. Benne, Dr. P. Sloof and Dr. H.F. Tabak for critical reading of the manuscript and Prof. P. Borst for many useful discussions. This work was supported in part by grants from the Netherlands Foundation for Chemical Research (SON) with financial aid from the Netherlands Organization for the Advancement of Pure Research (ZWO).

REFERENCES

Arnberg, A.C., Van Ommen, G.J.B., Grivell, L.A., Van Bruggen, E.F.J. and Borst, P., 1980, Some yeast mitochondrial RNAs are circular. Cell, 19:313-319.

Arnberg, A.C., Van der Horst, G. and Tabak, H.F., 1986, Formation of lariats and circles in self-splicing of the precursor to the large ribosomal RNA of yeast mitochondria. Cell, 44:235-242

Cech, T.R. and Bass, B.L., 1986, Biological catalysis by RNA. Ann. Rev. Biochem., 55:599-629.

Grivell, L.A., Bonen, L. and Borst, P., 1983, Mosaic genes and RNA processing in yeast mitochondria. in: "Genes: Structure and Expression", Kroon, A.M., ed., Wiley, Chichester, pp 279-306.

Jacquier, A. and Rosbash, M., 1986a, RNA splicing and intron turnover are greatly diminished by a mutant yeast branchpoint. Proc. Natl. Acad. Sci. USA, 83:5835-5839.

Jacquier, A. and Rosbash,. M., 1986b, Efficient trans-splicing of a mitochondrial RNA group II intron implicates a strong 5'-exon-intron interaction. Science, 234:1099-1104.

Michel, F. and Dujon, B.(1983, Conservation of RNA secondary structures in two intron families including mitochondrial-, chloroplast- and nuclear-encoded members. EMBO J., 2:33-38

Peattie, D.A., Douthwaite, S., Garrett, R.A. and Noller, H.F., 1981, A "bulged" double helix in a RNA-protein contact site. Proc. Natl. Acad. Sci. USA, 78:7331-7335.

Peebles, C.L. ,Perlman, P.S., Mecklenburg, K.L., Petrillo, M.L., Tabor, J.H., Jarrell, K.A. and Cheng, H-L., 1986, A self-splicing RNA excises an intron lariat. Cell, 44:213-223.

Peebles, C.L., Dietrich, R.C., Romiti, S.L., Jarrell, K.A., Benatan, E.J. and Perlman, P.S., 1986b, Mutational analysis and alternative splicing reactions of a group II self-splicing intron. Yeast, 2:S290.

Schmelzer, C. and Schweyen, R.J., 1986, Self-splicing of group II introns in vitro: mapping of the branch point and mutational inhibition of lariat formation. Cell, 46:557-565.

Schmelzer, C., Schmidt, C. and Schweyen, R.J., 1982, Identification of splicing signals in introns of yeast mitochondrial split genes: mutational alterations in intron bI1 and secondary structures in related introns. Nucl. Acids Res., 10:6797-6808.

Van der Veen, R., Arnberg, A..C, Van der Horst, G., Bonen, L., Tabak, H.F. and Grivell, L.A., 1986, Excised group II introns in yeast mitochondria are lariats and can be formed by self-splicing in vitro. Cell, 44:225-234.

THE EVOLUTION OF MITOCHONDRIALLY CODED CYTOCHROME GENES:

A QUANTITATIVE ESTIMATE

Cecilia Saccone*, Marcella Attimonelli*, Cecilia Lanave**,
Raffaele Gallerani* and Graziano Pesole*

* Dipartimento di Biochimica e Biologia Molecolare, Università
di Bari, Italy
** Centro Studi Mitocondri e Metabolismo Energetico, CNR
Bari, Italy

INTRODUCTION

It is well known that all mitochondrial (mt) genomes contain the information for a number of proteins which are part of the inner mitochondrial
membrane among which the three subunits of cytochromeoxidase (CoI, CoII,
CoIII) and the apocytochrome b (Cyt b). In spite of the rather constant information content other features of mtDNA, such as the genome size and the
gene structure and organization, appear to be very different in the various
organisms. With regard to the evolutionary rate of mt genes we have only a
limited number of data, particularly in some classes of organisms, which
however already suggest that also this parameter is extremely variable.
In this paper we report our quantitative analyses on the evolution of the
mitochondrially coded cytochrome genes in animals and in a few plants applying a method recently developed in our laboratory for the measurement of
the base substitution rate[1].
The results show that the rate of evolution of mitochondrial genes is very
different in the two kingdoms, fast in the animals and very slow in the
plants particularly at level of the third silent codon position.

METHOD

We have recently proposed a new method for the quantitative analysis of
the molecular evolution[2,3]. The method is based on a general "stationary
Markov process". The prerequisite for our quantitative analysis is, in fact,
that the homologous nucleotide sequences under consideration must obey the so
called "stationarity condition". By this we denote that the frequencies of the
four nucleotides in the homologous sequences compared must be equal for each
codon position (first, second or third respectively). In other words we do
not introduce any a priori assumption about the structure of the substitution
rate matrix of the four nucleotides as in previous methods proposed by other

authors[4-6] and we simply discard from our calculation those genes whose base population has been drastically changed.

Reliable quantitative estimates of the base substitution rate in gene evolution strongly depends on two parameters: $\underline{i}$ a trustworthy determination of the divergence time between species, $\underline{ii}$ a correct calculation of the nucleotide substitution number. The latter value is derived, in our method, through a sophysticated statistical analysis which plays particular attention to the measurement of statistical fluctuations. For the determination of the divergence time (T) our method proposes a simple way to calculate the divergence time ratios (T/T') between couples of species (i.e. species AB versus species AC). From the T/T' values we can calculate the absolute divergence time values between species giving a single external input, namely the divergence times between the members of one couple (i.e. the value T_{AB} between the species A and B) determined by other means, for example from paleontological data. Using this method we determine the average silent substitution rate at the third silent codon positions and the average replacement rates at the first or second codon position in gene sequences.

RESULTS

Gene evolution in animals

We have analyzed the sequences of the cytochrome genes from four mammals, namely rat(R), mouse(M), cow(B = bovine) and man(H = human), from Xenopus laevis (X) and from the invertebrate Drosophila yakuba(D). The sequences were taken from the GenBank collection by ACNUC software retrieval system[7]. The GenBank locus names are listed in Table 1 and can be used for determining sequence references and other information. The nucleotide sequences of homologous genes were aligned and the stationarity condition check was performed using the χ^2 test as described in our previous paper[8].

Table 1 shows the genes which, in pairwise comparison, obey the stationarity conditions. As previously shown[1] in third silent codon position only R, M and B are stationary. In the first and second codon position all the vertebrate genes are stationary except the apocytochrome b and CoIII of xenopus in the first codon position. On the other hand for the genes of drosophila we found stationarity with all the vertebrates only for the second position of the CoI and CoIII genes. This means that our method can be applied to all the mt genes of xenopus (first position of CoIII and Cyt b excluded) and only to the second positions of the CoI and CoIII genes of Drosophila.

In Table 2 the average substitution rates at the first and second codon position of the four mitochondrial genes in various animal couples are reported. The most conserved gene is the subunit 1 of the cytochrome oxidase, the most variable the apocytochrome b and CoII. The values reported are comparable with those of many nuclear genes (results not shown) and demonstrate that mt protein coding genes do not evolve faster than nuclear genes. On the contrary the silent substitution rate in mitochondria greatly exceeds that of nuclear genes. The mt process is from 4 to 10 times faster, according to our results[2] and those of various authors[9,10]. In our opinion, it is responsible of the lack of stationarity conditions at the third silent codon position which is observed among the vertebrates when man and xenopus are enclosed (see Table 1).

104

Table 1. Results of the chi-square test for stationarity for the genes Cyt b (1), CoI (2), CoII (3), CoIII (4). The stationarity is assumed (Y) if chi2 < 1. The GenBank locus names are also listed.

Codon position	Human				Cow				Mouse				Rat				Xenopus				Drosophila				Locus names
	1	2	3	4	1	2	3	4	1	2	3	4	1	2	3	4	1	2	3	4	1	2	3	4	
Human																									HUMMT (1,2,3,4)
1st	-	-	-	-	Y	Y	Y	Y	Y	Y	Y	Y	Y	Y	Y	Y	N	Y	Y	N	N	N	N	N	
2nd	-	-	-	-	Y	Y	Y	Y	Y	Y	Y	Y	Y	Y	Y	Y	N	Y	Y	Y	N	Y	N	Y	
3rd	-	-	-	-	N	N	N	N	N	N	N	N	N	N	N	N	N	N	N	N	N	N	N	N	
Cow																									BOVMT (1,2,3,4)
1st					-	-	-	-	Y	Y	Y	Y	Y	Y	Y	Y	N	Y	Y	Y	N	N	N	N	
2nd					-	-	-	-	Y	Y	Y	Y	Y	Y	Y	Y	Y	Y	Y	Y	N	Y	N	Y	
3rd					-	-	-	-	Y	Y	Y	Y	N	N	N	N	N	N	N	N	N	N	N	N	
Mouse																									MUSMT (1,2,3,4)
1st									-	-	-	-	Y	Y	Y	Y	Y	Y	Y	N	N	N	N	N	
2nd									-	-	-	-	Y	Y	Y	Y	Y	Y	Y	Y	Y	Y	Y	Y	
3rd									-	-	-	-	Y	Y	Y	Y	N	N	N	N	N	N	N	N	
Rat																									RATMTCYBT (1) RATMTCYOS (2,3,4)
1st													-	-	-	-	Y	Y	Y	Y	N	N	N	N	
2nd													-	-	-	-	Y	Y	Y	Y	Y	Y	Y	Y	
3rd													-	-	-	-	N	N	N	N	N	N	N	N	
Xenopus																									XENMTCG (1,2,3,4)
1st																	-	-	-	-	N	N	N	N	
2nd																	-	-	-	-	N	Y	N	Y	
3rd																	-	-	-	-	N	N	N	N	
Drosophila																									DRYMTTGB (1) DROMTM1 (2) DROMTY2 (3,4)
1st																					-	-	-	-	
2nd																					-	-	-	-	
3rd																					-	-	-	-	

Table 2. Average evolutionary replacements rates (V_r) and their standard
deviations at the first and second codon positions in the genes:
CoI, CoII, CoIII and Cyt b for the couples rat-human (RH), mouse-
-human (MH), cow-human (BH), xenopus-human (XH) and drosophila-
-human (DH).

Gene	Codon position	Evolutionary rate (V_r) (10^{-9}sub/site · year)				
		RH	MH	BH	XH	DH
CoI	1st	0.76±0.26	0.73±0.25	0.72±0.25	0.72±0.25	-
	2nd	0.26±0.11	0.28±0.13	0.25±0.10	0.23±0.12	0.24±0.10
CoII	1st	1.74±0.74	1.79±0.76	1.87±0.76	1.28±0.63	-
	2nd	0.94±0.43	0.91±0.42	0.88±0.39	0.56±0.30	-
CoIII	1st	0.90±0.39	0.77±0.37	0.91±0.41	-	-
	2nd	0.62±0.28	0.57±0.26	0.48±0.22	0.37±0.21	0.41±0.19
Cyt b	1st	1.63±0.55	1.68±0.56	1.62±0.56	-	-
	2nd	0.80±0.27	0.73±0.27	0.86±0.30	0.63±0.27	-

According to our base-drift hypothesis[2] two homologous genes belonging to
the species A and B remain stationary when their distance, d, defined as

$$d_{AB} = V_p \cdot T_{AB}$$

V_p = average rate of the process p
T_{AB} = divergence time between A and B
is below a well defined d_O value which, according to our calculation[2,3],
is equal to 0.5 ÷ 1 substitution/site · year. When $d_{AB} > d_O$, some drift
effects, yet to be understood, come into play and spoil the stationarity of
the process. In other words we postulate that gene evolution is subject both
to continuous variations, proportional to the time within well defined
limits, and to discontinuous changes.The limits of continuous variations are
defined by both the rate of the process and the divergence time. The slower
the process, the broader the time in which there is a regular gene variation
and the DNA sequences can behave as molecular clocks.
The data of Table 1 confirm our hypothesis and explain also the lack of stationarity observed among highly divergent animals (i.e. mammals - drosophila
and xenopus - drosophila) at the first and second codon position of some
cytochrome genes.

Gene evolution in plants

We have analyzed the evolution of the CoII genes among the following
species: three monocotyledons, rice (Oryza sativa), maize (Zea mays) and
wheat (Triticum aestivum) and two dicotyledons, oenothera (Oenothera
berteriana) and pea (Pisum sativum) and the evolution of Cyt b among
oenothera, maize and wheat. In both genes the stationarity conditions are
verified for the three codon positions (results not shown).
Among the monocot plants the gene variation is extremely low (up to 99% of
homology) and the evolutionary rate can be calculated with extreme diffi-

culty. Assuming a distance of 50 MY between wheat and maize[15] the silent substutition rate for the CoII gene among maize, rice and wheat results to be about 0.8×10^{-10} substitutions/site·year more than two order of magnitude lower than the silent substitution rate among rat, mouse and cow which turns out to be 1.4×10^{-8} substitutions/site·year[1].

The average substitution rate of first, second and third codon position for CoII and Cyt b between monocots and dicots are reported in Table 3. The values are definitely lower than those calculated in animal mitochondria codon position. The silent substitution rate appears to be also much slower than in any nuclear genes where a $V_s = 0.4 \times 10^{-8}$ sub/site·year was calculated with our method[2].

Table 3. Average evolutionary base substitution rates (v) and their standard deviation at the first, second and third silent codon positions in the genes CoII and Cyt b between the species: Zea mays (Mz), Oenothera berteriana (Oe), Oryza sativa (Ri), Pisum sativum (Pe), Triticum aestivum (Wh). The locus names from GenBank collection are respectively: MZEMTMOX1, MZEMTCOB, OBEMTCYO2, RICMTCYO2, PEAMTCOII, WHTMTCOII, WHMTCYBB. The sequences were extracted by ACNUC software retrieval system[7]. The Cyt b gene sequence for Oenothera b was as reported by Schuster[11]. The divergence time between dicot and monocot plants was estimated from indirect data reported in reference 13.

| Couple | Codon position | Evolutionary rate (v) (10^{-9} sub/site · year) | |
		CoII	Cyt b
Mz-Oe	1st	0.41+0.27	0.15+0.09
	2nd	0.35+0.22	0.16+0.10
	3rd	0.84+0.46	0.29+0.18
Mz-Pe	1st	0.48+0.36	-
	2nd	0.59+0.40	-
	3rd	0.70+0.48	-
Oe-Pe	1st	0.56+0.41	-
	2nd	0.53+0.38	-
	3rd	0.98+0.56	-
Oe-Ri	1st	0.42+0.28	-
	2nd	0.38+0.23	-
	3rd	0.80+0.46	-
Oe-Wh	1st	0.46+0.30	0.14+0.09
	2nd	0.40+0.24	0.13+0.09
	3rd	0.71+0.41	0.24+0.15
Pe-Wh	1st	0.55+0.38	-
	2nd	0.59+0.39	-
	3rd	0.64+0.43	-
Ri-Pe	1st	0.49+0.38	-
	2nd	0.65+0.43	-
	3rd	0.73+0.48	-

DISCUSSION

It has been widely reported that mitochondrial genes evolve faster than nuclear genes. The results reported here and others previously published by us[2] clearly demonstrate that in animal cells the replacement rates of mt protein coding genes are comparable to those of many nuclear genes. On the contrary the silent substitution rate in mitochondria highly exceeds that in nuclei. Our data are in agreement with the results reported by Gillespie using another method[12] and confirm that the evolution of replacement and silent sites are somewhat uncoupled because, for whatever reason the mitochondrial silent sites evolve more rapidly, it does not cause a speed up of the protein evolution. Since the rate of evolution depends on both the rate of mutation and the rate of mutation fixation[14]: $E = M \cdot F$, it may be argued that in mitochondrial genes the faster rate of silent substitution depends on looser functional constraints on the codon strategy which is presumably linked to the transcription apparatus and to the protein synthesizing machinary of the organelles. However it cannot be excluded that the rate of mutation is higher in animal mitochondria but it does not affect proportionally the rate of replacement since mitochondrially coded proteins possess higher functional constraints. The extremely slow rate of evolution in plant mitochondria is remarkable. It suggests that the system is highly constrained and/or that the rate of mutation in plants is much lower than in animals. The latter property can be linked to the different metabolism of mitochondria from the two kingdoms. It is interesting to stress that also the chloroplast genes in plants display a slow rate of evolution (G. Hauska, personal communications).

ACKNOWLEDGEMENTS

This work was supported partially by Progetto Strategico Biotecnologie, and Progetto Finalizzato Ingegneria Genetica e Basi Molecolari delle Malattie Ereditarie, C.N.R., Italy and partially by M.P.I. (40%).

REFERENCES

1. C. Lanave, G. Preparata, C. Saccone, and G. Serio, A new method for calculating evolutionary substitution rates, J. Mol. Evol. 20:86 (1984).
2. C. Lanave, G. Preparata, and C. Saccone, Mammalian genes as molecular clocks?, J. Mol. Evol. 21:346 (1985).
3. C. Lanave, S. Tommasi, G. Preparata, and C. Saccone, Transition and transversion rate in the evolution of animal mitochondrial DNA, BioSystems 19:273 (1986).
4. T. H. Jukes, and C.R. Cantor, Evolution of protein molecules, in: "Mammalian Protein Metabolism", H.N. Munro, ed., Academic Press, New York (1969).
5. N. Takahata, and M. Kimura, A model of evolutionary base substitutions and its application with special reference to rapid change of pseudogenes, Genetics 98:641 (1981).
6. T. Gojobori, K. Ishii, and M. Nei, Estimation of average number of nucleotide substitutions when the rate of substitution varies with nucleotide, J. Mol. Evol. 18:414 (1982).

7. M. Gouy, C. Gautier, M. Attimonelli, C. Lanave, and G. Di Paola, ACNUC: a portable retrieval system for nucleic acid sequence databases: logical and physical designs and usage, Cabios 1:167 (1985).

8. G. Preparata, and C. Saccone, A simple quantitative model of molecular clock, J. Mol. Evol., in press (1986).

9. W. M. Brown, E.M. Prager, A. Wang, and A.C. Wilson, Mitochondrial DNA sequences of primates: tempo and mode of evolution, J. Mol. Evol. 18:225 (1982).

10. T. Miyata, H. Hayashida, R. Kikuno, M. Hasegawa, M. Kobayashi, and K. Koike, Molecular clock of silent substitution: at least a six-fold preponderance of silent changes in mitochondrial genes over those in nuclear genes, J. Mol. Evol. 19:28 (1982).

11. W. Schuster, and A. Brennicke, TGA – Termination codon in the apocyto-chrome b gene from oenothera mitochondria, Current Genetics 9:157 (1985).

12. J. H. Gillespie, Variability of evolutionary rates of DNA, Genetics 113:1077 (1986).

13. A. Cronquist, in: "The evolution and classification of flowering plants", W.C. Steere and H.B. Glass eds, T. Nelson and sons LTD, London (1970).

14. A. C. Wilson, S.S. Carlson, and T.J. White, Biochemical evolution, Annu. Rev. Biochem. 46:573 (1977).

15. P. H. Boer, J.E. McIntosh, M.W. Gray and L. Bonen, The wheat mitochon-drial gene for apocytochrome b: absence of a prokaryotic ribosome binding site, Nucleic Acid Res. 13:2281 (1985).

INVOLVEMENT OF NUCLEAR GENES IN SPLICING OF THE MITOCHONDRIAL COB TRANSCRIPT IN S. CEREVISIAE

Jan Kreike[1], Gaby Krummeck[2], Thomas Söllner[2],
Cornelia Schmidt[2] and Rudolf J. Schweyen[1]

[1])Institut für Mikrobiologie und Genetik, Universität
Wien, Althanstrasse 14, A-1090 Wien, Austria
[2])Institut für Genetik und Mikrobiologie, Universität
München, Maria Ward Strasse 1a, D-8000 München, F.R.G.

INTRODUCTION

The long form of the mitochondrial COB gene consists of six exons (B1 - B6), separated by five introns (bI1 - bI5). The number of known nuclear genes in yeast specifically involved in the expression of this single mitochondrial gene, is steadily increasing. To date at least four nuclear genes (CBS1, CBS2, CBP1 and CBP6) have been shown to influence the stability of the COB transcript and its translation (Dieckmann et al., 1984; Dieckmann and Tzagoloff, 1985; Rödel, 1986). Also four genes are known to be involved in the excision of single introns from these transcripts: CBP2, MRS1, NAM2 and SUP-101. CBP2 and MRS1 gene products are essential for the excision of intron bI5 and bI3, respectively (McGraw and Tzagoloff, 1983; Kreike et al., 1986; Kreike et al., 1987). NAM2 and SUP-101 are nuclear sup-pressors of splice mutations in the COB introns bI4 and bI1, respectively (Dujardin et al., 1983; Schmelzer et al., 1983).

In our search for nuclear genes involved in mitochondrial splicing, we used two different approaches: (i), we characterized nuclear pet⁻ mutants defective in splicing of COB RNA and we screened a yeast gene bank for plasmids complementing them; (ii), we searched for a nuclear mutation (SUP-101) suppressing the defect in the mitochondrial cis-acting splice-mutant M1301, established a gene bank from this strain and screened it for plasmids conferring suppression activity.

Here we will discuss some recent results on MRS1 and MRS3, the two nuclear genes involved in the excision of intron bI3 and bI1, resp. MRS1 is indispensable for yeasts having the optional intron bI3. It appears to be absent in some yeasts lacking this intron. MRS3 is dispensable even for yeast strains having the optional intron bI1. As this intron is capable of autocatalytic splicing in vitro (Schmelzer and Schweyen, 1986), the MRS3 gene product might have an accessory function for the process of RNA splicing.

RESULTS AND DISCUSSION

The yeast nuclear MRS1 gene product is essential for the excision
of COB intron bI3

      In our first approach we have characterized several nuclear
mutants, defective in the expression of the mitochondrial COB
gene (Pillar et al., 1983). One of these mutants (mrs1-1) is
unable to excise two introns (bI3 and bI4) from the COB pre-RNA,
as well as intron aI4 from the OXI3 transcript (Kreike et al.,
1986). We named the mutation in this strain mrs1-1 (mitochondrial
RNA splicing). The primary defect in this mutant is the non-
excision of intron bI3; as a secondary effect of this also bI4
and aI4 cannot be excised. This became obvious, when we combined
the nuclear mrs1-1 mutation with a mitochondrial genome lacking
intron bI3 but still having retained the other four introns in
its COB gene. This strain was found to be respiratory competent.
So, we concluded, that in the presence of the nuclear mrs1-1
mutation COB introns bI1, bI2, bI4 and bI5 can be excised
correctly. We did not observe revertants of the mrs1-1 mutant
with a deletion of this mitochondrial intron, as other authors
reported (Hill et al., 1985). This may be a strain specific
effect, or it may be due to the absence in this mutant of a
functional form of the putative intron bI3 maturase, which may be
involved in this intron deletion process.

      From a yeast gene bank (Fasiolo et al., 1981) a recombinant
plasmid was isolated, which complements the mrs1-1 mutant. The
location and the DNA sequence of the MRS1 gene have been determined. We found two long open reading frames, which are on opposite strands and overlap more than 600 base-pairs. In vitro mutagenesis was used to determine which one of them is responsible
for complementation of the mrs1-1 mutation. We found, that a
premature stopcodon in the longer one (ORF1) abolishes complementation by the plasmid, whereas a stopcodon in ORF2 does not
(Kreike et al., 1987). Apparently, the ORF1 product is needed for
the splicing of the COB transcript. However, on basis of these
results, we did not know, whether this is the only function of
the gene. In order to answer this question, the MRS1 gene in the
chromosomal DNA of a respiratory competent strain was disrupted
by insertion of the TRP1 gene at a central site in the gene. We
compared the phenotype of this strain with that of the mrs1-1
mutant, having probably only a point mutation at some distance
from the site of disruption. Both strains are respiratory deficient and accumulate the same COB (and OXI3) RNA precursors. On
glucose medium they grow with comparable generation times. This
result reveals, that the MRS1 gene (ORF1) is essential for intron
bI3 excision, but it has no other vital functions. We do not know
yet whether ORF2 has any functions at all. The gene disruption
experiment, which also interrupts ORF2, suggests, that it has no
vital functions in the cell and no direct function in the splicing of COB transcripts (Kreike et al., 1987). These results are
summarized in Figure 1.

Yeasts lacking the MRS1 gene.

Since the nuclear MRS1 gene is essential for the excision of the
mitochondrial intron bI3 , we wanted to test, whether this
nuclear gene is conserved in strains, which possess or lack
intron bI3 in their mitochondrial DNA. Southern hybridi-zation
were performed with digested chromosomal DNA from seven yeast

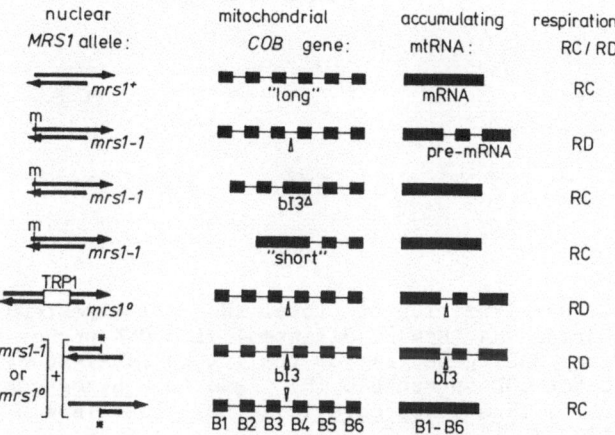

Figure 1. Combination of MRS1 alleles and different mitochondrial COB genes and their effect on COB RNA splicing. RC: respiratory competent; RD: respiratory deficient. Right arrow: ORF
1; left arrow: ORF 2; open block: TRP1 gene inserted at a central
site of the chromosomal MRS1 gene; black bars: COB exons; lines:
COB introns; m: the presumable approximate site of the mrs1-1 mutation; *: stopcodons introduced by in vitro mutagenesis; open
arrowheads indicate the position of intron bI3. Figure not drawn
to scale.

strains, using an MRS1 specific DNA probe. The strains were a
gift of H.F. Tabak (Amsterdam) and K. Wolf (Munich). As shown in
Figure 2A a 1.2 kb fragment could be identified in DNA from four
strains (S. cerevisiae D273-10B, S. cerevisiae DBY747, S. unisporus and S. florentinus. S. diarensis gave only a very weak
signal, visible after long exposure. Since the length of the
fragment and the intensity of the band are the same for the four
strains, the gene appears to be well conserved. With the DNA's
from Schizosaccharomyces pombe 50h- and K. lactis no signal could
be detected.

We have asked the question, whether strains having MRS1,
would also have intron bI3 in their mitochondrial genomes. This
was indeed the case. In Fig. 2B the results are shown of the
Southern hybridization with total or mitochondrial DNA using the
1.4 kb BamHI-EcoRV fragment as an intron bI3 specific probe. All
the strains having the MRS1 gene, also had an intron bI3 homologous sequence, with the exception of strain S. cerevisiae D273-
10B. A plausible explanation for the presence of the MRS1 gene
and the absence of intron bI3 in this strain is, that its origin
is too recent to eliminate its "useless" MRS1 gene. S. diarensis
again gave only very weak signals with the probe. This may be
interpreted, that S. diarensis has an MRS1-like gene and an
intron bI3 homologous sequence, which are, however, highly

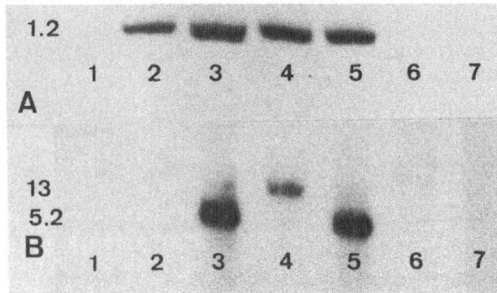

Figure 2. Hybridization of total (Hae III digested), total or
mitochondrial DNA (Bam HI digested) with DNA probes specific for
the nuclear MRS1 gene (A), or the 1.4 kb BamHI-EcoRV fragment
specific for COB intron bI3 (B). Lane 1: Schizosaccharomyces
pombe 50h⁻ ; lane 2: S. cerevisiae D273-10B; lane 3: S. cerevisiae DBY747; lane 4: S. unisporus; lane 5: S. florentinus; lane
6: S. diarensis; lane 7: K. lactis. Length of the DNA-fragments
in kilobasepairs.

diverged from the corre-sponding sequences in S. cerevisiae. Thus
it appears to be the case, that yeast strains having intron bI3,
also posses the nuclear MRS1 gene, in line with the finding, that
this nuclear gene is essential for bI3 excision. The study of
more yeast strains and the use of low stringency hybridization
are underway.

The nuclear gene MRS3 in high copy suppresses the mitochondrial splice mutation M1301

In our second approach we looked for suppressors of the
mitochondrial mutation M1301. This mutation is located in COB
intron bI1 and it blocks the excision in vivo of this intron
completely. A revertant of this mitochondrial mutant was found to
carry a dominant nuclear mutation, SUP-101, which efficiently
suppresses the splice defect exerted by mutation M1301 only
(Schmelzer and Schweyen, 1986). From a gene bank of this suppressor strain a DNA fragment (N3) was isolated, which in a high copy
plasmid confers suppression, when transformed into a M1301
strain. The N3 fragment carries a single open reading frame of
942 bp, starting with ATG, the intactness of which is essential
for bI1 excision. Therefore, we refer to this ORF as the MRS3
gene (Schmidt et al., submitted). As the N3 fragment originates
from the SUP-101 revertant, we expected, that it had the SUP-101
suppressor allele. However, this is unlikely, since from DNA of a
non-suppressor strain a homologous fragment could be isolated,
which had the same suppressor activity when present in a high
copy plasmid (YEp13)(Koll et al., submitted). But transformation
of M1301 with the fragment present in a low copy plasmid (e.g.
the CEN/ARS plasmid YCp50) or an integrating plasmid (pEMBLYi27)
gave two classes of transformants (Söllner et al., submitted):
(i), a majority of splicing deficient transformants, having one
or few copies of the YCp50/N3 recombinant plasmid or one or few
pEMBLYi27/N3 copies integrated in the chromosomal DNA.; (ii), a
minority of transformants (up to 20%), which are respiratory
competent and have multiple copies of the autonomous or integrated plasmids. An example of a Southern hybridization of the
two classes of pEMBLYi27/MRS3 transformants with part of the N3

114

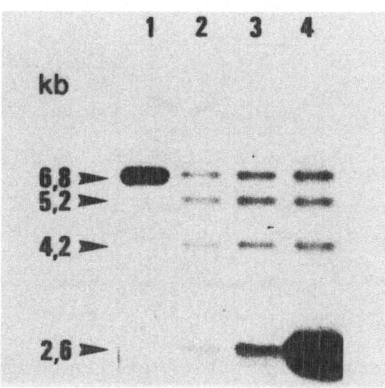

Figure 3. Southern hybridization of Bam HI digested chromosomal
DNA from strain AH215/M1301 (lane 1); or from transformants with
the integrated plasmid pEMBLYi27/MRS3 (RD, lanes 2,3; RC, lane 4)
using a MRS3 specific probe.

fragment as probe, is shown in Figure 3. Single integration of
this plasmid gives a 5.2 kb and a 4.2 kb BamHI fragment, instead
of a 6.8 kb band in untransformed cells. After two or more in
tandem integrations a band of 2.6 kb appears, the intensity of
which is related to the number of integrated plasmid copies
(Figure 4). The highest intensity signifies over 20 copies per
haploid genome. After growth of these respiratory competent
transformants on glucose medium for two days respiratory deficient colonies were found, in which this number had decreased to
only four copies per cell (data not shown). This suggests a
direct correlation between copy number of the MRS3 gene and
suppression of the M1301 mutation.

It thus appears, that selection for splicing competent
transformants results in: (i), a most unusual high copy number of
the recombinant CEN/ARS plasmid YCp50/MRS3, or (ii), the presence
of multiple in tandem array integrated recombinant pEMBLYi27/MRS3
plasmids in the chromosomal DNA. The amplification of the nuclear
MRS3 gene may lead to an increased number of MRS3 transcripts in
the cell. In the SUP-101 revertant, in which the MRS3 gene is not
amplified, it is unlikely, that suppression is caused by a mutation in the protein coding sequence. A more likelypossibility is,
that suppression is due to a mutation in a far upstream regulatory sequence, which leads to unusual high expression of this
gene. Interestingly, we were able to isolate from AH215 DNA two
other fragments (carrying the putative MRS2 and MRS4 genes),
which also suppress mutation M1301, when present in a high copy
number plasmid. These fragments do not crosshybridize with each
other nor with MRS3, and the three genes have completely different restriction maps. It is our current hypothesis, that the
MRS2, MRS3 and MRS4 genes code for accessory proteins involved in
mitochondrial RNA splicing. In line with this hypothesis is our
observation, that disruption of the MRS3 gene in the chromosomal
DNA of a respiratory competent strain does not lead to a splice
defect of intron bI1 or to respiratory deficiency (Söllner et
al., submitted).

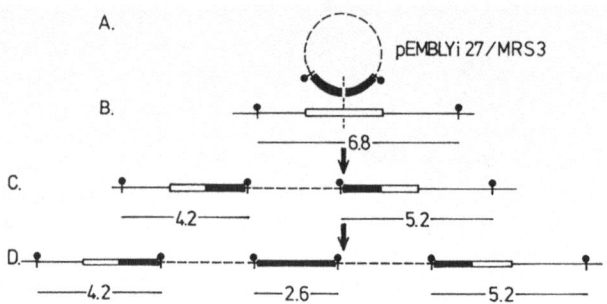

Figure 4. Schematic representation of linearized plasmid
pEMBLYi27/MRS3 (A) and of chromosomal DNA (B) after a single (C)
or two (D) integrations of the plasmid at the MRS3 locus. Only
the Bam HI restriction sites are shown here (●). Solid line:
chromosomal DNA; dotted line: plasmid sequences; black bar: MRS3
region in the plasmid; open bar: MRS3 region in the chromosomal
DNA. Length in kilobasepairs.

CONCLUDING REMARKS

     We have used two different approaches to identify nuclear
genes, which are specifically involved in the excision of single
mitochondrial introns. Both approaches, (i) functional complementation of nuclear mutants defective in mitochondrial splicing
by a recombinant plasmid, and (ii) isolation of nuclear suppressor mutations, restoring splicing in mitochondrial splice defective mutants, have lead to the identification of two completely
different classes of nuclear genes in S. cerevisiae, which both
are involved specifically in mitochondrial splicing. One class,
including MRS1, CBP2 and probably NAM2, is indispensable for
mitochondrial splicing. Mutations in these genes or their
disruption lead to a splice defect, or, in the case of NAM2
disruption, to complete loss of the mitochondrial DNA (Hill et
al., 1985; Labouesse et al., 1985; Kreike et al., 1987). The
second class, including the gene carrying the SUP-101 allele and
probably the MRS2, MRS3 and MRS4 genes, is involved in mitochondrial RNA splicing, but disruption of one of these genes has no
phenotypic effect. The MRS3 gene product may be dispensable,
since other genes may substitute for its function in bI1 excision. Concomitant disruption of all these genes may be necessary
to block the excision of intron bI1.

     Amplification of nuclear genes has been observed in higher
eukayotes. Also in yeast some genes (e.g. the genes coding for
ribosomal RNA's) are present in more than one copy per haploid
genome. By studying suppressors like MRS3, the amplification of
which may give a selective advantage to the cell, the mechanism
of such amplification in yeast may be studied.

REFERENCES

Dieckmann, C.L., Koerner, T.J. and Tzagoloff, A. (1984) J.
      Biol. Chem., 259, 4722-4731.

Dieckmann, C.L. and Tzagoloff, A. (1985) J. Biol. Chem., 260,
      1513-1520.

Dujardin, G., Labouesse, M., Netter, P. and Slonimski, P.P.
      (1983) in: Mitochondria 1983, Nucleo-mitochondrial
      Interactions, (Schweyen, R.J., Wolf, K. and
      Kaudewitz, F., eds.) De Gruyter, Berlin - New York,
      pp. 233-250.

Fasiolo, F., Bonnet, J. and Lacroute, F. (1981) J. Biol.
      Chem., 256, 2324-2328.

Hill, J., McGraw, P. and Tzagoloff, A. (1985) J. Biol. Chem.,
      260, 3235-3238.

Kreike, J., Schulze, M., Pillar, T., Körte, A. and Rödel, G.
      (1986) Curr. Genet., 11, 185-191.

Kreike, J., Schulze, M., Ahne, A. and Lang, B.F. (1987) EMBO
      J., 7, in the press.

Labouesse, M., Dujardin, G. and Slonimski, P.P. (1985) Cell,
      41, 133-143.

McGraw, P. and Tzagoloff, A. (1983) J. Biol. Chem., 258,
      9459-9468.

Pillar, T., Lang, B.F., Steinberger, I., Vogt, B. and
      Kaudewitz, F. (1983) J. Biol. Chem., 258, 7954-7959.

Rödel, G. (1986) Curr. Genet., 11, 41-45.

Rödel, G., Michaelis, U., Forsbach, V., Kreike, J. and
      Kaudewitz, F. (1986) Curr. Genet., 11, 47-53.

Schmelzer, C., Schmidt, C., May, K. and Schweyen, R.J. (1983)
      EMBO-J., 2, 2047-2052.

Schmelzer, C. and Schweyen, R.J. (1986) Cell, 46, 557-565.

INTRONS AS KEY ELEMENTS IN THE EVOLUTION OF MITOCHONDRIAL GENOMES IN LOWER EUKARYOTES

Klaus Wolf[1], Alfred Ahne[2], Luigi Del Giudice[3],
Güler Oraler[4], Feryal Kanbay[1], Ana Maria Merlos-Lange[1],
Franz Welser[1], and Manfred Zimmer[1]

[1]Institut für Gentik und Mikrobiologie der Universität
Maria-Ward-Strasse 1a, 800 Müchen 19
Federal Republic of Germany

[2]Gesellschaft für Strahlen- und Umweltforschung
Ingolstädter Landstrasse 1 8042 Neuherberg
Federal Republic of Germany

[3]Istituto Internazionale di Genetic e Biofisica
CNR, Via G Marconi 10, 80125 Napoli, Italia

[4]Department of Biology, University of Istanbul
Vezneciler-Istanbul, Turkey

INTRODUCTION

It is now well documented that mitochondrial (mt) genomes
of all eukaryotes contain genes encoding elements of mt protein synthesis (rRNAs and tRNAs) as well as a few proteins
for respiration and energy conservation. Genes encoding apocytochrome b (cob) or subunit I of cytochrome c oxidase (cox1)
can be found, with no exception, in every mt genome. These
genes are sufficiently similar in sequence, that comparison
of DNA sequences allows to assign their functions in the different organisms. This set of genes is referred to as the
"basic set" of mt genetic information (Kotylak et al., 1985).
Lower eukaryotes possess additional genetic information in
their mt genomes, which has been termed by Slonimski and
collaborators (Kotylak et al., 1985) the "extra set" of mt
genetic information. This information is deposited as introns
of the genes forming the "basic set". It is, however, important to note, that not all mt introns contain the genetic information for a protein.

The sequence of the human mt genome (Anderson et al.,
1981) has revealed an economy of genome organization never
before encountered in the world of eukaryotes, with genes so
tightly packed that there are few or no non-coding bases between them. This compact organization is highly conserved among
mammals (Bibb et al., 1981) and is shared with other lower eukaryotes such as sea urchins, flatworms and insects even including the relative sizes and positions of genes. An entirely
different situation has been found in the group of ascomycetes,
where the genomes of mitochondria are highly divergent both
in size and in gene order.

The extreme conservation of mammalian mt genomes on the one hand and the immense variability of fungal mt genomes on the other hand, has been attributed to the presence of introns in the latter and the absence in the former group of organisms. The proteins encoded by some of these introns have been termed "Nucleid Acid Wielding Proteins" (Kotylak et al., 1985), since they are very likely involved in the process of deletion of introns from the gene, in transposition events, and in homologous recombination between mt genes. All these events are believed to be responsible for shaping the mt genomes in lower eukaryotes.

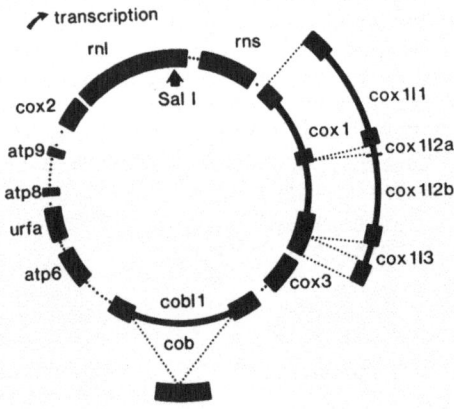

Figure 1. Circular map of the mt genome of strain 50 of *S. pombe* (inner circle) and the cox1 region of strain EF1 (outer circle). Thick bars represent exons, thinner bars introns. tRNA genes are indicated by dots. The gene symbols are the following: rnl and rns - genes for the large and small ribosomal RNA; cox1, cox2, cox3 - genes for subunits of cytochrome oxidase; cob - gene for apocytochrome b; atp6, atp8, atp9 - genes for subunits of ATPase; urfa - unassigned reading frame. The genetic nomenclature of nuclear and mt genes of *S. pombe* is found in Kohli (1987).

In this paper we shall give a brief overview of experiments designed to demonstrate the mobility of introns and the fluidity of the mt genome. The model used for this study is the small mt genome of the fission yeast *Schizosaccharomyces pombe (S. pombe)*, which has been sequenced entirely (Lang, 1984; Lang et al., 1985; Trinkl et al., 1985; Trinkl and Wolf, 1986; Merlos-Lange et al., 1987; B. F. Lang, unpublished results.

120

THE MITOCHONDRIAL GENOME OF *SCHIZOSACCHAROMYCES POMBE*

The genome (depicted in Figure 1) contains genes for the large and small ribosomal RNA (rnl and rns; for the genetic nomenclature see Kohli, 1987 and Wolf, 1987), which are separated by three tRNA genes. The three subunits of ATPase map in the genes atp6, atp8, and atp9. The latter two genes are separated by one of the two main tRNA clusters. Two of the three genes encoding subunits of cytochrome c oxidase, cox2 and cox3, are continuous. The cob gene is continuous in strain EF1 (Trinkl et al., 1985), but mosaic in strain 50 (Lang et al., 1984). The cox1 gene also shows a strain dependent variation in the number of introns (2-4) (Trinkl and Wolf, 1986). A single intergenic open reading frame (urfa) is located between atp6 and atp8. It potentially encodes a polypeptide of 227 amino acids (Kornrumpf, 1984). The 25 tRNA genes are organized in two main clusters (between atp8 and atp9, and cob and atp6), and with the exception of the regions between cox1 and cox3, and cox2 and rnl, respectively, tRNA genes are found to separate the different genes. In this study we have concentrated on the two mosaic genes cob (with 0-1 group II introns) and cox1 (with 2-4 group I introns).

THE OPTIONAL GROUP II INTRON IS A LATE ACQUISITION OF THE COB GENE

The cob gene in strain 50 is interrupted by a 2526 bp group II intron with an open reading frame (orf) of 2421 bp (Lang et al., 1985). The location of this intron is different from cob introns in *Saccharomyces cerevisiae* (*S. cerevisiae*), *Aspergillus nidulans* (*A. nidulans*) and *Neurospora crassa* (*N. crassa*). For strain EF1, Trinkl et al. (1985) could show that the cob gene is continuous. Its comparison with the exons of the mosaic gene in strain 50 has revealed a series of base pair changes in the splice point region of the otherwise highly homologous gene. The same situation has been described for the exons 5a and 5b in the cox1 gene of two *S. cerevisiae* strains (Hensgens et al., 1983). Altogether 11 base pair changes are found between the exons of the two strains. It is interesting that, with one exception, the changes lead to codons rarely if ever used in the mt genome of the strain with the continuous exon 5. The authors propose that these base pair changes are the consequence of a recombination event between a mt genome and a distantly related DNA, and that not enough time has elapsed to permit back-mutation to more commonly used codons. In essence, this result suggests that the mosaic form of the gene is the older one, and that the intron has been excised recently, since the rare codons are found in the genome with the continuous exon. In contrast to the situation in *S. cerevisiae*, the comparison between the cob genes in strain 50 (mosaic cob gene) and in strain EF1 (continuous cob gene) did not allow to assign the rare codons to the continuous or the mosaic gene. As a consequence it was not possible to decide whether these nucleotide changes are the result of an intron insertion or an intron deletion. This decision was possible after the sequence analysis of five further strains with continuous cob gene and a second strain with mosaic cob gene. The flanking exons of the mosaic cob gene of strain UCD-FstI (isolated 1965 by Prof. M. W. Miller from a slime flux of *Angophora costata* in Australia, kindly provided by Prof. H. J. Phaff, Davis, California). The flanking exons of the mosaic

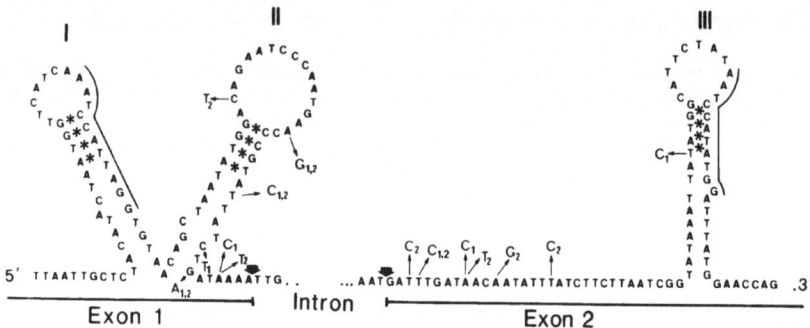

Figure 2. Possible secondary structure of the exon parts flanking the cob intron in the mt genome of strain 50 (adapted from Lang et al., 1985). The asterisks indicate short helical segments common to all three helices. (An exchange of a T by a G, leading to a G-U pairing in the RNA is permitted). The lines mark direct repeats in the two outer helices. The arrows mark base changes. Subscript 1: base change in the short cob genes, subscript 2: base change in the mosaic cob gene of strain UCD-FstI.

cob gene of this strain show other base pair changes than those found in strain 50. In contrast, all six continuous cob genes exhibited identical sequences. From this data it is plausible to propose that the present day group II intron-containing cob gene is the result of an intron integration.

Lang et al. (1985) have shown, that the flankin exon regions of the cob gene in strain 50 can form three helices, which contain direct repeats in the two outer helices and very similar base-paired regions in the upper part of all three helices (Figure 2). Here the base pair changes for the short cob genes and in the mosaic cob gene of strain UCD-FstI, compared with the cob gene of strain 50, are indicated. They are found in the regions immediately adjacent to the splice point for "short" and "long" genes, in addition in helix II for UCD-FstI and in helices II and III for the "short" genes. In this context it is worth to recall the two direct repeats located in the helices I and III in the cob gene, and it is interesting to note that none of the base changes occurs in the long direct repeats. These structures are reminiscent of the long direct repeats of transposons or the long terminal repeats of retroviruses, and, in a speculative view, the intron with adjacent exon sequences could be viewed as the relic of a transposable element.

HOMOLOGY BETWEEN MITOCHONDRIAL INTRONS OF *SACCHAROMYCES CEREVISIAE; ASPERGILLUS NIDULANS* AND *SCHIZOSACCHAROMYCES POMBE* SUGGESTS HORIZONTAL GENE TRANSFER

In strain 50, the mosaic cox1 gene contains two group I introns (cox1I1 and cox1I2b) with orfs in phase with their upstream exons. In strain EF1, the cox1 gene contains two additional small introns, which do not contain orfs (introns cox1I2a and cox1I3). Intron cox1I3 is inserted at the same position as intron 5β in the homologous *S. cerevisiae* gene. It is common to both introns that the conserved sequence elements E and P are not adjacent, and that both introns contain a stretch of A and U residues, which is 20 b in the case of

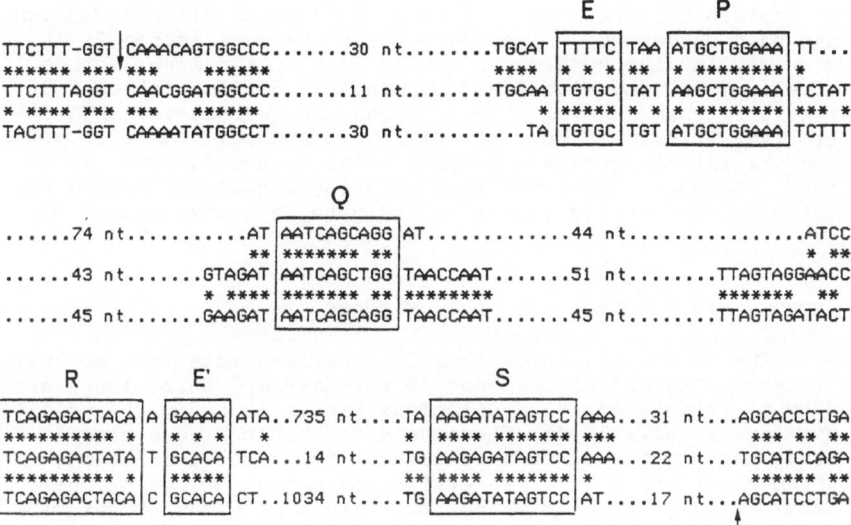

```
                                              E           P
TTCTTT-GGT|CAAACAGTGGCCC.......30 nt........TGCAT TTTTC TAA ATGCTGGAAA TT...
****** ***|***  ******                      ****  * * *  **  * ******** *
TTCTTTAGGT CAACGGATGGCCC.......11 nt........TGCAA TGTGC TAT AAGCTGGAAA TCTAT
* **** *** ***  ******                          * ***** * * * ******** *** *
TACTTT-GGT CAAAATATGGCCT.......30 nt...........TA TGTGC TGT ATGCTGGAAA TCTTT


                       Q
......74 nt..........AT AATCAGCAGG AT.............44 nt...............ATCC
                        ** ******* **                               * **
......43 nt.......GTAGAT AATCAGCTGG TAACCAAT.......51 nt........TTAGTAGGAACC
                   * **** ******* ** ********                      ******* **
......45 nt.......GAAGAT AATCAGCAGG TAACCAAT.......45 nt........TTAGTAGATACT


   R          E'                              S
TCAGAGACTACA A GAAAA ATA..735 nt....TA AAGATATAGTCC AAA...31 nt...AGCACCCTGA
********** * *  * * *      *          * **** *******  ***          *** ** **
TCAGAGACTATA T GCACA TCA...14 nt....TG AAGAGATAGTCC AAA...22 nt...TGCATCCAGA
********** * *  *****                 ** **** *******  *           ****** **
TCAGAGACTACA C GCACA CT..1034 nt....TG AAGATATAGTCC AT....17 nt...AGCATCCTGA
```

Figure 3. Comparison of the flanking exon sequences and the conserved sequence elements P, Q, R, S, E, and E' (boxed) from the *S. pombe* intron cox1I2a (middle line) with the homologous sequences of the cox1 intron 4 (upper line) and the cob intron 4 (lower line) from *S. cerevisiae*, which are very similar in their architecture and their intronic orfs. Identical bases are marked with asterisks, distances between conserve sequence elements are given in nucleotides. Arrows point to splice sites (Taken from Trinkl and Wolf, 1986)

the *S. pombe* intron and 160 b in the *S. cerevisiae* intron.

The other *S. pombe* intron, cox1I2a, is only 258 bp long and is the shortest group I intron so far found in lower eukaryotes. It is located at the same point where intron 4 is inserted in *S. cerevisiae*. It is remarkable (Figure 3) that the conserved sequence elements P, Q, R, S, E, and E' are not only well conserved among the two cox1 introns, but also a high degree of homology is found with the group I intron 4 of the cob gene of *S. cerevisiae*. This homology is found also in the regions adjacent to the conserved sequence blocks. If one admits an insertion of an A in the *S. pombe* sequence, there is an identity of 15 out of 17 bp between cox1I4 of *S. cerevisiae* and cox1I2a of *S. pombe*, and more astonishing, also 14 out of 17 bp between the *S. cerevisiae* cob intron 4 and intron cox1I2a of *S. pombe* in the flanking exon sequences.

On the one hand, location of homologous introns at the same place in genes of different organisms suggests that these introns may have been present in an ancestral gene before the divergence of the two organisms. Examples of identical location of introns in different organisms have been already described for several instances (Dujon, 1980; Nomyama et al., 1981; Lazowska et al., 1981; Burke and RajBhandary, 1982; Kan and Gall, 1982; Burke et al., 1984; Lang, 1984; Waring et al., 1984). On the other hand, this phenomenon is more readily explained as being due to recent insertions as suggested by Burke et al. (1984) for two introns in the *N. crassa* cob gene. One possibility to explain the presence of similar introns in different organisms has been suggested by Lang (1984) for the cox1 intron 2b of *S. pombe* and the homologous intron 3 of *A. nidulans* (Waring et al., 1984), by Michel and Cummings (1985) for intron 1 of *Podospora anserina (P. anserina)* and the *Tetrahymena* rRNA intron, by Trinkl and Wolf (1986) for intron cox1I2a of *S. pombe* and the introns cox1I4 and cobI4 of *S. cerevisiae*, and by Michel and Dujon (1986) for the *Tetrahymena* rRNA intron and the intron in the thymidylate synthase gene of bacteriophage *T4*.

INTRONS CAN BE REMOVED BY DNA SPLICING

Due to an extrachromosomally inherited mutation, so called "mutator strains" of *S. pombe* (Seitz-Mayr and Wolf, 1982) produce mt mutants carrying deletions between roughly 30 and 1500 bp (Ahne et al., 1984). These deletion mutants were used to study the process of "DNA splicing". By use of a deletion, the three classical ways of reversion (backmutation, mt or nuclear suppression) were eliminated. Starting with a mutant carrying a deletion of 162 bp in intron cox1I2b, we selected respiratory competent revertants. These revertants, which appeared at a frequency of $1.5 - 5 \times 10^{-6}$ were shown to have correctly spliced out the intron with the mutation from the cox1 gene. Intron DNA splicing was first described by Gargouri et al. (1983). It has been observed for the *S. cerevisiae* introns cobI1 (a group II intron without orf), cobI2 and cobI3 (both group I introns with orfs; Gargouri et al., 1983), for the introns cobI4 and cobI5 (group I; Perea and Jacq, 1986), and for intron cox1I1 (group II intron with orf; Carignani et al., 1986). It has been hypothesized (Gargouri et al., 1983) that the respective gene is processed by recombination between a cDNA reverse transcribed from a (partially) spliced mRNA precursor and the intron containing gene. Michel and Lang (1985) have shown that the deduced amino acid sequences of group II introns bear a dispersed but significant resemblance to reverse transcriptase of retroviruses. Steinhilber and Cummings (1986) could detect a reverse transcriptase activity in senescent mycelia of *P. anserina*. During senescence, the cox1 intron 1 (group II) is excised from the gene, circularized, and amplified (Kück et al., 1985). The structure of the *Mauriceville* and *Varkud* mt plasmids of *N. crassa* also suggests that they were generated via an RNA intermediate and a reverse transcription step (Akins et al., 1986). A direct proof for a group II intron product with reverse transcriptase activity is still missing. Merlos-Lange et al. (1987) have also found that the group II intron in the cob gene can be spliced out at the DNA level. By genetic analysis it could be shown that the process of DNA splicing of both group I and II introns is under the control of nuclear genes. Up to now it is impossible to eliminate the first cox1 intron, but viable deletions mapping in this intron demonstrate its optionality. If it would be possible to eliminate this intron, a genome without any intron could be constructed. This strain could then be used to test a hypothesis of Slonimski and collaborators by an experiment called "from yeast to mammalian mt DNAs". This experiment could provide direct evidence for the role of introns in mt DNA recombination.

```
                                5' splice point
                                      |
                                      ↓
Wild type      5' - CCGTATTATCTGATAAAA ttgcgcgttg - 3'
                    ** *** * ******    ** * *
EB 4, 7, 11    5' - GTATAATATTTAATAAAA -AGCTCATCA -3'
                                      |
                                      ↓
                                3' deletion end point
                                   in exon 2
```

Figure 4: Alignment of the 5' splice point region in the wild-
tpye cob gene with the 3' terminus of the deletion in mutants
EB 4, EB 7, and EB 11 (exon 2). Asterisks indicate identical
bases; arrows mark the 5' splice point and the 3' deletion
end point.

A POSSIBLE LINK BETWEEN RNA SPLICING AND DNA DELETION

In order to get insight into the process of deletion formation in the mt genome, we have analyzed several deletion
mutants by DNA sequence analysis of the deletion termini (Ahne
et al., manuscript submitted). Three independently isolated deletions in the cob gene are of interest in this context:
mutants EB 4, EB 7, and EB 11. Their 5' deletion endpoint coincides with the 3' splice site of the cob intron, and the
3' deletion endpoint exhibits a considerable sequence homology
with the 5' splice site (Figure 4). The process of deletion
formation could be viewed as the consequence of a false RNA
splicing followed by reverse transcription, as suggested for
the exact removal of an intron by DNA splicing. Imprecise
excision has been reported by Belcour and Vierny (1986) for
long-lived mutants of *P. anserina*. DNA sequencing of three deletion mutants has revealed that the 3' border of the deletion
is located inside the cox1 intron 1, while the 5' border is
located in the adjacent exon, a few nucleotides upstream of
the intron-exon junction. Site-specific deletion was also observed in cauliflower mosaic virus DNA by Hirochika et al.
(1985). Sequence analysis has shown that the deletion was promoted at sequences similar to the donor and acceptor consensus
sequences of RNA splicing. These authors present evidence that
RNA splicing followed by reverse transcription is an obligatory
or major pathway in the generation of site-specific deletions.

ACKNOWLEDGEMENTS

We thank B. F. Lang for providing sequence data prior to publication. We also thank our collegues from the Institute of Genetics and Microbiology for stimulating discussions and critical comments to the manuscript. The skilled technical assistence
of Mrs. M. Schropp and Mrs. E. Praetzel is appreciated. Work
was supported by a grant of the Deutsche Forschungsgemeinschaft
to K. W.

REFERENCES

Ahne, F., Merlos-Lange, A. M., Lang, B. F. and Wolf, K. (1984)
    The mitochondrial genome of the fission yeast *Schizosac-
    charomyces pombe*. Characterization of mitochondrial de-
    letion mutants. Curr. Genet. 8, 517-524.

Akins, R. A., Kelley, R. L. and Lambowitz, A. M. (1986) Mitochondrial plasmids of *Neurospora*: Integration into mitochondrial DNA and evidence for reverse transcription in mitochondria. Cell 47, 505-516.

Anderson, S., Bankier, A. T., Barell, B. G., de Bruijn, M. H. L., Coulson, A. R., Sanger, F., Schreier, P. H., Smith, A. J. H., Staden, R. and Yound, I. G. (1981) Sequence and organization of the human mitochondrial genome. Nature (London) 290, 457-464.

Belcour, L. and Vierny, C. (1986) Variable DNA splicing sites of a mitochondrial intron: relationship to the senescence process in *Podospora*. EMBO J. 5, 609-614.

Bibb, M. J., Van Etten, R. A., Wright, C. T., Walberg, M. W., Clayton, D. A. (1981) Sequence and gene organization of mouse mitochondrial DNA. Cell 26, 167-180.

Burke, J. M., Breitenberger, C., Heckman, J. E., Dujon, B. and RajBhandary, U. (1984) Cytochrome b gene of *Neurospora crassa* mitochondria. Partial sequence and location of introns at sites different from those in *Saccharomyces cerevisiae* and *Aspergillus nidulans*. J. Biol. Chem. 259, 504-511.

Burke, J. M. and RajBhandary, U. L. (1982) Intron within the large rRNA gene of *N. crassa* mitochondria: a long open reading frame and a consensus sequence possibly important in splicing. Cell 31, 509-520.

Carignani, G., Netter, P., Bergantino, E. and Robineau, S. (1986) Expression of the mitochondrial split gene coding for cytochrome oxidase subunit I in *S. cerevisiae*: RNA splicing pathway. Curr. Genet. 11, 55-64.

Dujon, B. (1980) Sequence of the intron and flanking exons of the mitochondrial 21S rRNA gene of yeast strains having different alleles of the omega and rib-1 loci. Cell 20, 185-197.

Gargouri, A., Lazowska, J. and Slonimski, P. P. (1983) DNA-splicing of introns in a gene: a general way of reverting intron mutations, in: Mitochondria 1983, pp 259-268, R. J. Schweyen et al., eds., Walter de Gruyter, Berlin-New York.

Hensgens, L. A. M., Bonen, L., de Haan, M., Van der Horst, G. and Grivell, L. A. (1983) Two intron sequences in yeast mitochondrial cox1 gene: Homology among URF-containing introns and strain-dependent variation in flanking exons. Cell 32, 379-389.

Hirochika, H., Takatsuji, H., Ubasawa, A. and Ikeda, J.-E. (1985) Site-specific deletion in cauliflower mosaic virus DNA: possible involvement of RNA splicing and reverse transcription. EMBO J. 4, 1673-1680.

Kan, M. C. and Gall, J. G. (1982) The intervening sequence of the ribosomal RNA gene is highly conserved between two *Tetrahymena* species. Nucl. Acids Res. 10, 2809-2822.

Kohli, J. (1987) Genetic nomenclature of *Schizosaccharomyces pombe*. Curr. Genet., in press.

Kornrumpf, D. (1984) Charakterisierung des mitochondrialen urf a Gens in *Schizosaccharomyces pombe* durch Klonierung und Sequenzierung eines Mutatorstammes. Diploma thesis, University of Munich.

Kotylak, Z., Lazowska, J. and Slonimski, P. P. (1985) Intron encoded proteins of mitochondria: Key elements of gene expression and genomic evolution, in: Achievements and Perspectives of Mitochondrial Research. Vol. II. Biogenesis. pp 1-20, E. Quagliarello et al., eds., Elsevier Science Publishers, Amsterdam-New York-Oxford.

Kück, U., Osiewacz, H. D., Schmidt, U., Kappelhoff, B., Schulte, E., Stahl, U. and Esser, K. (1985) The onset of senescence is affected by DNA rearrangements of a dicontinuous mitochondrial gene in *Podospora anserina*. Curr. Genet. 9, 373-382.

Lang, B. F. (1984) The mitochondrial genome of the fission yeast *Schizosaccharomyces pombe*: highly homologous introns are inserted at the same position in *Schizosaccharomyces pombe* and *Aspergillus nidulans*. EMBO J. 3, 2129-2136.

Lang, B. F., Ahne, F. and Bonen, L. (1985) The mitochondrial genome of the fission yeast *Schizosaccharomyces pombe*: The cytochrome b gene has an intron closely related to the first two introns in the *Saccharomyces cerevisiae* cox1 gene. J. Mol. Biol. 184, 353-366.

Lazowska, J., Jacq, C. and Slonimski, P. P. (1981) Splice points of the third intron in the yeast mitochondrial cytochrome b gene. Cell 27, 12-14.

Merlos-Lange, A. M., Kanbay, F., Zimmer, M. and Wolf, K. (1987) DNA splicing of mitochondrial group I and II introns in *Schizosaccharomyces pombe*. Molec. Gen. Genet. 206, 273-278.

Michel, F. and Cummings, D. J. (1985) Analysis of class I introns in a mitochondrial plasmid associated with senescence of *Podospora anserina* reveals extraordinary resemblance to the *Tetrahymena* ribosomal intron. Curr. Genet. 10, 69-79.

Michel, F. and Dujon, B. (1986) Genetic exchanges between bacteriophage *T4* and filamentous fungi? Cell 46, 323.

Michel, F. and Lang, B. F. (1985) Mitochondrial class II introns encode proteins related to the revers transcriptase of retroviruses. Nature (London) 316, 641-643.

Nomiyama, H., Sakaki, Y. and Takagi, Y. (1981) Nucleotide sequence of a ribosomal RNA gene intron from slime mould *Physarum polycephalum*. Proc. Natl. Acad. Sci. USA 78, 1376-1380.

Perea, J. and Jacq, C. (1985) Role of the 5' hairpin structure in the splicing accuracy of the fourth intron of the yeast cob-box gene. EMBO J. 4, 3281-3288.

Seitz-Mayr, G. and Wolf, K. (1982) Extrachromosomal mutator inducing point mutations and deletions in mitochondrial genome of fission yeast. Proc. Natl. Acad. Sci. USA 79, 2618-2622.

Steinhilber, W. and Cummings, D. J. (1986) A DNA polymerase activity with characteristics of a reverse transcriptase in *Podospora anserina*. Curr. Genet. 10, 389-392.

Trinkl, H., Lang, B. F. and Wolf, K. (1985) The mitochondrial genome of the fission yeast *Schizosaccharomyces pombe*. 7. Continuous gene for apocytochrome b in strain EF1 (CBS 356) and sequence variation in the region of intron insertion in strain ade7-50h⁻. Molec. Gen. Genet. 198, 360-363.

Trinkl, H. and Wolf, K. (1986) The mosaic cox1 gene in the mitochondrial genome of *Schizosaccharomyces pombe*: minimal structural requirements and evolution of group I introns. Gene 45, 289-297.

Waring, R. B., Brown, T. A., Ray, J. A., Scazzocchio, C. and Davies, R. W. (1984) Three variant introns of the same general class in the mitochondrial gene for cytochrome oxidase 1 in *Aspergillus nidulans*. EMBO J. 3, 2121-2128.

Wolf, K. (1987) Mitochondrial genes of the fission yeast *Schizosaccharomyces pombe*, in: Gene Structure in Eukaryotic Microbes. J. R. Kinghorn, ed., IRL Press, Oxford, in press.

I. GENETICS: Short Reports

CORE PROTEIN DEFICIENCY IN COMPLEX III OF THE RESPIRATORY CHAIN, IN A MISSENCE EXONIC MITOCHONDRIAL YEAST MUTANT OF CYTOCHROME B GENE

P. Chevillotte-Brivet, G. Salou, and D. Meunier-Lemesle

Laboratoire de Chimie Bactérienne

C.N.R.S., Marseille, France

In the mitochondrial complex III, cytochrome b is the only product of the mitochondrial genetic system. In a yeast strain carrying a mutation (W7) in the gene coding for cytochrome b, the level of core protein I and subunit VI (17KDa) of complex III was found to be greatly diminished. A low level of Rieske's iron-sulfur cluster has previously been observed in connection with this mutation (1). Wild type isolated complex III (2) was employed as a control for electrophoresis and for immuno-transfer assays (3). The missence mutant (W7) was also characterized by a low level of cytochrome b and a loss of activity in the b-c_1 segment of the respiratory chain (Table I).

This mutant W7 was compared to another one, V384, with similar biochemical characteristics, but which has integrated core protein I, as shown by antibody binding experiments with mitochondria isolated from the two mutants. The two missence mutations W7 and V384 result in neighbouring modifications in the polypeptide chain of cytochrome b, since genetic mapping (4) showed mutation W7 to be located at the end of exon B1 (AA 120 to 138) and mutation V384 in exon B2 (AA 139 to 143). The present study indicates that a missence exonic mutation of cytochrome b gene may result not only in apoprotein modification of cytochrome b and a decrease in its synthesis, but also, as in the case of mutant W7 in a deficiency in several other polypeptides of complex III coded for on nuclear DNA: these were core protein I, subunit VI, Rieske's iron-sulfur protein and to a lesser extent, cytochrome c_1 and core protein II. The extent to which complex III is properly assembled and structured seems to depend on the nature of the structural modification of cytochrome b.

The phenotype of mutant W7 looks like that described by Darley-Usmar et al. (5) concerning mitochondria isolated from a patient with mitochondrial myopathy: several complex III components (core proteins, Fe:S and subunit VI) in addition to cytochrome b were greatly diminished and activity was lossed in the b-c_1 segment. Mitochondrial myopathies are putative hereditary diseases of mit DNA, as most of them have non-mondelian maternal inheritance (6). The results presented here suggest that deficiencies in complex III involving polypeptides coded for by both nuclear and mitochondrial DNA are not incompatible with a missence exonic mutation in cytochrome b gene.

Table I. Characteristics of the mitochondria isolated from the wild strain and from the two missence box mutants W7 and V384.

strains	cyt.b (%)	Activity of: Succ. oxidase	Activity of: NADH oxidase	CPI	Cyt. b reduction: Succ.	Cyt. b reduction: NADH
box+	100	80	116	+	+	+
W7	15	0	8	–	–	+
V384	35	0	11	+	+	+

CPI : core protein I ; activities in μmole O_2/min/mg prot.

The two missence mutants W7 and V384 exhibit no succinate oxidase activity and a slight NADH oxidase activity (Table I). With succinate as substrate, cytochrome b alone is reduced in V384, not in W7. However, cytochrome b heme of W7 is not altered, since it is reducible by NADH or dithionite; its non-reducibility with succinate may be due either to direct structural modification of the cytochrome or to the loss of core protein I resulting from the W7 mutation. This suggests that electrons from NADH or succinate take two different pathways inside complex III before reaching cytochrome b heme(s).

Restoration of succinate activity by vitamin K_3 was important enough in wild type mitochondria inhibited by antimycin, low in mutant V384, nil in mutant W7. Restoration of NADH activity by K_3 was very important in the three cases.

REFERENCES

1. C. Capeillere-Blandin and T. Ohnishi (1982) Eur. J. Biochem. 122, 403-413.
2. P. Chevillotte-Brivet, G. Salou, N. Forget, and D. Meunier-Lemesle (1987) Biochimie 69, 25-36.
3. P. Chevillotte-Brivet, G. Salou, and D. Meunier-Lemesle, Current Genetics (in press).
4. J. Lazowska, C. Jacq, and P.P. Slonimski (1980) Cell 22, 333-348.
5. C.M. Darley-Usmar, N.G. Kennaway, N.R.H. Buist, and R.A. Capaldi (1983) Proc. Natl. Acad. Sc. USA 80, 5103-5106.
6. D.C. Wallace, G. Singh, L.C. Hopkins, and E.J. Novotny (1985) in Achievements and Perspectives of Mitochondrial Research, Vol. II Biogenesis (E.C. Quagliariello et al., ed.) pp 427-436, Elsevier Science Publisher, Amsterdam, New York, Oxford.

LOCALIZATION AND PARTIAL SEQUENCING ANALYSIS OF MITOCHONDRIAL GENE FOR APOCYTOCHROME B IN SUNFLOWER

D. Pacoda[1], A.S. Treglia[1], L. Siculella[2], C. Perrotta[2], and R. Gallerani[3]

[1]C.S.M.M.E. Università di Bari, Sezione di Trani, Italia
[2]Dipartimento di Biologia, Università di Lecce, [3]Dipartimento di Biochimica e Biologia Molecolare, Università di Bari

In higher plants the gene for cytochrome b (CYB gene) has been sequenced on mt DNA of maize (1) and wheat (2) (monocotyledonous plants) and oenothera (3) (dicotyledonous). The gene is continuous and codes for a protein of 388, 394, and 398 amino acids respectively.

The study of the organization of such a gene revealed interesting features related mainly with regions localized upstream the 5' termini of the gene. Among monocot plants in particular, for a region of about 500 nucleotides it has been observed a very high homology level (93%) only slightly lower than that of coding region (98%). In the dicot oenothera, upstream the 5' termini of the gene, only a region of about 50 nucleotides, very rich in A/G is well conserved, comparing the equivalent in maize and wheat.

The analysis of sequences adjacent to the initiation codon of CYB gene at a distance of 13-18 nucleotides, allowed the identification of a putative eukaryote ribosome binding site on the basis of the homology of this region with 3' termini of 18S ribosomal RNA. The binding site has been identified in the octanucleotide 5' -AGT TGTCA-3', perfectly conserved in maize and oenothera.

As far as the coding regions are concerned the high level of nucleotide homology among the three CYB genes studied so far (more than 98%) and that of their deduced amino acid sequences (94 to 96%) confirm the high conservation of mitochondrial genes (both for proteins and RNAs) characteristic of higher plants.

With the aim to better understand the organization of CYB gene in higher plants and those of 5' and 3' adjacent regions we extended the study of such a gene to another dicot plant: the sunflower. By hybridization experiments, carried out by using a specific probe of maize mitochondrial genome (gift of Prof. C.J. Leaver) and southern blots of total sunflower mtDNA digested with HindIII and SaII restriction enzymes, we were able to identify two distinct HindIII (3.8 kbp) and SaII (8.8 kbp) restriction fragments bearing the sunflower mitochondrial CYB gene. The 8.8 kbp SaII fragment was cloned in the pUC8 vector and the recombinant plasmid pLS35S (see Fig. 1) was subjected to further restriction and hybridization analysis. The position of the gene was localized around an HindIII site whose distance from one of the two SaII sites was estimated to be about 1.9 kbp. The

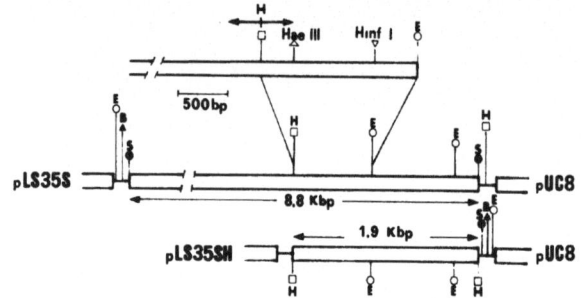

Fig. 1. Restriction map of plasmid pLS35S and sequencing
strategy for the sunflower CYB gene.

sequencing analysis of this region, carried out by using the Sanger procedure modified according to Korneluk et al. (4), allowed the identification
of about 250 nucleotides showing a very high homology level with the corresponding regions of maize, wheat and oenothera genes (from 94 to 98%). The
eighty amino acid residues coded for by this nucleotide stretch result part
of hydrophobic domains III, IV, and V (see Saraste (5)). Among them, 25
out of 31 invariant amino acids are confirmed, in particular histidines
189 and 203 which, according to the structure proposed by Saraste, should
be two of the four heme binding sites of cytochrome b.

REFERENCES

1. A.J. Dawson, V.P. Jones, and C.J. Leaver (1984) The EMBO Journal 3,
   210-213.
2. P.H. Boer, J.E. McIntosh, M.W. Gray, and L. Bonen (1985) Nucl. Ac.
   Research 13, 2281-2292.
3. W. Schuster and A. Brennicke (1985) Current Genetics 9, 157-163.
4. R.G. Korneluk, F. Quan, and R.A. Gravel (1985) Gene 40, 317-323.
5. M. Saraste (1984) FEBS Letters 166, 367-372.

MOLECULAR BASIS FOR RESISTANCE TO INHIBITORS OF THE MITOCHONDRIAL

UBIQUINOL-CYTOCHROME c REDUCTASE IN Saccharomyces cerevisiae

A.-M. Colson, B. Meunier, and J.-P. di Rago

University of Louvain, Laboratoire de Génétique Microbienne

Place Croix du Sud, 4, B-1348 Louvain-la-Neuve, Belgium

In the mitochondrial respiratory chain, the bc_1 complex transfers electrons from ubiquinol to the cytochrome c oxidase complex. There are two pathways for oxidation-reduction of cytochrome b (1). It is thought that cytochrome b is a transmembranous protein which forms a transmembrane electron circuit, carrying two ubiquinone redox sites responsible for proton uptake and release across the inner mitochondrial membrane. The current hypothesis is that these two ubiquinone redox sites, referred to as Q_i and Q_o sites, are proximal to the b-562 and b-566 hemes of cytochrome b, respectively. It is likely that the Q_i and Q_o reaction domains are on the cytochrome b protein, or are formed by the interaction of portions of the b protein with other proteins of the bc_1 complex. Presently, ∂ genes have been identified with code for subunits of the yeast ubiquinol-cytochrome c oxido-reductase complex (cytochrome bc_1 or complex III).

There are numerous drugs which inhibit respiration by blocking one of the two pathways of cytochrome b oxido-reduction, at either Q_i or Q_o site. Antimycin and funiculosin appear to block b oxidation-reduction at the Q_i site, and cause changes in the optical properties of heme b-562 (2). Myxothiazol, mucidin (strobilurin) and stigmatellin appear to block oxidation-reduction at the Q_o site, and cause changes in the properties of heme b-566 (3). Diuron inhibits also cytochrome b oxido-reduction (4) but the exact site of action of diuron is not known yet. It has been shown however, to reverse the redshift induced by HQNO which is supposed to act at the antimycin site (5).

Numerous yeast mutants resistant to antimycin, funiculosin, myxothiazol and mucidin (strobilurin) and diuron have been isolated, and all these mutants have been mapped in the cytochrome b gene (6, 7, 8, 9, 10). The mitochondrial gene from five diuron-resistant yeast mutants has been sequenced and the altered amino acid residues in the protein deduced from the change within the DNA sequence (10). The DNA base substitutions in three additional diuron-resistant mutants as well as in one antimycin-resistant mutant will be presented. Three mutated sites, two closely linked, in the cytochrome b gene were found for eight independent diuron-resistant mutations sequenced. The correlation between the genetic mapping and the molecular localization, the absence of polymorphism and the limited number of mutated sites provide strong supports that diuron-resistance was caused by these identified mutated sites.

In thylakoid membrane, the subunit of photosystem II responsible for herbicide binding was found to be the 32 kDa polypeptide (13). A correlation between the mutated sites of herbicide-tolerant mutants (e.g., DCMU or diuron-tolerant mutants) in the 32 kDa gene, the herbicide binding niche and the plastoquinone (Q_A/Q_B) binding niche of D-1 and D-2 subunits of photosystem II (PS II) has been proposed by Trebst and Draber (11). In yeast and according to the Widger (12) folding model of the cytochrome b, the identified mutated sites appeared to belong to either side of the membrane within hydrophylic amino acid sequences. One antimycin-resistant mutation has been located in a transmembrane helix close to a diuron-resistant mutated site at the presumed outer membrane side. Since antimycin is supposed to act at the Q_i site, thus near the inner side of the mitochondrial inner membrane, it is tempting to think that the present Widger folding model of the cytochrome b need to be somewhat adjusted. Full characterization of our diuron antimycin and other inhibitor resistant mutants will be reported in detail somewhere else. More recently, we have identified diuron-resistant mutations of nuclear heredity. They exhibit in vitro resistance to diuron at the level of the mitochondrial respiratory chain. Therefore, they are most likely located in one of the nuclear genes coding for bc_1 subunits. Tetrad analyses revealed a linkage of less than 1 cM between a nuclear diuron-resistant locus and the gene coding for cytochrome c_1. Wheter the nuclear diuron-resistant locus belong to the cytochrome c_1 gene or to an adjacent gene is presently under investigation.

REFERENCES

1. H. Tang and B.L. Trumpower (1986) J. Biol. Chem. 261, 6209-6215.
2. P.L. Dutton, M. Erecinska, N. Sato, Y. Mukai, M. Pring, and D.F. Wilson (1972) Biochem, Biophys. Acta 267, 15-24.
3. W.F. Becker, G. von Jagow, T. Anke, and W. Steglish (1981) FEBS Lett. 132, 329-333.
4. B. Convent and M. Briquet (1978) Eur. J. Bioche, 82, 473-481.
5. B. Convent, M. Briquet, and A. Goffeau (1978) Eur. J. Biochem. 92, 137-145.
6. G. Thierbach and G. Michaelis (1982) Molec. gen. Genet. 186, 501-506.
7. A.M. Colson and P. P. Slonimski (1979) Molec. gen. Genet. 167, 287-298.
8. A.M. Colson, G. Michaelis, E. Pratje, and P.P. Slonimski (1979) Molec. gen. Genet. 167, 299-300.
9. A.M. Colson, Luu The Van, B. Convent, M. Briquet, and A. Goffeau (1977) Eur. J. Biochem. 74, 521-526.
10. J.P. di Rago, X. Perea, and A.M. Colson (1986) FEBS Lett. 208-210.
11. A. Trebst and W. Draber (1986) Photosynthesis Res. 10, 381-392.
12. W.R. Widger, W.A. Cramer, R.G. Herrman, and A. Trebst (1984) Proc. Natl. Acad. Sci. 81, 674-678.
13. K. Pfister, K.E. Steinback, G. Gardner, and C.J. Arntzen (1981) Proc. Natl. Acad. Sci. USA 78, 981-985.

A.M. Colson is Research Associate to the F.N.R.S. Belgium and J.-P. di Rago is supported by I.R.S.I.A. Belgium.

STRUCTURE OF THE PROTEINS AND GENES FOR THE NUCLEAR-ENCODED

SUBUNITS OF N. CRASSA CYTOCHROME OXIDASE

M.D. Suárez, M. Sachs, M. David, and U.L. RajBhandary

Department of Biology, Massachusetts Institute of Technology

Cambridge, Massachusetts 02139

Cytochrome oxidase is a multisubunit protein of complex structure and function. The smaller subunits are encoded by nuclear DNA, synthesized in the cytoplasm and transported into the mitochondria; whereas the three largest subunits are made in the mitochondria. As a part of our efforts at studying the organization, expression and regulation of the nuclear genes for cytochrome oxidase, we are in the process of isolating and characterizing the genes and proteins for the nuclear-encoded subunits in Neurospora crassa.

We have isolated cDNA (1) and genomic DNA clones containing the complete genes for subunits V and VIII and parts of the genes for subunits IV and VI of N. crassa cytochrome oxidase. In addition, the amino terminal sequences of subunit VII and VIII have been determined.

Information obtained from characterization of the proteins and genes indicates that there is significant homology between the primary amino acid sequences of the nuclear-encoded subunits of N. crassa, yeast and bovine subunits. Comparison of the amino acid sequence deduced from the DNA sequence with protein sequence data reveals that subunits IV and V are made as larger precursors (1). Their signal sequences share structural features with those of other N. crassa mitochondrial proteins encoded by nuclear genes (2, 3). In contrast, subunit VIII is made without an N-terminal extension, as is the case for a homologous subunit (VIIa) in yeast (4).

Sequence analysis of cDNA and genomic clones revealed that the N. crassa gene for subunit V contains two introns (5). The first intron is the longest (398 bp) described thus far in a Neurospora gene. Two different types of short repeat elements are found upstream of the subunit V gene. These sequences resemble short upstream repeats which are involved in the regulation of several yeast genes. The gene for subunit VIII also contains at least one intron. The chromosomal location of the genes for subunits IV, V, and VI was determined by restriction fragment length polymorphism (6). These genes map to different linkage groups and roughly to the same chromosomal loci as some of the cytochrome oxidase deficient mutants. Transformation of cya-4-23, one of the cytochrome oxidase deficient mutants, with DNA containing the gene for subunit V, resulted in transformants which grew rapidly and contained cytochrome aa_3 (5). This suggests (a) that the cya-4 locus specifies structural information for cytochrome oxidase subunit V in Neurospora and (b) that subunit V is essential for cytochrome oxidase function in Neurospora. Currently, we are completing the characterization of the genes for subunit IV, VI, and VIII. These will be used as tools in the characterization of cytochrome oxidase deficient mutants and as probes for studying the regulation of nuclear genes for cytochrome oxidase under a variety of conditions.

REFERENCES

1. M.S. Sachs, M. David, S. Werner, and U.L. RajBhandary (1986) J. Biol. Chem. 261, 869-873.
2. V. Harnisch, H. Weiss, and W. Sebald (1985) Eur. J. Biochem. 149, 95-99.
3. A. Viebrock, A. Perz, and W. Sebald (1982) EMBO J. 1, 565-571.
4. R.M. Wright, L.K. Dircks, and R.O. Poyton (1986) J. Biol. Chem. 261, 17183-17191.
5. M.S. Sachs and U.L. RajBhandary (1987) manuscript in preparation.
6. R.L. Metzenberg, J.N. Stevens, E.U. Selker, and E. Morzycka-Wroblewska (1985) Proc. Natl. Acad. Sci. USA 82, 2067-2071.

PARTIAL SEQUENCE OF GENE FOR CYTOCHROME OXYDASE SUBUNIT II OF SUNFLOWER MITOCHONDRIAL DNA

L.R. Ceci[1], C. De Benedetto[2], C.M. Perrotta[3]. L. Siculella[3], and R. Gallerani[2]

[1]Sezione di Trani del Centro di Studio sui Mitocondri e Metabolismo Energetico del Consiglio Nazionale delle Ricerche, Trani Italia
[2]Dipartimento di Biochimica e Biologia Molecolare, Università di Bari
[3]Dipartimento di Biologia, Università di Lecce

The mitochondrial DNA (mtDNA) in higher plants is larger than that of animals and fungi for 1-2 orders of magnitude (1). Despite its unusual complexity its informational content is very similar to that of other eukaryote organisms studied so far and it includes genes for 26S, 18S, and 5S ribosomal RNAs and tRNAs and for some proteins which are components of respiratory chain and F_1-Fo ATP--ase complex (2). Among these the gene for cytochrome oxydase subunit II (COXII gene) has been sequenced both in monocotyledonous (3-5) and dicotyledonous plants (6-7). The comparative analysis of the organization of COXII genes in the five systems studied so far reveals interesting features concerning coding, non coding and putative regulatory regions of the genes:
1) in monocot plants (maize (3), wheat (4), and rice (5)) an intron of various length interrupts the coding region at exactly the same position;
2) the coding sequences are highly conserved (nucleotide homology is higher than 88%), in contrast with animal mitochondrial genes which evolved more rapidly;
3) common regions of the introns, characteristic of maize, wheat and rice, show also high level of homology (98%) suggesting a possible structural or functional role for the untranslated region of the gene;
4) 5' non coding regions appear to be highly homologous only in the comparison rice/wheat (97%);
5) 3' non coding sequences are well conserved among monocot genes (90%) but very different from those of pea and oenothera;
6) the codon usage is quite similar to the universal code, only the CGG codon has probably a different meaning: triptophane vs arginine.
The COXII gene of the dicot plant Helianthus annus has been localized in a specific clone (798) of a genomic library of sunflower mitochondrial DNA fragments obtained by cloning total HindIII and Sal I restriction digests in the homologous sites of pUC8 plasmid vector. Restriction and hybridization anlaysis of pCP798 plasmid, carried out by using several restriction enzymes in single and double combination allowed the identification of COX II gene on a DNA stretch of about 1.8 kbp. Surprisingly, despite the sunflower belongs to the dicotyledonous classe of angiosperms, the sequencing analysis of such a DNA segment revealed the presence of both regions highly homologous (from 85 to 94%) to the coding and non-coding part of maize COXII gene.

The analysis of sequencing data so far available (70% of the gene has been sequenced) revealed the presence of an intron of about 1.2 kbp very similar to that of rice and wheat. Nevertheless in these two monocot plants there is a small difference in the structure of two genes; in the rice intron a stretch of about 50 bp having at its termini two direct repeats CTTTCC is present. The same segment, perfectly conserved, has been found in the sunflower gene.

The comparative analysis of amino acid sequences relative to bovine cytochrome oxidase subunit II and those deduced from maize and sunflower COXII genes, allowed the identification of specific regions of the protein such as the first and the second hydrophobic transmembrane domain, some acid amino acid residues involved in the binding of the protein to the cytochrome C and a particular cluster of aromatic amino acids supposed to be involved in the electron transfert (8).

ACKNOWLEDGMENTS

This work was supported by M.P.I. (40% funds).

REFERENCES

1. C.J. Leaver and M.W. Gray (1982) Ann. Rev. Plant Phys. 33, 373-402.
2. L.R. Ceci, C. De Benedetto, L. Siculella, C.M. Perrotta, and R. Gallerani In: E. Quagliariello, G. Bernardi, and A. Ullman Eds.: Jacques Monod and Molecular Biology, yesterday and today, Elsevier Amsterdam (1987) In press.
3. T.D. Fox and C.J. Leaver (1981) Cell 26, 315-323.
4. L. Bonen, P.H. Boher, and M.W. Gray (1984) The EMBO Journal 3, 2531-2536.
5. T. Kao, E. Moon, and R. Wu (1984) Nucl. Ac. Research 12, 7305-7315.
6. R. Hiesel and A. Brennicke (1983) The EMBO Journal 2, 2173-2178.
7. E. Moon, T. Kao, and R. Wu (1985) Nucl. Ac. Research 13, 3195-3212.
8. R.A. Capaldi, F. Malatesta, and V.M. Darley-Usmar (1983) Bioch. Bioph. Acta 726, 135-148.

UNUSUAL FEATURES OF KINETOPLAST DNA FROM TRYPANOSOMES: NOVEL MECHANISM OF
GENE EXPRESSION (RNA-EDITING), THE ABSENCE OF tRNA GENES AND THE VARIABLE
PRESENCE OF A CYTOCHROME OXIDASE SUBUNIT GENE

P. Sloof, R. Benne, B. de Vries, T. Hakvoort*, and A. Muijsers*

Sections for Molecular Biology and Enzymology*
Laboratory of Biochemistry, University of Amsterdam
AMC, Meibergdreef 15, 1105 AZ Amsterdam, The Netherlands

Kinetoplast DNA is the unorthodox mitochondrial (mt)DNA of Trypanosomes
which consists of a network of catenated circular DNAs of two types: about
10^4 minicircles (1-3 kb, depending on the species) and 25-50 maxicircles
(20-40 kb). The coding capacity of this mtDNA resides in the maxicircle
component. The nucleotide sequences of large portions of the maxicircles
of Trypanosoma brucei, Crithidia fasciculata and Leishmania tarentolae
have been determined. So far, genes coding for mitochondrial rRNAs,
apocytochrome b, cytochrome oxidase subunits (cox) I, II and III (present
in C.fasciculata and L.tarentolae but absent in T.brucei), NADH dehydrogenase
subunits (ND) I, IV and V and some unassigned reading frames (URF) have
been identified (reviewed in 1). A comparison of trypanosomal mitochondrial
genes with those of other organisms reveals a wealth of unusual features not
only with respect to the genes themselves, but also to the way they are
organized and expressed. Four of these unusual aspects will be discussed.

(i) The gene for cox II contains a -1 frameshift, which is conserved in the
three trypanosome species. Studying gene expression, we have shown that the
cox II mRNA contains 4 extra nucleotides at the frameshift position, which
are not DNA-encoded. Since a second cox II gene version, with the 4 extra
nucleotides, could not be detected in trypanosome DNA, we concluded that
nucleotide insertion occurred during or after transcription by a novel RNA-
editing mechanism (2). Here we present evidence for a second example of
RNA-editing in trypanosome mitochondria. We have found that the C.URF2/1
gene from C.fasciculata maxicircle DNA, which is strongly conserved in
L.tarentolae (97% at the amino acid level) but is absent in T.brucei (3),
contains a conserved +1 frameshift that is corrected by insertion of 5
extra, non DNA-encoded, nucleotides in C.URF2/1 mRNA.

(ii) tRNA-genes appear to be absent in trypanosomal maxicircle DNA, as
judged from a search for conserved nucleotide sequences which can be
folded as tRNAs in the three trypanosome species. Since aberrant tRNAs
may excape detection by this approach we have hybridized blots of T.brucei
(t)RNA with maxicircle DNA segments. Hybridization was not found in the
small RNA region (< 200 nt) under conditions that allowed detection of a
single mitochondrial tRNA gene in Saccharomyces cerevisiae mtDNA. The
absence of tRNA genes on maxicircle DNA suggests the possibility that
mitochondrial tRNAs are nuclearly encoded and are imported into mitochondria.

(iii) The cox I and cox II genes in the three trypanosome species are
strongly conserved (73-79% at the nucleotide level; 1) and also the cox III

141

genes of C.fasciculata and L.tarentolae are highly homologous (85% at the nucleotide level; 3). It is therefore remarkable that a homologous cox III gene could not be detected in T.brucei, using the C.fasciculata gene as a probe. This implies that in cytochrome oxidase of T.brucei either a drastically divergent version of subunit III is present or that it is absent. Results of an analysis of purified oxidase will be presented. Furthermore, the unusual high number of cysteine residues in mitochondrially encoded proteins of trypanosomes, as predicted from the nucleotide sequences of their genes (see 1), has been confirmed in purified cytochrome oxidase of C.fasciculata.

(iv) Comparison of N-terminal amino acid sequences of corresponding protein encoding maxicircle genes in the three trypanosome species revealed that amino acid homology starts either at the classical AUG codon (in 6 out of 10 genes) or at leucine triplets (UUA, CUG, UUG, in the remaining 4 genes). This result suggests the use of leucine codons, apart from AUG, as initiator triplets in trypanosome mitochondria.

REFERENCES

1. R. Benne, (1985) Trends in Genetics 1, 117-121.
2. R. Benne, J. Van den Burg, J. Brakenhoff, P. Sloof, J. Van Boom, and M. Tromp (1986) Cell 46, 819-826.
3. P. Sloof, J. Van den Burg, A. Voogd, and R. Benne (1987) Nucl.Acids Res. 15, 51-65.

II. BIOSYNTHESIS

HETEROGENEOUS EFFICIENCIES OF mRNA TRANSLATION
IN HUMAN MITOCHONDRIA

Anne Chomyn and Giuseppe Attardi

Division of Biology
California Institute of Technology
Pasadena, CA 91125

The recently completed elucidation of the informational content of the human mitochondrial genome (Chomyn et al., 1986), taken as a prototype of all mammalian mitochondrial genomes, has set the stage for an analysis of the mechanisms and regulation of gene expression in this system. The well established mode of mitochondrial DNA (mtDNA) transcription and RNA processing in mammalian mitochondria (Ojala et al., 1981), while admirable in its simplicity and economy, raises questions as concerns the mechanisms which control the differential expression of mitochondrial genes. In particular, one would like to know how the regulation of the steady state amounts of the different RNA species is achieved in a genome where both strands are transcribed in the form of polycistronic molecules comprising rRNA, mRNA and tRNA sequences (Fig. 1). Furthermore, one can ask whether, in addition to a control at the transcriptional and RNA processing levels, there is also a control at the translational level.

Some insight has recently been obtained concerning gene regulation operating in mammalian mitochondria at the level of mtDNA transcription. There is good evidence indicating that the 15- to 60-fold higher rate of transcription of the rRNA genes and adjacent tRNA genes situated in the promoter proximal region of the heavy (H)-strand relative to the transcription of the remainder of the H-strand (containing all but one of the reading frames and many tRNA genes) (Gelfand and Attardi, 1981) is achieved through the existence of two overlapping transcription units with distinct, though closely located promoters (Fig. 1) (Montoya et al., 1983). Of these transcription units, one produces RNA molecules starting about 90 nt upstream of the 12S rRNA gene and terminating near the 3'-end of the 16S rRNA gene; the other transcription unit, much less active, produces molecules starting near the 5'-end of the 12S rRNA gene and covering almost the entire length of the H-strand. There is also evidence that differential stability accounts for the much higher copy number of the individual tRNAs relative to the mRNAs (M. King and G. Attardi, unpublished observations). Very little is known, on the contrary, about how the differential expression of the protein coding genes is achieved. The evidence that the mRNAs derived from processing of the H-strand polycistronic transcripts (Fig. 1) have quite different steady state amounts, irrespective of the positions of their coding sequences relative to the promoter (Gelfand and Attardi, 1981; Attardi et al., 1982) (Fig. 2a, Table 1), suggests that mRNA stability may be involved in differential gene expression. The recent identification of the polypeptide products corresponding to all reading frames of human mtDNA (Mariottini et al., 1983, 1986; Chomyn et al., 1983, 1986) has made it possible to approach the question of whether regulation of gene expression in

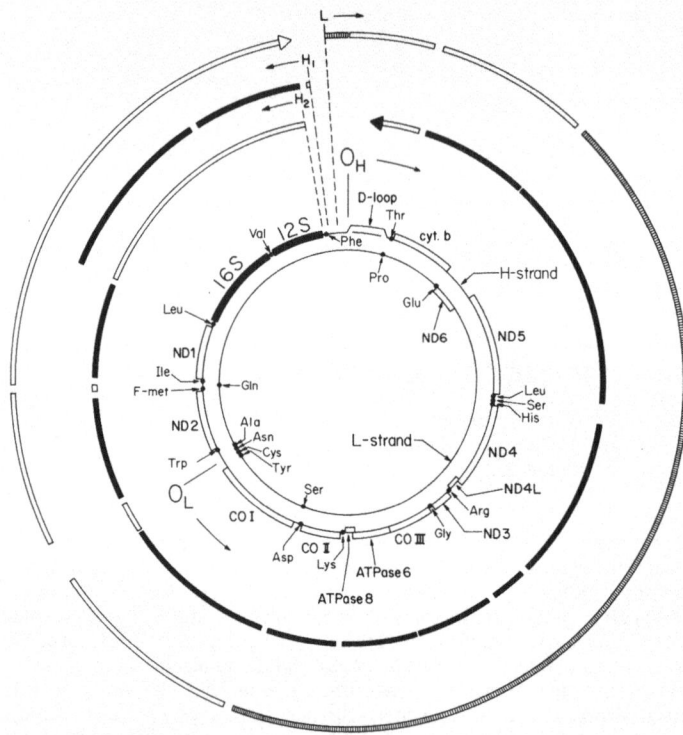

Fig. 1. Genetic and transcription maps of the human mitochondrial genome. The two inner circles show the positions of the two rRNA genes, the tRNA genes (black circles) and the reading frames. In the outer portion of the diagram, the identified functional RNA species other than tRNAs are represented by black bars [those deriving from the two H-strand transcription units, starting at H_1 (rDNA) and H_2 (total H-strand)] or cross-hatched bars (those deriving from the L-strand transcription unit). The white bars represent unstable, presumably non-functional by-products. COI, COII, COIII: subunits I, II and III of cytochrome c oxidase; CYT b: apocytochrome b; ATPase 6 and ATPase 8: subunits 6 and 8 of H^+-ATPase; ND1, ND2, ND3, ND4, ND4L, ND5 and ND6: subunits of NADH dehydrogenase; O_H, O_L: origin of H-strand and, respectively, L-strand synthesis (from Attardi, 1986).

mammalian mitochondria occurs also at the level of translation. In this paper we present the preliminary results obtained in this analysis.

The Human Mitochondrial mRNAs and Their Translation Products

Figure 2a displays the polyadenylated RNA species encoded in HeLa cell mtDNA, visualized by labeling *in vivo* with [^{32}P] orthophosphate for 2.5 hr in the absence of inhibitors (Gelfand and Attardi, 1981). Each of these species has been precisely mapped on the mitochondrial genome (Ojala *et al.*, 1980) and well characterized in its metabolic and structural properties (Gelfand and Attardi, 1981; Montoya *et al.*, 1981; Ojala *et al.*, 1981). Among them, the mature mRNAs corresponding to the 13 reading frames of the mitochondrial genome are designated according to their functional identity, determined from their mapping

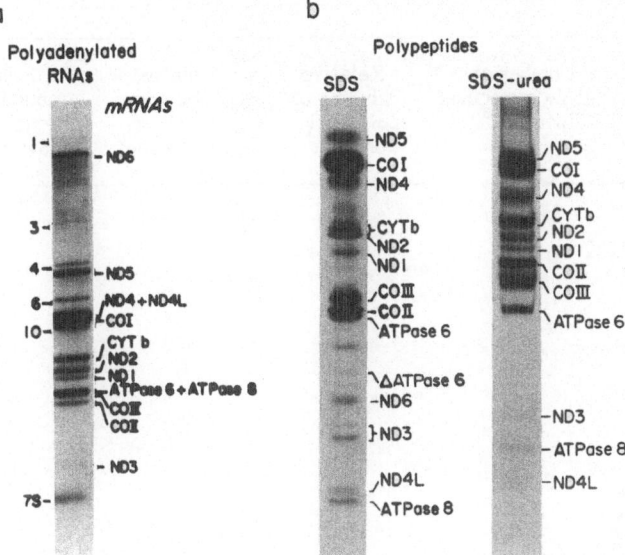

a

Polyadenylated
RNAs

mRNAs

1 –   – ND6

3 –

4 –   – ND5

6 –   ND4+ND4L
10 –   COI

       CYT b
       ND2
       NDI
       ATPase 6+ATPase 8
       COⅡ
       COⅠ

       – ND3

7S –

b

Polypeptides

SDS

–ND5
–COI
–ND4

CYTb
ND2
NDI

COⅢ
COⅡ
ATPase 6

ΔATPase 6
–ND6

}–ND3

ND4L
ATPase 8

SDS-urea

ND5
COI
ND4

CYTb
ND2
NDI
COⅡ
COⅢ

ATPase 6

–ND3

–ATPase 8

–ND4L

Fig. 2. Display of mitochondrial messenger RNAs and translation products from
HeLa cells. a) Electrophoretic fractionation of ^{32}P-labeled poly(A)-containing
RNAs in an agarose-methylmercuric hydroxide gel. RNAs 1, 3 and 7S and ND6
mRNA are L-strand products, all the other RNAs are H-strand products (from
Gelfand and Attardi, 1981). b) Electrophoretic fractionation of ^{35}S-methionine-
labeled mitochondrial translation products in an SDS-polyacrylamide gradient gel
or in an SDS-urea-polyacrylamide gel. ΔATPase 6: COOH-terminal fragment of
ATPase 6 (Chomyn et al., 1983). The two bands designated as ND3 represent the
two forms of this gene product identified in HeLa cells (Oliver et al., 1983).

position and from the functional assignment of the corresponding reading frames
(Anderson et al., 1981) or polypeptide products (Chomyn et al., 1985, 1986; see
below), while the other species are designated according to Amalric et al. (1978).
There is one mRNA for each reading frame, with the exception of two pairs of
overlapping reading frames (for subunits 6 and 8 of the H$^+$-ATPase and for
subunits ND4L and ND4 of the NADH dehydrogenase), which are represented each
by a single mRNA (Ojala et al., 1980; Anderson et al., 1981) (Figs. 1 and 2a). It
appears from the intensity of labeling in Figure 2a that the various mRNAs
labeled during the 2.5 hr [^{32}P] orthophosphate pulse are not present in equimolar
amounts. This apparent variability in molar representation of the mRNAs has
been confirmed by an analysis of their steady state amounts in exponentially
growing cells (Table 1) (Gelfand and Attardi, 1981; Attardi et al., 1982).

Figure 2b shows the electrophoretic patterns in an SDS-polyacrylamide
gradient gel and in an SDS-urea-polyacrylamide gel of the HeLa cell mitochondrial
translation products which had been labeled in vivo with [^{35}S]-methionine for 2 hr

Table 1. Rates of translation of mRNAs in HeLa cell mitochondria

Gene	Number of mRNA molecules per cell[a]	Relative labeling of polypeptide product[b]	Relative efficiency of mRNA translation[c]	Relative abundance of enzyme complex (bovine heart)[d]
NADH dehydrogenase				1
ND1	650	1.0	1.0	
ND2	720	2.0	1.8	
ND3	225	2.8	8.0	
ND4L	960	1.7	1.1	
ND4		1.8	1.2	
ND5	165	0.9	3.6	
ND6	<50[e]	0.4	>5.8	
Ubiquinone-cytochrome c reductase				3
apocytochrome b	570	4.6	5.3	
Cytochrome c oxidase				6-7
COI	950	5.9	4.0	
COII	1190	7.0	3.8	
COIII	980	5.2	3.4	
H^+-ATPase				3-5
ATPase 8	770	4.7	3.9	
ATPase 6		6.7	5.6	

[a]Taken from Attardi et al. (1982).

[b]Determined after a 15 min ^{35}S-methionine pulse in the presence of 100 µg/ml emetine, and corrected for differences in methionine content.

[c]Rate of translation (estimated from the 15 min pulse data) per mRNA molecule, in arbitrary units.

[d]Taken from Hatefi et al. (1985).

[e]Estimated for the most abundant polyadenylated L-strand transcript containing the ND6 reading frame (RNA #2).

in the presence of emetine (to inhibit cytoplasmic protein synthesis) (Ching and Attardi et al., 1982; Attardi et al., 1986). The translation products are designated according to their functional identification. This was made by the use of antibodies directed against peptides derived from the DNA sequence and of enzyme-specific polyclonal antibodies (Chomyn et al., 1985, 1986), or by the isolation of enzyme complexes and characterization of their subunit composition and site of synthesis (Hare et al., 1980; Doersen and Attardi, in preparation). It is clear that the relative migration of these polypeptides differs considerably in the two gel systems: this results in different subsets of components having optimum resolution in the two systems.

Relative Rates of Labeling of Mitochondrial Translation Products

The capacity of resolving by gel electrophoresis all the mitochondrial translation products from HeLa cells has made it possible to estimate the labeling of the various polypeptides after a short pulse of $[^{35}S]$methionine. Table 1 shows data concerning the relative labeling of the mitochondrially synthesized polypeptides during a 15 min exposure of the cells to the labeled amino acid in the presence of emetine, after correction for differences in their methionine content. It appears from Table 1 that the various HeLa cell mitochondrial translation products are labeled to a different extent, covering a more than ten-fold range. Furthermore, there is a clear tendency for polypeptides of the same complex to be labeled to a more similar degree than polypeptides of different complexes. The length of the pulse used in these experiments was about one-hundredth of the generation time of the cells (~22 hrs), and also much shorter than the half-lives of the mitochondrial translation products in a rat hepatoma cell line [ranging between 35 hr and >100 hr (Hare and Hodges, 1982)]. Therefore, it is reasonable to assume that the relative labeling of the various polypeptides measured here reflects their relative rates of synthesis. Preliminary observations on the rate of labeling of the mitochondrial translation products after short pulses of $[^{35}S]$methionine in the absence of inhibitors have confirmed this conclusion. The cytochrome c oxidase subunits are the most actively synthesized, followed by the H^{+}-ATPase subunits and apocytochrome b, and finally by the NADH dehydrogenase subunits. The differences in rate of synthesis among subunits of the same complex are not necessarily reflected in the molar representation of these subunits in the complex because of possible differences in their effective utilization.

Also in Table 1 is shown the relative abundance of different complexes of the oxidative phosphorylation system in beef heart mitochondria (Hatefi et al., 1985). It appears that the lowest among the estimated rates of synthesis of the subunits of each complex in HeLa cells is roughly proportional to the relative abundance of the same complex in beef heart mitochondria. If the relative steady state amounts of the various complexes in HeLa cell mitochondria are similar to those found in beef heart mitochondria, the data of Table 1 suggest that the main factor that determines the different molar abundance of these complexes is the rate of synthesis of their subunits.

Relative Efficiencies of Translation of Mitochondrial mRNAs

A comparison of the relative rates of synthesis of the individual HeLa cell mitochondrial translation products with the abundance of the corresponding mRNAs reveals interesting differences in the efficiency of translation of the mRNAs. In fact, while the mRNAs coding for apocytochrome b, cytochrome c oxidase subunits and H^{+}-ATPase subunits have a remarkably similar efficiency of translation, the mRNAs coding for four NADH dehydrogenase subunits (ND1, ND2, ND4 and ND4L) are translated three or four times less effectively; the mRNAs for the three remaining NADH dehydrogenase subunits have an efficiency of translation similar to that of the mRNAs for subunits of the other complexes of the oxidative phosphorylation system (ND5 and ND6) or twice as high (ND3).

A surprising finding is that, in the two cases where a single mRNA codes for two overlapping reading frames (i.e., mRNA7 for ND4L and ND4 and mRNA14 for ATPase subunits 8 and 6), the second reading frame is translated equally or more efficiently than the first reading frame. The possibility that the block of cytoplasmic protein synthesis, even for the short duration of the pulse, would affect the rate of translation of one or both the overlapping reading frames, was investigated in the case of mRNA14. For this purpose, immunoprecipitation experiments were carried out using an excess of antibodies against the COOH-terminal nonapeptide of the ATPase 8 subunit or against the COOH-terminal nonapeptide of the ATPase 6 subunit and a mitochondrial lysate from exponentially growing cells labeled with [^{35}S]-methionine for 15 or 30 min in the absence of inhibitors. After both pulses, the ratio of the rates of labeling of ATPase 6 and ATPase 8 was ~2 (A. Chomyn, M. Strathman and G. Attardi, unpublished observation). These results strongly suggest that, in HeLa cells, under physiological conditions, the ATPase 6 subunit is synthesized at a rate approximately twice as high as the ATPase 8 subunit.

Possible Mechanisms of Translational Control

The conclusions reached above concerning the relative efficiencies of translation of different mitochondrial mRNAs in human mitochondria are based upon the assumption that the distribution of the various mRNAs extracted from the total mitochondrial fraction reflects that of the mRNAs actively involved in protein synthesis. Previous observations (Amalric *et al.*, 1978; Gelfand and Attardi, 1981; Attardi *et al.*, 1982) indicate that this is the case.

There is not much information available concerning the possible mechanisms underlying the phenomena of translational control discussed above. From an analysis of the codon usage in the synthesis of the different mtDNA-encoded polypeptides one can exclude that the presence of rarely used codons is responsible for the low efficiency of translation of some of the mitochondrial mRNAs (unpublished observations). A possibility is that differences among the various mRNAs in degree of secondary structure and/or accessibility of the initiator codon determine the efficiency of their utilization. Although no such differences have been observed in comparing the most stable potential secondary structures of the molecules, as determined by the Nussinov-Jacobson algorithm (1980), there is uncertainty as to the validity of extrapolating these observations to the *in vitro* situation. Another possibility is that the affinity of the small ribosomal subunit for the initiator codon and surrounding sequences may differ among different mRNAs.

Apart from the factors discussed above, which are all related to the structure of the mRNAs, the possibility has to be considered that specific translation factors exist which modulate the rate of translation of the individual mRNAs, presumably at the initiation step. In yeast, there is evidence suggesting that specific nuclear-coded factors play a role in the control of translation of individual mitochondrial mRNAs, in particular COIII mRNA (Ebner *et al.*, 1973; Mueller *et al.*, 1984; Costanzo and Fox, 1986; Costanzo *et al.*, 1986), CYT *b* mRNA (Dieckmann and Tzagoloff, 1985; Rödel *et al.*, 1985; Rödel, 1986), and possibly COII mRNA (Fox, 1986). In the case of COIII mRNA, the available evidence is compatible with the idea that the specific factor(s) interacts with the 5'-untranslated region of the mRNA, promoting initiation of protein synthesis. It is possible that the differential modulation of expression of the various mRNAs by these factors, under different physiological conditions, affects the rate of respiration and the degree of coupling. Mammalian mitochondrial mRNAs all lack a significant 5'-untranslated region (Montoya *et al.*, 1981). On the other hand, experiments in which the interaction of artificial or natural mitochondrial mRNAs from human source with bovine mitochondrial ribosomes was investigated have strongly suggested that the small ribosomal subunits interact with the 5'-end proximal 80 nt of the mRNAs (N.D. Denslow, T. W. O'Brien, G. S. Michaels, J. Montoya, and G. Attardi, in preparation). It is tempting to speculate that also in mammalian cells specific factors play a role in this interaction and/or initiation of protein synthesis, and thus adjust the expression of the individual mRNAs to the level required by the cells under different physiological conditions.

The mechanism of translation of the two overlapping reading frames encoded in mRNA 14 and mRNA 7 is unknown. The results reported here pose constraints on the possible mechanisms operating in the synthesis of two polypeptides on the same mRNA. In particular, they exclude a mechanism in which the same ribosome is used for the synthesis of the two complete polypeptides, i.e., one in which the ribosome would remain on the mRNA after release of the first polypeptide and by backward diffusion would reach the AUG of the second reading frame. In fact, this model would require the rate of translation of the second reading frame to be lower or at most equal to the rate of translation of the first reading frame.

It is clear that the elucidation of the mechanisms of translational control operating in mammalian mitochondria will require the development of an *in vitro* submitochondrial system for protein synthesis programmed by exogenous mRNA.

ACKNOWLEDGEMENTS

These investigations were supported by N.I.H. grant GM-11726 to G.A.

REFERENCES

Amalric, F., Merkel, C., Gelfand, R., and Attardi, G., 1978 : Fractionation of mitochondrial RNA from HeLa cells by high-resolution electrophoresis under strongly denaturing conditions, *J. Mol. Biol. 118*, 1-25.

Anderson, S., Bankier, A. T., Barrell, B. G., de Bruijn, M. H. L., Coulson, A. R., Drouin, J., Eperon, I. C., Nierlich, D. P., Roe, B. A., Sanger, F., Schreier, P. H., Smith, A. J. H., Staden, R., and Young, I. G., 1981, Sequence and organization of the human mitochondrial genome. *Nature 290*, 457-465.

Attardi, G., Cantatore, P. Chomyn, A., Crews, S., Gelfand, R., Merkel, C., Montoya, J., and Ojala, D., 1982, A comprehensive view of mitochondrial gene expression in human cells, in *Mitochondrial Genes*, P. Slonimski, P. Borst, and G. Attardi, eds., pp. 51-71. Cold Spring Harbor Laboratory, Cold Spring Harbor, New York.

Attardi, G., Chomyn, A., Doolittle, R. F., Mariottini, P., and Ragan, C. I., 1986, Seven unidentified reading frames of human mitochondrial DNA encode subunits of the respiratory chain NADH dehydrogenase, *Cold Spring Harbor Symp. Quant. Biol. 51*, 103-114.

Attardi, G., 1986, The elucidation of the human mitochondrial genome: A historical perspective, *Bioassays 5*, 34-39.

Ching, E., and Attardi, G., 1982, High resolution electrophoretic fractionation and partial characterization of the mitochondrial translation products from HeLa cells, *Biochemistry 21*, 3188-3195; Corr. *Biochemistry 24*, 7853 (1985).

Chomyn, A., Mariottini, P., Gonzalez-Cadavid, N., Attardi, G., Strong, D. D., Trovato, D., Riley, M., and Doolittle, R. F., 1983, Identification of the polypeptides encoded in the ATPase 6 gene and in the unassigned reading frames 1 and 3 of human mtDNA, *Proc. Natl. Acad. Sci. USA 80*, 5535-5539.

Chomyn, A., Mariottini, P., Cleeter, M. W. J., Ragan, C. I., Matsuno-Yagi, A., Hatefi, Y., Doolittle, R. F., and Attardi, G., 1985, Six unidentified reading frames of human mitochondrial DNA encode components of the respiratory chain NADH dehydrogenase, *Nature 314*, 592-597.

Chomyn, A., Cleeter, M. W. J., Ragan, C. I., Riley, M., Doolittle, R. F., and Attardi, G., 1986, URF6, the last unidentified reading frame of human mitochondrial DNA, codes for an NADH dehydrogenase subunit, *Science 234*, 614-618.

Costanzo, M. C., Seaver, E. C., and Fox, T., 1986, At least two nuclear gene products are specifically required for translation of a single yeast mitochondrial mRNA, *The EMBO Journal 5*, 3637-3641.

Costanzo, M. C., and Fox, M., 1986, Product of *Saccharomyces cerevisiae* nuclear gene *PET494* activates translation of a specific mitochondrial mRNA, *Molec. Cell. Biology 6*, 3694-3703.

Dieckmann, C. L., and Tzagoloff, A., 1985, Assembly of the mitochondrial membrane system: CBP6, a yeast nuclear gene necessary for synthesis of cytochrome *b*, *J. Biol. Chem. 260*, 1513-1520.

Ebner, E., Mennucci, L., and Schatz, G., 1973, Mitochondrial assembly in respiration-deficient mutants of *Saccharomyces cerevisiae*. I. Effect of nuclear mutations on mitochondrial protein synthesis, *J. Biol. Chem. 248*, 5360-5368.

Fox, T. D., 1986, Nuclear gene products required for translation of specific mitochondrially-coded mRNAs in yeast, *Trends in Genetics 2*, 97-100.

Gelfand, R., and Attardi, G., 1981, Synthesis and turnover of mitochondrial ribonucleic acid in HeLa cells: The mature ribosomal and messenger ribonucleic acid species are metabolically unstable, *Molec. Cell. Biol. 1*, 497-511.

Hare, J. F., Ching, E., and Attardi, G., 1980, Isolation, subunit composition, and site of synthesis of human cytochrome c oxidase, *Biochemistry 19*, 2023-2030.

Hare, J. F., and Hodges, R. 1982, Turnover of mitochondrial inner membrane proteins in hepatoma monolayer cultures, *J. Biol. Chem. 257*, 3575-3580.

Hatefi, Y., Ragan, C. I., and Galante, Y. M., 1985, The enzymes and the enzyme complexes of the mitochondrial oxidative phosphorylation system, in *The Enzymes of Biological Membranes*, Vol. 4, A. Martonosi, ed., pp. 1-70, Plenum Press, New York.

Mariottini, P., Chomyn, A., Attardi, G., Trovato, D., Strong, D. D., and Doolittle, R. F., 1983, Antibodies against synthetic peptides reveal that the unidentified reading frame A6L, overlapping the ATPase 6 gene, is expressed in human mitochondria, *Cell 32*, 1269-1277.

Mariottini, P., Chomyn, A., Riley, M., Cottrell, B., Dootlittle, R. F., and Attardi, G., 1986, Identification of the polypeptides encoded in the unassigned reading frames 2, 4, 4L and 5 of human mitochondrial DNA, *Proc. Natl. Acad. Sci. USA 83*, 1563-1567.

Montoya, J., Ojala, D., and Attardi, G., 1981, Distinctive features of the 5'-terminal sequences of the human mitochondrial mRNAs, *Nature 290*, 465-470.

Montoya, J., Gaines, G., and Attardi, G., 1983, The pattern of transcription of the human mitochondrial rRNA genes reveals two overlapping transcription units, *Cell 34*, 151-159.

Mueller, P. P., Reif, M. K., Zonghou, S., Sengstag, C., Mason, T. L., and Fox, T. D., 1984, A nuclear mutation that posttranscriptionally blocks accumulation of a yeast mitochondrial gene product can be suppressed by a mitochondrial gene rearrangement, *J. Mol. Biol. 175*, 431-452.

Nussinov, R., and Jacobson, A. B., 1980, Fast algorithm for predicting the secondary structure of single-stranded RNA, *Proc. Natl. Acad. Sci. USA 77*, 6309-6313.

Ojala, D., Merkel, C., Gelfand, R., and Attardi, G., 1980, The tRNA genes punctuate the reading of genetic information in human mitochondrial DNA, *Cell 22*, 393-403.

Ojala, D., Montoya, J., and Attardi, G., 1981, The tRNA punctuation model of RNA processing in human mitochondria, *Nature 290*, 470-474.

Oliver, N. A., Greenberg, B. D., and Wallace, D. C., 1983, Assignment of a polymorphic polypeptide to the human mitochondrial DNA unidentified reading frame 3 gene by a new peptide mapping strategy, *J. Biol. Chem. 258*, 5834-5839.

Rödel, G., Koerte, A., and Kandewitz, F., 1985, Mitochondrial suppression of a yeast nuclear mutation which affects the translation of the mitochondrial apocytochrome b transcript, *Curr. Genet. 9*, 641-648.

Rödel, G., 1986, Two yeast nuclear genes, CBS1 and CBS2, are required for translation of mitochondrial transcripts bearing the 5'-untranslated COB leader, *Curr. Genet. 11*, 41-45.

REGULATION OF THE EXPRESSION OF COI AND COIII mRNAs IN RAT LIVER MITOCHONDRIA

Palmiro Cantatore, Flavio Fracasso, Angela Maria Serena Lezza
and Maria Nicola Gadaleta
Dipartimento di Biochimica e Biologia Molecolare, Università di
Bari and Centro di Studio sui Mitocondri e Metabolismo Energetico, Consiglio Nazionale delle Ricerche, Via Amendola 165/A
70126 Bari, Italy

INTRODUCTION

Recent work in several laboratories has produced a great deal of information on the structure of mitochondrial (mt) genomes of some mammalian species. MtDNA sequence of man, cow and mouse as well as large part of rat has
been determined and the transcription products of these DNAs have been identified and mapped[1,2]. Mammalian mtDNA codes for 2 rRNAs, 11 mRNAs specifying
13 polypeptides for respiratory complexes and 22 tRNAs. Despite the complete
transcription of both strands, the location of the structural genes is asym-
metrical: the L-strand codes only for ND6 mRNA and eight tRNAs, while the
rest of the genes is coded for by the H-strand. The tRNA genes are inter-
spersed with almost absolute regularity among the rRNA and the mRNA coding
sequences; this arrangement is consistent with a RNA processing mechanism
in which the cloverleaf structure of the tRNA genes is used as a recognition
signal for RNAse P-like enzymes involved in mtRNA processing. The gene organization of rat liver mtDNA is reported in Fig.1. The mammalian mt transcription starts from three initiation sites, one placed on the L-strand
and two on the H-strand: this means that while the L-strand contains only
one transcription unit, the H-strand is transcribed according to two different modes. Data obtained mainly in human cells[3,4] have generated an H-strand
transcription mechanism which implies that one transcription unit initiates
16 nt upstream of the tRNA[Phe] gene, giving rise to the two rRNAs 16S and 12S
and to the tRNA[Phe] and tRNA[Val]. The other transcriptional event starts in
proximity of the 5' end of the 12S rRNA; it originates a polycistronic
transcript that is processed in correspondence of the tRNA genes.

The different mode of transcription of the rRNA and mRNA genes probably
represents one of the crucial steps in the regulation of their expression. To
obtain more information about this subject studies have been performed on the levels of mt RNAs in different cell types. In HeLa cells an analysis of the kinetics of synthesis and degradation of mtRNA[5,6] showed that the level of the mt mRNA
species is about 1/10 - 1/30 that of the rRNAs. In adult and developing rat liver

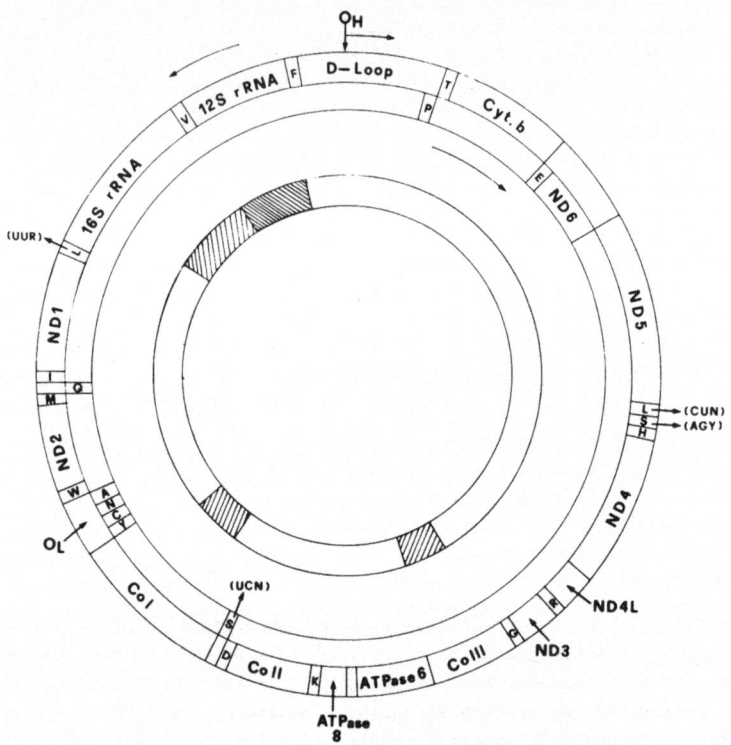

Fig. 1. Gene organization of mammalian mtDNA. The two outer
circles show the position of the rRNA genes, of the
protein coding genes and of the tRNA genes, as derived
from DNA and RNA sequence. Dashed areas in the two inner circles indicate the probes used in the hybridization experiments. Left and right arrows indicate the
direction of H and L strand transcription respectively
(H-strand transcripts are in the outer circle).

Cantatore et al.[7,8] measured the content of several mtRNA species by hybridizing total mtRNA to specific DNA probes. The results obtained in the adult
tissue showed that the rRNAs were about 10 times more abundant with respect
to the mRNAs. Comparison between HeLa cells and rat liver mtRNA levels
showed a similar rRNA content but a higher mRNA concentration in the rat
liver. By considering that the mtRNA species decay with first order
kinetics[5,6] their steady-state level is given by the ratio between the
rate of synthesis K_s, and that of degradation K_d. Knowledge of such parameters and comparison with those of other systems may throw light on the fac-

tors controlling the relative abundance of the mRNA and rRNA species in the same and different cell types. In this communication we will report recent results concerning the synthesis rates and the metabolic half lives of four rat liver mt RNA species. The data will be discussed in the light of the regulation of mitochondrial gene expression.

RESULTS AND DISCUSSION

Calculation of the Synthesis and Degradation Rates of Four Rat Liver mt RNAs

The experimental plan used to estimate the metabolic parameters of the rat liver mtRNA consists in measuring the kinetics of incorporation of [3H]-Uridine in the mtRNA extracted from rat primary hepatocytes cultures. This is accomplished by hybridizing with specific DNA probes total rat mtRNA extracted from hepatocytes labelled for different times and measuring the kinetics of labelling of the mitochondrial UTP pool. The RNA species analysed are the two rRNAs 16S and 12S and the mRNAs for the subunits I and III of the cytochrome oxidase (CoI and CoIII). The data obtained are used to calculate K_s and K_d by utilizing the following equations[9]:

$$M (t) = \frac{K_s}{K_d} (1-e^{-K_d t}) \qquad (1)$$

where M (t) is the number of the newly synthesized RNA molecules which accumulate in the mitochondria, K_s is the apparent entry rate of the transcripts in the mitochondrial compartment (molecules/min/cell) and K_d is the decay rate of the transcripts (min^{-1}). The amount of the [3H] UMP incorporated in the specific transcripts at each time point is given by:

$$R (t) = K_s \int_0^t S (t') \exp \left[(-t'-t) K_d \right] dt' \qquad (2)$$

where S (t) is the specific activity of the precursor [3H]-UTP pool at each time point (dpm/pg UMP) and t is the variable of integration. The equation (2) is numerically resolved by using a program[10] which, by considering two arbitrarly chosen values of K_s and K_d, recalculates R (t) changing the values of K_s and K_d until the root mean square difference between the measured and the calculated value of R (t) is minimized. At the end of calculation the program generates the best fit curves for R (t) and S (t) as well as the newly synthesized RNA accumulation curve M (t).

Experimental Data

The two sets of data that must be provided to the MESSAGE program are the specific activity of the precursor pool at different times, S (t) and the amount of [3H]-UMP incorporated in the specific transcript at each time point, R (t). To generate these data rat hepatocytes prepared by liver perfusion and collagenase treatment[11] were labelled up to 5 hr with [3H]-Uridine. At fixed times samples of the cells were removed and used for the measurement of the cellular and of the mitochondrial UTP pool specific activity and for the preparation of total mtRNA. The Fig.2 reports the kinetics of labelling of the mitochondrial pool. It saturates at around 30 min.

and declines over the next 60 min. The decline is probably due to the entering in the UTP pool of unlabelled UMP produced by the degradation of RNA
synthesized by cold precursors.

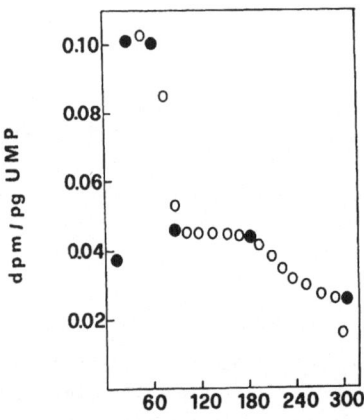

LABELLING TIME (min)

Fig. 2. Variation of the mt UTP pool specific activity during
the labelling period. Specific activity values
(dpm/pg UMP), obtained as reported[12] were normalized
for counting efficiency of the scintillation system
used (0.3) divided by 4 and supplied to the computer
program. (●) measured pool specific activities; (o)
interpolated form of the time function S (t) used for
synthesis rate calculation.

The kinetics of incorporation of $[^3H]$-Uridine in the four mtRNA species
was measured by hybridizing mtRNA from each time point with filters containing an excess of specific DNA probes (see Fig.1 for probe identification).
The hybridized cpm were normalized for the counting and hybridization efficiency. Then they were reduced as dpm/cell, by measuring, as reported by
Bestwick et al.[13], the amount of mtDNA coextracted with the mtRNA, assuming
a mean content of 0.1 μg of mtDNA per 10^6 liver cells[14]. The values of K_s,
K_d and $t_{\frac{1}{2}}$ of the RNA species analysed are listed in Table 1. The rate of
appearance of the mt rRNAs is about ten times that of the mRNAs.

Table 1. Metabolic Parameters of Some Rat Liver mt RNAs

RNA species	Rate of Synthesis K_S (N° of molecules/min per cell)	Rate of Degradation K_d (min^{-1})	Half life[a] (min)	Steady state content (N° of molecules/cell) K_S/K_d	Direct[b] Determination
12S	402	$6.7 \cdot 10^{-3}$	102	60000	80000
16S	276	$5.3 \cdot 10^{-3}$	131	52000	80000
COI	17	$6.0 \cdot 10^{-3}$	115	2800	8000
COIII	41	$11.0 \cdot 10^{-3}$	63	3700	8000

[a] Half life is $\ln 2/K_d$.

[b] Data calculated from Cantatore et al.[7], assuming a mean content of 1000 mitochondria per rat liver cell.

The K_d values of all the RNA species analysed are however similar with half lives of about 100 min for both rRNAs and mRNAs. The ratios K_S/K_d which give an estimate of the steady state amount of the individual RNAs are also reported in Table 1. They are in good agreement with the molar amount per cell previously calculated by us, titrating rat mtRNA with labelled DNA probes[7]. The results support the conclusion that the higher rat mt rRNAs content with respect to the mRNAs is mainly due to a higher rRNA synthesis rate. This is in agreement with the data reported in HeLa cells[5,6] and with the existence of two different transcription units for rRNAs and mRNAs respectively[3]. Data obtained in several systems[15,16] raised the possibility that, as for some cytoplasmic mRNA species (the mRNAs for casein, globin and histones[17-19]) at least one control of mitochondrial gene expression may take place at level of RNA stability. According to this hypothesis it could have been expected that the higher level of the rat mt mRNAs with respect to the corresponding HeLa cells species might be mainly due to a stabilization of rat mt mRNAs. The comparison of the kinetic parameters of HeLa cells and rat liver mt mRNAs, shown in Table 2, seems to exclude this hypothesis: both HeLa cells and rat liver mRNAs have a comparable stability, so that the higher content of rat mt mRNAs seems mainly due to an overall higher synthesis rate.

Table 2. Metabolic Characteristics of Some HeLa Cells and Rat Liver mtRNAs[a]

RNA species	K_S(mol/min/cell)		K_d(min^{-1})		STEADY STATE LEVEL (N° mol/cell) K_S/K_d		Direct Determination	
	Rat	HeLa	Rat	Hela	Rat	HeLa	Rat	HeLa
16S	276	n.d.	$5.3 \cdot 10^{-3}$	$2.4 \cdot 10^{-3}$	52000	n.d.	80000	n.d.
12S	402	265	$6.7 \cdot 10^{-3}$	$3.0 \cdot 10^{-3}$	60000	88000	80000	n.d.
CoI	17	10	$6.0 \cdot 10^{-3}$	$10.0 \cdot 10^{-3}$	2800	1000	8000	n.d.
CoIII	41	9	$11.0 \cdot 10^{-3}$	$9.8 \cdot 10^{-3}$	3700	900	8000	n.d.

[a] HeLa cells values are from Ref.[5] and [6]. Rat liver steady state data are from Ref.[7].

The higher mt mRNA level in cells with an active oxidative metabolism (rat liver) compared to cells which generate ATP essentially by glicolysis (HeLa cells), is an observatiion which suggests the existence of a relationship between mitochondrial transcriptional levels and cellular metabolism. Other data agree with this view. The content of CoI mRNA increases during development with a peak at birth, in coincidence with the rise of cytochrome oxidase activity[8]. Moreover it has been demonstrated that the concentration of CoI and CoIII mRNAs in rat liver and HeLa cells well correlates with their respective cytochrome content[20,21]. The change in the levels of the mt transcripts in dependence of the cell conditions has been reported also in other organisms such as in yeast mitochondria. In this system Mueller and Getz[22] have shown that the mtRNA levels are 3-4 times higher in derepressed with respect to respiratory repressed cells and that they also correlate with the subunit stoichiometry of the respiratory enzymes. On the other hand it is likely that the transcription is only one of the steps at which the mt gene expression may be affected. The ratio of the number of synthesized CoI molecules/mRNA molecule per min. calculated as reported by Kim and Warner[23] gives a translation efficiency that in both rat liver and HeLa cells is less than 10%. The inefficiency or underutilization of the mt mRNAs suggests the existence of further controls, probably at level of the translation and it opens the way toward investigations on the factors involved in this process.

REFERENCES

1. G. Attardi, Animal mitochondrial DNA: an extreme example of genetic economy, Int. Rev. Cytol. 93:93 (1985).
2. P. Cantatore and C. Saccone, Organization, structure and evolution of mammalian mitochondrial genes, Int. Rev. Cytol. (in press) (1987).
3. J. Montoya, R. Christianson, D. Levens, M. Rabinowitz and G. Attardi, Identification of initiation sites for heavy-strand and light-strand transcription in human mitochondrial DNA, Proc. Natl. Acad. Sci. USA 79:7195 (1982).
4. D. D. Chang and D.A. Clayton, Precise identification of individual promoters for transcription of each strand of human mitochondrial DNA, Cell 36:635 (1984).
5. R. Gelfand and G. Attardi, Synthesis and turnover of mitochondrial ribonucleic acid in HeLa cells: the mature ribosomal and messenger ribonucleic species are metabolically unstable, Mol. Cell. Biol. 1:497 (1981).
6. G. Attardi, P. Cantatore, A. Chomyn, S. Crews, R. Gelfand, C. Merkel, J. Montoya and D. Ojala, A comprehensive view of mitochondrial gene expression in human cell, in: "Mitochondrial Genes", P. Slonimski, P. Borst and G. Attardi, eds., 51, Cold Spring Harbor, N.Y. (1982).
7. P. Cantatore, M.N. Gadaleta and C. Saccone, Determination of some mitochondrial RNAs concentration in adult rat liver, Biochem. Biophys. Res. Commun. 13:284 (1984).
8. P. Cantatore, P. Loguercio Polosa, F. Fracasso, Z. Flagella and M.N. Gadaleta, Quantitation of mitochondrial RNA species during rat liver development: the concentration of cytochrome oxidase subunit I (CoI) mRNA increases at birth, Cell Diff. 19:125 (1986).

9. G. A. Galau, E.D. Lipson, R.J. Britten and E.M. Davidson, Synthesis and turnover of polysomal mRNAs in sea urchin embryos, *Cell* 10:415 (1977).

10. C. V. Cabrera, J.J. Lee, J.W. Ellison, R.J. Britten and E.M. Davidson, Regulation of cytoplasmic mRNA prevalence in sea urchin embryos. Rates of appearance and turnover for specific sequences, *J. Mol. Biol* 174:85 (1984).

11. H. Sies, The use of perfusion of liver and other organs for the study of microsomal electron-transport and cytochrome P-450 systems, in: "Methods in Enzimology", S. Fleischer and L. Packer, eds. Vol.52:48, Academic Press, New York (1978).

12. P. Cantatore, Z. Flagella, F. Fracasso, A.M.S. Lezza, M.N. Gadaleta and A. de Montalvo, Synthesis and turnover rates of four rat liver mitochondrial RNA species, *FEBS Letters* 213:144 (1987).

13. R. K. Bestwick, G.L. Moffett and C.K. Mathews, Selective expansion of mitochondrial nucleoside triphosphate pools in antimetabolite-treated HeLa cells, *J. Biol. Chem.* 257:9300 (1982).

14. D. Neubert, C.T. Gregg, R. Bass and H.J. Merker, Occurrence and possible functions of mitochondrial DNA in animal development, in: "The Biochemistry of Animal Development",R. Weber ed., Vol.III:387, Academic Press, New York (1975).

15. J. England, P. Costantino and G. Attardi, Mitochondrial RNA and protein synthesis in enucleated african green monkey cells, *J. Mol. Biol.* 119:455 (1978).

16. R. A. Lansman and D.A. Clayton, Mitochondrial protein synthesis in mouse L-cells: effect of selective nicking of mitochondrial DNA, *J. Mol. Biol.* 99:777 (1975).

17. W. A. Guyette, R.J. Matusik and J.M. Rosen, Prolactin-mediated transcription and post-transcriptional control of casein gene expression, *Cell* 17:1013 (1979).

18. H. F. Lodish and B. Small, Different lifetimes of reticulocyte messenger RNA, *Cell* 7:59 (1976).

19. L. M. Hereford, M.A. Osley, J.R. Ludwig and C.S. McLaughlin, Cell-cycle regulation of yeast histone mRNA, *Cell* 24:367 (1981).

20. J. N. Williams Jr., A comparative study of cytochrome ratios in mitochondria from organs of the rat, chicken, and guinea pig, *Biochem. Biophys.* Acta, 162:175 (1968).

21. J. F. Hare, E. Ching and G. Attardi, Isolation, subunit composition and site of synthesis of human cytochrome c oxidase, *Biochemistry* 19:2023 (1980).

22. D. M. Mueller and G.S. Getz, Steady state analysis of mitochondrial RNA after growth of yeast *Saccharomyces cerevisiae* under catabolite repression and derepression, *J. Biol. Chem.* 261:11816 (1986).

23. C. H. Kim and J.R. Warner, Messenger RNA for ribosomal proteins in yeast, *J. Mol. Biol.* 165:79 (1983).

TWO CONSENSUS SEQUENCES FOR RNA PROCESSING IN *Neurospora crassa*

MITOCHONDRIA

Giuseppe Macino and Mary Anne Nelson

Dipartimento Biopatologia Umana, Sezione di Biologia Cellulare
Università di Roma, La Sapienza
Policlinico Umberto I, I-00161 Rome, Italy

INTRODUCTION

The structure of the mitochondrial genome of the filamentous fungus *Neurospora crassa* has been extensively characterized, and its DNA sequence has been largely determined (as reviewed by Breitenberger and RajBhandary[1]; see also recent works by De Vries *et al.*[2] and Nelson and Macino[3, 4]). However, less is known about the expression of the mitochondrial genes. No promoter has yet been identified, and analysis of precursor transcripts has suggested that transcription of the *Neurospora* mitochondrial genome initiates at a very small number of promoters, perhaps as few as two. Large precursor transcripts, some of which correspond to 20% or more of the genome, have been detected[5, 6, 7]. In many cases, messenger RNAs are generated from precursor transcripts by the simple removal of transfer RNA sequences, in a process that is quite similar to that used by mammalian mitochondria[8, 9]. However, in *Neurospora* mitochondria 5' and 3' end processing has also been observed at sites that do not correspond to transfer RNAs or tRNA-like sequences[3, 6, 7, 10-13, this paper]; a few of these sites share limited homology[6]. We have examined the sites of RNA processing near the ATPase subunit 6 and 8 genes (*oli2* and URFA6L, respectively), and present evidence for the existence of two classes of "Consensus" sequences for RNA processing in *Neurospora crassa* mitochondria.

MATERIALS AND METHODS

Preparation of Mitochondrial DNA and RNA

N. crassa mitochondria were prepared from exponentially-growing cells of the wild type strain SL74A[14]. A recombinant plasmid containing the Eco11 fragment of mitochondrial DNA was prepared as previously described[15]. Mitochondrial RNA was purified as described by Bonitz *et al.*[16].

5'- and 3'-end-labelling Procedures

Restriction fragments were labelled at their 5' ends with $[\gamma-^{32}P]$ dATP and T4 polynucleotide kinase[17]. 3'-end-labelling of restriction

GAATTCTGCATGATCCACTGCCCCGATCTACCCATCCAACTCCCGAGGCGTAGGXXXTACCCTACGTCCTTGGT
EcoRI   74

ATAGGGATCGATGATCCCGTGGAGCCCAACTGGATTCACGTATCTTCTCCCATACAACTTCCACTCCGCTTCCA
                              HinfI   148

TTGTATGAGGTAGTAAGCCTTTACGATTCTTTAATTACTTTCCATTAGCGGGTTTCATTAAAGATACCAAAAGG
                         HinfI   222

CTAGACCGCCTTACCTTTCCTATTTGGTGCACCGCTCTGGCCGGGGGTTGAGAAGTAATGAGACGCTGGXXXAC
                                                                           296

TTTTCAGACGCCTCGCAAATCATAATATATCCTTTTACTAAATATAATAGAAACTAGTCTCTACTTCTATTAGA
                                        *****   370

AGATTCACTTCAACATTATGCTTCCTCCGAAGGCAGGCAGGACCCTTCGGCAGGAGGAGGAAGAAAAAAGGATA
 HinfI   AsuI   444

AAATTAAGGTATTCTTTAAAAGGTXXXCAACTCTACGAGTGGAATCCACCCCXXXCGAATAXXXCACGAAGGTG
                                            HinfI   518

TGTGGGGTATTCGTGGGGCCCTAGTAGTGAAGCAGCGAGGGGAGCCGAGGCTAAGAATTC
        AsuI   DdeI EcoRI   578

Fig. 1. Nucleotide sequence of the Ecoll fragment of *Neurospora
        crassa* mito- chondrial DNA. The sequence of the non-
        transcribed (sense) strand is shown. X's indicate the
        positions of a few nucleotides of uncertain sequence.
        Relevant restriction sites are marked. The Ecoll fragment is
        present immediately upstream from and contiguous with the
        Eco7b fragment, whose sequence has been previously
        reported[18]. The 5' end of the URFA6L transcripts
        (determined by S1 mapping, Figure 2) is indicated by
        asterisks around nucleotide 344.

fragments was carried out with *Escherichia coli* DNA polymerase I and [α-
^{32}P]dATP. The single strands were separated on polyacrylamide gels, and
strands were identified by sequencing.

DNA Sequencing

DNA sequencing was performed as described by Maxam and Gilbert[17].

S1 Nuclease Mapping

Experiments were performed as previously described[10]. In control
experiments with the complementary strands of DNA, the restriction
fragments were totally degraded, indicating that the mitochondrial RNA
preparations were not contaminated by mitochondrial DNA that could protect
the labelled probes (not shown).

RESULTS

Nucleotide Sequence of the Ecoll Fragment

We have investigated the sites of RNA processing in the region of
the *Neurospora* mitochondrial genome containing the ATPase subunit 6 and 8
genes. Since the published sequence in this region included only eighty

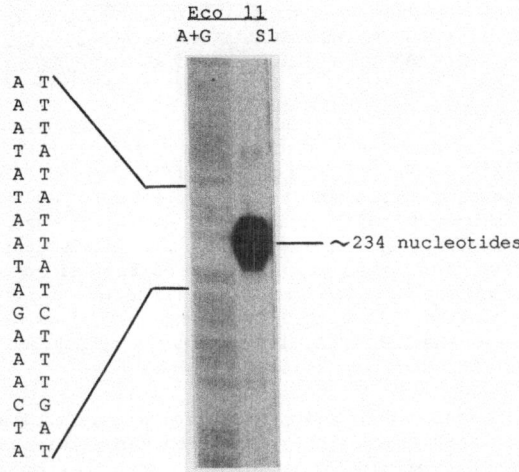

Fig. 2. Mapping of the 5' end of the URFA6L tran- scripts.
The Eco11 fragment of *Neurospora* mitochondrial DNA
was labelled at its 5' end, hybridized with total
mitochondrial RNA and treated with S1 nuclease. The
reference ladder contains a purine-specific reaction
of the Eco11 fragment. The DNA sequence of both
strands is shown to the left; the arrows indicate
the 5' processing site.

nucleotides upstream from the subunit 8 (URFA6L) gene[18], we first extended
the known sequence by analyzing the Eco11 fragment of mitochondrial DNA,
thus increasing the available sequence upstream from the URFA6L gene to
about 650 nucleotides. The nucleotide sequence of the Eco11 fragment is
shown in Figure 1.

The Eco11 fragment does not contain any long open reading frames,
and stop codons as well as codons not normally used in *Neurospora*
mitochondrial genes are present very frequently in all three potential
frames. Therefore, this fragment most likely does not include even a
portion of a coding region for any structural gene. Also, no transfer RNA
sequences were detected. However, when the Eco11 fragment was labelled
and hybridized to Northern blots of mitochondrial RNA, many discrete
transcripts were detected (not shown), indicating that this region is
transcribed. S1 nuclease mapping experiments (discussed below) confirmed
and extended the Northern hybridization results.

5' Ends of the URFA6L Transcripts

The 5' ends of transcripts from the URFA6L region were investigated
in S1 mapping experiments with single-stranded, 5'-end-labelled probes.
When probes corresponding to the URFA6L coding sequence and the region
immediately upstream were used, no signals were observed (not shown),
indicating that RNA processing and/or transcriptional initiation do not
occur very close to the URFA6L coding sequence. When the Eco11 fragment
was used as a probe, a strong signal mapping about 310 nucleotides
upstream from the URFA6L start codon was detected (Figure 2; indicated in
Figure 1 by asterisks). The intact Eco11 fragment was also protected from
S1 nuclease digestion, suggesting that precursor transcripts extending
further upstream are also present among the mitochondrial RNAs. This
supposition was supported by Northern hybridization experiments (not

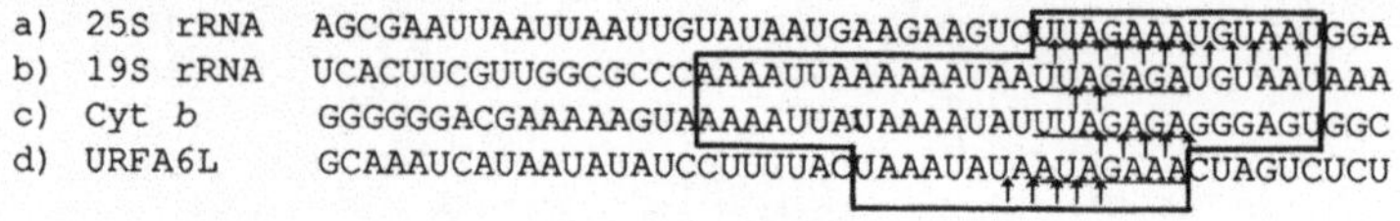

a) 25S rRNA   AGCGAAUUAAUUAAUUGUAUAAUGAAGAAGUC⎡UUAGAAAUGUAAU⎤GGA
b) 19S rRNA   UCACUUCGUUGGCGCCC⎡AAAAUUAAAAAAAUAAUU⎤AGAGAUGUAAU⎤AAA
c) Cyt b   GGGGGGACGAAAAAGUA⎡AAAAUUAUAAAAAUAUUU⎤AGAGAGGGAGU⎤GGC
d) URFA6L   GCAAAUCAUAAUAUAUCCUUUUAC⎡UAAAUAUAAUAGAAA⎤CUAGUCUCU

Fig. 3. Homology at 5' end processing sites. The sequences flanking four sites of RNA processing are shown: a) the 5' end of the 25S rRNA[12]; b) the 5' end of the 19S rRNA[11]; c) the processing site about 717 nucleotides upstream from the cytochrome b coding sequence[6]; d) the processing site about 310 nucleotides upstream from the URFA6L gene (Figure 2). Arrows indicate approximate sites of processing, as determined by S1 mapping and/or primer extension experiments. Homologous sequences are boxed. The homology between the 25S rRNA, 19S rRNA and cytochrome b processing sites has been previously described[6].

shown). The S1 mapping and Northern hybridization results indicate that the 5' end of URFA6L transcripts identified here arose as the result of RNA processing of a precursor transcript. No sites of transcriptional initiation were detected in the region under study. Since a unique 5' end of URFA6L transcripts was determined in these experiments, we suggest that this 5' extremity is most likely the actual 5' end of the mature URFA6L transcript(s).

The URFA6L 5' RNA processing site shares a limited homology with three previously-described sites of RNA processing; this homology is shown in Figure 3. The $^U/_AUAGA^G/_AA$ sequence (underlined in Figure 3) present at the sites of processing is well conserved, while the flanking sequences are more or less divergent in the four sites. All four sites are preceded by AU-rich sequences of varying lengths. "PstI palindromes"[19] (GC-rich palindromic sequences containing two closely-spaced PstI restriction sites that are present in perhaps from 50 to 100 copies in the Neurospora mitochondrial genome) are located from thirty to forty nucleotides upstream from the 25S rRNA and cytochrome b sites of 5' end processing. No strong RNA secondary structures or tRNA-like structures were noted in the regions surrounding these 5' processing sites. The primary structures in these regions might be sufficient in themselves to serve as signals for RNA processing.

Processing Sites Between the ATPase Subunit 6 and 8 Genes

In S1 nuclease mapping experiments, three sites of RNA processing were detected between the ATPase subunit 6 and 8 genes (not shown); the positions of these sites are indicated in Figure 4. Signals at all three sites were detected when either 3'-end-labelled or 5'-end-labelled single-stranded probes were used, indicating that different transcripts corresponding to the URFA6L gene terminate at each of these three sites, and that the 5' ends of transcripts from the region upstream from the oli2 gene (and perhaps including oli2 coding sequences) map at the same three sites. Thus, RNA processing events at these sites generate the 3' ends of potential mature URFA6L transcripts, and the 5' ends of either precursor or mature transcripts from the downstream (oli2) region. The complex pattern of oli2 transcripts has been previously described[18], but the properties of a potential oli2 messenger RNA have not been determined. Recent re-sequencing of the oli2 gene has shown that this gene is not interrupted by the previously-postulated short intervening sequence, and instead contains one long intron (previously called intron 2[18]).

The three sites of RNA processing between the URFA6L and oli2 genes

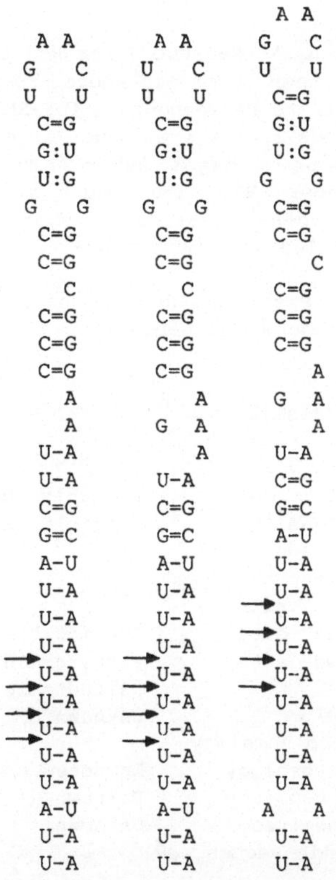

```
                                    A A
        A A          A A           G   C
       G   C        U   C          U   U
       U   U        U   U          C=G
       C=G          C=G            G:U
       G:U          G:U            U:G
       U:G          U:G           G   G
      G   G        G   G           C=G
       C=G          C=G            C=G
       C=G          C=G              C
        C            C             C=G
       C=G          C=G            C=G
       C=G          C=G            C=G
       C=G          C=G              A
        A            A            G   A
        A          G   A              A
       U-A            A             U-A
       U-A          U-A             C=G
       C=G          C=G             G=C
       G=C          G=C             A-U
       A-U          A-U             U-A
       U-A          U-A          →  U-A
       U-A          U-A          →  U-A
    →  U-A       →  U-A          →  U-A
    →  U-A       →  U-A          →  U-A
    →  U-A       →  U-A             U-A
    →  U-A       →  U-A             U-A
       U-A          U-A             U-A
       U-A          U-A             U-A
       A-U          A-U            A   A
       U-A          U-A             U-A
       U-A          U-A             U-A
```

UAAUUUGUC   UAUGUC   UAUGUC   UAAGC...535 nucleotides...AUG
URFA6L stop codon   *oli2* start codon

Fig. 4. RNA Processing at Conserved Palindromic Sequences.
The sequence of part of the region between the URFA6L
(ATPase subunit 8) and *oli2* (ATPase subunit 6) genes is
shown[18]. The potential structures of three palindromic
sequences (with free energies of -27.6, -28.4 and -24.3
kcal, respectively[20]) are diagrammed, and the sites of
RNA processing that were identified in S1 nuclease
mapping experiments are indicated by arrows.

share extensive homology, both at the level of primary and of secondary
structure (Figure 4). They share perfect homology for a region of fifteen
nucleotides, but the highly-conserved region extends for more than sixty
nucleotides. These sites are similar to the previously-described "PstI
palindromes"[19], although they lack the closely-spaced PstI restriction
sites. A sequence similar to the eighteen nucleotide core sequence of
"PstI palindromes" (CCCTGCAGTACTGCAGGG; PstI sites are underlined) is
present in the "PstI-like palindromes" diagrammed in Figure 4 (CCGTGCT^T/
_GAACTGTGGGG). Several of the nucleotides that are differ- ent in these
"PstI-like palindromes" cause disruption of the perfect palindromic
sequence characteristic of "PstI palindromes". However, the "PstI-like"
and "PstI palindromes" share similar flanking sequences; they have quite
pyrimidine-rich upstream and purine-rich downstream sides.

DISCUSSION

Two possible "Consensus" sequences for RNA processing in *Neurospora crassa* mitochondria have been described above. One "Consensus" sequence, shown in Figure 3, appears to be recognized for RNA processing events that generate the mature 5' ends of the small and large ribosomal RNAs, as well as the 5' extremities of a major cytochrome *b* transcript and the postulated URFA6L messenger RNA. The length of the perfectly-conserved sequence at these 5' processing sites is short, but they share other similarities as well, including upstream AU-rich sequences.

Table 1. Properties of Presumed RNA Processing Sites 5' and 3' to *Neurospora   crassa* Mitochondrial Genes

Gene[a]	5' Processing Site(s)[b]	3' Processing Site(s)	Ref.
CO I	tRNA^{Cys}	tRNA^{Arg}	6, 21
CO III	tRNA^{Asn}	Probably tRNA^{Lys}	7
ND6	Perhaps tRNA^{Trp}	Probably tRNA^{Val}	7
Cyt *b*	1) "Consensus" site	tRNA^{Cys}	6
	2) No noted homology		6
19S rRNA	"Consensus" site	tRNA^{Tyr}	6,7,11
25S rRNA	"Consensus" site	GC-rich "PstI palindrome"[c]	6, 12
URFA6L	"Consensus" site	Three conserved palindromic sequences[d]	This paper
ND1	1) tRNA^{Arg}	Unknown	6, 13
	2) No noted homology		6, 13
ND4L/ND5	No noted homology	No noted homology	3
CO II	No noted homology	Unknown	10
oli2	Three conserved palindromic sequences[d]	Unknown	This paper

[a]Genes are as follows: the three cytochrome oxidase subunit genes (CO I, CO II   and CO III),   NADH dehydrogenase subunit genes (ND6, ND1, ND4L and ND5, previously called "URFs" or unidentified reading frames), cytochrome *b* (Cyt *b*),   the small and large ribosomal RNA genes (19S and 25S rRNA) and the ATPase   subunit   6 and 8 genes (*oli2* and URFA6L, respectively). (ND6 was previously   called URF-N11, 7.

[b]The "Consensus" site is discussed in the text and shown in Figure 3. Two sites   of 5' end processing have been found for the cytochrome *b* and ND1 genes.

[c]These conserved GC-rich palindromic sequences, which contain two closely-spaced PstI restriction sites, were initially described by Yin *et al.*[19].

[d]The three conserved palindromic sequences are diagrammed in Figure 4.

The second potential "Consensus" sequence for RNA processing (shown in Figure 4) consists of a long palindromic sequence, or "PstI-like palindrome". Processing events at three such contiguous palindromes generate the 3' ends of possible mature URFA6L transcripts, and perhaps also the 5' ends of the downstream *oli2* messenger RNA(s). The three "PstI-like palindromes" share extensive homology for more than sixty nucleotides, and differ significantly from the previously-described "PstI palindromes"[19] that are present in many copies in the *Neurospora* mitochondrial genome. When the "PstI palindromes" themselves were initially identified, it was thought that they might play a role in the processing of large precursor transcripts[10], [19]. However, later work showed clearly that these palindromes do not serve as signals for RNA processing[6], [7]; indeed, in several cases, "PstI palindromes" are present in mature transcripts.

A summary of the RNA processing sites that have been identified to date in *Neurospora* mitochondria is presented in Table 1. Many of these sites consist in transfer RNA sequences; in this sense, RNA processing in *Neurospora* mitochondria resembles that in human mitochondria[8], [9]. Also, in both human and *Neurospora* mitochondria, large precursor transcripts are synthesized and the mature transcripts are generated by RNA processing events. In *Neurospora*, transcripts corresponding to 20% or more of the mitochondrial genome have been detected[5], [6]. This situation differs dramatically from that observed in mitochondria of *Saccharomyces cerevisiae*, where numerous, much shorter, primary transcripts are synthesized, and tRNA sequences do not play major roles in the processing of precursor transcripts[22].

Since most or all of the *Neurospora* mitochondrial genes are transcribed as parts of large precursor transcripts, any eventual control of the relative amounts of the different transcripts might be exercised by regulating the processing of the precursor transcripts. The multiplicity of RNA processing sites (Table 1) could permit a fairly fine-tuned regulation of the amounts of different RNA species.

ACKNOWLEDGEMENTS

We thank Mr. T. Aversa and Dr. A. Colonna for excellent technical assistance. This work was supported by grants from the "Istituto Pasteur/ Fondazione Cenci Bolognetti" and "Progetti Finalizzati, Ingegneria Genetica del C.N.R.".

REFERENCES

1. C. A. Breitenberger and U. L. RajBhandary, Some highlights of mitochondrial research based on analysis of *Neurospora crassa* mitochondrial DNA, Trends in Biochem. Sci. 10:478 (1985).
2. H. De Vries, B. Alzner-DeWeerd, C. A. Breitenberger, D. Chang, J. C. De Jonge, and U. L. RajBhandary, The E35 stopper mutant of *Neurospora crassa*: Precise localization of deletion endpoints in mitochondrial DNA and evidence that the deleted DNA codes for a subunit of NADH dehydrogenase, EMBO J. 5:779 (1986).
3. M. A. Nelson and G. Macino, Structure and expression of the overlapping ND4L and ND5 genes of *Neurospora crassa* mitochondria, Mol. Gen. Genet. 206:307 (1987).
4. M. A. Nelson and G. Macino, Three class I introns in the ND4L/ND5 transcriptional unit of *Neurospora crassa* mitochondria, Mol. Gen. Genet. 206:318 (1987).
5. M. R. Green, M. F. Grimm, R. R. Goewert, R. A. Collins, M. D. Cole, A. M. Lambowitz, J. E. Heckman, S. Yin, and U. L. RajBhandary, Transcripts and processing patterns for the ribosomal RNA and transfer RNA region of *Neurospora crassa* mitochondrial DNA, J. Biol. Chem. 256:2027 (1981).
6. G. Burger, M. Helmer Citterich, M. A. Nelson, S. Werner, and G. Macino, RNA processing in *Neurospora crassa* mitochondria: transfer RNAs punctuate a large precursor transcript, EMBO J. 4:197 (1985).

7. C. A. Breitenberger, K. S. Browning, B. Alzner-De Weerd, and U. L. RajBhandary, RNA processing in *Neurospora crassa* mitochondria:Use of transfer RNA sequences as signals, EMBO J. 4:185 (1985).

8. J. Montoya, D. Ojala, and G. Attardi, Distinctive features of the 5' terminal sequences of the human mitochondrial mRNAs, Nature 290:465 (1981).

9. D. Ojala, J. Montoya, and G. Attardi, tRNA punctuation model of RNA processing in human mitochondria, Nature 290:470 (1981).

10. G. Macino and G. Morelli, Cytochrome oxidase subunit 2 gene in *Neurospora crassa* mitochondria, J. Biol. Chem. 258:13230 (1983).

11. R. A. Akins and A. M. Lambowitz, The *poky* mutant of *Neurospora* contains a 4-base-pair deletion at the 5' end of the mitochondrial small RNA, Proc. Nat. Acad. Sci. 81:3791 (1984).

12. G. Garriga, H. Bertrand, and A. M. Lambowitz, RNA splicing in *Neurospora* mitochondria: Nuclear mutants defective in both splicing and 3' end synthesis of the large rRNA, Cell 36:623 (1984).

13. G. Burger and S. Werner, The mitochondrial URF1 gene in *Neurospora crassa* has an intron that contains a novel type of URF, J. Mol. Biol. 186:231 (1985).

14. P. Terpstra, M. Holtrop, and A. M. Kroon, A complete cleavage map of *Neurospora crassa* mtDNA obtained with endonucleases EcoRI and BamHI, Biochim. Biophys. Acta 475:571 (1977).

15. M. Helmer Citterich, G. Morelli, and G. Macino, Nucleotide sequence and intron structure of the apocytochrome *b* gene of *Neurospora crassa* mitochondria, EMBO J. 2:1235 (1983).

16. S. G. Bonitz, G. Coruzzi, B. E. Thalenfeld, A. Tzagoloff, and G. Macino, Assembly of the mitochondrial membrane system: Structure and nucleotide sequence of the gene coding for subunit 1 of yeast cytochrome oxidase, J. Biol. Chem. 255:11927 (1980).

17. A. M. Maxam and W. Gilbert, Sequencing end-labelled DNA with base-specific chemical cleavages, Methods Enzymol. 65:499 (1980).

18. G. Morelli and G. Macino, Two intervening sequences in the ATPase subunit 6 gene of *Neurospora crassa*. A short intron (93 base-pairs) and a long intron that is stable after excision, J. Mol. Biol. 178:491 (1984).

19. S. Yin, J. Heckman, and U. L. RajBhandary, Highly conserved GC-rich palindromic DNA sequences flank tRNA genes in *Neurospora crassa* mitochondria, Cell 26:325 (1981).

20. I. Tinoco, P. N. Borer, B. Dengler, M. D. Levine, O. C. Uhlenbeck, D. M. Crothers, and J. Gralla, Improved estimation of secondary structure in ribonucleic acids, Nature New Biol. 246:40 (1973).

21. H. De Vries, P. Haima, M. Brinker, and J. C. De Jonge, The *Neurospora* mitochondrial genome: the region coding for the polycistronic cytochrome oxidase subunit I transcript is preceded by a transfer RNA gene, FEBS Lett. 179:337 (1985).

22. L. A. Grivell, Mitochondrial gene expression 1983, in: "Mitochondria 1983: Nucleo-Mitochondrial Interactions", R. J. Schweyen, K. Wolf, and F. Kaudewitz, eds., de Gruyter, Berlin (1983).

PRIMARY STRUCTURE OF THE YEAST NUCLEAR CBS1 GENE PRODUCT,

NECESSARY TO ACTIVATE TRANSLATION OF MITOCHONDRIAL COB mRNA

Vera Forsbach and Gerhard Rödel

Institut für Genetik und Mikrobiologie
Universität München
Maria-Ward-Strasse 1a, 8000 München 19, F.R.G.

INTRODUCTION

A number of yeast nuclear mutations prevent the accumulation of specific mitochondrial gene products by interfering with a post-transcriptional step in the expression of the respective genes (for review see: Fox, 1986). At least six nuclear genes have been identified which are specifically required for the expression of the mosaic COB gene, coding for apocytochrome b, the only mitochondrially synthesized subunit of the ubichinol-cytochrome c oxidoreductase. Production of stable 5´ ends of the COB mRNA is dependent on the gene CBP1 (Dieckmann et al., 1982), while the genes CBP2 and MRS1 are specifically required for the excision of introns 5 (bI5) and 3 (bI3), respectively, from the COB pre mRNA (McGraw and Tzagoloff, 1983; Hill et al., 1985; Kreike et al., 1986). Mutations in the nuclear genes CBP6, CBS1 and CBS2 have been shown to interfere with the translation of COB transcripts (Dieckmann and Tzagoloff, 1985; Rödel et al., 1985; Rödel, 1986). cbs1- and cbs2-mutants can be suppressed by a fusion of the COB structural gene to the 5'-untranslated leader of other mitochondrial genes, e.g. OLI1 (Rödel et al., 1985; Rödel, 1986). From this observation it was concluded that the CBS1- and CBS2-gene products or something under their control act in the COB mRNA 5' leader to activate translation of the COB coding sequences. This notion has been extended by the demonstration that the CBS1 gene is also required for translation of cytochrome oxidase subunit III (coxIII) from a chimeric coxIII gene bearing the 5' COB leader (Rödel and Fox, 1987).
Disruption of the CBS1 and CBS2 wild type genes by insertion of a marker gene (URA3) results in a phenotype which is indistinguishable from that of the original cbs1 and cbs2 mutants with respect to mitochondrial transcription- and translation products (Rödel et al., 1986). This observation suggests that stimulation of translation of COB transcripts may be the only function of these gene products. However, additional functions of these PET gene products cannot be excluded, e.g. as structural components of the bc_1-complex. Only recently, examples for an interplay between various subunits of this complex have been reported: Analysis of cor1 mutants, which are defi-

cient in the 44 kD subunit, provided strong evidence that this
subunit is necessary for the addition of heme to apocytochrome
b (Tzagoloff et al., 1986). Gene disruptions of the two genes
coding for the 14 and the 11 kD subunits result in the complete
absence of immunologically detectable cytochrome b (Schoppink
et al., 1986). It was suggested that these subunits are required for proper integration of cytochrome b into the membrane
and that the lack of cytochrome b is due to proteolytic breakdown of unassembled apocytochrome b.

To test whether CBS1 may represent a known gene (with the
yet unknown function as a positive modulator of cytochrome b
synthesis) we determined the nucleotide sequence of a DNA fragment which contains the functional CBS1 gene. In addition we
tested whether introduction of a chimeric COB gene with the 5'
untranslated leader of the OLI1 gene is able to suppress the
effect of a disruption of the nuclear CBS1 gene.

Our results show i) that this rearrangement in the mitochondrial DNA is able to suppress the CBS1 disruption and ii)
that the CBS1 gene product is a hydrophilic polypeptide with
an estimated molecular weight of 20.5 kD, which is not identical
to any of the known yeast nuclear gene products.

RESULTS AND DISCUSSION

Primary structure of the CBS1 gene

We have recently shown that the insert of plasmid pVF1,
a 1.9 kb BglII/ClaI fragment, contains the functional CBS1 gene
(Rödel et al., 1986). DNA-sequence of a 0.9 kb HaeIII/NsiI sub-
clone was determined by the strategy outlined in Fig. 1. The
only open reading frame (orf) of considerable length is shown
in Fig. 2. Evidence that this orf constitutes the CBS1 gene
comes from the finding that the unique EcoRI site (at position
465 in Fig. 2) must be located in the functional gene. Insertion
of a marker gene (URA3) into this site of the wild type gene
leads to respiratory deficient mutants which are no longer able
to complement cbs1 mutants and which exhibit a phenotype identical to that of the original cbs1 mutants (Rödel et al., 1986).

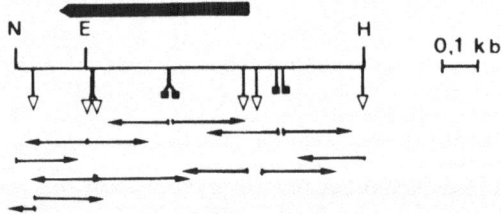

Fig. 1. Strategy for sequencing the CBS1 gene
         The NsiI (N)/HaeIII (H) fragment con-
         taining the CBS1 gene is shown. The
         orf is represented by the black bar
         on the top. TaqI (∇)-, RsaI (■)-
         and EcoRI (E) used for further sub-
         cloning are shown. Replicative forms
         of M13 derivatives mp18 and mp19 were
         isolated and used for cloning (Mes-
         sing et al.,1981). DNA was sequenced
         by the method of Sanger et al., 1977.

```
        Met Asn Leu Asp Met Leu Arg Thr Lys Val Phe Ala Thr Thr Val Ala Arg Ile Ser Gly
   1    ATG AAT CTC GAC ATG TTG AGG ACA AAA GTG TTT GCA ACT ACT GTT GCT CGA ATA TCT GGG    60


        Ile Arg Arg Tyr Ile Pro Ile Arg Thr Ile Asn Thr Val Thr Lys Lys Asn Ile Ser Lys
  61    ATT CGC AGG TAT ATT CCC ATC AGA ACT ATA AAC ACG GTG ACG AAA AAG AAT ATT AGT AAG   120


        Ile Glu Lys Leu Cys Glu Val Leu Glu Val Asn Pro Asp Gly Tyr Lys Gly Lys Glu Arg
 121    ATA GAA AAA CTG TGT GAA GTC CTT GAA GTT AAT CCT GAC GGA TAT AAA GGA AAG GAA CGC   180


        Ile Pro Thr Lys Glu Leu Thr Lys Leu Leu Tyr Thr Thr Ser Arg Asn Met Leu Val Arg
 181    ATA CCG ACT AAA GAA CTA ACT AAA CTG CTA TAT ACC ACA AGC AGG AAT ATG TTG GTA CGA   240


        Val Pro Met Thr Gly Asp Leu Ser Thr Gly Asn Thr Phe Glu Thr Arg Asn Glu Thr Leu
 241    GTA CCA ATG ACT GGA GAC TTG AGC ACA GGA AAT ACA TTT GAA ACA AGA AAC GAA ACT TTA   300


        Gln Lys Leu Gly Glu Gln Leu Ile His Leu Glu Ile Asn Lys Met Leu Thr Ile Thr Phe
 301    CAA AAA TTG GGT GAA CAG CTC ATT CAC TTG GAA ATT AAT AAG ATG CTT ACA ATA ACA TTT   360


        Thr Asn Phe Asn Gln Phe Asn Ile Met Asn Lys Asn Phe Asn Tyr Ile His Asn Leu Asp
 361    ACG AAT TTC AAT CAG TTT AAT ATA ATG AAC AAA AAC TTC AAT TAC ATT CAT AAC TTA GAT   420


        Arg Ala Arg Val Val Asn Met Asp Ser Ile Ser Trp Leu Ile Lys Asn Ser Leu Lys Ile
 421    CGA GCT CGA GTA GTG AAC ATG GAC TCG ATA AGC TGG CTT ATC AAG AAT TCG TTG AAA ATT   480


        Asn Gln Leu Ala His Leu Arg Ile Pro Ala Asn Leu Pro Lys Lys Trp Asp ###
 481    AAC CAA TTA GCT CAT TTG CGA ATA CCT GCC AAT TTG CCG AAG AAA TGG GAT TAA
```

Fig. 2. Sequence of the orf in the pVF1-insert.
Only the sequence of the sense strand is shown.
The derived amino acid sequence is indicated
above the nucleotide sequence.

The orf is not interrupted by an intron, as splicing
signals typical of yeast nuclear genes (Langford et al., 1984)
are absent. In the upstream and downstream sequences, motifs
characteristic for transcription initiation and termination
are found (e.g. the TATAAT – box (Breathnach and Chambon, 1981)
and the sequence TAGT...TTT (Zaret and Sherman, 1982). The sequence context around the presumptive initiation codon shows
several of the features typically found in yeast genes: at
position -3 (with respect to the first nucleotide of the initiation codon) an adenine residue is found. A purine at that position is among the best conserved features of the sequences
upstream from the initiator codon of eukayotic genes (Kozak,
1984). The purine at position +4 (A) and the pyrimidine at position +6 (T) are also frequently found in yeast genes (Dobson
et al., 1982).
    The orf encodes a protein of 177 amino acids, with a
calculated molecular weight of 20.5 kD. The overall nature of
the polypeptide is hydrophilic (polarity: 53 %). No long continuous stretch of hydrophobic residues is found (Fig. 3).
Charged amino acids are spaced through the sequence. Positively
charged amino acids (17.5 %) are in excess over negatively
charged amino acids (8.5 %). The aminoterminal stretch of 40
amino acids exhibits features typically found in mitochondrial
targeting sequences (Hurt and van Loon, 1986; Allison and
Schatz, 1986): it is rich in serine and threonine (20 %), contains 9 positively and only one negatively charged residues.The
codon usage is shown in Table 1. The codon bias index which -
in yeast - is indicative of the level of expression (Bennetzen
and Hall, 1982; Sharp et al., 1986) is extremely low (CBI =

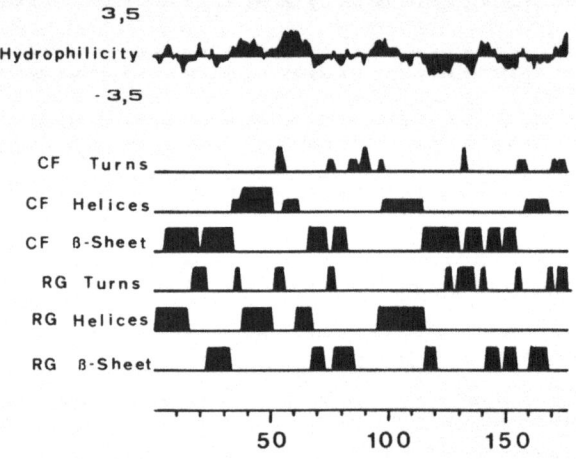

Fig. 3. Structural prediction of the CBS1 protein
From the nucleotide sequence (Fig.2) the
secondary structure of the corresponding
gene product was predicted using a computer program written for VAX750, using the
algorithms of Chou and Fasman (1974) (CF)
and of Garnier et al.(1978) (RG), respectively. Parameters were averaged over 7
amino acid residues.

- 0.03). This is in accordance with the very low concentration
of the CBS1 transcript in wild type yeast cells (V. Forsbach,
unpublished results). Comparison with available sequence data
revealed no extensive homology to any one. Although probably
not statistically significant, it may be worth noting that a
short stretch of 12 amino acids of the CBS1 gene product shows
a high degree of homology to a sequence of the yeast heat shock
protein HSP90 (Farrelly and Finkelstein, 1984) and of the Tn3
transposon encoded transposase (Chou et al., 1979) (Fig. 4).
Interestingly, there is also a low degree of homology to the

TABLE I

Amino acid composition and codon usage of CBS1

UUU	Phe	4	UCU	Ser	1	UAU	Tyr	3	UGU	Cys	1
UUC	Phe	2	UCC	Ser	0	UAC	Tyr	1	UGC	Cys	0
UUA	Leu	3	UCA	Ser	0	UAA	Stp	1	UGA	Stp	0
UUG	Leu	8	UCG	Ser	2	UAG	Stp	0	UGG	Trp	2
CUU	Leu	3	CCU	Pro	2	CAU	His	2	CGU	Arg	0
CUC	Leu	2	CCC	Pro	1	CAC	His	1	CGC	Arg	2
CUA	Leu	2	CCA	Pro	1	CAA	Gln	2	CGA	Arg	5
CUG	Leu	2	CCG	Pro	2	CAG	Gln	2	CGG	Arg	0
AUU	Ile	7	ACU	Thr	7	AAU	Asn	12	AGU	Ser	1
AUC	Ile	2	ACC	Thr	1	AAC	Asn	7	AGC	Ser	3
AUA	Ile	8	ACA	Thr	7	AAA	Lys	10	AGA	Arg	2
AUG	Met	7	ACG	Thr	3	AAG	Lys	6	AGG	Arg	3
GUU	Val	2	GCU	Ala	3	GAU	Asp	2	GGU	Gly	1
GUC	Val	1	GCC	Ala	1	GAC	Asp	4	GGC	Gly	0
GUA	Val	3	GCA	Ala	1	GAA	Glu	9	GGA	Gly	4
GUG	Val	3	GCG	Ala	0	GAG	Glu	0	GGG	Gly	1

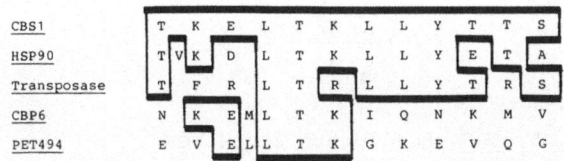

CBS1	T	K	E	L	T	K	L	L	Y	T	T	S
HSP90	T	V	K	D	L	T	K	L	L	Y	E	T	A
Transposase	T	F	R	L	T	R	L	L	Y	T	R	S
CBP6	N	K	E	M	L	T	K	I	Q	N	K	M	V
PET494	E	V	E	L	L	T	K	G	K	E	V	Q	G

Fig. 4. Sequence alignement of amino acid residues 63 to 74 of the CBS1 gene product with the yeast heat shock protein HSP90 (a.a. 638-650), the transposon Tn3 encoded transposase (a.a. 134-145), the yeast CBP6 gene product (a.a. 80-92) and the yeast PET494 gene product (a.a. 226-238). Sequence data are from Farrelly and Finkelstein, 1984 (HSP90), Chou et al., 1979 (Transposase), Dieckmann and Tzagoloff, 1985 (CBP6) and Costanzo et al., 1986 (PET494). The database searched was the protein sequence database (8/86) of the National Biomedical Research Foundation, Washington, D.C.

yeast nuclear genes CBP6 and PET494 which both have been shown to be essential for translation of specific mitochondrial transcripts (Dieckmann and Tzagoloff, 1985; Mueller et al., 1984).

Fusion of the COB structural gene to the OLI1 5' -untranslated leader suppresses a CBS1 disruption

We recently described that a rearrangement in the mitochondrial genome which leads to a fusion of the COB structural gene to the OLI1 5' -untranslated leader is able to restore respiratory competence to mutant strains carrying the original cbs1 mutation (Rödel et al., 1985). This suppressor information is contained in a rho⁻ genome which must be present in addition to a rho⁺ genome. By transfer of this rho⁻ genome into a cbs2/rho⁺ mutant strain it was possible to demonstrate that the original cbs2 mutation can also be suppressed by this chimeric OLI1/COB gene (Rödel, 1986). Using the same technique of cytoduction, we introduced this rho⁻ genome into the nuclear background of strain GDV0 in which the chromosomal CBS1 wild type gene is replaced by the disrupted form of CBS1 (CBS1::URA3) (Rödel et al., 1986). Again we obtained heteroplasmic respiratory competent cytoductants, which rapidly segregated homoplasmic respiratory deficient cells when grown under non selective conditions (i.e. YPD medium). This result strongly argues in favor of the idea that the only function of the CBS1 gene product is to stimulate translation of COB transcripts. In case of a dual function of the gene product one had to assume that the gene disruption (as well as the original mutation) has no consequence for the second function.

CBS1 homologous genes in other yeasts

The COB gene is among the set of genes invariably found in all mitochondrial genomes. While the structural gene from

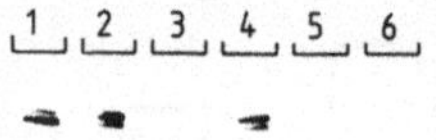

Fig. 5. CBS1-homologous sequences in various
yeast strains
Nuclear DNA of S. cerevisiae strains
D273-10B (1) and DBY747 (2), S.dairen-
sis (3), S. unisporus (4), K. lactis
(5) and S.pombe (6) was cut with EcoRI
and separated on a 0.9 % agarose gel.
After transfer onto nitrocellulose membrane the DNA was hybridized at 62° C
against the nick-translated BglII/ClaI
fragment (the insert of pVF1) which
covers the CBS1 gene.

various organisms shows a high degree of homology (e.g. Widger
et al., 1984), there is little or no homology in the 5' - untranslated part of the COB genes. As this region has been identified as the target region of the CBS1 gene product, we looked
for the presence of CBS1 homologous DNA sequences in various
yeast species. As shown in Fig. 5, hybridization of labelled
DNA fragments from the S. cerevisiae CBS1 gene is observed
with nuclear DNA from different S. cerevisiae strains and from
S. unisporus. No signal was observed with DNA from S. pombe
which according to several criteria is thought to be evolutionary very distant of S. cerevisiae (Huysmans et al., 1983).
Surprisingly, however, K. lactis and one Saccharomyces strain,
S. dairensis, also gave no hybridization signal. CBS1 therefore may represent a class of genes which allow several yeast
species to optimize regulation of mitochondrial gene expression.

Acknowledgements

We thank Prof. H. Wolf and Dr. S. Modrow, Max-von-Pettenkofer
Institut München for performing the secondary structure analysis, and Dr. D. Kamp, Max-Planck-Institut für Biochemie,
Martinsried for the protein sequence database search. This work
was supported by the Deutsche Forschungsgemeinschaft.

References

Allison, D.S. and Schatz, G., 1986, Artificial mitochondrial
        presequences, Proc. Natl. Acad. Sci. USA, 83: 9011-9015
Bennetzen, J.L. and Hall, B.D., 1982, Codon selection in yeast,
        J. Biol. Chem., 257: 3026-3031
Breathnach, R. and Chambon, P., 1981, Organization and expres-
        sion of eucaryotic split genes coding for proteins, Ann.
        Rev. Biochem., 50: 349-383
Chou, P.Y. and Fasman, G.D., 1974, Prediction of protein con-
        formation, Biochemistry, 13: 3026-3031
Chou, J., Lemaux, P.G., Casadaban, M.J., and Cohen, S.N., 1979,
        Transposition protein of Tn3: identification and charac-
        terization of an essential repressor-controlled gene

product, Nature, 282: 801-806

Costanzo, M.M., Mueller, P.P., Strick, C.A., and Fox, T.D., 1986, Primary structure of wild-type and mutant alleles of the PET494 gene of Saccharomyces cerevisiae, Mol. Gen. Genet., 202: 294-301

Dieckmann, C.L., Pape, L.K. and Tzagoloff, A., 1982, Identification and cloning of a yeast nuclear gene (CBP1) involved in expression of mitochondrial cytochrome b, Proc. Natl. Acad. Sci. USA, 79: 1805-1809

Dieckmann, C.L. and Tzagoloff, A., 1985, Assembly of the mitochondrial membrane system: CBP6, a yeast nuclear gene necessary for synthesis of cytochrome b, J. Biol. Chem., 260: 1513-1520

Dobson, M.J., Tuite, M.F., Roberts, N.A., Kingsman, A.J., and Kingsman, S.M., 1982, Conservation of high efficiency promoter sequences in Saccharomyces cerevisiae, Nucl. Acids Res., 10: 2625-2637

Farrelly, F.W. and Finkelstein, D.B., 1984, Complete sequence of the heat shock-inducible HSP90 gene of Saccharomyces cerevisiae, J. Biol. Chem., 259: 5745-5751

Fox, T.D., 1986, Nuclear gene products required for translation of specific mitochondrially coded mRNAs in yeast, Trends Genet., 2: 97-100

Garnier, J., Osguthorpe, D.J., and Robson, B., 1978, Analysis of the accuracy and implications of simple methods for predicting the secondary structure of globular proteins, J. Mol. Biol., 120: 97-120

Hill, J., McGraw, P., and Tzagoloff, A., 1985, A mutation in yeast mitochondrial DNA results in a precise excision of the terminal intron of the cytochrome b gene, J. Biol. Chem., 260: 3235-3238

Hurt, E.C. and van Loon, A.P.G.M., 1986, How proteins find mitochondria and intramitochondrial compartments, Trends Biochem. Sci., 11: 204-207

Huysmans, E., Dams, E., Vandenberghe, A., and DeWachter, R., 1983, The nucleotide sequences of the 5S rRNAs of four mushrooms and their use in studying the phylogenetic position of basidiomycetes among the eukaryotes, Nucl. Acids Res., 11: 2871-2879

Kozak, M., 1984, Compilation and analysis of sequences upstream from the translational start site in eukaryotic mRNAs, Nucl. Acids Res., 12: 857-872

Kreike, J., Schulze, M., Pillar, T., Körte, A., and Rödel, G., 1986, Cloning of a nuclear gene MRS1 involved in the excision of a single group I intron (bI3) from the mitochondrial COB transcript in S. cerevisiae, Curr. Genet., 11: 185-191

Langford, C.J., Klinz, F.-J., Donath, C., and Gallwitz, D., 1984, Point mutations identify the conserved, intron-contained TACTAAC box as an essentiell splicing sequence in yeast, Cell, 36: 645-653

McGraw, P. and Tzagoloff, A., 1983, Assembly of the mitochondrial membrane system: characterization of a yeast nuclear gene involved in the processing of the cytochrome b pre-mRNA, J. Biol. Chem., 258: 9459-9468

Messing, J., Crea, R., and Seeburg, P.H., 1981, A system for shotgun DNA sequencing, Nucl. Acids Res., 9: 309-321

Mueller, P.P., Reif, M.K., Zonghou, S., Mason, T.L. and Fox, T.D., 1984, A nuclear mutation that post-transcriptionally blocks accumulation of a yeast mitochondrial gene product can be suppressed by a mitochondrial gene rearrangement, J. Mol. Biol., 175: 431-452

Rödel, G., 1986, Two yeast nuclear genes, CBS1 and CBS2, are
required for translation of mitochondrial transcripts
bearing the 5' -untranslated COB leader, Curr. Genet.,
11: 41-45

Rödel, G. and Fox, T.D., 1987, The yeast nuclear gene CBS1 is
required for translation of mitochondrial mRNAs bearing
the cob 5' untranslated leader, Mol. Gen. Genet., 206:
45-50

Rödel, G. Körte, A., and Kaudewitz, F., 1985, Mitochondrial
suppression of a yeast nuclear mutation which affects
the translation of the mitochondrial apocytochrome b
transcript, Curr. Genet., 9: 641-648

Rödel, G., Michaelis, U., Forsbach, V., Kreike, J., and Kaudewitz, F., 1986, Molecular cloning of the yeast nuclear
genes CBS1 and CBS2, Curr. Genet., 11: 47-53

Sanger, F., Nicklen, S., and Coulson, A.R., 1977, DNA sequencing with chain-terminating inhibitors, Proc. Natl. Acad.
Sci. USA, 74: 5463-5467

Schoppink, P.J., Berden, J.A., and Grivell, L.A., 1986, Construction and characterization of yeast mutants deficient
in one of the genes coding for subunits of QH_2:Cyt c
oxidoreductase, Abstract of the Fourth European Bioenergetics Conference, p. 106

Sharp, M.P., Tuohy, T.M.F., and Mosurski, K.R., 1986, Codon
usage in yeast: cluster analysis clearly differentiates
highly and lowly expressed genes, Nucl. Acids Res., 14:
5125-5143

Tzagoloff, A. and Myers, A.M., 1986, Genetics of mitochondrial
biogenesis, Ann. Rev. Biochem., 55: 249-285

Tzagoloff, A., Wu, M., and Crivellone, M., 1986, Assembly of the
mitochondrial membrane system: characterization of COR1,
the structural gene for the 44 kD core protein of yeast
coenzyme QH_2-cytochrome c reductase, J. Biol. Chem., 261:
17163-17169

Widger, W.R., Cramer, W.A., Herrmann, R.G., and Trebst, A.,
1984, Sequence homology and structural similarity between
cytochrome b of mitochondrial complex III and the chloroplast b_6-f complex: position of the cytochrome b hemes in
the membrane, Proc. Natl. Acad. Sci. USA, 81: 674-678

Zaret, K.S. and Sherman, F., 1982, DNA sequence required for
efficient transcription termination in yeast, Cell, 28:
563-573

A CALMODULIN-LIKE PROTEIN IN THE CYTOCHROME bc_1 COMPLEX REQUIRED FOR SYNTHESIS OF BOTH CYTOCHROME bc_1 AND CYTOCHROME c OXIDASE COMPLEXES IN YEAST MITOCHONDRIA

Mark E. Schmitt and Bernard L. Trumpower

Department of Biochemistry
Dartmouth Medical School
Hanover, NH   03756

Introduction

The cytochrome bc_1 complexes of eukaryotic mitochondria contain nine to eleven polypeptides (1-3). The cytochrome bc_1 complex of *Paracoccus denitrificans*, a gram negative bacterium which elaborates a respiratory chain which appears to be functionally equivalent to its mitochondrial counterpart, consists of only three polypeptides (4). Photosynthetic bacteria, as exemplified by *Rhodobacter sphaeroides* and *Rhodobacter capsulata*, contain bc_1 complexes which consist of only four polypeptides (5). The cytochrome bf complex of chloroplasts, which resembles the bc_1 complex in most respects, consists of only five polypeptides (6). The subunit compositions of the bc_1 complexes of mitochondria from beef heart and yeast and those of *Paracoccus* and a photosynthetic bacterium are shown in Figure 1.

From these examples we conclude that electron transfer and energy transduction in the bc_1 complex requires only four polypeptides. The required polypeptides are cytochrome b, which carries two heme groups, cytochrome c_1, the Rieske iron-sulfur protein, and a fourth polypeptide, typically of low molecular weight (5), of unknown function, which may be a ubiquinone binding protein (8). The three subunit composition of the *Paracoccus* complex probably results from a gene fusion between the genes for cytochrome c_1 and the gene for the putative Q binding protein (4), resulting in a cytochrome c_1 protein of approximately 62 kDa in this bacterium. In all other species examined to date, cytochrome c_1 and the analogous cytochrome f of chloroplasts have molecular weights of 30-35 kDa (6). The five subunit compositon of the chloroplast bf complex is attributable to the fact that cytochrome b is split into two gene products in this case (9).

We have thus begun to investigate what function may be served by those polypeptides of the mitochondrial bc_1 complex which have no obvious role in electron transfer or energy transduction. One obvious possibility is that these proteins have some role in controlling the rate of respiration in this region of the respiratory chain(10-13). However, the only convincingly documented control on respiration is "respiratory control," which is mediated by the protonmotive force and imposed as a rate constraint on electron transfer through the pH dependence of the iron-sulfur protein catalyzed oxidation of ubiquinol to ubisemiquinone (14), and through the electrogenic transfer of electrons through the b cytochromes, which is subject to opposition by the membrane potential (15). On a purely theoretical basis, there is no need to invoke the participation of any proteins other than the three redox components, and possibly the Q binding protein, to account for respiratory control. Furthermore, the three subunit bc_1 complex of *Paracoccus denitrificans* exhibits respiratory control ratios of approximately eight when reconstituted into liposomes (X. Yang and B. Trumpower, unpublished results).

A second possible role for these "extra" polypeptides is that they are required for assembly of the bc_1 complex. However, assembly of the bc_1 complexes in the cytoplasmic membrane of the bacteria appears to proceed without the participation of any such proteins, although the possibility can not be excluded that such proteins may exist in bacteria but not copurify with the redox components of the complex.

It is also conceivable that the "extra" polypeptides are uniquely required for assembly of the bc_1 complex in eukaryotes because the redox proteins originate from different sides of the energy transducing membrane in these organisms. In mitochondria cytochrome b is encoded by the organelle genome (16), while cytochrome c_1 (17), iron-sulfur protein (18), and the presumed Q binding protein (19) are encoded in the nucleus. One can envision that the bipolar nature of the assembly process in mitochondria is more complicated than that which occurs in the cytoplasmic membrane of a bacterium, and thus the "extra" polypeptides may provide a scaffold for coordinating this assembly. However, it seems inefficent to have five to seven extra proteins required for the oligomeric assembly of four. Furthermore, assembly of the cytochrome bf complex in chloroplasts is also a bipolar process, since cytochrome b is encoded on the chloroplast genome (20), and this complex is apparently assembled without the need for extra "scaffolding" proteins.

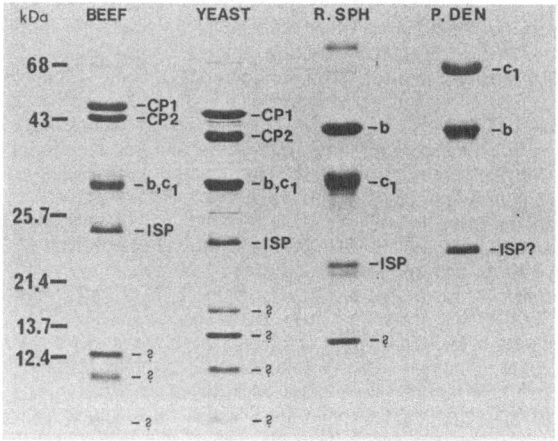

Figure 1   Comparison of the subunit compositions of the cytochrome bc_1 complexes of beef heart and yeast mitochondria with those of Rhodobacter sphaeroides and Paracoccus denitrificans. The purified complexes from beef heart and yeast mitochondria contain 11 and 9 polypeptides, respectively. Cytochromes b and c_1 of the mitochondrial complexes migrate together under the conditions of this electrophoresis. On a different electrophoresis gel system, designed to optimize resolution of low molecular weight peptides, 11 polypeptides are observed in the beef heart complex, as first reported by Von Jagow and coworkers (7). The bc_1 complexes of R. sphaeroides and P. denitrificans consists of 4 and 3 subunits, respectively. The high molecular weight band in the R. sphaeroides sample is incompletely denatured cytochrome b, which was revealed by staining for heme, and by cross-reactivity to P. denitrificans cytochrome b antibodies (results not shown).

178

Properties of a 17 kDa protein of the cytochrome bc₁ complex

In this paper we describe experiments in which we have started to examine the possible function of a protein of the bc_1 complex of yeast mitochondria which has no obvious counterpart in the bc_1 complexes of bacteria, and thus may have a uniquely "eukaryotic" function. This protein migrates on SDS gel electrophoresis with an apparent molecular weight of 17 kDa. The gene for the 17 kDa protein was cloned and sequenced by Van Loon and coworkers (21), and provided to us by Dr. Grivell. We purified the mature protein from the yeast bc_1 complex, thus allowing the identification of a "presequence," which is apparently removed post-translationally as discussed below.

The amino acid sequence, deduced from the sequence of the cloned gene, is shown in Figure 2. The 17 kDa protein is translated as a protein of 147 amino acids. The sequence of the N-terminal portion of the mature protein (Figure 2) matches a sequence of ten residues starting at glutamate-26. The inferred sequence of the mature protein thus consists of 121 residues, and has a molecular mass of 14.5 kDa.

The "17 kDa protein" has several unusual properties, the first of which is that this protein contains a presequence which does not conform to the properties expected of a presequence for targeting a cytoplasmically encoded protein to the inner mitochondrial membrane. In Figure 3 are shown the presequences for five cytoplasmically encoded proteins, including two of the subunits of cytochrome c oxidase ("oxi 5" and "oxi 4"), the beta subunit of the proton translocating ATP synthase, cytochrome c_1, and the Rieske iron-sulfur protein ("ISP"). These five proteins are all constituents of oligomeric protein complexes of the inner mitochondrial membrane. The presequences of all of these proteins are positively charged, devoid of acidic amino acids, enriched in hydroxy-amino acids, and exhibit an amphipathic character when projected in an alpha helical configuration. These common properties have been proposed as essential for targeting proteins to the inner mitochondrial membrane (for references, see 22,23).

In contrast, the presequence of the 17 kDa protein is enriched in acidic residues, contains only one positively charged residue and only one threonine. The presequence is amphipathic when cast as an alpha helical wheel. It thus seems likely that this protein is "targeted" to the inner mitochondrial membrane by a different mechanism than that which operates with the other inner membrane proteins thus far characterized.

One possible explanation for how the 17 kDa is targeted is that "presequence" and "targeting sequence" are not synonomous in the instance of this protein. Rather, the targeting sequence may be internal to the sequence of the mature protein, and the presequence may be a structural determinant which is post-translationally removed in order to lock the protein into its native conformation. However, examination of the sequence of the protein fails to reveal any region which is enriched in positively charged residues, serines or threonines, or which is amphipathic when cast on an alpha helical wheel.

A second possibility is that the 17 kDa protein may be co-imported as a hetero-dimer with some other protein which is enriched in positive charges. In similar fashion, divalent cations such as calcium may bind and promote import by conferring a net positive charge on some region(s) of the 17 kDa protein. At present we can not exclude either of these possibilities.

A third possibility is that the 17 kDa protein is targeted to the mitochondria in the absence of a mitochondrial membrane potential, and that the specificity of targeting of this protein is controlled by properties other than its net charge. This possibility would allow the 17 kDa protein to be localized in situ under conditions where the membrane is not competent for energy transduction.

The 17 kDa protein is also unusual in that it is highly acidic. Approximately 50 percent of the amino acids are glutamates or aspartates (Figure 2), and there is one sequence of 24 uninterrupted acidic residues, beginning with aspartate-49 and extending through glutamate-73. Van Loon and coworkers (21) pointed out that this is the longest uninterrupted stretch of acidic residues in any naturally occurring protein sequenced to date. In addition, and partly because of the high content of acidic residues, the protein has a high content of alpha helix structure. According to the secondary structure prediction algorithm used here, approximately 85 percent of the sequence of the mature protein is alpha helical. Although there is a generally recognized element of uncertainty in such structural predictions, it seems likely that this protein is highly helical, since predictions

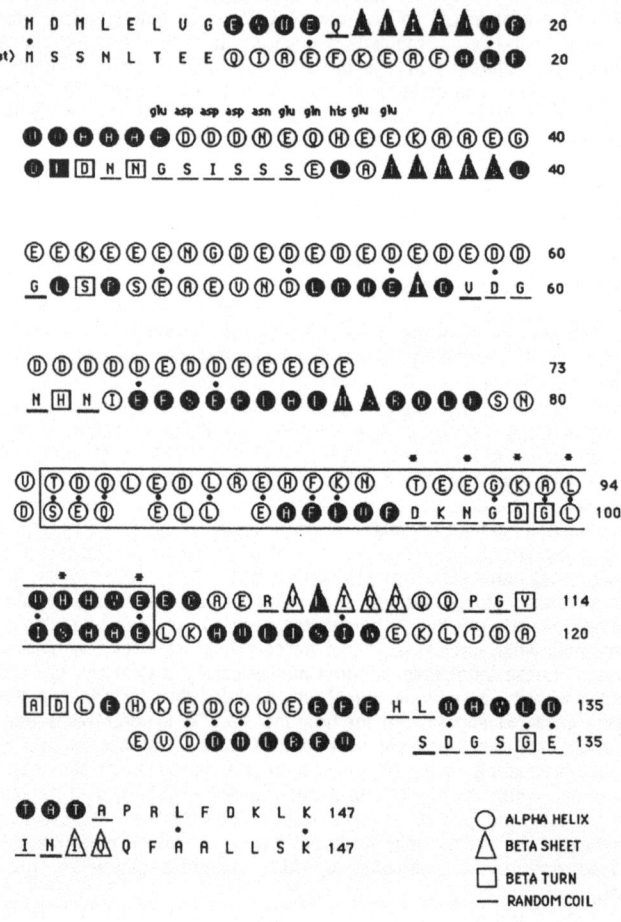

Figure 2 *Comparison of amino acid sequences and secondary structures of the 17 kDa protein and yeast calmodulin.* Amino acid sequences of the 17 kDa protein (21) and calmodulin (24) were inferred from the sequences of the cloned genes. Secondary structures were predicted by the method of Garnier et al (25), using a commerically available program and a MacIntosh computer. The prediction method calculates "information functions" for alpha helix (circles), beta strands (triangles), beta turns (squares), and random coils (underline). The values of these information functions are then compared, and the structure having the highest value is assigned. Hydropathy was calculated according to Kyte and Doolittle (26), using a "window" setting of 11 residues. Hydrophilic residues, predicted to be externally disposed to solvent, are indicated by open symbols, while hydrophobic or internal residues are indicated by solid symbols. The program does not predict structure for approximately 8 residues at the N- and C-termini. The region of sequence homology between the two proteins is boxed; conserved residues are identified by a black dot between the two sequences. Calcium binding coordinates of calmodulin (24) are marked by asteriks (*). The amino acid sequence of the ten N-terminal residues of the mature 17 kDa protein, which begins at residue 26 in the 17 kDa protein sequence, is indicated above the sequence with three letter abbreviations.

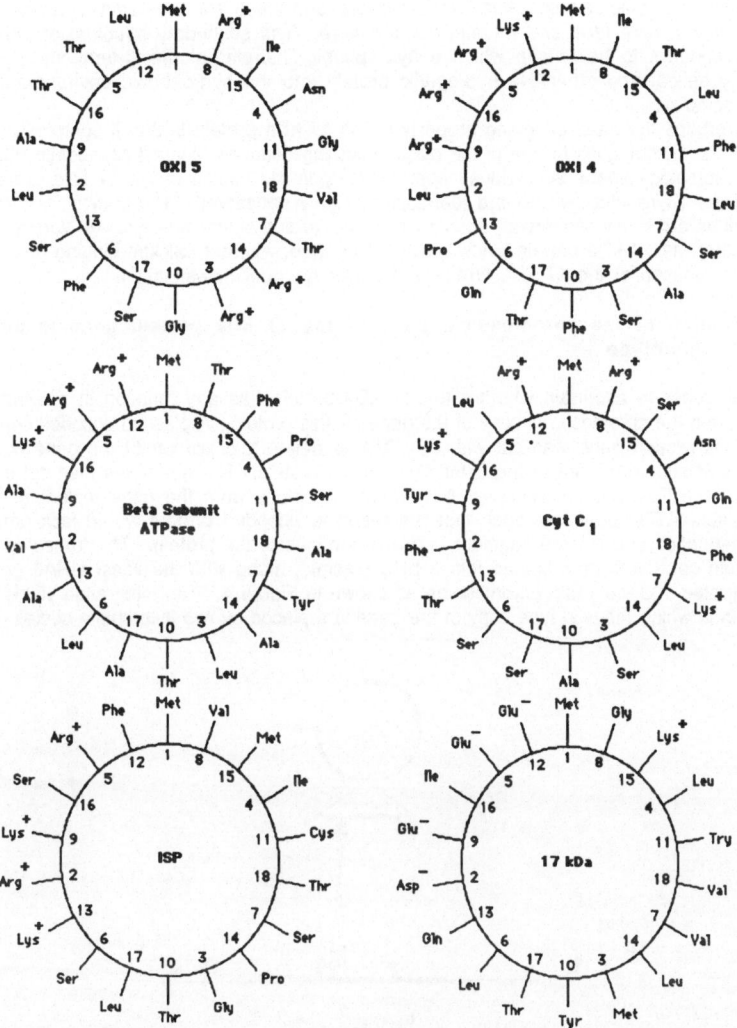

Figure 3 *Comparison of the presequence of the 17 kDa protein with presequences of other mitochondrial proteins encoded in the nucleus and imported from the cytoplasm.* The presequence of the 17 kDa protein was determined by sequencing the N-terminus of the mature 17 kDa protein (see Figure 2). Other presequences are from the literature (17,18,27-29). The sequences are plotted on a helical wheel , which approximates the two dimensional juxtaposition of amino acid residues in an alpha helix (30,31). Charged residues are indicated by a + or - sign.

of alpha helix are more reliable than other secondary features, especially when applied to hydrophilic proteins.

There are only three short hydrophobic regions in the sequence of the 17 kDa protein. One of these is in the N-terminal presequence, and is removed post-translationally (Figure.2). It is conceivable that this property of the presequence may operate in initially adhering the premature protein to the membrane. The remaining mature protein has two short hydrophobic sequences in the C-terminus, and these are separated by a sequence of beta sheet, beta turn, and random coil structure. The secondary structure of the protein thus appears to be one in which a hydrophobic "hairpin" at the C-terminus anchors a highly helical and otherwise hydrophilic protein into the hydrophobic environment of the bc_1 complex.

Perhaps the most intriguing property of the 17 kDa protein is that it contains a domain which is homologous to one of the calcium binding domains of yeast calmodulin (Figure 2). This homology spans 24 residues approximately in the middle of the 17 kDa protein, and includes 13 residues which are identical or highly conserved. In addition, several other residues are quasi-conserved, such as histidine versus serine and tyrosine versus alanine. Whether the 17 kDa protein binds calcium and, if so, whether calcium binding has any role in the function of the 17 kDa protein are currently under investigation.

Disruption of the chromosomal copy of the 17 kDa protein gene results in a *pet⁻* phenotype

In order to ascertain whether the 17 kDa protein has any function in respiration, we disrupted the chromosomal copy of the gene for this protein. A plasmid encoded copy of the 17 kDa protein gene was cut with Sau 3A1 to delete that portion of the gene coding for approximately one third of the C-terminus of the protein. The gene was then cut a second time, with Spe 1 which removes 6 N-terminal residues from the gene including the only available ATG sequence, such that the resulting encoded protein would lack part of the presequence and a large segment of the C-terminus of the protein. The truncated 17 kDa protein gene was then ligated into a pUC plasmid, along with the yeast URA3 gene, and integrated into the yeast chromosome as shown in Figure 4. The integration yields a yeast strain in which the wild type copy of the gene is replaced by two incomplete copies.

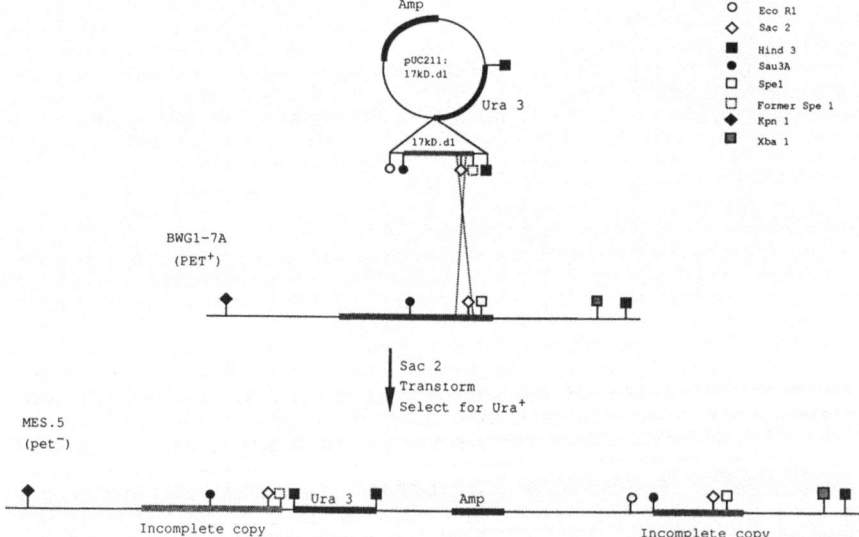

Figure 4 Disruption of the chromosomal copy of the gene encoding the 17kDa protein. *The plasmid pUC211:17kD.d1 was constructed from pUC18 and contains a 1.1 kb URA3 gene, allowing selection in yeast, and an internal portion of the gene encoding protein gene and used to transform, BWG1-7A, a ura3⁻ yeast strain. Since the plasmid does not contain sequences permitting autonomous replication in yeast, it can only be retained and complement the ura3⁻ auxotroph by integration into the yeast chromosome. Integration occurs by crossover and recombination at homolgous regions of the plasmid and chromosomal copies of the17 kDa protein gene. The resulting integrant includes the URA3 gene along with the vector, and results in disruption of the chromosomal gene and formation of two incomplete copies.*

182

In order to confirm that the truncated 17 kDa protein gene was integrated at the expected locus, chromosomal DNA from the disrupted strain was analyzed by Southern hybridization (32). Genomic DNA was purified from the wildtype, BWG1-7A, and the disrupted strain, MESΔ5, and digested as in Figure 5. Fragments carrying portions of the gene for the 17 kDa protein were then detected by hybridization with a P32 labeled probe corresponding to that part of the gene in the plasmid pUC211:17kD.d1. Chromosomal DNA from the wildtype strain gives a single band of approximately 4200 bp when digested with Xba1 and Kpn1 and a single band of 4800 bp when digested with Hind 3 and Kpn1. Chromosomal DNA from the disrupted strain, MESΔ5, gives one enlarged band of approximately 8000 bp when digested with Xba1 and Kpn1, and two bands of approximately 4400 and 2800 when digested with Hind 3 and Kpn1. The sizes of these fragments are consistent with an integration event occurring as in Figure 4.

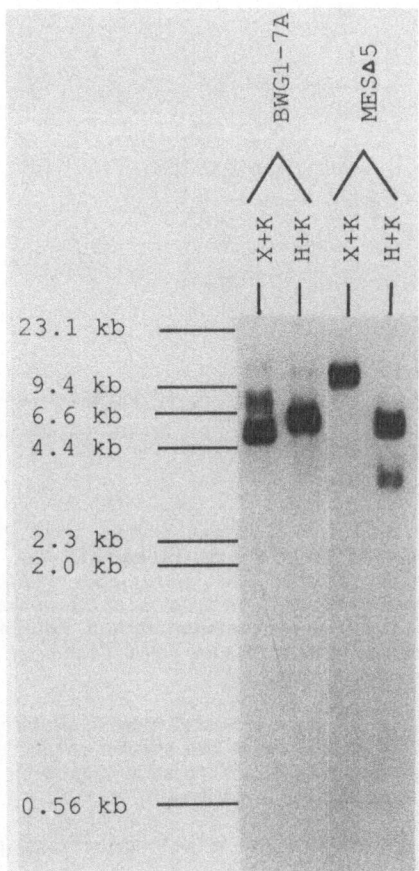

Figure 5 *Southern hybridization analysis demonstrating disruption of the chromosomal copy of the 17 kDa protein gene. Genomic DNA's from the wild type strain, BWG1-7A, and the disrupted strain, MESΔ5, were purified, digested with either Xba1 and Kpn1(X+K), or Hind 3 and Kpn 1(H+P) and the digests fractionated by agarose gel electrophoresis. Fragments of the genomic DNA carrying portions of the gene for the 17kDa protein were then detected by Southern hybridization (32) with a labeled probe corresponding to the internal fragment of the 17 kDa gene in the plasmid pUC211::17kD.d1 (see Figure 4).*

183

After disrupting the chromosomal copy of the gene for the 17 kDa protein, the resulting haploid yeast is unable to grow on non-fermentable carbons sources, including glycerol, ethanol, or lactate. The results of such an experiment, testing for growth on glycerol, are shown in Figure 6. The curves in Figure 6a are controls, showing growth on dextrose. The wild type parent, BWG1-7a, the strain in which the 17 kDa protein gene was disrupted, MESΔ5, and a rho^0 strain, DV147, grow on dextrose with essentially identical doubling times. A diploid strain, formed by crossing MESΔ5 with the rho^0 strain grows slightly faster than the haploids, as expected.

As shown in Figure 6b, MESΔ5 is unable to grow on glycerol. As a control, to exclude the possibility that the pet^- phenotype of MESΔ5 is not due to spontaneous formation of a rho^- mutant due to loss or rearrangement of mitochondrial DNA, we crossed MESΔ5 with the rho^0 strain. The latter haploid is also unable to grow on glycerol (Figure 6b). When MESΔ5 is crossed with the rho^0 strain, the resulting diploid is respiratory competent, and grows slightly faster than the wild-type haploid (Figure 6b). This experiment establishes that MESΔ5 contains a normal mitochondrial genome.

(a)   (b)

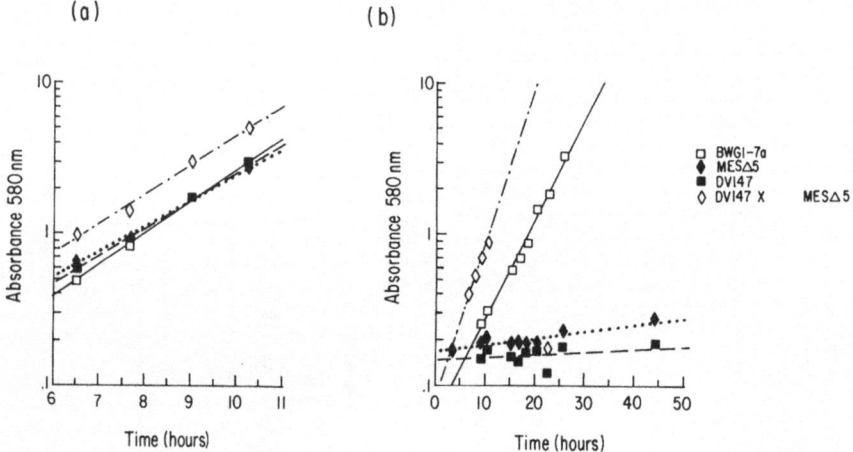

Figure 6 *Growth curves of wild type yeast(BWG1-7a), yeast in which the gene for the 17 kDa protein was disrupted (MESΔ5), a rho° strain (DV147), and a diploid strain derived from a cross between DV147 and MES Δ5 on fermentable and non-fermentable carbon sources. The curves in (a) show growth on dextrose and those in (b) show growth on glycerol. Growth was monitored by light scattering (absorbance) at 580 nm.*

To confirm that the pet^- phenotype of MESΔ5 is due to disruption of the gene for the 17 kDa protein, we transformed this mutant with plasmid carrying a wild-type copy of the gene. The resulting transformant regained the ability to grow on glycerol, and recovered the optical spectra of the parent, wild-type strain.

The mutant, MESΔ5, is deficient in both cytochrome bc$_1$ and cytochrome c oxidase complexes

An optical spectrum of the wild-type strain, BWG1-7A, is shown in the upper trace of Figure 7. The spectrum shows the typical absorption at 600-605 nm due to cytochromes a and a$_3$, a peak at approximately 562 nm due to the b cytochromes, and a pronounced shoulder at 553 nm due to cytochrome c$_1$. A spectrum of the mutant, MESΔ5, is shown in the bottom trace of Figure 7. The spectrum consists of a single absorption band at approximately 553 nm attributable to cytochrome c$_1$. The spectrum of the mutant lacks the absorption bands of cytochromes a and a$_3$ in the 600-605 nm region, and also lacks the 562 nm absorption band due to the b cytochromes.

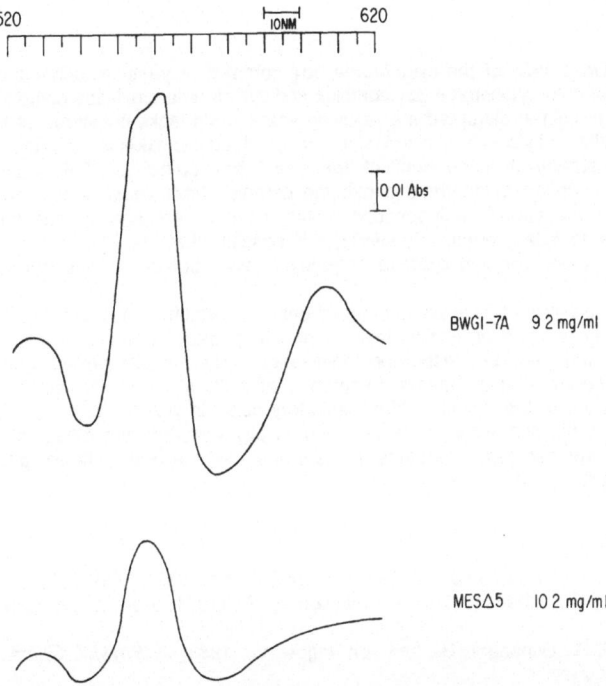

520   10NM   620

0 0I Abs

BWGI-7A   9 2 mg/ml

MES∆5   I0 2 mg/ml

Figure 7   *Optical spectra of submitochondrial particles from the wild type yeast(BWG1-7a) and the strain (MES∆5) in which the gene for the 17 kDa protein was disrupted.*   Submitochondrial particles were solubilized in dodecyl maltoside and suspended at the indicated protein concentrations. Spectra of samples oxidized with potassium ferricyanide and then reduced with dithionite were recorded on an Aminco DW-2A spectrophometer in the dual wavelength mode. Spectra were stored and dithionite reduced minus ferricyanide oxidized difference spectra were calculated with a digital storage oscilloscope (33).

Electron transfer activities associated with the cytochrome bc_1 and cytochrome c oxidase complexes are also absent in mitochondria from the strain in which the gene for the 17 kDa protein was disrupted. Ubiquinol-cytochrome c reductase and cytochrome c oxidase activities of the wild type strain, BWG1-7A, and the disrupted strain, MES∆5, are shown in Table 1.

Table 1

Ubiquinol-cytochrome c reductase and cytochrome c oxidase activities
of mitochondria from wild type yeast and from the disrupted strain

Strain	Cytochrome c Reductase	Cytochrome c Oxidase
BWG1-7A	1.22	1.25
MES∆5	<0.01	0.02

Activities were measured at 30 °C and are in μmoles of cytochrome c reduced or oxidized per minute per milligram of mitochondria extract.

Summary

The 17 kDa protein of the cytochrome bc_1 complex of yeast mitochondria is required for synthesis of both cytochrome bc_1 complex and cytochrome c oxidase complex. When the gene for this protein is disrupted the resulting yeast strain lacks cytochromes b, a, and a_3, and has virtually no cytochrome c reductase or cytochrome c oxidase activities. The 17 kDa protein is a structural component of the yeast bc_1 complex. This protein is not a constituent of purified cytochrome c oxidase complex from yeast, since the amino acid sequences for the subunit polypeptides of this complex are known, and none of these resembles the 17 kDa protein. However, it is possible that the 17 kDa protein may be a constituent of cytochrome c oxidase complex *in vivo*, but lost during purification of the complex.

If the 17 kDa protein is a constituent of only the cytochrome bc_1 complex, this is the first example in which a protein intrinsic to one respiratory complex affects the synthesis of two structurally separate respiratory complexes. The 17 kDa protein thus appears to coordinately control the synthesis, assembly, or maturation of the entire cytochrome-containing portion of the mitochondrial respiratory chain in yeast. How the 17 kDa protein is implicated in the synthesis of the cytochrome bc_1 complex and cytochrome c oxidase complex, and whether it has the same function in the synthesis of both complexes, remains to be elucidated.

References

1. Sidhu, A., and Beattie, D. S. (1982) *J. Biol. Chem.* **257**, 7879-7886
2. Gellerfors, P., Johansson, T., and Nelson, B. D. (1981) *Eur. J. Biochem.* **115**, 275-278
3. Engel, W. D., Schagger, H., and von Jagow, G. (1983) *Z. Physiol. Chem.* **364**, 1753-1763
4. Yang, X., and Trumpower, B. L. (1986) *J. Biol. Chem.* **226**, 12282-12289
5. Ljungdahl, P. O., Pennoyer, J. D., Robertson, D. E., and Trumpower, B. L. (1987) *Biochim. Biophys. Acta* **891**, 227-242
6. Hurt, E., and Hauska, G. (1981) *Eur. J. Biochem.* **117**, 591-599
7. Shaggler, H., Link, T. A., Engel, W. D., and Von Jagow, G. (1986) *Methods in Enzymol.* **126**, 224-237
8. Yu, L., Mei, Q., and Yu, C. (1984) *J. Biol. Chem.* **259**, 5753-5760
9. Hauska, G., Hurt, E., Gabellini, N. and Lockau, W. (1983) *Biochim. Biophys. Acta* **726**, 97-133
10. Jenson, C., Sistare, F., Hamman, H. and Haynes, R. (1983) *Biochem. J.* **210**, 819-827
11. Hamman, H. and Haynes, R. (1983) *Biochim. Biophys. Acta* **724**, 241-250
12. Halestrap, A., Quinlan, P., Armston, A. and Whipps, D. (1985) *Biochem. Soc. Trans.* **13**, 659-663
13. Haynes, R. (1985) *Biochem. Soc. Trans.* **13**, 655-656
14. Trumpower, B. L. (1981) *Biochim. Biophys. Acta.* **639**, 129-155
15. Wikstrom, M. K. F. (1973) *Biochim. Biophys. Acta.* **301**, 155-193
16. Nobrega, F. G., and Tzagoloff, A. (1980) *J. Biol. Chem.* **255**, 9828-9837
17. Sadler, O., Suda, K., Shatz, G., Kaudewitz, K. and Haid, A. (1984) *EMBO J.* **3**, 2137-2143.
18. Beckmann, J. D., Ljungdahl, P. O., Lopez, J. L., and Trumpower, B. L. (1987) *J. Biol. Chem.* **262**, in press
19. De Haan, M., Van Loon, A., Kreike, J., Vaessen, R., and Grivell, L.A. (1984) *Eur. J. Biochem.* **138**, 169-177
20. Bendall, D. S. (1982) Biochim. Biophys. Acta **683**, 119-151
21. Van Loon, A., DeGroot, R., Haan, M., Dekker, A., and Grivell, L. (1984) *EMBO J.* **3**, 1039-1043
22. Von Heijne, G. (1986) *EMBO J.* **5**, 1335-1342
23. Smeekens, S., de Groot, M., van Binsbergen, J., and Weisbeek, P. (1985) *Nature* **317**, 456-458
24. Davis, T., Urdea, M., Masiarz, F., and Thorner, J. (1986) *Cell* **47**, 423-431
25. Garnier, J. Ogsthorpe, D. J. and Robson, B.(1978) *J. Mol. Biol.* **120**, 97-120
26. Kyte, J. and Doolittle, R. (1982) *J. Mol. Biol.* **157**, 105-132

27. Koerner, T.J., Hill, J., and Tzagoloff, A. (1985) *J. Biol. Chem.*, **260**, 9513-9515
28. Maarse, A.C., van Loon, A., Riezman, H., Gregor, I., Schatz, G., and Grivell, L. A. (1984) *EMBO J.* **3**, 2831-2837
29. Vassarotti, A., Chen, W., Smagula, C., and Douglas, M. G. (1987) *J. Biol. Chem.* **262**, 411-418
30. Schiffe, M., and Edmundson, A. B. (1967) *Biophys. J.* **7**, 121-135
31. Argos, P., Rao, J.K., and Hargrave, P. A. (1982) *Eur. J. Biochem.* **128**, 565-575
32. Southern, E. M. (1975) *J. Mol. Biol.* **98**, 503-517
33. Tang, H. and Trumpower, B. L. (1986) *J. Biol. Chem.* **261**, 6209-6215

IMPORT OF CYTOCHROMES b_2 AND c_1 INTO MITOCHONDRIA IS DEPENDENT

ON BOTH MEMBRANE POTENTIAL AND NUCLEOSIDE TRIPHOSPHATES

Franz-Ulrich Hartl, Joachim Ostermann, Nikolaus Pfanner,
Maximilian Tropschug, Bernard Guiard* and Walter Neupert

Institut für Physiologische Chemie, Goethestr. 33
8000 München 2, FRG, and
* Centre de Genetique Moleculaire, 91190 Gif-sur-Yvette
France

SUMMARY

Import of precursors of cytochromes b_2 and c_1 into mitochondria requires a mitochondrial membrane potential. We show here that in addition to $\Delta\Psi$, nucleoside triphosphates (NTPs) are necessary for protein translocation. At low concentrations of NTPs, intermediate-sized cytochrome b_2 was accumulated spanning the outer and inner membranes at contact sites. For complete translocation into mitochondria, higher concentrations of NTPs were necessary. We conclude that different levels of NTPs are required for distinct steps in the import pathway.

INTRODUCTION

Most mitochondrial proteins are coded for by the nucleus and are synthesized as precursors on cytoplasmic polysomes. Transport of proteins into mitochondria can be subdivided into several steps (for reviews see: Harmey and Neupert, 1985; Pfanner and Neupert, 1987; Hartl et al., 1987): (i) specific interaction with receptors on the mitochondrial surface; (ii) transport into mitochondria at translocation contact sites between outer and inner membranes; (iii) processing of precursors having N-terminal extensions by the processing peptidase in the matrix; (iv) additional modifications, including covalent or non-covalent attachment of cofactors or, in certain cases, a second proteolytic processing step; and (v) assembly into active supramolecular protein complexes.

Transport into or translocation across the inner membrane is dependent on an energized inner membrane (Hallermayer and Neupert, 1976; Nelson and Schatz, 1979; Zimmermann et al., 1981; Schleyer et al., 1982; Gasser et al., 1982; Kolanski et al., 1982). Energy is required in the form of the electrical component $\Delta\Psi$ of total protonmotive force (Pfanner and Neupert, 1985). For long, however, it could not be decided whether high energy phosphate compounds, such as ATP, are necessary in addition to $\Delta\Psi$. Indeed, this was recently shown for the import of the ß subunit of F_oF_1-ATPase ($F_1\beta$) (Pfanner and Neupert, 1986), the ADP/ATP-translocator of the inner membrane, and fusion proteins between F_oF_1-ATPase subunit 9 and dihydrofolate reductase (Pfanner et al., 1987).

In the present report we investigated whether the import of

cytochromes b_2 and c_1 was dependent on NTPs. Cytochrome b_2 is a soluble component of the intermembrane space (Daum et al., 1982a). Cytochrome c_1 is anchored to the inner membrane but contains a large hydrophilic domain which protrudes into the intermembrane space (Li et al., 1981). Compared to ß subunit of F_oF_1-ATPase their import and sorting pathways are more complex in that both precursor proteins are proteolytically processed in two steps (Daum et al., 1982b; Ohashi et al., 1982; Teintze et al., 1982). The first processing step is performed by the matrix peptidase, i.e. precursors have to be translocated either completely or at least partially across the inner membrane. The second processing event occurs at the outer surface of the inner membrane by a so far uncharacterized protease(s) (Pratje and Guiard, 1986). On addition both proteins have to acquire heme, which is covalently attached in case of cytochrome c_1.

Selective and independent manipulation of NTP levels and the membrane potential showed that import of cytochromes b_2 and c_1 required both NTPs and $\Delta\Psi$. Interestingly, at low levels of NTPs precursors were only partially translocated into mitochondria: they accumulated in translocation contact sites (Schleyer and Neupert, 1985).

MATERIALS AND METHODS

Growth of Neurospora crassa (wild type 74A) (Schleyer et al., 1982) and isolation of mitochondria by Percoll (Pharmacia) density gradient centrifugation was done as described (Hartl et al., 1986). Yeast cells of wild type Saccharomyces cerevisiae (D273-10B) were grown on 2% lactate and mitochondria were isolated according to Daum et al. (1982a). Mitochondria were finally suspended in SEM buffer (250 mM sucrose, 1 mM EDTA, 10 mM MOPS/KOH, pH 7.2) at a protein concentration of 2.5 mg/ml.

Precursor proteins were synthesized by coupled transcription/ translation. For cytochrome c_1, a full length cDNA was isolated from a N. crassa library and cloned into pGEM4. For cytochrome b_2, the genomic clone described previously (Guiard, 1985) was used. Transcription/translation of the cloned sequences followed the methods of Krieg and Melton (1984) and Stueber et al. (1984), respectively. Postribosomal supernatants were prepared and supplemented as published (Schleyer et al., 1982).

Labelled reticulocyte lysates and isolated mitochondria were treated with apyrase (Sigma, grade VIII) essentially as described before (Pfanner and Neupert, 1986). Afterwards reticulocyte lysates were cooled to 0°C and diluted with BSA buffer (250 mM sucrose, 80 mM KCl, 5 mM $MgCl_2$, 10 mM MOPS, 3% (w/v) BSA, pH 7.2). Antimycin A, oligomycin or valinomycin (8 µM, 20 µM and 1 µM, respectively) were added from 100-fold concentrated stock solutions in ethanol when indicated. Mixtures for import into N. crassa mitochondria contained 8 mM potassium ascorbate and 0.2 mM N,N,N',N'- tetramethylphenylenediamine (TMPD) as an energy source, whereas mixtures for yeast mitochondria included 20 mM potassium succinate. Then mitochondria (50 µg of protein) were added. In order to supplement NTPs, either ATP or GTP (8 mM final concentration) were added from 200 mM stock solutions in water. For neutralization sufficient amounts of 1 M MOPS/NaOH, pH 7.2, were included. Incubation was for 30 min at 25°C in a total volume of 100 µl. Mitochondria were then reisolated by centrifugation (15 min 27,000 x g), resuspended in SEM buffer and treated with proteinase K (15 µg/ml final concentration) as described (Hartl et al., 1986). Reisolated mitochondria were lysed in SDS sample buffer. SDS polyacrylamide electrophoresis and fluorography were carried out according to published methods (Laemmli, 1970; Hartl et al., 1986).

RESULTS

Import of cytochromes b_2 and c_1 requires nucleoside triphosphates

Reticulocyte lysates containing the ^{35}S-methionine labelled precursor of cytochrome b_2 and freshly isolated yeast mitochondria were pretreated with different concentrations of apyrase, an adenosine 5'-triphosphatase and adenosine 5'-diphosphatase which caused rapid depletion of endogenous ATP and ADP. Mitochondria and reticulocyte lysate were mixed in the presence of succinate (as a respiratory substrate) and oligomycin (which inhibits the F_oF_1-ATPase, Wikstrom and Krab, 1982). The latter was included to prevent reduction of the mitochondrial membrane potential by ATPase activity. Following incubation for 30 min at 25°C, the samples were treated with proteinase K to digest cytochrome b_2 that had not been imported into mitochondria. Then mitochondria were reisolated and dissolved in SDS-containing buffer for subsequent

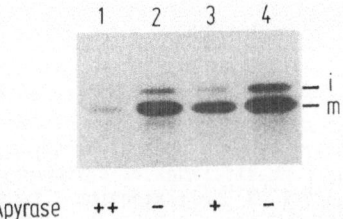

Fig. 1. Import of cytochrome b_2 into yeast mitochondria is inhibited by apyrase treatment.
Reticulocyte lysates containing labelled precursor of cytochrome b_2 were incubated for 15 min at 30°C and 15 min at 25°C with apyrase: reactions 1 and 3 received 1 and 0.25 U/ml, respectively; reactions 2 and 4 received corresponding amounts of inactivated apyrase. Mitochondria were added to the lysate in presence of succinate and oligomycin. Incubation for import was for 30 min at 25°C. Afterwards the samples were cooled to 0°C and diluted 1:2 with SEM. Proteinase K treatment was then performed (30 min at 0°C). Protease activity was stopped by adding PMSF to 1 mM. Then mitochondria were reisolated by centrifugation and dissociated in SDS-containing buffer. The samples were analyzed by electrophoresis and fluorography. Abbreviations: i, intermediate; m, mature cytochrome b_2.

electrophoresis and fluorography. A fluorograph of the dried gel is shown in Fig.1. Control samples received an apyrase preparation which had been inactivated by heating to 95°C for 10 min. In these reactions, cytochrome b_2 precursor was imported into a protease protected location and processed to the mature form. Besides mature cytochrome b_2, a small quantity of the intermediate sized form (about 20% of total) was observed which was also protected against externally added protease (Fig.1, lanes 2 and 4). When lysate and mitochondria had been pretreated with apyrase, import was clearly diminished (Fig.1, lanes 1 and 3). Apyrase per se did reduce neither the protease resistance of endogenous mitochondrial proteins nor the amount of precursor proteins in the reticulocyte lysate (Pfanner and Neupert, 1986; Pfanner et al., 1987). We conclude that pretreatment with apyrase causes inhibition of import of cytochrome b_2 into mitochondria.

To test whether the apyrase effect was due to depletion of NTPs, experiments were performed where ATP or GTP were included during import (Fig.2).

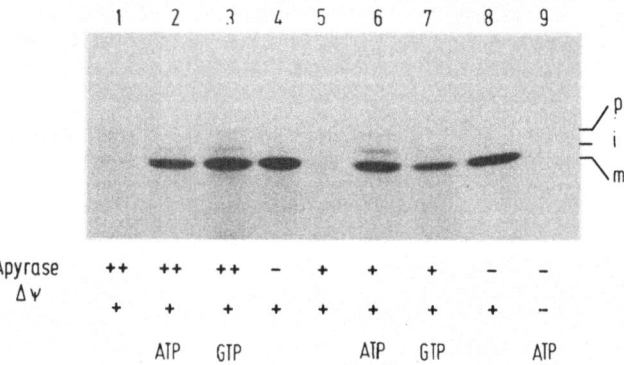

Fig. 2. Import of cytochrome b_2 from apyrase treated reticulocyte lysate is restored by addition of ATP or GTP.
Reticulocyte lysates and mitochondria were incubated with the following concentrations of apyrase: reactions 1- 3, 4 U/ml; reactions 5-7, 1 U/ml; reaction 4 received 4 U inactivated apyrase/ml and reactions 8 and 9 1 U/ml. Import and protease treatment was performed as described in legend to Fig.1, except that in reactions 2,6 and 9, 8 mM ATP and in reactions 3 and 7, 8 mM GTP were added during import. In reaction 9, 1 μM valinomycin was added prior to ATP. A fluorograph of the dried gel is shown.
Abbreviations as in Fig.1. p, precursor of cytochrome b_2.

Under these conditions the import of cytochrome b_2 could be fully restored (Fig.2, lanes 2,3 and 6,7). This import, however, was completely abolished when valinomycin plus potassium ions were added to destroy the membrane potential across the inner membrane (Fig.2, lane 9). In this case, addition of ATP did not restore import.

The same result was obtained with import of cytochrome c_1 into mitochondria of N. crassa. Experimental conditions were essentially as described for import of cytochrome b_2, except that ascorbate/TMPD was used to establish a membrane potential and NADH was included, which is required for the second maturation step of cytochrome c_1 (Schleyer and Neupert, 1985, see accompanying article by Nicholson et al.). A fluorograph corresponding to the experimental design presented in Fig.2 was quantified by densitometry (Fig.3).

Again apyrase treatment drastically reduced import and processing (Fig.3, lanes 1,5) which could be restored by addition of ATP or GTP (Fig.3, lanes 2,3,6,7). Import was completely blocked after inhibition of the membrane potential with antimycin A and oligomycin and could not be restored by including ATP in the reaction (Fig.3, lane 9). Consequently, the presence of NTPs and a membrane potential are two separate requirements. NTPs cannot substitute for the requirement of $\Delta\psi$. At present, however, it is unknown which form of high energy phosphate is actually needed since nucleoside phosphate kinases present in mitochondria can lead to formation of various nucleoside triphosphates.

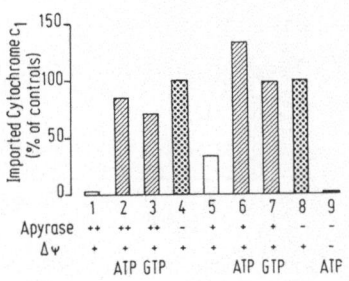

Fig. 3. Import of cytochrome c_1 is inhibited by apyrase treatment and restored by ATP or GTP.
The experimental design was essentially as described in the legend to Fig.2, except that mitochondria from N. crassa were used and import was performed in the presence of ascorbate/TMPD and NADH instead of succinate. Antimycin A was included in addition to oligomycin. Formation of mature cytochrome c_1 was quantified by densitometry of the fluorograph. The amount of mature c_1 formed in controls (inactivated apyrase) was set at 100%.

Intermediate-sized cytochrome b_2 spanning outer and inner membranes at contact sites can be accumulated at low levels of NTPs

For precursors of ß subunit of F_0F_1-ATPase, cytochrome c_1 and the Fe/S-protein of complex III, it has been previously shown that import into mitochondria performed at lower temperatures results in the formation of so called "contact site intermediates" (Schleyer and Neupert, 1985; Hartl et al., 1986). Such an intermediate is characterized as follows: the N-terminal presequence of the precursor has been translocated across both membranes in a $\Delta\psi$ dependent manner and is cleaved off by the processing peptidase in the matrix. A large part of the polypeptide, however, is still outside the mitochondrion where it can be digested by externally added protease. It follows that these features can be only fulfilled at regions where outer and inner membranes are close enough together to be spanned by a single polypeptide chain.

Experiments with apyrase pretreatment indicated that after depletion of ATP the formation of intermediate-sized cytochrome b_2 was not reduced to the same extent as was processing to the mature form. In contrast to mature b_2, more than 85% of which were protease-resistent, this intermediate was largely sensitive to externally added protease. This effect could be clearly demonstrated when apyrase concentrations were titrated over a wider range (0 to 100 U apyrase/ml of lysate or mitochondrial suspension). After import, one half of each reaction was treated with proteinase K. Following electrophoresis and fluorography the amounts of intermediate-sized b_2 formed were quantified by densitometry (Fig. 4).

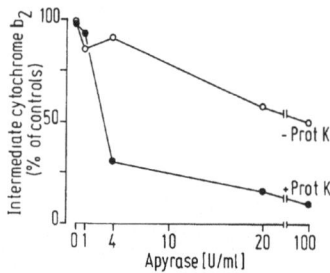

Fig 4. Intermediate sized cytochrome b_2 is accumulated in contact sites at low levels of NTPs.
Reticulocyte lysates and mitochondria were incubated with apyrase (0-100 U/ml). Controls received corresponding amounts of inactivated apyrase. Import and protease treatment were performed as described in the legend to Fig.1, except that only half of each sample received protease. Formation of intermediate cytochrome b_2 was quantified by densitometry of the fluorograph. The amount of intermediate b_2 formed in controls (inactivated apyrase) was set at 100%.

At apyrase concentrations between 4 and 20 U/ml, the formation of intermediate b_2 was reduced by 10 to 40% compared to controls that had received inactivated apyrase. Most of this intermediate sized b_2, however, was digested by externally added proteinase K thus fulfilling the criteria for a contact site intermediate described above. Only with very low concentrations of apyrase was intermediate-sized b_2 protected against externally added protease. Within a narrow range of 1 to 4 U apyrase/ml, protease protection decreased from 95 to 30% indicating that only above a distinct level of NTPs import into protease protected position did take place. When the membrane potential was dissipated, no processing to intermediate b_2 was observed. We conclude that partial translocation of the precursor can occur at low levels of NTPs; this step depends on the potential across the inner membrane. For complete translocation, however, higher levels of NTPs are required.

DISCUSSION

The import of precursors of cytochromes b_2 and c_1 into mitochondria needs NTPs in addition to $\Delta\Psi$. At low levels of NTPs, a translocational intermediate of cytochrome b_2 could be accumulated in contact sites.
Owing to the presence of nucleoside phosphate kinases it is unclear so far which form of high energy phosphate compound (eg. ATP or GTP) is the

direct energy source. Non-hydrolyzable ATP-analogues could not restore import after depletion of NTPs with apyrase (Pfanner and Neupert, 1986) indicating that the mechanism of action of NTPs involves the hydrolysis of high energy phosphate bonds. The dependence of protein import into mitochondria on NTPs seems to be a general phenomenon. Similar effects have been recently observed with the precursors of ß subunit of F_oF_1-ATPase (Pfanner and Neupert, 1986) and the ADP/ATP-translocator (Pfanner et al., 1987). Interestingly, the insertion of porin into the outer membrane (which is independent of $\Delta\Psi$) also seems to need NTPs (Kleene et al., in preparation).

What could be the role of NTPs? Previous results had already suggested that NTPs modify the conformation of cytosolic mitochondrial precursor proteins (Pfanner et al., 1987). Eilers and Schatz (1986) have demonstrated that lack of tertiary structure is a prerequisite for protein import into mitochondria. Taking the resistance against digestion by protease as a measure for the degree of tertiary structure it could be shown that the presence of NTPs results in the unfolding of precursor molecules (Pfanner et al., 1987) thus rendering them competent for translocation across the mitochondrial membranes. In the present study, $\Delta\Psi$ dependent partial translocation of the precursor of cytochrome b_2 was possible at very low concentrations of NTPs resulting in an intermediate reaching into the matrix with its aminoterminus but having a large part of the molecule still outside the mitochondrion. Complete translocation into a protease protected position was then achieved by adding ATP or GTP and was independent of $\Delta\Psi$ (Hartl and Neupert, unpublished). These findings are consistent with the idea that the membrane potential is only necessary for the translocation of the aminoterminal part of the precursor across the inner membrane. It is assumed to exert an electrophoretic effect on the positive charges contained in the presequence (Pfanner and Neupert, 1985; Roise et al., 1986). Complete translocation of the precursor across both membranes is only possible when the polypeptide is kept in an unfolded state, the energy source for the unfolding reaction being NTPs. Specific binding of the precursor to receptors on the surface of mitochondria, insertion into and partial translocation across the mitochondrial membranes is possible at very low levels of NTPs; thus, it seems likely that the presequence folds independently of the mature part of the precursor and can be recognized by the mitochondrial import machinery. On the other hand it cannot be excluded that besides the unfolding of cytosolic precursors the role of NTPs includes functions such as the modification of mitochondrial membranes e.g. by phosphorylation of mitochondrial transport components.

The existence of "unfolding proteins" in the cytosol has been proposed (Rothman and Kornberg, 1986; Zimmermann and Meyer, 1986) that could bind to precursor proteins and whose action would involve the hydrolysis of high energy phosphate bonds. The role of NTPs in preventing (mis)folding of precursor proteins into an import incompetent conformation could explain the general importance of NTPs for the translocation of proteins across membranes in both procaryotic and eucaryotic systems (for review see Zimmermann and Meyer, 1986).

ACKNOWLEDGEMENTS
    The authors wish to thank S. Meier for expert technical assistance and Dr. D. Nicholson for critically reading the manuscript. This work was supported by the Deutsche Forschungsgemeinschaft (SFB 184, B2).

REFERENCES

Daum, G., Böhni, P.C., and Schatz, G. (1982a). J. Biol. Chem. 257, 13028-13033.

Daum, G., Gasser, S.M., and Schatz, G. (1982b). J. Biol. Chem. 257, 13075-13080.

Eilers, M., and Schatz, G. (1986). Nature 322, 228-232.

Gasser, S.M., Daum, G., and Schatz, G. (1982). J. Biol. Chem. 257, 13034-13041.

Guiard, B. (1985). EMBO J. 4, 3265-3272.

Hallermayer, G., and Neupert, W. (1976). In "Genetics and Biogenesis of Chloroplasts and Mitochondria" (Bücher, T., Neupert, W., Sebald, W., and Werner, S., eds.) pp. 807-812. North Holland, Amsterdam.

Harmey, M.A. and Neupert W. (1985). In: The Enzymes of Biological Membranes (Martonosi A. ed.) Plenum Publ. Co. New York, Vol.4, p. 431-464.

Hartl, F.-U., Schmidt, B., Wachter, E., Weiss, H., and Neupert, W. (1986). Cell 47, 939-951.

Hartl, F.-U., Pfanner, N., and Neupert, W. (1987). Biochem. Soc. Trans. 15, 95-97.

Kolanski, D.M., Conboy, J.G., Fenon, W.A., and Rosenberg, L. (1982). J. Biol. Chem. 257, 8467-8471.

Krieg, P.A., and Melton, D.A. (1984). Nuc. Acid Res. 12, 7057-7070.

Laemmli, V.K. (1970). Nature (Lond.) 227, 680-685.

Li, Y., Leonard, W., and Weiss, H. (1981a). Eur. J. Biochem. 116, 199-205.

Nelson, N., and Schatz, G. (1979). Proc. Natl. Acad. Sci. USA 76, 4365-4369.

Ohashi, A., Gibson, J., Gregor, I., and Schatz, G. (1982). J. Biol. Chem. 257, 13042-13047.

Pfanner, N., and Neupert, W. (1985). EMBO J. 4, 2819-2825.

Pfanner, N., and Neupert, W. (1986). FEBS Lett. 209, 152-156.

Pfanner, N., and Neupert, W. (1987). In "Current Topics in Bioenergetics" (C.P. Lee, ed.), Vol. 15, Academic Press, New York, in press.

Pfanner, N., Tropschug, M., and Neupert, W. (1987). Cell, in press.

Pratje, E., and Guiard, B. (1986) EMBO J. 5, 1313-1317.

Roise, D., Horvath, S.J., Tomich, J.M., Richards, J.H., and Schatz, G. (1986). EMBO J. 5, 1327-1334.

Rothman, J.E., and Kornberg, R.D. (1986). Nature 322, 209-210.

Schleyer, M., Schmidt, B., and Neupert, W. (1982). Eur. J. Biochem. 125, 109-116.

Schleyer, M. and Neupert, W. (1985). Cell 43, 339-350.

Stueber, D., Ibrahimi, I., Cutler, D., Dobberstein, B., and Bujard, H. (1984) EMBO J. 3, 3143-3148.

Teintze, M., Slaughter, M., Weiß, H., and Neupert, W. (1982). J. Biol. Chem. 257, 10364-10371.

Wikstrom, M., and Krab, K. (1982). Biochim. Biophys. Acta 549, 177-222.

Zimmermann, R., Hennig, B., and Neupert, W. (1981). Eur. J. Biochem. 116, 455-460.

Zimmermann, R., and Meyer, D.I. (1986). Trends. Biochem. Sci. 11, 512-515

NADH: A COMMON REQUIREMENT FOR THE IMPORT

AND MATURATION OF CYTOCHROMES c AND c_1

Donald W. Nicholson, Joachim Ostermann and Walter Neupert

Institut für Physiologische Chemie der Universität München
Goethestrasse 33
D-8000 München 2
Federal Republic of Germany

SUMMARY

The covalent attachment of heme to apocytochrome c, which is catalyzed by the mitochondrial enzyme cytochrome c heme lyase, was dependent on NADH. In addition, a cofactor present in reticulocyte lysate or a Neurospora crassa cytosol fraction was required for the NADH-dependent step. In the absence of NADH, apocytochrome c was bound to the mitochondrial surface and remained accessible to externally added proteases. In the presence of NADH, covalent attachment of heme occurred with concomitant translocation of cytochrome c across the outer mitochondrial membrane to a protease-resistant location. Both heme attachment and translocation were inhibited by the heme analogue deuterohemin.

The second proteolytic-processing step during cytochrome c_1 import, from the intermediate to mature-size protein, was also dependent on NADH and could also be inhibited by deuterohemin. We suggest that this occurs as a result of conditions which affect the heme-attaching reaction for cytochrome c_1 and that heme attachment must precede the second processing step. Models are presented to account for these observations.

INTRODUCTION

The majority of mitochondrial proteins are encoded by nuclear genes and are synthesized as precursors on free ribosomes in the cell cytosol. They are then imported into mitochondria along pathways which can be subdivided into a consecutive series of distinct steps (for review see 1-4). Most mitochondrial proteins, particularly those which must be directed to the inner membrane or matrix, are imported by the following sequence of events: i) synthesis in the cytosol as a precursor containing an N-terminal targeting sequence; ii) binding to specific receptors on the mitochondrial surface; iii) membrane-potential-dependent insertion into the inner membrane via translocation contact sites where the inner and outer membrane come close enough together to be spanned simultaneously by the imported protein; iv) removal of the N-terminal prepiece by the chelator-sensitive processing peptidase located in the matrix; v) sorting of the protein to its final sub-mitochondrial location; and vi) assembly into functional complexes. In a number of cases, the import pathway is accompanied by covalent modification

197

or the acquisition of non-covalently bound prosthetic groups.

Energy is required for protein import in three known forms. First, it has been well established that all proteins which must be translocated into or across the inner membrane require the presence of a membrane potential (5,6). Recently, it has also been demonstrated that ATP is required for the maintenence of an import-competent conformation during all steps which precede and include interaction of the precursor protein with the outer membrane (7, see accompanying article by Hartl et al). Finally, NAD(P)H is required for the maturation of cytochromes c (8,9) and c_1 (10,11), for the Fe/S protein of the bc_1 complex (Hartl and Neupert, unpublished), and for cytochrome oxidase subunit II (Driever, Cook and Neupert, unpublished).

The requirement for NADH by cytochromes c and c_1 appears to be a common feature of the later stages of their respective import pathways. Despite a number of similarities between the two proteins (e.g. both mature proteins are exposed to the mitochondrial intermembrane space; they are the only two mitochondrial proteins to which heme is covalently·bound; they both require NADH during import), cytochromes c and c_1 follow markedly different import pathways. Cytochrome c is synthesized in the cytosol as apocytochrome c, which differs from its mature counterpart in conformation and by the absence of covalently-bound heme. It does not contain a cleavable N-terminal prepiece and does not require a membrane potential for import (12-18). Apocytochrome c is transferred from a cytoplasmic pool to specific receptors at the outer mitochondrial membrane (18-21). Heme is attached to the apoprotein, by the enzyme cytochrome c heme lyase (8,9,20,22-24), in a step which is coupled to the translocation of cytochrome c across the outer membrane to its final location in the intermembrane space. Cytochrome c_1, on the other hand, follows a somewhat more complicated sequence of events during import. The precursor of cytochrome is synthesized in the cytosol and contains an unusually long N-terminal prepiece which is processed in two steps (10,11,25,26). The precursor binds to receptors at the outer membrane and the N-terminus is then translocated through the inner membrane via contact sites (11) in a step which is dependent on a membrane potential. The hydrophilic first half of the prepiece is removed by the matrix peptidase followed by removal of the second part by another processing activity which is presumed to be located in the intermembrane space. The latter step is dependent on heme (25,26) and therefore might be coupled to the heme attaching reaction or might have to be preceded by heme linkage. The mature protein is then assembled into the bc_1 complex, anchored to the inner membrane by a hydrophobic stretch of amino acids at the C-terminus (27,28).

In this report we have examined the common requirement for NADH during the import of cytochromes c and c_1 into mitochondria. We demonstrate that NADH is required for the covalent attachment of heme to apocytochrome c and that the NADH-dependent step is mediated by a cytosolic cofactor. Since the second processing step of cytochrome c_1 has nearly identical requirements, we suggest that NADH is needed for a similar import event; namely, for the activity of cytochrome c_1 heme lyase.

MATERIALS AND METHODS

Cell Growth and Subcellular Fractionation

Neurospora crassa wild type 74A was grown for 14 h at 25°C as previously described (29). Mitochondria were isolated from freshly harvested hyphae by Percoll-gradient centrifugation (Pharmacia) and suspended in buffer A (250 mM sucrose, 10 mM Mops/KOH (pH 7.2), 2 mM EDTA, 1 mM phenylmethylsulphonyl fluoride (PMSF)) at a protein concentration of 5 mg/ml (8). PMSF was not included in buffer A during any of the fractionation or import steps if proteinase K digestion was included in the experimental procedure. A cytosol fraction was prepared by grinding hyphae with quartz sand in buffer A and then preparing a post-ribosomal supernatant (8).

Cell-Free Protein Synthesis

Precursor proteins of N. crassa cytochromes c and c_1 were synthesized in rabbit reticulocyte lysates (30) in the presence of L-(^{35}S)cysteine as previously described (8). Synthesis of apocytochrome c was directed by N. crassa poly(A)-containing RNA (31). Synthesis of the precursor to cytochrome c_1 was directed by a full-length cDNA clone of pre-cytochrome c_1 in pGEM-4 that was transcribed with SP6 RNA-polymerase (Ostermann and Neupert, unpublished).

Import of Cytochrome c

1. Direct import: Mitochondria (75 µg protein) were incubated for 10 min at 25°C in a total volume of 200 µl buffer A in the presence of 50 µl (^{35}S)cysteine-labelled reticulocyte lysate plus other additions as indicated. Holocytochrome c formation was determined by re-isolating the mitochondria by centrifugation, immunoprecipitating total cytochrome c (holo plus apo), dissociation of the immunocomplexes with urea, digestion with trypsin, and analysis of the resulting peptides by reverse-phase HPLC (8). The holocytochrome c cysteine-containing tryptic peptide was collected and its radioactivity determined as a measure of holocytochrome c formation.

2. Chase of pre-bound apocytochrome c to holocytochrome c: Apocytochrome c was bound to mitochondria in the absence of conversion to holocytochrome c (by withholding NADH) by incubating mitochondria (75 µg protein) with 50 µl (^{35}S)cysteine-labelled reticulocyte lysate in a total volume of 200 µl buffer A for 10 min at 25°C. The mitochondria were re-isolated by centrifugation at 17,400 xg for 12 min and resuspended in fresh buffer A. The bound apocytochrome c was then chased to holocytochrome c during a second incubation for 10 min at 25°C in a mixture containing 75 µg mitochondrial protein, plus additions as indicated, in 200 µl buffer A. Holocytochrome c formation was then determined as described above.

Import of Cytochrome c_1

1. Direct import: Mitochondria (50 µg) were incubated for 30 min at 25°C in a mixture (total volume 100 µl) containing 3% (w/v) bovine serum albumin, 70 mM KCl, 220 mM sucrose, 10 mM Mops/KOH (pH 7.2) in the presence of 20 µl (^{35}S)cysteine-labelled reticulocyte plus other additions as indicated. The samples were cooled to 0°C and proteinase K was added to a final concentration of 20 µg/ml. Following incubation for 30 min at 0°C, the mitochondria were re-isolated as above and dissociated in SDS sample buffer. The samples were then resolved by SDS polyacrylamide gel electrophoresis and visualized by fluorography of the dried gel.

2. Chase of intermediate to mature-size cytochrome c_1: The precursor was imported into mitochondria as above but in the presence of 2.5 mM $MgCl_2$ and absence of NADH to accumulate the intermediate-size protein. The mixtures were then treated with proteinase K (Fig. 4D) or not (Fig 4C) as described above. The mitochondria were re-isolated and suspended in buffer A then incubated for 30 min at 25°C in the presence of additions, as indicated, in a total volume of 100 µl. The samples were diluted with 1 ml buffer A and the mitochondria were sedimented by centrifugation and then dissociated in SDS sample buffer as above.

Miscellaneous Methods

Cytochrome c was purified from N. crassa and specific antibodies were raised in rabbits as previously described (29). Radioactivity determinations

were performed by scintillation counting in 0.1 ml of 10% (w/v) SDS, 1 M
Tris/HCl (pH 8.0), plus 10 ml ACS II (Amersham). SDS polyacrylamide gel
electrophoresis was performed using standard techniques (32). Gels were
prepared for fluorography by soaking them for 30 min in Amplify (Amersham)
followed by drying and then exposure to X-ray films at -80°C. The bands were
quantified by laser densitometry (LKB-GSXL). Protein was determined as
described previously (33).

RESULTS

Covalent Attachment of Heme to Apocytochrome c Requires NADH and a Cofactor from Reticulocyte Lysate or Cell Cytosol

In the absence of reducing agents, the import of cytochrome c into
mitochondria and formation of holocytochrome c occurred at only very low
rates. In the presence of NADH, however, holocytochrome c formation was
stimulated 8 to 12-fold (figure 1). The NADH-dependent activity of
cytochrome c heme lyase was not affected by the presence of valinomycin/K^+
(which dissipates the membrane potential) or by antimycin A/oligomycin (which
blocks the generation of a membrane potential). Other reducing agents could
substitute for the NADH requirement to varying degrees. NAD^+ alone
stimulated activity to 22% (at 2 mM) of the optimum observed with NADH (at
5 mM). In the presence of an NADH-regenerating system (L(+)lactate plus
lactate dehydrogenase), NAD^+ behaved essentially the same as NADH.

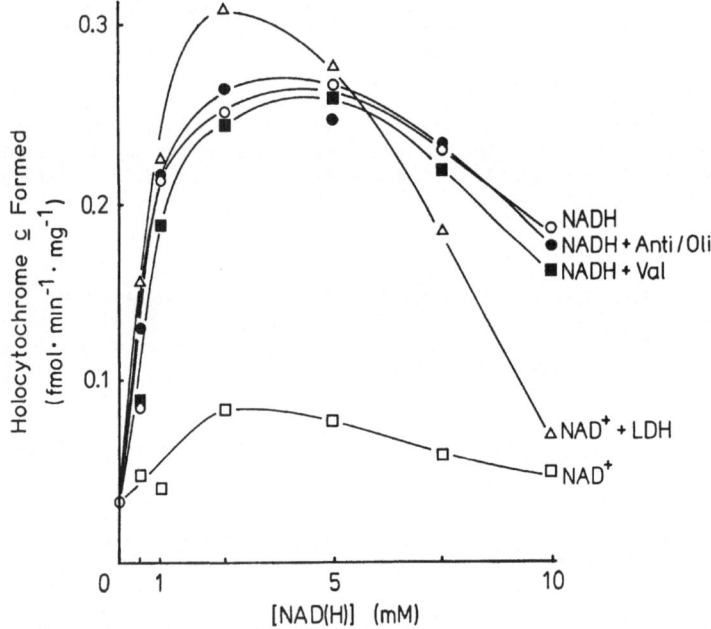

Fig. 1 Holocytochrome c Formation Depends on NADH. Apocytochrome c,
synthesized in reticulocyte lysate, was imported into mitochondria in
the presence of varying amounts of either NAD^+ (□,△) or NADH
(O,●,■) plus other additions as follows: O,□, no further
additions; △, 45 mM L(+)lactate, 3 U lactate dehydrogenase (EC
1.1.1.27) per ml; ●, 8 µM antimycin A, 20 µM oligomycin; ■, 0.5 µM
valinomycin. Holocytochrome c formation was determined following
incubation for 10 min at 25°C.

NADPH (at 1 mM), which has been reported to be required for holocytochrome c formation in yeast (9), stimulated activity to 45% of the NADH optimum (8), as did glutathione (43% at 25 mM)(8), Na dithionite (100% at 1 mg/ml, unpublished), and 2-mercaptoethanol (7% at 50 mM, unpublished).

We have previously investigated the role of NADH in the covalent attachment of heme to apocytochrome c (8). NADH was not required for the binding of apocytochrome c to mitochondria and, unlike the majority of imported mitochondrial proteins, a membrane potential was not necessary for any of the stages of cytochrome c import. NADH was not involved in the reduction of the cysteine thiols to which heme is covalently attached. Preliminary experiments indicate that reduction of the heme iron from Fe(III) to Fe(II) must occur before the enzymatic linkage of heme to apocytochrome c, and that this reduction step requires NADH (Nicholson and Neupert, in preparation).

Apocytochrome c could be bound to mitochondria in the absence of conversion to holocytochrome c by not including NADH in the incubation mixtures. When the mitochondria were re-isolated and washed, to remove constituents from the reticulocyte lysate, the bound apocytochrome c was inefficiently chased to holocytochrome c after adding NADH unless the mixtures were supplemented with either unlabelled reticulocyte lysate or a cell cytosol fraction (figure 2). Neither the reticulocyte lysate or cytosol fraction had any stimulatory activity in the absence of NADH, and there was no measurable cytochrome c heme lyase activity in these preparations alone. The cofactor was a heat-stable, protease-insensitive, dializable component which could presumably reach the intermembrane space, where heme attachment occurs, via the channels formed by porin (8).

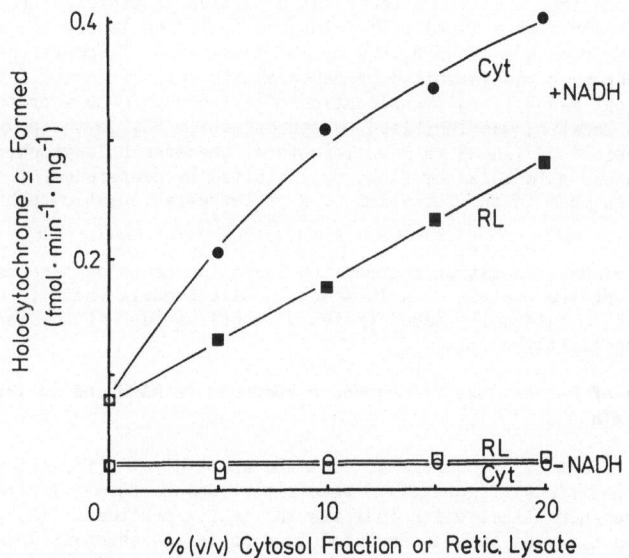

Fig. 2 NADH-Dependent Holocytochrome c Formation Depends on a Cofactor. Apocytochrome c, synthesized in reticulocyte lysate, was pre-bound to mitochondria in the absence of NADH (to prevent conversion to holocytochrome c). The mitochondria were reisolated and the bound apocytochrome c was chased to holocytochrome c for 10 min at 25°C in the presence (●,■) or absence (O,□) of 5 mM NADH, plus varying amounts of either cytosol fraction (●,O) or unlabelled reticulocyte lysate (■,□). Holocytochrome c formation was then determined.

Covalent attachment of heme to apocytochrome c, by the enzyme cytochrome c heme lyase, requires NADH in a step which is also dependent on a factor present in reticulocyte lysate or N. crassa cell cytosol. This step appears to be the reduction of the heme iron and the cofactor probably mediates this reduction. The conformation of the heme group and/or its ability to form critical alignments with apocytochrome c may be essential for the cytochrome c heme lyase reaction.

The Translocation of Cytochrome c to a Protease-Resistant Location Depends on NADH and is Inhibited by Deuterohemin

We have previously demonstrated that the apocytochrome c associated with mitochondria in the presence of deuterohemin (an analogue of heme which does not contain the vinyl groups at positions 3 and 8 of the porphyrin ring that are necessary for formation of the thioether linkages with apocytochrome c) could be displaced by excess added apocytochrome c; e.g. import was blocked at the stage of high-affinity receptor binding (20). We therefore proposed that the translocation of cytochrome c across the outer mitochondrial membrane during import is intrinsically coupled to the covalent attachment of heme (8,20).

Translocation of cytochrome c across the outer mitochondrial membrane was determined by the accessibility of the protein to externally added proteases which did not penetrate the outer membrane under the conditions used here (figure 3). In the presence of NADH, formation of holocytochrome c occurred at 23-times the rate compared to samples which did not contain NADH (mixtures II and I, respectively). Translocation of the cytochrome c to a protease-resistant location also depended on NADH (cf. lane 1 vs 3). As a control, the imported cytochrome c was sensitive to protease treatment when the mitochondria were lysed with detergent following import (lanes 2 and 4). In the presence of NADH, 80% of the conversion of apocytochrome c to holocytochrome c was inhibited by deuterohemin (cf. mixture III vs IV). In an identical manner, the translocation of cytochrome c to a protease-resistant location was inhibited by approximately 80% in the presence of deuterohemin (cf. lane 5 vs 7). Therefore, whenever holocytochrome c formation was stimulated by NADH, or inhibited by deuterohemin, there were parallel changes in the formation of a protease-resistant cytochrome c species.

The close correlation between the formation of holocytochrome c and the transport of the protein to a location in mitochondria where it was not accessible to externally added proteases confirms our hypothesis that the two events are tightly coupled.

Formation of Mature-Size Cytochrome c_1 Depends on NADH and is Inhibited by Deuterohemin

The import of cytochrome c_1 could be arrested at different stages under various conditions (figure 4A). When import was performed in the presence of EDTA/o-phenanthroline, which inhibits the matrix peptidase, the precursor of cytochrome c_1 (p-C_1) was accumulated in a protease-resistant location (lane 1). In the presence of $MgCl_2$, the imported cytochrome c_1 was processed to the intermediate-size protein (i-C_1; lane 2). Processing to the mature-size cytochrome c_1 (m-C_1) depended on the presence of NADH in addition to $MgCl_2$ (lane 3). The second processing step, or events tightly coupled to the second processing step (e.g. covalent attachment of heme), therefore appear to require NADH.

To determine whether the second processing step of cytochrome c_1 maturation is coupled to heme linkage, cytochrome c_1 was imported in the presence or absence of deuterohemin (figure 4B). In the absence of NADH, cytochrome c_1 accumulated as the intermediate-size protein with negligible formation of $m-C_1$ (lane 1). In the presence of NADH, more than 65% of the imported cytochrome c_1 appeared as $m-C_1$ (lane 2). When deuterohemin was included in import mixtures that were otherwise identical to that in lane 2, formation of $m-C_1$ was inhibited (lane 3). Formation of $m-C_1$ in the presence of deuterohemin occurred at 39% of the rate compared to that in the absence of deuterohemin (cf. lane 2 vs 3). Although the total amount of imported cytochrome c_1 was lower in the presence of deuterohemin, the ratio of $m-C_1$ to $i-C_1$ in the presence of deuterohemin (0.66) was considerably lower than the ratio in the absence of deuterohemin (2.1) indicating that the second processing step was specifically blocked.

Similar results were observed when cytochrome c_1 was imported from reticulocyte lysate into mitochondria in the absence of NADH, then the mitochondria were reisolated and the bound cytochrome c_1 was chased under various conditions (figure 4C). Low amounts of the bound cytochrome c_1 were chased to $m-C_1$ in the absence of NADH (lane 1). In the presence of NADH, however, $m-C_1$ formation was stimulated 3.2-fold (lane 2). This NADH-dependent chase to $m-C_1$ was blocked when deuterohemin was added to the incubation mixture (lane 3). When unlabelled reticulocyte lysate was added during the chase incubation, the NADH-dependent $m-C_1$ formation was stimulated a further 39% (cf. lane 4 vs 2). Processing to $m-C_1$ under these conditions

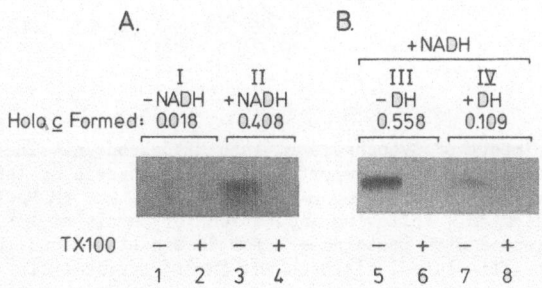

Fig. 3 **A.** Translocation of Cytochrome c to a Protease-Resistant Location Depends on NADH. Apocytochrome c, synthesized in reticulocyte lysate, was imported into mitochondria in the absence (pool I) or presence (pool II) of 5 mM NADH. Aliquots of the two samples were removed for determination of holocytochrome c formation (expressed as fmol x min^{-1} x mg^{-1}). The samples were then divided into two aliquots, one of which received Triton X-100 (1% (w/v) final concentration)(lanes 2 & 4). All four samples were treated with 40 µg proteinase K/ml for 25 min at $25^{o}C$ at a mitochondrial protein concentration of 1 mg/ml. (Using this procedure, less than 5% of adenylate kinase activity, a marker for the intermembrane space, was lost in the absence of Triton X-100 while more than 90% was lost in the presence of detergent.) Total cytochrome c was immunoprecipitated from the samples, resolved by SDS-PAGE, and visualized by fluorography. **B.** Translocation of Cytochrome c to a Protease-Resistant Location is Inhibited by Deuterohemin. Apocytochrome c was imported into mitochondria in mixtures containing 5 mM NADH and in either the absence (pool III) or presence (pool IV) of 100 µM deuterohemin. Holocytochrome c formation and translocation to a protease-resistant location were then determined as described for panel A.

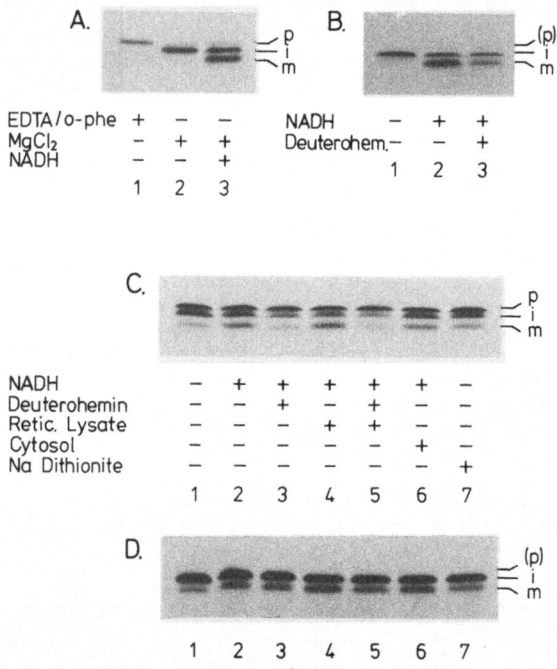

Fig. 4 **A.** Import of Cytochrome c_1 into Mitochondria. The precursor of
cytochrome c_1 was imported into mitochondria in the presence of either
5 mM EDTA plus 0.2 mM o-phenanthroline, 2.5 mM $MgCl_2$, or 5 mM NADH as
indicated. Following incubation for 30 min at $25^{\circ}C$, the samples were
digested with proteinase K for 30 min at $0^{\circ}C$ and then the mitochondria
were reisolated, dissociated in SDS sample buffer and processed as
described in Methods. p, precursor; i, intermediate; m, mature.
B. The NADH-Dependent Second Processing Step of Cytochrome c_1 is
Inhibited by Deuterohemin. The precursor of cytochrome c_1 was
imported into mitochondria, as described in panel A, in the presence
of 2.5 mM $MgCl_2$, plus 5 mM NADH or 0.1 mM deuterohemin as indicated.
C. Chase of Mitochondrial-Bound Cytochrome c_1. The precursor of
cytochrome c_1 was imported into mitochondria in the presence of 2.5 mM
$MgCl_2$ for 30 min at $25^{\circ}C$. The mitochondria were re-isolated by
centrifugation and suspended in buffer A. The bound cytochrome c_1 was
chased for 30 min at $25^{\circ}C$ in buffer A alone or in the presence of 5 mM
NADH, 0.1 mM deuterohemin, 25% (v/v) unlabelled reticulocyte lysate,
20% (v/v) cytosol fraction, or 1 mg Na dithionite/ml as indicated.
Mitochondria were reisolated and analyzed as above. **D.** Chase of
Protease-Resistant Intermediate-Size Cytochrome c_1. The experiment
was performed as described for panel C except that following the first
incubation period the samples were treated with proteinase K as
described in panel A.

was also inhibited by deuterohemin (lane 5). The additional stimulation of m-C_1 formation observed in the presence of reticulocyte lysate (lane 4) occurred only marginally (about 5%) when a cell cytosol fraction was used instead (lane 6). Like the NADH-requiring step of cytochrome c import, Na dithionite could be used as a reducing agent for m-C_1 formation with comparable efficiency (cf. lane 7 vs 2).

A similar experiment as described in figure 4C was attempted to examine only the chase from i-C_1 to m-C_1. The intermediate-size cytochrome c_1 was accumulated by importing p-C_1 into mitochondria in the absence of NADH followed by treatment with proteinase K to remove p-C_1 that might be bound to the mitochondrial surface. Under these conditions the mitochondria contained mostly i-C_1 and very little protease resistant p-C_1 (figure 4A, lane 2). The mitochondria were then re-isolated and i-C_1 was chased to m-C_1 under various conditions (figure 4D). Although the efficiency of the chase was low following this treatment, the same basic features described in figure 4C were observed, namely: m-C_1 formation was stimulated by NADH (2.2-fold; lane 2) and somewhat further in the presence of unlabelled reticulocyte lysate (40% over NADH alone; lane 4) or cytosol fraction (26% over NADH alone; lane 6); this stimulation over NADH-independent m-C_1 formation was inhibited by deuterohemin (lanes 3 and 5); formation of m-C_1 in the presence of Na dithionite (lane 7) was 85% of the amount observed with NADH (lane 2).

It therefore appears that the second processing step of cytochrome c_1 is affected by conditions which affect heme attachment to cytochrome c and thus, by analogy, might affect heme attachment to cytochrome c_1. It is possible then that heme attachment to cytochrome c_1 enhances the rate of the second processing step, though it might not be obligatory.

DISCUSSION

Cytochromes c and c_1 are imported into mitochondria by distinctly different mechanisms. They do, however, share the common requirement for covalent heme attachment during the final stages of their respective import pathways. During the import of cytochrome c, this step occurs in the mitochondrial intermembrane space (8) and is responsible for the completion of translocation of the protein across the outer membrane, probably owing to a conformational change resulting from the covalently attached heme group. To account for previous observations and those presented here we propose the following model. Apocytochrome c spontaneously inserts part way into the lipid bilayer of the outer membrane with low affinity (34-39). The partially inserted protein is then bound with high affinity by a binding protein which is localized in the intermembrane space (Köhler, Stuart and Neupert, in preparation). Heme is covalently attached to the cysteine thiols at positions 14 and 17 (universal numbering) in a reaction which is catalyzed by the enzyme cytochrome c heme lyase and is dependent on NADH plus a cytosolic cofactor. The NADH appears to be required for reduction of the heme iron to Fe(II) before this step, though it is unclear where and how this might occur (Nicholson and Neupert, in preparation). The covalently attached heme group is presumably then the nucleus around which the rest of the polypeptide chain folds, drawing the remainder of the molecule across the outer membrane as it does so to its final location in the intermembrane space.

Since cytochrome c_1 maturation shares so many common features with the heme-attaching step in cytochrome c import, it might be expected that the same enzyme catalyzes the reaction for both. Cytochrome c_1, like cytochrome c, is also exposed to the intermembrane space where heme attachment occurs in the latter case. Furthermore, there is sequence homology between the two proteins in the heme-binding region, e.g. in N. crassa (40-42):

```
Cytochrome c      (n)...KTRCAQCHILEEG...(c)
Cytochrome c₁     (n)...REVCASCHSLSRV...(c)
```

Despite these likely circumstances, however, a yeast mutant which lacks the
heme lyase enzyme for cytochrome c (cyc3⁻) contains normal levels of
cytochrome c_1 (43,44). We have found this to also be the case for a mutant
of N. crassa (cyt-2-1) that is deficient in cytochrome c heme lyase activity,
and therefore contains no cytochrome c, but which has normal levels of
cytochrome c_1 (Nargang, Nicholson and Neupert, in preparation). It therefore
appears that two separate enzymes are involved, perhaps because of
topological requirements during import and maturation.

How might the covalent attachment of heme to cytochrome c_1 be related to
the second proteolytic processing event? It is apparent that heme attachment
must precede processing of $i\text{-}C_1$ to $m\text{-}C_1$. This is indicated by the
requirement of this step for NADH and its inhibition by deuterohemin.
Similarly, a heme-deficient mutant of yeast accumulates $i\text{-}C_1$ in vivo (25-26).
One possibility is that heme attachment affects the conformation of $i\text{-}C_1$
around the region of the second processing site which enables recognition by
the second processing protease. A more likely possibilty is that following
heme attachment and the ensuing conformational changes, the second processing
site becomes accessible to the peptidase. For example, applying the
principles of the 'stop transport' model (45), the following sequence of
events might occur. The precursor of cytochrome c_1 binds to its receptor at
the outer mitochondrial membrane and the N-terminus is translocated through
the inner membrane, via contact sites, in a step which is dependent on a
membrane potential. The positively charged first part of the prepiece is
removed by the chelator-sensitive matrix peptidase leaving the more
hydrophobic 'stop transport' domain (the second part of the prepiece)
inserted through the inner membrane. At some point following translocation
of the remainder of the protein across the outer membrane, the C-terminus
(which anchors the mature protein to the inner membrane) becomes embedded in
the inner membrane. At this stage the second processing site is presumably
not accessible to the intermembrane-space-localized second processing
protease. Following covalent heme attachment, however, the resulting
conformational change might expose this site allowing the removal of the
remainder of the prepiece to occur.

Another possibility is that cytochrome c_1 follows a 'conservative
sorting' pathway similar to that of the Fe/S protein of the bc_1 complex (46)
in which $p\text{-}C_1$ would be transported completely into the matrix where the first
part of the prepiece is removed. The second part of the prepiece might then
redirect $i\text{-}C_1$ back to the inner membrane. Covalent heme attachment and the
ensuing conformational change is then responsible for drawing the protein
back across the inner membrane, exposing the second processing site in the
meantime. As the C-terminus is pulled through it anchors the protein to the
inner membrane. If this pathway were to be the case, then the coupling of
translocation to heme attachment for cytochrome c_1 might be analogous to the
same event during cytochrome c import, except that instead of being
translocated across the outer membrane into the intermembrane space (as is
the case for cytochrome c), cytochrome c_1 is translocated from the matrix
across the inner membrane to the intermembrane space. The intermembrane
space $i\text{-}C_1$ should therefore have heme attached to it while the matrix
localized $i\text{-}C_1$ species should not. Further work is required in this regard
to determine the exact route that cytochrome c_1 takes during import. Where
and how the heme attaching step occurs, and how it compares with the
equivalent step of cytochrome c import will also be of considerable interest.

REFERENCES

1. Neupert, W. & Schatz, G. (1981) Trends Biochem. Sci. 6:1-4.
2. Hay, R., Böhni, P. & Gasser, S. (1984) Biochim. Biophys. Acta 779:65-87.
3. Harmey, M.A. & Neupert, W. (1985) in The enzymes of biological membranes (Martonosi, A., ed.) 4:431-464, Plenum Press, New York.
4. Nicholson, D.W. & Neupert, W. (1987) in Protein transfer and organelle biogenesis (Das, R.C. & Robbins, P.W., eds.) Academic Press, New York (in press).
5. Schleyer, M., Schmidt, B. & Neupert, W. (1982) Eur. J. Biochem. 125:109-116.
6. Pfanner, N. & Neupert, W. (1985) EMBO J. 4:2819-2825.
7. Pfanner, N. & Neupert, W. (1986) FEBS Lett. 209:152-156.
8. Nicholson, D.W., Köhler, H. & Neupert, W. (1987) Eur. J. Biochem. 164:147-157.
9. Basile, G., DiBello, C. & Taniuchi, H. (1980) J. Biol. Chem. 255:7181-7191.
10. Teintze, M., Slaughter, M., Weiss, H. & Neupert, W. (1982) J. Biol. Chem. 257:10364-10371.
11. Schleyer, M. & Neupert, W. (1985) Cell 43:339-350.
12. Zimmermann, R., Paluch, V. & Neupert, W. (1979) FEBS Lett. 108:141-146.
13. Stewart, J.W., Sherman, F., Shipman, N.A. & Jackson, M. (1971) J. Biol. Chem. 246:7429-7445.
14. Zitomer, R.S. & Hall, B.D. (1976) J. Biol. Chem. 251:6320-6326.
15. Smith, M., Leung, D.W., Gillam, S., Astell, C.R., Montgomery, D.L. & Hall, B.D. (1979) Cell 16:753-761.
16. Matsuura, S., Arpin, M., Hannum, C., Margoliash, E., Sabatini, D.D. & Morimoto, T. (1981) Proc. Natl. Acad. Sci. USA 78:4368-4372.
17. Scarpulla, R.C., Agne, K.M. & Wu, R. (1981) J. Biol. Chem. 256:6480-6486.
18. Zimmermann, R., Hennig, B. & Neupert, W. (1981) Eur. J. Biochem. 116:455-460.
19. Korb, H. & Neupert, W. (1978) Eur. J. Biochem. 91:609-620.
20. Hennig, B. & Neupert, W. (1981) Eur. J. Biochem. 121:203-212.
21. Hennig, B., Köhler, H. & Neupert, W. (1983) Proc. Natl. Acad. Sci. USA 80:4963-4967.
22. Veloso, D., Basile, G., & Taniuchi, H. (1981) J. Biol. Chem. 256:8646-8651.
23. Taniuchi, H., Basile, G., Taniuchi, M. & Veloso, D. (1983) J. Biol. Chem. 258:10963-10966.
24. Visco, C., Taniuchi, H. & Berlett, B.S. (1985) J. Biol. Chem. 260:6133-6138.
25. Gasser, S.M., Ohashi, A., Daum, G., Böhni, P.C., Gibson, J., Reid, G.A., Yonetani, T. & Schatz, G. (1982) Proc. Natl. Acad. Sci. USA 79:267-271.
26. Ohashi, A., Gibson, J., Gregor, I. & Schatz, G. (1982) J. Biol. Chem. 257:13042-13047.
27. Wakabayashi, S., Matsubara, H., Kim, C.H., Kawai, K. & King, T.E. (1980) Biochem. Biophys. Res. Commun. 97:1548-1554.
28. Li, Y., Leonard, K. & Weiss, H. (1981) Eur. J. Biochem. 116:199-205.
29. Hennig, B. & Neupert, W. (1983) Methods Enzymol. 97:261-274.
30. Pelham, H.R.B. & Jackson, R.J. (1976) Eur. J. Biochem. 67:247-256.
31. Zimmermann, R. & Neupert, W. (1983) Methods Enzymol. 97:275-286.
32. Laemmli, U.K. (1970) Nature (Lond.) 227:680-685.
33. Bradford, M. (1976) Anal. Biochem. 72:248-254.
34. Rietveld, A., Sijens, P., Verkleij, A.J. & de Kruijff, B. (1983) EMBO J. 6:907-913.

35. Dumont, M.E. & Richards, F.M. (1984) J. Biol. Chem. 259:4147-4156.
36. Rietveld, A. & de Kruijff, B. (1984) J. Biol. Chem. 259:6704-6707.
37. Rietveld, A., Ponjee, G.A.E., Schiffers, P., Jordi, W., van de Coolwijk, P.J.F.M., Demel, R.A., Marsh, D. & de Kruijff, B. (1985) Biochim. Biophys. Acta 818:398-409.
38. Rietveld, A., Jordi, W. & de Kruijff, B. (1986) J. Biol. Chem. 261:3846-3856.
39. Berkhout, T.A., Rietveld, A. & de Kruijff, B. (1987) Biochim. Biophys. Acta 897:1-4.
40. Heller, J. & Smith, E.L. (1966) J. Biol. Chem. 241:3165-3180.
41. Lederer, F. & Simon, A.M. (1974) Biochem. Biophys. Res. Commun. 56:317-323.
42. Römisch, J., Tropschug, M., Sebald, W. & Weiss, H. (1987) Eur. J. Biochem. 164:111-115.
43. Rothstein, R.J. & Sherman, F. (1980) Genetics 94:871-889.
44. Dumont, M.E., Ernst, J.F., Hampsey, D.M. & Sherman, F. (1987) EMBO J. 6:235-241.
45. Hurt, E.C. & van Loon A.P.G.M. (1986) Trends Biochem. Sci. 11:204-207.
46. Hartl, F.-U., Schmidt, B., Wachter, E., Weiss, H. & Neupert, W. (1986) Cell 47:939-951.

IMPORT OF PROTEINS INTO MITOCHONDRIA: STRUCTURAL

AND FUNCTIONAL ROLE OF THE PREPEPTIDE

David Roise

Biocenter, University of Basel
Klingelbergstrasse 70
CH-4056 Basel, Switzerland

Nuclear-encoded proteins which are destined for import into mitochondria face at least two major problems during the course of transport from their site of synthesis in the cytoplasm to their site of function in the mitochondria. First, they must be sorted specifically to the mitochondrial outer membrane and must avoid being targeted to any of the other cytosol-exposed membranes. Second, they must somehow overcome the hydrophobic barrier of the mitochondrial membranes and pass one or both of the organelle's lipid bilayers. A molecular understanding of the mechanism of these processes is the ultimate goal of current research on this topic. This paper will present ideas about how the presequence portion of a mitochondrial precursor protein may function both in the sorting and translocation stages of import.

Many ideas about the pathway of protein import into mitochondria have been developed by analogy with the secretory pathway of eukaryotic cells (review, Wickner and Lodish, 1985). Like secreted proteins, most mitochondrial proteins are synthesized as larger precursors containing amino-terminal extensions (presequences, prepeptides, prepieces) which are cleaved by a matrix-localized metalloprotease upon energy-dependent uptake of the proteins into mitochondria (reviews, Douglas et al., 1986; Hay et al., 1984). The advent of gene fusion techniques has allowed the primary sequence requirements for functional presequence activity to be determined (Hurt and van Loon, 1986). The major result of these experiments was the demonstration that the attachment of a presequence to a non-mitochondrial protein can be sufficient for correct import of that protein into mitochondria, and therefore that presequences can act independently of their attached proteins. This suggested that the presequence probably forms a separate structural and possibly functional domain within a precursor protein.

An analysis of the primary sequences for prepeptides which target proteins to the matrix space of mitochondria has shown that they have comparable chemical compositions, but no primary sequence homology (von Heijne, 1986). The sequences are highly basic, normally are completely devoid of acidic residues, usually contain large numbers of hydroxylated amino acids, show an average overall hydrophobicity, and lack long stretches of hydrophobic residues. This contrasts with the "signal" sequences of secreted proteins in bacteria and rough ER-targeted proteins in eukaryotes which generally contain an uncharged and fairly hydrophobic

Table 1. The limiting pressure of insertion of the synthetic CoxIV presequence peptide (p25) into negatively charged phospholipid monolayers is comparable to those of small peptide toxins.

Peptide	Monolayer Lipid	Limiting Pressure (mN/m)	Reference
p25	Mitochondrial lipid	49	Roise et al. 1986
d-lysin	DPPG	31.4	Bhakoo et al. 1982
Melittin	DPPG	40.0	
CTX I	DLPS	32.0	Bougis et al. 1981
CTX II	DLPS	32.5	
CTX III	DLPS	33.0	
CTX IV	DLPS	45.0	
Melittin	DLPS	42.5	
NTX I	DLPS	15	
NTX III	DLPS	15	

CTX = Cardiotoxin, NTX = Neurotoxin, DPPG = Dipalmitoyl phosphatidylglycerol, DLPS = Dilauryl phosphatidylserine

stretch of amino acids (Briggs and Gierasch, 1986). The lack of primary sequence homology suggests that a higher order structure may be important for the function of the presequences in targeting proteins to the mitochondrial membranes.

Examination of the known matrix-targeting sequences suggested to us (Roise et al., 1986) that these sequences could potentially form a-helices of high hydrophobic moment (Eisenberg, 1984) and a statistical analysis of the sequences gave further support for this idea (von Heijne, 1986). In the case of the cytochrome c oxidase subunit IV (CoxIV) presequence, the potential for forming a helix with separate hydrophilic and hydrophobic faces is striking (Figure 1). Such an amphiphilic structure would be expected to have chemical properties of a surfactant (Kaiser and Kézdy, 1984), and synthetic peptides corresponding to the CoxIV presequence have indeed been shown to behave as amphiphiles (Roise et al., 1986). Figure 2 shows the influence of a 25-residue CoxIV peptide (p25) on the surface pressure of a monolayer of mitochondrial phospholipids at various peptide concentrations (A) and at various initial monolayer surface pressures (B). Comparison of the peptide's limiting pressure of insertion with those of several small peptide toxins which are thought to act via direct membrane interaction is shown in Table 1. These experiments revealed that the presequence peptides could strongly interact with phospholipids,

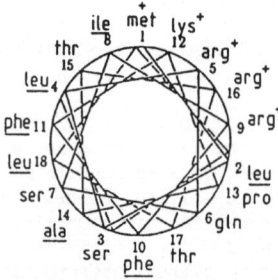

Fig. 1. A helical wheel representation of the amino-terminus of the precursor to yeast CoxIV.

presumably via a combination of ionic and hydrophobic effects, and
suggested that an initial binding of mitochondrial precursors to the
mitochondrial outer membrane may occur via hydrophobic contacts between
the amphiphilic presequence and phospholipid and/or hydrophobic proteins
within the membrane bilayer. That the effect is not due simply to ionic
binding of the highly cationic prepeptide with negative charges on the
phospholipid is suggested by the lack of surface activity of the
neurotoxins NTXI and NTXIII. These peptides are also basic, but lack
exposed hydrophobic domains and are not thought to function by direct
binding to the phospholipid bilayer. There is also an effect of the
phospholipid head group on binding of the mitochondrial prepeptide to
synthetic phospholidid monolayers; the 25-residue prepeptide has a higher
affinity for lipid monolayers containing a net negative charge (Tamm,
1986). This has been interpreted as showing that the peptide's binding to
a monolayer is a combination of ion-pairing between the peptide's basic
residues and the phospholipid head groups in addition to direct
hydrophobic interaction.

The relevance of the high surface activity of a presequence for the
import of a protein into mitochondria is not known. Clearly, binding of
the presequence to mitochondria is a necessary first step in the import
process, but the problem remains as to what determines the specificity of
binding of the presequence to only mitochondrial and not to other
membranes exposed to the cytoplasm. One possible explanation for the lack
of precursor missorting to other membranes in a growing cell is that the
binding interaction is reversible, and since only mitochondria contain a

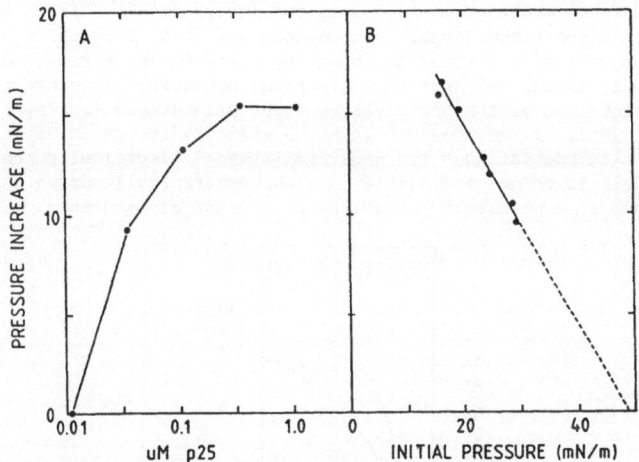

Figure 2. A synthetic CoxIV presequence peptide binds
strongly to a pure phospholipid monolayer. A) A monolayer of
yeast mitochondrial phospholipid was spread from
hexane:ethanol (9:1) onto the surface of a Langmuir trough
containing 25 mL 5 mM KP_i pH 7.0. The initial surface
pressure was 20 mN/m, and the surface area was held constant
at 40 cm^2. Various concentrations of a 25-residue peptide
corresponding to the amino-terminus of the yeast CoxIV
precursor protein were injected into the sub-phase, and the
final increase in surface pressure was measured. B) A
similar experiment was performed, except that the amount of
lipid spread was varied to give different initial surface
pressures at a constant 40 cm^2 surface area. The peptide
concentration used in this case was 0.14 uM.

functional import machinery, all precursors are eventually driven
kinetically into the mitochondria. There is some evidence that prepeptide
binding to a phospholipid monolayer can be reversible (Tamm, 1986).
Alternatively, there may be components within mitochondria which increase
a precursor's affinity for the organelle by tightly binding the precursor
after its initial interaction with the bilayer. Such components have been
postulated from experiments showing protease sensitivity for both binding
and import activities of isolated mitochondria and mitochondrial outer
membranes (Zwizinski et al., 1983,1984; Riezman et al., 1983; Ohba and
Schatz, 1987).

An additional chemical property of the synthetic presequence peptides
is their ability to disrupt phospholipid bilayers (Roise et al., 1986).
Figure 3 shows the effect of various concentrations of the 25-residue
prepeptide on sonicated vesicles containing the self-quenching dye,
carboxyfluorescein. Increasing fluorescence is due to release of trapped
dye upon vesicle disruption by the peptide. The rate of fluorescence
dequenching is dependent on the peptide concentration, and is also
accelerated by application of a valinomycin-induced potassium diffusion
potential having a negative internal polarity (Roise et al., 1986). This
result could be important for two reasons. First, the bilayer-perturbing
effect of a presequence may play a role in forming a pathway for the rest
of the protein to follow. It is not yet known what sort of protein import
apparatus is associated with the mitochondria itself, but perhaps by
partial disruption of one or both of the mitochondrial bilayers, a low
energy route for protein translocation could be created. The second point
concerns the role of the membrane potential in protein import. An
energized inner membrane is necessary for import of all matrix-localized
proteins. Pfanner and Neupert have determined that it is the electrical
($\Delta\Psi$) component of the total protonmotive force which is required (Pfanner
and Neupert, 1985), and that this eletrical potential is necessary only
for translocation of the positively-charged presequence (Schleyer and
Neupert, 1985). Taken together with the vesicle-disruption experiments,
these results suggest that the negative internal electrical potential of
mitochondria is being used simply to electrophoretically drive the
presequence of a precursor across the mitochondrial membranes, and that an

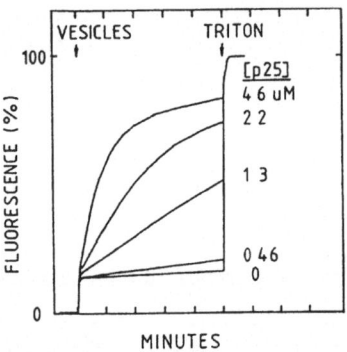

Figure 3. The synthetic prepeptide induces release of trapped
dye from sonicated vesicles. Vesicles containing entrapped
carboxyfluorescein were prepared by sonication of synthetic
palmitoyl oleoyl phosphatidyl choline: bovine brain
cardiolipin (2:1) as described (Roise et al., 1986). Release
of trapped dye from the vesicles in the presence of various
peptide concentrations was followed as fluorescence increase
versus time. Detergent was added to determine 100% release
values.

analogous process may be occurring in the model system with vesicles. It remains to be determined what components in the mitochondria modulate the perturbing effect of the prepeptides on a membrane. Several model presequence peptides have been shown to have a disruptive effect on the mitochondrial membrane potential (Gillespie et al., 1985; Ito et al., 1985; Roise et al., 1986), but presumably this is only due to the large concentrations of model peptides presented to the mitochondria.

An interesting system which may be relevant to the possible role of the mitochondrial membrane potential in the sorting of proteins to mitochondria has been developed by Chen et al.. Using the cationic, membrane-permeable dye, rhodamine 123, these workers show massive and specific accumulation of the dye in mitochondria of living cells (Chen et al., 1982). This demonstrates clearly that cations which are able to penetrate mitochondrial membranes will be specifically concentrated there. As long as there exists a facile pathway for transfer of precursors into mitochondria, the positively-charged presequence should effect their specific accumulation in the organelle. Other basic, non-mitochondrial proteins would be excluded from mitochondria because their positively-charged regions lack the amphiphilicity necessary to bind to mitochondria and to interact with the mitochondrial import machinery.

Mitochondrial targeting sequences therefore seem ideally suited for their job in guiding proteins to the organelle and getting the protein started in its transfer across the mitochondrial membranes: they are located in exposed positions at the amino-termini of transported proteins to allow their interaction with the mitochondrial surface; they can directly insert into phospholipid bilayers to effect binding to the mitochondrial outer membrane; and they are highly basic to interact with the internal negative inner membrane potential and to be pulled specifically into mitochondria. Further work should determine components associated with mitochondria which participate in the process, and structural or conformational requirements of the mature protein which are also important for its ability to be transported.

Acknowledgement. The author is a fellow of the Jane Coffin Childs Memorial Fund for Medical Research.

References

Bhakoo, M., Birkbeck, T. H., and Freer, J. H., 1982, Biochem., 21:6879-6883.
Bougis, P., Rochat, H., Pierni, G., and Verger, R., 1981, Biochem., 20:4915-4920.
Briggs, M. S. and Gierasch, L. M., 1986, Adv. Prot. Chem., 38:109-180.
Chen, L. B., Summerhayes, I. C., Johnson, L. V., Walsh, M. L., Bernal, S. D., and Lampidis, T. J., 1982, CSH Symp. Quant. Biol., 46:141-155.
Douglas, M. G., McCammon, M. T., and Vassarotti, A., 1986, Microbiol. Rev., 50:166-178.
Eisenberg, D., 1984, Annu. Rev. Biochem., 53:595-623.
Gillespie, L. L., Argan, C., Taneja, A. T., Hodges, R. S., Freeman, K. B., and Shore, G. C., 1985, J. Biol. Chem., 260:16045-16048.
Hay, R., Boehni, P., and Gasser, S., 1984, Biochim. Biophys. Acta, 779:65-87.
Hurt, E. C. and van Loon, A. P. G. M., 1986, TIBS, 11:204-207.
Ito, A., Ogishima, T., Ou, W., Omura, T., Aoyagi, H., Lee, S., Mihara, H., and Izumiya, N., 1985, J. Biochem. (Tokyo), 98:1571-1582.
Kaiser, E. T. and Kézdy, F. J., 1984, Science, 223:249-255.
Ohba, M. and Schatz, G., 1987, submitted.
Pfanner, P. and Neupert, W., 1985, EMBO J., 4:2819-2825.
Riezman, H., Hay, R., Witte, C., Nelson, N., and Schatz, G., 1983, EMBO J., 2:1113-1118.

Roise, D., Horvath, S. J., Tomich, J. M., Richards, J. H., and Schatz, G., 1986, EMBO J., 5:1327-1334.

Schleyer, M. and Neupert, W., 1985, Cell, 43:339-350.

Tamm, L. K., 1986, Biochem., 25:7470-7476.

Von Heijne, G., 1986, EMBO J., 5:1335-1342.

Wickner, W. T. and Lodish, H. F., 1985, Science, 230:400-407.

Zwizinski, C., Schleyer, M., and Neupert, W., 1983, J. Biol. Chem., 258:4071-4074.

Zwizinski, C., Schleyer, M., and Neupert, W., 1984, J. Biol. Chem., 259:7850-7856.

INTERACTION OF THE MITOCHONDRIAL PRECURSOR PROTEIN APOCYTOCHROME C WITH

MODEL MEMBRANES AND ITS IMPLICATIONS FOR PROTEIN TRANSLOCATION

B. de Kruijff[1], A. Rietveld[2], W. Jordi[2], T.A. Berkhout[2], R.A. Demel[2], H. Görrissen[3] and D. Marsh[3]
1Inst. Mol. Biol. and Medical Biotechnol., 2Dept. Biochem., Univ. of Utrecht, Padualaan 8, 3584 CH Utrecht, NL and 3Max-Planck Inst. Biophysikalische Chemie, Abt. Spektroskopie, D-3400 Göttingen, FRG

INTRODUCTION

The majority of mitochondrial proteins are synthesized in the cytosol on free ribosomes in the form of precursors which are subsequently imported into the organelle by a posttranslational transport step[1]. Depending on the final destination of the protein, either insertion into or translocation across one or two membranes has to occur. During this process the precursor (apoprotein) is converted into the mature holoprotein.

Apocytochrome c (apo-c), the heme-free precursor of cytochrome c, has been extensively used to study the molecular details of posttranslational protein import. These studies have not only given insight into the import possible mechanism of protein translocation across the outer mitochondrial membrane but also might serve as a more general model for protein insertion and translocation. Apo-c and cytochrome c have identical polypeptide chains of 104 amino acids (Fig. 1), but they differ in secondary and tertiary structure. Cytochrome c is a highly structured, nearly spherical protein, whereas apo-c has virtually no structure[2]. After synthesis on free polysomes apo-c binds to the mitochondrial outer membrane possibly involving a specific receptor[3]. During transport across this membrane the heme group is attached[4], whereafter the cytochrome c reaches its final location at the outside of the inner mitochondrial membrane[5].

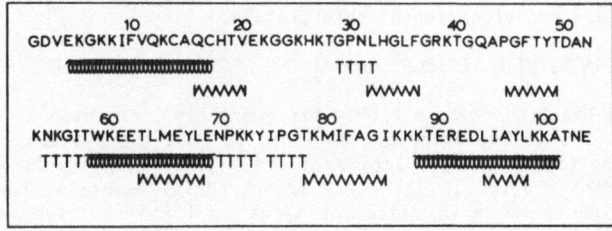

Fig. 1. Primary structure of apo-c and predicted secondary structure according to[8].

The molecular details of the actual insertion and translocation steps of apo-c and for precursor proteins in general are obscure. In principle, transport can occur either via protein tunnels, protein-lipid complexes or solely through the lipid part of membranes (Fig. 2). Protein tunnels are at yet fully hypothetical. However, there are several arguments[6,18], which suggest that membrane lipids are involved in the insertion and translocation processes.

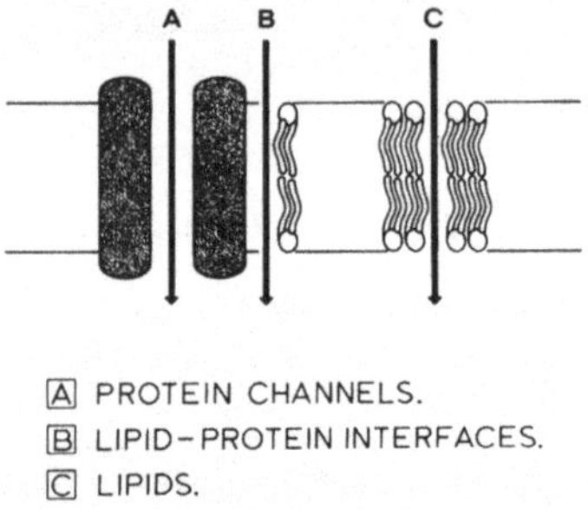

Fig. 2. Possible protein insertion/ translocation pathways in membranes.

A PROTEIN CHANNELS.
B LIPID-PROTEIN INTERFACES.
C LIPIDS.

Potential sites for protein insertion and translocation involving membrane lipids in a bilayer organization are for instance[6] the structural defects which can occur at the interface of integral membrane proteins and lipids or at the interface between lipids in the gel and liquid-crystalline state (Fig. 3). Also inverted non-lamellar lipid structures[6] of the kind schematically illustrated in Fig. 4 for instance might provide transient sites especially for the translocation of the more polar parts of proteins.

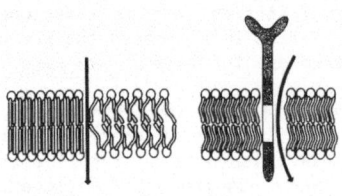

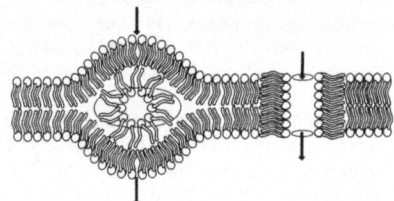

Fig. 3. Packing defects are potential sites for protein insertion and translocation in a bilayer.

Fig. 4. Potential non-bilayer structures involved in protein insertion and translocation.

Apo-c can be readily made in large quantities by the chemical removal of the heme group from the holoprotein[2]. This allows for detailed biophysical investigations of this precursor protein. It is the aim of this chapter to review our recent studies on interactions between apo-c and lipids and to construct from the results of these studies a model for the membrane insertion and translocation of this protein.

APO-C INTERACTS WITH VESICLES CONTAINING NEGATIVELY CHARGED LIPIDS

Horse heart apo-c is a highly basic protein containing a net +9 charge at neutral pH. It therefore can be expected that the protein will strongly bind to negatively charged lipids of which phosphatidylserine (PS) is the most abundant species in the outer mitochondrial membrane. The results of binding experiments with different types of lipid vesicles indeed demonstrated[7-9] that the protein can bind with very high affinity to PS vesicles, but virtually not to vesicles of the neutral phosphatidylcholine (PC). In the physiological range of ionic strength and pH the binding is accompanied by vesicle aggregation but not by vesicle fusion[8]. In case of small unilamellar PS vesicles, a dissociation constant of 0.04 µM was determined by fluorescence measurements of the single Trp-59[9]. This value is very close to the value of binding to the mitochondrial outer membrane[3]. The affinity of the protein for the bilayer of the less curved large unilamellar vesicles (LUV) is less but still in the μM range (Table I).

Table 1. Apo-c binding to PC/PS vesicles. For details see[8].

PC/PS (M/M)	Kd (μM)	n(PS/apo-c)
85/15	21 ± 4	10 ± 2
70/30	14 ± 6	11 ± 2
50/50	23 ± 5	8 ± 1
30/70	16 ± 5	10 ± 1
0/100	15 ± 4	9 ± 1

This binding is nearly charge stoichiometric and thus primarily electrostatic and interestingly nearly independent of the PS fraction suggesting that the protein creates its own micro domain which is enriched in PS. Direct evidence for the creating of such micro domains came from fluorescence spectroscopy[9,10] and electron spin resonance (ESR) measurements[10]. For instance, when apo-c is titrated with mixed PC/PS vesicles in which either the PC or PS component contained a parinaric acid chain at the 2-position[10] the fluorescence of the Trp-59 residue was quenched by an energy transfer mechanism, most when the parinaric acid was present in the PS component (Fig. 5). Thus, the immediate environment of the protein in the model membrane is enriched in the PS component.

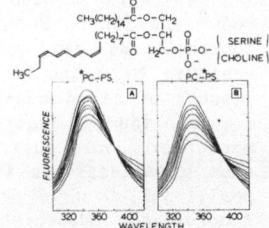

Fig. 5. Quenching of Trp-59 fluorescence of apo-c by 1-palmitoyl-2-parinaroyl-PC/PS in mixed PC/PS (1:1) LUV. In A and B the parinaric acid is in PC or PS, respectively. The top traces represent the fluorescence emission spectra of a 50 μg/ml apo-c solution. Subsequent traces are in the presence of increasing amounts of vesicles. For details see[10].

APO-C PENETRATES INTO THE HYDROPHOBIC PART OF A MODEL MEMBRANE

Injection of apo-c under a monolayer of either PS or PC results in a large increase in surface pressure only in case of negatively charged lipids[11], demonstrating that following the electrostatic interaction the protein penetrates into the hydrophobic part of the lipid monolayer (Fig. 6).

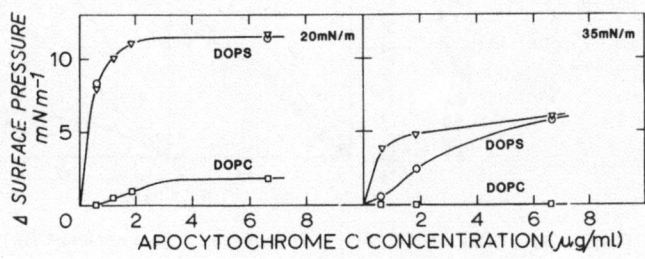

Fig. 6. Apo-c penetration in monolayers of cardiolipin (∇-∇), DOPS (o-o) and DOPC (□-□) at initial surface pressures of 20 and 35 mN/m. For details see[11].

217

The area of the protein occupied in the monolayer was determined by quantifying the surface expansion at constant surface pressure and by determining the amount of protein in the monolayer by using radiolabelled proteins and was found to be 700-900 $Å^2$/molecule[12]. The existence of extensive hydrophobic interactions between apo-c and the acyl chains of negatively charged lipids could also be demonstrated using differential scanning calorimetry (DSC). Figure 7 illustrates this for the synthetic dimyristoylphosphatidyl glycerol (DMPG), a negatively charged lipid which resembles PS in its interactions with apo-c. Addition of relatively small amounts of protein causes a drastic reduction in the energy content of the gel to liquid-crystalline phase transition. From the proportional decrease in ΔH as a function of the apo-c/PG ratio it can be concluded that one apo-c molecule can prevent 150 PG molecules from undergoing the cooperative phase transition. Such strong effects are typical for integral membrane proteins or very hydrophobic polypeptides and thus support the view that apo-c penetrates the hydrocarbon part of the bilayer.

Fig. 7. Apo-c eliminates the cooperative gel -> liquid-crystalline transition of DMPG (mid point transition temperature 23°C). For details see[11].

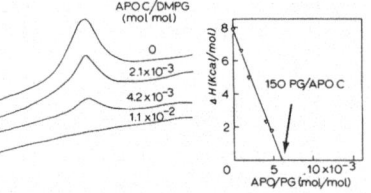

The depth of penetration can be monitored with fluorescence spectroscopy[9] and ESR[13]. Bromine atoms covalently attached to the acyl chain of phospholipids can quench the fluorescence of nearby polypeptide Trp residues by means of a collisional quenching process. When increasing amounts of mixed non-bromine PC/PS (1:1) vesicles are added to an apo-c solution the Trp fluorescence intensity increases[9,11] most likely due to a more hydrophobic environment of the indole ring system (Fig. 8). When in such mixed vesicles the 2-sn-acyl chain of PC contains bromine atoms at position 2, 6 and 7 or 11 and 12, the fluorescence increase is less due to fluorescence quenching[9]. The quenching efficiency is strongest when the bromines are present at position 6, 7, suggesting a penetration of the Trp-containing part of the protein some 7-8 Å deep in the bilayer[9].

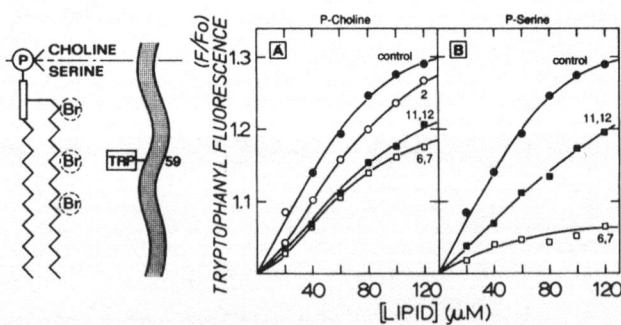

Fig. 8. Quenching of apo-c (4 μM) tryptophanyl fluorescence by PS/PC (1:1) vesicles containing non-brominated (control) or brominated acyl chains. The bromine atoms are located at the indicated positions in either PC (P-choline) or PS (P-serine). The left part gives the rationale of the experiment. For details see[9].

218

The quenching is much more obvious when the bromine atoms are present on the acyl chain of the PS component in line with the preferential interaction between apo-c and the negatively charged lipids.

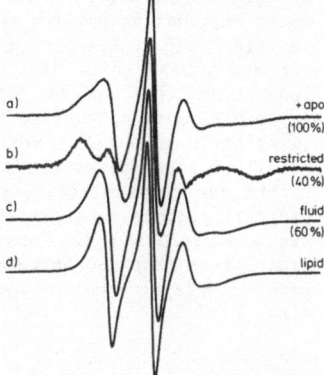

Fig. 9. ESR spectra of 12-PG spin label in bovine PS dispersions containing a saturating amount of apo-c (a), difference spectrum (b) obtained by subtracting (c) from (a), (d) experimental spectrum in the absence of apo-c. For details see[13].

ESR measurements of phospholipids spin-labelled at different positions on the sn-2 chain indicate a generalized decrease in mobility of the lipids while the characteristic flexibility gradient towards the terminal methyl end of the chain is maintained on binding of apo-c to PS dispersions[13]. In addition, a second, more motionally restricted component is observed with lipids labelled close to the terminal methyl ends of the chains (Fig. 9). This second component is not observed on binding of the holocytochrome c and can be taken as direct evidence for deep penetration of apo-c into the lipid bilayer.

APO-C CAN (PARTIALLY) TRANSLOCATE ACROSS A PURE LIPID BILAYER

Figure 10 illustrates a translocation assay for apo-c in a lipid vesicle system[8,14,15]. PC/PS (1:1) LUV are prepared containing enclosed trypsin[8]. Outside trypsin is washed away by centrifugation and the residual outside trypsin activity is blocked by soy bean trypsin inhibitor (SBTI).

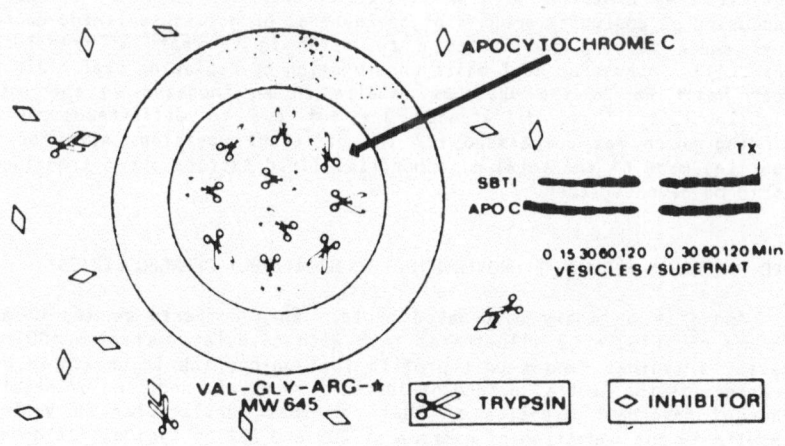

Fig. 10. Schematic representation of the apo-c translocation assay with LUV of PS/PC (1:1). For details see text and[8].

When apo-c is added to these vesicles a time-dependent degradation of apo-c in the vesicles could be demonstrated[8]. This is for instance illustrated by a time-dependent decrease in intensity of the apo-c band after gel electrophoresis (compare with constant SBTI band). This is not due to apo-c degradation outside the vesicles as incubation of supernatant of such vesicles with a similar amount of apo-c does not result in a decrease in the apo-c band (Fig. 10). Apo-c degradation is also not due to transient rupture of the vesicle bilayer by the protein causing rapid release of trypsin because disrupting the bilayer with the detergent Triton X-100 (TX) immediately after the addition of the protein to the vesicle does not result in apo-c digestion due to the large excess of SBTI which immediately blocks the trypsin activity. Simultaneous addition of apo-c and a chromogenic tripeptide substrate of trypsin to the vesicles only results in apo-c digestion proving the specificity of the translocation process[8]. These experiments thus demonstrate that a substantial amount of apo-c reaches the inner monolayer surface upon external addition to these pure lipid vesicles.

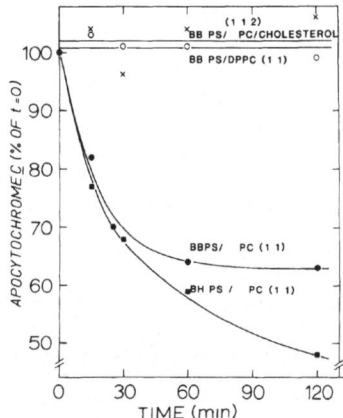

Fig. 11. Influence of lipid composition on apo-c translocation. For details see[8]. BBPS: PS from beef brain, PC: PC from egg, DPPC: dipalmitoyl-PC.

The apo-c translocation is dependent on the lipid composition of the vesicles. As expected no translocation occurs for pure PC vesicles[8,15]. Inclusion of equimolar amounts of cholesterol or gel state lipids decreases acyl chain packing and causes a reduction in the rate of translocation (Fig. 11). Increasing acyl chain unsaturation by replacing beef brain PS by beef heart PS in the vesicles results in an increase in the rate of translocation. These differences are not due to differences in apo-c binding which was comparable for the different vesicles. Also for lipid vesicles made of the total mitochondrial lipid extract apo-c translocation could be demonstrated[8].

APO-C CHANGES STRUCTURE UPON BINDING TO NEGATIVELY CHARGED LIPIDS

Apo-c is a highly disordered protein when compared to the holocytochrome c[2]. Figure 12 illustrates this with circular dichroism (CD) which reveal a typical random coil profile for apo-c which is unaltered by the presence of the neutral detergent lubrol[11]. However, addition of negatively charged detergent micelles of SDS[11] or small unilamellar PS vesicles[16] results in the induction of extrema at 209 and 222 nm typical for α-helical structures (α-helix ± content 27%). For comparison, the CD spectrum of cytochrome c in buffer is included which is characterized by a similar content of α-helix. The α-helices of apo-c induced after interaction with

220

negatively charged lipids are probably located at residues 4-17, 58-69 and 88-101 because their structure prediction methods indicate the highest probability for α-helix (▨▨▨▨) formation[11]. In addition, some small stretches of β-strand (ᴡᴡᴡ) and β-turns (TT) are predicted. Nowhere in the primary structure (Fig. 1) continuous stretches of hydrophobic amino acid residues occur which are long enough to span either as α-helix or β-strand the hydrophobic part of a bilayer.

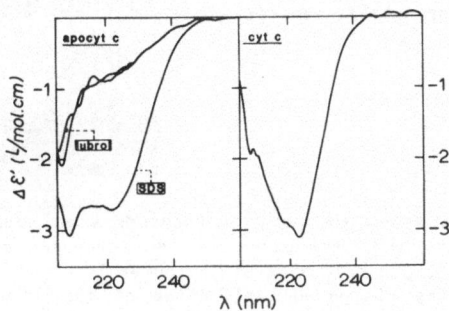

Fig. 12. CD spectra of cytochrome c and apo-c in the absence and presence of lubrol and SDS. For details see[11].

APO-C-LIPID VERSUS THE CYTOCHROME C-LIPID INTERACTION

The net charge of the polypeptide part of both proteins is similar, therefore it is not unexpected that both proteins bind electrostatically to model membranes of negatively charged lipids[7]. However, apo-c binding to PS is stronger. More interesting differences are found in the interaction of these proteins with the phospholipid acyl chains. DSC experiments demonstrate more significant acyl chain perturbation of the apo-protein[7]. ESR experiments revealed that only the apo-protein can deeply insert into the bilayer[13]. Accordingly only the apo-c[7,14,15] and not cytochrome c[17] can translocate across a vesicle bilayer. The covalent coupling of the heme group thus renders the cytochrome c translocation incompetent, probably because it fixes the protein into a specific folded conformation.

AN APO-C MEMBRANE TRANSLOCATION MODEL

Figure 13 is a pictorial description of the apo-c-lipid interaction in model membranes and schematically represents the insertion and translocation process[18]. The initially non-structured protein binds electrostatically to the negatively charged phospholipids causing them to cluster and to form a translocation site. Subsequently, the protein penetrates into the hydrophobic part of the bilayer which probably is accompanied by the formation of 3 α-helical segments. In order to accommodate the charged amino acid residues into the bilayer either some of the negatively charged phospholipids have to adopt temporarily a non-bilayer conformation (shown in this figure) or alternatively polypeptide-polypeptide interactions cause a favorable hydrophobic exterior of part of the polypeptide aggregate (not shown in Fig. 13).

In this respect the observation of PS induced oligomer formation of apo-c in model membranes could be of relevance. After the insertion process the C-terminus is assumed to be still located at the exterior surface of the vesicle. The N-terminus where at cysteine 14 and 17 the heme group has to be covalently coupled is assumed to cross the bilayer. In extrapolation

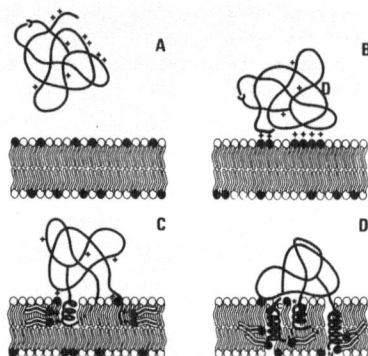

Fig. 13. Schematic representation of the interaction of apo-c with mixed PC (o)/ PS (●) bilayers. For details see text and[18].

this model to the apo-c import in mitochondria we suggested[18] that the interaction of apo-c with the outer membrane proceeds similarly but that subsequently cardiolipin molecules of the outer layer of the inner membrane are involved in the charge neutralization of the penetrated positively charged apo-c segments, possibly in the form of (transient) contact sites between the outer and inner membrane. Subsequent enzymatic heme coupling and folding of the polypeptide chain around the heme moiety results in formation of cytochrome c which then is attached to the outside of the inner membrane by high affinity binding to the cytochrome c oxidase and cardiolipin. We furthermore proposed[18] that apo-c import and possibly import of other mitochondrial precursor protein with positively charged N-terminal presequences might (in part) be coupled to the inward flow of PS molecules from endoplasmic reticulum to inner mitochondrial membrane.

REFERENCES

1. R. Hay, P. Böhni and S. Gasser, Biochim. Biophys. Acta 779:65 (1984).
2. W.R. Fisher, H. Taniuchi and C.B. Anfinsen, J. Biol. Chem. 248: 3188 (1973).
3. B. Hennig, H. Koehler and W. Neupert, Proc. Natl. Acad. Sci. USA 80:4963 (1983).
4. B. Hennig and W. Neupert, Eur. J. Biochem. 121:203 (1981).
5. R.A. Capaldi, Biochim. Biophys. Acta 694:291 (1982).
6. B. de Kruijff, P.R. Cullis, A.J. Verkleij, M.J. Hope, C.J.A. van Echteld, T.F. Taraschi, P. van Hoogevest, J.A. Killian, A. Rietveld and A.T.M. van der Steen, in "Progress in Protein-Lipid Interactions", A. Watts and J.J.H.M. de Pont, eds., Elsevier Publ. Co., Amsterdam, Vol. 1, pp. 89-142 (1985).
7. A. Rietveld, P. Sijens, A.J. Verkleij and B. de Kruijff, EMBO J. 2:907 (1983).
8. A. Rietveld, W. Jordi, B. de Kruijff, J. Biol. Chem. 261:3846 (1986).
9. T.A. Berkhout, A. Rietveld and B. de Kruijff, Biochim. Biophys. Acta 897:1 (1987).
10. A. Rietveld, T.A. Berkhout, A. Roenhorst, D. Marsh and B. de Kruijff, Biochim. Biophys. Acta 858:38 (1986).
11. A. Rietveld, G.A.E. Ponjee, P. Schiffers, W. Jordi, P.J.F.M. van de Coolwijk, R.A. Demel, D. Marsh and B. de Kruijff, Biochim. Biophys. Acta 818:398 (1985).
12. M. Pilon, W. Jordi, B. de Kruijff and R.A. Demel, Biochim. Biophys. Acta, submitted (1987).
13. H. Görrissen, D. Marsh, A. Rietveld and B. de Kruijff, Biochemistry 25:2904 (1986).

14. M.E. Dumont and F.M. Richards, J. Biol. Chem. 259:4147 (1984).
15. A. Rietveld and B. de Kruijff, J. Biol. Chem. 259:6704 (1984).
16. E. Walter, D. Margolis, R. Mohan and R. Blumenthal, Membrane Biochem. 6:217 (1986).
17. B.L. Geller and W. Wickner, J. Biol. Chem. 260:13281 (1985).
18. A. Rietveld and B. de Kruijff, Biosci. Reports 6:775 (1986).

INFLUENCE OF THYROID HORMONES ON THE EXPRESSION OF NUCLEAR

GENES ENCODING SUBUNITS OF THE CYTOCHROME bc$_1$ COMPLEX

Vigg Joste and B. Dean Nelson

Department of Biochemistry
Arrhenius Laboratory
University of Stockholm
Stockholm, Sweden

INTRODUCTION

Thyroid hormone is the most important physiological regulator of mammalian mitochondrial biosynthesis known to date. It is well accepted that thyroid hormone acts via nuclear receptors (Tata, 1980) to regulate the expression of selected nuclear genes (Seelig et al., 1981; Ivarie et al., 1981; Liaw et al., 1983; Dillmann et al., 1983; Magnuson et al., 1985). However, the hormone also activates mitochondrial protein synthesis (Freeman et al., 1963; Roodyn et al., 1965; Nelson et al., 1980; Nelson et al., 1984), leading to an increase in translation of all mitochondrial gene products (Nelson et al., 1980; Nelson et al., 1984).

We have initiated studies to elucidate the relative importance of nuclear and mitochondrial gene expression during mitochondrial biogenesis in thyroid hormone treated rats (Nelson et al., 1980; Nelson et al., 1984; Nelson et al., 1987). We have shown that, under conditions where mito-chondrial numbers (Gustafsson et al., 1965) and inner membrane area (Gustafsson et al., 1965; Jakovcic et al., 1978) are increased, the syn-thesis of only a limited set of inner membrane proteins is induced by thyroid hormone (Nelson et al., 1984). Thus, accumulation of new mito-chondrial membrane in thyroid hormone treated animals is not associated with general activation of the many genes coding for inner membrane polypeptides. The present study describes our initial attempts to iden-tify this limited set of nuclear genes and their translation products.

METHODS AND MATERIALS

Male Sprague-Dawley rats made hypothyroid by administration of Tapazole (Nelson et al., 1980) were given daily injections of 20 μg triiodothyronine/100 g body weight for 3-6 days. Free polysomes prepared by the method of Ramsey and Steele (1976) were translated in rabbit reticulocyte lysates (Pelham and Jackson, 1976). Immunoabsorption of samples from hypothyroid and hormone-treated rats was carried out in parallel. Methods for immunoabsorption, electrophoresis and fluorography were described earlier (Kuzela et al., 1986). Densitometric scans of fluorographs were done with an LKB Ultroscan Laser Densitometer.

RESULTS

Since mitochondrial proteins are translated almost exclusively on free polysomes, these preparations were used for in vitro translation. The yield of free polysomes (mg polysomal RNA/g tissue) from livers of hypothyroid rats or hypothyroid rats treated with triiodothyronine is summarized in Table 1. Although small hormone-dependent increases were observed in all paired experiments, these differences were obscured in a larger sample population by the variation between experiments (Table 1). These results suggest that, in spite of the lack of statistical significance, small increases in polysome yield might occur after hormone treatment (Dillmann et al., 1978). In contrast, the efficiency of translation of the polysomes was not significantly altered by hormone treatment as judged by the incorporation of ^{35}S-methionine by equal amounts of polysomes under identical translation conditions (Table 1). This is also confirmed by the intensity of the labeled polypeptides detected by fluorography of lysates programmed with equal amounts of polysomes and resolved on SDS-PAGE (Fig. 1A).

Fig. 1 shows, in addition to the total polypeptides translated in vitro from free polysomes, polypeptides immunoabsorbed from the translation mixtures using antibodies against total rat liver cytosolic proteins (Fig. 1B) or against mitochondrial matrix proteins (Fig. 1C). The pattern of translated polypeptides in all samples is only slightly changed by triiodothyronine treatment. Although the majority of the translated polypeptides are, admittedly, not resolved on one dimensional gels, this experiment shows, in accordance with our previous results for inner membrane proteins (Nelson et al., 1984) and results of others on general cellular proteins (Seelig et al., 1981; Ivarie et al., 1981; Dillmann et al., 1983; Magnuson et al., 1985), that only a limited set of mRNA species are affected by hormone treatment.

Since both the numbers of mitochondrial profiles (Gustafsson et al., 1965) and the area of the inner membrane (Gustafsson et al., 1965; Jakovcic et al., 1978) are expanded by thyroid hormone treatment, it must be assumed that an accumulation of all inner membrane polypeptides takes

Table 1. The Effects of Thyroid Hormone on the Yield of Liver Polysomes and Their Ability to Support In Vitro Translation

	Yield of Polysomes (mg RNA/g liver)	In Vitro Translation (cpm/mg polysomal RNA)
Hypothyroid	0.43 ± 0.05 (6)	111,000 ± 15,000 (11)
Hypothyroid, hormone-treated	0.51 ± 0.06 (6)	117,000 ± 11,000 (11)

Free polysomes from hypothyroid and thyroid hormone-injected, hypothyroid rats were isolated and the yield was calculated assuming an absorbance at 260 nm of 25 for 1 mg polysomal RNA/ml. Equal amounts of polysomes from both groups were translated for 30 min in reticulocyte lysates. Values are expressed as the mean ± S.E. Numbers of experiments are given in parentheses.

place. However, since the synthesis of only a limited number of nuclear-
encoded inner membrane polypeptides is regulated by thyroid hormone
(Nelson et al., 1984), their identification could lead to a better understanding of genetic control of mammalian mitochondrial biosynthesis. To
this end, the effects of thyroid hormone on a number of specific mitochondrial polypeptides was analyzed (Fig. 2).

Several polypeptides were quantitatively immunoabsorbed from lysates
programmed with polysomes from hypothyroid rats or from hypothyroid,
hormone-treated rats (Fig. 2). A second immunoabsorption of the same
sample removed no, or only barely detectable, amounts of the translated
polypeptide. Paired samples were used in which polysomes from treated and
untreated hypothyroid rats were isolated, translated and immunoabsorbed
in parallel.

Table 2 summarizes the results obtained from several experiments. An
induction factor was calculated for each polypeptide from the densitometric
scans of paired samples such as shown in Fig. 2. The largest and most consistent increase was seen in cytochrome c_1 which was induced about 2.6-fold
All samples were induced, and 70% of the samples were induced more than
2-fold. The difference in induction between cytochrome c_1 and the other

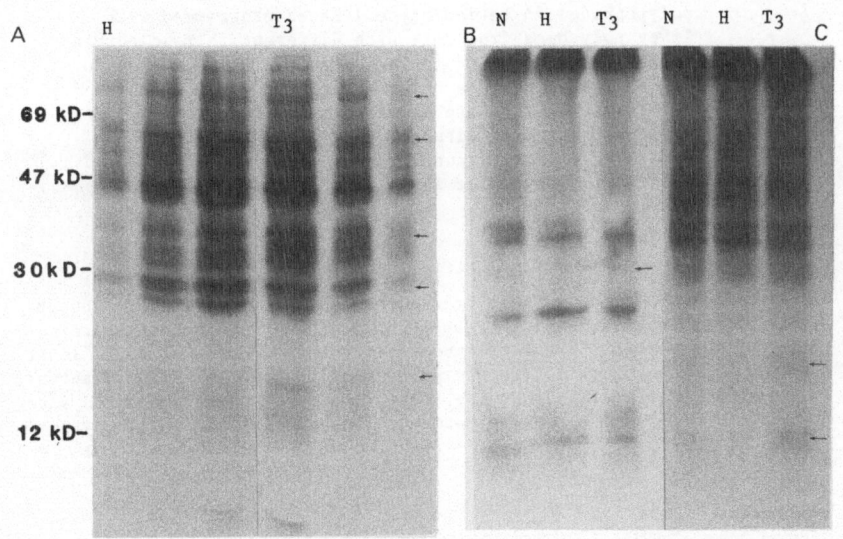

Fig. 1   Analysis of the polypeptides translated in reticulocyte lysates
         programmed with liver polysomes from rats with different thyroid
         hormone states. Polysomes from hypothyroid (H), hormone-treated
         hypothyroid (T_3) or euthyroid (N) rats were translated in reticulo-
         cyte lysates. The resultant labeled lysates were either electro-
         phoresed directly (A) or immunoabsorbed with antisera raised against
         cytoplasmic proteins (B) or mitochondrial matrix proteins (C) from
         rat liver. The individual lanes in (A) represent increasing but
         corresponding amounts of radioactivity in both samples. Arrows
         indicate polypeptides responding to hormone-treatment.

227

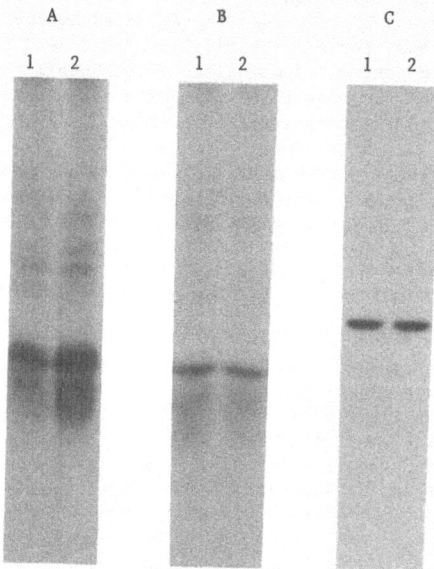

Fig. 2 Translation of specific mitochondrial inner membrane
polypeptides in reticulocyte lysates programmed with
liver polysomes from rats with different thyroid hormone
states. Cytochrome c_1 (A) and the iron sulphur protein
(B) of the cytochrome bc_1 complex, and the β-subunit of
the F_1-ATPase (C) were immunoabsorbed from reticulocyte
lysates programmed with polysomes from livers of
hypothyroid rats (lanes 1) or hypothyroid rats treated
with triiodothyronine for 6 days (lanes 2). Fluorographs
are shown.

polypeptides analyzed was statistically significant. A smaller, though
statistically significant, increase was also observed in core protein, for
which all samples but one were induced more than 1-fold. No significant
changes were observed for the Rieske iron sulphur protein, the β-subunit
of F_1-ATPase, or transhydrogenase. The above results were obtained after
both 3 and 6 days of hormone treatment. Thus, the response with cytochrome c_1 occurs within 3 days of treatment.

DISCUSSION

The number of mitochondrial profiles (Gustafsson et al., 1965),
the area of the mitochondrial inner membrane (Gustafsson et al., 1965;
Jakovcic et al., 1978) and the number of respiratory chain components,
including cytochromes (Tata et al., 1963; Kadenbach, 1966), decrease in
hypothyroid animals and return to normal after hormone treatment. However, triiodothyronine induced the biosynthesis of only a small population of the nuclear-encoded inner membrane polypeptides (Nelson et al.,
1984). To explain these results, we proposed that thyroid hormone exerts
its main effect on mitochondrial protein synthesis and that accumulation
of functional inner membrane respiratory chain units is set by the production of mitochondrial translation products (Nelson et al., 1987). We
also suggested, in view of the well established role of thyroid hormone

228

Table 2. Effect of Thyroid Hormone on the Levels of Translatable
mRNA for Selected Nuclear-Encoded Mitochondrial
Proteins in Rat Liver

Protein	n	Increase over Hypothyroid[a]	% Experiments Induced more than:	
			1-fold	2-fold
Cytochrome c_1	10	2.62 ± 0.42[b]	100	70
FeS protein	10	1.30 ± 0.29	50	20
Core I	11	1.25 ± 0.05[b]	91	0
F_1-ATPase β-subunit	10	1.49 ± 0.40	70	10
Transhydrogenase	1	-	0	0

Polysomes from livers of hypothyroid or hypothyroid hormone-
treated rats were translated in reticulocyte lysates. Translation products were immunoabsorbed and separated on SDS-PAGE.
Fluorographs were quantitated by densitometric scanning.
n = number of experiments. [a] mean $\pm$ S.E. [b] Significant increase
calculated from Student's t-test.

in regulating the expression of nuclear genes (Seelig et al., 1981;
Ivarie et al., 1981; Dillmann et al., 1983; Magnuson et al., 1985), that
hormone-regulated nuclear genes are probably responsible for the control
exerted over the mitochondrial genome (Nelson et al., 1987).

The present study shows that certain polypeptides of the respiratory
chain complexes are also induced by triiodothyronine within 3 days of
treatment. The clearest result was obtained with cytochrome c_1, the mRNA
of which is elevated approximately 3-fold after thyroid hormone treatment.
It remains to be shown if the nuclear-encoded subunits of other respiratory
chain complexes, such as those in cytochrome oxidase, are equally affected. However, of the Complex III subunits tested, cytochrome c_1 is by far
the most highly induced. This was recently confirmed in our laboratory in
experiments in which endogenous mRNA in a postmitochondrial fraction from
the livers of hypothyroid and hypothyroid, hormone-treated rats was translated in vitro (Joste and Nelson, unpublished observations). In this system, an early (12 hours) and large (maximum of 15-fold) induction of cytochrome c_1 was measured. In addition, a smaller but less reproducible increase was observed in the translation of the FeS protein.

It is of interest that although only 10 percent of the inner membrane proteins are induced by thyroid hormone (Nelson et al., 1984) one
of these is cytochrome c_1. The significance of this remains obscure. One
possibility is that cytochrome c_1 is important for assembly of the cytochrome bc_1 complex and that its synthesis must be coordinated with that
of cytochrome b in the mitochondria. Indeed, it has been shown that
cytochrome c_1 and cytochrome b are the most rapidly synthesized and
assembled subunits of yeast Complex III (Sidhu and Beattie, 1983). It
is also of interest that cytochrome c is induced by thyroid hormone

(Matsuura et al., 1981). Whether or not the two c-type cytochromes are regulated in the same way is not known.

The results reported here show that the steady state levels of translatable cytochrome c_1 mRNA are elevated after triiodothyronine treatment. This is widely accepted as a measure of increased transcription. However, we can not eliminate the possibility at the present time that specific mRNA species are stabilized in hormone treated rats. Although this seems unlikely, since it implies a mechanism by which individual mRNAs are stabilized, further work is required to elucidate the mechanism and physiological significance of thyroid hormone regulation of cytochrome c_1.

ACKNOWLEDGEMENTS

Antisera against the β-subunit of F_1-ATPase was kindly supplied by T. Hundal, that against nicotinamide nucleotide transhydrogenase by E. Carlenor and J. Rydström. This work was supported by the Swedish Natural Science Research Council.

REFERENCES

Freeman, K. B., Roodyn, D. B., and Tata, J. R., 1963, Stimulation of amino acid incorporation into protein by isolated mitochondria from rats treated with thyroid hormones, Biochim. Biophys. Acta, 72:129.

Dillmann, W. H., Mendecki, J., Koerner, D., Schwartz, H. L., and Oppenheimer, J. H., 1978, Triiodothyronine-stimulated formation of poly(A)-containing nuclear RNA and mRNA in rat liver, Endocrinology, 102:568.

Dillmann, W. H., Barrieux, A., Neeley, W. E. and Contreras, P., 1983, Influence of thyroid hormone on the in vitro translational activity of specific mRNAs in the rat heart, J. Biol. Chem., 258:7738.

Gustafsson, R., Tata, J. R., Lindberg, O., and Ernster, L., 1965, The relationship between the structure and activity of rat skeletal muscle mitochondria after thyroidectomy and thyroid hormone treatment, J. Cell Biol., 26:555.

Ivarie, R. D., Baxter, J. D., and Morris, J. A., 1981, Interaction of thyroid and glucocorticoid hormones in rat pituitary tumor cells, J. Biol. Chem., 256:4520.

Jakovcic, S., Swift, H. H., Gross, N. J., and Rabinowitz, M., 1978, Biochemical and stereological analysis of rat liver mitochondria in different thyroid states, J. Cell. Biol., 77:887.

Kadenbach, B., 1966, Effect of thyroid hormone on mitochondrial enzymes, in: "Regulation of Metabolic Processes in Mitochondria", J. M. Tager, S. Papa, E. Quagliariello, and E. C. Slater, eds., Elsevier Publishing Co., Amsterdam.

Kuzela, S., Joste, V. and Nelson, B. D., 1986, Rhodamine 6G inhibits the matrix-catalyzed processing of precursors of rat-liver mitochondrial proteins, Eur. J. Biochem., 154:553.

Liaw, C., Seelig, S., Mariash, C. N., Oppenheimer, J. H., and Towle, H. C., 1983, Interactions of thyroid hormone, growth hormone and high carbohydrate, fat-free diet in regulating several rat liver messenger ribonucleic acid species, Biochemistry, 22:213.

Magnuson, M. A., Dozin, B., and Nikodem, V. M., 1985, Regulation of specific rat liver messenger ribonucleic acids by triiodothyronine, J. Biol. Chem., 260:5906.

Matsuura, S., Arpin, M., Hannum, C., Margolish, E., Sabatini, D. D., and
Morimoto, T., 1981. In vitro synthesis and posttranslational uptake of cytochrome c into isolated mitochondria: role of a specific
adressing signal in the apocytochrome, Proc. Natl. Acad. Sci.
78:4368.

Nelson, B. D., Joste, V., Wielburski, A., and Rosenqvist, U., 1980, The
effect of triiodothyronine on the synthesis of mitochondrial proteins in isolated rat hepatocytes, Biochim. Biophys. Acta, 608:422.

Nelson, B. D., Mutvei, A., and Joste, V., 1984, Regulation of biosynthesis
of the rat liver inner mitochondrial membrane by thyroid hormone,
Arch. Biochem. Biophys., 228:41.

Nelson, B. D., Mutvei, A., Joste, V., Wielburski, A., and Kuzela, S.,
1987, Factors regulating the biogenesis and assembly of mammalian
mitochondria, in: "Nobel Symposium 66, Membrane Proteins: Structure, Function, Assembly", Chemica Scripta, in press.

Pelham, H. R. B. and Jackson, R. J., 1976, An efficient mRNA-dependent
translation system from reticulocyte lysates, Eur. J. Biochem.,
67:247.

Ramsey, J. C. and Steele, W. J., 1976, A procedure for the quantitative
recovery of homogenous populations of undegraded free and bound
polysomes from rat liver, Biochemistry, 15:1704.

Roodyn, D. B., Freeman, K. B., and Tata, J. R., 1965, The stimulation
by treatment in vivo with triiodothyronine of amino acid incorporation into protein by isolated rat liver mitochondria, Biochem.
J., 94:628.

Seelig, S., Liaw, C., Towle, H. C. and Oppenheimer, J. H., 1981, Thyroid
hormone attenuates and augments hepatic gene expression at a pre-
translational level, Proc. Natl. Acad. Sci., 78:4733.

Sidhu, A., and Beattie, D. S., 1983, Kinetics of assembly of Complex III
into the yeast mitochondrial membrane. J. Biol. Chem., 258:10649.

Tata, J. R., Ernster, L., Lindberg, O., Arrhenius, E., Pedersen, S., and
Hedman, R., 1963, The action of thyroid hormones at the cell level,
Biochem. J., 86:408.

Tata, J. R., Thyroid hormone receptors, in: "Cellular Receptors for
Hormones and Neurotransmitters", D. Schulster and A. Levitzki,
eds., John Wiley & Sons Ltd., New York.

II. BIOSYNTHESIS: Short Report

IMPORT OF CYTOCHROME c_1 AND CYTOCHROME b_2 INTO MITOCHONDRIA

J. Ostermann, F.-U. Hartl, M. Tropschug, B. Guiard*, and
W. Neupert

Institut für Physiologische Chemie, Universität München, BRD
*Centre de Genetique Moleculaire, 91190 Gif-sur-Yvette, France

We have investigated the import pathways of the two mitochondrial proteins, cytochrome c_1 (Neurospora crassa) and b_2 (yeast). These proteins are synthesized in the cytosol as larger precursor molecules, posttranslationally imported into mitochondria and processed in two steps to their respective mature sized forms (1). Cytochrome c_1 is a protein of the inner mitochondrial membrane with a large hydrophilic domain exposed to the intermembrane space. Cytochrome b_2 is a soluble protein of the intermembrane space. Both proteins enter mitochondria via translocation contact sites (2).

We have isolated a full-length cDNA clone for the cytochrome c_1, which is used in a coupled in vitro transcription/translation system for the synthesis of precursor molecules (3). These can be imported into isolated mitochondria of Neurospora crassa. With cytochrome b_2 a genomic clone is used (4).

Import of cytochrome c_1 can be blocked at two distinct steps. By adding EDTA and o-phenanthroline to the import buffer, the matrix peptidase can be inhibited and the precursor accumulates inside the mitochondria, where it is not accessible to externally added protease. The second processing step to the mature protein depends on NADH. Omitting NADH during the import results in the accumulation of the intermediate sized form. Both the precursor and intermediate can be chased to the mature protein by adding Mn^{2+} and NADH. Import of cytochrome b_2 at low temperature in the presence of EDTA/o-phe leads to the accumulation of precursor in a protease protected localization. Fractionation of mitochondria with digitonin after import showed that a small part of the precursor is still resistant to protease, under conditions where most of the intermembrane space marker is released. When mitoplasts were formed by digitonin treatment import was still possible and again a part of the imported precursor is in a protease protected localization.

We discuss these results in the context of the question whether cytochrome c_1 and b_2 contain a "stop-transfer" sequence which blocks translocation of the mature sequence into the matrix (5), or if these cytochromes are first translocated into the matrix and then reexported to the surface of the inner membrane or the intermembrane space. With the Fe/S protein of complex III, which has a localization similar to cytochrome c_1, it could be shown that the precursor is first imported into the matrix and then retranslocated across the inner membrane (6).

A truncated form of cytochrome c_1 has been constructed. This protein does not contain the hydrophobic domain at the carboxy-terminus, which is thought to serve as a membrane anchor. Import and processing of this construct is analysed to study the role of this hydrophobic domain in intramitochondrial sorting and heme attachment.

REFERENCES

1. M. Teintze, M. Slaughter, H. Weiss, and W. Neupert (1982) J. Biol. Chem. 257, 10364-10371.
2. M. Schleyer and W. Neupert (1985) Cell 43, 339-350.
3. P.A. Krieg and D.A. Melton (1984) NAR 12, 7057-7070.
4. B. Guiard (1985) EMBO J. 4, 3265-3272.
5. A.P.G.M. Van Loon, A.W. Brändli, and G. Schatz (1986) Cell 44, 801-806.
6. F.-U. Hartl, B. Schmidt, E. Wachter, H. Weiss, and W. Neupert (1986) Cell 47, 939-951.

III. PROTEIN STRUCTURE

CYTOCHROME C OXIDASE: PAST, PRESENT AND FUTURE

Michele Müller, Nestor Labonia, Beatrice Schläpfer and
Angelo Azzi

Institut für Biochemie und Molekularbiologie
Universität Bern
Bühlstrasse 28
CH-3012 Bern, Switzerland

In the present report the last ten years of scientific research in our laboratory will be reviewed. A particular accent will be given to the data being presently elaborated and to the future lines which can be already forseen. The work with cytochrome c oxidase has experienced the same evolution as the general field of bioenergetics: Studies centered largely on function have developed into more structural research to end up in the beginning of the molecular biology of such a complex enzyme.

AFFINITY CHROMATOGRAPY PURIFICATION OF MAMMALIAN AND BACTERIAL ENZYMES

Affinity chromatography based isolation of mitochondrial cytochrome c oxidase and reductase resulted to be generally successful also for bacterial enzymes (1,2). Saccharomyces cerevisiae cytochrome c was used as a ligand, bound to a thiol-Sepharose 4B gel through cysteine 107. Through this binding, the interaction of cytochrome c with cytochrome oxidase and reductase was unaltered. As a consequence of this, binding and isolation was rendered possible of a number of other enzymes (3) having in common the property of a high affinity to cytochrome c, e.g. cytochrome c oxidase, reductase, and peroxidase, sulfite oxidase, and reaction centers of photosynthetic bacteria (4). The development of this affinity chromatography technique has permitted the isolation of three new bacterial oxidases and their structure-function characterization: Rhodopseudomonas sphaeroides (5), Bacillus subtilis (6), Micrococcus luteus (Artzatbanov et al., unpublished). These enzymes posess a limited number of subunits (2 to 3) relative to the eukaryotic enzymes and, as documented for Rps. sphaeroides immunological cross reactivity with the analogous subunits of eukaryotes (yeast) and other prokaryotes (Paracoccus denitrificans) (7). Rps. sphaeroides and B. subtilis enzymes cannot be reconstituted in lipid vesicles in such a way to show proton pumping activity (7,8). It is probable that the lack of such a function is to be attributed rather to the extrinsic requirements of the enzyme (special lipid environment, type of cytochrome c or reductant employed, presence of ions) than to an intrinsic inability to perform proton pumping, as indicated by a certain activity present in the P. denitrificans enzyme.

LOCALIZATION OF THE ACTIVE CENTERS IN BACTERIAL AND MAMMALIAN CYTOCHROME
OXIDASES

The limited number of subunits of bacterial enzymes and in particular of that isolated from P. denitrificans (two subunits) restricts
the localization of the reaction centers (two heme-irons and two
coppers) to those polypeptides. Due to the presence of a large number of
polypeptides associated with the purified mammalian enzyme a gradual
elimination of them was necessary to permit localization of the hemes
(9). Bovine heart cytochrome c oxidase has been partially denatured
under mild conditions with 0.1-0.25% lithium dodecyl sulfate and 0.05%
Triton X-100.

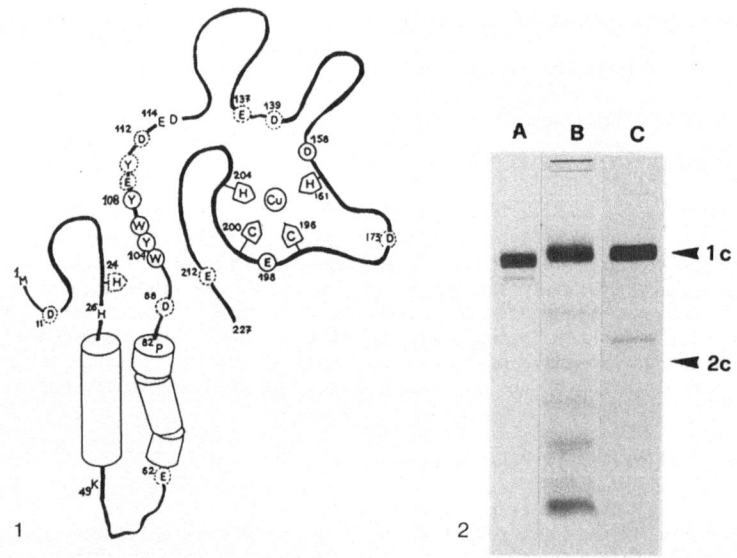

Fig. 1. Evolutionary conserved residues in subunit II. This scheme is
derived from that of Millett, F., de Jong, C., Paulson, L. and
Capaldi, R.A. (Biochemistry 22, 546-552, 1983) and contains the
conserved aromatic, acidic residues, cysteins and histidines
considered to play a functional role in the polypeptide. The
present version of the diagram includes the recent analyses of
Trypanosoma oxidases (Benne, R., Van den Burg, J., Brakenhoff,
J.P.J., Sloof, P., van Boom, J.H. and Tromp, M.C. (Cell, 46,
819-826, 1986).

Fig. 2. Enzymatic digestion of P. denitrificans oxidase. Silver staining
of a SDS polyacrylamide gel electrophoresis. A: 2 μg ovalbumin;
M_r = 43000. B: Chymotrypsin and S.aureus V8 protease treated
oxidase. C: as B after purification with HPLC (Baker Bond column
PEI widebore, eluted with a gradient 0-1 M NaCl in 20 mM Hepes
pH 7.2, 0.1% Triton X-100 R). 1c, 2c: chymotrypsinized subunit 1
and 2 respectively.

By gel filtration of the partially denatured enzyme the following
complexes of subunits were obtained: I-III, I-II-III, II-IV-V-VI-VII and

IV-V-VI-VII. The first three complexes retained almost all the heme, and
their spectral characteristics were very similar to those of the
partially denatured cytochrome c oxidase. The data, in combination with
the information that subunit III does not contain heme suggest that the
hemes are attached to subunit I and/or II. A more detailed delimitation
of the domains which bind the metals has been achieved more recently.
The study of evolutionary conserved residues which may be considered
candidates to the role of metal ligands has brought to the conclusion
that subunit II cannot ligate heme iron with imidazol nitrogens as
indicated by precise spectroscopic studies. Recent finding on the
subunit II gene of cytochrome c oxidase from Trypanosoma brucei,
Crithidia fasciculata and Leishmania tarentolae (cf ref in Fig. 1) have
in fact indicated that the only possible histidine (after the binding of
copper to a cluster of residues typical of copper proteins) is not
conserved in this species leaving subunit I as the only polypeptide
responsible for heme binding. Direct proof for this conclusion has been
afforded by the serial proteolytic degradation of P. denitrificans
oxidase by chymotrypsin and Staphilococcus aureus V8 protease resulting
in a single polypeptide (subunit I) active cytochrome c oxidase (Fig.
2).

THE SITE OF CYTOCHROME C BINDING

Cytochrome c was modified by introducing a 3-nitrophenylazido group
at lysine 13, at lysine 22, or at both residues (10). The cytochrome c
modified at lysine 13 in the presence of ultraviolet light formed a
covalent complex with cytochrome c oxidase subunit II. Using the lysine
22 derivative, the polypeptide composition of the oxidase was not
modified (11). The data were consistent with a specific covalent
interaction of the lysine 13 derivative of cytochrome c with the
polypeptide of molecular weight 23,700 (subunit II) of cytochrome c
oxidase (12). This finding does not imply that other subunits are
totally excluded from the binding site. On the contrary, it appears
probable that other subunits are involved in the delimitation of
cytochrome c binding site, such as subunit III and the low molecular
weight components of the mammalian enzyme. The recent finding that the
single polypeptide enzyme resulting from digestion of the subunit II of
P. denitrificans oxidase is capable of oxidizing reduced cytochrome c
with affinity higher than that of the two subunits complex suggests that
subunit I may play an important role in binding not only of one
substrate, oxygen, but also the other, cytochrome c. It seems at least
possible that, through subunit II, the contact is realized necessary to
the passage of electrons between cytochrome c and one of the cytochrome
c oxidase coppers.

LOCALIZATION OF THE DOMAINS OF THE ENZYME IN CONTACT WITH THE
PHOSPHOLIPID MEMBRANE USING PHOTOLABELING

Phospholipid derivatives labeled with an arylazido (13) group at
the end of the fatty acid or close to the glycerol (the "deep" and
"shallow" probes respectively) reacted with all subunits of cytochrome c
oxidase except V and VI: Subunits I, III and VII were heavily labeled,
subunit II was labeled to a lesser extent, and subunit IV was poorly
labeled. Subunit I was labeled more by the deep label and subunit VII by
the shallow one. The other subunits were equally labeled by the two
probes. This technique has revealed which subunits of cytochrome c
oxidase interact with the lipid and their approximate position in the
membrane (14).
A more detailed picture of the polypeptides in contact with the

phospholipid can be derived from the amino acid sequences available for all subunits.

THE BOVINE ENZYME AND THAT FROM PARACOCCUS DENITRIFICANS ARE ACTIVE AS MONOMERS

Gel filtration chromatography on Ultrogel AcA 34 in the presence of dodecylmaltoside (15-19) separated the monomeric and dimeric forms of bovine cytochrome c oxidase, both of them containing all 12-13 subunits described for this enzyme. Sucrose density centrifugation analysis and analytical centrifugation gave sedimentation coefficients of 15.5 and 9.6 S for the dimer and the monomer respectively. With the Stokes radius (measured by laser light-scattering to be 7 nm for the dimeric detergent-lipid-protein complex) and the partial specific volumes of the detergent and the enzyme (determined densitometrically), the molecular weights of 400,000 for the protein moiety of the dimer and 170,000-200,000 for the monomer were calculated. The monomer/dimer equilibrium was found to be dependent (under very low ionic strength conditions) on the protein concentration: Monomers were predominant at low (10^{-9} M) and dimers (plus aggregates) at high ($> 5 \times 10^{-6}$ M) enzyme concentrations. The dimeric enzyme showed a biphasic activity and monomers gave monophasic kinetics as a function of cytochrome c concentration (measured spectrophotometrically and analyzed by Eadie-Hofstee plots), compatible with a homotropic negative cooperative mechanism for the dimer of cytochrome c oxidase (20). From observations that in bidimensional crystals the bovine heart oxidase is dimeric the conclusion was inferred that the enzyme is only active in such a form. The conclusions reported above indicate that in detergent dispersed cytochrome oxidase not only dimers but also monomers are efficient catalysts, leaving the question open as to the activity of the enzyme as a proton pump, due to the lack of information on the state of aggregation of the enzyme in the phospholipid membrane (21). The enzyme from Paracoccus denitrificans was always found monomeric, at whatever salt and protein concentration in dodecylmaltoside and Triton X-100 which may point to an intrinsic difficulty of this enzyme to form aggregates (16,19): still the enzyme reconstituted in lipid vesicles was able to pump, although with a limited efficiency.

QUANTITATIVE ANALYSIS OF THE VECTORIAL PROTON TRANSLOCATION

For a quantitative analysis of the proton pump associated with bovine cytochrome c oxidase (22-25) we have synthesized fluorescein-phosphatidylethanolamine which, after reconstitution with cytochrome c oxidase into phospholipid vesicles, has been used as a specific and sensitive indicator of the intravesicular pH (26-29). It was observed that cytochrome c oxidase catalyzed the abstraction of almost 2 protons from the intravesicular medium per molecule of ferrocytochrome c oxidized while in the external medium approximately 1.0 proton per molecule appeared. The fact that cytochrome c oxidase behaves as a proton pump seems to be strongly supported by the above data. It was also shown that apparent anomalies in the kinetics of H^+ reentry (26) resulted from insufficient transmembrane charge equilibration during oxidase turnover (27) and were fully normalised by appropriately adjusting K^+ and valinomycin concentrations.

242

INHIBITION OF THE PROTON PUMP: THE EFFECT OF WATER INSOLUBLE
CARBODIIMIDES AND THEIR BINDING TO SUBUNIT III

Dicyclohexylcarbodiimide (DCCD) was found to bind to cytochrome c
oxidase with a parallel inhibition of ferrocytochrome c-induced H^+
translocation (28,29). The maximal overall stoichiometries of DCCD
molecules bound per cytochrome c oxidase was 1 for the reconstituted
enzyme. The DCCD- binding site was identified to be in a non polar
sequence (the hydrophilic carbodiimide, 1-ethyl-(3-dimethyl-amino-pro-
pyl)-carbodiimide affected to a minor extent H^+ translocation) located
in the subunit III of the oxidase (30, 31-33). It appears, from these
observations that subunit III of cytochrome c oxidase plays an important
role in H^+ translocation by the enzyme. An evolutionary conserved
glutamic acid residue was found to be the specific target of DCCD.

The experiment shown in Fig. 3 suggests that the role of subunit
III is that of protecting the enzyme from a loss of efficiency of the
proton pump when the enzyme is subjected to multiple turnovers. It is
apparent in fact that while the native enzyme is able to undergo
repeated turnovers without a great loss of efficiency, the subunit III
depleted enzyme has a high efficiency only when a substoichiometric
amount of cytochrome c is oxidized. Since valinomycin and K^+ are present
to guarantee full collapse of the membrane potential the only change
which can be produced by subsequent turnovers is an increase of the
transmembrane pH difference.

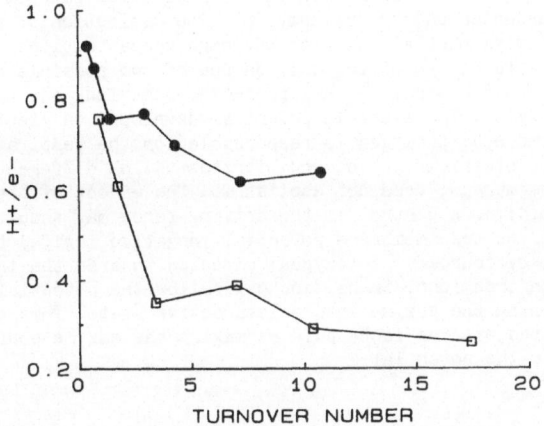

Fig. 3. The effect of subunit III depletion on the H^+/e^- ratio of
        reconstituted oxidase. The subunit III depletion was carried out
        according to Malatesta, F., Georgevich, G., and Capaldi, R.A.
        (1983) in Structure and function of membrane proteins
        (Quagliarello, E., and Palmieri, F. eds.) pp. 223-235, Elsevier,
        Amsterdam.

The observation that the detergent dispersed enzyme catalyzes as
the native enzyme electron transport excludes that the inhibition of the
proton pump is the consequence of an inhibition of the H^+ translocation.
It is evident that the extractions of protons becomes more and more
difficult, after each turnover, due to the decrease in the concentration
of the transported substrate, the proton itself. What subunit III may do
is to increase by creating the appropriate environment (through the

evolutionary conserved glutamate 90, whose block inhibits the proton pump?), the pK value of a protonatable group associated with the proton pump. Such a conclusion is also supported by the observation that the midpoint potential of the heme a becomes pH insensitive after subunit III extraction (Pentillä T., Eur. J. Biochem. 133, 355-361 (1983)).

A MECHANISM FOR MODULATION OF CYTOCHROME C OXIDASE ACTIVITY

The system of cytochrome c oxidase reconstituted in phospholipid vesicles has been used to study the regulation of the enzyme by free fatty acids (34). The proton pump of the redox complex was found not to be affected, even at concentrations of 10 µM by the presence of palmitic acid (Na salt). The H^+/e^- ratio remained at values close to 0.9 in the presence or absence of the fatty acid. The proton permeability of the vesicles was studied under three conditions: 1. passive re-entry of protons following the active H^+ extrusion 2. Passive re-entry of H^+ following and acid pulse. 3. Passive entry of H^+ driven by a diffusion potential (negative inside). In all cases, under the experimental conditions employed, no increase of the passive H^+ permeability was produced by concentrations of palmitic acid known to uncouple oxidative phosphorylation. Also the permeability for potassium ions was not affected by palmitic acid. Despite the lack of proton permeability changes and of molecular uncoupling of the pump (slippage) the respiratory control index was constantly diminished in the presence of the fatty acid due to an increased basal respiration rate (in the absence of uncoupler and/or valinomycin). The diminution of respiratory control was always partial, despite the high concentrations employed, as if the fatty acid had an effect only on one of two possible components of the respiratory control. Such a paradoxal behaviour can be described by a model (Fig 4). The electric potential developed on electron flow from cytochrome c to dioxygen is responsible for the respiratory control, since nigericin, which equilibrates the pH differential across the coupling membrane, does not abolish it. The effect of the potential may be two-fold: 1. A control of the driving force may result from the opposition of the transmembrane potential (negative inside) to electron transfer from cytochrome c to oxygen, directed towards the inside as well. 2. A conformational transition may follow the potential onset which would bring the enzyme into a less active state. This second event may be prevented by free fatty acid by making the enzyme conformation insensitive to the potential.

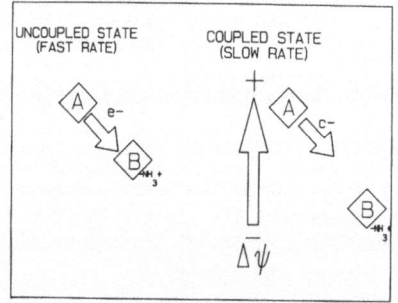 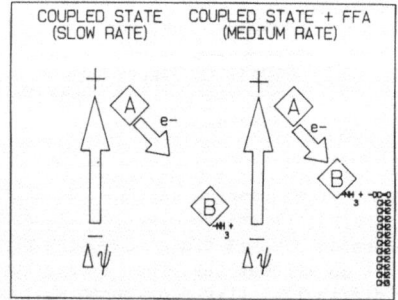

Fig. 4. A schematical model of the effect of the membrane potential and of free fatty acids on the electron transfer step between cytochromes a and a_3. The model is explained in the text.

244

The enzyme may thus have, in the membranous situation, when exposed to a potential two control levels, a thermodynamic and a kinetic one. When both are present the electron transfer rate is slow (maximal respiratory control). In the presence of a FFA the kinetic control would be abolished, resulting in a lower respiratory control which would never decline to 1 due to the persistence of the thermodynamic control. This latter could be abolished only by the collapse of the transmembrane potential. Such a control of the terminal oxidase may have important physiological functions in the activation of the respiratory chain without loss of efficiency.

References

1. A. Azzi, K. Bill, and C. Broger, Affinity chromatography purification of cytochrome c binding enzymes, Proc. Natl. Acad. Sci USA 79: 2447 (1982).
2. K. Bill and A. Azzi, Interaction of reduced and oxidized cytochrome c with the mitochondrial cytochrome c oxidase and bc_1-complex, Biochem. Biophys. Res. Commun. 120: 124 (1984).
3. K. Bill, R.P. Casey, C. Broger, and A. Azzi, Affinity chromatography purification of cytochrome c oxidase: Use of a yeast cytochrome c-thiol-sepharose 4B column, FEBS Lett. 120: 248 (1980).
4. K. Bill, C. Broger, and A. Azzi, Affinity chromatography purification of cytochrome c oxidase and $b-c_1$ complex from beef heart mitochondria. Use of thiol-Sepharose-bound Saccharomyces cerevisiae cytochrome c, Biochim. Biophys. Acta 679: 28 (1982).
5. A. Azzi and R.B. Gennis, Purification of the aa_3-type cytochrome-c oxidase from Rhodopseudomonas sphaeroides, Methods Enzymol. 126: 138 (1986).
6. W. deVrij, B. Poolman, W.N. Konings, and A. Azzi, Purification, enzymatic properties, and reconstitution of cytochrome-c oxidase from Bacillus subtilis, Methods Enzymol. 126: 159 (1986).
7. R.B. Gennis, R.P. Casey, A. Azzi, and B. Ludwig, B. Purification and characterization of the cytochrome c oxidase from Rhodopseudomonas sphaeroides, Eur. J. Biochem. 125: 189 (1982).
8. W. deVrij, A. Azzi, and W.N. Konings, Structural and functional properties of cytochrome c oxidase from Bacillus subtilis W23, Eur. J. Biochem. 131: 97 (1983).
9. M.J. Corbley and A. Azzi, Resolution of bovine heart cytochrome c oxidase into smaller complexes by controlled subunit denaturation, Eur. J. Biochem. 139: 535 (1984).
10. R. Bisson, H. Gutweniger, and A. Azzi, Photoaffinity labeling of yeast cytochrome oxidase with arylazido cytochrome c derivatives, FEBS Lett. 92: 219 (1978).
11. R. Bisson, A. Azzi, H. Gutweniger, R. Colonna, C. Montecucco, and A. Zanotti, Interaction of cytochrome c with cytochrome c oxidase. Photoaffinity labeling of beef heart cytochrome c oxidase with arylazido-cytochrome c, J. Biol. Chem. 253: 1874 (1978).
12. R. Bisson, H. Gutweniger, C. Montecucco, R. Colonna, A. Zanotti, and A. Azzi, Covalent binding of arylazido derivatives of cytochrome c to cytochrome oxidase, FEBS Lett. 81: 147 (1977).
13. R. Bisson, C. Montecucco, H. Gutweniger, and A. Azzi, Hydrophobic labelling of bovine heart cytochrome c oxidase with an azido-phosphatidylcholine, Biochem. Soc. Trans. 7: 156 (1979).
14. R. Bisson, C. Montecucco, H. Gutweniger, and A. Azzi, Cytochrome c oxidase subunits in contact wit phospholipids. Hydrophobic photo-labeling with azidophospholipids, J. Biol. Chem. 254: 9962 (1979).
15. R. Bolli, K.A. Nałęcz, and A. Azzi, The aggregation state of bovine heart cytochrome c oxidase and its kinetics in monomeric and dimeric form, Arch. Biochem. Biophys. 240: 102 (1985).

16. K.A. Nałęcz, R. Bolli, B. Ludwig, and A. Azzi, The role of subunit III in bovine cytochrome c oxidase. Comparison between native, subunit III-depleted and Paracoccus denitrificans enzymes, Biochim. Biophys. Acta 808: 259 (1985).

17. R. Bolli, K.A. Nałęcz, and A. Azzi, The interconversion between monomeric and dimeric bovine heart cytochrome c oxidase, Biochimie 67: 119 (1985).

18. K.A. Nałęcz, R. Bolli, and A. Azzi, Preparation of monomeric cytochrome c oxidase: its kinetics differ from those of the dimeric enzyme, Biochem. Biophys. Res. Commun. 114: 822 (1983).

19. R. Bolli, K.A. Nałęcz, and A. Azzi, Cytochrome c oxidase from Paracoccus denitrificans in Triton X-100: Aggregation state and kinetics, J. Bioenerg. Biomembr. 18: 277 (1986).

20. K.A. Nałęcz, R. Bolli, and A. Azzi, Techniques for the study of bovine cytochrome-c oxidase monomer-dimer association, Methods Enzymol. 126: 45 (1986).

21. R.P. Casey, P.S. O'Shea, J.B. Chappell, and A. Azzi, A quantitative characterisation of H^+ translocation by cytochrome c oxidase vesicles, Biochim. Biophys. Acta 765: 30 (1984).

22. A. Azzi, Cytochrome c oxidase. Towards a clarification of its structure, interactions and mechanism, Biochim. Biophys. Acta 594: 231 (1980).

23. M. Mueller, M. Thelen, P.S. O'Shea, and A. Azzi, Functional reconstitution of proton-pumping cytochrome-c oxidase in phospholipid vesicles, Methods Enzymol. 126: 78 (1986).

24. R.P. Casey, C. Broger, M. Thelen, and A. Azzi, Studies on the molecular basis of H^+ translocation by cytochrome c oxidase, J. Bioenerg. Biomembr. 13: 219 (1981).

25. A. Azzi, Mitochondria: the utilization of oxygen for cell life, Experientia 49: 901 (1984).

26. R.P. Casey and A. Azzi, An evaluation of the evidence for H^+ pumping by reconstituted cytochrome c oxidase in the light of recent criticism, FEBS Lett. 154: 237 (1983).

27. M. Thelen, P.S. O'Shea, G. Petrone, and A. Azzi, Proton translocation by a native and subunit III-depleted cytochrome c oxidase reconstituted into phospholipid vesicles. Use of fluorescein-phosphatidylethanolamine as an intravesicular pH indicator, J. Biol. Chem. 260: 3626 (1985).

28. A. Azzi, M. Mueller, P.S. O'Shea, and M. Thelen, Molecular properties of reconstituted cytochrome c oxidase: New evidence supports vectorial proton translocation, J. Inorg. Biochem. 23: 341 (1985).

29. M. Thelen, P.S. O'Shea, and A. Azzi, New insights on the cytochrome c oxidase proton pump, Biochem. J. 227: 63 (1985).

30. R.P. Casey, M. Thelen, and A. Azzi, Dicyclohexylcarbodiimide binds specifically and covalently to cytochrome c oxidase while inhibiting its H^+-translocating activity, J. Biol. Chem. 255: 3994 (1980).

31. R.P. Casey, C. Broger, and A. Azzi, Structural studies on the cytochrome c oxidase proton pump using a spin-label probe, Biochim. Biophys. Acta 638: 86 (1981).

32. A. Azzi, R.P. Casey, and M.J. Nałęcz, The effect of N,N'-Dicyclohexylcarbodiimide on enzymes of bioenergetic relevance, Biochim. Biophys. Acta 768: 209 (1984).

33. M.J. Nałęcz, R.P. Casey, and A. Azzi, Use of N,N'-dicyclohexylcarbodiimide to study membrane-bound enzymes, Methods Enzymol. 125: 86 (1986).

34. R.P. Casey, B.H. Ariano, and A. Azzi, Studies on the transmembrane orientation of cytochrome c oxidase in phospholipid vesicles, Eur. J. Biochem. 122: 313 (1982).

UNIVERSAL FEATURES IN CYTOCHROME OXIDASE

Moshe Finel, Tuomas Haltia, Liisa Holm, Tuulikki Jalli,
Tuula Metso, Anne Puustinen, Mirja Raitio, Matti Saraste,
and Mårten Wikström

Department of Medical Chemistry, University of Helsinki
Siltavuorenpenger 10A, SF-00170 Helsinki, Finland

Mitochondrial cytochrome c oxidase (cytochrome aa_3) and its equivalent in aerobic bacteria are known to be closely related in function as well as in structure (1-3). Recent cloning and sequencing of the genes for this enzyme in Paracoccus denitrificans (4,5) allows us now to make conclusions on some invariant features in cytochrome oxidase that have prevailed throughout evolution. Evolutionary conservation helps to focus the attention to the functionally most important parts in structure and guides us in attempts to make models for active centres.

We discuss here two central aspects of the cytochrome oxidase: (1) that its functional core seems to be made of three subunits I, II and III universally, and (2) where the active (redox) centres may be located within subunits I and II.

CYTOCHROME OXIDASE GENES IN Paracoccus: THE THIRD SUBUNIT IS UNIVERSAL ?

Fig. 1 shows the maps around two oxidase loci in the genomic DNA of Paracoccus denitrificans. Three subunits of the enzyme have been identified by their clear homology to the equivalent subunits in the eukaryotic enzyme (5). In addition two unidentified genes are flanked in the cox1 locus by the COII and COIII genes (coxB and coxC in Figure 1). The COI gene (coxE) is found in a second locus. It is preceded by a short open reading frame (marked with ? in Fig. 1) which may also be a coding gene.

The presence of the third subunit (COIII) in this enzyme was not clear before (1). It was anticipated, however, because the proton transport properties of the isolated Paracoccus enzyme deviated from the cytochrome oxidase in situ (2,6) as well as from those of the intact mitochondrial enzyme (7). The stoicheiometry of transported protons to transfered electrons is 1 H^+ / e^- in cytochrome oxidase (8). This stoicheiometry was demonstrated for the bacterial enzyme in the cytoplasmic membrane (6) but has not been reached in reconstituted systems (7).

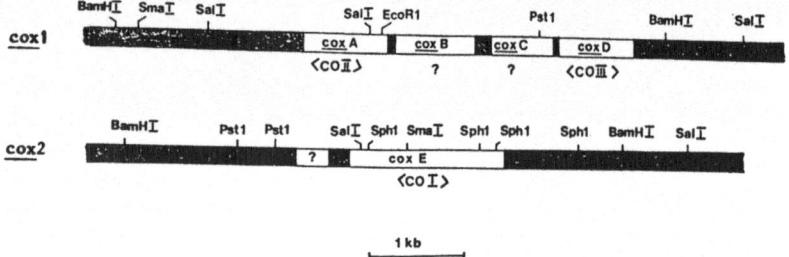

<u>Fig. 1</u> Restriction sites and location of the cytochrome oxidase genes in two loci in <u>Paracoccus</u> <u>denitrificans</u>. The first locus contains the genes for COII (<u>cox</u>A) and COIII (<u>cox</u>D). Two unidentified genes <u>cox</u>B and C are flanked by these. The second locus <u>cox</u>2 contains the COI gene (<u>cox</u>E). It is preceded by a short open reading frame (shown with ?) that could code for a small protein of 111 amino acid residues (5).

COIII has been suggested to have a role in assisting the enzyme to acquire a proper conformation for proton translocation (8), but this activity can be demonstrated also with the COIII-depleted cytochrome oxidase, although with a lower stoicheiometry (9). Thus the exact role of COIII in the oxidase is obscure; it can be now studied by deleting the COIII gene from <u>Paracoccus</u>. It should be added that an isolated bacterial cytochrome oxidase from <u>Thermus</u> <u>thermophilus</u>, which appears to have no COIII, has been reported to translocate protons with a high stoicheiometry in liposomes (10).

The protein is characterized by an invariant glutamic acid residue residing in a hydrophobic segment that can be modified by dicyclohexyl carbodiimide (DCCD) in the membrane-bound enzyme (11). This residue is present in the bacterial enzyme (Fig. 2).

We have found a way to modify the purification procedure of Berry and Trumpower (12) so that a three-protein complex of cytochrome aa_3 without an associated cytochrome <u>c</u> is obtained from <u>Paracoccus</u>. When this complex was incorporated into liposomes and the protein reacted with radioactive DCCD, the third band was selectively labelled (Fig. 3). Thus we think that this protein is COIII. Further studies to identify it and study its effect on the proton translocation are underway.

Cu_A IS BOUND TO SUBUNIT II

Four redox centres are found in cytochrome oxidase. Cu_A is the low-potential copper ion that is associated with subunit II. The ligands of this metal ion are probably two cysteines (sulphurs) and two histidines (nitrogens), see ref. 14. Two regions of COII show similarity in primary structure to azurins and plastocyanines (15,16). One of these is a sequence containing two invariant cysteines and a histidine; the other is centred at a histidine residue. We show in Figure 4 these four ligands binding a copper-ion (Cu_A).

248

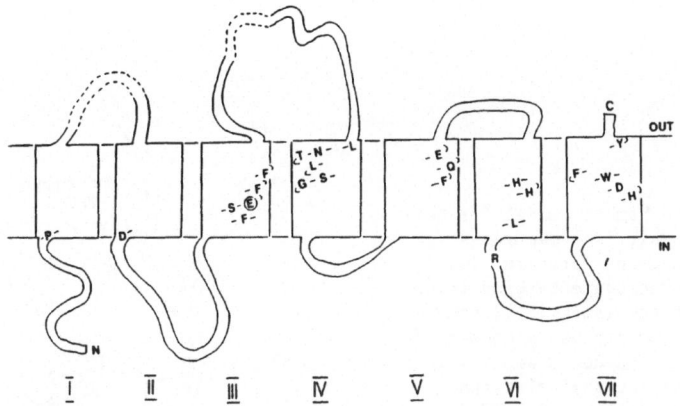

Fig. 2 A schematic model for COIII in the membrane. Seven transmembrane helices are shown with the strictly invariant amino acids.
The DCCD-binding glutamic acid residue is circled. Sequences of several
mitochondrial proteins (15), one derived from Leischmania kinetoplast
(13) and the Paracoccus COIII are included in this comparison.

We have built a model for this centre fitting the COII sequences
into the known 3-D structure of Pseudomonas azurin (17). An interesting
finding is that two strictly invariant carboxylic acids (circled negative
charges in Fig. 4) are located very close to this centre. They are
expected to have a function of cytochrome c binding to the oxidase (15,18).
If these residues are involved in the binding site for cytochrome c, it
resides very close to Cu_A, which thus may be the primary electron
acceptor in the enzyme. Preliminary attemps in docking of the cytochrome
c to the site indicate that its haem edge comes to ca. 15 Å apart from
Cu_A.

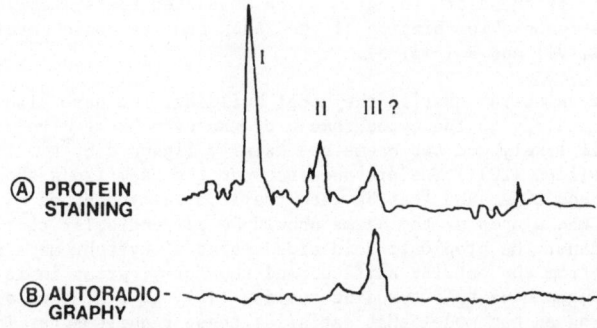

Fig. 3 Cytochrome oxidase was purified from aerobically grown Paracoccus
denitrificans by a modification of the procedure in (12), incorporated   .
into liposomes, labelled with radioactive DCCD, delipidated and analysed
by gel electrophoresis. (A) shows the scanning of Coomassie Blue stained
protein, (B) of the autoradiograph.

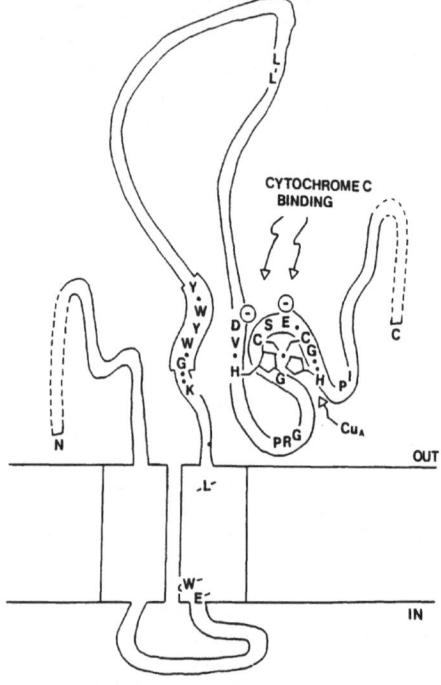

Fig. 4 Schematic model for COII
This subunit is a membrane-
anchored copper protein. Two
hydrophobic segments bind it to
the membrane (see (15)), the C-
terminal domain has a conserved
aromatic sequence G*WYW*Y* (involved in internal electron
transfer reactions ?) and four
conserved ligands for a copper
ion. Two invariant carboxylic
acids are marked with $\ominus$.

CYTOCHROME a AND THE OXYGEN-REDUCING CENTRE ARE IN SUBUNIT I

From a number of studies it has been clear that the two coppers and
two haems reside in subunits I and II (see (1,15)). The possible ligands
for these centres in COII are exhausted when Cu_A is accomodated in it
(above). The other centres should therefore be located in COI. Haem a
is a bisimidazole complex, the proximal ligand to haem a_3 is also a
histidine and Cu_B is liganded by three histidines and an oxygen (15,19).
Thus we have to employ six invariant histidines in COI for the binding
of these redox centres. There are nine such residues in COI (circled in
Fig. 5); six of these are found in three predicted trans-membrane segments.
A minimal structure for binding of the redox centres could involve these
segments VI, VII and X (Fig. 5).

Some parameters restrict the model building. (We have also relied
here on an analogy to the cytochrome b of the cytochrome c reductase,
where in all likelyhood two haems are axially liganded by two transmembrane helices (20).) The distance between the haem irons should be
between 12 and 20 Å, and that between the iron in cytochrome a_3 and Cu_B
about 4 Å; the planes of the haems should be perpendicular to the
membrane plane; the propionic acid side chains of cytochrome a should be
accessible from the outside surface, and the formyl group in it might
form a hydrogen bond to a tyrosine residue (15). In Fig. 6 we show the
design for an ad hoc model that satisfies these requirements. This model
has been further developed using computer graphics which unfortunately
cannot be shown in black and white. The haems in it are slightly tilted
relative to each other and roughly perpendicular to the membrane; Fe-Fe
distance is 16 Å; Cu_B is at a 4 Å distance from haem iron of cytochrome
a_3 and forms the centre where dioxygen is reduced with this. The formyl
group of cytochrome a finds an invariant tyrosyl residue in segment X
and forms a hydrogen bond to its phenolic OH-group.

250

We are refining this model at the moment. Although it is based on educated guesses, it offers a possible structure where the accumulated knowledge is nicely crystallised into a plausible model. This model as well as other features of the enzyme discussed here that try to link the structure to the function, will be tested in future using mutagenesis on the cloned Paracoccus oxidase genes.

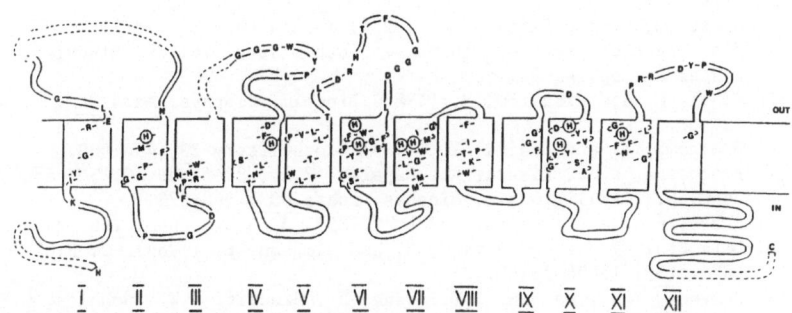

Fig. 5 A schematic model for COI. This protein is predicted to have twelve trans-membrane segments. The strictly invariant residues are shown; in membrane they are drawn on helical surfaces, supposing that the membrane-penetrating segments are α-helical. The invariant histidines are circled.

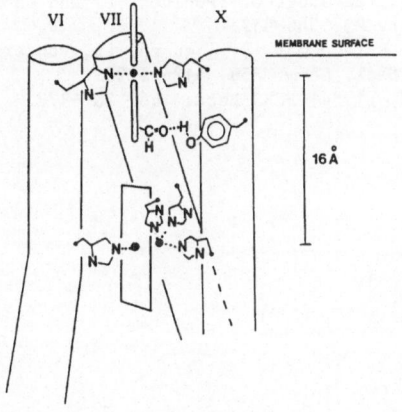

Fig. 6 A model for active centre. Segments VI, VII and X of Fig. '5 are used to bind two haems and a copper. This model has been further amended using Chem-X program and Evans & Sutherland PS 300 computer graphics and will be shown in detail elsewhere (17). Cytochrome a is on the top and bound between two histidines in segments VI and X. Its propionic side chains are pointing upwards (not shown) out from the membrane surface. The haem is slightly tilted to the membrane plane, and ca. 30 degrees around its z-axis. Its formyl group makes a hydrogen bond to the invariant tyrosine in segment X. The proximal ligand to the haem of cytochrome a_3 is the bottom histidine in segment VI. Two histidines in VII and the bottom one in X ligate Cu_B.

251

REFERENCES

1. Ludwig, B. (1980) Biochim. Biophys. Acta 594, 177-189.
2. Ludwig, B. (1987) FEMS Microbiol. Rev., in press.
3. Poole, R.K. (1983) Biochim. Biophys. Acta 726, 205-243.
4. Saraste, M., Raitio, M., Jalli, T. and Perämaa, A. (1986) FEBS Lett. 206, 154-156.
5. Raitio, M., Jalli, T. and Saraste, M. (1987) submitted.
6. Van Verseveld, H.W., Krab, K. and Stouthamer, A.H. (1981) Biochim. Biophys. Acta 635, 525-534.
7. Solioz, M., Carafoli, E. and Ludwig, B. (1982) J. Biol. Chem. 257, 1579-1582.
8. Wikström, M. and Saraste, M. (1984) In Ernster, L. (ed.): Bioenergetics. New Comprehensive Biochemistry. Vol. 9, Elsevier, Amsterdam, pp. 49-94.
9. Finel, M. and Wikström, M. (1986) Biochim. Biophys. Acta 851, 99-108.
10. Hon-nami, K. and Oshima, T. (1984) Biochemistry 23, 454-460.
11. Prochaska, L.J., Bisson, R., Capaldi, R.A., Steffens, G.C.M. and Buse, G. (1981) Biochim. Biophys. Acata 637, 360-373.
12. Berry, E.A. and Trumpower, B.L. (1985). J. Biol. Chem. 260, 2458-2467.
13. Dela Cruz, V.F., Neckelmann, N. and Simpson, L. (1984). J. Biol. Chem. 259, 15136-15147.
14. Stevens, T.H., Martin, C.T., Wang, H., Brudvig, G.W., Scholes, C.P. and Chan, S.I. (1982) J. Biol. Chem. 257, 12106-12113.
15. Wikström, M., Saraste, M. and Penttilä, T. (1985). In Martonosi, A.N. (ed.): The Enzymes of Biological Membranes, Plenum, New York, Vol. 4, pp. 111-149.
16. Chothia, C. and Lesk, A. (1982) J. Mol. Biol. 160, 309-323.
17. Holm, L., Saraste, M. and Wikström, M. (1987) in preparation.
18. Millett, F., de Jong, C., Poulson, L. and Capaldi, R.A. (1983) Biochemistry 23, 546-552.
19. Cline, J., Reinhammar, B., Jensen, P., Venters, R. and Hoffman, B.M. (1983) J. Biol. Chem. 258, 5124-5128.
20. Saraste, M. (1984) FEBS Lett. 166, 367-372.

POLYPEPTIDE SUBUNITS ENCODED BY NUCLEAR GENES ARE ESSENTIAL

COMPONENTS OF EUKARYOTIC CYTOCHROME C OXIDASE

Thomas E. Patterson, Cynthia E. Trueblood, Richard M. Wright
and Robert O. Poyton

Department of Molecular, Cellular and Developmental Biology
University of Colorado at Boulder
Boulder, CO 80309-0347

INTRODUCTION

Eukaryotic cytochrome c oxidase spans the inner mitochondrial membrane and is a complex protein composed of: 4 redox centers (Fe_a, Cu_a, and the Fe_{a3}-Cu_{a3} binuclear center)[1]; cardiolipin[2,3]; and as many as 13 polypeptides[4,5]. During the past several years, Saccharomyces cerevisiae cytochrome c oxidase has been used extensively for studies of mitochondrial biogenesis and genetics[6] while bovine heart cytochrome c oxidase has provided most of the structural and functional data for the enzyme[7]. Recent work on the isolation and sequencing of the polypeptides of both enzymes[8-21] as well as the cloning and sequencing of their genes[22-31] has provided the complete primary sequences of the polypeptides in the holoenzymes from both bovine heart and yeast. The three largest polypeptides (designated subunits I, II, and III) in both enzymes are encoded on mitochondrial DNA. The remaining polypeptides (6 in yeast[4] and 9-10 in bovine heart[5]) are encoded by nuclear genes.

Despite these recent advances in isolating, characterizing, and sequencing the subunits and their genes, surprisingly little is known about subunit function in cytochrome c oxidase from any species. Currently, it is assumed that the catalytic functions of eukaryotic cytochrome c oxidases are performed by the three mitochondrially-encoded subunits. This is based on several types of evidence. First, subunit-specific antisera against yeast subunit II inhibits cytochrome c oxidase activity[32]. Second, mutations in any one of the structural genes for subunits I, II, and III or in nuclear genes that affect the expression of these structural genes lead to cytochrome c oxidase deficient yeast cells[33-36] and can lead to shifts in the absorption spectrum of heme a[37]. Third, heme a appears to be associated with subunits I and II in partially dissociated cytochrome c oxidase molecules[38]. Fourth, there is primary sequence homology between a region of subunit II and the copper binding proteins, plastocyanin and azurin, suggesting that one (or both) of the copper ions of the holoenzyme is (are) associated with subunit II[9]. Fifth, subunit III appears to function in proton pumping[1, 39]. Finally, procaryotic aa3-type cytochrome c oxidases contain only 2 or 3 polypeptides[40]. These exhibit partial homology to the mitochondrially-coded subunits of eukaryotic cytochrome c oxidases.

Although indirect and largely circumstantial, the above observations have raised questions concerning the relevance of the nuclear-coded poly-

peptides to holocytochrome c oxidase. If, as implied from the above
observations, the mitochondrially-coded subunits are sufficient for catalysis, what is the function of the nuclear-coded polypeptides? Are they
essential constituents of the holoenzyme or merely contaminating polypeptides that adventitiously co-purify with it? In principle, it is
possible to address these questions in two ways: through biochemical
reconstitution studies, with purified polypeptides, or through genetic
studies, with strains that carry either deletion of missense mutations in
the genes for each polypeptide. While reconstitution studies have been
useful for identifying essential polypeptides and defining their function
in other oligomeric protein complexes (e.g., RNA polymerases), they have
not been applied successfully to cytochrome c oxidase from any species
yet. Fortunately, the second approach to the "subunit problem" is feasible with a genetically-tractable eukaryote, like Saccharomyces
cerevisiae. Using cloned genes from this yeast, it is possible to:
1) establish the essentiality of a polypeptide by creating a null mutation
in its structural gene; and 2) identify essential domains or amino acid
residues within it by creating site-, or region-, directed missense
mutations. Both null and missense mutations are useful for examining the
function of the nuclear-coded subunits of cytochrome c oxidase.

In this paper we will summarize the results obtained recently with
null mutants created in all but one of the nuclear COX genes which encode
the subunits of yeast cytochrome c oxidase. Using these results, in conjunction with computer searches for homologous polypeptides in bovine
heart cytochrome c oxidase, we then address the possibility that the
nuclear-coded subunits in this latter enzyme are also essential.

CONSTRUCTION AND ANALYSIS OF NULL MUTATIONS IN COX4, COX5a COX5b, COX6,
COX8, AND COX9 FROM SACCHAROMYCES CEREVISIAE

Null mutations have been constructed in one of two ways: either by
1) disrupting or 2) removing the coding region of each gene[29-31,41,42].
From Table I, it is clear that null mutations in COX4, COX6, and COX9--the
structural genes for subunits IV, VI, and VIIa respectively--lead to the
complete loss of cellular respiration and absorption bands corresponding
to cytochromes aa_3. In principle, this phenotype could result if these
subunits play an essential role in catalysis, serve to facilitate folding
of a catalytic subunit (e.g., subunits I, II, or III), or function in
assembly. In contrast to the complete loss of cytochrome c oxidase
activity observed in GD4, GD6, and GD9 null mutants, a null mutation in
COX8, the structural gene for subunit VIII only reduces cellular respiration to 80% of that in JM43 and has little effect on the level of intracellular aa_3. Because this mutant, GD8, has cytochromes aa_3 and respiration, subunit VIII obviously cannot play an indispensible role in holoenzyme assembly or electron transport. Possible roles it might have are
in regulation (as a modulator of electron transport) or proton translocation.

STRUCTURALLY DIFFERENT ISOLOGS FOR SUBUNIT V ARE FUNCTIONAL IN YEAST
HOLOCYTOCHROME C OXIDASE

As discussed elsewhere[42, 46], subunit V is the only subunit of
yeast cytochrome c oxidase for which isologous forms have been identified. These isologs, V_a and V_b, are encoded by the single copy genes
COX5a and COX5b, and have 67% primary sequence homology[28]. Isolog V_a is
the polypeptide that has been isolated and sequenced. It is routinely
found assembled in holocytochrome c oxidase molecules from aerobically-
grown yeast cells. While the V_b isolog is not found assembled in holoenzyme molecules from aerobically-grown yeast cells, its structural gene

254

Table 1. Null Alleles of Individual Nuclear COX Genes in S. cerevisiae Lead to a Decrease in Cytochrome c Oxidase

Strain[a]	Subunit Deleted	aa$_3$ Content (% of JM43)	[b]CN-Sensitive Respiration Rate (% of JM43)
JM43 (Wild Type)	None	100	100
GD4	IV	0	<2
GD6	VI	0	<2
GD9	VIIa	0	<2
GD8	VIII	100	80
GD5a	Va	86	96
GD5b	Vb	6	10
GD5ab	Va+Vb	0	<2

[a]All mutated strains were derived from and are isogenic with JM43 (MAT , his-4-580, trp1-289, leu2-3, leu2-112, ura3-52) except at their COX loci. Their COX genotypes are wild type except for the disrupted gene: GD4 (cox4 Δ::LEU2)[41]; GD6 (cox6::URA3)[48]; GD9 (cox9 Δ::URA3)[30]; GD8 (cox8 Δ::LEU2)[31]; GD5a (cox5a Δ::URA3)[42]; GD5b (cox5b::LEU2)[42]; and GD5ab (cox5a Δ::URA3; cox5b::LEU2)[42].
[b]CN-sensitive respiration and aa$_3$ content were determined as described[42].

is expressed, albeit at low levels[27,42]. Moreover, it assembles and functions in holocytochrome c oxidase molecules in cox5a structural gene mutants grown aerobically[27,42].

In order to analyze the contribution of each COX5 gene to cytochrome c oxidase activity, we have disrupted the chromosomal COX5a and COX5b genes, either singly or together (Table 1). When both genes are disrupted (in strain GD5ab), cells have no detectable cytochrome aa$_3$ and hence no cyanide-sensitive respiration. When only COX5b is disrupted (in strain GD5b), cells exhibit wild type levels of cytochrome aa$_3$ and respiration. In contrast, when only COX5a is disrupted (in strain GD5a), cells exhibit only 6-10% of the wild type level of cytochrome aa$_3$ or cellular respiration. These results indicate: 1) that either V$_a$ or V$_b$ is required for cytochrome c oxidase and 2) that a single copy of COX5a is more effective in supporting cytochrome c oxidase activity than a single copy of COX5b.

To determine if the differential effectiveness of COX5a and COX5b is due to a difference in level of expression of each gene or to a difference in stability, assembly, or function of the V$_a$ and V$_b$ polypeptides themselves, we constructed the chimeric COX genes, COX5ab and COX5ba. These genes were constructed by joining COX5a and COX5b at a common restriction site at codon 13 of each mature subunit V isolog[42]. COX5ab encodes the 5' flanking region, leader peptide and first 13 amino acids of COX5a, and the codons for amino acids 14 through 134 of mature subunit V$_b$. COX5ba encodes the 5' flanking region, leader peptide and first 13 amino acids of COX5b, and the codons for amino acids 14 through 133 of mature subunit V$_a$. By analyzing the level of cyanide-sensitive respiration in strains carrying these chimeric genes, it is clear that when the coding region of COX5b is put under the control of the COX5a promoter, it is as effective as COX5a in supporting respiration. Conversely, when the coding region of COX5a is put under control of the COX5b promoter it is as ineffective as COX5b in supporting respiration. From these in vivo assays it is clear that amino acids 13-133 and 13-134 in V$_a$ and V$_b$, respectively, are equivalent in their ability to support respiration. For reasons discussed elsewhere[42], it is also likely that the first 12 amino acids in V$_a$ and V$_b$ are equivalent in their ability to support respiration in aerobic cells. These findings suggest that V$_a$ and V$_b$ do not differ in their ability to assemble and function in the holoenzyme and that the effectiveness of their genes results primarily from differences in their expression.

YEAST IV/BOVINE VIa

34.0% identity in 100 aa overlap

```
  1' MLSLRQSIRFFKPATRTLCSSRYLLQQKPVVKTAQNLAEVNGPETLIGPGAKEGTVPTDL
                                                 :.:.:::::
  1"                                              ASGGGVPTDE

 61' DQETGLARLELLGKLEGIDVFDTKPLDSSRKGTMKDPIIIESYDDYRYVGCTGSPAGSHT
     .:.:::.:  .:.  .:....:  ..  .::..::  .:.. : :::. ...
 11" EQATGLEREVMLAARKGQDPYNILA-PKATSGTKEDPNLVPSITNKRIVGCI-CEEDNST

121' IMWLKPTVNEVARCWECGSVYKLNPVGVPNDDHHH
     ..:.  .:..::  .::.  ::: : ...
 69" VIWFWLHKGEAQRCPSCGTHYKLVPHQLAH
```

YEAST Va/BOVINE IV

19.2% identity in 99 aa overlap

```
  1' MLRNTFTRAGGLSRITSVRFAQTHALSNAAVMDLQSRWENMPSTEQQDIVSKLSERQKLP
                                              :.:..:  .
  1"                              AHGSVVKSEDYALPSYVDRRDYPLPDVAHVKNLSASQKALKEKEKAS

 61' WAQLTEPEKQAVWYISYGEWGPRRPVLNKGDSSFIAKGVAAGLLFSVGLFAVVRMAG---
     :.  :.  ::  ...  ...  :    .  .  .:......  .    ::  ....  .  ...
 48" WSSLSIDEKVELYRLKFKE---SFAEMNRSTNEWKTVVGAAMFFIGFTALLLIWEKHYVY

118' GQDAKTMNKEWQLKSDEYLKSKNANPWGGYSQVQSK
     :..  ..:..::  :  ...  .....:  :.:
105" GPIPHTFEEEWVAKQTKRMLDMKVAPIQGFSAKWDYDKNEWKK
```

YEAST Vb/BOVINE IV

18.6% identity in 97 aa overlap

```
  1' MLRTSLTKGARLTGTRFVQTKALSKATLTDLPERWENMPNLEQKEIADNLTERQKLPWKT
                                                 :.:..:  .:..
  1"                              AHGSVVKSEDYALPSYVDRRDYPLPDVAHVKNLSASQKALKEKEKASWSS

 61' LNNEEIKAAWYISYGEWGPRRPVHGKGDVAFITKGVFLGLGISFGLFGLVRLLANPETPK
     :..  .:  ...  .  ....  :  .  ....  .  ...  :  .  .  .  .:.
 51" LSIDEKVELYRLKFKESFAEMNRSTNEWKTVVGAAMFF-IGFTALLLIWEKHYVYGPIPH

121' TMNREWQLKSDEYLKSKNANPWGGYSQVQSK
     :...  ::  : ...  .....:  :.:
110" TFEEEWVAKQTKRMLDMKVAPIQGFSAKWDYDKNEWKK
```

YEAST VI/BOVINE V

40.0% identity in 100 aa overlap

```
  1' MLSRAIFRNPVINRTLLRARPGAYHATRLTKNTFIQSRKYSDAHDEETFEEFTARYEKEF
                                              .::  :::.::.  .  :
  1"                              SHGSHETDEEFDARWVTYF

 61' DEA-YDLFEVQRVLNNCFSYDLVPAPAVIEKALRAARRVNDLPTAIRVFEALKYKVENED
     ...  :  .:...  .:.  .:::::.:  .:.  ::::  ::.::..:.:.:..:  :..  ..
 20" NDPDIDAWELRKGMNTLVGYDLVPEPKIIDAALRACRRLNDFASAVRILEVVKDKAGPHK

120' QYKAY-LDELKDVRQELGVPLKEELFPSSS
     .  .:  .::.  ..:::..  :::
 80" EIYPYVIQELRPTLNELGISTPEELGLDKV
```

YEAST VIIa/BOVINE VIc

19.2% identity in 52 aa overlap

```
  1'    TIAPITGTIKRRVIMDIVLGFSLGGVMASYWWWGFHMDKINKREKFYAELAERKKQ
        ...  :  .  ::.  ..:: ...  .  .:...  .  ..  .  ..:: . ...:
  1" STALAKPQMRGLLARRLRFHIVGAFMVSLGFATFYKFAVAEKRKKAYADFYRNYDSMKDF

 57' EN

 61" EEMRKAGIFQSAK
```

Figure 1.   Sequence alignment of nuclear-coded polypeptides from
yeast and bovine cytochrome c oxidases. For each set
the top line is the yeast sequence (including leader
peptides where they exist); the bottom line is the
bovine sequence. Homology values are given only for
the regions of overlap. A colon denotes identity and a
dot denotes a conservative replacement (ref 43).
Bovine subunits are named according to ref 47.

Studies are currently underway to determine if these isologs change the kinetic properties of holoenzyme molecules into which they assemble.

SEQUENCE SIMILARITIES BETWEEN NUCLEAR-CODED YEAST AND BOVINE HEART SUBUNIT POLYPEPTIDES

Are the nuclear-coded subunits of other eukaryotic cytochrome c oxidases also essential? Because genetic studies like those described above are not yet feasible with most other eukaryotes, this question is currently unanswered. However, before extrapolating data obtained with yeast to other eukaryotes one must demonstrate that these other organisms contain polypeptides that have significant homology to those of yeast. Toward this end we previously used partial sequences of the nuclear-coded yeast subunits to tentatively identify subunit homologs in yeast, bovine heart, and Neurospora crassa cytochrome c oxidases[20]. This preliminary analysis has been refined further here by use of the complete polypeptide sequences of all subunits of yeast and bovine heart cytochrome c oxidases and a new algorithm[43] (which aligns sequences for optimal homology after scoring for amino acid identity, the presence of insertions and deletions, and amino acid replacements based on the frequency with which similar replacements occur in the Dayhoff data base[43]). The best alignments are shown in Figs. 1 and 2. All yeast subunits except VII show homology with at least one of the subunits in the bovine heart enzyme. Interestingly, yeast subunit VIII can be aligned with both bovine VIIIa and VIIIc (Fig. 2).

To address the question of whether the alignments shown in Figs. 1 and 2 are significant, we have used the RDF program[43], an algorithm that evaluates the statistical significance of each match by comparing each yeast sequence with randomly permuted versions of the related bovine sequence. This program gives a Z-valve that is comparable to a probability value (Table 2). Using the guidelines established by Lipman and Pearson[43]--it is possible to recognize 3 classes of alignments. The matches between the mitochondrially-coded subunits (I, II, III) in both organisms and between yeast subunit IV - bovine V and yeast subunit VI - bovine VIa are highly significant. The match between yeast VIII and bovine VIIIa is significant. And the matches between yeast subunit V_a or V_b and bovine subunit IV, yeast subunit VIIa - bovine VIa and yeast subunit VIII - bovine VIIIa are probably significant. In Table 2 we have also shown the results of a match between yeast subunit VII and bovine VIIIc, a pair of subunits recently proposed to be homologous[45]. The Z values determined for this subunit pair can not be considered significant.

From the alignments shown in Figs. 1 and 2 and their Z-values it appears likely that all of the nuclear-coded subunits of yeast cytochrome c oxidase, except subunit VII, have counterparts among the nuclear-coded subunits of bovine heart cytochrome c oxidase (Fig. 3). While yeast

BOVINE VIIIa/YEAST VIII/BOVINE VIIIc

```
1'  LGYQQGPGKNIPFSVENKWRLLAMMTL-FFGSGFAAPFFIVRGQLLKK
       ...: .::::.:...  :.  .  .  ::. .:::.::  . :: :
1"  VHFKLGVYENIPFKVKGRKCPYALSHFGFFAIGFAVPFVATYVQLKK
       ::.:.:.  .::  ...:  :  .  . ....:
1''' FENRVAEKQKLFQEDNGLPVHLKGGATDNILYRVTMTLC-LGGTLYSLYCLGHASKKYVQLKK
```

Figure 2. Sequence alignment of yeast subunit VIII (middle line) with bovine subunit VIIIa (top line) and bovine subunit VIIIc (bottom line). A colon denotes identity and a dot denotes a conservative replacement.

Table 2. Homologies of Yeast and Bovine Cytochrome c Oxidase Subunits

Yeast	Bovine	Homology[a]	Z-value[b]
I	I	58.4% in 510 AA	113.1 ± 34.1
II	II	43.8% in 201 AA	28.9 ± 0.42
III	III	45.0% in 260 AA	37.1 ± 0.66
IV	VIa	34.0% in 100 AA	17.9 ± 5.0
Va }	IV	19.2% in 99 AA	4.4 ± 1.47
Vb }		18.6% in 97 AA	4.8 ± 0.40
VI	V	40.0% in 100 AA	19.6 ± 3.56
VII	VIIIc	23.9% in 46 AA	2.4 ± 0.41
VIIa	VIc	19.2% in 52 AA	4.4 ± 0.33
VIII	{ VIIIa	37.8% in 45 AA	7.7 ± 2.73
	{ VIIIc	27.3% in 33 AA	4.5 ± 0.75
No Known Counterparts	{ VIb { VII { VIIb		

[a]Homology is given only for the regions of overlap.

[b]$Z = \dfrac{(\text{similarity score} - \text{mean of random scores})}{(\text{standard deviation of random scores})}$; calculated as described[43]

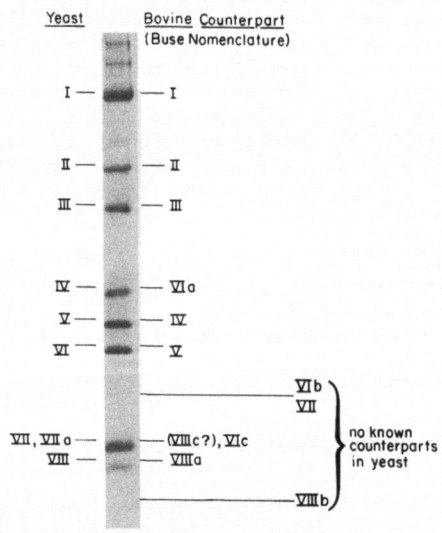

Figure 3. Bovine heart cytochrome c oxidase subunit polypeptides which are proposed to be equivalent to the nine polypeptides of yeast cytochrome c oxidase. The enzyme displayed on a "high resolution" SDS-gel[4] is from yeast. The nomenclature used for the yeast and bovine enzymes are from refs 4 and 47, respectively.

subunit VIII exhibits homology to both bovine subunit VIIIa and VIIIc it is more similar to VIIIa. No counterparts for bovine heart subunits VIb, VII, or VIIIb exist among the nuclear-coded subunits of yeast cytochrome c oxidase.

CONCLUSIONS

The results summarized here clearly indicate that the nuclear-coded subunits of yeast cytochrome c oxidase are essential constituents of the holoenzyme. They now provide a basis for studies on the role of these polypeptides in holoenzyme function, assembly, and regulation. These studies will be performed using the techniques of site-directed mutagenesis, in conjunction with the cloned genes for these polypeptides and the null mutants described in Table 1. In extrapolating the findings with yeast null mutants to cytochrome c oxidases from other organisms, it is essential to realize that computer alignments, like those shown in Figs. 1 and 2, can only suggest functional homology. They cannot prove it. One possible approach toward establishing that polypeptide subunits in other organisms have similar functions to those in yeast is through heterologous complementation in yeast (cf., ref. 45). This would involve either: 1) the introduction of cloned genes for a nuclear-coded subunit (e.g., subunit V) from an organism like bovine into a yeast strain that carries a null mutation in one of the structural genes for its proposed yeast counterpart (e.g., GD6); or 2) the use of a cDNA library from any organism to identify genes that complement mutants (like those described in Table 1) in the structural genes for yeast cytochrome c oxidase.

ACKNOWLEDGEMENTS

This work was supported by grant GM 34827 from the National Institutes of Health.

REFERENCES

1. M. Wikstrom, K. Krab, and M. Saraste, "Cytochrome Oxidase," Academic Press, New York (1981).
2. R. Walenga and R. O. Poyton, Fed. Proc. 37:2326 (1978).
3. N. C. Robinson, Biochemistry 21:184 (1982).
4. S. D. Power, M. A. Lochrie, K. A. Sevarino, T. E. Patterson, and R. O. Poyton, J. Biol. Chem. 259:6564 (1984).
5. B. Kadenbach and P. Merle, FEBS Lett. 135:1 (1981).
6. A. Tzagoloff and A. M. Myers, Ann. Rev. Biochem. 55:248 (1986).
7. A. Naqui, B. Chance, and E. Cadenas, Ann. Rev. Biochem. 55:137 (1986).
8. G. Buse and G. J. Steffans, Hoppe-Seyler's Z. Physiol. Chem. 359:1005 (1978).
9. G. J. Steffans and G. Buse, Hoppe-Seyler's Z. Physiol. Chem. 360:613 (1979).
10. R. Sacher, G. J. Steffans, and G. Buse, Hoppe-Seyler's Z. Physiol. Chem. 360:1385 (1979).
11. M. Tanaka, M. Hanin, K. T. Yasunobu, C-A. Yu, L. Yu, Y-H. Wei, and T. E. King, J. Biol. Chem. 254:3879 (1979).
12. G. C. M. Steffans, G. J. Steffans, and G. Buse, Hoppe-Seyler's Z. Physiol. Chem. 360:1641 (1979).
13. R. Biewald and G. Buse, Hoppe-Seyler's Z. Physiol. Chem. 363:1141 (1982).
14. L. Meinecke, G. J. Steffans, and G. Buse, Hoppe-Seyler's Z. Physiol. Chem. 365:313 (1984).

15. L. Meinecke and G. Buse, Biol. Chem. Hoppe-Seyler's 366:687 (1985).
16. M. Erdweg and G. Buse, Biol. Chem. Hoppe-Seyler's 366:257 (1985).
17. L. Meinecke and G. Buse, Biol. Chem. Hoppe-Seyler's 367:67 (1986).
18. I. Gregor and A. Tsugita, J. Biol. Chem. 257:13081 (1982).
19. S. D. Power, M. A. Lochrie, T. E. Patterson, and R. O. Poyton, J. Biol. Chem. 259:6571 (1984).
20. S. D. Power, M. A. Lochrie and R. O. Poyton, J. Biol. Chem. 259:6575 (1984).
21. S. D. Power, M. A. Lochrie and R. O. Poyton, J. Biol. Chem. 261:9206 (1986).
22. S. Anderson, M. H. L. deBruijn, A. R. Coulson, I. C. Eperon, F. Sanger, and I. G. Young, J. Mol. Biol. 156:683 (1982).
23. S. G. Bonitz, G. Coruzzi, B. E. Thalenfeld, A. Tzagoloff, and G. Macino, J. Biol. Chem. 255:11927 (1980).
24. G. Coruzzi and A. Tzagoloff, J. Biol. Chem. 254:9324 (1979).
25. B. E. Thalenfeld and A. Tzagoloff, J. Biol. Chem. 255:6173 (1980).
26. A. C. Maarse, A. P. G. M. Van Loon, H. Riezman, I. Gregor, G. Schatz and L. A. Grivell, EMBO J. 3:2831 (1984).
27. M. G. Cumsky, C. Ko, C. E. Trueblood, and R. O. Poyton, Proc. Natl. Acad. Sci. USA 82:2235 (1985).
28. M. G. Cumsky, C. E. Trueblood, C. Ko, and R. O. Poyton, Mol. Cell Biol., submitted (1987).
29. R. M. Wright, C. Ko, M. G. Cumsky, and R. O. Poyton, J. Biol. Chem. 259:15401 (1984).
30. R. M. Wright, L. K. Dircks, and R. O. Poyton, J. Biol. Chem. 261:17183 (1986).
31. T. E. Patterson and R. O. Poyton, J. Biol. Chem. 261:17192 (1986).
32. R. O. Poyton and G. Schatz, J. Biol. Chem. 250:762 (1975).
33. A. Tzagoloff, A. Akai, R. B. Needleman, and G. Zulch, J. Biol. Chem. 250:8236 (1975).
34. P. P. Slonimski and A. Tzagoloff, Eur. J. Biochem. 61:27 (1976).
35. F. Cabral, M. Solioz, Y. Rudin, G. Schatz, L. Clavilier, and P. P. Slonimski, J. Biol. Chem. 253:297 (1978).
36. J. E. McEwen, C. Ko, B. Kloeckener-Gruissem, and R. O. Poyton, J. Biol. Chem. 261:11872 (1986).
37. F. Cabral, M. Solioz, D. Deters, Y. Rudin, G. Schatz, L. Clavilier, O. Groudinsky, and P. P. Slonimski, in "Mitochondria 1977," W. Bandlow, R. J. Schweyen, K. Wolf, and F. Kaudewitz, ed., Gruyter, Berlin (1977).
38. D. B. Winter, W. J. Bruyninckx, F. G. Boulke, N. P. Grnich, and H. S. Mason, J. Biol. Chem. 255:11408 (1980).
39. M. Thelen, P. S. O'Shea, G. Petrone, and A. Azzi, J. Biol. Chem. 260:3626 (1985).
40. B. Ludwig, FEMS Microbiol. Rev. 46:41 (1987).
41. J. M. McEwen, unpublished observation.
42. C. E. Trueblood and R. O. Poyton, Mol. Cell Biol., submitted (1987).
43. D. J. Lipman and W. R. Pearson, Science 227:1435 (1985).
44. M. Dayhoff, "Atlas of Protein Sequence and Structure," National Biomedical Research Foundation, Silver Spring, MD, vol. 5. (1978).
45. R. A. Capaldi, D. Gonzalez-Halphen, and S. Takamiya, FEBS Letts. 207:11 (1986).
46. R. M. Wright, J. D. Trawick, C. E. Trueblood, T. E. Patterson, and R. O. Poyton, this volume (1987).
47. G. Buse, L. Meinecke, and B. Bruch, J. Inorgan. Biochem. 23:149 (1985).
48. R. M. Wright and R. O. Poyton, in preparation.

RESPIRATORY COMPLEX IV AND CYTOCHROME a,a_3

G. Buse, G.C.M. Steffens, R. Biewald, B. Bruch and
S. Hensel

RWTH Aachen
Abteilung Physiologische Chemie
Fachgebiet Molekulare Biologie der Proteine
Klinikum, Pauwelsstraße
5100 Aachen .

INTRODUCTION

If one asks, which criteria might be mandatory for the
opinion on an enzyme complex, the function of which is not yet
fully understood, the integral stoichiometry of all components of
the isolate must be considered a guideline for preparation and
purification besides known enzymatic activities and pertinent
spectral properties. Application of this principal chemical rule
is especially necessary in those fields of work, where our
methods leave doubt, whether what we obtain is a faithful
representation of what exists in nature. This is the case with
the respiratory enzyme complexes, e.g. mitochondrial cytochrome c
oxidase. The solubilisation and purification of this enzyme from
the mitochondrial (or bacterial) membrane has in many cases not
met the above criterion. The complete proteinchemical
description of the so far most complex type of this enzyme,
obtained from bovine heart, and its comparison with simpler
eucaryotic and procaryotic oxidases defines the structure of
integral preparations more precisely and at the same time is a
guide to the function.

THE RESPIRATORY COMPLEX IV FROM BOVINE HEART MITOCHONDRIA

If cytochrome c oxidase is isolated from beef heart
mitochondria via disruption of the membrane and solubilisation by
deoxycholate, successive purification by fractionated
precipitation with ammoniumsulfate in different concentrations of
cholate can produce an enzyme which is a stoichiometric
arrangement of 13 subunits with 7 metal centres besides less well
defined amounts of phosphate components (phospholipids, ATP?) and
detergents[1,2]. This is called the respiratory complex IV. If
reconstituted in phospholipid vesicles it exhibits the well known
activities of coupled electron transport, oxygen activation and
proton translocation. In contrast to its complexity only two to

three subunits and four metal centres of this array have been claimed for this function.

The protein components of complex IV[*]

The complete primary structures of the 12 protein components constituting the 13 subunits of bovine heart complex IV are listed in table 3. In the following we point to a few characteristics of structural and functional importance.

I.   The amino acid sequence of subunit I (514 residues, Mr 56.993) was first obtained from the mtDNA gene[3] with the aid of structural information from the protein. Investigation of the latter has now proved this structure (S. Hensel and G. Buse, in prep.). This chain, as that of subunit II, is among the few examples of mammalian proteins with persistent N-formyl-methionine in the mature protein indicating the bacterial like mitochondrial origin. The hydrophobic protein may have up to 12 membrane penetrating helices. Investigation of subunit I genes obtained from phylogenetically distant organisms shows a set of invariant histidine residues (pos. according to bovine sequence His 61, 138, 151, 233, 240, 290, 291, 368, 376, 429) but absence of invariant cysteines in this rather conservative protein. In an attempt to find the minimal cytochrome oxidase among the much simpler bacterial enzymes, the c_1,a,a_3 terminal oxidase from Thermus thermophilus[4] is presently sequenced in the authors' lab (S. Hensel, J.A. Fee and G. Buse, in prep.). As can be seen from the example in table 1 the larger subunit of this enzyme shows clear homology to subunit I of known cytochrome c oxidases.

Table 1: Alignment of sequences from the a,a_3 subunit of Thermus thermophilus to subunits I of cytochrome oxidase

	293	437
bovine	FTVGMDVDTRAYFTSATMIIAIPTGVKVFS	PRRYSDYPDAYTMW
maize	FTVGLDVDTRAYFTAATMIIAVPTGIKIFS	PRRIPDYPDAYAGW
yeast	YIVGLDADTRAYFTSATMIIAIPTGIKIFS	PRRIPDYPDAFAGW
Trypanos.b.	FVVGMDVDSRAYFGSITVLIGLPTCIKLFN	PRRISDYPISFLFW
Thermus th.	FTVGESTLFQIAFAFFTALIAVPTGVKLFN	PRRYYTYNADIAGW

The second subunit seems to be a c_1-cytochrome and thus it is likely that subunit I binds both heme a and heme a_3 and is the only "cytochrome" also in the respiratory complex IV (see also[5]).

II.   The structure of subunit II (227 residues, Mr 26.049) also supports this suggestion. This protein was the first to be sequenced from the mitochondrially coded subunits of the enzyme,[6] and had already been suggested to be a copper protein distantly related to plastocyanines and azurines. Sequences obtained from

---

[*]The authors suggest to introduce a nomenclature which lists the proteins of the bovine (mammalian) type of the enzyme from I to XII mainly according to molecular mass. Subunits derived from less complex enzymes may be listed in the same way and homology to mammalian subunits added in parenthesis. Thus yeast VIII,(XI) indicates the second smallest subunit among the nine proteins of the yeast complex and its homology to subunit XI of the bovine enzyme. Clearly, I, II, III are the subunits coded for in mitochondria or bacteria.

the mtDNA genes coding for subunit II show that two cysteines (pos.196,200) and histidines, the suggested copper ligands, are among the invariant residues of this chain.

Comparison of subunits II from Paracoccus denitrificans (P. Steinrücke, G.C.M. Steffens, G. Pankus, G. Buse and B. Ludwig, Eur. J. Biochem. submitted) and the exprimed Trypanosoma brucei oxidase[6] reduces the number of invariant histidine residues to 3 (pos.24,161,204) or 2 (pos.161,204) respectively, and thus do not allow for a binding of an imidazol coordinated heme a iron besides copper.

Table 2: Sequence alignment of the proposed copper binding site in subunit II and the C-terminus of the mature Paracoccus protein

	161	196 200 204	227
bovine	EDVLHSW	YYGQCSEICGSNHSFMPIVLELVPLKYFEKWSASML	
maize	ADVPHSW	YYGQCSEICGTNHAFTPIVVEAVTLKDYADWVSNQLILQTN	
yeast	ADVIHDF	FYGACSELCGTGHANMPIKIEAVSLPKFLEWLNEQ	
Tryp.b.	VDVIHSF	LYGQCSELCGVLHGFMPIVINFI	
Par.den.	TDVIHAW	YFGQCSELCGINHAYMPIVVKAVSQEKYEAWLAGAKEEFAA	

Since subunit II has been identified as cytochrome c binding site,[8] the copper in this subunit must function as first electron conductor to the terminal enzyme unit.

III. Description of the function of cytochrome c oxidase makes so far only use of subunits I and II, which bind all redox active centres. They represent the core of the larger membrane domain of the y shaped enzyme and correspond to the fully functional two subunit form of the enzyme isolated from Paracoccus denitrificans [9,10]. The in reality second largest chain of mitochondrial oxidases, subunit III (261 residues, Mr 29.918),[3] a proteinchemically characterized mtDNA product, is a hydrophobic protein with 5-7 membrane intercalating sequences - one containing the DCCD reactive Glu (pos.90)[11]. It may represent the core of the second membrane domain of the mitochondrial enzymes. The N-terminus of this subunit is deformylated and therefore probably excessible to the cytoplasmic surface. Among the non-invariant cysteine residues there is an in situ reactive species at pos.115[12]. The function of this subunit is not known.

The nuclear coded subunits of the bovine heart enzyme represent 44,3% of the protein molecular mass of complex IV. Eight of the nine mature polypeptides have been sequenced in the authors' lab. There is no safe information about the function of any of these proteins, however, the indication of a tissue specific structure has led to suggestions of a regulatory function [13]. Isoenzyme expression in different tissues would point to an even more complex organization of the corresponding nuclear genome.

IV. Subunit IV (147 residues, Mr 17.153)[14] has been identified as the largest nuclear coded subunit in the mammalian oxidases - probably without exhibiting tissue specifity. Two forms of this chain were analysed from yeast[15]. The bovine protein has one membrane sequence and a large charged N-terminal part directed towards the matrix space of the mitochondria[16]. The chain does not contain cysteine residues. The C-terminus -Lys-Lys points to a specific processing site as in several other cytoplasmically synthesized subunits[17].

V.   The sequence of subunit V (109 residues, Mr 12.436) was first published by Tanaka et al.[18]. It has also been analysed from yeast[19]. The protein has no hydrophobic membrane section and contains one cysteine residue (pos.55).

VI.   In most SDS gel-systems a polypeptide termed VIa (98 residues, Mr 10.668)[20] runs with larger apparent Mr than V. The chain has no hydrophobic sequence. Among the 4 cysteine residues of the bovine protein 2 represent sulfhydryls (pos.60,62) and 2 (pos.82 to 85) are arranged as a disulfide bond similar to the cysteine center of thioredoxins. These latter residues are also present in the homologous yeast subunit IV (VI)[21]. The chain contains a sequence which may arrange to a metal complexing site. This protein is therefore a candidate for the binding of zinc found in mitochondrial oxidases.

VII.   The chain of polypeptide VII (85 residues, Mr 10.063)[22] is the only N-terminally blocked protein among the cytoplasmically synthesized subunits of the bovine heart enzyme. Also this chain has 4 cysteine residues, these form 2 disulfide linkages from pos.29 to 64 and 39 to 53. With 4 tryptophan residues it exhibits the most extensive UV absorption among the nuclear coded subunits. This subunit as well as the following is accessible to trypsin cleavage in the intact enzyme.

VIII. Subunit VIb in our original nomenclature (84 residues, Mr 9.419)[23] contains one cysteine in its membrane intercalating sequence. The protein is rich in histidine residues in its hydrophilic part. A homologous subunit has not been found in yeast cytochrome c oxidase.

IX.   With polypeptide VIc (73 residues, Mr 8.480)[24] we have described a positively charged protein which may include a membrane sequence with one lysine residue. The chain does not contain cysteine. Lack of tryptophan leads to a low 280 nm absorption. Again no homologous subunit has been found in the yeast enzyme.

The beef as well as the yeast enzyme each contains three small membrane penetrating polypeptides exhibiting different degrees of homology to their respective counterparts[25]. This is, however, obvious only with the pair listed as XI; while it may be simulated by the close structural analogy in the other cases.

X.   The largest, polypeptide VIIIc (56 residues, Mr 6.243)[26] contains 2 cysteine residues within its membrane sequence and ends in a short positively charged sequence with terminal -Lys-Lys.

XI.   A similar construction is found in VIIIa (47 residues, Mr 5.441)[27], which has no cysteine and aspartic acid residues, but again a similar C-terminus, indicating a site specific processing.

XII.   The shortest polypeptide in the bovine enzyme is VIIIb (46 residues, Mr 4.962)[28]. It does not contain arginine and cysteine residues. It is the only chain which has been found with the stoichiometry 2 in the monomer of complex IV.

Table 3. Amino acid sequences of cytochrome c oxidase from beef heart. Hydrophobic sequences in boldface type.

I   Subunit I
                        20   30   40   50
        fMFINRWLFST NHKDIGTLYL LFGAWAGMVG TALSLLIRAE LGQPGTLLGD
                60   70   80   90   100
        DQIYNVVVTA HAFVMIFFMV MPIMIGGFGN WLVPLMIGAP DMAFPRMNNM
               110   120   130   140   150
        SFWLLPPSFL LLLASSMVEA GAGTGWTVYP PLAGNLAHAG ASVDLTIFSL
               160   170   180   190   200
        HLAGVSSILG AINFITTIIN MKPPAMSQYQ TPLFVWSVMI TAVLLLLSLP
               210   220   230   240   250
        VLAAGITMLL TDRNLNTTFF DPAGGGDPIL YQHLFWFFGH PEVYILILPG
               260   270   280   290   300
        FGMISHIVTY YSGKKEPFGY MGMVWAMMSI GFLGFIVWAH HMFTVGMDVD
               310   320   330   340   350
        TRAYFTSATM IIAIPTGVKV FSWLATLHGG NIKWSPAMMW ALGFIFLFTV
               360   370   380   390   400
        GGLTGIVLAN SSLDIVLHDT YYVVAHFHYV LSMGAVFAIM GGFVHWFPLF
               410   420   430   440   450
        SGYTLNDTWA KIHFAIMFVG VNMTFFPQHF LGLSGMPRRY SDYPDAYTMW
               460   470   480   490   500
        NTISSMGSFI SLTAVMLMVF IIWEAFASKR EVLTVDLTTT NLEWLNGCPP
               510 514
        PYHTFEEPTY VNLK

II   Subunit II
                        20   30   40   50
        fMAYPMQLGFQ DATSPIMEEL LHFHDHTLMI VFLISSLVLY IISLMLTTKL
                60   70   80   90   100
        THTSTMDAQE VETIWTILPA IILILIALPS LRILYMMDEI NNPSLTVKTM
               110   120   130   140   150
        GHQWYWSYEY TDYEDLSFDS YMIPTSELKP GELRLLEVDN RVVLPMEMTI
               160   170   180   190   200
        RMLVSSEDVL HSWAVPSLGL KTDAIPGRLN QTTLMSSRPG LYYGQCSEIC
               210   220   227
        GSNHSFMPIV LELVPLKYFE KWSASML

III   Subunit III
                        20   30   40   50
        MTHQTHAYHM VNPSPWPLTG ALSALLMTSG LTMWFHFNSM TLLMIGLTTN
                60   70   80   90   100
        MLTMYQWWRD VIRESTFQGH HTPAVQKGLR YGMILFIISE VLFFTGFFWA
               110   120   130   140   150
        FYHSSLAPTP ELGGCWPPTG IHPLNPLEVP LLNTSVLLAS GVSITWAHHS
               160   170   180   190   200
        LMEGDRKHML QALFITITLG VYFTLLQASE YYEAPFTISD GVYGSTFFVA
               210   220   230   240   250
        TGFHGLHVII GSTFLIVCFF RQLKFHFTSN HHFGFEAGAW YWHFVDVVWL
                261
        FLYVSIYWWG S

                                                        (CONTINUED)

265

IV   Subunit IV

```
               20         30         40         50
AHGSVVKSED YALPSYVDRR DYPLPDVAHV KNLSASQKAL KEKEKASWSS
       60         70         80         90        100
LSIDEKVELY RLKFKESFAE MNRSTNEWKT VVGAAMFFIG FTALLLIWEK
      110        120        130        140     147
HYVYGPIPHT FEEEWVAKQT KRMLDMKVAP IQGFSAKWDY DKNEWKK
```

V   Subunit V

```
               20         30         40         50
SHGSHETDEE FDARWVTYFN KPDIDAWELR KGMNTLVGYD LVPEPKIIDA
       60         70         80         90        100
ALRACRRLND FASAVRILEV VKDKAGPHKE IYPYVIQELR PTLNELGIST
      109
PEELGLDKV
```

VI   Subunit VIa

```
               20         30         40         50
ASGGGVPTDE EQATGLEREV MLAARKGQDP YNILAPKATS GTKEDPNLVP
       60         70         80         90      98
SITNKRIVGC ICEEDNSTVI WFWLHKGEAQ RCPSCGTHYK LVPHQLAH
```

VII   Subunit VII

```
                  20         30         40         50
acAEDIQAKIKN YQTAPFDSRF PNQNQTRNCW QNYLDFHRCE KAMTAKGGDV
          60         70         80       85
SVCEWYRRVY KSLCPISWVS TWDDRRAEGT FPGKI
```

VIII   Subunit VIb

```
               20         30         40         50
ASAAKGDHGG TGARTWRFLT FGLALPSVAL CTLNSWLHSG HRERPAFIPY
       60         70         80      84
HHLRIRTKPF SWGDGNHTFF HNPRVNPLPT GYEK
```

IX   Subunit VIc

```
               20         30         40         50
STALAKPQMR GLLARRLRFH IVGAFMVSLG FATFYKFAVA EKRKKAYADF
       60         70  73
YRNYDSMKDF EEMRKAGIFQ SAK
```

X   Subunit VIIIc

```
               20         30         40         50
FENRVAEKQK LFQEDNGLPV HLKGGATDNI LYRVTMTLCL GGTLYSLYCL
       56
GHASKK
```

XI   Subunit VIIIa

```
               20         30         40       47
SHYEEGPGKN IPFSVENKWR LLAMMTLFFG SGFAAPFFIV RHQLLKK
```

XII   Subunit VIIIb

```
               20         30         40     46
ITAKPAKTPT SPKEQAIGLS VTFLSFLLPA GWVLYHLDNY KKSSAA
```

The purified enzyme complex

Criteria for the purification of the bovine heart cytochrome
c oxidase complex can be obtained from the proteinchemical
analysis. Taken together the monomeric respiratory complex IV is
arranged stoichiometrically from 3 mitochondrial and 10
cytoplasmic subunits with 1.793 amino acids and a protein
molecular mass of 202.787 Da[29]. Since this unit binds one species
each of the a and a_3 hemes the theoretical heme A to protein
ratio for an integral complex can be calculated. A molar
absorption coefficient close to 12.000 $l \cdot mol^{-1} \, cm^{-1}$ for the
reduced minus oxidized absorption at 604 nm has proven to be
correct by independent determination of the protein and iron
contents of purified enzyme preparations. On this basis a
stoichiometric complex should have 9,86 nmol heme a/mg protein.
The 12 different polypeptides, which stain without visable
impurity in SDS gels of the best preparations should, upon Edman
degradation of the entire enzyme, produce no phenylthiohydantoin
amino acids other than 3 Ala, 3 Ser, 2 Ile, 1 Phe and 1 Met/Thr
from the chains with free N-termini[30].

THE CATALYTIC UNIT

If enzyme preparations which fulfill the above criteria are
investigated for their metal contents by inductively coupled
plasma atomic emission spectroscopy (ICP-AES), a stoichiometric
relation is also observed for the metal contents: 3 Cu, 2 Fe, 1
Zn, 1 Mg . The metal contents can directly be correlated to the
simultaneously determined sulfur contents, which originate from
the 92 sulfur containing amino acids (75 Met + 17 Cys) of the
protein moiety.

Table 4: Stoichiometries of Cu, Fe, Zn, Mg and S determined by
ICP-AES in preparations of cytochrome c oxidase from
bovine heart and Paracoccus denitrificans

Bovine heart

Cu	Fe	Zn	Mg	S	heme a/mg
2,83±0,07	1,94±0,12	1,01±0,04	0,98±0,05	86,70±5,82	9,63±0,56

Paracoccus denitrificans

Cu	Fe	Zn	Mg	S	heme a/mg
2,97±0,08	2,09±0,10	0,33±0,07	0,70±0,27	42,98±1,00	23,32±1,39

Since also a purified Paracoccus denitrificans cytochrome c
oxidase, the preparation of which follows a completely different
protocol, contains 3 Cu and 2 Fe, three copper atoms must be
intrinsic constituents of cytochrome c oxidase. Together with the
metal contents and protein data described for the Thermus
thermophilus enzyme this led us to the conclusion, that subunit I
of the mitochondrial (and many bacterial) enzymes is the
principal 2 Cu, heme a,a_3 catalytic unit of complex IV and the
universal terminal oxidase of this spectral type[2].

ACKNOWLEDGEMENT

This work was supported by Sonderforschungsbereich 160
"Biologische Membranen" of the Deutsche Forschungsgemeinschaft.

REFERENCES

1. G. Steffens and G. Buse, Studien an Cytochrom-c-Oxidase, I; Reinigung und Charakterisierung des Enzyms aus Rinderherzen und Identifizierung der im Komplex enthaltenen Peptidketten, Hoppe-Seyler's Z. Physiol. Chem. 357:1125 (1976).

2. G.C.M. Steffens, R. Biewald and G. Buse, Cytochrome c oxidase is a three copper, two heme a protein, Eur. J. Biochem., in press.

3. S. Anderson, M.H.L. De Bruijn, A.R. Coulson, I.C. Eperon, F. Sanger and I.G. Young, Complete Sequence of Bovine Mitochondrial DNA; Conserved Features of the Mammalian Mitochondrial Genome, J. Mol. Biol. 156:683 (1982).

4. T. Yoshida, R.M. Lorence, M.G. Choc, G.E. Tarr, K.L. Findling and J.A. Fee, Respiratory Proteins from the Extremely Thermophilic Aerobic Bacterium, Thermus thermophilus; Purification Procedures for Cytochromes c_{552}, $c_{555,549}$ and $c_1 aa_3$ and Chemical Evidence for a Single Subunit Cytochrome aa_3, J. Biol. Chem. 259:112 (1984).

5. G. Buse, R. Biewald, G. Raabe and J. Fleischhauer, Structural Facts for the Site of e^- and H^+ Translocation in Cytochrome c Oxidase, in: "3rd European Bioenergetics Conference Reports", Hannover, 3A:119 (1984).

6. G.J. Steffens and G. Buse, Studies on Cytochrome c Oxidase, IV; Primary Structure and Function of Subunit II, Hoppe-Seyler's Z. Physiol Chem. 360:613 (1979).

7. L.A.M. Hensgens, J. Brakenhoff, B.F. De Vries, P. Sloof, M.C. Tromp, J.H. Van Boom and R. Benne, The sequence of the gene for cytochrome c oxidase subunit I, a frameshift containing gene for cytochrome c oxidase subunit II and seven unassigned reading frames in Trypanosoma brucei mitochondrial maxi-circle DNA, Nucl. Acid. Res. 12:7327 (1984).

8. J.F. Deatherage and R. Henderson, Three-dimensional Structure of Cytochrome c Oxidase; Vesicle Crystals in Negative Stain, J. Mol. Biol. 158:487 (1982).

9. M. Solioz, E. Carafoli and B. Ludwig, The Cytochrome c Oxidase of Paracoccus denitrificans Pumps Protons in a Reconstituted System, J. Biol. Chem. 257:1579 (1982).

10. G.C.M. Steffens, G. Buse, W. Oppliger and B. Ludwig, Sequence homology of bacterial and mitochondrial cytochrome c oxidases; Partial sequence data of cytochrome c oxidase from Paracoccus denitrificans, Biochem. Biophys. Res. Commun. 116:335 (1983).

11. L.J. Prochaska, R. Bisson, R.A. Capaldi, G.C.M. Steffens and G. Buse, Inhibition of Cytochrome c Oxidase Function by Dicyclohexylcarbodiimide, Biochim. Biophys. Acta 637:360 (1981).

12. F. Malatesta and R.A. Capaldi, Localization of Cysteine 115 in Subunit III of Beef Heart Cytochrome c Oxidase to the C-Side of the Mitochondrial Inner Membrane, Biochem. Biophys. Res. Commun. 109:1180 (1982).

13. B. Kadenbach, R. Hartmann, R. Glanville and G. Buse, Tissue-Specific Genes Code for Polypeptide VIa of Bovine Liver and Heart Cytochrome c Oxidase, FEBS Lett. 138:236 (1982).

14. R. Sacher, G.J. Steffens and G. Buse, Studies on Cytochrome c Oxidase, VI; Polypeptide IV - The Complete Primary Structure, Hoppe-Seyler's Z. Physiol. Chem. 360:1385 (1979).

15. M.G. Cumsky, C. Ko, C.E. Trueblood and R.O. Poyton, Two Nonidentical Forms of Subunit V are Functional in Yeast

Cytochrome c Oxidase, <u>Proc.</u> <u>Nat.</u> <u>Acad.</u> <u>Sci.</u> <u>USA</u> 82:2235 (1985).

16. F. Malatesta, V. Darley-Usmar, C. de Jong, L.J. Prochaska, R. Bisson, R.A. Capaldi, G.C.M. Steffens and G. Buse, Arrangement of Subunit IV in Beef Heart Cytochrome c Oxidase Probed by Chemical Labeling and Protease Digestion Experiments, <u>Biochemistry</u> 22:4405 (1983).

17. T.E. Patterson and R.O. Poyton, Cox 8, the Structural Gene for Yeast Cytochrome c Oxidase Subunit VIII; DNA Sequence and Gene Disruption Indicate that Subunit VIII is Required for Maximal Levels of Cellular Respiration and is Derived from a Precursor Which is Extended at Both its NH_2 and COOH Termini, <u>J.</u> <u>Biol.</u> <u>Chem.</u> 261:17192 (1986).

18. M. Tanaka, M. Haniu, K.T. Yasunobu, C.-A. Yu, L. Yu, Y.-H. Wei and T.E. King, Amino acid sequence of the heme a subunit of bovine heart cytochrome oxidase and sequence homology with hemoglobin, <u>Biochem.</u> <u>Biophys.</u> <u>Res.</u> <u>Commun.</u> 76:1014 (1977).

19. I. Gregor and S. Tsugita, The amino acid sequence of cytochrome c oxidase subunit VI from <u>Saccharomyces</u> <u>cerevisiae</u>, <u>J.</u> <u>Biol.</u> <u>Chem.</u> 257:13081 (1982).

20. R. Biewald and G. Buse, Studies on Cytochrome c Oxidase, IX; The Primary Structure of Polypeptide VIa, <u>Hoppe-Seyler's</u> <u>Z.</u> <u>Physiol.</u> <u>Chem.</u> 363:1141 (1982).

21. A.C. Maarse, A.P.G.M. van Loon, H. Riezman, I. Gregor, G. Schatz and L.A. Grivell, Subunit IV of Yeast Cytochrome c Oxidase, Cloning and Nucleotide Sequencing of the Gene and Partial Amino Acid Sequencing of the Mature Protein, <u>EMBO</u> <u>J.</u> 3:2831 (1984).

22. G.C.M. Steffens, G.J. Steffens and G. Buse, Studies on Cytochrome c Oxidase, VIII; The Amino Acid Sequence of Polypeptide VII, <u>Hoppe</u> <u>Seyler's</u> <u>Z.</u> <u>Physiol.</u> <u>Chem.</u> 360:1641 (1979).

23. L. Meinecke and G. Buse, Studies on Cytochrome c Oxidase, XII; Isolation and Primary Structure of Polypeptide VIb from Bovine Heart, <u>Biol.</u> <u>Chem.</u> <u>Hoppe-Seyler</u> 366:687 (1985).

24. M. Erdweg and G. Buse, Studies on Cytochrome c Oxidase, XI; The Amino Acid Sequence of Bovine Heart Polypeptide VIc, <u>Biol.</u> <u>Chem.</u> <u>Hoppe-Seyler</u> 366:257 (1985).

25. R.A. Capaldi, D. Gonzales-Halphen and S. Takamiya, Sequence Homologies and Structural Similarities Between the Polypeptides of Yeast and Beef Heart Cytochrome c Oxidase, <u>FEBS</u> <u>Lett.</u> 207:11 (1986).

26. L. Meinecke and G. Buse, Studies on Cytochrome c Oxidase, XIII; Amino Acid Sequence of the Small Membrane Polypeptide VIIIc from Bovine Heart Respiratory Complex IV, <u>Biol.</u> <u>Chem.</u> <u>Hoppe-Seyler</u> 367:67 (1986).

27. G. Buse and G.J. Steffens, Studies on Cytochrome c Oxidase, II; The Chemical Constitution of a Short Polypeptide from the Beef Heart Enzyme, <u>Hoppe-Seyler's</u> <u>Z.</u> <u>Physiol.</u> <u>Chem.</u> 359:1005 (1978).

28. L. Meinecke, G.J. Steffens and G. Buse, Studies on Cytochrome c Oxidase, X; Isolation and Amino Acid Sequence of Polypeptide VIIIb, <u>Hoppe-</u> <u>Seyler's</u> <u>Z.</u> <u>Physiol.</u> <u>Chem.</u> 365:313 (1984).

29. G. Buse, L. Meinecke and B. Bruch, The Protein Formula of Beef Heart Cytochrome c Oxidase, <u>J.</u> <u>Inorg.</u> <u>Biochem.</u> 23:149 (1985).

30. G. Buse, G.J. Steffens, G.C.M. Steffens, L. Meinecke, S. Hensel and J. Reumkens, Sequence Analysis of Complex Membrane Proteins (Cytochrome c Oxidase), <u>in</u>: "Advanced Methods in Protein Microsequence Analysis", B. Wittmann-Liebold et al., eds., Springer Verlag (1986).

AN AMINO ACID SEQUENCE REGION OF SUBUNIT II OF CYTOCHROME OXIDASE WHICH
MAY BE RESPONSIBLE FOR EVOLUTIONARY CHANGES IN REACTIVITY WITH DIFFERENT
CYTOCHROMES c

Thomas L. Luntz and E. Margoliash

Dept. of Biochemistry, Molecular Biology and Cell Biology
Northwestern University
Evanston, Illinois 60201 USA

INTRODUCTION

The information encoded in the amino acid sequence of a protein, the
major expression of the genetic make-up of the organism in that particular
protein, has been interpreted in many ways in attempts to understand important structural and functional characteristics. At the simplest level
and particularly with the development of computational procedures for the
prediction of secondary structures from amino acid sequences (Chou and
Fasman, 1978), one can estimate which segments of a membrane-bound protein
are likely to be within the membrane and which are probably on one or the
other surface (Garoff, 1985). This is likely to become particularly useful
for respiratory chain membrane-bound components which have so far not
readily yielded to direct determinations of spatial structure requiring
crystallization. Furthermore, that type of analysis may serve to direct
experiments designed to verify an initial structural hypothesis, by indicating what residue modifications will yield significant conclusions, whether they are to be carried out chemically, on the protein itself, or by
directed mutagenesis of the relevant segment of the genetic apparatus.
    As the mutagenic approach to structure-function relations of proteins
is sure to become increasingly widespread, it might be useful to inject a
note of caution in regard to the interpretation of such experiments. Artificially obtained mutants of proteins, in which one amino acid residue
has replaced another, are just as much derivatives of the native structure,
a structure that has been filtered through eons of evolutionary selection,
as are chemically-modified proteins. As such, satisfactory interpretations of the functional concomitants of these changes depend on understanding the structural consequences, if any, of the mutation. In this regard,
it is expected that the considerable work being done on approaches to the
crystallization of membrane proteins, which, to date, has had its most sig-
gnal success in the determination of the spatial structure of an entire
bacterial photosynthetic reaction center (Diesenhofer et al., 1985), will
shortly lead to the crystallization of many of the membrane proteins that
that make up the typical mitochondrial respiration chain. This in turn
should provide a solid basis for the understanding of how single or multiple residue substitutions influence function.
    At the other extreme, if one develops the amino acid sequences of an
individual protein from a large taxonomic spread of organisms, one already
has available the results of many amino acid residue modification experiments carried out by the evolutionary process itself. At this time, the

development of effective gene cloning and nucleotide sequencing procedures, has made the accumulation of amino acid sequence information for many proteins enormously simpler than in the past two decades, during which amino acid sequences were generally laboriously established on the protein itself (Dayhoff, 1972, 1978). This is especially significant in regard to hydrophobic membrane proteins which are difficult objects for amino acid sequence determination. As a result, we are faced with an increasingly massive amount of sequence information. On such an extensive basis, the conservation of certain features of the amino acid sequence may serve to strengthen, in a convincing fashion, conclusions as to structure and function reached by other approaches, such as by secondary structure or membrane domain predictions. On the other hand, the evolutionary variations of certain features are generally much more difficult to interpret, because it is often impossible to determine whether such variation indicates that these features are of little or no significance to the structure of the protein, or whether, quite the contrary, they represent a precise selective adaptation to each species in which the protein is found. The argument between proponents of neutral mutations playing a major role in protein evolution and proponents of the view that evolutionary adaptation is the predominant factor in amino acid sequence changes has not been resolved [see, for example, the exchange of letters between Kimura (1981) and Goodman (1981)], though it does seem that so-called non-Darwinian processes of evolutionary descent of proteins tend to fade when enough precise information becomes available as to the detailed structural concomitants of functional changes.

In this connection, the major problem with the evolutionary approach to structure-function relations is that the only products that are available for observation are the results of successful experiments, and it is far more difficult to discern details of functional activities with a set of perfectly operating mechanisms, than if one could interfere with them in several different ways. Only when there is a concomitant change of some functional parameter and some structural factors is it sometimes possible to interpret them to be related, and thus explain the evolutionary amino acid sequence change as a result of a selective adaptation to a change in functional activity. These cases tend to be rare. It is interesting that the relation between the changes in the kinetic reactivities of primate, mammalian non-primate, and yeast cytochrome oxidases with various cytochromes c appear to be amenable to this type of analysis, as described below.

Finally, it should not be forgotten that the amino acid sequences of sets of homologous proteins are very rich repositories of the evolutionary history of the species making them and that is possible to unravel it, as was done first with cytochrome c (Fitch and Margoliash, 1967), using statistical approaches. To discuss the numerous types of biological information that can be derived from such statistical phylogenetic trees is well beyond the scope of these introductory remarks. (See, for example, Fitch and Margoliash, 1970; Margoliash, 1972; Dayhoff, 1972, 1978; George et al., 1985).

DIFFERENCES IN CYTOCHROME c - CYTOCHROME OXIDASE INTERACTIONS

There are at least three cases in which major differences have been observed in the interactions of cytochrome oxidase with the cytochromes c from appropriate homologous and heterologous sources.

In a comparison of the reactions of primate and non-primate mammalian cytochrome oxidases, by the polarographic technique, it was found that while the homologous pairs had the same kinetic behaviour, the heterologous combinations gave distinctly different results (Osheroff et al., 1983). Thus, a

non-primate cytochrome c, the horse protein, reacting with a primate oxidase yielded the same apparent K_m for the high affinity phase of the reaction, but only half the V_{max} recorded for a primate cytochrome c, the
human protein. The difference was even more dramatic with a non-primate
oxidase, the reaction with primate cytochrome c showing both a 6-fold
lower K_m and close to a 7-fold lower V_{max} than for the non-primate cytochrome c. These relationships occurred even though the second order rate
constant for the presteady state reaction of the reduced cytochrome c with
purified beef cytochrome oxidase was about two times larger for human
cytochrome c than it was for the horse protein. Even more remarkable, the
2,4,6-trinitrophenyl derivative of lysine 13 human cytochrome c, a modification which is located near the center of the enzymic interaction domain
on the 'front' surface of the molecule and causes major decreases in activity in the reactions of the homologous pairs (Koppenol and Margoliash,
1982), shows a decrease in K_m and an increase in V_{max} as compared to unmodified human cytochrome c reacting with beef cytochrome oxidase. With
this modification, the apparent high affinity K_m for human cytochrome c is
fully restored to that for the horse protein reacting with the beef oxidase, while the V_{max} goes from 15% to 58% of that for non-primate cytochrome c. These kinetic analysis are depicted in Fig. 1.

Furthermore, it was shown that though N,N,N',N'-tetramethylphenyl-
enediamine (TMPD), the reducing agent used in the polarographic assay,
reacted at the same rate with primate and non-primate cytochromes c
in solution, it reduced ferric human cytochrome in a preformed 1:1

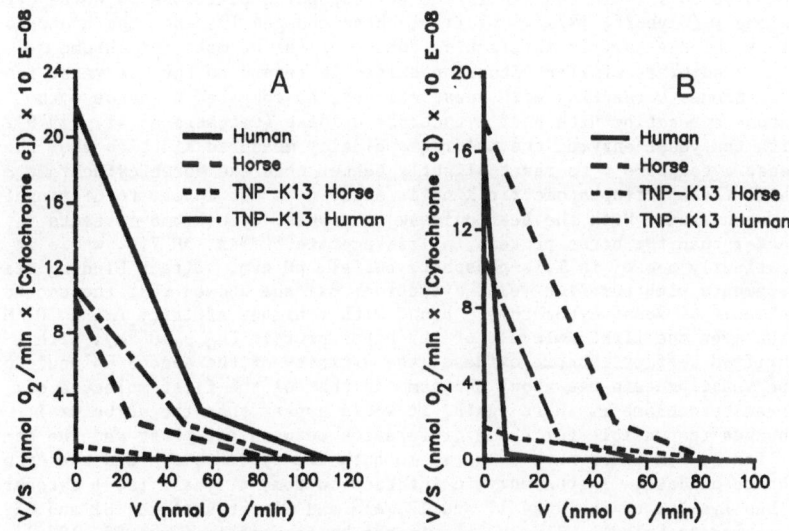

Fig. 1.   Panel A: Eadie-Hofstee representation of the steady state
oxidation of primate (human) and non-primate (horse) ferro-
cytochromes c by a Keilin-Hartree mitochondrial particle
preparation from rhesus monkey hearts, monitored polarographically. TNP-K13 refers to the 2,4,6-trinitrophenyl lysine
13 derivatives of the cytochromes c indicated. According to
Osheroff et al. (1983).
Panel B: An experiment similar to that depicted in Panel A,
but employing a mitochondrial particle preparation from beef
hearts. According to Osheroff et al. (1983).

complex with beef cytochrome oxidase at about one third the rate that it reduced the complex with horse cytochrome c. Similarly, with the preformed 1:1 complex of human ferricytochrome c with purified beef cytochrome oxidase, added ferrocytochrome c, whether human or horse, was oxidized 3 times slower than if the complex had contained horse ferricytochrome c (Osheroff et al., 1983).

All of these results were taken to indicate that the high affinity complex formed between non-primate mammalian cytochromes c and their homologous oxidase, just like the complex of primate cytochromes c with primate oxidase, define a 'normal' interaction, but that in both cases each member of the pair contributed differently to the binding affinity and to the nature of the forces involved in maintaining the complex. This was revealed when the kinetics of reaction of the heterologous pairs were examined, as described above. It appeared that the primate cytochrome c bound too tightly to the non-primate oxidase to attain the usual V_{max}, and in a way which hindered the usual reaction of TMPD, or of another molecule of cytochrome c, with the complex, while the non-primate cytochrome c carried out a less effective reaction with the primate than with the non-primate oxidase.

These observations made it clear that functionally significant evolutionary changes had occurred with both the cytochrome c and the oxidase of primates as compared to the non-primate proteins. Primate cytochromes c indeed show what appear to be significant differences in the amino acid side chains located in the enzymic interaction domain (Koppenol and Margoliash, 1982), as compared to non-primate mammalian cytochromes c. Thus, the human protein has an Ile-Met at Residues 11 and 12, and a Val at Residue 83, as compared to Val-Gln and Ala in the corresponding positions in horse cytochrome c (Dayhoff, 1972). Clearly, these changes increase the hydrophobicity of the enzymic interaction domain of the primate cytochrome c.

A somewhat similar situation exists in regard to the two yeast iso-cytochromes c reacting with yeast oxidase, as compared to horse cytochrome c reacting with beef cytochrome oxidase (Dethmers et al., 1979). With the yeast enzyme, the polarographically measured kinetics show the yeast cytochrome c to react slightly better than the horse cytochrome c, while the spectrophotometric kinetic assay does not appear to distinguish between them. With the beef oxidase, the yeast cytochrome c reacts better than the horse protein in Tris-acetate buffer, pH 7.8, while it is distinctly poorer in Tris-phosphate buffer, pH 6.5. Direct binding measurements with purified yeast cytochrome oxidase showed that the second molecule of yeast cytochrome c bound with a higher affinity ($K_D \cong 10^{-7}$M) than even the first molecule of the horse protein ($K_D \cong 10^{-6}$M). With purified beef cytochrome oxidase, the affinity of the second molecule of the yeast protein was about the same as that of the first molecule of horse cytochrome c. Here again, it would appear that the structural changes responsible for these differences between the yeast and the mammalian system, must have occurred in both the cytochrome c and the cytochrome oxidase. In the enzymic interaction domain, yeast iso-1 cytochrome c has Lys-Thr at Residues 11 and 12, Ala and Gly at Residues 81 and 83, as compared to Val-Gln, Ile and Ala in the horse protein (Dayhoff, 1972). These changes make the yeast cytochrome c interaction domain less hydrophobic and contribute an extra positively charged residue, as compared to the mammalian protein.

IDENTIFICATION OF A PROBABLE CYTOCHROME c BINDING DOMAIN ON SUBUNIT II

In an attempt to further explore the source of these kinetic phenomena, attention was turned to cytochrome oxidase and some simplifying assumptions were made. Despite the presence of 13 subunits (Kadenbach et al., 1983) and uncharacterized tissue-specific subunits (Kuhn-Nentwig and Kadenbach, 1985), for simplicity, the possibility that the behaviour was due to anything other than an alteration at the site, or part of the site, at which cytochrome   reacts with high affinity with cytochrome oxidase, was rejected. Since cross-linking reactions with cytochrome c and chemical modification of several residues in Subunit II (Bisson et al., 1980, 1982; Millet et al., 1983) have indicated that Subunit II contains at least part of the high affinity binding site for cytochrome c on the enzyme, attention was focused on the known amino acid sequences of this subunit. Indeed, it was anticipated that the alteration in functional behaviour would be reflected in changes of amino acid sequence. Further, since a comparison of all the corresponding reading frames from the human, beef and mouse mitochondrial genomes indicated the lowest level of positional evolutionary conservation was of alanines, serines, methionines, isoleucines, valines and threonines (Anderson et al., 1982), it was expected that elimination of changes involving these residues would tend to reveal a class of alterations related to functional differences.

Alignment of human, beef and mouse Subunit II sequences is straightforward, because they are identical in size and have a high degree of similarity. Mouse and beef Subunit II are 90% identical at the amino acid level; there are 22 differences in the total of 227 amino acids (Anderson et al., 1982; Bibb et al., 1981). Of these 22, 17 involve at least one of the six variable amino acids mentioned above. The remaining five are scattered along the polypeptide chain at positions 9, 22, 127, 192 and 221.

Mouse and human Subunit II are about 70% identical, with 65 differences (Bibb et al., 1981; Anderson et al., 1981). Fifty-one of these are excluded, again, because they involve one of the six variable amino acids, and the 14 which remain are at positions 3, 52, 92, 114, 115, 119, 126, 127, 129, 132, 137, 157, 192 and 222. It can be clearly seen that there is a cluster of sequence alterations between positions 114 and 137. In fact, there are 8 such changes in 24 amino acids—60% of this type in 10% of the protein. The region also contains 3 of the changes in the so-called variable residues, two less than expected if all of those differences were distributed evenly across the sequence.

```
             113                 117  118                      132      139
Human    WYWTYEYTDY   -----   G G L I   F N S Y M L P P L F L E P G D   LRLLDVD


Mouse        S        -----   E D C       D     I T N D K         E     E


Cow          S        -----   E D S       D     I T S E K         E     E


Yeast        K        INDSG   E T V E     E V I D E L     P Q             T
             133                142 143                       157      164
```

Fig. 2. Proposed cytochrome c binding domain on cytochrome oxidase Subunit II. The single letter code for amino acid residues is used to list the amino acid sequences of segments of the cytochrome oxidase Subunit II of the species indicated, the numbers referring to sequence positions. Blank spaces denote identity of the corresponding residue to that in the human Subunit II sequence at the top of the figure. Each dash represents a gap introduced into the mammalian sequences to maintain maximal similarity with the yeast subunit sequence.

If the beef Subunit II is compared to the human Subunit II, a similar result is obtained. Sixty-one differences in total, of which 46 are excluded, leaving 15 changes, at positions 3, 9, 52, 92, 114, 115, 119, 127, 129, 132, 137, 157, 184, 221 and 222. The set of positions at which the human subunit differs from both the beef and mouse subunits consists of 3, 52, 92, 114, 115, 119, 127, 129, 132, 137, 157 and 222 (see Fig. 2).

A closer look at this portion of the sequence reveals that the only change between the mouse and beef proteins not occurring at a variable residue is a conservative one, aspartate 127 to glutamate 127. From the human sequence, on the other hand, it can be seen that there is a pattern in which acidic groups at positions 114, 115, 119 and 127 in the mouse and beef subunits have been replaced by uncharged residues and a basic amino acid, lysine 129, is replaced by a glutamate. The net charge of the segment between positions 114 and 137 has been reduced from -4 to -2 in going from the mouse to the human oxidase. Furthermore, the distribution of charges in this region has been drastically altered, resulting in the creation of an uncharged stretch from position 113 to position 128. Without three dimensional information it is difficult to relate these observations to the structure of cytochrome c, but the sequence variation in this small segment of Subunit II would seem significant, not only with regard to charge, but also in hydrophobicity. Indeed, it is known that human Subunit II is more hydrophobic than the beef subunit, as evidenced by both its unusual mobility in SDS gels and by computation of a hydrophobicity index (Sinjorgo et al., 1987). This index, which consists of the summed mole percents of aspartate, asparagine, glutamate, glutamine, lysine, histidine, arginine, serine and threonine, shows that the human protein contains a net of 11 less hydrophilic residues than does the beef Subunit II. When the sequence differences between positions 114 and 137 were examined in this regard, it was observed that there were 6 relevant changes, all of which result in a loss of hydrophilic residues in the human protein. In fact, these alterations at positions 114, 115, 117, 125, 126 and 127 account for more than 50% of the difference in the hydrophobicity index between human and beef Subunits II in a segment which comprises only 6% of the protein. To be effective, the increased hydrophobicity of the enzymic interaction domain of human cytochrome c, as compared to that of horse cytochrome c, must relate to an increased hydrophobicity in the corresponding area of the oxidase. Examination of the human sequence, as noted above, indicates that it is much less acidic and more hydrophobic than the beef and mouse oxidase Subunits II in just one small region, between residues 114 and 137.

The suggestion that the differences in this region account for the discrimination by the cytochrome oxidases between homologous and heterologous cytochromes c is supported by a further comparison with the corresponding region of yeast oxidase Subunit II. Restricting the examination to this region is necessary because the much greater total divergence between mammalian and yeast sequences renders useless the simple approach of excluding the six most highly variable amino acids.

There is clearly strong similarity between the yeast (Coruzzi and Tzagoloff, 1979) and mammalian sequences when a gap totalling five amino acids is introduced. The exact location of the gap is not obvious; the position shown in Fig. 2 is only one possibility. Although there is apparently not a significant difference in hydrophobicity between the proposed cytochrome c binding domains of yeast and mouse or beef Subunits II, the yeast sequence is far more acidic, with a net charge of -6. The presence of an extra lysine in the interaction domain of yeast iso-1-cytochrome c may be a functional complement to this increased acidity.

Attention has been directed to the same area on Subunit II by other studies. Chemical modification of carboxylates on Subunit II suggests that bovine residues 112, 114 and 198 are located at the high affinity binding site for cytochrome c (Millet et al., 1983). The proximity of two of these

276

residues to the conserved Trp-Tyr-Trp-X-Tyr-Glu-Tyr sequence at positions 104 to 110 (postulated to participate in electron transfer, in part because of its unusual nature) adds to the inclination to include them in the cytochrome c binding site, and extending further, the possibly significant region from residues 114 to 137. Another location of contact between cytochrome c and Subunit II is presumably histidine 161, as shown by crosslinking to arylazidolysine 13-cytochrome c in the high affinity site (Bisson et al., 1982). This brackets the region from 114 to 137 between residues which are presumed to interact with cytochrome c. The amino acid comparisons in this study suggest that the same segment of Subunit II which is between those residues is in all likelihood also important in cytochrome c binding and may be the region which is responsible for the specificities of reaction of primate, non-primate mammalian and yeast cytochrome oxidases with homologous and heterologous cytochromes c.

SUMMARY

It is proposed that a small region, between Residues 114 and 137, of cytochrome oxidase Subunit II makes up all or part of the binding domain for the high affinity interaction with cytochrome c. The amino acid composition of this region has been shown to differ strikingly between the primate, mammalian non-primate and yeast proteins and varies in concert with changes observed in the interaction domains for cytochrome oxidase on the molecular surface of the homologous cytochromes c. Thus, the presence of Ile, Met and Val at positions 11, 12 and 83, respectively, which makes the interaction domain of human cytochrome c more hydrophobic than that of horse cytochrome c, and the lack of hydrophilic or charged residues at positions 114, 115, 119, 125, 126 and 127 in human cytochrome oxidase Subunit II, as compared to the beef or mouse protein, combine to make the human subunit a suitable partner for its cognate cytochrome c. Yeast iso-1-cytochrome c, with a more hydrophilic interaction domain containing an extra positive charge at position 11 as compared to horse cytochrome c, is adapted to yeast subunit II, which is more negatively charged in the proposed cytochrome c binding domain than the mammalian proteins. Thus, the proportions and magnitudes of the hydrophobic and electrostatic binding forces which hold the various homologous cytochrome c-cytochrome oxidase high affinity complexes together are different and these intrinsic differences are revealed in the kinetics of the heterologous interactions.

Supported by Grants GM-19121 and GM-29001 from the National Institutes of Health.

REFERENCES

Anderson, S., Bankier, A. T., Barrell, B. G., de Bruijn, M. H. L., Coulson, A. R., Drouin, J., Eperon, I. C., Nierlich, D. P., Roe, B. A., Sanger, F. A., Schreier, P. H., Smith, A. J. H., Staden, R. and Young, I. G., 1981, Sequence and organization of the human mitochondrial genome, Nature, 290:457-465.

Anderson, S., de Bruijn, M. H. L., Coulson, A. R., Eperon, I. C., Sanger, F. A. and Young, I. G., 1982, Complete sequence of bovine mitochondrial DNA. Conserved features of the mammalian mitochondrial genome, J. Mol. Biol., 156:683-717.

Bibb, M. J., Van Etten, R. A., Wright, C. T., Walberg, M. W. and Clayton, D. A., 1981, Sequence and gene organization of mouse mitochondrial DNA, Cell, 26:167-180.

Bisson, R., Jacobs, B. and Capaldi, R. A., 1980, Binding of arylazido-cytochrome *c* derivatives to beef heart cytochrome *c* oxidase: Cross-linking in the high- and low-affinity binding sites, <u>Biochem.</u>, 19:4173-4178.

Bisson, R., Steffens, G. M., Capaldi, R. A. and Buse, G., 1982, Mapping of the cytochrome *c* binding site on cytochrome *c* oxidase, <u>FEBS Lett.</u>, 144:359-363.

Chou, P. Y. and Fasman, G. D., 1978, Prediction of secondary structure of proteins from their amino acid sequence, <u>Adv. in Enzymol.</u>, 47:45-148.

Coruzzi, G. and Tzagoloff, A., 1979, Assembly of the mitochondrial membrane system. DNA sequence of subunit 2 of yeast cytochrome oxidase, <u>J. Biol. Chem.</u>, 254:9329-9330.

Dayhoff, M. O., 1972, "Atlas of protein sequence and structure 1972, Vol. 5," National Biomedical Research Foundation, Washington, D. C.

Dayhoff, M. O., 1978, "Atlas of protein sequence and structure 1978, Vol. 5, Supplement 3," National Biomedical Research Foundation, Washington, D. C.

Dethmers, J. K., Ferguson-Miller, S. and Margoliash, E., 1979, Comparison of yeast and beef cytochrome *c* oxidases. Kinetics and binding of horse, fungal and euglena cytochromes *c*, <u>J. Biol. Chem.</u>, 254:11973-11981.

Diesenhofer, J., Epp, O., Miki, K., Huber, R. and Michel, H., 1985, Structure of the protein subunits in the photosynthetic reaction centre of *Rhodopseudomonas viridis* at 3Å resolution, <u>Nature</u>, 319:618-624.

Fitch, W. M. and Margoliash, E., 1967, Construction of phylogenetic trees, <u>Science</u>, 155:279-284.

Fitch, W. M. and Margoliash, E., 1970, The usefulness of amino acid and nucleotide sequences in evolutionary studies, <u>in</u> "Evolutionary Biology Vol. 4," T. Dobzhansky, M. K. Hecht and W. C. Steere, eds., Appleton-Century-Crofts, New York.

Garoff, H., 1985, Using recombinant DNA techniques to study protein targeting in the eukaryotic cell, <u>Ann. Rev. Cell Biol.</u>, 1:403-445.

George, D. G., Hunt, L. T., Yeh, L-S. L. and Barker, W. C., 1985, New perspectives on bacterial ferrodoxin evolution, <u>J. Mol. Evol.</u>, 22:20-31.

Kadenbach, B., Jaraush, J., Hartmann, R. and Merle, P., 1983, Separation of a mammalian cytochrome *c* oxidase into 13 polypeptides by a sodium dodecyl sulfate-gel electrophoretic procedure, <u>Anal. Biochem.</u>, 129:517-521.

Kimura, M., 1981, Was globin evolution very rapid in its early stages?: A dubious case against the rate constancy hypothesis, <u>J. Mol. Evol.</u>, 17:110-113. Goodman, M., 1981, Globin evolution was apparently very rapid in early vertebrates: A reasonable case against the rate constancy hypothesis, <u>J. Mol. Evol.</u>, 17:114-120. Kimura, M., 1981, Doubt about the studies of globulin evolution based on maximum parsimony codons and the augmentation procedure, <u>J. Mol. Evol.</u>, 17:121-122.

Koppenol, W. H. and Margoliash, E., 1982, The asymmetric distribution of charges on the surface of horse cytochrome *c*: Functional implications, <u>J. Biol. Chem.</u>, 257:4426-4437.

Kuhn-Nentwig, L. and Kadenbach, B., 1985, Isolation and properties of cytochrome *c* oxidase from rat liver and quantification of immunological differences between isozymes from various rat tissues with subunit-specific antisera, <u>Eur. J. Biochem.</u>, 149:147-158.

Margoliash, E., 1972, The molecular variations of cytochrome *c* as a function of the evolution of species, <u>Harvey Lectures</u>, Series 66:177-247.

Millet, F., de Jong, C., Paulson, L. and Capaldi, R. A., 1983, Identification of specific carboxylate groups on cytochrome *c* oxidase that are involved in binding cytochrome *c*, <u>Biochem.</u>, 22:546-363.

278

Osheroff, N., Speck, S. Margoliash, E., Veerman, E. C. I., Wilms, J., König, B. W. and Muijsers, A. O., 1983, The reaction of primate cytochromes *c* with cytochrome *c* oxidase. Analysis of the polarographic assay, J. Biol. Chem., 258:5731-5738.

Sinjorgo, K. M. C., Hakvoort, T. B. M., Durak, I., Draujer, J. W., Post, J. K. P. and Muijsers, A. O., 1987, Human cytochrome *c* oxidase isoenzymes from heart and skeletal muscle; purification and properties, Biochem. Biophy. Acta, 850:144-150.

EVIDENCE FOR A FUNCTIONAL ROLE OF NUCLEAR ENCODED SUBUNITS IN MITOCHONDRIAL CYTOCHROME c OXIDASE

Roberto Bisson and Barbara Bacci

Centro C.N.R. Fisiologia dei Mitocondri e Laboratorio di Biologia e Patologia Molecolare, Istituto di Patologia Generale, via Loredan 16, 35131 Padova Italy

INTRODUCTION

In recent years a significant progress on several aspects concerning the structure-function relationship in cytochrome c oxidase has been obtained[1-3]. On the contrary, problems concerning subunit composition and possible role have become more complicated. Improvements on the electrophoretic techniques and other analytical methods have demonstrated the complexity of mitochondrial oxidases, leading to the discovery of tissue-specific differences[4]. Moreover, the development of chromatographic procedures for enzyme purification has reinforced the idea that the oxidase polypeptide composition is strongly related to the evolutionary stage of the organism[5-8]. The reasons for this structural heterogeneity remains obscure. Indeed, only the two-three largest subunits are sufficient for the electron transfer and proton pumping catalyzed by cytochrome c oxidase. Hence two different hypothesis have been proposed to explain the presence of the additional components. The first one suggests that some of these polypeptides may represent copurified contaminants[3] while a regulative role is implied by the alternative view[4]. A relevant, though indirect, support to the latter suggestion is given by studies on cytochrome c oxidase deficiencies found in some mitochondrial myopathies[9].

Molecular genetics is expected to shed light on the problem of subunit function. Mutation and gene disruption experiments have shown that four nuclear encoded polypeptides of yeast oxidase are necessary for its assembly, while a fifth smaller component seems to be required for maximal levels of cellular respiration[10]. These findings demonstrate that the cytoplasmic subunits are essential components of oxidase but the question concerning their possible role in the intact oxidase remains open. Information from site directed *muted* polypeptides could be limited by assembly problems. Moreover if the hypothetical regulative role of the cytoplasmic subunits is exerted through interaction with specific molecules present in the intracellular melieu, it may be difficult to correlate activity changes with subunit function.

This work presents two quite different situations which, however, share common features, since in both cases the environment appears to affect the enzyme structure and the cytoplasmic polypeptides seems to play a role in these events. In this context, the problem of oxidase purification, related to the possibility of loosing important interactions present in the native membrane, is briefly considered.

MATERIALS AND METHODS

Cytochrome c oxidase was prepared as reported elsewhere[7,8,11]. *T. thermophilus* oxidase was a kind gift of dr. G.C.M. Steffens. Antibody preparations against *D. discoideum* oxidase and other immunological procedures were as described by Bisson et al.[7] and Bisson and Schiavo[23]. Chemical modification and photoaffinity labelling experiments were performed according to Bisson et al.[12] and Bisson and Montecucco[13]. Other details are in figure legends.

RESULTS AND DISCUSSION

Tight and loose interactions: what is a pure cytochrome *c* oxidase?

Early methods of isolation of cytochrome *c* oxidase were based essentially on repeated ammonium sulfate fractionations of detergent-solubilized, enzyme-enriched membrane fractions[11]. These procedures, which generally last for days, need large amounts of starting material and usually they require *ad hoc* modifications depending on the particular biological source under investigation. These limitations have hampered the study on the enzyme from different organisms and also have raised the possibility that its polypeptide composition might depend on the protocol used for purification[2]. More recently, fast and efficient chromatographic techniques applicable to milligrams of membranes have been developed; as a consequence, cytochrome c oxidase from sources as divergent as thermophilic bacteria, slime molds and human tissues has been isolated[5,7,14].

Fig. 1A shows the electrophoretic pattern of cytochrome *c* oxidase isolated from six evolutionary distant organisms. All the enzymes were purified by column chromatography using, with the exception of the *T. thermophilus* oxidase, an identical procedure[7]. The figure offers a pictorial view of one of the major problems concerning the structure-function relationship in oxidase, namely the dramatic increase in its complexity throughout evolution which, consequently, poses the question of the function of the additional polypeptides.

As can be seen the subunit composition of bovine oxidase does not appear to be linked to the two purification procedures considered here and the same is true for the yeast enzyme (data not shown). This suggests that the electrophoretic patterns reported in the figure represent polypeptides *tightly* associated with the enzyme. Nevertheless, it is well known that under defined, though non-physiological conditions, the interaction of certain subunits with the rest of the complex is loosened and eventually they can be dissociated[2]. Very recently evidence indicating that similar dissociations can also occur at physiological pH and in the presence of a mild detergent have been provided[17]. Hence, at least in relative terms, some subunits can be considered *loosely* bound to the enzyme. Figure 1 (panel B) indicates that for certain polypeptides, this aspect may be particularly pronounced; *D. discoideum* oxidase subunit III, for example, does not copurify with the enzyme[7] and the same may hold for *P. denitrificans* oxidase[18]. Whether the differences in the strength of interaction have a physiological meaning, remains to be established. Noteworthy, the depletion of the subunit III (and other smaller polypeptides) of the bovine enzyme seems not only to influence the proton pumping efficiency[19,20], but also to reduce the heterogeneity in some kinetic and spectroscopic properties promoting the protein complex to a configuration closer to the pulsed state[17].

Loose associations could be at the origin of some discrepancies concerning the polypeptide composition of the same enzyme isolated with different procedures (compare for example the bird cytochrome *c* oxidase shown in fig. 1 with the more complex pattern found by Kadenbach[21]), or

282

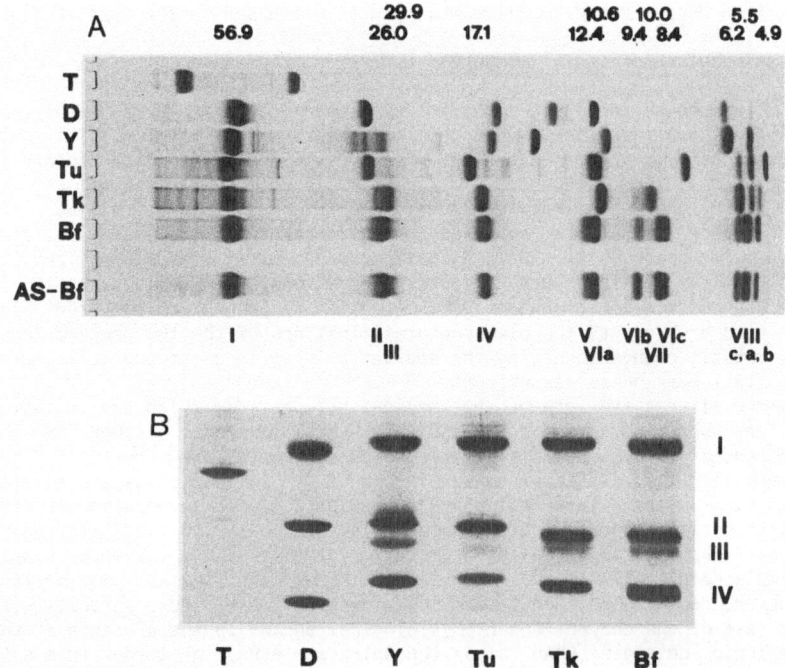

Fig. 1. A close look throughout cytochrome *c* oxidase evolution. Panel A: SDS-polyacrylamide gel electrophoresis[15] of cytochrome *c* oxidase isolated from *T. thermophilus* (T), *D. discoideum* (D), *S. cerevisiae* (Y), and tuna (Tu), turkey (Tk) and beef (Bf) hearts. With the exception of the bacterial enzyme, the chromatographic procedure used for purification[7,8] was identical. For comparison a sample of beef oxidase isolated by ammonium sulfate fractionation[11] is shown (AS-Bf). Subunit nomenclature and molecular weights (top figure) for bovine oxidase are according to Buse et al.[10]. Panel B: separation of subunit II and III in a Swank and Munkres SDS-urea gels system[28].

the changes in the enzyme electron transfer kinetics during purification. For example, a decrease in the apparent Km and increase in Vmax of one order of magnitude has been found in *D. discoideum* oxidase, from the membranous to the isolated detergent-solubilized form[7]. Similar changes have been usually interpreted as an alteration of lipid-protein interaction operated by the detergents used for purification[22]; however, it should be stressed that there are no reasons to exclude *a priori* similar perturbations at the level of other weak (relatively to the conditions used for the enzyme isolation) intermolecular interactions present in the native membrane. An interesting observation has been made during the purification of *T. thermophilus* oxidase, which is normally isolated with a bound *c*-type cytochrome. It was found that about half of the enzyme does not interact with the ion-exchange column and it appears strictly associated, in a 1:1 molar ratio, to a b-type cytochrome[5]. Although not extensively investigated, a similar situation is found during the purification of cytochrome *c* oxidase from different eukaryotic sources where 20-40% of the enzyme in detergent solubilized membranes does not interact with the resin in the hydrophobic chromatography step[7,8].

The possibility of structural heterogeneity in cytochrome c oxidase has been demonstrated in slime mold and is discussed in the next section.

Subunit switching in *D. discoideum* cytochrome c oxidase

As shown in fig.1, eukaryotic oxidases show the presence of two-three polypeptides in the 5 kD molecular weight region. The only exception is represented by the *D. discoideum* enzyme which appears to contain only one polypeptide of comparable molecular weight and is therefore the simplest eukaryotic oxidase so far purified. The electrophoretic pattern reported in fig. 1 refers to the enzyme isolated from slime mold cells in the stationary phase. A surprising result, however, is obtained when oxidase preparations from cells harvested in the log and stationary phases of the vegetative growth are compared. Fig. 2 a and b, reports the electrophoretic pattern of the two preparations: the subunit change involving the smaller polypeptides, as the cells enter the stationary phase, is evident.

The two alternative form of the smallest polypeptide, which are indicated by the subscript e and s to indicate their presence either in the exponential or in the stationary phase of growth, are structurally and immunologically different. Subunit specific antibodies against VIIs demonstrate that this polypeptide begins to be integrated in the mitochondrial membrane only when cells are entering the stationary phase[23]. Whether this implies a *de novo* synthesis of the enzyme or simply a replacement of VIIe by VIIs is not known. The latter possibility, however, could be related to the loose interaction of these subunits with the rest of the enzyme. Under physiological pH and in the presence of the non ionic detergent LDAO at a concentration equal or larger than 0.5% both VIIe and VIIs dissociate giving rise to an active five-subunits enzyme (fig. 2c).

The lack of differences in the enzyme electron transfer kinetics of the two purified slime mold oxidase forms is puzzling[23], but nevertheless these observations raise the possibility that the subunit change might be an adaptive response to modified growth conditions in the cell environment. This possibility has been already described in some

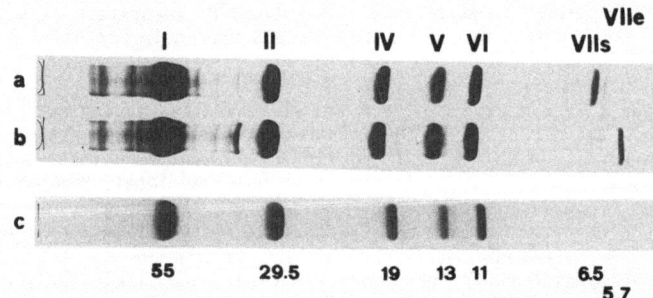

Fig. 2. SDS gel electrophoretic pattern of *D. discoideum* oxidase isolated from cells in the stationary (a) and in the middle log (b) phase of the vegetative stage of growth. Lane c shows the electrophoretic pattern of the purified enzyme after treatment with 1% lauryl dimethylamine oxid (LDAO) in 10 mM NaCl, 10 mM Tris-Cacodylate buffer pH 7.5 and recovery by affinity chromatography. Subunit nomenclature (top) and apparent molecular weight (bottom figure) are according to Bisson and Schiavo[23].

prokaryotes such as *E. coli* where two terminal oxidases alternatively prevail in response to different oxygen concentrations. The fact that *D. discoideum* oxidase switch to a different form close to the stationary phase when oxygen and other metabolites may become limited, prompted us to test the effect of a reduced supply of oxygen under condition where, normally, only one form is present (exponential growth). The results obtained are shown in fig. 3.

Under the experimental conditions used, oxygen appears to influence the expression of the two alternative oxidase forms of this strictly aerobic organism (fig. 3, panel A, lanes a-c). Although to a much lower extent, the same phenomenon can be detected during the developmental stage of the organism (G. Schiavo and R. Bisson, unpublished observations) when thousands of cells, because of the lack of nutrients, aggregate in a single migrating slug where an elementary differentiation process takes place, eventually leading to the formation of spores. Although these observations do not say anything about the molecular mechanisms involved in the process, they do emphasizes the importance of the smaller polypeptides in the structural organization and function of the enzyme and stress the problems which may rise by studying the enzyme properties *in vitro*. The latter approach, in fact, inevitably looses all the interactions that in a complex system like the cell might exist. The next example will perhaps better clarify this idea.

ATP modulates charge distribution on the protein surface of cytochrome *c* oxidase

The possibility that ATP and other ions may affect the interaction between oxidase and the substrate cytochrome c was carefully studied by Ferguson-Miller et al.[24]. Millimolar concentrations of ATP influence both the so called high and, though to a lower extent, low affinity phase of the reaction with cytochrome *c*. The molecular aspects of these process have been recently investigated by using chemical and photoaffinity labelling techniques[12].

It is known that the modification of the exposed carboxyl residues on bovine heart cytochrome *c* oxidase by water soluble carbodiimides leads to loss of enzyme activity and lowers the affinity for the substrate[13,25]. These effects are largely reduced when the same reaction is performed in the presence of cytochrome c and the result is explained as a shielding of the acidic residues forming the substrate binding site operated by cytochrome $c^{[3,13,25]}$.

Fig. 3. The synthesis of the two different forms of *D. discoideum* oxidase depends on growth conditions. In these experiments the expression of the two D. discoideum oxidase forms was monitored by immunoblotting of mitochondrial membranes using an antiserum against the holoenzyme raised in rabbits and ^{125}I-labeled goat-anti-rabbit IgG for autoradiographic detection[20]. Since anti-oxidase antibodies do not cross react with VIIe, the appearance of a band in the 5 kD molecular weight region is directly correlated to the synthesis of the alternative enzyme form.

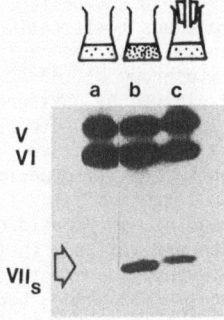

The figure shows the effect of limiting oxygen supply to exponentially growing cells; membranes are from cells in the middle log phase (a), stationary phase (b), middle log phase but with growth limited to 70% of the control, by reducing the opening of the culture flask for 20 hours (c).

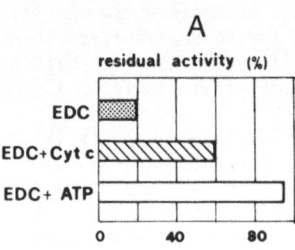

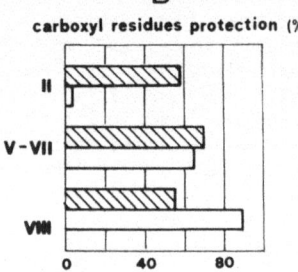

Fig. 4. Effect of cytochrome *c* and ATP on chemical modification of bovine
cytochrome *c* oxidase by EDC. Panel A shows the enzyme activity
after reaction in the presence of horse heart cytochrome *c* in
1:1 molar ratio to oxidase (▨) and 3 mM ATP (▢); (▩) is
the residual activity after treatment with 1-ethyl-3-(3-
dimethylaminopropyl)carbodiimide (EDC). Oxidase concentration
was 1 mg/ml. Other conditions as published elsewhere[12,25].
Panel B reports the protection against carboxyl group
modification analyzed by comparing the EDC-mediated
[14C]glycine ethyl ester incorporation into the enzyme
subunits, in the absence and in the presence of cytochrome *c* or
ATP (symbols as in panel A).

As shown by fig. 4A, under similar reaction conditions, ATP is even
more efficient in protecting the enzyme activity while AMP or phosphate,
at similar ionic strength are not (data not shown)[12]. In fig. 4B the same
phenomenon is investigated by analyzing the protection against chemical
modification of the reactive carboxyl residues present in the different
subunits. As it is shown, there is a strong reduction in the extent of
chemical modification of cytoplasmic subunits operated by ATP. This
phenomenon cannot be explained as a direct protection of the acidic
residues present on the substrate binding site (at variance with
cytochrome *c*, ATP is negatively charged) rather it can be interpreted as
the result of an allosteric conformational change induced by ATP upon
interaction with the enzyme. The consequent altered distribution of the
negative charges would influence the interaction of the enzyme with
cytochrome *c* increasing the Km of the high affinity phase[12].
An unexpected result of fig. 4B concerns subunit II whose acidic
residues modification does not appear to be differently influenced by ATP
in spite of the central role of this polypeptide for the interaction with
cytochrome c[13,25,26]. This latter finding is surprising but it is
explained by evidence, presented elsewhere[12], suggesting a compensating
exposure and protection of carboxyl groups in the same polypeptide.
A selective binding of ATP to the enzyme is supported by
photoaffinity experiments with ATP and one of its photoreactive azido-
analogue[12,27]. In the case of bovine oxidase, subunit IV and one of the
smallest polypeptides are selectively labelled while most of the subunits
are derivatized in the SDS denatured enzyme[12]. In spite of this result,
however, the exact location of the ATP binding site on oxidase remains to
be established because of the intrinsic limitations of these
photolabelling experiments. Photocross-linking in fact occurs through the
adenine ring of ATP which, as shown by parallel experiments with AMP, it
is not responsible for triggering of the conformational changes described
above[12]. Hence, until the location of the triphosphate group is not

defined, a direct interaction with the mitochondrial subunits cannot be excluded. Nevertheless, these experiments demonstrate that the interaction of ATP with the enzyme is specific, causing a conformational change which involves the cytoplasmic subunits and ultimately alters the interaction with the substrate.

CONCLUSIONS

Growing evidence are suggesting a role for the nuclear encoded subunits of cytochrome c oxidase which appears to be different from a simply structural one. The data presented in this work add further, though still indirect, support to this view. One of the major problems seems to be the definition of conditions which *in vivo* can affect the energetic metabolism of the cell and their correct transfer to the *in vitro* system. This goal may be further complicated by the loss of important interactions that the enzyme may experience in the native membrane.

ACKNOWLEDGEMENTS

We thank C. Montecucco, E. Papini and G. Schiavo for useful discussions. This work was partially supported by a grant of Regione Veneto.

REFERENCES

1. A. Azzi, K. Bill, R. Bolli, R. P. Casey, K. A. Nalecz and P. O'Shea, Molecular aspects of the structure-function relationship in cytochrome c oxidase, in: "Structure and properties of cell membranes", G. Bengha ed., CRC Press, Boca Raton Fl.
2. M. Wikstrom, K. Krab and M. Saraste, "Cytochrome c oxidase. A synthesis", Academic Press, New York (1981).
3. R. A. Capaldi, F. Malatesta and V. M. Darley-Usmar, Structure of cytochrome *c* oxidase, Biochem. Biophys. Acta 726:35 (1983).
4. B. Kadenbach, Structure and evolution of the "Atmungsferment" cytochrome *c* oxidase, Angew. Chem. Int. Ed. Engl. 22:275 (1983).
5. T. Yoshida, R. M. Lorence, M. G. Choc, G. E. Tarr, K. L. Findling, and J. A. Fee, Respiratory proteins from the extremely thermophilic aerobic bacterium *Thermus thermophilus*, J. Biol. Chem. 259:2 (1984).
6. W. DeVrij, A. Azzi and W. N. Konings, Structural and functional properties of cytochrome *c* oxidase from Bacillus subtilis W23, Eur. J. Biochem. 13:97 (1983).
7. R. Bisson, G. Schiavo and E. Papini, Cytochrome *c* oxidase from the slime mold *Dictyostelium discoideum*: purification and characterization, Biochemistry 24:7845 (1985).
8. C. Montecucco, G. Schiavo, B. Bacci and R. Bisson, Isolation and characterization of cytochrome *c* oxidase from bird and fish heart mitochondria, Comp. Biochem. Physiol. (1987) in press
9. S. DiMauro, E. Bonilla, M. Zeviani, M. Nakagawa, D. C. DeVivo, Mitochondrial Myopathies, Ann. Neurol. 17:521 (1985).
10. T. E. Patterson and R. O. Poyton, COX8, the structural gene for yeast cytochrome *c* oxidase, J. Biol. Chem. 261:17192 (1986).
11. B. Errede, M. D. Kamen and Y. Hatefi, Preparation and properties of complex IV, Meth. Enz. 53:40 (1978).

12. R. Bisson, G. Schiavo and C. Montecucco, ATP induces conformational changes in mitochondrial cytochrome *c* oxidase: effect on the cytochrome *c* binding site, <u>J. Biol. Chem (1987)</u> in press.

13. R. Bisson and C.Montecucco, Different polypeptides of bovine heart cytochrome *c* oxidase are in contact with cytochrome *c*, <u>FEBS Lett.</u> 150:43 (1982).

14. K. M. C. Sinjorgo, T. B. M. Hakvoort,I. Durak, J. W. Draijer, J. K. P. Post and A. O. Muijsers, Human cytochrome *c* oxidase isoenzymes from heart and skeletal muscle; purification and properties, <u>Biochim. Biophys. Acta</u> 850:144 (1987).

15. B. Kadenbach, J. Jaraush, R. Hartmann and P. Merle, Separation of mammalian cytochrome *c* oxidase into 13 polypeptides by an SDS-gel electrophoretic procedure, <u>Anal. Biochem.</u> 129:517 (1983).

16. G. Buse, G. C. M. Steffens and L. Meinecke, Cytochrome oxidase: the primary structure of electron and proton translocation subunits and their hints at mechanisms, <u>in</u> "Structure and function of membrane proteins" E. Qualiariello and F. Palmieri eds., Elsevier, New York (1983).

17. B. C. Hill and Robinson N. C., Cyanide binding to bovine heart cytochrome *c* oxidase depleted of subunit III by treatment with lauryl maltoside, <u>J. Biol. Chem.</u> 261:15356 (1986).

18. M. Saraste, M. Raitio, T. Jalli and A. Peramaa, A gene in *Paracoccus* for subunit III of cytochrome oxidase, <u>FEBS Lett.</u> 206:154 (1986).

19. L. J. Prochaska and K. A. Reynolds, Characterization of electron-transfer and proton-translocation activities in bovine heart mitochondrial cytochrome *c* oxidase deficient in subunit III, <u>Biochemistry</u> 25:781 (1986).

20. P. Sarti, M. G. Jones, G. Antonini, F. Malatesta, A. Colosimo, M. T. Wilson and M. Brunori, Kinetics of redox-linked proton pumping activity of native and subunit III-depleted cytochrome *c* oxidase: a stopped flow investigation, <u>Proc. Natl. Acad. Sci. USA</u> 82:4876 (1985).

21. P. Merle and B. Kadenbach, On the heterogeneity of vertebrate cytochrome *c* oxidase polypeptide chain composition, <u>Hoppe-Seyler's Z. Physiol. Chem.</u> 361:257 (1980).

22. D. A. Thompson and S. Ferguson-Miller, Lipid and subunit III depleted cytochrome *c* oxidase purified by horse cytochrome *c* affinity chromatography in lauryl maltoside, <u>Biochemistry</u> 22:378 (1983).

23. R. Bisson and G. Schiavo, Two different forms of cytochrome *c* oxidase can be purified from the slime mold *Dictyostelium discoideum*, <u>J. Biol. Chem.</u> 261:4373.(1986).

24. S. Ferguson-Miller, D. L. Brautigan and E. Margogliash, Correlation of the kinetics of electron transfer activity of various eukaryotic cytochromes *c* with binding to mitochondrial cytochrome *c* oxidase, <u>J. Biol. Chem.</u> 25:1104 (1976).

25. F. Millett, V. M. Darley-Usmar and R. A. Capaldi, Cytochrome *c* is cross-linked to subunit II of cytochrome *c* oxidase by a water-soluble carbodiimide, <u>Biochemistry</u> 21:3857 (1982).

26. R. Bisson, A. Azzi, H. Gutweniger, R. Colonna, C. Montecucco and A. Zanotti, Interaction of cytochrome *c* with cytochrome *c* oxidase. Photoaffinity labeling of beef heart cytochrome *c* oxidase with arylazido cytochrome *c*, <u>J. Biol. Chem.</u> 253:874 (1978).

27. C. Montecucco, G. Schiavo and R. Bisson, ATP binding to bovine heart cytochrome *c* oxidase. A photoaffinity labelling study, <u>Biochem. J.</u> 234:241 (1986).

28. R. T. Swank and K. Munkres, Molecular weight analysis of oligo-peptides by electrophoresis in polyacrylamide gel with sodium dodecyl sulfate, <u>Anal. Biochem.</u> 39:462 (1971).

288

STRUCTURAL ANALYSIS OF THE BC_1 COMPLEX FROM BEEF HEART MITOCHONDRIA BY THE SIDED HYDROPATHY PLOT AND BY COMPARISON WITH OTHER BC COMPLEXES

Thomas A. Link, H. Schägger, and G. Von Jagow

Institut für Physikalische Biochemie
der Universität München
8000 München 2, FRG

INTRODUCTION

The bc_1 complex from beef heart mitochondria consists of eleven protein subunits, only three of which contain the four redox centres.[1] Since the primary structures of several subunits of the bc complexes from various species have been determined by amino acid sequencing or deduced from the DNA sequence, an attempt is made to gain more insight into the general structure of the complex by a comparative approach, i.e., by sequence comparisons and by hydropathy analyses. To achieve this, we have not only used the method of Kyte and Doolittle,[2] but developed our own graphic method for the analysis of amphipathic secondary structures, i.e., amphipathic α-helices or ß-sheets.

STRUCTURE PREDICTION METHODS

All programmes were written in BASIC or FORTRAN and run on a Kontron PSI 80 microcomputer linked to a Graphtec MP 1000 plotter.

Hydropathy plots were made according to Kyte and Doolittle,[2] whose hydropathy indices were used throughout.

The sided hydropathy values of segments of the surface of sided α-helices and ß-sheets and the corresponding averaged hydropathy values were obtained by summing up the hydropathy indices of the respective residues, using the weights given in brackets:

Weighted average: residues n (1.0), n±1 (0.5), n±2 (0.5), and n±3 (0.5);

Sided ß-sheet: residues n (1.0), n±2 (1.0), and n±4 (0.5);

Sided α-helix: residues n (1.0), n±3 (0.5)•(distance 1 turn, 40°), n±4 (0.5) (1 turn, 60°), and n±7 (0.5) (2 turns, 20°).

Thus three values were obtained for each residue n and plotted above the number of the residue. The comparison of the three traces allows the prediction of different structural domains (for an example, cf. Fig. 4). In the weighted average plot, hydrophobic domains are detected, while amphipathic segments appear to be neither hydrophobic nor hydrophilic. Possible amphipathic α-helices show an alternation between hydrophobic and hydrophilic residues every third or fourth residue in the sided α-helical plot, i.e., at the frequency with which an α-helix turns around its central axis (3.6 residues per turn). Possible sided β-sheets can be detected in the sided β-sheet profile by an alternation between hydrophobic and hydrophilic values every second residue.

Helical wheels were obtained according to the method of Schiffer and Edmundson.[3] Sequence comparison was performed according to McLachlan.[4] The alignment was done by inserting necessary residues by hand.

AMINO ACID SEQUENCES

An overview shows which amino acid sequences of subunits of various bc complexes have been determined so far (Fig. 1).

	M_r (beef)	Vertebrates		Fungi		Plants		Bacteria		Trypanosoma
		Beef	other	yeast	N. crassa	mito	chloro	Rb. caps.	P. denitr.	
Core I	47 kD	-	-	DNA	-	-				
Core II	45 kD	-	-	DNA	-	-				
Cyt. b	43 847	DNA	DNA	DNA	DNA	DNA	DNA	DNA	DNA	DNA
Cyt. c₁	27 902	AAS	-	DNA	DNA	-	DNA	DNA	DNA	?
ISP	21 708	AAS	-	DNA	DNA	-	AAS + DNA	DNA	DNA	?
VI	13 389	AAS	-	DNA	-	?	?	?		
VII	9 507	AAS	-	DNA	-	↓	?			
VIII	9 172	AAS	-	DNA	-					
IX	7 998	AAS	-	-	-					
X	7 189	AAS	-	-	-					
XI	6 363	AAS	-							

Fig. 1. Elucidated sequences of subunits of bc complexes from various species. The figure shows the increasing complexity of the bc complexes going from bacteria (3 subunits) to mammalia (11 subunits). The numbering of the subunits corresponds to the beef heart complex. In chloroplasts, cytochrome b is split into two proteins (cytochrome b_6 and the 17 kDa protein). AAS: sequence determined by amino acid sequencing; DNA: deduced from the DNA sequence; -: sequence not determined; ?: existence of subunit unclear. The underlined sequences have been determined by our group.

290

The complexity of the bc complexes increases in the course of evolution. The three subunits carrying the four redox centres, present in all known bc complexes, are: cytochrome b, containing two heme centres; cytochrome c_1 (cytochrome f in chloroplasts); and a 'Rieske' iron sulfur protein (ISP) with a Fe_2S_2 cluster that has an unusually high redox potential (+280 mV). The sequences of these subunits from species as different as bacteria, plants, fungi, and mammalia have been determined, so that at present the sequences of about 18 cytochromes b, 5 cytochromes c_1, and 6 ISPs have been elucidated.

THE SUBUNITS WITHOUT REDOX CENTRES

The bc complexes of chloroplasts and mitochondria contain additional subunits without redox centres which are lacking in the bacterial bc_1

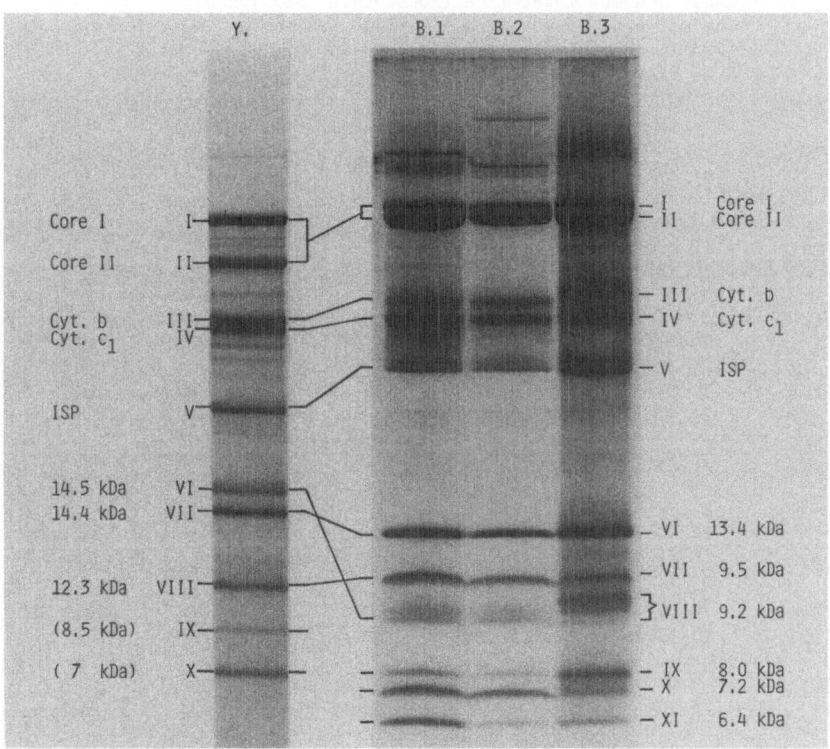

Fig. 2. Comparison of three different preparations of beef heart bc_1 complex (B.1: Hatefi;[24] B.2: Engel et al.;[25,1] B.3: Ljungdahl et al.[26]) with the yeast bc_1 complex. Homologous subunits are indicated. The SDS-PAGE was performed according to Schägger and Von Jagow[22] (acrylamide concentration: Y: 13.3% T; B.1-B.3: 15% T).

complexes. The best known mitochondrial bc_1 complexes are those from yeast and from beef heart. In both cases, the sequences of all 10 (yeast) and 11 (beef heart) subunits have been determined[5-21] with the exception of two subunits in each case, i.e., the two smallest subunits in yeast and the two 'core' proteins in beef heart (Fig. 1).

A comparison of the yeast bc_1 complex with three different preparations of the beef heart bc_1 complex is shown in Fig. 2. The SDS-PAGE was performed by a new method using Tricine as trailing ion,[22] allowing a separation of all small subunits in the range of 6 to 15 kDa. The occurence of the same eleven subunits in three completely different preparations of the beef heart complex[23-25] (using either cholate, Triton X-100, or

Table 1. Comparison of the Subunits of Beef Heart and Yeast bc_1 Complexes
In each case, the upper line represents the subunit from beef heart and the lower line the subunit from yeast.
The polarity values were calculated according to Vanderkooi and Capaldi.[26]

	M_r	AA	Residues +	Residues −	Net charge	Arom. (%)	Polarity (%)	Hydrophobic (%)
Core I	47 kDa							
	48 347	441	80	90		9	43	40
	38 704		86	93	7 −	8.3	44.9	38.3
Core II	45 kDa							
	38 704	352						
Cyt. b	43 847	379	18	17	0	13.7	28.8	47.8
	44 668	384	16	14	1 +	16.7	27.9	50.8
Cyt. c_1	27 902	241	27	29	2 −	10.8	41.1	33.2
	28 386	248	28	31	3 −	10.9	42.3	32.3
ISP	21 708	196	25	24	1 +	8.2	42.9	34.2
	20 271	185	19	22	3 −	8.1	40.5	36.8
VI ('QP-C')	13 389	110	24	21	2 +	10.9	55.5	29.1
VII	14 433	126	16	18	3 −	8.1	40.5	36.8
VII	9 507	81	14	5	9 +	14.8	43.2	33.3
VIII	12 326	108	12	4	8 +	15.7	37.0	38.0
VIII	9 172	78	11	24	13 −	2.6	57.7	25.6
VI	14 528	122	11	55	44 −	5.7	69.7	19.7
IX	7 998	78	9	3	5 +	2.6	30.8	46.2
	8.5 kDa							
X	7 189	62	9	6	3 +	14.5	41.9	41.9
	7 kDa							
XI	6 363	56	8	4	4 +	12.5	39.3	39.3

laurylmaltoside as detergent and based on either ammonium sulfate precipitation, hydroxyapatite, or ion exchange chromatography as main purification principle, respectively) clearly demonstrates that all of these subunits are true constituents of the bc_1 complex. The small subunits are conserved in the beef heart and yeast complexes; a comparison of the main properties of the subunits of these two bc_1 complexes is given in Table 1.

The individual subunits show distinct properties:
- The 'core' proteins[5,6] are mainly hydrophilic;
- Cytochrome b[7,8] is the hydrophobic core of the complex with nine predicted membrane-spanning helices;
- Cytochrome c_1[9,10] and the ISP[11,12] are largely hydrophilic, but each have a membrane anchor;
- Subunit VI (beef),[13] homologous to subunit VII (yeast),[14] was named 'Q-binding protein' ('QP-C') by Yu and Yu since it was specifically labelled by the photoaffinity label NAPA-quinone;[27]
- Subunits VII (beef)[15] and VIII (yeast)[16] have a net positive charge of 8+ or 9+, respectively, and a high content of aromatic residues;
- Subunits VIII (beef)[17] and VI (yeast)[18] have a large excess of negative charges, located mainly in the N-terminal part of the sequence;
- The three smallest subunits of the beef heart complex[19-21] are rather hydrophobic.

The individual properties of the subunits are maintained in the homologous subunits. This can be analysed more thoroughly by comparing the sequences in the alignment of the small subunits of the beef heart and yeast complexes shown in Fig. 3.

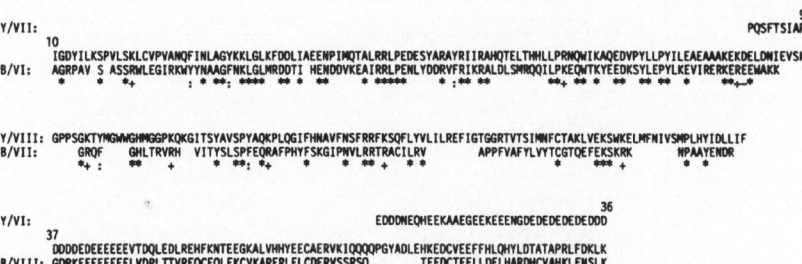

Fig. 3. Alignment of the sequences of three small subunits from beef heart (lower rows: B/VI, 13.4 kDa = 'QP-C'; B/VII, 9.5 kDa; B/VIII, 9.2 kDa) and yeast (upper rows: Y/VII, 14.4 kDa; Y/VIII, 12.3 kDa; Y/VI, 14.5 kDa). The two cystine bridges of the 9.2 kDa subunit of beef heart[28] are shown. Conserved residues are indicated by *, + and - indicate conserved charges, and : indicates an exchange of one aromatic residue against another.

The 13.4 kDa (= 'QP-C') and 9.2 kDa subunits (VI and VIII) of beef heart have a higher degree of homology with the respective yeast subunits VII and VI (37% and 40% conserved residues) than the 9.5 kDa subunit (VII) of beef heart with yeast subunit VIII (23% conserved residues).

Subunit VI of yeast has a N-terminal extension which contains most of the extra negatively charged residues of the yeast compared to the beef heart subunit while the rest of the protein is homologous. The homologous part of the protein includes the only two cysteine residues of the yeast subunit. Both these cysteines are conserved in the beef heart subunit (Fig. 3) and have been shown to form a cystine bridge.[28] The residues that form the other cystine bridge in beef heart are not conserved in the yeast subunit. This is an indication that not only the amino acid sequence but also structural properties are conserved in the two subunits. A further indication for this strucural consideration is the fact that the hydropathy patterns of the two subunits are very similar.

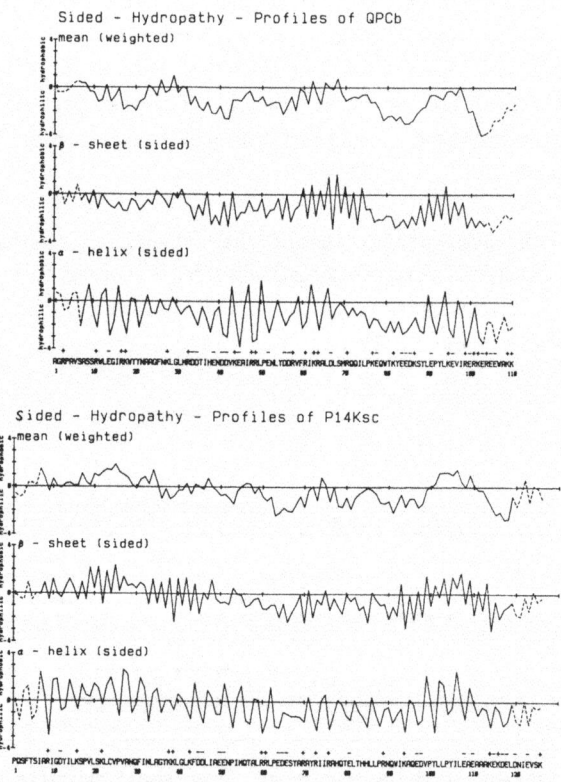

Fig. 4. Sided hydropathy patterns of subunit VI ('QP-C') of the beef heart complex[13] and of subunit VII of the yeast complex.[14] The adjustment of the plots is such that the sequences are well-nigh aligned.

The same holds for 'QP-C' (subunit VI of beef heart) and the homologous subunit (14 kDa = VII) of yeast. Furthermore, the sided hydropathy patterns, indicating the existence of possible sided α-helices or β-strands, are also very alike (Fig. 4). While neither of the proteins has strongly hydrophobic regions, several regions of the two proteins show an alternation between hydrophobic and hydrophilic residues every third or fourth residue in the sided α-helical profile, i.e., at the frequency with which an α-helix turns around its central axis (3.6 residues per turn). Three of these possible amphipathic α-helical structures are found in each of the two proteins, one at the N-terminus, one in the middle part of the proteins (although less pronounced in the yeast subunit), and one near the C-terminus. Therefore, both proteins may have a strongly amphipathic structure and could be situated between hydrophobic and hydrophilic parts of the complex (Fig. 5). This may explain the quinone-binding properties of the subunit, since it may form part of one of the quinone reaction sites, the other part of which is supplied by the hydrophobic domains of cytochrome b. Thus, 'QP-C' would form a 'lid' on top of part of cytochrome b, most probably at the Q_i site.

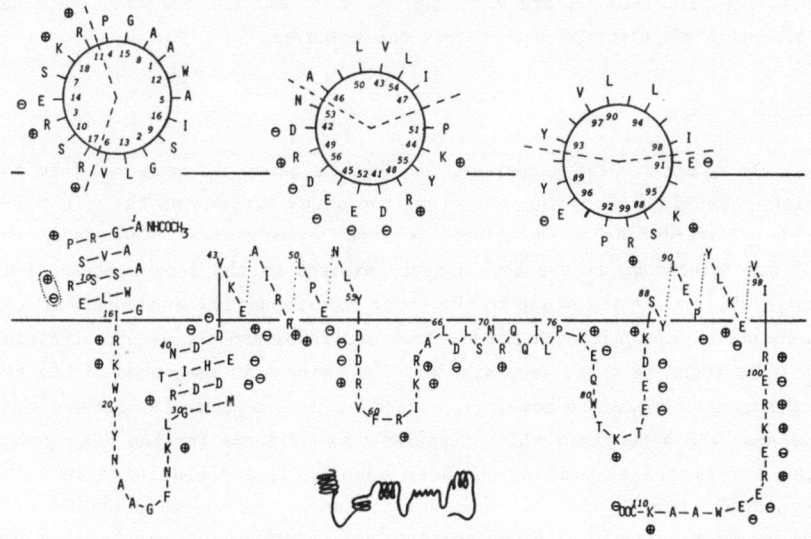

Fig. 5. Predicted folding pattern of beef heart subunit VI ('QP-C'). The inserts show helical wheel plots[3] of the predicted amphipathic helices.

THE THREE 'CATALYTIC' SUBUNITS CONTAINING THE FOUR REDOX CENTRES

The arrangement of the 'catalytic' subunits and of the four redox centres reflects the bifurcation of the path of electrons through the bc_1 complex (for a review, see Von Jagow et al.[29]). On oxidation of a hydroquinone molecule at the Q_o centre, one electron is transferred to the ISP (+280 mV) and from there via cytochrome c_1 (+275 mV) to cytochrome c, while the second electron goes to the b_1 centre of cytochrome b (-50 mV) and from there to the b_h centre (+50 mV).

Cytochrome b

Cytochrome b is a hydrophobic protein of about 400 residues, embedded mainly in the membrane. In the hydropathy profiles of all cytochromes b, nine hydrophobic segments have been detected which are predicted to form nine membrane-spanning α-helices.[30,31] Cytochrome b_6 of the chloroplast b_6f complex is considerably shorter (about 210 residues) and contains only the first five predicted membrane-spanning helices.[31] However, a 17 kDa polypeptide is homologous to the C-terminal half of cytochrome b and the gene is located on the chloroplast DNA behind the b_6 gene, indicating that the cytochrome b gene has been split during the evolution of chloroplasts. Cytochrome b and cytochrome b_6 contain the two heme centres and four histidine residues are conserved in all cytochromes b, two each in helices II and V. The two hemes are ligated between helices II and V in a transmembrane arrangement, probably within a '4-α-helical-bundle' formed by helices II, III, IV, and V.[32] Thus the two heme centres constitute the 'low-potential' electron path across the membrane.

Cytochrome c_1

The other two redox centres, the Fe_2S_2 cluster and heme c_1, form the 'high-potential' electron path along the outer surface of the membrane, leading towards the water-soluble acceptor cytochrome c. Therefore, the ISP and cytochrome c_1 are both largely exposed to the intermembrane bulk phase while they are bound to the inner mitochondrial membrane through membrane anchors. Although the spectral and redox properties of cytochrome c_1 and cytochrome c are very similar, the amino acid sequences of the two proteins show almost no homology, except for the sequence Cys-Ser-Ser-Cys-His near the N-terminus which supplies three ligands for the heme group, i.e., two cysteines binding the heme covalently and histidine as axial ligand. The second axial ligand in cytochrome c is a methionine residue and one methionine is also conserved in all cytochrome c_1 sequences (residue 160 in beef heart), which is not the methionine that has been proposed in the original sequence paper (residue 208).[9]

The 'Rieske' Iron Sulfur Protein

We have recently determined the amino acid sequence of the beef heart ISP[11]. A comparison of all known 'Rieske' ISP sequences is given in Fig. 6. All ISPs except the spinach b_6f ISP contain over 20% of charged residues and have a polarity index of 40% or more, indicating large hydrophilic domains (spinach: 15.6% charged residues, polarity index 36%). Only 14% of the residues are conserved in all species (but 32%, when the spinach is excluded). However, the C-terminal segment is more strongly conserved (35% in all 6 species, 55% when the spinach is excluded). Although the single amino acid conservation through all 6 ISPs is not very strong, the hydropathy patterns are very well conserved (Fig. 7). In each case, there is a long hydrophobic segment near the N-terminus, while the rest of the protein is rather hydrophilic, except for a short hydrophobic domain in the strongly conserved region near the C-terminus. The structure can be divided into the catalytic domain (C-terminal) and the membrane anchor (N-terminal) (Fig. 8).

```
                                                : :             *                        *
Spinach:            ATSIPADNVPDMQKRETLNLLLLGALSLPTGYMLLPYASFFVPPGGGAGTGGTIAKD          ALGND
                                                                                           67
Beef:      SHTDIKVPDFSDY  RRPEVLDSTKSSKESSEA      RKGF SYLVTATTTVGVAYA AKNVVSQFVSSMSASAD

N. crassa: GSSSSTFESPFKGESKAAKVPDFGKTMSKAPPSTNM      LF SYFMVGTMGAITAAG AKSTIQEFLKNMSASAD
S. carlsb.:            KSTY  RTPNFDDVLKENNDADKG      RSYA YFMVGAMGLLSSAG AKSTVETFISSMTATAD
P. denitr.:   MSHADEHAGDHGATRR                        DFL YYATAGAGTVAAGA A  AWTLVNQMNPSAD
Rb. caps.:    MSHAEDNAG    TRR                        DFL YHATAATGVVVTGA A  VWPLINQMNASAD
                  +                                     : *             *        *   * **


             * *                       * * :                               -  +
Spinach:   VIAA  EWLKTHAPGDRTLTQGLKGHPTYL                         VVESDKTLATF GIN
                                                                               130
Beef:      VLAMAKIEIKLSDIPEGKNMAFKWRGKPLFVRHRTKKEIDQEAAVEVSQLRDPQH   DLERVKKP    E

N. crassa: VLAMAKVEVDLNAIPEGKNVIIKWRGKPVFIRHRTPAEIEEANKVNVATLRDPET   DADRVKKP    E
S. carlsb.:VLAMAKVEVNLAAIPLGKNVVVKWQGKPVFIRHRTPHEIQEANSVDMSALKDPQT   DADRVKDP    Q
P. denitr.:VQALASIQVDVSGVETGTQLTVKWLGKPVFIRRRTEDEIQAGREVDLGQLIDRSAQNSNKPDAPATDENRTMDEA   GE
Rb. caps.: VKAMSSIFVDVSAVEVGTQLTVKWRGKPVFIRRRDEKDIELARSVPLGALRDTSAENANKPGAEATDENRSLAAFDGTNTGE
             * *       *   ** *** * *   -*    *  * *              * *


                 *******       -  : ****** *  **  +**** *
Spinach:   AVCTHLGCVVPFN AAE NKFICPCHGSQYNNQGRVVRGPAPLSLALAHCD VDDGKVVFVPWTETDFRTGEAPWWSA
                                                                                    196
Beef:      WVILIGVCTHLGCVPIAN AGDFGGYYCPCHGSHYDASGRIRKGPAPLNLEVPSYEFTSDGMVIVG

N. crassa: WLVMLGVCTHLGCVPIGE AGDYGGWFCPCHGSHYDISGRIRKGPAPLNLEIPLYEFPEEGKLVIG
S. carlsb.:WLIMLGICTHLGCVPIGE AGDFGGWFCPCHGSHYDISGRIRKGPAPLNLEIPAYEF DGDKVIVG
P. denitr.:WLVMIGVCTHLGCVPIGDGAGDFGGWFCPCHGSHYDTSGRIRRGPAPQNLHIPVAEFLDDTTIKLG
Rb. caps.: WLVMLGVCTHLGCVPMGDKSGDFGGWFCPCHGSHYDSAGRIRKGPAPRNLDIPVAAFVDETTIKLG
             *    *  ********   **:**::*********  ****+**** **   *   *        *
                            ▲ ▲ ▲              ▲ ▲▲          ▲
```

Fig. 6. Alignment of the sequences of 'Rieske' iron sulfur proteins from spinach b_6f,[33,34] beef heart,[11] N. crassa,[35] S. carlsbergensis,[12] Rb. capsulatus,[36] and P. denitrificans.[37] The top line above the spinach sequence shows residues conserved in all six sequences while the bottom line below the Rb. caps. sequence shows residues conserved in the mitochondrial and bacterial sequences (excluding the spinach). * indicates conserved residues, + and - indicate conserved charges, and : indicates an exchange of one aromatic residue against another.

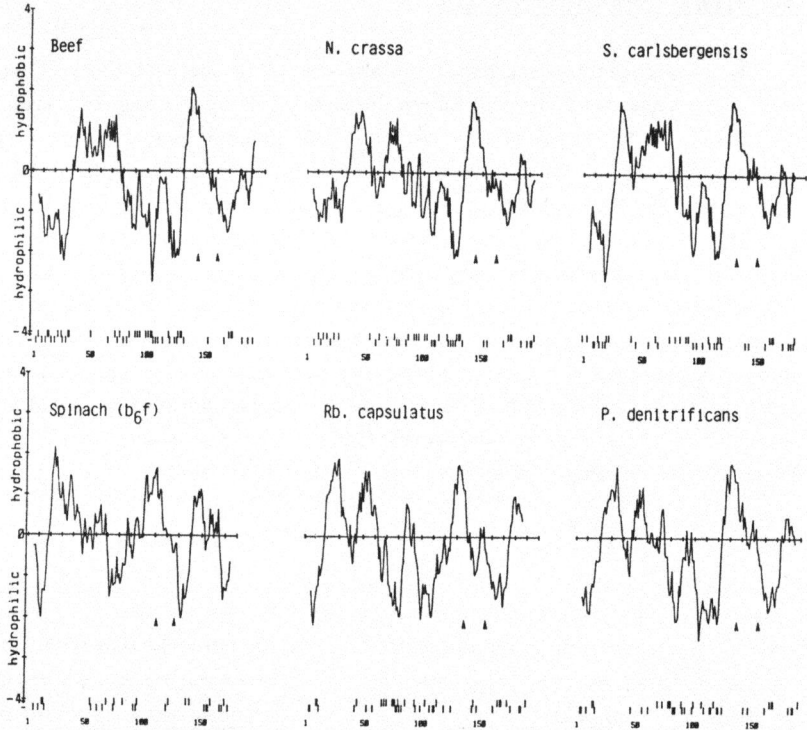

Fig. 7. Comparison of the hydropathy profiles of the six 'Rieske' iron
sulfur proteins according to Kyte and Doolittle[2] using a span
setting of 11. The arrows indicate the approximate positions of
the two pairs of cysteine residues.

The long hydrophobic segment (about 40 residues) seems to form the
membrane anchor; since its length allows for two membrane-spanning
α-helices, we assume that it forms a 'hairpin' structure (Fig. 8). This
would be in agreement with the facts that (i) the N- and the C-termini are
both on the outside of the mitochondrial membrane (W. Neupert, personal
communication); (ii) the beef heart ISP is in an dissociation-association
equilibrium in the detergent-solubilised complex,[38] since it does not have
large protein domains on the matrix side of the membrane, in contrast to
the situation found in cytochrome c_1. The ISP of the b_6f complex is a
noteworthy exception since it seems to contain only one membrane-spanning
segment. Considering its orientation in the chloroplast membrane, where
the iron sulfur cluster faces to the inside, while it is directed outwards
in the mitochondrial membrane, the absence of a second membrane-spanning
helix in the chloroplast ISP would bring the N-termini of both the mitochondrial and the chloroplast ISP to the cytosolic side of the respective

298

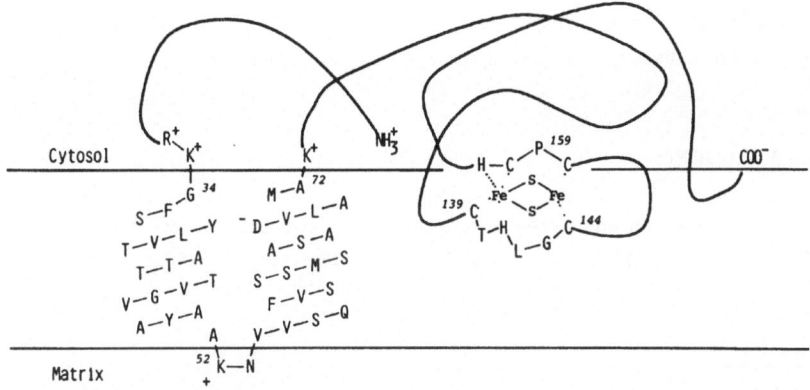

Fig. 8. Predicted folding pattern of the beef heart iron sulfur protein in the inner mitochondrial membrane. Since the co-ordination of the iron sulfur cluster has not been firmly established, merely possible ligands are indicated, two of which may bind to each iron atom (see text).

membranes. This may be relevant considering the import pathways of these nuclear coded proteins.[39]

The catalytic domain is located in the strongly conserved region of the protein near the C-terminus. The iron sulfur cluster is bound between a short hydrophobic and a more hydrophilic domain which reveals strong amphipathy in the sided hydropathy plot (not shown). Therefore, the iron sulfur cluster seems to be located at the interface between the hydro-phobic and hydrophilic domains of the complex near the heme b_1 centre of cytochrome b and may act as 'lid' of the Q_o reaction site formed by these two redox centres.[40] The location of the iron sulfur cluster near the membrane surface has been confirmed by EPR measurements (T. Ohnishi, personal communication).

It had been assumed that the four conserved cysteine residues might bind the Fe_2S_2 cluster in analogy to the situation found in plant ferre-doxins. However, this possibility can now be excluded, since a 'Rieske' type ISP from <u>Thermus thermophilus</u> with spectral properties identical to the mitochondrial ISPs[41] was found to contain two apparently identical Fe_2S_2 clusters, but only four cysteines,[42] so that the iron sulfur cluster has to be ligated by two non-sulfur ligands, probably by two histidines.[43] Besides the four cysteine residues, two histidines and one arginine are conserved in all six ISPs, within the same domain. Mössbauer spectra have confirmed that the Fe^{2+} site of the reduced complex has non-sulfur ligands while the Fe^{3+} site is tetrahedrally coordinated by four sulfur atoms.[44] Therefore, the left iron atom in Fig. 8 would correspond to the Fe^{2+} and the right iron atom to the Fe^{3+} of the reduced cluster. However, since it has not been shown which of the four cysteines are involved in binding the iron sulfur cluster, the above arrangement is tentative.

ACKNOWLEDGEMENTS

This work was supported by grants from the Deutsche Forschungsgemein-schaft (Ja 284/6-10) and from the Fonds der Chemischen Industrie to GVJ.

REFERENCES

1. H. Schägger, T.A. Link, W.D. Engel, and G. Von Jagow, Methods Enzymol. 126:224 (1986).
2. J. Kyte and R.F. Doolittle, J. Mol. Biol. 157:105 (1982).
3. M. Schiffer and A.B. Edmundson, Biophys. J. 7:121 (1967).
4. A.D. McLachlan, J. Mol. Biol. 61:409 (1971).
5. A. Tzagoloff, M. Wu, and M. Crivellone, J. Biol. Chem. 261:17163 (1987).
6. P. Oudshoorn, H. Van Steeg, B.W. Swinkels, P. Schoppink, and L.A. Grivell, Eur. J. Biochem. 163:97 (1987).
7. S. Anderson, M.H.L. de Bruijn, A.R. Coulson, I.C. Eperon, F. Sanger, and I.G. Young, J. Mol. Biol. 156:683 (1982).
8. F.G. Nobrega and A. Tzagoloff, J. Biol. Chem. 255:9828 (1980).
9. S. Wakabayashi, H. Matsubara, C.H. Kim, K. Kawai, and T.E. King, Biochem. Biophys. Res. Commun. 97:1548 (1980).
10. I. Sadler, K. Suda, G. Schatz, F. Kaudewitz, and A. Haid, EMBO J. 3:2137 (1984).
11. H. Schägger, U. Borchart, W. Machleidt, T.A. Link, and G. Von Jagow, FEBS Lett., submitted (1987).
12. J.D. Beckmann, P.O. Ljungdahl, J.L. Lopez, and B.L. Trumpower, J. Biol. Chem. 262:129 (1987).
13. S. Wakabayashi, T. Takao, Y. Shimonishi, S. Kuramitsu, H. Matsubara, T.-y. Wang, Z.-p. Zhang, and T.E. King, J. Biol. Chem. 260:337 (1985).
14. M. De Haan, A.P.G.M. Van Loon, J. Kreike, R.T.M.J. Vaessen, and L.A. Grivell, Eur. J. Biochem. 138:169 (1984).
15. U. Borchart, W. Machleidt, H. Schägger, T.A. Link, and G. Von Jagow, FEBS Lett. 200:81 (1986).
16. A.C. Maarse and L.A. Grivell, Eur. J. Biochem., in press (1987).
17. S. Wakabayashi, H. Takeda, H. Matsubara, C.H. Kim, and T.E. King, J. Biochem. 91:2077 (1982).
18. A.P.G.M. Van Loon, R.J. De Groot, M. De Haan, A. Dekker, and L.A. Grivell, EMBO J. 3:1039 (1984).
19. U. Borchart, W. Machleidt, H. Schägger, T.A. Link, and G. Von Jagow, FEBS Lett. 191:125 (1985).
20. H. Schägger, G. Von Jagow, U. Borchart, and W. Machleidt, Hoppe-Seyler's Z. Physiol. Chem. 364:307 (1983).
21. H. Schägger, U. Borchart, H. Aquila, T.A. Link, and G. Von Jagow, FEBS Lett. 190:89 (1985).
22. H. Schägger and G. Von Jagow, Anal. Biochem., accepted for publication (1987).
23. G. Vanderkooi and R.A. Capaldi, (1972) Ann. N.Y. Acad. Sci. 195:135 (1972).
24. Y. Hatefi, A.G. Haavik, and D.E. Griffiths, J. Biol. Chem. 237:1681 (1962).

25. W.D. Engel, H. Schägger, and G. Von Jagow, <u>Hoppe-Seyler's</u> <u>Z. Physiol.</u> <u>Chem.</u> 364:1753 (1983).
26. P.O. Ljungdahl, J.D. Pennoyer, and B.L. Trumpower, <u>Methods Enzymol.</u> 126:181 (1986).
27. L. Yu and C.-A. Yu, <u>J. Biol. Chem.</u> 257:10215 (1982).
28. K. Mukai, T. Miyazaki, S. Wakabayashi, S. Kuramitsu, and H. Matsubara, <u>J. Biochem.</u> 98:1417 (1985).
29. G. Von Jagow, T.A. Link, and T. Ohnishi, <u>J. Bioenerg. Biomembr.</u> 18:157 (1986).
30. M. Saraste, <u>FEBS Lett.</u> 166:367 (1984).
31. W.R. Widger, W.A. Cramer, R.G. Herrmann, and A. Trebst, <u>Proc. Natl.</u> <u>Acad. Sci. U.S.A.</u> 81:674 (1984).
32. T.A. Link, H. Schägger, and G. Von Jagow, <u>FEBS Lett.</u> 204:9 (1986).
33. B. Pfefferkorn and H.E. Meyer, <u>FEBS Lett.</u> 206:233 (1986).
34. J. Steppuhn, J. Hermans, T. Janson, J. Vater, G. Hauska, and R.G. Herrmann, <u>Mol. Gen. Genet.,</u> submitted (1987).
35. U. Harnisch, H. Weiss, and W. Sebald, <u>Eur. J. Biochem.</u> 149:95 (1985).
36. N. Gabellini and W. Sebald, <u>Eur. J. Biochem.</u> 154:569 (1986).
37. B. Kurowski and B. Ludwig, <u>J. Biol. Chem.,</u> submitted (1987).
38. W.D. Engel, C. Michalski, and G. Von Jagow, <u>Eur. J. Biochem.</u> 132:395 (1983).
39. F.-U. Hartl, B. Schmidt, E. Wachter, H. Weiss, and W. Neupert, <u>Cell</u> 47:939 (1986).
40. G. Von Jagow and T. Ohnishi, <u>FEBS Lett.</u> 185:311 (1985).
41. J. Telser, B.M. Hoffman, R. LoBrutto, T. Ohnishi, A.-L. Tsai, D. Simpkin, and G. Palmer, <u>FEBS Lett.</u> 214:117 (1987).
42. J.A. Fee, K.L. Findling, T. Yoshida, R. Hille, G.E. Tarr, D.O. Hearshen, W.R. Dunham, E.P. Day, T.A. Kent, and E. Münck, <u>J. Biol. Chem.</u> 259:124 (1984).
43. J.F. Cline, B.M. Hoffman, W.B. Mims, E. LaHaie, D.P. Ballou, and J.A. Fee, <u>J. Biol. Chem.</u> 260:3251 (1985).
44. J.A. Fee, D. Kuila, M.W. Mather, and T. Yoshida, <u>Biochim. Biophys.</u> <u>Acta</u> 853:153 (1987).

CRYSTALLISATION OF WATER-SOLUBLE PREPARATIONS OF THE IRON-SULFUR-PROTEIN AND CYTOCHROME C_1 OF UBIQUINOL:CYTOCHROME REDUCTASE FROM NEUROSPORA MITOCHONDRIA

Jürgen Römisch, Uwe Harnisch, Ulrich Schulte and Hanns Weiss

Institut fur Biochemie der Universitat Dusseldorf, Universitátsstraße 1, Federal Republic of Germany

INTRODUCTION

The proton translocating ubiquinol-cytochrome c reductase, (EC 1.10.2.2) of mitochondria, is composed of the Rieske iron-sulfur protein, cytochrome c_1, cytochrome b, and six to nine (depending on the source of mitochondria) subunits without redox-centres (for a review see Weiss, 1987). The low-resolution 3-D structure of the enzyme from Neurospora crassa, the arrangement of the structure in the mitochondrial inner membrane and the subunit topography within the structure (Fig. 1) have been determined by electron microscopy of membrane crystals (Leonard et al., 1981, Karlsson et al. 1983), neutron diffraction of enzyme-detergent preparations (Perkins and Weiss, 1983), biochemical characterisation of isolated subunits (Li et al., 1981 a and b) and sequencing of subunits (Citterich et al. , 1983, Harnisch et al. 1985, Römisch et al., 1987).

The studies have shown that the iron-sulfur protein and cytochrome c_1 protude with their catalytic domains approximately 3 nm into the intermembrane space of mitochondria and are anchored to the membrane each by only one protein stretch.

These two subunits transfer the "high potential electron" from ubiquinol to cytochrome c. The molecular details underlying this reaction are largely unknown because no high resolution structural informations on the two subunits are available. In this article we report that after clipping the membrane spanning part of the two subunits, the proteins can be crystallized.

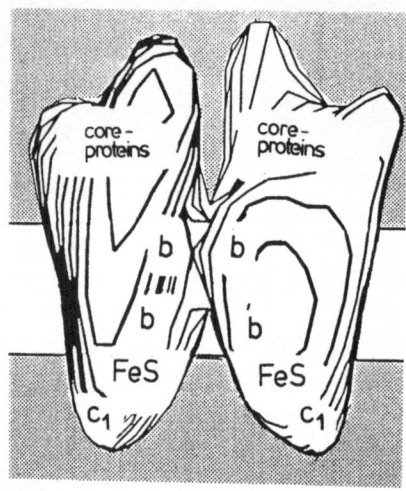

Fig. 1. Topographic model of cytochrome reductase from Neurospora mitochondria. The projected view of the enzyme parallel to the plane of membrane is shown. The density map has been contoured at a level that the volume of the model corresponds to 80 % the molecular mass of the enzyme which is about 550 000 Da. The white section indicates the membrane, the upper dark area the matrix space of mitochondria and the lower dark area the intermembrane space. Core refers to the subunits I and II (historically called core-proteins), b, c_1 and FeS, to the redox-groups of cytochrome b (subunit III), cytochrome c_1 (subunit IV) and the Rieske iron-sulfur protein (subunit V). The four small subunits (VI to IX) are not included into the model because their location is not yet known.

THE PRIMARY STRUCTURES OF THE IRON-SULFUR PROTEIN AND CYTOCHROME C_1

The iron-sulfur subunit consists of 199 amino acids corresponding to the molecular mass of 21 600 Da. The primary structure is characterized by a small N-terminal hydrophilic part of 29 residues, a hydrophobic stretch of 25 residues and a large C-terminal hydrophilic domain of 145 residues. The only four cysteines of the protein, which are assumed to bind the 2Fe-2S cluster are located in a moderate hydrophobic region of this large domain (Harnisch et al., 1985).

Cytochrome c_1 consists of 262 amino acids and has the molecular mass of 29 500 Da. The sequence is characterized by an N-terminal hydrophilic domain of 211 residues with the heme covalently linked by two cysteines and one histidine, a hydrophobic stretch of 15 residues, and a C-terminal hydrophilic part of 36 residues (Römisch et al., 1987).

PREPARATION OF THE WATER-SOLUBLE IRON-SULFUR PROTEIN AND CYTOCHROME C_1

Ubiquinol:cytochrome reductase was prepared by chromatography of Triton-solubilized mitochondrial membranes on cytochrome c Sepharose (Weiss and Kolb, 1979). By treatment with NaCl, the iron-sulfur protein was released from the enzyme as protein-Triton complex (Li et al., 1981b, Karlsson et al., 1983). Without further purification it was incubated for 30 min at 20 ^{O}C with 0.01 mg chymotrypsin per mg total protein. This lead to digestion of the N-terminal hydrophilic part and the membrane spanning part of the subunit. The probably compact C-terminal hydrophilic part remained intact and was isolated from the mixture of the other proteins by gel chromatography in detergent-free buffer.

Preparation of water-soluble cytochrome c_1 was started from a crude cytochrome c_1-detergent preparation obtained by chromatography of total mitochondrial protein on DEAE-Sepharose. The negatively charged cytochrome c_1 eluted at about 0.4 M NaCl far behind the bulk of the other proteins. The small hydrophilic C-terminal part and the hydrophobic part of the subunit were digested by chymotrypsin and the large N-terminal hydrophilic domain was isolated essentially as described above for the iron-sulfur protein.

PROPERTIES OF THE WATER-SOLUBLE IRON-SULFUR PROTEIN AND CYTOCHROME C_1

In the Table , the molecular masses and the sequence regions of the two water soluble preparations are compared to the corresponding data of the membrane bound subunits.

Table. Sequence regions and molecular masses of the water-soluble preparations of the iron-sulfur protein and cytochrome c_1.

Preparation	Molecular mass (Da)	Sequence region	Residues to which the redox-centres are linked
Membrane-bound iron-sulfur protein	21 600	1 - 199	Cys-142, Cys-147 Cys-161, Cys-163
Water-soluble iron-sulfur protein	14 200	72 - 199	
Membrane-bound Cytochrome c_1	29 500	1 - 262	Cys-40, Cys-43 His-44, Met-164
Water-soluble Cytochrome c_1	22 300	1 - 193	

The two most conserved regions of the iron-sulfur subunit are part of the water-soluble preparation. They are located between residues 134 to 186 and 93 to 104. The former region contains four cysteines which bind the 2Fe-2S-cluster. The homology to the corresponding region of Rhodopseudomonas sphaeroides (Gabellini and Sebald, 1986) and Paraccocus denitrificans (B. Ludwig, personal communication) amounts to 85 %. The latter region includes 6 positively charged residues and is assumed to be the contact site to the negative cytochrome c_1. The homology of this region to that of Rhodopseudomonas and Paraccocus amounts to 90 % and 83 %, respectively.

Also the water-soluble preparation of cytochrome c_1 includes the most conserved sequences. The region around the heme binding residues Cys-40, Cys-43, His-44 shows homology to yeast (Sadler et al. 1984), bovine (Wakabayashi et al., 1980), Rhodopseudomonas (Gabellini and Sebald, 1986) and Paraccocus (Ludwig et al., 1983), of 87 %, 77 %, 67 % and 67 %, respectively. The other two regions which are assumed to be the contact sites to cytochrome c are located from Asp 62 to Glu 84 (Stonehuerner et al., 1985) and Asp 170 to Asp 177 (Broger et al., 1983).

The EPR spectrum of the 2Fe-2S cluster of the water-soluble iron-sulfur protein is indistinguishable from the spectrum of the intact subunit. The $g_{z,y,x}$ values are 2.03, 1.90 and 1.75 at 36 K and 9.26 GHz. The light absorption spectrum of the oxidized and ascorbate reduced water-soluble forms of cytochrome c_1 show no difference to the corresponding spectra of intact cytochrome c_1. The ratio of the absorbance at 278 nm and 410 nm of the oxidized protein lies between 0.3 and 0.4 depending on its purity (Li et al., 1981 a and b).

The water-soluble iron-sulfur protein catalyses a single-turnover electron transfer from duroquinol to cytochrome c_1. This reaction, however, is myxothiazol-insensitive in contrast to that in cytochrome reductase. Binding of ferricytochrome c to the water-soluble cytochrome c_1 was studied by gel filtering ^{14}C-leucine labelled cytochrome c_1 with ^{3}H-leucine labelled cytochrome c both from Neurospora. Similar binding parameters are found as with cytochrome c_1 in cytochrome reductase (Li et al., 1981a).

CRYSTALLISATION OF WATER-SOLUBLE IRON-SULFUR PROTEIN AND CYTOCHROME C_1

The iron-sulfur protein was concentrated by binding to a small DEAE-Sepharose column, followed by batch-elution with NaCl and by ammonium sulfate-precipitation. The protein was dissolved at 20 mg/ml protein concentration in 10 mM Tris-Cl, pH 6 - 7 and 2 mM Na-ascorbate. Residual ammonium sulfate was removed by dialysis against the same buffer. Crystals grew within 2 - 3 days at room temperature when the protein was further concentrated by vapour-diffusion using the hanging-drop-method. Reservoirs contained 60 - 80 % ammonium sulfate in 10 mM Tris-Cl, pH 6 - 7 (Fig. 2).

Concentration and crystallisation of cytochrome c_1 were carried out as above but omitting the ammonium sulfate-precipitation step. Starting from 20 mg/ml protein, crystals grew at $4^{\circ}C$ within 7 days (Fig. 2).

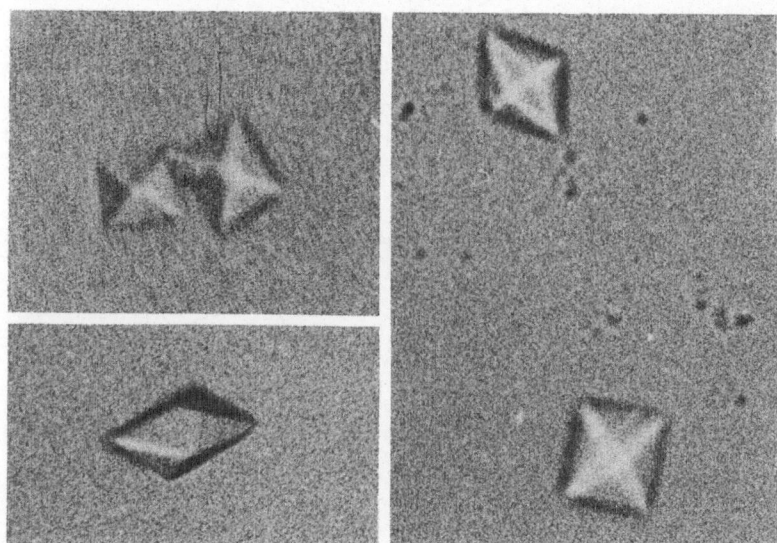

Fig. 2. Crystals of the catalytic domains of the iron-sulfur protein (left) and cytochrome c_1 (right). Both crystals grew as tetragonal bipyramides. The edge lengths are 30 - 40 um.

This work was supported by the Deutsche Forschungsgemeinschaft and the Fonds der Chemischen Industrie.

References

Broger, C., Salardi, S. and Azzi, A., 1983, Interaction between isolated cytochrome c_1 and cytochrome c, Eur. J. Biochem. 131, 349

Citterich, M.H., Morelli, G. and Macino, G., 1983, Nucleotide sequence and intron structure of the apocytochrome b gene of Neurospora crassa mitochondria, EMBO J., 2, 1235

Gabellini, N. and Sebald, W., 1986, Nucleotide Sequence and transcription of the fbc operon from Rhodospseudomonas sphaeroides. Evaluation of the deduced amino acid sequences of the FeS-protein, cytochrome b and cytochrome c_1, Eur. J. Biochem. 154, 569

Harnisch, U., Weiss, H. and Sebald, W., 1985, The primary structure of the iron-sulfur subunit of ubiquinol-cytochrome c reductase from Neurospora determined by cDNA and gene sequencing, Eur. J. Biochem. 149, 95

Karlsson, B., Hovmöller, S., Weiss, H. and Leonard, K., 1983, Structural studies of cytochrome reductase. Subunit topography determined by electron microscopy of membrane crystals of a subcomplex, J. Mol. Biol. 165, 287

Leonard, K., Wingfield, P., Arad, T. and Weiss, H., 1981, Three-dimensional structure of ubiquinol:cytochrome c reductase from Neurospora mitochondria determined by electron microscopy of membrane crystals, J. Mol. Biol. 149, 259

Li, Y., Leonard, K. and Weiss, H., 1981a, Membrane-bound and water-soluble cytochrome c_1 from Neurospora mitochondria, Eur. J. Biochem. 116, 199

Li, Y., De Vries, S., Leonard, K. and Weiss, H., 1981b, Topography of the iron-sulfur subunit in mitochondrial ubiquinol:cytochrome c reductase, FEBS Lett. 135, 277

Ludwig, B., Suda, K., Cerletti, N., 1983, Cytochrome c_1 from Paraccocus denitrificans, Eur. J. Biochem. 137, 597

Perkins, S.J. and Weiss, H., 1983, Low resolution structural studies of mitochondrial ubiquinol:cytochrome c reductase in detergent solution by neutron scattering, J. Mol. Biol. 168, 847

Römisch, J., Tropschug, M., Sebald, W. and Weiss, H., 1987, The primary structure of cytochrome c_1 from Neurospora crassa, Eur. J. Biochem., in press

Sadler, J., Suda, K., Schatz, G., Kaudewitz, F. and Haid, A., 1984, Sequencing of the nuclear gene for the yeast cytochrome c_1 precursor reveals an unusually complex amino-terminal presequence, EMBO J. 3, 2137

Stonehuerner, J., O'Brien, P., Geren, L., Millett, F., Steidl, J., Yu, L. and Yu, C.A., 1985, Identification of the binding site on cytochrome c_1 for cytochrome c_1, J. Biol. Chem. 260, 5392

Wakabayashi, S., Matsubara, H., Kim, C.H., Kawai, K. and King, T.E., 1980, The complete amino acid sequence of bovine heart cytochrome c_1, Biochem. Biophys. Res. Commun. 97, 1548

Weiss, H. and Kolb, H.J., 1979, Isolation of mitochondrial succinate:ubiquinone reductase, cytochrome c reductase and cytochrome c oxidase from Neurospora crassa using nonionic detergent, Eur. J. Biochem. 99, 139

Weiss, H., 1987, Structure of mitochondrial ubiquinol:cytochrome c reductase (complex III), Curr. Top. Bioenerg. 15 (in press)

IRON CLUSTER SITES OF CARDIAC Ip-SUBUNIT OF SUCCINATE DEHYDROGENASE

Tsoo E. King, N. S. Reimer, M. T. Seaman, L. Q. Sun, Q. W. Wang, K. T. Yasunobu and S. H. Ho

Department of Chemistry, Laboratory of Bioenergetics
State University of New York at Albany
Albany, New York 12222 USA, and
Department of Biochemistry and Biophysics
University of Hawaii Medical School
Honolulu, Hawaii 96822 USA

SUMMARY

Comparison of the amino acid sequence worked out for the Ip subunit of succinate dehydrogenase from cardiac mitochondria with that of microbial enzyme and fumarate dehydrogenase as well as ferredoxins suggests that all iron sulfur clusters in heart SDH may originally exist in the Ip.

It is now generally agreed that mitochondrial succinate dehydrogenase (SDH) (1) consists of two subunits which are separable by SDS-PAGE. The larger subunit contains covalently linked FAD with molecular weight of about 70,000 known as Fp and the smaller one approximately 27,000 called Ip contains only an iron-sulfur cluster without flavin. On the other hand, the distribution of iron-sulfur clusters is somewhat still not completely settled. Previously, it was thought that Fp contains FAD together with two 2Fe2S centers and that Ip contains one 4Fe4S center (4). Very recently, from physical methods, a claim has been made that Fp consists of a 2Fe2S center and a 4Fe4S cluster, whereas Ip consists of a 3FeXS cluster (2, 3).

This communication inquires how much information can be obtained about the positions of prosthetic groups bound to a protein from its amino acid sequence. Ip from cardiac mitochondria has been used to deduce some knowledge in this aspect.

EXPERIMENTAL PROCEDURES

Ip was prepared by extensive modification of the method reported (1) from reconstitutively active and pure (>99%) SDH. The SDH was prepared by the method developed in this laboratory as published (5) with some modifications from succinate-cytochrome c reductase made by adoption of a previous method (6, 7). The amino acid sequence determined chemically was by conventional methods (8-13).

```
1            10              20                30      35
A Q T A A A A A P R I K K F A I Y R W D P D K T G D K P H M Q T Y E I

36    40              50                60              70
D L N N C G P M V L D A L I K I K N E I D S T L T F R R S C R E G I C

71          80              90              100     105
G S C A M N I N G G N T L A C T R R I D T N L S K   - - I Y P L P

106   110              120              130              140
H M Y V I K D L V P D L S N F Y A Q Y K S I E P Y L K K K D E S Q G G

141         150              160              170     175
K E Q Y L Q S I E D R E K L D G L Y E C I L C A C C S T S C P S Y W W

176   180              190              200              210
D G D K Y L G P A V L M Q A Y R W M I D S R D D F T E E R L A K L Q D

211         220              230              241     245
P F S L Y R C H T I M N C T Q T C P K G L N P G K A I A E I K

246         257
  (M) A T Y K E K Q A S A


unpositioned
    tryptic: V S K                    chymotryptic: E K M
             A N L E K
             E V V Y R
```

Fig. 1. Sequence of Ip of mitochondrial SDH from heart.

RESULTS AND DISCUSSION

Five cysteine-containing peptides have been isolated and are designated as peptides T-5, T-9, T-10, T-20 and T-29. Similarly a separate S. aurease protease and a CNBr digest led to the isolation of peptides S-3 and CNBr-3 which were needed to complete the sequence of peptides T-5 and T-10, respectively. The sequence is shown in Fig. 1. It may be noted that some overlapping work in two segments is still to be completed[*].

Comparison of the primary structure of Ip subunits between mitochondrial SDH and bacterial SDH as well as fumarate reductase reveals that the most probable membrane binding site of the mammalian enzyme is the alanine rich hydrophobic segment. The latter has a sequence of Ala-Gln-Thr-Ala-Ala-Ala-Ala-Ala-Pro- and is unique. It is absent in microbial enzymes or ferredoxins. The segment may be attached to the membrane as diagrammatically shown in Fig. 2.

The recent proposal (2, 3, 20) of the distribution of the iron-sulfur clusters require a total iron in SDH of 9. Review of the literature reveals the ratio of Fe to FAD not larger than 7.5 ± 0.6 (see also p. 254 of

---

[*] After the work was completed, a report of amino acid sequence of Ip prepared from SDS dissociation came to our attention (26). Their results with one or two segments to be confirmed agree with our finding as shown in Fig. 1 except for some minor differences.

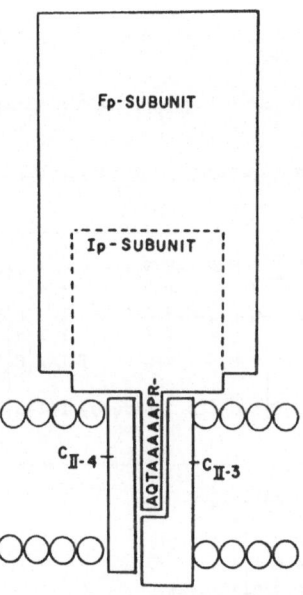

Fig. 2. Schematic representation of subunits of succinate-Q reductase modeled from Girdlestone et al. (15). II-3 is apparently QP-S and II--4 is either an artifact or another QP-S (Xu and King, in preparation).

ref. 20) not until very recently a value has been reported on 8.6 ± 0.3 based on three determinations of Fe, FAD and protein on a SDH preparation (3). The sequence of the Ip of E. coli SDH (22) and E. coli fumarate reductase are 44% homologous and have very similar conformations (23), yet only one out of 11 cysteine residues is in homologous sequence positions. The cysteine residues are important since they are chelated to the iron of FeS-clusters in iron-sulfur proteins. However, 9 out of 11-13 cysteine residues of the Ip of mitochondrial heart SDH, E. coli SDH (14) and the analogous E. coli fumarate reductase (16) are located at homologous positions. This makes it very likely that all of the FeS-clusters are present in the Ip subunit and not within the Fp. It is possible that while under the drastic conditions used to dissociate the subunits of SDH by high concentrations of trichloroacetic acid (1) the Fe atoms might well be redistributed in both Fp and Ip subunits. Unpublished results from this laboratory showed completely different EPR behavior of Ip and native SDH for S-3.

Darlison and Guest (14) noted Ip of the E. coli SDH and Cole et al. (16) with fumarate reductase, that the cysteine residues of these subunits, which are most probably chelated to the iron of the FeS clusters, occur in three different groups. The first cluster of cysteine residues (from the N-terminal end) was proposed to bind a 2Fe2S cluster as in the plant ferredoxins. The second cluster had cysteine residues situated similarly to those of certain bacterial 3FeXS or 4Fe4S cluster containing proteins. A third group of cysteines were placed like the 4Fe4S cluster

A   17V-D-T-A-P-H-S-A-F-Y-E-V——P-Y-D-A——T-T-S-L-L-D-A-L-G-Y
       * *   * *   *   * * * * *

B   13V-D-D-A-P-R-M-Q-D-Y-T-L-E-A-D-E-G-R-D-M-M-L-L-D-A-L-I-Q
       *   *   * *   *   *   *   * * * *

C   T-G-D-K-P-H-M-Q-T-Y-E-I-D-L-N-N-[C]-G-P-M-V-L——D-A-L-I-K

A   56S-[C]-R-M-A-I-[C]-G-S-[C]-G-M-M-V-N-N-V-P-K-L-A-[C]-K-T-   CYSTEINE
       * | * *   * | * *   * | * | *

B   53S-[C]-R-E-G-V-[C]-G-S-D-G-L-N-M-N-G-K-N-G-L-A-[C]-K-T-   CLUSTER
       * | * * * * | * *   *   * *   * * | *

C₁   63S-[C]-R-E-G-I-[C]-G-S-[C]-A-M-N-I-N-G-G-N-T-L-A-[C]-T-R——   I

D   38S-[C]-R-A-G-S-[C]-S-S-[C]-A-G-(25 residues) L-T-[C]-A-A-

---

A   148[C]-I-N-[C]-G-L-[C]-Y-A-A-[C]-P-Q-F-G   CYSTEINE
         | * * | * | *   * | * *   *

B   148[C]-I-L-[C]-A-[C]-C-S-T-S-[C]-P-S-F-W   CLUSTER
         | * * * | * | * * * *   * | * *

C₂   157[C]-I-L-[C]-A-[C]-C-S-T-S-[C]-P-S-Y-K   II
         | * | *   *   * |

E   8[C]-V-S-[C]-G-A-[C]-A-S-E-[C]-P-V-N-A
        | * | * * * * | * * *

F   8[C]-I-A-[C]-G-A-[C]-K-P-E-[C]-P-V-I

A   204[C]-T-F-V-G-Y-[C]-S-E-V-[C]-P-K   CYSTEINE
         | *   * | *   * | * *

C₃   214[C]-H-T-I-M-N-[C]-T-Q-T-[C]-P-K   CLUSTER
         | *   * | *   * | *

E   37[C]-I-D-C-G-N-[C]-A-N-V-[C]-P-V   III
        | * * * *   * | * *   * | *

F   34[C]-I-D-C-G-S-[C]-A-S-V-[C]-P

Fig. 3. Comparison of sequence of various iron-sulfur proteins. (A), Ip
of fumarate reductase of E coli (22); (B), SDH of E. coli
(14); From Ip of SDH are (C), T-5; (C₁), T-9 + T-10; (C₂),
T-20; (C₃), T-29; (D), plant ferredoxin of Lucaena glauca
(17); (E), bacterial ferredoxin of Clostridium pasteurianum
(18); and (F), bacterial ferredoxin of Peptococcus aerogenes
(19). Boxed, identical; *homologous - 11 of 13; homo. = 60%.

containing proteins. However, this third cluster contains only 3 cysteine
residues and not 4.

The present study shows that the mitochondrial Ip of SDH contains 13
cysteine residues of which 11 are in constant, conserved positions when
compared to the E. coli Ip of SDH as well as the E. coli Ip of fumarate reductase, as shown in Fig. 3. The mammalian cluster I like the
E. coli fumarate reductase has the $CysX_4CysX_2CysX_3Cys$ sequence
like 2Fe2S cluster containing plant ferredoxins (17). However, it should
be noted that the E. coli SDH lacks the second cysteine. In order for
a 2Fe2S cluster to exist, there must be an OH or H_2O in place of the
second cysteine or cluster I does not exist. The second cysteine cluster
resembles in sequence and relative cysteine position the 4Fe4S cluster of
bacterial ferredoxin (18, 19). The cysteine sequence being $CysX_2CysX_2$

312

CysXCys may possibly be a HiPIP type 4Fe4S cluster configuration having a Cys-Pro sequence following the fourth cysteine.

The third cluster of relevant residues consists of only three cysteines which may represent either of two types of Fe-clusters. One possible structure is similar to the 4Fe4S cluster of Azotobacter I ferredoxin (24) as well as Peptococcus aerogenes (19) in which one cysteine is replaced by a μ-oxo bridge, or possibly by an OH⁻ ion or H_2O molecule. The other possible structure is one previously proposed by Beinert and Thomson (2) and described as a 3Fe4S cluster.

In summary, the Fp-subunit probably contains no FeS-cluster; that is, Ip contains all of the FeS-clusters in native SDH. A 2Fe2S may be bound by the first group of cysteine residues, a 4Fe4S cluster by the second group of cysteines and a 3Fe4S by the third group of cysteine residues.

Sequence data alone cannot conclusively determine the iron-sulfur chelation structures of FeS-proteins. However, many studies with ferredoxins and certain other FeS-proteins have shown that the sequence positions of the cysteine residues involved in binding the various types of FeS-clusters are strongly conserved (18-25). The present sequence study brought up new proposals to be tested concerning the structure of both Fp and Ip. From the evolutionary standpoint, it is interesting to note a very high (50%) degree of sequence homology in Ip of SDH of the mammalian mitochondria, E. coli, and other 2Fe2S and 4Fe4S ferredoxins. At any rate, it is worthwhile to serve as a fecund exercise for inductive reasoning.

ACKNOWLEDGMENT

Supported in part by National Institutes of Health research grants HLB-12576 and GM-16767 and American Heart Association grant 86-1425.

REFERENCES

1. Davis, K. A. and Hatefi, Y. (1971) Biochemistry 10, 2509-2576.
2. Beinert, H. and Thomson, A. J. (1983) Arch. Biochem. Biophys. 222, 333-361.
3. Johnson, M. K., Morningstar, J. E., Bennett, D. E., Ackrell, B. A. C. and Kearney, E. B. (1985) J. Biol. Chem. 260, 7368-7378.
4. Ohnishi, T., Salerno, J. C., Winter, D. B., Lim, J., Yu, C. A., Yu, L. and King, T. E. (1976) J. Biol. Chem. 251, 2094-2104.
5. Yu, C. A. and Yu, L. (1980) Biochim. Biophys. Acta 591, 409-420.
6. Takemori, S. and King, T. E. (1964) J. Biol. Chem. 239, 3546-3558.
7. Yu, L., Yu, C. A. and King, T. E. (1978) J. Biol. Chem. 253, 2657-2663.
8. Crestfield, A. M., Moore, S. and Stein, W. H. J. (1963) J. Biol. Chem. 238, 618-621.
9. Tarr, G. E. (1977) Meth. Enzymol. 47E, 335-357.
10. Ambler, R. P. (1967) Meth. Enzymol. 11, 155-166.
11. Spackman, D. H., Moore, S. and Stein, W. H. J. (1958) Anal. Chem. 30, 1190-1206.
12. Reimer, N. S., Yasunobu, C. L., Yasunobu, K. T. and Norton, T. R. (1985) J. Biol. Chem. 260, 8690-8693.
13. Reimer, N. S., Yasunobu, K. T., Wei, Y. H. and King, T. E. (1983) Biochem. Biophys. Res. Commun. 110, 8-14.
14. Darlison, M. G. and Guest, R. (1984) Biochem. J. 223, 507-517.
15. Girdlestone, J., Bisson, R. and Capaldi, R. A. (1981) Biochemistry 20, 152-156.

16. Cole, S. T., Grundstrom, T., Jaurin, B., Robinson, J. J. and Weiner, J. H. (1982) Eur. J. Biochem. 126, 211-216.
17. Benson, A. M. and Yasunobu, K. T. (1969) Proc. Natl. Acad. Sci. U.S.A., 1269-1273.
18. Yasunobu, K. T. and Tanaka, M. (1973) Systematic Zool. 22, 570-589.
19. Adams, E. T., Sieker, L. C. and Jensen, L. H. (1973) J. Biol. Chem. 248, 3989-3996.
20. Beinert, H. and Albracht, S. P. J. (1982) Biochim. Biophys. Acta 683, 245-277.
21. King, T. E., Ohnishi, T., Winter, D. B. and Wu, J. T. (1976) In Iron and Copper Proteins (K. T. Yasunobu, H. F. Mower and O. Hayaishi, eds.) Plenum Press, New York, p. 182-227.
22. Wood, D., Darlison, M. G., Wilde, R. J. and Guest, J. R. (1984) Biochem. J. 222, 519-534.
23. Cole, S. T. (1982) Eur. J. Biochem. 122, 479-484.
24. Gosh, D., O'Donnell, S., Furey, E. Jr., Robbins, A. H. and Stout, D. C. (1982) J. Mol. Biol. 158, 73-109.
25. Tsukihara, T., Fukuyama, K., Nakamura, M., Katsube, Y., Hase, T., Wada, K. and Matsubara, H. (1982) Biosystems 15, 2443-257.
26. Wakabayashi, S., Matsuda, S., Matsubara, H., Yu, L. and Yu, C. (1987) In Iron sulfur Protein Research (H. Matsubara, Y. Katsube and K. Wada, eds.) Japan Scientific Societies Press, Tokyo, p. 240-244.

POLYPEPTIDES IN MITOCHONDRIAL ELECTRON-

TRANSFER COMPLEXES

Takayuki Ozawa, Morimitsu Nishikimi, Hiroshi Suzuki,
Masashi Tanaka, and Yoshiharu Shimomura

Department of Biomedical Chemistry, Faculty of Medicine
University of Nagoya, Nagoya, Japan

SUMMARY

We established an isolation method for ubiquinone-binding proteins
(QPs) from either mitochondria or electron-transfer particles, and found
that at least 29% of the total coenzyme Q in the inner membrane was bound
to QPs. The QP from Complex I (QP-I) was identified with a 13-kDa
polypeptide, and the QP from Complex III (QP-III) with a 12.4-kDa
polypeptide. We also isolated subunits of Complex III: the iron-sulfur
protein, cytochrome c_1, cytochrome $\underline{b}$, and QP-III, and core proteins in
their functional states. In vitro translation of rat liver poly(A)$^+$ RNA
followed by immunoprecipitation with antibody directed against QP-III
yielded a polypeptide with a molecular weight that was the same as that of
the mature protein. It was also found that this polypeptide was imported
into mitochondria and became resistant to trypsin treatment, and that the
import required the energized state of the inner membrane. A cDNA for
human cytochrome c_1 was cloned using the λgt11 expression vector, and the
sequence analysis showed that the amino acid sequence deduced from the DNA
sequence was quite similar to that of bovine heart cytochrome c_1
determined by amino acid sequence analysis. Together with the structural
data from the crystallographic analysis of Complex III, the sequence data
would provide a basis for elucidation of structure and function of the
complex. Immunoblotting technique gave us information on the molecular
level regarding the deficiency of subunits of complexes in patients with
mitochondrial cytopathies.

INTRODUCTION

Mitochondrial electron-transfer chain was fragmented into four
complexes by Hatefi et al.[1,2], and the tripartite particles of the inner
membrane were discovered by Fernandez-Moran et al.[3]. These works opened
a new era for investigation of the molecular architecture of the mitochondrial energy-transducing units. MacLennan and Tzagoloff isolated the
oligomycin-sensitive ATPase and established that it is the seat of ATP
hydrolysis and synthesis[4-6]. Concurrently, Racker, in a series of
studies, identified the head-piece of the tripartite unit as oligomycin-
insensitive ATPase (F_1) and the membrane sector (base piece) of the
tripartite unit as F_0 which carries out coupled ATP hydrolysis and
synthesis with F_1[7-10]. Thus, all of the units that participate in energy

coupling could be isolated and defined, namely the four electron-transfer complexes and the F_0-F_1 tripartite system. However, details of the molecular architecture of each unit and the three dimensional arrangement of the units and F_0-F_1 system have not been fully clarified. As Mitchell has nominated the F_0-F_1 system as H^+-pump ATPase in his chemiosmotic coupling hypothesis[11-13], investigation on the reality of three dimensional interaction between the electron-transfer units and H^+-pump ATPase is especially important to assess the hypothesis.

With this view in mind, it was intended to clarify the detailed molecular architecture and three dimensional arrangement of the mito-chondrial energy-transducing system by characterization of its constituents.

CONSTITUENTS OF THE ENERGY TRANSDUCING SYSTEM

1. NADH-Coenzyme Q Oxidoreductase (Complex I). Complex I transfers electrons and protons from NADH to coenzyme Q (CoQ) and is the energy coupling site I. However, the information on Complex I is still limited because it is a high molecular weight enzyme of considerable structural and functional complexity[14]. We have been attempting to isolate and characterize individual polypeptides and subfragments of Complex I. As the first step, Complex I was fractionated into three subfragments — the hydrophobic proteins (HP), the soluble iron-sulfur proteins (IPs), the flavoprotein (FP) with NADH dehydrogenase activity — by using deoxy-cholate and cholate instead of chaotrope[16]. They were further purified by hydrophobic affinity chromatography and gel filtration. Iron-sulfur clusters were found to be associated with 51- and 23-kDa polypeptides in the FP subfraction[17].

2. CoQ-Binding Proteins. CoQ is an essential constituent of the energy-transducing respiratory chain in mitochondria. No one had estimated definite number of either free or bound CoQ in the mitochondria. We have established an isolation method for CoQ-binding proteins (QPs) from either mitochondria or electron-transfer particles[15]. By this method, at least 29% (0.87 nmol/mg of protein) of the total CoQ in the mitochondrial inner membrane was found to be bound to QPs[18]. Furthermore, QPs were isolated from Complex I and Complex III in the form of protein-CoQ complexes. As shown in Fig. 1, QP from Complex I (QP-I) was identified with a 13-kDa polypeptide, a constituent of IP, and QP from Complex III (QP-III) with a 12.4-kDa polypeptide[19]. It is now recognized that QP-I and QP-III are new constituents of Complexes I and III. The observation of one or two stable ubisemiquinone species[20] and the presence of QP-I would propose a mechanism of energy tranduction in Complex I analogous to the Q-cycle or b-cycle hypothesized in Complex III.

3. Ubiquinol-Cytochrome c Oxidoreductase (Complex III). Complex III transfers electrons from ubiquinol to cytochrome c and is the energy coupling site II. It was postulated that the complex plays a central role in H^+ pumping from inside to outside of the mitochondrial inner membrane. It was found that Complex III closely interacts with phospholipids[21] and that the iron-sulfur protein in the complex can be isolated from the complex when the boundary phospholipids, especially cardiolipin, were depleted by washing the complex with detergent on a hydrophobic interaction affinity column of phenyl-Sepharose[22-24]. This presented the notion that boundary cardiolipin plays a role as a hoop in the complex, integrating the subunits into a functional unit[25]. In fact, after removal of the boundary cardiolipin, all of the subunits could be separated from a single source of the complex by detergent-exchange chromatography, as shown in Fig. 2[26]. After the purification, cytochrome c_1 was demonstrated to be coupled to the iron-sulfur protein, resulting in reconstitution of

316

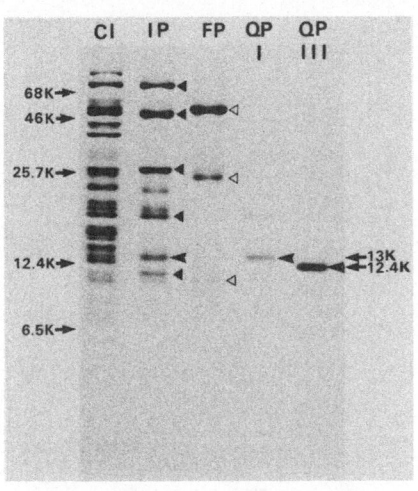

Fig. 1. Subunits in Complex I. Beef heart
mitochondrial Complex I (CI) and its iron–sulfur
protein (IP) and flavoprotein (FP) subfractions were
subjected to SDS–urea polyacrylamide gel electrophoresis. CoQ-binding protein purified from Complex
I (QP-I) and that from Complex III (QP-III) are
shown by arrows. QP-I was identified with one of
the polypeptides in IP subfraction with a molecular
mass of 13 kDa[19]. Solid arrowheads indicate the
subunits of IP, and open arrowheads those of FP.

the antimycin-insensitive pathway of electrons in the complex[26]. Cytochrome b was very labile when it was purified to a single polypeptide, but
was stable when it formed a complex with subunit IX, suggesting that
subunit IX stabilizes the cytochrome[28].

Antibody against the iron–sulfur protein[29] was used to quantify this
protein in submitochondrial particles by radioimmunoassay and immunoblotting[30]. The results showed that the mitochondrial inner membrane
contains two times as much of the immunoreactive iron–sulfur protein as is
expected for Complex III.

In vitro translation products programed with poly(A)$^+$ RNA of rat
liver were precipitated with anti-QP-III antiserum, and analyzed by
SDS-gel electrophoresis and fluorography[31]. An immunoprecipitated labeled
protein showed apparently the same mobility on a SDS-gel as purified beef
heart QP-III (Fig. 3, lanes 1 and 6). Thus, it is clear that the
translation product formed in the cell-free system has a molecular mass
that is indistinguishable from that of the mature form of QP-III. The
translation product of QP-III is incorporated into mitochondria, and it
disappears from the postmitochondrial supernatant after incubation (Fig.
3, lanes 2 and 5). The imported labeled protein becomes resistant to
trypsin treatment by which the protein can be completely fragmented when
the mitochondria have been solubilized with Triton X-100 (Fig. 3, lanes 3
and 4). In accord with the finding that in vitro synthesized QP-III has
the same apparent Mr as that of purified QP-III, the size of the labeled
protein do not change to any appreciable degree in the process of import.

Fig. 4 shows that the import of the translation product of QP-III

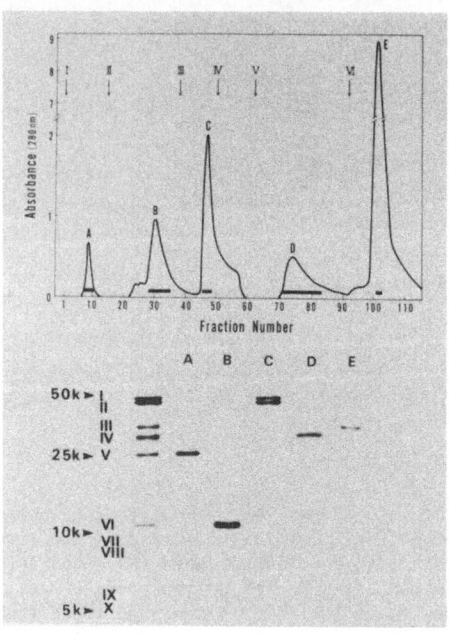

Fig. 2. Isolation of subunits of Complex III by
detergent-exchange chromatography. Upper: After
removal of phospholipids from Complex III on a
phenyl-Sepharose CL-4B column, an iron-sulfur
protein fraction (peak A) was eluted with buffer
containing 1% deoxycholate (I). Subsequently, two
fractions of subunit VI (peak B) and core proteins
(peak C) were eluted with 1.5 M (II) and 3 M (III)
guanidine hydrochloride, respectively. After
equilibration of the column with buffer without
guanidine (IV), a cytochrome c_1 fraction (peak D)
was eluted with buffer containing 1% $C_{12}E_8$ (V).
Finally, a cytochrome b-rich fraction (peak E) was
eluted with buffer containing 2% SDS (VI). Arrows
indicate the change of buffers. Lower: SDS-
polyacrylamide gel electrophoretic patterns of
original Complex III (leftmost lane) and the
fractions (A–E) from the phenyl-Sepharose CL-4B
column are shown.

requires the energized state of mitochondrial inner membrane. Carbonyl
cyanide p-(trifluoromethoxy)phenylhydrazone, an uncoupler, completely
blocked the incorporation of the labeled protein into the mitochondria
(compare lanes 1 and 2). The translation product in the postmitochondrial
supernatant was almost completely fragmented during the incubation with
mitochondria (lane 3). This phenomenon appears to be due to contamination
of lysosomal proteinase in the mitochondrial preparation, and indicates
that the newly translated QP-III is highly sensitive to proteolytic
digestion.

A cDNA for cytochrome c_1 was cloned from a human liver cDNA library in

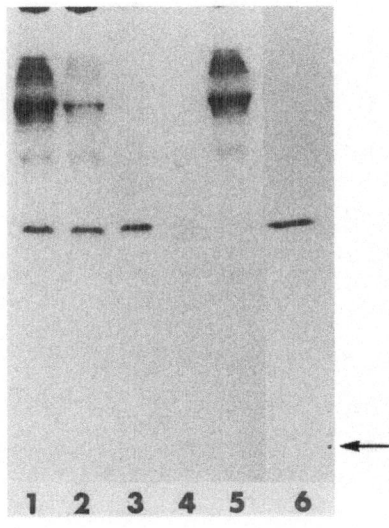

Fig. 3. Cell-free synthesis of QP-III and its import into mitochondria. Poly(A)$^+$ RNA isolated from rat liver was translated in the presence of [^{35}S]methionine in a rabbit reticulocyte lysate system. A portion of the translation mixture (10 µl) was used for direct immunoprecipitation with anti-QP-III antiserum (lane 1). The other portion of the mixture (60 µl) was mixed with 60 µl of a suspension of mitochondria (7 mg of protein/ml) and incubated at 30°C for 1 h. The mixture was divided into three portions (40 µl each), and mitochondria were spun down. The mitochondrial pellet from one of the samples was suspended in 100 µl of a solution for mitochondria isolation (solution A) and further incubated with trypsin (20 µg/ml) at 4°C for 30 min. After the digestion was stopped by addition of soybean trypsin inhibitor (1.1 mg/ml), the mitochondria were dissolved in 400 µl of an immuno-precipitation buffer (solution B) (lane 3). The second mitochondrial pellet was previously dissolved in 100 µl of a solution for mitochondrial isolation containing 2% Triton X-100, and treated with trypsin as above (lane 4). The third mitochondrial pellet was directly dissolved in 400 µl of solution B (lane 2). These samples and the postmitochondrial supernatant (lane 5) were immuno-precipitated and subjected to SDS-gel electrophoresis followed by fluorography. Purified QP-III (1.2 µg) was electrophoresed on the same gel and stained with Coomassie blue (lane 6). Arrow indicates the position of bromo-phenol blue.

λgt11[32]. The amino acid sequence deduced from the nucleotide sequence of the insert (Fig. 5) showed a high degree of homology with that of bovine cytochrome c_1 determined by amino acid sequence analysis reported by Wakabayashi et al.[33].

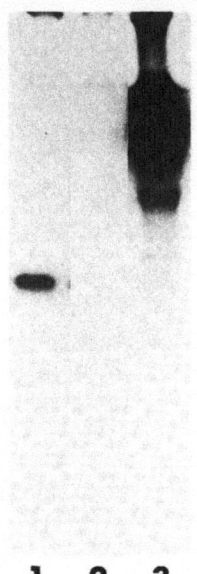

1 2 3

Fig. 4. Energy-dependent import of QP-III into
mitochondria. The translation products, prepared
in the same manner as in the experiment of Fig. 3,
were incubated with mitochondria in the presence
of carbonyl cyanide p-(trifluoromethoxy)phenylhy-
drazone at 30 °C for 1 h. The mixture was separated
into the mitochondria (lane 2) and supernatant
(lane 3) fractions, which were carried through the
same procedures as specified for lanes 3 and 5 in
Fig. 3, respectively. As a control (lane 1), the
translation mixture was incubated with mitochondria in the absence of the uncoupler, and
processed as specified for lane 3 in Fig. 3.

4. Cytochrome c-Oxygen Oxidoreductase (Complex IV). Cytochrome c
oxidase, located at the terminus of the mitochondrial electron-transfer
chain, transduces the redox energy into the driving force for ATP
production. We have succeeded in crystallizing the oxidase in a form of
complex with a ligand, cytochrome c[34]. By using a detergent as another
ligand, crystals of the oxidase alone were obtained[35]. The electron
microscopic observations and electron diffraction studies revealed the
dimensions and angles of the unit cell in the crystal. The three-
dimensional structure of the oxidase to be elucidated by X-ray diffraction studies will give us fundamental information on the mechanism of
energy transduction. Other examples of membrane protein crystals obtained
by the principle of crystallizing ligand-protein complexes[36] are Complex
III[37,38] and the calcium-binding protein in sarcoplasmic reticulum[39].

```
           CGT GGC CTC CTC TCT TCC TTG GAC CAC ACC AGC ATC CGG AGG GGT TTC CAG GTA TAT AAG
Human      Arg Gly Leu Leu Ser Ser Leu Asp His Thr Ser Ile Arg Arg Gly Phe Gln Val Tyr Lys
Bovine     -   -   -   -   -   -   -   -   -   -   -   -   -   -   -   -   -   -   -   -
           15              20              25              30


           CAG GTG TGC GCC TCC TGC CAC AGC ATG GAC TTC GTG GCC TAC CGC CAC CTG GTG GGC GTG
           Gln Val Cys Ala Ser Cys His Ser Met Asp Phe Val Ala Tyr Arg His Leu Val Gly Val
           -   -   -   Ser -   -   -   -   -   -   Tyr -   -   -   -   -   -   -   -   -
           35              40              45              50


           TGC TAC ACG GAG GAT GAA GCT AAG GAG CTG GCT GCG GAG GTG GAG GTT CAA GAC GGC CCC
           Cys Tyr Thr Glu Asp Glu Ala Lys Glu Leu Ala Ala Glu Val Glu Val Gln Asp Gly Pro
           -   -   -   -   -   -   -   -   Ala -   -   Glu -   -   -   -   -   -   -   -
           55              60              65              70


           AAT GAA GAT GGG GAG ATG TTC ATG CGG CCA GGG AAG CTG TTC GAC TAT TTC CCA AAA CCA
           Asn Glu Asp Gly Glu Met Phe Met Arg Pro Gly Lys Leu Phe Asp Tyr Phe Pro Lys Pro
           -   -   -   -   -   -   -   -   -   -   -   -   -   Ser -   -   -   -   -   -
           75              80              85              90


           TAC CCC AAC AGT GAG GCT GCT CGA GCT GCC AAC AAC GGA GCA TTG CCC CCT GAC CTC AGC
           Tyr Pro Asn Ser Glu Ala Ala Arg Ala Ala Asn Asn Gly Ala Leu Pro Pro Asp Leu Ser
           -   -   -   Pro -   -   -   -   -   -   -   -   -   -   -   -   -   -   -   -
           95              100             105             110


           TAC ATC GTG CGA GCT AGG CAT GGT GGT GAG GAC TAC GTC TTC TCC CTG CTC ACG GGC TAC
           Tyr Ile Val Arg Ala Arg His Gly Gly Glu Asp Tyr Val Phe Ser Leu Leu Thr Gly Tyr
           -   -   -   -   -   -   -   -   -   -   -   -   -   -   -   -   -   -   -   -
           115             120             125             130


           TGC GAG CCA CCC ACC GGG GTG TCA CTG CGG GAA GGT CTC TAC TTC AAC CCC TAC TTT CCT
           Cys Glu Pro Pro Thr Gly Val Ser Leu Arg Glu Gly Leu Tyr Phe Asn Pro Tyr Phe Pro
           -   -   -   -   -   -   -   -   -   -   -   -   -   -   -   -   -   -   -   -
           135             140             145             150


           GGC CAG GCC ATT GCC ATG GCC CCT CCC ATC TAC ACA GAT GTC TTA GAG TTT GAC GAT GGC
           Gly Gln Ala Ile Ala Met Ala Pro Pro Ile Tyr Thr Asp Val Leu Glu Phe Asp Asp Gly
           -   -   -   Gly -   -   -   -   -   -   Asn Glu -   -   -   -   -   -   -   -
           155             160             165             170


           ACC CCA GCT ACC ATG TCC CAG ATA GCC AAG GAT GTG TGC ACC TTC CTG CGC TGG GCA TCT
           Thr Pro Ala Thr Met Ser Gln Ile Ala Lys Asp Val Cys Thr Phe Leu Arg Trp Ala Ser
           -   -   -   -   -   -   -   Val -   -   -   -   -   -   -   -   -   -   -   Ala
           175             180             185             190


           GAG CCA GAG CAC GAC CAT CGA AAA CGC ATG GGG CTC AAG ATG TTG ATG ATG ATG GCT CTG
           Glu Pro Glu His Asp His Arg Lys Arg Met Gly Leu Lys Met Leu Met Met Met Ala Leu
           -   -   -   -   -   -   -   -   -   -   -   -   -   Leu -   -   Gly -
           195             200             205             210


           CTG GTG CCC CTG GTC TAC ACC ATA AAG CGG CAC AAG TGG TCA GTC CTG AAG AGT CGG AAG
           Leu Val Pro Leu Val Tyr Thr Ile Lys Arg His Lys Trp Ser Val Leu Lys Ser Arg Lys
           -   Leu -   -   -   -   Ala Met -   -   -   -   -   -   -   -   -   -   -   -
           215             220             225             230


           CTG GCA TAT CGG CCG CCC AAG TGA CCC TGT CCA GTG TCT GCT TGC CAT CCT GCC AGA ACA
           Leu Ala Tyr Arg Pro Pro Lys ***
           -   -   -   -   -   -   -
           235             240


           GGC CCT AAG CCA AGA GCA ······
```

Fig. 5. Nucleotide sequence of the cDNA insert that codes for human cytochrome c_1 and its deduced amino acid sequence. The amino acid sequence of bovine cytochrome c_1[33] is included for comparison. The dashes represent homologous amino acids. Numbering for the amino acid sequence is based on that for the sequence of mature bovine cytochrome c_1. The typical amino acid sequence for covalent binding of heme is placed in the boxes. The underlined nucleotides represent the TaqI sites.

MITOCHONDRIAL CYTOPATHY

We have analyzed the mitochondria from more than 20 patients with mitochondrial cytopathies. Most of the patients had deficiency of Complex I and/or Complex IV[40,41]. In some cases of Complex IV deficiency[42], deficiency of Complex IV subunits was accompanied by partial deficiency of Complex I subunits. Conversely, in patients with Complex I deficiency, partial deficiency of Complex IV subunits was observed concomitantly with deficiency of Complex I subunits[43]. In contrast, deficiency of subunits in Complex III or Complex V was rare[40,42]. These results indicate that in mitochondrial cytopathies, Complexes I and IV are more susceptible than the other enzyme complexes in the inner membrane. Since seven subunits in Complex I and three in Complex IV are encoded by mitochondrial DNA while only one subunit in Complex III and two in Complex V are of mitochondrial origin[44], the susceptibility might be related to the length of respective structural genes in the mitochondrial DNA.

Our knowledge on the interaction between the mitochondrial and nuclear genes in their expression is still limited, although we recognize it as a primary determinant of the structure and function of mitochondria. Development of various basic researches, such as molecular cloning of subunits in the electron transfer enzymes, immunochemical identification of subunits, and in vitro synthesis of components in the respiratory chain, would help to elucidate the regulatory mechanism of biosynthesis of the components which build the structure of mitochondrial inner membrane.

REFERENCES

1. Y. Hatefi, A. G. Haavik, L. R. Fowler, and D. E. Griffiths, Studies on the electron transfer system, J. Biol. Chem. 237: 2661 (1962).
2. Y. Hatefi, A. G. Haavik, and D. E. Griffiths, Studies on the electron tranfer system, J. Biol. Chem. 237: 1676 (1962).
3. H. Fernandez-Moran, T. Oda, P.U. Blair, and D. E. Green, Macromolecular repeating unit of mitochondrial structure and function, J. Cell. Biol. 22: 63 (1964).
4. A. Tzagoloff, K. H. Byington, and D. H. MacLennan, Studies on the mitochondrial adenosine triphosphatase system, J. Biol. Chem. 243: 2405 (1968).
5. D. H. MacLennan, J. M. Smoly, and A. Tzagoloff, Studies on the mitochondrial adenosine triphosphatase system, J. Biol. Chem. 243: 1589 (1968).
6. A. Tzagoloff, D. H. MacLennan, and K. H. Byington, Studies on the mitochondrial adenosine triphosphatase system, Biochemistry 7: 1596 (1968).
7. M. E. Pullman, H. S. Penefsky, A. Datta, and E. Racker, Partial resolution of the enzymes catalyzing oxidative phosphorylation, J. Biol. Chem. 235: 3322 (1962).
8. Y. Kagawa, and E. Racker, Partial resolution of the enzyme catalyzing oxidative phosphorylation, J. Biol. Chem. 246: 5477 (1971).
9. Y. Kagawa, and E. Racker, Partial resolution of the enzyme catalyzing oxidative phosphorylation, J. Biol. Chem. 241: 2461 (1966).
10. E. Racker, and L. L. Horstman, Partial resolution of the enzyme catalyzing oxidative phosphorylation, J. Biol. Chem. 242: 2547 (1967).
11. P. Mitchell, Coupling of phosphorylation to electron and hydrogen transfer by a chemi-osmotic type of mechanism, Nature(London) 191: 144 (1961).
12. P. Mitchell, "Chemiosmotic coupling in oxidative and photo-synthetic phosphorylation," Glynn Research Ltd, Bodmin, England (1966).
13. P. Mitchell, Chemiosmotic molecular mechanism for proton-translocating adenosine triphosphatases, FEBS Lett. 43: 189 (1974).
14. Y. Hatefi, Y. M. Galante, L. Frigeri, and D. L. Stiggall, Structure and compositon of the mitochondrial energy transduction system, in

"Biomembranes," K. Yagi, ed.,   Japan Sci. Soc. Press, Tokyo (1979).

15. H. Suzuki, and T. Ozawa, Novel isolation of ubiquinone proteins located in different sites of beef heart mitochondrial respiratory, Biochem. Int. 9: 563 (1984).

16. Y. M. Galante, and Y. Hatefi, Resolution of Complex I and isolation of NADH dehydrogenase and an iron-sulfur protein, in: "Methods in Enzymology," S. Fleischer, and L. Packer, eds., Academic Press, New York (1978).

17. M. Nishikimi, Y. Shimomura, H. Yamada, and T. Ozawa, Detection of iron-sulfur center-containing subunits of mitochondrial NADH dehydrogenase by sodium dodecyl sulfate-polyacrylamide gel electrophoresis and by high-performance gel permeation chromatography, Biochem. Biophys. Res. Commun. 120: 237 (1984).

18. H.Suzuki, and T. Ozawa, Quantities of ubiquinone bound to proteins in beef heart mitochondria, Biochem. Biophys. Res. Commun. 124: 889 (1984).

19. H. Suzuki, and T. Ozawa, An ubiquinone-binding protein in mitochondrial NADH-ubiquinone reductase (Complex I), Biochem. Biophys. Res. Commun. 138: 1237 (1986).

20. H. Suzuki, and T. E. King, Evidence of an ubisemiquinone radical(s) from the NADH-ubiquinone reductase of the mitochondrial respiratory chain, J. Biol. Chem. 258: 352 (1983).

21. Y. Shimomura, and T. Ozawa, Preferential dissociation of iron-sulfur protein from Complex III of mitochondrial electron-transfer chain by depletion of boundary cardiolipin, Biochem. Int. 5: 1 (1982).

22. Y. Shimomura, and T. Ozawa, Integral polypeptide of Complex III of the mitochondrial electron-transfer chain, Biochem. Int. 8: 187 (1984).

23. Y. Shimomura, M. Nishikimi, and T. Ozawa, Novel isolation and reconstitution of the iron-sulfur protein of mitochondrial Complex III, Biochem. Int. 8: 19 (1984).

24. Y. Shimomura, M. Nishikimi, and T. Ozawa, Isolation and reconstitution of the iron-sulfur protein in ubiquinol-cytochrome c oxidoreductase complex, J. Biol. Chem. 259: 14059 (1984).

25. T. Ozawa, Mitochondrial electron transport system, in: "Transport and bioenergetics in biomembranes," R. Sato, and Y. kagawa, eds., Japan Sci. Soc. Press, Tokyo (1982).

26. Y. Shimomura, M. Nishikimi, and T. Ozawa, Purification of the iron-sulfur protein, ubiquinone-bining protein, and cytochrome c_1 from a single source of mitochondrial Complex III, Anal. Biochem. 153: 126 (1986).

27. Y. Shimomura, M. Nishikimi, and T. Ozawa, Novel purification of cytochrome c_1 from mitochondrial Complex III, J. Biol. Chem. 260: 15075 (1985).

28. H. Nakahara, Y. Shimomura, and T. Ozawa, Purification of cytochrome b from complex III of beef heart mitochondria, Biophys. Res. Commun. 132: 1166 (1985).

29. M. Nishikimi, Y. Shimomura, and T. Ozawa, Immunochemical demonstration of the iron-sulfur protein in Complex III of mitochondrial electron-transfer chain, Biochem. Int. 7: 793 (1983).

30. M. Nishikimi, Y. Shimomura, and T. Ozawa, The iron-sulfur protein of cytochrome bc_1 complex, J. Biol. Chem 260: 10398 (1985).

31. M. Nishikimi, Y. Shimomura, and T. Ozawa, Cell-free synthesis of ubiquinone-binding protein of mitochondrial cytochrome bc_1 complex, Biochem. Biophys. Res. Commun. 138: 1291 (1986).

32. M. Nishikimi, H. Suzuki, S. Ohta, T. Sakurai, Y. Shimomura, M. Tanaka, Y. Kagawa, and T. Ozawa, Isolation of a cDNA clone for human cytochrome c_1 from a λgtll expression library, Biochem. Biophys. Res. Commun. submitted (1987).

33. S. Wakabayashi, H. Matsubara, C.H. Kim, and T.E. King, Structural studies of bovine heart cytochrome c_1, J. Biol. Chem. 257: 9335 (1982).

34. T. Ozawa, H. Suzuki, and M. Tanaka, Crystallization of part of the mitochondrial electron transfer chain: Cytochrome c oxidase-cytochrome c complex, Proc. Natl. Acad. Sci. USA 77: 928 (1980).
35. T. Ozawa, M. Tanaka, and T. Wakabayashi, Crystallization of mitochondrial cytochrome oxidase, Proc. Natl. Acad. Sci. USA 79: 7175 (1982).
36. T. Ozawa, Crystallization of intrinsic membrane proteins, J. Bioenerg. Biomembr. 16: 321 (1984).
37. T. Ozawa, M. Tanaka, and Y. Shimomura, Crystallization of the middle part of the mitochondrial electron transfer chain: Cytochrome bc_1-cytochrome c complex, Proc. Natl. Acad. Sci. USA 77: 5084 (1980).
38. T. Ozawa, M. Tanaka, and Y. Shimomura, Crystallization of cytochrome bc_1 complex, Proc. Natl. Acad. Sci. USA 80: 921 (1983).
39. A. Maurer, M. Tanaka, T. Ozawa, and S. Fleischer, Purification and crystallization of the calcium binding protein of sarcoplasmic reticulum from skeletal muscle, Proc. Natl. Acad. Sci. USA 82: 4036 (1985).
40. M. Tanaka, M. Nishikimi, H. Suzuki, T. Ozawa, Y. Koga, and I. Nonaka, Partial deficiency of subunits in Complex I or IV of patients with mitochondrial myopathies, Biochem. Int. 14: 525 (1987).
41. M. Tanaka, M. Nishikimi, H. Suzuki, Y. Koga, and I. Nonaka, Deficiency of subunits of Complex I or IV in mitochondrial myopathies: Immuno-chemical and immunohistochemical study, J. Inher. Metab. Dis. (in press)
42. M. Tanaka, M. Nishikimi, T. Ozawa, S. Miyabayashi, and K. Tada, Lack of subunit II of cytochrome c oxidase in a patient with mitochondrial myopathy, Ann. N.Y. Acad. Sci. 488: 503 (1987).
43. M. Tanaka, M. Nishikimi, H. Suzuki, T. Ozawa, M. Nishizawa, K. Tanaka, and T. Miyatake, Deficiency of subunits in heart mitochondrial NADH-ubiquinone oxidoreductase of a patient with mitochondrial encephalo-pathy and cardiomyopathy, Biochem. Biophys. Res. Commun. 140: 88 (1986).

THE FATTY ACID-ANCHORED FOUR HEME CYTOCHROME
OF THE PHOTOSYNTHETIC REACTION CENTER FROM
THE PURPLE BACTERIUM RHODOPSEUDOMONAS VIRIDIS

K.A.Weyer, F.Lottspeich, W.Schäfer and H.Michel

Max-Planck-Institut für Biochemie
D-8033 Martinsried
West Germany

INTRODUCTION

The photosynthetic bacteria use a single photosystem for the
absorption and conversion of solar energy. The simple structural
organization of the bacterial photosynthetic reaction centers makes them
useful for studying the light-driven electron transfer across the
photosynthetic membrane. Photosynthetic reaction centers are complexes of
pigments and integral membrane proteins. The well characterized reaction
centers from the purple bacteria contain three protein subunits, which are
called H (heavy), M (medium) and L (light) subunits according to their
apparent molecular weights as determined by SDS-polyacrylamide gel
electrophoresis[1-3]. In addition, the reaction centers from several purple
bacteria, e.g. Rhodopseudomonas viridis contain a tightly bound cytochrome
subunit, which re-reduces the photo-oxidized primary electron donor. Early
work has shown that the cytochrome is of the c type and contains four (to
five) heme groups. Redox potentiometry and spectroscopic studies led to
the conclusion that two of these heme groups ("C558") operate at +330 mV
and the other two ("C553") at -12mV[4,5].
After the successful crystallization[6] of the photosynthetic reaction center
from Rhodopseudomonas viridis[6] an X-ray structure analysis became possible
and showed the arrangement of the photosynthetic pigments and confirmed
the presence of four heme groups[7]. Following the elucidation of the amino
acid sequences of H, M and L subunits[8,9], the amino acid sequence of the
cytochrome subunit was determined[10] and allowed a detailed interpretation
of the protein part of the electron density map. At present the structure
has been refined at 2,3 Å resolution[11].

RESULTS AND DISCUSSION

Structure and function of the heme-binding domains

73 % of the primary structure of the cytochrome subunit was obtained
by protein sequencing. The complete amino acid sequence was elucidated by
sequencing the DNA coding for the cytochrome subunit[10].
The crystallographic analysis[12] showed that the structure of the
cytochrome subunit is different from all other cytochromes whose
three-dimensional structures are known[13,14]. A helix runs parallel to the
plane of each heme group. After the C-termini of the helices the peptide

chains turn back towards the hemes, and then the heme attachment sites
-Cys-X-X-Cys-His- are found. This motif is repeated four times. The
arrangement of the hemes and their parallel helices ("heme-binding
domains") is symmetric with respect to a twofold rotation axis which
relates heme binding domains 1 and 3 as well as 2 and 4 (For arrangement
of the hemes with respect to the primary donor see figure 1).

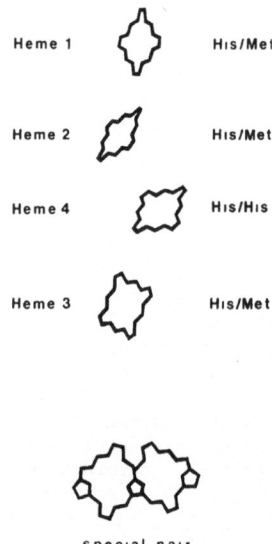

Fig. 1. Arrangement of the hemes and nature of the axial iron ligands
in the cytochrome subunit with respect to the primary donor.
The hemes are numbered according to their position in the amino
acid sequence.

The fourfold repeated structure suggests that the cytochrome subunit gene
may have been evolved from an ancestral gene coding for a one-heme
cytochrome by two subsequent gene duplications: A first one which gave
rise to a two-heme cytochrome (domains 1 plus 2 or domains 3 plus 4) and a
second one which resulted in the formation of a four-heme cytochrome. In
figure 2 those amino acid sequences are aligned which are found in
equivalent positions in the X-ray structure. The observed sequence
homology is low. Only the two cysteine residues which are needed for the
covalent linkage of the heme groups and the subsequent histidine residues,
which are the fifth ligands to the heme-iron, are conserved in all four
heme binding domains. In the helices facing the heme planes not a single
residue is conserved. The sequence homologies between heme-binding domains
1 and 3 as well as between 2 and 4 are considerably higher, supporting the
hypothesis of two subsequent gene duplications.

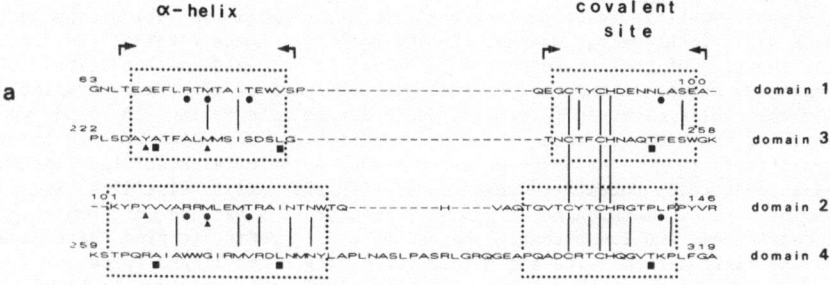

a

α-helix   covalent site

```
63                                                              100
GNLTEAEFLRTMTAITEWVSP----------------------QEGCTYCHDENNLASEA-    domain 1

222                                                       258
PLSDAYATFALMMSISDSLG------------------TNCTFCHNAQTFESWGK          domain 3

101                                                             146
KYPYVVARRMLEMTRAINTNWTQ----------H------VAGTGVTCYTCHRGTPLPPYVR   domain 2

259                                                             319
KSTPQRAIAWWGIRMVRDLNMNYLAPLNASLPASRLGRQGEAPQADCRTCHQGVTKPLFGA    domain 4
```

b

	domain 1	domain 2	domain 3	domain 4
domain 1				
domain 2	28 (4,6 SD)			
domain 3	55 (6,2 SD)	39 (5,1 SD)		
domain 4	10 (3,2 SD)	50 (6,3 SD)	13 (3,9 SD)	

Fig. 2. a) Alignment of the amino acid sequences of the heme binding
domains. Each domain consists of the covalent binding site
for the heme and the parallel α-helix. The structurally
equivalent amino acid sequences are surrounded by the dotted line.

     labels identical amino acids between symmetrical domains

     labels identical amino acids between domains 1 and 2

     "   "   "   "   "   domains 2 and 3

     "   "   "   "   "   domains 3 and 4

     the regions of α-helices and covalent sites between the
arrows were taken for the calculation of the similarity
matrix of the heme-binding domains

b) Similarity matrix of the heme binding domains. The first
values in the matrix indicate the segment score obtained
by the Dayhoff-matrix (MDM78, 250 PAM)[15]. The values in
brackets indicate the segment score expressed in units of
standard deviation (SD) as calculated using the program
"PirRelate"[15]. The highest values for the segment score
were obtained from the comparison of domain 1 with domain 3,
respectively domain 2 with domain 4.

The only known function of the cytochrome subunit is to re-reduce the photooxidized primary electron donor, which is a dimer of two nearly parallel bacteriochlorophyll b molecules ("special pair"). At medium redox potentials (50 - 300 mV) only the ascorbate reducible hemes ("C558") of the cytochrome subunit are reduced and can donate electrons to the photooxidized special pair[4,5]. C558 which is reduced by the soluble cytochrome c_2 in vivo[16] is involved in the cyclic flow of electrons from the photosynthetic reaction center to the bc_1-complex via ubiquinone and back via cytochrome c_2, whereas the low potential hemes ("C553") are not. The function of the low potential hemes may be to oxidize substrates of low redox potential and thus to replenish the pool of electrons available for the cyclic electron flow[17]. It would now be interesting to find out which of the hemes operate at low redox potentials and which at high redox potentials. In general, heme groups possessing two axial histidine ligands have lower redox potentials than groups with one axial histidine ligand and one axial methionine ligand[18]. From the existence of two high potential and two low potential hemes one would predict to find histidine as the sixth ligand twice and methionine as the sixth ligand twice.
As shown in figure 1 this is not the case. A histidine residue is found as the sixth ligand only for heme 4, but a methionine residue is the sixth ligand for hemes 1,2 and 3. At least in one of the hemes 1-3 other environmental influences must lower the redox potential. For instance, a decrease of the redox potential by approximately 400 mV could possibly be achieved by shortening the Fe-S (methionine) distance by 0,1 Å [18], which is certainly below the accuracy of the crystallographic data. Since C558 re-reduces the special pair we consider heme 3 (which is closest to the special pair) as the most likely candidate for a high potential heme. Heme 4, which is the next one in the linear chain of hemes is most likely a low potential heme due to the two histidine ligands. We are not aware of any report where a c-type cytochrome with two histidine ligands has such a positive redox potential. No considerations can be made for hemes 1 and 2. Due to the existence of the twofold rotation axis it will be extremely difficult to find out unambiguously which are the high and which are the low potential hemes, even if one takes into account that the C558 hemes can be split into a more positive and a more negative high potential heme[19].

The fatty acid membrane-anchor

The existence of a fatty acid acylation of the N-terminal amino acid residue of the cytochrome subunit e.g. a "fatty acid anchor" has been established by the following observations[20]: After automated Edman degradation of the N-terminal amino acid of the cytochrome subunit a phenylthiohydantoin (PTH)-derivative could never be detected using standard HPLC methods. Upon manual-degradation of the N-terminal amino acid a thiazolidine-derivative could be extracted with methanol and then converted to the PTH-derivative. After transesterification in methanol/HCl primarily two types of fatty acids (18:OH and 18:1) could be detected in this derivative by GC/MS. An HPLC analysis of the PTH-derivative showed the characteristic pattern of a molecule with two covalently linked fatty acids and from mass spectroscopical data evidence for an S-modified cysteine as the N-terminal amino acid was obtained. Therefore a structure similar to the structure of the N-terminal amino acid residue of the bacterial lipoproteins became apparent[21]. These lipoproteins contain an N-terminal cysteine which is modified by a diglyceride at the sulfhydryl-group and acylated by a third fatty acid at the amino group. A third fatty acid could not exist in our structure, since the N-terminus was unblocked. Figure 3 presents the proposed structure. Further support for this structure came from the "Fast Atom Bombardement" mass spectra obtained

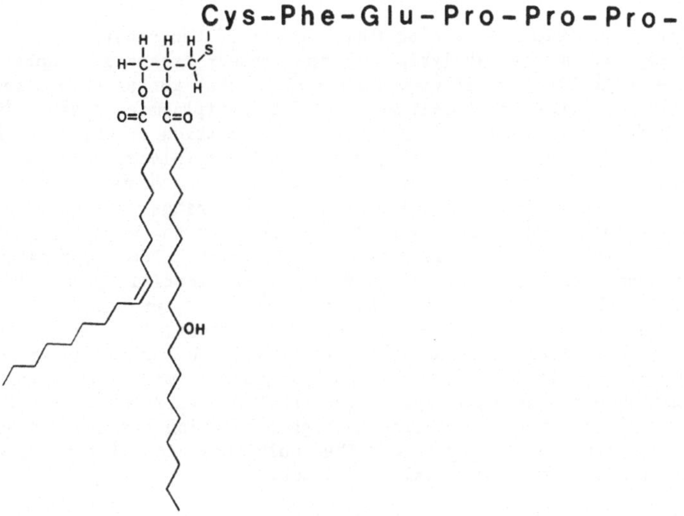

Cys–Phe–Glu–Pro–Pro–Pro–

Fig. 3. The N-terminus of the cytochrome subunit. Two fatty acids are esterified to the N-terminal S-glycero-cysteine. The fatty acids are a mixture of 18:OH (2 isomers) and 18:1 (3 isomers) acids roughly in a 1:1 ratio, which are represented by oleic-acid and 11-hydroxy-stearic acid in the figure.

with the material from the peak, which contained two 18:1-fatty acids. The calculated relative molecular mass for a PTH-cysteine modified by a diglyceride containing two 18:1 fatty acid is 840 ($C_{49}H_{80}N_2O_5S_2$). This value agreed with the obtained relative mass of 841 for the quasi molecular ion $(M+H)^+$ of the component.

Additional evidence for the proposed structure was given by the characteristics of the signal peptide preceding the mature cytochrome subunit. The amino acid sequence could be deduced from the DNA sequence. The DNA indeed coded for a cysteine as the N-terminal amino acid of the mature cytochrome subunit. The peptide preceding the mature N-terminus consists of 20 amino acids and exhibits all features characteristic of a signal peptide[22], e.g. a positive charge in the N-terminal region followed by a highly hydrophobic region of 15 amino acids. But the most striking characteristic for bacterial prolipoproteins is the nature of amino acids in the three positions before the cleavage site of the signal peptide. This sequence is known to be the recognition site for the signal peptidase II[23,24,25] which removes signal peptides when the cysteine is modified by a diglyceride. The comparison with ten lipoproteins[20] for which the sequences of the signal peptides were available showed that the glycine (position -1) preceding the cleavage site is conserved in nine of ten cases. The alanine in position -2 is conserved in eight cases. The valine in position -3 is conservatively exchanged in the cytochrome subunit; leucine is found in nine of ten cases of the other lipoproteins.

Leucine in position -4 is also found in six of ten cases.
The X-ray structure analysis of the intact reaction center complex
together with biochemical experiments shows that the protein moiety of the
cytochrome subunit is localized in the periplasmic space. The X-ray
structure analysis also indicates that the position of the N-terminus of
the cytochrome subunit is near the presumed periplasmic surface of the
membrane. The fatty acids seem to anchor the cytochrome subunit in the
photosynthetic membrane. A calculation of the change of free energy by
transferring an hydrocarbon with 34 C-atoms from the water phase to the
hydrocarbon-phase gives a gain of 32 kcal/mol[26]. The importance of an
energy change of this size relative to the substantial polar interaction
of the cytochrome subunit with the rest of the protein, can only be
deduced after an exact calculation of this interaction energy has been
done. The principal function of the fatty acid anchor may be to retain the
cytochrome subunit bound to the photosynthetic membrane prior to its
association with the main part of the reaction center complex. The fatty
acids itself are not visible in the high resolution electron density map
due to disorder in the crystals. The only way to firmly prove their
existence was by protein chemical methods.

REFERENCES

1. Feher, G. & Okamura, M.Y. (1978) in "The Photosynthetic Bacteria", eds.
   Clayton, R.K. & Sistrom, W.R. (Plenum Press, New York), pp. 349-386.
2. Hoff, A.J. (1982) in "Molecular Biology, Biochemistry, and Biophysics",
   Vol. 35, ed. Fong, F.K. (Springer, Berlin), pp. 80-151, 322-326.
3. Parson, W.W. (1982). Ann. Rev. Biophys. Bioeng. 11:57-80.
4. Thornber, J.P. & Olson, J.M. (1971) Photochem. Photobiol. 14:329-341.
5. Thornber, J.P., Dutton, P.L., Fajer, J., Forman, A., Holten, D., Olson,
   J.M., Parson, W.W., Prince, R.C., Tiede, D.M. & Windsor, T.W. (1977) in
   "Proc. of the Fourth International Congress on Photosynthesis", eds.
   Hall, D.O., Coombs, J. & Goodwin, T.W., (The Biochemical Society,
   London), pp. 55-70.
6. Michel, H. (1982) J. Mol. Biol. 158:567-572.
7. Deisenhofer, J., Epp, O., Miki, K., Huber, R. & Michel, H. (1984)
   J. Mol. Biol. 180:385-398.
8. Michel, H., Weyer, K.A., Gruenberg, H. & Lottspeich, F. (1985) EMBO J.
   4:1667-1672.
9. Michel, H., Weyer, K.A., Gruenberg, H., Dunger, I., Oesterhelt, D. &
   Lottspeich, F. (1986) EMBO J. 5:1149-1158.
10. Weyer, K.A., Lottspeich, F., Gruenberg, H., Lang, F., Oesterhelt, D. &
    Michel, H., in preparation
11. Deisenhofer, J., Epp, Sinning, I. & Michel, H., in preparation
12. Deisenhofer, J., Epp, O., Miki, K., Huber, R. & Michel, H. (1985)
    Nature 318:618-624.
13. For review see: Meyer, T. & Kamen, M.D. (1982) Adv. Prot. Chem.
    35:105-212.
14. For review see: Mathews, F.S. (1985) Prog. Biophys. molec. Biol.
    45:1-56.
15. Dayhoff, M.O., Barker, W.. & Hunt, L.T. (1983) Methods Enzymol.
    91:524-545.
16. Shill, D.A. & Wood, P.M. (1984) Biochim. Biophys. Acta 764:1-7
17. Michel, H. & Deisenhofer, J. (1986) in "Encyclopedia of Plant
    Physiology: Photosynthesis III", Vol. 19, eds. Staehelin, A.C. &
    Arntzen, C.J., (Springer, Berlin), pp. 371-381.
18. Moore, G.R. & Williams, R.J.P. (1971) FEBS Lett. 79:229-232.
19. Dracheva, S.M., Drachev, L.A., Zaberezhnaya, S.M., Konstantinov, A.A.,
    Semenov, A.Yu. & Skulachev, V.P. (1986) FEBS Lett. 205:41-46.

20. Weyer, K.A., Schaefer, W., Lottspeich, F. & Michel, H. (1987) _Biochemistry_, in press
21. Hantke, K. & Braun, V. (1973) _Eur. J. Biochem._ 34:284-296.
22. For review see: Duffaud, G.D., Lehnhardt, S.K., March P.E., & Inouye, M. (1985) _Current Topics in Membranes and Transport_ 24:65-105.
23. Lai, J.S., Sarvas, M., Brammar, W.J., Neugebauer, K., & Wu, H.C. (1981) _Proc. Natl. Acad. Sci. USA_ 78:3506-3510.
24. Inouye, S., Franceschini, T., Sato, M., Itakura, K., & Inouye, M. (1983) _EMBO J._ 2:87-91.
25. Politt, S., Inouye, S., Inouye M. (1986) _J. Biol. Chem._ 261:1835-1837.
26. Tanford, C. (1980) in "The Hydrophobic Effect: Formation of Micelles and Biological Membranes", ed. Tanford, Ch. (John Wiley & Sons, New York), pp. 7.

III. PROTEIN STRUCTURE: Short Reports

MEMBRANE PROTEIN IN <u>PARACOCCUS</u> <u>DENITRIFICANS</u> RESEMBLES SUBUNIT III OF BEEF

HEART CYTOCHROME OXIDASE

Tuomas Haltia and Moshe Finel

Department of Medical Chemistry
University of Helsinki
Helsinki, Finland

The aa_3-type cytochrome oxidase purified from <u>Paracoccus</u> (1) consists of two proteins corresponding to the subunits I and II of the mitochondrial cyto-chrome oxidase. However, it was recently found that the genome of <u>Para-coccus</u> contains a gene encoding a protein homologous to subunit III (su̅I̅I̅I̅) of the mitochondrial enzyme (2). The absence of this subunit in the pre-parations of purified oxidase may have two explanations: either it is lost during the purification or the gene is not expressed in the growth condi-tions employed.

The suIII gene in <u>Paracoccus</u> contains a sequence homologous to the DCCD-binding site in the mitochondrial oxidase suIII (2). This sequence also includes the glutamic acid residue that reacts with DCCD (2, 3). We have made use of this to study whether there is a suIII-like protein in the <u>Paracoccus</u> membranes.

The spectra shown in Fig. 1 demonstrate clearly that the aerobically grown cells contain a large amount of aa_3-type cytochrome in their membranes while cells grown anaerobically do not. Fig. 2 shows that aerobically grown cells contain a DCCD-binding protein that migrates similarly to the beef heart enzyme suIII (lane 2). This protein is almost completely absent from the anaerobically grown cells (lane 3). So there is a clear correlation between the aa_3 spectrum shown in Fig. 1 and the presence of a DCCD-binding 23 kD protein in the membranes. On the basis of heme staining, the labelled protein is located just above a 22 kD cyt c present abundantly in the mem-branes (not shown). This may have prevented its discovery earlier (1, 4).

These results prompt us to suggest that the suIII gene is expressed under aerobic conditions. This would mean that the <u>Paracoccus</u> oxidase is actually a three subunit oxidase, and suIII is lost during the purification procedure used (1). This necessarily calls for less perturbing purification methods. Recently a three polypeptide cyt aa_3 was isolated from <u>Paracoccus</u>. The smallest polypeptide (23 kD) is labelled by DCCD both in detergent solubi-lized and in membrane reconstituted enzyme (T. Haltia and M. Finel, unpub-lished).

ACKNOWLEDGMENTS

This study was supported by the Finnish Academy (M.R.C.) and the Sigrid Jusèlius Foundation.

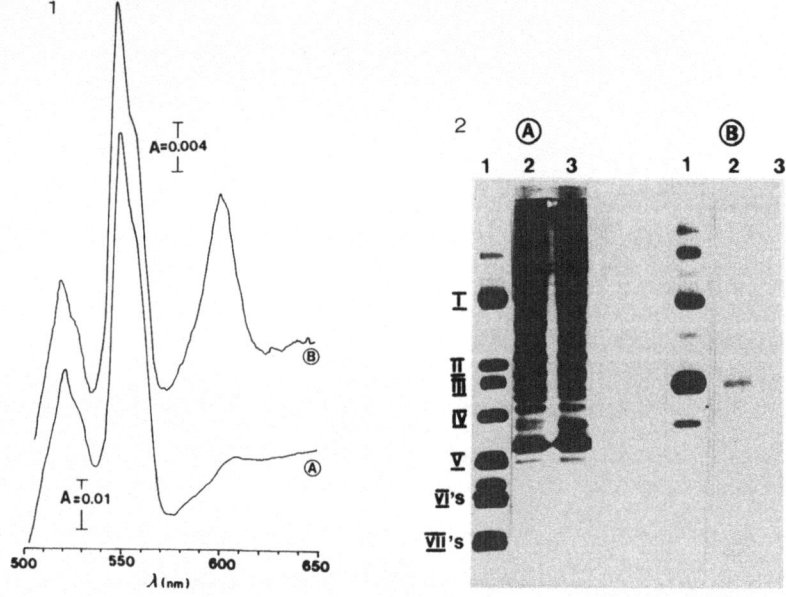

Fig. 1. Reduced minus oxidised spectra of Paracoccus (S1657) membranes. Cells were grown aerobically or anaerobically in the media described in (5), harvested in early log phase and alkaline washed membranes were prepared as described in (4). (A) Membranes of anaerobically grown cells. (B) Membranes of aerobically grown cells.

Fig. 2. SDS-PAGE (14-20% acrylamide in the presence of 6 M urea) of [^{14}C]-DCCD labelled membranes. Membranes (1 mg prot. in 0.1 ml) were incubated with 0.35 µCi [^{14}C]-DCCD for 4 h at 25 C followed by cholate extraction. A. Coomassie blue staining of the gel. B. Autoradiography of the same gel. Lane 1 = [^{14}C]-DCCD labelled isolated beef heart oxidase, lane 2 = membranes of aerobically grown cells, lane 3 = membranes of anaerobically grown cells. The Roman numerals on the left refer to the subunits of beef enzyme.

REFERENCES

1. B. Ludwig and G. Schatz (1980) Proc. Natl. Acad. Sci. USA 77, 196-200.
2. M. Saraste, M. Raitio, T. Jalli, and A. Perämaa (1986) FEBS Lett. 206, 154-156.
3. L.J. Prohaska, R. Bisson, R.A. Capaldi, G.C.M. Steffens, and G. Buse (1981) Biochem. Biophys. Acta 637, 360-373.
4. E.A. Berry and B.L. Trumpower (1985) J. Biol. Chem. 260, 2458-2467.
5. J.P. Chang and J.G. Morris (1962) J. Gen. Microbiol. 29, 301-310.

THE CIRCULAR DICHROISM PROPERTIES OF THE RIESKE PROTEIN AND THE b AND c_1

CYTOCHROMES OF THE MITOCHONDRIAL bc_1 COMPLEX

G. Solaini, M. Crimi, F. Ballester, M. Degli Esposti,
and G. Lenaz

Department of Biochemistry and Department of Biology
University of Bologna, 40126 Bologna, Italy

The circular dichroism (CD) spectrum of the mitochondrial ubiquinol cytochrome c reductase (bc_1 complex) isolated from beef heart has been resolved
in the visible region into the contributions from the individual prosthetic
groups: cytochrome c_1, the "Rieske" iron-sulfur center and cytochrome(s) b.

The reduction of the bc_1 complex by either ascorbate or ubiquinol is
accompanied by the formation of a negative band at about 500 nm, corresponding in its properties to the specific dichroic absorption of the reduced
Rieske protein isolated by the method of Shimomura et al. (1). This band
is lacking in the complex depleted of the Rieske protein (2); reconstitution with the isolated protein leads to the reappearance of the negative
peak around 500 nm. The CD features of both the oxidized and reduced forms
of the isolated Rieske protein strongly resemble those reported for a
Rieske-type iron-sulfur protein purified from Thermus thermophilus (3).

The CD contribution of cytochrome c_1 in the Soret region has been resolved
from that of cytochrome b by using a bc_1-subcomplex devoid of cytochrome b
by guanidine-HCl cleavage (4). The difference spectrum between the whole
oxidized enzyme and the subcomplex is a bilobe with maximum at 411 nm and
crossovers at 402 and 416.5 nm. Subtraction of the CD spectrum of the
oxidized Rieske protein and of oxidized cytochrome b in the whole complex
reveals the contribution of the

Table 1. Characteristics of the CD spectra of the electron-transfer components of the mitochondrial bc_1 complex in the Soret region.

Component	λ_{max} (nm)	$\Delta\varepsilon$ $(M^{-1}cm^{-1})$	crossover (nm)
Oxidized Iron-Sulphur protein	375	- 16.5	408
Reduced Iron-Sulphur protein	384	- 19.0	412
Oxidized cytochrome c_1	414	+ 74.5	441
Reduced cytochrome c_1	415	+ 76.0	441
Oxidized cytochrome b (two hemes)	411	+ 39.5	402,416.5
	426	- 37.0	
Reduced cytochrome b (two hemes)	423	+ 58.0	408,428.5
	434	- 101	

native oxidized cytochrome c_1. Since ascorbate reduces only cytochrome c_1 and the Rieske protein, the spectrum of reduced cytochrome c_1 can be resolved by subtractions of the reduced Rieske protein and the oxidized cytochrome b. The specific CD absorption of reduced cytochrome b may be obtained either by the difference spectrum, dithionite-reduced minus ascorbate-reduced, or by subtracting the contributions of reduced cytochrome c_1 and the Rieske protein from that of the dithionite-reduced complex, or finally by obtaining the difference spectrum between reduced bc_1 complex and reduced c_1 subcomplex. The properties of the redox centers are summarized in Table 1.

The CD properties of cytochrome c_1 within the complex differ from those of isolated cytochrome c_1 and can be restored by formation of a c_1-iron-sulfur protein subcomplex catalyzing the antimycin-insensitive oxidation of ubiquinol. The characteristics of cytochrome b within the complex are suggestive of exciton splitting mediated by an electron bridge between the two b-hemes via conserved aromatic aminoacid residues. We propose a model for the interaction of the two heme groups of cytochrome b with surrounding aromatic aminoacids that is shown in Fig. 1.

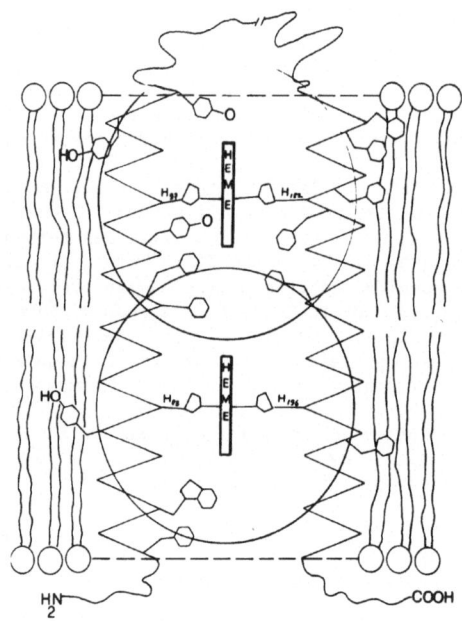

Fig. 1. A model for cytochrome b heme's region.

REFERENCES

1. Y. Shimomura, M. Nishikimi, and T. Ozawa (1984) J. Biol. Chem. 259, 14059-14063.
2. M. Degli Esposti, G. Solaini, F. Ballester, and G. Lenaz (1987) J. Biochem. 241, 285-290.
3. J.A. Fee, K.L. Findling, T. Yoshida, R. Hille, G.E. Tarr, D.D. Hearshen, W.R. Dunham, E.P. Day, T.A. Kent, and E. Munck (1984) J. Biol. Chem. 269, 124-133.
4. J.S. Rieske, H. Baum, C. Stoner, and S.H. Lipton (1967) J. Biol. Chem. 242, 4854-4866.

MONOMERIZATION OF CYTOCHROME OXIDASE MIGHT BE ESSENTIAL FOR SUBUNIT III

REMOVAL

Moshe Finel

Department of Medical Chemistry
University of Helsinki
Helsinki, Finland

A present discrepancy in the study of proton translocation by cytochrome oxidase is whether removal of subunit III (suIII) abolishes proton pumping (1) or not (2). We have recently suggested that monomerization of the dimeric enzyme rather than suIII removal reduces the pumping efficiency (3). The present report tries to clarify the interaction between suIII removal and monomerization of cytochrome oxidase and suggests that monomerization might be a prerequisite for suIII removal.

Figure 1 shows that different incubation conditions used by different laboratories during the first steps of their suIII removal procedures causes at least partial monomerization. It should be emphasized that Fig. 1 shows oligomeric state analysis before, or without, the steps that actually remove suIII like chromatography and chymotrypsin. Incubation at high pH in Triton (Fig. 1b) is the only one almost fully monomerizing. The incomplete monomerization by incubating according to other procedures (Fig. 1c-e) may explain why addition of protease is necessary (2, 4). Otherwise suIII is removed only from a fraction of the oxidase population (3).

If monomerization must precede suIII removal then application of fully monomeric enzyme to the anion-exchange FPLC column is expected to yield a larger fraction of suIII-less oxidase in comparison with application of partially monomerized population (Fig. 1d) which was used before (3). Figure 2 shows that the fraction of suIII-less enzyme (which is eluted first from the MONO-Q column, Ref. 3) is indeed much larger when the enzyme was first monomerized by sucrose gradient centrifugation in the presence of LDAO (3), which does not remove any subunit.

The association of monomerization with the initial steps of all the treatments to remove suIII (Fig. 1), the improved removal of that polypeptide from the monomerized enzyme (Fig. 2) and the reports of monomeric enzyme containing all the subunits (e.g. 5) suggest that monomerization makes suIII susceptible for removal rather than suIII removal making the dimer susceptible to monomerization.

The results do not mean, however, that redimerization after removal of suIII is impossible or that suIII would or would not play an important role in determining the oligomeric state of cytochrome oxidase.

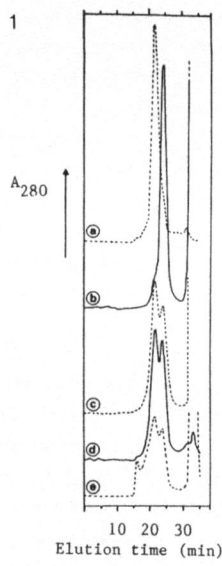

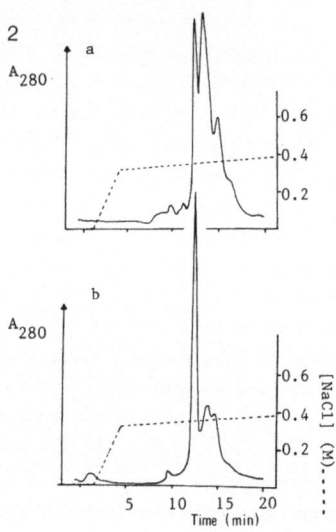

Fig. 1. Gel filtration FPLC of cytochrome oxidase after incubation in different conditions. Chromatography was performed on Suprose 12 column in 1% cholate, 0.1M KPi, 0.3M NaCl pH 7.4 at 0.5 ml/min. The peak eluted after 22 min represent dimeric and after 24 min monomeric cytochrome oxidase. The incubations conditions of 0.01 mM enzyme in 0.2 ml were: A. Control, stock enzyme; B. 1% Triton, pH 9.5, 18 hours at 4°C (6); C, 1% Triton, pH 8.5, 3h at 22°C (4); D. 2% LDAO, pH 7.4, 1h on ice (3); E. First 2% cholate plus 0.05% SDS, pH 8.5, 25 min at 37°C then transfer (by centricolumn) to 1% Triton, 0.2M NaCl, pH 7.2, 18h at 4°C.

Fig. 2. Anion-exchange FPLC of cytochrome oxidase on MONO-Q column. A. Sample prepared as in (3). B. The enzyme was first centrifuged 18h in sucrose gradient in the presence of LDAO (3) and the green fractions collected from the tube were diluted prior to chromatography.

ACKNOWLEDGMENTS

This study was supported by the Academy of Finland (M.R.C.) and the Sigrid Juselius foundation.

REFERENCES

1. M. Thelen, P.S. O'Shea, G. Petrone, and A. Azzi (1985) J. Biol. Chem. 260, 3626-3631.
2. I. Puettner, E. Carafoli, and F. Malatesta (1985) J. Biol. Chem. 260, 3719-3723.
3. M. Finel and M. Wikström (1986) Biochem. Biophys. Acta 851, 99-108.
4. F. Malatesta, G. Georgevich, and R.A. Capaldi (1983) in (E. Quagliariello and F. Palmieri, eds.) Structure and Function of Membrane Proteins, Elsevier, Amsterdam. pp. 223-235.
5. N.C. Robinson and L. Talbert (1986) Biochemistry 25, 2328-2335.
6. T. Penttilä (1983) Eur. J. Biochem. 133, 355-361.
7. K. Bill and A. Azzi (1982) Biochem. Biophys. Res. Commun. 106, 1203-1209.

FOURIER-TRANSFORM INFRA-RED STUDIES OF CYTOCHROME c OXIDASE

Michael F. Grahn, Parvez I. Haris*, John M. Wrigglesworth,
and Dennis Chapman*
Department of Biochemistry, King's College London, Kensington
W8 7AH, United Kingdom
*Department of Biochemistry and Chemistry, Royal Free
Hospital School of Medicine, London NW3 2PF, United Kingdom

Kinetic studies using isolated cytochrome oxidase have shown that two distinct functional forms of the enzyme exist (1). The fully oxidised (resting) enzyme, as isolated, oxidises cytochrome c relatively slowly and binds cyanide with low affinity. However, if the enzyme is fully reduced prior to reaction with oxygen for at least one catalytic cycle, then a "pulsed" form is produced in which both cytochrome c oxidation and cyanide binding is markedly increased (1, 2). The "pulsed" form of the enzyme is unstable and, depending on the conditions of incubation, decays back to the resting form within minutes. If the transition between resting and pulsed enzyme were to involve any changes in the conformation of the protein then it might be expected that these changes would also be seen between the oxidised (resting) enzyme and the fully reduced enzyme, since full reduction followed by re-oxidation is one method for producing the pulsed enzyme.

Infra-red spectroscopy using hydrogen-deuterium exchange is a powerful tool for investigating small changes in protein structure (3, 5). Previous work on cytochrome oxidase was carried out in D_2O using a dispersive infra-red spectrophotometer (4). The extent of exchange of peptide hydrogens with solvent deuterium was used to estimate the relative exposure of the poly-peptide chain to the aqueous milieu surrounding the protein. This showed that the oxidised (resting) enzyme contains a high proportion of helical structure and about 60% of the polypeptide is exposed to the solvent.

In the present work we have taken advantage of the increased sensitivity of Fourier-transform infra-red spectroscopy to obtain spectra of the enzyme in aqueous solvent (H_2O and D_2O) and to monitor structural differences between the oxidised (resting) form of the enzyme and the fully reduced form. The spectra were recorded at a resolution of 4 wavenumbers using a Perkin-Elmer 1750 FTIR spectrophotometer at pH 7 and 20°C.

The oxidised form of cytochrome oxidase in H_2O (Figure 1a, solid line) shows bands in the amide region. A precise assignment of the position of these bands was made from the second derivative spectrum (Figure 1b) in which over-lapping components are separated. The amide I band lies at 1658 cm^{-1} and the amide II band is at 1550 cm^{-1}. The position of the amide I band is indicative of either α-helical or of unordered structure. The position of this band does not shift significantly when D_2O is the solvent (1654 cm^{-1}

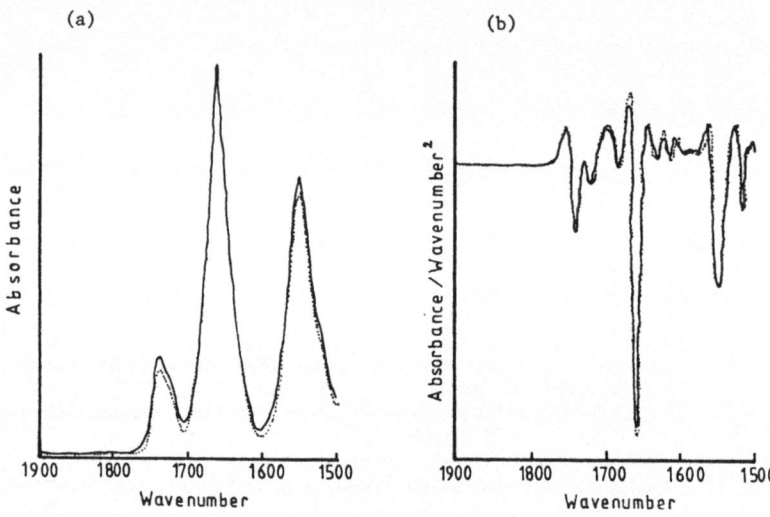

(a)   (b)

Absorbance

Wavenumber

Absorbance / Wavenumber^2

Wavenumber

1900 1800 1700 1600 1500   1900 1800 1700 1600 1500

FIGURE 1

for the oxidised enzyme, spectra not shown). It may be concluded therefore, that the α-helical conformation predominates (5). The dotted lines in the figure show the absolute (Figure 1a) and the second differential (Figure 1b) spectra of dithionite-reduced cytochrome oxidase in H_2O. As these spectra are virtually identical to those of the oxidised enzyme it appears that there is no major change in secondary structure on reduction.

This work is supported by a grant from the S.E.R.C.

REFERENCES

1. E. Antonini, M. Brunori, A. Colosimo, C. Greenwood, and M.T. Wilson (1977) Proc. Natl. Acad. Sci. USA 74, 3128-3132.
2. M. Wikstrom, K. Krab, and M. Saraste (1981) "Cytochrome Oxidase: A Synthesis" Academic Press.
3. P.I. Haris, D.C. Lee, and D. Chapman (1986) Biochem. Biophys. Acta. 874, 255-265.
4. R.A. Capaldi (1973) Biochem. Biophys. Acta 303, 237-241.
5. D.C. Lee and D. Chapman (1986) Bioscience Rep. 6, 235-250.

ISOENZYMES OF HUMAN CYTOCHROME c OXIDASE

T.B.M. Hakvoort, G.J.C. Ruyter, K.M.C. Sinjorgo, and
A.O. Muijsers

Laboratory of Biochemistry, University of Amsterdam, Plantage
Muidergracht 12, 1018 TV Amsterdam, The Netherlands

Cytochrome c oxidase is a protein of 2.10^5 consisting of 3 large subunits,
encoded by mtDNA, and at least 10 smaller ones of nuclear origin. The
largest subunits contain the catalytic center. The function of the small
subunits is still under discussion, they may have structural and or regulatory functions. For the mammalian oxidase the presence of organ-specific
isoenzymes has been shown. The maternally inherited mtDNA contains single
copies of the genes coding for the large subunits, multiple copies may be
present for the genes of the small subunits. Several cases of fatal in-
fantile myopathy have been associated with complete or partial deficiency
of the oxidase in skeletal muscle leading to respiratory arrest [1].

We developed a HPLC technique to purify the human oxidase, starting with
laurylmaltoside-solubilized mitochondrial membrane fractions (from heart,
kidney, liver, and skeletal muscle). With size exclusion chromatography
we could separate the oxidase from other membrane proteins [2]. An even
better resolution of cytochromes was obtained with hydrophobic interaction

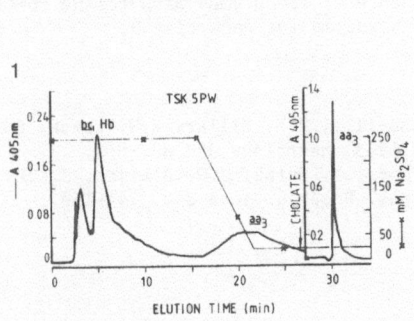
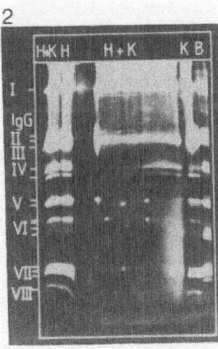

Fig. 1. Purification of human heart cytochrome c oxidase by hydrophobic
interaction HPLC.

Fig. 2. Isoelectric focusing (pH 5-10) followed by SDS-urea PAGE of a
mixture of human heart (H) and kidney (K) oxidase. As a reference
bovine heart (B) oxidase. The subunits are given as groups with
roman numerals according to Kadenbach.

HPLC, as shown in Figure 1. A crude laurylmaltoside extract of human heart mitochondrial membranes was applied on a TSK-5PW column at high ionic strength. Upon elution and decreasing the ionic strength there is a release of protein. The oxidase is only released from the column after introduction of a second detergent into the eluens. Comparison of the HPLC-purified oxidases with a classical bovine oxidase preparation showed that: (1) The human oxidase from heart, kidney and muscle were fully enzymically active and showed the biphasic steady state kinetics as was found for the bovine oxidases. (2) Normal UV-vis spectra were recorded. (3) On SDS-urea PAGE at least 13 subunits were detected. The human subunits II and III had a higher mobility and subunit VIa was stained more intense than their bovine heart counterparts. Comparison of the human heart, kidney, and muscle oxidase revealed similar subunit patterns. Differences in peptide composition at subunit IV level are explained by proteolysis of subunit IV.

By means of immuno-affinity the oxidase was directly isolated from laurylmaltoside solubilized membrane fractions. In these studies an immobilized anti holo bovine heart cytochrome c oxidase antiserum was used. With SDS-urea PAGE we found that : (1) All cytoplasmatic subunits could be detected. (2) Differences were present in the relative staining intensities of the components in the subunit VI fraction for human heart, kidney, and skeletal muscle.

The subunit bands could still be visualized upon starting the immunoaffinity procedure with a 2 mg sample of human skeletal muscle or 3 mg liver solubilized with laurylmaltoside.

Although the SDS-urea PAGE system has a high resolution some small subunits migrate close together. Therefore, we developed a two-dimensional high resolution system. Isoelectric focusing of the urea denatured oxidases, followed by SDS-urea PAGE in the second dimension showed that: in the first dimension the subunits of bovine heart oxidase migrated according to their respective IEP as estimated from their known amino acid sequences. The human oxidase showed a similar behavior and is shown in Figure 2. In the two-dimensional system the human heart, muscle, and kidney oxidases show: (1) All subunits could be detected. (2) One extra band in subunit fraction VIabc. (3) Subunit Va represents two peptides. (4) More than one peptide in subunit VIII. (5) No clear differences between the human oxidases (on 2D gels of mixtures).

Our experiments suggest the presence of isoenzymes with tissue specific ratios, rather than a specific isoenzyme for each tissue.

REFERENCES

1. N. Bresolin, M. Zeviani, E. Bonilla, R.H. Miller, R.W. Leech, S. Shanske, M. Nakagawa, and S. DiMauro (1985) Neurology 35, 802-812.
2. K.M.C. Sinjorgo, T.B.M. Hakvoort, I. Durak, J.W. Draijer, J.K.P. Post, and A.O. Muijsers (1987) Biochem. Biophys. Acta 850, 144-150.

FOLDING OF INTEGRAL MEMBRANE PROTEINS: RENATURATION EXPERIMENTS WITH

BACTERIORHODOPSIN SUPPORT A TWO-STAGE MECHANISM

Jean-Luc Popot* and Donald M. Engelman

Department of Molecular Biophysics and Biochemistry
Yale University, New Haven, CT 06511
*Permanent address: Institut de Biologie Physico-Chimique
13, rue P. and M. Curie, 75005 Paris, France

It has become frequent to know the amino acid sequence of integral membrane proteins on which little other structural data are available. Predictive schemes have been developed to try to predict their transmembrane folding from the sequence (reviewed in ref. 1). The topology of the protein is thought to derive directly from the position and number of sequence segments that could partition into a lipid bilayer in the form of hydrophobic α-helices. Yet, most integral membrane proteins that are not simply anchored, whether they be monomeric or oligomeric, appear to contain multihelical assemblies in which protein/protein contacts are as numerous if not more than protein/lipid contacts.

Implicit in this approach, there are therefore two assumptions: (1) the native fold of the protein lies at a thermodynamic free energy minimum, and therefore can be predicted independently of its biosynthetic history; (2) the transmembrane domain can be considered as resulting from the packing of elements - helices - that would be stable as isolated entities in a lipid bilayer. In the recent years, these hypotheses have been tested using bacteriorhodopsin (BR) as a model system. Huang et al. (2) showed that BR could be renatured to a spectroscopically and functionally native state, starting from the completely unfolded polypeptide. Liao et al. (3) extended these studies to the complex of two chymotryptic fragments of BR.

We have developed renaturation conditions that permit to refold BR in lipid bilayers, starting from the denatured chymotryptic fragments, at a very low lipid-to-protein ratio (1:1 w/w) (4, 5). These conditions induce two-dimensional crystallization of BR trimers into a hexagonal lattice. The structure of the renatured molecule can thus be studied crystallographically. Using x-ray and neutron diffraction, we have shown it to be undistinguishable from that of native BR to 7 Å resolution (4). These observations bring further strong support to the first hypothesis, namely, that the native structure of BR lies at a free energy minimum (2).

The renaturation procedure lends itself to separate refolding of the two fragments into distinct lipid vesicles. Circular dichroism spectra indicate that each fragment has recovered a highly α-helical structure. Addition of retinal to such 'renatured' samples does not lead to a spectral change, indicating that the chromophore of BR is not reformed. No spectral changes occur following mixing of the two populations of vesicles. If the vesicles are fused by freeze-thaw, however, the two fragments interact and bind retinal. The resulting complex exhibits the spectrum of native BR. These experiments suggest that the two isolated fragments have recovered structures close to those which the corresponding sequence segments adopt in the native structure of BR (5). This is consistent with the second hypothesis presented above, namely, that hydrophobic helices fold largely independently of the rest of the molecule.

In summary, our experiments support a two-stage mechanism for the folding of BR and similar integral membrane proteins, according to which the final structure essentially results from the packing of preformed hydrophobic helices.

REFERENCES

1. D.M. Engelman, T.A. Steitz, and A. Goldman (1986) Ann. Rev. Biophys. Chem. 15, 321-353.
2. K.-S. Huang, H. Bayley, M.-J Liao, E. London, and H.G. Khorana (1981) J. Biol. Chem. 256, 3802-3809.
3. M.-J. Liao, E. London, and H.G. Khorana (1983) J. Biol. Chem. 258, 9949-9955.
4. J.-L. Popot, J. Trewhella, and D.M. Engelman (1986) EMBO J. 5, 3039-3044.
5. J.-L. Popot, S.-E. Gerchman, and D.M. Engelman (1987) J. Mol. Biol., in press

IV. REACTION DOMAINS AND OXIDO-REDUCTION MECHANISMS

THE NATURE OF FERRYL, Fe(IV)=O, HAEM IN PEROXIDASES

A.J. Thomson, C. Greenwood*, P.M.A. Gadsby and N. Foote*

Schools of Chemical and Biological Sciences*, The
University of East Anglia, Norwich NR4 7TJ, U.K.

Haem containing peroxidases comprise a range of enzymes which catalyse the two electron, two proton reduction of hydrogen peroxide,[1] viz

$$H_2O_2 + 2H^+ + 2e^- \rightarrow 2H_2O$$

The oxidizing equivalents are used to oxidise variously, organic amines
and phenols (horseradish peroxidase, HRP), proteins such as cytochrome
c and c_{551} (cytochrome c peroxidase, CCP, ex. yeast and Pseudomonas
aeruginosa respectively), and inorganic ions such as chloride (myelo-
peroxidase) and thiocyanate (lactoperoxidase). The peroxidase must therefore be capable of storing two oxidising equivalents of electrons. Two
compounds, called I and II, which are, respectively, two and one
oxidising equivalent above the ferric state, have been isolated. It appears
quite general that one oxidising equivalent is stored by oxidation of the
ferric ion of the haem group to give an oxene or ferryl ion, Fe(IV)=O.
The second equivalent may be lost either from the porphyrin ring itself, as
is the case of compound I of HRP, or from a protein side-chain to generate
an organic radical as in compound ES of CCP, yeast, or in the case of the
di-haem CCP from Ps.aeruginosa from the second haem centre, initially
ferrous, to give ferric haem. A number of haemoproteins without significant
peroxidatic activity, such as myoglobin (Mb) and leghaemoglobin (Lb), will
also react with H_2O_2 to give a ferryl form of the haem group.[2]

In this account we examine the nature of the ferryl form of the haem
ring in various protein environments in order to determine whether the
nature of the ferryl haem is the same in all peroxidases. Since this
species is a crucial one in the catalytic cycle it is important to understand how the protein environment can control the reactivity of this
species. We report the optical absorption and magnetic circular dichroism
(MCD) spectra of a range of haemoproteins in the ferryl state. The
objective is to use MCD spectroscopy to identify spin-states, to measure
ground-state zero-field splittings and to provide an optical fingerprint
of the haem state.

The evidence for the structure of the ferryl haem comes from a
number of techniques. EXAFS identifies a short Fe-O bond, with a value of
1.6 Å in HRP.[3,4] This testifies to the multiple character of this bond.
Raman spectroscopy shows a resonantly enhanced vibration of Fe=O at 790
cm^{-1},[5] also evidence for a multiple-bonded oxygen atom. The electronic
structure is known to be formally Fe(IV) d^4, in the low-spin state of S=1.

This spin state undergoes a large positive axial zero-field splitting with D in the range 20-30 cm^{-1}. Mössbauer spectroscopy has shown this clearly in a large number of cases.[6,7] All of the above evidence has been concerned with haem peroxidases that have histidine as the proximal axial haem ligand. The crystallographic evidence[8] on CCP, yeast, shows a distal histidine group which is likely to have catalytic importance as well. Spectroscopic evidence suggests that a distal histidine group is present in many if not all peroxidases.

Although the evidence for ferryl haem as the one-electron oxidation product of ferric haem in many proteins is incontrovertible experiments on the oxidation of iron porphyrins in organic solvents under anaerobic conditions has shown oxidation of the porphyrin ring to generate [por.$^{+}$-Fe(III)], that is, a ring oxidised product as opposed to a metal-oxidised species. Examples have been reported in which the Fe(III) ion is high spin (S=5/2) and in which there is a coupling between the odd electron of the porphyrin radical and the d-electrons of Fe(III) ion. It has been proposed that the nature of the axial ligand to the iron controls whether the oxidising equivalent is localised in the metal ion, giving Fe(IV), or on the porphyrin ring to generate a radical species.[9] There is NMR evidence that an unstable ring oxidised species can be generated with Fe(III) in the low-spin state in the presence of two imidazole ligands.[10]

There is, to our knowledge, no well authenticated case of species such as those just described in proteins. One of the objectives of this study is to seek evidence for the presence of such species in peroxidases themselves.

EXPERIMENTAL

EPR spectra and MCD spectra have been measured as previously described.[11] Horse heart myoglobin was obtained from Sigma (type III); other proteins were isolated by published methods and further purified where necessary using a Pharmacia FPLC system. All samples contained glassing agent (glycerol or ethanediol) at 50% (v/v).

Compound X was prepared at pH 10.7 by the addition of a slight molar excess of sodium chlorite to ferric horseradish peroxidase.[13] HRP compound II was prepared by adding hydrogen peroxide to HRP; impurities in the sample caused the slow decay of the green compound I so formed to a stable, red compound II state. Yeast CCP compound ES was formed by adding 1.1 molar equivalents of H_2O_2 to the ferric enzyme. Myoglobin at the Fe(IV) level was prepared by adding 2-4 molar equivalents of H_2O_2 to the ferric protein at pH 8-9. In order to obtain the short-lived acid form of this species, the stable alkaline form in 5 mM TAPS buffer at pH 8.5, containing 50% ethanediol, was rapidly mixed with 0.1 M acetic acid, also containing 50% ethanediol, and frozen within 5 sec. The final pH was measured as 3.5. Compound I of Pseudomonas CCP was prepared by rapidly mixing and freezing half-reduced PsCCP and excess H_2O_2 in 25 mM Mes pD 5.6 containing 50% ethanediol.

RESULTS

This section presents the MCD spectra of ferryl haem species in the following proteins, namely, cytochrome c peroxidase (yeast) compound ES, horseradish peroxidase compounds II and X, the peroxide compounds of myoglobin at two pH values, and the di-haem cytochrome c peroxidase (Pseudomonas aeruginosa).

Compound ES of CCP (Yeast)

We illustrate the major features of the spectrum by reference to compound ES of CCP (Yeast) which is well established to contain ferryl haem. Figure 1 shows the absorption spectrum and Figure 2 the MCD spectrum of this compound. The only EPR signal detected in this sample was the organic radical ion at $g \sim 2.0$. It is clear from the MCD spectrum that there are two haem species present with different temperature dependences. The spectral forms of the two can be separated by means of a temperature difference spectrum. At 100 K the MCD spectrum is dominated by one species and the difference spectrum between the 50 K and 1.6 K eliminates the major peaks at 555, 564 and 643 nm. The resulting spectra of the two species are given in Figure 5 and 6 along with the data for other compounds. The magnetic properties of these two species can be obtained by a study of the field and temperature dependences of the MCD intensity at wavelengths where one or other dominates.

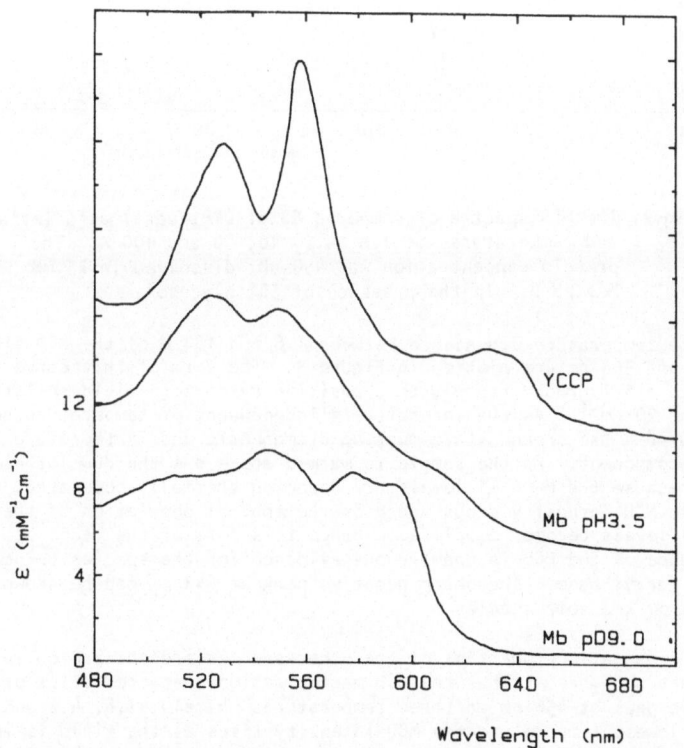

Fig.1. The absorption spectra, at 1.6 K, of CCP (yeast) compound
ES at pH 6.5 and the hydrogen peroxide compounds of
myoglobin at pH 3.5 and pD 9.0. Samples were in 50:50
(v:v) mixtures of buffer and glycerol (yeast CCP) or
ethanediol (Mb).

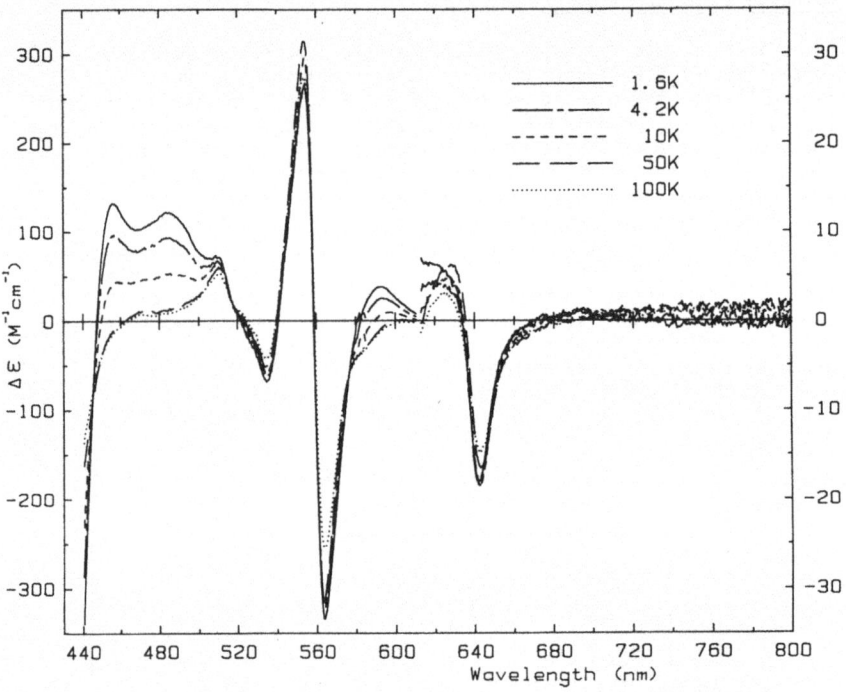

Fig.2. The MCD spectra of compound ES of CCP(Yeast) at 5 Tesla
and temperatures of 1.6, 4.2, 10, 50 and 100 K. The
protein concentration was 450 μM, dissolved in 25 mM
Mes pH 6.5 in the presence of 50% glycerol.

The temperature dependence between 1.6 and 100 K of the MCD signals
at 555 and 564 nm are plotted in Figure 3. The form of this curve corresponds to a S=1 ground state with a positive axial zero-field splitting of
at least 20 cm^{-1}. As the intensity is independent of temperature between
1.6 and ~8 K the ground state must be diamagnetic and is therefore the
M_S = 0 component. As the sample is warmed above 8 K the MCD intensity
grows because the M_S = ±1 levels are becoming thermally populated. Above
25 K the MCD intensity drops again as the thermal population of the
M_S = ±1 levels becomes equalised. Hence this form of the temperature
dependence of the MCD is unambiguous evidence for the species being
S = 1, ferryl haem. The sharp negative peak at 643 nm can be shown to
arise from the same species.

The magnetic properties of the other species present are quite
different. Figure 4 shows the MCD magnetisation characteristics of the
positive peak at 456 nm at three temperatures, namely, 1.6, 4.2 and 10 K.
At the lowest temperature the MCD intensity rises as the field is increased
and levels off. This is characteristic of a ground state which is an
electronic doublet. Since there appears to be no EPR signal associated
with this species it is likely to be an even electron paramagnet. The
most plausible assignment is to a S=1 species with a large negative axial
zero-field splitting parameter D. For a pure spin state S=1 a large
negative D value leaves a doublet M_S=±1 with $g_{\parallel}$ = 4.0, $g_{\perp}$ = 0.0 as the
ground state. This will be EPR silent, since the selection rule is
ΔM_S=±1. By using the method of intercepts introduced by Thomson and
Johnson[11] a prediction can be made of the intercept value, I, from the

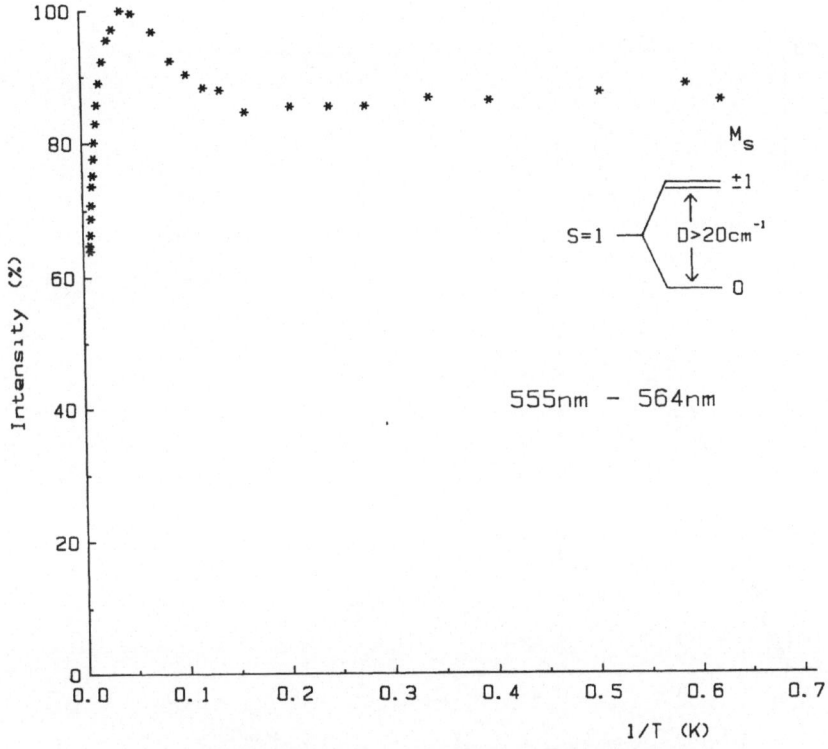

Fig.3. The intensity of the MCD signals in compound ES of
CCP(Yeast) at 5 Tesla as a function of temperature
between 1.6 and 100 K. The intensity was measured as
the peak-to-trough separation, 555-564 nm, and normalised
to the maximum intensity. The inset shows the splitting
of an S=1 electronic state experiencing a positive axial
zero-field.

relationship $g_{\parallel}$ = 3/2I. Hence for a value of $g_{\parallel}$ = 4.0 an intercept
value, I, of 0.375 is predicted. The value found from Figure 4 is
0.38. Hence we conclude that this species is S=1 with a negative
axial zero-field splitting parameter. Our analysis of the magnitude of D
is not yet completed but D must be larger than $\sim$2 cm^{-1} for the ground
doublet to approximate so well to a pure $M_S=\pm1$ state. The form of the
MCD spectrum of this novel species is shown in Figure 6. There are bands
throughout the wavelength range 400-600 nm with a form characteristic
of many haem MCD spectra. Therefore we conclude that this new species is
a ferryl haem, S=1 with a negative D, in contrast to the well known ferryl
haem, S=1 with a positive D. We call these two species ferryl$^-$ and ferryl$^+$,
respectively. We return later to a discussion of the nature of the
structural change which can switch the axial zero-field parameter from a
large positive to a large negative value.

Hydrogen Peroxide Compound of Myoglobin

The peroxide compound of myoglobin at alkaline pH is relatively stable
and has an absorption spectrum, Figure 2, quite different from that of
compound ES of CCP(Yeast).[12] By jumping the pH to 3.5 in a flow apparatus
followed by rapid freezing we have been able to trap an acid form of the

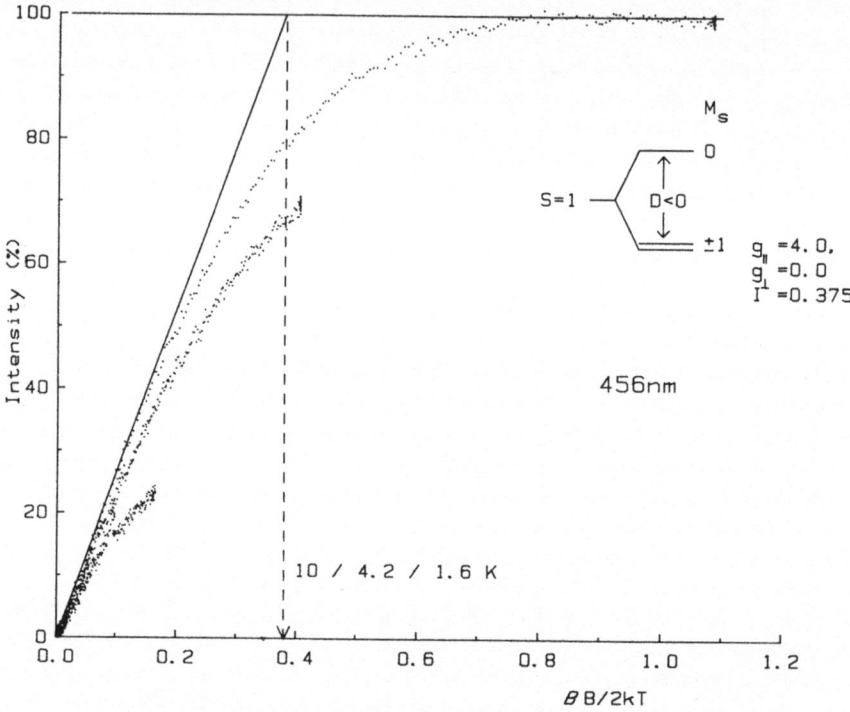

Fig.4. The MCD magnetisation curves of the peak at 456 nm in
the spectrum of compound ES of CCP(Yeast) at temperatures
of 1.6, 4.2 and 10 K. On the abscissa axis $\mathcal{B}$ is Bohr
magneton; B, the magnetic field (Tesla); k, Boltzmann's
constant and T, absolute temperature. The inset shows the
splitting of an S=1 electronic state experiencing a
negative, axial zero-field. The predicted intercept
value is I = 0.375 for $g_{//}$ = 4.0 and $g_{\perp}$ = 0.0 and the
measured value is 0.38.

peroxide compound of Mb. The sample was squirted into a cooled MCD cuvette
which allowed us to measure both the optical absorption spectrum, Figure 1,
and the MCD spectrum, Figures 5 and 6. The absorption spectrum shows an
overall similarity to that of compound ES but is quite different from
that of the alkaline form of the Mb peroxide compound. The MCD spectra
are very similar to those of compound ES. By using temperature difference
spectra the form of the two ferryl species can be obtained. They are
compared in Figures 5 and 6 with those of compound ES. The spectra are
similar but not identical. The MCD magnetisation and temperature dependences of the two species are virtually identical to those of compound ES.
Hence we conclude that the acid form of the peroxide compound of Mb
contains the two species of Fe(IV)=0, namely, ferryl[+] and ferryl[-].

The high pH form of the peroxide compound of Mb is different again
from its acid forms and from compound ES. Figure 5 compares the forms at
100 K. The temperature dependence of the pronounced negative feature at
595 nm shows clearly that the electronic ground state of this species is
S=1, with a large, positive, axial zero-field splitting parameter, that is,

354

a D value of at least 20 cm^{-1}. There is also a minor species with a different temperature dependence whose form is given in Figure 6. However, this is too weak for us to draw any useful conclusion about its nature.

Hence, we conclude that the peroxide compound of Mb has an acid and an alkaline form of ferryl haem both with a large positive D but with distinct MCD spectra. The acid form contains both the ferryl^{+} and ferryl^{-} forms in about the same proportions as has been observed in compound ES.

Horseradish Peroxidase, Compounds II and X (HRPII and HRPX)

These two compounds can be made from oxidised HRP following reaction with hydrogen peroxide (HRPII) or with chlorite (HRPX).[13] The spectra are shown in figures 5 and 6 in the high-temperature (50 K) forms and as the temperature difference spectra. The temperature dependence of the MCD intensity at 543 nm in both cases shows that the form at 50 K is dominated by the species with S=1, positive D value. The form of the MCD spectrum shows them to be similar to the peroxide compound of Mb in the acid form. Hence we conclude that both HRP compounds contain ferryl^{+} haems.

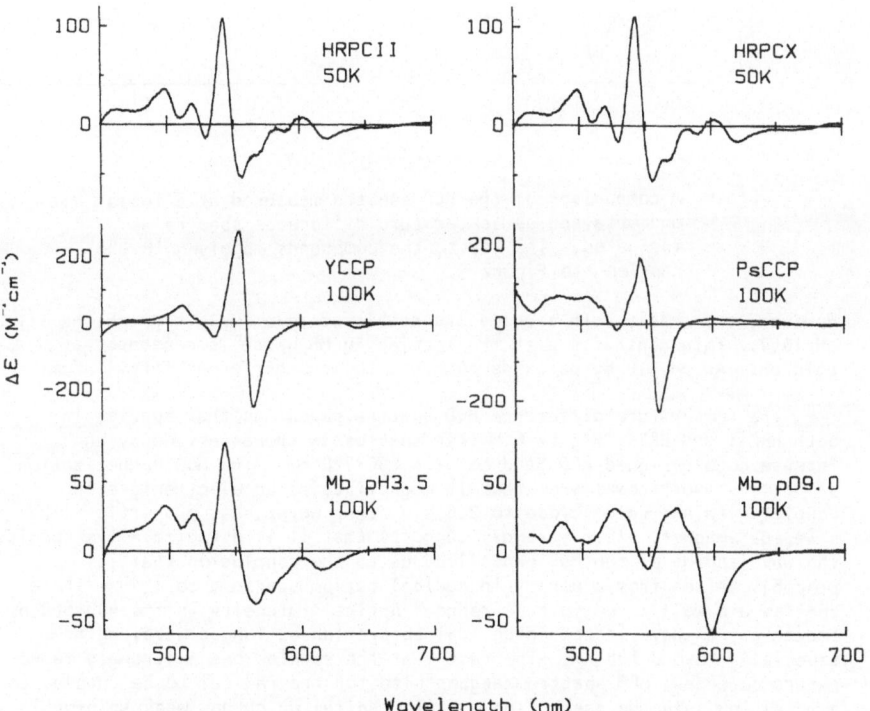

Fig.5. A comparison of the MCD spectra at 5 Tesla and high
      temperature, as indicated, of several haemoproteins
      containing the ferryl haem. YCCP, compound ES of yeast CCP;
      HRPCII and HRPCX, Horseradish peroxidase, compound II and
      compound X; PsCCP, compound I of the di-haem cytochrome
      c peroxidase from Ps.aeruginosa; Mb, the peroxide adduct
      of horse myoglobin at the indicated pH values.

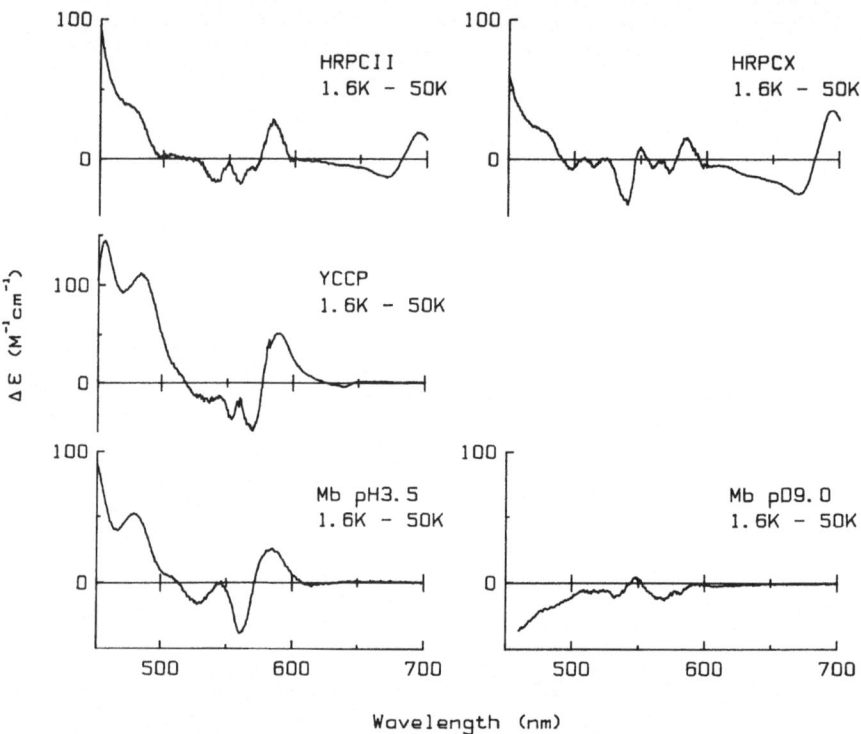

Fig.6. A comparison of the MCD spectra measured at 5 Tesla
and obtained as temperature difference spectra as
indicated. The key to the compounds is given in the
caption to Figure 5.

However, remarkably both species are stable at relatively high pH, namely,
pH 10.7. This contrasts with the species in Mb which is generated at
acid pH. At pH 9.0 Mb peroxide compound forms a different ferryl haem.

The temperature difference MCD spectra reveal another species in
both HRPII and HRPX, Figure 6. This species is characterised by an
intense double-signed MCD band between 650-720 nm. The MCD magnetisation
properties (not shown) show that it magnetises as an electronic spin
doublet with a g-value close to 2.0, in other words, has properties like
a $S=\frac{1}{2}$ paramagnet. This strongly suggests that it is a radical-like species.
The wavelengths of the MCD bands lead us to the conclusion that it
probably arises from a porphyrin radical cation species, por^{+}.[14] These
species are well known to have reduced optical intensity in the 400-600 nm
region but to have increased optical absorption at longer wavelengths
especially beyond 600 nm, The fact that the species has a strongly temperature dependent MCD spectrum argues also for the radical to be coupled to
a metal ion. In the case of an organic radical which has weak spin-orbit
coupling the MCD intensity and temperature dependence is very weak.[15]
Coupling to iron is therefore necessary to produce appreciable MCD intensity
and temperature dependence. These arguments lead us to propose that this
species is probably an example of a ring oxidised haem at an oxidation level
equivalent to that of ferryl haem, viz. [Fe(III)por^{+}]. We have no evidence
from our experiments as to the spin state of the ferric ion, whether high-

and low-spin, in this species. We favour low-spin ferric ion weakly coupled in the ground state to the odd electron on the porphyrin ring. But this remains to be established definitively.

This represents the first evidence for the existence of a ferric porphyrin ring oxidised species in a protein environment. It is perhaps not surprising that it can be found in HRP since compound I of this peroxidase is well established to be [Fe(IV) por^{+}]. Thus the environment of the haem is conducive to oxidation of the porphyrin ring. This species may have significance for the catalytic cycle of HRP which we discuss later.

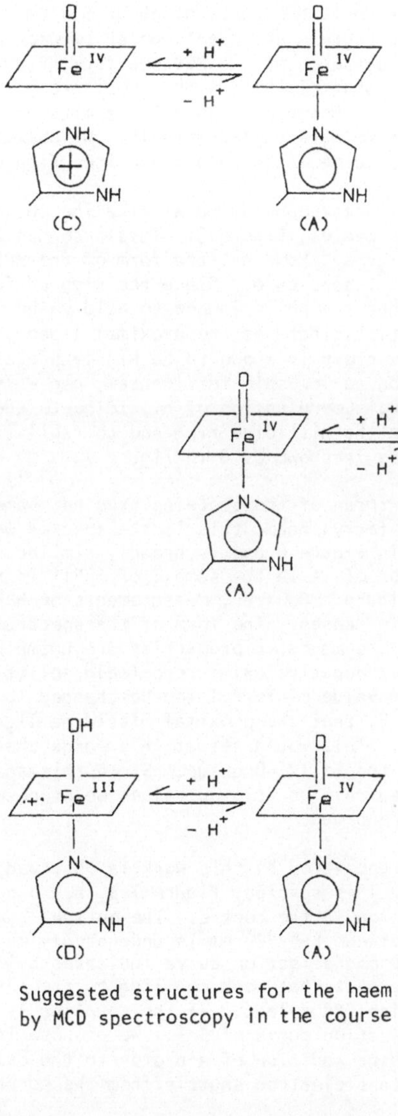

Fig.7. Suggested structures for the haem centres identified by MCD spectroscopy in the course of this work.

DISCUSSION

This survey of the MCD spectra of haemoproteins which contain the ferryl form of protoporphyrin IX has shown that this oxidation level of the haem can exist in a number of forms depending upon the protein environment and the pH of the external medium. Since the species are highly oxidising and unstable it is not possible to carry out a study of the pH dependences of the concentration of the several species discovered. In order to discuss the nature of the various species identified some possible structures are shown in Figure 7.

Species A is without doubt the well characterised ferryl species known from Raman and Mössbauer to have a Fe(IV)=O structure, and to be low-spin d^4, S=1 with a large, positive axial zero-field splitting parameter D. This species is seen in the spectra of all the proteins examined in this work and is best observed at 50-100 K in the MCD spectrum. It shows characteristic intense bi-signate MCD bands at about 550 nm. Weaker negative features which are protein dependent appear between 550 and 650 nm. The temperature dependence of the MCD spectrum, Figure 3, is unambiguous that the ground state is S=1, with a positive D value, probably between 30-40 cm^{-1} rather than between 20-30 cm^{-1} as fits of the Mössbauer spectra suggest. This form we have called ferryl$^+$. We assign this to ferryl haem liganded by histidine in the proximal site, Figure 7, species A.

In the hydrogen peroxide compound of Mb at alkaline pH, pD 9.0, there is a closely related species, Figure 5. This also has a positive D value and an S=1 ground state. However, the form of the MCD spectrum is quite unlike that of ferryl$^+$, species A. Since the high pH form is converted into species A when the pH is jumped to acid value we propose that the high pH form has histidinate as the proximal ligand. The pK$_a$ of the N-1 of the histidine group is known to be highly protein dependent and, in the case of ligation to low-spin ferric haem, can vary between extremes of pH 7.0 and 11.0. Coordination of histidine to the Fe(IV)=O group is likely to polarise the histidine ring and to facilitate proton loss from N-1. This species is shown as B in Figure 7.

We have discovered in three of the proteins studied, namely, HRP, CCP and Mb a novel form of ferryl haem, this is the species we call ferryl$^-$. It has the MCD form shown in Figure 6 and is broadly similar in all three proteins. The concentration of it in the sample of HRPII is rather low at the high pH shown in the figure. However, measurements on HRPII at neutral pH show its concentration increases. The form of the spectrum strongly indicates it is haem like. The magnetic properties are unambiguous that it is a S=1 state with a large, negative axial zero-field splitting parameter, D, Figure 4. How can the D value of ferryl ion be changed in sign? We suggest, Figure 7, species C, that the proximal histidine ligand has been lost on protonation of N-3. This would result in a large change in the axial field experienced by the Fe(IV)=O group. Since this species is observed most clearly at neutral and acid pH values we propose the protonation of the histidine group.

The third new species uncovered by this work is observed only in HRPII and HRPX at high pH. This species, Figure 7 D, has a porphyrin radical cation with ferric ion in the centre. The optical band giving rise to the MCD spectrum between 650-720 nm is undoubtedly due to a porphyrin radical. The MCD magnetisation curve indicates S=½ with a g-value close to 2.0. We expect that weak coupling to the ferric ion spins will render the species EPR silent. If the coupling is weak it will not perturb the MCD magnetisation curve of S=½. We propose in Figure 7 that this species involves the addition of a proton to the oxide ion of the ferryl group and a concomitant electron shuttle from the porphyrin ring to the Fe(IV) ion. This places the oxidising equivalent on the porphyrin ring.

The identification of this species leads us to propose that it is involved in the catalytic cycle of HRP. It is now known from NMR studies that the organic aromatic substrate is located $\sim$10-12 Å from the periphery of the porphyrin ring,[16,17] the plane of the aromatic ring being perpendicular to that of the porphyrin ring. The aromatic substrate does not approach the iron atom either to ligand it or to add electrons to it. Thus we envisage a two electron cycle as follows:

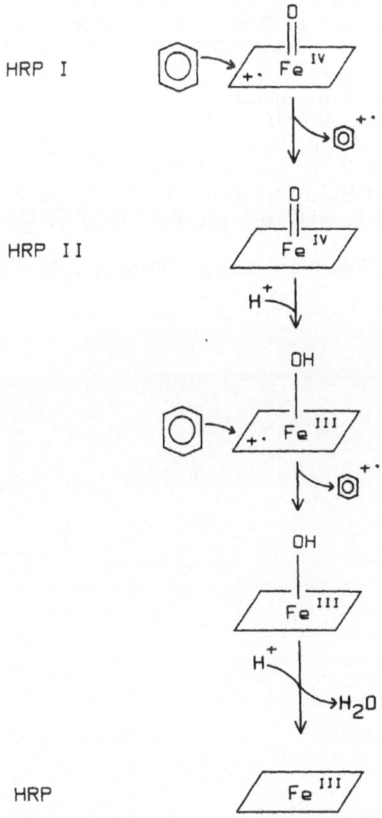

This mechanism involves an electron shuttle between Fe(IV)=O and the porphyrin ring which is controlled by the proton density at the oxide ion of the ferryl froup. It could be that this mechanism is widely used in peroxidases.

It remains to be established what role, if any, the other new ferryl forms discovered by this work play in peroxidatic catalysis.

REFERENCES

1. H.B. Dunford, J.S. Stillman, Coord.Chem.Rev. 19:187 (1976).
2. J.B. Wittenberg, J.Biol.Chem. 253:5694 (1978).
3. J.E. Penner-Hahn, K.S. Eble, T.J. McMurray, M. Renner, A.L. Balch, J.T. Groves, J.H. Dawson and K.O. Hodgson. J.Amer.Chem.Soc. 108:7819 (1986).
4. B. Chance, L. Powers, Y. Ching, T. Poulos, G.R. Schonbaum, I. Yamazaki and K.G. Paul. Arch.Biochem.Biophys. 235:596 (1984).
5. J. Terner, A.J. Sitter, C.M. Reczek. Biochem.Biophys.Acta, 828:73 (1985).
6. C.E. Schulz, R. Rutter, J.T. Sage, P.G. Debrunner and L.P. Hager, Biochem. 23:4743 (1984) and references therein.
7. G. Lang, K. Spartalian and T. Yonetani, Biochim.Biophys.Acta, 451:250 (1976).
8. T.L. Poulos, S.T. Freer, R.A. Alden, S.L. Edwards, U. Skoglund, K. Takio, B. Eriksson, Ng. H. Xuang, T. Yonetani and J. Kraut. J.Biol.Chem. 255:575 (1980).
9. P. Gans, G. Buisson, E. Duee, J-C, Marchon, B.S. Erler, W.F. Scholz and C.A. Reed, J.Amer.Chem.Soc. 108:1223 (1986).
10. H.M. Goff and M.A. Phillippi, J.Amer.Chem.Soc. 105:7567 (1983).
11. A.J. Thomson and M.K. Johnson, Biochem.J. 191:411 (1980).
12. N.K. King and M.E. Winfield, J.Biol.Chem. 238:1520 (1963).
13. S. Shahangian and L.P. Hager, J.Biol.Chem. 257:11529 (1982).
14. D. Dolphin and R.H. Felton, Acc.Chem.Res. 7:26 (1974).
15. W.R. Browett and M.J. Stillman, Inorg.Chim.Acta, 491:1 (1981).
16. P.S. Burns, R.J.P. Williams and P.E. Wright, Chem.Commn. 1975:795 (1975).
17. J. Sukurada, S. Takahashi and T. Hosoya, J.Biol.Chem. 261:9657 (1986).

POLARIZATION IN HEME PROTEINS AND CYTOCHROME C OXIDASE

James O. Alben

Department of Physiological Chemistry
Ohio State University, College of Medicine
Columbus, Ohio, U.S.A.

INTRODUCTION

Communication at the molecular level is the basis for all forms of biological control. This may range from simple dipole interactions that alter a chemical equilibrium to a complex series of interactions that lead to control of electron transport in the cytochrome system in mitochondria. All of these processes can be analyzed into a series of steps, which in turn can be described in terms of simple molecular force fields. Infrared spectroscopy[1] has been an excellent tool for the study of molecular interactions in biological molecules, since chemical bonding, and therefore vibrational force constants, are very sensitive to changes in local molecular interactions. Our understanding of cytochrome c oxidase has been greatly enhanced by direct spectroscopic studies, and by comparisons with metal coordination complexes and simpler heme proteins and hemocyanins.

LOCAL MOLECULAR PROBES OF POLARIZATION EFFECTS

A central theme that emerges from all of these studies is that because of the compactness of structures, information in terms of polarization effects can be transfered over long distances. These interactions have been described in terms of local solvation shells, with non-bonding molecular interactions, or polarization effects in aromatic compounds, or in longer distance effects associated with tertiary or quaternary structures in proteins. It is thus possible to define vibrating groups which are sensitive to changes in surroundings, and can be used as local molecular probes for more distant alterations. A simple example of this is in the iron porphyrin derivatives[2], in which carbon monoxide coordinated axially to iron porphyrins has a vibrational frequency that is sensitive to substituent groups on the porphyrin ring which are cis- to the coordinated carbon monoxide, or to substituents on a pyridine ligand that is trans- to the carbon monoxide. The vibrational frequency of the coordinated carbon monoxide is modified by the basicity of the pyrrole nitrogens or of the trans-ligand (Figure 1). Thus, the entire iron-porphyrin complex, including its trans-ligands, is sensitive to structural modifications anywhere in the metal-porphyrin coordination complex.

Metal porphyrins serve as an ideal sensing device, whereby more distant structural modifications may modulate a reaction that occurs at the iron. Such is the case with hemoglobin, where the effects of structural modifications at remote protein sites have been extensively studied in

361

relation to their effects on oxygen affinity at the iron. At least three discrete anion binding sites have been shown to affect oxygen affinity[3]. Thus the entire process of oxygen transport in the lungs and in the peripheral tissues are controlled by such molecular modifications. This information transfer occurs in both directions, from the protein to the metal complex, and from the metal complex back throughout the protein. The latter has been studied extensively by means of cysteine sulfhydryl groups[4,5,6] in the non-polar interface between alpha and beta chains in hemoglobin (α-104 and β-112 cysteines at the $\alpha^1\beta^1$ interface), and near the protein surface at the β-93 cysteine.

The information transferred is mediated through steric repulsions (van der Waals interactions), by non-covalent interactions between the porphyrin and surrounding protein groups, through dipole or H-bond interactions with the coordinated ligand, and through covalently mediated steric effects through the proximally coordinated histidine, and from there to the F-helix and its amino acid side chains. The effects of ligation at the iron transmitted through the G-helix and measured at the α-104 cysteine SH absorption, are greatly accentuated by quaternary interactions in the hemoglobin tetramer[5], whereas those effects that are transmitted through the proximal (F8) histidine to the β93 (F9) cysteine SH group are already maximal in the isolated β-chain (β_4), and are not further accentuated by quaternary interactions in the $\alpha_2\beta_2$ tetramer[6]. These conformational changes

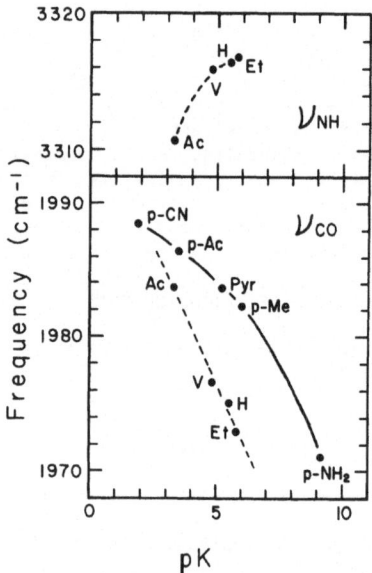

Figure 1. Polarization of Fe(C-O) measured as v(CO), is compared with basicity of the coordinating groups. pK is the pK3 of the corresponding metal-free 2,4-disubstituted porphyrin derivatives, showing cis-effects through the porphyrin ring (------), or the pK of 4-substituted pyridine corresponding to the trans-coordinated ligand (———). Porphyrin 2,4-disubstituents are Ac, acetyl; V, vinyl; H, hydrogen; Et, ethyl. Trans-ligands are p-cyano, p-acetyl, pyridine, p-methyl, and p-aminopyridine. Pyrrole NH frequencies of the metal-free porphyrins are compared in the upper section of the Figure. Data from Alben and Caughey[2] as arranged by Alben and Fiamingo[1].

result in a frequency shift in the α-104 cysteine SH absorption due to change in the strength of its H-bond with rotation of the G-helix, whereas at the β93 cysteine, a change in SH absorptivity is observed, which appears to be due to a change in the dipolar interaction between the sulfur and the HC2 tyrosine ring.

PHOTODISSOCIATION OF Fe-CO

Photodissociation in the iron-coordinated carbon monoxide at low temperatures has been studied extensively by use of Fourier transform infrared spectroscopy. This has provided information about non-covalent interactions in the heme pocket that may help to modify biological reactivity. In the case of myoglobin[7] or hemoglobin[8] (Figure 2), photodissociated carbon monoxide shows a single vibrational absorption (B_1) above 30 K near 2131 cm^{-1}, that is only slightly perturbed from the free gas frequency of 2144 cm^{-1}. Below 20 K, a second population (B_2) appears that absorbs near 2118 cm^{-1}. The small deviation from the free gas frequency of carbon monoxide indicates that B_1 is perturbed by a weak dipole-dipole or induced dipole interaction, while B_2 may be perturbed by two such interactions. B_2 dissociates at a lower temperature than does B_1, indicating a more labile interaction, whereas lower $v(CO)$ frequencies are associated with greater absorptivities and stronger bonds. This seeming paradox is resolved if B_2 represents a second weak dipole association of photodissociated CO. Possible interactions of photodissociated CO with the distal histidine and porphyrin ring have been discussed by Fiamingo and Alben[8]. Photodissociation of heme carbonyls has been studied in many laboratories by Moessbauer[9], mid-infrared[7,8,10], near infrared[8,11], magnetic circular dichroism[12], visible[13,14], and Raman[15,16,17] spectroscopic measurements, and by magnetic susceptibility[18]. All are consistent with transformation from a low spin tetragonal iron(II) complex

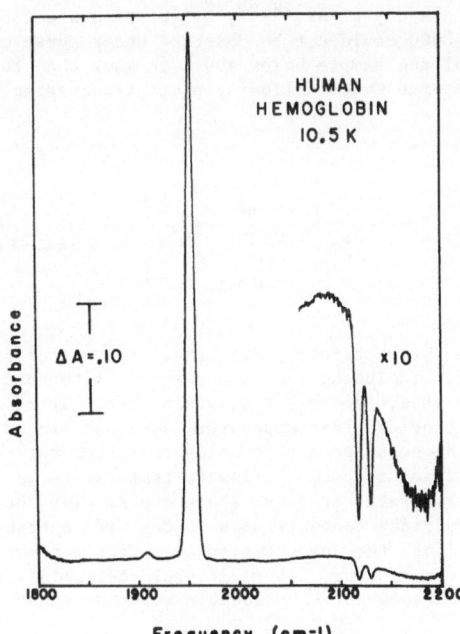

Figure 2. Infrared absorbance difference spectrum[8] of carboxyhemoglobin showing the iron carbonyl complexes in the dark (pointing upward) minus the photodissociated carbon monoxide populations in the light (pointing downward) at 10.5 K.

to a high spin square pyramidal (five coordinate) iron(II) complex with loss of CO from the coordination sphere. That excess kinetic energy is available to photodissociated CO is evident from consideration of the difference in energy of the absorbed visible radiation and that of the iron carbonyl bond which absorbs in the far infrared. Indeed, studies of photodissociation of carboxyhemoglobin suggest that large increases occur in the local temperature of iron porphyrins with absorption of visible light, which must then be dissipated as kinetic energy[19,20]. Similar excess kinetic energy is observed with photodissociation of cytochrome c oxidase carbonyl[21,22,23], where CO must travel from its location at the heme to a copper complex that is sufficently distant that it cannot be in van der Waal's contact with the iron carbonyl, at least in the α-form of cytochrome c oxidase. These conclusions are in good agreement with energy minimization studies of Case and Karplus[24] and of Sassaroli and Rousseau[25] who suggest that upon breaking the iron-carbon bond at low temperatures, the CO moves to a position about 4 Å away from the iron. The latter simulation was driven only by van der Waal's interactions. A different picture has been suggested by Powers and Chance[26,27] to interpret data observed by X-ray absorption spectroscopy. Their suggestion that CO photodissociated from carboxymyoglobin at low temperatures results in an increased Fe-(CO) distance of only 0.05 Å appears to be inconsistent with other types of spectroscopic data. Possible reasons for these differences have been discussed by Fiamingo and Alben[8].

PHOTODISSOCIATION OF CYTOCHROME C OXIDASE CO COMPLEX

The heme pocket of cytochrome c oxidase is quite different from that of myoglobin or hemoglobin, in that a reactive copper complex (Cu_B) is also present in the vicinity of the heme (a_3Fe)[21,22,23]. We consider here the ligand-reactive portion of cytochrome c oxidase, cytochrome a_3, and its heme pocket which contains iron and copper, both of which have been observed to bind carbon monoxide, and together are taken to be the site of reduction of molecular oxygen to water. The Fe-CO complex of cytochrome c oxidase was first observed by Caughey et al.[28,29], by infrared spectroscopy close to room temperature, but CuCO could not be observed under these conditions. It was necessary to cool the sample below 200 K to slow the thermal dissociation sufficiently to observe Cu_BCO following photodissociation of a_3FeCO complex.

This reaction has been repeated many times with cytochrome c oxidase in a variety of forms, including purified enzyme, mitochondrial preparations, isolated heart myocytes, and heart tissue slices. It may be quantitatively cycled many times provided the temperature does not exceed 210 K. CO does not escape from the heme-copper pocket below this temperature. It is readily photodissociated from iron to the lowest temperature we have used (8.5 K), and thermally dissociates from CuB above 140 K. This demonstrates that a clear space or corridor connects a_3Fe to Cu_B in cytochrome oxidase, and provides support for the expectation that dioxygen may form a bridging complex between a_3Fe and Cu_B, where it could be rapidly reduced to water. Figure 3 appears to represent a reasonable reaction sequence[22].

ALPHA- AND BETA-FORMS OF CYTOCHROME C OXIDASE

Multiple populations of a_3FeCO and Cu_BCO were observed in our early infrared studies with low temperature photodissociation. These were divided into a major component, with νCO for a_3FeCO at 1963 cm-1, and at 2062 cm-1

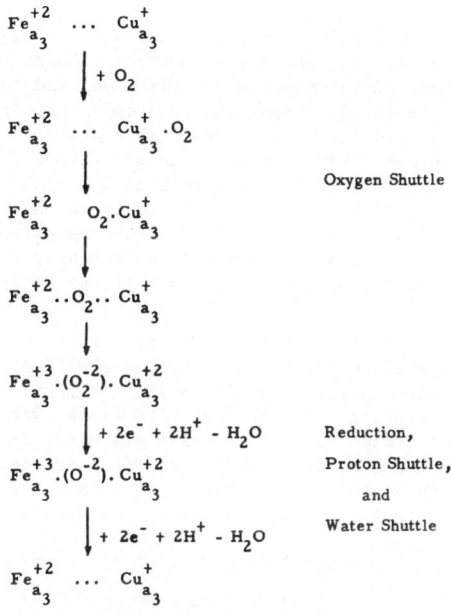

$$Fe_{a_3}^{+2} \ \cdots \ Cu_{a_3}^{+}$$

$$\downarrow \ + \ O_2$$

$$Fe_{a_3}^{+2} \ \cdots \ Cu_{a_3}^{+} \cdot O_2$$

Oxygen Shuttle

$$Fe_{a_3}^{+2} \ \ O_2 \cdot Cu_{a_3}^{+}$$

$$Fe_{a_3}^{+2} \cdots O_2 \cdots Cu_{a_3}^{+}$$

$$Fe_{a_3}^{+3} \cdot (O_2^{-2}) \cdot Cu_{a_3}^{+2}$$

$$\downarrow \ + \ 2e^- \ + \ 2H^+ \ - \ H_2O$$

Reduction,

Proton Shuttle,

$$Fe_{a_3}^{+3} \cdot (O^{-2}) \cdot Cu_{a_3}^{+2}$$

and

$$\downarrow \ + \ 2e^- \ + \ 2H^+ \ - \ H_2O$$

Water Shuttle

$$Fe_{a_3}^{+2} \ \cdots \ Cu_{a_3}^{+}$$

Figure 3. Possible reaction sequence for oxygen reduction by cytochrome a₃. From Alben, et al.[22].

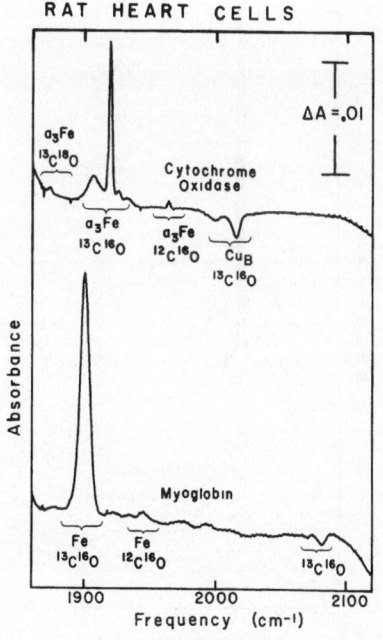

Figure 4. Infrared absorbance difference spectra (dark – light) of CO complexes in rat heart myocytes, measured as described in the text. Cytochrome oxidase was measured at 120 K, and myoglobin at 10 K after prephotolysis at 120 K.[10]

for Cu_BCO, and minor a_3FeCO absorptions and a minor Cu_BCO absorption at 2043 cm^{-1}. The similarity of the copper carbonyl bands to those previously observed[30] for hemocyanin copper carbonyls (2062 and 2063 cm^{-1} for molluscan hemocyanins from squid and limpet and 2043 cm^{-1} for crustacean hemocyanins from marine crab and fresh-water crayfish) suggests that similar copper coordination complexes may be present in cytochrome c oxidase. The major a_3FeCO absorption is clearly distinguished by its narrow half-bandwidth (FWHM) of about 2.5 cm^{-1}, which is less than half the width of the corresponding CuCO absorption. This led to the suggestion that Cu_B is held in a much more flexible coordination shell and may help to "shuttle" oxygen in to the more structurally ordered a_3Fe where it can be reduced without loss of reactive oxygen radicals.

The previous studies were conducted with cytochrome oxidase in mitochondrial preparations from beef heart or purified enzyme, and therefore may have represented a selection of enzyme fractions not representative of the whole, or perhaps the "minor" fractions were artifacts of the preparation. That this was not the case was established[10] by studies with tissue slices from perfused rat heart and with isolated rat heart myocytes. These preparations contained all of the cytochrome oxidase and most of the myoglobin. The spectral contributions of CO coordinated to

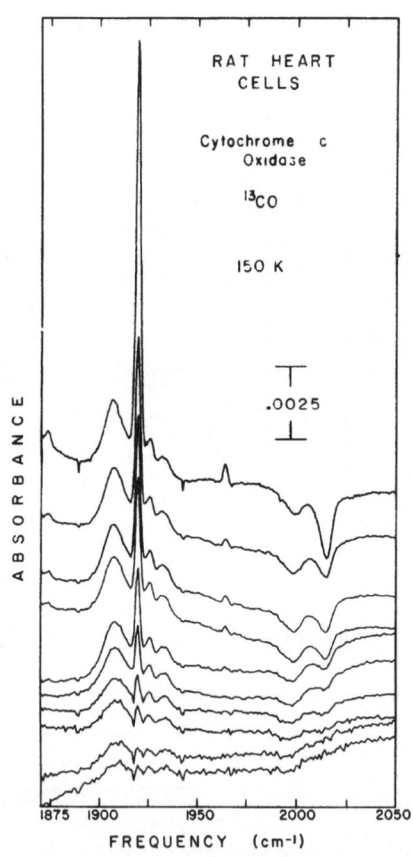

Figure 5. Relaxation kinetics after photolysis of cytochrome c oxidase show faster recovery in beta-forms than in alpha-forms of iron and copper carbonyl complexes. Reproduced with permission from Fiamingo, et al.[10]

cytochrome c oxidase were separated from those of carboxymyoglobin by the greatly different temperature dependence of relaxation of photodissociated CO to reform the corresponding iron carbonyl. Photodissociated cytochrome oxidase is quite stable below 140 K, while photodissociated carboxymyoglobin relaxes rapidly above 100 K. Therefore, cytochrome oxidase absorbance difference spectrum (dark minus light) is clearly observed following a short photolysis at 120 K, and the carboxymyoglobin difference spectrum is observed at 10 K following a pre-photolysis of the oxidase at 120 K. The results are illustrated in Figure 4. The heavy isotope of carbon (^{13}C) produces absorption bands at lower frequencies than ^{12}C, but which are otherwise similar, which positively identifies all absorption bands as due to added carbon monoxide. Bands due to iron carbonyl point upward and those due to copper carbonyl point downward in the absorbance difference spectrum.

The relative amounts of the "major" and "minor" forms of cytochrome c oxidase vary over a considerable range. In beef heart mitochondria or in "skinned" rat heart myocytes, values range between 0 and 25%, whereas the "minor" forms represent as much as 50% of the total carbonyl absorption band area in intact rat heart myocytes. In every case, the relative area of the sharp absorption band near 1964 cm^{-1} (1919.5 cm^{-1} for ^{13}CO) for a$_3$FeCO corresponds closely to that of the Cu$_B$CO absorption at 2062 cm^{-1} (2015 cm^{-1} for ^{13}CO). We therefore designate this pair of absorptions as due to the alpha-form of cytochrome c oxidase. The multiple broad absorptions of a$_3$FeCO correlate with the Cu$_B$CO at 2043 cm^{-1} (1999 cm^{-1} for ^{13}CO), and are designated as multiple beta-forms of the oxidase. Support for this designation comes from relaxation kinetics after photolysis, with reformation of the a$_3$FeCO complexes (Figure 5). The beta-forms of cytochrome c oxidase are 50% relaxed in about one tenth of the time required for the alpha-forms.

Both alpha- and beta-forms of cytochrome c oxidase react with carbon monoxide to form iron carbonyls that can be photodissociated at low temperatures to form copper carbonyls that can thermally dissociate to reform the iron carbonyls. The alpha form a$_3$FeCO produces a sharp, narrow absorption that indicates that its heme a is in a highly ordered, non-polar protein surrounding, whereas its copper complex has a broader CO absorption which indicates greater vibronic coupling with the surrounding protein (Figure 6). The alpha form relaxes more slowly than the beta-form, consistent with a more restrictive local environment. This description would suggest that the alpha-form of cytochrome c oxidase may partake in highly controlled electron

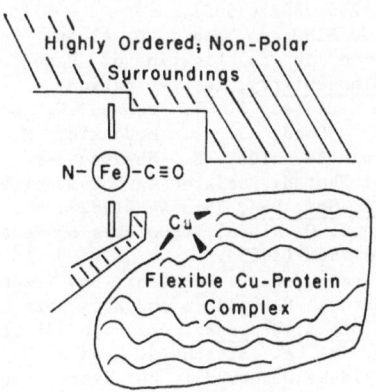

Figure 6. Representation of CO binding sites in the alpha-form of cytochrome a$_3$. In the beta-forms, the heme a is also embedded in more polar and flexible surroundings.

transfer reactions, and may be the form that is primarily involved with energy conservation with ultimate synthesis of ATP. The beta-forms have multiple iron carbonyl populations, but a single Cu_BCO absorption that is similar to that found in crustacean hemocyanins. These forms are not interchangeable below 210 K, but we have no information about this possibility at higher temperatures. The large amounts of beta-forms present in isolated myocytes (or tissue slices) suggest their importance in heart metabolism. Their differences in reactivity from the alpha-form are sufficient to severely complicate all studies that do not quantitatively distinguish contributions of each form.

CONCLUSIONS

The cyclical photodissociation of a_3FeCO to form Cu_BCO and thermal dissociation of Cu_BCO to reform a_3FeCO demonstrate the proximity of these metal centers and their availability for ligand binding. This makes highly probable a bridged peroxo complex (Figure 3) as a transient intermediate in dioxygen reduction. Alpha- and multiple beta-forms of cytochrome c oxidase are present in heart tissue and variously purified oxidase preparations. They have different kinetic properties, but it is not known whether these forms are interconvertable and subject to metabolic control. The differences in CO vibrational frequency, half-bandwidth, and relaxation rates after photodissociation, are all consistent with important differences in polarization of the heme a and Cu_B coordination complexes by the surrounding protein. The detailed manner in which this affects the metabolic control of oxygen reduction and energy conservation remains to be determined.

REFERENCES

1. J. O. Alben and F. G. Fiamingo, Fourier Transform Infrared Spectroscopy, in "Optical Techniques in Biological Research," D. L. Rousseau, ed., Academic Press, New York (1984).
2. J. O. Alben and W. S. Caughey, An Infrared Study of Bound Carbon Monoxide in the Human Red Blood Cell, Isolated Hemoglobin, and Heme Carbonyls, Biochemistry, 7:175 (1968).
3. A. M. Nigen, J. M. Manning, and J. O. Alben, Oxygen-linked Binding Sites for Inorganic Anions to Hemoglobin, J. Biol. Chem., 255:5525 (1980).
4. J. O. Alben and G. H. Bare, Fourier Transform Infrared Spectroscopic Study of Molecular Interactions in Hemoglobin, Applied Optics, 17:2985 (1978).
5. J. O. Alben and G. H. Bare, Ligand-dependent Heme-Protein Interactions in Human Hemoglobin Studied by Fourier Transform Infrared Spectroscopy, J. Biol. Chem., 255:3892 (1980).
6. P. P. Moh, F. G. Fiamingo, and J. O. Alben, Conformational Sensitivity of b-93 Cysteine SH to Ligation of Hemoglobin Observed by FT-IR Spectroscopy, Biochemistry, in preparation.
7. J. O. Alben, D. Beece, S. F. Bowne, W. Doster, L. Eisenstein, H. Frauenfelder, D. Good, J. D. McDonald, M. C. Marden, P. P. Moh, L. Reinisch, A. H. Reynolds, E. Shyamsunder, and K. T. Yue, Infrared Spectroscopy of Photodissociated Carboxymyoglobin at Low Temperatures, Proc. Natl. Acad. Sci. USA, 79:3744 (1982).
8. F. G. Fiamingo and J. O. Alben, Structures of Photolyzed Carboxymyoglobin, Biochemistry, 24:7964 (1985).
9. K. Spartalian, G. Lang, and T. Yonetani, Low Temperature Photodissociation Studies of Ferrous Hemoglobin and Myoglobin Complexes by Moessbauer Spectroscopy, Biochim. Biophys. Acta, 428:281 (1976).
10. F. G. Fiamingo, R. A. Altschuld, and J. O. Alben, α and β Forms of Cytochrome c Oxidase Observed in Rat Heart Myocytes by Low Temperature Fourier Transform Infrared Spectroscopy, J. Biol. Chem., 261:12976 (1986).
11. T. Iizuka, H. Yamamoto, M. Kotani, and T. Yonetani, Low Temperature Photodissociation of Hemoproteins: Carbon Monoxide Complex of Myoglobin

and Hemoglobin, Biochim. Biophys. Acta, 371:126 (1974).

12. Y. A. Sharonov, N. A. Sharonova, V. A. Figlovsky, and V. A. Grigorjev, A comparison of the Heme Electronic States in Equilibrium and Nonequilibrium Protein Conformations of High-Spin Ferrous Hemoproteins. Low Temperature Magnetic Circular Dichroism Studies, Biochim. Biophys. Acta, 709:332 (1982).

13. R. H. Austin, K. W. Beeson, L. Eisenstein, H. Frauenfelder, and I. C. Gunsalus, Dynamics of Ligand Binding to Myoglobin, Biochemistry, 14:5355 (1975).

14. N. Alberding, S. S. Chan, L. Eisenstein, H. Frauenfelder, D. Good, I. C. Gunsalus, T. M. Nordland, M. F. Perutz, A. H. Reynolds, and L. B. Sorensen, Binding of Carbon Monoxide to Isolated Hemoglobin Chains, Biochemistry, 17:43 (1978).

15. D. L. Rousseau and P. V. Argade, Metastable Photoproducts from Carbon Monoxide Myoglobin, Proc. Natl. Acad. Sci. USA, 83:1310 (1986).

16. M. Sassaroli, S. Dasgupta, and D. L. Rousseau, Cryogenic Stabilization of Myoglobin Photoproducts, J. Biol. Chem., 261:13704 (1986).

17. S. Dasgupta and T. G. Spiro, Resonance Raman Characterization of the 7-ns Photoproduct of (Carbonmonoxy)hemoglobin: Implications for Hemoglobin Dynamics, Biochemistry, 25:5941 (1986).

18. H. Roder, J. Berendsen, S. F. Bowne, H. Frauenfelder, T. B. Sauke, E. Shyamsunder, and M. B. Weissman, Comparison of the Magnetic Properties of Deoxy- and Photodissociated Myoglobin, Proc. Natl. Acad. Sci. USA, 81:2359 (1984).

19. V. M. Molleran, F. G. Fiamingo, A. A. Croteau, and J. O. Alben, Local Molecular Temperature in Carboxy-Hemoglobin Photolyzed at Low Temperature, Biophys. J., 51:292a (1987).

20. E. R. Henry and W. A. Eaton, Molecular Dynamics Simulations of Cooling in Laser-Excited Heme Proteins, Biophys. J., 51:404a (1987).

21. J. O. Alben, R. A. Altschuld, F. G. Fiamingo, and P. P. Moh, Structure of Cytochrome c Oxidase Heme Pocket: Low-Temperature FTIR Spectroscopy of the Photolyzed CO Complex, in "Electron Transport and Oxygen Utilization," C. Ho, ed., Elsevier North Holland, new York (1982).

22. J. O. Alben, P. P. Moh, F. G. Fiamingo, and R. A. Altschuld, Cytochrome oxidase (a_3) Heme and Copper Observed by Low-Temperature Fourier Transform Infrared Spectroscopy of the CO Complex, Proc. Natl. Acad. Sci. USA, 78:234 (1981).

23. F. G. Fiamingo, R. A. Altschuld, P. P. Moh, and J. O. Alben, Dynamic Interactions of CO with a_3Fe and Cu_B in Cytochrome c Oxidase in Beef Heart Mitochondria Studied by Fourier Transform Infrared Spectroscopy at Low Temperatures, J. Biol. Chem., 257:1639 (1982).

24. D. A. Case and M. Karplus, Dynamics of Ligand Binding to Heme Proteins, J. Mol. Biol., 132:343 (1979).

25. M. Sassaroli and D. L. Rousseau, Simulation of Carboxymyoglobin Photodissociation, J. Biol. Chem., 261:16292 (1986).

26. B. Chance, R. Fischetti, and L. Powers, Structure and Kinetics of the Photoproduct of Carboxymyoglobin at Low Temperatures: An X-ray Absorption Study, Biochemistry, 22:3820 (1983).

27. L. Powers, J. L. Sessler, G. L. Woolery, and B. Chance, CO Bond Angle Changes in Photolysis of Carboxymyoglobin, Biochemistry, 23:5519 (1984).

28. J. A. Volpe, M. C. O'Toole, and W. S. Caughey, Quantitative Infrared Spectroscopy of CO Complexes of Cytochrome c Oxidase, Hemoglobin and Myoglobin: Evidence for One CO per Heme, Biochem. Biophys. Res. Commun. 62:48 (1975).

29. S. Yoshikawa, M. G. Choc, M. C. O'Toole, and W. S. Caughey, An Infrared Study of CO Binding to Heart Cytochrome c Oxidase and Hemoglobin A, J. Biol. Chem., 252:5498 (1977).

30. L. Y. Fager and J. O. Alben, Structure of the Carbon Monoxide Binding Site of Hemocyanins Studied by Fourier Transform Infrared Spectroscopy, Biochemistry, 11:4786 (1972).

EFFECTS OF FREEZING ON THE COORDINATION STATE AND LIGAND ORIENTATION IN HEMOPROTEINS

Helen Anni and Takashi Yonetani

Department of Biochemistry and Biophysics, University of

Pennsylvania, Philadelphia, PA 19104-6089, USA

INTRODUCTION

Some spectroscopic and kinetic measurements of hemoproteins have been carried out in cryogenic temperatures in order to achieve a number of specific objectives such as trapping transient intermediates, retarding decay processes and electron/nuclear relaxation rates, controlling reaction rates, expanding a range of temperature, increasing signal-to-noise ratios of spectroscopic data, etc. It is generally assumed in these measurements that freezing would not adversely alter the sites and properties of interest. The absence of obvious changes in the frozen sample after thawing is sometimes taken as a proof that freezing has not irreversibly modified the protein. However, this does not exclude the possibility that a hemoprotein may be reversibly altered in frozen states due to the physical stress exerted by crystallized solvent water molecules. In addition, it is well known that pH and other physical properties of aqueous solutions could be significantly changed upon freezing[1].

Adverse effects of solvent freezing on hemoproteins are well recognized. Abrupt changes in the paramagnetic susceptibility of hemoglobin near freezing point[2], the loss of the ordered intermolecular arrangement in crystals of cytochrome c peroxidase upon freezing[3], multiple reorientation of bound gaseous ligands in crystals of myoglobin-nitric oxide[4] and oxy cobalt-substituted myoglobin[5,6] on freezing, temperature-dependent equilibria between two forms of myoglobin-nitric oxide at low temperatures[7], temperature-dependent spin transitions in horseradish

1. Douzou, P. (1977) **Cryobiochemistry**, Academic Press, New York.
2. Iizuka, T. and Kotani, M. (1969) **Biochim. Biophys. Acta** 194, 351-363.
3. Yonetani, T. and Schleyer, H. (1967) J. Biol. Chem. 242, 3919-3925.
4. Hori, H., Ikeda-Saito, M., and Yonetani, T. (1981) J. Biol. Chem. 256, 7849-7855.
5. Hori, H., Ikeda-Saito, M., and Yonetani, T. (1980) **Nature** 288, 501-502.
6. Hori, H., Ikeda-Saito, M., and Yonetani, T. (1982) J. Biol. Chem. 257, 3636-3642.
7. Morse, R. H. and Chan, S. I. (1980) J. Biol. Chem. 255, 7876-7882.

peroxidase[8] and cytochrome c peroxidase[9] at cryogenic temperature are some of such examples. It is, therefore, important to recognize that freezing may cause major alterations in the molecular structure and some properties of hemoproteins, though they may be reversible and that certain precautionary measures should be taken prior to interprete experimental data obtained at cryogenic temperatures.

Several cryo-protective/anti-freezing agents such as glycerol, ethylene glycol, propylene glycol, methanol and dimethylsulfoxide have been used to avoid freezing injury of certain cells and for protection against crystallization of solvent water[1]. Glycerol and ethylene glycol also partially prevent the anomalous spin transitions of some hemoproteins at cryogenic temperatures[10,11,12].

In this paper, we show that freezing does induce significant changes in the coordination/spin state and the ligand orientation of several hemoproteins. Such changes can be effectively eliminated by the use of antifreezing agents like glycerol.

MATERIALS AND METHODS

Cytochrome c peroxidase was purified from baker's yeast according to the method of Yonetani and Ray[13] and crystallized by dialysis against distilled water[14]. Metmyoglobin from sperm whale muscle was purchased from Calbiochem and purified by repeated recrystallization from ammonium sulfate solution[15]. Myoglobin nitric oxide was prepared by reduction with excess dithionite in the presence of nitrite[16].

EPR measurements were carried out with a Varian X-band E-109 EPR spectrometer with a liquid nitrogen Dewar and an Air Product helitran LTD-13 cryostat for 77-K and 10-K measurements, respectively. Absorption spectrophotometry was performed with a Hitachi 557 recording spectrophotometer.

RESULTS AND DISCUSSION

Cytochrome c peroxidase, a monomeric protoheme-containing peroxidase of yeast, was shown by spectrophotometry[17] and magnetic susceptibility measurements[9] to undergo a spin transition from an essentially high-spin state at ambient temperature to a predominantly low-spin state at cryogenic temperature. Fig. 1 (top) illustrates an EPR spectrum of cytochrome c peroxidase at 77 K to show a predominantly low-spin character of the

8. Tamura, M.(1979) Biochim. Biophys. Acta 243, 249-258.
9. Iizuka, T., Kotani, M., and Yonetani, T. (1968) Biochim. Biophys. Acta 167, 257-267.
10. Blum, H., Chance, B., and Litchfield, W. J. (1978) Biochim. Biophys. Acta 534, 317-321.
11. Schulz, C. E., Rutter, R., Sage, J. T., Debrunner, P. G., and Hager, L. P. (1984) Biochemistry 23, 4743-4754.
12. Manthey, J. A., Boldt, N. J., Bocian, D. F., and Chan, S. I. (1986) J. Biol. Chem. 261, 6734-6741.
13. Yonetani, T. and Ray, G. S. (1965) J. Biol. Chem. 240, 4503-4508.
14. Yonetani, T., Chance, B., and Kajiwara, S. (1966) J. Biol. Chem. 241, 2981-2982.
15. Kendrew, J. C. and Parish, R. G. (1956) Proc. Roy. Soc. London A. 238, 305-324.
16. Yonetani, T. Yamamoto, H., Erman, J. E., Leigh, J. S., Jr., and Reed, G. H. (1972) J. Biol. Chem. 247, 2447-2455.
17. Yonetani, T., Wilson, D. F., and Seamonds, B. (1966) J. Biol. Chem. 241, 5347-5352.

372

enzyme, with EPR absorption extrema at $g_x = 2.70$, $g_y = 2.20$ and $g_z = 1.78$. The 1.7-Å X-ray structure of this peroxidase[18] shows that there is no internal strong-field ligand available in an inner-sphere coordination distance from the heme iron. This indicates that the low-spin state observed at 77 K may be produced by a "forced" axial bonding of a strong-field ligand to the heme iron in the distal crevice, as a result of a freezing-induced distortion or compression of the heme crevice.

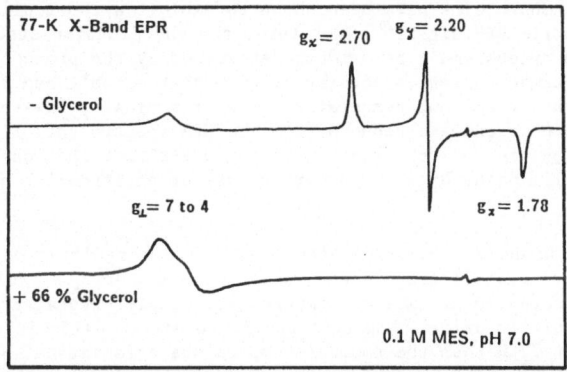

Fig. 1. X-band EPR spectra at 77 K of cytochrome c peroxidase (0.1 M Mes buffer, pH 7.0) in the absence and presence of 66% glycerol. Microwave frequency: 9.10 GHz, Modulation amplitude: 10 G, Microwave power: 20 mW.

The same preparation exhibits no low-spin EPR signals in the presence of 66% glycerol (Fig. 1, bottom). The disappearance of the low-spin signals is proportionally compensated by an increase in an ill-defined broad high-spin signal around $g = 7$ to 4. The line shape of this broad high-spin signal resembles that of the quantum-mechanical mixed-spin state reported by Maltempo and Moss[19]. EPR measurements at or near liquid helium temperature (Fig. 2) show also the transition from low-spin to high spin state upon addition of glycerol.

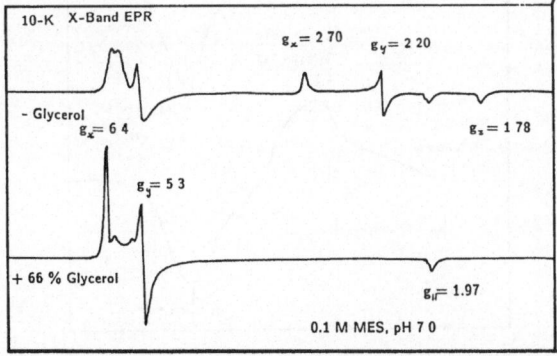

Fig. 2. X-band EPR spectra at 10 K of cytochrome c peroxidase (0.1 M Mes buffer, pH 7.0) in the absence and presence of 66% glycerol. Microwave frequency: 9.33 GHz, Modulation amplitude: 20 G, Microwave power: 1 mW.

18. Finzel, B. C., Poulos, T. L., and Kraut, J. (1984) J. Biol. Chem. 259, 13027-13036.
19. Maltempo, M. M., and Moss, T. H. (1976) Quart. Rev. Biophys. 9, 181-215.

However, the broad g = 7 to 4 EPR signal seen at 77 K is clearly derived from the temperature-dependent broadening of a rhombically-distorted axially symmetric high-spin signal with maxima at g_x = 6.4, g_y = 5.3 and g_z = 1.97 (Fig. 2, <u>bottom</u>).

The X-ray structure of cytochrome c peroxidase[18] shows that the ferric heme iron is essentially penta-coordinated, as the H_2O-595 in the distal crevice is at least 2.4 A away from the heme iron. Penta-coordinated high-spin ferric hemoproteins have been shown to exhibit a rhomically-distorted axially symmetric EPR signal[20]. Therefore, the coordination state of the heme group in cytochrome c peroxidase determined by the present EPR results at cryogenic temperatures is consistent with that established by the X-ray crystallography at ambient temperature. The predominatly low-spin character of cytochrome c peroxidase deduced from the EPR spectra (cf. Fig. 1, <u>top</u> and Fig. 2, <u>top</u>) is due to a freezing-induced artifact that can be effectively eliminated by the appropriate use of antifreezing agents like glycerol.

The heme-bound nitric oxide ligand in hemoglobin-nitric oxide has been shown by X-ray crystallographic analysis[21] to have a unique Pauling-type 145°-bent orientation at ambient temperature. Single-crystal EPR studies of myoglobin-nitric oxide[4] show that the bound nitric oxide is oriented differently at 77 K than the ambient-temperature orientation. However, the latter can gradually be shifted to the 77-K one by lowering the temperature[4]. Powder EPR studies of myoglobin-nitric oxide and model heme complexes[7,16,22] indicate that myoglobin-nitric oxide consists of two different states/species, high-temperature (HT) and low-temperature (LT) ones, which are in a temperature-dependent equilibrium. Thermodynamic

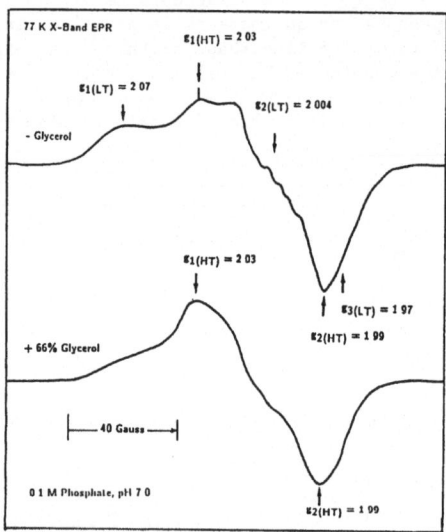

Fig. 3. X-band EPR spectra at 77 K of the myoglobin-nitric oxide complex (0.1 M phosphate buffer, pH 7.0) in the absence and presence of 66% glycerol. Microwave frequency: 9.1 GHz, Modulation amplitude: 6.3 G, Microwave power: 10 mW.

20. Yonetani, T. and Anni, H. (1987) J. Biol. Chem., submitted.
21. Deatherage, J. F. and Moffat, K. (1979) J. Mol. Biol. 134, 401-417.
22. Yoshimura, T., Ozaki, T., Shintani, Y., and Watanabe, H. (1979) Arch. Biochem. Biophys. 193, 301-313.

parameters of the equilibrium have also been determined[5]. Fig. 3 (top) illustrates the EPR spectrum of myoglobin-nitric oxide, which exhibits both HT and LT signals in agreement with previous reports[7,16].

In the presence of 66% glycerol (Fig. 3, bottom), the EPR spectrum of myoglobin-nitric oxide is essentially a HT type, which is indistinguishable from that measured at 20°C. The EPR spectrum of myoglobin-nitric oxide in the presence of glycerol is practically temperature-independent from ambient temperature to 77 K. This suggests that the LT species observed at cryogenic temperatures may be a freezing-induced artifact, which is again effectively eliminated in the presence of 66% glycerol.

These two examples of freezing-induced artifacts in hemoproteins and their circumvention with glycerol point to a previously neglected aspect of cryogenic-temperature studies. Obviously inclusion of anti-freezing agents at high concentrations, in hemoprotein systems under consideration, would impose in some cases serious technical difficulties. Especially noted are increased viscosity, dilution of samples, and possible adverse effects of anti-freezing agents themselves. High concentrations of methanol and ethylene glycol tend to denature proteins at ambient temperature, whereas glycerol appears to be the mildest of all, though it increases the viscosity.

ACKNOWLEDGEMENTS

This investigation has been supported in part by Research Grant PCM83-16935 from the National Science Foundation and Research Grant HL 14508 from the National Heart, Lung and Blood Institute.

CATALYTIC MECHANISM OF O_2 REDUCTION BY CYTOCHROME OXIDASE

Mårten Wikström

Department of Medical Chemistry, University of Helsinki
Siltavuorenpenger 10 A, SF-00170 Helsinki, Finland

In the past it has been thought that the reduction of O_2 to water catalysed by cytochrome oxidase would constitute an irreversible reaction step in the respiratiry chain. More recently it was shown that this is not the case, but that two consecutive one-electron steps of the catalytic cycle may be reversed at a high electrochemical proton gradient (1,2). This enabled identification of two spectrally distinct forms of the binuclear haem a_3-copper centre, as probable intermediates of the catalytic process of O_2 reduction. On the basis of such data a possible mechanism of catalysis has been proposed (1,2).

This paper deals with the approach to resolve the molecular mechanism of O_2 reduction through its reversal.

THE MISSING "PEROXY" INTERMEDIATE

Fig. 1 shows our view of the major intermediates of the catalytic cycle, based on its partial reversal in mitochondria (1,2). The states termed O, F and P are observed during the reversed reaction. We will return to these shortly.

In the upper part of the figure we have summarised our view (1-3) of the initial events in low-temperature kinetics of the forward reaction (4-6). Such studies have employed the "triple-trapping" technique (4), where the binuclear centre is initially in its reduced carbonmonoxy form. The primary intermediate generated on flash-photolysis in the presence of O_2 was called Compound A (4; Fig. 1), and was proposed to be an "oxy" compound.

With the fully reduced enzyme the next discernible intermediate is one in which electron transfer from cytochrome a and Cu_A has already occurred (4,5,6). (Note that this is not the case for Intermediate P in Fig. 1). This led to the sugestion that intramolecular electron transfer has already occurred in Compound A, for which a "peroxy" structure was therefore proposed (8-10). The "oxy" state was assumed to be too unstable to be detected (contrast 4).

However, when the "mixed valence" enzyme (with cytochrome a and Cu_A oxidised) is photolysed in the presence of O_2, Compound A is still formed

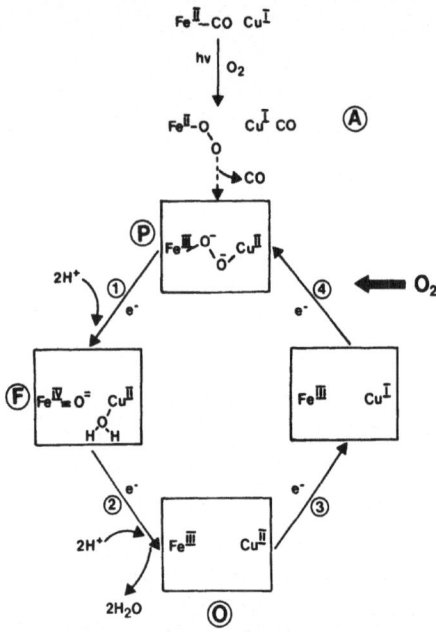

Figure 1. Model of catalytic mechanism of O_2 reduction at the binuclear centre of cytochrome oxidase (2; modified from refs. 1,3). For details, see the text.

primarily, but is followed by a "dead-end" state, Compound C, with peculiar properties. Compound C was not found on photolysis of the fully reduced enzyme, and was indeed not given any role in the catalytic cycle (4,6).

The first clue for a role of Compound C came from the finding that a species with spectral properties identical to it (see Fig. 2) was formed from the oxidised binuclear centre (O in Fig. 1) by reversed transfer of two electrons at room temperature (1,3). This strongly suggested that C (or P) is a "peroxy" species.

But two problems remained: Why is Compound C not observed in the forward reaction between fully reduced enzyme and dioxygen, but only with "mixed valence" enzyme ? And what is, then, the nature of Compound A ?

Alben et al. (11) demonstrated that photolysis of CO from Fe(II) of haem a_3 leads to binding of CO to Cu(I) at low temperatures. We therefore proposed the "oxy/carbonmonoxy" structure shown in Fig. 1 for Compound A (1,3; cf. 7). It seems very likely now that Compound C (or P, Fig. 1) is not generally observed in the forward reaction with the fully reduced enzyme because dissociation of CO from Cu_B in Compound A (Fig. 1) is much slower than subsequent electron transfer from cytochrome a or Cu_A (see also 7).

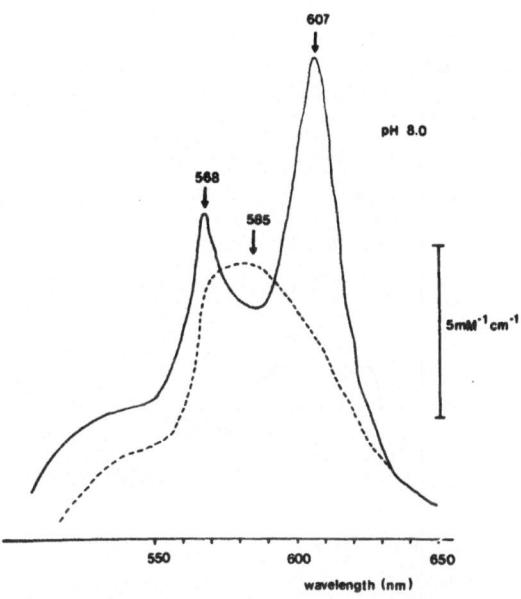

Figure 2. Difference spectra of Compound P (solid line) and Compound F (dashed line) vs. fully oxidised enzyme, as generated by reversed electron transfer in mitochondria (2; cf. 1).

BREAKING THE O-O BOND AND THE "FERRYL" COMPOUND

One-electron oxidation of the oxidised binuclear centre (plus water), as a result of reversed electron transfer (1-3), produced a species which was suggested to have a ferryl iron-cupric structure (F; Figs. 1,2).

Karlsson et al. (12) also proposed this structure for the low-temperature intermediate discernible next after Compound A (Intermediate II; see ref. 5). More recently Blair et al. (7) have suggested that one-electron reduction of the "peroxy" compound (P in Fig. 1) in fact first yields a ferrous-peroxy-cupric intermediate (not shown in Fig. 1), after which follows intramolecular electron transfer, breaking of the O-O bond, and formation of the ferryl species (F). The properties of the ferrous-peroxy intermediate are such that it would not be expected to be observed at room temperature where the equilibrium would lie far towards F (7).

Recently Witt et al. (13,14) have provided strong support for the proposal that F has a ferryl iron structure. They also showed that the optical spectrum seen during the forward reaction corresponds closely to that described in the reversed reaction (1,2). They have further clarified the relationship between "hydrogen peroxide adducts" or "oxyge-nated" enzyme observed earlier in various laboratories and the inter-mediates P and F (cf. below).

Fig. 2 shows the difference spectra of intermediates F and P, as generated by reserved electron transfer. The differential extinction coefficients (versus O) are about 6 and 12 $mM^{-1}cm^{-1}$, respectively. Wrigglesworth (15) and others have shown that addition of H_2O_2 to the oxidised enzyme yields the "peroxy" species P, and that F is formed at high peroxide concentrations. It is important to note, however, that the occupancy of P achieved this way is only about 10%, and that the spectra suggest admixtures of P, F and O states

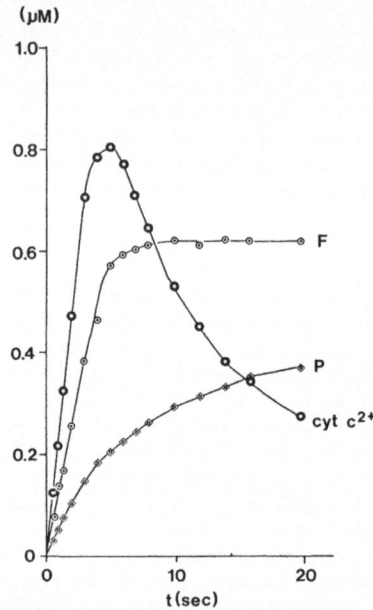

Figure 3. Kinetics of formation of P and F, and oxidoreduction of cytochrome c during reversed electron transfer. Rat liver mitoplasts (0.92 μM cytochrome oxidase) in 0.2M sucrose, 20 mM KCl, 20 mM HEPES-Tris, pH 8.3, with 2 μM rotenone, 5 μM myxothiazol, 0.1 mM EGTA, and 11 μM ferricytochrome c. Temperature 15°. At t=0 the reaction was started by adding 3 mM ATP. Cytochrome c(+c_1) was measured at 550-540 nm (16.5 mM^{-1}cm^{-1}). P and F were determined at 607-630 and 583-630 nm by spectral deconvolution, and using 12 cm^{-1} and 6 cm^{-1} as millimolar extinction coefficients (vs. oxidised enzyme; ref. 2).

KINETICS OF REVERSED ELECTRON TRANSFER

Fig.3 shows the ATP-induced kinetics of reduction of cytochrome c and formation of F and P from 0 (cf. Fig. 1) in mitoplasts supplemented with ferric cytochrome c. Addition of ferric cytochrome c augments the reaction (2), but it is still transient and incomplete in comparison with the case where an excess of ferricyanide serves as high-potential electron acceptor (1,2). However, this experiment proves that reversed electron transfer is indeed taking place. Moreover, as Fig. 3 shows, the occupancies of both F and P are substantial even in these conditions.

It may be seen from Fig. 3 that there is further generation of P during reoxidation of cytochrome c (2). This is due to forward electron transfer (see Fig. 1) from previously reduced cytochrome c to the binuclear centre in state 0, which yields P in the presence of dioxygen. P is relatively stable against conversion into F due to the optimal conditions for reversing reactions 1 and 2 (Fig. 1). As shown elsewhere (2), both F and P relax later more slowly into 0.

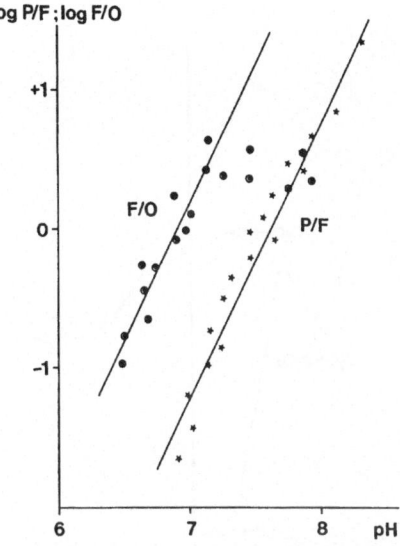

Figure 4. pH-dependence of the P/F and F/O equilibria. Rat liver mitochondria were suspended in sucrose-KCl-HEPES-Tris-EGTA with rotenone and myxothiazol (see legend to Fig. 3). In addition 4 mM potassium ferricyanide and 30 ng/ml nigericin were present. Temperature 25°. The reaction was started by 3 mM ATP. Concentrations of Compounds P and F were determined as in the legend to Fig. 3. The concentration of oxidised enzyme (0) was assumed to be equal to total enzyme minus (F+P). The straight lines have slopes of 2. Note the deviation of the F/O data from this slope above pH=7 (see the text).

PROTON UPTAKE IN REDUCTION OF DIOXYGEN

Both the conversion of 0 to F and of F to P (Fig. 1) are highly pH-dependent (1,2), and this pH-dependence is strictly specific for pH of the mitochondrial matrix (unpublished). Fig. 4 demonstrates the pH-dependence of the F/O and P/F equilibria. Both are consistent with uptake of 2 H^+ upon reduction, as indicated in Fig. 1. However, the behaviour of the F/O equilibrium above pH 7 may indicate that two protonable groups of the 0 state have similar pK values in the neighbourhood of 7.0. More data is required to ascertain this possibility.

This provides the first identification of the catalytic steps in which reduced dioxygen is protonated to water (see Fig. 1).

THERMODYNAMIC PROPERTIES OF THE CATALYTIC CYCLE

Fig. 5 summarises the $E_{m,7}$ values of the individual couples involved in one-electron reduction of O_2 to water (A), and for the first time provides an estimate of the $E_{m,7}$ values for the four one-electron couples of the catalytic cycle (Fig. 5B). The latter can be estimated (see refs. 1,2) from redox titrations of F and P in ATP-supplemented mitochondria, assuming that the binuclear centre resides roughly half-way within the membrane.

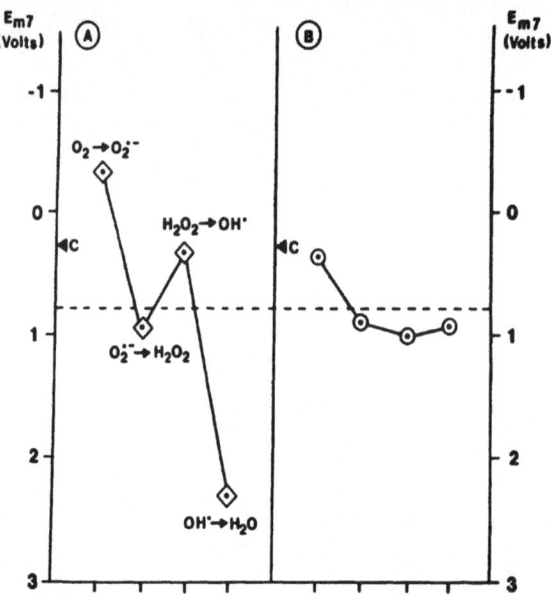

Figure 5. Midpoint redox potentials at pH=7 and 0.2 atm partial dioxygen pressure for the one-electron couples involved in O_2 reduction to water (A; ref. 3), and as estimated for the four one-electron couples of the catalytic cycle of cytochrome oxidase (B). In B the $E_{m,7}$ values are plotted in the order 3, 4, 1, and 2 (cf. Fig. 1 for the numbering).

It is clear from Fig. 5 that the catalytic metals of the binuclear centre have achieved considerable "smoothening" of the free energies of the individual one-electron steps. This is due to binding of intermediates to the metal centre, to its bimetallic nature, and to the property of iron allowing wide changes in valence. All this has made a unique catalytic path possible that maximises the velocity of the reduction of dioxygen in cell respiration. Simultaneously, the catalytic mechanism avoids release of toxic partially reduced oxygen intermediates (Fig. 1). Three of the four couples (1,2 and 4 in Fig. 1) are roughly equipotential at pH 7 and 0.2 atm dioxygen pressure, whereas the fourth (no. 3; Fig. 1) has a more negative $E_{m,7}$. This is consistent with the fact that it is the oxidised (O) state of the binuclear centre that accumulates in aerobic steady states.

REFERENCES

1. Wikström, M. (1981) Proc. Natl. Acad. Sci. USA 78, 4051-4054.
2. Wikström, M. (1987) Chemica Scripta, in press.
3. Wikström, M., Krab, K. and Saraste, M. (1981) Cytochrome Oxidase - A Synthesis, Academic Press, London and New York.
4. Chance, B., Saronio, C. and Leigh, J.S., Jr. (1975) J. Biol. Chem. 250, 9226-9237.
5. Clore, G.M., Andreasson, L.-E., Karlsson, B., Aasa, R. and Malmström, B.G. (1980) Biochem. J. 185, 139-154.
6. Clore, G.M., Andreasson, L.-E., Karlsson, B., Aasa, R. and Malmström, B.G. (1980) Biochem. J. 185, 155-167.
7. Blair, D.F., Witt, S.N. and Chan, S.I. (1985) J. Am. Chem. Soc. 107, 7389-7399.
8. Malmström, B.G. (1982) Annu. Rev. Biochem. 51, 21-59.
9. Wilson, M.T., Jensen, P., Aasa, R., Malmström, B.G. and Vänngård, T. (1982) Biochem. J. 203, 483-492.
10. Blair, D.F., Martin, C.T., Gelles, J., Wang, H., Brudvig, G.W., Stevens, T.H. and Chan, S.I. (1983) Chemica Scripta 21, 43-53.
11. Fiamingo, F.G., Altschuld, R.A., Moh, P.P. and Alben, J.O. (1982) J. Biol. Chem. 257, 1639-1650.
12. Karlsson, B., Aasa, R., Vänngård, T. and Malmström, B.G. (1981) FEBS Lett. 131, 186-188.
13. Witt, S.N., Blair, D.F. and Chan, S.I. (1986) J. Biol. Chem. 261, 8104-8107.
14. Witt, S.N., and Chan, S.I. (1987) J Biol. Chem. 262, 1446-1448.
15. Wrigglesworth, J.M. (1984) Biochem. J. 217, 715-719.

THE ELECTRON-TRANSFER REACTIONS IN AND SUBSTRATE BINDING TO
CYTOCHROME C OXIDASE

B.F.van Gelder, A.C.F.Gorren, L.Vlegels and R.Wever

Department of Biochemistry, University of Amsterdam
Plantage Muidergracht 12, 1018 TV Amsterdam
The Netherlands

INTRODUCTION

Cytochrome $\underline{c}$ oxidase, containing the redox centres: cytochrome $\underline{a}$, Cu_A and the binuclear centre cytochrome $\underline{a}_3$-Cu_B, transfers electrons from cytochrome $\underline{c}$ to dioxygen.

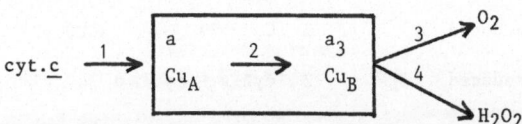

Fig.1 Scheme of electron transfer between cytochrome $\underline{c}$ oxidase
and its substrates. Numbers denote reaction steps.

Fig.1 shows schematically the various steps in the electron transfer
reaction. The first step (marked 1) is the binding of cytochrome $\underline{c}$ to the
oxidase followed by a fast electron transfer from the heme of cytochrome $\underline{c}$
to that of cytochrome $\underline{a}$. The latter reaction is so fast that the rate constant of the electron transfer could not be determined. The binding reaction the rate of which was measured by stopped flow and the radiolysis
technique [1-5], is also fast (cf Table I). The rate is strongly pH dependent and decreases at higher ionic strength, indicating that attractive
electrostatic forces affect the interaction between cytochrome $\underline{c}$ and the
oxidase. Although it has been suggested that the attraction is governed
by dipole-dipole interactions between the cytochromes [6], there is recent
data available, suggesting that the binding is ruled by local charges on
the cytochromes.

The Cu_A depicted close to cytochrome $\underline{a}$ in the scheme (Fig.1) accepts
an electron from cytochrome $\underline{a}$. Both redox centres are in rapid equilibrium.

The second observable phase in the reaction, marked 2 in Fig.1, is
the electron transfer from cytochrome $\underline{a}$ or Cu_A to the binuclear redox
centre cytochrome $\underline{a}_3$-Cu_B. The rate of the internal electron transfer in
cytochrome $\underline{c}$ oxidase is variable and modulated by the state of cytochrome $\underline{c}$
oxidase. In "resting" enzyme, i.e. the oxidized species as isolated, the

385

electron transfer to cytochrome $\underline{a}_3$ is extremely slow (0.5 s^{-1}). Upon changing the conformation of the enzyme to the "pulsed" state by reduction and subsequent oxidation as shown by Brunori and Antonini [7], the electron transfer of the second phase increases by a factor of about 5. However, this rate and that of the resting ezyme are too small to explain the turn-over number of 100 s^{-1} of the steady-state oxidation of cytochrome $\underline{c}$ by dioxygen mediated by cytochrome $\underline{c}$ oxidase.

Table I Kinetic constants of electron transfer in and substrate binding to cytochrome $\underline{c}$ oxidase.

substrate	state of oxidase	reaction*	value	ref.
cyt.$\underline{c}$	oxidized	1	10^8 M$^{-1}\cdot$s^{-1}	1-5
+	"resting"	2	0.5 s^{-1}	1-5
O_2	pulsed	2	2-5 s^{-1}	7
	enzymic	TN	100 s^{-1}	8
_	mixed valence anaerobic + CO	2 (Cu$_A$←cyt.$\underline{a}_3$)	7000 s^{-1}	10
	reduced	2 (Cu$_A$→cyt.$\underline{a}_3$)	6000 s^{-1}	9
O_2	reduced	2 (cyt.$\underline{a}$→cyt.$\underline{a}_3$)	700 s^{-1}	1
	reduced	3	10^8 M$^{-1}\cdot$s^{-1}	11
	reduced	2	16 s^{-1}	19,this paper
	reduced (peroxy.comp.)	2	$>10^2$ s^{-1}	this paper
H_2O_2	reduced	4	$2\cdot10^4$M$^{-1}\cdot$s^{-1}	18,19
	mixed valence (centre red.)	4	$2\cdot10^4$M$^{-1}\cdot$s^{-1}	18
	mixed valence (centre ox.)	4	700 M$^{-1}\cdot$s^{-1}	this paper
	oxidized	4	700 M$^{-1}\cdot$s^{-1}	19

* the numbers refer to the reaction phase in Fig.1.

In the presence of oxygen, however, the rate of electron transfer of the second phase increases considerably. Gibson and Greenwood found a value of 700s^{-1} for the rate constant of the electron flow from cytochrome a to the binuclear centre [1] and of 6000 s^{-1} between Cu$_A$ and the centre [9]. The internal electron flow in cytochrome $\underline{c}$ oxidase is also extremely rapid when under anaerobic conditions mixed valence carboxy-cytochrome $\underline{c}$ oxidase (centre reduced, cytochrome $\underline{a}$ and Cu$_A$ oxidized) is photolysed. Due to a change of redox potential of the centre, a redistribution of electrons occurs in cytochrome $\underline{c}$ oxidase. Boelens et al [10] found upon illumination a value of 7000 s^{-1} for the rate of electron transfer from the centre to Cu$_A$.

It has been suggested [7,12-14] that the rapid internal electron transfer rate is caused by the peroxy compound of cytochrome c oxidase. However, since the internal electron transfer in the presence of carbomonoxyde under anaerobic conditions is as rapid as in the presence of oxygen, it is concluded that not only the peroxy compound but also a compound that stabilizes the conformation, in which the centre is reduced and has a high redox potential, increases the internal electron transfer rate of cytochrome c oxidase.

It has been shown [15-19] that hydrogen peroxide can oxidize cytochrome c oxidase and that the compound can be used as electron acceptor in cytochrome c oxidase mediated oxidation of cytochrome c. The study of the oxidation of fully reduced cytochrome c oxidase (4 electrondonor) by hydrogen peroxide (2 electronacceptor) is of interest, since the reaction occurs in two steps, is much slower than the oxygen reaction and takes place at the binuclear centre, to which also dioxygen (4 electron acceptor) binds.

In this paper we will discuss mainly the data from our laboratory reported by Gorren et al. [18,19] about the oxidation of cytochrome c oxidase by hydrogen peroxide and moreover we will add some new data.

The reaction with hydrogen peroxide

Gorren et al. [19] showed that at low hydrogen-peroxide concentration (µM range) the oxidation rate of cytochrome a (measured at 428 nm), Cu_A (at 830 nm), cytochrome a_3 (at 436 nm) and of the binuclear centre (at 655 nm) is equally fast and linearly dependent on the hydrogen-peroxide concentration. This result indicates that the binding of hydrogen peroxide to the oxidase is the rate determining step in the reaction. The rate constant of binding was found to be $2 \cdot 10^4$ $M^{-1} \cdot s^{-1}$. The value of this constant is the same as that determined after photodissociation of mixed valence carboxy-cytochrome c oxidase in the presence of hydrogen-peroxide [18]. This shows that the reduced binuclear centre of cytochrome c oxidase has the same affinity for the oxidant whether or not cytochrome a and Cu are reduced or oxidized. However, when the binuclear centre is oxidized, such as in "pulsed" cytochrome c oxidase, the rate of binding of hydrogen peroxide is much slower and a value for the rate constant of 700 $M^{-1} \cdot s^{-1}$ could be calculated from the data [19].

The rate of oxidation of cytochrome a_3 by dioxygen is much faster than with hydrogen peroxide. Greenwood and Gibson [11] found for this reaction a value of the rate constant which is about 4 orders of magnitude greater than that for the reaction with hydrogen peroxide. Therefore, we conclude that the feature of cytochrome c oxidase to function as a peroxidase is of little physiological importance.

At higher hydrogen-peroxide concentrations (mM range), however, the rate of oxidation of cytochrome a and Cu_A lag behind that of the binuclear centre [19]. This shows that under these conditions the binuclear centre is oxidized faster than cytochrome a and Cu_A. Thus, the internal electron-transfer step in cytochrome c oxidase seems to become rate determining. Furthermore, it can be concluded that the site of binding of hydrogen peroxide is at the binuclear centre of cytochrome c oxidase.

Fig. 2 displays the relationship between the observed first-order rate constant of the oxidation of cytochrome a and the hydrogen peroxide concentration in the mM range. A biphasic curve was obtained with a linear dependence of the rate constant at the higher hydrogen-peroxide concentrations. The rate constant, calculated from the straight part of the curve, was found to be 700 $M^{-1} \cdot s^{-1}$. This value is the same as that found in the reaction of oxidized cytochrome c oxidase with hydrogen peroxide. Therefore, we attribute

the rate constant to the binding of a second molecule of hydrogen peroxide to
mixed valence cytochrome c oxidase in which the binuclear centre is oxidized
and cytochrome a and Cu_A are reduced.

It should be pointed out that the redox state of the centre is of
importance for the rate of binding of hydrogen peroxide to cytochrome c
oxidase. Apparently, when the centre is oxidized the access of ligands to the
centre is more difficult than when the centre is reduced. This phenomenon has
also been observed with cyanide by Van Buuren et al. [20,21]. They proposed a
closed (more compact) conformation for the oxidized species and an open one
for the reduced enzyme.

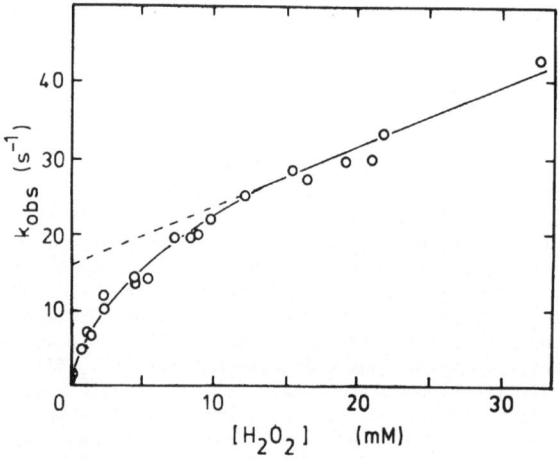

Fig.2 Dependence of the rate of oxidation of cytochrome a
on the H_2O_2 concentration.
For experimental details cf. Material and Methods of Ref.19.

Extrapolating the straight part of the curve in Fig.2 to zero hydrogen
peroxide concentration reveals a rate constant of 16 s^{-1}. We assign this
rate constant to the internal electron transfer after that the first molecule
of hydrogen peroxide has reacted with reduced cytochrome c oxidase. After complete reduction of the oxidant by donation of both electrons from the binuclear centre, the centre becomes oxidized and a slow electron transfer occurs
from cytochrome a and Cu_A. The transfer is slightly faster (factor 3) than
when the internal electron transfer was studied by rapid kinetics between
reduced cytochrome c and pulsed cytochrome c oxidase. Interestingly, in both
reactions no peroxy intermediate of cytochrome c oxidase is present.

The linear dependence of the observed rate constant of cytochrome a oxidation and hydrogen peroxide at the higher concentrations indicates that the
binding of hydrogen peroxide to the oxidized binuclear centre, whereby the

peroxy intermediate might be formed, increases considerably the internal electron transfer rate of cytochrome $\underline{c}$ oxidase. From the data it could be estimated that upon formation of the peroxy compound the internal electron-transfer rate constant increases to a value greater than 10^2 s^{-1}.

It would be of interest to increase the hydrogen peroxide concentration in order to obtain conditions in which the internal electron flow to the peroxy compound becomes rate determining. Since the binding reaction of hydrogen peroxide with the oxidized binuclear centre is slow, the kinetic measurements should be carried out in the molar concentration range of the oxidant. Under these extreme conditions, cytochrome $\underline{c}$ oxidase is too unstable for measuring accurate rate constants. However, it is evident from our data that the peroxy compound of the oxidized binuclear centre stimulates greatly the internal electron flow in cytochrome $\underline{c}$ oxidase.

Fig.3 shows a scheme for the oxidation of cytochrome $\underline{c}$ oxidase by hydrogen peroxide. For simplicity the redox centre of Cu_A and Cu_B, associated with cytochrome $\underline{a}$ and cytochrome $\underline{a_3}$, respectively, are left out.

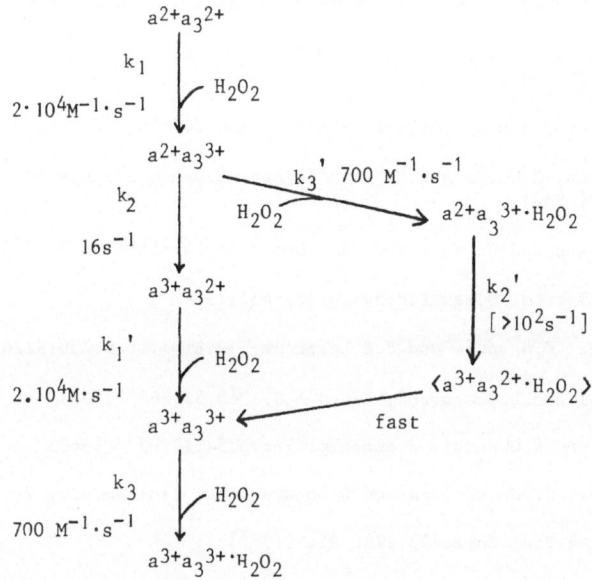

Fig. 3 Scheme for the oxidation of cytochrome $\underline{c}$ oxidase by H_2O_2 $\cdot$ $\underline{a}$ and $\underline{a_3}$ represent the redox centres of cytochrome $\underline{a}$ and cytochrome $\underline{a_3}$, respectively. For the simplicity the Cu_A and Cu_B are deleted.

At low hydrogen peroxide concentrations the reaction steps at the left occur. At higher concentrations of hydrogen peroxide, the reaction of the oxidized binuclear centre with hydrogen peroxide (k_3') is faster than the internal electron flow to the binuclear centre to which no oxygen compound is bound (k_2). Due to the stimulation of the internal electron transfer by the peroxy compound, the electrons from cytochrome $\underline{a}$ and Cu_A will mainly take the shunt for the complete oxidation of cytochrome $\underline{c}$ oxidase. This path is also followed when oxygen is the substrate for cytochrome $\underline{c}$ oxidase and under enzymical conditions.

References

1. Q.H.Gibson, C.Greenwood, D.C.Wharton and G.Palmer, J.Biol.Chem. 240: 888-894(1965).

2. K.J.H.van Buuren, B.F.van Gelder, J.Wilting and R.Braams, Biochim.Biophys.Acta 333:421-427(1974).

3. M.T.Wilson, C.Greenwood, M.Brunori and E.Antonini, Biochem.J. 147: 145-153(1975).

4. E.C.I.Veerman, J.Wilms, G.Casteleijn and B.F.van Gelder, Biochim.Biophys.Acta 590:117-127(1980).

5. T.M.Antalis and G.Palmer, J.Biol.Chem. 257:6194-6206(1982)

6. W.H.Koppenhol, Biophys.J. 29:493-508(1980)

7. M.Brunori, A.Colosimo, G.Rainoni, M.T.Wilson and E.Antonini, J.Biol.Chem. 254:10769-10775(1979)

8. J.Wilms, J.L.M.L.van Rijn and B.F.van Gelder, Biochim.Biophys.Acta 593:17-23(1980)

9. C.Greenwood and Q.H.Gibson, J.Biol.Chem. 240:2694-2698(1965)

10. R.Boelens, R.Wever and B.F.van Gelder, Biochim.Biophys.Acta 682: 264-272(1982)

11. Q.H.Gibson and C.Greenwood, Biochem.J.86:541-554(1963)

12. B.G.Malmström, Q.Rev.Biophys.6:389-431(1974)

13. B.Chance, C.Saronio and J.S.Leigh Jr., J.Biol.Chem.250:9226-9237(1975)

14. B.C.Hill and C.Greenwood, Biochem.J. 215:659-667(1983)

15. Y.Orii and K.Okunuki, J.Biochem.(Tokyo)54:207-213(1963)

16. D.Bickar, J.Bonaventura and C.Bonaventura, Biochemistry 21:2661-2666(1982)

17. Y.Orii, J.Biol.Chem.257:9246-9248(1982)

18. A.C.F.Gorren, H.Dekker and R.Wever, Biochim.Biophys.Acta 809:90-96 (1985)

19. A.C.F.Gorren, H.Dekker and R.Wever, Biochim.Biophys.Acta 852:81-92 (1986)

20. K.J.H.van Buuren, P.F.Zuurendonk, B.F.van Gelder and A.O.Muijsers, Biochim.Biophys.Acta 256:243-257(1972)

21. K.J.H.van Buuren, P.Nicholls and B.F.van Gelder, Biochim.Biophys.Acta 256:258-276(1972)

CONTROL OF CYTOCHROME OXIDASE IN PROTEOLIPOSOMES:

FLUX AND STOICHIOMETRY

P. Nicholls, S. Shaughnessy*, and A.P. Singh+

Department of Biological Sciences
Brock University, St. Catharines
Ontario, Canada L2S 3A1

ABSTRACT

The fluorescent pH indicator pyranine was trapped in sonicated proteoliposomes containing cytochrome c oxidase. The steady state pH gradient (alkaline inside) is directly proportional to the oxidase turnover. A maximum ΔpH of between 0.35 and 0.45 pH units is obtained. The rate of pH gradient formation is increased by valinomycin; at low valinomycin levels a corresponding increase is seen in steady state ΔpH. Either nigericin or FCCP prevent ΔpH formation, but nigericin stimulates an increase in membrane potential, $\Delta\psi$, an effect partially reversed by valinomycin. Levels of valinomycin which abolish $\Delta\psi$ but increase ΔpH, also inhibit proteoliposomal respiration. Conversion of $\Delta\psi$ into ΔpH may thus increase respiratory control. Both steady state ΔpH and the rate of alkalinization were decreased by 50% upon treatment of the vesicles with DCCD, both in the presence and absence of valinomycin. Two separable oxidase-mediated processes may thus contribute to this alkalinization: proton uptake due to the reduction of molecular oxygen and vectorial proton translocation. The DCCD inhibition suggests (i) that these processes are intrinsic and not ionophore-induced, and (ii) that H^+-pumping occurs continuously in steady state and not merely as a transient following oxidant or reductant pulses.

INTRODUCTION

Cytochrome oxidase generates an electrochemical gradient by translocating electrons from cytochrome c at the 'C' face of the inner mitochondrial membrane to oxygen at the $^{'}M'$ face (1). When counterion movement is permitted the oxidase can also be seen to function as a proton pump, moving protons across the membrane (2-5). Although the vectorial origin of these protons was originally questioned by Mitchell and Moyle (6), its reality is now generally accepted (7). Nevertheless, the extent of H^+ pumping is variable (5), its steady state action has yet to be shown, and Archbold et al (8) suggested that H^+ appearance is dependent upon the presence of K^+ plus valinomycin.

*Present address: Dept. of Pathology,
                  McMaster University   +Deceased 23 June 1985
                  Hamilton, Ontario L8N 3Z5.

Wikström (2) and coworkers (9) monitored the establishment of ΔpH in mitochondria and in submitochondrial particles with neutral red, while Hinkle and Wrigglesworth (10-13) used phenol red to follow respiration-dependent internal alkalinization of cytochrome c oxidase vesicles. Pyranine (14, 15, 16) is an alternative fluorescent pH probe. Its trianion character at all physiological pH values renders it less permeable and more reliable than the phthaleins. DiS-C$_3$-(5) can similarly be used to monitor membrane potential changes (17, 18).

We use these two probes to follow pH gradients and membrane potentials in cytochrome oxidase-containing proteoliposomes. Under steady state conditions, both in presence and absence of valinomycin, the observed internal alkalinization depends upon two processes: (a) the consumption of protons when oxygen is reduced to water, and (b) proton pumping by the oxidase. These processes may be distinguished using DCCD, which inhibits proton translocation (19), perhaps by binding to a glutamyl residue of subunit III of the oxidase (20), although this latter interpretation has been questioned by Puettner et al (21). Our experiments show that internal vesicle alkalinization is also inhibited 50% by DCCD, both in presence and absence of valinomycin, supporting the concept of a binary process of charge transfer across the membrane. We have also examined the action of ionophores and uncouplers on respiration rate, pH gradient, and membrane potential. With Moroney et al (22), we conclude that these two components of the p.m.f. are not kinetically interchangeable. In proteoliposomes ΔpH may be more important than $\Delta\psi$ in controlling oxidase turnover.

MATERIALS AND METHODS

Chemicals: Cytochrome c (type VI, horse heart), sodium ascorbate, TMPD, DCCD, and valinomycin were Sigma products, and pyranine was from Eastman Kodak. Nigericin was from Calbiochem-Behring, FCCP was a gift of Dr. P. G. Heytler (Dupont Chemical Co.), and the carbocyanine dye diS-C$_3$-(5) was a gift of Dr. Alan Waggoner (Carnegie-Mellon University).

Preparation of cytochrome c oxidase and pyranine entrapped cytochrome oxidase vesicles: Beef heart cytochrome oxidase was prepared according to Kuboyama et al., (23), as described (5). The enzyme had a haem a:protein ratio of not less than 8.5 μmole/g and a maximal turnover (electrons/cyt. aa$_3$/s) of 430 s^{-1} at 30°C and pH 7.4. Pyranine-containing cytochrome oxidase vesicles were prepared according to Proteau et al. (5), using asolectin (40% L-α-phosphatidylcholine, Sigma type IV-S) and cytochrome oxidase to give a phospholipid/protein weight ratio of 80:1. External pyranine was removed by passage through G-25 Sephadex. For the DCCD treatment, cytochrome oxidase vesicles containing 2.3 μM cytochrome aa$_3$ and 50 mg lipid/ml with entrapped pyranine were pretreated with the indicated concentrations of DCCD at 4°C for 12-15 hrs, prior to assay.

Fluorescence and Polarographic Measurements: Pyranine and diS-C$_3$-(5) measurements were carried out in a multipurpose cuvette system (24), exciting pyranine fluorescence at 460 nm and following the resulting emission as in (18), or exciting carbocyanine fluorescence at 622 nm with measurement using a 670 nm cut-off filter. The pK of internally trapped pyranine was 7.5, compared with the pK of 7.2 reported for free pyranine (15). Simultaneous oxygen uptake measurements were carried out using a Clark oxygen electrode inserted horizontally into the wall of the cuvette.

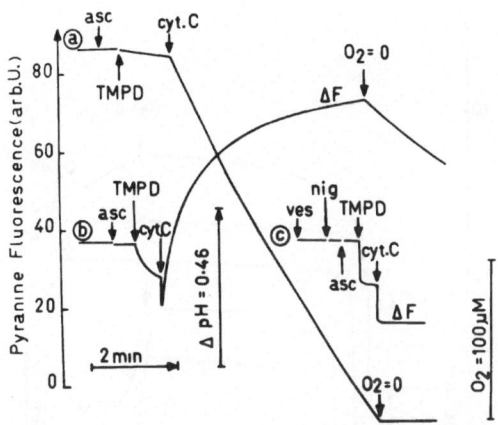

Fig. 1: Respiration-dependent internal alkalinization and oxygen uptake of proteoliposomes. Vesicles containing pyranine (1.8 mg lipid ml^{-1} and 0.11 μM cytochrome aa_3) in 2.8 ml 5mM (K$^+$) MOPS, pH 7.2, 100 mM KCl, 30°C. Oxidase turnover with 14mM ascorbate, 0.26mM TMPD, and 3.7 μM c. (a) O_2 electrode, (b) and (c), pyranine fluorescence; (b) control, (c) + 0.7 μg ml^{-1} nigericin.

RESULTS

Fig. 1 shows a typical experiment in which oxygen uptake and pyranine fluorescence were followed synchronously. Ascorbate and TMPD addition give little respiratory stimulation (trace a) but promote a decrease in pyranine fluorescence (trace b). Activation of turnover by addition of cytochrome c induces a rapid increase in pyranine fluorescence which reaches a steady state corresponding to an internal alkalinization of about 0.35 units and then collapses upon anaerobiosis (trace b).

As shown previously (13, 25), the internal alkalinization is modulated by ionophores and uncouplers. In the absence of valinomycin, the internal alkalinization rate is slow (Fig. 2, trace a) and the subsequent collapse upon anaerobiosis is also slow. In the presence of low levels of valinomycin (Fig. 2, trace b) the initial rate of alkalinization is about 5 times greater, and the collapse upon anaerobiosis is slightly faster. A maximal pH gradient of not more than 0.4 pH units is increased to a value of 0.6 units in the presence of valinomycin (cf. Fig. 2, traces a and b), when the latter is added in small amounts. When the valinomycin concentration is increased, a dramatic change is seen in the pattern (Fig. 2, traces c-e). While the initial rate of alkalinization is unchanged, the steady state ΔpH is sharply diminished, and while at high valinomycin levels the respiration rate increases, at low levels it is diminished (cf. anaerobiosis times in traces (b) through (e) in Fig. 2).

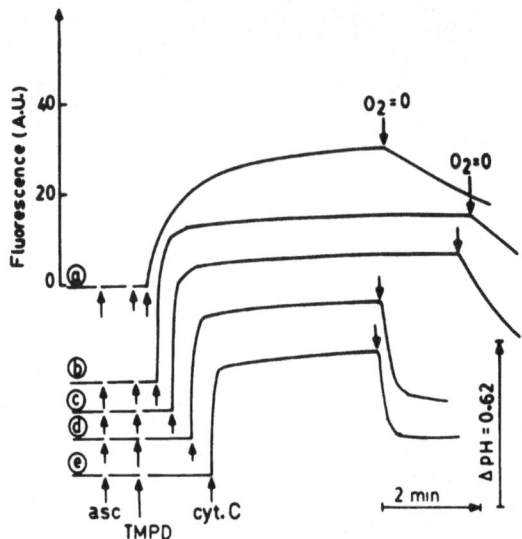

Fig. 2: Effect of valinomycin concentration on ΔpH. Pyranine fluorescence monitored as in Fig. 1. (a) Control; (b) + 3.6 ng/ml valinomycin; (c) + 36 ng/ml valinomycin; (d) + 360 ng/ml valinomycin; (e) + 700 ng/ml valinomycin.

The effect of nigericin (in the presence and absence of valinomycin) on the respiratory rate and upon pyranine fluorescence is shown in Fig. 3. Preincubation of cytochrome c oxidase-containing proteoliposomes in a KCl containing buffer with nigericin results in an inhibition of steady state alkalinization. Nigericin also stimulates respiration yet promotes an increased $\Delta\psi$ (cf. ref. 25). Electroneutral H^+/K^+ exchange by nigericin reduces the ΔpH, as shown by the data in Fig. 3. Stimulation of respiration by nigericin alone parallels its effect on ΔpH (Fig. 3). On addition of valinomycin, the respiration rates increase compared to those with nigericin alone (Fig. 3, upper traces), although ΔpH is now larger (Fig. 3, lower traces). Valinomycin reverses the effect of nigericin by permitting a electrogenic entry of K^+, allowing ΔpH to reform.

Fig. 4 shows that the rate of internal alkalinization and the steady state ΔpH are proportional to cytochrome c oxidase turnover, whether respiratory rate was adjusted by varying ascorbate (Fig. 4a) or by adding cyanide (Fig. 4b). However, if respiration is stimulated by addition of lauryl maltoside (cf. ref. 26), the measured pH gradient declines as the activity increases (Fig. 5). The latter effect occurs over a narrower concentration range than the former, suggesting a critical ΔpH for release of oxidase activity. But release of intrinsic activity (26) complicates the interpretation.

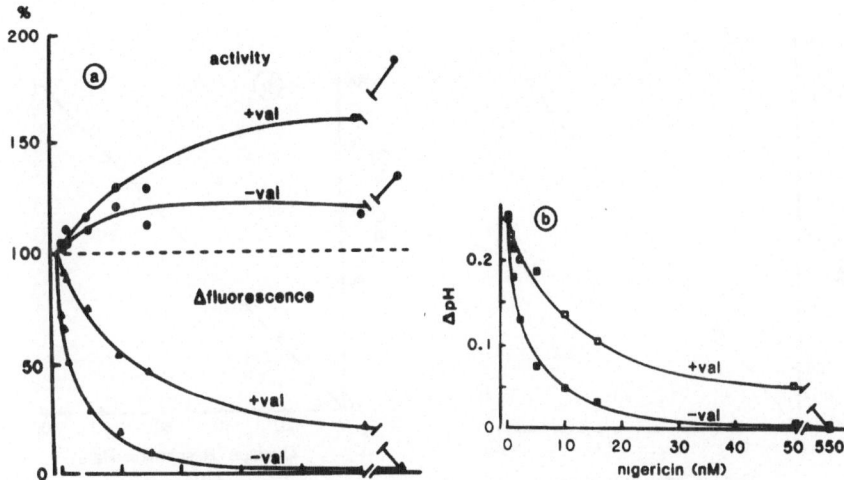

Fig. 3: Effect of nigericin on oxidase activity and ΔpH. Pyranine-
containing vesicles (3.7 mg/ml lipid, 0.19 μM cytochrome aa_3)
in 2.7 ml 5 mM (K^+) MOPS plus 100mM KCl buffer, pH 7.2, 30°C.
Reaction initiated with 14.8mM sodium ascorbate, 0.26 mM TMPD,
and 3.7 μM cytochrome c. ΔpH formation in absence and presence
of 0.38 μg/ml valinomycin. (a) oxidase activity (upper traces)
and pyranine fluorescence (lower traces): (b) calculated pH
gradients.

The effects of incubation with DCCD on oxidase turnover and on
internal alkalinization are summarized in Table I. Both in the presence
and absence of valinomycin, the effects are biphasic, showing sensitive
and less sensitive phases, with an intermediate plateau between 0.2 and
0.5 mM DCCD. The second phase is accompanied by declines in respiratory
rates and respiratory control values, indicating nonspecific effects. But
the early inhibition of internal alkalinization, approximating 50% at
relatively low DCCD levels (Table I), resembles the early inhibition of
$\Delta\psi$-dependent $BTPP^+$ (permeant cation) accumulation seen under similar
conditions (27).

Table 1. Effect of DCCD on oxidase activity and on pH gradient formation.

[DCCD] mM	Activity (μMO_2/s/μM aa_3)	ΔF (%)	ΔpH
0	28.3	40	0.46
0.04	28.3	29	0.33
0.08	29.3	25	0.29
0.12	30.0	18	0.20
0.16	31.0	18	0.20
0.20	28.3	18	0.20

Pyranine-loaded vesicles (5 mg. lipid, 0.1 μM cytochrome aa_3) in
2.4 ml. 5 mM K^+/Tricine/MES buffer pH 7.4, 30°C. Respiration on 15 mM
ascorbate, 0.26 mM TMPD, 3.7 μM cyt. c.

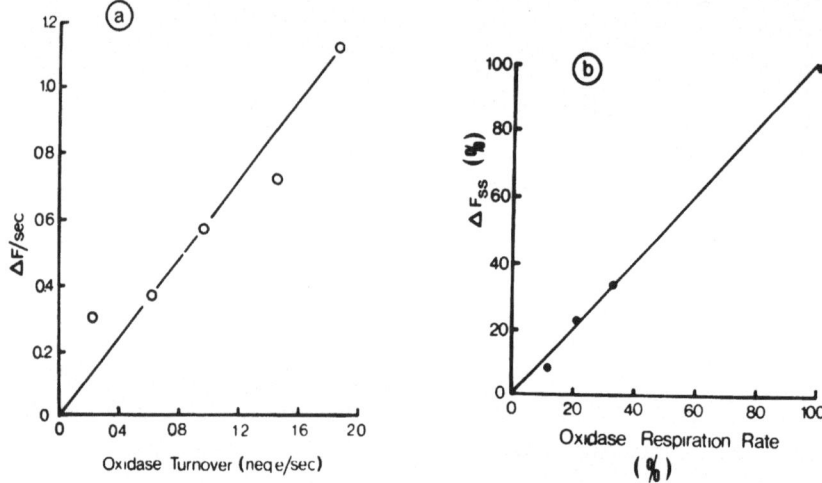

Fig. 4: Effect of electron flux on internal alkalinization. Pyranine-containing vesicles (0.75 mg lipid ml^{-1} and 0.19 μM cytochrome aa$_3$) in 2.7 ml 5mM Tricine/Mes buffer, pH 7.4, 7.5 mM choline chloride, 0.4 mM KCl, and 1.9 μg/ml valinomycin. Oxidase turnover initiated with 3.7 μM cytochrome c: (a) altering ascorbate concentration between 0.35 mM and 5.7 mM; (b) adding 15 mM ascorbate + 0.26 mM TMPD, and altering KCN concentrations from 0 to 36 μM.

DISCUSSION

In the absence of valinomycin the observed rate of proteoliposomal alkalinization is limited by the slowness of the charge compensating influx of cations (28). In its presence, potassium moves freely and the alkalinization rate reflects the respiration rate (13). At high levels of valinomycin there is a stimulation of potassium/proton exchange. The maximal ΔpH observed was 0.6 pH units in the presence and 0.4 to 0.5 pH units in the absence of valinomycin, as found with phenol red (11-13). Under limited turnover conditions Casey et al. (29) reported an internal alkalinization of 0.23 pH units. Hinkle obtained a ΔpH of 0.8 pH units in dialysed reconstituted cytochrome c oxidase vesicles (10). An indirect measure of ΔpH obtained from the partial collapse of Δψ assuming constancy of ΔμH$^+$, is of a similar magnitude to that obtained directly.

The ΔpH generated in the steady state is a linear function of respiration rate (Fig. 4), whereas Krishnamoorthy and Hinkle (30) found a nonlinear relationship between ΔμH$^+$ and respiration rate in rat liver mitochondria. Variation in Δψ may be responsible for the nonlinearity; O'Shea et al. (31) reported that Δψ is indeed a nonlinear function of respiration rate in pyranine-containing proteoliposomes. ΔpH, rather than Δψ, may be the major component of ΔμH$^+$ responsible for respiratory control of vesicular cytochrome c oxidase is suggested; in the absence of nigericin, addition of a small amount of valinomycin, sufficient to collapse Δψ, and to increase pH inhibits respiration (Fig. 2). With increasing valinomycin levels turnover increases, and simultaneously ΔpH decreases. Moroney et al. (22) have shown that ΔpH has specific spectroscopic effects on the oxidase that cannot be duplicated by a thermodynamically equivalent membrane potential.

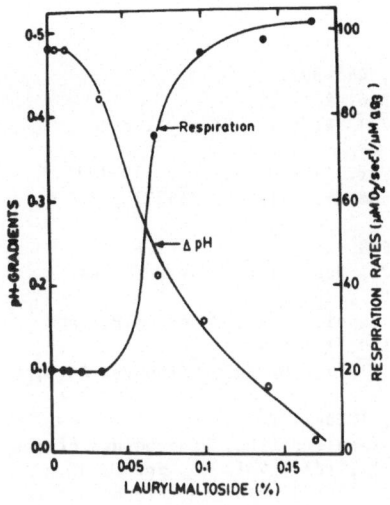

Fig. 5: Effect of lauryl maltoside
on pH gradient and activity.
Pyranine-containing vesicles
monitored as in Fig. 1 in
presence of increasing levels
of lauryl maltoside.
o ---- o, left ordinate:
pH gradient; ● ---- ●,
right ordinate: oxidase
turnover.

The transmembranous pumping of protons, but not the reduction of
oxygen to hydroxyl ions, is sensitive to inhibition by DCCD (19). An
inhibition of internal alkalinization is seen in vesicles treated with
DCCD (Table I), which reaches a maximum of 50% between 0.2 and 0.6 mM
DCCD, supporting the model according to which the alkalinization has a
dual origin. In the absence of valinomycin, the same phenomenon occurs as
in its presence, despite the fact that when it is not present, proton
translocation is not observed to accompany oxygen pulses in anaerobic
systems (2-5), and some workers question its occurrence in the absence of
charge compensation (8). Why therefore is 50% inhibition of internal
alkalinization observed after DCCD preincubation, in the absence of
valinomycin? In the absence of valinomycin proton translocation must still
occur, with one proton extruded externally for every electron transferred.
Under these conditions, the $\Delta\psi$ created induces the influx of two
compensating positive charges. In order for proton translocation not to
be seen (8), at least one proton must enter for every proton pumped out;
in addition, up to one potassium ion may flow in (28). In order for
internal alkalinization to be observed, <u>less than</u> two protons must
move in for every pumped proton. The H+ influx/K+ influx ratio depends on
the ratios of concentrations and permeability coefficients. In the DCCD-
treated system, proton pumping is inhibited; only one positive charge is
required internally to compensate for the passage of one electron.
Therefore, half as many protons are needed as well as half as many
potassium ions, compared to the uninhibited system. Since only half as
many potassium ions move, the internal alkalinization will be reduced by
50% even in the absence of valinomycin. The DCCD inhibition therefore
supports (i) the idea that the internal alkalinization is a consequence of
two separable processes, and (ii) the previously implicit conclusion that
both processes occur in the absence of charge-compensating ionophores as
well as in their presence.

ACKNOWLEDGMENTS

This work was supported by Canadian NSERC Grant No. A-0412 to P.N. We
thank Mr. G.A. Chanady and Mr. J. Kjarsgaard for skilled technical assistance and Dr. J.M. Wrigglesworth for discussions. Two of us (P.N. & S.S.)
acknowledge our loss in the death of our coauthor (A.P.S.), who initiated
this work, in the Air India disaster on 23rd. June 1985.

REFERENCES

1. Mitchell, P. (1966). Biol. Rev. 41, 445-502.
2. Wikstrom, M. K. F. (1977). Nature 266, 271-273.
3. Krab, K. and Wikstrom, M. K. F. (1978) Biochim. Biophys. Acta, 504, 200-214.
4. Sigel, E. and Carafoli, E. (1978) Eur. J. Biochem. 89, 119-123.
5. Proteau, G., Wrigglesworth, J. M., and Nicholls, P. (1983) Biochem. J. 210, 199-205.
6. Mitchell, P. and Moyle, J. (1983) FEBS Lett. 151, 167-178.
7. Mitchell, P., Mitchell, R., Moody, J., West, I.C., Baum, H. and Wrigglesworth, J.M. (1985) FEBS Lett., 188, 1-7.
8. Archbold, G.P.R., Farrington, C.L., Lappin, S.A., McKay, A.M., and Malpress, F. H. (1979) Biochem. J. 180, 161-174.
9. Wikstrom, M. K. F. and Saari, H. T. (1977) Biochim. Biophys. Acta, 462, 347-361.
10. Hinkle, P. C. (1973) Fed. Proc. 32, 1988-1991.
11. Wrigglesworth, J. M. (1978) In Membrane Proteins, Proceedings of the 11th FEBS Meeting, (P. Nicholls et al., eds.) Vol. 45, pp. 95-103.
12. Wrigglesworth, J. M. and Nicholls, P. (1979) Biochim. Biophys. Acta 547, 36-46.
13. Nicholls, P., Verghis, E. and Singh, A. P. (1984) EBEC Reports Vol. 3A, 251-252.
14. Kano, K., and Fendler, J. H. (1978) Biochim. Biophys. Acta 509, 289-299.
15. Clement, N. R. and Gould, J. M. (1981a) Biochem. 20, 1534-1538.
16. Clement, N. R. and Gould, J. M. (1981b) Biochem. 20, 1539-1543.
17. Waggoner, A. S. (1979) Ann. Rev. Biophys. Bioeng. 8, 47-68.
18. Singh, A. P., Chanady, G. A. and Nicholls, P. (1985) J. Memb. Biol. 84, 183-190.
19. Casey, R. P., Thelen, M. and Azzi, A. (1980) J. Biol. Chem. 255, 3994- 4000.
20. Prochaska, L. J., Bisson, R., Capaldi, R. A., Steffens, G. C. M. and Buse, G. (1981) Biochim. Biophys. Acta, 637, 360-373.
21. Puettner, I., Carafoli, E. and Malatesta, F. (1985) J. Biol. Chem. 260, 3719-3723.
22. Moroney, P. M., Scholes, T. A. and Hinkle, P. C. (1984) Biochemistry 23, 4991-4997.
23. Kuboyama, M., Yong, F. C., and King, T. E. 1972) J. Biol. Chem. 247, 6375-6383.
24. Kraayenhof, R., Schuurmans, J. J., Valkier, L. J., Veen, J. C. P., Van-Marun, D. and Jasper, C. G. G. (1982) Anal. Biochem. 127, 93-99.
25. Singh, A. P. and Nicholls, P. (1986) Biochem. Cell Biol. 64, 647-655.
26. Nicholls, P. and Shaughnessy, S. (1985) Biochem. J. 228, 201-210.
27. Singh, A. P. and Nicholls, P. (1986) Arch. Biochem. Biophys. 245, 436-445.
28. Singh, A. P. and Nicholls, P. (1984) Biochim. Biophys. Acta 777, 194-200.
29. Casey, R. P., O'Shea, P. S., Chappell, J. B., and Azzi, A. (1984) Biochim. Biophys. Acta 765, 30-37.
30. Krishnamoorthy, G. and Hinkle, P. C. (1984) Biochem. 23, 1640-1645.
31. O'Shea, P. S., Petrone, G., Casey, R. P., and Azzi, A. (1984) Biochem. J. 219, 719-726.

CYTOCHROME C OXIDASE ACTIVITY IS REGULATED BY NUCLEOTIDES AND ANIONS

Bernhard Kadenbach, Annemarie Stroh, Fritz-Joachim Hüther
and J. Berden*

Biochemie, Fachbereich Chemie, Philipps-Universität
D-3550 Marburg, F.R.G.
*Laboratory of Biochemistry, University of Amsterdam
1000 HD Amsterdam, Holland

INTRODUCTION

The mammalian cytochrome c oxidase complex is composed of 13 subunits
(1) and occurs in multiple, tissue- and developmental-specific isozymes (2).
In contrast the enzyme from procaryotes contains only 2-3 subunits, which
are homologous to the 3 mitochondrial-encoded subunits of the eukaryotic
enzyme (3,4). The kinetic properties of the enzyme from Paracoccus denitrificans and bovine heart are almost the same (5), but recent work on yeast
mutants, defective in nuclear-coded subunits, established the essential
requirement of all subunits for the formation of an active enzyme (6).
What is the function of nuclear-coded subunits in the eucaryotic enzyme
complex? In a recent hypothesis we have suggested that in addition to
respiratory control, respiration is regulated by allosteric modification
of respiratory chain enzyme complexes, in particular of cytochrome c
oxidase (7). The following results demonstrate an influence of nucleotides
and anions on cytochrome c oxidase activity and, by comparison of the
mammalian with the Paracoccus enzyme, suggest a modulatory involvement
of nuclear-encoded subunits.

METHODS

Mitoplasts were prepared from rat liver mitochondria using digitonin
(0.12 mg/mg protein) according to Schnaitman and Greenawalt (8). Bovine
heart cytochrome c oxidase was reconstituted (80 % right side out) by the
cholate-dialysis method, in a buffer containing 100 mM Hepes, pH 7.4,
50 mM KCl as previously described (9). The photometric assay of activity
in proteoliposomes was carried out in 100 mM Hepes, pH 7.4, 50 mM KCl,
1 µg/ml valinomycin, 3 µM CCCP, 1-80 µM ferrocytochrome c and 20 nM heme
aa_3. In the polarographic assay the medium contained in addition 25 mM
K-ascorbate, 0.1 mM EDTA and 0.7 mM TMPD (9). The activity of the isolated
enzyme or of mitoplasts, mitochondria, or membranes was measured polarographically in 250 mM sucrose, 10 mM K-Hepes, pH 7.5, 7 mM K-ascorbate,
0.14 mM EDTA, 0.7 mM TMPD, 40 µM cytochrome c, and inhibitors as indicated
in the legends. The indicated anions were added as concentrated solutions
of the sodium salts except chloride and Hepes, which were added as
potassium salts.
Photoaffinity-labelling of the isolated enzyme with $[\gamma-^{32}P]-8-N_3ATP$
(ICN Biochemicals, Cleveland, Ohio) was performed in 25 mM Tris-cacodylate,

pH 7.5 according to Montecucco et al. (10). Labelling with 8-N$_3$ATP (synthesized by A.F. Hartog according to (11)) was done as described (9). The non-radioactive labelled enzyme was reconstituted in liposomes prior to activity assay. The radioactive labelled enzyme was separated by SDS-PAGE, stained, dried, autoradiographed, and the radioactive bands were cut out, dissolved in 1 ml 30 % H$_2$O$_2$ and counted in a liquid scintillation counter.

Photoaffinity-labelling of proteoliposomes with [γ-^{32}P]-8-azido-ATP was carried out in 100 mM Hepes, pH 7.4, 50 mM KCl according to (9). The lipids were removed from the enzyme by discontinuous density gradient centrifugation (a) 3 % sucrose, b) 5 % sucrose, 2 % Triton X-100, 1 % Na-cholate, pH 8.1, c) 10 % sucrose, 0.2 M NaCl) for 15 h. SDS-PAGE and radio-activity counting were done as described above. Kinetic measurements of non-radioactive 8-N$_3$ATP-labelled proteoliposomes were performed after removal of unbound nucleotide by dialysis.

Table 1: Influence of various anions on the kinetic parameters of reconstituted bovine heart cytochrome c oxidase.
The anions were added to the assay buffer at 10 mM final concentrations. The 8-azido-compounds were preincubated for 15 min at 0°C with proteoliposomes at 10 mM final concentrations, and illuminated for 40 min as described (1). Unbound compounds were removed by dialysis.

| | Polarographic assay | | Photometric assay | |
	K_m	V_{max}	K_m	V_{max}
	μM	s^{-1}	μM	s^{-1}
None	2.7	300	10.4	150
8-N$_3$-adenosine			10	135
Cl$^-$	2.6	314		
Acetate	3.6	280		
AMP	5.6	308		
P$_i$	5.2	310		
ADP	8.3	315		
PP$_i$	11.6	306		
8-N$_3$-ATP			21.8	180
ATP	13.0	312	27.1	190
ITP	13.6	315		
PPP$_i$	18.5	305	41.2	210

RESULTS AND DISCUSSION

Cytochrome c oxidase activity is influenced by anions and nucleotides, which interact with the complex from the cytosolic side. This follows from table 1, where the kinetic parameters (determined from Eadie-Hofstee plots) of the reconstituted enzyme were measured by the polarographic or photo-metric assay. The increase of the K_m for cytochrome c (low affinity phase) is proportional to the charge of the anion.

In order to differentiate between an interaction of anions with cytochrome c and with the oxidase proteoliposomes were photoaffinity-labelled with 8-N$_3$ATP. The increase of K_m by covalently bound ATP (table 1) suggests a specific interaction with the oxidase. This is corroborated by results shown in fig. 1, where the soluble enzyme was photolabelled in the absence and presence of 10 mM ATP or ADP. A protection of the increase of K_m by 8-N$_3$ATP is found with ATP but not with ADP. The same results were obtained when proteoliposomes were photolabelled with 10 mM 8-N$_3$ATP but not with 1 mM 8-N$_3$ATP (not shown).

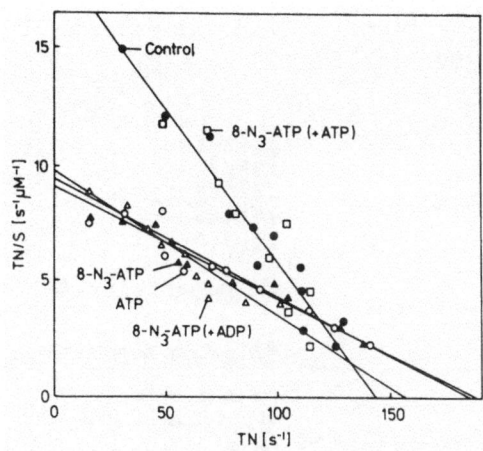

Fig. 1: Modification by photolabelling with 8-N$_3$ATP of kinetics of reconstituted cytochrome c oxidase. The isolated enzyme was photolabelled, reconstituted in liposomes as described under Methods, and the activity was
measured by the photometric assay at various cytochrome c concentrations.
The data are present in an Eadie-Hofstee plot ●——●: Control; ▲——▲: photolabelling with 8-N$_3$ATP; □——□ : photolabelling with 8-N$_3$ATP in the presence
of 10 mM ATP; △——△ : photolabelling in the presence of 10 mM ADP; ○——○:
control, assayed in the presence of 10 mM ATP.

Table 2: Influence of ATP and ADP on photolabelling of isolated and reconstituted bovine heart cytochrome c oxidase with [γ-^{32}P]-8-N$_3$ATP.
For details see Methods.

A. Proteoliposomes + 0.05 mM [γ-^{32}P]-8-N$_3$ATP

Subunit	bound ATP/aa$_3$		
	Control	+ 10 mM ATP	+ 10 mM ADP
	nmole/mole	% of control	
II + III	11	64	120
IV	6	66	85
VIIa+c	5	60	100

B. Soluble enzyme + 0.1 mM [γ-^{32}P]-8-N$_3$ATP

Subunit	bound ATP/aa$_3$		
	Control	+ 10 mM ATP	+ 10 mM ADP
	nmole/mole	% of control	
II + III	10	140	170
IV	14.5	83	103
VIIa+c	23	117	100

C. Soluble enzyme + 10 mM [γ-^{32}P]-8-N$_3$ATP

Subunit	bound ATP/aa$_3$		
	Control	+ 10 mM ATP	+ 10 mM ADP
	mole/mole	% of control	
II + III	0.48	178	172
IV	0.45	122	118
VIIa+c	0.55	167	156

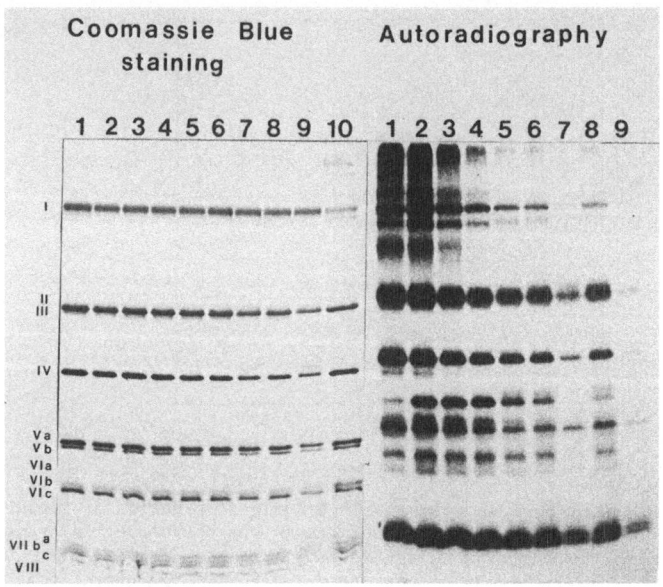

Fig. 2: ATP does not prevent photoaffinity-labelling of isolated bovine heart cytochrome c oxidase with $[\gamma-^{32}P]$-8-N3ATP. Photolabelling was done as described under Methods in the absence (lane 1) or presence of 10 mM ATP (lanes 2-10) with 0.8 μM (lanes 1,2), 10 μM (lane 3), 100 μM (lane 4), 400 μM (lane 5), 750 mM (lane 6), 1 mM (lane 7), 5 mM (lane 8), and 10 mM (lane 9) $[\gamma-^{32}P]$-8-N3ATP. For each incubation $2 \cdot 10^6$ dpm were applied. Lane 10: Control enzyme.

An apparently unspecific labelling of laurylmaltoside-dissolved cytochrome c oxidase is obtained with $[\gamma-^{32}P]$-8-N3ATP (fig. 2). Radioactivity is found in subunits II, III, IV, Va+b, VIa, VIb, VIIa, VIIc but only little in subunits I, Vb, VIc (fig. 2, lane 1). This contrasts the results of Montecucco et al. (10), who observed radioactivity only in subunits IV and VII. The presence of 10 mM ATP does not protect but increases the labelling of all subunits (fig. 2, lane 2), which contrasts the protecting effect of ATP on the increase of K_m by 8-N3ATP (fig. 1). A 5000-fold dilution of the labelled compound with 8-N3ATP and the presence of 10 mM ATP results in the same labelling pattern (fig. 2, lane 8) and almost the same radioactive intensity, indicating no saturation of labelling.

A quantitation of labelling with $[\gamma-^{32}P]$-8-N3ATP of 3 selected bands is shown in table 2. With proteoliposomes, e. g. binding of ATP to the cytosolic domain of the complex, a protective effect by 10 mM ATP but not by ADP is found in all bands (table 2A). In contrast an increase of labelling with $[\gamma-^{32}P]$-8-N3ATP is found in the presence of 10 mM ATP as well as ADP with the soluble enzyme (table 2B); this becomes even more prominent at higher concentration of the label (table 2C). Apparently nucleotides stimulate the binding of 8-N3ATP to the soluble enzyme, but not to the cytosolic domain of the reconstituted enzyme.

The influence of various anions on cytochrome c oxidase activity in mitoplasts under uncoupled conditions and in the presence of various inhibitors is shown in fig. 3. At very high anion concentrations only a slight

402

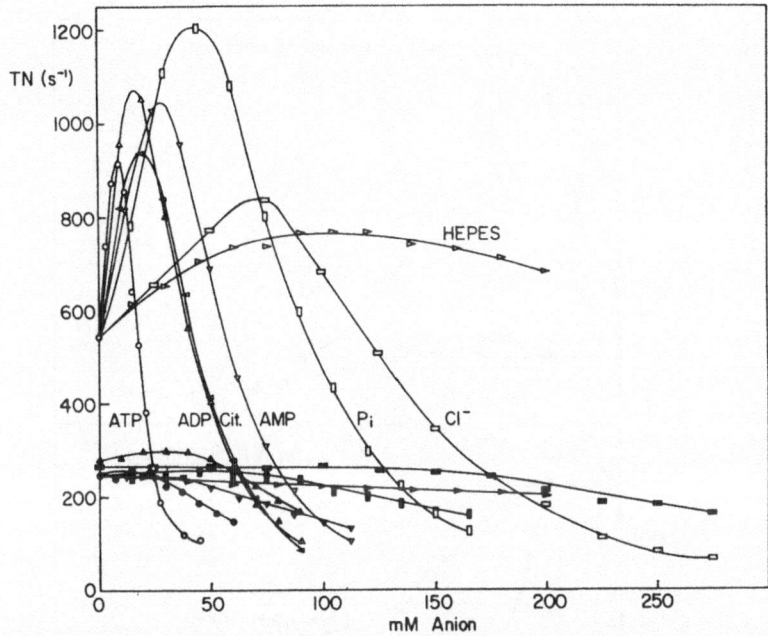

Fig. 3: Effect of increasing concentrations of anions on the activity of cytochrome c oxidase in intact rat liver mitoplasts and after solubilization by laurylmaltoside. Oxygen uptake was measured as described under Methods with the following inhibitors: 1 μM rotenone, 0.1 μM antimycin A, 1 μg/ml oligomycin, 5 μM carboxyatractyloside, 40 μM mersalyl, 1 μg/ml valinomycin, 3 μM CCCP. Open symbols with, closed symbols without 0.8 mM laurylmaltoside.

inhibition is observed. However, after addition of laurylmaltoside a biphasic effect of anions is found: stimulation at low and inhibition at high concentrations. The effect is independent of the type but proportional to the charge, indicating a general, electrostatic effect of anions on the electron transfer from cytochrome c to oxygen.

In order to investigate the involvement of nuclear-coded subunits in the anion sensitivity of cytochrome c oxidase, membranes of Paracoccus denitrificans were studied (fig. 4). Again anions inhibited the dissolved enzyme at high concentrations proportional to their charge. But there are two differences in Paracoccus: 1. No inhibition of activity is found at low anion concentrations, and 2. half-maximal inhibition of activity is obtained at almost half concentrations required for the beef heart enzyme. Because cytochrome c oxidase from Paracoccus contains only 2 or 3 (4) sub-units, we conclude that nuclear-coded subunits modify the anion sensitivity of the laurylmaltoside-dissolved enzyme.

For the understanding of electrostatic interactions, knowledge of netto charges on the enzyme complex is of interest. In table 3 are presented the numbers of charged amino acids of 9 transmembraneous subunits on both sides of the membrane as calculated from hydropathic plots (12), assuming a matrix-orientation of the amino-terminal region of the trans-membraneous nuclear-coded subunits, and from the folding pattern of the mitochondrial-encoded subunits as suggested by Wikström and coworkers (13).

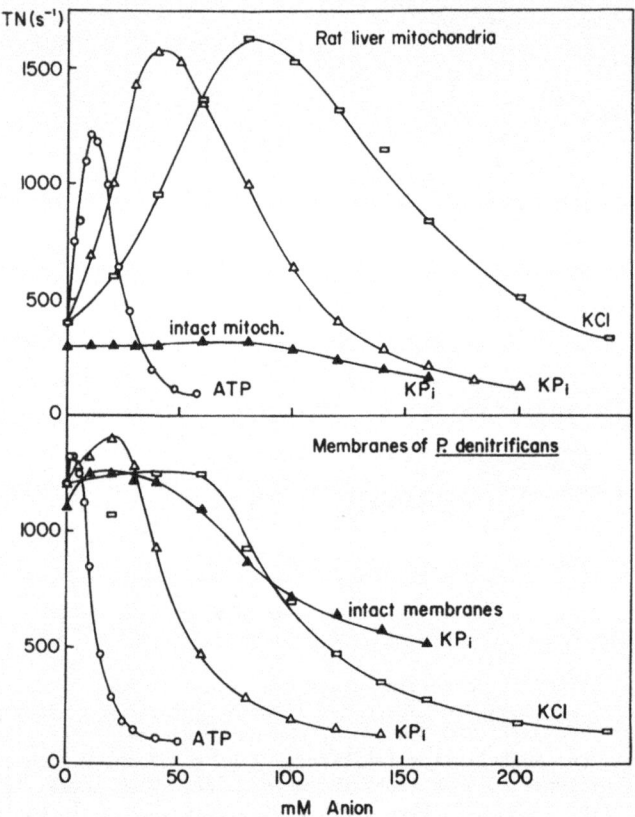

Fig. 4: Comparison of the effect of anions on cytochrome c oxidase activity from rat liver and Paracoccus. Cytochrome c oxidase activity of rat liver mitochondria and Paracoccus denitrificans membranes was measured polarographically in the absence (closed symbols) or presence (open symbols) of 0.8 mM laurylmaltoside under uncoupled conditions (1 µg/ml valinomycin, 3 µM CCCP).

From the data a dipol structure of the complex, negative on the cytosolic and positive on the matrix side is concluded. From electron microscopy of cytochrome c oxidase vesicle crystals a Y-shaped structure was deduced for the monomer, where the large domain, the stem of the Y, projects over 50 Å into the cytosolic phase, and two smaller domains, separated by lipids and penetrating the lipid bilayer, extend to the matrix phase (14). Since all subunits listed in table 3 contain excess positive charges on the matrix side, except subunit II, we postulate excess positive charges for both matrix-oriented domains. The biphasic effect of anions on the laurylmaltoside-dissolved enzyme then could be explained, assuming repulsion of the two arms in the absence of anions, accompanied with low activity. Increasing concentrations of anionic charges could attract the two arms leading to the biphasic effect on activity, where the intermediate distance corresponds to maximal activity. Cytochrome c oxidase from Paracoccus does not contain nuclear-coded subunits. The lack of inhibition of activity at very low anion concentration, and the lower concentration of anions required for half-maximal inhibition could thus be explained by a diminished repulsion of two positively charged protein domains. Further experiments are necessary to prove this model.

404

Table 3: Sidedness of charged amino acids of cytochrome c oxidase subunits in the inner mitochondrial membrane. The number of charged amino acids on both sides of the membrane was calculated from the folding pattern suggested by Wikström et al. (13) for mitochondrial coded subunits I-III, and from hydropathy plots of nuclear-coded subunits (12), assuming a matrix orientation of the N-terminal part of transmembraneous nuclear coded subunits.

Sub-unit	Cytosol		Matrix		Membrane	
	negative	positive	negative	positive	negative	positive
I	13	5	11	11	1	1
II	23	12	3	1	0	0
III	5	0	3	9	5	0
IV	9	9	13	15	0	0
VIa	4	7	1	4	0	0
VIc	7	10	0	6	0	0
VIIa	1	2	5	6	0	0
VIIc	1	3	3	4	0	0
VIII	2	2	1	4	0	0
total	65	50	40	60	6	1
difference	15 (-)		20 (+)		5 (-)	

CONCLUSIONS

A new influence of anions on the activity of cytochrome c oxidase is described, characterized by its effective concentration in the millimolar range. The effects occur by electrostatic interactions and modify the kinetics of the enzyme differently when interacting from the cytosolic side with the reconstituted enzyme or with the dissolved enzyme. ATP may have a specific regulatory effect due to its high negative charge and preponderance in the cell.

ACKNOWLEDGEMENTS

We thank Dr. B. Ludwig for a sample of membranes from Paracoccus, and C. Thiel for kinetic measurements. This work was supported by grants from the Deutsche Forschungsgemeinschaft (SFB 103, A2) and from Fonds der Chemischen Industrie.

REFERENCES

1. B. Kadenbach, J. Jarausch, R. Hartmann, and P. Merle, Separation of mammalian cytochrome c oxidase into 13 polypeptides by a sodium dodecyl sulfate-gel electrophoretic procedure, Anal. Biochem. 129:517 (1983).
2. L. Kuhn-Nentwig, and B. Kadenbach, Isolation and properties of cytochrome c oxidase from rat liver and quantification of immunological differences between isozymes from various rat tissues with subunit-specific antisera, Eur. J. Biochem. 149:147 (1985).
3. G.C.M. Steffens, G. Buse, W. Oppliger, and B. Ludwig, Sequence homology of bacterial and mitochondrial cytochrome c oxidases, Biochem. Biophys. Res. Commun. 116:335 (1983).
4. M. Saraste, M. Raitio, T. Jalli, and A. Perämaa, A gene in Paracoccus for subunit III of cytochrome oxidase, FEBS Lett.206:154 (1986).
5. J.K.V. Reichardt, and Q.H. Gibson, Turnover of cytochrome c oxidase from Paracoccus denitrificans, J. Biol. Chem. 258:1504 (1983).

6. J.E. McEwen, C. Ko, B. Kloeckner-Gruissem, and R.O. Poyton, Nuclear functions required for cytochrome c oxidase biogenesis in Saccharomyces cerevisiae, J. Biol. Chem. 261:11872 (1986).

7. B. Kadenbach, Regulation of respiration and ATP synthesis in higher organisms: hypothesis, J. Bioenerg. Biomembr. 18:39 (1986).

8. C. Schnaitman, and J.W. Greenawalt, Enzymatic properties of the inner and outer membranes of rat liver mitochondria, J. Cell Biol. 38:158 (1968).

9. F.-J. Hüther, and B. Kadenbach, Specific effects of ATP on the kinetics of reconstituted bovine heart cytochrome c oxidase, FEBS Lett. 207:89 (1986).

10. C. Montecucco, E. Schiavo, and R. Bisson, ATP binding to bovine heart cytochrome c oxidase, Biochem. J. 234:241 (1986).

11. J.-J. Schäfer, P. Scheurich, and K. Dose, Eine einfache Darstellung von 8-Azidoadenosin-5'-triphosphat; ein Agenz zur Photoaffinitätsmarkierung von ATP-bindenden Proteinen, Liebigs Ann. Chem. 2:1749 (1978).

12. B. Kadenbach, L. Kuhn-Nentwig, and U. Büge, Evolution of a regulatory enzyme: cytochrome c oxidase (complex IV), in: "Curr. Topics Bioenerg.", Vol. 15, C.P. Lee, ed., Academic Press, New York, in press.

13. M. Wikström, M. Saraste, and T. Penttilä, Relationships between structure and function in cytochrome oxidase, in: "The Enzymes of Biological Membranes", Vol. 4, A.N. Martonosi, ed., Plenum Publishing Corporation, 111 (1985).

14. J.F. Deatherage, R. Henderson, and R.A. Capaldi, Relationship between membrane and cytoplasmic domains in cytochrome c oxidase by electron microscopy in media of different density, J. Mol. Biol. 158 : 501 (1982).

CYTOCHROME OXIDASE AND NEUROMUSCULAR DISEASES

C. P. Lee*, M. E. Martens#, P. L. Peterson# and J. S. Hatfield**

Departments of Biochemistry* and Neurology#, School of Medicine, Wayne State University; and Department of Pathology**, Harper Hospital, Detroit, MI 48201, U.S.A.

INTRODUCTION

The pioneer work of Luft, Ernster and associates more than 2 decades ago on a patient with hypermetabolism of non-thyroid origin has clearly illustrated the critical role of mitochondrial respiratory control in the energy metabolism of living organisms[1]. Since then there have been a growing, though not very large, number of reports of mitochondrial deficiencies identified by direct investigation of biopsied tissue. These advances have stemmed partly from an increasing awareness of the clinical and metabolic consequences of impaired oxidative metabolism in humans, and partly from the introduction of improved methods for assessing the functional integrity of these pathways in intact and disrupted cells, and in isolated mitochondrial preparations. A number of biochemical defects have been identified which have recently been reviewed by DiMauro[2] and Morgan-Hughes[3]. Based on biochemical characteristics, Morgan-Hughes has classified the defects into the following 4 major groups: (A). defects of mitochondrial substrate transport; (B). defects of substrate utilization; (C). defects of the respiratory chain components; and (D). defects of energy conservation and transduction[3].

There have been an increasing number of reports that deficiency of cytochrome oxidase in muscle mitochondria is associated with a variety of neurological diseases[4-14] (also articles cited in ref. 10). In most cases (if not all), the defect was identified as a decrease in the cytochrome oxidase activity estimated histochemically with tissue slices, or measured biochemically with tissue homogenates or isolated mitochondrial fractions from either fresh or frozen tissues of patients as compared to controls. In all cases, the rates of only the partial reaction catalyzed by cytochrome oxidase were determined. More recently, immunological and immunocytochemical techniques, which estimate the amount of material cross-reacting with antibodies to cytochrome oxidase, have also been applied as a diagnostic tool in determining the content of cytochrome oxidase. In no case, were the respiratory rates with either succinate, NADH (with mitochondrial fragments) or NAD-linked substrates (intact mitochondria) determined. This raises a very important question, since it is well established that cytochrome oxidase possesses a very high turn-over number. Namely, is cytochrome oxidase the rate limiting step of respiratory chain-linked oxidative metabolism in these patients?

In this paper a brief summary of our recent studies on the oxidative metabolism of isolated skeletal muscle mitochondria of patients suffering from Kearns-Sayre syndrome (KSS) is presented. Our data indicate a partial deficiency (30% of control) of cytochrome oxidase in skeletal muscle mitochondria of KSS, which is in line with other reports in the literature[4-7,15,16]. Our data further indicate that in addition to an excess of cytochrome c (150% of control), the rate-limiting step in respiratory chain-linked electron transfer lies between cytochrome c and cytochrome oxidase, as revealed by steady state kinetic analysis. The implications of these alterations for mitochondrial oxidative metabolism as a whole will also be discussed. Details of these studies are described by Martens et al [17].

RESULTS AND DISCUSSION

Kearns Sayre syndrome (KSS) is a metabolic disorder of unknown etiology which was first described by Kearns and Sayre in 1958[18]. The disorder has been more recently classified as a progressive multisystem disease[19]. The clinical features of KSS include ophthalmoplegia, retinal degeneration, bilateral facial weakness, proximal limb weakness, heart block, short stature, neurosensory hearing loss, elevated cerebrospinal fluid protein and lactic acidosis. Histochemical studies of muscle biopsies showed "ragged red" fibers, the morphological hallmark of mitochondrial myopathy. Further support has been provided at the ultrastructural level. An increased population of mitochondria tightly embedded in glycogen-rich sarcoplasm and exhibiting a variety of changes in their fine structure have been seen under the electron microscope. In addition, many of the mitochondria were enlarged and contained rectangular paracrystalline inclusions or unusual concentrically-arranged cristae. This leaves little doubt that a mitochondrial metabolic disorder is associated with Kearns Sayre syndrome. However, to date no systematic biochemical studies of this disease have been described in the literature.

Intact skeletal muscle mitochondrial preparations were isolated from fresh biopsy specimens according to the methods developed in our laboratory[20,21]. It was noted that the recovery of mitochondrial protein was considerably higher (on the basis of muscle wet weight: 4 mg protein/gram muscle for KSS vs 2 mg protein/gram muscle for controls), in line with the results derived from ultrastructural studies[5,16-19]. As shown in Table 1, the mitochondrial preparations exhibited decent respiratory control and phosphorylating efficiencies with both succinate and NAD-linked substrates. An excellent Ca^{++} transport efficiency supported by succinate oxidase was also seen. However, the State 3 rates with either succinate or NAD-linked substrates were considerably lower than those of controls. Although the cytochrome oxidase activity (measured with ascorbate + PMS as substrate) in KSS was also lower than that of controls, it was considerably faster than the rate with either

Table 1. Respiratory and phosphorylating activities of isolated skeletal muscle mitochondria from KSS patients and controls.*

Substrates	State 3 Resp. Rate (natoms O/min/mg prot.)	RCI	ADP/O
Pyruvate + Malate			
Patients (n = 4)	36 ± 9^3	3.2 ± 0.2	3.2 ± 0.2
Controls (n = 6)	154 ± 8	4.2 ± 0.4	3.1 ± 0.2
Glutamate + Malate			
Patients (n = 2)	43 ± 1^3	2.2 ± 0.6^1	2.6 ± 0.05^2
Controls (n = 3)	165 ± 13	7.4 ± 1.5	3.2 ± 0.1
Succinate + Rotenone			
Patients (n = 4)	59 ± 12^3	2.5 ± 0.5	1.9 ± 0.1
Controls (n = 6)	175 ± 13	3.2 ± 0.2	1.8 ± 0.1
Succinate + Rotenone + Ca^{+2}			
Patients (n = 4)	90 ± 15^3	6.6 ± 1.1	$4.8 \pm 0.8**$
Controls (n = 6)	206 ± 13	6.4 ± 0.8	$4.2 \pm 0.3**$
Ascorbate + PMS			
Patients (n = 4)	1038 ± 546		
Controls (n = 3)	2158 ± 706		

* Values are mean $\pm$ SEM; ** Ca^{+2}/O ratio.
  Statistical significance: $^1 P < 0.10$; $^2 P < 0.05$; $^3 P < 0.01$

pyruvate + malate, glutamate + malate or succinate as substrate. This would indicate that the site of impairment causing the depressed respiratory rates in KSS skeletal muscle mitochondria with either succinate or NAD-linked substrates cannot be in cytochrome oxidase and/or on the path of electron transfer from cytochrome oxidase to oxygen.

Figure 1 shows the difference spectra (reduced _minus_ oxidized) of skeletal muscle mitochondria derived from a KSS patient (Figure 1B) and a control (Figure 1A) recorded at aerobic steady state and anaerobiosis with succinate and pyruvate + malate as substrates. A cross over point between cytochrome c and cytochrome oxidase is clearly seen (Figure 1B) where more than 50% of the cytochrome c was reduced at steady state (Spectrum I) in KSS, in contrast to controls in which less than 15% was reduced. A deficiency of cytochrome oxidase (approximately 30% of control) and an enrichment of cytochrome c are clearly seen (Figure 1B, Spectrum II). Subsequent addition of dithionite after anaerobiosis showed no significant increase in the reduction of any of the respiratory chain pigments (data not shown).

In conclusion, our data clearly show that although the cytochrome oxidase of KSS mitochondria is deficent, the depressed rate of the respiratory chain-linked electron transfer is not due to the deficiency of cytochrome oxidase. The site of impairment is on the path of electron transfer from cytochrome c to cytochrome oxidase. The precise mechanism of the impairment is not known at the present time. It is possible that the binding affinity of cytochrome c towards cytochrome oxidase has been retarded because of an alteration of either cytochrome oxidase or the cytochrome c molecule. In addition, the inhibition of electron transfer from cytochrome c to cytochrome oxidase will cause the accumulation of reduced forms of the respiratory chain carriers on the substrate side of cytochrome c and, consequently, promote and/or accelerate the formation of hydroperoxides, causing injury to mitochondrial structure and function.

There is no evidence, thus far, indicating maternal inheritance in Kearns Sayre syndrome. This would suggest that the mutation affects the nuclear genome system responsible for the synthesis of either cytochrome c and one or more subunit(s) of cytochrome oxidase, protein(s) responsible for the assembly of the subunits into an active oxidase or for the proper insertion of the enzymes into the mitochondrial inner membrane. One is also tempted to ask: are the biosynthesis of cytochrome c and subunit(s) of cytochrome oxidase controlled by a single common factor, or by two or more closely related ones?

ACKNOWLEDGEMENT

This work has been supported by grants from the Muscular Dystrophy Association of America and the National Institutes of Health of U.S. Public Health Service.

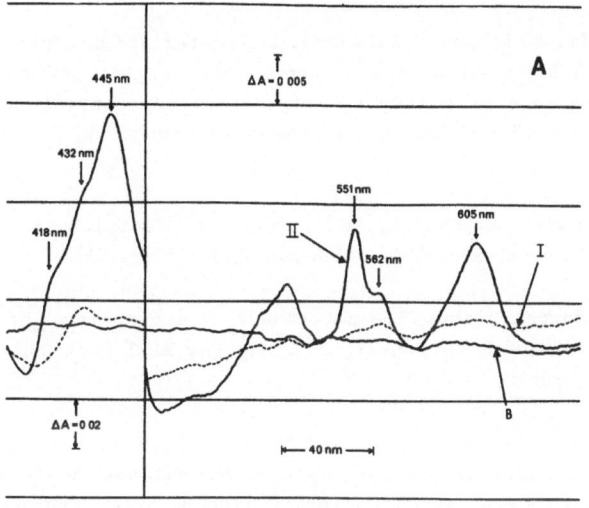

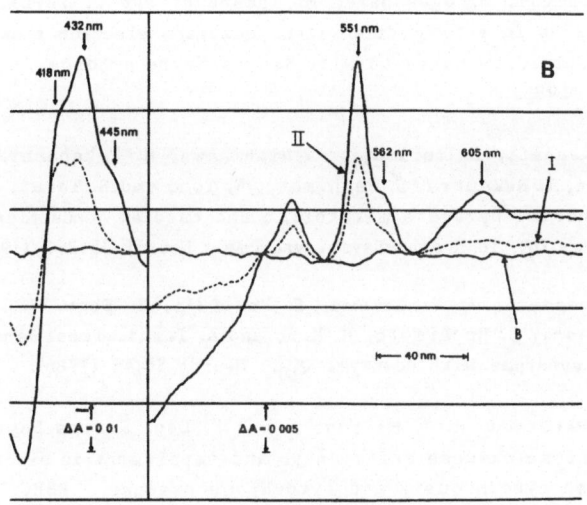

Figure 1. Substrate-reduced <u>minus</u> oxidized difference spectra of
skeletal muscle mitochondria isolated from KSS-patient (B)
and control (A). B: Baseline (oxidized <u>minus</u> oxidized);
I: reduced <u>minus</u> oxidized spectrum recorded under state 3
conditions immediately upon addition of substrates
(succinate, pyruvate and malate) into the sample cuvette;
II: reduced <u>minus</u> oxidized spectrum recorded following
anerobiosis. $T = 25^{\circ}C$. Protein concentrations were 1.2
and 1.1 mg/ml for patient and control, respectively.

REFERENCES

1. R. Luft, D. Ikkos, G. Palmieri, L. Ernster and B. Afzelius, A case of severe hypermetabolism of nonthyroid origin with a defect in the maintenance of mitochondrial respiratory control: a correlated clinical, biochemical and morphological study, J Clin Invest 41:1776 (1962).

2. S. DiMauro, E. Bonilla, M. Zeviani, M. Nakagawa and D. C. DiVivo, Mitochondrial myopathies, Ann Neurol 17:521 (1985).

3. J. A. Morgan-Hughes, The mitochondrial myopathies, in: "Myology", A. G. Engel and B. Q. Banker, eds., McGraw Hill Book Co., New York, p. 1709 (1986).

4. D. M. Turnbull, M. A. Johnson, D. J. Dick, N. E. F. Cartlidge, and H. S. A. Sherratt, Partial cytochrome oxidase deficiency without subsarcolemmal accumulation of mitochondria in chronic progressive external ophthalmoplegia, J Neurol Sci 70:93 (1985).

5. S. Yorifuji, S. Ogasahara, M. Takahashi and S. Tarui, Decreased activities in mitochondrial inner membrane electron transport system in muscle from patients with Kearns-Sayre syndrome. J Neurol Sci 71:65 (1985).

6. S. Ogasahara, S. Yorifuji, Y. Nishikawa, M. Takahashi, K. Wada, T. Hazama, Y. Nakamura, S. Hashimoto, N. Tono and S. Tarui, Improvement of abnormal pyruvate metabolism and cardiac conduction defect with coenzyme Q_{10} in Kearns-Sayre syndrome. Neurol 35:372 (1985).

7. S. Ogasahara, Y. Nishikawa, S. Yorifuji, F. Soga, Y. Nakamura, M. Takahashi, S. Hashimoto, N. Kono and A. Tarui, Treatment of Kearns-Sayre syndrome with coenzyme Q_{10}. Neurol 36:45 (1986).

8. P. L. Peterson, M. E. Martens and C. P. Lee, Kearns Sayre syndrome: cytochrome oxidase deficiency, and impairment in electron transfer between cytochrome c and cytochrome oxidase. EBEC Reports 4:81 (1986).

9. M. E. Martens, P. L. Peterson, C. P. Lee, M. Weisenfeld and S. S. Yang, Congenital fatty metamorphosis of the viscera: cytochrome oxidase deficiency, and defective electron transfer between the flavoproteins and CoQ. EBEC Reports 4:404 (1986).

10. S. DiMauro, M. Zeviani, S. Servidei, E. Bonilla, A. F. Miranda, A. Prelle and E. A. Schon, Cytochrome oxidase deficiency: clinical and biochemical heterogeneity, Ann New York Acad Sci, 488:19 (1986).

11. M. Zeviani, D. H. Van Dyke, S. Servidei, S. Bauserman, E. Bonilla, E. T. Beaumont, J. Sharda, K. Vanderlaan and S. DiMauro, Myopathy and fatal cardiopathy due to cytochrome c oxidase deficiency, Arch Neurol 43:1198 (1986).

12. S. Servidei, R. P. Lazaro, E. Bonilla, K. D. Barron, M. Zeviani and S. DiMauro, Mitochondrial encephalomyopathy and partial cytochrome c oxidase deficiency, Neurol 37:58 (1987).

13. M. Zeviani, P. L. Peterson, S. Servidei, E. Bonilla and S. DiMauro, Benign reversible muscle cytochrome c deficieny: a second case. Neurol. 37:64 (1987).

14. S. DiMauro, S. Servidei, M. Zeviani, M. DiRocco, D. C. DeVivo, S. DiDonato, G. Uziel, K. Berry, G. Hoganson, S. D. Johensen and P. C. Johnson, Cytochrome c oxidase deficiency in Leigh syndrome, Ann Neurol In press.

15. M. A. Johnson, D. M. Turnbull, D. J. Dick, and H. S. A. Sherratt, A partial deficiency of cytochrome c oxidase in chronic progressive ophthalmoplegia. J Neurol Sci 60:31 (1983).

16. H. Mitsumoto, J. R. Aprille, S. H. Wray, R. Nemni, W. G. Bradley, Chronic progressive external opthalmoplegia (CPEO): clinical, morphological, and biochemical studies. Neurol. 33:452 (1983).

17. M. E. Martens, P. L. Peterson, C. P. Lee, J. Hatfield, C. H. Chang, Z. Hart, M. A. Nigro, and M. Glassberg, Biochemical studies of ocular myopathy: abnormal mitochondrial oxidative metabolism in skeletal muscle of four patients. In preparation.

18. T. Kearns and G. Sayre, Retinitis pigmentosa, external ophthalmoplegia and complete heart block. Unusual syndrome with histologic study in one of two cases. Arch. Ophthalmol. 60:280 (1958).

19. F. M. S. Tome and M. Fardeau, Ocular myopathies, in: "Myology", A. G. Engel and B. Q. Banker, eds., McGraw Hill Book Co., New York, p. 1327 (1986).

20. M. W. Makinen and C. P. Lee, Biochemical studies of skeletal muscle mitochondria: I. Microanalysis of cytochrome content, oxidative and phosphorylative activities of mammalian skeletal muscle mitochondria. Arch Biochem Biophys 126:75 (1968).

21. C. P. Lee, M. E. Martens, L. Jankulovska and M. A. Neymark, Defective oxidative metabolism of myodystrophic skeletal muscle mitochondria. Muscle & Nerve 2:340 (1979).

ELECTRON TRANSFER BETWEEN CARDIAC CYTOCHROME c_1 AND c

Chong H. Kim, Claude Balny*, and Tsoo E. King

Department of Chemistry and Biology and Laboratory of
Bioenergetics, State University of New York at Albany
Albany, New York 12222, USA

*Institut National de la Santé et de la Recherche Médicale
U 128, CNRS, B.P. 5051
34033 Montpellier Cedex, France

INTRODUCTION

The molecular mechanism for electron transfer between cytochrome c_1 and cytochrome c remains to be clarified. It has been based only on a *priori* consideration that cytochrome c is an immediate electron acceptor of cytochrome c_1 in mitochondria. The discovery of cytochrome c_1-cytochrome c complex (1, 2) which is later found to be actually c_1-Hp-c complex[1] (3, 4), has suggested that the c_1-Hp-c complex may be an intermediate in the interaction of these two cytochromes in the mitochondrial respiratory chain. The kinetics of this reaction were first studied (5) using cytochrome c_1 preparations (6) that contained two polypeptides, the cytochrome c_1 and a small colorless protein, which was recently isolated and named the hinge protein (Hp) (3, 4). The electron transfer reaction between cytochrome c_1 and c has been reinvestigated by König et al. (7), using a c_1 preparation claimed to contain only one heme peptide (8). They suggested the stable c_1-Hp-c complex as an intermediate in the electron transfer reaction between cytochrome c_1 and c (7).

The unique structural feature of the hinge protein (4, 9, 10) which is essential for the formation of the stable cytochrome c_1-Hp-c complex, led us to investigate for its genuine function or the action of the c_1-Hp-c complex in mitochondrial electron transport. To clarify the role of the hinge protein (4, 9, 10), which is also one of the constituents of b-c_1 complex, we have performed comparative study on the reactions of electron transfer between cytochrome c_1 and c in the presence and absence of the hinge protein, using pure monomeric cytochrome c_1 without the hinge protein ("one band" c_1,) monomeric cytochrome c_1 bound with the hinge protein ("two band" c_1) and one band c_1 plus the hinge protein ("reconstituted two band" c_1) (3,11,12).

---

[1]The c_1-Hp-c complex in oxidized, reduced or mixed oxidation forms represent the stable complex and is sensitive to ionic strength. The c_1-Hp•c and c_1•c complexes in oxidized, reduced or mixed oxidation forms indicate the transient complex and are not affected by ionic strength.

The purpose of this communication is to summarize our recent findings on the electron transfer reaction between cytochrome c_1 and c (13, 14), that are somewhat different from those previous studies by this laboratory (5) and by König et al. (7). Our results suggest that the electron transfer reaction between cytochrome c_1 and cytochrome c is not through a simple mechanism of redistribution of charges between c_1 and c, but it involves a number of transient intermediates. The hinge protein may be involved in regulation of electron transfer between these two cytochromes.

TRANSIENT INTERMEDIATE COMPLEX IS SUGGESTED IN ELECTRON TRANSFER BETWEEN CYTOCHROME c_1 and c

Our result for the studies (13) of electron transfer reaction between cytochrome c and pure monomeric cytochrome c_1, which is completely free of the hinge protein, suggested a minimum mechanism for electron transfer between these two cytochromes as in the following Eq. 1.

$$c_1^{2+} + c^{3+} \underset{k_{-2}}{\overset{K_1}{\rightleftharpoons}} (c_1^{2+} \bullet c^{3+}) \overset{k_2}{\underset{k_{-2}}{\rightleftharpoons}} (c_1^{3+} \bullet c^{2+}) \overset{K_3}{\rightleftharpoons} c_1^{3+} + c^{2+} \qquad (1)$$

where K_1 and K_3 sympolize a rapid equilibria with association constants for the first and last steps to be $>> 10^6$ M^{-1}, and $(c_1^{2+} \bullet c^{3+})$ and $(c_1^{3+} \bullet c^{2+})$ are postulated to be possible kinetic intermediates. These $(c_1 \bullet c)$ complex species differ from the stable c_1-Hp-c complex (1-4) which is ionic strength-dependent and can be obtained only in the presence of the hinge protein (3, 4) in a medium of low ionic strength. Our evidence shows that the electron transfer reaction between cytochrome c_1 and c does not require the c_1-Hp-c complex, which has been generally considered as one of the characteristic interactions between these two cytochromes (11). Our experimental evidence (see ref. 13) are briefly described below.

Reactions of c_1^{2+} and c^{3+} were measured during stopped-flow rapid mixing of the two cytochromes in 20 mM and 500 mM sodium cacodylate buffer, pH 7.4 at 2°C. Optical difference spectra of the reaction mixture of $(c_1^{2+} + c^{3+}) - (c_1^{3+} + c^{2+})$ yielded an absorbance decrease at 416 ± 1 nm. These observed spectral deviations are not those expected if the reaction proceeds as simple as $c_1^{2+} + c^{3+} \rightleftharpoons c_1^{3+} + c^{2+}$. Instead, the spectral variations observed during electron transfer between these two cytochromes were comparable to the difference spectra of $[(c_1^{2+} \bullet c^{2+}) - (c_1^{2+} + c^{2+})]$ and $[(c_1^{3+} \bullet c^{3+}) - (c_1^{3+} + c^{3+})]$ (Fig. 1.). When the c_1^{2+} concentration was higher or equal to the c^{3+} concentration, the observed spectral variations were corresponding to spectrum A in Fig. 1, which is the difference spectrum of $[(c_1^{2+} \bullet c^{2+}) - (c_1^{2+} + c^{2+})]$ and when the c_1^{2+} concentration was lower than that of c^{3+}, an absorbance increase at 408 ± 1 nm was observed and these spectral variations are comparable to spectrum B in Fig. 1, which is the difference spectrum of $[(c_1^{3+} \bullet c^{3+}) - (c_1^{3+} + c^{3+})]$. For the back reaction (c_1^{3+} with c^{2+}) the phenomena observed in the forward reaction (c_1^{2+} with c^{3+}) were reversed; that is, when the concentration of c_1^{3+} was higher than that of c^{2+}, the absorbance at 408 ± 1 nm decreased as a function of time, corresponding to the formation of the ferricytochrome complex $(c_1^{3+} \bullet c^{3+})$, and when the concentration of c_1^{3+} was lower than that of c^{2+}, only the increase of absorbance at 416 ± 1 nm was observed, corresponding to supposedly the formation of the ferro-cytochrome complex $(c_1^{2+} \bullet c^{2+})$. The rate constant is slightly higher for the back reaction compared with that for the forward reaction.

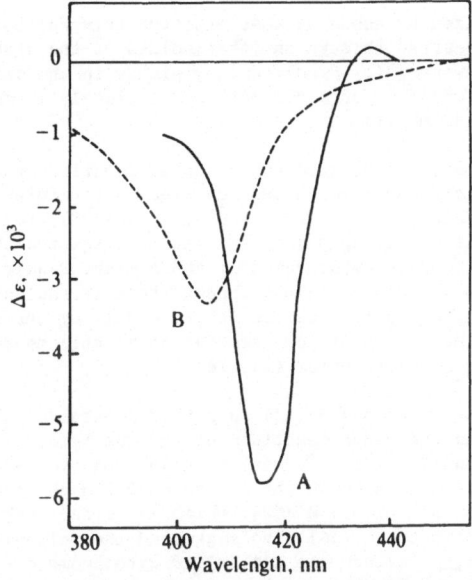

Fig. 1. Difference spectra of the cytochrome complexes. Spectrum A, $(c_1^{2+} \cdot c^{2+}) - (c_1^{2+} + c^{2+})$; spectrum B, $(c_1^{3+} \cdot c^{3+}) - (c_1^{3+} + c^{3+})$. Spectra were traced in 20 mM cacodylate buffer at 2°C. Tandem cuvettes were used. Overall light path was 0.875 cm. Spectrum A was obtained using 3.45 µM each c_1^{2+} and c^{2+}. Spectrum B was obtained using 2.55 µM each c_1^{3+} and c^{3+}.

There is no ionic strength effect for either the forward reaction or the back reaction. This is consistent with the fact that the electron transfer reaction cannot be modulated with the variation of the ionic strength, even though cytochromes c_1 and c can be in the electrostatic interaction (cf. the isoelectric points (pI) of c_1 and c are 5.8 (12) and 10.3, respectively (15)).

The temperature effect on the rate of reactions was performed by lowering the temperature step by step and using 40% ethylene glycol (v/v). At both 2°C and -5°C, the same characteristic spectral variations were observed at 416 nm as in pure aqueous buffer (20 mM cacodylate buffer, pH 7.4). However, when the temperature was lower than -20°C, the spectral variations at 416 nm were not observed; instead, the spectral characteristics with maximum at 408 nm were appeared. At -10°C, practically no signal was evident. These observations may be the consequence of a variation of equilibrium between the two complexes as in $(c_1^{2+} \cdot c^{3+})$ and $(c_1^{3+} \cdot c^{2+})$ through possible intermediates such as $(c_1^{2+} \cdot c^{2+})$ and $(c_1^{3+} \cdot c^{3+})$. The measured constant (k_{obs}) does not depend on the concentration of c_1, but the amplitude is proportional to it. We consider that when $[c_1^{2+}] < [c^{3+}]$, all c_1^{2+} is completely complexed with (or saturated by) c^{3+} with only an excess of c^{3+} free, and that for the reverse reaction c^{2+} is completely complexed with c_1^{3+}.

Our results are quite different from those reported (6) in which a second order rate constant of the forward reaction (c_1^{2+} with c^{3+}) was determined to be decreased from 3.0×10^7 M^{-1}s^{-1} at ionic strength, 223 mM to 1.8×10^5 M^{-1}s^{-1} at ionic strength, 450 mM, at 10°C. Such a result

417

could be rationalized by assuming that electron transfer between these two cytochromes occurred through an intermediate of the stable complex (c_1-Hp-c) (1). However, (c_1-Hp-c) complex either in the oxidized, reduced, or mixed valence forms dissociates completely in media with ionic strength > 100 mM (1).

Our proposal is that the electron transfer reaction between isolated cytochrome c_1 and c, does require the transient intermediate, $(c_1 \bullet c)$ complex species, such as $(c_1^{2+} \bullet c^{2+})$, $(c_1^{3+} \bullet c^{3+})$, $(c_1^{2+} \bullet c^{3+})$, and $(c_1^{3+} \bullet c^{2+})$, but not c_1-Hp-c complex. It is suggested that electron transfer between cytochromes c_1 and c might require some special conformational rearrangement through these transient complexes because $(c_1 \bullet c)$ complex species can be observed only by the spectral variation during the course of low temperature kinetic measurement and cannot be observed at equilibrium (13, 14).

The scheme that we proposed (13) is rather general (16-18). In refs. 16-18 are discussed the redox reactions of various types of cytochrome c with iron hexacyanides and intermediate complexes, $(c^{3+} \bullet Fe^{2+})$, $(c^{2+} \bullet Fe^{3+})$ are suggested even in the medium of 0.1 M phosphate buffer, pH 7.0, containing 0.3 M KNO_3, which is rather high ionic strength. Creutz and Sutin (16) also suggested the following scheme: cytochrome c + Im. $\rightleftarrows$ (cytochrome c) $\bullet$ (Im) $\rightleftarrows$ cytochrome c — Im. in the kinetics of ligand binding studies of cytochrome c_1. This type of reaction scheme must be postulated in order to explain our observation, in that k_{obs} is not dependent on the cytochrome c or c_1 concentration but the amplitude is proportional to their concentration. For this reason, the simplest mechanism postulated by König et al. (7) cannot be considered a feasible one (13).

ROLE OF THE HINGE PROTEIN ON THE ELECTRON TRANSFER REACTION OF CYTOCHROME c_1 AND c

The kinetic investigation (13) of the electron transfer reaction between cytochrome c_1 and c in the presence of the hinge protein, using two band c_1 (c_1 isolated with the hinge protein) and one band c_1 plus the hinge protein (c_1 with the added hinge protein) indicates that our proposed mechanism (13) for electron transfer between one band cytochrome c_1 and c appears to be applicable to the electron transfer reaction between these two cytochromes in the presence of the hinge protein. At high ionic strength, at which the c_1-Hp-c complex does not form, the measured rate constant, k_{obs}, is not affected by the hinge protein. However, the results observed at low ionic strength are somewhat different from those at high ionic strength; the presence of the hinge protein increases the rate constant (k_{obs}) for the forward reaction (c_1^{2+} with c^{3+}) but have little effect for the back reaction (c_1^{3+} with c^{2+}).

The observed spectral variations during electron transfer reaction between two band cytochrome c_1 and cytochrome c indicate that the reaction occurs via the formation of transient intermediates, $(c_1^{2+}-Hp \bullet c^{3+})$ and $c^{3+}-Hp \bullet c^{2+})$ as similar as that shown in equation 1. The rate constant, k_{obs}, was about 20% lower for the back reaction $(c_1^{3+}-Hp$ with $c^{2+})$ as compared with that for the forward reaction $(c_1^{2+}-Hp$ with $c^{3+})$. With increasing ionic strength the rate constant decreased slightly, 30% for the forward reaction and 17% for the back reaction.

The electron transfer reactions between one band c_1 plus the hinge protein and cytochrome c was also very similar to that of two band c_1

and cytochrome c for both of the forward reaction and the back reaction; the rate constant was decreased about 20% when ionic strength was increased from 0.02 M to 0.5 M cacodylate buffer, pH 7.4. The rate constant for the back reaction, that is, one band c_1^{3+} plus the hinge protein with c^{2+}, was about 28% lower than that of the forward reaction. It is noteworthy that the increase of the amount of the hinge protein to the reaction system (up to 2.5 times of molar ratio of the hinge protein to cytochrome c_1) did not have further effect on k_{obs} at both of low and high ionic strength.

Our results show that the hinge protein does not affect the electron transfer reaction between cytochrome c_1 and c at high ionic strength, but it does at low ionic strength. The effect of the hinge protein is not great but seems to be significant for the forward reaction (c_1^{2+} with c^{3+}) with little effect for the back reaction (c_1^{3+} with c^{2+}). Since the hinge protein does not seem to affect the rate constant of electron transfer reaction between c_1 and c, at least at high ionic strength, it is plausible to state that the hinge protein, or c_1-Hp-c complex, may not directly participate to the electron transfer reaction between cytochromes c_1 and c. Nevertheless, they may control some conformational rearrangement during electron transfer between these two cytochromes.

Previously we have proposed (4, 13) that the hinge protein functions as a bridge between cytochrome c_1 and c, and as a result the heme moiety of these two cytochromes are in close proximity to transfer electrons from each other. This may accord with a report (19) that the hinge protein could be crosslinked with both cytochromes c_1 and c in the presence of cross-linking agent.

A complete reaction scheme (14) is postulated depicting the role of the hinge protein for the electron transfer reaction between cytochrome c_1 and c as shown in Eq. 2.

$$c_1^{2+} + c^{3+} \underset{k_{-1}}{\overset{K_1}{\rightleftharpoons}} (c_1^{2+}\bullet c^{3+}) \underset{k_{-2}}{\overset{k_2}{\rightleftharpoons}} (c_1^{3+}\bullet c^{2+}) \underset{}{\overset{K_3}{\rightleftharpoons}} c_1^{3+} + c^{2+}$$

$$+ \text{Hp} \downarrow\uparrow - \text{Hp} \qquad\qquad + \text{Hp} \downarrow\uparrow - \text{Hp} \qquad\qquad (2)$$

$$(c_1^{2+}\text{-Hp}\bullet c^{3+}) \underset{k_{-2}'}{\overset{k_2'}{\rightleftharpoons}} (c_1^{3+}\text{-Hp}\bullet c^{2+})$$

$$\downarrow\uparrow \qquad\qquad\qquad \downarrow\uparrow$$

$$(c_1^{2+}\text{-Hp-}c^{3+}) \longrightarrow (c_1^{3+}\text{-Hp-}c^{2+})$$

In the absence of the hinge protein, $k_2 \leq k_{-2}$ and in the presence of the hinge protein, $k_2' \geq k_{-2}'$ at high ionic strength but at low ionic strength $k_2' > k_{-2}'$.

EQUILIBRIUM CONSTANT FOR THE REACTION OF CYTOCHROME c_1 AND c

The equilibrium of equation 3 was studied by direct spectrophotometric measurements (14).

$$c_1^{2+} + c^{3+} \rightleftharpoons c_1^{3+} + c^{2+} \qquad\qquad (3)$$

The equilibrium constants, Keq, were 1.10 for one band c_1, 1.52 for two band c_1, and 1.65 for one band c_1 plus the hinge protein at 2°C in 20 mM cacodylate buffer containing 1% Emasol 1130. Additional amount of the hinge protein to one band c_1 plus the hinge protein (c_1 to Hp in a ratio between 1 and 2) does not significantly change Keq. The increase of ionic strength has almost no effect on Keq of one band c_1 (1.1 at 0.02 M and 0.95 at 0.5 M) but a rather significant effect on Keq of two band c_1 and one band c_1 plus the hinge protein showing 1.02 and 1.1 at 0.5 M of the ionic strength for two respective cases at 2°C.

In contrast to the effect of ionic strength, a large effect of temperature on Keq was observed for both one band c_1 and two band c_1 showing the decrease to less than half of Keq from 2°C to 20°C (see ref. 14).

The equilibrium constants were also reported, 3.5 by Yu et al. (5) and 0.7 by König et al. (7). Keq measurement of König et al. was in a medium of 0.1 M phosphate buffer, pH 7.0 at 10°C and their result of Keq = 0.7 is comparable to our result at 0.5 M cacodylate buffer, pH 7.4 at 2°C. Although we cannot clearly explain the difference between the result of Keq = 3.5 by Yu et al. (5) and our present data, it is most probably due to the fact that c_1 preparation of Yu et al. (6) is different from our present preparation of two band c_1; their preparation may contain other small protein of 15,000 Da in addition to the hinge protein and is in a higher polymerized form.

The equilibrium constant for two band c_1 seems to be affected with the increase of ionic strength. At 2°C Keq is decreased in ≈33% from 0.02 to 0.5 M of the ionic strength, whereas, at 20°C the change was ≈26% showing less effect than at 2°C. Although more experiments may be needed to clarify this, it could indicate that electrostatic interactions involved in the stable c_1-Hp-c complex formation are also modulated with temperature. It is generally understood that an increase of temperature weakens the electrostatic or ionic interactions. The low value of Keq at 20°C with less ionic strength effect, comparing to Keq at 2°C, may indicate that the electrostatic interaction is weakened at 20°C.

TEMPERATURE AND SOLVENT DEPENDENCE

The ethylene glycol increases the rate constant for the reaction of cytochrome c_1^{2+} with c^{3+} about 60% in the absence of the hinge protein, but slightly increases the rate constant, ≈18%, for the reaction of two band c_1 and c. Although there is no general rule for the ethylene glycol effect on the rate constant, cryosolvents can change the thermodynamic parameters influencing the conformation of the proteins.

The temperature effect from +2 to –24°C on the rate constant for the reaction between two band c_1 and c shows a "break" between –15 and –21°C in the Arrhenius plot (14), whereas in the reaction of one band c_1 and c, the break was observed at higher temperature (between –5 and –10°C) (13). This "break" or "jump" was considered to be the consequence of a variation of equilibrium resulting from a conformational change of the cytochrome c_1, which is modulated by the hinge protein.

These results from both the ethylene glycol and temperature effects explain that cytochrome c_1 without the hinge protein is more sensitive to the physico-chemical environment than two band c_1. This is consistent with our observations in various other experiments such as photoreduction and autooxidation of cytochrome c_1, in which one band c_1 is more easily autooxidized and photoreduced than two band c_1.

It seems that the hinge protein is necessary for stabilizing the structure of cytochrome c_1 and inducing an active conformation of cytochrome c_1.

CONCLUDING REMARKS

The mechanism of the electron transfer reaction between cytochrome c_1 and c may be postulated as follows: 1) Transient intermediates $c_1 \bullet c$) or (c_1-Hp$\bullet c$) complexes are formed during the electron transfer, either in the absence or the presence of the hinge protein. 2) The hinge protein or (c_1-Hp-c) complex may function as a regulator for the reaction of electron transfer with no direct participation. 3) The regulating process by the hinge protein can be postulated in such a way that the hinge protein induce a special conformational arrangement of cytochrome c_1 in which the electron transfer from c_1^{2+} to c^{3+} is favored.

However, there may be a possibility of electron flow from c_1^{2+} through the hinge protein to c, as demonstrated in the recent report of "long-range electron transfer in heme protein", by Gray and coworkers (20). In this report it is claimed that electron transfer can take place over large distances through a protein. This was evidenced from their kinetic experiments with a ruthenium derivative of cytochrome c (a_5Ru^{2+}(His-33)cyt.c^{3+}). It is suggested that this long range (Ru^{2+} Fe^{3+}) electron transfer rate does not depend strongly on temperature (21). It is also mentioned that this weak temperature dependence of the ong range electron transfer rate suggests that the energy for reorganization of the heme c in the protein is relatively small (0.3 eV) (21).

Considering the less temperature effect on the reaction between cytochrome c_1 with the hinge protein and c than that of cytochrome c_1 and c, a long-range electron transfer mechanism may be involved in the reaction between cytochrome c_1 and c in the presence of the hinge protein. Particularly, the electron transfer between cytochrome c_1 and c in mitochondrial membrane will be different from that of isolated cytochrome c_1 and c in aqueous medium due to the properties of membrane proteins as discussed recently by Moore and Rogers (22). Further study with the reaction between liposome inlaid cytochrome c_1 and cytochrome c may be able to give more definitive answer to the mechanism of electron transfer between these two cytochromes.

ACKNOWLEDGMENTS

This work was supported by grants GM 16767 and HL 12576 from the National Institutes of Health and grant BC 349 from the American Cancer Society (TEK) and by Grant-in-Aid from American Heart Association (CHK).

REFERENCES

1. Chiang, Y. L., Kaminsky, L. S., and King, T. E. (1976) *J. Biol. Chem.* 251, 29-36
2. Kaminsky, L. S., Chiang, Y. L., Yu, C. A., and King, T. E. (1974) *Biochem. Biophys. Res. Commun.* 59, 688-692
3. Kim, C. H., and King, T. E. (1981) *Biochem. Biophys. Res. Commun.* 101, 607-614
4. Kim, C. H., and King, T. E. (1983) *J. Biol. Chem.* 258, 13543-13551

5. Yu, C. A., Yu, L., and King, T. E. (1973) *J. Biol. Chem.* <u>248</u>, 528-533

6. Yu, C. A., Yu, L., and King, T. E. (1972) *J. Biol. Chem.* <u>247</u>, 1012-1019

7. König, B. W., Wilms, J., and van Gelder, B. F. (1981) *Biochim. Biophys. Acta* <u>636</u>, 9-16

8. König, B. W., Schilder, L. T. M., Tervoort, M. J., and van Gelder, B. F. (1980) *Biochim. Biophys. Acta* <u>121</u>, 283-295

9. Wakabayashi, S., Takeda, H., Matsubara, H., Kim, C. H., and King, T. E. (1982) *J. Biochem.* (Tokyo) <u>91</u>, 2077-2085

10. Kim, C. H., and King, T. E. (1986) *Meth. Enzymol.* <u>126</u>, 238-253

11. King, T. E. (1983) *Adv. Enzymol. Relat. Areas Mol. Biol.* <u>54</u>, 267-366

12. Kim, C. H., and King, T. E. (1987) *Biochemistry* <u>26</u>, *1955-1961*

13. Kim, C. H., Balny, C., and King, T. E. (1984) *Proc. Natl. Acad. Sci. U.S.A.* <u>81</u>, 2026-2029

14. Kim, C. H., Balny, C., and King, T. E. (1987) *J. Biol. Chem.* <u>262</u>, 8103-8108

15. Flatmark, T. (1966) *Acta Chem. Scand.* <u>20</u>, 1476-1486

16. Creutz, C., and Sutin, N. (1974) *J. Biol. Chem.* <u>249</u>, 6788-6795

17. Kihara, M. (1981) *Biochim. Biophys. Acta* <u>634</u>, 93-104

18. Stellwagen, E., and Schulman, R. G. (1973) *J. Mol. Biol.* <u>80</u>, 559-573

19. Millet, F., Stonehuyerner, J., O'Brien, P., Geren, L., Steidl, J., Yu, L. and Yu, C. A. (1985) *Biophys. J.* <u>47</u>, 197a

20. Mayo, S. L., Ellis, Jr., W. R., Crutchley, R. J., and Gray, H. B. (1986) *Science* <u>233</u>, 948-952

21. Nocera, D. G., Winkler, J. R., Yocom, K. M., Bordignon, E., Gray, H. B. (1984) *J. Am. Chem. Soc.* <u>106</u>, 5145-5150

22. Moore, G. R., and Rogers, N. K. (1985) *J. Inorg. Biochem.* <u>23</u>, 219-226

HEME CLUSTER STRUCTURES AND ELECTRON TRANSFER

IN MULTIHEME CYTOCHROMES C3

Richard Haser and Jacques Mossé

CRMC2-CNRS, Campus Luminy
Case 913, 13288 Marseille cedex 09
France

INTRODUCTION

Cytochromes c_3 (molecular weight around 14000) form a class of multi-heme cytochromes which are present in all anaerobic sulfate-reducing bacteria belonging to the genus Desulfovibrio (1). They are essential electron carriers in several electron transfer processes and their oxidation-reduction properties have been studied in some detail (2). Their main function within the electron transport chain is to act as the natural electron donor and acceptor for hydrogenase, the iron-sulfur enzyme responsible for the reversible oxidation of molecular hydrogen. They contain four hemes covalently bound to the polypeptide chain through thioether bonds provided by cysteinyl residues. The 5th and 6th iron axial ligands are histidinyl side chains, an iron coordination typical of the cytochromes b_5. Electrochemical and spectroscopic studies are consistent with four heme sites of non identical and pH dependent low redox potential. The oxido-reduction midpoint potential for cytochrome c_3 from various species of Desulfovibrio ranges from about -400mV to -120mV (to be compared with the range +100mV to +450mV observed for cytochrome c).

Nuclear magnetic resonance studies of these proteins in solution have provided a large body of information on the kinetic characteristics of the oxido-reduction process (3,4). In order to gain further insight into the understanding of the intra- and inter-molecular electron transfer mechanisms, it is important to underline the structural factors which may control the heme-heme interactions.

The X-ray structure determinations of two tetra-heme cytochromes c3 from two species of Desulfovibrio have led to the detailed features of this class of redox proteins (5,6).

CYTOCHROME C_3 FOLD

Cytochrome c_3, from Desulfovibrio desulfuricans, Norway strain, (hereafter D.d.N.), consists of a single polypeptide chain of 118 amino acids and binding four heme groups. Its crystal structure has already been described in some detail (5) and that of cytochrome c_3 from Desulfovibrio vulgaris Miyazaki F. (D.v.M.) has been refined at high resolution (6).

As it is shown in Figure 1 the molecule is folded in two structural parts, different in size (residues 1 to 72 and 73 to 118) with one heme in each domain, the two others (hemes 3 and 2) filling the groove dividing the molecule. The polypeptide chain is wrapping around a compact four heme cluster which presents a quite high overall exposure to the external medium. The sole alpha-helix (residues 84 to 101) is in domain 2 and runs nearly parallel to the planes of hemes 4 and 3. It provides the attachment sites Cys92, Cys95 and His96 for heme 4 and one iron axial ligand (His89) for heme 3. The chain folding is also characterized by a large number of reverse turns which comprise about 45% of the structure. The charged side chains are fairly evenly distributed over the molecular surface. However there is a significant cluster of positive charges (Lys99, Lys100, Lys101, Asp102, Lys103, Lys104) at the C-terminal end of the helix which, as shown later on, may be important in the recognition process of redox partners.

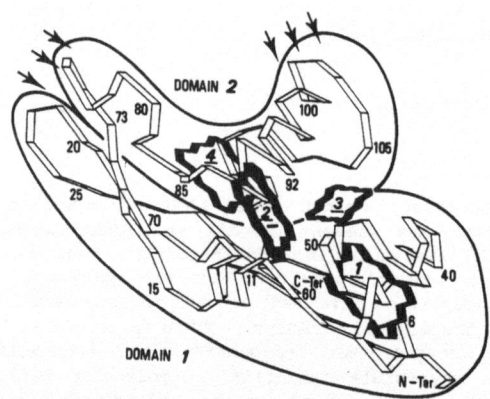

Fig. 1 - The α-carbon chain with the heme cluster of cytochrome c_3 D.d.N. Heme numbering is as in (7). The arrows point to the presumed recognition sites for other redox partners. Iron to iron distances are : Fe1-Fe3 10.9 Å ; Fe1-Fe2 12.8 Å ; Fe2-Fe3 16.8 Å ; Fe4-Fe2 16.3 Å ; Fe1-Fe4 17.3 Å ; Fe3-Fe4 12.7 Å.

HEME CORE

In figure 2 is shown the heme cluster with some of the intervening amino acid residues. Indeed the folding of the polypeptide chain creates a specific environment and solvent exposure of each redox center. The heme pockets have in common the following structural characteristics :

- the cysteinyl thioether links and the axial histidinyl iron ligands

- at least one aromatic side chain in close contact with the porphyrin ring

- a relatively high solvent accessibility of each heme (the accessible area being 125 Å^2 on average (6), to be compared to 40 Å^2 for a heme in a typical monoheme c-type cytochrome) and one cysteinyl thioether bridge (Cysteines 44, 66, 95 and 111) exposed at the surface of the molecule.

The orientations of the porphyrin moieties are dictated mainly by the thioether bonds to the backbone, by the axial iron ligands and also by the

424

hydrogen bonds in which the latter residues are involved. The first three heme groups along the chain are nearly perpendicular to one another, and the fourth adopts an orientation roughly parallel to the first (the angle between the corresponding porphyrin planes being about 35°, see also Figure 3).

As already underlined, the overall solvent exposure of the redox centre is a remarkable feature of the structure, the accessibility of the individual hemes increasing in the order 1,4,3,2. Each porphyrin ring has one edge protruding at the surface of the protein. The location of the eight propionate groups reflects also the various heme exposures : - both propionic groups of heme 2 participate in intermolecular electrostatic interactions, (Figure 3) in contrast those of hemes 3 and 4 are extending into external medium.

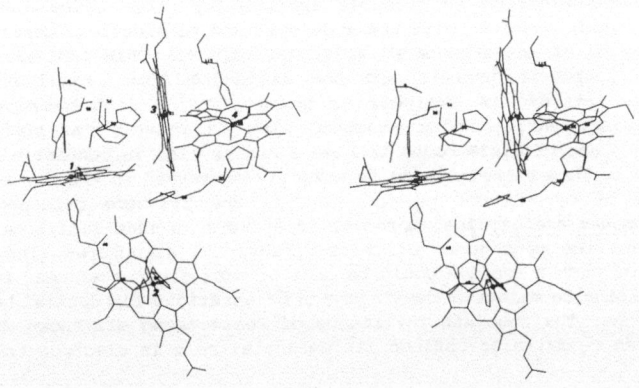

Fig. 2 - Stereoscopic view of the heme core in cytochrome c_3 D.d.N. with the nearby aromatic residues. For clarity the cysteine thioether bridges to the backbone have been omitted.

Despite a poor degree of sequence homology (about 30%, 36 strictly conserved residues including the 16 amino acids involved in heme binding), the two cytochrome c_3 three-dimensional structures reveal an overall similarity and particularly the redox cores are remarkably conserved in terms of iron to iron distances and also of relative heme orientations. The iron-iron separations differ only by 0.4 Å on the average. Details of this comparison and diagrams are given in a recent review by Mathews (7). A more accurate description for cytochrome c_3 D.d.N. can be made when refinement of the model and addition of diffraction data at higher resolution are completed. A set of diffraction data at 1.7 Å resolution has now been collected using synchrotron radiation. On the other hand the preliminary refinement of our model at 2.5 Å resolution (8) has already led to the conclusion that the hemes present a significant puckering, the porphyrin rings having a saddle shape, like in cytochrome c_3 D.v.M. (6) and in tuna cytochrome c (9). There is also evidence for about 40 specific water molecule sites, some of them being in the vicinity of the redox groups.

Extension of the analysis up to 1.7 Å resolution will allow a detailed comparison with the refined high resolution structure of cytochrome c_3 D.v.M. It should also provide clues concerning the subtle differences between these proteins, like the differences in midpoint redox potentials.

ROLE OF PROTEIN IN HEME-HEME INTERACTIONS

Intramolecular heme-heme interactions

The crystallographic results strongly suggest that hemes are interacting within the redox cluster. First of all owing to the close proximity of the hemes which favors overlap between the pi electron orbitals from adjacent porphyrin rings, it has been suggested that direct electron transfer can take place (10). For example some edge to edge distances are about 6 Å (as between hemes 1 and 2). This heme-heme electron communication is probably assisted by some nearby intervening aromatic residues which, with their delocalized pi electrons contribute to the formation of an extended pi molecular orbital. This orbital involves also the porphyrin pyrrole and the imidazole iron ligand rings. Of particular interest is the pair of hemes 1 and 3 with between them a phenylalanine, Phe34, whose aromatic ring is roughly parallel to the imidazole plane of His39 bound to heme 3 and is also in contact within 4 Å with heme 1. This phenylalanine is strictly conserved in the six available sequences of cytochromes c_3 and also in the tri-heme cytochrome from Desulfuromonas acetoxidans. Moreover it appears in identical localization within both the cytochrome c_3 three-dimensional structures. The primary function of such a residue could be that of excluding water near the hemes and of helping to maintain the porphyrin orientations for optimal heme-heme interactions. The absolute invariance of Phe34 among all known multiheme cytochromes c_3 may also reflect its essential role in electron transfer.

The demonstration that a phenylalanine lying between two interacting heme groups can affect the rate of electron transfer has been given very recently in the case of the cytochrome c-cytochrome c peroxidase complex (11). Previous computer modeling studies of this association have suggested the functional importance of a specific phenylalanine residue. Its replacement with other non aromatic amino acid residues, using site directed mutagenesis, leads to a dramatic decrease in the rate of electron transfer reaction. Moreover these experiments show that the electron transfer process in this system is directional.

A similar arrangement, but with obviously weaker heme-heme interactions owing to the iron to iron distance (16.3 Å), exists between hemes 2 and 4 with the intervening Phe88. However this residue is not conserved and has no structural equivalent in the cytochrome c_3 D.v.M. three-dimensional structure.

Hemes 3 and 4 (iron to iron distance is 12.7 Å) appears as a possible pair of strong interacting groups. Both porphyrin rings are approximately parallel to the alpha-helix running from residues 84 to 101 and providing an iron ligand for each heme (His89 and His96). No significant pi orbital overlap between these hemes seems possible as the helix is intervening. However we have suggested that a strong interaction between these groups could be mediated by the large internal electric field generated by the alpha-helix dipole and might be transmitted through the iron histidine ligands which protrude from this "active site helix" (12). Along these lines, it is of interest to note that for hemoglobin the alpha-helix dipole is suggested to be responsible for the high pka of a histidine residue (13). The comparison of the cytochrome c_3 spatial structures has led us to suggest also that the helical segment could act as a modulator of the redox potentials. Moreover as proposed earlier the cluster of positively charged residues (some of them being highly conserved) at the carboxy end of the helix may function as a potential recognition site for redox partners of the electron transport chain. If this is the case, interaction of these redox components (hydrogenase, ferredoxin ...) with the helix could affect its electrical properties and therefore could perturb the attached heme groups.

Intermolecular heme-heme interactions

The importance of the heme binding helix is reinforced when one considers its role in the intermolecular contacts. The lysines 100 and 101 form salt bridges with the propionate groups of heme 2 of a symmetry related molecule (hemes 1',2',3',4' Figure 3). The structural consequence of these interactions is a close approach between heme 1' and heme 4 (Fe1'-Fe4 18.7 Å, edge to edge distance 12.5 Å) at the molecular interface. Most striking is the nearly parallel alignment of these hemes.

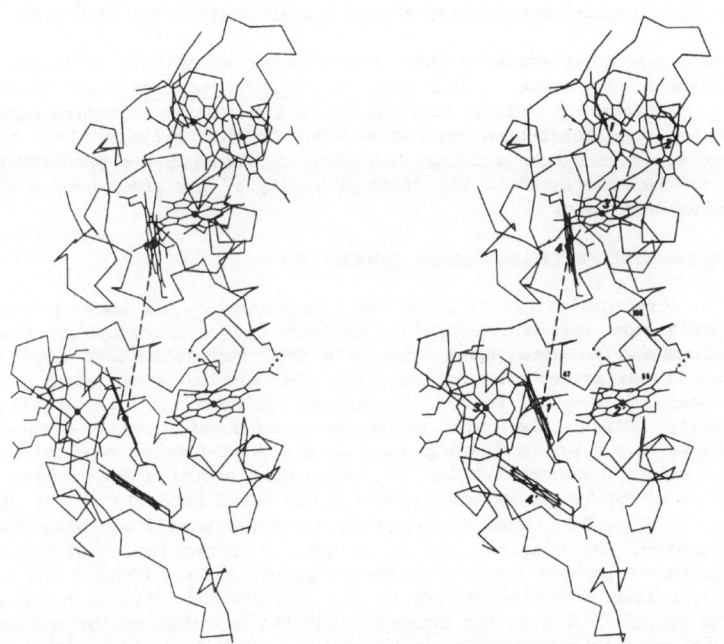

Fig. 3 - Stereoscopic view of the intermolecular association. The distance Fe1'-Fe4 is 18.7 Å. The dots indicate the intermolecular salt bridges formed between Lys 100, Lys 101 and the propionate side chains of Heme 2'.

There are a number of reasons to believe that this intermolecular heme arrangement has a functional importance :

- on the basis of ^{1}H-NMR studies, there is strong evidence for a fast intermolecular electron exchange between heme moieties of cytochrome c_3 (14)

- the high electrical conductivity observed for this type of electron transferring protein (15) may be explained by the observed interlocked heme-heme system

- this redox organisation may be consistent with the presumed electron storage properties of cytochrome c_3 (16), electrons being delivered by the storage unit when redox partners have to bind to the specific sites inferred from structure and sequence comparisons of various cytochromes c_3

- the fact that hemes 1' and 4 are roughly parallel is a characteristic common to all computer-generated hemoprotein associations studied so far(7)

- computer-graphic docking and analysis of a cytochrome c_3.ferredoxin complex (8,17) have shown that the heme group interacting with the iron sulfur cluster of the ferredoxin corresponds precisely to one of the hemes (heme 4) involved in donor-acceptor coupling interactions within the intermolecular redox core of cytochrome c_3

- recently in a series of kinetic experiments it has been conclusively shown that significant electron transfer rates occur in protein systems, under physiological conditions, across distances of 10 to 20 Å (18)

- we have now clear evidence that the redox center spatial arrangement of the tri-heme cytochrome c_3 from Desulfuromonas acetoxidans (or cytochrome $c_{551.5}$, previously named c_7) corresponds to the cluster formed by hemes 1, 3 and 4 in the tetra-heme cytochromes c_3. In this protein also, a fast intermolecular electron exchange has been observed (19), a property which again may be associated to the close proximity of the redox groups at the molecular interface.

STRUCTURAL SIMILARITY WITH OTHER CYTOCHROMES

The structural elucidation of two cytochromes c_3 has shown a tertiary fold and a redox center organisation that are unique among cytochromes. It is interesting to note again that this fold can accomodate many local structural variations without altering the spatial arrangement of the functional redox unit. However we already pointed out (12) a striking similarity between the heme arrangement observed in the crystal of cytochrome c_3 D.d.N. and the heme core in the tetra-heme c-type cytochrome of the reaction center complex of the purple bacteria R. viridis, the structure of this complex having been established recently at the atomic levels (20,21). When these arrangements are superimposed and when the fit is optimized, the reaction center is seen to share the c_3 D.d.N. heme cluster formed by heme 1 of one protein molecule and the hemes 3 and 4 of a symmetry-related molecule (Figure 3). Not only are the inter-iron distances similar (within 1.6 Å on the average), but the orientations of homologous hemes are roughly retained. It is therefore tempting to propose that there is a common multi-heme architecture which allows efficient electron transfer in very distinct systems operating in such different organisms as strictly anaerobic bacteria and photosynthetic bacteria.

Finally, the sequence comparison between the protein binding fragment of heme 3 in cytochrome c_3 D.d.N. (about 32 amino acids) and an eucaryotic cytochrome c reveals a high extent of homology : around 44% of the residues are strictly conserved and a much higher value is found if one takes into account conservatively substituted amino acids (Figure 4). This homology is significantly higher than that observed between the six available cytochromes c_3 from different <u>Desulfovibrio</u> species (22) : there are about 25% strictly invariant residues or 30% if a pairwise sequence comparison is made.

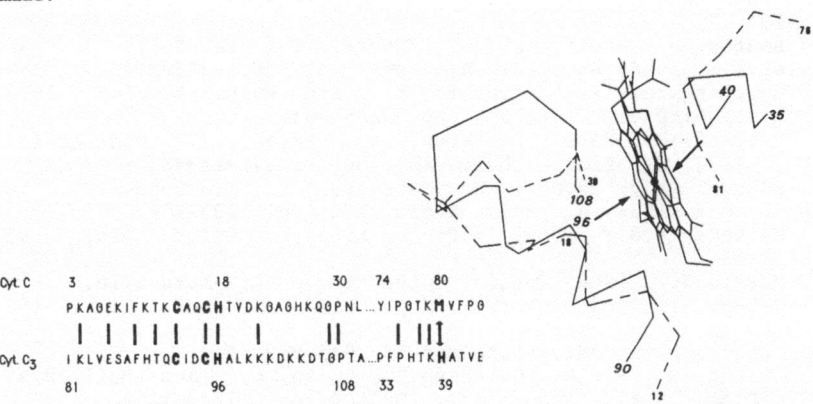

Cyt. C   3   18   30   74   80

P K A G E K I F K T K C A Q C H T V D K G A G H K Q Q P N L ... Y I P G T K M V F P G

Cyt. C_3 I K L V E S A F H T Q C I D C H A L K K K D K K D T G P T A ... P F P H T K H A T V E

    81   96   108   33   39

Fig. 4 – Sequence comparison between the heme binding segments of cytochrome c (rice sequence, numbering according to (23)) and of cytochrome c_3 D.d.N.. Residues in bold-faced type are the heme attachment sites.

Fig. 5 – Superimposition between hemes and their protein binding fragments. Dashed lines correspond to cytochrome c. The carbonyl oxygen atoms of Pro 108 and Pro 30 are hydrogen bonded to His 96 and His 18 respectively.

Among the four redox groups of cytochrome c_3 D.d.N., it is clear that heme 3 with its binding fragment bears the highest resemblance to cytochrome c. Aside from conservation of amino acids involved in heme attachment, spacing of cysteine residues is maintained. Particularly noteworthy is the conservation of the hydrogen bond interaction between the axial iron histidinyl ligand and a proline residue : in both proteins the delta nitrogen of the histidine is hydrogen bonded to the carbonyl oxygen of a proline and spacing between these two amino acids is identical. On Figure 5 we represent a best fit between the alpha carbon chains and the heme groups.

These findings support the idea that cytochrome c_3, with its inter-domain heme 3, contains the essential features required for the structure and function of the less sophisticated cytochrome c.

It is tempting to speculate that cytochrome c_3, a current representative of very ancient microorganims, may be the primitive precursor of the cytochrome c family.

ACKNOWLEDGEMENTS

We thank Mrs D. Laporte, J.P. Astier for technical help and Mrs D. Destre for expert typing.

The authors gratefully acknowledge financial support from the CNRS.

REFERENCES

1. Odom, J.M. and Peck, H.D.: 1984, Ann. Rev. Microbiol. 38, pp. 551-592.
2. Niki, K., Kawasaki, Y., Nishimura, N., Higuchi, Y., Yasuoka, N. and Kakudo, M.: 1984, J. Electroanal. Chem. 168, pp. 275-286.
3. Santos, H., Moura, J.J.G., Moura, I., Le Gall, J. and Xavier,A.: 1984, Eur. J. Biochem. 141, pp. 283-296.
4. Guerlesquin, F., Bruschi, M. and Wuthrich, K.: 1985, Biochim. Biophys. Acta 830, pp. 296-303.
5. Pierrot, M., Haser, R., Frey, M., Payan, F. and Astier, J.P.: 1982, J. Biol. Chem. 257, pp. 14341-14348.
6. Higuchi, Y., Kusunoki, M., Matsuura, Y., Yasuoka, N. and Kakudo, M.: 1984, J. Mol. Biol. 172, pp. 109-139.
7. Mathews, F.S.: 1985, In Prog. Biophys. Molec. Biol. 45, pp. 1-56.
8. Mosse, J.: 1986, Thesis, University of Aix-Marseille.
9. Takano, T. and Dickerson, R.E.: 1981, J. Mol. Biol. 153, 79-94
10. Haser, R.: 1981, Biochimie 63, 945-949.
11. Liang, N., Pielak, G., Mauk,G., Smith, M. and Hoffman,B.: 1987, Proc. Natl. Acad. Sci. USA 84, pp. 1249-1252.
12. Haser, R. Frey, M. and Payan, F.: 1987, In Crystallography and Molecular Biology, pp.425-437, Plenum Publishing Corporation, New York.
13. Perutz, M.F., Gronenborn, A.M., Clore, G.M., Fogg, J.H. and Shih, D.T.- b.: 1985, J. Mol. Biol. 183, 491-498.
14. Guerlesquin, F., Noailly, M. and Bruschi, M.: 1985, Biochem. Biophys. Res. Comm. 130, pp. 1102-1108.
15. Kimura, K. Nakahara, Y., Yagi, T. and Inokuchi, H.: 1979, J. Chem. Phys. 70, pp. 3317-3321.
16. Dobson, C.M., Hoyle, N.J., Geraldes, C.F., Wright, P.E., Williams, R.J.P, Bruschi, M. and Le Gall, J.: 1974, Nature 249, pp. 425-429.
17. Cambillau, C. et al., to be published.
18. Mayo, S.L., Ellis, W.R., Crutchley, R.J. and Gray, H.B.: 1986, Science 233, pp. 948-952.
19. Moura, J.J.G., Moore, G.K., Williams, R.J.P., Probst, I., Le Gall, J. and Xavier, A.V.: 1984, Eur. J. Biochem. 144, pp. 433-440.
20. Deisenhofer, J., Epp,O., Miki, K., Huber, R. and Michel, H.: 1984, J. Mol. Biol. 180, pp. 385-398.
21. Deisenhofer, J., Epp, O., Miki, K., Huber, R. and Michel, H.: 1985, Nature 318, pp. 618-624.
22. Bruschi, M.: 1981, Biochim. Biophys. Acta 671, pp. 219-226.
23. Dickerson, R.E.: 1980, Sci. Amer. 242, pp. 99-110.

IV. REACTION DOMAINS AND OXIDO-REDUCTION MECHANISMS: Short Reports

ELECTRON EXCHANGE BETWEEN CYTOCHROMES a

P. Sarti, F. Malatesta, G. Antonini, M.T. Wilson, and
M. Brunori

Department of Biochemical Sciences and CNR Center of Molecular
Biology, University of Rome "La Sapienza", Department of
Experimental Medicine and Biochemical Sciences, University of
Rome "Tor Vergata", Rome, Italy. Department of Chemistry
University of Essex, Colchester, United Kingdom

When the carbon monoxide complex of fully reduced cytochrome c oxidase is
mixed with oxygen containing buffer, complex kinetic progress curves are
observed. The wavelength dependence of the amplitudes of a slow (k' 0.02
s-1) and a faster autocatalytic processes were interpreted by Gibson and
Greenwood by attributing the fast phase to the oxidation of cytochrome a
that is completed before full oxidation of cytochrome a3 (1-2).

Cytochrome a (and possibly Cu A) of a monomer having the corresponding
cytochrome a3 still reduced and bound to CO can be oxidized by giving
electrons to another enzyme molecule already fully oxidized. To test
this hypothesis we have performed experiments with two different preparations of cytochrome oxidase monomers. The figure shows the dependence
of cytochrome a oxidation rate on monomer concentration.

Concentration dependence of the maximum cytochrome a oxidation rate constant
in a CO displacement experiment with monomeric cytochrome oxidase. (●) refers
to the III-less enzyme obtained by chymotryptic digestion of the beef heart
enzyme, having a sedimentation coefficient of 6; (O) refers to the shark
(Sphyrna lewini) enzyme, having an S = 7. The arrow indicates the CO-off
rate constant.

The III-less enzyme was obtained as in (3); shark oxidase, purified as in
(4) was a kind gift of Dr. D. Bickar. Oxygen free enzyme, dissolved in

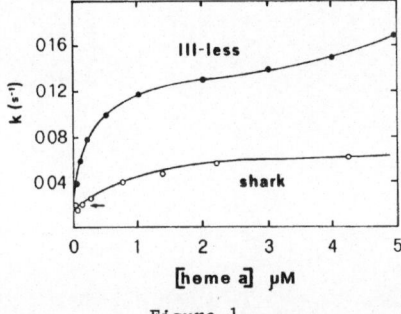

Figure 1

25 mM phosphate buffer, 0.5% Tween 80, pH 7.3, was reduced with 0.5 mM
dithionite in the presence of 0.1 mM CO and mixed in a stopped-flow apparatus
with oxygen saturated buffer. The observation wavelength was 450 nm, which
is isosbestic for cytochrome a3. Temperature 20°C.

It should be noticed that the maximal rate of oxidation of cytochrome a in
both the shark enzyme and the III-less oxidase approaches at very low concentration the CO-off rate.

It may be concluded that:
i) at sufficient low concentration the oxidation of cytochrome a in a monomeric species proceeds only via oxidation of cytochrome a3 and thus cytochrome a is not oxidized directly by oxygen;
ii) the concentration dependence of the rate of oxidation of cytochrome a
in a population of monomers involves complex kinetics;
iii) other solution components were found to be important in controlling
the rate of electron exchange between cytochromes a.

REFERENCES

1. Q. Gibson and C. Greenwood (1963) Biochem. J. 86, 541.
2. Q. Gibson and C. Greenwood (1964) J. Biol. Chem. 239, 586.
3. I. Puettner et al. (1985) J. Biol. Chem. 260, 3719.
4. M.T. Wilson et al. (1980) J. Biol. Chem. 255, 2722.

PULSED, RESTING AND PEROXY FORMS OF CYTOCHROME OXIDASE

G. Antonini, F. Malatesta, P. Sarti, M.T. Wilson,
and M. Brunori

Department of Experimental Medicine and Biochemical Sciences
University of Rome "Tor Vergata", Department of Biochemical
Sciences and CNR Center of Molecular Biology, University of
Rome "La Sapienza", Rome, Italy, Department of Chemistry
University of Essex, Colchester, UK

Two functionally distinct states of cytochrome oxidase were initially
demonstrated by kinetic experiments and the difference in the catalytic
activity between these two states was attributed to a faster internal
electron transfer observed in the so-called "pulsed" enzyme, which is
obtained by exposing the reduced enzyme to molecular oxygen (1). This
result was supported by the finding that the rate of reduction of cytochrome a is the same in the two functional states of the enzyme (2).

The optical properties of the two states have been for a long time misunderstood. As a matter of fact, when the enzyme reduced with dithionite is
pulsed a variable amount of the peroxy form is obtained with the maximum
of the Soret band moving towards 428 nm (3). This very same spectroscopic
species can be obtained by treating the enzyme with hydrogen peroxide (4).
We present here an experiment performed to distinguish between the optical
properties of the resting, pulsed and peroxy forms of the enzyme.

Cytochrome oxidase was degassed and reduced with 1.5 excess dithionite in
the presence of carbon monoxide. The enzyme was then diluted 100-fold in
a cuvette with oxygen-saturated buffer containing, or not, catalase. Spectra
were successively collected at various times after dilution using a Cary 219
thermostated spectrophotometer. In some cases, the cuvette was flashed
immediately after the dilution of cytochrome oxidase.

When the displacement of CO by oxygen is strongly autocatalytic (5, 6, ourselves), the peak in the Soret region was centered around 428 nm and was
insensitive to the presence of catalase. On the other hand, when rapid CO
dissociation was induced by the flash, the reaction with oxygen, which takes
place immediately, yields a form of oxidase which has a Soret maximum at
425 nm.

It is of interest to note that the slow displacement of CO by oxygen may
lead to the 428 nm form (peroxy form) possibly according to the following
reaction scheme (written for a monomeric cytochrome oxidase) where Step 1
reports the CO dissociation from reduced cytochrome oxidase as described
by Gibson and Greenwood (5), $k=0.02$ s-1. Step 2 is of a very complex
nature and involves electron redistribution among functional units (6).

$$1)\quad \begin{matrix} a^{2+}\ a_3^{2+}\text{-CO} \\ Cu_A^{1+}\ Cu_B^{1+} \end{matrix} + O_2 + 4\,H^+ \longrightarrow \begin{matrix} a^{3+}\ a_3^{3+} \\ Cu_A^{2+}\ Cu_B^{2+} \end{matrix} + 2\,H_2O + CO$$

$$2)\quad \begin{matrix} a^{3+}\ a_3^{3+} \\ Cu_A^{2+}\ Cu_B^{2+} \end{matrix} + \begin{matrix} a^{2+}\ a_3^{2+}\text{-CO} \\ Cu_A^{1+}\ Cu_B^{1+} \end{matrix} \longrightarrow \begin{matrix} a^{2+}\ a_3^{3+} \\ Cu_A^{1+}\ Cu_B^{2+} \end{matrix} + \begin{matrix} a^{3+}\ a_3^{2+}\text{-CO} \\ Cu_A^{2+}\ Cu_B^{1+} \end{matrix}$$

$$3)\quad \begin{matrix} a^{2+}\ a_3^{3+} \\ Cu_A^{1+}\ Cu_B^{2+} \end{matrix} + O_2 \longrightarrow \begin{matrix} a^{3+}\ a_3^{3+}\text{-}O_2^{2-} \\ Cu_A^{2+}\ Cu_B^{2+} \end{matrix}$$

The overall kinetics of this reaction (extensively reinvestigated by us (7)) depends on the aggregation state of the protein and can occur via intermolecular and/or intramolecular electron exchange (rate=0.2-0.5 s-1). Step 3 generates the peroxy form whose yield depends on the efficiency of electron redistribution step 2.

On the other hand, when reduced cytochrome oxidase in combination with CO is flashed in the presence of dioxygen, the resulting species can be iden-tified with the true pulsed one, without contamination of the peroxy form, ng according to the reaction:

$$\begin{matrix} a^{2+}\ a_3^{2+}\text{-CO} \\ Cu_A^{1+}\ Cu_B^{1+} \end{matrix} \xrightarrow[CO]{h\nu} \begin{matrix} a^{2+}\ a_3^{2+} \\ Cu_A^{1+}\ Cu_B^{1+} \end{matrix} + O_2 + 4\,H^+ \longrightarrow \begin{matrix} a^{3+}\ a_3^{3+} \\ Cu_A^{2+}\ Cu_B^{2+} \end{matrix} + 2\,H_2O$$

After several hours, both the pulsed and peroxy forms of cytochrome oxidase shift the maximum of the Soret peak to 418 nm, corresponding to the resting cytochrome oxidase.

REFERENCES

1. M.T. Wilson et al. (1981) Proc. Natl. Acad. Sci. USA 78, 7115.
2. M. Brunori et al. (1979) J. Biol. Chem. 254, 10769.
3. C. Kumar et al. (1984) J. Biol. Chem. 259, 2073.
4. D. Bickar et al. (1982) Biochemistry 21, 2661.
5. Q. Gibson and C. Greenwood (1963) Biochem. J. 86, 541.
6. Q. Gibson and C. Greenwood (1964) J. Biol. Chem. 239, 586.
7. M.T. Wilson et al. Chem. Scripta (1987) in press.

EFFECT OF pH AND TEMPERATURE ON ELECTRON TRANSFER IN MIXED-VALENCE CYTO-CHROME c OXIDASE

Peter Brzezinski and Bo G. Malmström

Department of Biochemistry and Biophysics, Chalmers University of Technology and University of Göteborg
S-412 96 Göteborg, Sweden

Cytochrome c oxidase is the terminal, dioxygen-reducing enzyme in the respiratory chain of mitochondria. The enzyme contains four active metal centers. Two heme groups (cytochrome a and a_3) and two copper ions (Cu_A and Cu_B). Cytochrome oxidase catalyzes a vectorial reaction in which electron transport is coupled to the translocation of protons from the matrix to the cytosol side of the inner mitochondrial membrane (1-3). The requirement of such a pump is that it can exist in two different conformations with different access for protons to the two sides of the membrane. The pump must also control the electron flow through the protein. Such electron gating requires that reduction and the subsequent oxidation of certain metal centers in the protein must take place in different conformations (1, 2).

The existence of redox-linked conformational changes is evident from the redox interactions observed between a and a_3 (4). Cytochrome a accepts an electron from cytochrome c at a reduction potential of 285 mV in the fully oxidized enzyme. When a_3 becomes reduced the potential of a drops to 220 mV whereas that of a_3 is raised to 350 mV. This suggests that there exist two conformations of the enzyme with different driving force for electrons.

Cytochrome oxidase can be prepared in several different states. The mixed valence state, in which the a_3Cu_B pair is reduced whereas a and Cu_A are oxidized, is stabilized by carbon monoxide, which binds to $(a_3Cu_B)^{3+}$ (5). Cu_A has the same EPR-spectrum in this state as in the fully oxidized enzyme (5, 6).

After flash photolysis of the CO-mixed valence complex, electrons are transferred from the a_3Cu_B pair to other metal centers in the enzyme. This reaction has earlier been observed by Boelens et al. (7).

The absorbance change at 830 nm corresponds to 5.8±0.8% reduction of Cu_A. The change at 445 nm corresponds to 3.8±0.8% oxidation of a_3. This suggests that there must exist a very fast equilibrium between a_3 and Cu_B. The half-time for the electron transfer reaction between a_3Cu_B and Cu_A is ~50 μs. The reaction shows a very small temperature dependence (0-25°C) and it is pH-independent (pH 5.0-9.0).

There is also a slower phase (half-time ~100 ms), which represents reduction of a. The slower phase shows a pH (pK ~7.6) and temperature dependence.

If no interaction between a_3 and Cu_B is assumed in this conformation the potential of a, a_3 and Cu_B was found to be 225, 345, and 355 mV (± 10 mV) respectively. The enzyme is thus in a conformation in which the driving force for electrons is considerable. According to electron-transfer theory (8) a small temperature dependence is obtained when the enthalpy change associated with electron transfer is close to zero and the reorganizational barrier is very low. Therefore, we would like to suggest that two-electron reduction of cytochrome c oxidase triggers a conformational change. In the two-electron reduced enzyme the driving force for electrons is high and the structure of the a_3Cu_B site is different from that in the fully oxidized enzyme so that the reorganizational barrier is removed. The fact that the a_3Cu_B site can exist in two different conformations is supported by studies of the transition between the open and closed form, observed in the reactions with cyanide (9).

The distance between Cu_A and a_3Cu_B can be calculated (8) from these experiments. It was found to be ~15 Å, which is consistent with other observations (10).

REFERENCES

1. M. Wikström, K. Krab, and M. Saraste (1981) Cytochrome Oxidase, Academic Press, London.
2. B.G. Malmström (1985) Biochem, Biophys. Acta 811, 1-12.
3. P. Brzezinski and B.G. Malmström (1986) Proc. Natl. Acad. Sci. USA 83, 4282-4286.
4. L.C. Petersen and L.-E Andréasson (1976) FEBS Lett. 66, 52-57.
5. C. Greenwood, M.T. Wilson, and M. Brunori (1974) Biochem. J. 137, 205-215.
6. G.M. Clore, L.-E. Andréasson, B. Karlsson, R. Aasa, and B.G. Malmström (1980) Biochem. J. 185, 155-167.
7. R. Boelens, R. Wever, and B.F. van Gelder (1982) Biochem. Biophys. Acta 682, 264-272.
8. R.A. Marcus and A. Sutin (1985) Biochem. Biophys. Acta 811, 265-322.
9. P. Jensen, M.T. Wilson, R. Aasa, and B.G. Malmström (1984) Biochem. J. 224, 829-837.
10. G.W. Brudvig, D.F. Blair, and S.I. Chan (1984) J. Biol. Chem. 259, 11101-11009.

THE pH-DEPENDENCE OF THE REDUCTIONAL LEVELS OF CYTOCHROME c AND CYTOCHROME

a DURING TURNOVER OF CYTOCHROME c OXIDASE

Per-Eric Thörnström, Brigitta Maison-Peteri, Peter Brzezinski
Lars Arvidsson, Per-Olof Fredriksson, and Bo G. Malmström

Department of Biochemistry and Biophysics, Chalmers University
of Technology and University of Göteborg
S-412 96 Göteborg, Sweden

The four redox centers of cytochrome oxidase (the cytochromes a and a_3 and the coppers Cu_A and Cu_B) are since long known to be involved in electron transport through the enzyme, leading to the reduction of dioxygen. Now it is also known that the enzyme is a proton pump. The energy needed for pumping protons is derived from electron transport, so that the requirements for a redox-linked proton pump must be fullfilled. Namely: 1. Two different conformations must account for an alternating access of a proton-translocating group to the two different sides of the membrane. 2. A redox center must be reduced in one conformation and reoxidized in the other conformation. This also means that there is an obligatory coupling between electron transfer and proton pumping (1, 2).

We here present a model for electron transfer and its coupling to proton uptake and release in the oxidase. The model is based on the following assumptions: The electrons from ferrocytochrome c enter the enzyme via cytochrome a, which is in rapid equilibrium with Cu_A. Both these redox centers have to be reduced to allow further electron transfer to the oxygen-reducing entity, cytochrome a_3-Cu_B. The reduction of both cytochrome a and Cu_A triggers a conformational transition, so providing an alternating access of the H^+ translocating groups.

With this type of model we can semi-quantitatively simulate the behavior of cytochrome a and cytochrome c in kinetic experiments where pulsed enzyme reacts with a limited amount of reduced cytochrome c at different pH values from 5.4 to 8.4. It is not necessary to change the rate constants for these simulations, only the proton concentration is varied with pH. The rate constants used are known or measured constants as far as possible. Other constants are chosen to fit the constraints put by known k_{cat} and k_{cat}/K_m values. These simulations are strongly in favour of a mechanism that is of the transition-state type (2).

The same type of experiments, but with cytochrome oxidase incorporated into phospholipid vesicles were also performed. It seems that both cytochrome c and cytochrome a show essentially the same type of behavior as can be seen in experiments with the pulsed enzyme. On addition of uncouplers and ionophores, both the rate of oxidation of ferrocytochrome c and the rate of reoxidation of cytochrome a increase at most pH values.

We can also see that the reoxidation of cytochrome a is markedly slower

439

in the vesicle experiments than in those with the enzyme present in detergent. This is in accordance with our view (3-5) that the remaining partial reoxidation of cytochrome a, when all ferrocytochrome c is oxidised shows that both a and Cu_A need to be reduced for the conformational change and subsequent electron transfer to occur. The intermolecular transfer of electrons between oxidase molecules must be much slower when the enzyme is incorporated into vesicles.

In steady-state experiments, ascorbate-TMPD-cytochrome c reacted with pulsed oxidase, at different pH values, until oxygen was exhausted. When the total rate of electron flow was not too fast an "overshoot" of the initial phase of the 605 nm absorption change was seen. This phenomenon provides further strong evidence that reduction of both cytochrome a and Cu_A must take place prior to internal electron transfer.

The overshoot, as well as the reductional levels of both cytochrome c and cytochrome a could be simulated almost quantitatively at different pH values and with different cytochrome c concentrations with exactly the same parameters that were used in the simulations of the limited turnover experiments. We consider this as strong support for our model.

REFERENCES

1. M. Wikström, K. Krab, and M. Saraste (1981) Cytochrome Oxidase, Academic Press, London.
2. B.G. Malmström (1985) Biochem. Biophys. Acta 811, 1-12.
3. P. Brzezinski, P.-E. Thörnström, and B.G. Malmström(1986) FEBS Lett. 194, 1-5.
4. E. Antonini, M. Brunori, C. Greenwood, and B.G. Malmström (1970) Nature 228, 936-937.
5. M. Fabian, P.-E. Thörnström, P. Brzezinski, and B.G. Malmström (1987) FEBS Lett. 213, 396-400.

V. Fe-S CENTERS

STUDIES OF BACTERIAL NADH-UBIQUINONE (OR MENAQUINONE)

OXIDOREDUCTASE SYSTEMS

Tomoko Ohnishi, Steven W. Meinhardt, and
Kazunobu Matsushita*

Department of Biochemistry and Biophysics, University of
Pennsylvania, Philadelphia, PA 19104, U.S.A.

*Roche Institute of Molecular Biology, Roche Research
Center, Nutley, New Jersey 07110, U.S.A.[1]

INTRODUCTION

The mitochondrial NADH-ubiquinone (Q) oxidoreductase (Complex I)
contains the highest number of subunit polypeptides, some 25, (1,2) and
redox components (3-5) among the four respiratory chain complexes. It is
generally accepted that Complex I contains 22-24 nonheme iron atoms (6-9)
and equivalent acid labile sulfides, together with 1 FMN and 2-4
ubiquinone (1,2). Three tetranuclear, N-2, N-3, and N-4, and one
binuclear iron-sulfur cluster, N-1b, in Ohnishi's nomenclature, have been
established as intrinsic EPR detectable components of Complex I (10-15),
while the binuclear cluster N-1a remains as a controversial redox
component because it has an extremely low and variable redox midpoint
potential (E_m) in different Complex I preparations (3,4,12).

Because of the complexity of mammalian Site I, we have searched for
useful bacterial Site I model systems for comparative studies. We have
shown that both Escherichia coli (16-18) and Thermus thermophilus cells
contain (16,19,20) an energy transducing NADH-Q oxidoreductase system
with a simpler composition of redox components than the mammalian
counterpart. Another useful bacterial system is Paracoccus denitrificans
which has a "mitochondria-like" Site I system. The cytochrome oxidase
(21) and the cytochrome bc_1 complex (22) of P. denitrificans have been
shown to contain far fewer polypeptides than their mitochondrial
counterparts while retaining all of the redox components (22-24). The
NADH-Q oxidoreductase also appears to follow this rule (25-28). Recent
work on these bacterial Site I systems will be briefly reviewed below.

I. P. DENITRIFICANS SYSTEM

The NADH-Q oxidoreductase in membrane vesicles from P. denitrificans
has been previously shown to contain iron-sulfur clusters similar to

[1]Present Address, Department of Agricultural Chemistry, Faculty of
Agriculture, Yamaguchi University, Yamaguchi 753, Japan

mitochondrial N-1b, N-2, N-3, and N-4 (25,26). This enzyme is sensitive to rotenone and forms $\widetilde{\Delta\mu}_{H+}$ with high $H^+/2e$ stoichiometry analogous to that of the mitochondrial enzyme (29-33). Although the presence of iron-sulfur clusters spectrally similar to those found in mitochondria has been reported, the thermodynamic properties of these clusters have never been studied, leaving the possibility that these clusters may be functionally different from their mitochondrial counterparts.

We have conducted detailed potentiometric analysis and spectral resolution of iron-sulfur clusters using P. dentrificans membrane vesicles (19,27). As summarized in Table I, we have found that the Paracoccus system has 2 binuclear and 3 tetranuclear clusters, N-1a, N-1b, N-2, N-3, and N-4, similar to the mammalian system. Cluster N-1a and N-2 are shown to have pH dependent redox midpoint potentials with pK values near 7.7 while other clusters show pH independent E_m values, again in analogy to the mammalian counterpart. We have revealed, however, some interesting differences between these two systems. Cluster N-1a has much higher E_m value ($E_{m7.0}$=-150 mV) which is close to the E_m of the cluster N-2 (-130 mV). In addition the line shape of cluster N-1a and N-1b are distinguishable due to their differing spectral rhombicity, in contrast to the two bovine heart binuclear clusters. Clusters N-3 and N-4 show EPR spectra with somewhat different spectral parameters from mitochondrial counterparts. These clusters elicit relative spin relaxation properties, which are the reverse of the spectrally similar clusters in mitochondria, as previously reported by Albracht et al. (26). We have also noticed the very labile nature of the cluster N-1a which may have caused controversies over the identity and function of the cluster N-1a. The Paracoccus Site I system is unique because of its general similarities in prosthetic groups to the mammalian system. Recently the NADH dehydrogenase complex from P. denitrificans has been isolated and shown to consist of only 10 polypeptides, containing one FMN, and multiple nonheme iron and acid labile sulfides (28). It also has advantages provided by the bacterial systems, i.e. manipulation of growth conditions (25,34), and in the future genetic manipulation, which are not available from the bovine heart systems.

Table I

Spectral simulation Parameters and other Properties of the Iron-Sulfur clusters N-1a, N-1b, N-2, N-3, and N-4 in P. denitrificans

Component	g_x	g_y	g_z	E_{m7}	E_m/pH	cluster-type
N-1a	1.92	1.94	2.03	-150	-60	[2Fe-2S]
N-1b	1.93	1.94	2.02	-260	0	[2Fe-2S]
N-2	1.92	1.92	2.05	-130	-60	[4Fe-4S]
N-3	1.86	1.94	2.01	-240	0	[4Fe-4S]
N-4	1.88	1.94	2.09	-270	0	[4Fe-4S]

II. ESCHERICHIA COLI SYSTEM

A question as to whether Site I energy coupling is present in E. coli membrane or not, has been unresolved. In spite of earlier suggestions (35) of the presence of Site I in E. coli, Young's group showed that the NADH dehydrogenase isolated from genetically amplified cells is composed of a single polypeptide containing FAD and no iron sulfur clusters (36). Independently, Kaback's group reported the presence of at least two different types of NADH dehydrogenase in the E. coli, one containing iron (37,38). They also demonstrated that these two dehydrogenases can be distinguished by the capacity to react with an NADH analog deamino-(d)-NADH. Matsushita et al. (18) have clearly demonstrated the presence of the two types of NADH dehydrogenases, designated [NADH dehydrogenase (dh) I] and [NADH dh II]. (See Fig. 1) The former oxidizes both d-NADH and NADH and is energy coupled, while the latter complex exclusively oxidizes NADH and is not energy coupled. The d-NADH-Q_1 reductase activity is more sensitive than NADH-Q_1 reductase activity towards various Q analog inhibitors, such as piericidin A, UHNQ, or myxothiazol. The [NADH dh I] is extremely labile and its activity is almost completely lost, even by the overnight storage of the membrane vesicles in the refrigerator. The $\Delta\widetilde{\mu}_{H+}$ generation is observed during the turnover of [NADH dh I], using either d-NADH or NADH as a reductant and Q_1 as an electron acceptor. However $\Delta\widetilde{\mu}_{H+}$ is not formed in the membrane vesicles from GR-19N strain in which d-NADH-Q_1 reductase is inactivated. Using membrane vesicles of GR-19N, we have resolved the EPR spectra arising from at least two distinct iron-sulfur clusters, one binuclear and one tetranuclear, with the E_m values in the range of -230 to -260 mV (16,17). The tetranuclear cluster with $g_{x,y,z}$ (1.90, 1.92, 2.05) was clearly shown to be located on the substrate side of the piericidin A inhibition site. A binuclear type cluster with $g_{x,y,z}$ =1.92, 1.94, 2.02, however, exhibits very slow reduction kinetics with either d-NADH and NADH ($t_{1/2}$ of 2 min. at room temperature). Thus its location in the NADH dh I could not be definitively shown. Its most likely presence in the NADH dh I was indicated by the UHNQ sensitive reduction of this cluster by L-lactate via Q (17).

III. T. THERMOPHILUS SYSTEM

The NADH-Q oxidoreductase segment of the T. thermophilus HB-8 respiratory chain provides a very useful system for the comparative studies of Site I. The thermophilic membrane vesicles oxidize d-NADH with a slightly higher rate than that of NADH oxidation (0.9 nmoles/mg protein, min) and these two activities are much more stable than that of the E. coli system. Both activities show high sensitivity towards piericidin A inhibition as in the case of the bovine heart system. In order to demonstrate the presence of iron-sulfur clusters in the NADH-Q segment of the respiratory chain, we have examined EPR signals of T. thermophilus HB-8 membrane vesicles which were reduced with NADH after pretreatment with Piericidin A. We have detected EPR signals from two distinct iron-sulfur clusters, one each of the binuclear and tetranuclear type. Fig. 2A is the EPR spectra recorded at 26 K with a microwave power of 2 mW, under this condition binuclear type iron-sulfur signals predominate. It elicits the "g=1.94" type spectrum with the g_z peak at g=2.019 and the Cu_A signal in the central region of the spectrum which demonstrates that these piericidin A treated membrane vesicles remained in an aerobic state until the sample was frozen in the EPR tube. We have obtained spectrum of the [2Fe-2S]$^{+1}$ cluster after subtracting Cu_A signal (Fig. 2B). A reasonable computer fit to spectrum A-B was obtained with $g_{x,y,z}$ values of (1.927, 1.940, 2.019) and line widths $L_{x,y,z}$ of (7.5, 12.0, 8.0 x 10^{-4} tesla).

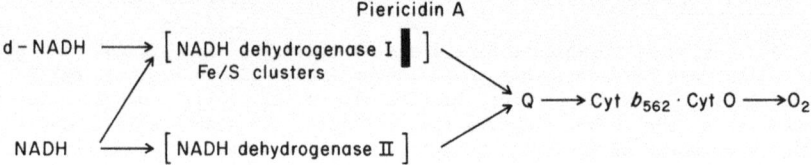

Figure 1. NADH Dehydrogenase System of E. coli GR-19 N.

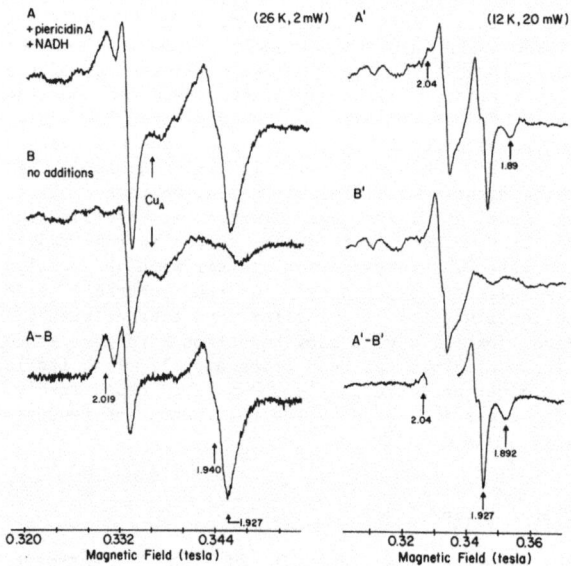

Figure 2. Spectral resolution of binuclear and tetranuclear clusters in
Thermus thermophilus membrane vesicles under two different EPR
conditions. Membrane vesicles (37 mg protein/ml) were preincubated with piericidin A (4.6 nmoles/mg protein) were reduced
with 5mM NADH in spectra A and A'. In spectra B and B', membrane vesicles were used as isolated without addition of reductants. The Cu$_A$ spectra seen in spectra B and B' were subtracted
from spectra A and A', respectively.

The EPR spectrum of the tetranuclear type cluster was obtained using the same samples shown in Fig 2A' and 2B' recorded at a lower temperature. Additional EPR signals at g_x=1.89 and g_z=2.04 are clearly seen (spectrum A'-B'). This iron-sulfur species is reminiscent of the cluster N-3 or N-4 in the mitochondrial system. We obtained a reasonable spectral simulation using parameters of $g_{x,y,z}$=1.891, 1.950, 2.042 and $L_{x,y,z}$=15.0, 8.0, 11.5 x 10^{-4} tesla. Under the EPR conditions employed, we cannot completely resolve the overlapped signals from the binuclear type cluster in the g_y region. We have reported similar resolved iron-sulfur spectra for these two clusters using difference spectra between membrane vesicles reduced with NADH and with succinate plus glycerol-1-phosphate (19,20).

Both clusters have similar low midpoint redox potentials (about -260 mV region) and their relative spin concentrations are approximately in 1:1 ratio. Coupled with NADH-Q_1 reductase activity, the formation of $\Delta\psi$ was shown, which is inhibited by piericidin A and is dissipated by valinomycin in the presence of potassium. We have also obtained preliminary data on the presence of a stable ubisemiquinone species with $E_{m9.0}$ of approximately -160 mV which can be easily titrated directly in the membrane vesicles as will be reported by Meinhardt et al. in this volume (39). Yagi and Ohnishi (unpublished data) have isolated the NADH dehydrogenase complex from T. thermophilus HB-8 membranes which contain one FMN and consists of about 10 polypeptides, retaining a partial rotenone sensitivity (c. f. ref. 40). An almost pure FAD- containing single polypeptide NADH dehydrogenase was also isolated, which is analogous to the [NADH dh II] of the E. coli system.

ACKNOWLEDGEMENT

We would like to thank Drs. T. Yagi, T. Kula, K. Hon-nami, and T. Oshima, for the gift of bacterial membranes or cells used in the works presented in this paper. Reported studies were partly supported by NIH grant GM-30763.

References

1. Y. Hatefi, The Mitochondrial Oxidative Phosphorylation System, Ann. Rev. Biochem. 54:1015 (1985)

2. C.I. Ragan, Structure and Function of Respiratory Complex I in "Coenzyme Q," G. Lenaz ed., pp. 315, John Wiley and Sons Inc., New York (1985)

3. T. Ohnishi, Mitochondrial Iron-Sulfur Flavodehydrogenases in "Membrane Proteins in Energy Transduction" R.A.Capaldi ed., Marcel Dekker, New York, (1979)

4. T. Ohnishi, and J. Salerno, Iron-Sulfur Clusters in the Mitochondrial Electron Transport Chain in "Iron-sulfur Proteins" vol. 4, T.G. Spiro, ed., pp.285, John Wiley and Sons, Inc., New York (1982)

5. H. Beinart, and S.P.J. Albracht, New Insights, Ideas and Unanswered Questions Concerning Iron-Sulfur Clusters in Mitochondria, Biochim. Biophys. Acta 683:245 (1982)

6. Y. Hatefi, Flavoproteins of the Electron Transport System and the Site of Action of Amytal, Rotenone, and Piericidin A, Proc. Natl. Acad. Sci. U.S.A. 60:733 (1968)

7. M.C. Fry and D.E. Green, Cardiolipin Requirement for Electron Transfer in Complex I and III of the Mitochondrial Respiratory Chain, J. Biol. Chem. 256:1874 (1981)

8. C.I. Ragan, Y.M. Galante, and Y. Hatefi, Purification of Three Iron-Sulfur Proteins from the Iron Protein Fragment of Mitochondrial NADH-Ubiquinone Oxidoreductase, Biochemistry 21:2518 (1982)

9. C. Paech, A. Friend, and T.P. Singer, Simplified Isolation and Molecular Composition of NADH Dehydrogenase of the Respiratory Chain, Biochem. Journ. 203:477 (1982)

10. N.R. Orme-Johnson, R.E. Hansen, and H. Beinert, Electron Paramagnetic Resonance Detectable Electron Acceptors in Beef Heart Mitochondria, J. Biol. Chem. 249:1922 (1974)

11. S.P.J. Albracht, G. Dooijwaard, F.J. Leeuwerkid, and B. Van Swol, EPR Signals of NADH: Q Oxidoreductase Shape and Intensity, Biochim. Biophys. Acta 459:300 (1977)

12. T. Ohnishi, H. Blum, Y.M. Galante, and Y. Hatefi, Iron Sulfur N1 Clusters studied in NADH-Ubiquinone Oxidoreductase and in Soluble NADH Dehydrogenase, J. Biol. Chem. 256:9216 (1981)

13. D.O. Hearshen, W.R. Dunham, S.P.J. Albracht, T. Ohnishi, and H. Beinert, EPR Spectral Simulation on Cluster N-1b in NADH-Ubiquinone Oxidoreductase of Bovine Heart Mitochondria, FEBS Lett. 133:287 (1981)

14. W.R. Hagen, D.O. Hearshen, L.J. Harding, and W.R. Dunham, Quantitative Numerical Analysis of g Strain in the EPR of Distributed Systems and Its Importance for Multicenter Metalloproteins J. Magnetic Resonance 61:233 (1985)

15. A.T. Kowal, J.E. Morningstar, M.K. Johnson, R.R. Ramsey, and T.P

Singer, Spectroscopic Characterization of the number and type of Iron-Sulfur Clusters in NADH:Ubiquinone Oxidoreductase, J. Biol. Chem. 261:9239 (1986)

16. T. Ohnishi, K. Matsushita, H.R. Kaback, K. Hon-nami, and T. Oshima, Comparative Studies of the NADH-Q Oxidoreductase System of Bacterial Respiratory Chain, in: "Iron-Sulfur Protein Research," eds. H. Matsubara et al., pp. 232, Japan Sci. Soc. Press, Tokyo/Springer Verlag, Berlin (1986)

17. T. Ohnishi, S.W. Meinhardt, K. Matsushita, and H.R. Kaback, Studies of the NADH-UQ Oxidoreductase System of the E. coli in: "Structure and Function of Energy Transducing Systems," eds. T. Ozawa and S. Papa, Japan Sci. Soc. Press, Tokyo/Springer Verlag, Berlin, (1986) in press

18. K. Matsushita, T. Ohnishi, H.R. Kaback, manuscript submitted for publication

19. T. Ohnishi, S.W. Meinhardt, T. Yagi, and T. Oshima, Comparative Studies on the NADH-Q Oxidoreductase Segment of the Bacterial Respiratory Chain, in: "Advances in Membrane Biochemistry and Bioenergetics," C. Kim, et al. eds., Plenum, New York, in press

20. T. Ohnishi, S.W. Meinhardt, D.C. Wang, K. Hon-nami, and T. Oshima, Studies on the NADH-Q Oxidoreductase Segment of the Respiratory Chain in Thermus thermophilus HB-8, manuscript submitted for publication

21. B. Ludwig and G. Schatz, A Two-subunit Cytochrome c Oxidase (Cytochrome aa$_3$) from Paracoccus denitrificans, Proc. Natl. Acad. Sci. U.S.A. 77:196 (1980)

22. X. Yang and B.L. Trumpower, Purification of a Three-subunit Ubiquinol-Cytochrome c Oxidoreductase Complex from Paracoccus denitrificans, J. Biol. Chem. 261:12282 (1986)

23. B. Ludwig, Heme aa$_3$-type Cytochrome c Oxidase from Bacteria, Biochim. Biophys. Acta 594:177 (1980)

24. S.W. Meinhardt, X. Yang, B.L. Trumpower, and T. Ohnishi, Identification of a Stable Ubisemiquinone and Characterisation of the Effects of Ubiquinone Oxidation-Reduction Status on the Rieske Iron-Sulfur Protein in the Three Subunit Ubiquinol-Cytochrome c Oxidoreductase Complex of Paracoccus denitrificans, J. Biol. Chem., in press, (1987)

25. E.M. Meijer, R. Wever, and A.H. Stouthamer, The Role of Iron Sulfur Center 2 in Electron Transport and Energy Conservation in the NADH-Ubiquinone Segment of the Respiratory Chain in Paracoccus denitrificans, Eur. J. Biochem. 81: 276 (1977)

26. S.P.J. Albracht, H.W. Van Verseweld, W.R. Hagen, and M.L. Kalkman, A Comparison of the Respiratory Chain in Particles from Paracoccus denitrificans and Bovine Heart Mitochondria by EPR Spectroscopy, Biochim. Biophys. Acta 593:173 (1980)

27. S.W. Meinhardt, T. Kula, T. Yagi, T. Lillich, and T. Ohnishi, EPR Characterization of the NADH:Ubiquinone Oxidoreductase Segment of the Respiratory Chain in Paracoccus denitrificans, J. Biol. Chem., in press (1987)

28. T. Yagi, Purification and Characterization of NADH Dehydrogenase Complex from Paracoccus denitrificans, Arch. Biochem. Biophys. 250:302 (1986)

29. A.H. Stouthamer, Bioenergetic Studies on Paracoccus denitrificans, Trends in Biochem Sci. 5:164 (1980)

30. T. Pozzan, V. Miconi, F., DiVirgilio, and G.F. Azzone, H^+/Site, Charge/Site, and ATP/Site Ratios at Coupling Sites I and II in Mitochondrial e^- Transport, J. Biol. Chem. 254:10200 (1979)

31. M. Wikstrom, Two Protons are Pumped from the Mitochondrial matrix per electron transferred between NADH and Ubiquinone, FEBS Lett. 169:300 (1984)

32. T.A. Scholes and P.C. Hinkle, Energetics of ATP Driven Reverse Electron Transfer from Cytochrome c to Fumarate and from Succinate to NAD in Submitochondrial Particles, Biochem. 23: 3341 (1984)

33. J.J. Lemasters, The ATP- to Oxygen Stoichiometries of Oxidative Phosphorylation by Rat Liver Mitochondria, An Analysis of ADP-induced Oxygen Jumps by Linear Nonequilibrium Thermodynamics, J. Biol. Chem. 259:13123 (1984)

34. M.K. Phillips and D.B. Kell, A Novel Inhibitor of NADH Dehydrogenase in Paracoccus denitrificans, FEBS Lett., 104:248 (1982)

35. Poole, R.K., and Haddock, B.A., Energy-linked Reduction of Nicotinamide Adenine Dinucleotide in Membranes Derived from Normal and Various Respiratory-deficient Mutant Strains of E. coli K12, Biochem. J. 152:537 (1975)

36. A. Jaworowski, H.D. Campbell, M.I. Poulis, and I.G. Young, Genetic Identification and Purification of the Respiratory NADH Dehydrogenase of Escherichia coli, Biochemistry 20:2041 (1981)

37. P. Owen and H.R. Kaback, Immunochemical Analysis of Membrane Vesicles from Esherichia coli, Biochemistry 18:1413 (1979)

38. Owen, P., Kaczorowski, G.J., and Kaback, H.R. Resolution and Identification of Iron-Containing Antigens in Membrane Vesicles from Escherichia coli, Biochemistry 19:596 (1980)

39. Meinhardt, S.W., Yang, X., Trumpower, B.L., and Ohnishi, T. (this volume)

40. M.G. Choc, R.M. Lorence, T. Oshida, W.R. Dunham. and J.A. Fee, Resolution and Partial Characterization of Electron Transport Components of Thermus thermophilus: NADH-Flavoprotein-Menaquinone-Rieske Fe/S Protein, in Flavins and Flavoproteins, eds. V. Massey and C.H. Williams, pp. 746, Elsevier North Holland Inc., (1982)

LOCALIZED VALENCE STATES IN IRON-SULFUR CLUSTERS AND THEIR
POSSIBLE RELATIONSHIP TO THE ABILITY OF IRON-SULFUR CLUSTERS
TO CATALYZE REACTIONS OTHER THAN ELECTRON TRANSFER

Helmut Beinert

Department of Biochemistry and National Biomedical ESR Center
Medical College of Wisconsin
Milwaukee, WI 53226

INTRODUCTION

The last few years have seen great progress in our knowledge of the
large variety and wide distribution of iron-sulfur (Fe-S) clusters as
biocatalysts. A priori one might predict that a structure made up of four
atoms of a transition metal that can be found in several stable valency and
spin states plus four atoms of a "soft" chalcogen that can occur in stable
ionic forms with oxidation states 2- to 6+ should yield a device of
remarkable properties. We are learning that this is indeed the case,
particularly for the larger, i.e. 4Fe clusters. They are surprisingly
malleable entities which readily respond to subtle influences from the
surrounding ligands furnished by the protein and (or) from additional
ligands approaching from the medium. Intuitively, these would seem exactly
conditions required for producing a potential active site of an enzyme and
there is evidence that nature indeed makes use of these circumstances.

Up until very recently, Fe-S clusters have generally been looked at as
agents for net electron (e^-) transfer between redox groups of proteins or
cofactors. It was clear from results of spectroscopies and theoretical
calculations that e^- density is delocalized widely over the whole Fe-S
cluster structure, including ligands. Thus 4Fe clusters, e.g., appear to
be ideal devices for transmitting electronic charges efficiently over
distances of ~ 10 Å - the approximate distance across the cluster - and
also by different pathways through the Fe-S cube, if the protein were to
impose particular constraints on the geometry, thus favoring a specific
pattern of charge distribution. It now seems plausible that this very
capability of Fe-S clusters to localize or delocalize charge in specific
ways within the cluster structure can be used to advantage by nature not
only in e^- transfer but also in providing sites of high or low e^- density
as required in certain catalytic processes, without the result of net e^-
transfer. I would now like to discuss experimental results which prompted
me to make the above statements.

STUDIES ON THE FE-S PROTEIN ACONITASE

Advantages of Aconitase as an Experimental Object

The reason for the choice of this particular Fe-S protein are the advantages that it offers to the experimenter: 1) It is an _enzyme_ which has an easily measurable activity that depends on a specific state of the Fe-S cluster; thus there is always a measure of the integrity of the protein [1], 2) It contains a single Fe-S cluster in a single-chain protein of manageable size, M_r = 81 kD [2,3], 3) It can be purified in fair quantity without great difficulty [1,3], 4) Its Fe-S cluster is of intermediate stability, i.e., it can be manipulated without excessive losses and the products of such manipulation have a lifetime that allows convenient measurements and other experiments to be done [4], 5) The ready interconversion between the 3Fe and 4Fe forms of the cluster allows easy incorporation of isotopes as required for Mössbauer (MB) and ENDOR spectroscopies [5,6]. Sulfide and, to some extent, iron can also be exchanged into the enzyme [7], 6) A viable apoenzyme can be prepared which can be reconstituted in up to 75% yield, providing additional means of isotope incorporation, 7) The site of the protein where the cluster is anchored - presumably by cysteine ligands - allows the presence of the [4Fe-4S], as well as the cubane - type and linear [3Fe-4S] clusters [4,6], thus permitting, in a sense, model chemistry of protein-bound clusters.

Properties of the Fe-S Cluster of Aconitase

Points 5) to 7) above call for somewhat more detailed comment, which follows. Aconitase was one of the first clear cut examples of a 3Fe cluster in a protein [5,8]. The 3Fe form is the most stable form under aerobic conditions, but it is readily converted to the 4Fe form under reducing conditions [1,9]. This conversion proceeds spontaneously by rearrangements of clusters between protein molecules.[1,7] Neither extraneous iron or sulfide is required in this process [1,7]; however, in the presence of extra iron, the yield of 4Fe form from the 3Fe form approaches 100% instead of 75% in its absence. Even in this case S^{2-} is not needed, which provided the first hint that S^{2-} may never be lost during the 4Fe to 3Fe conversion.[2,10] Indeed, analysis shows that four labile S^{2-} are present in the 3Fe form [2,10]. This was the basis for the proposal that the 3Fe form has the stoichiometry of components [3Fe-4S] and not [3Fe-3S] as previously assumed [5,8,11,12]. Different structures are possible for [3Fe-4S], requiring 4 or 3 protein ligands, respectively [12]. The availability of the apoenzyme together with the facility with which the 3Fe and 4Fe forms can be interconverted allows labeling with pure ^{56}Fe or highly purified ^{57}Fe. This labeling can be made specific for the site of the labile iron (called Fe_a in our publications) versus the three other sites (Fe_b). These are important conditions for discrimination of individual sites by MB and ENDOR spectroscopies. Concerning EPR and ENDOR, it must be remembered that the active form of aconitase with a [4Fe-4S]$^{2+}$ cluster is diamagnetic, i.e. EPR silent. However, this form can be reduced to the [4Fe-4S]$^{+}$ state, which shows the usual EPR signal of reduced 4Fe clusters as, e.g. in reduced ferredoxins. This form binds substrate at least as strongly as the 2+ form and has, to the best of our knowledge [5], about 30% of the activity of the 2+ form. Thus, while we must keep in mind that it is not the naturally occurring form of the enzyme which we are studying by EPR and ENDOR spectroscopies, we can still hope to derive important clues from studying its behavior.

---

* In the presence of active aconitase a mixture of the three substrates, viz. _cis_-aconitate, citrate and isocitrate will always be present. While the composition of the equilibrium mixture in solution is known for this situation, it is not known what species are bound to the enzyme. Unless it is otherwise specified we designate, therefore, with the name "substrate" any of the three acids or any mixture thereof.

Function of the Fe-S Cluster of Aconitase

Mössbauer spectroscopy. What did we specifically learn from this enzyme? What is the function of the Fe-S cluster in aconitase, which is a hydratase, not an enzyme of oxido-reduction? MB spectra indicated that when substrate was added to active enzyme, the specific iron atom that is built into the cluster on activation (Fe_a) and only this Fe atom, underwent drastic changes [6,13]. While, among the four iron atoms present, the spectral parameters (the isomeric shift δ and the quadrupole moment ΔE_Q) of Fe_a tended most toward those of a ferric ion, Fe_a showed the most ferrous character among the four iron atoms after substrate addition. Also, the characteristics of this ion were no longer those typical of iron in a tetrahedral environment, but such that expansion of its coordination sphere was indicated [6,13]. This was most readily interpreted as binding of substrate to Fe_a, while, and this is important to stress, this iron atom remained an integral part of the cluster, according to its magnetic behavior. Thus we have with aconitase the first case of a typical non-gaseous substrate molecule apparently bound to cluster iron in an Fe-S protein (The binding of CO to Fe-S clusters has been observed with CO-dehydrogenase and hydrogenases [14,15]). Although shifts of e^- density in the Fe-S cluster-substrate complex are apparent from the MB spectra, namely from substrate to Fe_a [6,13], net e^- transfer, generally assumed to be the function of Fe-S proteins, does not occur in the aconitase reaction.

EPR and ENDOR Spectroscopy. While MB spectroscopy allows us to look at the active site of aconitase as perceived by the four Fe nuclei, it cannot provide any information as to the groups of the substrates that may be involved. Here hyperfine structure (hfs) from magnetic nuclei close to the Fe-S cluster and observable by EPR approaches might be useful. The reduced active form of the enzyme, $[4Fe-4S]^+$, lends itself to such studies. When substrate is added to this form of the enzyme in $H_2^{17}O$, the lines of the EPR signal are broadened by unresolved hfs from ^{17}O ($I = 5/2$) [6]. Since in the presence of active aconitase the OH of citrate or isocitrate is readily exchanged with solvent water, the broadening can be interpreted in two ways. Either water or OH^- (henceforth called H_xO) from the solvent or OH from the substrate or both together are bound to the cluster (there is no effect in $H_2^{17}O$ without substrate). To decide between these possibilities, the inhibitor trans-aconitate was bound to the enzyme in $H_2^{17}O$. Again, line broadening in the EPR signal was observed. In this case the hydration reaction does not proceed, because of the unsuitable geometry of trans-aconitate. This means, in this instance, that the hfs must be contributed by bound $H_x^{17}O$.

Ia   Ib

Citrate (Ia) and isocitrate (Ib) analogs in which one carboxyl group is replaced by a nitro group are tight-binding and powerful inhibitors of aconitase[16]. Studies on the isocitrate analog by EPR and ENDOR have been reported[17]. It was added to the enzyme under several conditions of ^{17}O labeling: 1) the inhibitor was labeled in the OH group, which is not exchangeable with water from the medium (in contrast to the situation with the true substrates); 2) the OH of the inhibitor was unlabeled but the solvent was $H_2^{17}O$; 3) both inhibitor and solvent were labeled with ^{17}O. By both EPR (hfs broadening) and ENDOR it was found that both $H_x^{17}O$ and the ^{17}OH of the labeled analog were bound and apparently simultaneously at the same enzyme molecule. However, an ENDOR signal of the kind attributed to labeled ^{17}OH of the analog was not observed when citrate was added to the enzyme in $H_2^{17}O$, that is, there was no evidence that, at equilibrium, substrate was bound by its OH group. From a synopsis of this work it was concluded, therefore, that with reduced active enzyme, [4Fe-4S]$^+$, at equilibrium neither citrate nor isocitrate is bound to the active site to any appreciable extent, but <u>cis</u>-aconitate and H_xO [17].

With citrate labeled in all three carboxyl groups with ^{17}O no broadening of the EPR signal had been observed[6]. Thus, there was no evidence for substrate binding to aconitase via one of its carboxyl groups. Therefore, further work along the lines reported appeared of doubtful value. At this point of our investigation two events occurred which gave our search for an answer to the function of the Fe-S cluster in aconitase new impetus: First, an ENDOR study of ^{17}O carboxyl-labeled citrate in the presence of active enzyme ([4Fe-4S]$^+$) showed that there was indeed an ENDOR signal , contrary to the indications from EPR, meaning that at least one of the substrate carboxyls was also bound to the Fe-S cluster. Second, Gahan <u>et al.</u>[18] published a paper on "Metal Ion Promoted Hydration of Pendant Alkenes and its Possible Relationship to Aconitase", in which these authors drew attention to the analogy of a model system which they had

II   III

studied and the aconitase reaction. In this model an ethylenediamine complex of Co(III) substantially facilitates the hydration of the

J. Telser, B.M. Hoffman, M. Werst, M.C. Kennedy, M.H. Emptage and H. Beinert, to be published.

monomethylester of maleic acid. The key intermediate is a five membered
cyclization product (II) in which both, OH^- from the solvent and the free
carboxyl of maleate, are bound to the metal center, with the carbon
adjacent to the carboxyl furnishing the fifth member of the ring. This
latter carbon is also part of the alkene structure of maleate. Gahan et
al. proposed that an analogous cyclization involving Fe, OH^- from the
solvent, one of the methylene carbons of cis-aconitate and the carboxyl
attached to that same carbon (III) could be the crucial intermediate in the
mechanism of the aconitase reaction. The product of the reaction would
then be determined by the identity of the carboxyl group adjacent to the
double bond of cis-aconitate that happened to bind to the cluster (cf.
III).

    In search for evidence for such a mechanism, we set out to label the
oxygen or carbon atoms of the three carboxyl groups individually with [17]O
or ^{13}C, respectively.[#] ENDOR signals were only observed when the
central carboxyl was labelled. This together with the ENDOR data obtained
previously (see above)[17] indicates then that, at equilibrium, in the
overwhelming majority of enzyme molecules cis-aconitate is bound to the
cluster with the protein in the "citrate"-conformation, i.e. the center
carboxyl bound to Fe_a in addition to H_xO from the solvent (cf. III).

Localized and Delocalized Valence States in Fe-S Proteins

    I had mentioned above that one of the initial observations by MB
spectroscopy that indicated substrate binding to the Fe-S cluster was the
dramatic increase in δ and ΔE_Q[6,13]. These results were no longer
compatible with a tetrahedral environment of Fe_a and also pointed to an
increased ferrous character of this Fe-ion while it remained part of the
cluster. This was then amply confirmed by the observation of hfs from
constituent atoms of the substrate as seen by EPR[6,17] and ENDOR
spectroscopies[17]. I am coming back to this because I want to emphasize a
fact implicit in these observations, viz. the appearance of a localized
valence state in a cubane type cluster of four metal ions, where generally
charge delocalization had been expected and indeed observed[19]. We know
from the now classical studies on ferredoxins that there is almost complete
delocalization of charge in oxidized 2Fe clusters, but pronounced
localization of valence in the reduced form with one Fe-ion showing clearly
ferrous and the other one ferric character[20]. There is also complete
delocalization in oxidized [3Fe-4S] clusters but not in the reduced state,
where two Fe ions share the extra electron while the third is essentially
unchanged from the oxidized state, i.e. ferric[5]. From earlier work on
4Fe clusters in the 3+ and 1+ states it had been concluded that, while
there is extensive delocalization of valence over these clusters, the Fe
ions are equivalent only in pairs (cf.19), whereas in the 2+ state all iron
sites are essentially equivalent. This no longer holds for the Fe-S
cluster of aconitase, particularly in the presence of substrate, where one
Fe ion, namely the most labile one, Fe_a, is different from the others
[6,13]. It has the most pronounced ferric character in the substrate-free
2+ state and the most ferrous when substrate is bound. The inequality
between Fe ions even increases when going to the 1+ state in the presence
of substrate (we have not obtained yet the substrate-free reduced form in
sufficient spectral purity for a comparison)[13]. In this case, two Fe
ions are equivalent, whereas Fe_a, where substrate is bound, tends most
toward ferrous and the remaining Fe ion shows an intermediate state of
localization of valence[13].

    We are tempted to search for a possible relationship of this behavior

[#] M. Werst, B.M. Hoffman, M.C. Kennedy, M.H. Emptage and H. Beinert
    unpublished.

with much of the behavior of the Fe-S cluster that we observe in biochemical experimentation. It is the detailed protein structure and subtle changes in that structure around the cluster which bring about the delocalized or localized valence states. It has been shown, for instance, in theoretical work that the orientation of the cysteine ligands bound to the iron atoms has a significant influence on the Fe-S bonding interactions[21]. In turn, these protein-cluster interactions are likely to contribute to or even determine the catalytic capabilities of the Fe-S protein, as suggested by our example of aconitase.

OUTLOOK

Without going into further detail, I would like to venture here the prediction that we are reaching the point where the studies by the various physical techniques are beginning to converge with those made by biochemical approaches toward a joint interpretation of the observed phenomena. I would like to close by quoting from the final discussion in one of the most interesting and promising theoretical studies on Fe-S clusters[21]:

"Upon reduction of . . . the "oxidized" clusters . . . most of the added charge (56 to 70%) migrates to the sulfur atoms, as a result of changes in orbitals other than those which formally accept the extra electron. Both S and S* bear a negative charge, even in the oxidized complexes . . . .

The close proximity in energy of the filled S orbitals and empty Fe 3d orbitals may be important for the electron-transfer function of ferredoxins. In both 2-Fe an 4-Fe ferredoxins the iron sites are buried in the protein interior, wheras the cysteine sulfurs are more exposed to solvent. Internal electron transfer from cysteine S to Fe could be induced by the electrostatic field of a charged donor and might be the initial step in electron transfer; this would be followed by electron transfer from the donor to the more accessible hole in the S 3p band. . . . A two-step electron-transfer model, such as that outlined above, could allow electrons to move over significant distances (10 Å or more) while still maintaining specificity at both the metal and the ligand sites. These characteristics are important for electron-transfer proteins and for multielectron oxido-reductases."

Acknowledgments. I am indebted to Drs. M.H. Emptage, B.M. Hoffman, M.C. Kennedy and E. Münck for many discussions and to Dr. L. Noodleman for permission to quote from his publication. The experimental work was supported by NIH research grants GM-12394 until 1984 and GM-34812 and by the Medical College of Wisconsin. I am also indebted to the Institute For Enzyme Reseach of the University of Wisconsin, Madison, for the use of equipment and facilities.

REFERENCES

1. M. C. Kennedy, M. H. Emptage, J.- L. Dreyer, and H. Beinert, The Role of Iron in the Activation-Inactivation of Aconitase, J. Biol. Chem. 258:11098 (1983).
2. L. Rydén, L.- G. Öfverstedt, H. Beinert, M. H. Emptage, and M. C. Kennedy, Molecular Weight of Beef Heart Aconitase and Stoichiometry of the Components of Its Iron-Sulfur Cluster, J. Biol. Chem. 259:3141 (1984).
3. H. Scholze, Studies on Aconitase From Saccharomyces Cerevisiae, Porcine and Bovine Heart Obtained by a Modified Isolation Method, Biochem. Biophys. Acta. 746:133 (1983).
4. M. C. Kennedy, T. A. Kent, M. Emptage, H. Merkle, H. Beinert, and E.

Münck, Evidence for the Formation of a Linear [3Fe-4S] Cluster in Partially Unfolded Aconitase, J. Biol. Chem. 259:14463 (1984).

5. T. A. Kent, J.- L. Dreyer, M. C. Kennedy, B. H. Huynh, M. H. Emptage, H. Beinert, and E. Münck, Mössbauer Studies of Beef Heart Aconitase: Evidence for Facile Interconversions of Iron-Sulfur Clusters, Proc. Natl. Acad. Sci. U.S. 79:1096 (1982).

6. M. H. Emptage, T. A. Kent, M. C. Kennedy, H. Beinert, and E. Münck, Mössbauer and EPR Studies of Activated Aconitase: Development of a Localized Valence State at a Subsite of the [4Fe-4S] Cluster on Binding of Citrate, Proc. Natl. Acad. Sci. U.S. 80:4674 (1983).

7. M. C. Kennedy, M. H. Emptage, and H. Beinert, Incorporation of [^{35}S] Sulfide Into the Fe-S Cluster of Aconitase, J. Biol. Chem. 259:3145 (1984).

8. T. A. Kent, J.- L. Dreyer, M. H. Emptage, I. Moura, J.J.G. Moura, B. H. Huynh, A. V. Xavier, J. LeGall, H. Beinert, W. H. Orme-Johnson, and E. Münck, Evidence for a Novel Three-Iron Center in Two Ferredoxins and Aconitase, in: "Electron Transport and Oxygen Utilization," Chien Ho, ed., Elsevier Holland, Inc., pg. 371 (1982).

9. M. H. Emptage, J.- L. Dreyer, M. C. Kennedy, and H. Beinert, Optical and EPR Characterization of Different Species of Active and Inactive Aconitase, J. Biol. Chem. 258:11106 (1983).

10. H. Beinert, Semi-micro Methods for Analysis of Labile Sulfide and of Labile Sulfide plus Sulfane Sulfur in Unusually Stable Iron-Sulfur Proteins, Anal. Biochem. 131:373 (1983).

11. H. Beinert, M. H. Emptage, J.- L. Dreyer, R. A. Scott, J. E. Hahn, K. O. Hodgson, and A. J. Thomson, Iron-sulfur Stoichiometry and Structure of Iron-Sulfur Clusters in Three-Iron Proteins: Evidence for [3Fe-4S] clusters, Proc. Natl. Acad. Sci. 80:393 (1983).

12. H. Beinert and A. J. Thomson, Three-Iron Clusters in Iron-Sulfur Proteins, Arch. Biochem. Biophys. 222:333 (1983).

13. T. A. Kent, M. H. Emptage, H. Merkle, M. C. Kennedy, H. Beinert, and E. Münck, Mössbauer Studies of Aconitase, J. Biol. Chem. 260:6871 (1985).

14. S. W. Ragsdale, H. G. Wood, and W. E. Antholine, Evidence That an Iron-Nickel-Carbon Complex is Formed by Reaction of CO with the CO Dehydrogenase From Clostridium thermoaceticum, Proc. Natl. Acad. Sci. 82:6811 (1985).

15. J. Telser, M. J. Benecky, M.W.W. Adams, L. E. Mortenson, And B. M. Hoffman, An EPR and ENDOR Investigation of Carbon Monoxide Binding to Hydrogenase I (Bidirectional) From Clostridium pasteurianum W5, J. Biol. Chem. 261:13536 (1986).

16. J. V. Schloss, D. J. T. Porter, H. J. Bright, and W. W. Cleland, Nitro Analogues of Citrate and Isocitrate as Transition-State Analogues for Aconitase, Biochem. 19:2358 (1980).

17. J. Telser, M. H. Emptage, H. Merkle, M. C. Kennedy, H. Beinert, and B. M. Hoffman, ^{17}O Electron Nuclear Double Resonance Characterization of Substrate Binding to the [4Fe-4S]$^{+}$ Cluster of Reduced Active Aconitase, J. Biol. Chem. 261:4840 (1986).

18. L. R. Gahan, J. M. Harrowfield, A. J. Herlt, L. F. Lindoy, P. O. Whimp, and A. M. Sargeson, Metal Ion Promoted Hydration of Pendant Alkenes and Its Possible Relationship to Aconitase, J. Am. Chem. Soc. 107:6231 (1985).

19. E. Münck and T. A. Kent, Structure and Magnetism of Iron-Sulfur Clusters in Proteins, Hyperfine Interact. 27:161 (1986).

20. W. R. Dunham, G. Palmer, R. H. Sands, and A. J. Bearden, On the Structure of the Iron-Sulfur Complex In the Two-Iron Ferredoxins, Biochim. Biophys. Acta. 253:373 (1971).

21. L. Noodleman, J. G. Norman, Jr., J. H. Osborne, A. Aizman, and D. A.

Case, Models for Ferredoxins: Electronic Structures of
Iron-Sulfur Clusters with One, Two, and Four Iron Atoms, _J. Am._
Chem. _Soc_. 107:3418 (1985).

PROBING THE Fe/S DOMAIN WITH EPR: PANDORA'S BOX AJAR

Wilfred R. Hagen

Department of Biochemistry, Agricultural University
De Dreijen 11, NL-6703 BC Wageningen, The Netherlands

INTRODUCTION

The lack of detail in the optical absorbance of iron-sulfur proteins is
well balanced by their magnetic colorfulness. The study of Fe/S clusters
usually involves the study of its (para)magnetism. Among the many tools
provided by magnetic-resonance spectroscopy EPR, MCD and Mössbauer
spectroscopy are protagonistic. The EPR technique bears the potential to
come up with the major part of the biochemically relevant information that
one can expect to extract from a probing of the magnetism of the Fe/S site,
i.e. the type of cluster, the cluster stoichiometry, and also its
thermodynamic and kinetic characterization. There are several examples of
iron-sulfur proteins for which other methods, notably Mössbauer and MCD
spectroscopies, proved to be complementary or even vital to solve a magnetic
puzzle. Yet the EPR experiment has always provided at least the convenient
initial exploration.

In the following I reassess the combination of iron-sulfur proteins and
conventional EPR spectroscopy for two reasons. First, although the EPR
experiment is by now a straightforward procedure in the biochemistry
department, the methodology of the data reduction has kept a small group of
specialists preoccupied up to this date. Second, while Fe/S biochemistry
for a long time encompassed only few different structures, which were
effectively ether two-level systems (S=1/2) or diamagnets, a research effort
is now developing on Fe/S clusters characterized by different magnetic
properties. Ground states have been detected with S=3/2, 2, 5/2, 7/2, and
several cases of "inverted multiplets" (i.e. negative zero-field splittings)
associated with complex temperature dependencies, have been found. For most
of these clusters the structure is not established, their reported Fe and S
numbers vary, and the proteins show no significant amino-acid sequence
homology with well characterized iron-sulfur proteins.

In the many details of these recent results there are two underlying
questions of general interest. First, there is the question to the
applicability of the technique: is EPR spectroscopy of iron-sulfur proteins
still the principal, straightforward method that we thought it to be; have
the recent developments in theoretical analysis of Fe/S EPR made the method
more powerful; or have they rather limited applicability by revealing
limitations that we were previously not aware of. Second, there is the
question as to the unity of Fe/S biochemistry: are these novel EPR
signals an announcement that we be at the verge of drastically enlarging our
inventory of biologically possible Fe/S structures, or are they different
magnetic manifestations of the familiar 2Fe, 3Fe or 4Fe structures.

459

G-STRAIN; THE STATISTICAL APPROACH

Paramagnetic forms of the majority of known Fe/S clusters are S=1/2. Their EPR spectra are among the simplest that one encounters for biochemical systems. The g-values do not change with the microwave frequency and the spectral intensity is proportional to 1/T. At the common X-band frequency of 9 GHz hyperfine interactions (from [57]Fe and from ligands) are quite small and always unresolved. Data analysis here means just to get a fingerprint by reading-out the three g-values and to get the concentration number by doubly integrating the spectrum versus that of an external standard.

Off and on the question has arisen whether things are really as simple as outlined above. The key word for these inspective discussions has been "g-strain". The term has a history of two decades now, yet its explicit meaning is still to be defined. Originally cast by the Ann Arbor group in 1971 to describe the linearly field dependent EPR line width of 2Fe ferredoxins, g-strain has subsequently been a loose denominator for indications that there is intrinsically more to the EPR spectrum of a metalloprotein that just three g-values. Phenomenologically, g-strain is the observation at low temperature of a linewidth of considerable magnitude, not related to relaxation, and the observation of asymmetries or skewings in the spectrum not obviously related to any multiplicity or inhomogeneity of the biological preparation. We have tried to develop an accurate mathematical description of these phenomena - on the basis of a few general statistical arguments - which is not necessarily directly deduced from a physical picture of the system[1]. In other words, we want to be able to now describe what we see, to reduce spectral data to a few defined numbers, while we may defer to the future to obtain a physical explanation of why this set of numbers per center is always larger than three g-values. There is considerable biochemical relevance in this numerical game.

EPR is frequently used to study the role of individual Fe/S centers in the biological action of a complex Fe/S protein. A g-strain analysis, i.e. a description of the spectra up to the fine details using the statistical theory of g-strain[1], tells whether a specific detail is likely to be an expression of g-strain, and thus contains only information on the cause of g-strain (a general physical property of all proteins) or alternatively, whether the detail is not possibly caused by g-strain and thus contains information on a biochemically relevant variation specific to the system under study.

In addition to a number of model testings[2,3,4] we have published five examples of a g-strain analysis, illustrating applicability of the method for the solution of biochemical problems. All cases dealt with were Fe/S clusters, namely in NADH dehydrogenase[5], Rieske protein[5], a 7Fe ferredoxin[6], xanthine oxidase[7] and nitrogenase Fe-protein[8]. Conclusions were drawn on stoichiometry and/or homogeneity of the clusters and on (the absence of) magnetic interaction with other paramagnets. These conclusions were at variance with several previous interpretations ignoring g-strain.

These succesful applications might create the impression that the g-strain phenomenon is well understood by now. This is not true. The theory[1] has been rigorously tested to satisfaction only on [2Fe-2S] ferredoxins[4]. Here, a "rigorous test" means that, previous to a detailed fitting, the g-strain contribution is separated from other broadening mechanisms, as unresolved (super)hyperfine splittings, by comparison of data taken at sufficiently different microwave frequencies. Only one such a multifrequency test has been made for a [4Fe-4S] ferredoxin with the result that the fine spectral details were not completely reproduced[9]. This is a very disturbing observation since the statistical theory of g-strain was intended to be a generally applicable effective description of powder EPR in proteins irrespective of the molecular composition of the paramagnet. If it does not apply to a simple cubane system then we either do not understand cubanes or we do not understand g-strain. A rigorous test has not yet been carried out on other type of Fe/S clusters or on any other paramagnetic protein, including cytochromes. For systems with resolved hyperfine interactions the situation is probably even more complicated because g-strain is different for different nuclear orientations. An early version of the statistical theory of g-strain was employed in an attempt to reproduce multifrequency data from the hydrated cupric ion. The g-strained EPR of this utterly simple model system proved to be not describable in detail[10], leaving few hopes for similar work on, e.g., Cu, Mn, Mo, Co, V proteins.

As things stand, whether or not it pays off for a biochemist to worry about g-strain strongly depends on the nature of the system under study. For [2Fe-2S] spectra reliable deconvolutions may be made into S=1/2 component spectra of well defined g-values and intensities whereas weak magnetic coupling may be identified as such. At the other extreme, e.g., a shoulder in the spectrum of a copper protein should be left for what it is: at present uninterpretable. In between is a gray area of effective S=1/2 systems (e.g., Fe/S other than 2Fe, cytochromes, Ni proteins) where the theory may or may not give a fully satisfactorily description of the g-strain.

An example of the dillemmatic situation that one is to encounter in practice, is given in Figure 1. The X-band spectrum of the model prismane [6Fe6S6Cl] has been simulated as a g-strained S=1/2 system. The spectrum from 700 μM cluster is not completely noise-free because it extends over an unusually large magnetic field range. Noise cannot be reduced by increasing the concentration because this leads to dipolar broadening[11]. Similarly, collection of a multifrequency data set of high quality is not possible since the X-band frequency is optimal. Thus, rigorous testing of the statistical theory of g-strain for prismanes is at present impossible. The g-strain fit is not perfect, but is unique with respect to the g-values. Although the distinct spectral features are around g=2, the simulation tells that one of the effective g-values is as low as 1.2. Only with this number as the third g-value in the Aasa-Vänngard intensity expression quantitation of the spectrum gives a spin concentration equal to the weighed-in amount of prismane (independent measurements proved that all the prismane was S=1/2[11]). This example illustrates that employing the g-strain algorithm may provide one with important chemical information where the parameterization of the g-strain itself is still insufficiently accurate to deduce information on the physical nature of the g-strain.

G-STRAIN; THE PHYSICAL APPROACH

As an alternative to the exact description of g-strain, in several studies on metalloproteins the approach of the simplified physical model has been taken. One assumes that a distribution in g-values exists which is approximately describable in terms of a distribution in a single crystal - field parameter. This means that one assumes a higher symmetry of the paramagnet than is justifiable by inspection and/or experimental observation, and this is bound to lead to approximate simulations.

Does this approach produce information useful to the biochemist? The harvest thus far has been limited. In their elegant studies on the EPR of [3Fe-xS] proteins Gayda et al.[12] have shown that the effective g-values of the cluster are related to the real g-value of the individual ferric ions by the Fe zero-field splitting (D) and the Fe-Fe exchange coupling (J). They have subsequently roughly reproduced the g-strain of 3Fe single-frequency spectra in terms of a distribution in D/J[12]. Unfortunately there is not much to be learned here for the biochemist since D itself is a parameter in an effective Hamiltonian and a physical interpretation of its magnitude is not available.

For the only example of the physical approach to g-strain that has produced relevant biochemical information, we have to side-step to the EPR of cytochromes. The model of Griffith describes the g-values of low-spin hemes in terms of the axial and rhombic crystal-field parameters, V and Δ. Salerno[13] has used the model of Griffith to show that certain asymmetries in the low-field EPR feature of cytochromes with extremely anisotropic spectra are describable in terms of a symmetric distribution in the axial crystal-field parameter V. Therefore, it is not allowed to interpret these asymmetries as reflections of heme multiplicity and this is a crucial point in the biochemical interpretation of EPR from the mitochondrial bc1 complex[13].

Unfortunately, Salerno overestimates the applicability of his approach when he states that "clearly, the line shapes of the ESR spectra of b- and c-type cytochromes are easily modeled using Griffith's model and a symmetric distribution of the crystal field parameter V"[13]. He has only tested his model on the single low-field peak of the cytochrome spectra which he simulates as if it were an absorption line for a single molecular orientation. I have made a more realistic test of the model by incorporating it into a full-blown powder simulator. I have used the numbers published by Salerno to try to reproduce the complete powder spectrum of cytochrome c. The result is given in Figure 2. It is immediately obvious that this model is not capable of accounting for the pronounced asymmetry in the g-y feature of the spectrum. This asymmetry is present in all low-spin heme spectra[2]. One can also make a theoretical argument why the model is not expected to be ever succesful in describing the fine details of g-strain: the ferric ion crystal field has the same tensorial properties as its g-value. Contrarily, our g-stain analyses on Fe/S centers and on cytochromes show that the cause of g-strain, when described as a three-dimensional tensor, is in general rotated away from the g-tensor axis system.

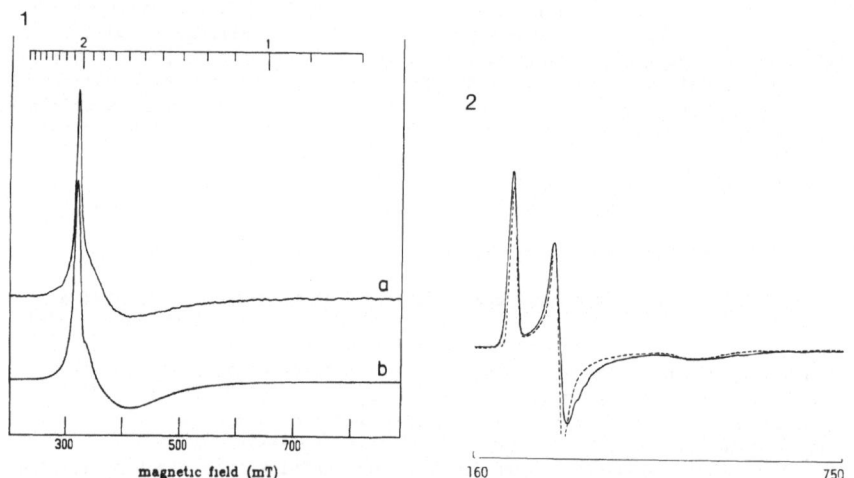

Fig. 1 EPR spectrum (a) and g-strain simulation (b) of the [6Fe6S6Cl]3- cluster at 9 K and 9.20 GHz. The g-values are 2.038, 1.71 and 1.2

Fig. 2 EPR spectrum[2](—) and simulation[13] (--) of equine-heart cytochrome c at 20 K and 9.33 GHz. The crystal-field parameter V=1.5λ, δV=0.17λ, Δ=2.5λ.

HIGH-SPIN FeS CLUSTERS

A variety of high-spin EPR has been reported recently for iron-sulfur proteins. The spectra are intrinsically more complex than those from the S=1/2 systems. Determination of the spin, the g-values and the spin concentration - a triviality for S=1/2 systems - are major problems here. G-strain analyses, be it precise or approximative, are beyond what we currently seek to attain in high-spin studies.

Several of the recently detected high-spin signals are from FeS clusters that used to be labeled "EPR silent" or "EPR undetectable". I assumed that increasing the protein concentration and/or turning up the knobs on the spectrometer should ultimately render any paramagnetic metalloprotein EPR detectable. This naive approach has been remarkably yielding as all the systems I tried proved ultimately to be positive, except one (i.e. ferrous heme). Sucessful examples are S=2 systems in cytochrome oxidase[14], ferrous transferrin[15], 7Fe ferredoxin[6], hydrogenase[16], S=3/2 in nitrogenase Fe-protein[17], and S=7/2 in nitrogenase MoFe-protein[18].

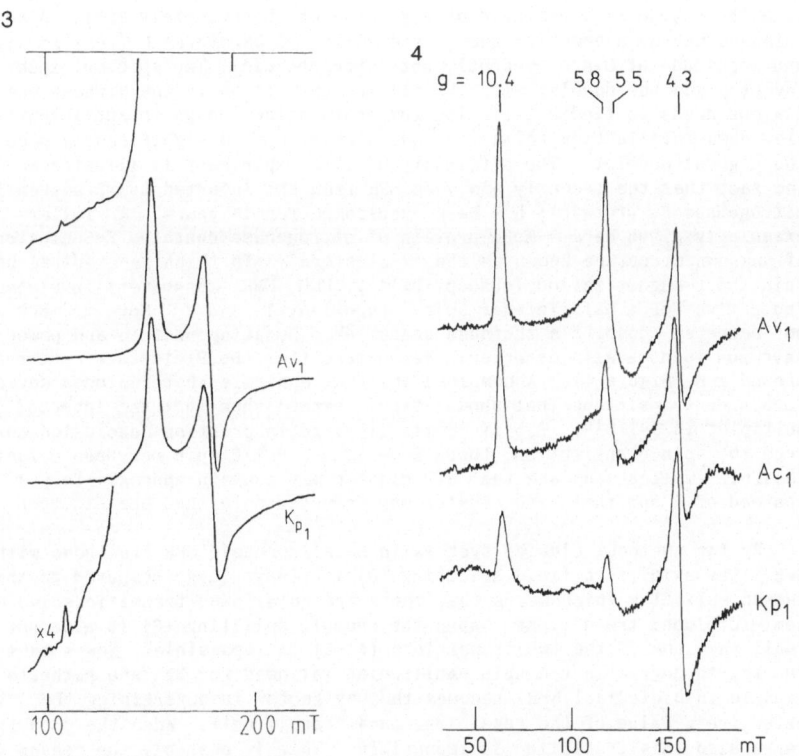

Fig. 3 $\Delta m=3$ transition (g=6.11) at 13 K and 9.2 GHz from the reduced MoFe cofactor (S=3/2) in nitrogenase from <u>Azotobacter vinelandii</u> and <u>Klebsiella pneumoniae</u>. For the regular signal (g=4.3; 3.7) the power was -20 dB.

Fig. 4 S=7/2 EPR at 31 K and 9.45 GHz from oxidized P-clusters in nitrogenase from <u>A.vinelandii</u>, <u>A.chroococcum</u> and <u>K.pneumoniae</u> (45, 27 and 25 mg/ml).

Another example is given here. The FeMo cofactor in dithionite-reduced nitrogenase is an S=3/2 system with large zero-field splitting (i.e. a two-doublet system). The allowed Δm=1 transition within the ground doublet is readily detected[19]. A transition with g-z~6 is possible within the other doublet, but this one is forbidden (Δm=3) in axial symmetry and semi-forbidden in lower symmetry. However, axial symmetry is incongruous with polypeptide structure, and a semi-forbidden transition means a finite transition probability, therefore intensity. This is the physical basis for putting into the EPR cavity more milligrams of protein and more milliWatts of microwave power. Thus, although Münck et al. in their analysis of the EPR of this system conclude that "the transition probability at g-z=6 is vanishingly small compared to the transition probability of the other doublet"[19], I find that the resonance is readily detectable when employing maximal microwave power, as seen in Figure 3. The effective g-value of this peak is 6.11. Since a value of 6.00 or lower is expected for a system of axial or lower symmetry with a real g-value of 2.00, this result means that the deviation from axial symmetry is very small and that the real g-z~2.04. This confirms that the analysis of the ground doublet EPR by Munck et al. is correct, and thus their conclusion is strenghtened that the spectrum integrates to roughly one spin system per Mo atom[19].

Assignment of the spin is for half-integer spin systems usually straightforward since the peak of highest intensity commonly is the g-xy from the ± ½ doublet centered at a g-value of approximately 2S+1. A serious nuisance may be a negative zero-field splitting parameter D (recall: sign and magnitude of D are presently not interpretable). The spin multiplet is inverted and the doublet with the allowed transition is the highest one. Now one needs to find a detection temperature low enough to sufficiently slow down spin-lattice relaxation and high enough to significantly populate the highest doublet. The difficulty of this experiment is illustrated by the fact that the recently analysed EPR from the inverted S=3/2 system in nitrogenase Fe-protein[17] has been overlooked for 13 years. A similar example is given here. MoFe-protein of nitrogenase contains FeS clusters of unknown structure known as the "P-clusters". In thionine-oxidized protein their magnetization (susceptibility, MCD, NMR, Mössbauer) is strongly indicative for a half-integer spin, approximately S=5/2. However, EPR was not detected "despite a thorough search"[20]. Boosting protein and power we have now found easily detectable resonances from the P-clusters centered around g~8 (Figure 4). A complete spectral analysis that includes several forbidden transitions (not shown) firmly establishes that the inverted multiplet is S=7/2[18]. The biochemically more interesting conclusion comes from the spin quantitation: there is only one S=7/2 spin per MoFe cofactor. Possible implications are that a P-cluster may contain approximately 8 FeS instead of 4 and that each cluster may transfer more than one electron.

By far the most elusive systems in metalloprotein EPR are those with S=2. The axial zero-field splitting (D) is always large compared to the Zeeman splitting which means that there are no allowed transitions and 0-2 semi-forbidden transitions. When the rhombic splitting (E) is also not small then one of the two transitions (Δm=2) is impossible. Now a term of the fourth degree in the spin Hamiltonian (allowed for S≥2 and hitherto ignored in biological EPR) becomes the key factor in determining the effective g-value of the remaining, Δm=4 transition[14]. When the term is large also this transition is impossible. This is possibly the reason why ferrous hemes are EPR silent. For not too large a fourth degree zero field interaction (another quantity whose sign and magnitude are presently not amenable to interpretation for biological systems) a g-z may be observed anywhere from about g~8 down to zero field, i.e. g approaches infinity. All the systems detected thus far show this resonance as a weak, broad and usually extremely assymmetric feature at low field. This is at present the EPR fingerprint for S=2.

464

The single exception to this rule was the observation of a sharp resonance with g=5 in an Fe-hydrogenase which I ascribed to the Δm=2 transition of an S=2 system[16]. We have now looked at this enzyme more closely, namely we have boosted the protein concentration of the EPR sample 20x. The "fingerprint line" is now also detectable as shown in Figure 5. The spectra of Figure 5 clearly illustrate the complexity of this system. The shape of the Δm=4 spectrum changes with the temperature, however this is not caused by relaxational broadening since the much sharper g=5 line is unaffected. We are probably still a long way from understanding these spectra in detail. Spin quantitation on the semi-forbidden transitions is an involved matter and the theory is at present in a rudimentary stage. We will not pursue the argument here except to conclude that our attempts at quantitation have thus far not yet resulted in gross (>50%) inconsistencies with chemical determinations leaving hopes for the technique to be mastered in the future.

Is it worth the effort for biochemists to try and detect these weak resonances? For the example of Figure 5 the answer is affirmative. The data is from oxidized enzyme, therefore the FeS cluster involved is non-standard. When the strucural genes for this enzyme were cloned and expressed in E.coli the resulting protein was identical to the native one except for the absence of activity and the absence of the S=2 EPR[21]. Chemically we find some 14 Fe in these enzymes eight of which are in two regular cubanes. Thus it appears that the hydrogen activating site is a novel, single FeS cluster containing some 6 Fe. Since the reaction catalyzed involves 2 electrons we think we may have found here another FeS cluster that contains more than 4 Fe and that transfers more than 1 electron.

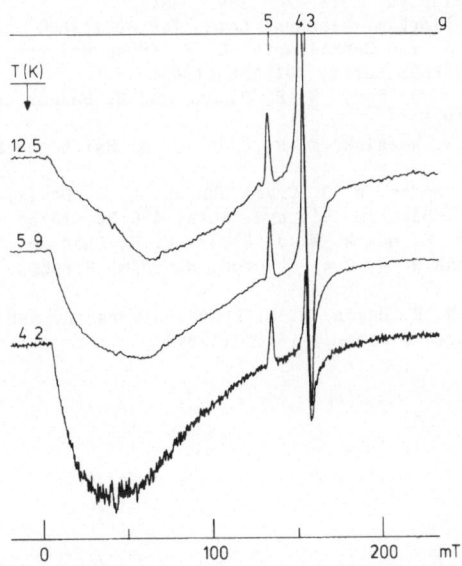

Fig. 5   S=2 EPR at 9.37 GHz in 119 mg/ml reoxidized Fe-hydrogenase from Desulfovibrio vulgaris H.

THE BOTTOM LINES

EPR of iron-sulfur proteins continues to be a straightforward and highly informative technique, however it requires an understanding of g-strain effects for S=1/2 systems and zero-field interaction effects for high-spin systems. The variety of association of iron and sulfur in proteins appears not to be limited to $\leqslant$ 4 Fe/S structures and $\leqslant$ 1 electron transfer.

REFERENCES

1. W. R. Hagen, D. O. Hearshen, R. H. Sands and W. R. Dunham, J. Magn. Reson., 61:220 (1985)
2. W. R. Hagen, J. Magn. Reson., 44:447 (1981)
3. W. R. Hagen and S. P. J. Albracht, Biochim. Biophys. Acta, 702:61 (1982)
4. D. O. Hearshen, W. R. Hagen, R. H. Sands, H. J. Grande, H. L. Crespi, I. C. Gunsalus and W. R. Dunham, J. Magn. Reson., 69:440 (1968)
5. W. R. Hagen, D. O. Hearshen, L. J. Harding and W. R. Dunham, J. Magn. Reson., 61:233 (1985)
6. W. R. Hagen, W. R. Dunham, M. K. Johnson and J. A. Fee, Biochim. Biophys. Acta, 828:369 (1985)
7. R. Hille, W. R. Hagen and W. R. Dunham, J. Biol. Chem., 260:10569 (1985)
8. W. R. Hagen, W. R. Dunham, A. Braaksma and H. Haaker, FEBS Lett., 187:146 (1985)
9. D. O. Hearshen, Ph.D. thesis, University of Michigan (1983)
10. W. R. Hagen, Ph.D. thesis, University of Amsterdam (1982)
11. M. G. Kanatzidis, W. R. Hagen, W. R. Dunham, R. K. Lester and D. Coucouvanis, J. Amer. Chem. Soc., 107:953 (1985)
12. B. Guigliarelli, J. P. Gayda, P. Bertrand and C. More, Biochim. Biophys. Acta, 871:149 (1986)
13. J. C. Salerno, J. Biol. Chem., 259:2331 (1984)
14. W. R. Hagen, W. R. Dunham, R. H. Sands, R. W. Shaw and H. Beinert, Biochim. Biophys. Acta, 765:339 (1984)
15. W. R. Hagen, Biochim. Biophys. Acta, 708:82 (1982)
16. W. R. Hagen, A. van Berkel-Arts, K. M. Kruse-Wolters, W. R. Dunham and C. Veeger, FEBS Lett., 201:158 (1986)
17. W. R. Hagen, R. R. Eady, W. R. Dunham and H. Haaker, FEBS Lett., 189:250 (1985)
18. W. R. Hagen, H. Wassink, R. R. Eady, B. E. Smith and H. Haaker, submitted
19. E. Munck, H. Rhodes, W. H. Orme-Johnson, L. C. Davis, W. J. Brill and V. K. Shah, Biochim. Biophys. Acta, 400:32 (1975)
20. R. Zimmermann, E. Munck, W. J. Brill, V. K. Shah, M. T. Henzl, J. Rawlings and W. H. Orme-Johnson, Biochim. Biophys. Acta, 537:185 (1978)
21. G. Voordouw, W. R. Hagen, K. M. Kruse-Wolters, A. van Berkel-Arts and C. Veeger. Eur.J.Biochem., 162:31(1987)

ASPECTS OF SPIN COUPLING BETWEEN EVEN AND ODD ELECTRON SYSTEMS:

APPLICATIONS TO SUCCINATE: Q REDUCTASE

J.C. Salerno and Xu Yan*

Biology Department & Center for Biophysics, Rensselaer
Polytechnic Institute, Troy, NY, USA 12180
*Chemistry Department & Laboratory for Bioenergetics, State
University of NY at Albany, Albany, NY, USA 12205

Summary
    The spin coupling between the iron sulfur centers of SDH can
be modeled in terms of interactions between two spins of 1/2
(S-1/S-2) and between a spin of 1/2 and a spin of 2 (S-3). Physical
considerations of half integral-integral spin interactions are
discussed.

    Succinate dehydrogenase (SDH), a flavo-iron sulfur enzyme of
the inner mitochondrial membrane, has long been known to contain
multiple metal centers which interact. The iron sulfur cluster S-1
is succinate reducible and contains two iron atoms and two acid
labile sulfides. The then unusual electron paramagnetic resonance
(epr) spectrum of the cluster, reported by Beinert and Sands in
1960 (1), was eventually shown to result fron stong spin coupling
between the two iron atoms, one of which is ferric and the other
ferrous in the reduced state (2).

    Progress in interpreting the experimental results obtained from
the enzyme has often depended on results obtained in simpler
systems, and work has often been impeded by the differences in
preparations used by variuos groups. A breakthrough in the study
of the mitochondrial respiratory chain was made by the introduction
of liquid helium cooled epr methods. Preparation dependent changes
in the epr spectra of SDH upon reduction with dithionite were
attributed to a second cluster, S-2 (3). At about the the same time,
the dicovery of the epr spectrum of the four iron cluster of
Chromatium HiPIP caused the somewhat similar resonance in SDH to
be attributed by all workers in the field to an analogous cluster,
S-3 in the nomenclature of Ohnishi et al (4). The then generally
accepted iron/flavin ratio of eight led to the assumption that
center S-2 was, like S-1, a two iron cluster. S-2 was not generally
accepted by all workers; two different two cluster models of the
enzyme were put forward, one featuring two four iron clusters and
one in which a four iron cluster and a two iron cluster were the
only metal containing groups (5,6).

    The discovery of three iron clusters in several simpler iron
sulfur proteins had obvious ramifications for SDH. The epr spectrum

of S-3 much more closely resembles those of known three iron
clusters than the epr spectrum of HiPIP. Linear electric field
effects, mossbauer and magnetic circular dichroism results (7,8,9)
have provided conclusive evidence that S-3 is a trinuclear cluster.
In addition, cluster S-2 has been detected and evidence has been
presented that it is a four iron cluster. This suggests that the
intact enzyme has nine iron atoms per molecule.

Reexamination of the epr spectrum of the fully reduced enzyme
indicated that signals near g=2.06 and 1.87 are present (4,9);
similar signals have been observed previously in impure preparations
and attributed to contaminating fragments of complex I. The
persistence of the signals in the very pure `two band' preparations
now available demonstrate that they arise from integral components
of SDH. In addition, weak broad wings can be observed near g=2.2
and g=1.6-1.7 in dithionite reduced reconstitutively active
preparations. The destruction of S-3 by incubation in air causes
these wings to vanish, suggesting that they result from S-2/S-3
coupling (4).

Results
The epr spectrum of dithionite reduced succinate-Q reductase
is shown in figure 1. The wings are typical of those observable
in complex II type preparations, succinate cytochrome c reductase,
and resconstitutively active SDH. Incubation of the solubilized
enzyme (BS-SDH) under conditions known to cause destruction of
center s-3 causes loss of the wings, as does air exposure and
incubation with 50% DMSO. Unexpectedly, KCN or solvent treatment
also caused the appearance of epr features near g=2 characteristic
of Mn^{+2} which must have been bound in the preparation in an epr
inactive form. The origin of the Mn^{+2} is unknown; although it is
almost certainly adventitious, we are checking other preparations
for signs of it.

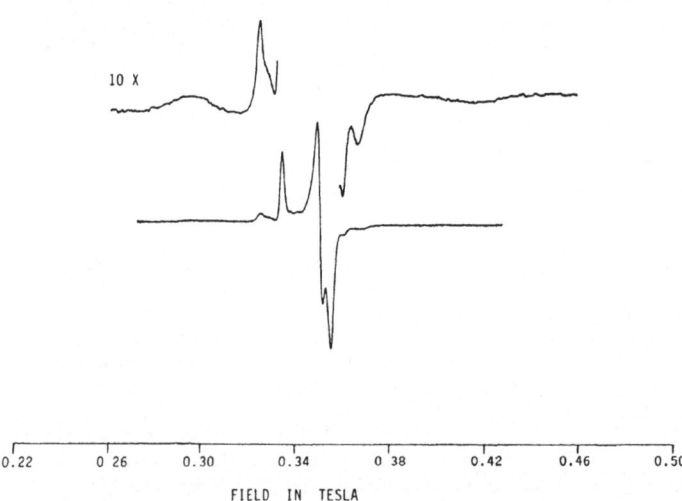

Figure 1
X band epr spectrum of dithionite reduced SQR;
T = 7.5k, power = 20.5 mW.

468

In order to model the epr spectra of SDH, we need to consider possible interactions between the three clusters. Previously, the epr spectrum of the spin coupled pair S-1/S-2 in BS-SDH and B-SDH was modeled by assuming that the two clusters had similar g tensors and were primarliy dipole-dipole coupled (10). If we substitute new values for the g tensor of center S-2 as suggested by the most recent data (princpal values of 2.05,1.93 and 1.87), we find that most of the intensity previously observed and simulated is from the spectrum of S-1. The small changes in the g tensor of S-2 move most of the S-2 intensity out of the way without much change in the dipolar splitting of the S-1 resonance. Thus the S-1 to S-2 distance implied by the simulation is still about 10-12 angstroms. We will present detailed simulations of the S-1/S-2 system at a later date.

The wings of the spectrum of the dithionite reduced SDH must, as previously mentioned, arise from interaction between reduced S-3 and reduced S-2. The ground state of a reduced ferredoxin type four iron cluster has a net spin of 1/2. Reduced HiPIP type clusters have a net spin of zero in the ground state, but trinuclear clusters have an integral spin when reduced; the most probable value appears to be S=2.

Spin 2 systems have been treated by a number of workers in the past (11); like the better studied and more common triplet sytems, which they resemble in some respects, they are non Kramers systems. The degeneracy of the five sublevels can be entirely lifted by zero field terms; not even the upper levels (for D positive) are Kramers doublets, and these can be separated by terms in E. Therefore, S=2 need not have any epr detectable transitions, but such transitions may be sometimes observed if the values of the zero field splitting parameters are not too large. Recently, integral/half integral spin interactions have been discussed in terms of the expectation values for an integral spin as a function of the zeeman field vector (12). While some insight has been gained from these arguements, it is more instructive to consider the coupled system explicitly.

When a system containing an integral spin and a spin of 1/2 is considered, Kramers theorem comes into play and there are 2S+1 doublets, where S is the value of the integral spin. Figure two shows energy levels for a system with spin 1 coupled to spin 1/2 with zeeman fields along all three axes. The non linear dependence of the energy on the field will be seen even as the coupling goes to zero. The allowed transitions in the absence of coupling will be obseved at the same fields as for the spin of 1/2 alone, however. In the presence of coupling, the ground state doublet for positive D cannot be split in zero field since it is a Kramers doublet. Instead, the coupling terms will mix in excited states and shift the dependence of the energy levels on field. This will appear as an effective g value shift, which will be at least slightly field dependent. The degree of field dependence will depend in turn on the separation of the doublets relative to the off-diagonal zeeman terms connecting them.

The upper levels will split into Kramers doublets by the coupling if they have not already been split by the rhomic terms in E. While we have shown a rhombic case in the illustration, it is easiest to understand the upper states in the axial system. There are four such states, which we can name by the Ms values of the two spins along a molecular z axis. These are (1,1/2,), (1,-1/2),

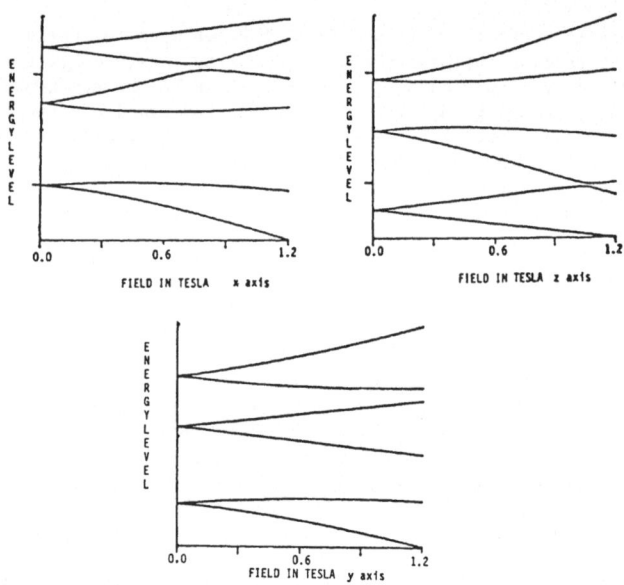

Figure 2
Energy level diagram for spin of 1 coupled to spin of 1/2
D = 2, E = .5, J = .1.

(-1,1/2), (-1,-1/2), which will be called w3,w4,w5,and w6
respectively. In the absence of a rhombic term but with D>>J, w3
and w6 will form one Kramers doublet and w4 and w5 the other.
However, allowed transitions with the microwave magnetic field
perpendicular to the zeeman field will occur only between w3 and
w4 and between w5 and w6. Therefore, transitions can be observed
between these states which again correspond to flipping the spin
of 1/2, but now the transitions will be split by a term representing
the separation of the doublets by the coupling.

In the presence of a strong rhombic term and no coupling, new
linear combinations would be formed of w3 with w4 and w5 with w6.
The allowed transitions would be within the Kramers doublets and
the resonances would be observed at the S=1/2 field positions with
no effect of the integral spin. When both E and J are present, all
four transitions will be observed with the relative intensity
determined by the relative importance of J and E.

The spin 2- spin 1/2 system is similar in many respects. It
consists of five Kramers doublets which are separated by terms in
D and J or E. As in the simpler system described above, the ground
state doublet for positive D cannotr be split by interactions, but
for reasonably strong coupling apparent g value shifts can be
observed. The upper doublets can be split, and in particular the
levels corresponding to Ms=2,-2 for the integral spin will be more
sensitive to J than to E. This is because they are not directly
connected by the terms in E, but are coupled through the Ms=0
(integral spin) states. Their separation by E terms depends on the
admixture of these states, separated from them by diagonal terms
of strength 4D.

470

We expect the wings of the spectrum of dithionite reduced SDH to be due to transitions within the quartet corresponding to the two Kramers doublets formed primarily from the states with integal spin Ms values of 2 and -2. The well resolved splitting of the S-1/S-2 interaction in non reconstitutively active enzyme is due to dipolar coupling between the two S=1/2 systems, much as previously proposed. The loss of resolution in intact enzymes is probably not due to a change in distance or orientation, but can instead be attributed to the effects of spin state admixture by interaction with S-3. This also gives rise to the wings and to the complicated and broadened S-2 spectrum observable just outside the S-1 features. The splitting of the wings is a function of E as well as J; the coupling strength must be substantial, however, and will be estimated in the future by detailed simulation of the intensity of the wings. Weak coupling also exists between FAD and S-1, S-1 and S-3 and S-3 and Qs· as shown by relaxation enhancement; the two Qs radicals are strongly dipole-dipole coupled, and relaxation effects suggest that Qs is coupled to cytochrome $\underline{b}_{560}$. The series of magnetic couplings described here is extensive but too weak to play a role in catalysis. However, the proximity implied by these observations suggests that electrical interactions could play a substantial role. It has been previously suggested that cooperativity may explain the anomolously low redox potential of S-2. Now that S-2 can be reliably distinguished from S-1 by epr measurements, it is possible to test such a hypothesis. Preliminary measurements show that the intrinsic midpoint potential of S-2 must be more negative than -60 mV., but seem to indicate that some reduction (10%) may occur at relatively high potential. This would allow S-2 to function in sequential but not simultaneous electron transfer with S-1. It is also possible that S-2 functions as a `voyeur' cluster in order to modify the wavefunctions of its neighbors; it could in this way be involved in electron transfer without itself being reducible by succinate.

Acknowledgement: This work was supported by NIH grant GM34306.

REFERENCES
1. Beinert,H.,and Sands,R.H.,(1960) Biochem. Biophys. Res. Commun. 3, 41-46
2. Gibson,J.F.,Hall,D.O.,Thornley,J.F.,and Whatley,F.(1966) Proc. Nat. Acad. Sci. U.S.A. 56, 987-990
3. Ohnishi,T, Salerno,J.C., Winter,D., Lim,J., Yu,C.A., Yu,C.A. and King, T.E. (1976) J. Biol. Chem. 251, 2094-2104
4. Ohnishi, T (1987) Current Topics in Bioenergetics in press
5. Beinert,H. and Thomson,A.J. (1983) (Arch. Biochem. Biophys.) 222,333-361
6. Beinert,H. and Albracht,S.P.J. (1982) Biochim. Biophys. Acta. 683,245-277
7. Ackrell, B.A.C., Kearney, E.B., Mims, W.B., Peisach, J. and Beinert, H. (1984) J. Biol. Chem. 259,4015-4018
8. Johnson,M.K., Morningstar, J.E., Bennet,D.E., Ackrell, B.A.C. and Munck, E. (1985 J. Biol. Chem. 260, 7368-7378
9. Johnson, M.K., Morningstar, J.E., Cecchini,G. and Ackrell, B.A.C. (1985) Biochem. Biophys. Res. Commun. 131, 653-658
10. Salerno,J.C., Lim,J., King,T.E., Blum,H., and Ohnishi,T. (1979) J.Biol. Chem. 254,4828-4835
11. Hagen,W.R. (1982) Biochim. Biophys. Acta 708, 82-98
12. Hagen,W.R., Dunham, W.R., Johnson,M.K. and Fee, J.A. (1985) Biochim. Biophys. Acta 828,369-374

THE IRON-SULFUR CLUSTERS IN SUCCINATE DEHYDROGENASE

Michael K. Johnson[a], Joyce E. Morningstar[b], Edna B. Kearney[c],
Gary Cecchini[c], and Brian A. C. Ackrell[c]

[a]Department of Chemistry, University of Georgia, Athens, GA
30602, U.S.A. [b]Department of Chemistry, Louisiana State
University, Baton Rouge, LA 70803, U.S.A. [c]Molecular Biology
Division, Veterans Administration Medical Center, San Francisco
CA 94121, and Department of Biochemistry and Biophysics
University of California, San Francisco, CA 94143, U.S.A.

INTRODUCTION

Succinate-ubiquinone oxidoreductase (Complex II) is a membrane-bound
enzyme that couples the oxidation of succinate to fumarate to the reduction
of ubiquinone in the mitochondrial respiratory chain. It is composed of four
subunits (1); two hydrophilic subunits, a flavoprotein containing covalently
bound FAD (M_r = 70,000) and a smaller iron-sulfur protein (M_r = 27,000), that
together constitute the enzyme succinate dehydrogenase (2), and two small
hydrophobic subunits which are associated with a b-type cytochrome (3). The
two small peptides are required for anchoring the enzyme to the membrane and
for the reduction of ubiquinone, but are not required for the catalytic
oxidation of succinate in the presence of artificial electron acceptors
(4,5).

This brief review focuses on our recent investigations into the number,
type, and subunit location of the multiple iron-sulfur centers in bovine
heart succinate dehydrogenase. The combined application of low temperature
magnetic circular dichroism (MCD) and electron paramagnetic resonance (EPR)
spectroscopies, coupled with the availability of pure, reconstitutively-
active* enzyme preparations, has afforded new insights into this much debated
and controversial topic (for comprehensive reviews prior to the commencement
of this work see, refs. 6 and 7). These studies have been greatly enhanced by
parallel spectroscopic investigations of the fumarate-menaquinone oxidoreductase enzyme complex from Escherichia coli. Whereas succinate dehydrogenase catalyses the oxidation of of succinate to fumarate in aerobic respiration, fumarate reductase catalyses the reverse reaction, with fumarate
serving as the terminal electron acceptor during anaerobic growth. Both
enzymes have similar subunit compositions as well as iron and FAD contents,
and appear to be simple oxidoreductases, in the sense that they have not been
implicated directly in the formation of transmembrane chemiosmotic
potentials. The possibilities for genetic modification and amplification of

---

*Reconstitutive activity refers to the ability of samples to recombine with
submitochondrial particles, depleted of SDH activity by alkaline treatment,
and restore electron transport from succinate to oxygen.

fumarate reductase enzyme complex in E. coli, coupled with the fact that the amino acid sequence of all four subunits has been established by the DNA sequence of structural genes (8-11), makes this enzyme particularly attractive for comparative spectroscopic characterization.

This review is organized into four sections. The results of our spectroscopic studies into the number and type of iron-sulfur clusters in mammalian succinate dehydrogenase and E. coli fumarate reductase are presented first. This is followed by a discussion of their subunit location and a conclusion which summarizes the current state of knowledge and outlines current problems and areas of active investigation.

MAMMALIAN SUCCINATE DEHYDROGENASE

Extensive low temperature MCD studies of both reconstitutively-active (BS-SDH) and reconstitutively-inactive (P-SDH) preparations of bovine heart succinate dehydrogenase revealed the presence of three distinct types of iron-sulfur cluster, S1, S2, and S3 (12). Unfortunately it is not possible to investigate the nature of the iron-sulfur clusters in Complex II itself by MCD spectroscopy because the spectra are completely dominated by transitions originating from cytochrome b. Fig. 1 shows low temperature spectra in the UV-visible region for dithionite-reduced BS-SDH. In contrast to the featureless, monotonically-increasing absorption spectrum, the MCD spectra reveal

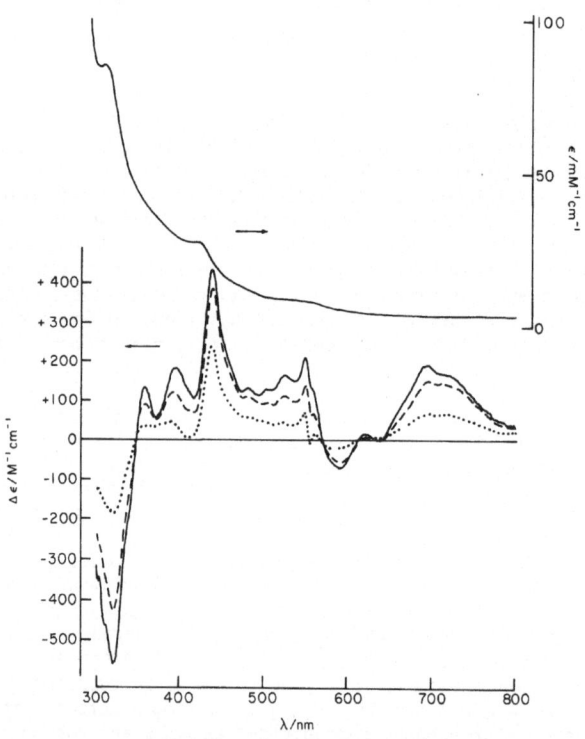

Fig. 1. MCD and absorption spectra of dithionite-reduced BS-SDH. Upper spectrum: room temperature absorption. Lower spectra: MCD recorded at 1.56 K (————), 4.22 K (- - - -) and 14.0 K (·······) at a magnetic field of 4.5 T. Taken from ref. 12.

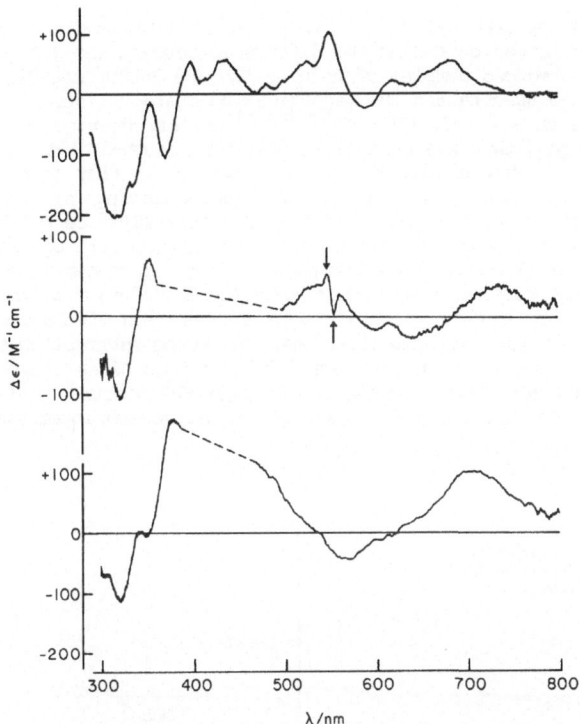

Fig. 2. MCD spectra of reduced S1, S2, and S3 in SDH.
Conditions: temperature, 4.22 K; magnetic
field, 4.5 T. Top: Reduced S1 (succinate-
reduced minus as isolated P-SDH). Middle:
Reduced S2 (dithionite minus succinate-reduced
BS-SDH). Arrows indicate sharp derivative due
to a trace of cytochrome impurity. Bottom:
Reduced S3 (succinate-reduced BS-SDH minus
reduced S1. Broken line represents regions
where Soret MCD from cytochrome impurities
overlap. Taken from ref. 12.

numerous, temperature-dependent transitions originating both from paramagnetic iron-sulfur centers and traces of cytochrome impurities. Spectral
deconvolution, to obtain the form of the spectrum from each paramagnetic
reduced iron-sulfur clusters, was achieved by exploiting differences in the
cluster composition of BS-SDH and P-SDH as well as differences in the redox
potentials and magnetization characteristics of the constituent chromophores.
The resulting MCD spectra for the succinate-reducible S1 and S3, and the
dithionite-reducible S2, are shown in Fig. 2.

In accord with previous EPR studies (13-15), the low temperature MCD and
room temperature CD characteristics of reduced S1 are indicative of an S =
1/2, $[2Fe-2S]^{1+(1+,2+)}$ center. Quantitation of the EPR resonance (g = 2.026,
1.935, 1.912) shows this center to be stoichiometric with FAD and almost
completely reduced in the presence of a large excess of succinate, in both
types of preparation.

The MCD results gave the first definitive evidence for the existence of
a low potential iron-sulfur center, S2, that is reducible by dithionite, but

not by succinate, (12). MCD bands indicative of a paramagnetic iron-sulfur center were observed on taking the difference between the dithionite-reduced and succinate-reduced samples of both BS-SDH and P-SDH, see Fig. 2. Moreover, the form of the spectra and the magnetization characteristics indicate that reduced S2 is an S = 1/2, $[4Fe-4S]^{1+(1+,2+)}$ center. Previous studies had either questioned the existence of S2 (16), or assigned it to an additional $[2Fe-2S]^{1+(1+,2+)}$ center with EPR parameters very similar to those of reduced S1 (17). Our MCD results were initially rather puzzling, since no EPR resonance that could be attributed to an S = 1/2, $[4Fe-4S]^{1+}$ center had been reported. However, careful examination of the EPR spectra of dithionite-reduced Complex II and soluble SDH preparations, at temperatures below 20 K, revealed broad, complex signals from reduced S2, underlying that from reduced S1 (18), see Fig. 3. While accurate spin quantitation of the broad resonance is difficult, approximate quantitations, involving subtraction of the signal from reduced S1 prior to integration, indicate that S2 is stoichiometric with FAD to within ± 20%. Similar broad and complex EPR spectra have been observed for fully reduced 8Fe ferredoxins and attributed to weak intercluster spin-spin

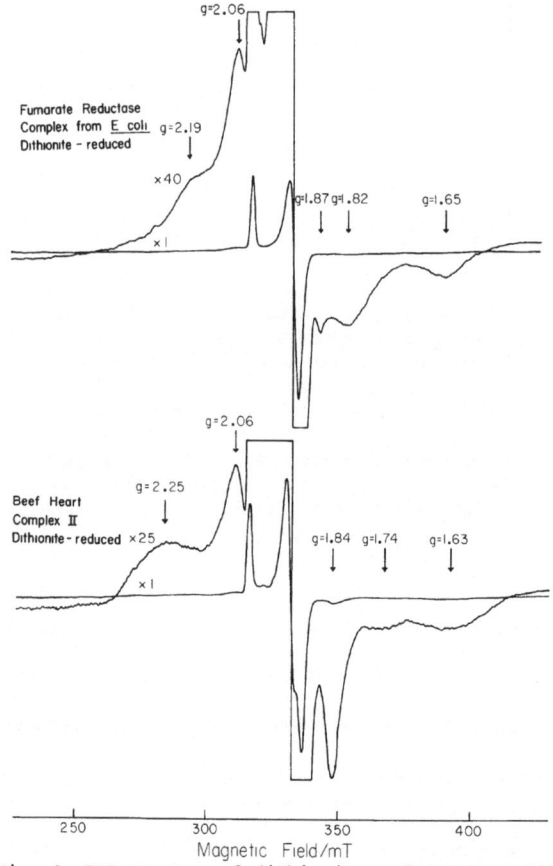

Fig. 3. EPR spectra of dithionite-reduced E. coli
fumarate reductase complex and bovine heart
Complex II. Conditions: temperature, 10 K;
modulation amplitude, 0.63 mT; microwave
power, 5 mW; frequency, 8.99 GHz. Multiplication factors indicate the relative gains for
the two spectra of each individual sample.
Taken from ref. 33.

interactions between two $S = 1/2$ [4Fe-4S]$^{1+}$ centers (20). Likewise we attribute the complex EPR spectrum from reduced S2 to intercluster spin coupling involving one or both of the two other paramagnetic clusters in dithionite-reduced Complex II (i.e. S1, $S = 1/2$ [2Fe-2S]$^{1+}$, and S3, $S = 2$ [3Fe-4S]^{0} (see below)).

Direct evidence for spin-spin interaction between reduced S1 and S2 was obtained by EPR redox titrations (18). For both Complex II and BS-SDH, the appearance of the EPR signal associated with reduced S2 occurred at the same midpoint potential as the enhancement of the spin relaxation of reduced S1. However, since the S1-S2 spin coupling produces negligible effects on the form of the EPR spectrum of S1, it seems improbable that this interaction alone is responsible for the breadth and complexity of the S2 resonance. More likely an additional spin interaction between reduced S2 and reduced S3 (paramagnetic, but effectively EPR silent as a result of zero field splitting of the $S = 2$ ground state) is primarily responsible. Support for a spin interaction between reduced S2 and S3 comes from the observation that the EPR signal from S2 becomes progressively narrower with less pronounced low and high field features at $g = 2.27$ and 1.63 in soluble preparations which are partially (BS-SDH) or almost totally (P-SDH) depleted in center S3 (M. K. Johnson, J. E. Morningstar, B. A. C. Ackrell, and E. B. Kearney, unpublished observations).

The discovery in 1980 of a new type of iron-sulfur cluster containing three iron atoms (21,22) has been of crucial importance in establishing the identity of the third iron-sulfur center in SDH, S3. The first indication that S3 was a [3Fe-4S]$^{0,1+}$ center, rather than a HiPIP-type [4Fe-4S]$^{2+,3+}$ center as originally postulated (23,24), came from a study of the magnetic field dependence of the linear electric field effect (LEFE) for the isotropic EPR signal at $g = 2.01$ in air-oxidized Complex II (25). However, [3Fe-4S]$^{1+}$ clusters exhibiting similar EPR signals had been shown to be produced by oxidative degradation of [4Fe-4S]$^{2+,1+}$ centers, first in Clostridium pasteurianum ferredoxin (26) and subsequently in aconitase (27). Therefore, by analogy with aconitase, there was a possibility that the $S = 1/2$ [3Fe-4S]$^{1+}$ center in oxidized Complex II was an artifact of aerial oxidation. This raises the possibility of rapid trinuclear to tetranuclear cluster conversion under reducing conditions, with the latter being the catalytically active form. Low temperature MCD measurements provide an effective method of addressing this question, since reduced [3Fe-4S] clusters exhibit intense temperature dependent MCD spectra with characteristic magnetization properties (28,29).

Both the form of the low temperature MCD spectrum of reduced S3 in BS-SDH, see Fig. 2, and the observed magnetization data, provide unambiguous evidence for the presence of $S = 2$ [3Fe-4S]^{0} clusters in samples reduced with either succinate or dithionite. Unfortunately it is not possible to assess accurately the number of [3Fe-4S]^{0} centers that are responsible for the MCD signal. However, comparison with the MCD spectra reported for [3Fe-4S]^{0} centers in well characterized ferredoxins (29), would suggest that this center and FAD are in an approximate 0.5:1 ratio in BS-SDH. We believe this deficiency is a consequence of the extreme oxygen lability of this cluster in soluble preparations (30), rather than any cluster conversion on reduction by substrate. This assertion is based on two lines of evidence. First, we have been unable to effect any significant trinuclear to tetranuclear iron-sulfur cluster conversion on incubating samples of BS-SDH with Fe(II) ions and dithiothreitol under anaerobic, reducing conditions. Second, the four subunit fumarate reductase complex from E. coli has approximately double the number of [3Fe-4S]^{0} centers, as judged by the intensity of the MCD signals for dithionite-reduced samples (31). Moreover, loss of approximately half of the [3Fe-4S] clusters accompanies isolation of soluble fumarate reductase in this instance (31).

Comparison of the MCD and EPR results for reduced samples of P-SDH and BS-SDH attest to analogous cluster compositions, except that the former is almost completely deficient in $[3Fe-4S]^0$ centers (12). Both samples are catalytically-competent in oxidizing succinate in the presence of artificial electron acceptors, but only BS-SDH exhibits significant reconstitutive capacity. Therefore, we conclude that the physiological function of the $[3Fe-4S]^{0,1+}$ center, S3, lies in mediating electron transfer to ubiquinone.

E. COLI FUMARATE REDUCTASE

Prior to our spectroscopic investigations, EPR studies of the fumarate reductase enzyme complex from E. coli had been interpreted in terms of three clusters, i.e. two $[2Fe-2S]^{1+,2+}$ centers, FR1 and FR2, and one high potential center probably of the $[4Fe-4S]^{2+,3+}$-type, FR3 (32). In contrast, the low temperature MCD and EPR studies conducted in our laboratories (31,33,34), point to an analogous cluster composition to that deduced for mammalian SDH. Moreover, spin quantitation data for the EPR signals observed in the fumarate reductase complex indicate an approximate 1:1:1 stoichiometry for the constituent prosthetic groups, i.e. $[2Fe-2S]^{1+,2+}$ (FR1), $[4Fe-4S]^{1+,2+}$ (FR2), $[3Fe-4S]^{0,1+}$ (FR3), and covalently-bound FAD (31,33). In contrast to Complex II, the fumarate reductase complex does not appear to be associated with an endogenous cytochrome b. This facilitates MCD studies of the more intact enzyme complex and permits spectroscopic characterization of the oxidized, high potential center, FR3. As discussed above, this cluster becomes oxidatively labile in the two subunit soluble preparations of mammalian SDH and E. coli fumarate reductase.

Fig. 4 shows a comparison of the EPR and MCD spectra of oxidized FR3 in

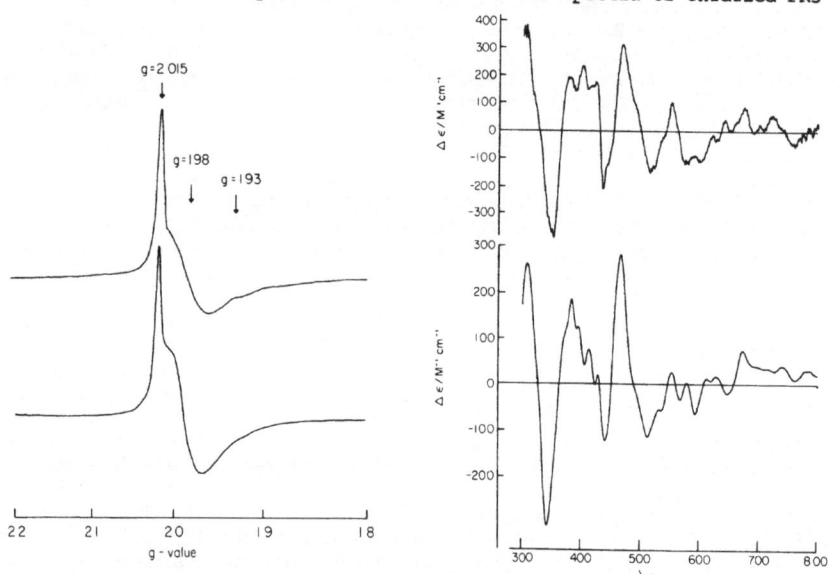

Fig. 4. Comparison of the MCD and EPR spectra of the high potential iron-sulfur center in as prepared fumarate reductase complex (upper spectra) and the oxidized trinuclear iron-sulfur cluster in T. thermophilus ferredoxin (lower spectra). Left panel: EPR spectra. Conditions: temperature, 13 K; frequency, 8.99 GHz; microwave power, 1 mW; modulation amplitude 0.63 mT. Right panel: MCD spectra at 1.5 K and 4.5 T. (The MCD spectrum of the fumarate reductase complex has been corrected for contributions from low spin ferricytochrome). Taken from Ref. 31

as isolated fumarate reductase complex with those of the well characterized S = 1/2 [3Fe-4S]$^{1+}$ cluster in the 7Fe ferredoxin from Thermus thermophilus (29). The close similarity of the spectra in terms of both form and intensity, as well as the spin quantitation of the EPR signal, provide convincing evidence that the fumarate reductase complex as prepared contains one [3Fe-4S]$^{1+}$ center.

Low temperature MCD and room temperature absorption spectra of the dithionite-reduced fumarate reductase complex are shown in Fig. 5. As yet it has not been possible to deconvolute the MCD signals from individual paramagnetic clusters in the dithionite-reduced enzyme complex. The deconvolution procedure utilized for mammalian SDH samples is not feasible, since our experiments indicate that neither FR1 nor FR3 is completely reduced by succinate alone (31). However, based on the MCD magnetization data, we conclude that the low temperature MCD spectrum of the dithionite-reduced complex is dominated by the S = 2 [3Fe-4S]^{0} cluster, i.e. reduced FR3. Moreover, the intensity of spectrum is entirely consitent with one [3Fe-4S]^{0} center, suggesting that the trinuclear cluster remains intact on reduction.

The observation that this type of cluster could be formed readily by oxidative degradation of a tetranuclear center had led workers to speculate that all biological trinuclear clusters could be artifacts of the isolation procedure (35). Despite the overwelming evidence for [3Fe-4S] centers that

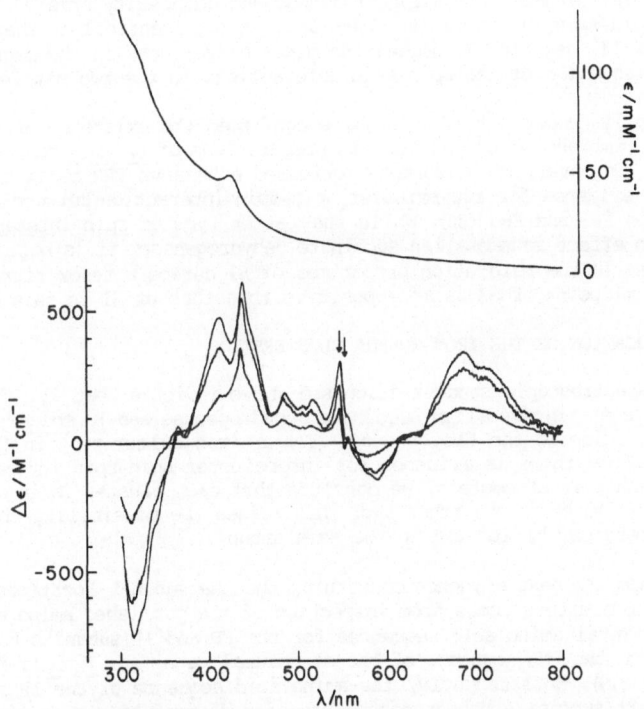

Fig. 5. MCD and absorption spectra of dithionite-reduced
fumarate reductase complex from E. coli. Upper
spectrum: room temperature absorption. Lower spectra:
MCD recorded at 1.53 K, 4.22 K, and 12.4 K (intensity
of all transitions increasing with decreasing temperature) at a magnetic field of 4.5 T. Arrows indicate
sharp derivative from low spin ferrocytochrome. Taken
from Ref. 31.

do not undergo ready conversion to [4Fe-4S] clusters in enzymatically active samples of both mammalian succinate dehydrogenase and E. coli fumarate reductase (12,31), the question of whether or not this cluster is present in vivo still remained. The ability to grow cells of E. coli with plasmid amplified expression of the fumarate reductase complex, and thereby generate samples in which the EPR signals of the iron sulfur clusters could be observed in whole cells, permitted a timely answer to this question. Samples of whole cells of E. coli with plasmid amplified expression of fumarate reductase were found to exhibit the EPR resonance characteristic of the $S = 1/2$ $[3Fe-4S]^{1+}$ cluster, FR3, on incubation under anaerobic conditions with the natural substrate, fumarate. This result suggests that the [3Fe-4S] centers in fumarate reductase and succinate dehydrogenase are indeed functioning components of the enzymes in vivo (34).

EPR studies of the dithionite-reduced fumarate reductase complex show broad features to high and low field of the almost axial signal from the $[2Fe-2S]^{1+}$ center ($g = 2.026$, 1.934, and 1.920), see Fig. 3. A similar broad signal (although without the feature at $g = 1.87$) was also detected in highly purified samples of dithionite-reduced soluble fumarate reductase (33), indicating that it does not arise from a contaminating iron-sulfur protein. Preliminary attempts to quantify this new signal gave values between 0.7 and 1.0 spins/FAD. As for Complex II, we attribute this new resonance to an $S = 1/2$ $[4Fe-4S]^{1+}$ cluster, with the broadness and complexity arising from inter-cluster spin-spin interactions. The signal is not identical to that observed in Complex II, see Fig. 3, suggesting minor differences in the magnitude and/or orientation of the spin-spin interactions in the two samples.

Recently Cammack et al. (36) have confirmed the existence of this new signal in membrane-bound and soluble preparations of E. coli fumarate reductase. Moreover, these workers performed extensive EPR redox titrations that gave evidence for intercluster spin-spin interaction between FR1 and FR2 and between FR1 and FR3 (36). While the latter type of spin interaction may also be in effect in mammalian succinate dehydrogenase, it is not observable via changes in the relaxation properties of S1 during a redox titration, since the midpoint of S3 is more positive than that of S1 in this enzyme.

SUBUNIT LOCATION OF THE IRON-SULFUR CLUSTERS

The spectroscopic studies discussed above indicate that all three iron-sulfur clusters in mammalian succinate dehydrogenase and E. coli fumarate reductase reside in the flavoprotein (FP) or iron-sulfur protein (IP) subunits. Since there is evidence for intercluster spin-spin interactions between each pair of centers, we conclude that each cluster is in close proximity (< 20 Å) to the other two. This raises the possibility that all three centers may be located in the same subunit.

Perhaps the best evidence concerning the the subunit locations of the iron-sulfur clusters comes from inspection of the published amino acid sequences. Total amino acid sequences for the FP and IP subunits have been deduced from the DNA sequence of the structural genes for E. coli fumarate reductase (8,9). More recently, the amino acid sequence of the IP subunit of bovine heart succinate dehydrogenase has been deduced by direct determination (37). While the cysteine residues in the FP subunit appear to be randomly dispersed, those in the IP subunits are conserved in three "ferredoxin-like" clusters, see Fig. 6. The marked similarity between the first cluster of cysteines and the arrangement of cysteines bound to [2Fe-2S] centers in plant ferredoxins suggests that it is the site for the [2Fe-2S] centers, S1 or FR1. The remaining two clusters of cysteines closely resemble those observed for [4Fe-4S] centers in bacterial ferredoxins. However, since facile interconversion between [3Fe-4S] and [4Fe-4S] clusters is now well established for many bacterial ferredoxins and aconitase (35), the same

```
E. coli        FRD IP      56 S C R M A I C G S C G M M V N N V P K L A C 77
Bovine Heart   SDH IP      63 S C R E G I C G S C A M N I N G G N T L A C 86
S. plantensis  [2Fe-2S] Fd 40 S C R A G A C S T C A  (26 residues)  L T C 79


E. coli        FRD IP     147 G C I N C G L C Y A A C P Q F G 162
Bovine Heart   SDH IP     156 E C I L C A C C S T S C P S Y(W) 173
P. aerogenes   [4Fe-4S] Fd  7 S C I A C G A C K P E C P V N I 22


E. coli        FRD IP     203 S C T F V G Y C S E V C P 215
Bovine Heart   SDH IP     213 R C H T I M N C T E T C P 227
P. aerogenes   [4Fe-4S] Fd 33 S C I D C G S C A S V C P 45
```

Fig. 6. Comparison of the cysteine clusters in the IP subunits of E. coli
fumarate reductase (8) and bovine heart succinate dehydrogenase (37)
with those of the [2Fe-2S] center in S. plantensis (38) and the 2
[4Fe-4S] centers in P. aerogenes (39).

sequence must also be able to accommodate a [3Fe-4S] center. The number of
cysteines required to coordinate a [3Fe-4S] cluster is presently unknown and
awaits further structural elucidation. Resonance Raman studies of [3Fe-4S]
centers in a range of bacterial ferredoxins suggest a common structure (40),
and two plausible structures requiring 3 and 4 cysteines have been proposed
(35,40). Certainly no more than 4 cysteines are necessary, since a [3Fe-4S]
center is readily formed under oxidizing conditions in Bacillus stearothermophilus ferredoxin (35), which comprises a single polypeptide containing only
four cysteine residues. Such considerations lead to the conclusion that all
three iron-sulfur clusters could be accommodated in the IP subunit, with only
three cysteines coordinating the [3Fe-4S] center, S3 or FR3. However, the
possibility of non-cysteine coordination for this center, or of residues
being suppied by the FP subunit, cannot be ruled out at this stage.

Recently we have obtained definitive spectroscopic evidence to show that
both FR1 and FR3 are located in the IP subunit of the fumarate reductase
complex. Fig. 7 shows EPR spectra for wild type whole cells of E. coli as
well as whole cells that have been amplified with plasmids encoding for all
four fumarate reductase subunits, the FP and IP subunits, and the FP and IP
subunit with the latter truncated after the first two clusters of cysteines.
Clearly FR1 has been amplified in all three types of the plasmid amplified
cells, showing that this cluster is not associated with the cysteines 204,
210, or 214. In contrast, these three cysteines do appear to be involved
coordinating FR3, since amplification of FR3, as evidenced by the appearance
of the characteristic EPR signal of the [3Fe-4S]$^{1+}$ cluster in fumarate-
treated cells, was observed with the plasmids encoding for all four subunits
and the FP and IP subunits, but not for the plasmid encoding for FP and the
truncated IP subunits. Subsequent EPR studies of whole cells that had been
amplified with a plasmid encoding for only the IP subunit provided
unambiguous evidence for the presence of FR1 in this subunit (data not shown)

CONCLUSIONS

Our conclusions are summarized by Fig. 8 which shows a schematic representation of the topographical distribution of the redox active centers of
mammalian Complex II. The proposed iron-sulfur cluster composition of one
each of [2Fe-2S], [3Fe-4S], and [4Fe-4S] center is consistent with the available spectroscopic and analytical information and provides a rational explanation of the earlier results by the iron-sulfur core extrusion method
(12,41). All the available evidence at the present time points to the

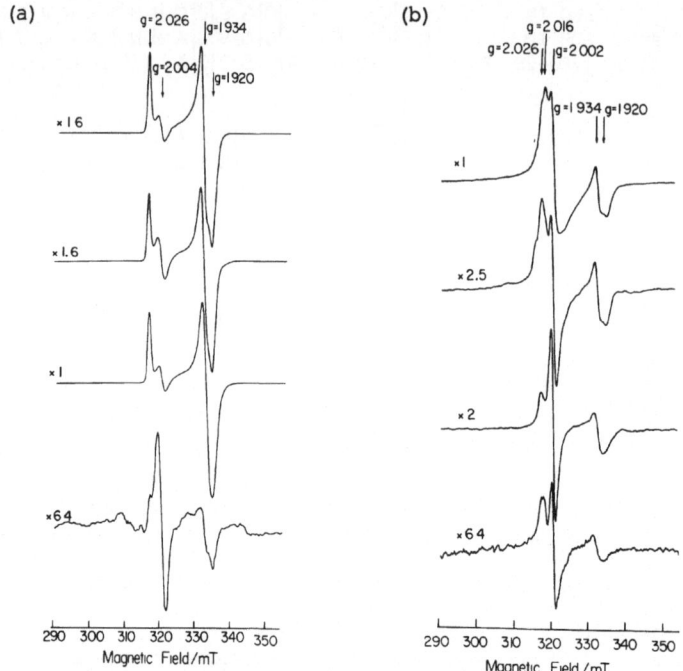

Fig. 7. EPR spectra of whole cells of E. coli fumarate reductase. (a) Whole
cells suspended in anaerobic 50 mM potassium phosphate buffer, pH
7.8. Conditions: temperature, 70 K; microwave power, 1 mW; modulation
amplitude, 0.63 mT; frequency, 8.99 GHz. (b) Whole cells suspended in
anaerobic 50 mM potassium phosphate buffer, pH 7.8, with 50 mM
fumarate. Conditions: as for (a), except temperature, 15 K. In both
(a) and (b) the samples are (from top to bottom): cells with plasmid
amplification of all four fumarate reductase subunits; cells with
plasmid amplification of FP and IP subunits; cells with plasmid
amplification of FP and truncated IP subunits; wild-type cells

trinuclear cluster being an intrinsic component of of both fumarate reductase
and succinate dehydroganse rather than artifact of the isolation procedure.
Moreover its requirement for reconstitutive activity suggests a role in
mediating electron transfer to ubiquinone or menaquinone. Based on the available sequence data and the observed intercluster spin-spin interactions it
seems likely that all three clusters are located in the IP subunit in both
mammalian succinate dehydrogenase and E. coli fumarate reductase.

While the spectroscopic studies discussed in this review represent a
major step forward, numerous important questions remain for future studies.
For example the detailed pathway of electron tranfer through Complex II is
still to be elucidated. Any mechanism must also explain the apparent requirement for two components, cytochrome $\underline{b}$ and the $[4Fe-4S]^{1+,2+}$ center, S2, with
midpoint potentials far below that of the fumarate/succinate couple. Fortunately the availability of cloned fumarate reductase genes has opened up new
avenues of research. Biochemical studies of genetically modified forms of
fumarate reductase, coupled with spectroscopic studies of the type discussed
above, should provide answers to many of the remaining questions.

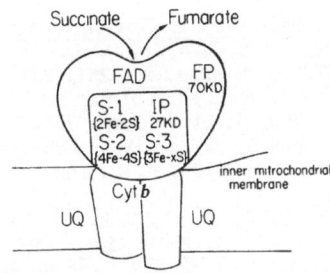

Fig. 8. Schematic representation of the proposed topographical
distribution of the redox active centers in Complex II.
FP, flavoprotein subunit; IP, iron-sulfur protein
subunit; Q, ubiquinone.

ACKNOWLEDGEMENTS

This work was supported by National Institutes of Health Grant GM-33806
(M. K. J.) and National Institutes of Health Grant HL-16251 and the Veterans'
Administration (G. C., B. A. C. A., E. B. K.)

REFERENCES

(1) Capaldi, R. A., Sweetland, J., and Merli, A. (1977) Biochemistry 16,
    5707-5710.
(2) Davis, K. A., and Hatefi, Y. (1971) Biochemistry 10, 2509-2516.
(3) Davis, K. A., Hatefi, Y., Poff, K. L., and Butler, W. L. (1972) Biochem.
    Biophys. Res. Commun. 46, 1984-1990.
(4) Ackrell, B. A. C., Ball, M. B., and Kearney, E. B. (1980) J. Biol. Chem.
    255, 2761-2769.
(5) Hatefi, Y., and Galante, Y. M. (1980) J. Biol. Chem. 255, 5530-5537.
(6) Ohnishi, T., and Salerno, J. C. (1982) in Iron-Sulfur Proteins (Spiro.
    T. G., ed.) pp. 285-327, John Wiley and Sons, New York.
(7) Beinert, H. and Albracht, S. P. J. (1982) Biochim. Biophys. Acta 683,
    245-277.
(8) Cole, S. T., Grundstrom, T., Jaurin, B., Robinson, J. J., and Weiner, J.
    H. (1982) Eur. J. Biochem. 126, 211-216.
(9) Cole, S. T. (1982) Eur. J. Biochem. 122, 479-484.
(10) Grundstrom, T., and Jaurin, B. (1982) Proc. Natl. Acad. Sci. U.S.A. 79,
     1111-1115.
(11) Cole, S. T., Condon, C., Lemire, B. D., and Weiner, J. H. (1985)
     Biochim. Biophys. Acta 811, 381-403.
(12) Johnson, M. K., Morningstar, J. E., Bennett, D. E., Ackrell, B. A. C.,
     and Kearney, E. B. (1985) J. Biol. Chem. 260, 7368-7378.
(13) Beinert, H., and Sands, R. H. (1960) Biochem. Biophys. Res. Commun. 3,
     41-46.
(14) Salerno, J. C., Ohnishi, T., Blum, H., and Leigh, J. S. (1977) Biochim.
     Biophys. Acta 494, 191-197.
(15) Albracht, S. P. J., and Subramanian, J. (1977) Biochim. Biophys. Acta
     462, 36-48.

483

(16) Albracht, S. P. J. (1980) Biochim. Biophys. Acta **612**, 11-28.
(17) Ohnishi, T, Salerno, J. C., Winter, D. B., Lim, J., Yu, C. A., Yu, L., and King, T. E. (1976) J. Biol. Chem. **251**, 2094-2104.
(18) Maguire, J. J., Johnson, M. K., Morningstar, J. E., Ackrell, B. A. C., and Kearney, E. B. (1985) J. Biol. Chem. **260**, 10909-10912.
(19) Singer, T. P., and Johnson, M. K. (1985) FEBS Lett. **190**, 189-198.
(20) Mathews, R, Charlton, S., Sands, R. H., and Palmer, G. (1974) J. Biol. Chem. **249**, 4326-4328.
(21) Emptage, M. H., Kent, T. A., Huynh, B. H., Rawlings, J., Orme-Johnson, W. H., and Munck, E. (1980) J. Biol. Chem. **255**, 1793-1796.
(22) Stout, C. D., Ghosh, D., Pattabhi, B., and Robbins, A. H. (1980) J. Biol. Chem. **255**, 1797-1800.
(23) Beinert, H., Ackrell, B. A. C., Kearney, E. B., and Singer, T. P. (1974) Biochem. Biophys. Res. Commun. **58**, 564-572.
(24) Beinert, H., Ackrell, B. A. C., Kearney, E. B., and Singer, T. P. (1975) Eur. J. Biochem. **54**, 185-194.
(25) Ackrell, B. A. C., Kearney, E. B., Mims, W. B., Peisach, J., and Beinert, H. (1984) J. Biol. Chem. **259**, 4015-4018.
(26) Thomson, A. J., Robinson, A. E., Johnson, M. K., Cammack, R., Rao, K. K., and Hall, D. O. (1981) Biochim. Biophys. Acta **637**, 423-432.
(27) Kent, T. A., Dreyer, J.-L., Kennedy, M. C., Huynh, B. H., Emptage, M. H., Beinert, H., and Munck, E. (1982) Proc. Natl. Acad. Sci. U.S.A. **79**, 1096-1100.
(28) Johnson, M. K., Robinson, A. E., and Thomson, A. J. (1982) in Iron-Sulfur Proteins (Spiro, T. G. ed.) pp. 367-406, John Wiley and Sons, New York.
(29) Johnson, M. K., Bennett, D. E., Fee, J. A., and Sweeney, W. V. (1987) Biochim. Biophys. Acta **911**, 81-94.
(30) Beinert, H., Ackrell, B. A. C., Vinogradov, A. D., Kearney, E. B., and Singer, T. P. (1977) Arch. Biochem. Biophys. **182**, 95-106.
(31) Morningstar, J. E., Johnson, M. K., Cecchini, G., Ackrell, B. A. C., and Kearney, E. B. (1985) J. Biol. Chem. **260**, 13631-13638.
(32) Simpkin, D., and Ingledew, W. J. (1984) Biochem. Soc. Trans. **12**, 500-501.
(33) Johnson, M. K., Morningstar, J. E., Cecchini, G., and Ackrell, B. A. C. (1985) Biochem. Biophys. Res. Commun. **131**, 756-762.
(34) Johnson, M. K., Morningstar, J. E., Cecchini, G., and Ackrell, B. A. C. (1985) Biochem. Biophys. Res. Commun. **131**, 653-658.
(35) Beinert, H., and Thomson, A. J. (1983) Arch. Biochem. Biophys. **222**, 333-361.
(36) Cammack, R., Patil, D. S., and Weiner, J. H. (1986) Biochim. Biophys. Acta **870**, 545-551.
(37) Yao, Y., Wakabayashi, S., Matsubara, H., Yu, L., and Yu, C. A. (1986) in Iron-Sulfur Protein Research (Matsubara, H. et al., eds.) Japan Sci. Soc. Press, Tokyo Springer-Verlag, Berlin.
(38) Tsukihara, T., Kobayashi, M., Nakamura, M., Katsube, Y., Fukuyama, K., Hase, T., Wada, K., and Matsubara, H. (1982) Biosystems **15**, 243-257.
(39) Adman, E. T., Sieker, L. C., and Jensen, L. H. (1973) J. Biol. Chem. **248**, 3989-3996.
(40) Johnson, M. K., Czernuszewicz, R., Spiro, T. G., Fee, J. A., and Sweeney, W. V. (1983) J. Am. Chem. Soc. **105**, 6671-6678.
(41) Coles, C. J., Holm, R. H., Kurtz, D. M., Orme-Johnson, W. H., Rawlings, J., Singer, T. P., and Wong, G. B. (1979) Proc. Natl. Acad. Sci. U.S.A. **76**, 3805-3808.

MECHANISMS OF ELECTRON TRANSFER IN SUCCINATE DEHYDROGENASE AND FUMARATE
REDUCTASE: POSSIBLE FUNCTIONS FOR IRON-SULPHUR CENTRE 2 AND CYTOCHROME b

Richard Cammack*, John J. Maguire** and Brian A.C. Ackrell***

*Department of Biochemistry
King's College, London W8 7AH, U.K.

**Membrane Bioenergetics Group,
Lawrence Berkeley Laboratory, Berkeley, CA94720, USA

***Department of Biochemistry and Biophysics
Veterans Administration Medical Center, San Francisco
CA94121, USA

INTRODUCTION

Succinate dehydrogenase and fumarate reductase are membrane-bound
enzymes of similar structure which catalyze electron transfer between the
fumarate/succinate and quinone/quinol couples [1-3]. The involvement and
location of covalently-bound flavin and three iron-sulphur clusters,
[2Fe-2S] Centre 1, [4Fe-4S] Centre 2 and [3Fe-4S] Centre 3 [4], in the two
dissociable subunits are indicated by the amino-acid sequences [5]. The
flavin is attached to the largest subunit, $\sim$ 70kDa, and the iron-sulphur
clusters to the other soluble protein, $\sim$ 30kDa; these two subunits may be
isolated as soluble succinate dehydrogenase or fumarate reductase.

A b-type cytochrome has also been persistently reported to be
associated with the membrane-associated four-subunit form of Complex II
[6]. This has been confirmed by the identification of the E. coli sdhC
subunit with cytochrome b-556 [7]. A possible exception is E. coli
fumarate reductase, in which no cytochrome b has been detected; most of the
molecular characterization of this protein has been made with protein
isolated from over-producing strains, in which the haem might not be
inserted correctly. Certainly the haem is readily lost during extraction
of the succinate dehydrogenase and fumarate reductase complexes, and it has
been suggested [8] that it might be bound between two subunits.

MIDPOINT POTENTIALS OF THE ELECTRON CARRIERS

The flavin semiquinone and iron-sulphur clusters in succinate
dehydrogenase and fumarate reductase are detectable by EPR spectroscopy;
the low-potential Centre 2 has only recently been assigned as an unusually
broad spectrum [9,10]. The cytochrome yields an EPR signal at g=3.4
[11,12]. By a combination of optical and EPR spectroscopy it is possible
to estimate the midpoint reduction potentials of the centres. Values
obtained for various proteins are summarized in Table 1.

Table 1. Midpoint potentials of redox centres in succinate dehydrogenase and fumarate reductase.

Potentials are expressed relative to the standard hydrogen electrode, and were determined by mediator titrations unless otherwise stated.
UQ = ubiquinone, MQ = menaquinone.

	quinone used	Fe-S 1	Fe-S 2	Fe-S 3	cyt b	Ref
Succinate dehydrogenase						
Beef heart	UQ	0	-260	60	-180	13,14
Arum maculatum	UQ	-7	-240	90	-30	15
E. coli	UQ	10	-175	65		16
M. luteus	MQ	70	-295	10		17
Bacillus subtilis	MQ	80	-240	-25		18
Rhodospirillum rubrum	UQ	50	-160			33
Fumarate reductase						
E. coli	MQ	-20	-320	-70		10
		-50	-285	-50		19
Wolinella succinogenes	MQ	-125	-300	-130	-55, -250	20
Fumarate/succinate titration		-59		-24	-23	

It may be noted that the potentials of the [4Fe-4S] centre 2 and [3Fe-xS] centre 3 are within the normal range for iron-sulphur proteins, but the potential of centre 1 is exceptionally high for a [2Fe-2S] cluster. Typical ferredoxin potentials are in the range -155mV to -455mV [13]. The potential of Centre 1 is suitable for accepting electrons from succinate ($E=28$mV at pH 7.0). The mechanism by which its high potential is maintained by the protein is not clear. In all cases, except perhaps E. coli succinate dehydrogenase [5], the amino acid sequence indicates that there are four cysteine sulphurs available for coordination to the cluster in a similar way to the [2Fe-2S] ferredoxins. It seems unlikely that these ligands to the cluster are substituted by nitrogenous ligands, as in the Rieske iron-sulphur protein [22]. Spin-echo envelope modulation experiments on succinate dehydrogenase [23], and fumarate reductase (R. Cammack, J.H. Weiner, J. McCracken and J. Peisach, unpublished observations) indicate that the g=1.94 EPR signal of centre 1 in succinate dehydrogenase and fumarate reductase is associated with a nitrogen atom which is probably from the polypeptide chain and not in the first coordination sphere of the iron.

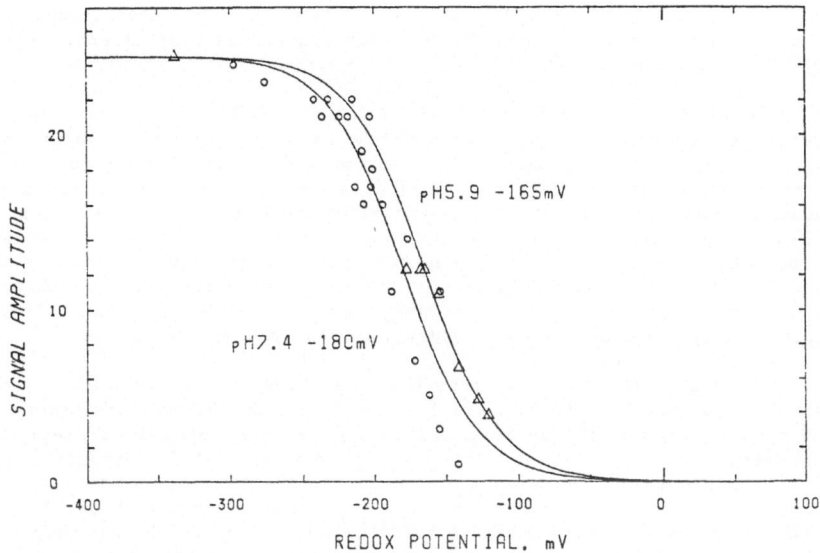

Fig. 1. Oxidation-reduction titrations of cytochrome b-560 in Complex II from beef heart. Points O, pH 7.4; Δ, pH 5.9.

The midpoint potentials of the b-type cytochrome have for long been uncertain, because of overlap of the optical spectrum with the cytochromes b of Complex III, and because of the suspicion that it represents a denatured b-type cytochrome, which would tend to have a low potential. Recently we have measured the midpoint potential of the cytochrome b in highly-purified Complex II from beef heart. The results (Fig. 1) indicate a low potential, around -180mV, similar to that reported recently by Yu et al. [12].

Table 1 includes data from the unusual mitochondria from the thermogenic spadix of the higher plant Arum maculatum, in which succinate dehydrogenase is the dominant iron-sulphur protein [15]. These mitochondria are capable of extremely high rates of cyanide-resistant respiration with externally-added NADH or succinate as substrates. It is noteworthy that these mitochondria also contain unusually high levels of a b-type cytochrome absorbing at 560nm [24], which is not reducible by succinate.

ELECTRON TRANSFER PATHWAYS IN SUCCINATE DEHYDROGENASE AND FUMARATE REDUCTASE

From a soluble hydrogen carrier in the aqueous environment (succinate) to a hydrophobic hydrogen carrier in the membrane (quinone), the redox equivalents are passed through iron-sulphur clusters and cytochromes. These are pure electron carriers, as shown by the fact that the redox potentials of the cytochrome b and of the iron-sulphur centres have only a small pH-dependence.

The structure and composition of succinate dehydrogenase and fumarate reductase appear to have been highly conserved in evolution. The differences in midpoint potentials between the equivalent centres in different proteins probably reflect the different directions of electron flow (the potential of Centre 1 tends to be lower in fumarate reductase than succinate dehydrogenase), and the interaction with either ubiquinone or menaquinone (Centre 3 tends to be lower in enzymes that interact with MQ).

The midpoint potentials of Centre 2 and cytochrome $\underline{b}$ in beef heart succinate dehydrogenase are apparently so low that they cannot be significantly reduced by succinate. For comparison, the midpoint potential of the fumarate/succinate couple is +28mV at pH 7.0, and the two-electron reduction potentials for ubiquinone and menaquinone are approx. +70mV and -80mV, respectively. There may be some uncertainty about the precise values obtained by mediator titrations, particularly when there may be intramolecular electron reorganization during freezing for EPR spectroscopy [25]. Nevertheless, all observations indicate that Centre 2 can only be substantially reduced by strong reducing agents such as dithionite.

In the absence of any evidence that they have any other function such as regulation, we have to consider how the low-potential carriers Centre 2 and cytochrome $\underline{b}$ might be involved in a kinetic mechanism of electron transfer, in which they are transiently reduced. It is important to distinguish between the midpoint potential of a centre and its working redox potential. Electron carriers such as Centre 2 and cytochrome $\underline{b}$ may work at considerably more positive redox potentials, in which case they are very substantially oxidized, provided that the rates of intramolecular electron transfer are rapid enough.

There are few multi-centred electron-transfer proteins, for which the mechanism of electron transfer has been determined in detail. In xanthine oxidase from milk [26], and the four-haem cytochrome $\underline{c}$-3 from Desulfovibrio sp. [27], it has been determined that intramolecular electron transfer is so rapid that the redox groups within the enzyme are close to equilibrium during catalysis. The average electron distribution within the enzyme at any stage would be determined by the midpoint potentials, and the total number of electrons within the molecule. In these two proteins, the redox potentials are all fairly close, so that all would become significantly reduced during the reaction cycle. In succinate dehydrogenase and fumarate reductase, the potentials of the constituent groups span a considerably wider range, and at equilibrium the average electron distribution would be highly asymmetric.

A reason for the disparity of potentials of the constituent groups may be found in the fact that flavin and quinones are all reduced in two steps, each involving one electron and one proton, via a semiquinone intermediate. The two potentials for the flavin in the beef heart succinate dehydrogenase were estimated to be -127 and -31mV respectively [28]. This is presumed to be the group which reacts directly with the fumarate/succinate couple in both succinate dehydrogenase and fumarate reductase. The semiquinone states of ubiquinone and menaquinone are also unstable, the first reduction potential in each case being significantly more negative than the second [29]. This difficulty may be overcome in two ways: by stabilizing the protein-bound semiquinone, or by arranging to have intermediate electron carriers which also have high and low potentials.

A mechanism involving low-and high-potential carriers has been outlined, and termed the "dual-pathway" model [30]. In one form of this model for succinate dehydrogenase, Centre 1 and Centre 2 are proposed to accept the first and second electrons from reduced flavin. These electrons are then passed to Centre 3 and cytochrome $\underline{b}$, and then reduce ubisemiquinone and ubiquinone respectively. In this way the low-potential carriers are matched with low-potential semiquinones, and the higher-potential carriers with the quinol forms, thereby ensuring the most efficient electron transport.

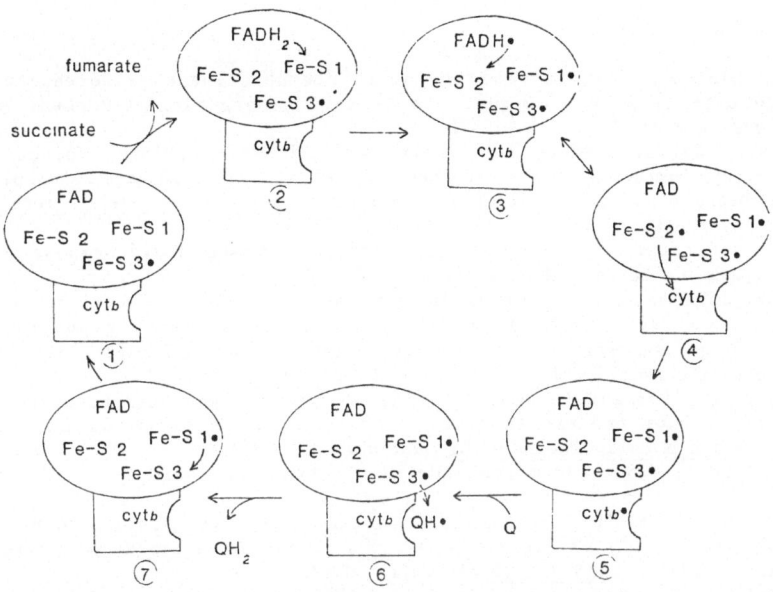

Fig. 2. A dual-pathway model of electron transfer in succinate dehydrogenase, and in the reverse direction, for fumarate reductase.

It seems unlikely that there is a strict channelling of electrons through the two pathways. The iron-sulphur clusters are all in the 30kDa subunit, and interact magnetically, so it would be difficult to prevent electrons on the low-potential Centre 2 and cytochrome b from "short-circuiting" to Centres 1 and 3. However, consideration of the electron distribution in the enzymes indicates that an electron should be displaced onto Centre 2 and/or cytochrome b, if the enzyme begins the reaction cycle with an odd number of electrons (Fig. 2). Then the electron transfer sequence is such that the high-potential centres 1 and 3 always beccme reduced <u>before</u> low-potential Centre 2 and cytochrome <u>b</u>. The one-electron-reduced state could be produced by reduction with, or release of, a ubisemiquinone molecule.

This scheme is presented as a working hypothesis, which can be tested against kinetic and spectroscopic data. One such observation is a complex EPR signal, which appears rapidly during reoxidation of succinate dehydrogenase. This signal is very labile, and is only observed in intact, membrane-bound Complex II in the presence of ubiquinone [31]. Ruzicka et al. [32] modelled the spectrum on an interaction between one or two ubisemiquinone radicals, interacting with another, faster-relaxing paramagnetic species. This latter paramagnetic species was assumed to be oxidized Centre 3. However it seems unlikely that this high-potential centre would remain oxidized while other centres were reduced. Other possibilities are reduced Centre 3, which is paramagnetic [4], or as we have suggested [8], oxidized cytochrome <u>b</u>. In the proposed mechanism this spectrum would be derived from step 6.

Acknowledgement

This work was supported by a grant to R.C. from the Wellcome Foundation.

REFERENCES

1. T. Ohnishi, Structure of the succinate-ubiquinone oxidoreductase (Complex II), in: "Current Topics in Bioenergetics" C.P. Lee, ed. Academic Press,New York (1987)

2. S.T. Cole, C. Condon, B.D. Lemire and J.H. Weiner, 1986, Molecular biology, biochemistry and bioenergetics of fumarate reductase, a complex membrane bound iron-sulphur flavoenzyme of Escherichia coli., Biochim. Biophys. Acta, 135:381.

3. L. Hederstedt and L. Rutberg, 1981, Succinate dehydrogenase - a comparative review, Microbiol. Rev., 45:542.

4. M.K. Johnson, J.E. Morningstar, D.E. Bennett, B.A.C. Ackrell and E.B. Kearney, 1985, Magnetic circular dichroism studies of succinate dehydrogenase. Evidence for [2Fe-2S], [3Fe-xS], and [4Fe-4S] centres in reconstitutively active enzyme., J. Biol. Chem., 260:7368.

5. M.G. Darlison and J.R. Guest, 1984, Nucleotide sequence encoding the iron-sulphur protein subunit of the succinate dehydrogenase of Escherichia coli, Biochem. J., 223:507.

6. Y. Hatefi, 1985, The mitochondrial electron transport and oxidative phosphorylation system, J. Biol. Chem., 54:1015.

7. H. Murakami, K. Kita, H. Oya and Y. Anraku, 1986, The E. coli cytochrome b556 gene, cybA, is assignable as sdhC in the succinate dehydrogenase gene cluster., FEMS Microbiol. Lett., 30:307.

8. R. Cammack, Iron-sulfur clusters in enzymes: pathways of electron transfer, in: "Iron-sulfur Protein Research," H. Matsubara, ed. Japan Scientific Societies Press/Spinger-Verlag,Tokyo and Berlin (1987)

9. J.J. Maguire, M.K. Johnson, J. Morningstar, B.A.C. Ackrell and E.B. Kearney, 1985, EPR studies of mammalian succinate dehydrogenase. Detection of the tetranuclear cluster S2., J. Biol. Chem., 260:10909.

10. R. Cammack, D.S. Patil and J.H. Weiner, 1986, Evidence that centre 2 in Escherichia coli fumarate reductase is a [4Fe-4S] cluster, Biochim. Biophys. Acta, 870:545.

11. N.R. Orme-Johnson, R.E. Hansen and H. Beinert, 1971, EPR studies of the cytochrome b-c1 segment of the mitochondrial electron transfer system, Biochem. Biophys. Res. Commun., 45:871.

12. L. Yu, J.X. Yu, P.E. Haley and C.A. Yu, 1987, Properties of bovine heart mitochondrial cytochrome b560, J. Biol. Chem., 262:1137.

13. T. Ohnishi, J.C. Salerno, D.B. Winter, J. Lim, C. Yu, L. Yu and T.E. King, 1976, Thermodynamic and EPR characterization of two ferredoxin-type iron-sulfur centers in the succinate-ubiquinone reductase segment of the respiratory chain, J. Biol. Chem., 251:2094.

14. T. Ohnishi, J. Lim, D.B. Winter and T.E. King, 1976, Thermodynamic and EPR characteristics of a HiPIP-type iron-sulfur center in the succinate dehydrogenase of the respiratory chain, J. Biol. Chem., 251:2105.

15. R. Cammack and J.M. Palmer, 1977, Iron-sulphur centres in mitochondria from Arum maculatum spadix with very high rates of cyanide-resistant respiration, Biochem. J., 166:347.

16. C. Condon, R. Cammack, D.S. Patil and P. Owen, 1985, The succinate dehydrogenase of Escherichia coli., J. Biol. Chem., 260:9427.

17. B.A. Crowe, P. Owen, D.S. Patil and R. Cammack, 1983, Characterisation of succinate dehydrogenase from Micrococcus luteus (lysodeikticus) by electron-spin-resonance spectroscopy, Eur. J. Biochem., 137:191.

18. J.J. Maguire, K. Magnusson and L. Hederstedt, 1986, Bacillus subtilis mutant succinate dehydrogenase lacking covalently bound flavin: identification of the primary defect and studies on the iron-sulfur clusters in mutated and wild-type enzyme, Biochemistry, 25:5202.

19. D. Simpkin and W.J. Ingledew, 1985, The membrane-bound fumarate reductase of Escherichia coli: an electron-paramagnetic resonance study, Biochem. Soc. Trans. 13:603.

20. G. Unden, S.P.J. Albracht and A. Krüger, 1984, Redox potentials and

kinetic properties of fumarate reductase complex from <u>Vibrio</u> <u>succinogenes</u>., <u>Biochim. Biophys. Acta</u>, 767:460.

21. R. Cammack, Midpoint potentials of iron-sulphur proteins - a survey., <u>in</u>: "Charge and field effects in biosystems.," M.J. Allen and P.N.R. Usherwood, ed. Abacus Press,Tunbridge Wells (1984)

22. J.F. Cline, B.M. Hoffman, W.B. Mims, E. LaHaie, D.P. Ballou and J.A. Fee, 1985, Evidence for N coordination to Fe in the (2Fe-2S) clusters of <u>Thermus</u> Rieske protein and phthalate dioxygenase from <u>Pseudomonas</u>., <u>J. Biol. Chem.</u>, 260:3251.

23. R. LoBrutto, P.E. Haley, C.A. Yu, T. Ohnishi and J.S. Leigh, 1986, <u>Biophys. J.</u>, 49:327a.

24. D.S. Bendall and R. Hill, 1956, Cytochrome components in the spadix of <u>Arum</u> <u>maculatum</u>, <u>New Phytol.</u>, 55:206.

25. A.G. Porras and G. Palmer, 1982, The room temperature potentiometry of xanthine oxidase, <u>J. Biol. Chem.</u>, 257:11617.

26. J.S. Olson, D.P. Ballou, G. Palmer and V. Massey, 1974, The mechanism of action of xanthine oxidase, <u>J. Biol. Chem.</u>, 249:4363.

27. H. Santos, J.J.G. Moura, I. Moura, J. LeGall and A.V. Xavier, 1984, NMR studies of electron transfer mechanisms in a protein with interacting redox centres: <u>Desulfovibrio</u> <u>gigas</u> cytochrome c-3, <u>Eur. J. Biochem.</u>, 141:283.

28. T. Ohnishi, T.E. King, J.C. Salerno, H. Blum, J.R. Bowyer and T. Maida, 1981, Thermodynamic and electron paramagnetic resonance characterization of flavin in succinate dehydrogenase, <u>J. Biol. Chem.</u>, 256:5577.

29. P.R. Rich, 1984, Electron and proton transfers through quinones and cytochrome <u>bc</u> complexes, <u>Biochim. Biophys. Acta</u>, 768:53.

30. R. Cammack, B.A. Crowe and N.D. Cook, 1986, Dual-pathway models of electron transfer in succinate dehydrogenase and fumarate reductase, <u>Biochem. Soc. Trans.</u>, 14:1207.

31. B.A.C. Ackrell, E.B. Kearney, C.J. Coles, T.P. Singer, H. Beinert, Y.P. Wan and K. Folkers, 1977, Kinetics of the reoxidation of succinate dehydrogenase, <u>Arch. Biochem. Biophys.</u>, 182:107.

32. F.J. Ruzicka, H. Beinert, K.L. Schepler, W.R. Dunham and R.H. Sands, 1975, Interaction of ubisemiquinone with a paramagnetic component in heart tissue, <u>Proc. Nat. Acad. Sci. USA</u>, 72:2886.

33. R.P. Carithers, D.C. Yoch and D.I. Arnon, 1977, Isolation and characterization of bound iron-sulfur proteins from bacterial photosynthetic membranes. II. Succinate dehydrogenase from <u>Rhodospirillum</u> <u>rubrum</u> chromatophores. <u>J. Biol. Chem.</u>, 252:7461.

VI. QUINONE BINDING SITES: STRUCTURE AND FUNCTION

STRUCTURAL AND MECHANISTIC ASPECTS OF THE QUINONE BINDING SITES OF THE bc

COMPLEXES

P.R. Rich

Glynn Research Institute
Bodmin
Cornwall PL30 4AU
U.K.

INTRODUCTION - THE GENERAL MECHANISM

The common genetic origin of the bc complexes from mitochondria, bacteria, fungi, and from higher plant chloroplasts has been revealed by striking similarities of their component redox centres[1], of the orientations of these redox centres[2], and of the amino acid sequences of the cytochrome b apoproteins[3].

The similarities also extend to mechanism. All bc complexes are able to pump protons, and exhibit features expected of a Q-cycle type of operation[4]; these have been reviewed elsewhere[5]. Most important of these features are that there are two different sites for interaction with quinones, each in protonic contact with only one of the bulk aqueous phases on either side of the membrane, and that charge separation occurs by electron transfer through the cytochrome b haems. Perhaps the most striking difference between the chloroplast bf and the other bc complexes is in the lack of antimycin A effects on the bf complex. An example of this is illustrated in figure 1 which shows that, whereas both bf and bc_1 complexes show a similar red shift of cytochrome b on binding of stigmatellin to the quinol oxidation site (the o site), the characteristic red shift caused by binding of antimycin A to the quinone oxidation site (the r site) of the bc_1 complex is not seen in the cytochrome bf complex. It seems most likely that the lack of effects of antimycin A are caused because it does not bind, rather than as a result of a different reaction mechanism of the cytochrome bf complex.

Wikström and Krab[6] have suggested a somewhat different reaction cycle of the bc complexes in which charge separation can also occur by the direct movement of a charged semiquinone from one quinone reaction site to the other. This modification was invoked in an attempt to explain how the complex was still able to turn over even when the route of charge separation through the cytochrome b haems had been blocked by their prereduction[7-9]. We have recently studied this phenomenon in detail in the chloroplast system[10]. Cytochrome b-563 oxidation after a flash can be shown to be rapid even at -220 mV at pH 8.0 ($t_\frac{1}{2}$ approx. 20 ms), has a weak but significant sensitivity to the r site inhibitor NQNO, and exhibits only a small lag in its onset[10]. This lag is at a minimum when the cytochrome b-563 haems are fully reduced, hence arguing the possibility[11] that oxidation might be initiated by turnover of a small residual fraction of partially oxidised complexes. Most importantly, the associated electrogenic charge separation is correlated with the kinetics of cytochrome b-563 oxidation and is equivalent to only one charge separation per turnover of the bf complex. We interpret these experiments as suggesting that oxidation is caused by a semiquinone which is produced at centre o but which acts at centre r to cause electrogenic cytochrome b oxidation. However, because an additional electrogenicity expected for movement of charged $(Q\cdot-)$ versus the uncharged $(QH\cdot)$ semiquinone is not observed experimentally, we suggest that it is the neutral semiquinone only which acts in this way. For these reasons, we consider it unlikely that the catalytic cycle could involve electrogenic semiquinone movement.

It might be noted that movement of only uncharged semiquinone would act to uncouple electron and proton transfers and so is unlikely to occur continuously during normal protonmotive functioning of the bc complexes. Nevertheless, it is somewhat surprising that the reaction can occur at rates only a little slower than the maximal turnover rates of the complex in optimal conditions. Under coupled 'state 4' conditions of high protonmotive force, this reaction is potentially much faster than the turnover time of the complex and could in principle produce a molecular 'slip'. Since such 'slip' has, however, not been demonstrated under any physiological condition, it remains to be seen whether it is of any physiological significance. I tentatively suggest that the reaction might act as a "safety mechanism" to prevent permanent blocking of functioning of complexes which occasionally become locked in a situation of both b haems reduced with no free quinone in the pool.

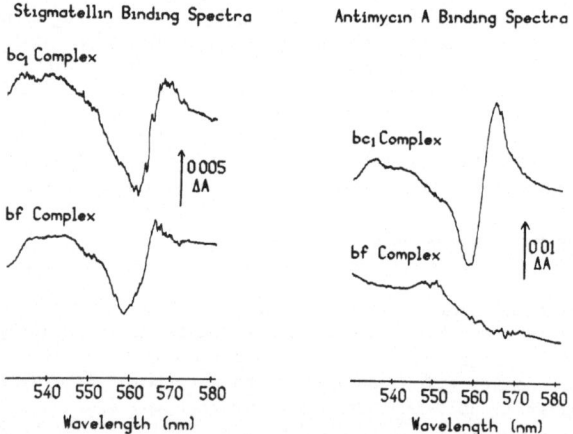

Fig. 1. Inhibitor binding to the bc complexes. The sample was either 5 μM bf complex or 5 μM beef heart mitochondrial succinate-cytochrome c reductase in 50 mM potassium phosphate and 2 mM EDTA at pH 7. Samples were reduced with sodium dithionite. Spectra are difference spectra on addition of either 7.5 μM antimycin A or 7.5 μM stigmatellin (data obtained in collaboration with G. von Jagow).

496

A DIMERIC OR A TWO STEP REACTION CYCLE?

All available evidence suggests that the bc complexes are structurally organised as dimers in their natural membranes[12,13] and speculations have been made that the reaction cycle might require this dimeric structure[12,14]. Indeed, some recent data have indicated that only one o site inhibitor might be required per dimer for full inhibition under some conditions[15]. The existence of functional monomers are difficult to reconcile with such observations. However, other data which have shown the presence of a quinol-quinone transhydrogenase activity of the r site[12] are less convincing of dimeric function since such activity could occur by alternative two electron reduction and reoxidation of the two haems of a single cytochrome b.

A two step reaction of a monomer is still most attractive to the present author. In chloroplasts, the intermediate state may actually be generated in stable ($t_\frac{1}{2}$ approx. 500 ms) form as shown in figure 2. This is achieved by preillumination of chloroplasts with far red light to fully oxidise all components, followed by a single saturating flash to generate one plasto-quinol per two photosystem II. Since there are more bf complexes than generated plastoquinol, statistically many bf complexes oxidise only a single quinol and become stranded in a state with only a single electron in the cytochrome b haems. This state normally requires a second catalytic turnover for rapid cytochrome b reoxidation (figure 2). Under appropriate

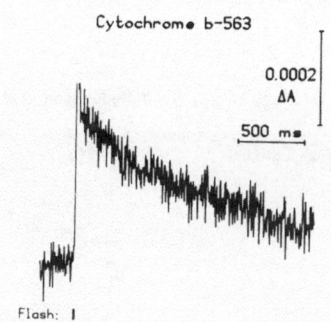

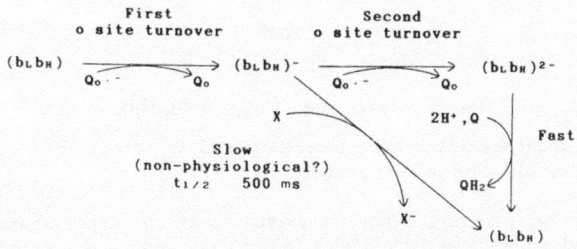

Fig. 2. The stable intermediate of the bf reaction cycle. Chloroplasts were resuspended to 75 µg/ml in 0.4 M sucrose, 40 mM KCl, 0.5 mM EDTA and 10 mM potassium phosphate at pH 7.25. 1 mM potassium ferricyanide and 0.3 µM nonactin were then added. The quinone pool was oxidised by far red preillumination. 10 s dark incubation was given before each flash. Data were deconvoluted as in [10] and are the average of 10 measurements at each wavelength.

conditions, a similar intermediate may be generated in the mammalian bc complex, and is even more stable.

The stability of the half-reduced intermediate is expected from the chemistry of the r site. It is likely that the electron is shared between b_H and a quinone bound at centre r. However, oxidation cannot occur readily since it would require semiquinone to be able to leave the site. This general model explains why reduced cytochrome b can be stable even in the presence of an oxidised quinone pool (reviewed in[6]) without the necessity of a "SQ cycle"[6]. It may also account for the phenomenon of triphasic redox changes of cytochrome b[16] in terms of the proportion of complexes with 0, 1 or 2 electrons in cytochrome b. It might also be noted that it makes the prediction that a singly-reduced cytochrome b should be ineffective in quinol-quinone transhydrogenase activity since a productive interaction with a quinone or with a quinol would require that a semiquinone could leave the site.

MOLECULAR SLIP IN THE CHLOROPLAST CYTOCHROME bf COMPLEX?

Although it is likely under physiological conditions that the mito-chondrial bc_1 complex is always coupled to proton translocation, it is widely believed that the chloroplast cytochrome bf complex functions protonmotively only under conditions of low light intensity and/or low membrane potential. A number of schemes can be invoked as to how such 'slip' might occur in a directly coupled system. All involve a novel reaction for the semiquinone produced at centre o:

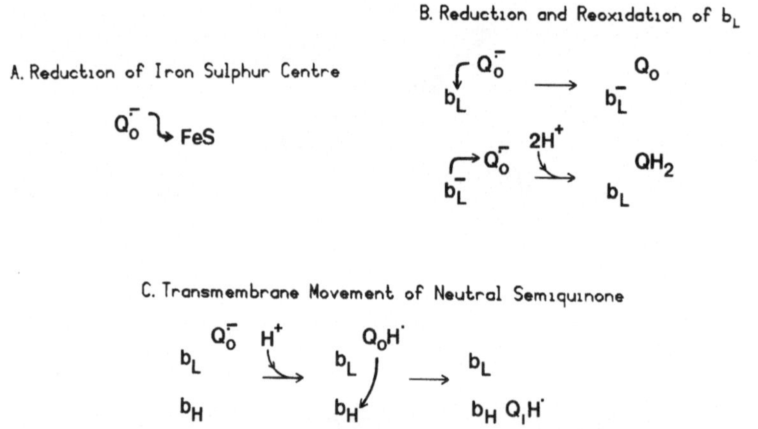

Fig. 3. Mechanisms which have been proposed for 'molecular slip' in a directly coupled bc complex.

Recently, however, I have suggested that the experimental evidence for such 'slip' is very weak[17]. Data which have been used to indicate influence of membrane potential[18,19] actually indicate when simulated that the electrogenic component of the bf complex is still present (although masked by decay) even in the presence of an electric field. Steady state data indicating a loss of proton pumping at high light intensity[20,21] can be explained by the presence of a DCMU-insensitive photochemical proton production at very high light intensities which only causes an apparent drop in the proton stoichiometry. My present conclusion is that, *at least under physiological conditions*, it is most likely that the bf complex, like other *bc* complexes, is obligatorily linked to proton translocation and that none of the three novel reactions of $Q \cdot \bar{}_o$ listed above occur to any great extent.

POSSIBLE STRUCTURAL CHEMISTRY

Understanding of the chemistry of the quinone reaction sites of the *bc* complexes is becoming quite detailed. Unfortunately, the crystal structure of an entire *bc* complex is not yet available and hence deliberations on the structural features which cause such chemistry can only be indirect and speculative at present. Nevertheless, the opening of discussion on possible structure might prove useful.

The binding of quinol to the *o* site is not strong and may be displaced by lipid. This is illustrated in figure 4 where reconstitution of the mitochondrial bc_1 complex into liposomes together with bacterial reaction centres causes loss of quinol at centre *o*. A great deal of quinol has to be co-incorporated into the vesicle to restore the activity to levels observed in the isolated complex (which generally purifies containing 1-2 UQ per complex). This ratio is larger than *in vivo* presumably because of the much greater ratio of lipid/protein (30:1 w/w) used for reconstitution. The enzymatic reaction itself is controlled by a protonatable group both in bf[5]

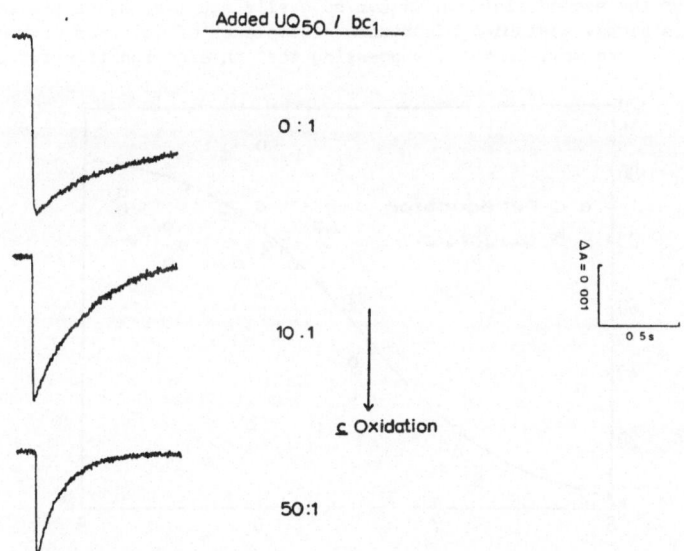

Fig. 4. The reaction of centre *o* with ubiquinol-50 in vesicle-reconstituted beef heart mitochondrial bc_1 complex. Soya bean asolectin vesicles were prepared by cholate dialysis at pH 7.8 of a mixture of 0.1 M K-phosphate, 30 mg/ml asolectin, 20 mg/ml K-cholate, 2 μM beef heart succinate -*c* reductase and 2 μM *R. sphaeroides* reaction centres, together with an appropriate amount of ubiquinone-50. Assays were carried out in 0.4 M sucrose, 40 mM KCl and 0.5 mM EDTA at pH 7.25 with 1 mM KCN, 7 μM cytochrome *c* and vesicles at 5 mg lipid/ml. Activation was with a saturating single turnover flash, after addition of 10 mM succinate.

and in *bc* complex (figure 5). I have suggested that this group must be protonated for activity and that the active form is positively charged. The basis for thinking that the protonated residue is necessary for activity, which is the opposite of the obvious interpretation of data such as that in figure 5, has been discussed in detail[22]. Since the semiquinone at this site is not highly thermodynamically stabilised, it may be that the active form of the group is the neutral -XH (rather than XH⁺) which forms a hydrogen bond with one quinol hydroxyl and so promotes the active anionic quinol intermediate:

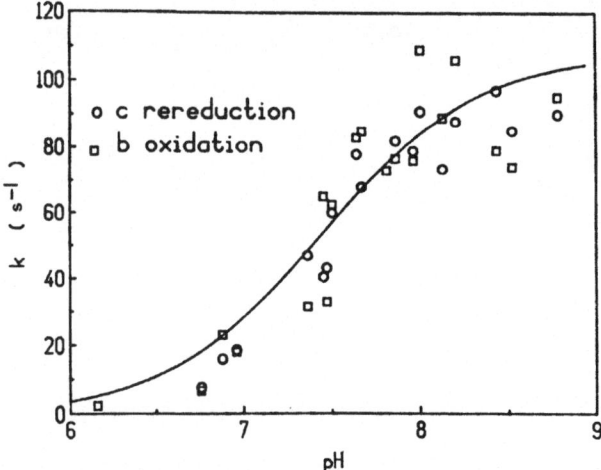

Removal of the second electron is not so easily studied, since the semiquinone is highly unstable. Inorganic π-complexes of quinones with metals such as iron are well known[23], suggesting that an electron transfer structure

Fig. 5. The pH dependency of quinol oxidation at centre *o* in a solubilised reconstructed system. Buffer was 50 mM TRIS, phosphate *or* MES, each together with 1 mM KCN, 2 mM EDTA, 2 μM beef heart succinate-*c* reductase, 2 μM *R. sphaeroides* reaction centres, 7 μM cytochrome *c* and 10 mM succinate *plus* 10 mM fumarate as a redox buffer to hold the *b* cytochrome approximately 50% reduced. The plot is the first order rate constant of *c* rereduction or of *b*-562 oxidation after flash oxidation. The curve is for a one proton change of pK 7.45. Details of why such a shape is thought to be characteristic of an active *protonated* enzyme system have been discussed previously[22].

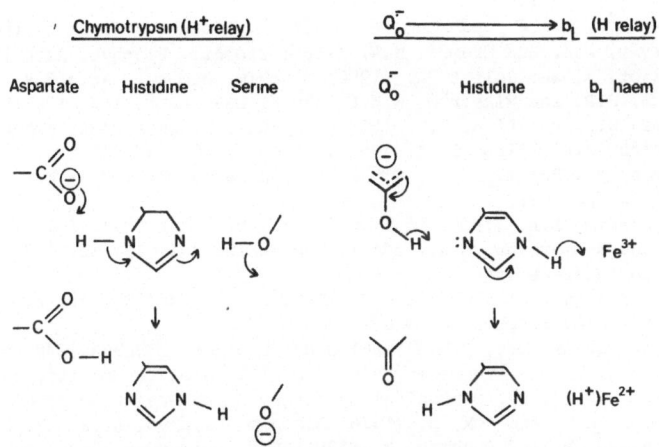

Fig. 6. The proton relay system of chymotrypsin and a speculative
hydrogen relay system for reaction between protonated $Q \cdot\bar{\bar{o}}$
and the low potential haem of cytochrome b.

involving direct electron transfer from quinone ring to Fe^{3+} (perhaps via
histidine) might be possible. However, the crystal structure of the
bacterial reaction centre indicates that electron transfer from Q_A to Q_B
is indirect and involves a hydrogen bonded chain[24] between the quinone
carbonyl groups of

$$Q_A \ldots \text{histidine} \ldots Fe^{2+} \ldots \text{histidine} \ldots Q_B$$

Consideration of this structure and of the well described 'charge relay'
mechanism of action of chymotrypsin, suggests an alternative possible
reaction mechanism where hydrogen bond rearrangement could lead to coupled
proton and electron transfer. An example of how this could occur, in
comparison to the proton transfer mechanism in chymotrypsin, is shown in
figure 6. These possible mechanisms, although highly speculative, have at
least suggested to us further methods of probing these active sites and
such studies are presently underway.

ACKNOWLEDGEMENTS

These developments have been aided by able technical assistance from
S. Madgwick, and by discussions with Dr. Mitchell, Moss and West. The work
is supported by the Venture Research Unit of British Petroleum plc.

REFERENCES

1. Hauska, G., Hurt, E., Gabellini, N. and Lockau, W. (1983) Biochim.
       Biophys. Acta 726, 97-134
2. Tiede, D.M. (1986) in *Encyclopedia of Plant Physiology* (Pirson, A. and
       Zimmermann, M.H., eds), new series vol. 19, pp. 344-352, Springer-
       Verlag
3. Widger, W.R., Cramer, W.A., Herrmann, R. and Trebst, A. (1984) Proc.
       Natl. Acad. Sci. U.S.A. 81, 674-678
4. Mitchell, P.D. (1976) J. Theor. Biol. 62, 327-367
5. Rich, P.R. (1986) J. Bioenerg. Biomemb. 18, 145-156

6. Wikström, M.K.F. and Krab, K. (1986) J. Bioenerg. Biomemb. 18, 181-193
7. Girvin, M.E. and Cramer, W.A. (1984) Biochim. Biophys. Acta 767, 29-38
8. Joliot, P. and Joliot, A. (1986) Biochim. Biophys. Acta 849, 211-222
9. Rich, P.R. and Wikström, M.K.F. (1986) FEBS Lett. 194, 176-182
10. Moss, D.A. and Rich, P.R. (1987) Biochim. Biophys. Acta *submitted*
11. Crofts, A.R. (1986) J. Bioenerg. Biomemb. 18, 437-445
12. Linke, P., Bechmann, G., Gothe, A. and Weiss, H. (1986) Eur. J. Biochem. 158, 615-621
13. Staehelin, L.A. (1986) in *Encyclopedia of Plant Physiology* (Pirson, A. and Zimmermann, M.H., eds.), new series vol. 19, pp. 1-84, Springer-Verlag
14. De Vries, S., Albracht, S.P.J., Berden, J.A. and Slater, E.C. (1982) Biochim. Biophys. Acta 681, 41-53
15. Graan, T. and Ort, D.R. (1986) Arch. Biochem. Biophys. 248, 445-451
16. Tang, H.-L. and Trumpower, B.L. (1986) J. Biol. Chem. 261, 6209-6215
17. Rich, P.R. (1987) Biological Chemistry Hoppe-Seyler *in press*
18. Fowler, C.F. and Kok, B. (1976) Biochim. Biophys. Acta 423, 510-523
19. Rathenow, M. and Rumberg, B. (1980) Ber. Bunsenges. Phys. Chem. 84, 1059-1062
20. Bouges-Bouquet, B. (1981) Biochim. Biophys. Acta 635, 327-340
21. van Kooten, O., Gloudemans, A.G.M. and Vredenberg, W.J. (1983) Photobiochem. Photobiophys. 6, 9-14
22. Rich, P.R. (1982) Faraday Discuss. Chem. Soc. 74, 349-364
23. Foster, R. and Foreman, M.I. (1974) in *The Chemistry of the Quinonoid Compounds* (Patai, S., ed.), part 1, pp. 257-333, John Wiley & Sons
24. Deisenhofer, J., Epp, O., Miki, K., Huber, R. and Michel, H. (1985) Nature 318, 618-624

QP-S — THE ELECTRON ACCEPTOR OF SUCCINATE DEHYDROGENASE

Tsoo E. King and Yan Xu

Department of Chemistry and Laboratory of Bioenergetics
State University of New York at Albany, Albany, N.Y. 12222
U.S.A.

SUMMARY

A ubiquinone protein called QP-S accepts electrons from succinate via succinate dehydrogenase (SDH). A method, different from the previously reported one from this laboratory (Biochemistry 19, 3579), produced a new preparation of QP-S. The old preparation has been found by chemical sequencing to be a mixture containing a significant amount of QP-C (another QP acting in the cytochrome b and c_1 region). The new QP-S is entirely different from the old QP-S by SDS-gel electrophoretic pattern and amino acid composition. These two aspects are similar to that reported by Hatefi and Galante (J. Biol. Chem. 255, 5530). However, the new QP-S contains only 0.2-0.6 nmol b/mg protein and its activity is completely independent of cytochrome b. The new QP-S has been shown to be structurally reconstitutive with SDH to form succinate-Q reductase.

* * * * * * *

QP-S is a ubiquinone (Q) protein which directly accepts electrons from succinate dehydrogenase (SDH). It was first reported from this laboratory in 1977 (1, 2) and since then several improvements and modifications for solubilization and purification have been made (e.g., 3, 4). The latest paper (4) presented two methods of preparation of QP-S. The one using deoxycholate solubilization gives the highest activity whereas the other yields the "highest purity." We have recently found that the "highest purity" preparation is actually a mixture containing also QP-C by chemical sequencing. Several other laboratories have also reported protein fractions which function as QP-S (5-7). All these preparations possess a molecular weight(s) in the neighborhood of 15,000 and contain various amounts of cytochrome b. One school (7) which employs Complex II by perchlorate extraction has prepared a sample with 14 nmol cytochrome b per mg protein and claims the cytochrome is the carrier from SDH to Q. Recently this protein has been prepared by a different method and con-

---

[1] Abbreviations: DCIP, 2,4-dichlorophenolindophenol; Fp, flavoiron protein subunit of SDH; Ip, iron-sulfur protein subunit of SDH; PMS, phenazine methosulfate; Q, ubiquinone, the subscript denotes the number of isoprene unit; QP-C, the Q-protein acts in the cytochromes b and c_1 region; QP-S, the Q-protein which accepts electrons directly from SDH; SDH, succinate dehydrogenase; TTFA, thenoyltrifluoroacetone.

tains 25 nmol cytochrome b_{560} per mg protein (8). In all the starting
materials for these methods, a large amount of cytochrome b exists, such
as succinate-c reductase used in preparation (3, 4, 8) and Complex II
used in (5, 7). Complex II consists of a SDH-flavin to cytochrome b
ratio of one. Thus the role of the heme or cytochrome b in QP-S has not
been settled and is indeed in vigorous dispute (cf. 7-9). This communication reports a preparation of QP-S that has been solubilized and purified from a starting material which contains no QP-C and 1.2 nmol cytochrome b per mg protein. It has been demonstrated the cytochrome b
does not participate in reconstitutive activity of QP-S with SDH to form
succinate-Q reductase. In the absence of SDH the isolated QP-S does not
catalyze the oxidation of succinate.

*   *   *

Samples of QP-S obtained from the old method (4) have been found, to
our astonishment, impure but containing at least two C-terminals and two
N-terminals by amino acid sequencing. After chemical derivatization, one
of two major components was isolated successfully whereas the other was
not. The sequence of the successfully isolated component was actually
identical to QP-C (10). Thus, after careful design and painstaking
trials, a dramatically different method was developed using a starting
material that is completely free of QP-C and contains about or less than
1.2 nmol of cytochrome b per mg of protein. The new QP-S thus prepared
is different from the old preparation.

The QP-S prepared from the new method is a lipoprotein and rather
stable. It is pure in SDS-gel electrophoresis (11). The densiometric
scan is depicted in Fig. 1. It might be noted that the QP-S band(s) is
different from the sample prepared according to a previous method (see
Fig. 1 of Ref. 4) but similar to that by the method prepared from Complex
II (7). Apparently two bands occur in SDS-gel patterns corresponding to
molecular weights of approximately 13,500 and 15,000. A comparison of the
amino acid compositions determined according to the method of Houston (12,
7) between our new and old preparations and those reported by Hatefi and
Galante (7) are presented in Table 1. The validity of the method used (7,
10) has been confirmed with QP-C by conventional procedure. Several sali-
ent facets may be pointed out here. The amino acid composition of these
two bands of QP-S is very similar. Indeed, the average amino acid contents of the 13,500 and 15,000 bands possess standard deviations within
the experimental errors perhaps except for alanine and serine. The possibility exists that the two bands are the result of dissociation of QP-S in
dissociation media. Alternatively, they may be formed from one peptide
but bound with different numbers of SDS molecules. Apparent multiple
bands have been reported from monodisperse proteins in gel electrophoresis in the presence of SDS or other highly charged ionic detergents due to
the numbers of the detergent molecules associated with the protein (see,
for example, ref. 13, especially p. 160; ref. 14, especially p. 241 and p.
246). At any rate, the gel pattern of the new QP-S is completely different from that reported previously (4), although the position of the
band(s) is also in the neighborhood of 15 K. Likewise, no similarity what-
soever with the amino acid composition of QP-C (10) can be found. However, the composition is similar to that of the "cytochrome b" isolated
(7). But it must be emphasized that various batches of the new QP-S preparation contain only 0.2-0.6 nmol b_{560} per mg protein.

From Fig. 1, it also may be noted, the SDH employed showed only Fp and
Ip subunits. The reconstituted succinate-Q reductase exhibits bands of
SDH subunits and QP-S, whereas evidently small amounts of impurities (la-
beled a, b, and c in the figure) also occur in the intact reductase.

Table 1. Amino Acid Composition of QP-S

	This paper				"QP-S" previously reported (4)	Hatefi & Galante (7)		QP-C (see also 10)
	15 K* subunit	13.5 K* subunit	Mean	(σ_n)		"Large" protein	"Small" protein	
Lysine	3.75	3.9	3.835	(0.083)	8.2	3.87	4.7	9.31
Histidine	6.8	6.85	6.835	(0.460)	3.4	4.44	4.17	1.43
Arginine	2.8	2.25	2.535	(0.482)	8.4	2.47	1.8	12.5
Aspartic acid	4.8	6.3	5.55	(0.876)	9.8	3.28	6.18	11.9
Threonine	5.8	5.8	5.80	(0.354)	4.6	6.97	6.58	2.45
Serine	10.35	8.55	9.45	(0.966)	6.3	10.91	8.32	4.53
Glutamic acid	5.65	4.6	5.13	(0.789)	11.9	5.57	3.35	17.4
Proline	3.85	3.35	3.60	(0.367)	7.7	4.76	2.95	4.28
Glycine	11.6	11.4	11.5	(0.308)	8.7	10.28	9.0	3.95
Alanine	9.4	12.6	11.	(1.639)	10.2	9.28	15.07	7.96
Valine	7.0	7.9	7.45	(0.550)	5.4	6.35	8.68	4.91
Methionine	3.0	1.8	2.4	(0.687)	ND	3.67	1.74	1.69
Isoleucine	4.0	3.35	3.68	(0.327)	5.8	4.56	2.88	5.07
Leucine	15.6	15.2	15.4	(0.515)	12.7	16.7	15.53	10.0
Tyrosine	2.15	2.8	2.48	(0.460)	4.7	1.12	4.14	5.20
Phenylalanine	3.55	3.3	3.43	(0.286)	3.9	3.8	2.92	2.13

σ_n, population standard derivation.

*The bands are separately cut out and amino acid content is determined according to method of Houston (12, 7). The results are the same if the cut out bands are eluted and then subjected to amino acid determination.

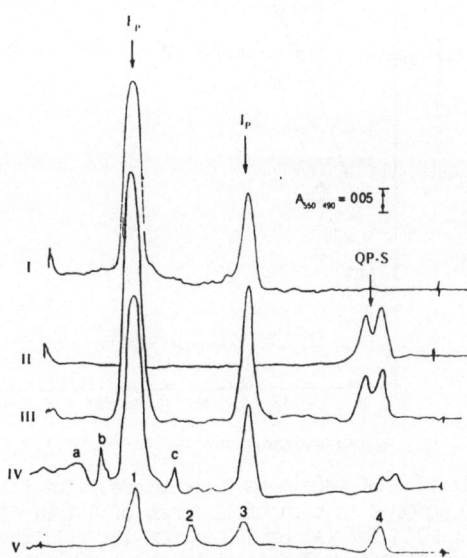

Fig. 1. Densiometric profiles of SDH (I), QP-S (II), reconstituted (III), and intact (IV) succinate-Q reductase. Peaks a, b, and c on the intact reductase pattern are apparently due to impurities. The standard proteins (V) used are bovine serum albumin (1), ovalbumin (2), chymotrypsinogen A (3) and horse cytochrome c (4) with molecular weights of 68 K, 45 K, 23 K and 12.4 K, respectively. SDS-gel electrophoresis is conducted according to Laemmli (11).

Samples of QP-S are active in reconstitution of succinate-Q reductase with soluble SDH. As shown in Fig. 2, when an excess of SDH is present and a limiting amount of QP-S is used, a rapid increase of the activity of succinate-Q reductase is observed by adding QP-S. Further addition of QP-S sharply flattens to a plateau. A similar result is obtained with an excess of QP-S and a limiting amount of SDH. The activity is found to be 16 μmol succinate oxidized at room temperature per min per mg of total protein present, using the same method as the one employed previously in this and other laboratories (4, 7, 9). This value is about the same as the intact succinate-Q reductase and that reported by Hatefi and Galante (7) after temperature correction. Very recently, Yu et al. (8) have reported a higher activity because they have used the QP-S protein as the base, not the total protein in the system. It should be mentioned our activity is about two or more times higher when Q_2 is used directly as final electron acceptor. At any rate, the intersections in the titration curves when either SDH or QP-S is a limiting component are the same giving a ratio of SDH to QP-S of approximately 1 SDH:2 QP-S (on the basis of 14 K).

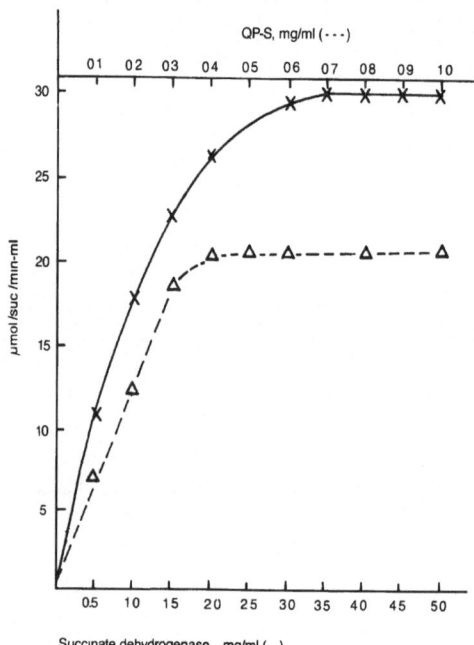

Fig. 2. Reconstitution of succinate-Q reductase. The titration system contains 78 μg QP-S in each of 11 tubes of 0.2 ml 50 mM phosphate buffer, pH 7.4 for (A) or 300 μg SDH for (B); the indicated amount of SDH and QP-S is added to each tube. The tubes are incubated at 0°C for 5 min. In both cases, the assay is conducted with 10 μl aliquots from the incubation mixture in the presence of 20 mM succinate, 60 μM DCIP, 16 μM Q_2, 0.01% Triton X-100, and 50 mM phosphate buffer in a final volume of 1.0 ml. The abscissa indicates amounts of QP-S or SDH added during incubation converted to per ml of the original incubation system and the ordinate is the activity at 23°C also expressed as per ml.

In the reconstitution, the properties of SDH are changed; for example, the low Km ferricyanide activity (15) is lost. The stability of the reconstituted succinate-Q reductase is dramatically different from the free SDH as shown in Fig. 3 and about the same as the intact reductase.

Table 2. Structural reconstitution of succinate–Q reductase
from QP–S and SDH

| | Eluting Agent | | |
| | 50 mM Tris acetate pH 7.4 | 0.3 M phosphate; pH 7.4 | SDS–Gel pattern |
System			
(a) Free SDH	—	SDH	Fp, Ip
(b) Free QP–S	QP–S		QP–S
(c) QP–S:SDH (1:1.4)	—	succinate–Q reductase	Fp, Ip, QP–S
(d) SDH + Excess QP–S	QP–S	succinate–Q reductase	Fp, Ip, QP–S

From hydroxyapatite column, Tris–acetate elutes QP–S but not SDH which is
eluted by 0.3 M phosphate buffer. However, QP–S in the succinate–Q reductase from reconstitution is not eluted by Tris–acetate but by 0.3 M phosphate, pH 7.4. SDS–gel analysis is performed by (11). —, not eluted.

The reconstitution is indeed a physical recombination and not just a
functional interaction. The SDH or QP–S once reconstituted cannot be separated by various kinds of chromatography which can be done while in free
form as detailed in Table 2.

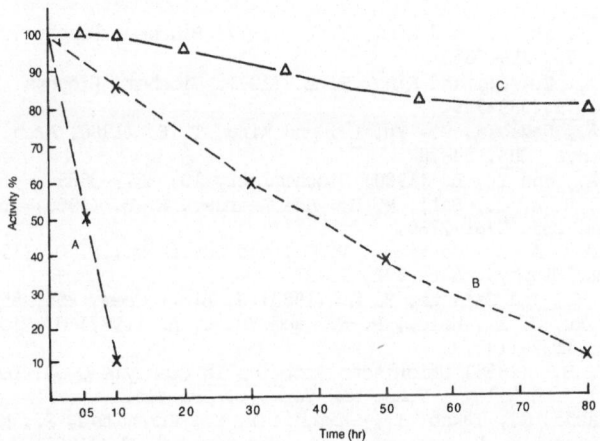

Fig. 3. Effect of QP–S on the stability of SDH. (A) soluble SDH, reconstitutive activity, (B), artificial (PMS) activity of soluble SDH,
(C), the activity of reconstituted succinate–Q reductase from
70 µg SDH and 80 µg QP–S in 0.2 ml, 50 mM phosphate buffer, pH
7.4. The systems are left standing in air at 0°C, at times indicated, aliquots are withdrawn for the activity determination. The
SDH activities are measured according to (16) and reductase activity as legend of Fig. 2.

In collaboration with Drs. J. Salerno and Y. H. Wei (in preparation)
QP–S ubisemiquinone radical, from EPR experiments, sensitive to TTFA or
3-nitro-N-methyl salicylamide has been demonstrated in the reconstituted
system with SDH and QP–S. The midpoint potential has been found to be
E_1 = 5 mV and E_2 = 125 mV. The cytochrome $\underline{b}$ signals in SQR can be

demonstrated in EPR spectroscopy in very concentrated ($\sim$40 mg protein per ml of protein) solutions. Their g values are found at 3.46 (main peak) and 3.07; upon addition of ethanol to 3%, all the cytochrome b_{560} is denatured as reflected by the shift of the EPR peaks from 3.46 as well as 3.07 to 2.92 completely. However, enzymatic activity of SQR has been found to be not affected by 1-4% ethanol. Likewise, the enzymatic activity from the EPR tubes has been found identical between the control and the ethanol treated. The details of these experiments will be reported elsewhere.

From the results presented, it is beyond any doubt that QP-S does reconstitute with SDH to form succinate-Q reductase and the binding is not just a func- tional interaction but true structural reconstitution. Although the QP-S has shown very similar amino acid composition with the so-called Complex II type cytochrome b, or sometimes known as b_{560}, the reconstitutive tivity is completely independent of the cytochrome. That the activity is not due to the lipid of QP-S has been discussed previously (17).

Acknowledgment--The generous assistance of Neil Reimer, Michael Seaman, L. Q. Sun, J. Q. Tan, and K. T. Yasunobu is gratefully acknowledged. Discussion with Professor Charles Tanford about the formation of multiple bands from pure monodisperse proteins in dissociation media is very much appreciated. This work was supported by grants from National Institutes of Health HL-12576, GM-16767 and American Cancer Society BC-349.

REFERENCES

1. Yu, C. A., Yu, L., and King, T. E. (1977) Biochem. Biophys. Res. Commun. 78, 259-265.
2. Yu, C. A., Yu, L., and King, T. E. (1977) Biochem. Biophys. Res. Commun. 79, 939-936.
3. Yu, C. A., Nagaoka, S., Yu, L., and King, T. E. (1980) Arch. Biochem. Biophys. 204, 59-70
4. Yu, C. A., and Yu, L. (1980) Biochemistry 19, 3579-3585.
5. Ackrell, B. A. C., Ball, M. B., and Kearney, E. B. (1980) J. Biol. Chem. 255, 2761-2769.
6. Vinogradov, A. D., Gavrikov, V. G., and Gavrikova, E. O. (1980) Biochem. Biophys. Acta 592, 13-27.
7. Hatefi, Y., and Galante, Y. M. (1980) J. Biol. Chem. 255, 5530-5537.
8. Yu, L., Xu, J. X., Haley, P. E., and Yu, C. A. (1987) J. Biol. Chem. 262, 1137-1143.
9. King, T. E. (1985) Ubiquinone Proteins in Coenzyme Q (G. Lenaz, ed.) John Wiley & Sons, New York, p. 391-408.
10. Wakabayashi, S., Takao, T., Shimonishi, Y., Kuramitsu, S., Matsubara, H., Wang, T. Y., Zhang, Z. P., and King, T. E. (1985) J. Biol. Chem. 260, 337-343.
11. Laemmli, U. K. (1970) Nature 227, 680-685.
12. Houston, L. L. (1971) Anal. Biochem. 44, 81-88.
13. Tanford, C. (1980) The hydrophobic effect, 2nd Ed., John Wiley, New York.
14. Steinhardt, J., and Reynolds, J. A. (1969) Multiple equilibria in proteins, Academic Press, New York.
15. Vinogradov, A. D., Gavrikova, E. V., and Goloveshkina, V. G. (1975) Biochem. Biophys. Res. Commun. 65, 1264-1269.
16. King, T. E. (1965) Meth. Enzymol. 10, 322-331.
17. King, T. E. (1982) Ubiquinone Proteins in Cardiac Mitochondria in Function of Quinones in Energy Conserving Systems (B. L. Trumpower, ed.) Academic Press, New York, p. 3-25.

CHARACTERISTICS OF QP-C AND RECONSTITUTION

OF THE QH$_2$-CYT C REDUCTASE*

Tsing-Ying Wang[1], Zhen-Ping Zhang[2] and Tsoo E. King[3]

1, Shanghai Institute of Biochemistry, Academia Sinica
Shanghai, China; 2, Institute of Biophysics, Academia
Sinica, Beijing, China; 3, Department of Chemistry and
Laboratory of Bioenergetics, State University of New
York, Albany, N.Y. 12222, U.S.A.

INTRODUCTION

Although the essential role of Q in electron transport has been generally accepted as respiratory or redox (electron or hydrogen) carrier
(1-3), the reaction mechanism and the sequence of the reaction in the region of the so-called phosphorylation site II are far from being understood.
In contrast to the other redox components of the respiratory chain such as
iron-sulfur protein or the cytochromes, Q is the only lipophilic molecule
and is aboundant in the inner membrane. These facts have led to the idea
that Q is a mobile component "swimming" in the phospholipid bilayer and
shuttle electrons among the electron-transfer lipoprotein complex; more
likely Q functions as a converging point in mitochondrial electron transport for NADH→Q, succinate→Q and Q→cyt c. Furthermore Q can carry out electron transfer either by one or two electron equivalent step process. The
fact that reduction of Q by each of its electron carriers yields fully reduced Q can not be used as evidence to support the two electron step mechanism because the dismutation rate of the free radical is too rapid (4). On
the other hand, reports on demonstration of Q radicals in mitochondrial reaction have gradually accumulated (5-7). Complex III and other highly purified
preparations of ubiquinone cyt c reductase such as cyt bc$_1$ III complex from
mitochondria contain significant amounts of Q which can not be easily removed (8). A ubisemiquinone radical concentration as high as 60% of the
total Q (9) present in bc$_1$ III complex has been detected at pH 9.0 and decreased drastically when the pH was higher than 9.0 and very little ubisemiquinone radical can be detected at pH 10.0. Demonstration of ubisemiquinone
suggests that the Q radical must bind something in order to be stabilized.
A mixture of Q and QH$_2$ in phospholipid vesicles will show the ubisemiquinone

*Key words: Q-binding protein, QP-C, QH$_2$-cyt. c reductase, quinol:ferri-
cytochrome c reductase, respiratory chain
**Abbreviation: Q, ubiquinone; QH$_2$, reduced Q; QP, Q-binding protein; QCR,
ubiquinone cyt c reductase; SQR, succinate ubiquinone reductase; SDS-PAGE,
sodium dodecyl sulfate polyacrylamide gel electrophoresis; SDH, succinate
dehydrogenase; DCPIP, dichlorophenolindophenol; PMSF, phenylmethyl-sulfonyl-
fluoride; AA, antimycin A; TTFA, thenoyltrifluoroacetone; PHMB, para-hydro-
xymercuric benzoic acid.

radical only above pH 12 (8) indicating that the stability of semiquinone radical in the cyt bc_1 III complex (9) is mainly due to the protein rather than phospholipid. Furthermore digestion of cyt bc_1 III complex with   - chymotrypsin abolished the ability to form the ubisemiquinone radical (10). From collective considerations of these results, it has been proposed that active forms of ubiquinone in electron hydrogen transfer of the respiratory chain is protein linked.

Evidence from many lines indicates that the mitochondria respiratory chain contains at least four QP acting at different loci of the chain. QP-S has been purified (11) which was involved in the electron tranfer from suc-cinate to Q. Two QP-N, QP in the NADH dehydrogenase segment (12) and QP-C, the QP functions in the region of bc_1 segment. We have obtained the QP-C in pure form from cyt bc_1 III complex. The procedure for purification has been described in the previous paper (13). The present paper deals with the cha-racterization of QP-C and reconstitution of QH_2-cyt c reductase.

PROPERTIES

The absorbance spectrum of the QP-C protein is shown in Fig.1,B. It exhibits a maximum only at 279 nm. When the eluate portions from ultragel AcA 44 chromatography (last step of purification, see Fig. 1 of Ref. 13) were subjected to analysis of the Q content by reduction with $NaBH_4$, only the QP-C peak causes absorbance change at 275 nm (Fig. 2B) while the other peak does not (Fig. 2A). The amount of Q in QP-C is calculated to be 1 mole/mole protein by using the extinction coefficient of Q as 12.2 mM^{-1} at 275 nm (14), and based on the monomeric molecular weight of QP-C as 13.4k (15). The high absorbance at 279 nm of QP-C is partly due to the Q bound in the preparation.

The molecular weight of this protein as determined from its elution pattern on an ultragel AcA column was about 63000 in 25 mM Tris-HCl buffer pH 8.0, containing 50 mM NaCl and 0.5% lubrol px as shown in Fig.2.

The sulfhydryl group was not detected in QP-C by the Ellmen reaction with 5,5'-dithio-bis (2-nitrobenzoic acid) (16).

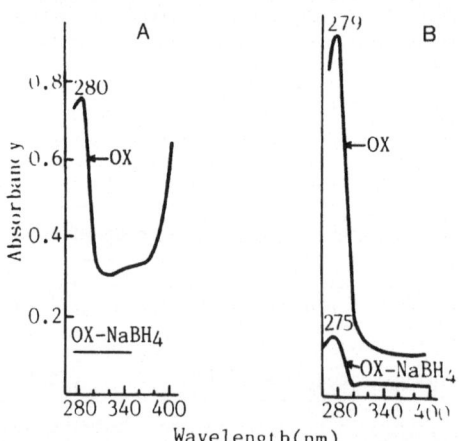

Fig.1. Estimation of Q-binding of the QP-C protein (A) absorption spectrum and $NaBH_4$ reduced differ-ence spectrum of the first peak from ultragel AcA 44 chromatography, (B) of the QP-C peak.

510

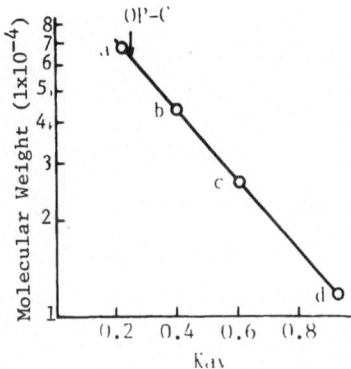

Fig.2. Estimation of the molecular weight
of the QP-C protein by filtration chromatography.
Ultragel AcA 44 column (1.4x59 cm) was used by
decending gel filtration chromatography. The proteins of known molecular weight were used for
establishing a standard curve. They are: (a), bovine serum albumin (Mr=67000); (b), ovalbumin
(43000); (c), chymotrypsinogen (25700); (d), cytochrome c (11700).

The protein has been shown to be stable at neutral to slightly alkaline
pH when stored at − 70°C for months.

RECONSTITUTION OF QP-C

QCR activity of cyt bc_1 III is sensitive to α-chymotrypsin (9). When
cyt bc_1 III was submitted to digestion with α-chymotrypsin, the QH_2-cyt c
reductase gradually decreased, as shown in Fig.3. The α-chymotrypsin used
was immobilized α-chymotrypsin coupled to CNBr-activated sepharose 4B.
After the QCR activity was lowered to 25-30% of the original, the digestion
procedure was stopped by removing the immobilized enzyme on a sintered-glass
funnel. The filtrate obtained is called cyt bc_1 IV complex. In the case of
using soluble α-chymotrypsin, the reaction is stopped by adding the inhibitor PMSF.

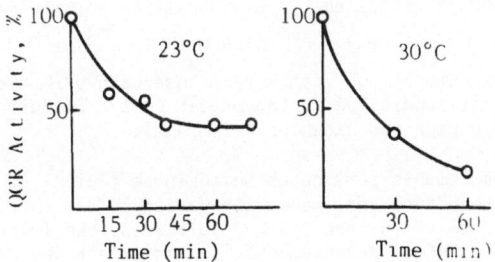

Fig.3. Effect of α-chymotrypsin on the
QH_2-cytochrome c reducatase.
Immobilized α-chymotrypsin coupled to
CNBr-activated Sepharose 4B was used.

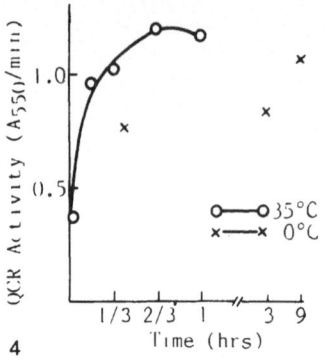
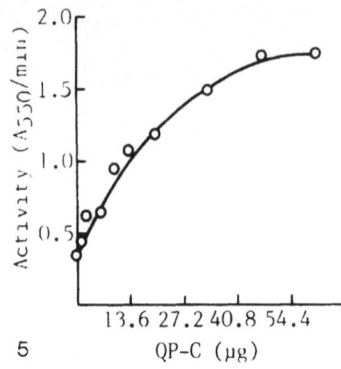

Fig.4. Effect of incubation temperature on reconstitution of ubiquinone cytochrome c reductase.

Fig.5. Reconstitution of ubiquinone cytochrome c reductase. 55 μg aliquots of cytochrome bc_1 IV complex were incubated with different amounts of QP-C at 35°C for 1 hr. Other details see text.

The isolated QP-C can be reconstituted with cyt bc_1 IV to recover the QCR activity. The reconstitution was carried out as follows: aliquots of 30-60 μg of bc_1 IV were mixed with varying amounts of QP-C in Tris-sucrose buffer pH 8.0 (0.05M-0.25M) in a total volume of 200 μl. These mixtures were incubated for a definite time & at a definite temperature and then diluted to 500 μl with the same Tris-sucrose buffer. 10 μl aliquots were drawn and QH_2-cyt c reductase activity was assayed in 1ml assay mixture by measuring the reduction of cyt c in the presence of 80-100 μm Q_2H_2 at 22-23°C Fig.4 shows the effect of incubation temperature and duration on the reconstitution at 35°C and 0°C. Fig.5 shows the restoration of QH_2-cyt c reductase of cyt bc_1 IV complex by reconstitution with QP-C at 35°C for 1 hour.

Since both QP-S and QP-C possess the same monomeric molecular weight in SDS-PAGE, we would like to test whether or not they are interchangeable. The experiment was carried out as follows : QP-C and QP-S were mixed separately with SDH at 0°C. After making up the volume to 0.75 ml with 0.02 M phosphate buffer pH 7.8, aliquots of 20 μl were withdrawn and SQR activity was assayed by measuring decrease of absorbance at 600 nm in 1 ml assay mixtures at 23°C in the presence of Q and DCPIP. The results are shown in Fig.6. It shows that QP-C failed to replace QP-S in the reconstitution Q reductase with SDH as witnessed by the inactivity to catalyze the succinate-DCPIP reaction.

The reconstitution of QH_2-cyt c reductase with QP-C and cyt bc_1 complex IV was strongly inhibited in the presence of NaCl during reconstitution (Fig.7). 50% inhibition was shown at 0.2 M NaCl.

The EPR measurements for the ubisemiquinone radical of the reconstituted QH_2-cyt c reductase were made with Varian E4. As the lubrol px has an inhibitory effect on ubiquinone radical formation, the lubrol px in the sample was removed before measurement. The experiment was carried out as follows: after reconstitution, the sample was subjected to concentration by going through PM 10 membrane (Pharmacia product) to about 5 ml and then passed through a Bio-Beads SM-2 column (1.6x6.5 cm) to remove lubrol px, concentrate again to the desired concentration for EPR measurement. A small amount of lubrol px remained in the sample so it had some inhibitory effect

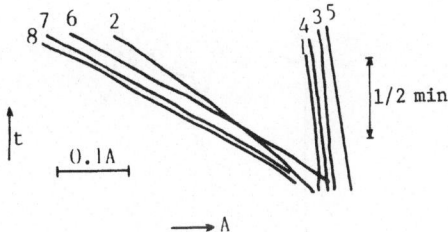

Fig.6. Reconstitution of succinate-ubiquinone reductase.
SDH, 1.2 mg/ml, prepared from SCR (17) to the stage of
gel elution.
QP-S. crude sample prepared according to Yu (11).
QP-C. 1.3 mg/ml at the stage of 0.23-0.48 ammonium
sulfate fraction (13). After dissolved in Tris-
sucrose buffer, pH 8.0 (0.05M-0.25M), it was passed
through Sephadex G-25 to remove ammonium sulfate.
curve 1. 0.15 ml SDH alone
      2. 0.15 ml SDH with 0.02 ml QP-S
      3. 0.15 ml SDH with 0.1 ml QP-C
      4. 0.15 ml SDH with 0.2 ml QP-C
      5. 0.15 ml SDH with 0.4 ml QP-C
      6,7,8, same as curves 3,4,5, with
      further addition of 0.02 ml QP-S

on the ubiquinone radical. But anyhow, the ubiquinone radicals of the reconstituted particle can be seen in Fig.8. Cyt bc_1 IV complex itself showed
no signal at all (curve a) after it was reconstituted with QP-C, the signal
reappeared (curve c) to about 60% of its control experiment (curve b). On
further increasing the QP-C amount for reconstitution the signal was conversely reduced (curve d & e). It may be due to the concomitant increase
of lubrol px with QP-C sample.

The reconstituted QH_2-cyt c reductase exhibited the same properties
as native cyt bc_1 III complex towards some respiratory inhibitors (Table 1).

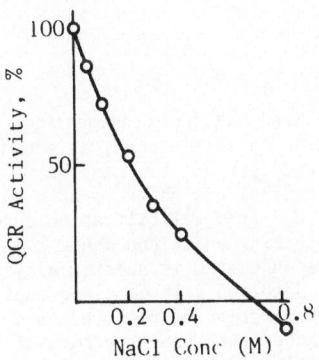

Fig.7. Effect of NaCl on the reconstitution
of ubiquinone cytochrome c reductase.
NaCl concentration was added as indicated
during icubation of bc_1 IV complex with QP-C.

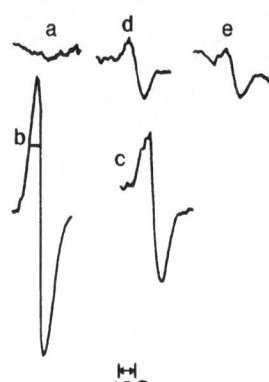

Fig.8. Reappearance of the ubiquinone radical after reconstitution of bc_1 IV complex with purified QP-C protein.

a. EPR spectrum of bc_1 IV complex containing 34 nmole cytochrome c_1 in 1 ml 0.05 M Tris-0.25 M sucrose-0.5 mM EDTA buffer (TSE).

b. EPR spectrum of bc_1 III complex. To 18 ml bc_1 III complex solution containing 62 nmole cytochrome c_1 in TSE buffer, an amount of 20% Lubrol px solution was added to a final concentration of 0.6%. The solution was passed through Bio-Beads SM-2 column (1.6x 6.5cm) equilibrated with TSE buffer and eluated with the same buffer, the collected portion was then concentrated to 2 ml.

c. EPR spectrum of reconstituted one. 4 ml bc_1 IV complex solution containing 34 nmole cytochrome c_1 was mixed with 15 ml QP-C rich solution, other details see text.

d. e. EPR spectra, same as spectrum c except the QP-C used was 34 ml and 38 ml respectively.

The instrument was set at field modulation frequency 100 KHz; microwave frequency 9.49 GHz; modulation amplitude 10 G; time constant 1 sec; scanning rate 50 G/min and micropower 100 mW. The temperature was about 23°C.

DISCUSSION

QP's have been isolated and characterized from mitochondria (11-13), and chromatophore (18-20). In this report, a reconstitution study of QP-C was made with QP-C depleted cyt bc_1 III complex to restore the QCR activity and the ubisemiquinone radical was shown to have an absolute requirement for QP-C. The QP-C obtained from gel filtration chromatography binds Q at about 1 mole per mole protein, while the other components besides QP-C do not contain Q. It indicates that Q is specifically bound to the protein even in the presence of detergent. It is clear that the active species of Q in the electron transfer reaction of the mitochondrial respiratory chain is the Q-protein complex rather than the free form of Q. It suggests that the Q radical has a functional role in electron transfer.

QP-C & QP-S possess approximately the same molecular weight but they are not interchangeable. From Fig.6 it is clearly shown that QP-C can not replace QP-S to mediate electron transfer from SDH to Q. They actually act at different sites.

514

Table 1. Inhibitory effect of some respiratory inhibitors on the activity of reconstituted ubiquinol-cytochrome c resductase.

Preparation	Protein (ug) based on bc_1 III or IV	Addition			QCR Activity A_{550}/min
		AA (ug)	TTFA (mM)	PHMB (mM)	
bc_1 III	0.3	--		--	0.821
	0.3	0.005	--	--	0.060
	0.3	0.001	--	--	0.086
	0.3	--	0.1	--	0.064
	0.3	--	--	4	0.079
Reconstituted bc_1 III	0.78	--	--	--	1.067
	0.78	0.005	--	--	0.069
	0.78	0.001	--	--	0.129
	0.78	--	0.1	--	0.082
	0.78	--	--	4	0.087

Calculating from the results in Fig.5 it can be seen that the molar ratio of QP-C to c_1 was greater than unity. As the molecular weight of QP-C determined by gel filtration was 63000, QP-C may be an active multiple form and it is quite possible that some inactivation has occurred during its preparation. More likely, whether there are more than one QP-C acting at Qo & Qi sites (21) of the Q cycle (22) or just the same QP-C is functioning at different sites is a question to be ascertained.

From the inhibitory effect of NaCl on the reconstitution QH_2:cyt c reductase with QP-C and Q-depleted particle (Fig.7), it is suggested that QP-C binds to the mitochondrial membrance primarily through ionic bonds. It may be that the negatively charged Cl^- would influence the enviroment of QP-C.

Acknowledgment: This research is supported by grants of NIH-HL 12576 & American Cancer Society BC-349. We express our gratitude to Dr Yau-Huei Wei & Dr Hiroshi Suzuki for kind help with running EPR Spectra, Michael Seaman for skillful assistance.

REFERENCE

1. D. E. Green, Coenzyme Q and electron transport, in "Quinones in transport" G. E. W. Wolstenholme and C. M. O'Conner, eds., Little Brown, Boston (1960).
2. I. W. Depierre and L. Ernster, Enzyme topology of intracellular membranes, Annu. Rev. Biochem. 46:201 (1977).
3. A. Kroeger and M. Klingenberg, Kinetics of the redox reactions of ubiquinone related to the electron transport activity in the respiratory chain, Eur. J. Biochem. 34:358 (1973).
4. E. J. Land and A. J. Swallow, One-electron reaction in biochemical systems as studied by pulse radiolysis, J. Biol. Chem., 245:1890 (1970).
5. H. Baum, J. S. Rieske, H. I. Silman and S. H. Lipston, On the mechanism of electron transfer in complex III of the electron transfer chain, Proc. Natl. Acad. Sci. U.S.A., 57:798 (1967).
6. A. A. Konstantinov and E. K. Ruuge, Semiquinone Q in the respiratory chain of electron transport particles, FEBS Letters, 81:137 (1977).
7. W. J. Ingledew, J. C. Dalerno and T. Ohnishi, Studies on electron paramagnetic resonance spectra manifested by a respiratory chain hydrogen carrier, Arch. Biochem. Biophys. 177:176 (1976).
8. L. Yu, C. A. Yu and T. E. King, The indispensability of phospholipid

and ubiquinone in mitochondrial electron transfer from succinate to cytochrome c, J. Biol. Chem. 253:2657 (1978).

9. C. A. Yu, S. Nagaoka, L. Yu and T. E. King, Evidence of ubisemiquinone radicals in electron transfer at cytochrome bc_1 region of the cardiac respiratory chain, Arch. Biochem. Biophys. 204:59 (1980).

10. T. E. King, Mitochondrial Coenzyme Q Linked enzymes, in "Biomedical and clinical aspects of coenzyme Q" K. Folkers, Y. Yamamura, eds., Elsevier, North Holland (1981).

11. C. A. Yu, L. Yu and T. E. King, Reconstitution of succinate-Q reductase, Biochem. Biophys. Res. Commun., 79:939 (1977).

12. T. E. King and H. Suzuki, Ubiquinone protein with emphasis of QP-N, in "Biomedical and clinical aspects of coenzyme Q" K. Folkers, Y. Yamamura, eds, Elsevier, North Holland (1984).

13. T. Y. Wang and T. E. King, Isolation of QP-C and reconstitution of the QH_2-cyt c reductase, Biochem. Biophys. Res. Commun. 104:591 (1982).

14. R. L. Lester, Y. Hatefi, C. Widmer and F. L. Crane, Studies on the electron transport system, Biochim. Biophys. Acta, 33:169 (1959).

15. S. Wakabayashi, T. Takao, Y. Shimonishi, S. Kuramitsu, H. Matsubara, T. Y. Wang, Z. P. Zhang and T. E. King, Complete amino acid sequence of the ubiquinone binding protein (QP-C), a protein similar to the 14000-Dalton subunit of the yeast ubiquinol-cytochrome c reductase complex, J. Biol. Chem. 260:337 (1985).

16. J. Janatova, J. K. Fuller and M. J. Hunter, The heterogeneity of bovine albumin with respect to sulfhydryl and dimer content, J. Biol. Chem. 243:3612 (1968).

17. C. A. Yu, L. Yu and T. E. King, Soluble cytochrome bc_1 and the reconstitution of succinate-cytochrome c reductase, J. Biol. Chem. 249:4905 (1974).

18. Q. S. Zhu, T. A. Berden and E. C. Slater, A myxothiazol-sensitive Q-binding protein isolated from Chromatium Vinosum, Biochim. Biophys. Acta, 724:184 (1983).

19. N. Nishi, M. Kataoka, G. Soe, T. Kakuno, T. Ueki, J. Yamashita and T. Hario, Disintegration of Rhodospirillum Rubrum chromatophore membrane into photoreaction units, reaction centers, and ubiquinone-10 protein with mixture of cholate and deoxycholate, J. Biochem., 86:1211 (1979).

20. M. Snozzi, S. Bodmer, A. Baccarini-Melandri and R. Bachofen, Characterization and function of protein-bound quinones in Rhodospirillum Rubrum, Dev. Bioenerg. Biomembr., 5:191 (1981).

21. Q. S. Zhu, J. A. Berden, S. De Vries, K. Folkers, T. Porter and E. C. Slater, Identification of two different Q-binding sites in QH_2-cytochrome c oxidoreductase, using the Q analogue, n-heptadecylmercapto-6-hydroxy-5, 8-quinolinequinone, Biochim. Biophys. Acta, 682:160 (1982).

22. P. Mitchell, Possible molecular mechanism of the protonmotive function of cytochrome systems, J. Theor. Biol., 62:327 (1976).

THE KINETICS OF OXIDATION OF CYTOCHROME B ARE IN AGREEMENT WITH

THE Q-CYCLE HYPOTHESIS

S. de Vries, A.N. van Hoek, A. ten Bookum and J.A. Berden

Lab. of Biochemistry, B.C.P. Jansen Institute, University of
Amsterdam, P.O. Box 20151, 1000 HD Amsterdam, The Netherlands

INTRODUCTION

Concerning the question of how electron transfer through the QH_2: cytochrome c or PQH_2: plastocyanin oxidoreductases is coupled to the translocation of protons across the energy-transducing membrane, two important hypotheses have been proposed in the last decade, the ubiquinone (Q) cycle by Mitchell (1) and the semiquinone (SQ) cycle by Wikström and Krab (2). With respect to electron transfer, both hypotheses may be considered as extensions of the original proposal by Wikström and Berden (3) in which the oxidation of quinol is suggested to occur in two one-electron steps with the semiquinone as an intermediate. In retrospect, it is somewhat curious that the reluctance to accept the model of Wikström and Berden was due to the belief that ubisemiquinone would be too unstable to be an intermediate in the catalytic cycle and not due to the results of experiments reported ten years earlier by Deul and Thorn (4). The latter authors had shown that reduction of cytochrome b in BAL ($+O_2$)-treated particles is sensitive to the addition of antimycin. Obviously, the outcome of these experiments was not fully understood and probably for that reason forgotten, but from a historical point of view this is a fortunate circumstance.

It is precisely the result of the type of experiment first performed by Deul and Thorn, however, that is nowadays regarded a strong support for both the Q cycle and the SQ cycle. Thus the removal (5) or destruction (6,7) of the Rieske 2Fe-2S protein or cluster, respectively, or the presence of the inhibitor UHDBT (8) or myxothiazol (9), all prevent the reduction of cytochrome b in the presence of antimycin indicating that there are two pathways of electron transfer leading to the reduction of cytochrome b. One is the so-called oxidant-induced reduction route, involving the Q_{out}-binding domain (conformation); the other one, normally operative to oxidize cytochrome b, involves the Q_{in}-binding domain (conformation).

The existence of two different semiquinones, the antimycin-sensitive $Q_{in}^{\cdot -}$ (10 - 12) and the $Q_{out}^{\cdot -}$, detected sofar only in the presence of antimycin, is in perfect agreement with the Q cycle. Although the b cycle does not explicitly account for the presence of two different semiquinones in our opinion, the SQ cycle does. Moreover, since both the Q cycle and the SQ cycle, but not the b cycle, start from the principle that electron transfer and proton translocation are coupled directly (as a consequence of the physico-chemical properties of Q and QH_2) the two 'cycles' are so similar that most of the currently available experimental data do not discriminate against the validity of one of the two models.

The difference between the Q cycle and the SQ cycle can be summarized as follows. According to the SQ cycle the bc_1 complex contains a single Q ($Q^{\cdot-}$, QH_2)-binding pocket and the enzyme alternately is in a state in which $Q^{\cdot-}$ is the reductant ($Q_{out}^{\cdot-}$) to cytochrome b or the oxidant ($Q_{in}^{\cdot-}$). The transition from one state into another, accomplished by a 'flip-flop' of $Q^{\cdot-}$ occurs as fast as or faster than turnover. According to the Q cycle the enzyme contains two separate Q ($Q^{\cdot-}$, QH_2)-binding sites, the $Q_{in}^{\cdot-}$ - and $Q_{out}^{\cdot-}$-binding domains. The transition of $Q_{out}^{\cdot-}$ into $Q_{in}^{\cdot-}$ (or vice versa) occurs as fast as or faster than turnover only as the result of <u>electron transfer</u> via the two b-type hemes and any other pathway yielding the same net result is excluded to occur on the timescale of turnover (1).

As a consequence of this difference between the two models one may argue (2,15) that the kinetics of oxidation of initially fully reduced cytochrome b following a pulse of oxidant would show a lag period according to the Q cycle whereas the SQ cycle predicts instantaneous oxidation of cytochrome b. Such an experiment has recently been performed by Rich and Wikström (16). These authors did not find any sign of a lag period, the kinetics of oxidation of cytochrome b being rapid and instantaneous in mitochondria reduced by succinate or succinate plus dithionite, thus favouring the SQ cycle. However, de Vries and Dutton (17) reported experiments performed with the so-called hybrid system that are inconsistent with the SQ cycle. It was found that at redoxpotentials at which the Q pool was less than half-reduced the kinetics of cytochrome c (re)reduction and cytochrome b oxidation matched, whereas at lower redox potentials the rate of oxidation of cytochrome b greatly decreased whilst the rate of cytochrome c reduction remained unchanged. According to the SQ cycle the rates of these two processes should match at any redox potential. In addition, it was observed that, in the presence of antimycin or myxothiazol, one molecule of UHDBT per molecule of enzyme was sufficient to inhibit all cytochrome b and c oxidation-reduction kinetics, but that two molecules of UHDBT per molecule of enzyme were required to completely block electron transfer in the absence of other inhibitors. This finding strongly suggests that the bc_1 complex contains two separate binding sites for UHDBT, just as it does for HMHQQ (18) and thus likely for ubiquinone.

In order to further resolve the question which of the two models, the Q cycle or the SQ cycle, most closely describes the pathway of electron transfer in the bc complexes we have studied the kinetics of oxidation of cytochrome b in mitoplasts from yeast by means of the stopped-flow technique. Oxidation was initiated by mixing with a solution saturated with pure oxygen in stead of an aerobic solution of ferricyanide (cf. 16). The degree of reduction of cytochrome b was varied by using succinate or succinate plus dithionite at different concentrations. It was observed that with succinate or succinate plus relatively low amounts of dithionite the oxidation of cytochrome b started immediately at a high rate. However, at higher concentrations of dithionite a <u>lag</u> in the oxidation of cytochrome b, maximally 80-100 ms, was observed. In addition, the kinetics of cytochrome c under these conditions show transient behaviour, i.e. after the initial rapid oxidation , the reduction level increases again at the time that cytochrome b becomes oxidized, asif only then the bc_1 complex is fully catalytically active. These results are in perfect agreement with the Q-cycle hypothesis and inconsistent with the SQ-cycle postulate.

MATERIALS AND METHODS

Yeast (commercially grown <u>Saccharomyces cerevisiae</u>) mitoplasts were prepared by breaking the cells with glass beads in a Dynomill. By means of differential centrifugation (impure) mitochondrial membranes were obtained at 35.000xg. The membranes were washed, suspended in a buffer of 50mM HEPES-KOH, 250mM KCl and 1mM EDTA (pH 7) and subsequently sonicated (4 times 10 seconds). By this procedure, the outermembrane (and cytochrome c) are

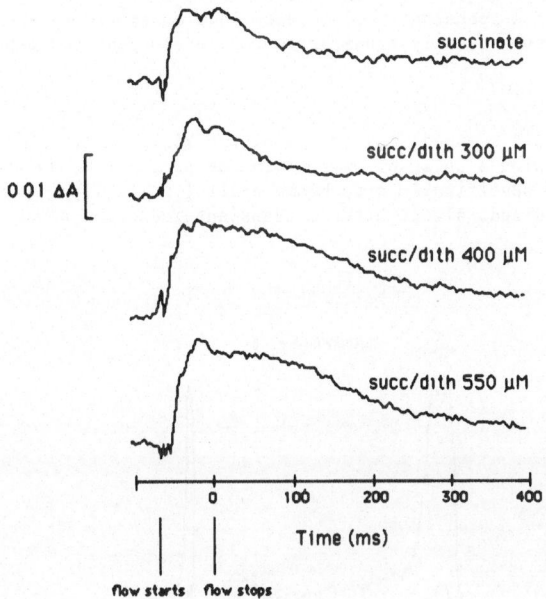

succinate

succ/dith 300 µM

001 ΔA

succ/dith 400 µM

succ/dith 550 µM

0   100   200   300   400

Time (ms)

flow starts   flow stops

Fig. 1. Kinetics of oxidation of cytochrome b in yeast mitoplasts measured by stopped-flow (pH 6.2). See Materials and Methods for details. In the upper trace 20mM succinate was added, in the other ones 6.7mM and, after anaerobiosis was reached, the indicated amount of dithionite. Cytochrome b was monitored at 560-575 nm. Traces are an average of 7 to 10. When the flow starts the optical chamber containing oxidized mitoplasts is filled with reduced mitoplasts leading to an increase of absorbance. Due to the abrupt stop of the flow (time zero) a spike in the trace is occasionally observed.

lost and the innermembrane retains the rightside-out conformation. After a
low speed run the mitoplasts were collected at 35.000xg, washed once and
suspended in an appropriate buffer. Experiments were performed with a home-
built stopped-flow apparatus (dead-time 2ms) connected to an Aminco DW-2
spectrophotometer. Reaction temperature was 28-29 ℃. Kinetics of cytochrome
b were monitored at 560-575 nm, those of cytochromes $c+c_1$ at 549.3-534 nm.
Mitoplasts (20 mg/ml, 2.5μM in bc_1 complex) were suspended in a buffer
containing 25mM MES-KOH, 125mM KCl and 0.5mM EDTA (pH 6.2). Subsequently,
12μM cytochrome c (from yeast) was added and succinate (20mM). Oxidation
was initiated by mixing with the same buffer saturated with pure oxygen. In
the experiments in which, in addition, dithionite was added to completely
reduce cytochrome b and ubiquinone, small amounts from a freshly prepared
sodium dithionite stock solution (0.65M in 1M KOH kept at 0 C under N_2)
were added to a suspension of mitoplasts made anaerobic by succinate
(6.7mM) and subsequently transferred to the stopped-flow apparatus.

RESULTS

Fig. 1 shows stopped-flow traces of the kinetics of oxidation of cytochrome b following a pulse of oxygen. In the presence of succinate, cytochrome b, more specifically cytochrome b-562 (initially reduced for 80-85%)
is rapidly oxidized, albeit after a transient reduction phase (19,20).

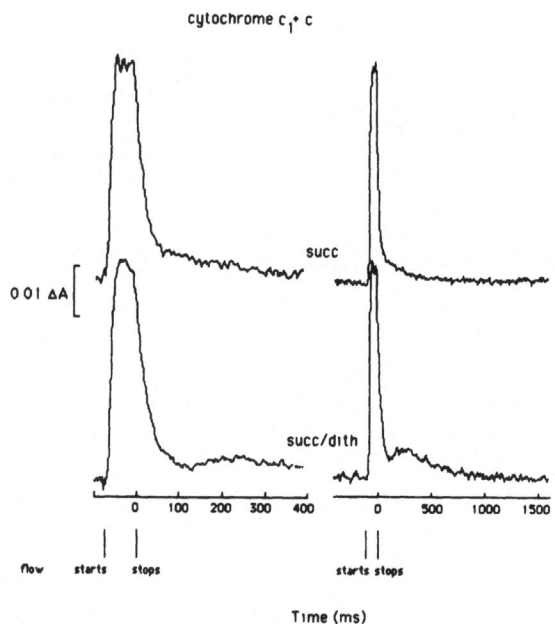

Fig. 2. Kinetics of oxidation of cytochromes $c+c_1$ in yeast mitoplasts (pH
6.2). See Materials and Methods and Fig. 1 for details. The kinetics were
monitored at 549.3-534 nm and at two different timescales. Upper traces:
20mM succinate (cf. upper trace of Fig. 1); lower traces: 6.7mM succinate
plus 550μM dithionite (cf. lower trace of Fig. 1).

When, in addition 300μM sodium dithionite is added (all cytochrome b-562 reduced, cytochrome b-566 largely oxidized) oxidation of cytochrome b is still rapid, following a transient or lag of about 20ms. At still higher concentrations of dithionite a long lag period (60-100ms) is observed after which cytochrome b (b-562 plus b-566) becomes relatively slowly oxidized.

In Fig. 2 the corresponding oxidation-reduction kinetics of cytochromes $c+c_1$ are shown. Following a pulse of oxygen these cytochromes are very rapidly oxidized. Although the traces do not follow a single exponential, the decay is monotonic when succinate (in the presence or absence of myxothiazol) or succinate plus dithionite, only in the presence of myxothiazol, were used (compare Figs. 2 and 3). However, a (net) rereduction phase is seen in the traces when succinate plus dithionite was employed (Fig. 2), indicating that, initially (i.e. during the lag period) the rate of electron transfer towards cytochromes $c+c_1$ is low (or even nil). After this lag period the bc_1 complex starts to rapidly oxidize QH_2 thereby slightly increasing the redox level of the c-type cytochromes and when (most of) the QH_2 is oxidized the redox level decreases again.

The control experiments in Fig. 3 indicate that oxidation of cytochrome b is completely inhibited by myxothiazol when succinate was used as a reductant, but not when a combination of succinate plus dithionite was used. However, this latter oxidation phase was (partially) abolished by the additional presence of antimycin.

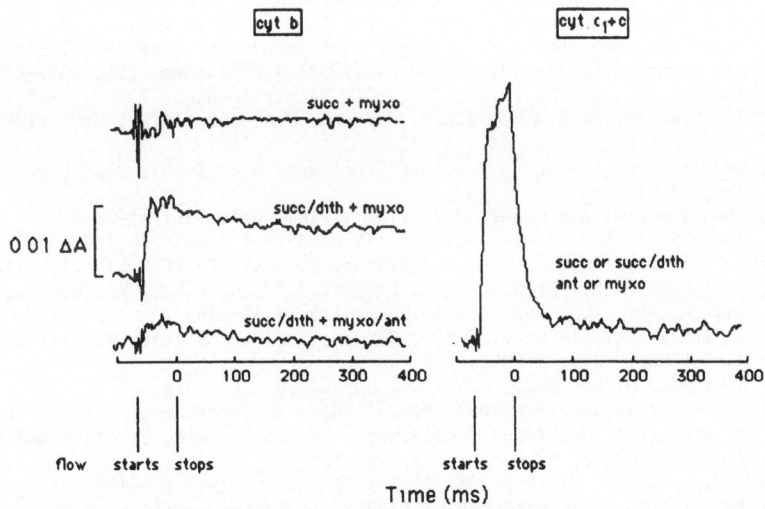

Fig. 3. Kinetics of oxidation of cytochromes b and c in yeast mitoplasts (pH 6.2) and the effect of myxothiazol and/or antimycin. Upper left: kinetics of cytochrome b reduced by 20mM succinate in the presence of myxothiazol. Middle left: as upper left but with 6.7mM succinate plus 550μM dithionite. Lower left: as middle left but in addition antimycin was added. Right: kinetics of cytochromes $c+c_1$ corresponding to the trace of cytochrome b of the middle left. The traces corresponding to the conditions of upper and lower left (not shown) are identical. See Materials and Methods and Figs. 1 and 2 for further details.

DISCUSSION

The experiments reported in this paper were intended to discriminate between the Q cycle and the SQ cycle. The results are in very good agreement with the original Q-cycle hypothesis (1) and inconsistent with the SQ cycle (2). The lag observed in the kinetics of oxidation of cytochrome $\underline{b}$, initially fully reduced, indicates that the rate of 'communication' between $Q_{in}^{\cdot -}$ and $Q_{out}^{\cdot -}$ is in fact much lower than the rate of turnover (6.6 ms per QH_2 at pH 6.2). In addition, the transient kinetics of cytochromes $\underline{c+c}_1$ under conditions that the system is initially fully reduced also very much speaks in favour of the Q-cycle model. Since the $\underline{bc}_1$ complex is postulated to be catalytically inactive when trapped in a state in which the cytochrome $\underline{b}$ and ubiquinone are fully reduced, the $\underline{c}$-type cytochromes are expected to become rapidly (relatively) highly oxidized. Then, after the lag, the $\underline{bc}_1$ complex starts to turn over at a very high rate, because of the high concentration of ubiquinol, and cytochromes $\underline{c+c}_1$ reach a new, more reduced, (steady-state) level. After a while, the concentration of QH_2 becomes so low that the rate of turnover decreases and the cytochromes $\underline{c+\bar{c}}_1$ adapt to a more oxidized level. This is precisely what is observed ($\overline{Fig}$. 2).

As a conclusion, the oxidation-reduction kinetics of both cytochrome $\underline{b}$ and cytochrome $\underline{c}$ are in excellent agreement with the Q cycle and exclude the SQ-cycle hypothesis.

REFERENCES

1) Mitchell, P. (1976) J.Theor.Biol. 62, 327-367
2) Wikström, M. and Krab, K. (1986) J.Bioenerg.Biomembr. Vol. 18, 181-193
3) Wikström, M. and Berden, J.A. (1972) Biochim.Biophys.Acta 283, 403-420
4) Deul, D.H. and Thorn, M.B. (1962) Biochim.Biophys.Acta 59, 426-436
5) Trumpower, B.L. and Edwards, C.A. (1979) J.Biol.Chem. 254, 8697-8706
6) Slater, E.C. and de Vries, S. (1980) Nature (London) 288, 717-718
7) de Vries, S., Albracht, S.P.J., Berden, J.A. and Slater, E.C. (1982) Biochim.Biophys.Acta 681, 41-53
8) Bowyer, J.R., Edwards, C.A. and Trumpower, B.L. (1981) FEBS Lett. 126, 93-97
9) von Jagow, G. and Engel, W.D. (1981) FEBS Lett. 136, 19-24
10) Ohnishi, T. and Trumpower, B.L. (1980) J.Biol.Chem. 255,3278-3284
11) de Vries,S., Berden, J.A. and Slater, E.C. (1980) FEBS Lett.122, 143-148
12) Robertson, D.E., Prince, R.C., Bowyer, J.R., Matsuura, K., Dutton, P.L. and Ohnishi, T. (1984) J.Biol.Chem. 259, 1758-1763
13) de Vries, S., Albracht, S.P.J, Berden, J.A. and Slater, E.C. (1981) J.Biol.Chem. 256, 11996-11998
14) Wikström, M. and Krab, K. (1980) Curr. Top. Bioenerg. 10, 51-101
15) Bowyer, J.R. and Trumpower, B.L. (1981). In Chemiosmotic Proton Circuits in Biological Membranes (Skulachev, V.P. and Hinkle, P. eds.) Addison-Wesley, Reading, Massachusetts, pp. 105-122
16) Rich, P.R. and Wikström, M. (1986) FEBS Lett. 194, 176-182
17) de Vries, S. and Dutton, P.L. (1985). In Achievements and Perspectives of Mitochondrial Research (Quagliariello, E., Slater, E.C., Saccone, C. and Kroon, A.M., eds.) Elsevier, Amsterdam, Vol. I pp. 103-110
18) Zhu, Q.S., Berden, J.A., de Vries, S., Folkers, K., Porter, T. and Slater, E.C. (1982) Biochim. Biophys. Acta 682, 160-167
19) Erecínska, M. and Wilson, D.F. (1972) FEBS Lett. 24, 269-272
20) Papa, S., Lorusso, M., Izzo, G. and Capuano, F. (1981) Biochem. J. 194, 395-306

THE Q-REACTION DOMAINS OF MITOCHONDRIAL QH$_2$:CYTOCHROME C OXIDOREDUCTASE

J.A. Berden, A.N. van Hoek, S. de Vries and P.J. Schoppink

Lab. of Biochemistry, B.C.P. Jansen Institute
University of Amsterdam, P.O.Box 20151
1000 HD Amsterdam, The Netherlands

INTRODUCTION

The proposal by Wikström and Berden (1) that the oxidation of ubiquinol by QH$_2$:cytochrome c oxidoreductase occurs in two steps with two different electron acceptors and the subsequent formulation of the Q-cycle by Mitchell (2) required specific sites on the oxidoreductase for the oxidation-reduction of ubiquinone and the stabilization of the intermediate semiquinone. The demonstration of the existence of a stable semiquinone with the properties of the postulated semiquinone at centre i (3,4) and of a less stable semiquinone with the properties of the postulated semiquinone at centre o (5) confirmed the postulate of specific Q-binding sites, stabilizing specifically the anionic forms of the semiquinone. Although the data were in full agreement with the Q-cycle model, Wikström and Krab formulated a b-cycle model as alternative (6), later modified to the semiquinone (SQ)-cycle (7). In this model only one Q-reaction domain exists with two possible conformations: in the one conformation bound semiquinone is electron acceptor for cytochrome b-562, in the other the bound semiquinone is electron donor for cytochrome $\overline{b}$-566. The transition between the two states is at least as fast as turnover of the oxidoreductase.

Evidence for the presence of two different quinone-reaction sites was obtained from experiments with the Q-analogue HMHQQ (8) and studies with UHDBT in the presence or absence of inhibitors of centre o or centre i (9). Kinetic evidence against the Q-cycle has been presented by Rich and Wikström (10) but recent experiments on the oxidation kinetics of cytochrome b in our group exclude the SQ-cycle and are in excellent agreement with the Q-cycle (11).

The localisation of the Q-binding sites has been a subject of study for several years now and especially the groups of King (12,13) Yu and Yu (14, 15) and Ozawa (16,17) have been involved in the identification of Q-binding proteins. In this paper we describe some results of experiments directed towards the localisation and properties of the Q-binding sites. Three approaches have been used: labeling of Q-binding sites with azido-quinone-analogues, correlation between activities of centre o and centre i in yeast mutants with the presence of various subunits of the cytochrome c reductase and pre-steady-state kinetics of reduction of ubiquinone by duroquinol in correlation with the reduction of the redox centres of the enzyme.

MATERIALS AND METHODS

Bovine-heart QH_2: cytochrome c oxidoreductase was isolated according to the procedure of Rieske (18). Yeast mutants, deficient in the gene for one of the subunits of the QH_2:cytochrome c oxidoreductase were constructed using the one step gene disruption method as essentially described in ref. 19. Also the preparation of mitochondria from yeast cells has been described in the same reference. Submitochondrial particles were prepared by sonication of mitochondria, followed by differential centrifugation.

Rapid-freeze and rapid-quench experiments were performed as described in refs. 20 and 21, respectively. The latter method is a modification of the procedure described by Tsai et al. (22), the essential difference being the use of acidic methanol in stead of neutral methanol as quenching solvent.

The reduction level of the Fe-S cluster was measured by EPR, the reduction level of the cytochromes by diffuse reflectance spectroscopy and the redox state of ubiquinone with HPLC (22). Reduction of ubiquinone-2 by duroquinol was measured with an Aminco DW-2 spectrophotometer at the wavelenght pair 300-284 nm. $[^3H]$ 3 azido-6-decyl-Q-0 was synthesized by A.F. Hartog in this laboratory.

RESULTS

Photoaffinity labeling of Q-binding sites

Especially Yu and Yu have been very active in the search for the Q-binding sites in mitochondrial QH_2:cytochrome c oxidoreductase, using photo-

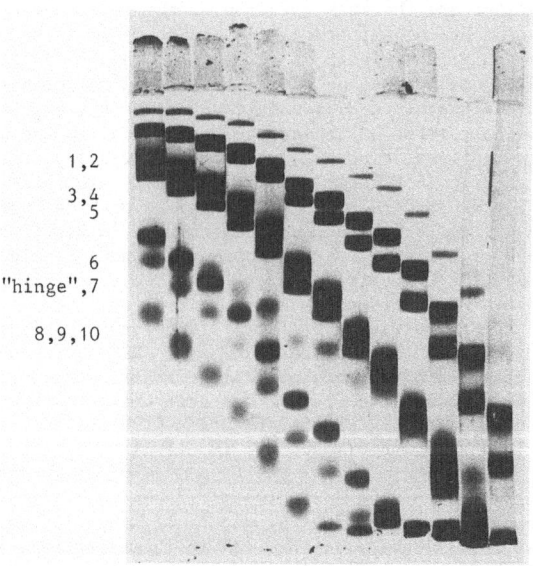

1,2
3,4
5

6
"hinge",7

8,9,10

Fig. 1 SDS polyacrylamide disc gel electrophoresis of bovine-heart QH_2: cytochrome c oxidoreductase. From left to right the concentration of polyacrylamide decreased from 18% to 6%. Electrophoresis was carried out as described by Laemmli (26) with the additional presence of 6M urea. Bands nr. 1 and 2 are the core proteins, 3 is cytochrome b, 4 cytochrome c_1 and 5 the Rieske Fe-S protein. The bands 8 and 10 are not well separated from the more intense band 9. The relative position of the hinge protein varies with the concentration of polyacrylamide.

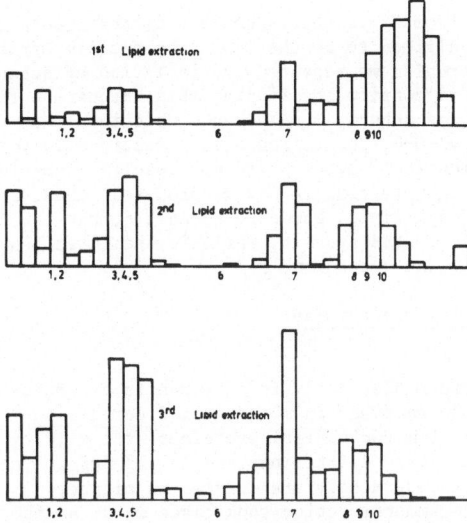

Fig. 2 Photoaffinity labeling of QH_2:cytochrome c oxidoreductase with
        [^3H] 3-azido-6-decyl-Q-0. Isolated QH_2:cytochrome c oxidoreductase
        was delipidated according to the procedure described in ref.15, in-
        cubated with the azido-Q analogue and illuminated for 20', with
        light of 360 nm so that the azido-compound was fully photolysed.
        Samples of 100 μg were put on 12% polyacrylamide gels for electro-
        phoresis according to Laemmli (26). After staining and destaining
        the gels were sliced and the radioactivity in each slice was deter-
        mined. Apart from the phospholipids only cytochrome b and subunit 7
        were labelled.

affinity labeling (14,15). We have used this approach as well, but have
reached different conclusions, using various Q-analogues as probe. One very
important point of agreement exists: intact QH_2:cytochrome c oxidoreductase,
isolated or in submitochondrial particles, can not be labeled with azido-
quinone analogues as far as the protein part is concerned. Bound label was
only found in the phospholipid part of the enzyme. Upon delipidation of the
enzyme the binding of ^3H nitreno-quinone analogues to the protein part of
the enzyme increased.
    To avoid confusion about the nomenclature of the subunits we have in-
cluded a figure (Fig. 1), representing the subunit pattern obtained with gel
electrophoresis at different acrylamide concentrations. The polypeptides
have been numbered 1-10, but the so called "hinge" protein (23) is not numbered. This polypeptide can have different relative positions depending on
the concentration of acrylamide: at the highest percentage of acrylamide it
migrates with subunit 7, but at low percentages it migrates even slower than
subunit 3 (cytochrome b). This subunit is analogous to the 17 kDa subunit of
the yeast enzyme. In Fig.2 it can be seen that upon delipidation of the
enzyme the photoaffinity labeling of the phospholipids with 3-azido-6-decyl-
Q-0 decreases, while labeling increases at the positions of subunit 3 (cytochrome b) and subunit 7. This latter result does not agree with the data of
Yu et al. (14) who detected labeling of a 17 kDa subunit. Such a 17 kDa subunit is not present in our preparations since it is different from the hinge
protein. A possibility is that the 17 kDa band of Yu et al. is a dimer of
subunit 7.

It is clear from Fig.2 that subunit 6 is not labeled, although this subunit has been claimed to be the Q-binding protein of the enzyme (13,17). To resolve this problem we repeated the isolation of subunit 6 as described in ref.17 and could confirm the finding that ubiquinone fractionates into the same fraction as subunit 6. Also when ubiquinone was replaced with [^{3}H]3-azido-6-decyl-Q-0, the radioactivity remained largely associated with subunit 6. Illumination, however, did not result in covalent binding of radioactivity to the protein. It may be proposed, then, that ubiquinone is present in the phospholipids bound to subunit 6, but the hydrophilic head-group is not close to the protein, while in the intact enzyme it is more close to subunit 7 and cytochrome b.

Deletion mutants of S.cerevisiae

Table 1. Western blot analysis of subunits of QH$_2$:cytochrome c oxidoreductase in mutants of S.cerevisiae
Equal amounts of mitochondrial protein of the wild type and the various mutants were electrophoresed on 15% SDS-polyacrylamide slab gels and subsequently transferred to nitrocellulose filters, whereafter the immunoreaction took place using antibodies against most of the subunits of Complex III. The antigen-antibody complex was visualized with the aid of ^{125}I-labelled protein A or the horse radish peroxidase colour assay.

SUBUNIT	MUTANT 11 kDa$^-$	14 kDa$^-$	17 kDa$^-$	40 kDa$^-$	17 kDa$^-$,* [1]
Core I	+	+	+	+	+
Core II	+	+	+	−	+
Cyt. b	−	−	+	o	o
Cyt. c$_1$	+	+	+	+	o
Fe-S	o	o	+	o	Δ
17 kDa	Δ	Δ	−	Δ	−
14 kDa	o	−	+	Δ	o
11 kDa	−	o	+	Δ	o

1) This mutant contains a secondary mutation causing the absence of heme groups in cytochromes b and aa$_3$.

+ : More than 70% of the wild type level.
Δ : Between 20 and 70% of the wild type level.
o : Less than 20% of the wild type level.
− : Not detectable.

Using cloned genes several mutants deficient in one of the genes for the subunits of QH$_2$:cytochrome c oxidoreductase have been constructed and were tested for the absence of both the gene in question and its product (19). In table 1 it can be seen that in these mutants not only the product of the missing gene was absent, but that also several other subunits were present in much lower amounts than in the wild type, as analysed by Western blot analysis, using various polyclonal antibodies and one monoclonal antibody (against the Rieske Fe-S protein). The two core proteins (subunits 1 and 2) were present at a nearly wild type level in all mutants, apart from the 40 kDa$^-$ mutant. This latter mutant still exhibited a low QH$_2$:cytochrome c oxidoreductase activity and the cells grew slowly on glycerol, indicating

Table 2.   Reduction of Q-2 by duroquinol catalysed by
                yeast submitochondrial particles
HR2 is the wild type strain, 17 kDa$^-$,* is a 17 kDa$^-$ mutant
containing an additional mutation as described in Table 1.
Conditions: 50 mM MES (pH 6.2), 0.25 M sucrose, 80 μM DQH$_2$,
10 μM Q-2 and 1 mM KCN. Temperature was 2° and the wavelength
pair 300-284 nm. An extinctioncoefficient of 5 mM^{-1} was used.

YEAST STRAIN	ACTIVITY μmol min^{-1} mg^{-1}	INHIBITORS
HR 2, w.t.	5.9	–
HR 2, w.t.	6.8	Antimycin
HR 2, w.t.	2.6	Myxothiazol
HR 2, w.t.	0.1	Antimycin and Myxothiazol
17 kDa$^-$,*	2.0	–
17 kDa$^-$,*	1.8	Antimycin
17 kDa$^-$,*	0.1	Myxothiazol

that subunit 2 is not essential for electron transfer activity of the enzyme.
Two 17 kDa$^-$ mutants are listed: one is a real 17 kDa$^-$ mutant and grows perfectly normal on glycerol. The QH$_2$:cytochrome c oxidoreductase activity of
this mutant was about half the wild type level and it is evident that the
17 kDa subunit is not essential for activity and assembly of the complex.
It will be further investigated whether its absence affects the electron
transfer from the Fe-S cluster to cytochrome c_1 or that from cytochrome c_1
to cytochrome c.
      The second 17 kDa$^-$ mutant contained an additional mutation and because
of the high frequency of such secondary mutation, 1 out of 4 at this moment,
there has to be some correlation. This mutant, containing very low levels
of the cytochrome b and cytochrome c_1 polypeptides, as well of the 14 and
11 kDa subunits, is used for the experiments reported in Table 2. It is the
only mutant in which the level of cytochrome c_1 is substantially lowered,
while of the Fe-S protein still a substantial amount is present. It can be
seen that in the wild type preparations (HR 2) the rate of reduction of Q-2
by duroquinol increased upon addition of antimycin. Since antimycin blocks
centre i activity, it has to be concluded that antimycin binding activates
centre o. The activity in the presence of antimycin was higher than that in
the presence of myxothiazol, indicating that in yeast, contrary to our results with the bovine-heart enzyme, centre o activity, at least in the presence of antimycin, is higher than centre i activity.
      The mutant showed no activity in the presence of myxothiazol, so centre
i was inactive. Centre o activity, however, was about 30% of the wild type
level and this result indicates that only the Fe-S protein can be responsible for this activity. All other subunits, apart from the core proteins,
were present in amounts much lower than 30% while cytochrome b also lacked
its hemegroup. It is likely that for centre i at least cytochrome b is required, but possibly the 14 and/or 11 kDa subunits as well.

Pre-steady-state reduction of ubiquinone and QH$_2$:cytochrome c oxidoreductase by duroquinol

      Using the rapid-quench technique in parallel with the rapid-freeze
technique the kinetics of the reduction of ubiquinone in submitochondrial
particles from bovine-heart by duroquinol could be measured and compared

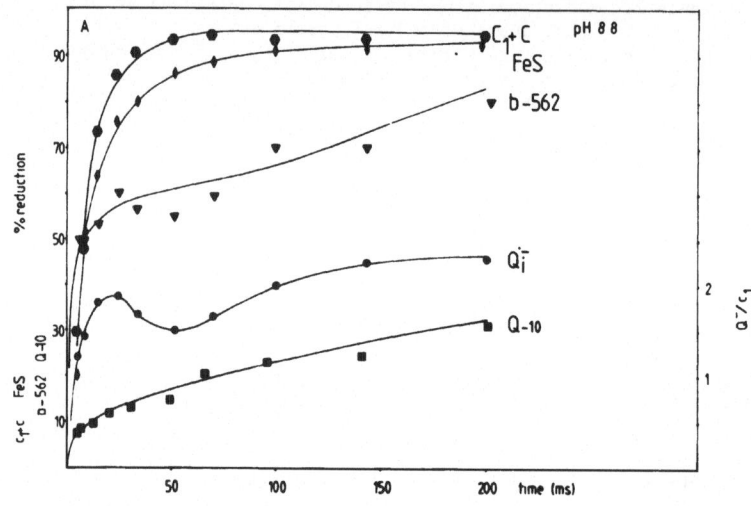

Fig. 3 Kinetics of reduction of the [2Fe-2S] cluster, cytochrome (c_1 + c)
cytochrome b, Q-10 and formation of $Q \cdot \overline{i}$ in submitochondrial particles, largely depleted of cytochrome c in the presence of 5 mM KCN.
EPR was used to detect [2Fe-2S] and $Q \cdot \overline{i}$ and low temperature diffuse
reflectance spectroscopy to detect cytochrome (c_1 + c) and cytochrome b, using the freeze-quench technique. The reduction of Q-10
was measured with reversed phase HPLC, using the chemical quench
technique as an extension of the freeze-quench method as described
in ref.21. The reaction was performed at room temperature. One
syringe contained 70-80 mg/ml particles suspended in 0.25 M sucrose,
50 mM Tris/HCL (pH 8.8). The other syringe contained 0.25 M sucrose,
1 mM HAc and 2 mM DQH$_2$. The DQH$_2$ solubilisation was facilitated with
the help of hot tap water. After mixing, the DQH$_2$ concentration was
1 mM. Diffuse-reflectance spectra were recorded at 110 K with a slit
width of 1 nm. Cytochrome (c_1 + c) was measured in the reduced-minus-
oxidised spectrum as 552 nm minus 542 nm. Cytochrome b-562 was
measured in the reduced-minus-oxidised spectrum as 559 nm minus
570 nm. The EPR measurements were performed at 9.25 GHz; T = 36K;
P = 6.3 mW; MA = 1.25 mT. The amount of reduced [2Fe-2S] cluster was
determined with the g_y amplitude. Semiquinone formation was measured
at 9.25 GHz; T = 36; P = 10 µW; MA = 0.5 mT; 100% reduction of cytochrome (c_1 + c) and [2Fe-2S] cluster was set with samples reduced
by ascorbate + TMPD. 100% reduction of cytochrome b-562 was set with
samples reduced by succinate. Samples at zero time, using only buffer in the substrate syringe, showed that the prosthetic groups were
fully oxidised and no semiquinone was present. The particles contained 12 mol of Q-10 per mole of cytochrome c_1.

with the kinetics of the reduction of cytochrome b, cytochrome c_1 and the
Rieske Fe-S cluster and the formation of semiquinone.
   Fig.3 shows the reduction kinetics of the various redox groups upon
mixing submitochondrial particles with duroquinol at pH 8.8 in the presence
of cyanide. To avoid disappearance of the cytochrome c_1 band due to cytochrome c the particles were prepared from cytochrome c-depleted mitochondria.
The reduction of cytochrome b, cytochrome c_1 and the Fe-S cluster, as well
as the formation of $Q \cdot \overline{i}$ showed the same kinetics as reported previously
(20). Concomitant with the initial (within 5 ms) reduction of cytochrome
b-562 and formation of semiquinone, 8% of the ubiquinone pool was reduced,

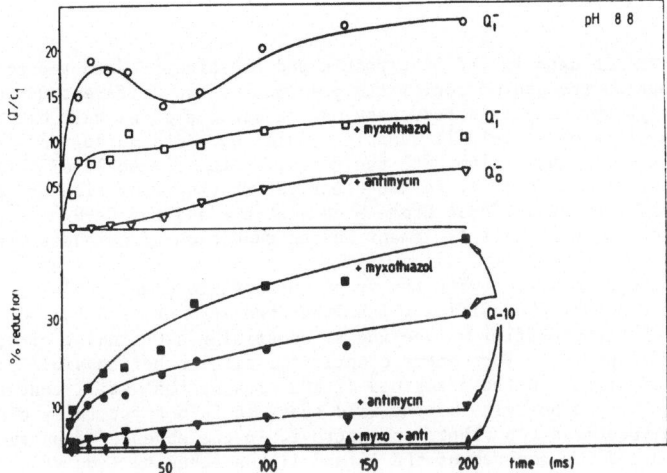

Fig. 4 Reduction of Q-10 and formation of semiquinones in the presence of KCN, myxothiazol, antimycin, or myxothiazol plus antimycin, measured as described in Fig.3. Open symbols: formation of semiquinone; filled-in symbols:reduction of Q-10. After long incubation the degree of reduction of Q-10 was increased till 90%, irrespective of the inhibitor present.

followed by a monophasic further reduction. The final level of reduction of Q-10 was 90%. The 8% of total Q-10, reduced initially, represents about 1 mol of ubiquinone per mol cytochrome c_1. It is evident that at t=5 ms no equilibrium exists between cytochrome b and the Q-pool. Only during the third phase of cytochrome b reduction ubiquinone and cytochrome b reach redox equilibrium.

The initial rapid reduction of about 1 mol Q-10 / mol cytochrome c_1 indicates that this amount of Q-10 is distinct from the rest of the Q-pool and that this amount is bound to the enzyme and is an intermediate in the reduction of the Q-pool by duroquinol. It is possible, but not certain, that dissociation of the bound QH_2 is the rate-limiting step in the reduction of the Q-pool. To investigate the localisation of the bound Q, the experiments were repeated in the presence of myxothiazol, antimycin or both inhibitors together. The results, as far as the reduction of Q-10 is concerned, are shown in Fig.4. Myxothiazol blocked the reduction of cytochrome c_1 and the Rieske Fe-S cluster, but hardly affected the amount of rapidly reduced Q-10 and enhanced the rate of reduction of the Q-pool. These results indicate that most of the Q-10 was bound to centre i and that centre i is influenced by the binding of myxothiazol at centre o: the reduction of Q-10 via centre i is faster in the presence of myxothiazol, similar to the effect described above for binding of antimycin to centre i on the reduction of Q-2 by DQH_2 at centre o in yeast particles. When antimycin is present, the amount of rapidly reduced Q-10 is strongly diminished, but not zero. Also the rate of reduction of the Q-pool is much lower, indicating that centre o contains less bound Q than centre i and has (for that reason?) a lower turnover, contrary to what is reported above for yeast. The experiment in the presence of both antimycin and myxothiazol shows that the rapidly reduced Q-10 in the presence of antimycin is indeed bound to centre o: it has disappeared when also myxothiazol is present and at the same time no reduction of the Q-pool occurs any more. The data clearly show that both centre o and centre i are Q-binding domains and that the Q-10 bound to these sites is not in (rapid) equilibrium with the Q-pool.

DISCUSSION

From the data in the litterature and the kinetic data reported in this contribution the assumption of the presence of two different Q-binding sites in QH_2:cytochrome c oxidoreductase may be considered as well established. At both sites bound Q-10 is rapidly reduced by added quinol and the bound QH_2 is not in equilibrium with the Q-pool at the timescale of turnover of the enzyme (a few ms). It is not clear yet whether reduction of redox groups of the enzyme (cytochrome b at centre i and the Fe-S cluster at centre o) is an essential element in the reduction of quinones via these centres.

The data obtained with the yeast mutants are clearly additive to the data obtained by photoaffinity labeling: the Fe-S protein has not been detected with photoaffinity labeling as containing a Q-binding site, but is clearly responsible for centre o activity, since other possible candidates can be dismissed in the described 17 kDa$^-$ mutant that still contains 30% of the centre o activity of the wild type. It is not yet fully clear how many polypeptides contribute to centre i. In the absence of active cytochrome b and low amounts of the 14 and 11 kDa subunits (equivalent to subunit 6 and 7 in the bovine-heart enzyme) no centre i activity was detectable. Our own photoaffinity labeling experiments indicate that not only cytochrome b but also subunit 7 is close to the headgroup of bound quinone. It should be remembered that subunit 7 is also involved in binding of antimycin (23) and of inhibitory DTNB (24). Additionally, the isolation of subunit 6 together with ubiquinone (17) indicates that the phospholipids bound to subunit 6 contain ubiquinone. The proposal that all three polypeptides are involved in the formation of centre i is supported by the finding that nor the 11 kDa$^-$ mutant, nor the 14 kDa$^-$ mutant show any QH_2:cytochrome c oxidoreductase activity, although no other subunit is completely absent in these mutants.

ACKNOWLEDGEMENTS

The work presented in this paper was supported in part by grants from the Netherlands Organization for the Advancement of Pure Research (Z.W.O.) under the auspices of the Netherlands Foundation for Chemical Research (S.O.N.).

REFERENCES

1. Wikström,M. and Berden,J.A. (1972) Biochim.Biophys.Acta, 283, 403-420.
2. Mitchell,P. (1976) J.Theor.Biol. 62, 327-367.
3. Ohnishi,T. and Trumpower,B.L. (1980) J.Biol.Chem. 255, 3278-3284.
4. de Vries,S., Berden,J.A. and Slater,E.C. (1980) FEBS Lett. 122, 143-148
5. de Vries,S., Albracht,S.P.J., Berden,J.A. and Slater,E.C. (1981) J.Biol.Chem. 256, 11996-11998.
6. Wikström,M. and Krab,K. (1980) Curr.Top.Bioenerg. 10, 51-101.
7. Wikström,M. and Saraste,M. (1984) in: Bioenergetics (Ernster,L. ed.) Elsevier, Amsterdam, pp.49-94.
8. Zhu,Q.S., Berden,J.A., de Vries,S., Folkers,K., Porter,T. and Slater, E.C. (1982) Biochim.Biophys.Acta 682, 160-167.
9. de Vries,S. and Dutton,P.L. (1985) in: Achievements and Perspectives of mitochondrial Research (Quagliariello,E., Slater,E.C., Saccone,C. and Kroon,A.M. eds.), Elsevier, Amsterdam, Vol.I, pp.103-110.
10. Rich,P. and Wikström,M. (1986) FEBS Lett. 194, 176-182.
11. de Vries,S., van Hoek,A.N., ten Bookum,A. and Berden,J.A. (1987) This volume.
12. Nagaoka,S., Yu,L. and King,T.E. (1981) Archives Biochem.Biophys. 209, 334-343.

13. Wang,T. and King,T.E. (1982) Biochem.Biophys.Res.Commun. 104, 591-596.
14. Yu,L., Yang,F.D. and Yu,C.A. (1985) J.Biol.Chem. 260, 963-973.
15. Yu,L., Yu,C.A. (1982) J.Biol.Chem. 257, 10215-10221.
16. Suzuki,H. and Ozawa,T. (1984) Biochem.Int. 9, 563-568.
17. Shimomura,Y., Nikishimi,M. and Ozawa,T. (1986) Anal.Biochem. 153, 126-131.
18. Rieske,J.S., Hansen,R.E. and Zang,W.S. (1964) J.Biol.Chem. 239, 3017-3022.
19. Schoppink,P.J., Grivell,L.A. and Berden,J.A. (1987) in: Membrane Biochemistry and Bioenergetics (Kim,C.H. ed.) in press.
20. de Vries,S., Albracht,S.P.J., Berden,J.A. and Slater,E.C. (1982) Biochim.Biophys.Acta 681, 41-53.
21. van Hoek,A.N., van Gaalen,M.C.M., de Vries,S. and Berden,J.A. (1987) Biochim.Biophys.Acta, in press.
22. Tsai,A.L., Kauten,R. and Palmer,G. (1985) Anal.Biochem. 151, 131-136.
23. Kim,C.H. and King,T.E. (1981) Biochem.Biophys.Res.Commun. 101, 607-614.
24. van Keulen,M.A. and Berden,J.A. (1985) Biochim.Biophys.Acta 808, 32-38.
25. Marres,C.A.M. (1983) Subunit structure and function of QH_2:cytochrome c oxidoreductase, PhD Thesis, University of Amsterdam.
26. Laemmli,U.K. (1970) Nature 227, 680-685.

EPR STUDIES OF THE QUINONE REACTION SITES IN BACTERIA

Steven W. Meinhardt, Xiaohang Yang[*], Bernard L. Trumpower[*]
and Tomoko Ohnishi

Department of Biochemistry and Biophysics
School of Medicine
University of Pennsylvania
Philadelphia, PA 19104   USA

[*]Department of Biochemistry
Dartmouth Medical School
Hanover, N.H. 03756   USA

INTRODUCTION

In the electron transport chain, the role of ubiquinone (UQ) as an electron and proton carrier has become more evident with the proposal of Q-cycle mechanisms for the cytochrome bc_1 complexes of photosynthetic bacteria (1-3) and mitochondria (4-6) and for the mitochondrial NADH:UQ oxidoreductase (7,8). An understanding of the interaction of ubiquinone, or menaquinone in some bacteria, with the protein complex is essential in defining its role in proton translocation and electron transport. In those complexes which react with ubiquinone the difficulty of converting from a two electron carrier, ubiquinone, to a single electron carrier, such as a cytochrome or an iron-sulfur cluster, has been solved by either the presence of two one electron acceptors which accept electrons in parallel from ubiquinol, as in the ubiquinol oxidase portion of the cytochrome bc_1 complex (1,6), or by the presence of a stabilized semiquinone species as in the case of Q_B in reaction center from the photosythetic bacteria (9,10) and Q_C in the cytochrome bc_1 complex (11). As an experimental medium in which to study electron transport, bacteria provide many advantages over both plants and animals. These advantages include a large diversity in the types of electron transport chains and complexes, the ease of controlling growth conditions, the possibility of genetic manipulation, and, in cases where complexes similar to those found in plants or mitochondria are present, the complexes are much simpler in subunit composition and often more stable. With these advantages in mind we have been investigating the electron transport chains of two bacteria. One, Paracoccus denitrificans, is very similar to the mitochondria in the number, types, and function of the complexes

---

Abbreviations: Modulation amplitude (MA), millitesla (mT), naphthoquinone (NQ), duroquinone (DQ), para-benzoquinone (PBQ), pyocyanine (PYO), 2,3,5,6 tetramethyl paraphenylene diamine (DAD), indigo disulfonate (IDS), indigo trisulfonate (ITS), phenosaphanine (PNS).

present. The other, Thermus thermophilus, which differs in many ways from mitochondria, has complexes which are stable and amenable to extreme experimental conditions. In this paper we will report on the quinone reaction sites found in the ubiquinol:cytochrome c oxidoreductase found in P. denitrificans and on a semiquinone species which we believe is associated with the NADH:quinone oxidoreductase of T. thermophilus HB-8.

THE UBIQUINOL: CYTOCHROME C OXIDOREDUCTASE OF P. DENITRIFICANS

The bacterium, P. denitrificans, has become of great interest to mitochondrial bioenergeticists looking for a bacterial model because it contains an aerobic electron transfer chain that has the same complexes as those found in mitochondria but that these complexes are composed of significantly fewer subunits. In P. denitrificans, the cytochrome c oxidase is composed of 2 subunits (12), rather than 7-8 in mitochondria (13), the ubiquinol: cytochrome c oxidoreductase is composed of 2 subunits rather than 8-11 (16-19) and the NADH:ubiquinone oxidoreductase if composed of only 10 subunits (20) while the mitochondrial complexes is composed of 25 subunits (21). This simplicity in subunit composition allows the clearer definition of the roles of each subunit in the function of the complex. In the mitochondrial cytochome bc_1 complex several subunits have been implicated to function in the binding of ubiquinone to the complex. Among these are the core protein II (22), the Rieske iron-sulfur protein (23,24), the cytochrome b apoprotein (25), a 15-17 kDa quinone binding protein (26,27), and a 12 KD protein which binds antimycin (25). In the isolated mitochondrial cytochrome bc_1 complex a thermodynamically stable ubisemiquinone species has been demonstrated and is referred to as Q_i or Q_c (11). The existence of a second ubiquinone binding site has been inferred from changes in the line shape of the Rieske iron-sulfur cluster EPR spectrum which coincides with changes in the redox poise of the ubiquinone pool (28). In addition a second semiquinone radical, Q_o, which is insensitive to antimycin and has a slightly different line shape from Q_i, has been shown in the isolated mitochondrial complex (29).

In P. denitrificans the cytochrome bc_1 complex is composed of the Rieske iron-sulfur protein, molecular weight (MW) 20 kDa, the cytochrom b apoprotein which contains both cytochromes b_{566} and b_{560}, MW 39 kDa, and cytochrome c_1, MW 62 kDa (15). The relatively large size of the cytochrome c_1 apoprotein has led to the suggestion that it may represent the gene fusion of the cytochrome c_1 apoprotein and the 12 kDa protein associated with antimycin binding (14). The demonstration of the ubisemiquinone species and the phenomena associated with their binding sites in the minimal three subunit cytochrome bc_1 complex of P. denitrificans would establish that the quinone reaction sites in the mitochondrial complex are contained, at least partly if not wholly, in these three subunits.

The isolated P. denitrificans cytochrome bc_1 complex exhibits an antimycin sensitive semiquinone radical at g=2.00, shown in Fig. 1, with a peak to trough width of (H)=0.8 millitesla. A potentiometric titration of the signal indicates a midpoint potential of +42 mV, at pH 8.5 and a maximal spin concentration of 0.57 per complex. This concentration represents a stability constant (Ks) of 0.22, assuming three quinones per complex (15). This concentration of ubisemiquinone is higher than previously reported for any isolated cyt. bc_1 complex (30-32) and indicates that the ubisemiquinone binding site has not been perturbed during the isolation procedure which is consistent with the high turnover of this preparation (15).

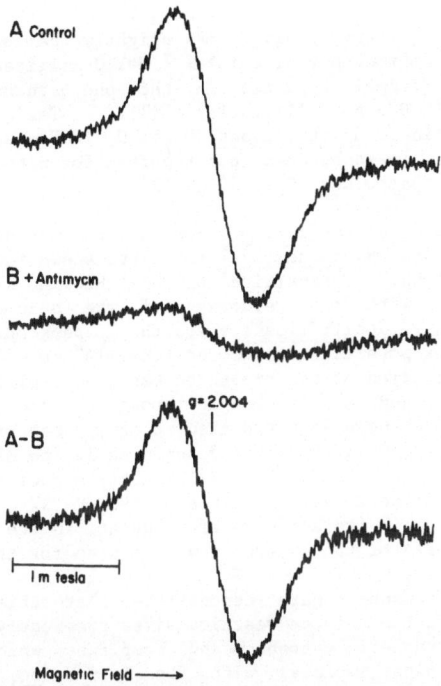

Fig. 1. EPR Sectrum of the Antimycin Sensitive Ubisemiquinone in the
Cytochrome bc_1 Complex of P. denitrificans.

The cyt. bc_1 complex, 21 uM, was suspended in 50 mM P_i-buffer, 350
mM KCl, $0.2g/L$ dodecylmaltoside and adjusted to pH 8.5 with 1M Tris.
Mediators present were 40 uM: 1.2 NQ, 1.4 NQ, 1.4 NQ-2-sulfonate, DQ,
DAD, PBQ, and PYO. EPR conditions: -133 C, MA 0.63 mT, and 10 uW.

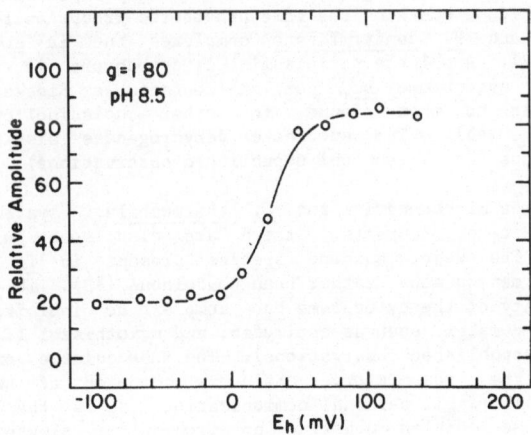

Fig. 2. Redox Titration of the Change in the Lineshape of the g_x
Transition of the Rieske Iron-Sulfur Cluster.
Samples were as in Fig. 1. The amplitude from the baseline to the
signal at g=1.80 is plotted.

This ubisemiquinone radical is slightly narrower than the one present in the mitochondrial complex (H=1.0 millitesla) (11,30) but is similar to the signal reported in the photosynthetic bacteria R. sphaeroides (H=0.8 millitesla) (31). The midpoint of the radical species in P. denitrificans, E_{m7}=130 10mV assuming a 60 mV/pH unit dependence, is in between that reported for mitochondria, E_{m7}=90 mV (33,34), and R. sphaeroides, E_{m7}=150 mV (31).

Previous studies of the cyt. bc_1 complex in bovine submitochondrial particles (34) and R. sphaeroides (35) have shown that there is a shift and sharpening of the g_x transition of the Rieske iron-sulfur cluster which correlates with the reduction of the quinone pool. A similar change is seen in P. denitrificans where the g_x peak shifts from 1.80 to 1.76 as the redox potential is lowered from +140 to -100 mV (36). Fig. 2 shows a redox titration of the trough to baseline amplitude of the g=1.80 signal as the potential is changed through the midpoint of the quinone pool. The signal changes as a two electron component with an $E_{m8.5}$ of 30 mV. Assuming a -60 mV/pH unit dependence in the midpoint, this would give a value of 120 mV, pH 7, which is slightly higher than that of the ubiquinone pool in bacterial membranes E_{m7}=90 mV (37). This may indicate a slight difference in the activity of ubiquinol in the detergent micell or a higher affinity of the quinone reaction site for the reduced form.

The results presented here demonstrate that this minimal complex contains both of the quinone reaction sites previously demonstrated with bovine and photosynthetic cytochrome bc_1 complexes which indicates that the other subunits isolated with the bovine bc_1 complex are not absolutely necessary for the quinone binding reactions and may play a role in regulating the function of this complex in mitochondria.

SEMIQUINONE SPECIES OF THE NADH:MENAQUINONE (OR UBIQUINONE) OXIDOREDUCTASE OF T. THERMOPHILUS

The electron transport chain of T. thermophilus is similar to that of mitochondrial and P. denitrificans in many ways. The aerobic electron transport chain is composed of a cytochrome c oxidase, cytochrome bc_1 complex, succinate dehydrogenase and an NADH dehydrogenase (38,39). The cytochrome c oxidase contains the same prosthetic groups as found in the mitochondrial and P. denitrificans complexes but is composed of 1-3 subunits (40-42). A soluble periplasmic c cytochrome is also present (43,44). The cytochrome bc_1 complex contains a Rieske iron-sulfur cluster similar to that found in other ubiquinol:cytochrome c oxidoreductase (45). The succinate dehydrogenase also has similar prosthetic groups (38, T. Ohnishi unpublished observations).

Although the mitochondrial and T. thermophilus systems are very similar in these respects, there are also some quite striking differences. The major quinone species present in T. thermophilus membranes is menaquinone rather than ubiquinone (39). This may explain the insensitivity of the cytochrome bc_1 complex to inhibitions of the mitochondrial complex such as antimycin, and myxothiazol (T. Ohnishi and G. Von Jagow, unpublished observations). The NADH:quinone oxidoreductase segment of the respiratory chain is composed of two different dehydrogenases (T. Yagi, personal communication) as is the case in E. coli (46). One complex contains no iron-sulfur clusters and is a single polypeptide. The other is rotenone sensitive and contains only 2 iron-sulfur clusters, one binuclear and one tetranuclear, both with

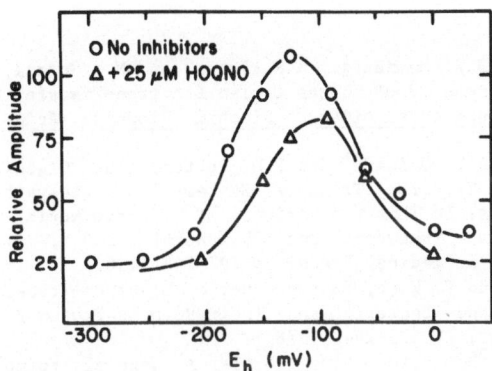

Fig. 3. Redox Titration of the g=2.00 signal in T. thermophilus
Membranes.

midpoint potentials near -260 mV (46). We have extended our direct
characterization of the electron transport chain of T. thermophilus to
the investigation of the semiquinone species present in the reductase.

T. thermophilus membranes (30 mg/ml) were adjusted to pH 8.0 with
1M EPPS and 60 uM of the following mediators were added: 1.2 NQ, 1.4 NQ,
DQ, PNS, DAD, IDS, and ITS. EPR conditions; -155 C, MA=0.63 mT, 1.0 mW.

At pH 8.0 we have identified three distinct semiquinone species
based on their redox midpoint potentials. The highest potential species
(E_{m9}=40 mV), is most likely associated with either the cytochrome $\underline{bc_1}$
complex or the succinate dehydrogenase complex, or may be a combination
of semiquinone species from both as in the case of submitochondrial
particles (11). A titration of the next lowest midpoint species, E_{m8} =
-125 mV, is shown in Fig. 3. The titration is wider than that
theoretically expected for a single species and is in fact composed of 2
species. When 25 uM 2-heptyl-4-hydrozyquinoline N-oxide (HOQNO) is added
there is a shift in the peak position of the titration. The midpoint of
the remaining species is near -100 mV. This species is much less
sensitive   to   HOQNO   and   is destabilized only at high inhibitor
concentrations, 250 uM HOQNO. Neither of these low potential species is
sensitive to the addition of 250 uM TTFA and probably do not arise from
the succinate:quinone oxidoreductase. Both of these species are
saturated at low microwave powers, with a $P_{1/2}$ of approximately 30 uW,
-150 C, with a peak to trough width (H) of 0.8 millitesla. At pH 9
these two species, combined, represent 0.7 spins per NADH dehydrogenase.
The concentration is much lower at pH 8.0 suggesting that they are
semiquinone anions. These preliminary studies indicate that the NADH
menaquinone (or ubiquinone) oxidoreductase has two stable semiquinone
species involved in the reduction of menaquinone. This then may provide
a mechanism by which this complex is able to pump protons with only two
iron-sulfur clusters present.

    This research partially supported by grants NIH GM 30736 and NSF
DBM85-11160.

REFERENCES

1. A.R. Crofts, S.W. Meinhardt, K.R. Jones, and M. Snozzi, The Role of the Quinone Pool in the Cyclic Electron-Transfer Chain of Rhodopseudomonas sphaeroides, Biochim Biophys. Acta, 723: 202-218 (1983)

2. R.C. Prince, D.P. O'Keefe, and P.L. Dutton, The Organization of the Cyclic Electron Transfer System in Photosynthetic Bacterial Membranes. Is This the Hardware of a Chemiosmotic System? , in: "Electron Transport and Phosphorylation" , J. Barber, ed., Elsevier Biomedical Press, pp 197-248 (1982)

3. A.R. Crofts and P. Wood, Photosynthetic Electron-Transport Chains of Plants and Bacteria and Their Role as Proton Pumps, Curr. Top. Bioenerg., 7: 175-244 (1978)

4. P. Mitchell, The Protonmotive Q Cycle: A General Formulation , FEBS Lett., 59: 137-139 (1975)

5. P. Mitchell, Possible Molecular Mechanism of the Protonmotive Cytochrome System , J. Theor. Biol., 62: 327-367 (1976)

6. B.L. Trumpower, Evidence for a Protonmotive Q Cycle Mechanism of Electron Transfer Through the Cytochrome bc_1 Complex, Biochem. Biophys. Res. Commun., 70: 73-80 (1976)

7. C.I. Ragan, T. Ohnishi, and Y. Hatefi, Iron-Sulfur Proteins of Mitochonrial NADH-Ubiquinone Reductase (Complex I), in: "Iron Sulfur Research" , H. Matsubara et al. eds., pp220-231, Japan Sci Soc. Press, Tokyo/Springer-Verlag, Berlin (1986)

8. C.I. Ragan, Structure of the NADH-Ubiquinone Reductase (Complex I), Curr Top. Bioenerg., in press (1987)

9. A. Vermeglio, Secondary Electron Transfer in Reaction Centers of Rhodopseudomonas sphaeroides. Out of Phase Periodicity of Two for the Formation of Ubisemiquinone and Fully Reduced Ubiquinone, Biochim. Biophys. Acta, 459: 516-514 (1977)

10. C.A. Wraight, Electron Acceptors of Photosynthetic Bacterial Reaction Centers. Direct Observation of Oscillatory Behavior Suggesting Two Closely Equivalent Ubiquinones, Biochim. Biophys. Acta, 459: 525-531 (1977)

11. T. Ohnishi and B.L. Trumpower, Differential Effects of Antimycin on Ubisemiquinone Bound in Different Enviroments in Isolated Succinate Cytochrome c Reductase Complex, J. Biol. Chem., 255: 3278-3284 (1980)

12. B. Ludwig and G. Schatz, A Two Subunit Cytochrome c Oxidase (Cytochrome aa_3) From Paracoccus denitrificans, Proc. Natl. Acad. Sci. U.S.A., 77: 196-200 (1980)

13. A. Azzi, Cytochrome c Oxidase. Towards a Clarification of Its Structure, Interactions, and Mechanism, Biochim. Biophys. Acta, 594: 231-252 (1980)

14. E.A. Berry and B.L. Trumpower, Isolation of Ubiquinol Oxidase From Paracoccus denitrificans and Resolution into Cytochrome bc_1 and Cytochrome $c-aa_3$ Complexes, J. Biol. Chem., 256: 2458-2467 (1985)

15. X. Yang and B.L. Trumpower, Purification of a Three Subunit Ubiquinol-Cytochrome c Oxidoreductase Complex From Paracoccus denitrificans, J. Biol. Chem., 261: 12282-12289 (1986)

16. J.S. Rieske, Composition, Structure, and Function of Complex III of the Respiratory Chain, Biochim. Biophys. Acta, 456: 195-247 (1976)

17. R.A. Capaldi, Arrangement of Proteins in the Mitochondrial Inner Membrane, Biochim. Biophys. Acta, 694: 291-306 (1982)

18. R. Gellerfors, T. Johnsson, and B.B. Nelson, Isolation of the Cytochrome bc_1 Complex From Rat-Liver Mitochondria, Eur. J. Biochem., 115: 275-278 (1981)

19. H. Weiss and H.J. Kolb, Isolation of Mitochondrial Succinate: Ubiquinone Reductase, Cytochrome c Reductase, and Cytochrome c Oxidase From Neurospora crassa Using Nonionic Detergent, Eur. J. Biochem., 99: 139-149 (1979)

20. T. Yagi, Purification and Characterization of NADH Dehydrogenase Complex From Paracoccus denitrficans, Arch. Biochem. Biophys., 250: 302-311 (1986)

21. Y. Hatefi, The Mitochondrial Electron Transport and Oxidative Phosphorylation System, Ann. Rev. Biochem., 54: 1015-1069 (1985)

22. M. LoRusso, D. Gatti, M. Marzo, D. Boffoli, T. Cocco, and S. Papa, Chemical Modification Studies of Beef-Heart Mitochondrial $b-c_1$ Complex. Effect of Modification by Ethoxyformic Anhydride, Eur. J. Biochem., 162: 231-238 (1986)

23. J.R. Bowyer, P.L. Dutton, R.C. Prince, and A.R. Crofts, The Role of the Rieske Iron-Sulfur Center as the Electron Donor to Ferrocytochrome c_2 in Rhodopseudomonas sphaeroides, Biochim. Biophys. Acta, 592: 445-460 (1980)

24. J.R. Bowyer, C.A. Edwards, T. Ohnishi, and B.L. Trumpower, An Analogue of Ubiquinone Which Inhibits Respiration by Binding to the Iron-Sulfur Protein of the Cytochrome bc_1 Segment of the Mitochondrial Respiratory Chain, J. Biol. Chem., 257: 8321-8330 (1982)

25. C.A. Yu and L. Yu, Identification of Ubiquinone Binding Proteins in Ubiquinol:Cytochrome c Reductase by Arylazido Ubiquinone Derivatives, Biochem. Biophys. Res. Commun., 96: 286-292 (1980)

26. Y. Wei, C.A. Yu, and T.E. King, Ubisemiquinone Radicals From the Cytochrome bc_1 Complex of the Mitochondrial Electron Transport Chain. Demonstration of QP-S Radical Formation, Biochem. Biophys. Res. Commun., 99: 1411-1419 (1981)

27. C.A. Yu, L. Yu, and T.E. King, The Existence of an Ubiquinone Binding Protein in the Reconstitutively Active Cytochrome bc_1 Complex, Biochem. Biophys. Res. Commun., 78: 259-262 (1977)

28. J.M. Siedow, S. Powers., F.F. De La Rosa, and G. Palmer, The Preparation and Characterization of Highly Purified, Enzymically Active Comlex III From Baker's Yeast, J. Biol. Chem., 253: 2392-2399 (1978)

29. S. DeVries, S.P.J. Albracht, J. Berden, and E.C. Slater, A New Species of Bound Ubisemiquinone Anion in QH_2:Cytochrome c Oxidoreductase, J. Biol. Chem., 256: 11996-11998 (1981)

30. T. Ohnishi, J.C. Salerno, and H. Blum, Ubisemiquinones in Electron-Transfer Systems of Mitochondria, in: "Function of Quinones in Energy Conserving Systems", B.L. Trumpower ed., pp. 247-262, Academic Press, New York (1982)

31. D.E. Robertson, R.C. Prince, J.R. Bowyer, K. Matsuura, P.L. Dutton, and T. Ohnishi, Thermodynamic Properties of the Semiquinone and Its Binding Site in the Ubiquinonl:Cytochrome c (c_2) Oxidoreductase of Respiratory and Phtosynthetic Systems, J. Biol. Chem., 259: 1758-1763 (1984)

32. S. Nagaoka, L. Yu, and T.E. King, Characterization of Ubisemiquinone Radical in the Cytochrome bc_1 Segment of the Mitochondrial Respiratory Chain, Arch. Biochem. Biophys., 208: 334-343 (1981)

33. S. De Vries, J.A. Berden, and E.C. Slater, Function and Properites of a Semiquinone Anion Located in the QH_2:Cytochrome c Oxidoreductase Segment of the Respiratory Chain, in: "Function of Quinones in Energy Conserving Systems", B.L. Trumpower ed., pp. 235-246, Academic Press, New York (1982)

34. S. De Vries, S.P.J. Albracht, and F. Leeuwerik, The Multiplicity and Stoichiometry of the Prosthetic Groups in QH_2:Cytochrome c Oxidoreductase as Studied by EPR, Biochim. Biophys. Acta, 546: 316-333 (1979)

35. K. Matsuura, J.R. Bowyer, T. Ohnishi, and P.L. Dutton, Inhibition of Electron Transfer by 3-Alkyl-2-Hydroxy-1,4-Naphthoquinones in the Ubiquinol-Cytochrome c Oxidoreductase of Rhodopseudomonas sphaeroides and Mammalian Mitochondria, J. Biol. Chem., 258: 1571-1579 (1983)

36. S.W. Meinhardt, X. Yang, B.L. Trumpower, and T. Ohnishi, Identification of a Stable Ubisemiquinone and Characterization of the Effect of Ubiquinone Oxidation-Reduction States on the Rieske Iron-Sulfur Cluster in the Three Subunit Ubiquinol-Cytochrome c Oxidoreductase in Paraccocus denitrificans, J. Biol. Chem., in press (1987)

37. K. Takamiya and P.L. Dutton, Ubiquinone in Rhodopseudomonas sphaeroides. Some Thermodynamic Properties, Biochim. Biophys. Acta, 546: 1-16 (1979)

38. J.A. Fee, K.L. Findling, A. Lees, and T. Yoshida, Respiratory Proteins of Some Extremely Thermophillic Bacteria, in: "Frontiers of Biological Energetics", P.L. Dutton, J.S. Leigh, and A. Scarpa eds., pp. 118-126, Academic Press, New York (1978)

39. M.G. Choc, R.M. Lorence, T. Yoshida, W.R. Dunham, and J.A. Fee, Resolution and Partial Characterization of Electron Transport Components of Thermus thermophilus: NADH -- Flavoprotein -- Menaquinone -- Rieske Iron-Sulfur Protein, in: "Flavins and Flavoproteins", pp 746-750, Elsevier North Holland Inc. (1982)

40. N. Sone, Y. Yanagita, K. Hon-Nami, Y Fukumori, and T. Yamanaka, Proton-Pump Activity of Nitrobacter agilis and Thermus thermophilus Cytochrome c Oxidases, FEBS Lett., 155: 150-154 (1983)

41. T. Yoshida, R.M. Lorence, M.G. Choc, G.E. Tarr, K.L. Findling, and J.A. Fee, Respiratory Proteins From the Extremely Thermophilic Aerobic Bacterium Thermus thermophilus, J. Biol. Chem., 259: 112-123 (1984)

42. J.A. Fee, M.G. Choc, K.L. Findling, R.M. Lorence, and T. Yoshida, Properites of a Copper-Containing Cytochrome c-aa_3 Complex: A Terminal Oxidase of the Extreme Thermophile Thermus thermophilus HB8, Proc. Natl. Acad. Sci. U.S.A., 77: 147-151 (1984)

43. R.M. Lorence, T. Yoshida, K.L. Findling, J.A. Fee, Observations on the c-Type Cytochromes of the Extreme Thermophile Thermus thermophilus HB8: Cytochrome c_{552} Is Located in the Periplasmic Space, Biochem. Biophys. Res. Commun., 99: 591-599 (1981)

44. K. Hon-Nami and T. Oshima, Purification and Some Properites of Cytochrome c_{552} From an Extreme Thermophile, Thermus thermophilus HB8, J. Biochem. (Tokyo), 82: 769-776 (1977)

45. J.A. Fee, K.L. Finding, T. Yoshida, R. Hille, G.E. Tarr, D.O. Hearshen, W.E. Dunham, E.P. Day, T.A. Kent, and E. Munck, Purification and Characterization of the Rieske Iron-Sulfur Protein From Thermus Thermohilus, J. Biol. Chem., 259: 124-133 (1984)

46. T. Ohnishi, S.W. Meinhardt, K. Matsushita, H.R. Kaback, Studies of the NADH-UQ Oxidoreductase System of the E. coli, in: "Structure and Function of Energy Transducing Systems", T. Ozawa and S. Papa eds., in press (1987)

EPR SIGNAL II IN PHOTOSYSTEM II : REDOX AND PARAMAGNETIC INTERACTIONS

WITH THE O_2 EVOLVING ENZYME

A. William Rutherford[1] and Stenbjörn Styring[1,2]

[1]Service de Biophysique, Département de Biologie
Centre d'Etudes Nucléaires de Saclay
91191 Gif-sur-Yvette cedex, France
[2]Present address : Department for Biochemistry and Biophysics
Chalmers Institute for Technology, S-41296 Göteborg, Sweden

INTRODUCTION

On the electron donor side of Photosystem II (PSII) there are two components, Z and D, which give rise to free radical EPR signals at g = 2.0046 (for a review, see ref. 1). These components appear to be spectroscopically identical but they have different kinetic properties. Firstly, Z gives rise to an EPR signal when it is oxidized by the photooxidized reaction center chlorophyll, $P680^+$. The EPR signal from Z^+ is designated Signal II very fast since Z^+ is rapidly reduced by electrons from water via the manganese cluster of the oxygen evolving enzyme. When the manganese cluster is destroyed or inhibited the decay rate of Z^+ becomes slower ; under these circumstances the EPR signal from Z^+ is designated Signal II fast (1). The component Z, then, is usually thought of as a transient electron carrier between $P680^+$ and the Mn of the oxygen evolving enzyme. In contrast, the second of the components, D^+, is very stable in the dark and present in virtually all intact PSII-containing material even after many hours of dark adaptation. The EPR signal arising from D^+ is designated Signal II slow. Despite its stability it is usually assumed that D/D^+ is a rather oxidizing redox couple with an estimated Em of 760 mV (2). Its stability probably arises from its location in a protein site inaccessible to reduction.

Although Signal II slow was one of the first EPR signals to be observed in photosynthetic material, the structure and function of D^+ has remained obscure. In this paper some new data on the redox and magnetic interactions of D^+ with the charge storage states (S-states, S_0-S_4) of the O_2 evolving enzyme are discussed along with speculation on the structure of Z^+ and D^+ based on the analogy with the bacterial reaction center.

D AS A DONOR TO S_2 AND S_3

Babcock and Sauer (3) and Velthuys and Visser (4) demonstrated that when D was present it could donate an electron to S_2 and S_3 with a $t\frac{1}{2}$ of about 1.5s at 20°C in chloroplasts. We have recently measured this reaction in PSII-enriched membranes and monitored not only D^+ but also the manganese multiline signal arising from S_2 (5). In these experiments D^+ was partially (50 %) reduced by ascorbate and the EPR signals were measured in samples frozen at given time intervals after 1 or 2 flashes (Fig. 1).

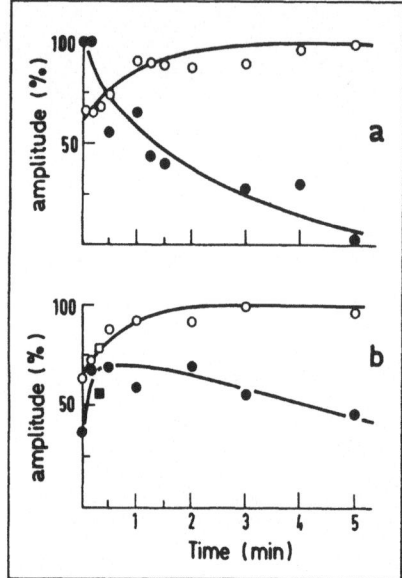
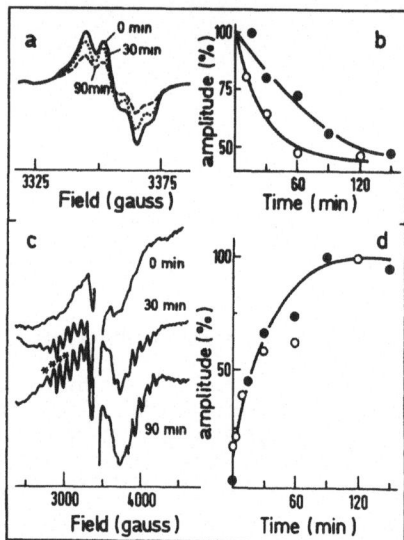

Figure 1 : Formation of Signal II slow (open circles) and changes in the amplitude of the S_2 multiline signal (solid circles) after 1 flash (a) and 2 flashes (b) in PSII-enriched membranes. Signal II slow was reduced to 50 % prior to illumination. Each point represents a different sample frozen with a variable interval after the flash illumination given at 20°C. The squares represent the same sample as that used for zero time, but which was thawed to room temperature and refrozen after 10-20 seconds. Samples contained 500 uM PPBQ. EPR conditions : S_2 multiline, 8 K, 8 dB, 22 G ; Signal II, 15 K, 0.5 uW, 2.8G.

Figure 2 a : EPR spectra of Signal II slow in PSII-enriched membranes after 3 flashes followed by 0, 30 and 90 min dark incubation at 20°C before freezing. b : Time course for the decay of Signal II slow in PSII-enriched membranes (closed symbols) and thylakoid membranes (open symbols) following 3 flashes. c : The S_2 -state multiline signal formed by illumination at 200 K in the same samples as in a. d : Formation of the S_2 -state multiline signal generated by illumination at 200 K of the same samples as in b. PSII-enriched membranes -closed symbols, thylakoid membranes- open symbols. Samples were given 1 preflash and 10 mins in the dark prior to flash illumination. EPR settings for Signal II slow and the multiline signal were as in Fig. 1.

After 1 flash an increase in the Signal II slow (D^+) amplitude was accompanied by a decrease in the S_2 multiline signal (Fig. 1A). The reaction is the following :

$$DS_1 \xrightarrow{\ 1F\ } DS_2 \longrightarrow D^+S_1$$

In a fraction of the centres a rapid oxidation of D takes place corresponding to the kinetics previously observed (3,4) but in the majority of centres the reaction is much slower ($t_{\frac{1}{2}} \sim 25s$). This is probably due to the isolation procedure. The slower kinetics, however allowed the reaction between D and S_3 to be studied using 2 flashes (the

542

minimum flash spacing for our laser is one second). Fig. 1B shows that the increase in Signal II slow (D^+) is accompanied by the formation of the S_2 multiline signal. The following reactions take place :

$$DS_1 \xrightarrow{1F} DS_2 \xrightarrow{2F} DS_3 \rightarrow D^+S_2$$

Again the electron donation from D to S_3 is slower in PSII enriched membranes than was reported for chloroplasts (5). Furthermore, fig. 1B is a direct demonstration of S_3 deactivation via S_2.

D^+ AS AN ELECTRON ACCEPTOR FROM S_0

Vermaas et al (6) showed that, contrary to the original model for the S state system (7), S_0 is not stable in the dark. Instead of the 25/75 distribution of S_0/S_1 which is commonly encountered in dark-adapted PSII centers, it was found that 100 % S_1 was present after long dark adaptation. However, in a fraction of the centers, D was present and could donate an electron to S_2 or S_3. These centers therefore required an extra reaction center turnover before oxygen was evolved, i.e. they appeared to be in the S_0 state before illumination (6). From these observations it was proposed that D^+ can accept an electron from S_0 forming D and S_1 (8).

We have recently verified this idea (5). Fig. 2 (A,B) shows that after S_0 has been formed by 3 flashes D^+ decreases in the dark ($t\frac{1}{2} \sim 20$ mins in thylakoids, ~ 50 mins in PSII-membranes) in a reaction in which S_1 is formed. S_1 formation was measured by the amplitude of the S_2 muliline signal photoinduced at 200 K (Fig. 2C,D). The following reactions take place :

$$D^+S_1 \xrightarrow{1F} D^+S_2 \xrightarrow{2F} D^+S_3 \xrightarrow{3F} D^+S_0 \xrightarrow{dark} DS_1 \xrightarrow{200K\ h\nu} DS_2$$

These results account for several previously unexplained phenomena : 1) the presence of 100 % S_1 in long dark adapted material, 2) the quantitative relationship between the centers in the D^+S_0 state prior to dark adaptation and those in the DS_1 state after long dark adaptation. 3) the decay of Signal II slow in a fraction of the centers (3). These and other phenomena are represented in scheme 1 in which real and apparent flash induced oxygen release patterns under different conditions are explained (5). Also in scheme 1 is shown the redox relationship between the S states and D.

This mechanism for the oxidation of S_0 to S_1 may exist to stabilize the Mn cluster if it is inherently less stable in S_0. This might be so, if for example Mn II is present in the S_0 state (see below) since Mn (II)

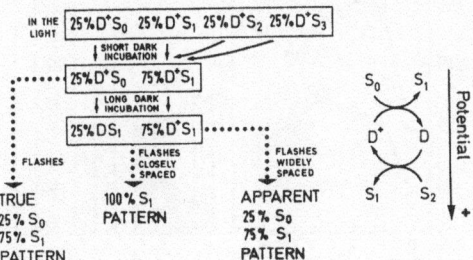

Scheme 1 : The redox interactions between D/D^+ and the S states. The left side of the Scheme shows the effect of dark adaptation and flash spacing on the oscillation pattern of the S states. The right side of the scheme shows the relative positioning of the redox couples on an arbitrary potential scale. Redrawn from ref (5).

often is more weakly bound to the protein than Mn III or Mn IV. It was also proposed that such an oxidation of Mn II by D^+ could play a role in the photoactivation process by which Mn is incorporated into the apoprotein (5).

D^+ AS A MAGNETIC PROBE OF THE S STATES

The saturation characteristics of Signal II very fast and fast (Z^+) change when the Mn is removed from the oxygen evolving enzyme (9,10). Using electron spin echo spectroscopy, Signal II slow (D^+) was recently shown to be sensitive to the presence of the Mn and to changes in the redox state of the Mn cluster during S state turnover (11). In this work the average spin lattice relaxation time (T_1) of D^+ was measured for each of the S states and it was reported that the relaxation rate became faster with increasing oxidation of the S states i.e. T_1^{-1} for $S_0 < S_1 < S_2 < S_3$ (11). This was interpreted in line with a model of Mn valence changes in which each of these S state transitions corresponds to a Mn III to Mn IV change (12). We have recently measured the microwave power saturation properties of Signal II slow (D^+) as a function of the S-states (13). Measurements of the S_2 multiline EPR signal induced by a sequence of flashes allowed a high degree of confidence in the states generated. The $P_{\frac{1}{2}}$ value for Signal II slow measured at 8 and 20 K after a series of flashes is plotted in Fig. 3A. The bar graphs (Fig. 3B) show the $P_{\frac{1}{2}}$ values for each S-state after correction for the photochemical miss factor (calculated to be 10 % from the oscillations of the multiline signal). $P_{\frac{1}{2}}$ for Signal II slow is low in the S_1 state but is increased upon formation of S_2. This agrees with the ESE measurements (11). However, in contrast to this earlier work the $P_{\frac{1}{2}}$ value (which is expected to be proportional to $1/T_1$) for Signal II slow in S_3 is virtually the same as in S_2 and, most strikingly, in S_0 the $P_{\frac{1}{2}}$ value is almost as high as in S_2 and S_3. At lower temperatures the $P_{\frac{1}{2}}$ is highest in S_0. The different temperature dependence of $P_{\frac{1}{2}}$ in S_0 as compared to S_2 and S_3 indicates that the fast relaxing species which interacts with Signal II slow changes between S_3 and S_0.

It is clear that these data do not correspond in a straightforward way with a model of manganese valence changes where an equivalent Mn III to Mn IV oxidation occurs on each of the S state transitions (11,12). Since the effects on the saturation of Signal II slow may reflect the magnetic properties of a cluster of up to 4 Mn atoms, the interpretation

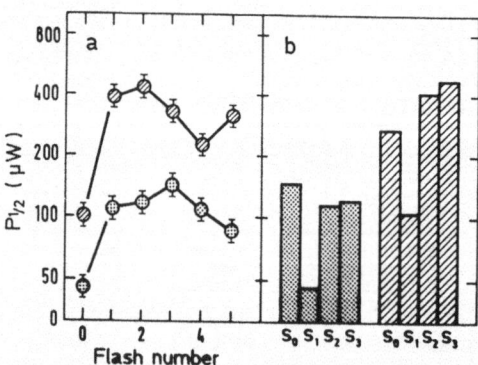

Figure 3 a : The $P_{\frac{1}{2}}$ of Signal II slow measured as a function of flash number in PS-II enriched membranes. b) The $P_{\frac{1}{2}}$ value for each S-state corrected for a 10 % miss factor. The lower plot in a and left hand bar graph were measured at 8 K. The upper plot in a and right hand bar graph were measured at 20 K. Experimental conditions were as in Fig. 2.

of these data in terms of redox states is rather difficult. Nevertheless a model with the following features might explain the EPR saturation data: 1) S_1, as the slowest relaxing state, consists of weakly or non coupled Mn ions (Mn III ?); 2) Mn is oxidized on the S_1 to S_2 transition* (Mn III to Mn IV ?); 3) no Mn is oxidized on the S_2 to S_3 transition; 4) S_0 represents the manganese in a different state (possibly a strongly coupled complex involving Mn II). Other data have indicated the absence of a redox change in the manganese cluster in the $S_2 \rightarrow S_3$ transition (reviewed in 1) and the presence of Mn II in the S_0 state (e.g. 14). It is worth pointing out the marked similarity between the Proton Relaxation Enhancement data (14) and power saturation data on Signal II (13). An unexpected rapid decay of the PRE in the long-lived S_0 state (14) also seems to be reflected in a similar change in the saturation measurements of Signal II slow (13). This could reflect a conformational change or a redox redistribution within the Mn complex.

THE STRUCTURE OF D^+ AND Z^+

The power saturation effects of the Mn cluster on D^+ and Z^+ indicate that these components are more equivalent relative to the Mn cluster than

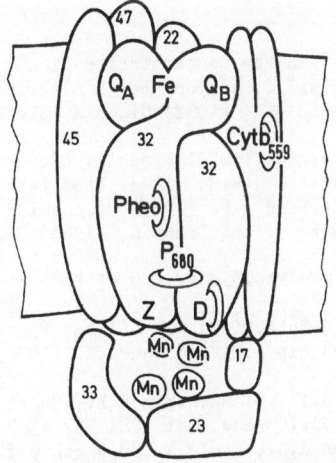

Figure 4 : A model of the PSII reaction center. The numbers represent the apparent molecular weight (KD) of the polypeptides. Q_A and Q_B are plastoquinone molecules molecules which act in series as electron acceptors and are associated with a ferrous ion, Fe. Pheo is a pheophytin molecule which acts as the primary electron acceptor. P680 is the primary electron donor chlorophyll. Other components are discussed in the text.

---

*Footnote : S_2 exhibits an EPR signal which arises from a strongly coupled mixed valence manganese complex.

was previously thought. This, taken with the fact that the two components are spectrally identical and yet functionally distinct leads to the proposition that Z and D may be located on the two halfs of the reaction center core i.e. on the D_1 and D_2 polypeptides. The model for the structure of PSII is based on the analogy to the bacterial reaction center obtained by X-ray crystallography (15). In the bacterial reaction center symmetrically located components have totally different functional properties despite being chemically similar (15).

As to the actual identity of Z^+ and D^+, the current view is that they are semiquinone cations since $\underline{in\ vitro}$ models have appropriate spectral and redox properties (1). However, extraction data have as yet provided no corrobative evidence and other candidates have not been ruled out. A favorite speculation currently circulating is again based on the bacterial analogy. In Rps. viridis a tyrosine molecule is located between P960 and the cytochrome c complex, indicating a role in the electron transfer reaction (16) ; in PSII, where $P680^+$ is much more oxidizing, a true oxidation of an analogous tyrosine could occur. A tyrosine cation could feasibly exhibit the spectral and redox characteristics of Z^+. Since D^+ may play a physiological role in photoactivation and redox priming of the S states, it could have been maintained throughout evolution as a tyrosine cation symmetrical to Z^+.

Other aspects of the structural model for PSII based on the analogy with the bacterial reaction centre have been discussed elsewhere (17-20).

ACKNOWLEDGEMENTS

We would like to thank Klaus Brettel and Orjan Hansson for useful discussion. A.W.R. is supported in part by the CNRS. S.S. is supported by a postdoctoral grant for biotechnological basic research provided from Knut and Alice Wallenbergs foundation, Stockholm.

REFERENCES

1. Babcock, G.T. (1987) in New Comprehensive Biochemistry, Photosynthesis (Amesz J., ed) Chapter 6 Elsevier, Amsterdam
2. Boussac A. and Etienne A.L. (1984) Biochim. Biophys. Acta 766, 576-581
3. Babcock G.T. and Sauer K. (1973) Biochim. Biophys. Acta 325, 483-503
4. Velthuys B.R. and Visser J.W.M. (1975) FEBS Lett. 55, 109-112
5. Styring S. and Rutherford A.W. (1987) Biochemistry 26, in press
6. Vermaas W.F.J., Renger G. and Dohnt G. (1984) Biochim. Biophys. Acta 764, 194-202
7. Kok B., Forbush B. and McGloin M. (1970) Photochem. Photobiol. 11, 457-475
8. Zimmermann J.-L. and Rutherford A.W. (1985) Physiol. Vég. 23, 425-434
9. Warden J.T., Blankenship R.E. and Sauer K. (1976) Biochim. Biophys. Acta 423, 462-478
10. Yocum C.F., Yerkes C.T., Blankenship R.E., Sharp R.R. and Babcock G.T. (1981) Proc. Natl. Acad. Sci. USA 78, 7507-7511
11. De Groot A., Plijter J.J., Evelo R., Babcock G.T. and Hoff A.J. (1986) Biochim. Biophys. Acta 848, 8-15
12. Dekker J.P., Plijter J.J., Ouwehand L. and Van Gorkom H.J. (1984) Biochim. Biophys. Acta 767, 176-179
13. Styring S. and Rutherford A.W. (1987) in preparation
14. Srinivasan A.N. and Sharp R.R. (1986) Biochim. Biophys. Acta 851, 369-376
15. Deisenhofer J., Epp O., Miki K., Huber R. and Michel, H. (1984) J. Mol. Biol. 180, 385-395
16. Michel H., Epp O. and Deisenhofer J. (1986) EMBO J. 5, 2445-2451
17. Rutherford A.W. (1986) Biochem. Soc. Trans. 14, 15-17

18. Trebst A. (1986) Z. Naturforsch 41c, 240-245
19. Rutherford A.W. (1987) Progress in Photosynthesis Research (Ed. J. Biggins) 1, 277-283
20. Deisenhofer J., Michel H. and Huber R. (1985) Trends Biochem. Sci. 10, 243-248

STUDIES ON THE UBIQUINONE POOL IN MITOCHONDRIAL ELECTRON TRANSFER

Giorgio Lenaz, Romana Fato and Giovanna Parenti Castelli*

Department of Biology and *Department of Biochemistry
University of Bologna
40126 Bologna, Italy

INTRODUCTION

Ubiquinone holds a central position in the mitochondrial electron transfer chain.[1] The majority of mitochondrial ubiquinone is dissolved in the lipid bilayer, constituting a functionally homogeneous pool, whereas an aliquot is bound to the respiratory complexes.[2] The most widely accepted organization of the respiratory chain is depicted in a random collisional model[3] of the complexes and their connecting substrates (ubiquinone and cytochrome c), whereby electron transfer between dehydrogenases and the bc_1 complex is assured by the lateral diffusion of the ubiquinone pool in the lipid bilayer, according to a kinetic behavior first described by Kröger and Klingenberg[4] (the so-called "pool equation"). In this model, the role of bound ubiquinone molecules would be confined to the electron transfer mechanisms within the individual complexes.

LATERAL DIFFUSION OF UBIQUINONE

In the random collisional model proposed by Hackenbrock[3], the diffusion of ubiquinone is explicitly postulated to control the rate of electron transfer: in agreement with this proposal, diffusion coefficients of the order of $\sim 10^{-9}$ cm^2/s were found by Gupte et al.[5] for a fluorescent quinone derivative by fluorescence photobleaching recovery (FPR) in fused megamitochondria. These low coefficients correspond to bimolecular collision constants of quinone interaction with the individual complexes of the order of 10^6 $M^{-1}s^{-1}$; this value seems "unconfortably close" to the second-order rate constant of ubiquinol oxidation by cytochrome b at center o or of ubiquinone reduction at center i determined in the bc_1 complex of Rps. sphaeroides chromatophores,[6] because it would assume a collisional efficiency very close to 100%; it may therefore be suggested, only on a kinetic basis, that the true values for diffusion coefficients of ubiquinone involved in electron transfer should be considerably higher. Diffusion coefficients greater than 10^{-6} cm^2/s were also suggested for plastoquinone diffusing between photosystem II and b_6f complex in chloroplasts[7] because of the distance involved, and on the basis of membrane viscosity;[8] the same reasoning concerning viscosity was also applied to ubiquinone in mitochondria.[9] Exploiting the collisional quenching of membrane-bound fluorophores by oxidized ubiquinone homologs, Fato et al.[9] obtained quenching collisional constants higher than 10^9 $M^{-1}s^{-1}$ both in lipid vesicles and mitochondrial membranes, corresponding to diffusion coefficients of $>10^{-6}$ cm^2/s.

The discrepancy of over three orders of magnitude between the results of Gupte et al.[5] and Fato et al.[9] has been the subject of recent debate between the two groups.[3,10] We have excluded that the fluorescence quenching method is grossly affected by static quenching or by other artifacts;[10] recently, M.F. Blackwell, K. Gounaris, S.J. Zara and J. Barber (personal communication) also employed collisional quenching of pyrene by plastoquinone and plastoquinol in lipid vesicles, developing an equation for calculation of quenching constants in two dimensions, and finding diffusion coefficients somewhat lower than those reported by our group, but still over 10^{-7} cm^2/s. Table 1 surveys diffusion coefficients reported up to now for ubiquinone and its analogs.

The reason for the discrepancy between the results obtained by FPR and those by fluorescence quenching may be ascribed to the range in which the two methods measure diffusion, viz. long-range and short-range diffusion, respectively.[10] Long-range diffusion in a membrane is retarded by obstruction of the diffusion path by the large protein complexes[11] (the so-called archipelago effect). Since electron transfer appears to be related more closely to short- or medium-range diffusion than to long-range diffusion,[10,12] the question whether ubiquinone diffusion controls electron transfer in the respiratory chain is open and requires direct demonstration by a kinetic approach.

LACK OF A DIFFUSION-LIMITED STEP IN UBIQUINOL CYTOCHROME c REDUCTASE

The kinetics of ubiquinol cytochrome c reductase is usually investigated with water-soluble ubiquinols as substrates[13] and is complicated by the fact that these molecules partition in a biphasic system, reaching the active site presumably from only one of the two phases (assumed to be the hydrophobic phase: lipid and/or detergent). We have developed a simple method

Table 1. Diffusion coefficients of quinones obtained by different methods.

System	Technique	Quinone	D (cm^2/s)	Reference
Fused mitochondria	FPR	"Q_2"[a]	3×10^{-9}	Gupte et al.[5]
Lipid vesicles	AS quenching	Q_3	6×10^{-6}	Fato et al.[9]
		Q_{10}	2×10^{-6}	Fato et al.[9]
			2.5×10^{-7}	recalculated[b]
SMP		Q_3	3.2×10^{-6}	Fato et al.[9]
Lecithin liposomes	pyrene			
	quenching	PQ	2.1×10^{-7}	Blackwell et al.
		PQH_2	2.1×10^{-7}	

[a]Abbreviations: AS, 12-(9-anthroyl)stearic acid; "Q_2", a fluorescent decyl quinone derivative; PQ, PQH_2, plastoquinone, plastoquinol.
[b]From ref. 9 by Blackwell et al. (personal communication).

to simultaneously determine the kinetic constants (V_{max} and K_m) of ubiquinol cytochrome c reductase and the partition coefficients of ubiquinols by performing saturation kinetics at different membrane fractional volumes (R.Fato, C.Castelluccio,G.Palmer and G.Lenaz,unpublished);the method allows to determine the minimal association constant,k_{cat}/K_m,in the lipid bilayer,and is therefore suitable for investigations related to a possible diffusion-limited step in the reaction.[14]

Determination of the true K_m of ubiquinol cytochrome c reductase

The method follows the outline given by Lakowicz[15] for the collisional quenching of membrane fluorophores by hydrophobic solutes,allowing the calculation of both the partition coefficient of the quencher and the true bimolecular quenching (rate) constant from simple fluorescence determinations at different membrane fractional volumes.

The ubiquinol concentration in the lipids $|QH_2|_L$ can be equated to:

$$[QH_2]_L = (P \cdot [QH_2]_{added})/(P \cdot \alpha + (1 - \alpha) \qquad (1)$$

where P is the partition coefficient,$[QH_2]_L/[QH_2]_{water}$, and α is the volume fraction of the membrane lipids in the assay medium. The Lineweaver-Burk equation with respect to ubiquinol (at saturating concentration of the second substrate,cytochrome c) can be written as:

$$1/v = 1/[QH_2]_L \cdot K_m'/V_{max} + 1/V_{max} \qquad (2)$$

where K_m' is the true K_m of the enzyme for the substrate dissolved in the membrane (in moles per liter of membrane lipids).Substitution of Eq. 1 into Eq. 2 gives:

$$1/v = \left\{ [P \cdot \alpha + (1 - \alpha)]/[P \cdot [QH_2]_{added}] \right\} \cdot K_m'/V_{max} + 1/V_{max} \qquad (3)$$

Putting $[P \cdot \alpha + (1 - \alpha) \cdot K_m']/P = K_{app}$ (the apparent K_m of the enzyme for the substrate in the total solution) and rearranging,we obtain:

$$K_{app} = \alpha \cdot (K_m' - K_m'/P) + K_m'/P \qquad (4)$$

Thus a plot of K_{app} vs. α allows the determination of both the partition coefficient and the true K_m of the enzyme. Double reciprocal plots of ubiquinol cytochrome c reductase activity at different α (obtained by addition of increasing amounts of asolectin vesicles to beef heart submitochondrial particles) and varying ubiquinol at fixed concentrations of cytochrome c, sufficient to saturate the enzyme,extrapolate to teh same V_{max},but K_{app} strongly increase with increasing α. Addition of phospholipids to the assay medium,increasing their volume fraction,decreases $[QH_2]$ in the lipid phase; thus the observation that the K_{app} increases with increasing the concentration of total lipids in the assay medium constitutes strong evidence that the substrate interacts with the enzyme by initially partitioning in the lipid bilayer.

Table 2 shows the kinetic constants obtained with different quinols.

Table 2. Kinetic constants of ubiquinol cytochrome c reductase
in submitochondrial particles*

	duroquinol	ubiquinol-1	ubiquinol-2
$K_m(QH_2)$ (μM in assay)	176	17.0	3.2
$K_m'(QH_2)$ (mM in lipids)	---	16.0	20.0
P (QH_2) (M_{lipids}/M_{water})	---	9.2×10^2	2.0×10^4
P (QH_2) (mole fraction)	---	3.8×10^4	8.5×10^5
k_{cat} (s^{-1})	42	283	1270
k_{cat}/K_m' ($M^{-1}s^{-1}$)	---	1.8×10^4	6.3×10^4
K_m(cyt.c)(μM in assay)	---	6.7	---
K_m'(cyt.c)(mM in lipids)	---	6.9	---
P(cyt.c)(mole fraction)	---	5.9×10^4	---

*Assay conditions:25 mM phosphate buffer,pH 7.5,25°C,following the
reduction of cytochrome c at 550 minus 540 nm.[13]

Note that K_{app} for duroquinol is independent of α,suggesting that this substrate analog may react with the enzyme from the water phase,and therefore
does not represent a good candidate to mimic the behavior of the natural
hydrophobic substrate,ubiquinol-10 (cf. ref. 16 for additional evidence that
duroquinol behaves differently from other quinols).

It is interesting that the same method can be applied titrating cytochrome c at saturating ubiquinol,indicating that also cytochrome c interacts
with the enzyme in a form bound to the lipid bilayer; a K_m of 6.9 mM cyt.c
with respect to the lipid bilayer (at 25 mM phosphate buffer) was obtained
by this method,corresponding to 9×10^{-3} cyt.c/lipid (mole fraction).The K_m
decreased by decreasing the ionic strength of the medium,indicating that
the "partition" of cytochrome c in the membrane is largely dictated by electrostatic interaction.

Evidence that ubiquinol cytochrome c reductase is reaction-limited

Since k_{cat} is higher with ubiquinol-2 than with ubiquinol-1,whereas
the K_m' remain roughly constant (Table 2),it is clear that the minimal second-
order rate constant for ubiquinol oxidation,k_{cat}/K_m',is also higher.It
therefore appears likely that the catalytic rate,at least with ubiquinol-1,
is reaction- and not diffusion-limited. Direct determination of the second-
order rate constant of ubiquinol oxidation at center o^6 yields a value of
3×10^5 $M^{-1}s^{-1}$ (in bacterial chromatophores). It seems therefore that the
rate constants of ubiquinol oxidation by the complex are higher for the
natural Q than with lower homologs,making it unlikely that the rates are
diffusion-controlled with any of the lower homologs.

The collisional frequency k_{coll} of ubiquinol with the enzyme can be
calculated from diffusion coefficients D of Q and bc_1 by the Smoluchowsky
equation:

$$k_{coll} = 4 \pi N' (D_Q + D_{bc})(R_Q + R_{bc}) \qquad (5)$$

where N' is Avogadro's number per millimole and R_Q and R_{bc} are the molec-

Table 3. Activation energies of some mitochondrial enzymes
and of ubiquinone diffusion and lipid viscosity.

Activity	Preparation	Activation energy* (Kcal/mol)	
Ubiquinol-2 cyt.c reductase	SMP	7.9	18.1
	Soluble	18.1	
	Proteoliposomes	11.3	18.2
	",+ cholesterol	18.1	
NADH Q$_2$ reductase	Complex I[30]	15	32
Succinate cyt.c reductase	Mitochondria[3]	12.9	
Succinate oxidase	Mitochondria[19]	9.1	17.0
ATPase	SMP[19]	12.0	22.0
Cytochrome oxidase	Mitochondria[19]	7.5	15.0
Ubiquinone-3 diffusion	Liposomes[9]	3.0	
	SMP[9]	1.7	
Viscosity**	Mitochondria	3.7	

* When two values are given,they are E$_A$ above and below break,respectively.
**Rotational correlation time of the lipid spin label 16-doxyl-stearate.

ular interaction radii of the two molecules.Using $D_Q = 10^{-6}$ cm^2/s and neg-
lecting the low value of D_{bc},and assuming molecular radii of 10 A for both
ubiquinol and the active site of the bc$_1$ complex,a k_{coll} over 10^9 M^{-1}s^{-1} is
obtained,at least three orders of magnitude greater than the second-order
rate constant of ubiquinol oxidation by the complex.

Diffusion-controlled reactions are characterized by low activation energies and by being viscosity-dependent.[17] Arrhenius plots of membranous
ubiquinol cytochrome c reductase exhibit a break at ca. 18°C,with increased
activation energy below the break [18](Table 3).Similar plots are obtained
with succinate cytochrome c reductase or succinate oxidase,[19] that use the
natural endogenous Q$_{10}$. The presence of a break in Arrhenius plots of membrane-linked enzymes is a well-known phenomenon usually ascribed to some
kind of phase change in the lipid bilayer,not corresponding,however,to the
main fluid-gel phase transition.[20]The activation energies of ubiquinol cytochrome c reductase,[18]succinate cytochrome c reductase,[3]and succinate oxidase[19] match closely with each other,suggesting that the activities may
have the same rate-limiting step.It appears unlikely that this step is ubiquinone diffusion,for two reasons:(i)we have demonstrated that the diffusion
of ubiquinol-1 is certainly not rate-limiting (see above);(ii)the activation
energy of ubiquinone diffusion is much lower than those of the enzyme activities (Table 3).Moreover,the activation energy of succinate cytochrome c
reductase[3] closely agrees with that of ubiquinol-10 oxidation by cytochrome
b in Rps. sphaeroides chromatophores,[6]suggesting that a rate-limiting component is comprised within this step;the fact that the physiological reaction using Q$_{10}$ has the same activation energy of the reaction using exogenous ubiquinols (and which is not diffusion-limited) and the observation
that the activation energies of enzymes not using ubiquinone are also within
the same ranges represent strong evidence for a catalytic mechanism of ubiquinol cytochrome c reductase where no diffusion-limited step is present.

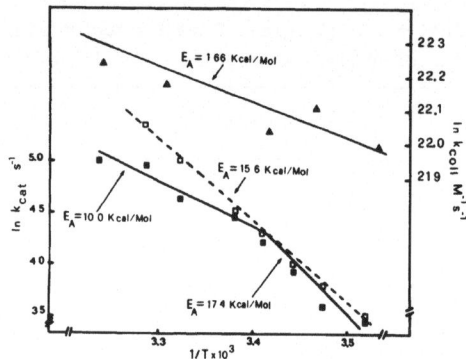

Fig.1.Arrhenius plot of ubiquinone lateral diffusion and of ubiquinol cyt.c
reductase activity in bc_1 proteoliposomes in presence and absence of
cholesterol.($\blacktriangle$),quenching constant of Q_3 in asolectin vesicles;($\blacksquare$),ubi-
quinol-2 cyt.c reductase (-cholesterol);($\square$),ubiquinol-2 cyt.c reduct-
ase (+cholesterol).The k_{cat}/K_m in the lipids was 3.3 x 10^4 and 3.1 x
10^4 $M^{-1}s^{-1}$,respectively.The fluorescence polarization of DPH,an index
of membrane viscosity,increased with cholesterol from 0.09 to 0.20.

The effect of viscosity was tested by incorporation of cholesterol in
the membranes;in spite of decreasing the diffusion coefficient of ubiquinones,[9]cholesterol resultes into an increase of ubiquinol cytochrome c reductase activity.The Arrhenius plot (Fig. 1) exhibits the disappearance of
the break,with increase of activation energy above the break.The fact that
the k_{cat}/K_m ratio is not decreased militates against the reaction being diffusion-limited. The increase of activity induced by cholesterol may find an
explanation in conformational changes of the enzyme by changed lipid environment;[20] the fact that k_{cat} can be increased represents evidence for
the removal of a rate-limiting step in the chemical reaction itself.

EFFECT OF INTERCOMPLEX DISTANCE ON NADH CYTOCHROME c REDUCTASE ACTIVITY

The time for a particle to diffuse to a small target of diameter d in
two dimensions is given by:[21]

$$t = (l^2/2D)(\ln l/d - 3/4) \qquad (6)$$

where l is the distance between the two objects.For a distance of 30 nm,the
average distance between Complexes I and III in the inner membrane,taking
$D = 10^{-6}$ cm^2/s and assuming a diameter of Complex III of 7 nm,the time for
a ubiquinone molecule reduced by Complex I to reach Complex III would be
5 μs. For a turnover of 100 s^{-1},close to the physiological rates of NADH
cytochrome c reductase,[22] this corresponds to 3300 collisions per turnover,
a very large excess.It may be asked,however,if conditions leading to enhanced respiratory rates,as an increased ATP request or loose coupling,could
render ubiquinone diffusion a control factor for respiratory activity.[23]

The problem of diffusional control in the ubiquinone region has been
approached experimentally by changing the distance between the redox com-

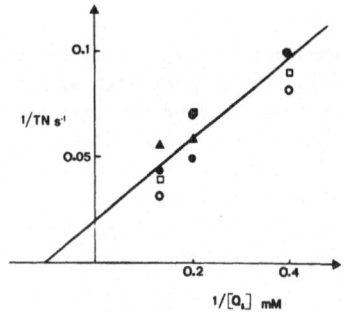

Fig. 2. Effect of increasing the distance between complex I and III on NADH
cyt.c reductase at different ubiquinone contents.The phospholipid
to protein ratios were:(o),10;(□),20;(▲),40;(●),80,corresponding to
38,54,76,and 108 nm average distance between the complexes.Data are
plotted as double reciprocal plots with respect to Q_6 concnetration.

plexes either by varying the phospholipid to protein ratio in reconstituted
systems or by phospholipid enrichment of mitochondrial membranes. Assuming
a random distribution of the complexes in the lipids,[3]an increase of phospholipid content results in increase of intercomplex distance;were ubiquinone diffusion the rate-limiting step,a proportional decrease of the overall
activity would be expected. Incorporating a crude NADH cytochrome c reductase (Complexes I plus III) in liposomes by cholate dialysis at different
phospholipid to protein ratios and ubiquinone contents (Fig. 2),the turnovers at each ubiquinone level are not affected,at least withın an experimental distance of 108 nm.

The phospholipid content of mitochondrial membranes was also increased
at different ubiquinone levels;[10,18]the loss of activity observed upon phospholipid enrichment was avoided by adding phospholipids plus ubiquinone,sug-
gesting that the decrease of NADH cytochrome c reductase,also observed by
others,[24,25] is due to dilution of the ubiquinone pool below the saturation
level of the enzymes,and not to a diffusion-limited step.Indeed the physiological concentration of ubiquinone is usually in the K_m range of the ubi-
quinone-reactive enzymes.[10]Accordingly,when the ubiquinone concentration is
kept constant,dilution of the complexes has no effect on electron transfer.
The physiological concentrations of ubiquinone are not sufficient to saturate electron transfer,[26] since the K_m of the bc_1 complex for ubiquinol-10
is 3.4 mM,[27] and the K_m of Complex I for Q_{10} is 10 mM.[28]This observation
raises the question whether one can artificially enhance electron transfer
by simply increasing ubiquinone concentration in the membrane.[23]

CONCLUSIONS

From the experimental evidence reviewed,it appears unlikely that ubiquinone diffusion is the rate-limiting step in electron transfer;the data
favor a random distribution of the complexes,with their redox interactions
coupled to,but not limited by ubiquinone diffusion.The observation[29] that
almost complete extraction of ubiquinone from the bc_1 complex has no effect

on cytochrome b oxidation by cytochrome c is incompatible with the cyclic schemes of intercomplex electron transfer so far proposed.We postulate that ubiquinone is required for the complex only as a reductant,with the pool in the lipid phase representing the free substrate and the bound ubiquinone as the enzyme-substrate complex meeting the steric and stability requirements for the two single electron transfer reactions,and not as a prosthetic group involved in the mechanism of electron transfer.

Acknowledgements. The research was supported by grants from the Ministero della Pubblica Istruzione and the CNR,Roma.Ubiquinones were kind gifts of Eisai Co.,Tokyo.

REFERENCES

1. G.Lenaz,Ed.,Coenzyme Q,Wiley,London (1985)
2. H.Suzuki and T.Ozawa,Biochem.Biophys.Res.Commun. 124:889 (1984)
3. C.R.Hackenbrock,B.Chazotte and S.S.Gupte,J.Bioenerg.Biomembr.,18:331 (1986)
4. A.Kröger and M.Klingenberg,Eur.J.Biochem.,34:358 (1973)
5. S.S.Gupte,E.S.Wu,L.Hoechli,M.Hoechli,K.Jacobson,A.E.Sowers and C.R. Hackenbrock, Proc. Natl. Acad. Sci. USA,81:2606(1984)
6. A.R.Crofts,J.Bioenerg.Biomembr.,18:437 (1986)
7. P.A.Millner and J.Barber,FEBS Lett.,169:1 (1984)
8. J.Z.Pedersen and R.P.Cox,4th EBEC Short Reports,Prague,p.413 (1986)
9. R.Fato,M.Battino,M.Degli Esposti,G.Parenti Castelli and G.Lenaz,Bio-chemistry,25:3378 (1986)
10. G.Lenaz and R.Fato,J.Bioenerg.Biomembr.,18:369 (1986)
11. J.Eisinger,J.Flores and W.P.Petersen,Biophys.J.,49:987 (1986)
12. S.Kawato and K.Kinosita,Biophys.J.,36:277 (1981)
13. M.Degli Esposti and G.Lenaz,Biochim.Biophys.Acta,682:189 (1982)
14. B.B.Hasinoff,Biochim.Biophys.Acta,704:52 (1982)
15. J.R.Lakowicz and D.Hogen,Chem.Phys.Lipids,26:1 (1980)
16. G.Lenaz,A.De Santis and E.Bertoli,In "Coenzyme Q",G.Lenaz,Ed.,Wiley, London (1985)
17. O.G.Berg and P.H.Von Hippel,Annu.Rev.Biophys.Biophys.Chem.,14:131 (1985)
18. G.Parenti Castelli,R.Fato,M.Battino,C.Castelluccio and G.Lenaz,Chem. Scripta,27 (1986),in press
19. A.M.Sechi,E.Bertoli,L.Landi,G.Parenti Castelli,G.Lenaz and G.Curatola, Acta Vitamin.Enzymol. (Milano),27:177 (1973)
20. G.Lenaz and G.Parenti Castelli,In "Structure and Properties of Cell Mem-branes",G.Benga,Ed.,Vol.1,CRC Press,Boca Raton (1985)
21. H.C.Berg and E.M.Purcell,Biophys.J.,20:199 (1977)
22. M.Gutman,In "Coenzyme Q",G.Lenaz,Ed.,Wiley,London (1985)
23. G.Lenaz and G.Parenti Castelli,Drugs Exp.Clin.Res.,10:481 (1984)
24. H.Schneider,J.J.Lemasters and C.R.Hackenbrock,J.Biol.Chem.,257:19789(1982)
25. R.Casadio,G.Venturoli,A.Di Gioia,P.Castellani,L.Leonardi and B.A.Melandri, J.Biol.Chem.,259:9149 (1984)
26. C.I.Ragan and I.R.Cottingham,Biochim.Biophys.Acta,811:13 (1985)
27. Q.S.Zhu,J.A.Berden,S.De Vries and E.C.Slater,Biochim.Biophys.Acta,680: 69 (1982)
28. B.Norling,E.Glazek,B.D.Nelson and L.Ernster,Eur.J.Biochem.,47:475(1974)
29. M.Degli Esposti,A.L.Tsai,G.Palmer and G.Lenaz,Eur.J.Biochem.,160:547(1986)
30. V.Poore and C.I.Ragan,In "Function of Quinones in Energy-Conserving Sys-tems",B.L.Trumpower,Ed.,Academic Press,New York (1982)

VI. QUINONE BINDING SITES: STRUCTURE AND FUNCTION: Short Reports

EFFECTS OF PROTEOLYTIC DIGESTION AND CHEMICAL MODIFICATION OF b-c$_1$ COMPLEX

ON THE Fe-S CENTER AND THE STABLE UBISEMIQUINONE (SQ$_c$)

T. Cocco, S. Meinhardt*, D. Gatti, M. Lorusso, T. Ohnishi*,
and S. Papa
Institute of Medical Biochemistry and Chemistry, University
of Bari, Bari. *Department of Biochemistry and Biophysics
University of Pennsylvania, Philadelphia, PA 19104

A study is presented on the effects of papain digestion on the activity and the EPR signals arising from the semiquinone radical (SQ$_c$) and the Fe-S center of bovine heart b-c$_1$ complex, these effects are compared with those exerted by the modification of the complex with ethoxyformic anhydride (EFA).

Papain digestion of the b-c$_1$ complex is affected by ascorbate reduction of the enzyme this showing that changes in the redox state of the electron carriers result in large conformational changes of the complex. Selective

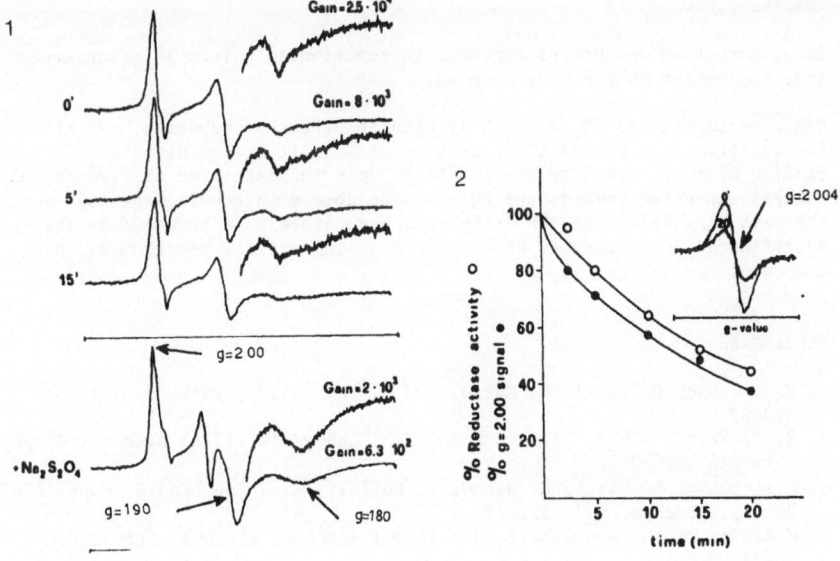

Fig. 1.   Effect of papain digestion on the EPR signal of the Rieske
          Fe-S cluster of the b-c$_1$ complex.

Fig. 2.   Effect of papain digestion on the height of g = 2.00 EPR signal
          of SQ$_c$ and reductase activity of b-c$_1$ complex.

digestion of core II and the 15 KDa protein in the oxidized enzyme, is accompanied by decoupling of proton pumping (1) without significant inhibition of electron flow. Digestion of the b-c$_1$ complex at high redox potential resulted in broadening of the line shape, of the EPR spectrum of the 2Fe-2S center, particularly evident at the g = 1.80 peak (Fig. 1). This spectral modification resembles that produced by full reduction of the complex by dithionite (2).

It appears then that the partial proteolytic cleavage of core II and/or the 15 KDa protein, effected by papain, results in modification of the protein environment of the 2Fe-2S cluster. Digestion of the core protein II seems to be primarily involved in this effects, in fact, broadening of the EPR spectrum of the 2Fe-2S cluster, similar to that caused by papain digestion, seems also to be produced by chemical modification by EFA of histidine residues in core protein II (3).

When the b-c$_1$ complex was reduced by ascorbate or when the enzyme was poised at 100 mV so that maximal formation of SQ_c was obtained, in addition to partial cleavage of core protein II and of the 15 KDa protein, the Fe-S center was extensively digested by papain. Under these conditions the content of SQ_c decreased along with the digestion of the FeS protein (Fig. 2). This shows that the FeS protein contributes to stabilize SQ_c. The cytochrome b apoprotein and the 12 KDa protein, tentatively identified as the antimycin binding component (4), don't seem to be involved in the binding of SQ_c. In fact, these two proteins were untouched by papain under conditions where the Fe-S protein was extensively digested and SQ_c was largely suppressed.

Furthermore, we have observed that papain digestion of the oxidized or reduced b-c$_1$ complex did not affect the red-shift of cytochrome b$_{562}$ induced by antimycin and promoted sigmoidicity in the titration curve of the inhibitor.

Thus, more than one protein appears to contribute to form an ubiquinone reaction pocket in the b-c$_1$ complex.

Since antimycin and SQ_c apparently bind to different subunits, but still the inhibitor suppresses the formation of SQ_c, it is conceivable that binding of antimycin A to the 12 KDa subunit induces large conformational changes extending towards the SQ_c binding domain in the Fe-S protein and the heme b$_{562}$ domain in the cytochrome b apoprotein as revealed by the specific red shift induced by antimycin in the optical spectrum of this component.

REFERENCES

1. M. Lorusso, D. Gatti, M. Marzo, and S. Papa (1985) FEBS Lett. 182, 370-374.
2. S. De Vries, S.P.J. Albracht, and F.Y. Leeuwerik (1979) Biochem. Biophys. Acta 546, 316-333.
3. M. Lorusso, D. Gatti, M. Marzo, D. Boffoli, T. Cocco, and S. Papa (1987) Eur. J. Biochem. 162, 231-238.
4. M.A. Van Keulen and J.A. Berden (1985) Biochem. Biophys. Acta 808, 32-38.

KINETICS OF UBIQUINOL CYTOCHROME c REDUCTASE: LACK OF A DIFFUSION-

LIMITED STEP WITH SHORT CHAIN UBIQUINOLS AS SUBSTRATES

R. Fato*, C. Castelluccio*, G. Lenaz*, M. Battino**,
and G. Parenti Castelli[**]

*Department of Biology and **Department of Biochemistry
University of Bologna, 40126 Bologna, Italy

The steady-state kinetics of mitochondrial ubiquinol-cyt.c reductase has
been investigated both in submitochondrial particles (SMP) and in the
isolated bc_1 complex using a new method to determine the concentrations
of ubiquinol in the lipid bilayer. The method, involving saturation
kinetics determinations at varying membrane phospholipid fractional
volumes α at saturating cyt.c, allows to simultaneously evaluate the
real K_m of the enzyme for ubiquinol-1 and -2 dissolved in the lipid
and their partition coefficients P, according to:

$$K_m(app) = \alpha \cdot (K_m - K_m/P) + K_m/P$$

where $K_m(app)$ is the apparent K_m in the total assay mixture and K_m is
expressed in mol/liter of lipid phase. Increases of phospholipid in the
medium decrease the actual QH_2 concentration in the lipids and therefore
increase $K_m(app)$. A plot of $K_m(app)$ vs. α allows determination of both
P and K_m. Table I shows that different $K_m(app)$ correspond to almost
identical K_m, a consequence of the different P. The K_m of duroquinol
is independent of lipid concentration, indicating that it may interact
with a different mechanism. The k_{cat} are independent of α, and much
higher with ubiquinol-2 than -1. It is also clear that the minimal second-
order rate constant for ubiquinol oxidation, k_{cat}/K_m, increases from
ubiquinol-1 to -2. It therefore appears likely that the catalytic rate,
at least with ubiquinol-1, is reaction- and not diffusion-limited.

Table I. Kinetic constants of ubiquinol-cyt.c reductase in SMP(25°)

	ubiquinol-1	ubiquinol-2
$K_m(app)$ (µM in total solution)	17.0	3.2
K_m (mM in lipid bilayer)	16.0	20.0
k_{cat} (s^{-1})	283	1270
k_{cat}/K_m $(M^{-1}s^{-1})$	1.8×10^4	6.3×10^4
P (M_{lipids}/M_{water})	9.2×10^2	2.0×10^4

The activation energies of ubiquinol cyt.c reductase above 18° are ca.
8-10 Kcal/mol with all ubiquinols tested, a value identical with those
reported for cyt.b reduction by endogenous ubiquinol-10 in Rps. sphaeroides

chromatophores $|1|$ and for succinate cyt.c reductase using endogenous Q_{10} in mitochondria $|2|$. The collisional frequency of ubiquinol with the enzyme, calculated from diffusion coefficients of ca. 10^{-6} cm^2/s directly measured by a fluorescence quenching method $|3|$, is 10^9 M^{-1}s^{-1}, i.e., at least three orders of magnitude higher than the second-order rate constant of ubiquinol oxidation by the complex (cf. $|1|$ for ubiquinol-10). The k_{cat}/K_m ratios are not decreased by increasing membrane viscosity through cholesterol incorporation (Table II).

Table II. Effect of cholesterol on the kinetics of ubiquinol-2 cyt.c reductase in bc$_1$ proteoliposomes (25°)

	Asolectin	Asolectin + cholesterol (2:1)
k_{cat}/K_m (M^{-1}s^{-1})	3.3 x 10^4	3.1 x 10^4
Activation energy (Kcal/mol)		
above 18°	10.0	15.6
below 18°	17.4	15.6
Fluorescence polarization (DPH)	0.09	0.20

This study allows the following conclusions: (i) Short chain ubiquinols interact with the enzyme from within the lipid bilayer, as does the physiological Q_{10} (with the possible exception of duroquinol). (ii) The oxidation of ubiquinol by the enzyme is reaction- and not diffusion-limited. The fact that the physiological reaction using Q_{10} has the same activation energy as the reaction with exogenous ubiquinols represents strong evidence for a catalytic mechanism where no diffusion-limited step is usually present.

The investigation was supported by grants from C.N.R. and Ministero della Pubblica Istruzione, Roma, Italy. Ubiquinones were kindly donated by Eisai Co., Tokyo, Japan.

REFERENCES

1. A.R. Crofts (1986) J. Bioenerg. Biomembr. 18, 437-451.
2. C.R. Hackenbrock, B. Chazotte, and S.S. Gupte (1986) J. Bioenerg. Biomembr. 18, 331-368.
3. R. Fato, M. Battino, M. Degli Esposti, G. Parenti Castelli, and G. Lenaz (1986) Biochemistry 25, 3378-3390.

VII. SPECIFIC REDOX SYSTEMS

BIOCHEMISTRY AND MOLECULAR BIOLOGY OF THE ESCHERICHIA COLI AEROBIC RESPIRATORY CHAIN

Yasuhiro Anraku

Department of Biology, Faculty of Science

University of Tokyo, Hongo, Tokyo 113, Japan

INTRODUCTION

The respiratory chains of mitochondria and aerobic bacteria play a fundamental role in the redox-linked proton pump (1). Cytochromes are the major functional units in the respiratory chain and are essential components in this energy transduction mechanism (2). Prior to this decade, remarkably little was known on a biochemical level about the cytochromes of the aerobic respiratory chain in E.coli. However, as reviewed recently (3), biochemical and molecular biological studies of the aerobic cytochromes have progressed rapidly, so the respiratory system has been mentioned as the most luxurious system to learn the biological and biophysical mechanisms of electron transport catalyzed by a ubiquinol oxidase. The main focus of this article is to describe the current status of biochemistry and molecular biology of the E.coli aerobic respiratory chain.

ORGANIZATION AND FUNCTION OF THE AEROBIC RESPIRATORY CHAIN

The respiratory chain of aerobically grown cells of E.coli K-12 contains seven main cytochromes, cytochrome b556, b561, b562-o, and b558-b595-d, which are arranged in the branched electron-carrying systems (3). Unlike aerobic bacterium Paracoccus denitrificance, E.coli, a facultative anaerobe, has dispenced entirely with a cytochrome c oxidase and its respiratory chain ends with two terminal oxidases, both possessing ubiquinol oxidase activities (3). The cytochrome b562-o complex is the sole terminal oxidase of cells in the early exponential phase of aerobic growth (4-9). Under culture conditions with a limited oxygen supply, the cytochrome b558-b595-d complex is synthesized adaptively as the major terminal oxidase (10-12) and these oxidase activities branch at the site of ubiquinone-8 (4,10). Both oxidase complexes function as coupling sites of the aerobic respiration (5,10,13).

Cytochrome b556 is a low-potential cytochrome that is a component of the succinate dehydrogenase complex (14-17). A membrane-bound diheme cytochrome b561 was found in a cytochrome b556-deficient mutant (18,19) and the structure gene, cybB, encoding this respiratory pigment was cloned (18) and sequenced (20).

Figure 1 shows a simple scheme for the functional organization of the respiratory chain and the coupling sites for oxidative phosphorylation in

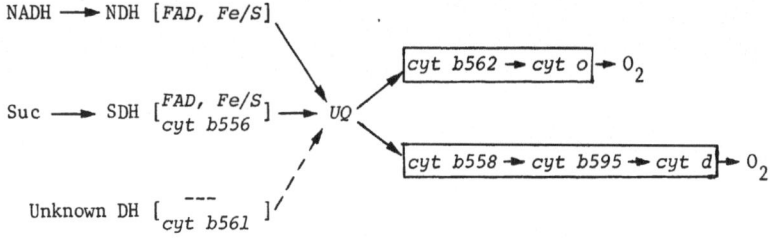

Figure 1. The aerobic respiratory chain of *Escherichia coli*

Abbreviations: NDH, NADH dehydrogenase; SDH, succinate dehydrogenase; DH, dehydrogenase; Suc, succinate; Fe/S, iron-sulfur protein; UQ, ubiquinone-8. Boxes represent the coupling sites of oxidative phosphorylation.

E.coli (see 3). Primary dehydrogenases, non-heme iron-sulfur components, ubiquinone-8 and all the cytochromes mentioned above are localized in the cytoplasmic membrane to organize the branched respiratory chains. Dehydrogenases such as NADH dehydrogenase, succinate dehydrogenase, D-lactate- and L-lactate dehydrogenases (not shown) oxidize respective substrate on the inner surface of the cytoplasmic membrane, and transfer the equivalent of 2 hydrogens ($2e^-$ plus $2H^+$) to ubiquinone-8. It is known that the ubiquinone present in the membrane of aerobically grown cells is about 50-fold per terminal oxidase complex, so that the ubiquinol-8 is thought to be a diffusible hydrogen carrier to reduce the terminal oxidase complexes. In other word, ubiquinone-8 serves as a two-electron carrier for branched ubiquinol oxidases (3).

The oxidation of ubiquinol on the molecule of terminal oxidases releases two protons and the two electrons liberated are transferred to molecular oxygen via sequential electron transport catalyzed by the oxidase complexes (Fig. 1). The electrogenic transfer of two electrons by the enzyme complex per vectorial liberation of two protons is responsible for the generation of a membrane potential across the cytoplasmic membrane. Formation of a membrane potential (about -150 mV) by the reconstituted ubiquinol oxidase complexes was observed with the fluorescence dye 3,3'-dipropylthiodicarbocyanine iodide on addition of an artificial electron donor ubiquinol-1 or ascorbate-phenazine methosulfate (5,10,13)

MOLECULAR PROPERTIES of LOW-POTENTIAL b-CYTOCHROMES

Two low-potential b-type cytochromes, cytochrome b556 and cytochrome b561, which both exist in the cytoplasmic membrane from aerobically grown E.coli cells and are reduced by several dehydrogenases, have been purified near homogeneity (14,19). Spectroscopic and protein-chemical properties of the two cytochromes are summarized in Table I. They are typical membrane proteins as judged by the polarity indices. Hydropathy analysis indicated that cytochrome b561 and cytochrome b556 have three and two membrane-spanning segments, respectively (20).

The cytochrome b556-deficient mutant E.coli K-12, strain TK3D11 could not grow with succinate as the sole carbon source, but could grow well on DL-lactate (16). Genetic studies indicated that the gene cybA encoding cytochrome b556 is located in the kdp-gltA region or at 16 min of the E.coli genetic map (15), very close to the location of the succinate dehydrogenase gene cluster, sdhCDAB (21). By comparison of the amino acid sequence of the amino-terminal of purified cytochrome b556 (16) with the nucleotide sequence of sdhC, one of the unassigned open reading frames in the sdh gene cluster(21), it was shown that the gene cybA is assignable as sdhC.

Table I. Molecular properties of *E.coli* cytochrome *b561* and *b556*

	Cytochrome *b561*	cytochrome *b556*
Gene	*cybB*	*cybA*
Map position (min)	31	16.7
α peak (nm)	561, 555	556
Heme content (mol/mol)	2	1
$E'm$ (mV)	+ 20	- 45
pI	9.6	8.5
Mr (SDS-PAGE)	18.0 KDa	17.5 KDa
(DNA sequence)	20,160	14,162
	(175 aa)	(128 aa)*
Polarity (%)	33.7	34.0
Function	Component of unknown gene cluster	Component of *sdh* gene cluster

* Purified cytochrome *b556* has lost the first three amino terminal residues, Met-Ile-Arg, with a molecular weight of 13,860.

   Cytochrome b561 was found as a minor b-type component in the cytoplasmic membrane from a mutant strain TK3D11 (cybA), which is deficient in biosynthesis of the cytochrome b556, and the structure gene encoding the cytochrome b561 was designated as cybB (18). A 20 kbp EcoRI fragment of the E.coli chromosomal DNA carrying the cybB gene was cloned by the plaque hybridization technique with Charon 4A as a vector. The gene was subcloned into pBR322 and was located in a 1.3 kbp DNA fragment(18). The nucleotide sequence of the cybB gene was determined and the amino acid sequence of the cytochrome b561 was deduced from it (20). The cytochrome b561 is predicted to consist of 175 amino acid residues, resulting in a molecular weight of 20,160 (see Table I).

   In order to examine the chromosomal location and physiological function of the cybB gene, a series of "Wreck and Check" experiments were carried out (Yamato & Anraku, unpublished). The kanamycin-resistant marker DNA was inserted into the unique Taq I site in the cybB gene on a plasmid pAM5167 to disrupt the gene. Then the disrupted gene was used for replacement of the intact cybB gene in a polA strain by in vivo recombination. The location of the disrupted gene was mapped at 31 min by P1 phage transduction with the co-transduction frequency of 95% with trg.

   The strain having the disrupted cybB gene did not show any notable defect of growth on various carbon sources such as glucose, glycerol, pyruvate, succinate, fumarate, malate, and D- and L-lactate, or of oxidase activities for respiratory substrates mentioned above and for oxalo-acetate, α-ketoglutarate, glutamate and proline.

SPECTRAL AND PROTEIN-CHEMICAL PROPERTIES OF UBIQUINOL OXIDASES

   Cytochrome b562-o complex ---- Purified cytochrome b562-o complex is composed of two major subunits with molecular weights of 33 KDa and 55 KDa, determined by gel electrophoresis in the presence of sodium dodecyl sulfate (6). These polypeptides are present in equimolar proportions, judging from the intensity of Coomassie Brilliant Blue staining of the bands. Chemical analysis indicated that the purified complex contained 1 mol of cytochrome b562, 1 mol of cytochrome o (b555), and 2 mol of Cu^{2+} per mol of a oxidase with minimum Mr of 88 KDa (Table II). A preparation of purified cytochrome b562-o complex by different procedure was reported to contain two addifinal minor polypeptides with Mr of 22 KDa and 17 KDa (9).

   Recently, an E.coli DNA fragment carrying the cyo gene cluster, which encodes the 33 KDa and 55 KDa polypeptides in this order, was cloned and

Table II. Molecular properties of *E.coli* ubiquinol oxidases

	Cytochrome *o* complex	Cytochrome *d* complex
Gene	*cyoA, cyoB*	*cyd*
Map position (min)	10.2	16.7
α peak (nm)	555, 562	558, 595, 624
Heme content (mol/mol)	1 heme *b*	2 heme *b*
	1 heme *o*	2 heme *d*
Copper content (mol/mol)	2	0
Mr, Subunit I	33 KDa (*cyoA*)	58 KDa (*b558*)
Subunit II	55 KDa (*cyoB*)	43 KDa (*b595,d*)
E'm (mV)	+ 125 (complex)	+ 140~180 (*b558*)
		+ 160 (*b595*)
		+ 240~260 (*d*)
ΔΨ formed (mV)	- 145	- 150~180
Function	coupling site	coupling site

the structure genes for the 33 KDa and 55 KDa subunits were designated as cyoA and cyoB, respectively (22).

The preparations of purified cytochrome b562-o complex were reconstitutively active in liposomes and formed a membrane potential of -145 mV with ubiquinol-1 as an electron donor (5).

The oxidation-reduction potential was determined by potentiometric titration (6). Cytochrome b562 and cytochrome o have apparently the same E'm value of +125 mV (pH 7.4), and this is pH dependent (-60 mV/pH) in medium of pH 6.0-7.4.

Cytochrome b558-b595-d complex ---- The complex has been purified to near homogeneity and contains two subunits in a ratio of 1:1 (10,11). Subunit I (Mr, 58 KDa) and subunit II (Mr, 43 KDa) are both encoded by the cyd locus, which appears to be a two-cistron operon (23,24). Recently, Lorence et. al (12) demonstrated that the purified complex contains two b type cytochromes (cytochrome b558 and b595) and two cytochrome d per minimal mass of the oxidase (Table II). Furthermore, they definitely showed that subunit I contains the cytochrome b558, while the cytochrome b595 and cytochrome d are located in subunit II.

The oxidation-reduction potential of each cytochrome in the complex was determined by the potentiometric titration of the ESR signals and the optical spectra (see Ref. 12,25 and Table II). The redox reaction catalyzed by the cytochrome b558-b595-d complex generates an electrochemical proton gradient of 150 mV~180 mV, negative inside, across the cytoplasmic membrane or the bilayer phospholipid membrane in reconstituded liposomes (10,13), showing that the physiological function of the complex is a coupling site of oxidative phosphorylation.

ENZYMATIC PROPERTIES OF UBIQUINOL OXIDASES

The enzymological studies of the two terminal oxidase complexes as ubiquinol oxidases have been performed and the results obtained are summarized in Table III. The ubiquinol oxidase activity of the purified cytochrome b562-o complex can be measured by following the absorbance change of ubiquinol-1 at 278 nm, or the rate of oxygen consumption using an oxygen electrode. Under the conditions used (6) the same Km value for ubiquinol-1 (48 μM) was obtained in both these assay systems. The Vmax values were 31.2 μmol ubiquinol-1 oxidized/min/nmol of cytochrome o and 15.0 μmol oxygen consumed/min/nmol cytochrome o, respectively (6). These values indicate that 2 mol of H_2O is formed from 1 mol of oxygen and 2 mol of ubiquinol-1 in the overall oxidation reaction, namely,

Table III. Enzymatic properties of *E.coli* ubiquinol oxidases

	Cytochrome *o* complex	Cytochrome *d* complex
Substrate (*K*m, μM)		
Ubiquinol-1	48	230
Menadiol	38	1.7
TMPD	9.5	18
O_2	2.9	0.38
Inhibitor (mM)*		
KCN	0.01	2
NaN_3	15	400
H_2O_2	300	120
HQNO	0.002	0.007
Piericidin A	0.002	0.015
$ZnCl_2$	0.001	0.060

* Concentration for 50% inhibition of the activity.
  Abbreviations: TMPD, N,N,N',N'-tetramethyl-p-phenylene-
  diamine dihydrochloride; HQNO, 2-heptyl-4-hydroxyquinoline
  N-oxide.

$$2UQ_1H_2 + O_2 \longrightarrow 2UQ_1 + 2H_2O$$

where UQ_1H_2 is ubiquinol-1. Similar but less stoichiometric relation
between the ubiquinol oxidation and the oxygen consumption was observed
for the overall oxidation reaction with the cytochrome b558-b595-d complex
in enriched membranes (10). From these observations, it was concluded that
both terminal oxidases function as ubiquinol oxidases.

Table III shows that the cytochrome b558-b595-d complex has the
highest affinity for oxygen of all the terminal oxidases so far known
(10). Similar to the mitochondrial cytochrome c oxidase, the E.coli
ubiquinol oxidase activities are inhibited by respiratory inhibitors. It
should be noted that the concentration of KCN required for 50% inhibition
is 10μM for cytochrome o and 2 mM for cytochrome d (Table III) whereas it
is 1μM for cytochrome a_3 (10). These results provide a new viewpoint in
considering the evolution of terminal oxidases with different heme
prosthetic groups in relation to atmospheric oxygen on the earth.

ASSIGNMENT OF THE SPIN STATES OF THE HEME-IRONS IN THE UBIQUINOL OXIDASE
COMPLEXES

Cytochrome b562-o complex ---- The ESR signals of the cytochrome
b562-o complex in purified enzyme and in enriched membranes have been
measured and assigned at liquid helium temperature (25). Under the air-
oxidized conditions the complex gives signals at g = 6.0, 3,0 and 2.26.
Since KCN is known to react with the cytochrome o (6), the effect of KCN
on the ESR spectra was measured. Upon addition of 10 mM KCN, the signal
intensity from the high spin heme (g = 6.0) decreased, and the rhombicity
of the g values of the two low-spin signals (g = 3.0 and 2.26) decreared
about 20 G. From this and other evidence (25), the ferric high spin
species of the complex was attributed to the cytochrome o.

The consistent result with this conclusion was obtained from a
resonance Raman study (26). For the complex in the dithionite-reduced
state, resonance Raman lines were observed at 1494 and 1473 cm^{-1} with a
406.7-nm excitation, indicating the occurrence of low spin and high spin
components. In the air-oxidized state with a 413.1-nm excitation, there
appeared 1372, 1503, and 1580 cm^{-1} lines, indicating that there is a

ferric low spin heme in the complex. In addition, a weak but appreciable Raman line was observed at 1480 cm^{-1} assignable to a ferric high spin heme. Accordingly, it has been concluded that the complex has low spin and high spin components in both of its reduced and air-oxidized states and the ferrous high spin component may be attributed to the cytochrome o. On the basis of these observations, it is indicated that the cytochrome o component is a high-spin species and the cytochrome b562 component is a low-spin species in both of the ferric and the ferrous states (26). This is a similar implication which was reached for the cytochrome aa$_3$(27); the cytochrome b562 corresponds to the cytochrome a and the cytochrome o corresponds to the cytochrome a$_3$. An ESR signal derived from cupric ions in the purified complex was observed near g = 2.0 (25).

In the CO-ligated state, with a defocused laser beam of 413.1-nm, two Raman bands assignable to the Fe-CO stretching mode have been observed at 489 and 523 cm^{-1}, as a major and a minor component, respectively (26). The " major" CO-binding site is labile to photodissociation and is similar to the known sites of "major" CO-ligated heme proteins, whereas the "minor" CO-binding site is an additional anomalous site in the complex and is resistant to photodissociation. Although no more detail of this anomalous site is known, one may speculate that the copper atoms in the oxidase complex may play a role in fixing CO in the site.

Cytochrome b558-b595-d complex ---- Measurements of the ESR spectra of the purified complex at cryogenic temperature were carried out under the air-oxidized and anaerobically oxidized cnditions (25,28). Potentiometric titration showed that the oxidized cytochrome b558 gives an axial high spin signal at g = 6.0 and that the oxidized cytochrome d gives low spin signals at g = 2.5 and 2.3. The oxidized cytochrome d shows the intense low spin signals, while the cytochrome d under the air-oxidized conditions gives corresponding signals of only very low intensity and is ESR-silent, indicating that under the air-oxidized conditions most of the cytochrome d contains a diamagnetic iron atom with a bound dioxygen (see Table IV).

Table IV. Molecular formulae and *g*-values of the heme components of the ubiquinol oxidase cytochrome *d* complex

	Molecular formula	*g*-value		
		b558	*b595*	*d*
Oxidized	$b558^{3+}b595^{3+}d^{3+}$	6.0	~6.3, ~5.5	2.5, 2.3
O$_2$-binding Intermediate I	$b558^{2+}b595^{2+}(d^{2+}.O_2)$	-^{a}	-	-
O$_2$-binding Intermediate II	$b558^{2+}b595^{3+}(d^{2+}.O_2)^-$	-	6.3, 5.5	2.15
O$_2$-binding Intermediate III	$b558^{3+}b595^{3+}(d^{2+}.O_2)^{2-}$	6.0	6.3, 5.5	-
O$_2$-binding Intermediate IV^b	$b558^{3+}b595^{3+}(d^{2+}.O_2)$	6.0	-	-

a, ESR-silent.   b, Air-oxidized form.

In addition to the results mentioned above, the weak rhombic signals at g = 6.3 and 5.5 - 5.7 were observed in enriched memrane preparations in the Eh range between 40 and 200 mV (25). The intensities and g values of the rhombic high spin signals changed when the electronic state of cytochrome d was changed from the oxidized state to the reduced or oxygen-binding or CO-binding state (28). These rhombic signals were therefore assigned to cytochrome b595 (see Table IV), which is located near cytochrome d in the oxidase complex (28).

ELECTRON TRANSPORT IN THE UBIQUINOL OXIDASE CYTOCHROME b558-b595-d COMPLEX

To study the roles of the three heme components in the reduction of ligated oxygen, redox intermediates of the complex were trapped under the conditions of controlled low temperature following photolysis and ligand exchange of the reduced CO-complex in the presence of oxygen. The ESR spectra of three intermediate forms were detected and those were designated as the O_2-binding intermediate I (ESR-silent), O_2-binding intermediate II (g=6.3, 5.5 and 2.15), and O_2-binding intermediate III (g=6.3, 5.5 and 6.0) (28). Assignment of the ESR signals including axial and rhombic high spin hemes and a low spin heme has been carried out and the result is shown in Table IV.

Namely, laser photolysis of the reduced CO-ligated cytochrome d complex in the presence of oxygen causes a ligand exchange reaction at -140°C (28):

$$(b558)^{2+}.(b595)^{2+}.(d^{2+}.CO) \xrightarrow{+O_2,-CO} (b558)^{2+}.(b595)^{2+}.(d^{2+}.O_2)$$

The cytochrome d becomes a diamagnetic O_2-binding form and the O_2-binding intermediate I is a starting cytochrome $d\text{-}O_2$ complex for the reduction of the ligated dioxygen. On incubation at -120°C, one electron transport from the cytochrome b595 to the cytochrome $d^{2+}.O_2$ occurs to form O_2-binding intermediate II as in Eqn. 2 of Fig. 2. The next step of electron

$$b558^{2+}\cdot b595^{2+}\cdot (d^{2+}\cdot O_2) \longrightarrow b558^{2+}\cdot b595^{3+}\cdot (d^{2+}\cdot O_2)^{-} \qquad \text{(Eqn. 2)}$$

$$b558^{2+}\cdot b595^{3+}\cdot (d^{2+}\cdot O_2)^{-} \longrightarrow b558^{3+}\cdot b595^{3+}\cdot (d^{2+}\cdot O_2)^{2-} \qquad \text{(Eqn. 3)}$$

$$b558^{3+}\cdot b595^{3+}\cdot (d^{2+}\cdot O_2)^{2-} \xrightarrow[UQH_2 \;\; UQ]{2H^+} b558^{2+}\cdot b595^{2+}\cdot (d^{2+}\cdot O_2)^{2-} \qquad \text{(Eqn. 4)}$$

$$b558^{2+}\cdot b595^{2+}\cdot (d^{2+}\cdot O_2)^{2-} \xrightarrow[4H^+ \;\; O_2]{2H_2O} b558^{3+}\cdot b595^{3+}\cdot (d^{2+}\cdot O_2) \qquad \text{(Eqn. 5)}$$

$$b558^{3+}\cdot b595^{3+}\cdot (d^{2+}\cdot O_2) \xrightarrow[UQH_2 \;\; UQ]{2H^+} b558^{2+}\cdot b595^{2+}\cdot (d^{2+}\cdot O_2) \qquad \text{(Eqn. 6)}$$

Figure 2. A redox reaction cycle catalyzed by the ubiquinol oxidase cytochrome *b558-b595-d* complex
Abbreviations: UQH_2, ubiquinol-8; UQ, ubiquinone-8.

transport occurs at about -40°C from the cytochrome b558 via cytochrome b595 to the reduced intermediate form of the cytochrome $d\text{-}O_2$ complex as in Eqn. 3. The O_2-binding intermediate III thus formed is assumed to react with ubiquinol-8 (UQH_2) to form a putative intermediate of highly reduced state as shown in Eqn. 4. This reaction takes place because the cytochrome b558 has a similar E'm value to that of the cytochrome b595 (see Table II).

Since the cytochrome d complex catalyzes the redox reaction cycle facilitating four electron chemistry with ubiquinol-8 and dioxygen (10), the putative intermediate in Eqn. 4 is assumed to accept 4 protons to generate 2 molecules of water followed by binding of dioxygen, leading to the formation of the air-oxidized cytochrome d complex or the O_2-binding intermediate IV (see Eqn. 5 and Table IV). The O_2-binding intermediate IV reacts with ubiquinol-8 to give the O_2-binding intermediate I for initiation of the next redox cycle as in Eqn. 6.

From all these results, electron flow in the cytochrome d complex is concluded to proceed in the order,

$$\text{cytochrome b558} \rightarrow \text{cytochrome b595} \rightarrow \text{cytochrome d} \rightarrow O_2$$

A model of the mechanism of four electron chemistry for oxidation of ubiquinol-8 and formation of water by the cytochrome d complex is plausible so far as the results of the present ESR study are concerned (28). Thermodynamically, the redox reaction can be expressed as ;

$$2UQH_2 + O_2 + 4H^+_{in} \longrightarrow 2UQ + 2H_2O + 4H^+_{out}$$

where H^+_{in} and H^+_{out} represent the proton species inside and outside the cytoplasmic membrane, respectively.

SUMMARY

The aerobic respiratory chain of E.coli is composed of two sets of the terminal oxidase cytochrome b562-o and cytochrome b558-b595-d complexes. The two terminal oxidases function as ubiquinol oxidases and generate an electrochemical proton gradient across the cytoplasmic membrane. The chemical and thermodynamic reactions catalyzed by the enzyems are established. The cytochrome b558-b595-d complex catalyzes four electron chemistry for oxidation of 2 mol of ubiquinol-8 and formation of 2 mol of water. The mechanism of electron transport in the complex and a model for the redox reaction cycle are proposed.

E.coli provides a luxurious genetic source for biochemical study of ubiquinol oxidases. Many structure genes encoding the heme proteins in the aerobic respiratory chain have been cloned and sequenced. The current status of molecular biology of E.coli aerobic cytochromes is described.

ACKNOWLEDGEMENTS

The author wishes to express his gratitude to his former and present colleagues who made the original work discussed in this article. Research quoted from the author's laboratory was supported by grants from the Ministry of Education, Science and Culture of Japan, Special Coordination Funds for Promotion of Science and Technology from the Science and Technology Agency of Japan, and the Yamada Science Foundation, Japan.

REFERENCES

1. P. Mitchell, Chemiosmotic coupling in oxidative and photosynthetic phosphorylation, Biol. Rev. Cambridge Philos. Soc., 11:445 (1966).
2. M. Wikström, K. Krab, and M. Saraste, Proton-translocating cytochrome complexes, Ann. Rev. Biochem., 50:623 (1981).
3. Y. Anraku, and R. B. Gennis, The aerobic respiratory chain of Escherichia coli, Trends Biochem. Sci., in press (1987).
4. K. Kita, and Y. Anraku, Composition and sequence of b cytochromes in the respiratory chain of aerobically grown Escherichia coli K-12 in the early exponential phase, Biochem. Int., 2:105 (1981).
5. K. Kita, M. Kasahara, and Y. Anraku, Formation of a membrane potential by reconstituted liposomes made with cytochrome b562-o

complex, a terminal oxidase of Escherichia coli K-12, J. Biol. Chem., 257:7933 (1982).

6. K. Kita, K. Konishi, and Y. Anraku, Terminal oxidases of Escherichia coli aerobic respiratory chain: I. Purification and properties of cytochrome b562-o complex from cells in the early exponential phase of aerobic growth, J. Biol. Chem., 259:3368 (1984).

7. K. Kita, H. Murakami, H. Oya, and Y. Anraku, Quantitative determination of cytochromes in the aerobic respiratory chain of Escherichia coli by high-performance liquid chromatography and its application to analysis of mitochondrial cytochromes, Biochem. Int., 10:319 (1985).

8. K. Kita, K. Konishi, and Y. Anraku, Purification and properties of two terminal oxidase complexes of Escherichia coli aerobic respiratory chain, in: Methods in Enzymol., S. Fleischer and B. Fleischer, eds., 126:94 (1986).

9. K. Matsushita, L. Patel, and H. R. Kaback, Cytochrome o type oxidase from Escherichia coli: Characterization of the enzyme and mechanism of electrochemical proton gradient generation, Biochemistry, 23:4703 (1984).

10. K. Kita, K. Konishi, and Y. Anraku, Terminal oxidases of Escherichia coli aerobic respiratory chain: II. Purification and properties of cytochrome b558-d complex from cells grown with limited oxygen and evidence of branched electron-carrying systems, J. Biol. Chem., 259:3375 (1984).

11. M. J. Miller, and R. B. Gennis, The purification and characterization of the cytochrome d terminal oxidase complex of the Escherichia coli aerobic respiratory chain, J. Biol. Chem., 258:9159 (1983).

12. R. M. Lorence, J. G. Koland, and R. B. Gennis, Coulometric and spectroscopic analysis of the purified cytochrome d complex of Escherichia coli: Evidence for the identification of cytochrome a_1 as cytochrome b595, Biochemistry, 25:2314 (1986).

13. M. J. Miller, and R. B. Gennis, The cytochrome d complex is a coupling site in the aerobic respiratory chain of Escherichia coli, J. Biol. Chem., 260:14003 (1985).

14. K. Kita, I. Yamato, and Y. Anraku, Purification and properties of cytochrome b556 in the respiratory chain of aerobically grown Escherichia coli, J. Biol. Chem., 253:8910 (1978).

15. H. Murakami, K. Kita, H. Oya, and Y. Anraku, Chromosomal location of the Escherichia coli cytochrome b556 gene, cybA, Mol. Gen. Genet., 196:1 (1984).

16. H. Murakami, K. Kita, H. Oya, and Y. Anraku, The Escherichia coli cytochrome b556 gene, cybA, is assignable as sdhC in the succinate dehydrogenase gene cluster, FEMS Microbiol. Lett., 30:307 (1985).

17. C. Condon, R. Cammack, D. S. Patil, and P. Owen, The succinate dehydrogenase of Escherichia coli: Immunochemical resolution and biophysical characterization of a 4-subunit enzyme complex, J. Biol. Chem., 260:9427 (1985).

18. H. Murakami, K. Kita, and Y. Anraku, Cloning of cybB, the gene for cytochrome b561 of Escherichia coli K-12, Mol. Gen. Genet., 198:1 (1984).

19. H. Murakami, K. Kita, and Y. Anraku, Purification and properties of a diheme cytochrome b561 of the Escherichia coli respiratory chain, J. Biol. Chem., 261:548 (1986).

20. H. Nakamura, H. Murakami, I. Yamato, and Y. Anraku, Nucleotide sequence of cybB, the cytochrome b561 gene of Escherichia coli K-12, submitted for publication.

21. D. Wood, M. G. Darlison, R. J. Wilde, and J. R. Guest, Nucleotide sequence encoding the flavoprotein and hydrophobic subunits of the succinate dehydrogenase of Escherichia coli, Biochem. J., 222:519 (1984).

22. H. Nakamura, I. Yamato, and Y. Anraku, Molecular cloning of the cyo

573

genes encoding the cytochrome o complex in <u>Escherichia</u> <u>coli</u> K-12, submitted for publication.

23. G. N. Green, and R. B. Gennis, Isolation and characterization of an <u>Escherichia</u> <u>coli</u> mutant lacking cytochrome d terminal oxidase, <u>J.</u> <u>Bacteriol.</u>, 154:1269 (1983).

24. G. N. Green, J. E. Kranz, and R. B. Gennis, Cloning the <u>cyd</u> gene locus coding for the cytochrome d complex of <u>Escherichia</u> <u>coli</u>, <u>Gene</u>, 32:99 (1984).

25. A. Hata, Y. Kirino, K. Matsuura, S. Itoh, T. Hiyama, K. Konishi, K. Kita, and Y. Anraku, Assignment of ESR signals of <u>Escherichia</u> <u>coli</u> terminal oxidase complexes, <u>Biochim</u>. <u>Biophys</u>. <u>Acta</u>, 810:62 (1985).

26. T. Uno, Y. Nishimura, M. Tsuboi, K. Kita, and Y. Anraku, Resonance Raman study of cytochrome b562-o complex, a terminal oxidase of <u>Escherichia</u> <u>coli</u> in its ferric, ferrous, and CO-ligated states, <u>J. Biol. Chem.</u>, 260:6755 (1985).

27. B. G. Malmström, Cytochrome c oxidase: Structure and catalytic activity, <u>Biochim</u>. <u>Biophys</u>. <u>Acta</u>, 549:281 (1979).

28. A. Hata-Tanaka, K. Matsuura, S. Itoh, and Y. Anraku, Electron flow and heme-heme interaction between cytochrome b558, b595 and d in a terminal oxidase of <u>Escherichia</u> <u>coli</u>, submitted for publication.

THE INTERPLAY BETWEEN PHOTOSYNTHESIS AND RESPIRATION IN FACULTATIVE ANOXYGENIC PHOTOTROPHIC BACTERIA

Davide Zannoni

Department of Biology, Institute of Botany,Univ. of Bologna

42 Irnerio, 40126 Bologna, Italy

INTRODUCTION

Green and purple non-sulphur bacteria (Chloroflexaceae and Rhodospirillaceae, respectively) are facultative anaerobes which utilize distinct membrane morphologies to accomodate the pigments and the redox components necessary for both respiration and anoxygenic photosynthesis [1] . When these phototrophs are grown aerobically in the light or the dark, the cells develop both respiratory and photosynthetic transport chains operating on the same continuous cytoplasmic membrane (CM). However, in all the purple non-sulphur bacteria the respiratory components are located mainly on the CM-peripheral part and the synthesis of the photosynthetic apparatus is associated with the elaboration of a complex intracytoplasmic membrane array (ICM) (chromatophores) [2] , which is regulated by external factors such as oxygen tension and light-energy flux. Conversely, the situation in green bacteria is quite different: the photosynthetic apparatus is composed of the chlorosomes (antenna structures similar to the phycobilisomes of red algae and cyanobacteria) plus the cytoplasmic membrane immediately adjacent to each chlorosome. The reaction centers as well as the other components forming the respiratory and the photosynthetic apparatuses are contained entirely within the CM [3] .

The interaction both in vivo and in vitro between the respiratory electron transport components of purple non-sulphur bacteria, has long been recognized [4-6] . Illumination of intact cells is seen to cause a reversible inhibition of the substrate dependent respiration, but in chromatophores the situation is more complex. Indeed, both light-induced stimulation and/or inhibition of respiration can be observed according to whether the experiments were performed in the presence or the absence of exogenous electron donors, respectively [7,8] . These observations suggest interactions between respiratory and photosynthetic electron transport systems.

Two types of hypothesis have been advanced to explain the light-induced inhibition of respiration in purple non-sulphur bacteria:
(a) The electrochemical proton gradient generated by photosynthetic electron transport exerts a thermodynamic control upon the rate of respiration[7,9]

(b) The photosynthetic and respiratory chains share redox components. Upon
illumination, oxidation of a common carrier, e.g. cytochrome c, prevents
subsequent reaction in the respiratory chain [10-11].

Although these two hypothesis are not preclusive, their intrinsic significance has a great inference on the apparent organization of the macromolecular complexes involved in photosynthesis and/or respiration. Indeed, proposal in (a) suggests that photosynthesis and respiration are not necessarily performed by the same redox components so to support the hypothesis of
a spatial separation of the two apparatuses on the cytoplasmic membrane
system. Conversely, proposal in (b) presumes that inhibition of respiration
is due to channelling of electrons from the respiratory chain towards the
photosynthetic reaction center and therefore these systems should be strictly intermingled.

The present work examines the most recent acquisitions on the organization of the electron transport components in some representative species
of purple- and green non-sulphur bacteria along with the controversial
aspects supporting either proposal in (a) or in (b), or both. It is concluded, that two modes of interactions between respiratory and photosynthetic
electron transport chains occur, namely: an indirect interaction (thermodynamic control) as proposed in (a) plus a direct interaction (redox control) as proposed in (b).

ON THE MECHANISM OF LIGHT-INDUCED INHIBITION OF RESPIRATION
(Thermodynamic control vs. Redox control)

It has been established, that light-generated membrane potential in
purple non-sulphur bacteria is higher than that produced by respiration
both in cells [11,12] and chromatophores [13]. Assuming an internal volume
of the cells of $102\mu l/\mu mol$ bacteriochlorophyll [14], the light- and oxygen-
induced membrane potentials measured by the lipid soluble ion-exchange
electrode technique, resulted to be close to -160mV and -120mV, respectively [10,15]. Thus whether illumination completely or partially inhibits respiration might simply depend on the magnitude of this thermodynamic control.
The latter explanation, recently favoured by McCarthy and Ferguson [8], is
clearly related to an earlier suggestion by Ramirez and Smith [16], that the
magnitude of a common intermediate of respiratory and photosynthetic electron
flow would be responsible for the inhibition. The intermediate is now identified as the proton electrochemical gradient according to the fact that
very low concentrations of FCCP $(0.5\mu M)$ seem to prevent both the inhibition
of respiration under continuous illumination and the formation of a membrane
potential [12]. The thermodynamic control upon the respiratory rate cannot
however adequately explain the following observation: the addition of an
uncoupler of phosphorylation to intact cells not only prevents the light-
inhibition, but also stimulates the oxygen uptake in the light. This phenomenon can be observed either in the presence or in the absence of inhibitors
of light-induced electron transfer, e.g.NQNO [10,11]. It is therefore obvious
that these effects are difficult to reconcile with a scheme where photosynthesis and respiration interact only at a membrane potential level. This
inconsistency is even more clear in experiments recently published by
Richaud et al. [17] using whole cells of Rhodobacter capsulatus, wild type
and mutants M6 and M7, which lack the 'alternative' and the cytochrome c_2
oxidase, respectively (see Table 1). These experiments show that the oxygen

576

Table 1. Properties of <u>Rhodobacter capsulatus</u> mutant strains

Strain designation	Genotype	Phenotype	Comments and References
M6	asr-1, aer-412r20-512	Ar^r, PS^+, Aer^+	Alternative-ox deficient [19] Derived from strain Z-1 by NTG mutagenesis
M7	asr-1 aer-412-512r34	Ar^r, PS^+, Aer^+, nadi$^-$	Cytochrome c_2-ox deficient [19] Derived from strain Z-1 by NTG mutagenesis
MT113	rif-10,crtD121, crtC113	Rif^r,green, PS^-, Aer^+	Deficient in cytochromes $c(c_2+c_1)$ and Rieske-FeS [29] constructed from strain SB1003 by tetracycline suicide selection(strain TL11) and by introducing the crtD marker from strain R121 into strain TL11 via GTA
R126	asr-1,crtD121, aer-103r11,bps-11	Ar^r, PS^-, green, Aer^+	Blocked in electron transfer at the myxothiazol binding site(Qz) [24] Derived from strain M50 by NTG mutagenesis and selection for regain of respiration;constructed by introducing the crtD marker from strain R121 into strain Y11

GENOTYPE: asr, arsenate resistance; aer, aerobic growth; bps, bacterial photosynthesis (normal pigments); crt, carotenoid synthesis; rif,rifampicin resistance. PHENOTYPE: Ar, arsenate resistance; PS, photosynthetic growth; nadi, oxidation of reduced TMPD; green, accumulate neurosporene,hydroxyneuro-sporene and methoxyneurosporene; Rif, rifampicin resistance; Aer, aerobic growth.

consumption is perturbed by short actinic flashes fired every second with an oscillatory pattern of two for wild-type and M6 cells: each flash induces an inhibition of respiration but a stimulation is observed after an even number of flashes. These oscillations are emphasized by addition of FCCP. For the strain M7, deficient in cytochrome c_2 oxidase, no flash-induced per-turbation of the oxygen consumption is observed. The latter result strongly suggest that under appropriate experimental conditions the interaction be-tween photosynthesis and respiration is manifested as a redox control of a component, presumably cyt.c_2, shared by the two apparatuses. On the other hand, Cotton et al. [15] measuring the carotenoid band shift as index of the membrane potential, have reported a good correlation between its extent and the inhibition by light in the presence of antimycin A and FCCP. These authors concluded that the light inhibition of respiration is dominated by the proton motive force and therefore photosynthesis and respiration share the same coupling membrane but not necessarily they share common redox components. The situation can be, however, more complex since it has widely been shown that in several species of purple non-sulphur bacteria, i.e. Rb.capsulatus, Rb.sphaeroides and R.rubrum, the respiratory chain branches at the level of UQ-b/c$_1$ complex into distinct pathways going to different oxidases, a cyt.c$_2$ oxidase sensitive to 10^{-5} M KCN and an alternative oxidase sensitive to 10^{-3} M KCN and to CO [18,19] . In other terms, the respiratory activity in the presence of FCCP and antimycin A could be sustained by the alternative oxidase and therefore would not be influenced by the redox components involved in cyclic electron flow as previously shown in chromatophores [7]. Indeed, as recently demonstrated in Rb.capsulatus M6,the mutant deficient in the alternative oxidase, addition of both antimycin A and CCCP does not prevent inhibition of respiration by light under experimental conditions in which the membrane potential is abolished.[17]

ON THE MECHANISM OF PHOTOSYNTHETIC AND RESPIRATORY ELECTRON TRANSFER IN FACULTATIVE PHOTOTROPHS

In purple non-sulphur bacteria such as Rb.capsulatus, Rb.sphaeroides and R.rubrum, photosynthesis or respiration involves, besides the photosynthetic reaction center, light-harvesting antenna complexes and cytochrome oxidases, a periplasmic diffusible c-type cytochrome (cyt.c$_2$) and a membrane bound complex, called ubiquinol-cyt.c$_2$ oxido-reductase (complex III or b/c$_1$ complex)[20]. The b/c$_1$ complex, constituted of the Rieske Fe-S protein, two b-type haems (designated bH and bL for high- and low-potential, respectively) and one c-type haem (cyt.c$_1$), catalyzes the conversion of quinols generated during respiration or photosynthesis, back to quinones and, as an energy coupling site , transport protons across the plasmamembrane. The key reaction associated with electron movement within the complex, is the concerted reduction of the Rieske Fe-S center and cyt.bL (b566, $E_{m7.0}$=-90mV) [21] by QH$_2$ at a special functional site designated Qz. Subsequently, one electron is delivered to cyt.c$_2$ through the high-potential part of the chain and the other returns to Qz via cyt.bH (b561, $E_{m7.0}$=+60mV) [21] to reduce a quinone at a second site designated Qc. This model, based upon the original 'Q-cycle' model of Mitchell [22] , requires therefore two functionally distinct sites to complete electron transfer and the vectorial transport of protons across the membrane by the Q/b-c$_1$ complex. Although there is excellent evidence from redox midpoints and the stabilities of quinone species, as well as the site specific effects of inhibitors, supporting the idea of two quinone binding sites in bacterial b/c$_1$ complexes [23] , the definitive proof supporting this model has recently been obtained by examining a non-photosynthetic mutant of Rb. capsulatus, designated R126 (see Table 1) [24]. Mutant strain R126 is only capable of aerobic growth and the lesion responsible has been localized to the function of the cytochrome b/c$_1$ complex [24]. More precisely, the evidence rising from flash-induced optical changes and from EPR spectroscopy points to a specific lesion related to quinone function at the Qz site. In addition, although Qz function is disrupted, antimycin-sensitive Qc function can readily be detected providing evidence for two separate binding domains as predicted by the 'Q-cycle' model. These results, besides their objective importance, have a great inference on the interpretation of previously published data indicating that strain R126 can performe ATP-synthesis linked to both light-induced oxygen uptake activity and succinate-dependent respiration in the presence of antimycin A [25] . The latter finding indicates that under experimental conditions in which the Qz and Qc sites are inactive, the energy transducing pathway is restricted to a segment formed by an indefinite 'quinol-oxidase' or 'alternative-oxidase' which is sensitive to KCN (Ki=0.5mM), UHDBT (5μM), mefloquine (Ki=15μM) and CO (Ki=0.6mM). In particular, it has been suggested that quinol respiration in chromatophores from Rb.capsulatus and R.rubrum is catalized by an oxidase of b type (formally designated as cyt.o) with a high redox mid-point potential (Em7.0=+260mV) [25,18]. Unfortunately, the exact mechanism of electron transfer and the associated proton movements catalyzed by the 'quinol-oxidase' pathway, along with its molecular composition, are currently unknown. Conversely, it is presently established that electrons can be passed from the photochemical reaction center to the 'alternative-oxidase' containing pathway and therefore these redox components must be strictly intermingled. Indeed, several lines of evidence show that under aerobic illuminated conditions two electron transport pathways coexist in membrane fragments from facultative phototrophs: a cyclic and a non-cyclic. They branch at the UQ-pool level and the non-cyclic electron flow leads to oxygen reduction through the 'alternative-oxidase' [7]. This light-activated 'quinol-oxidase', i.e. light-induced oxygen uptake, is blocked by KCN and it does not involve the b/c1 complex as shown by its insensitivity to both antimycin A and myxothiazol. The above reported data, taken altogether, unequivocally demonstrate that the b/c1 complex is not essential for aerobic growth due to the presence of an independent alternative oxidase. On the other hand, any residual doubt concerning the role of b/c1 in respiration, has recently been removed by the contruction in vitro of b/c1 deficient mutants through insertion-delition mutations affecting the b/c1 structural genes [26]. These mutants, were unable to grow photosynthetically, indicating that the b/c1 complex is essential for this growth mode, but they grew aerobically by means of the alternative pathway. The essential role of the alternative oxidase in respiration is strongly confirmed by the evidence that it was impossible to obtain a b/c1 derivative of strain M6, the mutant of Rb.capsulatus defective in quinol-oxidase, under either respiratory or photosynthetic growth conditions.

Similarly to purple non-sulphur bacteria, membrane fragments isolated from cells of the green photosynthetic thermophile Chloroflexus aurantiacus have been shown to performe light-dependent oxygen uptake [27]. The most intriguing aspect related with this latter finding is that antimycin A and/or myxothiazol, the most effective inhibitors of putative b/c1 complexes, did not significantly stimulate the light-driven respiration in membranes from Chloroflexus [27]. Indeed, it is well established that non-cyclic electron flow is greatly enhanced by blocking cyclic electron flow with antimycin[7].

Since it has previously been shown that Chloroflexus contains the redox elements (2 b-type haems, Rieske-center and 1 c-type haem) which are diagnostic of a putative b/c1 complex [28], the lack of sensitivity toward antimycin A and myxothiazol might suggest the presence of significative structural differences between the b/c1 complex of Chloroflexus and the b/c1 complexes of non-sulphur purple phototrophic bacteria. In other terms, the b/c1 complex of Chloroflexus might be structurally closer to the b_6/f of chloroplasts (which are insensitive to both antimycin A and myxothiazol), than to bacterial b/c1 complexes.

Concerning the role of cytochrome(s) c on photosynthesis and respiration of green and purple non-sulphur bacteria the situation appears to be complex.

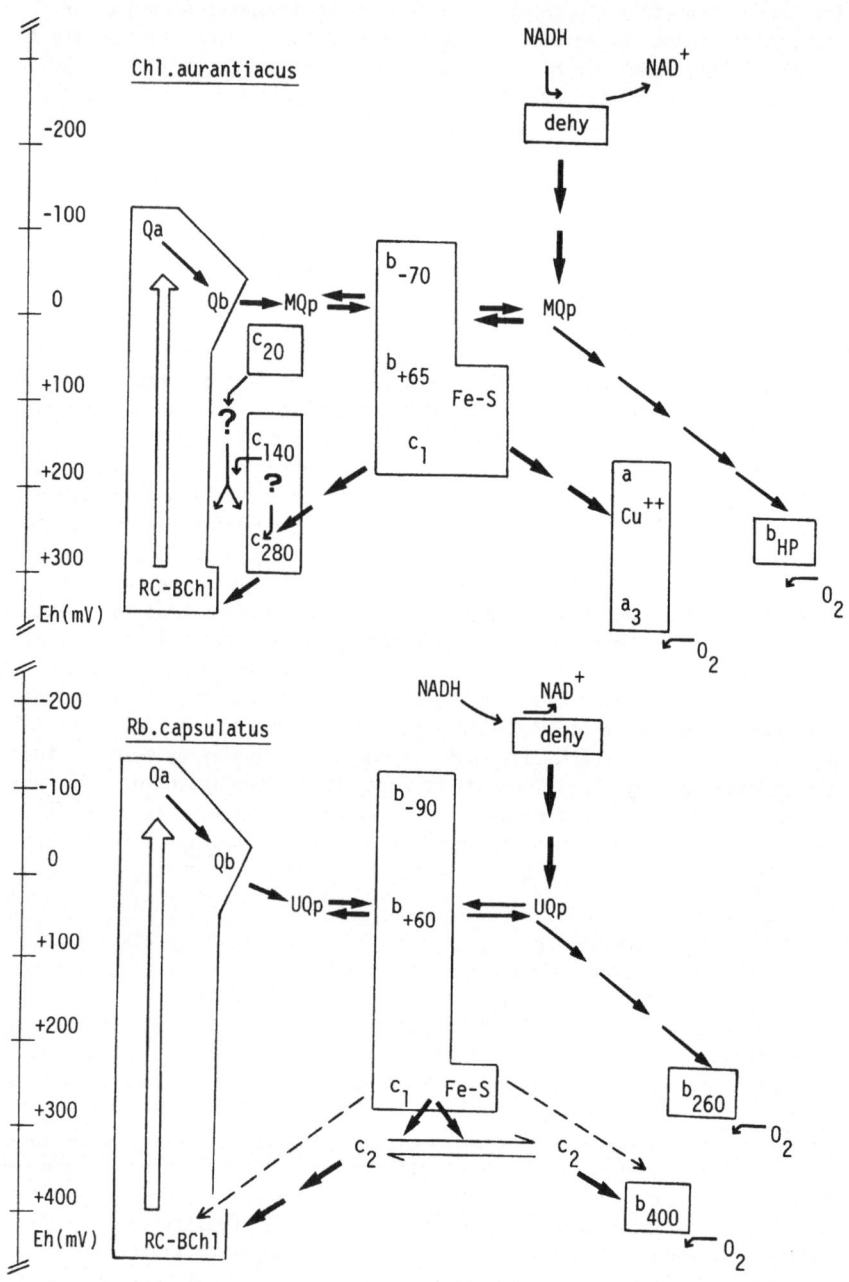

Fig.1. Schematic representation of the electron transfer chains operating
in green and purple non-sulphur bacteria. The thick arrows indicate
the main electron transport pathways while the dotted arrows suggest
possible secondary redox reactions. Many b- and c-type haems are labelled with their $Em_{7.0}$. The enclosed boxes simulate membrane-bound
components. Non standard abbreviations: b_{HP}, high-potential b-haem; UQp
and MQp, pools of ubiquinone and menaquinone, respectively.

In fact, until recently it has been generally accepted that soluble $\underline{c}$(formally cyt.$\underline{c}_2$) was essential for photosynthesis and respiration of purple non-sulphur bacteria based on spectroscopic analyses of wild type and mutant strains,such as MT113 (see also Tab.1),lacking it and defective in these processes.However, recent studies have demonstrated that MT113 lacks not only cyt.$\underline{c}_2$ but also cyt.c1, the Rieske iron-sulphur center and the antimycin-sensitive semiquinone Qc,all components of the b/c1 complex[29].Thus, the role of $\underline{c}_2$ on photosynthesis and respiration has recently been reexamined using $\underline{c}_2$-deficient mutants of Rb.capsulatus [26].These mutants are proficient in both respiration and photosynthesis (especially when high light intensity is provided) at a rate comparable to a wild type strain. This demonstrate that $\underline{c}_2$ is not essential for both photosynthetic and aerobic growth of this organism although spectroscopic analyses of electron pathways in the absence of $\underline{c}_2$ indicated that the kinetics clearly reflect a requirement for the diffusion of $\underline{c}_2$[21].In contrast to purple non-sulphur bacteria, the green non-sulphur bacteria (Chloroflexaceae) do not seem to contain soluble components functionally and structurally comparable to $\underline{c}_2$ or its counterpart in chloroplasts, plastocyanine. The recent isolation from membranes of Chloroflexus of a blue-copper protein[30] ,auracyanine (MW=12,000; $\mathcal{E}$ =2900 M^{-1} at 598nm; Em=+240mV), might suggest the possibility that a 'strong-hydrophobic' protein can operate as electron shuttle between the b/c1 complex and cyt.$\underline{c}$554 of Chloroflexus, the latter cytochrome being the direct electron donor to the reaction center.This hypothesis,however,does not preclude the necessity for a tight-coupling ,i.e.short-distance, between the b/c1 complex and cyt.c554. This consideration is based on the observation that following flash-induced oxidation of $\underline{c}$554, rapid re-reduction of this cytochrome can readily be observed also at relatively low temperature, the membrane being presumably close to a crystalline system[31].

The top scheme of Fig.1,represents a summary of our present acquisitions about the redox components functionally involved in photoactivated electron transport of Chloroflexus[28,31]. In this tentative model, at least 4 c-type haems are shown to be photooxidized by the RC-BChl, namely:$\underline{c}_{20}$,$\underline{c}_{140}$,$\underline{c}_{280}$ and $\underline{c}$1. Although the haems at 140mV and 280mV are thought to belong to the same cytochrome species($\underline{c}$554) [32] ,only $\underline{c}_{280}$ seems to clearly operate in series with cyt.$\underline{c}$1 while it is presently unclear whether $\underline{c}_{20}$ and $\underline{c}_{140}$ function in cyclic electron flow through cyt.$\underline{c}_{280}$ or they go directly oxidized by the RC-BChl bypassing the latter cytochrome. The lower scheme of Fig.1, combines the enormous amount of data on electron transport of Rb.capsulatus accumulated during the last decade.

REFERENCES

1. S.G.Sprague, and A.R.Varga,Membrane architecture of anoxygenic photo-synthetic bacteria,in:"Encyclopedia of Plant Physiology",C.J.Arntzen,ed., Springer-Verlag,Berlin-Heidelberg-New York-Tokyo (1986)
2. H.-H.Lampe, and G.Drews, Die Differenzierung des Membransystems von Rhodopseudomonas capsulata hinsichtlich seiner photosynthetischen und respiratorischen Funktionen, Arch.Mikrobiol. 84:1 (1972)
3. R.E.Blankenship, and R.C.Fuller, Membrane topology and photochemistry of the green photosynthetic bacterium Chloroflexus aurantiacus, in: "Encyclopedia of Plant Physiology",C.J.Arntzen,ed.,Springer-Verlag, Berlin-Heidelberg-New York-Tokyo (1986)

4. H.Nakamura, Uber die Photosynthese bei der schwefelfreien Purpubakterie Rhodobazillus palustris. Beitrage zur Stoffwechselphysiologie der Purpurbakterie .I. Acta Phytochem. 9:189 (1972)

5. C.B. van Niel, The bacterial photosyntheses and their importance for the general problem of photosynthesis, Adv. Enzymol. 1:263 (1941)

6. R.K.Clayton, Competition between light and dark metabolism in Rhodospirillum rubrum, Arch.Mikrobiol. 22:195 (1955)

7. D.Zannoni, P.Jasper, and B.L.Marrs, Light-induced oxygen reduction as a probe of electron transport between respiratory and photosynthetic components in membranes of Rhodopseudomonas capsulata,Arch.Biochem.Biophys. 191:625 (1978)

8. J.E.G.McCarthy, and S.J.Ferguson,Respiratory control and the basis of light induced inhibition of respiration in chromatophores from Rhodopseudomonas capsulata,Biochem.Biophys.Res.Comm. 107:1406 (1982)

9. N.P.J.Cotton,A.J.Clark,and J.B.Jackson,Interaction between the respiratory and photosynthetic electron transport chains in intact cells of Rhodopseudomonas capsulata mediated by membrane potential,Europ.J.Biochem. 130:581 (1983)

10. D.L.Keister, and M.J.Minton, Effect of light on respiration in Rhodospirillum rubrum chromatophores, in:"Energy Transduction in Respiration and Photosynthesis",E.Quagliariello,S.Papa and C.S.Rossi,eds.,Adriatica Editrice,Bari (1971)

11. M.Rugolo, and D.Zannoni, Oxygen-induced inhibition of light-dependent uptake of tetraphenylphosphonium ions as a probe of a direct interaction between photosynthetic and respiratory components in cells of Rhodopseudomonas capsulata,Biochem.Biophys.Res.Comm. 113:155 (1983)

12. A.J.Clark, and J.B.Jackson, The measurement of membrane potential during photosynthesis and during respiration in intact cells of Rhodopseudomonas capsulata by both electrochromism and by permeant ion redistribution, Biochem.J. 200:389 (1981)

13. S.J.Ferguson, O.T.Jones,D.B.Kell, and M.C.Sorgato, Comparison of permeant ion uptake and carotenoid band shift as methods for determining the membrane potential in chromatophores from Rhodopseudomonas sphaeroides Biochem.J. 180:75 (1979)

14. D.B.Kell,S.J.Ferguson, and P.John, Measurement by a flow dialysis technique of the steady state proton motive force in chromatophores from Rhodospirillum rubrum, Biochim.Biophys.Acta 502:111 (1978)

15. N.P.J.Cotton,A.J.Clark, and B.J.Jackson, The effect of venturicidin on light and oxygen-dependent electron transport and proton translocation. Membrane potential development and ATP-synthesis in intact cells of Rhodopseudomonas capsulata, Arch.Microbiol. 129:94 (1981)

16. J.Ramirez, and L.Smith, Synthesis of ATP in intact cells of R.rubrum and R.sphaeroides on oxygenation or illumination, Biochim.Biophys.Acta 153:466 (1968)

17. R.Richaud,B.L.Marrs, and A.Vermeglio, Two modes of interaction between photosynthetic and respiratory electron chains in whole cells of Rhodopseudomonas capsulata, Biochim.Biophys.Acta 850:256 (1986)

18. G.Venturoli,C.Fenoll, and D.Zannoni, On the mechanism of respiratory and photosynthetic electron-transfer in Rhodospirillum rubrum,Biochim. Biophys.Acta (in press)(1987)

19. D.Zannoni, and A.Baccarini-Melandri,Respiratory electron flow in facultative photosynthetic bacteria,in:"Diversity of Bacterial Respiratory

Systems, C.J.Knowles,ed. CRC Press,Inc.,Boca Raton Florida (1980)

20. G.Hauska, Composition and structure of cytochrome bc1 and b6f complexes, in:"Encyclopedia of Plant Physiology",L.A.staehelin and C.J.Arntzen,eds., Springer-Verlag,Berlin-Heidelberg-New York-Tokyo (1986)

21. W.A.Cramer, and A.R.Crofts, Electron and proton transport, in:"Energy Conversion by Plants and Bacteria, Govindjee,ed.,Academic Press New York (1982)

22. P.Mitchell, The proton motive Q-cycle:A general formulation, FEBS Lett. 59:137 (1975)

23. D.E.Robertson,R.C.Prince,J.R.Bowyer,K.Matsuura,P.L.Dutton, and T.Ohnishi Thermodynamic properties of the semiquinone and its binding site in the ubiquinol-cytochrome $c(c_2)$oxidoreductase of respiratory and photosynthetic systems, J.Biol.Chem. 259:1758 (1984)

24. D.E.Robertson,E.Davidson,R.C.Prince,W.H. van den Berg,B.L.Marrs, and P.L.Dutton, Discrete catalytic sites for quinone in the ubiquinol-cytochrome c_2 oxidoreductase of Rhodopseudomonas capsulata,J.Biol.Chem. 261:584 (1986)

25. D.Zannoni, ATP synthesis coupled to light-dependent non-cyclic electron flow in chromatophores of Rhodopseudomonas capsulata,Biochim.Biophys. Acta 680:1 (1982)

26. F.Daldal,Molecular genetics of c-type cytochromes and of ubiquinol-cytochrome c_2 oxidoreductase of R.capsulata, in:"Photosynthesis Research",J.Biggins,ed.,Martnus Nijhoff Publishers,Dordrecht (1987)

27. D.Zannoni,Respiration vs. Photosynthesis in membranes from the thermophilic green photosynthetic bacterium Chloroflexus aurantiacus, Fourth Europ.Bioen.Conf.4:139 (1986)

28. D.Zannoni, and J.W.Ingledew, A thermodynamic analysis of the plasma membrane electron transport components in photoheterotrophically grown cells of Chloroflexus aurantiacus,FEBS Lett. 193:93 (1985)

29. E.Davidson,R.C.Prince,F.Daldal,G.Hauska, and B.L.Marrs, Rhodobacter capsulatus MT113: a single mutation results in the absence of c-type cytochromes and in the absence of the cytochrome bc1 complex, Biochim. Biophys.Acta 890:292 (1987)

30. J.T.Trost,J.M.Freeman, and R.E.Blankenship,Purification and properties of auracynin, a blue-copper protein from Chloroflexus aurantiacus, Biophys.J. 51:309a (1987)

31. D.Zannoni and G.Venturoli,Thermodynamic and kinetic characterization of the photosynthetic electron transport system of Chloroflexus aurantiacus, in:"EMBO Workshop on Green Photosyn.Bacteria",Nyborg, Denmark (1987)(in press)

32. R.E.Blankenship,P.Huynh,H.Gabrielson, and L.J.Mancino,Purification, physical properties and kinetic behaviour of cytochrome c554 from Chloroflexus aurantiacus, Biophys.J. 47:M-AM-A2 (1985)

THE UBIQUINOL-CYTOCHROME C OXIDOREDUCTASE OF PHOTOTROPHIC BACTERIA

Mario Snozzi and Josef Kälin*

EAWAG/ETH, Dept. of Technical Biology, 8600 Dübendorf, Switzerland
* Institute of Plant Biology, University of Zürich, 8008 Zürich
Switzerland

INTRODUCTION

The wide use of phototropic bacteria to study electron transfer
pathway results from the fact that, in these bacteria, the electron
transport can be activated by actinic light. The amount of electrons
introduced into the cytochrome system, as well as the starting time of
the reactions, can be very precisely determined this way. Additionally,
the photosynthetic bacteria are able to grow using different energy
sources, e.g. beside anaerobic phototrophic growth, they are also able
to aerobically oxidize organic compounds in the dark and use the energy
by oxidative phosphorylation in a similar manner to mitochondria.

The membrane bound complexes for the electron transport chains of
the Rhodospirillales are similar to the corresponding enzymes in
mitochondria. This is also true for the ubiquinol-cytochrome c oxidoreductase (the b-c$_1$ complex). Protein composition and inhibitor action
of the two enzymes are comparable[1]. Therefore, results from photosynthetic bacteria may also apply to the mitochondrial system. The redox
components of Rhodobacter sphaeroides, which are involved in the cyclic
electron transport chain, have all been carefully characterized.

The light harvesting system of phototrophic bacteria is activated by light. The energy is transfered to the reaction centers, which are able to reduce quinone to quinol. The quinol is reoxidized by the $b-c_1$ complex and the electrons are ultimately used to reduce the soluble cytochrome c_2, which is then able to rereduce the light oxidized reaction centers. The $b-c_1$ complex, having two distinct quinone binding sites, acts in a modified Q-cycle[2]. The proton gradient which is produced during electron transfer reactions results from vectorial movements of quinones and quinols.

In the presence of antimycin A, the quinone reducing site Q_C is blocked and the inhibited $b-c_1$ complex is restricted to a maximum of two turnovers. Using redox poised chromatophore membrane suspensions, it was possible to control the concentration of reduced quinol and study their oxidation by the $b-c_1$ complex[2]. Variations in the concentration of quinones within the photosynthetic membranes from Rhodobacter sphaeroides GA (formerly called Rhodopseudomonas sphaeroides GA) were obtained by fusion of chromatophores with liposomes, either with or without additional quinones[3]. Since the ratio of protein to lipids is subject to drastic changes during the growth cycle of a cell[4], it was also possible to achieve a change in the quinone concentration by preparing chromatophores from synchronously grown cells[3]. Measurements of oxidation rates of quinols by the $b-c_1$ complex in these membrane systems all revealed a second order reaction between the two components. The second order reaction constant was determined to be about $1.4.10^5$ M^{-1} and the K_m of the reaction was around 10 mM, which corresponds to about 4 to 5 quinols reduced per reaction center to achieve half maximal oxidation rates.

More recently, Venturoli et al.[5] have reinvestigated earlier studies with partial extraction of the quinones from lyophilized chromatophores[6,7]. Measuring the quinol oxidation at different redox potentials in membranes containing different sizes of quinone pools, they were able to show that the quinone pool links the reducing side of the reaction centers with the $b-c_1$ complex.

It is now well established, that the model of Crofts et al.[2] is able to explain and predict the observed reaction sequences and kinetics of the

b-c$_1$ complex in <u>Rhodobacter</u> <u>sphaeroides</u>. The electrons of the quinols
oxidized are split, one going into the high potential chain with the Rieske
type iron sulphur center and cytochrome c$_1$, the other reducing first
cytochrome b$_{566}$ and then equilibrating between the two b cytochromes
according to their redox potentials. The electrons from the b cytochromes
are then used to reduce quinone at site Q$_C$.

Another important point of the model is the postulation of some sort
of cooperation of two reaction centers, such that a single saturating flash
yields one fully reduced quinol per pair of reaction center rather than
four semiquinones. The fact that the oscillations in the redox state of the
secondary quinone Q$_B$ are only visible in chromatophores at high ambient
redox potental has been reported by de Grooth <u>et</u> <u>al.</u>[8], Bowyer <u>et</u> <u>al.</u>[9] and
by O'Keefe <u>et</u> <u>al.</u>[10]. Whereas, isolated reaction centers display a flash
number dependent on the redox state at Q$_B$ at low potentials, the first
flash reducing to the semiquinone, and the second, to the fully reduced
quinol which is then replaced by a quinone. This behaviour disappears in
chromatophores at redox potential below 300 mV.

Chromatophores fused with liposomes to increase their phospholipid
content had at the same time an increased size, the inner volume being
increased by about 2.6 times and the inner membrane surface by 1.9. These
membranes showed a decrease in the oxidation rate of cytochrome c$_1$ by
cytochrome c$_2$ which corresponded roughly to the increase of the inner
membranes surface[11]. However, at the same time, the oxidation rate of
cytochrome c$_2$ by the reaction centers was unchanged. This suggests that
reduced cytochrome c$_2$ is preferably bound to the reaction center.

A reinvestigation of the oscillation of the secondary quinone acceptor
of the reaction centers lead to the following results. In chromatophores
with a stoichiometry of two reaction centers per b-c$_1$ complex and
cytochrome c$_2$, the oscillations were only present at potentials above 300
mV, titrating with the same midpotential as cytochrome c$_2$. When the
cytochrome c$_2$ content was markedly reduced, a fraction of the reaction
centers continued to oscillate at very low potentials. Sphaeroplast derived
vesicles, which have an opposite orientation of the membrane, with respect
to chromatophores, loose most of their cytochrome c$_2$ during their
preparation. Reaction centers in these membranes also displayed

oscillations at low potentials. Addition of small amounts of cytochrome c_2 or horse heart cytochrome c (in the order of 10 uM cytochrome) increased the oscillations at potentials below 300 mV. This effect was ascribed to the improvement of reaction center rereduction between the flashes, a prerequisite for a second turnover to produce the fully reduced quinol at Q_B. If the soluble c cytochrome concentration was increased above 30 uM, the extent of oscillation at potentials below 300 mV became smaller again. Addition of 70 uM cytochrome c_2 to sphaeroplast derived vesicles resulted in a titration curve which was similar to the one of chromatophores.

It was concluded that reduced cytochrome c_2, in sufficient high concentration, was responsible for the disappearance of the oscillations at the secondary quinone of the reaction centers. It is interesting to note, that Bosshard et al.[12] found, that in Rhodospirillum rubrum, cytochrome c_2 binds to isolated reaction centers by shielding a region of the cytochrome molecule opposite to the heme cleft (backside). Horse heart cytochrome c, which is able to replace c_2 as an electron acceptor, seems to bind by its front side[13]. Since electron transfer between reaction centers and cytochrome c_2 is not believed to occur via the backside of cytochrome c_2, the backward binding might have some function in the regulation of the oscillations of Q_B.

INCORPORATION OF REACTION CENTERS INTO SUBMITOCHONDRIAL PARTICLES

In mitochondria it is not possible to observe directly single turnovers of the $b-c_1$ complex as in membranes from photosynthetic bacteria. Since mixing of the membranes with substrates is necessary, the time resolution is restricted in experiments with mitochondria. To overcome this problem, isolated reaction centers have been mixed with isolated $b-c_1$ complexes from mitochondria[14,15]. Since it was shown that the quinone pool is involved in electron transfer it is more appropriate to incorporate the reaction centers into the mitochondrial membranes.

Isolated reaction centers from R. rubrum G9 can be incorporated into submitochondrial particles, if they are mixed with the membranes in

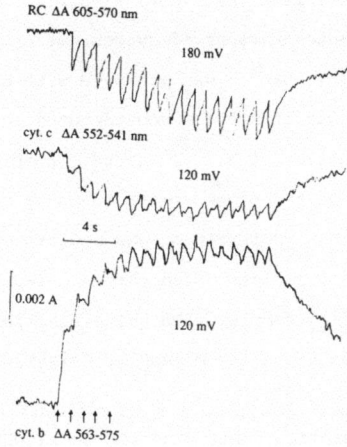

Fig. 1 Reaction centers incorporated into
submitochondrial particles. Flash induced changes of reaction centers, b
and c cytochromes were measured under
the conditiosn given in the figure.

the presence of 5 mM Ca^{2+} [16]. The reaction centers are oriented within the
mitochondrial membrane in both directions, as is evident from oxidation
kinetics after the addition of ferricyanide. Therefore, part of the
incorporated reaction centers have their reaction site with cytochrome c on
the same side of the membrane as the $b-c_1$ complex.

Figure 1 shows that the $b-c_1$ complex of particles with incorporated
reaction centers can be activated by flashing light. Although redox spectra
of the particles show normal concentrations of cytochrome c, the reaction
centers displayed oscillations at Q_B even at potentials as low as 50mV.
This means that only small amounts of quinols are produced in these
membranes by single turnover flashes. Consequently, the influence of the
ambient redox potential on the reduction rate of the b cytochromes in the
presence of antimycin A was rather small. But a severalfold increase of the
extent of cytochrome b reduction was found in accordance with the model.

ISOLATION OF THE UBIQUINOL-CYTOCHROME C_2 OXIDOREDUCTASE FROM R. RUBRUM

The electron transport of R. rubrum has received much less attention
than the one of Rhodobacter sphaeroides. Since chromatophores of R. rubrum

589

normally show only small light activated electron transport even in membranes with reasonable concentrations of cytochrome c_2, we decided to isolate the b-c_1 complex. Solubilisation was achieved with a mixture of LDAO and cholate, avoiding the use of octyl glucoside used in the isolation procedure described by Gabellini et al.[17]. The b-c_1 complex was then separated from a large fraction of the pigmented proteins by centrifugation in a sucrose gradient. Further purification was undertaken by ion exchange chromatography on DEAE cellulose. Such chromatography resulted in two fractions containing b-c_1 complex. SDS gel electrophoresis indicated that one of them did not contain a low molecular weight protein.

Whereas the preparation containing the small peptide showed normal inhibition of the ubiquinol cytochrome c oxidoreductase activity by antimicyn A, the second preparation was enhance in its activity by antimycin A. A possible explanation for this effect is that the quinol oxidizing site of this enzyme was modified, so that the splitting of electrons into the high and low potential chain of the complex was no longer obligatory. By blocking the Q_C site with antimycin, all the electrons of the quinols would then be transferred into cytochrome c.

Preliminary experiments using the same isolation procedure for b-c_1 complex from Rhodobacter sphaeroides also showed that with this organism two forms of the complex, which differ in their sensitivity towards antimycin, are found. This result shows that one has to be careful in interpreting results of isolated enzyme complex either in terms of Q-cycle models[2] or b-cycles[18].

ACKNOWLEDGEMENT

The authors are indepted to Prof. R. Bachofen for his support during the experiments of the b-c_1 isolation.

REFERENCES

1. G. Hauska, E. Hurt, N. Gabellini and W. Lockau, Comparative aspects of quinol-cytochrome c/plastocyanin oxidoreductases. Biochim. Biophys. Acta 726:97-133 (1983).
2. A. R. Crofts, S. W. Meinhardt, K. R. Jones and M. Snozzi, The role

of the quinone pool in the cyclic electron-transfer chain of
Rhodopseudomonas sphaeroides: a modified Q-cylce mechanism,
Biochim. Biophys. Acta 723:202-218 (1983).

3. M. Snozzi and A. R. Crofts, Electron transport in chromatosphores
from Rhodopseudomonas sphaeroides GA fused with liposomes,
Biochim. Biophys. Acta 766:451-463 (1984).

4. D. R. Lueking, R.T. Fraley and S. Kaplan, Intracytoplasmic membrane
syntheses in synchronous cell populations of Rhodopseudomonas
sphaeroides, J. Biol. Chem. 253: 451-457 (1978).

5. G. Venturoli, J. G. Fernandez-Velasco, A. R. Crofts and B. A.
Melandri, Demonstration of a collisional interaction of ubiquinol
with the ubiquinol cytochrome c_2 oxidoreductase complex in
chromatophores of Rhodobacter sphaeroides. Biochim. Biophys.
Acta 851:340-352 (1986).

6. K. Takamiya, R. C. Prince and P. L. Dutton, The recognition of a
special ubiquinone functionally central in the ubiquinone
cytochrome b cytochrome c_2 oxidoreductase. J. Biol. Chem.
254:11307-11311.

7. A. Baccarini-Melandri, N. Gabellini, B. A. Melandri, K. R. Jones, W.
Rutherford, A. R. Crofts and E. Hurt, Differential extraction and
structural specificity of specialized ubiquinone molecules in
secondary electron transfer in chromatophores from
Rhodopseudomonas sphaeroides GA. Arch. Biochem. Biophys.
216:566-580 (1982).

8. B. G. De Groth, R. Van Grondelle, J. C. Romijn and M. P. J. Pulles,
The mechanism of reduction of the ubiquinone pool in
photosynthetic bacteria at different redox potential. Biochim.
Biophys. Acta 503:480-490 (1978).

9. J. R. Bowyer, G. V. Tierney and A. R. Crofts, Secondary electron
transfer in chromatophores of Rhodopseudomonas capsulata Ala
pho$^+$. FEBS lett. 101:201-206 (1979).

10. D. P. O'Keefe, R. C. Prince and P. L. Dutton, The interaction of the
reaction center secondary quinone with the ubiquinone cytochrome
c_2 oxidoreductase in Rhodopseudomonas spaeroides chromatophores.
Biochim. Biophys. Acta 637:512-522 (1981).

11. M. Snozzi and A. R. Crofts, Kinetics of the c-cytochromes in
chromatosphores from Rhodopseudomonas sphaeroides as a function
of the concentration of cytochrome c_2. Influence of this
concentration on the oscillation of the secondary acceptor of the
reaction centers Q_B. Biochim. Biophys. Acta 809:260-270 (1985).

12. R. Rieder, V. Wiemken, R. Bachofen and H. R. Bosshard, Binding of
cytochrome c_2 to the isolated reaction center of Rhodospirillum
rubrum involves the "backside" of cytochrome c_2. Biochem.
Biophys. Res. Com. 128:120-126 (1985).

13. H. R. Bosshard, M. Snozzi, R. Bachofen, Interaction of horse
cytochrome c with the phtosyntehtic reaction center of
Rhodospirillum rubrum. J. Bioen. Biomemb., in press.

14. N. K. Packham, D.M. Tiede, P. Mueller and P. L. Dutton, Construction
of a flash-activated cyclic electron transport system by using
bacterial reaction centers and the ubiquinone-cytochrom b-c_1/c
segment of mitochondria. Proc. Natl. Acad. Sci. 77:6339-6343
(1980).

15. Q. F. Zhu, H. N. Van der Wal, R. Van Grondelle and J. A. Berden,
Kinetics of flash-induced electron transfer between bacterial
reaction centers, mitochondrial ubiquinol : cytochrome c
oxidoreductase and cytochrome c. Biochim. Biophys. Acta
725:121-130 (1983).

16. J. Hladik, M. Snozzi and R. Bachofen, Incorporation of reaction centers into submitochondrial particles, in preparation.

17. N. Gabellini, J. R. Bowyer, E. Hurt, B. A. Melandri and G. Hauska, A cytochrome b-c$_1$ complex with ubiquinol-cytochrome c$_2$ oxidoreductase activity from Rhodopseudomonas sphaeroides. Eur. J. Biochem. 126:105-111 (1982).

18. M. Wikström, K. Krab, The semiquione cycle. A hypothesis of electron transfer and proton translocation in cytochrome bc-type complexes, J. Bioenergetics and Biomembranes 18:181-193 (1986).

THE REDOX REACTION BETWEEN CYTOCHROME b_H AND THE
SEMIQUINONE-QUINOL COUPLE OF Q_C IS ELECTROGENIC IN
UBIQUINOLCYT c_2 OXIDOREDUCTASE

Dan E. Robertson and P.Leslie Dutton

Department of Biochemistry and Biophysics
University of Pennsylvania
Philadelphia, Pa. 19104 U.S.A.

INTRODUCTION

The ubiquinol-cyt c_2 oxidoreductase of *Rhodobacter
sphaeroides* acts in concert with the photosynthetic reaction
center (RC) to complete cyclic electron transfer in the
bacterial chromatophore membrane (for a review see 1,2).
Electron transfer between the complexes is mediated by a
mobile, membrane bound pool of quinone (Q_{pool}) and cyt c_2. The
cyt bc_1 uses the free energy difference between its substrate
quinol (QH_2) and product, ferricytochrome c_2 (cyt c_2) to
catalyze the formation of an electrochemical proton gradient
($\Delta\mu_H^+$).

The mechanism by which cyt bc_1 generates $\Delta\psi$ and ΔpH is
still controversial though most mechanisms are variants of the
Q-cycle (3,4). These models propose that charge separation,
hence $\Delta\psi$ formation, occurs during reduction and oxidation of
the two b-type cytochromes via two quinone functional sites.
In *Rhodobacter* these sites have been called Q_z, or the quinol
(QH_2) oxidation site and Q_C, the quinone (Q) reduction site.
Studies on the electron transfer mechanism using flash-
activated chromatophores have substantiated that one electron
from QH_2 at Q_z enters a high potential redox sequence which
includes an FeS center and cyt c_1 while the second reduces
first, cyt b_L and then cyt b_H. The b-cytochromes are
subsequently oxidized in a two-step reaction by quinone at
site Q_C (5). The reactions at Qz and Qc are inhibited
specifically by myxothiazol (6) and antimycin (7),
respectively.

Studies using the electrochromic bandshift of a set of $\Delta\psi$-sensitive carotenoids in the chromatophore have supported the suggestion of the Q-cycle that the redox reactions of the b-cytochromes are linked to charge separation by cyt bc_1 (8). The carotenoid spectrum responds to $\Delta\psi$ formation with a time constant within the flash duration, i.e., less than 5 usec, and thereby provide a tool for the kinetic resolution of discrete steps of charge separation.

Recent experiments of Glaser and Crofts (9) have resolved the electron transfer reactions from Q_z to cyt b_L and Q_z to cyt b_H using single turnover kinetics of antimycin-treated chromatophores poised at ambient redox potentials where cyt b_H is either reduced or oxidized before the flash. These studies showed that charge separation occurs during electron transfer between the b-cytochromes and not between Q_z and cyt b_L or Q_z, FeS and cyt c_1. The carotenoid bandshift accompanying this cyt b_L to cyt b_H event accounted for 35-50% of the full dielectric distance of the membrane, indicating that an additional charge separation occurs during quinone-catalyzed cyt b oxidation.

The mechanism of the redox interaction between cyt b_H and Q_c and the location of Q_c in the profile of the membrane dielectric remains undetermined. The approach to this problem, by activating cyt b_H and Q_c redox reactions via the Q_z site is complicated by uncertainties arising from multiple turnovers of cyt bc_1, the complex redox chemistry of Q_c and the difficulty of isolating the individual redox steps involved in reducing Q_c to the semiquinone and then to the quinol. This latter point is of particular importance. The location of Q_c relative to cyt b_H may determine whether charge separation occurs on both the first and second electron transfers and whether electrons or protons (or both) are the electrogenic species.

We have addressed this question by activating the redox interaction between cyt b_H and Q_c more directly and more specifically. It was predicted from E_m/pH relationships of the site-associated Q_c redox couples (10) and of cyt b_H that at high pH the Q_cH_2/Q_c- redox couple should be capable of reducing cyt b_H. This was subsequently demonstrated in a cyt bc_1 blocked at Q_z by myxothiazol (11,12); cyt b_H is reduced in milliseconds and the reaction is blocked by antimycin. Additional evidence from the RC/cyt bc_1 hybrid system confirmed that the reductant of cyt b_H is QH_2(12). The reaction may be written as follows:

$$Q_{pool}H_2 \; + \; Q_c \text{ site} \rightleftharpoons Q_cH_2 \qquad (1)$$

$$Q_cH_2 \; + \; \text{ferri cyt } b_H \rightleftharpoons Q_c^-(H^+) \; + \; \text{ferro cyt } b_H \; + \; H^+ \quad (2)$$

We have extended the study of Q_c-mediated cyt b_H reduction and show that this reaction is accompanied by charge transfer through the membrane dielectric.

METHODS

Chromatophores were prepared from *Rhodobacter sphaeroides* Ga as previously described (13). Rapid kinetics (13), redox poising (14). and the strategem for antimycin-sensitive cyt b_H reduction (12) were performed as outlined. Reaction center, cyt b and cyt c concentrations were determined using previously published extinction coefficients (13). See (12) for chemical sources.

RESULTS

Q_c-mediated cyt b_H reduction and the carotenoid bandshift

At pH 7.0, myxothiazol appears to inhibit all flash-induced cyt b reduction in chromatophores (not shown). Raising the ambient pH, however, reveals the antimycin-sensitive reduction of cyt b_H (11,12). Figure 1 shows cyt b reduction under these conditions and also documents a unique blue shift in the carotenoid spectrum associated with this reaction. On the left are two kinetic traces showing cyt b_H reduction following a flash delivered in the presence of myxothiazol alone or myxothiazol plus antimycin. At ph 9.6 and an E_h of 85 mV the extent of antimycin-sensitive cyt b_H reduction is maximal. Under these conditions 0.07 uM cyt b is reduced following flash-induced oxidation of 0.18 uM [BChl]$_2$. On the right are kinetic traces showing the change in the carotenoid bandshift measured under identical conditions. In the presence of both inhibitors only the bandshifts due to charge separating events in the RC are apparent (9). When antimycin-sensitive cyt b reduction is allowed to proceed i.e., myxothiazol alone, the red shift of the carotenoids is noticably less a few milliseconds after the flash. This difference continues to increase, reaching a maximum by approximately 30 msec.

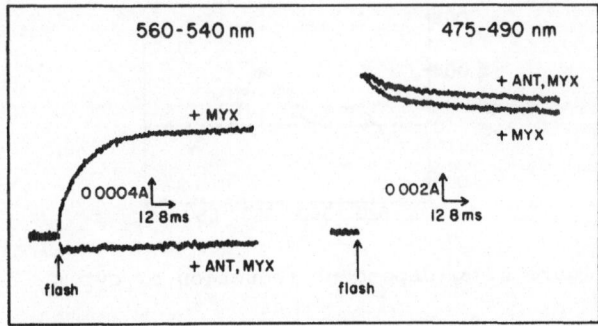

Figure 1. Kinetics of antimycin-sensitive cyt b_H reduction and of corresponding carotenoid bandshift development.

The kinetics of the blue bandshift development are very similar to those for antimycin-sensitive cyt b reduction (not shown). Furthermore, the redox potential-dependence of both phenomena are similar. A titration of the full extent of the carotenoid bandshift difference is complete between Eh values of 10 and 90 mV. The midpoint (E_m) for cyt b reduction at this pH has been reported to be approximately 20 mV (11). These

data, taken together, provide convincing evidence for a
transmembrane charge separation accompanying electron transfer
between the Q_CH_2/Q_C^- redox couple and cyt b_H.

Effect of electric field on the redox equilibrium between Q_C and cyt b_H

Previous studies have shown that Q_C mediated cyt b_H
reduction may be simulated as an equilibrium between Q_{pool} and
cyt b_H (12). At pH values where the reaction is favorable, the
E_m values of Q_{pool}, Q_C and cyt b_H are similar (10). This
situation provides an opportunity to alter the redox
equilibrium by imposition of membrane potentials across the
chromatophore membrane. The rapid $\Delta\psi$ generating reactions of
the RC permit an experiment of this kind using a strategem
similar to that of Takamiya and Dutton (14) who studied the
equilibrium between cyt c_2 and [BChl]$_2$.

The $\Delta\psi$ generated by a single turnover of the RC in
chromatophores of *Rhodobacter* may be measured by calibration
with artificially imposed K^+ diffusion potentials (8). The
corrected value for the first turnover is approximately 65 mV
(see also 15,16). A second flash delivered 24 msec after the
first increases $\Delta\psi$ to 100 mV. If cyt b_H reduction is observed
under conditions where $\Delta\psi$ is established after a single flash
and also under conditions where $\Delta\psi$ formation is prevented by
valinomycin, a significantly greater extent of cyt b_H
reduction is noted in the presence of $\Delta\psi$.

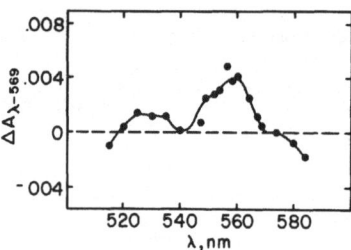

Figure 2. $\Delta\psi$-dependent reduction of cyt b_H.

Figure 2 shows a spectrum of the $\Delta\psi$-dependent cyt b_H
reduction following a single flash. This spectrum is the
difference between two independent spectral subtractions: 1) a
spectrum obtained in the presence of antimycin, myxothiazol
and valinomycin was subtracted from a similar experiment,
minus valinomycin; 2) a spectrum obtained in the presence of
myxothiazol and valinomycin was subtracted from one in the
presence of myxothiazol alone. The difference between 2 and 1

provides a spectrum free of contribution from carotenoid and showing only an antimycin-sensitive, $\Delta\psi$ dependent features. The spectrum is clearly that of a b-cytochrome with an -band maximum at 560nm. The spectral width is also that expected. There appears in the spectrum a reproducible shoulder near 550nm, which is due to the previously documented effect of $\Delta\psi$ on cyt c_2 oxidation by the RC (14). These data, taken together with the observation that $\Delta\psi$-dependent cyt b_H reduction kinetics ($t_{1/2}$ = 10 msec) are clearly much slower than those of the carotenoid bandshift (kinetically unresolved from the duration of the flash), argue strongly that the $\Delta\psi$-stimulated absorption increase at 560nm can be assigned to cyt b_H reduction.

The extra cyt b_H reduced in the presence of 65 mV of $\Delta\psi$ was calculated from a total of 0.083 uM cyt b_H reducible by multiple flashes delivered under optimal conditions for the reaction. This value was between 0.018 and 0.023 uM.

DISCUSSION

We show in this manuscript that antimycin-sensitive cyt b_H reduction is accompanied by a blue shift in the $\Delta\psi$-sensitive optical absorption bands of the membrane-bound carotenoids. The direction of the bandshift is opposite to the red bandshift that accompanies cyt b_H reduction via the Q_z site (9). Thus the blue shift indicates a charge transfer event opposite in direction to that normally identified with the physiological charge separating reactions of the cyt bc_1 and the RC. The magnitude of the blue shift measured under conditions which strongly favor cyt b_H reduction in the Q_c-cyt b_H equilibrium is approximately 23-28% as large as that measured in a complete transmembrane charge separation catalyzed by either the RC or the cyt bc_1 complex. This calculation was done by assuming that the bandshift observed in the presence of antimycin and myxothiazol represents charge separation events associated with two turnovers of photosynthetic RCs (see also 9).

Consistent with the idea that cyt b_H reduction via Q_c is coupled to transmembrane charge separation, we have shown that the membrane potential preformed by the RC after a flash acts to increase the extent of cyt b_H reduction. The magnitude of the effect of $\Delta\psi$ on the equilibrium of this reaction is a function of the charge transfer distance through the membrane dielectric (14). This may be quantitated using a simple relationship for the $\Delta\psi$-dependent change in the apparent E_h of cyt b_H if one assumes that the dielectric is linear with distance and that a single charge is transferred in the redox reaction. The relationship between the cyt b_H redox couple in the presence ($E_h{}'$) and absence (E_h) of $\Delta\psi$ is:

$$E_h{}' = E_h + x\,\Delta\psi \qquad (3)$$

where x is the fractional dielectric distance travelled by the charge. Values obtained for the extra cyt b_H reduced after a single flash i.e., in the presence of 65 mV $\Delta\psi$, gives a calculated x value of between 0.34 and 0.39.

The magnitude of the carotenoid bandshift also has direct implications for the distance of charge separation across the membrane dielectric. Moreover, if the identity of the charge, i.e., electron or proton, is known and assumptions are made concerning the properties of the membrane dielectric, more exact topological relationships of the redox centers involved may be defined. For example, turnover of the RC is accompanied by several charge separating reactions identified by direct voltage measurement, by field-induced equilibrium shifts and by carotenoid bandshifts (16). The positions of the redox centers derived from these measurements have been largely substantiated by x-ray structure analysis of crystals of the RC (17).

Similar assumptions (9) about the bandshift associated with the redox reaction between cyt b_L and cyt b_H led to the proposal that the two hemes are arranged across 35-50% of the full dielectric. These results are supported by analysis of primary protein sequences of cyt b using folding algorithms (18) and by data which relate the effect of $\Delta\psi$ on the redox equilibrium between the hemes as studied in submitochondrial particles (19).

There are no structural data available which directly address the location of the Q_C site in the membrane dielectric. We cannot therefore distinguish between protons and electrons in attempting to identify the species involved in the charge recombination event. We can however provide topological limits for the placement of Q_C by assuming that either an electron or proton is the sole contributor to charge separation in the redox interaction of Q_CH_2/Q_C^- and cyt b_H. From calibrated carotenoid bandshifts and from the effect of $\Delta\psi$, we can approximate the charge transfer distance to be between 23 and 39% of the dielectric distance. Figure 3 is a representation of the two extremes where either an electron or a proton is electrogenic. The figure shows a reaction scheme for the forward, physiological turnover of cyt bc_1 and the placement of cyt bc_1 redox centers in the profile of the membrane dielectric.

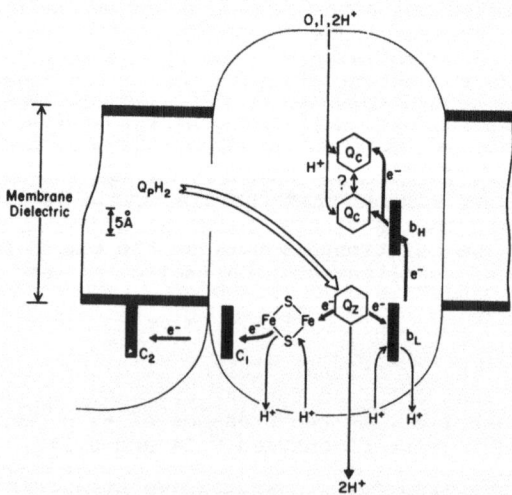

Figure 3. Possible positions of Q_C in the membrane dielectric.

Acknowledgements

Supported by PHS grant 27309

REFERENCES

1. Crofts, A.R. and Wraight, C.A. The Electrochemical Domain
   of Photosynthesis, Biochim. Biophys. Acta, 726:149
   (1983).

2. Rich, P.R., Electron and Proton Transfers Through Quinones
   and Cytochrome bc Complexes, Biochim. Biophys. Acta,
   768:53 (1984).

3. Mitchell, P., Possible Molecular Mechanisms of the Protonmotive Function of Cytochrome Systems, J. Theor. Biol.,
   62:327 (1976).

4. Rich, P.R., A Perspective on Q-cycles, J. Bioenerg.
   Biomemb.. 18:145 (1986).

5. Crofts, A.R., Meinhardt, S.W., Jones, K.R. and Snozzi, M.,
   The Role of the Quinone Pool in the Cyclic Electron
   Transport Chain of Rhodopseudomonas sphaeroides,
   Biochim. Biophys. Acta, 723:202 (1983).

6. Meinhardt, S.W. and Crofts, A.R. The Site and Mechanism
   of Action of Myxothiazol as an Inhibitor of Electron
   Transfer in Rhodopseudomonas sphaeroides, FEBS Lett.,
   149:217 (1982).

7. van den Berg, W.H., Prince, R.C., Bashford, C.L.,
   Takamiya, K., Bonner, W.D. and Dutton, P.L., Electron
   and Proton Transport in the Ubiquinone Cytochrome b-c_2
   Oxidoreductase of Rhodopseudomonas sphaeroides,
   J. Biol. Chem., 254:8594 (1979).

8. Jackson, J.B. and Crofts, A.R., The Kinetics of Light
   Induced Carotenoid Changes in Rhodopseudomonas
   Rhodopseudomonas sphaeroides and their Relation
   to Electrical Field Generation across the Chromatophore
   Membrane, Eur. J. Biochem., 18:120 (1971).

9. Glaser E.G. and Crofts, A.R. A New Electrogenic Step in
   the Ubiquinol:cyt c_2 Oxidoreductase Complex of
   Rhodopseudomonas sphaeroides, Biochim. Biophys. Acta,
   766:322 (1984).

10. Robertson, D.E., Prince, R.C., Bowyer, J.R., Matsuura, K.
    Dutton, P.L. and Ohnishi, T. Thermodynamic Properties
    of the Semiquinone and its Binding Site in the
    Ubiquinol-cyt $c(c_2)$ Oxidoreductase of
    Respiratory and Photosynthetic Systems. J. Biol. Chem.
    259:1758 (1984).

11. Glaser, E.G., Meinhardt, S.W. and Crofts, A.R. Reduction
    lof Cytochrome b_{561} through the Antimycin-sensitive site
    of the Ubiquinol-cyt c_2 Oxidoreductase Complex of
    Rhodopseudomonas sphaeroides, FEBS Lett.,178:336 (1984).

12. Robertson, D.E., Giangiacomo, K.M., Moser, C.C. and Dutton, P.L. Two Distinct Quinone Modulated Modes of Antimycin-sensitive Cytochrome b Reduction in the cyt bc_1 Complex, FEBS Lett., 178:343 (1984).

13. Dutton, P.L., Petty, K.M., Bonner, H.S. and Morse, S.D. Cytochrome c_2 and the Reaction Center of Rhodopseudomonas sphaeroides Ga Membranes. Biochim. Biophys. Acta, 387: 536 (1975).

14. Takamiya, K. and Dutton, P.L. The Influence of Transmembrane Potentials of the Redox Equilibrium Between cyt c_2 and the Reaction Center in Rhodopseudomonas sphaeroides Chromatophores, FEBS Lett., 80:279 (1977).

15. Packham, N.K., Berryman, J.A. and Jackson, J.B. The Charging Capacitance of the Chromatophore Membrane, FEBS Lett., 89:205 (1978).

16. Dutton, P.L. Energy Transduction in Anoxygenic Photosynthesis, Encyclopedia of Plant Physiology, vol 19 (Staehelin, L.A. and Arntzen, C.J., eds) pp 197-237. Springer, Berlin (1986).

17. Deisenhofer, J., Epp, O., Miki, K., Huber, R. and Michel, H. Structure of the Protein Subunits in the Photosynthetic Reaction center of Rhodopseudomonas viridis at 3A Resolution, Nature, 318:618 (1985).

18. Saraste, M. Location of Haem-binding Sites in the Mitochondrial cyt b. FEBS Lett., 166:367 (1984).

19. Gopher, A. and Gutman, M. Differentiation of C and M Side Reactions of Ubiquinone Using Imposed Electron-Electrochemical Potential Gradient, Function of Quinones in Energy Conserving Systems, (Trumpower, B.L., ed) pp 511-526. Academic Press, N.Y. (1982).

CONSTRUCTION AND CHARACTERIZATION OF MONOLAYER FILMS OF THE
REACTION CENTER CYTOCHROME-C PROTEIN FROM RHODOPSEUDOMONAS
VIRIDIS

Guillermo Alegria and P. Leslie Dutton

Department of Biochemistry and Biophysics
University of Pennsylvania, PA 19104 USA

INTRODUCTION

The x-ray crystal structure of the *Rhodopseudomonas viridis*
reaction center - cytochrome c complex (RC-cyt complex) has
stimulated considerable interest (1-4). One of the most
remarkable features of the protein is the linear array of the
four cytochrome c hemes which contrasts sharply with the
arrangement suggested from functional studies for the
analogous hemes of *Chromatium vinosum*.(5) How the four hemes,
two high potential and two low potential, are structurally
arranged around the bacteriochlorophyll dimer, $(BChl)_2$,
contained in the reaction center is a question of long
standing. This question is an important component of the
deeper issue that addresses the mechanism of electron transfer
not only from these hemes to the light generated $(BChl)_2^+$ but
also between the hemes (see 1-3). Of particular interest in
this regard is the finding that the low potential heme(s) of
photosynthetic bacteria are able to undergo oxidation at
cryogenic temperatures, while reactions of high potential
hemes tend to 'freeze out' with decreasing temperature (see
1,3, and 6).

One approach that we anticipate will clarify the
structure-function relationships in the RC-cyt c complex
involves the construction of Langmuir-Blodgett monolayer
films of the RC-cyt c complex deposited on planar conductive
supports (7, 8, and see 9 for a review). This arrangement
permits not only spectrophotometric determinations but also
direct electrical assays of the flash-activated redox
reactions within the cytochrome array as well as between the
cytochromes and $(BChl)_2$. Furthermore, the arrangement is
suitable for future plans to apply large electric fields to
modify the free energy of the reactions with the view to
obtain energetic and mechanistic information (10,11).

This paper describes the first efforts to fabricate and
characterize RC-cyt c protein monolayers from *Rhodopseudomonas
viridis*.

MATERIALS AND METHODS

Langmuir-Blodgett films of the RC-cyt c complex

RC-cyt c complex from <u>Rps</u>. <u>viridis</u> was prepared as described by Prince et al (12). The lauryl dimethylamine-N-oxide (LDAO) was replaced by <u>beta</u> octyl glucoside by extensively washing the LDAO-solubilized reaction centers on a DEAE column with a detergent-free buffer and then with a buffer containing 30mM beta octyl glucoside. Final elution was made with a 45mM beta glucoside, 10mM Tris HCl buffer at pH 8.0.

A Langmuir-Blodgett (LB) film balance (Lauda Type 1974) was used to make the films following the general procedure described elsewhere (7,10,11), but considerably improved (G. Alegria and P.L. Dutton; in preparation). The subphase contained 1 mM ascorbate, 1mM $CdCl_2$ in 5mM MES buffer at pH 6.5. Monolayer depositions onto glass slides were made at a surface pressure of 25mN/m.

Film Analysis by Redox Potentiometry and Spectroscopy

Redox titrations of the LB films were performed anaerobically with a homemade cuvette that permitted continuous spectrophotometric assay; otherwise the mediators (see figure 1 legend) and procedures were essentially as previously described (13). From 5 to 10 minutes for equilibration were allowed at each potential; the same results were obtained for oxidative and reductive titrations.

Both standard and linearly polarized light absorption spectra of the LB films on glass slides were recorded at defined redox potentials on a computer-driven, chopped Johnson Foundation scanning dual-beam apparatus that operated over the 350-1300nm range. Flash-induced absorbance changes in the cytochrome c <u>alpha</u>-band were monitored in a similar but unchopped single beam spectrophotometer with the slides tilted at 45 degrees to both the actinic and measuring beam.(7) Absorbance transients were stored and averaged using a computer scope (RC Electronics Inc., Santa Barbara, CA).

All experiments were done using a buffer (10mM Tris HCl; pH 8.0) containing 60% glycerol to decrease reflection losses and dispersion distortions.

RESULTS

Figure 1 shows a typical redox titration of the cytochrome c hemes associated with the <u>Rps</u>. <u>viridis</u> RC-cyt c complex in a five-monolayer LB film. The redox range -200 to +400 mV includes both the low and high potential hemes. However, instead of the familiar two waves for the two unresolved couples: high potential hemes (E_{m8} 300-350mV) and low potential hemes (E_{m8} approximately 10 mV) seen for the same preparation in solution there are four distinct waves. The experimental points are shown with four n=1 Nernst curves fitted to the absorption change at the <u>alpha</u>-band maxima

relative to the fully oxidized baseline between 540 and 572nm.
Moreover, the electrochemically resolved hemes in the film
display unique maxima that are more readily distinguishable
than is the case in solution. The four hemes in the film are
characterized as follows:

E_{m8}+340mV, λ_{max}558nm E_{m8}+90mV, λ_{max}553nm
E_{m8}+225mV, λ_{max}556nm E_{m8}-90mV, λ_{max}551nm

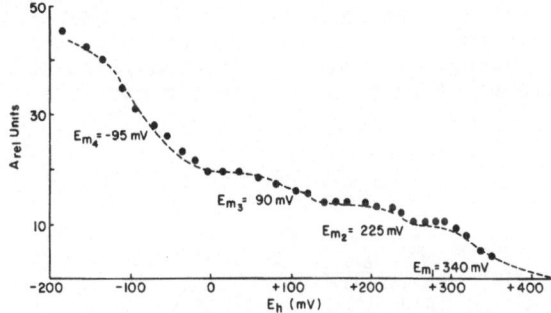

Figure 1

Redox titration of the alpha band of the cytochrome c
associated with the *Rhodopseudomonas viridis* RCs in a multilayer
LB film built up of five monolayer depositions. The slide was
submerged in a buffer containing 10mM Tris HCl 60% glycerol pH
8.0. The following dyes were used as redox mediators (2-5uM):
N,N,N,N-tetramethyl-p-phenylenediamine, 2,3,5,6-Tetramethyl-p-
phenylenediamine, N-methyl phenazonium methosulfate, N-ethyl
phenazonium ethosulfate, pyocyanine, and 2-hydroxy-1,4
naphthoquinone.

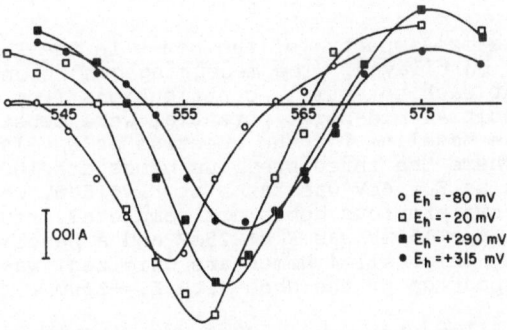

Figure 2

Spectra of the cytochrome c photo-oxidation in a *Rhodopseudomonas
viridis* RCs LB multilayer. The multilayer and measuring
conditions were as those in figure 1. The absorbance changes
were measured following flash activation.

Figure 2 shows that the four hemes are able to be
oxidized following flash-activation. Poised at different
redox potential values on each of the four plateaus revealed

603

in the titration in figure 1, flash-activation led to the stable oxidation of the lowest potential cytochrome of the ones reduced before activation.

No attempt at this stage was made to resolve the oxidation kinetics associated with each of the spectra shown in figure 2; in all cases oxidation was complete within 50 μs and once oxidized reduction occurred on the second time scale. At each potential a clearly different cytochrome species became oxidized; there were no obvious transients evident suggesting that any interheme electron transfer that occurs is not rate limiting. This is a characteristic of cytochrome oxidation in RC-cyt c complexes isolated in solution or in native membranes of many photosynthetic bacteria. (see 1-3,14,15)

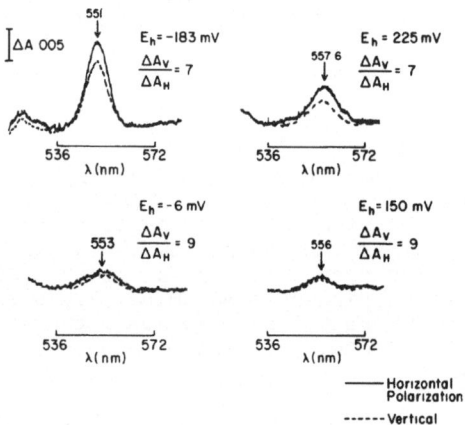

Figure 3.

Linearly polarized spectra of the hemes in the *Rhodopseudomonas viridis* RC LB multilayer. The measuring conditions were as in figure 1. At each potential, contributions from the hemes with more positive mid-point potential were substracted as follows: The baseline for the spectrum at E_h=-183mV was taken at E_h=-6mV where the three previous hemes are 100% reduced. The baseline at E_h=-6mV was taken at E_h=+150mV where, as before, the two previous hemes are completely reduced. The reference at E_h=+150mV was E_h=+225mV and a baseline at E_h=+400mV (at which all 4 hemes are oxidized) was used to obtain the spectrum of the heme with E_m=+340mV.

The LB films were examined in the visible and near IR regions with linearly polarized light (data not shown). The values of the dichroic ratios of the major bands of the reaction center and the high potential cytochromes agree well with those measured in whole cells (16), chromatophores (17), reaction centers in squeezed gels (18) and single crystals (19). Figure 3 shows the resolved spectra for each of the four cytochrome c <u>alpha</u>-bands for horizontally and vertically polarized light. The dichroic ratios associated with each of the four <u>alpha</u>-bands were computed at the maximum wavelength. Using a simplified model that treats the system as an array of uni-axially oriented molecules with plane-polarized transition moments, the angle that the heme plane makes with the slide plane can be calculated (20,21). It is clear that there are two pairs of orientationally equivalent hemes: One pair, characterized by a dichroic ratio close to 0.7, comprises the hemes with E_{m8}-95mV (λ_{max}551nm) and E_{m8}+340mV (λ_{max}558); the other pair, characterized by a dichroic ratio close to 0.9, comprises hemes with E_{m8}+90mV (λ_{max}553nm) and E_{m8}+225mV (λ_{max}556nm). Thus the lowest and highest potential hemes have their heme planes tilted out of the slide plane at least 15 degrees more than the hemes of intermediate potential values.

DISCUSSION

The work presented here focuses on the cytochrome c hemes of the *Rhodopseudomonas viridis* reaction center. The activity that is displayed by the films with respect to the cytochrome c oxidation shows considerable promise for the approach we are developing. Other views of the preparation are similarly encouraging: the orientation of chlorins and cytochromes appear similar to that encountered in native membranes. In addition to electron transfer from cytochromes c to $(BChl)_2$ and from $(BChl)_2$ through to Q_A, the Q_A to Q_B reaction is functional and inhibited by o-phenothroline. For these reasons we conclude the system presents us with a viable experimental vehicle that is usefully similar to the native system. (G. Alegria and P.L. Dutton in preparation) However, the small differences in the redox properties of the hemes that have recently been recognized in solution (14,15) appear amplified in the film. The sources of the altered redox properties may be environmental effects peculiar to the close-packed nature of the film that fortuitously enhances resolution. Indeed it may not be so surprising that the properties of the hemes are modified during film formation because they reside in a polypeptide that normally extends into the aqueous medium rather than being contained within the membrane. Hence exposure of the hemes to the aqueous medium may be greatly reduced, cutting off contact with ions, including hydrogen ions, and even water; also perhaps altering the dielectric properties around the heme (see ref 22).

The issue of identifying the low and high hemes in the linear array of the x-ray structure has been addressed by a number of laboratories but it is still an open and difficult question to answer (see refs 1,2,14,15 for discussions). The main contribution from the present study, made possible because of the clear spectral and redox resolution of the four hemes, comes from the assignments of the angular disposition of the hemes in the films, namely that the highest and the lowest potential hemes (high angle with respect to the film plane) and the intermediate potential hemes (lower angle) represent two angular populations. Judging from the x-ray crystal structure we can tentatively conclude that in the four heme array the highest and lowest potential hemes are placed at the ends and that the others represent the two central hemes. This cuts down the possibilities for the arrangement of the hemes and RC to just four, namely

(a) RC - high, low, high, low   (c) RC - low, high, low, high
(b) RC - high, high, low, low   (d) RC - low, low, high, high

Arguments based on the EPR studies by Tiede et al (5) on the structural organization of the Chromatium vinosum RC-cyt c complex can be used to reduce the number of possibilities to two. These workers revealed that magnetic interactions are observed neither between the two low potential cytochromes nor between the two high potential ones, implying that the distance between the cytochromes of the same pair is greater than 10 A; in contrast there was magnetic interaction between the high and low potential hemes. Similar although preliminary results have been obtained by EPR in oriented membranes of Rps. viridis (A.W. Rutherford, personal communication). Such results are consistent with an arrangement such as in (a) or (c) in which high and low potential hemes are adjacent but pairs of high and low potential hemes are not. This area of work now warrants further study.

Considerations on whether a high or low potential heme is proximal to the $(BChl)_2$ have mainly been based on kinetic properties and temperature dependency of the cytochrome c photo-oxidation (see 1,14,15,23). The most satisfactory in this regard would be arrangement (a) since ambient temperature kinetic properties are neatly explained with electron transfer occurring linearly through the four hemes. However, complications arise at cryogenic temperature where only the low potential heme oxidation is supported; here a separate electron transfer mechanism from the low potential heme to $(BChl)_2$ is required. On the other hand in the case of arrangement (c), while cryogenic temperature oxidation of the low potential heme is readily explained, the simple linear situation for the oxidation of the other hemes at higher temperature can be ruled out. (see ref 1)

Some considerations in favor of arrangement (a) come from the detailed structure of the RC-cyt c complex. Michel et al (24) have reported that the heme closest to the RC (number 3 in their nomenclature) appears to have a methionine as the sixth ligand, a characteristic of higher potential hemes; while the second heme (number 4) appears to have a histidine as the ligand, more characteristic of lower potential cytochrome c hemes. (Michel, Deisenhofer and Weyer personal communications) However, there is more to it than this since the outer two hemes (numbers 1 and 2) also include a low potential form for which no histidine sixth ligand is assigned. Environmental effects of the kind already alluded to and emphasized by Stellwagen (25) may be very important; a general rule discussed by Stellwagen is that the redox potential is raised as the heme is increasingly shielded from solvent water; however, in addition the nature of the contact of the exposed heme with ions in solution especially protons cannot be ignored. In this regard it may be pertinent that the third heme away from the RC is reported to be considerably more buried that its neighbors (26).

The results presented taken together with the above considerations suggest that the arrangement best accommodating the current information is the RC-high, low, high, low configuration. This is summarized below along with the preliminary redox and spectral assignments reported here for the RC-cyt c complex monolayer films.

	RC	heme	heme	heme	heme
x-ray nomenclature		3	4	2	1
Approx E_{m8} (mV)		+340	+90	+225	-90
alpha band max(nm)		558	553	556	551

We are currently planning to measure flash-induced voltage changes in the films potentiometrically poised at different redox states; we also intend to determine the effects of applied electric fields on the redox distribution in the heme array and on the electron transfer kinetics. Both approaches should provide insights into the function of this interesting system.

Acknowledgments

This work was supported by a grant from DOE DE-FG02-86ER 13476.

REFERENCES

1. Dutton, P.L. (1986) Encyclodpedia of Plant Physiology Vol 19 Ed. by L.A. Staehelin and C. Antzen Springer Verlag, Heidleberg, pp. 197-237.

2. Wraight, C.A. (To appear in Progress in Photosynthesis Research).

3. Dutton, P.L., and Prince, R.C. (1978) in The Photosynthetic Bacteria, Ed. by R.K. Clayton and W.R. Sistrom, Plenum Press, New York, pp. 525-570.

4. Antennas and Reaction Centers of Photosynthetic Bacteria, Ed. M.E. Michel-Beyerle, Springer Verlag, New York.

5. Tiede, D.M., Leigh, J.S., and Dutton, P.L. (1978) Biochim. Biophys. Acta 503: 524-544.

6. Dutton, P.L. (1971) Biochim. Biophys. Acta 681: 151-201.

7. Tiede, D.M., Mueller, and Dutton, P.L. (1982) Biochim. Biophys. Acta 681: 191-201.

8. Popovic, Z.D., Kovacs, G.J., Vincett, P.S., and Dutton, P.L. (1985) Chem. Phys. Lett 116: 405-410.

9. Tiede, D.M. (1985) Biochim. Biophys. Acta 811: 357-379.

10. Popovic, Z.D., Kovacs, G.J., Vincett, P.S., Alegria, G., and Dutton, P.L. (1986) Chem Phys. 110 : 227-237.

11. Popovic, Z.D., Kovacs, G.J., Vincett, P.S., Alegria, G. and Dutton, P.L. (1986) Biochim. Biophys. Acta 851: 38-48.

12. Prince, R.C., Tiede, D.M., Thornber, J.P. and Dutton, P.L. (1977) <u>Biochim</u>. <u>Biophys</u>. <u>Acta</u> 462: 467-490.

13. Dutton, P.L. (1978) <u>Meths</u>. <u>Enzymol</u>. Vol LIV, pp. 411-435.

14. Dracheva, S.M., Drachev, L.A., Zoberezhnaya, S.M., Konstantinov, A.A., Semenov, A.Y., and Skulachev, V.P. (1986) <u>FEBS Lett</u> 205: 41-46.

15. Shopes, R.J., Levine, L.M.A., Holten, D., and Wraight, C.A., to appear in <u>Photosynthesis Research</u>.

16. Paillotin, G. Vermeglio, A., and Breton, J. (1979) <u>Biochim</u>. <u>Biophys</u>. <u>Acta</u> 545: 249-264.

17. Vermeglio, A., Breton, J., Barouch, Y., and Clayton, R.K. (1980) <u>Biochim</u>. <u>Biophys</u>. <u>Acta</u> 593: 299-311.

18. Breton, J. (1985) <u>Biochim</u>. <u>Biophys</u>. <u>Acta</u> 810: 235-245.

19. Zinth, W., Kaiser, W., and Michel, H. (1983) <u>Biochim</u>. <u>Biophys</u>. <u>Acta</u> 723: 128-131.

20. Breton, J., Michel-Villaz M., and Paillotin, G. (1973) <u>Biochim</u>. <u>Biophys</u>. <u>Acta</u> 314: 42-56.

21. Hofrichter J., and Eaton, W.A. (1976) <u>Ann. Rev. Biophys. Bioeng.</u> 5: 511-560.

22. Senn H., and Withrich, K. (1985) <u>Quarterly Rev. of Biophys.</u> 18: 113-134.

23. DeVault, D., Chance, B. (1966) <u>Biophys</u>. <u>J</u>. 6: 825-847.

24. Michel, H., and Deisenhofer, J. (1986) <u>Encyclopedia of Plant Physiology</u> Vol 15, Ed. by L.A. Staehelin and C. Antzen Springer Verlag, Heidelberg, pp. 371-381.

25. Stellwagen E. (1978) <u>Nature</u> 275: 73-74.

26. Deisenhofer J., Epp, O., Miki, K., Hubber, R., and Michel, H. (1985) <u>Nature</u> 318: 19-26.

STRUCTURE-FUNCTION RELATIONSHIPS IN THE <u>Rhodopseudomonas viridis</u> REACTION CENTER COMPLEX: ELECTROGENIC STEPS CONTRIBUTING TO ΔΨ FORMATION

V.P. Skulachev, L.A. Drachev, S.M. Dracheva,
A.A. Konstantinov, A.Yu. Semenov and V.A. Shuvalov

Laboratory of Molecular Biology and Bioorganic Chemistry
Moscow State University, Moscow 119899, USSR

INTRODUCTION

The concept of transmembrane electron flow in the coupling sites of redox chains was put forward by Mitchell virtually simultaneously with the general chemiosmotic principle of energy coupling via protonmotive force (1).Whereas the general formulation of the chemiosmotic theory proved to be accepted by majority of bioenergeticists, there are still considerable debates on the electrogenic transmembrane electron transfer as a mechanism of $\Delta\bar{\mu}_H{}^+$ generation.

There are many indications that electron transfer across the coupling membrane does indeed occur in reaction center complexes of photosynthetic bacteria. These indications, however, can never be conclusive unless the 3-dimensional structure of the complex is known.

Recently such a structure has been established - and this is for the first time with respect to $\Delta\bar{\mu}_H{}^+$-generating protein - for reaction center (RC) complex from the purple photosynthetic bacterium <u>Rhodopseudomonas viridis</u> (2,3). Unfortunately, in this very bacterium, membrane potential generation coupled to RC electron transfer reactions was not studied until recently. In fact, <u>Rps.viridis</u> does not exhibit any electrochromic band-shift which was most widely used to monitor fast electrogenic events in membranes of some other photosynthetic bacteria.

In this group systematic studies on photoinduced ΔΨ generation across the coupling membranes of purple photosynthetic and halophilic bacteria were carried out with the aid of the direct electrometric method (4,5).

In particular, fast kinetics of the laser flash-induced ΔΨ generation in the collodion film-associated <u>R.rubrum</u> and <u>Rps.sphaeroides</u> chromatophores and RC complex proteoliposomes were measured. Three principal electrogenic steps were revealed:

(i) P-870 $\longrightarrow$ Q_A electron transfer,

(ii) Q_B^{2-} protonation to QH_2,

(iii) P-870$^+$ reduction by a soluble cytochrome <u>c</u> (6-8).

The electrogenic nature of the reaction (i) and (iii) was inferred from the earlier studied by means of some other methods as well.

Here we applied the proteoliposome-collodion film technique to investigate electrogenic events the <u>Rps. viridis</u> RC complex.

The RC complex from Rps. viridis includes a special bacteriochlorophyll pair $(BChl)_2$ serving as the photoexcitable primary electron donor,
2 molecules of the bacteriochlorophyll monomer (BChl), 2 bacteriopheophy-
tins(BPheo), menaquinone-9 (Q_A), ubiquinone-10 (Q_B) and tetraheme
cytochrome c (2,3).

METHODS

Rps. viridis cells were grown anaerobically (9). RC complexes were
isolated with the use of LDAO for chromatophore solubilization; subsequently, LDAO was replaced by Triton X-100 during the purification of
the RCs on a DEAE-cellulose column(9).

Proteoliposomes were prepared by the cholate dialysis method as
follows: a mixture containing asolectin (80 mg/ml) and sodium cholate
(4%) in 100 mM phosphate buffer (pH 7.5) was sonicated in an ultrasonic
desintegrator UZDN-2T in ~10 s outbursts (22 kHz, 50 mA) up to an overall sonication time of 1 min. The clear phospholipid solution was mixed
with an equal volume of the RC preparation $(A_{830} \sim 14)$ in 10 mM Tris-HCl
buffer (pH 7.0) containing 0.1% Triton X-100. The solution was then
dialyzed against 50 mM phosphate buffer (pH 7.5) overnight. The proteoliposomes were sedimented by centrifugation (165000 x g for 60 min) and
resuspended in an appropriate buffer. All the procedures were carried
out at 0-4°C.

RC concentration was determined spectrophotometrically using the
value $\mathcal{E}$ = 300 $mM^{-1}cm^{-1}$ at 830 nm.

Photoexcitation of RC was carried out with a YG-481 Quantel neodymium
laser (λ = 1064 nm; pulse half-width, 15 ns).

The photoelectric activity of proteoliposomes was measured electrometrically as described previously (6). The proteoliposome suspension
was added to one of the two compartments of a Teflon cuvette filled with
the incubation mixture (25 mM MOPS, 100 mM KCl, pH 7.0). A collodion film
impregnated with an asolectin solution in n-decane was used as a partition
between the compartments. Association of the vesicles (final RC concentration ~1 μM) with the collodion film was achieved upon 3-5 h incubation
in the presence of 20 mM $CaCl_2$ at room temperature. Subsequently, both
compartments were washed with a 10-fold volume of the incubation mixture
to remove the excess of $CaCl_2$ and proteoliposomes.

An electric potential difference generated across the collodion film
was measured with a pair of light-protected Ag/AgCl electrodes connected
via an operational amplifier (Burr Brown 3554 BM) with a transient recor-
der DL-1080 linked to the NOVA-3D computer.

All the measurements were carried out at 23-25°C.

RESULTS AND DISCUSSION

In order to measure electrogenic reactions associated with electron
transfer in Rps.viridis reaction centers, the isolated RC complexes were
reconstituted into asolectin proteoliposomes.

The experiments described and discussed below were carried out with
the proteoliposome preparations which showed uniform RC complex incorporation (cytochrome c outside).

Fig.1A shows a typical laser flash-induced photoelectric response
of the collodion film-associated RC proteoliposomes, measured with two
film-separated electrodes.

Before the flash, the system was stored in the dark for several min.

It is seen that the flash results in the generation of about 100 mV
electric potential difference ($\Delta \psi$) between two collodion film-separated
compartments, the proteoliposome-free side of film being charged negatively. Since the flash duration was about 30 ns, one may conclude that
the observed response was due to a single turnover of RC.

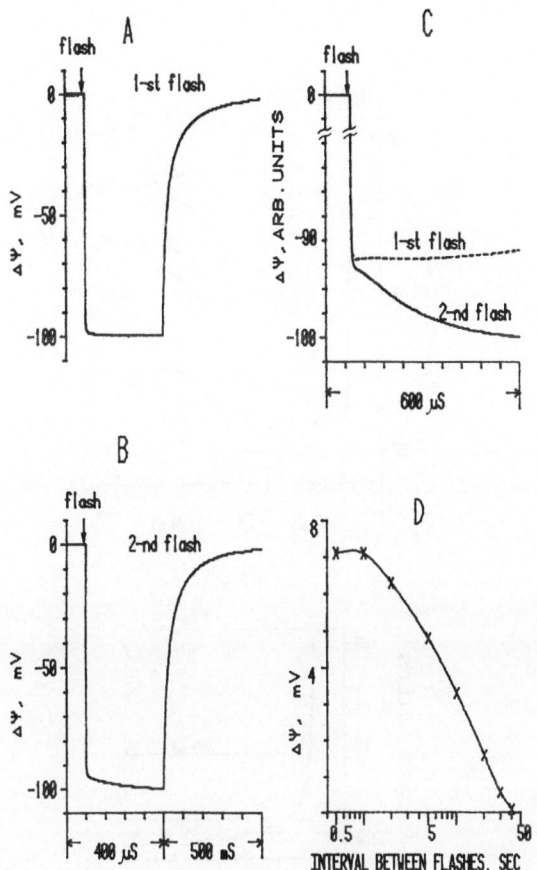

Fig. 1. Laser flash-induced electrogenic responses associated with
single and double reduction of Q_B in Rps. viridis RC proteoliposomes. (A) and (B) Photopotential traces observed upon the
1-st and 2-nd flashes, respectively.
Incubation mixture: 100 mM KCl, 25 mM MOPS-KOH, pH 7.0, 100 μM
diaminodurene, 100 μM vitamin K_3, 10 μM Methylene Blue and 2 mM
ferri/ferrocyanide in a proportion to obtain a 240 mV redox
potential. Before the flashes, the sample was preincubated for
2-3 min in the dark. The second flash was given 0.5 s after
the first one. (C) Expanded lower parts of the traces (A) and
(B). (D) Dependence of the second flash-induced slow electrogenic phase amplitude on the time interval between the 1-st
and 2-nd flashes.

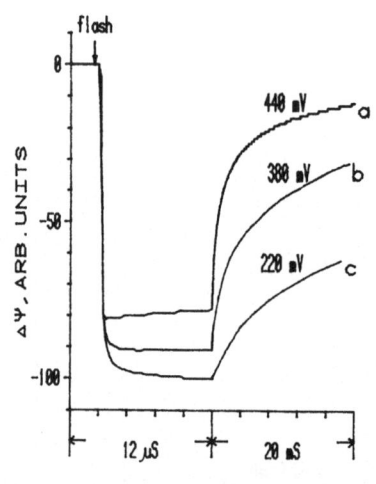

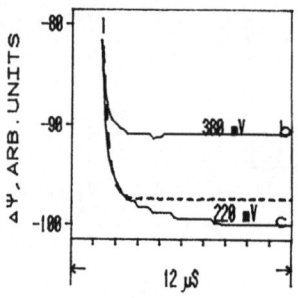

Fig. 2. Laser-flash induced electrogenesis associated with the c_{559} and
c_{559} oxidations in RC proteoliposomes.
Incubation mixure as in Fig.1. Redox potentials were adjusted at
440, 380 and 220 mV, as indicated. The photoelectric responses
at three redox potentials have been normalized with respect to
the amplitude of the fast electrogenic phase. The inset gives
expanded recordings of the lower parts of traces b, c, illustrating the cytochrome c associated electrogenesis; the dashed
line in the inset shows the contribution of the 0.3 μs phase
(c-559 oxidation) to the trace c as resolved by computer analysis.

The rate of the major portion of electrogenesis proved to be faster than the time resolution of the electrometer system (50 ns).

A much slower electrogenic process (τ = 400 μs) was detected when the second flash was added 0.5 s after the first one (Fig.1B). This step was found to contribute ~ 7% to the overall $\Delta\Psi$. Under conditions used, the degree of reconstitution of CoQ in the Q_B site of the RC complex was about 70% (9). Thus one may assume that contribution of the 400 μs electrogenic step in the intact RC complex should be 10%. Slow electrogenesis was absent if the interval between the two flashes was longer than 30 s (Fig.1D).

The simplest explanation of the above data consists in that the fast electrogenic step of τ < 50ns is due to the electron transfer from $(BChl)_2$ to Q_A whereas the slow one is caused by the transfer of H^+ from the water to the double reduced secondary quinone anion (Q_B^{2-}). In fact, $(BChl)_2 \longrightarrow Q_A$ electron transfer is the only process in the studied system which takes less than 50 ns (time resolution of the electrometer used). On the other hand, protonation of Q_B after the addition of two electrons (Q_B^{2-} + $2H^+ \longrightarrow Q_BH_2$) seems to be the only step which requires two consecutive flashes to be added. $Q_B^{\overline{\cdot}}$ which can be formed after the first flash does not accept H^+ since pK of ubisemiquinone is at acidic pH. The τ value of the slow stage is similar to that of Q_B^{2-} protonation (500 μs) and much slower than the rates of the $Q_A \longrightarrow Q_B$ electron transfer.

In agreement with the above reasoning, it was found that the 400 μs electrogenic step requires the collodion film-impregnating decane solution to be supplemented with CoQ_{10}. As it was previously shown in this group, decane extracts loosely-bound quinones from the RC proteoliposomes attached to the film (10). It was also shown that o-phenanthroline inhibiting the electron transfer at the level of quinones completely abolishes the slow $\Delta\Psi$ generation (not shown in the figures).

To study the contribution of cytochrome c to $\Delta\Psi$ formation, we varied the redox potential of the medium and, hence, the degree of reduction of hemes c. To avoid the electrogenic effect of Q_B^{2-} protonation, no CoQ_{10} was added to the collodion film-impregnating solution. At the 220 mV redox potential (hemes c_{556} and c_{559} are reduced, other two hemes are oxidized) a laser flash was found to induce oxidation of c-559 followed by its reduction by c-556 (not shown in the figure).

This process (τ = 300 ns and 3 μs for oxidation of hemes c_{559} and c_{556}, respectively (11)) was accompanied by an additional biphasic electrogenesis with the τ values similar to those of c_{559} and c_{556} oxidations. The contributions of these electrogenic steps to the overall $\Delta\Psi$ generation by the reaction center complex were about 15% and 5%. At 380 mV redox potential, when c_{559} is half-reduced and other hemes largely oxidized, only one additional electrogenic step (τ = 300 ns) was revealed. It disappeared at 440 mV (complete oxidation of all hemes) (Fig.2). An increase in the decay, which accompanies the redox potential rise, is explained by charge recombination in RC.

The fast monitoring of $\Delta\Psi$ generation by the Rps.viridis cells by electric measurements of the light-gradient type was quite recently made by Deprez et al (12). $\Delta\Psi$ measured with this method is lowered in magnitude by a factor of at least 100 but the time resolution appears to be as good as 40 ps. Two electrogenic steps ($\tau_1 \leq$ 40 ps, τ_2 = 125 ps) of almost equal contributions were observed. The former and the latter steps proved to be due to the electron transfer from $(BChl)_2$ to BPheo and from $BPheo^{\overline{\cdot}}$ to MQ, respectively. The data are in good agreement with the position of BPheo in the hydrophobic membrane core halfway from $(BChl)_2$ to Q (12).

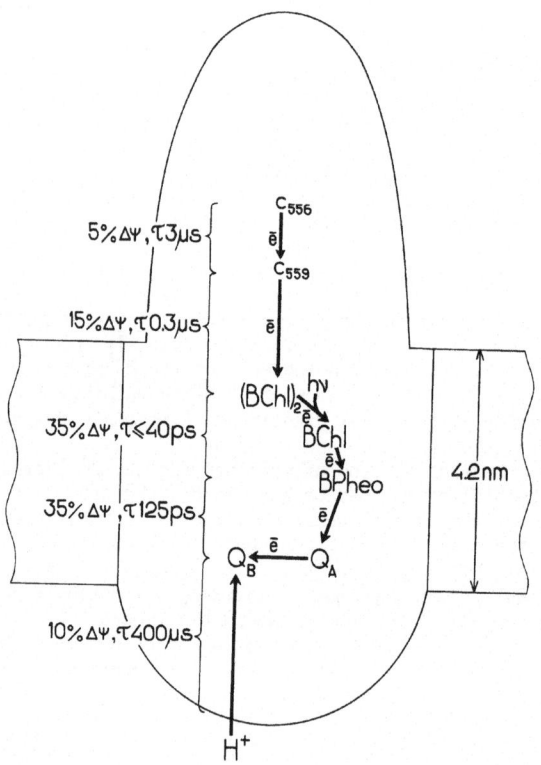

Fig. 3. Electrogenic steps of e⁻ and H⁺ transfer in the Rps.viridis
reaction center complex, revealed in this study and in that
by Deprez et al (12). The distances between the redox groups
are given according to the X-ray data by Deisenhofer et al (2,3),
assuming that it is heme $\underline{c}_{556}$ that is the closest redox
group to $\underline{c}_{559}$.

A scheme illustrating the structure-function relationships in the Rps.viridis reaction centers is shown in Fig.3. The distances between redox groups are given according to the X-ray data (2,3).

In the 1960s, as Mitchell postulated his chemiosmotic hypothesis, he suggested that an electron moving from cytocgrome $\underline{c}$ to CoQ via bacteriochlorophyll crosses the hydrophobic membrane barrier (the electron transfer half-loop), and this results in transmembrane charge separation (1). This assumption, quite speculative at that time, has now been directly proved. The only amendment which appeared to be necessary to the original Mitchell scheme consists in that besides the electron transfer-associated electrogenesis, there is a small but measurable electrogenic step arising because of the proton movement in the opposite direction.

CONCLUSION

The following conclusions can be made on the basis of the studies of light-induced $\Delta\Psi$ generation by the Rps.viridis reaction center complexes in proteoliposomes (this paper) and intact cells (11).

(A) The reaction center complex charges the membrane by means of the oppositely directed electron and proton transfers, the contribution of the former being predominant.

(B) Five discrete electrogenic steps can be revealed in the overall transmembrane charge transfer process. They are associated with:
(i) Electron transfer from $(BChl)_2$* to BPheo (τ $\leqslant$ 40 ps), which is responsible for $\sim$ 35% of the total $\Delta\Psi$ formation;
(ii) Electron transfer from BPheo to Q_A (τ 125 ps, $\sim$ 35% $\Delta\Psi$;
(iii) Electron transfer from heme $\underline{c}_{559}$ to $(BChl)_2^{+}$ (τ 300 ns, $\sim$15% $\Delta\Psi$);
(iv) Electron transfer from heme $\underline{c}_{556}$ to heme $\underline{c}_{559}$ (τ 3 µs, $2^{\sim 5\% \Delta\Psi}$);
(v) Proton transfer from the cytoplasmic membrane surface to Q_B (τ 400 µs, 10% $\Delta\Psi$).
Electron transfer from Q_A to Q_B seems to be non-electrogenic.

(C) As the X-ray analysis by Deisenhofer et al (2,3) showed, the centre-to-centre distance along the normal to the membrane plane between (i) Q_A and $(BChl)_2$, (ii) $(BChl)_2$ and the heme closests to $(BChl)_2$, and (iii) this heme and the next one is 2.9, 2.1 and 1.2 nm, respectively. If the electrogenesis were a linear function of the distance between the redox groups involved, the relative contributions of these electron transfer steps would be 1:00.7:0.4. In fact, they proved to be 1:0.2:0.07. This means that not only the distance between the redox groups but also the dielectric constant value of the corresponding membrane region where the reaction occurs affects the electrogenic efficiency. The efficiency is the higher, the deeper are these groups immersed into the membrane.

ACKNOWLEDGEMENTS

The authors would like to thank Dr. A.L. Drachev and S.M. Zaberezhnaya for their help in some experiments.

REFERENCES

1. P. Mitchell, Chemiosmotic coupling in oxidative and photosynthetic phosphorylation. Bodmin: Glynn Res. (1966).
2. J. Deisenhofer, O. Epp, K. Miki, R. Huber and H. Michel, X-ray structure analysis of a membrane protein complex. Electron density map of the photosynthetic reaction center from Rhodopseudomonas viridis. J.Mol.Biol. 180: 385 (1984).
3. J. Deisenhofer, O. Epp, K. Miki, R. Huber and H. Michel, Structure of the protein subunits in the photosynthetic reaction centre of Rhodopseudomonas viridis at 3Å resolution. Nature 318: 618 (1985).

4. L.A. Drachev, A.D. Kaulen, A.Yu. Semenov, I.I. Severina and V.P. Skula-chev, Lipid-impregnated filters as a tool for studying the electric current-generating proteins. Anal.Biochem. 96:250 (1979).

5. V.P. Skulachev, A single turnover study of photoelectric current-generating proteins. Methods Enzymol. 88: 35 (1982).

6. L.A. Drachev, A.Yu. Semenov, V.P. Skulachev, T.A. Smirnova, S.K. Chamorovsky, A.A. Kononenko, A.B. Rubin and N.Ya. Uspenskaya, Fast stages of photoelectric processes in biological membranes. III. Bacterial photosynthetic redox system. Eur.J.Biochem. 117: 482 (1981).

7. O.P. Kaminskaya, L.A. Drachev, A.A. Konstantinov, A.Yu. Semenov and V.P. Skulachev, Electrogenic reduction of the secondary quinone acceptor in chromatophores of Rhodospirillum rubrum. Rapid kinetics measurements. FEBS Lett. 202: 224 (1986).

8. A.Yu. Semenov, M.D. Mamedov, A.P. Mineev, S.K. Chamorovsky and N.P. Grishanova, Electrogenic stages in electron-transport chains of chromatophores from Rhodopseudomonas sphaeroides. Biol.Membrany (USSR) 3: 1011 (1986).

9. S.M. Dracheva, L.A. Drachev, A.A. Konstantinov, A.Yu. Semenov, V.P. Skulachev, A.M. Arutjunjan, V.A. Shuvalov and S.M. Zaberezhnaya, Vectorial electron and proton transfer in reaction centre complexes from Rhodopseudomonas viridis. Eur.J.Biochem. (1987).

10. L.A. Drachev, O.P. Kaminskaya, A.A. Konstantinov, M.D. Mamedov, V.D. Samuilov, A.Yu. Semenov and V.P. Skulachev, Effects of electron donors and acceptors on the kinetics of the photoelectric responses in Rhodospirillum rubrum and Rhodopseudomonas sphaeroides chromato-phores. Biochim.Biophys.Acta 850:1 (1986)

11. S.M. Dracheva, L.A. Drachev, S.M. Zaberezhnaya, A.A. Konstantinov, A.Yu. Semenov and V.P. Skulachev, Spectral, redox and kinetic characteristics of high-potential cytochrome c hemes in Rhodopseudomonas viridis reaction center. FEBS Lett. 205: 41 (1986).

12. J. Deprez, H.W. Trissl and J. Breton, Excitation trapping and primary charge stabilization in Rhodopseudomonas viridis cells, measured electrically with picosecond resolution. Proc.Natl.Acad.Sci USA 83: 1699 (1986).

CATALYTIC SITES FOR REDUCTION AND OXIDATION OF QUINONES

Antony Crofts, Howard Robinson, Kathe Andrews,
Steven Van Doren and Ed Berry

Biophysics Division, University of Illinois
Urbana, IL, 61801, USA

INTRODUCTION

The determination of the structure of the Rps. viridis reaction center at 3 Å resolution[1] has provided a great deal of information of direct relevance to the many other membrane proteins which are yet to be solved crystallographically. Two recent reviews[2,3] have discussed putative structures for the quinol oxidizing complexes, and independently suggested a structure (the Cramer-Widger-Saraste-Wikstrom or CWSW structure) for the main subunit of the complexes (the cytochrome b subunit) in which the major structural elements are a set of nine membrane spanning helices. Two of these helices have a special role in providing pairs of histine residues to ligand the two b-type hemes of the complex. In this brief paper, we wish to review the structure of the cytochrome b subunit in the light of additional information from the reaction center structure, and from inhibitor resistant mutants. We will discuss first the structure of the catalytic site of the reaction center at which quinone is reduced, and our attempts to predict a tertiary structure for the analogous site on the photosystem II reaction center. We will examine the location of lesions giving rise to inhibitor resistance, and the information these provide about mechanism. We will then discuss the structure of the ubiquinol:cyt c_2 oxidoreductases of R. capsulatus and R. sphaeroides, the location of the quinone reactive catalytic sites, and the role of inhibitor resistant mutants in elucidating the structure.

The Quinone Reductase Site of the Reaction Center

Although the atomic coordinates of the Rps. viridis reaction center are not available to us, we have been able to reconstruct a three dimensional model by triangulation from the stereo pair diagrams published by Michel and colleagues[1]. Because of the constraints of known structural elements, the model is likely to be accurate to within a few angstroms. The subunits D1 and D2 from the reaction centers of green plants show a marked homology with the subunits L and M respectively of Rps. viridis, and with those from the closely related R. capsulatus and R. sphaeroides, especially in those regions in which lesions linked with inhibitor resistance occur[4]. By homology, these are all found associated with the quinone reductase site of the Rps. viridis structure. Fig. 1 hows a preliminary hypothetical structure for the quinone reductase site of the reaction center of Anacystis nidulans, based on the sequence published by Golden and colleagues[5], and a slight modification of the homological alignment proposed by Michel et al.[4]. In aligning

617

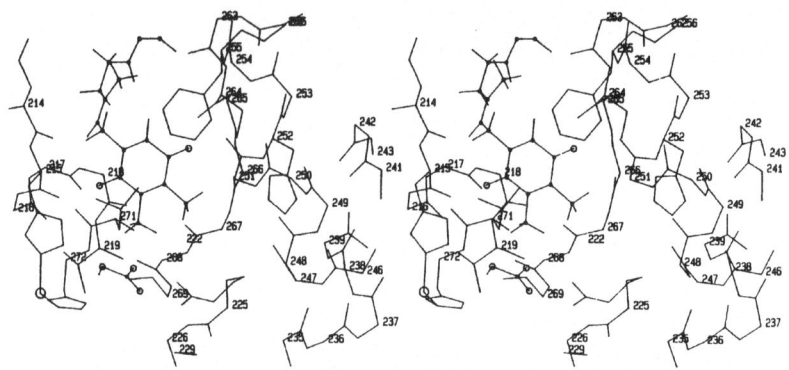

Fig. 1. Stereo pair diagram of a hypothetical structure for
the Q_B-site of Anacystis.

the hypothetical structure with that of Rps. viridis, we have overlaid the
peptide backbone in regions of high homology, and paid particular attention
to the alignment of groups modified in inhibitor resistant strains. Much of
the structure is then determined by the constraints of known secondary structural elements. Structure distal to the catalytic site and most side chains
have been ommitted for clarity. The side chains remaining (numbered from the
Anacystis sequence) are those thought to be of importance in function.

Met 214   the site of attachment of azido-atrazine;
His 215   the ligand to Fe from helix d;
Val 219   modified to Ile in a resistant Chlamydomonas strain;
Arg 225   putative salt bridge with bicarbonate.
His 252   putative ligand for the proton which stabilizes Q_B^-;
Phe 255   modified to Tyr in a herbicide resistant strain of Chlamydo
           monas;
Ser 264   modified to Gly or Ala in herbicide resistant strains;
Leu 271   homologous with Ile 229, modified to Met in a herbicide
           resistant strain of R. sphaeroides;
His 272   the ligand to Fe from helix e;

The consequences for the kinetic and thermodynamic properties of the two
electron gate of the lesions leading to herbicide resistance in green plants
have been examined in detail only for the Ser – Gly and Ser – Ala changes in
Amaranthus and Anacystis[6,7]. In both these cases, the herbicide resistant
strains showed an unchanged forward rate constant for electron transfer from
$Q_A^-.Q_B$ to $Q_A.Q_B^-$, but a decreased equilibrium constant for the sharing of an
electron between states with Q_A^- and states with Q_B^-. The modifications in
inhibitor binding have been much more thoroughly studied, and have shown
marked discimination between herbicides from different classes (see[8] for
review).

Space does not permit a lengthy discuss of these results, but we will
attempt to summarize some conclusions which are relevant to a general discussion of catalytic sites for quinone reactions.

1)   The residues involved in binding or catalytic mechanism are dispersed about the whole three dimensional volume of the Q_B-site.

2)   No herbicide resistant strains have shown lesions mapping outside
the catalytic site.

3)   Although the domains involved in binding the substrates and inhibitors are common, the effects of lesions depend on the chemical nature of the
liganded groups. It is this latter property which allows inhibitor resistance
without such drastic modification of substrate binding or catalytic mechanism
as to grossly impair function.

4)   In our previous kinetic studies we were able to suggest from the

618

effects of pH on the equilibrium constant for sharing an electron between states with Q_A^- and states with Q_B^-, that a group close to the catalytic site acted as a ligand to the proton which stabilized Q_B^-. We suggested that the charge on Q_B^- shifted the pK of this group from about pH 6.2 to about pH 7.9. In our tentative structure, the His residue at 252 provides an obvious candidate for this ligand.

5)   A feature of the green plant quinone reductase site which is not found in the bacterial mechanisms is the "bicarbonate effect",– the stimulation of electron transfer to the secondary quinone by added bicarbonate[9,10]. Although the ligand for the bicarbonate is not known, it has been shown that the bicarbonate anion is the active group[10], and Shipman[11] has suggested that an Arg residue is the most probable ligand. In our structure, the Arg at position 225 is a plausible candidate.

6)   Reduction of quinone at the catalytic site involves the following minimal steps[12,13,14,15]:

i)   Binding of the quinone;
ii) Photoreduction of Q_A;
iii) Electron transfer to Q_B;
iv) Stabilization of Q_B^- by binding of a proton;
v)   A second photoreduction of Q_A;
vi) Electron transfer to $Q_B^- \cdot (H^+)$;
vii) Binding of a second proton;
viii)Unbinding of QH_2.

With suitably intense illumination, the complete turn-over of the site takes about 2 ms[15,16].

It is obvious that the binding of the different forms of the quinone during this cycle will require different properties of the catalytic site. The forces involved in binding will be the non-covalent bonding forces;– H-bonding, London-van der Waals interactions, and electrostatic interactions. In order to accomodate the different quinone forms in the catalytic site, it seems likely that either the quinone is fairly mobile in the site, or that the site is fairly flexible, or that both of these apply. It is also clear that the changes in charge of the quinone in its different states of reduction require a fairly high dielectric in the neighbouring volume. We suggest that:

Plastoquinone in its various forms is liganded by H-bonding between His 215 and Ser 264, or neighboring groups, as in the Rps. viridis Q_A-site[1];

In the quinone and quinol forms, H-bonding is weakened by steric hinderance;

In the Q_B^- form, the structure is distorted by interaction of the charge so as to remove the steric hinderance, and to strengthen the H-bonding;

The charge on Q_B^- is compensated in part by the Fe-(His)$_4$ complex, and in part by protonation of His 252. The mechanism may involve net movement of the proton through the H-bond towards the semiquinone oxygens;

His 252 and Arg 225 are involved in H-exchanges with residues at either end of the quinone ring which enable the different H-bonding and proton requirements to be satisfied.

If His 252 is a ligand for the proton, as suggested above, and if the charges on Q_B^- and in His.(H^+) are regarded as point charges, then a "local" dielectric can be calculated from Coulomb's Law, and from the distance given in the model (7 Å). A value of about 23 is found, much higher than the commonly accepted value of about 4 for the dielectric constant of protein.

We will discuss mechanistic implications of this scheme in greater detail elsewhere[17].

The Structure of the Cytochrome b Subunit

Topology of the subunit.
In the structure previously proposed, the main topological features were nine membrane spanning helices, two of which (II and V in the nomenclature of

Widger and Cramer[2]) were involved in liganding the hemes of the two b-type
cytochromes of the complex. In reviewing the predicted structures for the
family of b-cytochromes, we have been struck by the homology of structure
pointed out by previous authors, but have noticed that helix IV is much less
strongly predicted as a transmembrane helix than are the others. Rao and
Argos[18] have recently analysed the probability parameters for occurence of
each amino acid in buried membrane helices, and have used these parameters to
predict membrane spanning helices. They have suggested that, in the family of
b-cytochromes, helix IV is not consistently predicted, and excluded it from
the "consensus" structure. A similar pattern is seen when hydropathy plots
are used. Ommitting helix IV resets the "sidedness" of the topology for all
structures after helix III. In a recent review, Cramer et al.[19] have found
support for the topology they predicted, in the distribution of lesions in
inhibitor resistant strains of yeast. The location of antimycin and mucidin
resistance according to the scheme of Subik et al.[20] fell with all antimycin resistant lesions on the C-terminal side, and all mucidin resistant
lesions on the N-terminal side. If helix IV does not span the membrane, then
the changed "sidedness" ruins this neat distribution. The mapping of lesions
to the sequence which they used then seems highly improbable, given the less-
ons from the Rps. viridis structure outlined above.

An alternative interpretation of the location of lesions in resistant
strains has been proposed by Mahler and Perlman[21]. They have taken account
of the organization of the cob gene as a series of exons and introns, and of
the additional information this brings to the mapping. Ommitting helix IV
gives the toplogical distribution shown in Fig. 2. Applying the location of
lesions suggested by Mahler nad Perlman now brings all the antimycin sites to
the N-side (proton negative) and the mucidin sites to the P-side. The putative structure includes additional information from application of hydropathy, amphipathy and acrophilicity analysis to the R. capsulatus sequence of
Gabellini et al.[22], using a set of programs developed in house (Fig. 3).

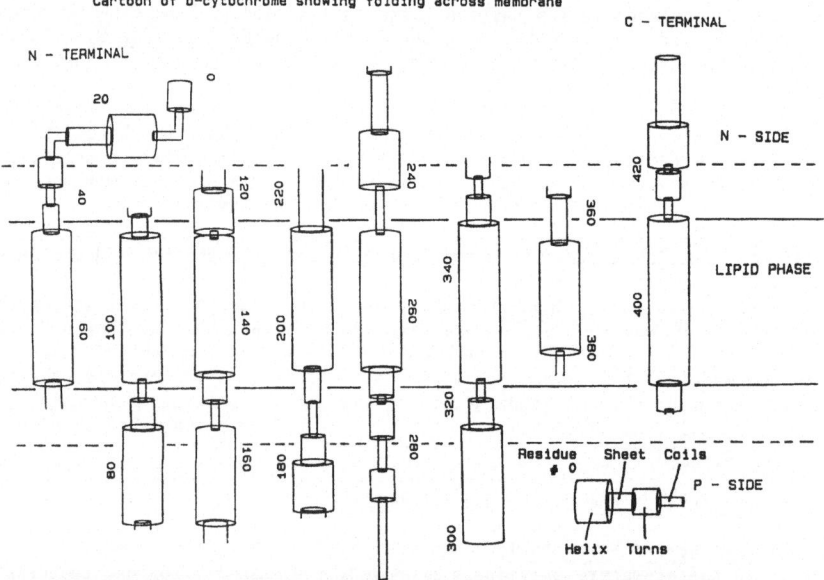

Fig. 2. Structural cartoon of the cytochrome b subunit.

620

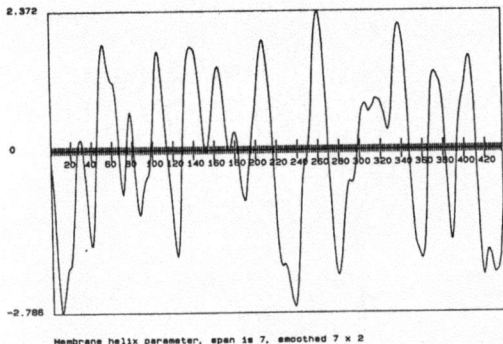

Membrane helix parameter, span is 7, smoothed 7 x 2

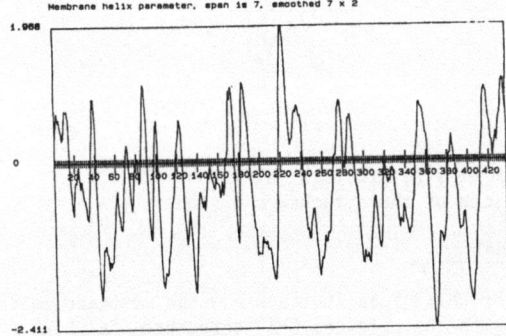

Hopp acrophilicity, span is 5, smoothed 5 x 1

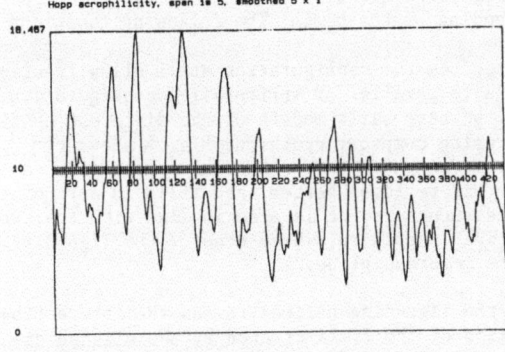

Amphiphilicity at 100 degrees, span is 11, smoothed 7 x 1

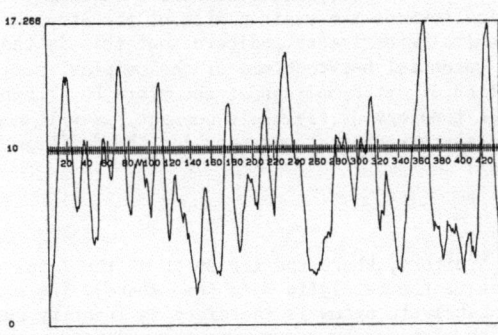

Amphiphilicity at 170 degrees, span is 11, smoothed 7 x 1

Fig. 3. Predictive profiles for the sequence of R. capsulatus.

A. Membrane helix parameter of Rao and Argos[18].

B. Acrophilicity using the parameters of Hopp[23].

C. Amphipathy measured with rotation of 100° along the sequence. This shows putative amphipathic helices.

D. Amphipathy measured with rotation of 170° along the sequence. This shows putative amphipathic sheets

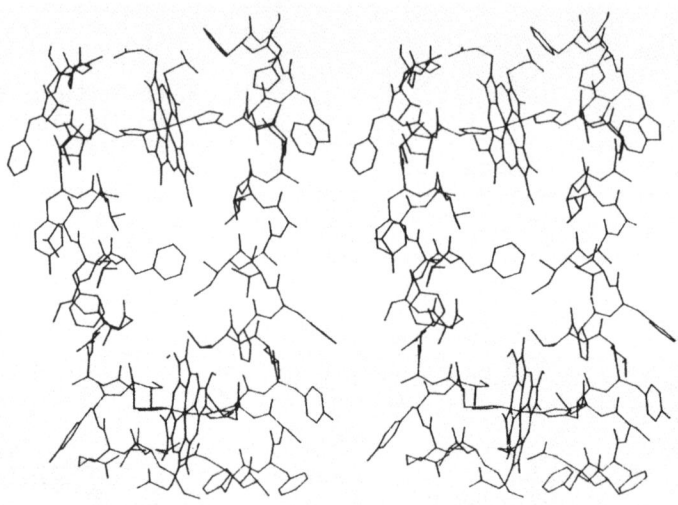

Fig. 4. Stereo pair diagram of a hypothetical structure for the
heme liganding helices of the cytochrome b subunit.

Folding of the heme-liganding helices

The reversal in direction of helix V as it traverses the membrane in the
scheme of Fig. 2 when compared with the original CWSW structure, in which the
helices were anti-parallel, brings into question the role of the highly conserved His residues in the liganding of the hemes. The following questions
seem pertinent:
a)   With parallel helices, does the configuration still allow ligation?
b)   Is there any advantage to parallel or antiparallel configuration?
To answer these questions, we have built models of the different config-
urations, and manipulated them using computer graphics. Fig. 4 shows two
views of a favorable configuration in which the helices have been given a
negative twist. This aligns the His residues better, and fills in more of the
anomalous space in the untwisted structure; it is also in line with the experience provided by the Rps. viridis structure, where none of the liganding
helices are perpendicular to the membrane plane.

The parallel direction of the liganding helices raises the interesting
question of the effect on function of the field created by the aligned di-
poles of the helices. The sign of the field (positive at the N-terminus)
would favor electron distribution towards the mucidin side of the structure.
However, biophysical and biochemical experiments indicate that this is the
site associated with the lower potential b-cytochrome of the complex, cyt b-
566. The greater ease of reduction of cyt b-561 cannot therefore be attributed to the dipole field. If the topology of Fig. 2 is correct, we will need
to search for other features in the structure to account for the differential
redox behavior of the two hemes.

Inhibitor Resistant Strains

In strains resistant to inhibitors, where the lesion is at the level of
the enzyme, all have so far been at the catalytic site (see above). The most
direct approach to mapping the catalytic sites is therefore to identify such
mutants for each site, and map the lesions by sequencing the modified gene.
In collaboration with the laboratories of Profs. Bob Gennis and Sam Kaplan,
we are at present sequencing the cloned genes for the subunits of the ubi-

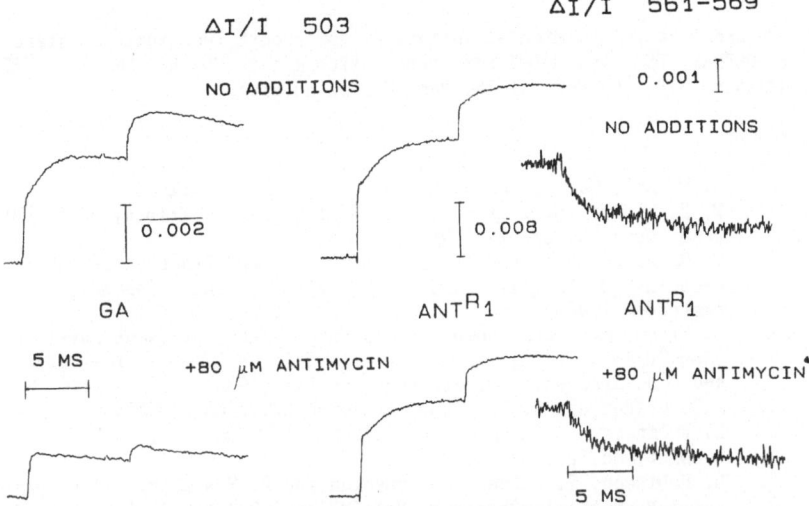

Fig.5. Traces showing the electrochromic carotenoaid change and cytochrome b-561 oxidation in whole cells of R. sphaeroides strains
Ga and ANT^{R}1, and the effect of antimycin. Cells were suspended in
RCV medium with 50 mM fumarate and 0.5 mM succinate. The dark-
adapted preparations were monitored under an atmosphere of nitrogen. Antimycin was added where indicated.

quinol:cyt c_2 oxidoreductase. We have generated a number of mutant strains
of R. sphaeroides Ga which are resistant to antimycin or myxothiazol. An
example of an antimycin resistant strain which we have investigated in
greater detail is shown in Fig. 5. The strain grows in media containing antimycin at 500 uM, and shows electron transfer rates in vivo only slightly
inhibited compared to the parent strain. In chromatophores, the turnover of
the complex shows titration with antimycin at concentrations more than 2
orders of magnitude higher than the parent strain.

Isolated Ubiquinol:Cytochrome c_2 Oxidoreductase

We have recently obtained a pure and highly active preparation of the
ubiquinol:cyt c_2 oxidoreductase from R. sphaeroides Ga[24]. The complex was
extracted from chromatophores with dodecyl maltoside in the presence of glycerol, and was purified by ion-exchange chromatography and gel filtration on
Sepharose CL-4B. Full spectrum redox titrations, in the presence or absence
of antimycin, showed two thermodynamically distinct b cytochromes, and cytochrome c_1, with spectra and mid-point redox potentials similar to those in
chromatophores. Redox titrations monitoring low temperature EPR spectra at g-
1.90 and g=2.00 shwed the presence of the Rieske Fe.S center and the antimycin sensitive semiquinone respectively. Ubiquinol, phospholipid, and iron
content have been determined, and the activity of the complex has been shown
to be enhanced by the presence of phospholipid. The procedure yields more
than 35 mg of purified complex from 4 g chromatophore protein, at a specific
heme content of 10 nmol c_1 per mg protein. The preparation catalyzes the
reduction of horse heart cytochrome c with a turnover in excess of 300 mol s$^-$
^{1} (mol c_1)$^{-1}$, in the presence of phospholipid. We are at present measuring
the pH dependence of the semiquinone signal in the complex, and are initiat-
ing a series of studies of the ENDOR-spectra in order to measure the interaction with protons at the catalytic site.

ACKNOWLEDGEMENTS

We are grateful to Michael Kulikowski for expert technical assistance, and to USDHHS, USDA and USDOE for support from grants PHS R01 GM26305, PHS R01 GM35438, USDA 84-CRCR-1-1476, and DE-AC02-80ER10701.

REFERENCES

1. H. Michel, O. Epp and J. Deisenhofer, EMBO J. 5:2445
2. W. R. Widger, W.A. Cramer, R.G. Herrman and A. Trebst, Proc. Natl. Acad. Sci. USA 81:674 (1984).
3. M. Saraste and M. Wikström, in Structure and Function of Membrane Proteins, E. Quagliariello and F. Palmieri, eds. Elsevier, Amsterdam (1983).
4. H. Michel and Deisenhofer, J. in Encyclopedia of Plant Physiology (New Series) Vol. 19 Photosynthesis III, pp.371-381. L.A. Staehelin and C.J. Arntzen, eds. Springer, Berlin (1986).
5. S.S. Golden and R. Haselkorn, Science 229:1104 (1985).
6. H. Robinson, in Advanced Agricultural Instrumentation, W.G. Gensler, ed. pp. 92-106 (1986).
7. H. Robinson, S. Golden, J. Brusslan and R. Haselkorn, in Progress in Photosynthesis Research, Vol IV, pp. 825-828, J. Biggins, ed. M. Nijhoff, Dordrecht (1987).
8. A. Trebst, Z. Naturforsch. 40c:237 (1986)
9. W.F.J. Vermaas and Govindjee, in Photosynthesis. Development, Carbon Metabolism and Plant Productivity, Vol. 2 pp. 541-558. Govindjee, ed. Academic Press, New York (1982).
10. D.J. Blubaugh and Govindjee, Biochim. Biophys. Acta, 848:147 (1986).
11. L.L. Shipman, J. Theor. Biol. 90:123 (1981).
12. B. Velthuys, in Function of Quinones in Electron Transfer Systems, pp. 401-408, B. Trumpower, ed. Academic Press, New York (1982).
13. A.R. Crofts and C.A. Wraight, Biochim. Biophys. Acta, 636:218 (1983).
14. A.R. Crofts, H.H. Robinson and M. Snozzi, in Advances in Photosynthesis Research, Vol. I, pp. 461-468, C. Sybesma, ed. M. Nijhoff/Dr. W. Junk, The Hague (1984).
15. H.R. Robinson and A.R. Crofts, in Progress in Photosynthesis Research, Vol II, pp. 429-432, J. Biggins, ed. M. Nijhoff, Dordrecht (1987).
16. H.H. Steihl and H. Witt, Z. Naturforsch. 24b:1588 (1969).
17. H.H. Robinson and A.R. Crofts, in preparation.
18. J.K. Rao and P. Argos, Biochim. Biophys. Acta, 869:197 (1986).
19. W.A. Cramer, W.R. Widger, M.T. Black and M.E. Girvin, in Topics in Photosynthesis Vol. 8, J. BArber, ed. in press (1987).
20. J. Subik, M. Briquet and A. Goffeau, Eur. J. Biochem. 119:613 (1981).
21. H.R. Mahler and P.S. Perlman, in The Enzymes of Biological Membranes, Vol. IV, pp. 195-234 A. Martonosi, ed. Plenum Publ. (1985).
22. N. Gabellini, U. Harnisch, J.E.G. McCarthy, G. Hauska and W. Sebald, EMBO J. 4:549 (1985).
23. T.P. Hopp, in Synthetic Peptides in Biology and Medicine (K. Alitalo, P. Partanen and A. Vaheri, eds. pp. 3-12. Elsevier, Amsterdam.
24. K.M. Andrews, A.R. Crofts and R.B. Gennis, Biophys. J. 51:493a (1987).

STUDIES OF THE ELECTROGENICITY OF THE REDUCTION OF CYTOCHROME b_{561}

THROUGH THE ANTIMYCIN-SENSITIVE SITE OF THE UBIQUINOL-CYTOCHROME

c_2 OXIDOREDUCTASE COMPLEX OF RHODOBACTER SPHAEROIDES

Elzbieta Glaser[*] and Antony R. Crofts

University of Illinois
Department of Physiology and Biophysics
Urbana, IL 61801, USA

INTRODUCTION

The electrochromic absorbance changes of carotenoids and bacterio-chlorophyll have been shown to be proportional to the membrane potential (Jackson and Crofts, 1969; Jackson and Crofts, 1971; Prince and Dutton, 1978; Wraight et al., 1978) and have been widely used as a measure of electrogenic processes in the membrane.

The flash-induced carotenoid change in chromatophores consists of three phases (Wraight et al., 1978; Dutton and Prince, 1978; Crofts and Wood, 1978) of which phase I and phase II are referred to as the fast phase, and are associated, respectively, with the photochemical reaction in the reaction center and the reduction of oxidized reaction center, P^+ by cytochrome c_2. Phase III is referred as the slow phase of the carotenoid change and is associated with the electrogenic processes involved in the electron transfer through the ubiquinol cytochrome c_2 oxidoreductase complex. The complex has been shown to contain two distinct sites at which oxidation of ubiquinol and reduction of ubiquinone take place (Bowyer and Crofts, 1981; Meinhardt and Crofts, 1982; Meinhardt and Crofts, 1983; Glaser et al., 1984; Robertson et al., 1984). Antimycin A, which binds to the ubiquinone-reductase site of the complex and inhibits cytochrome b_{561} oxidation, also inhibits a major portion of the carotenoid slow phase change (Meinhardt and Crofts, 1983). Myxothiazol, which is a specific inhibitor of the ubiquinol oxidase site of the complex (Von Jagow and Engel, 1981; Meinhardt and Crofts, 1982), inhibits totally the carotenoid slow phase change i.e. both the portion inhibited by antimycin plus an additional portion which has been shown (Glaser and Crofts, 1984) to be associated with the electron transfer between cytochrome b_{566} and cytochrome b_{561}.

In the present work we have studied the electrogenicity of a reverse reaction through the antimycin-sensitive site of the complex, i.e. the reduction of cytochrome b_{561} by ubiquinol in the presence of myxothiazol.

[*]Present address: Department of Biochemistry, Arrhenius Laboratory, University of Stockholm, S-106 91 Stockholm, Sweden

Our data point to the conclusion that the reverse reaction through the antimycin-sensitive site of the complex is electrogenic with polarity opposite to the normal forward reaction, and that it contributes about 60% of the total slow phase carotenoid change.

MATERIALS AND METHODS

Chromatophores of Rb. sphaeroides strain GA were prepared as described previously (Bowyer et al., 1979). The flash-induced reduction of cytochrome b_{561} and the electrochromic carotenoid change were measured using a computer-linked kinetic spectrophotometer as described earlier (Bowyer et al., 1981; Glaser and Crofts, 1984).

The reaction mixture consisted of chromatophores suspended in a medium, containing appropriate buffer for that pH at which the experiment was performed, KCl, redox mediators and ionophores and inhibitors when indicated. Detailed description of the media follows. The buffers used at different pH values were: MOPS at pH 7.0 and pH 7.6, HEPPS at pH 7.9 and pH 8.4, Bis-Tris-propane at pH 8.85, pH 9.4, and pH 9.5, glycin at pH 10.5 at the concentration of 50 mM in all cases. 100 mM KCl was present in all experiments. Concentrations of redox mediators were: 10 µM 1,2-naphtoquinone, 1,4-naphtoquinone, p-benzoquinone and duroquinone were present in the pH range between pH 7.0 and pH 9.5; each of phenazine methosulfate, phenazine ethosulfate, pyocyanine were present at concentration 1 µM at pH 7.0, 0.8 µM at pH 7.6, 0.5 µM at pH 7.9, 0.4 µM at pH 8.4 and 0.2 µM at pH > 8.85, 2,3,5,6-tetramethyl-p-phenylendiamine (DAD) was present at concentration 2 µM at pH 7.0, 1 µM at pH 7.6, 0.5 µM at pH 7.9 and pH 8.4 and 0.2 µM at pH > 8.85; 1 µM N,N,N',N'-tetra-methyl-p-phenylene diamine (TMPD) was included to the reaction mixture at pH > 9.4; ionophores, valinomycin and nigericin at concentrations 2 µM each and inhibitors, 10 µM antimycin and 3 µM myxothiazol were present when indicated. The reaction mixture was anaerobic and oxygen free argon passed over the mixture during the experiments. Redox poising was achieved by small additions of concentrated solutions of sodium dithonite or potassium ferricyanide. The concentration of chromatophores was adjusted so that a single flash induced turnover in more than 90% of the reaction centers. In all experiments, a dark period of 1 min was allowed between flashes or groups of flashes.

The concentration of reaction center, cytochrome b_{561}, cytochromes c_1 and c_2 and bacteriochlorophyll was estimated as described previously (Meinhardt and Crofts, 1983; Glaser and Crofts, 1984).

Myxothiazol was a kind gift from Drs. Reichenbach, Thierbach, and Trowitzsch, and nigericin was a gift from E. Lilly Pharmaceuticals. Valinomycin and antimycin A were obtained from Sigma.

RESULTS

Fig. 1 shows the flash-induced carotenoid bandshift change measured at 503 nm and the reduction of cytochrome b_{561} measured as difference at 561 nm and 569 nm in chromatophores in the presence of myxothiazol alone or both myxothiazol and antimycin or in the absence of the inhibitors.

Abbreviations: Bchl, bacteriochlorophyll; MOPS, 3-[N-morpholino]propane sulfonic acid; HEPPS N-2-hydroxyethyl-piperazine-N'-2-propane sulfonic acid; cyt, cytochrome; Q,QH_2, ubiquinone, ubiquinol

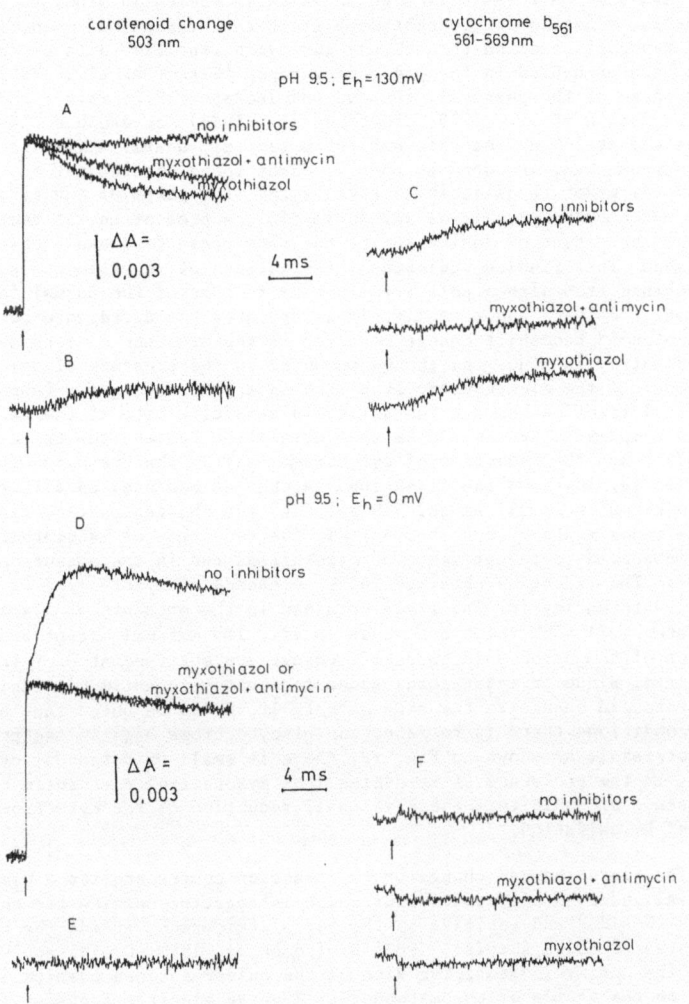

Fig. 1. Kinetics of the carotenoid electrochromic change and cytochrome b_{561} reduction. Chromatophores were suspended in the in 50 mM Bis-Tris-propane containing 100 mM KCl (pH 9.5) and redox mediators as described in Materials and Methods. Concentration of Bchl in the cuvette was 26 μM reaction center 0.25 μM; cytochrome b_{561} 0.16 μM; cytochrome ($c_1 + c_2$) 0.24 μM. Inhibitors were present when indicated at the concentrations as described in Materials and Methods. Traces A and D (average of four sweep 20 ms full scale, time constant 20 μs) show the change at 503 nm at 130 mV and 0 mV induced by excitation with a single flash; traces B and E show differences between traces with myxothiazol + antimycin minus traces with myxothiazol at 130 mV and 0 mV, respectively; traces C and F show the reduction of cytochrome b_{561} measured at 561 nm minus 569 nm, at 130 mV and 0 mV, respectively, (average of eight, 20 ms full scale, 20 μs time constant).

627

The traces show the change at pH 9.5, at two values of ambient potential, 130 mV and 0 mV. A relatively high pH value is chosen in order to achieve substantial reduction of cytochrome b_{561} in the presence of myxothiazol, in the reversal reaction through the antimycin-sensitive site of the complex, as has been presented in the preceeding paper (Glaser et al., 1984). The slower phase of the phase III (Dutton and Jackson, 1972; Prince and Dutton, 1977; De Grooth et al., 1978; Crofts et al., 1983) carotenoid change is observed at 130 mV. At this ambient potential, nearly maximal reduction of cytochrome b_{561} is noted at pH 9.5. Under these conditions, as shown in fig. 1A, myxothiazol inhibits totally the slow phase of the carotenoid change. When both myxothiazol and antimycin are present in the reaction mixture, the extent of inhibition of the slow phase carotenoid change is diminished. This finding indicates the existance of an antimycin-sensitive electrogenic step with a polarity opposite to that of the normal forward reaction. The trace shown in fig. 1B illustrates the difference between the carotenoid bandshift change measured in the presence of both myxothiazol and antimycin minus the change measured in the presence of myxothiazol alone. If the electrogenic step with an opposite polarity represents a reversal reaction through the antimycin-sensitive site of the oxidoreductase complex, there should be the correlation between the trace shown in fig. 1B and the reduction of cytochrome b_{561} in the presence of myxothiazol. Fig. 1C shows the flash-induced changes measured as difference between kinetics at 561 nm and 569 nm, i.e. the changes characteristic for the redox state of cytochrome b_{561}. The reduction of cytochrome b_{561} can be observed in the presence of myxothiazol and in the absence of inhibitors. The reduction obtained in the presence of myxothiazol is entirely sensitive to antimycin. The trace obtained in the presence of myxothiazol correlates well with the trace shown in fig. 1B. Maximal extent and rapid kinetics of the carotenoid bandshift change are observed at 0 mV (Fig. 1D). Myxothiazol alone or myxothiazol added together with antimycin inhibit the carotenoid change to the same extent. It should be noted that under these conditions there is no reduction of cytochrome b_{561} in the presence of myxothiazol. As shown in Fig. 1F, there is small oxidation of cytochrome b_{561} in the pre sence of myxothiazol or myxothiazol plus antimycin. In the absence of inhibitors there is small reduction of the cytochrome followed by oxidation.

The flash-induced change of the reaction center creates a membrane potential under coupled conditions which is negative outside the chromatophore (N-side) and positive on the periplasmic side, inside the chromatophores (P-side) (Crofts, 1983; Crofts et al, 1983; Crofts and Wraight, 1983). The antimycin-sensitive site of the oxidoreductase complex is placed on the N-side of chromatophores. Reverse electron transfer from ubiquinol to cytochrome b_{561} through the antimycin-sensitive site of the complex should be stimulated under coupled conditions. Fig. 2 shows the redox titration curves of cytochrome b_{561} in the presence of myxothiazol under coupled (closed circles) and uncoupled conditions (open circles). The change was measured at pH 8.4. Figs. 2A and 2B show the redox titration curves for the extent of reduction of cyt b_{561} at three values of ambient potential (110 mV, 160 mV and 200 mV) in the presence (A) and absence of ionophores (B). Figs. 2C and 2D show the change 20 msec after the first flash (C) and the maximal extent of the change after four flashes (D) at different values of ambient potentials. The extent of reduction of cytochrome b_{561} obtained in the absence of ionophores is higher than that obtained in the presence of ionophores. The extent of reduction of cytochrome b_{561} in the absence of ionophores is higher in the pH range $7.0 < pH < 9.5$ than when measured in the presence of ionophores (not shown). This is due to the electron pressure from the N-side to the P-side of chromatophores. The increase in reduction is constant over the range of pH from pH 7.0 to pH 8.5, both after the first flash and after four flashes.

The stimulation is slightly decreasing above pH 8.5 and disappears at pH 9.5. Above pH 9.5 the extent of reduction in the presence of ionophores is higher than in their absence. We do not have any explanation for this phenomenon. However, it may be due to the inhibiting effect of high membrane potential created under coupled conditions.

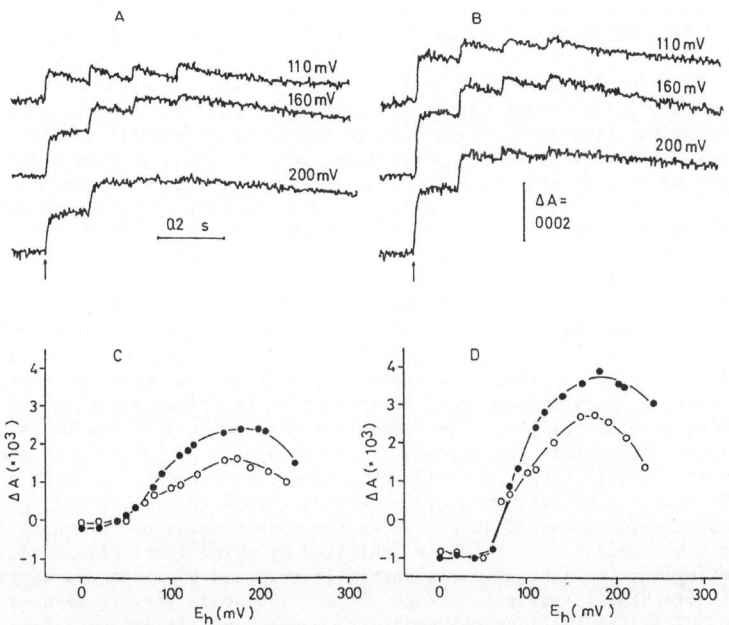

Fig. 2. Redox titration of the extent of reduction of cytochrome b_{561} in the presence of myxothiazol under uncoupled (A, open circles) and coupled conditions (B, closed circles). Experimental conditions were as described in Materials and Methods, at pH 8.4. Each point was an average of 2, at sweep of 1 s full scale and time constant 1 ms. Ionophores, 2 µM valinomycin and 2 µM nigericin were present under uncoupled conditions. The extent of reduction was measured 20 ms after the first flash (C) or at its maximal extent after the fourth flash (D).

DISCUSSION

Phase III of the electrochromic carotenoid change is attributed to electrogenic events involved in electron transfer through the ubiquinol-cytochrome c_2 oxidoreductase complex. The kinetics of Phase III, referred also as the slow phase of the carotenoid change, are dependent on the ambient redox potential. The faster kinetics appear on reductive titration below 150 mV at pH 7.0 and the slower kinetics are observed over the higher potential range, above 160 mV. Antimycin inhibits a major part of the slow phase carotenoid change (Meinhardt and Crofts, 1983; Glaser and Crofts, 1984). Since antimycin also inhibits oxidation of cytochrome b_{561}, it has been concluded that the antimycin-sensitive electrogenic event visualized by the slow phase of the carotenoid change is associated with the oxidation of cytochrome b_{561} and the reduction of ubiquinone, as described by the reaction:

$$\text{Cyt } b_{561}^- + Q \rightleftharpoons \text{Cyt } b_{561} + Q_c^{\cdot -}$$

$$\text{Cyt } b_{561}^- + Q_c^{\cdot -} + 2H^+ \rightleftharpoons \text{Cyt } b_{561} + QH_2$$

In recent work (Glaser and Crofts, 1984) we have shown that the additional part of the slow phase carotenoid change is inhibited by myxothiazol. Characterization of this electrogenic event suggests that the process is linked to electron transfer between cytochrome b_{566} and b_{561}. It has also been calculated that in this newly characterized electrogenic process electrons pass about 35-50% of the distance across the membrane.

The aim of the present work was to study the antimycin-sensitive electrogenic, slow phase carotenoid change. We have studied the electrogenicity of the reverse reaction through the antimycin-sensitive site of the complex. In the preceeding paper (Glaser et al., 1984) we have shown that cytochrome b_{561} is reduced after flash illumination in the presence of myxothiazol in a reaction which is antimycin sensitive. Reduction was observed in the redox range in which both cytochrome b_{561} and Q-pool are oxidized before the flash. Kinetic studies of the reaction show good correlation with the reaction at the ubiquinol oxidase site of the complex suggesting by analogy that cytochrome b_{561} is reduced by ubiquinol from the Q-pool. The extent of the reduction increases with increasing pH and is maximal at pH > 10.0 as shown in fig. 3. For the studies on the electrogenicity of this process, we have chosen conditions where a substantial portion of cytochrome b_{561} is reduced on the first flash in the presence of myxothiazol. For this reason the measurements of the carotenoid bandshift change were performed at relatively high pH (pH 9.5) in the high ambient potential range, E_h = 130 mV. Under these conditions about 50% of flash-reducible cytochrome b_{561} is reduced within 20 msec by a single flash. The carotenoid bandshift change shows the slower phase of the Phase III under these conditions, which is inhibited by myxothiazol. After addition of antimycin, the inhibition is partially reversed by about 30% of the total myxothiazol-sensitive change. Since cytochrome b_{561} is reduced to about 50% of the total extent when only myxothiazol is present, this finding indicate that the total antimycin-sensitive step contributes to about 60% of the total carotenoid change under these conditions. This value correlates well with our previous finding, that the additional electrogenic step between the b-type cytochromes is responsible for 35-50% of the carotenoid change.

REFERENCES

Bowyer, J. R. and Crofts, A. R., 1981, On the mechanism of photosynthetic electron transfer in Rhodopseudomonas capsulata and Rhodopseudommas sphaeroides, Biochim. Biophys. Acta, 636:218.
Bowyer, J. R., Meinhardt, S. W., Tierney, G. V., and Crofts, A. R., 1981, Resolved difference spectra of redox centers in photosynthetic electron flow in Rhodopseudomonas capsulata and Rhodopseudomonas sphaeroides, Biochim. Biophys. Acta, 635:167.
Bowyer, J. R., Tierney, G. V., and Crofts, A. R., 1979, Secondary electron transfer in chromatophores of Rhodopseudomonas capsulata Ala pho+. Binary out-of-phase oscillations in ubisemiquinone formation and cytochrome b_{50} reduction with consecutive light flashes, FEBS Lett. 101:201.
Crofts, A. R., 1983, The mechanism of the ubiquinol:cytochrome c oxidoreductases of mitochondria and of Rhodopseudomonas sphaeroides, in: "The Enzymes of Biological Membranes", A. N. Martonosi, ed., Plenum Publ. Corp., New York.

Crofts, A. R., Meinhardt, S. W., Jones, K.R., and Snozzi, M., 1983,
The role of the ubiquinone pool in the cyclic electron transfer chain
of Rps. sphaeroides: A modified Q-cycle mechanism, Biochim. Biophys.
Acta, 723:202.

Crofts, A. R., and Wood, P. M., 1978, Photosynthetic electron-transport
chains of plants and bacteria and their role as proton pumps,
Curr. Top. Bioenerg., 7:175.

Crofts, A. R., and Wraight, C.A., 1983, The electrochemical domain of
photosynthesis, Biochim. Biophys. Acta, 726:149.

De Grooth, B. G., Van Grondelle, R., Romijn, J. C., and Pulles, M. P.J.,
1978, The mechanism of reduction of the ubiquinone pool in photosynthetic bacteria at different redox potentials, Biochim. Biophys.
Acta, 503:480.

Dutton, P. L., and Jackson, J.B. 1972, Thermodynamic and kinetic characterization of electron-transfer components in situ in Rhodopseudomonas sphaeroides and Rhodospirillum rubrum, Eur. J. Biochem., 30:495.

Dutton, P. L., and Prince, R. C., 1978, Reaction-center-driven cytochrome
interactions in electron and proton translocation and energy coupling, in: "The Photosynthetic Bacteria", R. K. Clayton and W. R.
Sisтröm eds., Plenum Press, New York.

Glaser, E. G., and Crofts, A. R., 1984, A new electrogenic step in the
ubiquinol-cytochrome c_2 oxidoreductase complex of Rhodopseudomonas
sphaeroides, Biochim. Biophys. Acta, 766:322.

Glaser, E. G., Meinhardt, S. W., and Crofts, A. R., 1984, Reduction of
cytochrome b-561 through the antimycin-sensitive site of the ubiquinol-cytochrome c_2 oxidoreductase complex of Rhodospeudomonas
sphaeroides, FEBS Lett., 178:336.

Jackson, J. B., and Crofts, A. R., 1969, The high energy state in chromatophores from Rhodopseudomonas sphaeroides, FEBS Lett., 4:185.

Jackson, J. B. and Crofts, A. R., 1971, The kinetics of light-induced
carotenoid changes in Rhodopseudomonas sphaeroides and their relation to electrical field generation across the chromatophore membrane, Eur. J. Biochem., 18:120.

Meinhardt, S. W., and Crofts, A. R. 1982, The site and mechanism of action
of myxothiazol as an inhibitor of electron transfer in Rps. sphaeroides, FEBS Lett., 149:217.

Meinhardt, S. W., and Crofts, A. R., 1983, The role of cytochrome b-566
in the electron transfer chain of Rps. sphaeroides, Biochim. Biophys.
Acta, 723:219.

Prince, R. C., and Dutton, P. L., 1977, Single and multiple turnover
reactions in the ubiquinone-cytochrome b-c_2 oxidoreductase of
Rhodopspeudomonas sphaeroides. The physical chemistry of the major
electron donor to cytochrome c_2 and its coupled reactions, Biochim.
Biophys. Acta, 462:731.

Prince, R. C., and Dutton, P. L., 1978, Protonation and the reducing po-
tential of the primary electron acceptor, in: "The Photosynthetic
Bacteria", R. K. Clayton, and W. R. Sisтröm, eds., Plenum Press,
New York.

Robertson, D. E., Davidson, E., Prince, R., van der Berg, W. H., Marrs,
B. L. and Dutton, P. L., 1984, Discrete Q_z binding site in the
cytochrome bc_1 complex of Rhodopseudomonas capsulata, Fed. Proc.
43:2000.

Von Jagow, G. and Engel, W. D., 1981, Complete inhibition of electron
transfer from ubiquinol to cytochrome b by the combined action of
antimycin and myxothiazol, FEBS Lett., 136:19.

Wraight, C. A., Cogdell, R. J., and Chance, B., 1978, Ion transport and
electrochemical gradients in photosynthetic bacteria, in: "The
Photosynthetic Bacteria", R. K. Clayton, and W. R. Sisтröm, eds.
Plenum Press, New York.

MUTANTS AFFECTING THE QUINOL OXIDATION SITE OF UBIQUINOL-

CYT c_2-OXIDOREDUCTASE

D.E. Robertson, F. Daldal[*], and P.L. Dutton

University of Pennsylvania
Philadelphia, PA 19104
[*]Cold Spring Harbor Laboratories
Cold Spring Harbor, N.Y. 11724

INTRODUCTION

Ubiquinol-cyt c_2-oxidoreductase (cyt bc_1) is part of the cyclic electron transfer system of the purple, non-sulphur bacteria *Rhodobacter capsulatus* and *Rhodobacter sphaeroides*. The enzyme, like the cyt b_6f complex of plant chloroplasts and the cyt bc_1 of mitochondria, oxidizes quinol (QH_2) from a membrane-bound pool (Q_{pool}), reduces a c-type cytochrome, and, through a process of redox-linked charge separation, generates an electrochemical gradient of protons ($\Delta\mu_H+$;see 1,2 for reviews). A preponderance of evidence supports a Q-cycle-type mechanism (3,4) for the the formation of $\Delta\psi$ and ΔpH. In any Q-cycle variant (5) two quinone catalytic sites are postulated, one of them involved in net quinol oxidation (Q_o or Q_z) and the other in net quinone reduction (Q_i or Q_c). The sites are placed at opposite ends of a charge separating cyt b_H reduction and oxidation. In other words, one electron from QH_2 at Q_z passes to a high potential sequence including the FeS center and cyt c_1 while the other reduces first, cyt b_L and then cyt b_H. Cyt b_H is, in turn oxidized by Q at site Q_c.

These functional quinone sites involved in redox catalysis are distinguished by the selective inhibition of function at Q_c and Q_z by four separate classes of inhibitor. The structures and phenomenological observations accumulated for each class have recently been reviewed (6). Evidence from studies of the effects of these molecules on the quinone-linked function of cyt bc_1 indicates that they act as competitive-type inhibitors at the sites, Q_c and Q_z (6). In particular, antimycin specifically blocks both quinone reduction and oxidation at the Q_c site by binding to the site (8). Analogously, myxothiazol blocks quinol oxidation by occupying the Q_z site (9,10).

Questions regarding the topological relationships between the Q sites and the two cyt b hemes and the mechanism of electron transfer and proton involvement at these sites i.e., the charge separating mechanism of cyt bc_1, remain to be resolved. We have undertaken an approach which uses mutants

633

affecting the quinone-related functions of cyt bc_1. The cyt bc_1 of *Rhodobacter capsulatus* is ideal for a study of this kind for a number of reasons: 1) the bacterium may be grown via a number of modes, i.e., phototrophic anaerobic, aerobic or fermentative, thus allowing simple screening and growth of mutants; 2) a genetic system for the organism has been described (11) and used to sequence the *pet* operon for cyt bc_1 (12); 3) the redox changes of cyt c_1 and cyt c_2 and of cyt b_L and cyt b_H, as well as the kinetic changes in a group of membrane potential sensitive carotenoids, may be observed after light activated single turnover of the photosynthetic reaction center (RC).

We have used two types of mutant in recent studies: 1) A photosynthetic minus (Ps$^-$) strain, called R126, which is deficient in Q_z function and, appropriate to this study, completely blocked in Q_zH_2 mediated cyt c_1 and cyt b_L reduction (see 13), and; 2) Two Ps$^+$ mutants selected for their resistance to inhibitors of cyt bc_1. We show that each of these strains is impaired in QH_2 oxidation at the Q_z site.

METHODS

Cells were grown photosynthetically (14) or by respiration at low O_2 concentration (15) and chromatophores were prepared as previously described (16). Inhibitor-resistant strains were selected for photosynthetic growth on 5 x 10^{-5}M myxothiazol or 1 ug/ml stigmatellin (17). Single turnover light activated kinetics were obtained as described (16) as were EPR spectra of the Reiske 2Fe2S center (13). Redox poising was carried out as described by Dutton (18).

RESULTS

Reduction of cyts *b* and *c* in inhibitor-resistant mutants. Two mutants were chosen for this study, one resistant to both myxothiazol and stigmatellin, MXT102 (myx^{res},stg^{res}) and one resistant to myxothiazol alone, MXT103 (myx^{res},stg^{sens}). These mutations as well as that of strain R126 have been shown to map within the *pet* cluster coding for the cyt bc_1 complex (17). Mutant R126 is unable to reduce either cyt *c* or cyt *b* to any extent following a light flash (13). Both MXT102 and MXT103 are impaired in their ability to carry out these reactions though they retain their Ps$^+$ phenotype. Figure 1 is a collection of traces showing the progress of cyt c oxidation and rereduction following a light flash. In all experiments, results with mutants are compared to similar experiments done with the parent, wild-type strain, MT1131. The traces of figure 1 were obtained with the Q_{pool} poised reduced (i.e., $Q_{pool}H_2$;E_h = 85 mV) or oxidized (Q_{pool};Eh = 220mV).

Figure 2 shows the kinetics of reduction of the two b-type cytochromes. An experimental strategem was used in these experiments wherein the ambient pH was raised and samples poised with cyt b_H either reduced or oxidized prior to the flash (see Glaser and Crofts, 19).The half-times for reduction of cyt *c* and cyt b_L and cyt b_H are collected in table 1:

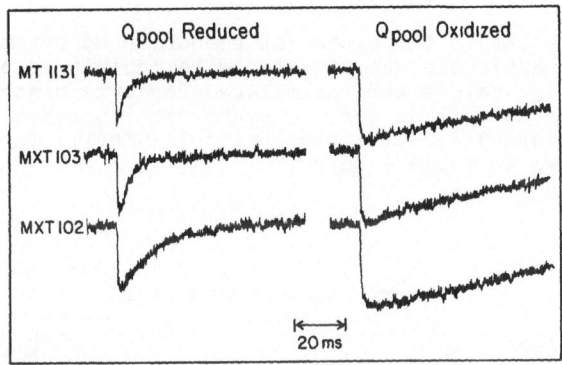

Figure 1. Kinetics of cyt c reduction via Q_z. Chromatophores plus valinomycin.

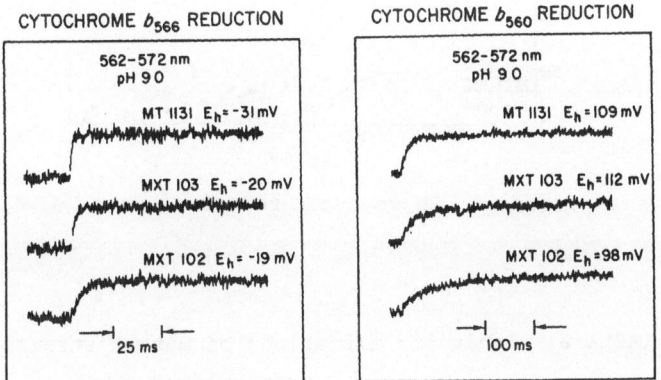

Figure 2. Kinetics of cyt b reduction via Q_z. Chromatophores plus antimycin and valinomycin.

TABLE 1.   Reduction kinetics of cyt $c_1 + c_2$ and cyt b_L and cyt b_H

$$\underline{t_{1/2}}$$

STRAIN	cyt c_1+cyt c_2 (Qpool ox)	cyt c_1+ cyt c_2 (Qpool red)	cyt b_L	cyt b_H
MT1131	65ms	3ms	4ms	13ms
MXT102	80ms	15ms	23ms	45ms
MXT103	65ms	4ms	9ms	20ms

In each strain the extent of reduction of cyt b in the presence of antimycin was titrated with inhibitors of quinol oxidation. I_{50} values were calculated for myxothiazol and stigmatellin as well as for the synthetic inhibitor 5-n-undecyl-6-hydroxy-4,7-dioxobenzothiazol (UHDBT). These results are collected in table 2 below.

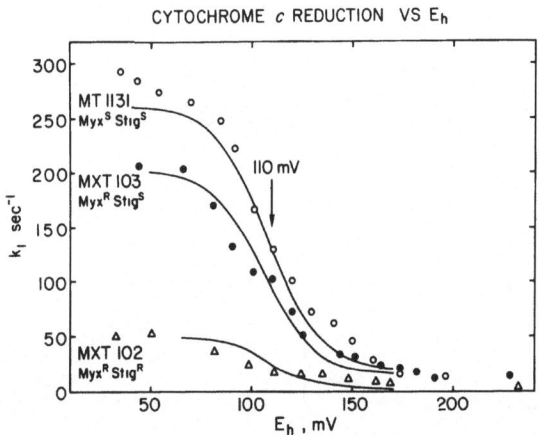

Figure 3. Eh vs cyt c reduction rate.

TABLE 2.   Inhibitor titrations of mutant strains.

$$I_{50}$$

STRAIN	Myxothiazol	Stigmatellin	UHDBT
MT1131	0.07uM	<0.01uM	0.7uM
MXT102	8.0uM	0.05uM	9.0uM
MXT103	8.0uM	<0.01uM	0.7uM

The reactions which lead to cyt c and cyt b reduction have been shown to be second-order and to be dependent on the diffusion of reductant i.e., quinol, to the site (17). The electrochemical midpoint potential apparent for reduction via Q_z (E_{m7} = 110 mV) presumably reflects either the midpoint potential of the site and its preference for binding QH_2 or simply the ambient potential of an oxidized Q_{pool} (E_{m7} = 90 mV) when a single QH_2 is donated by the RC ( ).

Figure 3 shows the dependence on E_h of the rate of reduction
of cyt c_1 + c_2 in wild-type and mutant strains. Data traces
were fit by a single exponential using a non-linear least
squares fit. It is clear from these data, as well as from
those shown in figures 1 and 2, that the mutation conferring
resistance to both inhibitors (i.e., MXT102) has a more
drastic effect on the rate of electron transfer from Q_z to
both cyts c and the cyts b than does the lesion in MXT103. The
midpoint potential for the reaction is, however the same for
all three strains. These data may be most simply explained by
postulating an impairment of binding at Q_z caused by
alteration of an essential residue at the site. This proposed
alteration lowers the site's affinity for QH_2. This conclusion
may be corroborated independently using the well-known
property of the FeS EPR lineshape (13).

EPR studies of the FeS center of inhibitor-resistant mutants

The lineshape of the Rieske FeS center of *Rhodobacter
capsulatus* is sensitive to the redox state of Q_{pool} (13). When
the ambient redox potential is adjusted to poise the Q_{pool} in
the fully reduced quinol state ($Q_{pool}H_2$), the lineshape is
broad while the spectrum narrows when Q_{pool} is fully oxidized.
Extraction of Q_{pool} has been shown to result in a broad
lineshape for FeS (22). A particularly prominent feature is
the g_x linewidth which goes from a g-value of 1.79 and a
linewidth of 13mT ($Q_{pool} H_2$) to g = 1.81 and 4mT (Q_{pool}) (see
13). Thus in the oxidized state the intensity of interaction
or presence of a Q in Q_z can be predicted from the FeS
lineshape.

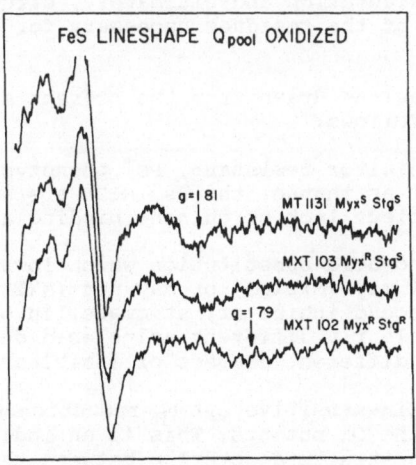

Figure 4. EPR lineshape of FeS center

Figure 4 shows the lineshape with Q_{pool} poised oxidized.
All strains exhibit the broad lineshape with Q_{pool} reduced
(not shown). MT1131 shifts and narrows as predicted. With
MXT102 the effect is intermediate while with MXT102 the broad

637

lineshape does not change from that observed when the Q_{pool} is reduced. The effect with MXT102 is similar to that observed with R126 (13).

These observations corroborate the suggestion that the lesions in MXT102 and MXT 103 as well as that of R126 (11) weaken binding of inhibitor and consequently, of substrate.

Antimycin-sensitive Cyt b_H Reduction

The structural locations of the quinone functional sites as well as their functional interrelationships are important for understanding the workings of cyt bc_1. Though the inhibitor resistant phenotypes affected the Q_z site it was of interest to examine their effects on the antimycin-sensitive site of cyt bc_1. In these experiments conditions were arranged to promote antimycin-sensitive reduction (8), i.e., high pH plus appropriate concentrations of myxothiazol. The rate and extent of reduction of cyt b_H in each inhibitor-resistant mutant or in R126 (13) was found to be nearly identical to the wild-type strain, MT1131 (data not shown).

CONCLUSIONS

Studies with inhibitor-resistant mutants are still at an early stage. The facets of protein structure which determine binding of inhibitors as well as binding and turnover of substrate in cyt bc_1 are as yet undetermined. Studies of functional alterations of mutants like MXT102 and MXT103 are a first step in a plan which includes sequencing, determination of amino acid alteration and ultimately, structural determinations of the residues necessary for binding and catalysis.

The conclusions drawn from the present studies may be summarized as follows:

1) The inhibitor resistant, Ps^+ phenotype of these mutants as well as that of the Ps^- R126 are accompanied by partial or complete lack of quinone binding at site Q_z;

2) An amino acid substitution which lowers the affinity for myxothiazol may (MXT102) or may not (MXT103) affect binding of a second inhibitor, stigmatellin or UHDBT. There are therefore clearly different amino acid determinants for the binding of different classes of inhibitors;

3) Antimycin-sensitive cyt b_H reduction via site Q_c is unaffected in the Q_z mutants. This is an indication that there is little or no structural overlap between the two sites, Q_z and Q_c.

Acknowledgments

Supported by PHS Grant 27309

REFERENCES

1. Crofts, A.R., and Wraight,C.A., The Electrochemical Domain of Photosynthesis, _Biochim. Biophys. Acta_, 726:149 (1983).

2. Rich, P.R., Electron and Proton Transfers Through Quinones and Cytochrome bc Complexes, _Biochim. Biophys. Acta_, 768:53 (1984).

3. Mitchell, P., The Protonmotive Q Cycle: A General Formulation, _FEBS Lett._, 59:137 (1975).

4. Mitchell, P., Possible Molecular Mechanisms of the Proton-motive Function of Cytochrome Systems, _J. Theor. Biol._, 62:327 (1976).

5. Rich, P.R., A Perspective on Q-cycles, _J. Bioenerg. Biomembranes_, 18:145 (1986).

6. von Jagow, G., and Link, T.A., Use of Specific Inhibitors on the Mitochondrial bc_1 Complex, _Meth. Enzymol._, 126:253 (1986).

7. van den Berg, W.H., Prince, R.C., Bashford, C.L., Takamiya, K., Bonner, W.D., and Dutton, P.L., Electron and Proton Transport in the Ubiquinone Cytochrome b-c_2 Oxidoreductase of _Rhodopseudomonas sphaeroides_, _J. Biol. Chem._, 254:8594 (1979).

8. Robertson, D.E., Giangiacomo, K., deVries, S., Moser, C.C., and Dutton, P.L., Two distinct quinone-modulated modes of antimycin-sensitive cytochrome b reduction in the cyt bc_1 complex, _FEBS Lett._, 178:343 (1984).

9. von Jagow, G., and Engels, W.D., Complete Inhibition of Electron Transfer from Ubiquinol to Cytochrome b by the Combined Action of Antimycin and Myxothiazol, _FEBS Lett._, 136:19 (1981).

10. Meinhardt, S.W., and Crofts, A.R., The Site and Mechanism of Action of Myxothiazol as an Inhibitor of Electron Transfer in _Rhodopseudomonas sphaeroides_, _FEBS Lett._, 149:217 (1982).

11. Yen, H.C., and Marrs, B.L., Map of the Genes for Carotenoid and Bacteriochlorophyll Biosynthesis in _Rhodopseudomonas capsulata_, _J. Bacteriol._, 126:619 (1986).

12. Davidson, E., and, Daldal, F., Primary Structure of the bc_1 Complex of _Rhodobacter capsulatus_, _J. Mol. Biol._, in press (1987).

13. Robertson, D.E., Davidson, E., Prince, R.C., van den Berg, W.H., Marrs, B.L., and Dutton, P.L., Discrete Catalytic Sites for Quinone in the Ubiquinone Cytochrome c_2 Oxidoreductase of _Rhodopseudomonas capsulata_ _J. Biol. Chem._, 261:584 (1986).

14. Weaver, D.F., Wall, J.D., and Gest, H., Characterization of *Rhodopseudomonas capsulata*, <u>Arch</u>. <u>Microbiol</u>., 105:207 (1975).

15. Zannoni, D., Jasper, P. and Marrs, B.L., Light-Induced Oxygen Reduction as a Probe of Electron Transport between Respiratory and Photosynthetic Components in Membranes of *Rhodopseudomonas capsulata*, <u>Arch. Biochem.</u> Biophys., 191:625 (1978).

16. Dutton, P.L., Petty, K.M., Bonner, H.S., and Morse, S.D., Cytochrome c_2 and Reaction Center of *Rhodopseudomonas sphaeroides* Ga membranes, <u>Biochim</u>. <u>Biophys</u>. <u>Acta</u>., 387:536 (1975).

17. Daldal, F., Davidson, E., Chang, S., Naiman, B., Rook, S., Genetic Analysis of the Structure and Function of Ubiquinone cyt c_2 oxidoreductase of *Rhodopseudomonas capsulata*, Current Commun. in Molec. Biol.; Microbial Energy Transduction (D.C. Youvan, F. Daldal eds) pg. 113-119, Cold Spring Harbor, 1986.

18. Dutton, P.L., Redox Potentionmetry Determination of Midpoint Potentials of Oxidation-Reduction Components of Biological Electron Transfer Systems, <u>Meths</u>. <u>Enzymol</u>., 54:411 (1978).

19. Glaser, E., and Crofts, A.R., A new electrogenic step in the Ubiquinol: cyt c_2 oxidoreductase complex of *Rhodopseudomonas sphaeroides*, <u>Biochim</u>. <u>Biophys</u>. <u>Acta</u>., 766:322 (1984).

20. Prince, R.C., and Dutton, P.L., Single and Multiple Turnover Reactions in the Ubiquinol-Cytochrome bc_2 oxidoreductase of *Rhodopseudomonas sphaeroides*, <u>Biochim</u>. <u>Biophys</u>. <u>Acta</u>., 462:731 (1977).

21. Crofts, A.R., Meindhart, S.W., Joner, K.R., and Nozzi, M., The role of the quinone pool in the cyclic electron transport chain of *Rhodopseudomonas sphaeroides*, <u>Biochim</u>. <u>Biophys</u>. <u>Acta</u>, 723:202 (1983).

22. deVries, S., Albracht, S.P.J., Berden, J.A., and Slater, E.C., The Pathway of Electrons through QH_2: Cytochrome c Oxidoreductase Studied by Pre-Steady State Kinetics, <u>Biochim</u>. <u>Biophys</u>. <u>Acta</u>., 681:41 (1982).

CYTOCHROME b558 OF *BACILLUS SUBTILIS*

Henrik Fridén and Lars Hederstedt

Department of Microbiology
University of Lund
Sölvegatan 21
S-223 62 Lund, Sweden

INTRODUCTION

The membranebound tricarboxylic acid cycle enzyme succinate dehydrogenase (SDH) is associated with a b-type cytochrome in many organisms.[1,2] The cytochrome b is often found in stoichiometric amounts in isolated succinate-ubiquinone oxidoreductase (complex II) from bovine heart,[3] *Neurospora crassa*,[4] *Ascaris suum*[5] and plant[6] mitochondria as well as in SDH complexes isolated from both Gram-negative[7] and Gram-positive[8,9] bacteria whereas yeast (*Saccharomyces cerevisiae*) apparently lacks this type of cytochrome.[10]

Cytochrome b of complex II is distinct from cytochrome b of the bc_1 complex (e.g. mitochondrial complex III and analogous plant and bacterial complexes) as judged by the size of the apoprotein(s), spectral properties and genetic organization.[23,11] In comparison to the bc_1 complex much less is known about the complex II b-type cytochrome. One reason may be that the identity or function of the complex II cytochrome has not always been clear. For example, bovine heart complex II preparations are often contaminated by complex III components.[3] Furthermore, the genetics of complex II is poorly known in eukaryotes where complex II cytochrome b and SDH are encoded by extramitochondrial genes.[4,11]

A unique combination of functional, structural, biosynthetic and genetic information on a complex II-type cytochrome has resulted from our studies on cytochrome b558 in the respiratory chain of *Bacillus subtilis*.[12] Previous results and more recent findings from this bacterial model system are summarized here.

FUNCTION IN *B. SUBTILIS*

Cytochrome b558 serves two functions in *B. subtilis*. It binds specifically SDH to the cytoplasmic membrane.[13] Mutants lacking the cytochrome therefore accumulate SDH subunits in the cytoplasm and have a SDH negative phenotype.[12] Furthermore, the cytochrome is the primary electron acceptor in the membrane for SDH at succinate oxidation.[14] The electron acceptor(s) for cytochrome b558 has not been identified.

GENETICS

The cytochrome $b558$ apoprotein is encoded by the $sdhC$ gene of the sdh operon, which also harbours the structural genes for the two SDH protein subunits; $sdhA$ (flavoprotein gene) and $sdhB$ (iron-sulfur protein gene). The operon has been cloned[15,16] and sequenced[17,18]. Recent transcription studies have shown that all three genes are transcribed from a sigma 43-type promoter yielding a 3.4 kbase $sdhCAB$ transcript.[19] Transcription starts 90 base pairs upstream the ATG translation initiation codon of $sdhC$. Mutants defective in transcription of sdh and in translation of $sdhC$, respectively have provided details regarding the expression of SDH in vivo.[20]

A functional membranebound SDH complex is not assembled when the _B. subtilis_ $sdhCAB$ operon is expressed in _Escherichia coli_ cells.[18] This is in part explained by a difference in the posttranslational processing of the flavoprotein subunit in the two bacteria, i.e. the protein is not flavinylated in _E. coli_.[21] _B. subtilis_ cytochrome $b558$ expressed in _E. coli_ is found in the inner membrane fraction and has physico-chemical properties identical to that of the cytochrome synthesized in _B. subtilis_.[15,22] Moreover, the heterologous cytochrome is reduced by succinate and NADH via _E. coli_ respiratory chain components (unpublished results). _B. subtilis_ cytochrome $b558$ can constitute up to 10% of total inner membrane protein in _E. coli_ containing _B. subtilis_ $sdhC$ on a multicopy plasmid. The colonies formed by such cells have a reddish color clearly visible by eye.[15]

STRUCTURE AND TOPOLOGY

A monodisperse SDH-cytochrome $b558$ complex can be solubilized from the _B. subtilis_ cytoplasmic membrane using Triton C-100. The complex, isolated by immunoprecipitation with antibodies against SDH, consists of three polypeptides in equimolar amounts; the flavoprotein (65 kDa) and iron-sulfur protein (28 kDa) subunits of SDH and the cytochrome $b558$ (23 kDa).[9,12]

Succinate rapidly reduces the cytochrome in the isolated complex.[14] Both in intact membranes and in the isolated complex the extent of reduction is about 50% of that obtained with dithionite. It is not established whether cytochrome $b558$ contains one or two hemes. Molecular and spectroscopic properties of cytochrome $b558$ are presented in Table 1.

The primary structure of cytochrome $b558$ has been determined from the DNA sequence[17] in combination with N-terminal amino acid sequence analysis.[21] No conclusive amino acid sequence homology to cytochrome of bc_1 complexes or any other cytochrome b has been detected.[17] Heme iron(s) in oxidized cytochrome $b558$ gives rise to an highly anisotropic low spin EPR signal (HALS-type signal), which suggests imidazoles as axial ligands to heme.[22] Of the six His present, four are located in stretches of hydrophobic amino acids and two in more hydrophilic parts (Figure 1). The His at position 113 (a hydrophobic region) can however be excluded as a ligand, since a mutant cytochrome which contains Tyr at position 113 shows normal cytochrome spectrum and heme content.[20] Assuming only one heme group in cytochrome $b558$ the His at position 28, 70 and 155 seem the most likely candidates as axial ligands to heme. These residues are located in separate predicted transmembrane segments and two of them would be able to ligate a heme group within the lipid bilayer.

Surface labeling and antibody adsorption experiments have demonstrated the transmembrane topology of the SDH-cytochrome $b558$ complex in _B. subtilis_.[23] SDH is anchored by the cytochrome on the inner (cytoplasmic) side. Cytochrome $b558$ is also exposed to the water-phase on the outer side

Table 1. Properties of *B. subtilis* Cytochrome *b*558[a]

Amino acid residues	202[b]
Molecular mass of apoprotein (Da)	22 901
Net charge	+5
Polarity index (%)	31
Protoheme per polypeptide	1.3 - 2
Light absorption spectra of reduced cytochrome (λ_{max}):	
at room temperature (nm)	426,529,558
at 77 K (nm)	426,526,555[c]
EPR spectrum of oxidized cytochrome (g_{max})	≈ 3.5

[a]Data from references.[14,17,20,22]
[b]About 50% of all polypeptides isolated from membranes lack the N-terminal Met and contain 201 residues.[21]
[c]The α-peak is a composite of two peaks with maximum at 553 and 558 nm.

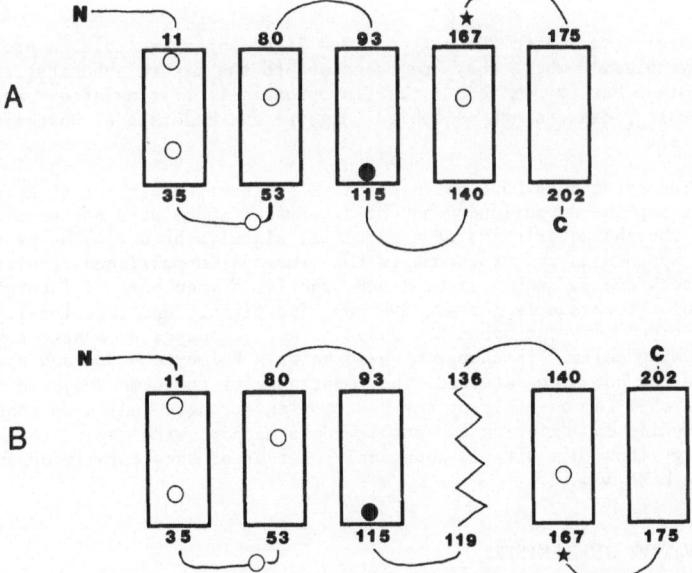

Fig.1. Alternative models of cytochrome *b*558 in the *B. subtilis* cytoplasmic membrane. ● and ★ indicate the location of residues 113 and 168 which are important for the binding of SDH (see text). ○ and ● indicate His residues. The 4th transmembrane segment from the N-terminal in model B is predicted to be a β-sheet with sided hydropathy (T.A. Link, personal communication).

of the membrane where it can react with diazobenzenesulfonate. Interestingly, chemical modification of the cytochrome from the outside with this reagent has a transmembrane effect in that it results in inactivation of SDH activity measured with phenazine methosulfate as artificial electron acceptor.[23] It has not been analyzed if electron transfer from SDH to cytochrome $b558$ is affected.

Up to six transmembrane segments in cytochrome $b558$ can be predicted from the hydropathy profile.[17] To study topology and to possibly indentify regions in the polypeptide important for SDH-binding we have characterized[20] cytochrome $b558$ mutants defective in the binding of SDH. Two such mutants, containing single missense mutations, synthesize a membranebound cytochrome of normal size and light absorption spectrum. One of the mutants has a Gly to Asp change at position 168, whereas the other mutant has His-113 replaced by Tyr (Figure 1).

If we return to the number of transmembrane segments in cytochrome $b558$, only a model with six such segments seems to place both the above mutations on the cytoplasmic,SDH binding, side of the membrane. A model with five segments leads to the conclusion that at least one of the mutations has a transmembrane effect on the structure of the SDH binding region. At this point we cannot decide between the two models. From the properties of the above mutants and from comparative biochemistry (see later) we can speculate that cytochrome $b558$ consists of two functionally separable domains; an N-terminal heme-binding and a C-terminal SDH-binding domain.

BIOSYNTHESIS

Newly translated SDH polypeptides first appear as soluble proteins in the cytoplasm[13] where they are processed to the mature subunits, i.e. the N-terminal Met is removed,[21] the flavoprotein is flavinylated[13] and the iron-sulfur centers are assembled (Maguire and Hederstedt, unpublished results).[24]

The cytochrome $b558$ polypeptide is synthesized without an N-terminal leader peptide extension[21] and the N-terminal amino acid sequence also lacks the characteristics of a bacterial signal peptide.[17] The protein first appears as apocytochrome in the membrane (unpublished results). This apocytochrome is unable to bind SDH tightly,[13] when heme is incorporated and holocytochrome is formed, SDH can bind tightly and functionally. Cytoplasmic and membrane-bound SDH subunits are exchanged at a detectable rate in growing cells.[13] Exchange of heme between holocytochrome and apocytochrome has not been detected. The importance of the heme group in cytochrome $b558$ for assembly of the SDH complex strongly indicates that the polypeptide can exist in two stable conformations with regard to the SDH-binding site. This site is apparently part of or structurally dependent on the heme domain.

COMPARATIVE BIOCHEMISTRY

One or two hydrophobic polypeptides, depending on the organism, co-purify with SDH in complex II-type preparations (Table 2). Two polypeptides of bovine heart mitochondria have been purified as cytochrome $b560$ or on their property to confer succinate-ubiquinone reductase activity when combined with the SDH enzyme proper.[26,27,28,29] Different procedures and starting materials have been used in the purifications and the resulting preparations contain various amounts of heme. The succinate-ubiquinone reductase activity of reconstituted complex seems correlated to the heme content, indicating a role of heme in SDH binding and/or quinone reduction.

644

Table 2. Polypeptides in the SDH membrane anchor of
different organisms with a complex II-type
cytochrome *b*

One polypeptide	MW[a]	(Ref)	Two polypeptides	MW[a]	(Ref)
Bacillus subtilis	23k	(12)	*Ascaris suum*	11k,12k	(5)
Neurospora crassa	14k	(4)	Bovine heart	7-14k,13-16k	(2)
			Escherichia coli	13k,14k	(7)
			Micrococcus luteus	15k,17k	(8)
			Mung bean	13k,15k	(6)

[a]Molecular weight as determined by SDS-polyacrylamide electrophoresis.
The MW of *E. coli* and *B. subtilis* polypeptides are those deduced from
the DNA sequence. [17, 25]

Cytochrome *b*560 of bovine heart and *B. subtilis* cytochrome *b*558 show
very similar light absorption and EPR spectra.[20,22,27,31] The cytochrome
in bovine complex II has a low midpoint redox potential and is not readily
reduced by succinate, but can be oxidized by fumarate or quinone.[2] Chemical
modification experiments have demonstrated the transmembrane orientation
of bovine SDH anchor protein.[32,33]

E. coli SDH solubilized from the membrane with detergent and purified
by immunoprecipitation contains a cytochrome *b* and two small polypeptides,
17 kDa and 15 kDa.[7] A structural and functional association of these polypeptides with SDH is supported by genetic data.[25,34] The *E. coli sdh* operon
contains four genes; the structural genes for SDH ($sdhA_{EC}$ and $sdhB_{EC}$) and
$sdhC_{EC}$ and $sdhD_{EC}$ which encode hydrophobic polypeptides of 14 kDa and
13 kDa, respectively. Anraku and coworkers recently showed that the N-
terminal amino acid sequence of *E. coli* cytochrome *b*556 exactly matches
residues 4 to 27 of the predicted $sdhC_{EC}$ gene product. In addition, they
demonstrated that a mutant deleted in the *sdh* region of the chromosome
and lacking cytochrome *b*556 could not grow on succinate. These results
strongly suggest that the *E. coli sdhC* product is (part of) cytochrome
*b*556 and corresponds to *B. subtilis* cytochrome *b*558.

Despite about 30% direct primary sequence homology between *B. subtilis*
and *E. coli* SDH subunits,[18] there is no apparent amino acid sequence
homology between the *B. subtilis* cytochrome *b*558 and the *E. coli sdhC* or
sdhD product.[17] However, these polypeptides share some properties: (i)
similar hydropathy profile, (ii) lack of cystein residues, (iii) the
genetic organisation of corresponding genes, (iv) multiple occurence of
the sequence His-X-X-X-Gly. One may speculate that the SDH-binding / cytochrome protein(s) originates from two separate hydrophobic polypeptides.
The genes encoding these polypeptides were later brought under joint
control with the structural genes for SDH flavoproteins and iron-sulfur
proteins by a rearrangement bringing all four genes into one operon. In
some organisms genes for the anchor and apocytochrome fused to code for
one protein. The suggested N-terminal heme-binding and the C-terminal
SDH-binding principal domains in *B. subtilis* cytochrome *b*558 (see structure and topology) together with the conserved *sdh* gene organisation and
direction of transcription in *E. coli* and *B. subtilis*, *sdhC*(cytochrome *b*)
sdhD (SDH binding, *E. coli* only) *sdhA sdhB*, support this view.

ACKNOWLEDGEMENTS

We are grateful to Thomas A. Link for a computer search for secondary structures in cytochrome *b*558, and to Inga Ohlsson for typing manuscript. This work was supported by grants from the Swedish Natural Research Council and the Emil och Wera Cornells Stiftelse.

REFERENCES

1. L. Hederstedt and L. Rutberg, Succinate dehydrogenase – a comparative review, Microbiol. Rev. 45:542 (1981).
2. Y. Hatefi, The mitochondrial electron transport and oxidative phosphorylation system, Ann. Rev. Biochem. 54:1015 (1985).
3. Y. Hatefi, Y.M. Galante, D.L. Stiggall and C.I. Ragan, Proteins polypeptides, prosthetic groups, and enzymic properties of complexes I,II,III,IV and V of the mitochondrial oxidative phosphorylation system, Meth. Enzymol. 56:577 (1979).
4. H. Weiss and H.J. Kolb, Isolation of mitochondrial succinate: Ubiquinone reductase, cytochrome *c* reductase and cytochrome *c* oxidase from *Neurospora crassa* using nonionic detergent, Eur. J. Biochem. 99:139 (1979).
5. S. Takamiya, R. Furushima and H. Oya, Electron-transfer complexes of *Ascaris suum* muscle mitochondria. II. Succinate-coenzyme Q reductase associated with substrate – reducible cytochrome *b*-558, Biochim. Biophys. Acta 848:99 (1986).
6. J.J. Burke, J.N. Siedow and D.E. Moreland, Succinate dehydrogenase. A partial purification from mung bean hypocotyls and soybean cotyledons, Plant Physiol. 70:1577 (1982).
7. C. Condon, R. Cammack, D.S. Patil and P. Owen, The succinate dehydrogenase of *Escherichia coli*, J. Biol. Chem. 260:9427 (1985).
8. B.A. Crowe and P. Owen, Molecular properties of succinate dehydrogenase isolated from *Micrococcus luteus*, J. Bacteriol. 153:1493 (1983).
9. L. Hederstedt, E. Holmgren and L. Rutberg, Characterization of a succinate dehydrogenase complex solubilized from the cytoplasmic membrane of *Bacillus subtilis* with the nonionic detergent Triton X-100, J. Bacteriol. 138:370 (1979).
10. R.J. Schilling, T. Baldwin and G. Palmer, The characterization of highly purified complex II fram baker's yeast, Fed. Proc. 41:3664 (1982).
11. H.R. Mahler and P.S. Perlman, Cytochrome *b* of the respiratory chain, in: The enzymes of biological membranes, vol 4. A.N. Martonosi ed. Plenum Press, New York (1985).
12. L. Hederstedt, Molecular properties, genetics and biosynthesis of *Bacillus subtilis* succinate dehydrogenase complex, Meth. Enzymol. 126:399 (1986).
13. L. Hederstedt and L. Rutberg. Biosynthesis and membrane binding of succinate dehydrogenase in *Bacillus subtilis*, J. Bacteriol. 144:941 (1980).
14. L. Hederstedt, Cytochrome *b* reducible by succinate in an isolated succinate dehydrogenase-cytochrome *b* complex from *Bacillus subtilis* membranes, J. Bacteriol. 144:933 (1980).
15. K. Magnusson, L. Hederstedt and L. Rutberg, Cloning and expression in *Escherichia coli* of *sdhA*, the structural gene for cytochrome *b*-558 of the *Bacillus subtilis* succinate dehydrogenase complex, J. Bacteriol. 162:1180 (1985).
16. S. Hasnain, R. Sammons, I. Roberts and C.M. Thomas, Cloning and deletion analysis of a genomic segment of *Bacillus subtilis* coding for the *sdhA, B, C* and *gerE* loci, J. Gen. Microbiol. 131:2269 (1985).

646

17. K. Magnusson, M.K. Phillips, J.R. Guest and L. Rutberg, Nucleotide sequence of the gene for cytochrome *b*–558 of the *Bacillus subtilis* succinate dehydrogenase complex, J. Bacteriol. 166:1067 (1986).

18. M.K. Phillips, L. Hederstedt, S. Hasnain, L. Rutberg and J.R. Guest, Nucleotide sequence encoding the flavoprotein and iron-sulfur protein subunits of the succinate dehydrogenase complex of *Bacillus subtilis*, J. Bacteriol. in press (1987).

19. L. Melin, K. Magnusson and L. Rutberg, Identification of the promoter of the *Bacillus subtilis sdh* operon, J. Bacteriol. in press (1987).

20. H. Fridén, L. Rutberg, K. Magnusson and L. Hederstedt, Genetic and biochemical characterization of *Bacillus subtilis* mutants defective in expression and function of cytochrome *b*–558. Submitted manuscript (1987).

21. L. Hederstedt, T. Bergman and H. Jörnvall, Processing of *Bacillus subtilis* succinate dehydrogenase and cytochrome *b*558 polypeptides, FEBS Lett. 213:000 (1987).

22. L. Hederstedt and K.K. Andersson, EPR spectroscopy of *Bacillus subtilis* cytochrome *b*558 in *Escherichia coli* membranes and in succinate dehydrogenase complex from *Bacillus subtilis* membranes. J. Bacteriol. 167:735 (1986).

23. L. Hederstedt and L. Rutberg, Orientation of succinate dehydrogenase and cytochrome *b*–558 in the *Bacillus subtilis* cytoplasmic membrane. J. Bacteriol. 153:57 (1983).

24. L. Hederstedt, J.J. Maguire, A.J. Waring and T. Ohnishi, Characterization by EPR and studies on subunit location and assembly of the iron-sulfur clusters of *Bacillus subtilis* succinate dehydrogenase, J. Biol. Chem. 260:5554 (1985).

25. D. Wood, M.G. Darlison, R.J. Wilde and J.R. Guest, Nucleotide sequence encoding the flavoprotein and hydrophobic subunits of the succinate dehydrogenase of *Escherichia coli*, Biochem. J. 222:519 (1984).

26. B.A.C. Ackrell, M.B. Ball and E.B. Kearney, Peptides from complex II active in reconstitution of succinate-ubiquinone reductase, J. Biol. Chem. 255:2761 (1980).

27. Y. Hatefi and Y.M. Galante, Isolation of cytochrome *b*560 from complex II and its reconstitution with succinate dehydrogenase, J. Biol. Chem. 255:5530 (1980).

28. A.D. Vinogradov, V.G. Gavrikov and E.V. Gavrikova, Reconstitution of succinate-ubiquinone reductase from the soluble components, Biochem. Biophys. Acta 592:13 (1980).

29. C.-A. Yu and L. Yu, Isolation and properties of a mitochondrial protein that converts succinate dehydrogenase into succinate-ubiquinone oxidoreductase, Biochemistry 19:3579 (1980).

30. Y. Hatefi, C.I. Ragan and Y.M. Galante, The enzymes and the enzyme complexes of the mitochondrial oxidative phosphorylation system, in: The enzymes of biological membranes, vol 4, A.N. Martonosi, ed. Plenum Press, New York (1985).

31. N.R. Orme-Johnson, R.E. Hansen and H. Beinert, EPR studies of the cytochrome *bc*, segment of the mitochondrial electron transfer system, Biochem. Biophys. Res. Comm. 45: 871 (1971).

32. A. Merli, R.A. Capaldi, B.A.C. Ackrell and E.B. Kearney, Arrangement of complex II in the mitochondrial inner membrane, Biochemistry 18: 1393 (1974).

33. J. Girdlestone, R. Bisson and R.A. Capaldi, Interaction of succinate-ubiquinone reductase with (arylazido) phospholipids, Biochemistry 20: 152 (1981).

34. M.G. Darlison and J.R. Guest, Nucleotide sequence encoding the iron-sulphur protein subunit of the succinate dehydrogenase of *Escherichia coli*, Biochem. J. 223:507 (1984).

35. H. Murakami, K. Kita, H. Oya and Y. Anraku, The *Escherichia coli* cytochrome *b*556 gene, *cyb*A, is assignable as *sdh*C in the succinate dehydrogenase gene cluster, FEMS Microbiol. Lett. 30:307 (1985).

MITOCHONDRIAL CYTOCHROME b_{560}

Chang-An Yu and Linda Yu

Department of Biochemistry
Oklahoma State University
Stillwater, Ok 74078

INTRODUCTION

Cytochrome b_{560} in the succinate-ubiquinone (Q) reductase region of the mitochondrial electron transfer chain was first reported by Davis *et al.* (1, 2). In spite of the detection of cytochrome b_{560} in various succinate -Q^1 reductase (3, 4), and Complex II (5-7) preparations, this cytochrome has often been regarded as a contaminant of the denatured cytochromes from ubiquinol-cytochrome *c* reductase because it is not reducible by succinate, and the spectra of dithionite reduced cytochrome b_{560} in these preparations resembles the spectra of a mixture of denatured cytochromes *b* and c_1 of ubiquinol-cytochrome *c* reductase. Thus, the importance of this particular cytochrome b_{560} has been slighted in the mammalian system. The participation of cytochrome b_{560} in succinate dehydrogenase (SDH) of *Bacillus subtilis* (8) and *Neurospora crassa* (9), however, is well recognized. Recently, a substrate reducible cytochrome b_{558} was detected in muscle mitochondrial succinate-Q reductase from *Ascaris suum* (10). In this paper we report the properties of mitochondrial cytochrome b_{560} and its possible function in succinate oxidation and fumarate reduction.

I. Preparations of Cytochrome b_{560}:

Several methods are available for the preparation of cytochrome b_{560} from complex II, succinate-Q reductase, or soluble cytochrome b-c_1 complex [succinate-cytochrome c reductase less SDH (11)]. Table I summarizes the reported preparations of cytochrome b_{560} and their heme content. The purest cytochrome b_{560} preparation contains two protein subunits with molecular weights of 15K and 13K[2]. Depending upon the starting material used, some preparations of cytochrome b_{560} contain ubiquinone. It should be mentioned that several terms have been used by different investigators for this two-subunit preparation, such as QPs (12) and CII-3,4 (13), in addition to cytochrome b_{560} (14). We prefer QPs because the main function of this preparation is for the Q binding and

---

[1] Abbreviations used: DCIP, dichlorophenolindophenol; GMD, N-D-gluco-N-methyldecamide; Q, ubiquinone; Q_2, 2,3-dimethoxy-5-methyl-6-geranyl-1,4-benzoquinone; QPs, a protein complex that converts SDH into succinate-Q reductase; SDH, succinate dehydrogenase; SDS, sodium dodecylsulfate; TTFA, 2-thenoyltrifluoroacetone.

[2] The electrophoretic properties of these two subunits were affected by detergents present in the preparation and the electrophoresis system used. The molecular weights of these two subunits were previously reported to be 17 K and 15 K (12).

Table I. Comparison of Various Cytochrome b_{560} Preparations.

Preparations	Prepared from	Cyt.b_{560}	Q	SA[1]	Ref.
		nmol/mg	nmol/mg	μmol/mg/min	
QPs, Method I	SCR[2]	1	10	17	12
QPs, Method II	SCR	8	17-25	79	12
CII$_{3,4}$	Complex II	2	0	40	13
Cytochrome b_{560}	Complex II	14	0	238[3]	14
QPs, b_{560}	SCR	20	25-35	105	15

[1] The specific activity is refered to succinate-Q reductase activity measured after the preparation is reconstituted with excess SDH, and is expressed by the protein of cytochrome b preparations. The activity was assayed at 23 $^{\circ}$C in the presence of 30 μM Q$_2$.

[2] The reconstituted succinate-Q reductase activity was measured at 37 $^{\circ}$C.

[3] SCR, succinate-cytochrome c reductase.

converting SDH into succinate -Q reductase. Cytochrome b$_{560}$ is only a part of QPs preparation and its catalytic function remains to be established.

II. Spectral Properties of Cytochrome b_{560}

Fig. 1A shows the absorption spectra of cytochrome b_{560} in the isolated QPs. The oxidized cytochrome shows broad absorption at the α- and β-regions with a Soret absorption at 412 nm. Cytochrome b_{560} is not reducible by succinate or ascorbate, even under anaerobic conditions. However, when the sample is reduced with dithionite, an α-absorption at 560 nm, a broad β-absorption peak at between 526 to 528 nm, and a Soret absorption at 424 nm are observed. The millimolar extinction coefficient of cytochrome b_{560} in isolated QPs or succinate-Q reductase is 20.5 for reduced minus oxidized absorbance at 560 nm minus 575 nm based on the heme content, is determined by pyridine hemochromogen spectra (16). The millimolar extinction coefficient for the oxidized Soret absorbance of cytochrome b_{560} in QPs is estimated to be 158.

It was reported (14) that the dithionite reduced spectra of isolated cytochrome b_{560} from Complex II deteriorated quickly at room temperature. The dithionite reduced spectra of cytochrome b_{560} in QPs, as prepared, without removing most of the Triton X-100 with Bio-Beads, also deteriorates rather quickly; about 80% of the reduced spectra disappears after 1.5 hrs at room temperature. The addition of more dithionite fails to regenerate the reduced form of the spectra, indicating that the sample has been irreversibly denatured. It is likely that the denaturation occurs at the heme moiety because the alkaline pyridine hemochromogen spectra is also diminished. The Soret absorption ratio between the reduced and oxidized cytochrome b_{560} in partially detergent free QPs is 1.3 (see Fig. 1A). However, this ratio varies from 0.9 to 1.3 with isolated QPs preparations without removing most of the Triton X-100. The rate of destruction of the dithionite reduced absorption characteristics and the ratio of Soret absorptions between reduced and oxidized cytochrome b$_{560}$ in isolated QPs are affected by the amount of Triton X-100 in the sample. When most of the Triton X-100 in QPs is removed, the dithionite reduced spectra of cytochrome b_{560} becomes more stable (15). The mechanism of the denaturation of cytochrome b_{560} in the presence of dithionite is not clear. Cytochrome b_{560} in QPs is also reducible by NADH in the presence of Type II NADH dehydrogenase (17) under anaerobic conditions. This reduced spectrum, which is the same as that obtained by dithionite reduction, is stable under anaerobic conditions.

When the absorpton spectra of cytochrome b_{560} in isolated QPs are compared with those of cytochrome b_{560} in succinate-Q reductase, slight differences in the α- and β-absorption regions are observed. Reduced cytochrome b_{560} in succinate-Q reductase exhibits an α-absorption maximum at 560.5 nm with a discernible shoulder at 553 nm (Fig. 1B) whereas in isolated QPs it has a symmetrical α-absorption peak at 560 nm (Fig. 1C). The 553 nm α-

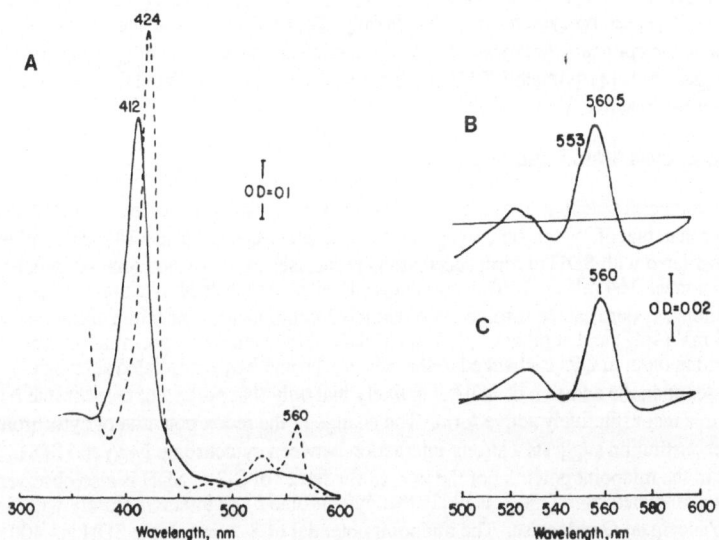

Fig. 1. Absorption spectra of cytochrome b_{560}. A, oxidized (—) and dithionite reduced (– –) forms of cytochrome b_{560} in isolated QPs. ; B, different spectra of dithionite reduced minus oxidized form of cytochrome b_{560} in isolated succinate-Q reductase; C, different spectra of dithionite reduced minus oxidized form of cytochrome b_{560} in isolated QPs.should be emphasized that the conversion of carbon monoxide reactive cytochrome b_{560} to carbon monoxide non-reactive cytochrome b_{560} is not merely the result of the presence of SDH. A specific interaction must occur because reconstitutively inactive SDH is not able to convert cytochrome b_{560} in isolated QPs into the carbon monoxide non-reactive form.

absorption shoulder is an intrinsic property of cytochrome b_{560} in succinate-Q reductase because when QPs is dissociated from SDH, the 553 nm shoulder of cytochrome b_{560} is lost; this shoulder is regenerated when QPs is reconstituted with SDH (15). It should, however, be mentioned that part of the 553 nm shoulder observed in a less pure preparation of succinate-Q reductase, such as Complex II (5-7), is due to contaminate denatured cytochrome c_1. Preparations of Complex II are reported to be contaminated with 15 to 20% of cytochrome b-c_1 complex (14).

Unlike cytochrome b_{560} in isolated succinate-Q reductase, in which the reduced form is not reactive toward carbon monoxide (2, 3), reduced cytochrome b_{560} in QPs is completely reactive (15). This carbon monoxide reactivity diminishes about 50% as the isolated cytochrome b_{560} (QPs) is recombined with SDH. This result indicates that the carbon monoxide reactivity of cytochrome b_{560} results from removal of its interacting partner. It should be emphasized that the conversion of carbon monoxide reactive cytochrome b_{560} to carbon monoxide non-reactive cytochrome b_{560} is not merely the result of the presence of SDH. A specific interaction must occur because reconstitutively inactive SDH is not able to convert cytochrome b_{560} in isolated QP into the carbon monoxide non-reactive form.

Since only about 50% of the cytochrome b_{560} in isolated QPs can be converted to the carbon monoxide non-reactive form by reconstitution with SDH, it is likely that only about 50% of the cytochrome b_{560} in the isolated QPs preparation is in the reconstitutively active form. This deduction is compatible with the fact that the specific reconstitutive activity of isolated QPs, based on cytochrome b_{560}, is only about 50% of that in succinate-Q reductase. Studies on the epr characteristics and redox potentials of cytochrome b_{560}, described below, also suggest that approximately 50% of the cytochrome b_{560} in isolated QPs is in the reconstitutively active form.

III. Redox Potential of Cytochrome b_{560}

The midpoint potential of cytochrome b_{560} in QPs is estimated to be -144 mV (15), which is higher than that of cytochrome b_{560} in intact succinate-Q reductase (-185 mV). When QPs is reconstituted with SDH to form succinate-Q reductase, the redox potential of cytochrome b_{560} becomes -164 mV (15). The redox potential titration curve of cytochrome b_{560} in the reconstituted system can be resolved into two $n = 1$ components: one with a midpoint potential of -185 mV (46%) and another of -144 mV (54%). Since the redox potential of about 46% of cytochrome b_{560} in QPs is changed to that of cytochrome b_{560} in isolated succinate-Q reductase, upon the addition of SDH, it is likely that only that portion of cytochrome b_{560} in QPs is in a reconstitutively active form. The change of the redox potential of cytochrome b_{560} upon reconstitution suggests a strong interaction between cytochrome b_{560} and SDH. Since a change in the midpoint potential of the iron sulfur center of S-2 of SDH is also observed when SDH is dissociated from QPs, it is likely that cytochrome b_{560} interacts closely with S-2 of SDH in succinate-Q reductase. The midpoint potential of S-2 in soluble SDH is - 400 mV, the midpoint potential of the corresponding iron sulfur cluster in succinate-Q reductase is - 260 mV (18).

The low redox potentials of cytochrome b_{560} observed in both succinate-Q reductase, reconstituted succinate-Q reductase, and isolated QPs are in line with the fact that cytochrome b_{560} is not reducible by succinate either in the isolated or complexed form. This low potential of cytochrome b_{560} is the main reason for skepticism about its direct participation in the catalytic function of succinate-Q reductase. A midpoint potential of less than - 80 mV was estimated for cytochrome b_{560} in Complex II by the putative reduction using a fumarate/succinate mixture (14). This estimation should be treated with caution because cytochrome b_{560} of beef heart mitochondrial succinate-Q reductase was shown (3) and reconfirmed by present study (15) to be not succinate reducible.

IV. EPR Characteristics of Cytochrome b_{560}:

As shown in Fig. 2. Cytochrome b_{560} in QPs preparation shows two epr signals, of roughly equal intensity, at $g = 3.07$ and $g = 2.92$ (15). These two signals also appear in the soluble cytochrome b-c_1 complex (11). In the soluble cytochrome b-c_1 complex preparation all three species of cytochromes b (b_{562}, b_{565}, and b_{560}) are epr detectable. Cytochrome b_{560} in isolated succinate-Q reductase exhibits mainly one epr signal at $g = 3.46$. This is different from those of cytochrome b_{562} ($g = 3.43$) and cytochrome b_{565} ($g = 3.76$) (19-21). A small second peak at $g = 3.07$ is also observed apparently due to the presence of a trace amount of denatured SDH in the succinate-Q reductase preparation. However, when QPs was reconstituted with soluble SDH to form succinate-Q reductase, a $g = 3.46$ signal appears, the g

= 3.07 signal disappears and the g = 2.92 signal remains unchanged. These results indicate that there are two forms of cytochrome b_{560} in the isolated QPs. One (g = 3.07) is reconstitutively active with succinate dehydrogenase; the other (g = 2.92) is reconstitutively inactive. The relative concentrations of cytochrome b_{560} with g = 3.07 and g = 2.92 in isolated QPs are estimated to be 47% and 53%, respectively, using the reported proportionality factors (20). This observation is consistent with the finding that only about 50% of the cytochrome b_{560} in QPs is in the reconstitutively active form, which is converted to carbon monoxide non-reactive cytochrome b_{560} and decreases its redox potential from - 144 mV to - 185 mV, by reconstitution with SDH. Although the evidence presented here clearly indicates that the properties of cytochrome b_{560} in QPs are changed upon binding to SDH, whether these effects on the heme environment are due to the direct binding of SDH to cytochrome b_{560} or due to an indirect effect of the binding of succinate dehydrogenase to the Mr = 13 Kd protein, or both, remains unclear.

Although the epr spectra of cytochrome b_{560} in succinate -Q reductase are very similar to those of cytochrome b_{562} of ubiquinol-cytochrome c reductase, the power saturation behavior

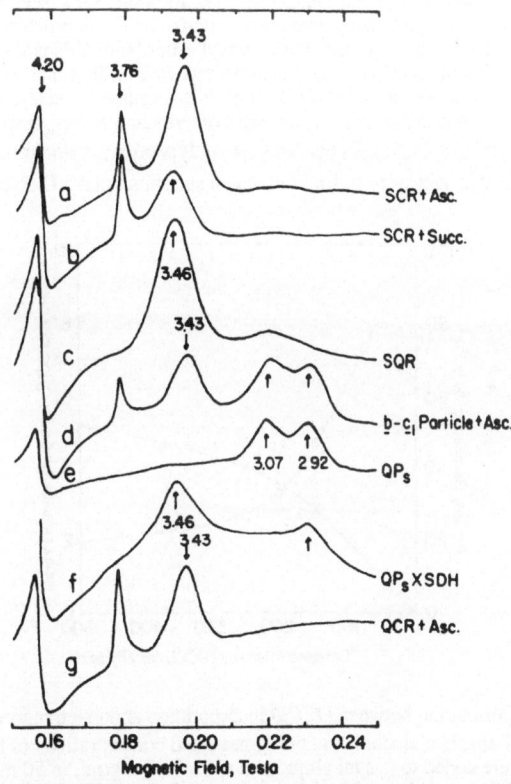

Fig. 2. EPR spectra of cytochromes b in isolated succinate-cytochrome c reductase, cytochrome b-c_1 particles, succinate-Q reductase, QPs, reconstituted succinate-Q reductase, and ubiquinol-cytochrome c reductase. The cytochrome b content of the preparations used, in μM, was 400, 400, 195, 70, 70, and 200 for succinate-cytochrome c reductase (SCR), cytochrome b-c_1 particles, succinate-Q reductase (SQR), QPs, reconstituted succinate-Q reductase, and ubiquinol-cytochrome c reductase (QCR), respectively. The epr instrument settings were: modulation frequency, 100 KHz; modulation amplitude, 20 gauss; time constant, 0.5 sec; microwave frequency, 9.42 GHz; microwave power, 20 mW; scan rate, 200 sec; and temperature, 11 K.

of these two cytochromes are quite different (15). Since cytochrome b_{560} is readily detectable in succinate-reduced succinate-cytochrome c reductase but not in ubiquinol-cytochrome c reductase, it is unlikely that cytochrome b_{560} is derived from cytochrome b_{562} of ubiquinol-cytochrome c reductase. By measuring the epr spectra of cytochromes b in different preparation of reductases at different stages of reduction, and using the reported proportionality factor (20), the relative distribution of cytochrome b_{566}, b_{562}, and b_{560} in succinate-cytochrome c reductase is estimated to be 38, 44, and 18%, respectively (15). Since the purified succinate-cytochrome c reductase contains 3.6 nmoles of cytochrome b per mole of flavin, this would translate into a molar ratio of flavin to cytochrome b of 0.65, which is close to that found in the isolated succinate-Q reductase. The epr spectra of cytochromes b in ubiquinol-cytochrome c reductase, QPs, and succinate-Q reductase are compared in Fig. 2.

V. Involvement of the Carboxyl Group(s) in the Interaction between QPs and SDH

When isolated QPs is reacted with increasing amounts of DCCD at pH 6.0, the reconstitutive activity of QPs decreases as the DCCD concentration increases, up to 200 molar excess DCCD is used, and the extent of decrease in the reconstitutive activity is correlated with the increase in the amount of [^{14}C]-DCCD incorporation into QPs (see Fig. 3). Beyond that, the increase in DCCD incorporation, presumably non-specific, is much slower and so is the activity loss. This result indicates that the carboxyl group(s) in QPs is involved in the interaction with SDH. This is consistent with the reported finding that an amino group in SDH is involved in reconstitution with QPs (22). Since the decrease in reconstitutive activity of QPs upon DCCD treatment also parallels the decrease of cytochrome b_{560} content in the preparation, and since isolated QPs contains two polypeptides, cytochrome b_{560} (15 K), and a Mr=13 K protein, it is necessary to find out which subunits uptake DCCD. When the [^{14}C]-

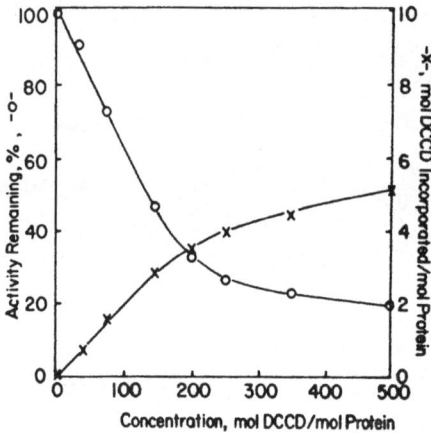

Fig. 3. Correlation between DCCD incorporation and inactivation of QPs. Five-μl of absolute alcohol containing indicated concentrations of [^{14}C]-DCCD were added to 0.2 ml aliquots of QPs, 0.18 mg/ml, in 50 mM Tris-MES, pH 6.0, containing 30 mM sucrose and 0.2% GMD. The specific radioactivity of DCCD used was 5,000 cpm/nmol. After incubation at room temperature for 10 min, 0.1 ml aliquots were withdrawn from each tube, cooled to 0 °C, and reconstituted with SDH. Succinate-Q reductase activity (-o-) was assayed after incubation at 0 °C for 20 min. For measurement of DCCD incorporation (x), 10 μl aliquots were withdrawn from samples and spotted on Whatman paper #3. The radioactivity of the original spots were determined after the paper was developed with chloroform : methanol (2:1) mixture.

DCCD treated samples were subjected to SDS-PAGE, the majority of radioactivity is found in the 13 K protein. These results suggest that modification of the carboxyl group(s) in the 13 K protein is the cause for the loss of reconstitutive activity of QPs and for change of the heme environment of cytochrome b. The observed decrease of the cytochrome b_{560} content in QPs upon DCCD treatment may result from cytochrome b_{560} being ligated to both subunits, thus modification of the 13 K protein affects the 15 Kd protein (cytochrome b). Since these two polypeptides are so closely related and the fact that the single-polypeptide QPs preparation is less active, it is not unreasonable to suggest that cytochrome b_{560} or its apoprotein (15 K) may play a structural role in succinate oxidation.

VI. The Role of Cytochrome b_{560} in the Reduction of Fumarate:

From evidence presented in the previous sections, it is clear that there is a strong physical association between cytochrome b_{560} and SDH. However, the inability of cytochrome b_{560} in succinate-Q reductase to be reduced by succinate, even under anaerobic conditions, rules out the catalytic role of this cytochrome in succinate oxidation. On the other hand, under anaerobic conditions dithionite- or NADH- reduced cytochrome b_{560} in succinate-Q reductase, or in QPs in the presence of SDH, is fully oxidized by fumarate (see Figure 4), suggesting that cytochrome b_{560} plays a role in fumarate reduction. The reduced form of cytochrome b_{560} in QPs is not oxidized by fumarate in the absence of SDH. In other words, cytochrome b_{560} apparently serves as the electron entrance for fumarate reduction but not as the electron exit for

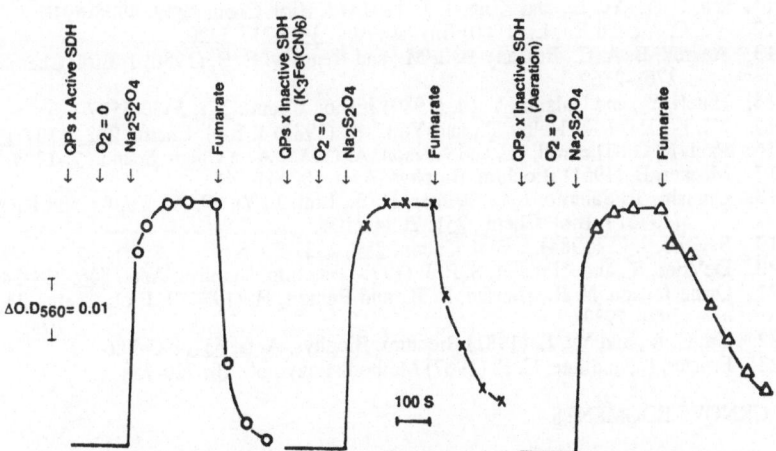

Fig. 4. Anaerobic re-oxidation of the dithionite-reduced cytochrome b_{560} by fumarate in the presence of reconstitutively active- and inactive SDH. 3 ml aliquots of QPs, 0.1 mg/ml, in 50 mM Tris-acetate buffer, pH 7.8, was mixed with 1.2 mg of reconstitutively active (-o-) or inactive (Δ, x) SDH. Reconstitutively inactive SDH was obtained either by following the same isolation procedure as that for active SDH except succinate was omitted under aerobic conditions (Δ), or by inactivation of active SDH with ferricyanide (x). The sample was placed in a two-arm thunberg cuvette with dithionite in one arm and fumarate in the other arm. Anaerobic condition was achieved by repeated evacuation and flushing with argon.

succinate oxidation. In the isolated system reduction of fumarate can only be demonstrated under anaerobic conditions, whereas in the intact mitochondrial inner membrane the reduction of fumarate may occur under specific conditions, such as when the membrane is in a highly energized state. The well established phenomenon of energy dependent reversed electron transfer is an example (23). Under anaerobic conditions, cytochrome b_{560} in QPs or succinate-Q reductase is reducible by NADH in the presence of Type II NADH dehydrogenase. This NADH reduced cytochrome b_{560} is oxidizable by fumarate only after SDH is added. In anaerobic organisms, fumarate serves as a terminal electron acceptor; in aerobic organisms no such function is needed. The reduction of fumarate at the expense of NADH might play a role in the regulation of electron transfer and oxidative phosphorylation. It is also possible that this particular cytochrome is a evolutionary vestige of fumarate reductase and its main function has been lost during the evolution process of mitochondria.

REFERENCES

1. Davis, K. A., Hatefi, Y., Poff, K. L., and Butler, W. L. (1972) Biochem. Biophys. Res. Commun., 46, 1984-1990.
2. Davis, K. A., Hatefi, Y., Poff, K. L., and Butler, W. L. (1973). Biochim. Biophys. Acta, 325, 341-356.
3. Yu, L., and Yu, C. A. (1982) J. Biol. Chem., 257, 2016-2021.
4. Tushurashvili, P. R., Gavrikova, E. V., Ledenev, A. N., and Vinogradov, A. D. (1985) Biochim. Biophys. Acta, 809, 145-159.
5. Ziegler, D. M., and Doeg, K. A. (1962) Arch. Biochem. Biophys., 97, 41-50.
6. Baginsky, M. L., and Hatefi, Y. (1969) J. Biol. Chem., 244, 5313-5319.
7. Hatefi, Y., and Stiggall, D. L. (1978) Methods in Enzymol, 53, 21-27.
8. Hederstedt, L., Holmgren, E., and Rutberg, L. (1979) J. Bacteriol., 138, 370-376.
9. Weiss, H., and Kolb, H. J.(1979) Eur. J. Biochem., 99, 139-149.
10. Takamiya S., Furushima, R., and Oya, H. (1986) Biochim. Biophys. Acta, 848, 99-107.
11. Yu, C. A., Yu, L., and King, T. E. (1974) J. Biol. Chem., 249, 4905-4910.
12. Yu, C. A., and Yu, L. (1980) Biochemistry, 19, 5717-5720.
13. Ackrell, B. A. C., Bethany-Ball, M., and Kearney, E. B. (1980) J. Biol. Chem., 255, 2761-2769.
14. Hatefi, Y., and Galante, Y. M. (1980) J. Biol. Chem., 255, 5530-5537
15. Yu, L., Xu, J-X., Haley, P., and Yu,C. A. (1987) J. Biol. Chem., 262, 1137-1143.
16. Paul, K. G., Theorell, H., and Akeson, A. (1953) Acta Chem. Scand., 7, 1284-1294.
17. Macker, B. (1961) Biochim. Biophys. Acta, 50, 141-146.
18. Ohnishi, T., Salerno, J. C., Winter, D. B., Lim, J., Yu, C. A., Yu, L., and King, T. E. (1976) J. Biol. Chem., 251, 2094-2104.
19. Salerno, J. C. (1984) J. Biol. Chem., 259, 2331-2336.
20. DeVries, S., and Albracht, S. P. J. (1979) Biochim. Biophys. Acta, 546, 334-340.
21. Orme-Jonson, N. R., Hansen, R. E., and Beinert, H. (1974) J. Biol. Chem., 249, 1928-1939.
22. Yu, C. A., and Yu, L. (1981) Biochim. Biophys. Acta, 637, 383-386.
23. Ernster, L., and Lee, C. P. (1967) Methods Enzymol., 10, 729-738.

ACKNOWLEDGMENTS

This work was supported by grants from the National Institutes of Health (GM 30721) and the Oklahoma Agriculture Experimental Station (J-5205). An instrumentation grant from NSF (8030271) which made possible the purchase of Bruker ER-200D EPR spectrometer is also acknowledged.

656

ISOLATION OF THE PHOTOSYSTEM TWO REACTION CENTRE AND THE LOCATION AND

FUNCTION OF CYTOCHROME b-559

J. Barber, K. Gounaris and D.J. Chapman

AFRC Photosynthesis Research Group
Department of Pure and Applied Biology
Imperial College of Science and Technology
London SW7 2BB, U.K.

INTRODUCTION

Although there have been numerous studies to understand the role of cytochrome b-559 in photosynthesis, no clear picture has yet emerged. The study of this cytochrome is complicated by the fact that there seems to be two distinctly different pools. One pool consists of a low potential form ($E \sim -30$ mV) and is located in the unappressed stromal regions of higher plant chloroplasts (1). This low potential form may be in some way linked to electron and proton translocation through the cytochrome b_6-f complex (2). The other pool is localized in the appressed regions which constitute the grana (3,4) and normally seems to exist in a high potential form ($E \sim 380$ mV). In the earlier literature there was some confusion about the redox properties of the high potential form because its midpoint potential can be significantly modified after certain treatments which affect membrane structure especially by the action of detergents (5,6). In this case the Em changes from 380 mV to about 80 mV. Apparently this shift is due to a perturbation of the environment around the cytochrome and can be reversed by adding back polar lipids derived from the thylakoid, particularly digalactosyldiacylglycerol (7,8). Reconstitution of a certain extrinsic polypeptide (23 kDa) associated with water oxidation, has also been reported to revert the cytochrome to its high potential form (9).

Despite the conclusion that two pools of cytochrome b-559 exist there seems to be no indication of two separate sets of genes encoding for the apoproteins. Biochemical (10) and molecular biological (11) data indicate that this cytochrome consists of two polypeptides having molecular weights of about 9 kDa and 4 kDa which are known as the alpha and beta subunits. These two subunits are the products of the psb E and psb F genes, respectively.

In this paper we report that cytochrome b-559$_{HP}$ is physically associated with the photosystem (PS2) reaction centre. Such a close association has previously been hinted from biochemical and biophysical studies. Isolation of membrane fragments and detergent solubilised preparations have consistently shown that cytochrome b-559, either in its high potential form, or in its modified low potential form, is present in PS2 enriched fractions (3,12). Knaff and Arnon (13) and later, Vermeglio and Mathis (14), showed that at low temperatures, when electron flow is

657

restricted to primary reactions, cytochrome b-559 can be photooxidised by the reaction centre chlorophyll of PS2 (P680). Despite these observations no clear picture has emerged regarding the function of cytochrome b-559 in PS2 activity. It has been proposed that this cytochrome is involved in water oxidation (15,16), possibly by acting as a proton carrier (17). Such suggestions are hampered because when it is in its modified low potential form oxygen evolution is still possible (18,19). Moreover when the water splitting reaction is operative there are no obvious indications of redox changes in this haem. On the contrary, photooxidation of the cytochrome only occurs when the water oxidation process is inhibited (13,20,21). It has often been speculated that the function of cytochrome b-559 is to catalyse cyclic electron flow around PS2 (22,23), either to generate a hydrogen ion gradient or to act as a protective mechanism. There is, however, no firm data to support these ideas (24). Recently Cramer et al. (24) suggested that this cytochrome may play a role in the process of photoactivation which involves the incorporation of oxidised manganese into the catalytic site of water oxidation. This postulate is attractive but experiments are needed to give it credibility.

Biophysical, biochemical, molecular biological and crystallographic studies have indicated that the PS2 reaction centre is similar to the reaction centre of purple bacteria (25). Both systems reduce primary and secondary quinone acceptors Q_A and Q_B via a route involving the initial reduction of a pheophytin molecule, and both contain non-haem iron which gives rise to characteristic EPR signals (26). The functional unit which generates primary charge separation within the bacterial reaction centre consists of two polypeptides known as L and M which together bind four bacteriochlorophylls, two bacteriopheophytin molecules, a non-haem iron and the two quinone molecules, corresponding to Q_A and Q_B (26). Two of the bacteriochlorophylls form a "special pair" which functions as the primary donor. The L and M subunits have closely related amino acid sequences (27) and also show localized sequence homologies with the two thylakoid membrane proteins D1 and D2 of PS2-containing organisms (27,28). D1 is the well characterised product of the _psb_ A gene and appears to be the site of Q_B binding (29). D2 is the product of the _psb_ D gene and has a similar amino acid sequence to D1 (30). The homology of the amino acid sequences of L and M subunits with those of D1 and D2, together with the analysis of X-ray diffraction data of crystals of the reaction centre of _Rhodopseudomonas viridis_ (31), led to the speculation that the latter two polypeptides form the reaction centre of PS2 (25,28,31). Prior to this suggestion the PS2 reaction centre had been assigned to a 47 kDa polypeptide (32) which is the product of the _psb_ B gene (33). In this communication we report data which supports the concept that D1 and D2 are the PS2 reaction centre polypeptides and that cytochrome b-559 is closely associated with the D1/D2 heterodimer.

MATERIALS AND METHODS

Membrane fragments enriched in PS2 were isolated from greenhouse grown pea plants (_Pisum sativum_ var. Feltham First) or from market spinach (_Spinacea oleracea_) according to the method of Berthold et al. (34). These membrane fragments were suspended at 4 mg ml^{-1} in 5 mM MgCl$_2$, 15 mM NaCl, 50 mM MES (pH 6.5) and 10% (w/v) glycerol, frozen at 77 K and stored at 190 K. PS2 reaction centres were prepared from a 50 mg sample of the stored membrane fragments using a method developed from the approach suggested by Nanba and Satoh (35) in which solubilization in Triton X-100 is followed by ion-exchange chromatography. Briefly the procedure was firstly to remove extrinsic membrane polypeptides by incubating the thawed sample on ice in the dark in 50 mM Tris pH 9.0 (0.8 mg Chl ml^{-1}) for 10 min followed by centrifugation at 40,000 x g at 4°C for 20 min. The pellets were resuspended in 50 mM Tris pH 7.2 (to about

50 mls) and 8 mls 30% Triton X-100 added to give a final Chl concentration of 0.8 mg ml^{-1}. A 60 min incubation with stirring, in the dark and on ice, was followed by centrifugation at 100,000 x g for 60 min. The supernatant was then applied to a column (20 x 120 mm), Fractogel TSK DEAE-650(S) (Merck-BDH). The column was then extensively washed with 30 mM NaCl in a running buffer containing 0.2% Triton X-100 and 50 mM Tris-Cl, pH 7.2 until no more chlorophyll could be eluted. This procedure removed more than 98% of the chlorophyll applied, taking up to 3 hours at 1.0 ml min^{-1}. The column was then subjected to a linear NaCl gradient from 30 to 200 mM in the same running buffer and the fraction eluted at about 110 mM NaCl and collected as 2.0 ml samples. These samples were pooled, diluted four-fold in running buffer and loaded onto a smaller column (10 x 60 mm) of the same DEAE-Fractogel. As before the column was washed extensively with 30 mM NaCl (about 2 h at 0.5 ml min^{-1}) and a linear NaCl gradient applied to obtain the PS2 reaction centre as a sharp peak at about 110 mM NaCl. For examination of the association of cytochrome b-559 to the D1/D2 proteins, the purified PS2 reaction centre was subjected to sucrose density centrifugation in the presence of varying amounts of detergents. The gradients were 0.1/1.0 M sucrose in 20 mM Tris pH 7.2 and were spun for 16 h at 180,000 x g. The absorption spectra and ratio of Chl to cytochrome b-559 were measured immediately to judge the success of the isolation. If samples were not used immediately they were stored at 190 K after addition of glycerol to 10% (w/v). Chlorophyll concentrations were assayed by the method of Arnon (36) while cytochrome b-559 was determined by recording the difference spectrum between the oxidised and reduced state (ferricyanide versus dithionite) and applying an extinction coefficient of 15 mM^{-1}. Absorption spectra and light-induced redox changes were monitored using either a Perkin-Elmer 554 or 557 UV/Vis spectrophotometer. Side illumination was provided by a quartze-iodine light source with an appropriate light guide and transmission filters (Calflex heat filter and Schott RG 610). The intensity of the actinic light at the cuvette surface was 100 W/m^2. The photomultiplier was shielded by a Schott B38, 4 mm filter. Emission spectra were measured with a Perkin-Elmer MPF 44A fluorimeter. Polypeptides were asssayed by SDS-polyacrylamide gel electrophoresis (SDS-PAGE) on a 12 to 17% gel or on a 10-20% gel containing 6 M urea and stained with Coomassie blue.

RESULTS

Isolation and characterisation of the PS2 reaction centre

Despite some minor differences in the isolation procedure we have obtained a preparation which seems to be the same as that reported by Nanba and Satoh (35). Our preparation shows an identical absorption spectrum (see Fig.1) to that given by the above workers. In addition we also confirm that this preparation contains 4 chl a, 2 pheo, 1 cyt b-559 and some beta-carotene (see Fig.2). As reported by Nanba and Satoh (35), the preparation contains no plastoquinone but we have detected at least one additional iron atom. As shown in Fig.1, according to SDS-PAGE followed by Coomassie blue staining, the complex is composed of four protein bands. The lower 9 kDa band was shown by Nanba and Satoh (35) to be the alpha-subunit of cytochrome b-559. The two bands in the region of 30-32 kDa were attributed to D1 and D2. We have confirmed this by preferentially labelling D1 with ^{35}S and by immunoblotting with antibodies raised to the psb D gene (Fig.3). This work also showed, in the absence of urea, that D2 runs with a lower apparent molecular weight than D1, but with 6 M urea present the reverse was true. Both radiolabelling and immunoblotting confirmed the speculation of Nanba and Satoh (35) that the higher molecular band, about 55 kDa on our gels, was an aggregate of D1 and D2. Studies involving the use of the lysine

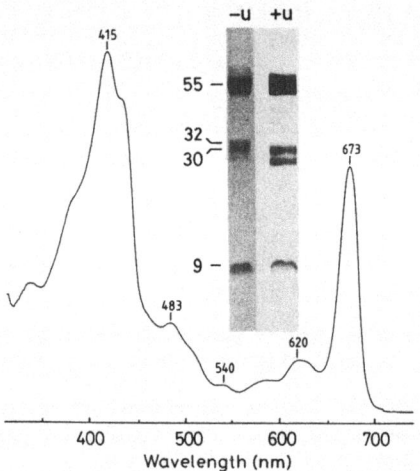

Fig. 1   Absorption and SDS-PAGE profile of purified pea PS2 reaction
centre. The absorption spectrum was measured after suspending in
60 mM Tris-Cl (pH 8.5) buffer at room temperature. Track -u was
SDS-PAGE on a 12-17% polyacrylamide gel with no urea and track +u
was SDS-PAGE using 10-20% gel containing 6 M urea.

specific protease, Lys C, have indicated that the aggregate is in the form
of a heterodimer (37). Immunoblotting with a monoclonal antibody raised
to the 47 kDa polypeptide of PS2 did not cross-react with any of the bands
in agreement with the results of Nanba and Satoh (35).

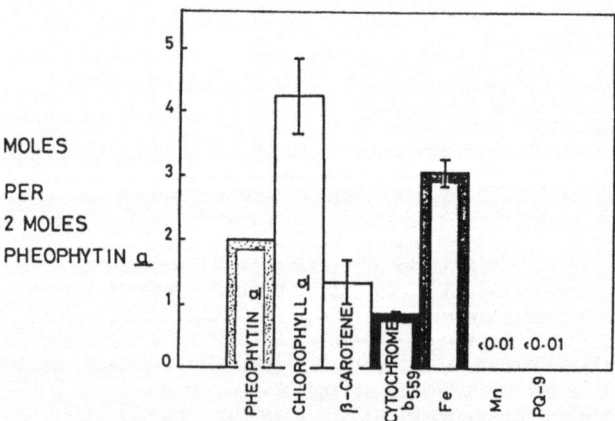

Fig.2   Composition of the purified PS2 reaction centre normalized to two
pheophytin a molecules. Pigment determinations were by HPLC,
cytochrome b-559 by optical spectroscopy and Fe and Mn levels by
atomic absorption.

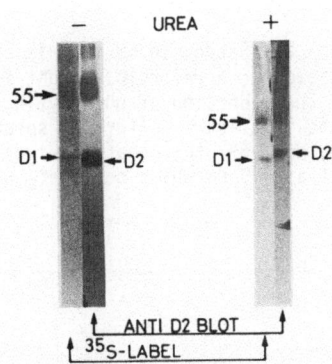

Fig.3 Identification of D1, D2 polypeptides and D1/D2 aggregate by
short-term labelling of D1 with ^{35}S methionine (29) and by
immunoblotting of same tracks using antibodies raised to the psb D
gene product expressed in E. coli (38). The gels were either urea
containing (+) or not (-).

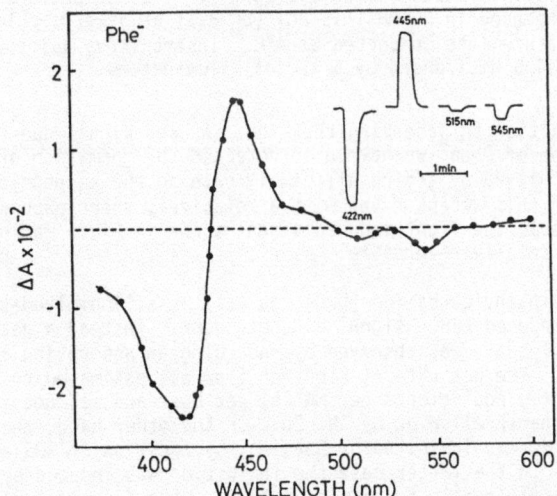

Fig.4 Light-dark difference spectrum obtained in the presence of excess
sodium dithionite plus 1 μM methyl viologen. The PS2 reaction
centre preparation was suspended in 60 mM Tris-HCl (pH 8.5) at 5
μg/ml chlorophyll and measurements made at 4°C. Insert shows
light induced absorption changes at four different wavelengths.

661

As reported by Nanba and Satoh, in 60 mM Tris (pH 8.0) and in dithionite and methyl viologen, a reversible light induced signal is observed, indicative of the reduction of pheophytin. A typical set of signals together with the light-dark difference spectrum are shown in Fig.4. In our spectrum, however, the negative signal at 422 nm is larger than the positive signal at 445 nm which contrasts with that published by Nanba and Satoh.

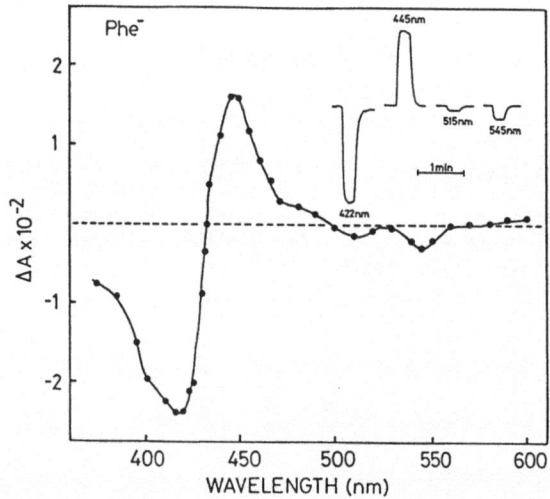

Fig.5   Light-dark difference spectrum obtained in the presence of silicomolybdate (about 200 μg/ml). The PS2 preparation was suspended in 60 mM Tris-HCl (pH 8.5) at 5 μg/ml chlorophyll and measurements conducted at 4°C. Insert shows absorption decrease at 435 nm induced by 5 sec of illumination.

In addition to observing the light induced signal due to the accumulation of Pheo$^-$ we have also detected the formation of P680$^+$. This was achieved by adding silicomolybdate to the suspension. In the presence of this acceptor and with a relatively short exposure to actinic light (5 sec), the light induced signal shown in Fig.5 was obtained which was almost totally reversible.

When diphenylcarbazide (DPC), as well as silicomolybdate, was present the light induced P680$^+$ signal did not occur. Instead a net reduction of silicomolybdate was observed by recording an absorption increase at 600 nm (Fig.6). The net rate of electron flow was estimated to be several thousands of μ equivalents per mg/Chl per hour and was not inhibited by DCMU, o-phenanthroline or by ANT 2p. On the other hand, the light induced electron flow was inhibited by heating, by addition of SDS and proteolytic digestion. In the latter case the inhibition was induced by treatment with 100 μg/ml Trypsin for 5 min at 25°C. When Trypsin inhibitor was also present with the Trypsin no inhibition was observed. Any degradation of the preparation indicated by blue shifts in the red absorption and chlorophyll fluorescence peaks, also led to a loss of the light induced signals including net electron flow from DPC to silicomolybdate. Normally the fluorescence emission at room temperature had a maximum of 682 nm while at 77 K the peak shifted to about 685 nm. There was no emission at 695 nm at 77 K as required by the Breton hypothesis (38).

Dissociation of cytochrome b-559 from the D1/D2 complex

Exposure of the purified PS2 reaction centre complex to mildly-denaturing SDS-PAGE (0.1% SDS) gave rise to a green band free of cytochrome b-559 as judged by second dimension electrophoresis under fully denaturing conditions. This result led us to explore whether the D1/D2 complex can be isolated in an active state free of the cytochrome. Sucrose gradient centrifugation procedures were adopted using various levels of Triton X-100 and SDS in the gradients. In this way fractions free of cytochrome b-559 were obtained with SDS while Triton X-100 gave rise to partial removal of the cytochrome as judged by difference spectroscopy and by SDS-PAGE (see Fig.7). In all cases the free cytochrome was located in the top fractions of the sucrose gradient. The SDS derived D1/D2 complex free of cytochrome was unable to catalyse the light induced reduction of pheophytin in the presence of methyl viologen and excess dithionite.

CONCLUSION

As indicated diagrammatically in Fig.8, it is now certain that cytochrome b-559 is physically associated with the D1 and D2 and that these latter polypeptides, like L and M subunits of bacterial photosystems, bind the reaction centre chlorophylls and the primary electron acceptors. The function of this cytochrome is unknown and no photochemical activity has yet been detected in the D1/D2/cyt b-559 complex. In the intact membrane, and in membrane fragments enriched in PS2, cytochrome b-559 can be photooxidised as long as electron donation from water has been inhibited. It could be that this component is normally kept in a reduced state in the light due to rapid electron donation from water. The problem is that its redox potential of about 380 mV is too low for a direct participation in electron flow from water to $P680^+$. Therefore alternative functions must be sort along the lines indicated in the Introduction. The fact that we have been able to remove the cytochrome from the D1/D2 complex suggests that the minimal unit for the PS2 reaction centre is the D1/D2 heterodimer binding four chlorophylls and two pheophytin molecules. Clearly there is a need to fully understand the role of high potential cytochrome b-559 in photosynthesis and isolation of the D1/D2/cyt b-559 complex is an important step towards this objective.

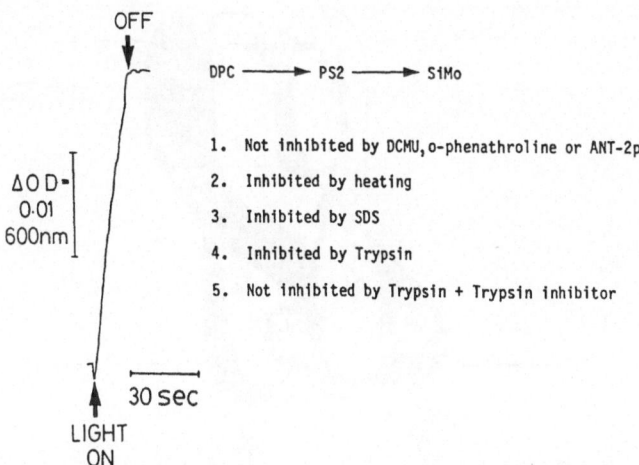

OFF

DPC ──────▶ PS2 ──────▶ SiMo

1. Not inhibited by DCMU, o-phenathroline or ANT-2p

2. Inhibited by heating

3. Inhibited by SDS

4. Inhibited by Trypsin

5. Not inhibited by Trypsin + Trypsin inhibitor

ΔOD = 0·01 600nm

30 sec

LIGHT ON

Fig.6   Net electron flow catalysed by PS2 reaction centre.

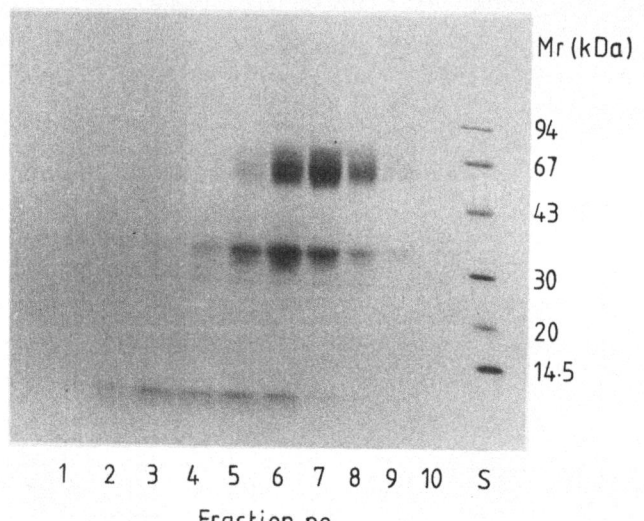

Fig.7   SDS-PAGE of fractions obtained from a sucrose density gradient
        containing 0.05% SDS. Top fraction is number one, other numbers
        refer to subsequent lower fractions. Also shown are molecular
        weight standards (S).

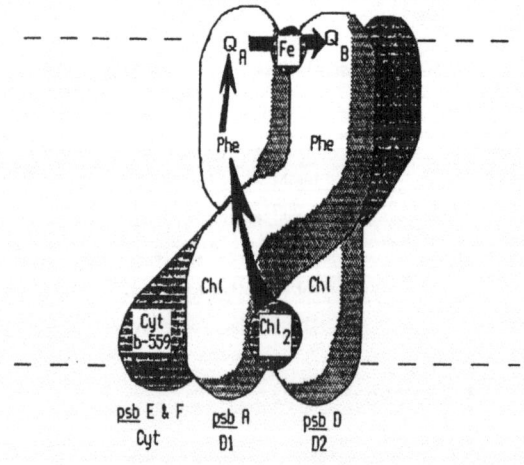

Fig.8   Diagrammatic representation of the PS2 reaction centre.

ACKNOWLEDGEMENTS

    We wish to thank our colleagues Jonathan Marder, Alison Telfer and
Peter Nixon for their support and particularly acknowledge the technical
assistance of Ken Davis and John DeFelice. Financial support is from the
Agricultural and Food Research Council and Science and Engineering
Research Council.

REFERENCES

1. Peters, F.A.L.J., Van Wielink, J.E., Wong Fong Sang, H.W., De Vries,
    A. and Kraayenhof, R. 1983, Biochim. Biophys. Acta 722, 460-470.
2. Hodges, M., Packham, N.K. and Barber, J. 1984, Photobiochem.
    Photobiophys. 7, 311-317.
3. Whitford, D. 1985, Ph.D. Thesis, University of London.
4. Murata, N., Miyao, M., Omata, T., Matsunami, H. and Kuwubara, T.
    1984, Biochim. Biophys. Acta 765, 363-370.
5. Wada, K. and Arnon, D.I. 1971, Proc. Natl. Acad. Sci. U.S.A. 68,
    3064-3068.
6. Ke, B., Vernon, L.P. and Chaney, T. 1972, Biochim. Biophys. Acta 256,
    345-357.
7. Matsuda, H. and Butler, W.L. 1983, Biochim. Biophys. Acta 725,
    320-324.
8. Whitford, D., Gounaris, K. and Barber, J. 1984, in: Advances in
    Photosynthesis Res. Vol.1, Sybesma, C. ed., Martinus Nijhoff/Dr. Junk
    Publ. pp 497-500.
9. Larsson, C., Jansson, C., Ljundberg, U., Akerlund, H-E. and
    Andersson, B. 1984, in: Advances in Photosynthesis Res. Vol.1,
    Sybesma. C. ed., Martinus Nijhoff/Dr Junk Publ. pp 363-366.
10. Widger, W.R., Cramer, W.A., Hermodson, M., Meyer, D. and Gullifor, M.
    1984, J. Biol. Chem. 259, 3870-3876.
11. Widger, W.R., Cramer, W.A., Hermodson, M. and Herrmann, R.G. 1985,
    FEBS Lett. 191, 186-190.
12. Cramer, W.A. and Whitmarsh, J. 1977, Ann. Rev. Plant Physiol. 28,
    133-172.
13. Knaff, D.B. and Arnon, D.I. 1969, Proc. Natl. Acad. Sci. U.S.A 63,
    956-962.
14. Vermeglio, A. and Mathis, P. 1974, Biochim. Biophys. Acta 368, 9-17.
15. Lundergardh, H. 1961, Proc. Natl. Acad. Sci. U.S.A. 53, 703-710.
16. Cox, R.P. and Bendall, D.S. 1972, Biochim. Biophys. Acta 283, 124-135.
17. Butler, W.L. 1979, FEBS Lett. 95, 19-25.
18. Briantais, J-M., Vernotte, C., Miyao, M., Murata, N. and Picaud, M.
    1985, Biochim. Biophys. Acta 808, 348-351.
19. Nakatani, H.Y., Mansfield, R., Whitford, D. and Barber, J. 1982,
    Photobiochem. Photobiophys. 4, 121-129.
20. Velthuys, B.R. 1981, FEBS Lett. 126, 272-276.
21. Packham, N.K. and Barber, J. 1984, Biochem. J. 221, 513-520.
22. Boardman, N.K., Anderson, J.M. and Hiller, R.G. 1971, Biochim.
    Biophys. Acta 234, 126-136.
23. Cramer, W.A. and Bohme, H. 1972, Biochim. Biophys. Acta 256, 358-369.
24. Cramer, W.A., Theg, S.M. and Widger, W.R. 1986, Photosynthesis Res.
    10, 393-403.
25. Trebst, A. 1985, Z. Naturforsch 41c, 240-245.
26. Rutherford, A.W. 1986, Biochem. Soc. Trans., Oxford 14, 15-17.
27. Williams, J.C., Steiner, L.A., Feher, G. and Simon, M.J. 1984, Proc.
    Natl. Acad. Sci. U.S.A. 81, 7303-7307.
28. Barber, J. and Marder, J.B. 1986, in: Biotechnology and Genetic
    Engineering Reviews, Vol.4, Russell, M. ed., Pub. Intercept,
    Newcastle-upon-tyne, U.K., pp 355-404.
29. Marder, J.B., Mattoo, A.R. and Edelman, M. 1986, Meths. in Enzymol.
    118, 384-396.

30. Rochaix, J-D., Dron, M., Rahire, M. and Malnoe, P. 1984, Plant Mol. Biol. 3, 363-370.
31. Deisenhofer, J., Epp, O., Miki, K., Huber, R. and Michel, H. 1985, Nature 318, 618-624.
32. Nakatani, H.Y., Ke, B., Dolan, E. and Arntzen, C.J. 1984, Biochim. Biophys. Acta 756, 347-352.
33. Morris, J. and Herrmann, R.G. 1984, Nucleic Acids Res. 12, 2837-2850.
34. Berthold, D.A., Babcock, G.T. and Yocum, C.J. 1981, FEBS Lett. 134, 231-234.
35. Nanba, O. and Satoh, K. 1987, Proc. Natl. Acad. Sci. U.S.A. 84, 109-112.
36. Arnon, D.I. 1949, Plant Physiol. 24, 1-15.
37. Marder, J.B., Chapman, D.J., Telfer, A., Nixon, P.J. and Barber, J. 1987, Plant Mol. Biol. submitted
38. Breton, J. 1982, FEBS Lett. 147, 16-20.
39. Nixon, P.J., Dyer, T., Barber, J. and Hunter, C.N. 1987, FEBS Lett. 209, 83-86

VII. SPECIFIC REDOX SYSTEMS: Short Reports

EFFECT OF ANTIMYCIN ON THE KINETICS OF REDUCTION OF b AND c_1 CYTOCHROMES IN SINGLE TURNOVER OF THE MITOCHONDRIAL b-c_1 COMPLEX

D. Boffoli, M. Lorusso, and S. Papa

Institute of Medical Biochemistry and Chemistry
Center for the Study of Mitochondria and Energy Metabolism
C.N.R. University of Bari
70124 Bari, Italy

It has been reported that antimycin lowers the apparent initial rate of reduction of cytochrome c_1 in a single turnover, both in succinate cytochrome c oxidoreductase and in the isolated b-c_1 complex (De Vries et al., 1982; Degli Esposti et al., 1982). This finding appears to be inconsistent with Q-cycle as formulated by Mitchell (1976), which envisaged a concerted and antimycin insensitive delivery of electrons from QH_2 to cytochrome b_{566} (b_L) and c_1 in the pre-steady-state. On these grounds, as well as on the basis of heterogenous kinetics of reduction of the prosthetic groups De Vries et al. (1982) have put forward a modified cyclic mechanism for the electron pathways in the b-c_1 complex, in which the enzyme operates as a dimer. In this double Q-cycle model, antimycin inhibits the reduction of cytochrome c_1 by QH_2 in one monomer, whereas the reduction in the other monomer would be antimycin-insensitive. A double cycle model was also proposed by Linke et al., (1986).

The isolation of an active cytochrome reductase in monomeric form appears, however, to be inconsistent with the various versions of double-cycle mechanisms (Nalecz et al., 1985).

Here we have re-examined, in experiments carried out at low temperature (0°C), the kinetics of reduction of b and c_1 cytochromes in the b-c_1 complex, as well as in a fraction enriched in b-c_1 complex (the S_1 fraction), under first turnover conditions.

Upon addition of DQH_2 to the fully oxidized b-c_1 complex, b cytochromes undergo a multiphasic reduction. A rapid phase followed by a lag and, finally, a second slower reduction phase are observed. Kinetic analysis of the first rapid phase gives under our experimental conditions, an apparent first order constant of about 0.55 sec^{-1}. Kinetic analysis of the reduction of cytochrome c_1 shows it to consist of two apparent first order processes contributing 70% and 30% respectively. The respective kinetic constants differ by one order of magnitude. The first rapid process correlates kinetically with the rapid phase of cytochromes b reduction (apparent k=0.66 sec^{-1}).

In the presence of antimycin the initial rate of cyt.c_1 reduction is markedly depressed. The process is still biphasic. Under these conditions the first rapid phase contributes only by 30% to the overall process but still shows an apparent kinetic constant close to that of the rapid phase in the absence of antimycin.

The reduction of cytochrome b in the presence of antimycin is also biphasic, with the fast phase correlated kinetically with the fast phase of cyt.c_1 reduction.

Analogous experiments carried out with the S_1 fraction (DQH_2 as substrate) give substantially the same results.

The kinetic characteristics of antimycin effect on the single turnover reduction of cytochromes c_1 and b have been explained by De Vries et al., (1982) in terms of a double quinone cycle. It seems to us that they are equally consistent with the Q-gated proton pump model in which quinone molecules tightly bound to proteins (Qc) (without significant exchange at the steady-state with quinone of the pool) provide a split pathway for transfer of the two electrons of the quinol substrate (Q_pH_2) to the Fe-S protein and cytochrome c_1 (Papa et al., 1983).

It is conceivable that the rapid phase of cytochrome c_1 reduction by duroquinol (and quinol of the pool) observed in single turnover experiments is mediated by Qc. Antimycin inhibits this process by displacing Qc from the binding sites in the reaction pocket. This results in suppression of electron transfer between cytochrome b_{562} (b_h) and Qc. The semiquinone in the pocket is rapidly oxidized by the Fe-S protein and mediates oxidation of Q_pH_2 to $\dot{Q}_p$, which in turn reduces b cytochromes. This pathway remains relatively rapid as long as oxidized b cytochromes are available to accept electron from Q_p, as it is the case of single turnover reduction of the fully oxidized enzyme and oxidant induced reduction of be cytochromes.

At the steady-state since of the block in the oxidation of b cytochromes and $\dot{Q}_p$, electron flow through the complex will be practically suppressed.

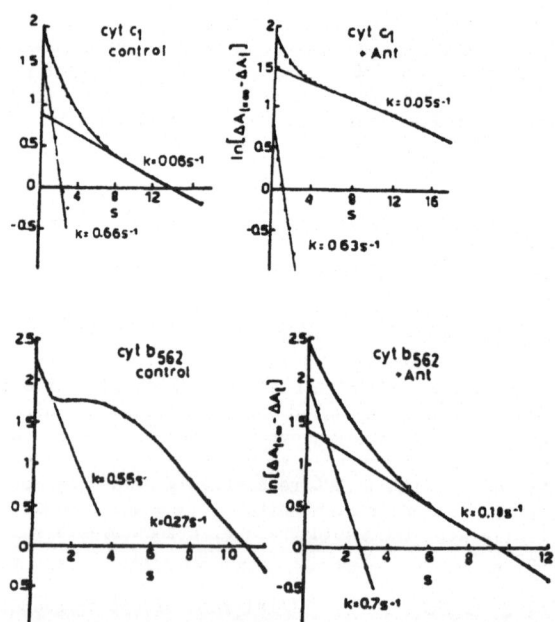

Fig. 1. First order plots of absorbance change (arbitrary units)of cyt.c_1 and b_{562} caused by the DQH_2 addition in b-c_1 complex.

REFERENCES

1. M. Degli Esposti and G. Lenaz (1982) FEBS Lett. 142, 49-53.
2. S. De Vries, S.P.J. Albracht, J.A. Berden, and E.C. Slater (1982) Biochem. Biophys. Acta 681, 41-53.
3. P. Linke, G. Bechmann, A. Gothe, and H. Weiss (1986) Eur. J. Biochem. 158, ·615-621.
4. P. Mitchell (1976) J. Theor. Biol. 62, 327-367.
5. M.J. Nalecz, R. Bolli, and A. Azzi (1985) Arch. Biochem. Biophys. 236, 619-628.
6. S. Papa, M. Lorusso, D. Boffoli, and E. Bellomo (1983) Eur. J. Biochem. 137, 405-412.

THE b-Q CYCLE, A NEW MODEL FOR THE PATHWAYS OF ELECTRONS AND PROTONS

THROUGH THE bc$_1$ COMPLEX.   ACTION OF ANTIMYCIN A AT CENTER O

D. Meunier-Lemesle and P. Chevillotte-Brivet

Laboratoire de Chimie Bactérienne
CNRS, BP 71
13277 Marseille Cedex 9, France

The b-Q cycle

According to the Q cycle, as to the SQ cycle, the cytochromes b species
(or cytochrome b hemes) are pictured as reacting in a linear sequence (1-5).
A model is presented here which, accounting for precedent results in a
yeast strain devoid of cytochrome b$_{565}$ (6-7) proposes that this b$_{565}$ species
is arranged in parallel with the b$_{562}$, within the Q cycle (Fig. 1). In this
model, the sequence of the reactions in the stationary state differs from
the classical Q cycle in the reactions 2, 4, and 5, at center o and i, which
have been expressed as follows:

$$Q^oH + b^{ox}_{562} \xrightleftharpoons{4} Q + H^+ + b^r_{562}$$

$$b^r_{562} + b^{ox}_{565} \xrightleftharpoons{5a} b^{ox}_{562} + b^r_{565}$$

$$b^r_{565} + b^{ox}_{562} \xrightarrow{5b} b^r_{562} + b^{ox}_{565}$$

$$b^r_{562} + Q^iH + H^+ \xrightleftharpoons{2} b^{ox}_{562} + QH_2$$

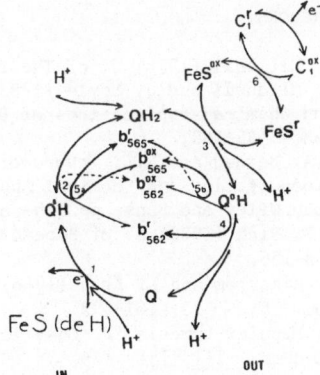

Fig. 1.   The b-Q cycle

Comparison between this reactional sequence and that of the Q cycle shows
the existence of great differences in the behavior of the b cytochrome
species in the electron transfer mechanism through the bc$_1$ complex.

1. In the b-Q cycle model, the couple QH$_2$/Q is the reductant for the cytochrome b$_{562}$ at center O (and not for the cytochrome b$_{565}$, as in the Q cycle)
and the oxidant for the same species b$_{562}$ at center i.

2. Moreover- and this is the most important characteristic of the b-Q cycle- the heme b_{562} can also act both as an oxidant (b^{ox}) and as a reductant (b^r) for heme b_{565}, which leads to a cyclic behavior for the two species. The interaction heme 562-heme 565 might take place fairly near the center i, in the case of the oxidation of b_{562} heme (and reduction of b_{565} heme) and fairly near the center o in the case of the reduction of b_{562} heme (and oxidation of b_{565} heme).

3. The thermodynamic problems at center o with the Q cycle formulation are irrelevant with the b-Q cycle.

Action of antimycin A at center O

The mitochondria are maintained in anaerobiosis in the presence of 40 mM ascorbate, 2μM CCCP, with or without 5μM rotenone, then an appropriate succinate/fumarate mixture is added (all reagents strictly deoxygenated). For different S/F ratios, leading to an appropriate reduction of the b_{562} species, the addition of antimycin A in strictly anaerobic conditions leads to a cytochrome b_{562} oxidation of about half of the initial value. This oxidation might be explained either through the reaction 2 at center i, or by the reverse reaction 4 at center O. The addition of fumarate (50 mM) in these conditions, leads to a rapid reduction of the cytochrome b; the value of the reduced cytochrome b is greater than the initial value, before the addition of antimycin A. This reduction is followed by a slow oxidation leading to a value for the cytochrome b reduced near than obtained before the addition of fumarate. The reduction of cytochrome b by fumarate in the presence of antimycin A can only be explained through the reverse of reaction 2, induced by fumarate, with antimycin A acting on the reaction 4, at center O, in these experimental conditions. After return to poise, the cytochrome b becomes more oxidized. These results show that, depending probably on the redox state of the electron transfer components, antimycin A can act also at center o in the bc_1 complex.

REFERENCES

1. P. Mitchell (1976) J. of Theor. Biol., 62, 327-367.
2. P. Mitchell and J. Moyle (1985) in Coenzyme Q: Biochemistry, Bioenergetics and Chemical Applications of Ubiquinone. Lenaz editor, John Wiley and Sons, 145-163.
3. E.A. Berden and B.L. Trumpower (1985) in Coenzyme Q: Biochemistry, Bioenergetics and Chemical Applications of Ubiquinone. Lenaz editor, John Wiley and Sons, pp 365-389.
4. P.R. Rich (1986) J. of Bioenergetics and Biomembranes, Vol. 18, No. 3, 145-156.
5. M. Wikström and K. Krab (1986) J. of Bioenergetics and Biomembranes, Vol. 18, No. 3, 181-193.
6. D. Meunier-Lemesle, P. Chevillotte-Brivet, and P. Pajot (1980) Eur. J. Biochem., 111, 151, 159.
7. P. Chevillotte-Brivet, D. Meunier-Lemesle (1980) Eur. J. Biochem., 111, 161-169.

RAPID OXIDATION KINETICS OF QUINOL-CYTOCHROME C OXIDOREDUCTASE:

QUINONE OR SEMIQUINONE CYCLE?

Alfred N. van Hoek, Jan A. Berden and Simon de Vries

Laboratory of Biochemistry, B.C.P. Jansen Institute
Plantage Muidergracht 12, 1018 TV Amsterdam, The Netherlands

The Q cycle (1) and SQ cycle (2) both describe the pathway of electrons through the quinol cytochrome c oxidoreductase. Both models have adopted the concept of two different semiquinone forms, which by now is firmly supported by experimental evidence (3,4). The two models differ with respect to the formation of an antimycin-sensitive oxidant for cytochrome b and with respect to the number of Q (SQ, QH_2)-binding sites, which is two in the Q cycle and one in the SQ cycle. According to the Q cycle, Q_i (first turnover) and SQ_i (formed after the first turnover, cf.5) alternately serve as the direct oxidant for cytochrome b_{562}, whereas according to the SQ cycle SQ_i, formed by reorientation of the SQ molecule at centre o, serves as the oxidant.

As pointed out previously (2) this difference between the two models can be experimentally tested by studying the kinetics of oxidation of cytochrome b in a fully reduced system. When under these conditions a pulse of oxidant is given, oxidizing cytochromes c_1+c and the FeS centre, rereduction of the FeS centre leads to the formation of SQ_o. According to the Q cycle SQ_o serves exclusively as a reductant for cytochrome b and hence cytochrome b cannot be rapidly oxidised but only after a lag in which via an unidentified mechanism an oxidant for cytochrome b is formed. According to the SQ cycle, however, this SQ_o is rapidly reoriented, becoming SQ_i, leading to the rapid oxidation of cytochrome b. Thus the rate of oxidation of cytochrome b is dependent on the redox state of the ubiquinone pool according to the Q cycle but not according to the SQ cycle. Rich and Wikström (6) have reported that there is not a significant difference in the rate of oxidation of cytochrome b whether cytochrome b (Q pool) is partly or fully reduced, favouring the SQ cycle. De Vries and Dutton (7) found that the rate of oxidation of cytochrome b is dependent on the redox potential in the system favouring the Q cycle. To solve this question we have studied the kinetics of oxidation of cytochrome b and QH_{2-6} in yeast mitoplasts with the stopped-flow and rapid quench technique (8).

In Fig. 1 the rate of oxidation of cytochrome b under different applied redox potentials is shown. In the presence of succinate (trace a) cytochrome b is firstly further reduced and then rapidly oxidised. With additional presence of dithionite (trace b), a lag (20-25 ms) in the oxidation is observed. Similar patterns of oxidation of cytochrome b were obtained by varying the redox potential using the NAD, EtOH and yeast alcohol dehydrogenase system. At relatively high redox potentials (cytochrome b_{562} almost fully reduced, trace c), a pattern similar to that in the presence of succinate was obtained. At lower redox potentials (cytochrome b_{566} about 20% reduced, trace d) a lag in the oxidation of cytochrome b is seen, similar to that obtained with dithionite. In the experiments of Fig. 1 cytochrome c was oxidised with a half time of 10 ms and more importantly the rate of steady-state electron transfer was kept low (at 1.5% of the capacity of the bc_1 complex), ensuring

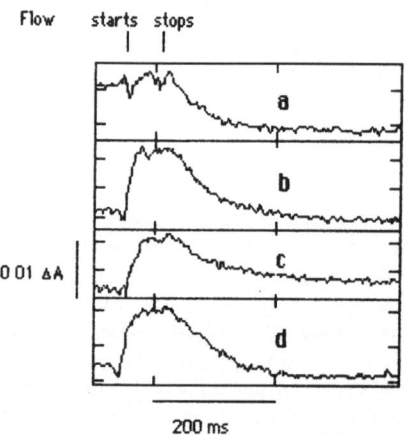

Figure 1. The kinetics of oxidation of cytochrome b in the quinol cytochrome c oxidoreductase of yeast mitoplasts using the stopped-flow method (dead time 2 ms). One syringe contained a buffer of 250 mM KCl, 1 mM EDTA, 50 mM Hepes-KOH (pH 7.0), 20 mg/ml mitoplasts, 12 µM yeast cytochrome c and an appropriate reductant, (a): 20 mM succinate; (b): 6.7 mM succinate, 1 mM dithionite; (c): 0.2% EtOH, 100 µM NAD, 5.1 µM yeast alcohol dehydrogenase; (d): as (c) but with 0.5% EtOH, 53 µM NAD. The other syringe contained aerobic buffer (a,c,d) or aerobic buffer supplied with 2 mM ferricyanide (b). Measurements were performed by monitoring the difference at 560 minus 575 nm, which is isosbestic for redox changes in cytochrome c.

that the observed differences in the traces of oxidation of cytochrome b are due to the applied redox potential and not due to different rates of electron input and output. Thus the lag found in the oxidation of cytochrome b (both b_{562} and b_{566}) is real. The fact that Rich and Wikström did not observe the lag is likely to be caused by slow mixing and slow response of their equipment. In our opinion the observed lag period of 20-25 ms is too long to be consistent with the SQ cycle, but intuitively a bit too short to rigorously confirm the Q-cycle arrangement of the semiquinone-binding domains. Determination of the redox state of the Q pool is in progress, and we are currently manipulating the system to vary the time of the lag period.

REFERENCES

1. Mitchell, P. (1976) J. Theor. Biol. 62, 327-367.
2. Wikström, M. and Krab, K. (1986) J. Bioenerg. Biomembr. 18, 181-193.
3. Ohnishi, T. and Trumpower, B.L. (1980) J. Biol. Chem. 255, 3278-3284.
4. De Vries, S., Albracht, S.P.J., Berden, J.A. and Slater, E.C. (1981) J. Biol. Chem. 256, 11996-11998.
5. Crofts, A.R., Meinhardt, S.W., Jones, K.R. and Snozzi, M. (1983) Biochim. Biophys. Acta 723, 202-218.
6. Rich, P.R. and Wikström, M. (1986) FEBS Lett. 194, 176-182.
7. De Vries, S. and Dutton, P.L. (1985) in "Achievements and Perspectives of Mitochondrial Research (Quagliariello, E., Slater, E.C., Saccone, C. and Kroon, A.M., eds.), Elsevier, Amsterdam, Vol. I, pp.103-110.
8. Van Hoek, A.N., van Gaalen, M.C.M., de Vries, S. and Berden, J.A. (1987) Biochim. Biophys. Acta (in press).

ELECTRON CONDUCTION BETWEEN b CYTOCHROMES OF THE MITOCHONDRIAL RESPIRATORY CHAIN IN THE PRESENCE OF ANTIMYCIN PLUS MYXOTHIAZOL

I.C. West

Glynn Research Institute
Bodmin, Cornwall
PL30 4AU
United Kingdom

The two b haems of the bc_1 complex lie approximately 20 Å apart on a line normal to the plane of the membrane and probably nearer to the outer surface.

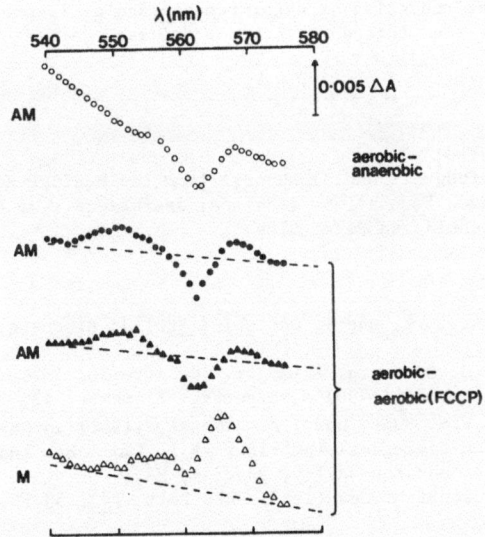

Fig. 1. The effect of membrane potential on b cytochromes. The spectrophotometer cuvette (10 mm lightpath) contained in a final volume
of 1.47 ml the following: beef heart mitochondria, 4.5 mg protein;
KCl, 100mM; Hepes, 50mM, pH 7.0; EGTA, 1mM; succinate, 1.7 mM;
fumarate, 1.7mM; hexammineruthenium chloride, 136µM; sodium ascorbate, 8.5mM; rotenone, 4µM; oligomycin, 7.5µg; antimycin, 2.5µg;
myxothiazol, 11.25µg; carbonylcyanide p-trifluoromethoxyphenyl-
hydrazone (FCCP, where indicated), 1µM. The cuvette rapidly went
anaerobic when not continuously stirred. Spectra were recorded
with a Sigma (Berlin) ZWS-11 dual-wavelength scanning spectrophotometer, and the difference spectra obtained manually.

The low potential b_{566} thus lies near the cytoplasmic surface and the high potential b_{562} near the center of the membrane [1]. It is widely assumed that the two $\underline{b}$ haems form a conducting pathway for the passage of electrons from the site of quinol oxidation (the myxothiazol-binding o-site) to the site of quinone reduction (the antimycin-binding i-site) [1, 2], but the transfer of an electron from one haem to the other has not yet been demonstrated.

It has previously been shown [3, 4] that, when the i-site is blocked by antimycin, a membrane potential will drive electrons from b_{562} out into the Q-pool with no detectable effect on b_{566}. The complementary experiment is illustrated in Fig. 1, in which an electric field was applied in the presence of myxothiazol. In that case electrons were forced from the Q-pool into b_{566} with little or no effect on the redox poise of b_{562}. These experiments are consistent with electron conduction between the $\underline{b}$ haems, but they are equally consistent with the two haems being connected in parallel to both the o and i sites, though positioned as described above.

In the present experiment, mitochondria were poised anaerobically with succinate/fumarate so that b_{562}, but not b_{566}, was reduced. Antimycin and myxothiazol were then added, and a membrane potential applied by aerating the suspension in the presence of ascorbate and hexammineruthenium chloride. The difference spectrum, aerobic minus aerobic-plus-uncoupler, showed (Fig. 1) the expected oxidation of b_{562} and reduction of b_{566}, and is consistent with the partial movement of the electron from b_{562} to b_{566}. The effect is distinguishable from the "energy-linked" spectral shift reported [5] previously. The slight reduction of cytochromes $\underline{c}$ and $\underline{c}_1$ is probably due to control of electron flux through cytochrome oxidase exerted by the membrane potential.

ACKNOWLEDGMENTS

I gratefully acknowledge financial support from the Medical Research Council and the Glynn Research Foundation, techincal assistance from Alan Jeal and help from Peter Mitchell and Peter Rich.

REFERENCES

1. G. von Jagow, T.A. Link, and T. Ohnishi (1986) J. Bioenerg. Biomembr. 18, 157-179.
2. P.R. Rich (1986) J. Bioenerg. Biomembr. 18, 145-156.
3. A. Gopher and M. Gutman (1980) J. Bioenerg. Biomembr. 12, 349-367.
4. A. Konstantinov, W.S. Kunz, and Y.A. Kamensky (1981) in Chemiosmotic Proton Circuits in Biological Membranes (V.P. Skulachev and P.C. Hinkle, eds.) pp. 123-146, Addison-Wesley, Reading, MA.
5. W.S. Kunz and A. Konstantinov (1983) FEBS Lett. 152, 53-56.

THE RELEASE OF NAD· RADICAL IS THE LIMITING STEP IN THE REDOX REACTION
BETWEEN Fe(III) CYTOCHROME C AND NADH

A. Ferri, P. Chiozzi, M.E. Cattozzo and D. Patti
Istituto di Chimica Biologica-Università di Ferrara-Italy

Water neutral solutions of Fe(III) Cytochrome c, in the presence of large excess of NADH gave the spectral changes typical of the reduction of the hemoprotein either in the absence or in the presence of oxygen.

The time course of the reaction showed a fast initial increase of the 550 nm absorbance followed by a slower steady-state during which the reduction rate was constant being negligible the reactants consumption. Both the initial and steady-state rates depended on the NADH concentration.

When aerated solutions of Fe(III) Cytochrome c were added with NADH in the presence of catalytic amounts of SOD, the steady-state rate of the cytochrome reduction was halved, whereas the initial rate was negligibly affected.

When the same experiment was performed on carefully deaerated samples, no SOD effects were observed on the reaction time course. The intercept of the slopes of the steady-state time courses depended on NADH concentration but did not depend on the presence of SOD.

By increasing the reaction temperature the slope of the steady-state time course was observed to increase whereas the intercept values of the slopes with the ordinate axis was unmodified. On the other hand ionic strength lowers both the slope and the intercept.

Results described above are consistent with the mechanism schematized below:

$$C_{III} + NADH \overset{1}{\rightleftharpoons} C_{III} - NADH \overset{2}{\rightleftharpoons} C_{II} - NADH·$$

$$C_{II} - NADH· \overset{3}{\longrightarrow} C_{II} + H^+ + NAD·$$

$$NAD· + O_2 \overset{4}{\longrightarrow} NAD^+ + O_2^-· \qquad k_4 = 1.9 \times 10^9 \ M^{-1}s^{-1} \qquad (1)$$

$$O_2^-· + C_{III} \overset{5}{\longrightarrow} O_2 + C_{II} \qquad k_5 = 10^6 \ M^{-1}s^{-1} \qquad (2)$$

$$O_2^-· + H^+ \overset{6}{\underset{SOD}{\longrightarrow}} 1/2 \ H_2O_2 + 1/2 \ O_2 \qquad k_6 = \text{Diffusion control} \quad (1)$$

in which reactions 4,5 and 6 are known to be very fast.

We calculated kinetic and thermodynamic parameters for steps 1,2 and 3:

$K_1 = 300 \ M^{-1}$ unaffected by temperature
affected by ionic strength

$K_2 = 5 \times 10^{-2}$ unaffected neither by temperature
nor by ionic strength

$K_3 = 6 \times 10^{-2} \ min^{-1}$ strongly affected by temperature
($E^* = 12$ Kcal/mol; $S^* = 19$ E.U.)

Step 3, during which the NADH· radical is detached from the reduced hemoprotein is so that the limiting step of the overall reaction described.

References

1) B.H.J. Bielski and P.C. Chan (1975) J. Biol. Chem. 250, 318.
2) J. Bulter, W.H. Koppenol and E. Margoliash (1982) J. Biol. Chem. 257, 10743.

PROPERTIES OF CYTOCHROME b558 IN COMPLEX II OF ASCARIS MUSCLE MITOCHONDRIA

AND ITS FUNCTION IN ANAEROBIC RESPIRATION

K. Kita, S. Takamiya, R. Furushima, Y. Ma, and H. Oya

Department of Parasitology
Juntendo University School of Medicine
Tokyo, Japan

The phosphoenolpyruvate carboxykinase (PEPCK)-succinate pathway is important in the energy metabolism of anaerobic organisms such as Ascaris suum, which resides in the host's small intestine where oxygen is fairly limited (1). The last step of this pathway is catalized by fumarate reductase activity of mitochondria, and our studies on the respiratory chain of mitochondria from Ascaris indicated that complex II (succinate-ubiquinone reductase) functions as fumarate reductase by its reverse reaction. Complex II contains b-type cytochrome and properties of this cytochrome of Ascaris was somewhat different from that of beef heart. Comparative characterization of these b cytochromes are described.

In the mitochondria of Ascaris muscle, relative content of cytochrome b is

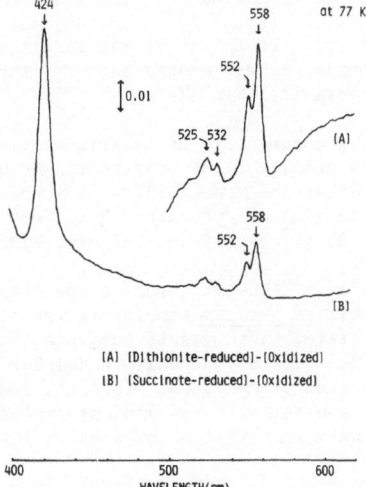

[A] [Dithionite-reduced]-[Oxidized]
[B] [Succinate-reduced]-[Oxidized]

Fig. 1. Low temperature difference spectra of the Ascaris complex II. A; spectrum of the succinate-reduced minus oxidized complex II. B; spectrum of the dithionite-reduced minus oxidized complex II.

683

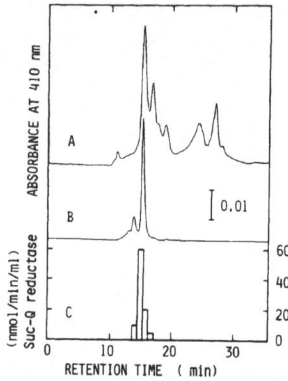

Fig. 2. Elution profiles from the HPLC of cytochromes and succinate-
ubiquinone reductase from <u>Ascaris</u> mitochondria. A; Cytochromes
in the red supernatant. B; Complex II was isolated from <u>Ascaris</u>
muscle and treated with 3% (W/V) Sarkosyl and injected. C;
Distribution of succinate-ubiquinone reductase from the red supernatant. During chromatogram, fractions were collected (1 ml each)
and activity was measured.

higher than other types of cytochromes. This b cytochrome was reduced by
respiratory substrates and reoxidized by fumarate. From the results of the
purification and characterization of complex II of <u>Ascaris</u>, it was clarified
that this b cytochrome is located in complex II of mitochondria (2, 3).
This b-type cytochrome had two α-absorption peaks at 552 (subpeak) and
558 (mainpeak) nm in the low temperature difference spectra (Fig. 1) and
was named as cytochrome b_{558}. Splitting of α-absorption peak of b cytochrome in complex II was also observed in beef heart complex II (cytochrome
b_{560}) (4), and <u>Paragonimus</u> <u>westermani</u> (5).

We have established a procedure for rapid, quantitative determination of the
composition and amount of cytochromes in the mitochondria by High Performance Liquid Chromatography (HPLC) (6). In the case of <u>Ascaris</u>, elution
profile was quite different from that of rat liver and beef heart and
cytochrome b_{558} in complex II was eluted as a major peak with succinate-
ubiquinone reductase activity (Fig. 2).

As described above, cytochrome b_{558} of <u>Ascaris</u> was reducible by succinate,
though b cytochrome in complex II of beef heart was hardly reduced by
succinate. This difference of reducibility by succinate is due to the
fact that midpoint potential of cytochrome b_{558} (-34 mV) is higher than
that of beef heart (<-80 mV: Hatefi and Galante, -190 mV: Yu et al.).

In the presence of <u>Ascaris</u> NADH-cytochrome c reductase (complex I-III),
cytochrome b_{558} of purified <u>Ascaris</u> complex II was also reduced by NADH
and reoxidized by fumarate. This result suggests that cytochrome b_{558}
functions as an electron carrier not only in complex II but also in the
<u>Ascaris</u> NADH-fumarate reductase system. In fact, complex II of <u>Ascaris</u>
showed fumarate reductase activity (24 µmol/min/mg) and its specific
activity was quite higher than that of beef heart (0.065 µmol/min/mg).

From these results, we conclude that complex II is a major component of
the respiratory chain in <u>Ascaris</u> muscle mitochondria, and cytochrome b_{558}
in the complex II functions as low potential electron carrier of fumarate
reductase activity.

684

REFERENCES

1. P. Köhler and H.J. Saz (1976) J. Biol. Chem. 251, 2217-2225.
2. S. Takamiya, R. Furushima, and H. Oya (1984) Mol. Biochem. Parasitol. 13, 121-134.
3. S. Takamiya, R. Furushima, and H. Oya (1986) Biochem. Biophys. Acta 848, 99-107.
4. Y. Hatefi and Y.M. Galante (1980) J. Biol. Chem. 255, 5530-5537.
5. Y. Ma, K. Kita, F. Hamashima, and H. Oya (1987) Jpn. J. Parasitol. 36, 107-117
6. K. Kita, Y. Murakami, H. Oya, and Y. Anraku (1985) Biochem. Int. 10, 319-326.

VIII.   COOPERATIVITY AND ALLOSTERIC TRANSITIONS

PULSED AND RESTING CYTOCHROME OXIDASE:

AN UPDATE OF OPTICAL AND MOLECULAR PROPERTIES

Maurizio Brunori, Paolo Sarti, Francesco Malatesta, Giovanni Antonini and Michael T. Wilson

Department of Biochemical Sciences and CNR Center of Molecular Biology, University of Rome "La Sapienza"; Department of Experimental Medicine and Biochemical Sciences, University of Rome "Tor Vergata", Rome, Italy and Department of Chemistry University of Essex, Colchester, United Kingdom

INTRODUCTION

The name "pulsed" oxidase was initially assigned to the transient species observed upon exposure of reduced cytochrome c oxidase, in the presence of cytochrome c and excess ascorbate, to a pulse of dioxygen (1). The pulsed species obtained according to this procedure was found to be several times more efficient, in terms of turnover number, than the resting enzyme i.e. the oxidized enzyme as obtained from the purification procedure (2).

The greater catalytic efficiency of the pulsed enzyme was attributed to the enhancement of the rate limiting step in turnover. Experiments designed to identify this step revealed that the internal electron transfer from cytochrome a/Cu a to the binuclear center is rate limiting in catalysis and is faster in the pulsed enzyme as supported by two set of experiments. Firstly, the rate of formation of the carbon monoxide-ferrocytochrome a3 complex, starting from the fully oxidized enzyme, was found to be increased in the pulsed enzyme (1); secondly, the initial bimolecular electron transfer to cytochrome a was found to be substantially the same in resting and pulsed oxidase (3). Moreover, kinetic analysis indicated that the resting to pulsed transition occurs during turnover (2). The oxidized pulsed enzyme, however, decays back to the resting form on a time scale strongly dependent on experimental conditions (1,2,3,4). Spectroscopic differences between resting and pulsed enzyme in the oxidized form were also reported.

EPR spectroscopy shows that resting oxidase displays signals only from oxidized Cu a (g= 2.18, 2.03, 1.99) and a low spin ferric heme, readily identified as cytochrome a (g= 3.03, 2.43, 1.45) (5); other EPR signals are thought to arise from conformational variants of the protein (possibly

689

at the binuclear site) resulting from different purification
procedures (6,7). In addition to the EPR signals described
for resting oxidase, pulsed cytochrome oxidase displays
transient EPR signals which disappear with time. Following
reoxidation of fully reduced oxidase with oxygen, Shaw et
al. (8) detected a transient species with resonances at g=
5, 1.78, 1.69 and, because of the reactivity of this
transient species with cyanide, it was assigned to a ferric
heme, possibly that of cytochrome a3.

EXAFS spectroscopy has also revealed differences
between resting and pulsed oxidase. In the fully oxidized
resting state Powers & Chance (9) have proposed that a
sulphur atom bridges the iron of cytochrome a3 and Cu a3;
this bridging ligand, although not unequivocally identified,
appears to be absent in pulsed, oxidized, cytochrome
oxidase.

The optical properties of pulsed oxidized cytochrome
oxidase are somewhat controversial. It is generally agreed
that the resting oxidized enzyme has a peak in the Soret
region centered at 418 nm, while pulsed oxidase was
initially associated with a Soret band at 428 nm (2),
similar to Okunuki's "oxygenated" derivative (10).
However, it is now established that the species with such a
Soret maximum is the adduct of the freshly pulsed enzyme
with hydrogen peroxide (11); if hydrogen peroxide formation
(produced by the reaction of dithionite with oxygen) is
minimized then the Soret band of the pulsed enzyme has been
reported at 420 nm (12). More recently, Young & Palmer
(13) reported a totally different result, i.e. that the
"redox cycled" enzyme displays a Soret maximum which is
blue-shifted compared to the resting enzyme.

In this paper we report novel experiments which clarify
and clearly distinguish between the optical properties of
the resting, pulsed and peroxy forms of the enzyme.

RESULTS

Cytochrome oxidase prepared according to Yonetani (14)
(100 uM total heme), in 10 mM Hepes buffer containing 39.6
mM KCl, 40.6 mM sucrose, 0.5% Tween 80, pH 7.3, was degassed
and equilibrated with CO (1 mM) in a Thunberg-type cuvette.
The ferrocytochrome a3-CO complex was prepared by adding
anaerobically oxygen-free dithionite (1.5 fold excess) by
means of a gas tight syringe, while reduction was monitored
spectrophotometrically via the alpha-band region.

The CO-complex of the enzyme was then rapidly diluted
100 fold into a cuvette containing oxygen-saturated buffer
and spectra were recorded as a function of time. In some
cases, immediately after dilution (3 seconds) the cuvette
was exposed to a 100 J/ 100 us flash of white light. A
single flash was sufficient to photodissoctiate fully the
carbon-monoxide complex and subsequent flashes had no
effect.

Spectra of the Soret region were successively collected
at various times after dilution using a Cary 219

690

thermostated spectrophotometer.   The results of   these
experiments are illustrated in figure 1.

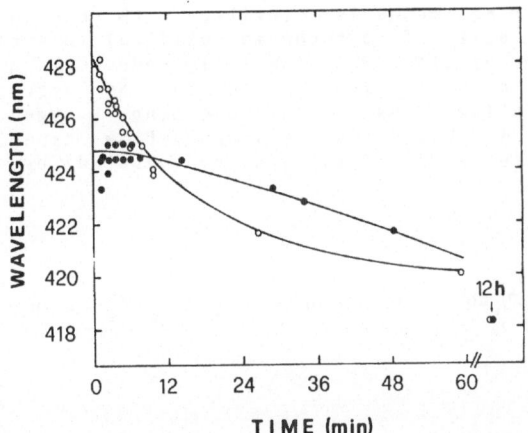

Figure 1:   Time dependent changes of the Soret peak
maximum   of   the   oxidized   enzyme   obtained   either   after
displacement of CO in the presence of pure oxygen (open
symbols),   or after photolytic removal of CO in the presence
of oxygen   (closed symbols)

     The final product of the displacement of CO by oxygen,
when the reaction takes place in the dark (no flash), has a
Soret peak centered at 428 nm.   On the other hand,   when
rapid CO dissociation was induced by the flash, the reaction
with   oxygen yielded a species of the oxidase with   a   Soret
maximum   centered   around   425 nm.   Both of these species
decay, over several hours to the 418 nm form, which
corresponds to the initial resting species (which has not
passed through a reduction-oxidation cycle).

     The   presence of catalase (25 nM) did not affect the
results,   suggesting   that   there   was   no   significant
involvement of free hydrogen peroxide, produced during
exposure of the excess dithionite to dioxygen.   However if
the   flash was fired approximately 1 minute after   dilution
with oxygen,   (i.e. after considerable displacement of CO by
oxygen had already occurred) the maximum of the Soret   band
was at   428 nm excluding any role of the flash other than
photodissociation.

     These results are interpreted in terms of the formation
of two enzyme species, with the two different protocols i.e.
the peroxy-pulsed form and the pulsed species.

DISCUSSION

     The   experiments   presented   above   were   designed   to distinguish between the multiple spectral forms of cytochrome oxidase using the Soret band which is a sensitive marker of the liganded state of the binuclear center. As shown in Fig. 1, the wavelength maximum of the Soret band is critically dependent on the experimental protocol used in the oxidation of the carbomonoxy adduct of the enzyme by dioxygen.

The following mechanism (written with reference to one functional unit of cytochrome oxidase) describes the processes taking place when the fully reduced CO complex of cytochrome oxidase is exposed, in the absence of a photodissociating flash, to molecular oxygen. This formulation is based on the stopped-flow experiments of Gibson & Greenwood (15,16) and corroborated by ourselves (17,18).

$$1 \quad \begin{matrix} a^{2+} & a_3^{2+} \\ Cu_a^{1+} & Cu_{a_3}^{1+} \end{matrix}\text{-CO} \;+\; O_2 \;+\; 4H^+ \;\longrightarrow\; \begin{matrix} a^{3+} & a_3^{3+} \\ Cu_a^{2+} & Cu_{a_3}^{2+} \end{matrix} \;+\; 2H_2O \;+\; CO$$

$$2 \quad \begin{matrix} a^{3+} & a_3^{3+} \\ Cu_a^{2+} & Cu_{a_3}^{2+} \end{matrix} \;+\; \begin{matrix} a^{2+} & a_3^{2+} \\ Cu_a^{1+} & Cu_{a_3}^{1+} \end{matrix}\text{- CO} \;\longrightarrow\; \begin{matrix} a^{2+} & a_3^{3+} \\ Cu_a^{1+} & Cu_{a_3}^{2+} \end{matrix} \;+\; \begin{matrix} a^{3+} & a_3^{2+} \\ Cu_a^{2+} & Cu_{a_3}^{1+} \end{matrix}\text{-CO}$$

$$3 \quad \begin{matrix} a^{2+} & a_3^{3+} \\ Cu_a^{1+} & Cu_{a_3}^{2+} \end{matrix} \;+\; O_2 \;\longrightarrow\; \begin{matrix} a^{3+} & a_3^{3+} \\ Cu_a^{2+} & Cu_{a_3}^{2+} \end{matrix}\text{-}\text{-}O_2^{2-}$$

Step 1 depicts the CO dissociation from, and oxidation of, reduced cytochrome oxidase as described by Gibson and Greenwood (15). These processes are rate limited at 0.02 s-1, the CO "off" rate.

Step 2 is very complex and involves electron redistribution among functional units (16). The overall kinetics of this reaction (extensively reinvestigated by ourselves (17,18)) depends on the aggregation state of the protein and can occur via intermolecular and/or intramolecular electron exchange (with rates up to 0.2-0.5 s-1).

Step 3 shows the overall reaction with oxygen of the species generated in step 2. This contains two electrons and the product is the peroxy form. It may be recalled (19) that the latter is also produced by displacement of CO from the mixed-valence form also generated in step 2.

We see therefore that such a mechanism generates both the fully oxidized, unliganded enzyme, and the peroxide bound form; the relative amount of these two species will be dictated by the relative rate constants for CO displacement in step 1 and electron redistribution in step 2. As indicated by unpublished data (from this lab), with dimeric oxidase, at the concentration employed in these experiments, electron redistribution is the fastest process, thus accounting for the observation that the majority of the enzyme absorbs at 428 nm, the maximum of the peroxy complex.

In the alternative type of experiments, when the carbon monoxide derivative of the fully reduced enzyme is photodissociated in the presence of oxygen, complete oxidation of the enzyme is known to occur very rapidly, yielding presumably water according to the following scheme:

$$
\begin{array}{c}
a^{2+} \quad a_3^{2+} - CO \\
Cu_a^{1+} \quad Cu_{a_3}^{1+}
\end{array}
\xrightarrow[CO]{h\nu}
\begin{array}{c}
a^{2+} \quad a_3^{2} \\
Cu_a^{1+} \quad Cu_{a_3}^{1+}
\end{array}
+ \; O_2 + 4H^+ \longrightarrow
\begin{array}{c}
a^{3+} \quad a_3^{3+} \\
Cu_a^{2+} \quad Cu_{a_3}^{2+}
\end{array}
+ 2H_2O
$$

In these experiments the enzyme exhibits a Soret band at 425 nm, which we therefore take as the spectrum of the pulsed (peroxide free) enzyme. Over a period of time (minutes to hours) both forms of the oxidized enzyme tend to shift their Soret maximum, and eventually decay back to the resting state (as described elsewhere (1,2,3,4)); however the peroxy-pulsed form decays with a biphasic time course, presumably reflecting both the dissociation of peroxide and the decay of the pulsed state back to resting.

So far attention has largely been paid to the resting and pulsed forms of the fully oxidized enzyme, distinguished both by their spectroscopic and functional properties. On the basis of multiturnover, steady-state experiments it has been proposed that transitions between these states may account for the activation of the enzyme during catalysis. This proposal has been formulated into a "two state model" (20), reminiscent of a general allosteric model. A feature of this model is that the fully reduced enzyme should also exist in the "resting" and "pulsed" states. The "pulsed" species now being thermodynamically favoured, a situation opposite to that found in the oxidized enzyme in which the resting state is the dominant species populated at equilibrium.

Although still preliminary, there is now evidence for the existance of (at least) two states of the reduced enzyme. Unfortunately, EPR spectroscopy cannot yield information on the reduced enzyme; however, there is other evidence from spectroscopy and reactivity which are consistent with this requirement of the model. Kornblatt (21) has reported that the spectrum of the reduced enzyme, presumed by us to be in the pulsed state, could be altered (Soret 445--->443 nm , alpha band 605--->603 nm) by addition of ferricytochrome c under conditions where no net electron transfer could take place between cytochrome a/Cu a and ferricytochrome c, in the absence of molecular oxygen.

More recently, Fiamingo et al. (22) have demonstrated, by low temperature Fourier transform infrared spectroscopy, that the reduced enzyme exists in at least two forms, called alpha & beta, distinguished by their rate of recombination with CO and the spectral properties of the resulting complexes.

It is also possible that the kinetic experiments of Hill & Greenwood (23), showing that electron transfer to oxygen within a stable cytochrome c-cytochrome oxidase complex follows more than one route, may similarly reflect different states of the reduced protein.

In conclusion, there is in our opinion sufficient evidence to support the requirement of the model (20) that (at least) two states of cytochrome oxidase can be detected not only in the oxidized state but also in the reduced derivative.

ACKNOWLEDGMENTS: A grant of M.P.I. of Italy (to M.B.) is gratefully ackowledged.

REFERENCES

1) E. Antonini, M. Brunori, A. Colosimo A, C. Greenwood and M.T. Wilson, Oxygen pulsed cytochrome c oxidase: functional properties and catalytic relevance, Proc. Natl. Acad. Sci. USA 74:3128 (1977)

2) M. Brunori , A. Colosimo, G. Rainoni, M.T. Wilson and E. Antonini, Functional intermediates of cytochrome oxidase. Role of pulsed oxidase in the pre-steady state reactions of the beef enzyme, J. Biol. Chem. 254:10769 (1979)

3) A. Colosimo, M. Brunori, P. Sarti, E. Antonini and M.T. Wilson, Pulsed cytochrome oxidase: a critical appraisal of properties and catalytic relevances, Israel J. Chem. 21:30 (1981)

4) M. Brunori, A. Colosimo, P. Sarti, E. Antonini and M.T. Wilson, Pulsed cytochrome oxidase may be produced without the advent of dioxygen, FEBS Lett. 126:195 (1981)

5) M.K.F. Wikstrom, K. Krab and M. Saraste "Cytochrome Oxidase. A synthesis", Academic Press, London (1981)

6) G.W. Brudwig, T.H. Stevens, R.H. Morse and S.I. Chan, Conformations of oxidized cytochrome c oxidase, Biochemistry 20:3912 (1981)

7) G.M. Baker, M. Noguchi and G. Palmer, The reaction of cytochrome oxidase with cyanide, J. Biol. Chem. 262:595 (1987)

8) R.W. Shaw, R.E. Hansen and H. Beinert, A novel electron paramagnetic resonance signal of "oxygenated" cytochrome c oxidase, J. Biol. Chem. 253:6637 (1978)

9) L. Powers and B. Chance, Multiple structures and functions of cytochrome oxidase, J. Inorg. Biochem. 23:207 (1985)

10) I. Sekuzu, S. Takemori, T. Yonetani and K. Okunuki, Studies on cytochrome a, J. Biochem. (Tokio) 46:43 (1959)

11) D. Bickar, J. Bonaventura and C. Bonaventura, Cytochrome c oxidase binding of hydrogen peroxide, Biochemistry 21:2661 (1982)

12) C. Kumar, A. Naqui and B. Chance, The identity of pulsed cytochrome oxidase, J. Biol. Chem. 259:2073 (1984)

13) L.J. Young & G. Palmer, Redox-cycled oxidase, J. Biol. Chem. 261:13031 (1986)

14) T. Yonetani, Studies on cytochrome oxidase, J. Biol. Chem. 236:1680 (1961)

15) Q. Gibson & C. Greenwood, Reaction of cytochrome oxidase with oxygen and carbon monoxide, Biochem J. 86:541 (1963)

16) Q. Gibson & C. Greenwood, The spectra and some properties of cytochrome oxiades components, J. Biol. Chem. 239:586 (1964)

17) G. Antonini, M. Brunori, F. Malatesta, P. Sarti and M. T. Wilson, Reconstitution of monomeric cytochrome c oxidase into phospholipid vesicles yields functionally interacting cytochrome aa3 units, J. Biol. Chem., submitted

18) M.T. Wilson, G. Antonini, F. Malatesta, P. Sarti and M. Brunori, manuscript in preparation

19) C. Greenwood, M.T. Wilson and M. Brunori, Studies on partially reduced mammalian cytochrome oxidase, Biochem. J. 137:205 (1974)

20) M.T. Wilson, J. Peterson, E. Antonini, M. Brunori, A. Colosimo and J. Wyman, A plausible two state model for cytochrome oxidase, Proc. Natl. Acad. Sci. USA 78:7115 (1981)

21) J. A. Kornblatt, Reduced cytochrome oxidase J. Biol. Chem. 255:7225 (1980)

22) F. G. Fiamingo, R. A. Altschuld and J. O. Alben, Alpha and beta forms of cytochrome c oxidase observed in rat heart myocytes by low temperature Fourier transform infrared spectroscopy, J. Biol. Chem. 261:12976 (1986)

23) B.C. Hill & C. Greenwood, Kinetice evidence for the re-definition of electron transfer pathways from cytochrome c to O2 within cytochrome oxidase, FEBS Letts. 166:362 (1984)

IS H_2O_2 INVOLVED IN ELECTRON TRANSPORT
BETWEEN CYTOCHROMES a AND a₃ IN CYTOCHROME OXIDASE?

John M. Wrigglesworth, Michael F. Grahn,
Jennifer Elsden and Harold Baum

Department of Biochemistry
King's College University of London
London W8 7AH

INTRODUCTION

The molecular mechanism by which cytochrome oxidase translocates protons across the inner mitochondrial membrane is unknown. Since the four redox centres in the oxidase (cytochromes a and a_3, Cu_A and Cu_B) are electron carriers, it has been assumed that the mechanism of proton pumping cannot involve direct ligand conduction, and must therefore be indirect, for example by a redox-linked Bohr effect (Papa, 1976). However, it has been pointed out that involvement of H_2O_2 as an intermediate in the oxidase reaction permits the formulation of theoretical O-loops or cycles, which could give rise to the observed stoichiometry, by a direct mechanism (Mitchell et al, 1985). The simplest such model is an O-loop (Fig.1), where two molecules of H_2O_2 sequentially generated at "centre A", diffuse to "centre O", from where they sucessively reduce oxygen at "centre B" to H_2O_2 and then to H_2O. This model makes the radical prediction of two sites of oxygen interaction with the oxidase, whereas spectroscopically only one site (associated with cytochrome a_3) has ever been demonstrated.

In the present experiments we have investigated the reported oxygen dependence of electron transfer between cytochromes a and a_3 (Antalis & Palmer, 1982; Bickar et al, 1986). Such a dependence might be predicted from the O-loop model shown in Figure 1, as O_2 would be necessary for the formation at "centre A" of H_2O_2, the hypothetical redox link between the two halves of the cytochrome oxidase complex. In addition, we have examined

697

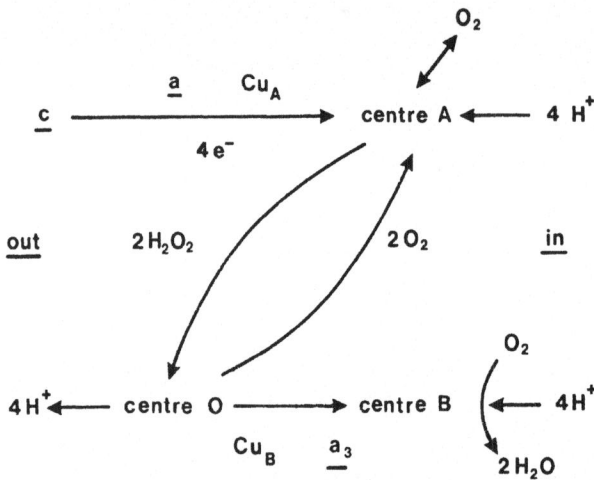

FIG.1. Proposed O-loop model for proton translocation by cytochrome
oxidase.   Reduction of a hypothetical centre A by electron
transfer from cytochrome c is associated with oxygen
reduction to peroxide with oxygen uptake of protons from the
matrix side.   Diffusion of H_2O_2 to centre O is followed by
reduction of oxygen at centre B, eventually to form a tightly
bound peroxy intermediate, oxidation of H_2O_2 to oxygen and
release of protons to the outside.   A repeat of the cycle
results in the reduction of the tightly bound peroxy
intermediate at centre B to water.   (Scheme adapted from
Mitchell et al (1985) and reproduced from Baum et al (1987)
with permission).

the reported ability of H_2O_2 to deliver reducing equivalents to the oxygen
reduction site (Wrigglesworth, 1984) as would also be predicted from the
O-loop model.

IS OXYGEN REQUIRED FOR ELECTRON TRANSFER BETWEEN CYTOCHROMES $\underline{a}$ AND $\underline{a}_3$?

It is a familiar observation that when soluble oxidase is reduced by the
addition of excess dithionite the enzyme takes several minutes to become
fully reduced (Jones et al, 1983).   From analysis of spectral changes in
the Soret and alpha band regions it can be seen that cytochrome $\underline{a}$ is rapidly
reduced, whereas there is a long time lag for the reduction of cytochrome a_3

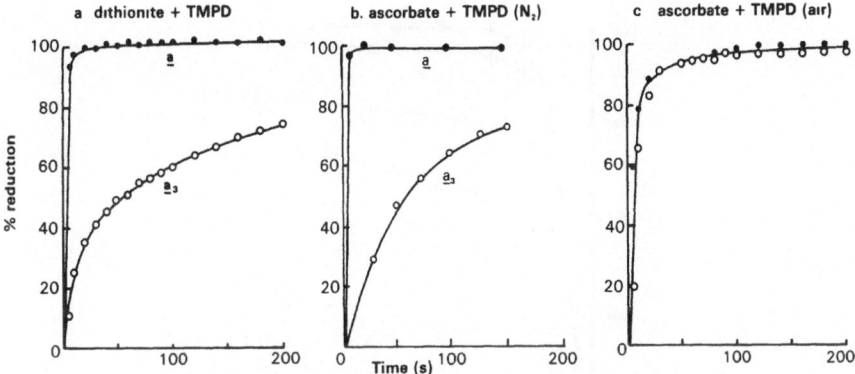

FIG.2. Rate of reduction of cytochromes a and a_3 following

    (a) dithionite plus TMPD addition to cytochrome oxidase,

    (b) ascorbate plus TMPD addition to the enzyme under N_2, and

    (c) anaerobiosis after a period of turnover with ascorbate

    plus TMPD as substrate.

(Fig.2a).   This observation is consistent with the requirement of oxygen
for electron transfer between the cytochromes, since presumably dithionite
acts as a reductant for the oxidase and it also renders the medium anaerobic
within a few milliseconds (Lambeth & Palmer, 1973).   TMPD was present in
the experiment shown in Figure 2a in order to make a direct comparison with
the experiments using ascorbate plus TMPD (Fig.2b).   In fact, as shown by
Bickar et al (1986), a slow rate of a_3 reduction occurs under anaerobic
conditions with several reductants used separately or in combination, with
the exception of cytochrome c.   This can be seen in Figure 2b where
ascorbate-TMPD is used as reductant in the absence of oxygen (Fig.2b).   On
the other hand, if the enzyme is alowed to turnover in the presence of
oxygen until the medium becomes oxygen-exhausted, then there is a rapid and
nearly synchronous reduction of both cytochromes (Fig.2c).   It would appear
therefore that an initial presence of oxygen is required for fast electron
transfer between cytochromes a and a_3.

However, as shown in Figure 3, addition of dithionite following initiation
of turnover (but before anaerobiosis) yields reduction rates for the two
cytochromes that depend upon how long turnover has been in progress.   Early
on, a reduction pattern is obtained very similar to that illustrated in
Figure 2a, but as turnover proceeds the effect of dithionite addition

699

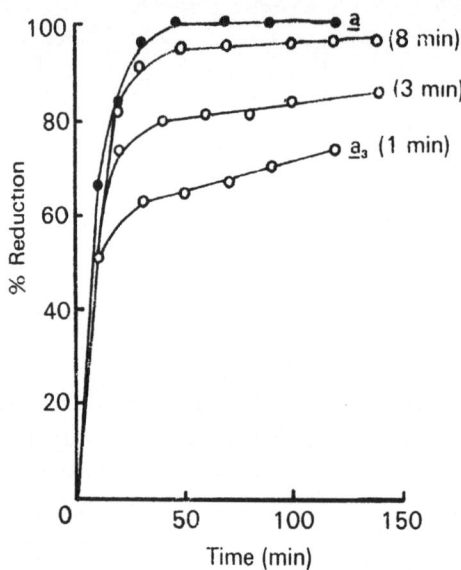

FIG.3. Rate of reduction of cytochromes a and a_3 following the addition of dithionite at different times to cytochrome oxidase turning over with ascorbate plus TMPD as substrate.

becomes composite and eventually is very similar to that occurring on turnover-induced anaerobiosis (Fig.2c). Since the rate of oxygen removal from the solution by dithionite under these conditions would largely be independent of how long turnover has proceeded, it would have to be concluded that oxygen is not required for intermolecular electron transport between cytochromes a and a_3, at least for enzyme under prolonged turnover conditions.

The simplest interpretation of the observations is that the population of oxidase moecules is gradually converted under turnover conditions from virtually inactive "resting" species (Antonini et al, 1977) to a "pulsed" form with full enzyme activity. The conversion of an individual complex might be very slow, requiring only one turnover or simply full reduction. If the 0-loop hypothesis were correct, then from the present results it would have to be asumed that the resting and pulsed forms of the enzyme differ by the fact that H_2O_2 is absent in the resting form of the enzyme but trapped at site A in the pulsed form. Addition of reductant to the resting enzyme in the absence of oxygen will therefore only result in an initial reduction of cytochrome $\underline{a}$.   However, a similar addition of reductant to the pulsed enzyme will result in the reduction of both $\underline{a}$ and $\underline{a}_3$ as reducing equivalents will be delivered by the internal H_2O_2 via centre O to the $\underline{a}_3/Cu_B$ centre.

CAN H_2O_2 DONATE ELECTRONS TO THE $\underline{a}_3/Cu_B$ CENTRE?

The reaction of cytochrome oxidase with H_2O_2 has a long history (see Naqui & Chance, 1986).   The enzyme can act as a peroxidase using H_2O_2 as an electron acceptor (Orii, 1982; Bickar et al, 1982), and the oxidised enzyme binds H_2O_2 to form a spectroscopically distinct species with an alpha band at 607nm (Wrigglesworth, 1984).   Purified preparations of cytochrome oxidase do not exhibit catalase activity (Orii & Okunuki, 1963; Wriggles-worth et al, 1985), but H_2O_2 can donate reducing equivalents to the enzyme if the reaction is carried out in the presence of cyanide to prevent immediate aerobic reoxidation (Wrigglesworth, 1984).   It would appear that under certain conditions, H_2O_2 can act as a reductant as well as an

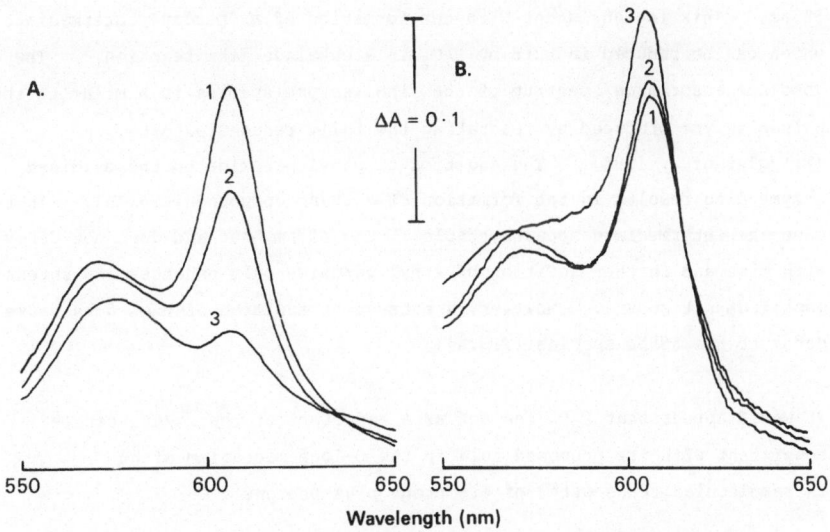

FIG.4. Effect of (A) H_2O_2, and (B) ethyl peroxide on ferric cytochrome oxidase.   Beef heart enzyme (13uM) was incubated in HEPES buffer (100mM), pH 7.4 plus potassium ferricyanide (1mM). H_2O_2 (200uM) or ethyl peroxide (280uM) was added and the spectra taken after 30s (1), 3min (2) and 10min (3). (Wrigglesworth and Nicholls, unpublished observations).

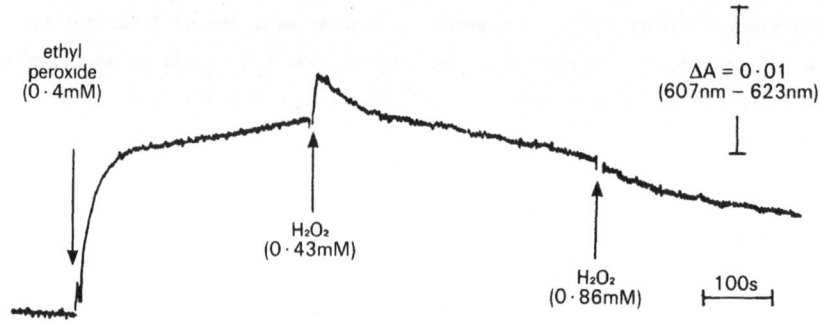

FIG.5. Effect of H_2O_2 on the 607nm intermediate formed by the
addition of ethyl peroxide to ferric cytochrome oxidase.
Conditions of incubation as in Figure 4.

oxidant for cytochrome oxidase.   To test this property further, we have
made use of ethyl peroxide which, for catalase, can act as an oxidant but
not as a reductant in the catalytic cycle.

It can be seen from Figure 4a that the 607nm compound produced by the
addition of H_2O_2 to oxidised (resting) cytochrome oxidase decays over a
period of minutes to an enzyme species with an alpha absorption band around
585nm.   This is consistant with the formation of a "peroxy" intermediate
which can be reduced in turn by H_2O_2 in a catalase-like reaction.   The
absolute absorbance spectrum of the final enzyme species is similar to the
pulsed enzyme produced by reaerating the fully reduced oxidase
(Wrigglesworth, 1984).   The addition of ethyl peroxide to the oxidised
enzyme also results in the formation of a 607nm compound (Fig.4b).   In this
case the intermediate appears stable.   The 607nm band and does not decay
with time and further addition of ethyl peroxide only enhances its intensity
(spectrum not shown).   However, a subsequent addition of H_2O_2 does cause a
decay to the 585nm species (Fig.5).

It would appear that H_2O_2 can act as a reductant at the a_3/Cu_B centre
consistant with its proposed role in the O-loop mechanism of an
intramolecular transporter of electrons plus protons.

ACKNOWLEDGMENTS

The experiments in Figures 4 and 5 were done by J.M.W. in the laboratory of
Peter Nicholls who kindly supplied the samples of ethyl peroxide.   We would
also like to acknowledge support from the SERC.

REFERENCES

Antalis, T.M. and Palmer, G. (1982) J.Biol.Chem. 257, 6194-6206

Antonini, E., Brunori, M., Greenwood, C., Colosimo, A. and Wilson, M.T.
    (1977) Proc.Natl.Acad.Sci.U.S.A. 74, 3128-3132

Baum, H., Grahn, M.F., Elsden, J. and Wrigglesworth, J.M. (1987) in:
    "Bioenergetics: Structure and Function of Energy Tansducing Systems",
    T.Ozawa and S.Papa, eds. Japan Sci.Soc.Press, Tokyo, pp.199-214

Bickar, D., Bonaventura, J. and Bonaventura, C. (1982) Biochemistry 21,
    2661-2666

Bickar, D., Turrens, J.F. and Lehninger, A.L. (1986) J.Biol.Chem. 261,
    14461-14466

Jones, G.D., Jones, M.G., Wilson, M.T., Brunori, M., Colosimo, A. and Sarti,
    P. (1983) Biochem.J. 209, 175-182

Lambeth, D.O. and Palmer, G. (1973) J.Biol.Chem. 248, 6095-6103

Mitchell, P., Mitchell, R., Moody, A.J., West, I.C., Baum, H. and
    Wrigglesworth, J.M. (1985) FEBS Lett. 188, 1-7

Naqui, A. and Chance, B. (1986) Ann.Rev.Biochem. 55, 137-166

Orii, Y. (1982) J.Biol.Chem. 257, 9246-9248

Orii, Y. and Okunuki, K. (1963) J.Biochem.(Tokyo) 54, 207-213

Papa, S. (1976) Biochim.Biophys.Acta 456, 39-84

Wrigglesworth, J.M. (1984) Biochem.J. 217, 715-719

Wrigglesworth, J.M., Elsden, J. and Baum, H. (1985) Biochem.Soc.Trans. 13,
    768-769

CONFORMATIONAL TRANSITIONS OF CYTOCHROME c OXIDASE

INDUCED BY PARTIAL REDUCTION

Charles P. Scholes, Chaoliang Fan, Janet Bank,
Roswitha Dorr, and Bo. G. Malmström†

Department of Physics, State University of New York
at Albany, Albany, NY 12222 USA
†Department of Biochemistry, Chalmers University of
Technology, S-412 96, Göteborg, Sweden

ELECTRONIC STRUCTURAL CHANGES AT CU_A AS PROBED BY ENDOR

The metal centers of cytochrome c oxidase obviously interact by transferring electrons. Potentiometric titrations of metal centers, as monitored optically and by EPR, indicate redox coupling between centers (1). This means that putting an electron on one redox center perturbs the redox potential of another center. It has been proposed that such redox interactions are in fact aspects of concomitant conformational change (2).

Of relevance to the present work are recent potentiometric titrations of Cu_A (3) and cytochrome a (4) in mixed-valence, CO-ligated cytochrome c oxidase where the a_3-Cu_B center was already reduced and ligated with carbon monoxide. Additional electrons were then added to cytochrome a and Cu_A, and there was evidence for anticooperative redox couplings between cytochrome a and Cu_A. In previous EPR studies slight changes in the g-values of the Cu_A center were seen in 3-electron-reduced cytochrome oxidase (5). Such 3-electron-reduced oxidase was prepared by adding a stoichiometric amount of reductant to cytochrome oxidase under a CO atmosphere (5), and the resultant EPR spectra showed cytochrome a preferentially reduced with respect to Cu_A.

Starting with cytochrome oxidase prepared by the methods of Refs. 6 and 7, we used a Dutton cell (8) and potentiometric monitoring to reduce cytochrome oxidase (through NADH plus catalytic amounts of PMS and TMPD) under an oxygen-free CO atmosphere. Then we slowly increased the potential by addition of ferricyanide. At a potential of about 200 mV we found similar EPR results to those reported for 3-electron-reduced oxidase (5); the overall Cu_A^{2+} EPR signal was about 1/3 of its intensity in the starting resting oxidase, and the ratio of a^{3+} to Cu_A^{2+} was about 40% of that in resting oxidase. Even in the absence of redox anticooperativity between cytochrome a and Cu_A, this would imply that the majority of Cu_A^{2+} centers do not have ferricytochrome a neighbors.

Abbreviations: EPR, electron paramagnetic resonance; ENDOR, electron nuclear double resonance; G, Gauss; p.t.p., peak-to-peak; NADH, nicotinamide adenine dinucleotide; TMPD, N,N,N',N'-tetramethyl-p-phenylenediamine; "spin amide", 3-carbamoyl-2,2,5,5-tetramethyl-3-pyrrolin -1-lyloxy; PMS, phenazine methosulfate.

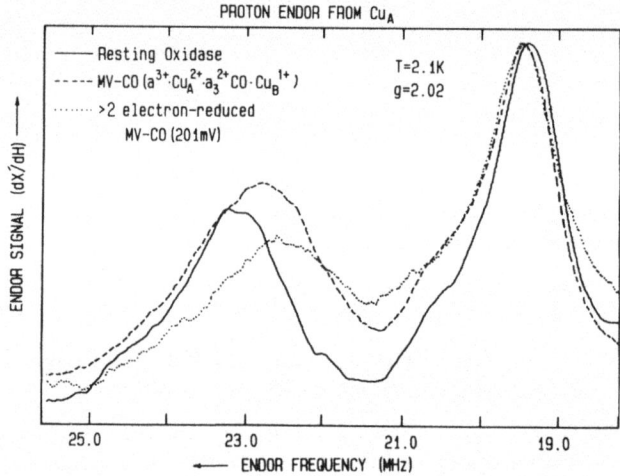

Fig. 1. ENDOR signals of hyperfine-coupled cysteine protons
from the Cu_A^{2+} center in cytochrome oxidase when
other metal centers are in various states of reduction. These samples were resting oxidase ($a^{3+} \cdot Cu_A^{2+}$
$a_3^{3+} \cdot Cu_B^{2+}$), mixed-valence CO ($a^{3+} \cdot Cu_A^{2+} \cdot a_3^{2+} CO \cdot Cu_B^{1+}$),
and the more completely reduced (200 mV) mixed-
valence CO, where the electron preferentially reduced cytochrome $\underline{a}$. ENDOR conditions were: ENDOR
RF field, 0.5 G p.t.p.; 100 KHz field modulation,
4 G p.t.p.; microwave power, 10 μW; T = 2.1 K;
electron resonance frequency, 9.37 GHz; H = 3.31
kG; ENDOR frequency sweep rate, 3 MHz/s. Samples
were approximately 0.4 mM in Cu_A and dissolved in
0.05 M potassium phosphate buffer, pH 7.4, with
0.5% Tween-20.

     To probe the structural basis for redox-linked cooperative interactions,
we studied how an aspect of the detailed electronic structure at Cu_A^{2+} is
changed by reduction of the other centers within the oxidase molecule. To
follow such strucural changes, we have the ENDOR technique which is highly
sensitive to electronic spin density at various nuclei near a paramagnetic
center. Our early ENDOR studies had shown large isotropic couplings
to protons in the vicinity of Cu_A^{2+}. (9). In later studies of selectively
deuterated yeast oxidase we assigned these as the Beta protons of cysteine
ligated through adjacent sulfur to the copper (10). Thus, ENDOR signals
from these protons report electron density localized near Cu_A. As shown in
Fig. 1, the ENDOR signals from resting oxidase, mixed-valence CO, and the
more completely reduced mixed-valence CO oxidase were compared. There was a
definite decrease in frequency of the peak near 23 MHz on going to the most
completely reduced species, and perhaps a slight decrease between resting
oxidase and the doubly reduced, mixed-valence CO oxidase. We consistently
have found the smallest splitting between the two proton peaks near 19 and
23 MHz from the most highly reduced material. This most highly reduced
material happens to have the smallest ratio of $\underline{a}^{3+}$ to Cu_A^{2+}. Therefore we
have shown that the electronic structure of Cu_A, specifically monitored by
hyperfine couplings to cysteine protons, changes in response to reduction
of metal centers elsewhere in cytochrome oxidase, especially at cytochrome
$\underline{a}$. This is the first in a series of studies where we will use ENDOR to
monitor electronic results from redox-related conformational change in
cytochrome $\underline{c}$ oxidase.

706

THE "CLOSED-TO-OPEN" CONFORMATIONAL CHANGE IN CYTOCHROME $\underline{c}$ OXIDASE AS
PROBED BY KINETIC MEASUREMENTS

Conformational changes may accompany and modulate electron transfer
from cytochrome $\underline{a}$ and Cu_A to the oxygen-binding $\underline{a}_3$-Cu_B center. Besides regulating oxygen binding, such conformational changes have been suggested to
provide the coupling between electron transport and proton pumping (2), a
phenomenon which can occur even within the time for the first oxygen molecule
to be consumed (11). The resting-to-pulsed transition is one such transition
that occurs on reduction and reoxidation with dioxygen, but it is slow on
the time scale of a single oxygen-consuming turnover of cytochrome oxidase
(12). A faster conformational change is the "closed-to-open" transition that
may be part of the mechanism that regulates electron transfer to the $\underline{a}_3$-Cu_B
center and thus regulates cytochrome $\underline{c}$ and oxygen consumption (2); it is most
straightforwardly shown in the rapid cyanide inhibition that follows partial
reduction (13). This rapid inhibition, suggested to occur when the oxidase
molecule "opens" after partial reduction (13-16), is to be contrasted with
the comparatively slow binding of cyanide to resting oxidase (14). Fig. 2,
showing oxidation of $\underline{c}^{2+}$ as monitored at 550 nm, indicates that after an initial burst of $\underline{c}^{2+}$ oxidation the subsequent oxidation is markedly slowed, well
within the time needed even for another $\underline{c}^{2+}$ to be consumed. Following inhibition, internal electron transfer to the $\underline{a}_3$-Cu_B center is blocked. There is
a characteristically increased extinction in the Soret, peaking at 430-437
nm, which is due to cyanide-ligated cytochrome $\underline{a}_3^{3+}$ (17), and this increased
extinction has also been shown in kinetic difference measurements (13). This
Soret extinction does not show itself immediately upon inhibition but builds
up slowly in time following inhibition. In the absence of reductant, the
time for build-up of this extinction is hours (14), while in the presence of

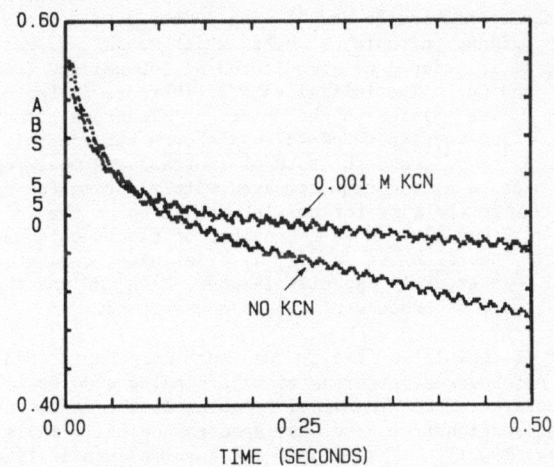

Fig. 2. The rapid onset of cyanide inhibition is shown
by diminishing cytochrome $\underline{c}^{2+}$ oxidation following an initial burst. The $\underline{c}^{2+}$ consumption can
be estimated from the absorbance change at 550
nm, where the extinction coefficient difference
between $\underline{c}^{2+}$ and $\underline{c}^{3+}$ is 21.1 X 10^3 M^{-1} cm^{-1} (18).
The $\underline{c}^{2+}$ concentration was initially 20 μM and
the oxidase concentration 5 μM.

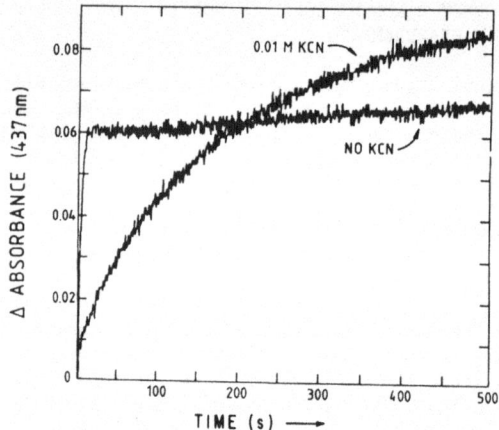

Fig. 3. This figure shows the build-up of absorbance
from the cytochrome a_3-cyanide complex. The
rapid initial change with the non-inhibited sample is due to non-inhibited consumption of c^{2+}. The c^{2+} concentration was
initially 20 μM, and the cytochrome oxidase concentration was 2.5 μM; the buffer
was air-saturated. This figure from Ref. 20.

reductant the time for build-up is minutes. [The build-up is not due to a
completely reduced, cyanide-liganded oxidase complex (19)].

A question related to the mechanism of the "closed-to-open" transition is: How many electrons must be accepted by the cytochrome oxidase
molecule for the transition to occur? The number of electrons donated
per cytochrome oxidase molecule, a number which we call N, was determined
from the decrease in reduced c^{++} (monitored at 550 nm) and from the increase
in reduced a^{2+} and Cu_A. The initial rate of increase in the extinction at
437 nm, called V, was related to the number of electrons consumed per oxidase molecule. (The wavelength of 437 was chosen because this wavelength is
isosbestic for a^{2+} - a^{3+}, and the rate of increase was measured at 20 s
after mixing which is a long time compared with the time for c^{2+} consumption
but slow compared to the time for complete build-up of the 437 nm extinction.) The rate V was plotted vs the number of electrons consumed per
oxidase molecule, and as shown in Fig. 4, a definite, quadratic dependence
was determined. In separate experiments ·where NADH-PMS was the reductant,
a similar non-linear dependence of V upon N was found.

The onset of inhibition (Fig. 2) was much more rapid than the optical
change at 437 nm; however, previous cyanide binding studies have shown
that the optically visible cyanide-a_3^{3+} complex is the result of a slow,
internal transformation from previous, spectroscopically invisible, cyanide-
inhibited forms (19,21). (These forms may involve cyanide ligation to Cu_B
(22).) Then it follows that the initial rate of increase of 437 nm extinction is directly proportional to the concentration of prior, "open" inhibited forms. Thus a correlation of V and N^2 would be a correlation of the
prior, "open" cyanide-bound forms with N^2.

A probabilistic model was devised to account for the number of non
$(a^{3+}Cu_A^{2+})$, singly $(a^{3+}Cu_A^+; a^{2+}Cu_A^{2+})$ and doubly $(a^{2+}Cu_A^+)$ reduced forms that
exist in a cytochrome oxidase molecule after reduction by N electrons per
molecule (20). The simplest model approximated $\underline{a}$ and Cu_A as non-interacting

708

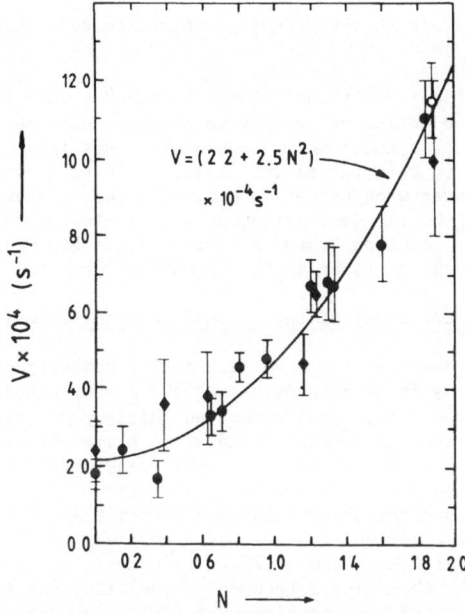

Fig. 4. Initial velocity, V, of cyanide-induced absorbance change at 437 nm as a function of the number, N, of electrons consumer per oxidase. The
electrons consumed were estimated from c^{2+} consumption and confirmed from the sum of $\underline{a}$ and Cu_A
reduction. Most points (●) were taken with 5 μM
oxidase, while the remainder (♦) were taken
with 2.5 μM oxidase. (The ordinates of the latter points were multiplied by 2.) The point
(○) was taken in the presence of excess reductant (ascorbate and TMPD) to ensure complete,
continuous reduction of $\underline{a}$ and Cu_A. (From Ref. 20).

sites with the same redox potentials and rates of reduction(23). This
model showed that the number of singly reduced sites should initially
increase linearly as N, while the number of doubly reduced sites should
increase as N^2. The model was easily modified to include moderate cooperativity or anticooperativity in the binding of the second electron (3,4) or
even to include a more elaborate multistep process designed to simulate
electron consumption by cytochrome oxidase (24). These more elaborate
models still predicted that the number of singly reduced sites should exhibit an initial linear dependence on N while the number of doubly reduced
sites should initially depend on N^2 and generally be non-linearly dependent
on N. Thus the concentration of doubly reduced forms of cytochrome oxidase
is suggested to have the same non-linear dependence on N as does V. This
experiment then provides evidence that two electrons must be added to the

---

* With this model we let P be the probability for having $\underline{a}$ reduced which
for the simplest case would be the same as the probability for having Cu_A
reduced. The probabilities for having cytochrome oxidase then in non,
singly and doubly reduced states would respectively be $(1 - P)^2$, $2P(1 - P)$,
and P^2. Since N = 2P, the fraction of doubly reduced forms would be
$(1/4)N^2$.

oxidase to convert it to the "open" conformation that leads to cyanide inhibition.

There is evidence that the "closed-to-open" transition is associated
with 2-electron reduction of cytochrome oxidase, not one-electron reduction.
Kinetic analysis of cytochrome c^{2+} consumption has indicated that two electrons at a time are transferred intramolecularly from cytochrome a and Cu_A
to the a_3-Cu_B center when oxygen is consumed (24). Internal electron transfer to the a_3-Cu_B center does not occur in the singly reduced enzyme (25).
Thus for internal electron transfer to the oxygen binding center, cytochrome
oxidase may be required to be in the "open" conformation.

Direction for Future Study of the "Closed-to-Open" Transition

It would be desirable to have methods for measuring the "closed-to-
open" transition as it affects events at the a_3-Cu_B center only on a faster
time scale than the slow, cyanide-induced build-up of extinction in the
Soret. Such faster measurements would be more amenable to a correlation of
the "closed-to-open" transition with oxygen binding and proton pumping. In
principle, the kinetics of oxygen binding at the a_3-Cu_B center, as monitored
by optical changes there, can yield such information, but optical changes
reflecting oxygen intermediates are fast, complex, and overlapped with concomitant changes of cytochrome a (26). Cytochrome c consumption is certainly affected by the "closed-to-open" transition, but it appears to reflect
an elaborate series of kinetic processes (24).

We are exploring a technique for measuring oxygen binding on the same
time scale as cytochrome c consumption is measured, i.e., much faster than
usual polarographic methods. We intend to quickly follow oxygen binding,
using a recently developed, ambient temperature EPR technique which uses
only microliter quantities of reactant. As developed by Hyde and co-workers,
this technique uses small, freely tumbling nitroxide spin probes whose sig-

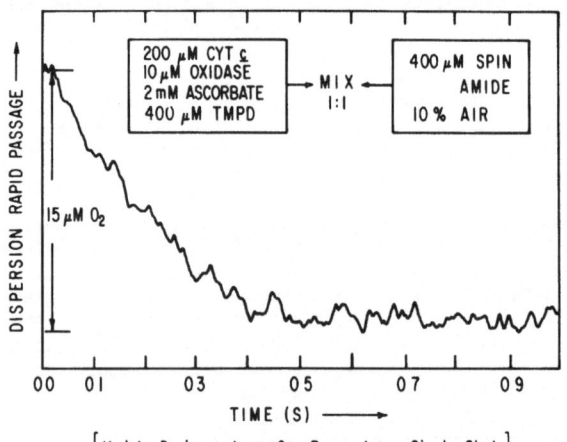

Fig. 5. Oxygen consumption observed by change in the
oxygen-sensitive spin probe dispersion EPR
signal following mixing oxidase containing
excess reductant with buffer that was 10% air-
saturated. The studies carried out at 23° C.

nals are sensitive to presence of oxygen in a non-destructive way because oxygen changes their relaxation times (27, 28). (The spin amide, also called CTPO, used in Fig. 5 is such a probe.) For high sensitivity of EPR and small sample volumes, a loop gap resonator is used (29). In the laboratory of Prof. W. Hubbell the loop gap resonator has been interfaced to an Update Instruments rapid mixing device for stopped flow EPR, which yields < 10 ms time resolution on sample volumes < 10 μl. In a preliminary experiment using this device, reduced oxidase containing excess reductant was mixed with 10% air-saturated buffer and the kinetics of oxygen consumption followed. This experiment shows the feasibility of measuring oxygen consumption on the same time scale as cytochrome c oxidation is followed in Fig. 2. We expect to use this device to obtain a different aspect of cytochrome c oxidase activity as viewed from its oxygen, as opposed to its cytochrome c consumption, and in particular to probe the "closed-to-open" transition as monitored by oxygen binding.

ACKNOWLEDGEMENTS

This work was supported by NIH Grant No. GM 35103 and by Visiting Scientist support from the Nobel Institute of Chemistry. We are particularly grateful to Prof. Y. P. Myer, SUNYA, for use of his Aminco-Morrow stopped flow system, to Prof. Tsoo E. King, SUNYA, for advice and starting materials in the preparation of cytochrome c oxidase, and to Prof. W. Hubbell, UCLA, for use of his loop gap resonator-stopped flow EPR system.

REFERENCES

1. Wikström, M., Krab, K., and Saraste, M. (1981) in: Cytochrome Oxidase A Synthesis, pp. 88- 116, Academic Press, London.
2. Malmström, B. G. (1985) Biochim. Biophys. Acta 811, 1-12.
3. Wang, H., Blair, D. F., Ellis, W. R., Gray, H. B., and Chan, S. I. (1986) Biochemistry 25, 167-171.
4. Ellis, W. R., Wang, H., Blair, D. F., Gray, H. B., and Chan, S. I. (1986) Biochemistry 25, 161-167.
5. Brudvig, G. W., Blair, D. F., and Chan, S. I. (1984) J. Biol. Chem. 259, 11001-11009.
6. Kuboyama, M., Yong, F. C., and King, T. E. (1972) J. Biol. Chem. 247, 6375-6383.
7. Yu, C. A., Yu, L., and King, T. E. (1975) J. Biol. Chem. 250, 1383-1392.
8. Dutton, P. L. (1978) in Methods in Enzymology, Vol. LIV, pp. 411-435, Academic Press, New York.
9. Van Camp, H. L., Wei, Y-H., Scholes, C. P., and King, Tsoo E. (1978) Biochim. Biophys. Acta 537, 238 - 246.
10. Stevens, T. H., Martin, C. T., Wang, H., Brudvig, G. W., Scholes, C. P., and Chan, S. I. (1982) J. Biol. Chem. 257, 12106-12113.
11. Sarti, P., Jones, M. G., Antonini, G., Malatesta, F., Colosimo, A., Wilson, M. T., and Brunori, M. (1985) Proc. Natl. Acad. Sci. USA 82, 4876-4880.
12. Brunori, M., Colosimo, A., Rainoni, O., Wilson, M. T., and Antonini, E. (1979) J. Biol. Chem. 254, 10769-10775.
13. Jones, M. G., Bickar, D., Wilson, M. T., Brunori, M., Colosimo, A., and Sarti, P. (1984) Biochem. J. 220, 57-66.
14. Van Buuren, K. J. H., Zuurendonk, P. F., Van Gelder, B. F., and Muijsers, A. O. (1972) Biochim. Biophys. Acta 256, 243-257.
15. Van Buuren, K. J. H., Nicholls, P., and Van Gelder, B. F. (1972) Biochim. Biophys. Acta 256, 258-276.
16. Jensen, P., Wilson, M. T., Aasa, R., and Malmström, B. G. (1984) Biochem. J. 224, 829-837.

17. Yonetani, T., and Ray, G. S. (1965) J. Biol. Chem. 240, 3392-3398.
18. Jensen, P., Aasa, R., and Malmström, B. G. (1981) FEBS Lett. 125 161-164.
19. Nicholls, P., and Hildebrandt, V. (1978) Biochem. J. 173, 65-72.
20. Scholes, C. P., and Malmström, B. G. (1986) FEBS Lett. 198, 125-129.
21. Wilson, D. F., Erecinska, M., and Brocklehurst, E. S. (1972) Arch. Biochem. Biophys. 151, 180-187.
22. Antonini, E., Brunori, M., Greenwood, C., Malmström, B. G., and Rotilio, G. C. (1971) Eur. J. Biochem. 23, 396-400.
23. Antalis, T. M., and Palmer, G. (1982) J. Biol. Chem. 240, 6194-6206.
24. Brzezinski, P., Thornstrom, P.-E., and Malmström, B. G. (1986) FEBS Lett. 194, 1-5.
25. Antonini, E. Brunori, M., Greenwood, C., and Malmström, B. G. (1970) Nature 228, 936-937.
26. Ref. 1, pp. 119-135.
27. Lai, C-S., Hopwood, L., Hyde, J. S., and Lukiewicz, S. (1982) Proc. Natl. Acad. Sci USA 79, 1166-1170.
28. Froncisz, W., Lai, C-S. and Hyde, J. S. (1985) Proc. Natl. Acad. Sci. USA 82, 411-415.
29. Froncisz, W., and Hyde, J. S. (1982) J. Magnetic Resonance 47, 515-521.

REDOX-LINKED CONFORMATIONAL CHANGES IN CYTOCHROME C OXIDASE

T. Alleyne and M.T. Wilson

Department of Chemistry
University of Essex
Colchester CO4 3SQ, U.K.

INTRODUCTION

It has been known for many years that cytochrome c oxidase can undergo changes in conformation. Sometimes these manifest themselves even when they are not the central point of an investigation. For example, those who have carried out rapid-quench EPR experiments will have noticed the difference in the packing properties of the fully oxidised and fully reduced enzyme. Such changes in a macroscopic property must presumably reflect redox-linked shape changes at the molecular level. More discriminating techniques have born out this conclusion, and it is now clear that conformational changes do accompany the enzyme's passage through its catalytic cycle. These changes may be monitored either through spectroscopic changes, such as CD measurements[1] or inferred from functional studies[2,3].

Whether these conformational changes can be described as "allosteric" in the same sense as this term is applied to haemoglobin, is perhaps debatable. If the electron can be compared to a ligand, then cytochrome c oxidase does apparently exhibit negative cooperativity[4], the redox potential of a haem being lowered by reduction of its partner. How much this property reflects electrostatic interactions and how much conformational transitions between states, remains, however, an open question.

Certainly, conformational states possessing different functional properties do exist (e.g. the "resting" and "pulsed" forms first described by Antonini et al.[5]) and transitions between them have been invoked to explain the activation of the enzyme during turnover[2] and the channelling of electrons into a limited number of oxidase molecules, thus diminishing the possibility of oxygen radical production[6].

Electron entry into the oxidase complex, that is into cytochrome a and Cu_A, triggers a dramatic change in the accessibility of ferric cytochrome a_3 to cyanide, allowing rapid binding of this ligand[3,7]. This stands in sharp contrast to the observed much slower combination rate to the fully oxidised (either "resting" or "pulsed") enzyme. Obviously this "opening" of the enzyme's ligand binding site, once electrons have entered the complex, must hold implications for the mechanism of reduction of molecular oxygen. This reduction of cytochrome a (together with Cu_A) is associated with a large negative entropy, consistent with a substantial conformational change[8]. In addition it has been proposed that this conformational change, linked to the "opening of the cytochrome a_3 cyanide/ oxygen binding site, is coupled to, and indeed may constitute, the mobile element of the redox-linked proton pump by which the enzyme transports a proton from the interior to the exterior of the mitochondrion for each electron passing through the complex[9].

Although it has become clear that conformational changes play an important role in the function of cytochrome c oxidase, our knowledge of the magnitude by which distances between sites change is, however, rudimentary. This paper reports the results of an investigation using the fluorescence emission spectrum of zinc cytochrome c, tightly bound to cytochrome c oxidase, to probe conformational changes in the enzyme as metal sites become reduced and/or bind ligands. The approach we have used is similar to that employed by others on a variety of protein systems and has been applied to cytochrome c oxidase itself[10,11]. The method relies on attributing quenching of the zinc cytochrome c fluorescence to resonance energy transfer to an acceptor centre (here a haem) within the enzyme. This process has been described and analysed by Förster[12], who has formulated the dependence of the fluorescence emission intensity on, among other factors, the donor/acceptor distance. Although it is possible using this methodology to obtain absolute distance measurements, and this we have endeavoured to do, our main emphasis has been to try to assess the size of changes in distance which accompany changes in the state of the enzyme. From the data presented below, we conclude that reduction of cytochrome a (and/or Cu_A) leads to an increase in the cytochrome c to cytochrome a distance of approx. 0.5 nm. Ligand binding to either the fully oxidised or fully reduced enzyme is not reported by changes in fluorescence intensity while cyanide binding to the half-reduced enzyme (a^{2+}-Cu_A^+-Cu_B^{2+}-CN-a_3^{3+}) enhances fluorescence emission relative to the fully reduced enzyme implying an increase in donor acceptor distance over and above that brought about by reduction of cytochrome a.

MATERIALS AND METHODS

All reagents used were of analar grade. Fluorescence measurements were made on a Baird Nova fluorimeter, and spectrophotometric studies were performed on a Perkin Elmer 575 spectrophotometer.

Zinc cytochrome c was prepared by the method of Dickinson and Chien[13] as modified by Vanderkooi et al.[14]. Bovine cytochrome c oxidase was isolated by the method of Yonetani[15]. The fully reduced enzyme was generated by the addition of ascorbate, 100 mM and N,N,N',N'tetramethylene phenylene diamine, 2 mM. The carbon monoxide adduct was obtained by bubbling carbon monoxide into fully reduced cytochrome c oxidase. The cyanide derivative was prepared by the method of Van Buuren et al.[16]. Monomeric (subunit III-depleted) cytochrome c oxidase was prepared as described by Puettner et al.[17].

Fluorimetric Titration

Zinc cytochrome c 0.7 μM in tris/acetate buffer (25 mM, pH 7.8, containing 0.1% lauryl maltoside) was titrated with cytochrome c oxidase, (either dimeric or monomeric) in a number of different redox and ligated states at identical ionic strengths. Titrations were first performed at low ionic strength (μ = 30 mM) where column chromatography demonstrates that an approximate 1:1 complex is formed. Control experiments were then performed in the presence of NaCl, 0.3 M, which abolishes complex formation. By subtracting the results of the latter from the former, fluorescence changes due to innerfiltering and absorbance changes were eliminated. The excitation wavelength was 432 nm and the emission wavelength was 590 nm. The temperature was 25°C.

RESULTS AND DISCUSSION

The fluorescence emission spectrum of zinc cytochrome c is given in Fig. la. This is in good agreement with that reported by others[18]. This spectrum was affected neither in intensity nor position by changes in ionic strength or pH (pH 6 - pH 8). At low ionic strength cytochrome c oxidase, in any of the derivatives studied here, forms tight complexes with zinc cytochrome c. The stoichiometry of these complexes determined spectrophotometrically, after passage through Sephadex G100 columns to remove unbound zinc cytochrome c, was approximately 0.8 moles zinc cytochrome c/1 mole of oxidase functional unit. This non-integral value, close to that found for native cytochrome c/oxidase complex (0.9) under similar conditions, we take to reflect some dissociation of a 1:1 complex occurring on the column. The measured stoichiometry was ionic strength dependent and at high salt concentrations (> 0.2 M NaCl) complexes did not form and complexes formed at low ionic strength and subjected to high salt dissociated. Column chromatography also revealed that zinc cytochrome c formed an electrostatic complex with bovine serum albumin.

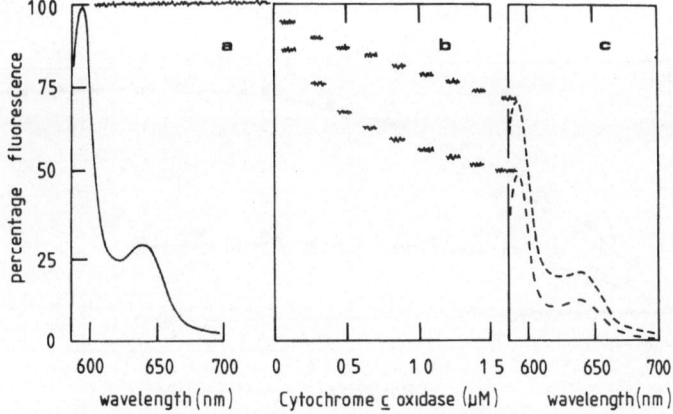

Fig. 1.   Titration of Zinc Cytochrome c with Cytochrome c Oxidase.

(a) The uncorrected fluorescence emission spectrum of zinc cytochrome c, 0.7 μM in the absence and presence of sodium chloride, 0.3 M. The emission maximum occurs at 590 nm and its intensity is arbitrarily set at 100%.

(b) Titration of zinc cytochrome c, 0.7 μM with cytochrome c oxidase (15 μl aliquots of 38 μM functional units). The lower traces occur under conditions of low ionic strength (μ = 10 mM). The upper traces are obtained when the experiment is repeated in the presence of NaCl 0.3 M which inhibits complex formation.

(c) The uncorrected fluorescence emission spectrum of zinc c on completion of both titrations.(N.B. the intensity, but not the position of the emission maximum is altered.)

Fig. 1 also shows the results of titrating zinc cytochrome c with fully oxidised cytochrome c oxidase at high and low ionic strength. At high salt, where no complex forms between the proteins, fluorescence is diminished by the presence of a chromophore which attenuates both the excitation beam and emitted fluorescence (i.e. innerfiltering). At low ionic strength additional quenching is observed which we take to be due to specific complex formation. The dependence on oxidase concentration of that quenching caused by complex formation (i.e. the difference between titrations performed at low and high ionic strength) is shown in Fig. 2 together with the data for similar titrations using a number of oxidase derivatives. The data for the fully oxidised enzyme in its "resting", "pulsed" and cyanide bound forms are identical and are consistent with a simple formulation for the production of a 1:1 complex and yields a value for the binding constant of 7×10^6 M^{-1}. This titration is the same whether performed with the dimeric or monomeric (subunit III - less) enzyme indicating that quenching is due to the functional unit to which the zinc cytochrome c is bound and not a neighbouring monomer within a dimer. The data for the fully reduced enzyme in its unliganded form or in combination with CO are identical and independent of whether the enzyme is dimeric or monomeric. The shape of the curve (Fig. 2) is again consistent with a 1:1 binding stoichiometry but with an association constant of 3×10^7 M^{-1}. The extent of quenching shown in Fig. 2 is clearly dependent on the state of reduction of the derivative, while ligand binding to the cytochrome a_3 and/or Cu_B site in either the fully oxidised or fully reduced enzyme has no effect.

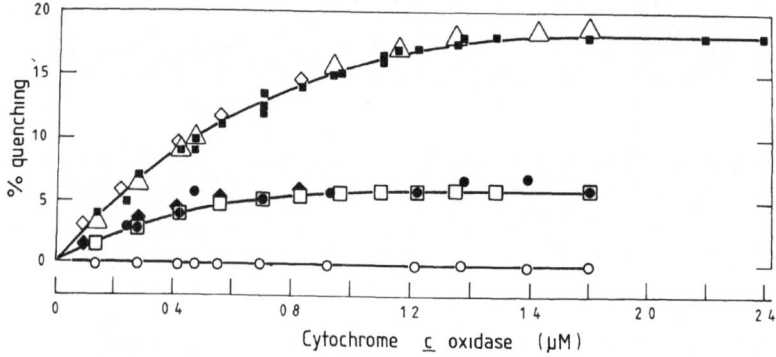

Fig. 2. Fluorimetric Titration of Zinc Cytochrome c with Cytochrome c Oxidase.

Zinc cytochrome c (0.7 μM) was titrated with dimeric and monomeric cytochrome c oxidase in different redox states and with cyanide or carbon monoxide present. ■ fully oxidised "resting"; △ fully oxidised "pulsed"; □ fully reduced; ● fully reduced carbon monoxide adduct; O half-reduced cyanide complex; ◇ fully oxidised monomer; ◆ fully reduced monomer.

The buffer was 25 mM tris/acetate pH 7.8 containing 0.1% lauryl maltoside. For the fully reduced enzyme, the buffer also contained sodium dithionite, 7 mM. This was replaced with sodium sulphate, 7 mM for all other species.

The difference spectrum between the zinc cytochrome c/oxidase complex and the sum of the spectra of the free components is shown in Fig. 3. This indicates that on binding both proteins experience a small diminution in absorbance at their maxima in the Soret region. The change in the absorption spectrum of oxidase, most clearly identified for the reduced protein, is, interestingly, not observed when native cytochrome c is substituted for the zinc derivative (Fig. 3, Inset). The difference in the spectrum of zinc cytochrome c, shown in Fig. 3, is very similar to that observed on binding to bovine serum albumin. However, it is important to note that, although the extinction coefficient at the absorption maximum (422 nm) was decreased by some 2% on complex formation with bovine albumin, neither the wavelength of the fluorescence emission maximum nor the quantum yield of fluorescence (ϕ) changed; binding per se does not therefore influence the fluorescence properties of zinc cytochrome c. We therefore conclude that the binding of cytochrome c oxidase to zinc cytochrome c, although it causes some perturbation of the absorption spectrum, does not lead to changes in ϕ, and consequently the observed fluorescence quenching must result from some other phenomenon.

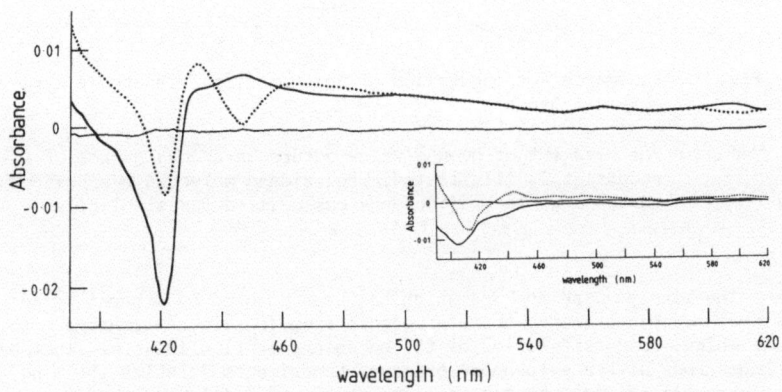

Fig. 3. Perturbation of the Absorption Spectra of Zinc Cytochrome c and Cytochrome c Oxidase on Complex Formation.

A pair of 10 mm path length cuvettes were divided into two equal chambers, 5 mm path length each. In each cuvette, zinc cytochrome c, 2.3 μM, was placed on one side of the glass barrier and cytochrome c oxidase, 1.5 μM, on the other side (i.e. mixing was prevented). One cuvette was used as the reference and the other as the sample.

────── The absorption spectrum obtained when the mixing is prevented. ━━━━ The absorption spectrum obtained when the contents of the sample cuvette were mixed, while keeping that of reference separated. The oxidase was in its oxidised state. ..... Spectrum obtained when the sample cuvette is mixed, but here the oxidase in both cuvettes is in its fully reduced state. Inset: The experiment repeated with native cytochrome c.

717

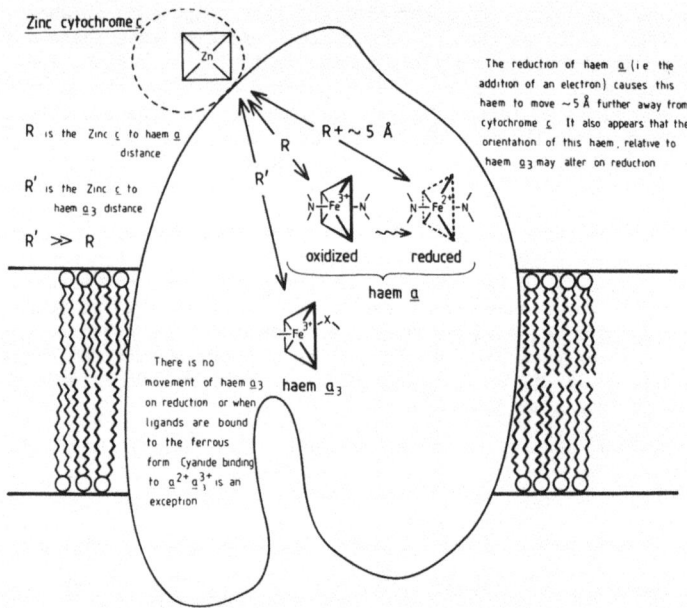

Fig. 4. Schematic Representation of Conformational Change in Cytochrome c Oxidase.

The movement of haem a which occurs as a consequence of its
reduction is illustrated. The oxidase molecule has been distorted and the two copper atoms omitted for simplicity.

The likely cause and one which has been invoked by others[10,19,20]
is that resonance energy transfer occurs from the zinc cytochrome c to a
site which, on consideration of the necessary overlap integral, must be
a haem group within cytochrome oxidase. Experiments in which the zinc
cytochrome c/oxidase complex was completely reduced in the absence or
partially reduced in the presence of cyanide (which traps the cytochrome a_3
site in the ferric state) showed that the decrease in quenching on reduction shown in Fig. 2, was quantitatively accounted for by reduction of
cytochrome a (and Cu_A).

Neither changes in the overlap integrals (overlap between the fluorescence emission spectrum of zinc cytochrome c and the absorption spectrum
of cytochrome c oxidase) nor in the association constants between the
proteins are able to account for the redox-linked change in fluorescence
emission, leaving conformation changes as the probable cause. Using
Förster's [12] theory for resonance energy transfer, we have calculated the
probable magnitude of this conformational change. The values of the parameters we have used are as following: ϕ the quantum yield of fluorescence
for zinc cytochrome c = 10^{-3}. The overlap integral (J) for the oxidised
and reduced enzyme is 0.92 x 10^{-13} and 1.21 x 10^{-13} cm^3 M^{-1}, respectively.
Given that haem groups have degenerate symmetry, we have taken K^2, the
factor describing the relative orientation of the donor (cyt c) and the
acceptor (cyt a) as either 1.5 or 2. The refractive index was 1.33. The
calculated values of R, the cytochrome c to cytochrome a distance, for

the oxidised and reduced enzyme were 2.4 nm and 3.2 nm, respectively giving $\Delta R = 0.8$ nm. If some reorientation is allowed such that K^2 cha on reduction[1], then ΔR falls to approximately 0.5 nm. This is shown schematically in Fig. 4.

Unlike ligand binding to the fully oxidised or fully reduced enzym combination of cyanide with the $Cu_B{}^{2+}$/cytochrome $a_3{}^{3+}$ binding site in an enzyme in which cytochrome $\underline{a}$ and Cu_A are reduced, does significantly enhance the fluorescence emission from the zinc cytochrome $\underline{c}$/oxidase comple relative to the fully reduced enzyme (see Fig. 2). This may indicate that in this species the quenching centre (cyt $\underline{a}$) is yet further removed from zinc cytochrome $\underline{c}$.

Although at present we cannot distinguish with certainty whether it is reduction of cytochrome $\underline{a}$ or Cu_A which triggers the conformational change, we have obtained some preliminary results using the p-(hydroxy-mercuri) benzoate derivative of the enzyme. Gelles and Chan[21] have shown that in this derivative the Cu_A site is significantly modified and is more difficult to reduce. This derivative, however, behaves in a very similar fashion to the unmodified enzyme in fluorescence quenching experiments, indicating that it is the reduction of cytochrome $\underline{a}$ which is responsible for the conformational change.

ACKNOWLEDGEMENTS

We thank the Science and Engineering Research Council, U.K. (Grant GR/80322) for financial support.

REFERENCES

1. T.E. King, P. M. Bailey and F. C. Young, Optical rotatory dispersion and circular dichroism of cytochrome oxidase, Eur. J. Biochem. 20:103 (1971).
2. M. Brunori, A. Colosimo, G. Rainoni, M. T. Wilson and E. Antonini, Functional intermediates of cytochrome $\underline{c}$ oxidase. J. Biol. Chem. 245:10769 (1979).
3. M. G. Jones, D. Bickar, M. T. Wilson, M. Brunori, A. Colosimo and P. Sarti, A re-examination of the reactions of cyanide with cytochrome $\underline{c}$ oxidase, Biochem. J. 220:57 (1984).
4. M.Wikström, K. Krab and M. Saraste, "Cytochrome Oxidase, a Synthesis", Academic Press, London/New York (1981).
5. E. Antonini, M. Brunori, A. Colosimo, C. Greenwood and M. T. Wilson, Oxygen "pulsed" cytochrome $\underline{c}$ oxidase: Functional properties and catalytic relevance, Proc. Natl. Acad. Sci. USA 74:3128 (1977).
6. D. Bickar, J. F. Turrens and A. L. Lehninger, The mechanism by which oxygen and cytochrome $\underline{c}$ increase the rate of electron transfer from cytochrome $\underline{c}$ to cytochrome a_3 of cytochrome $\underline{c}$ oxidase, J. Biol. Chem. 261:14461 (1986).
7. P. Jensen, M. T. Wilson, R. Assa and B. Malmström, Cyanide inhibition of cytochrome $\underline{c}$ oxidase. A rapid-freeze investigation, Biochem. J. 224:829 (1984).
8. D. F. Blair, W. R. Ellis, H. Wang, B. Gray and S. I. Chan, Spectroelectrochemical study of cytochrome $\underline{c}$ oxidase, J. Biol. Chem. 261:11524 (1986).
9. B. Malmström, Cytochrome $\underline{c}$ oxidase as a proton pump. A transition-state mechanism, Biochim. Biophys. Acta 811:1 (1985).

10. M. E. Dockter, A. Steinmann and G. Schatz, Mapping of yeast cytochrome c oxidase by fluorescence resonance energy transfer, J. Biol. Chem. 253:311 (1978).

11. T. Alleyne and M. T. Wilson, Conformational changes in cytochrome c oxidase, Biochem. Soc. Trans., in press.

12. Th. Förester, In: Fluorescenz organischer Verbindungen", Vandenhoeck and Ruprecht, Göttingen (1951).

13. L. C. Dickinson and J. C. W. Chien, Cobalt-cytochrome c. I. Preparation, properties and enzymic activity, Biochemistry 14:3526 (1975).

14. J. M. Vanderkooi and M. Erencińska, Cytochrome c interaction with membrane, Eur. J. Biochem. 60:199 (1975).

15. T. Yonetani, Studies on cytochrome oxidase, I., J. Biol. Chem. 235:845 (1960).

16. K. J. Van Buuren, P. F. Zuurendonk, B. F. Van Gelder and A. O. Muitsers, Biochemical and biophysical studies on cytochrome aa_3. V. Binding of cyanide to cytochrome aa_3. Biochim. Biophys. Acta 256:243 (1972).

17. I. Puettner, E. Carafoli and F. Malatesta, Spectroscopic and functional properties of subunit III-depleted cytochrome oxidase, J. Biol. Chem. 260:3719 (1985).

18. J. M. Vanderkooi, R. Landesberg, G. W. Hayden and C. S. Owen, Metal-free and metal-substituted cytochromes c. Use in characterization of the cytochrome c binding site, Eur. J. Biochem. 81:339 (1977).

19. J. M. Vanderkooi and M. Ericińska, Metallocytochromes c; characterization of electronic absorption and emission spectra, Eur. J. Biochem. 64:381 (1976).

20. J. A. Kornblatt and H. A. Luu, The interactions of cytochrome c and porphyrin cytochrome c with cytochrome c oxidase, Eur. J. Biochem. 159:407 (1986).

21. J. Gelles and S. I. Chan, Chemical modification of the Cu_A centre in cytochrome c oxidase by p-(hydroxymercuri) benzoate. Biochemistry 24:3963 (1985).

IX. PROTON-MOTIVE ACTIVITY

PROTONMOTIVE ACTIVITY OF THE CYTOCHROME CHAIN OF MITOCHONDRIA: MODELS AND

FEATURES

Sergio Papa and Nazzareno Capitanio

Institute of Medical Biochemistry and Chemistry

University of Bari, Bari, Italy

INTRODUCTION

Any model proposed to explain the mechanism of protonmotive redox systems has to cope with a minimum number of basic requirements(1): (i) the electron transfer process must be compulsorily coupled to transmembrane proton translocation. To achieve this:(ii) the redox centre has to alternate between electron input and output modes; (iii) protolytic group(s) has (have) to alternate (simultaneously to ii) between exposure with the N (protonic input) and P (protonic output) phases. The redox and protolytic input and output states may be merged together, with electrons and protons flowing combined as hydrogen atoms, conducted by diffusible hydrogen carriers. This is what predicts, in fact, the direct ligand conduction mechanism of chemiosmotic coupling of Mitchell (2-4). Electrons and protons may however, follow different pathways, the two processes being indirectly coupled by cooperative transitions in the enzyme. In this case the redox process could be thermodynamically linked to the protolytic process as proposed by Papa (5,6).

Indirect coupling could result in some loss of the energy provided by driving redox reactions (6) (molecular slipping, 7,8), unless conditions are met which make the rate of the transitions of the redox centre between the input and output states negligible when the protolytic center is unprotonated (1,9). Although it is generally conceded that in indirect mechanisms thermodynamic coupling (redox Bohr effects) can optimize energy conversion, this is not an absolute requirement (8,9). It is proposed that efficient coupling could also be provided by kinetic linkage (9) or gating of electron flow (8,10).

It should, at any event, be appreciated that direct ligand conduction and indirect co-operative mechanisms don't, necessarily, represent natural alternatives. Our group is working on the hypothesis that the protonmotive activity of respiratory chains derives from combination of vectorial protolytic redox reactions at the catalytic centers and co-operative proton transfer by proteins in the enzymes (11-13).

TABLE 1

DIRECT LIGAND CONDUCTION	INDIRECT (CO-OPERATIVE) H^+/e^- LINKAGE
Linear redox loops (Mitchell,1961)	
	Vectorial Bohr mechanism (Papa,1973) (thermodynamic coupling)
Quinone cycle (Mitchell,1975)	
	Proton pump of cytochrome oxidase (Wikström, 1977)
	Q-gated proton pump (Papa,1979)
	b cycle (Wikström, 1980)
Semiquinone cycle (Wikström,1984)	
	Transition state mechanism (kinetic linkage:Malmström,1985) (electron gating:Blair et al.,1986; Malmström, 1987)
Oxygen cycle (Mitchell,1985)	

Models

Table 1 lists the models so far proposed for protonmotive redox systems. Mitchell (2,4) developed in the sixties the linear redox-loop model for quinol oxidase, but was later led, by experimental observations produced in the seventies, to change this model into a cyclic protonmotive redox system, the Q cycle (3). The Q cycle explains the H^+/e^- stoicheiometry of quinol cytochrome c reductase which is two (15,16), and not 1 as predicted by the linear loop, as well as peculiar features of b cytochromes (3). At the same time Papa et al.(5,6) emphasized co-operative proton-electron linkage in cytochrome c reductase based on redox Bohr effects in b cytochromes (vectorial Bohr mechanism) (6). Other co-operative proton pump models were later developed by Wikström et al. (17) for cytochrome c oxidase and cytochrome c reductase (the b cycle) (see also Von Jagow et al., 18). Whilst other indirect models were more recently developed, like the kinetic linkage model (9) and gating of electron flow (8,10), our group proposed a mechanism, (Q-gated proton pump) (11-13,19), where indirect protolytic events of special quinone molecules in the cytochrome c reductase are combined in series with co-operative proton transfer in the proteins (redox Bohr effects).

Wikström et al., (20) moved, on the other hand, from the co-operative b cycle to a semiquinone cycle, which is essentially a direct type of mechanism. It may be noted that in the Q-cycle, the semiquinone cycle and the Q-gated proton pump, special protein bound quinone molecules and proton conducting wells represent essential elements for all of them, the differences residing in the details of the electron transfer pathways,cyclic in the first two models (rapid exchange of bound with free quinone molecules) and branched in the third one (negligible quinone exchange) and in the role attributed by the last to co-operative events.

724

Actual features of protonmotive activity

Quinone and semiquinone cycles have been discussed at length elwewhere (3,20-24) and by other authors in this volume (25-28). The basic elements and actual features of the Q-gated proton pump are described in accompanying papers by our group (29-31). We shall, thus, dwell here on the protonmotive activity of cytochrome c oxidase.

Reduction of O_2 to H_2O in the oxidase is organized anisotropically in the membrane so to result directly in the generation of transmembrane $\Delta\mu H^+$ with effective translocation of $1q^+/e^-$ from the inner side (where protons are taken up in the formation of H_2O) to the outer side of the osmotic barrier (1,2,6). This is a direct and general attribute of all the oxidases so far described (13,20). It is generally thought that eukaryotic and some prokaryotic oxidases are, in addition, capable to couple electron flow with electrogenic proton pumping from the N to the P side (1,20). Wikström et al.(20) and others (32,33) maintain that cytochrome oxidase pumps one H^+ per e^- (the overall process will thus result in the effective translocation of $2q^+/e^-$ from N to P). Mitchell after having refused for a long time a proton pumping activity of cytochrome oxidase, has now come to the same conclusion (4).

Our group has carried out in the last years a systematic study of the protonmotive activity of cytochrome oxidase (13,34-38). In this work previous observations from other laboratories on redox-linked proton ejection accompanying electron flow in cytochrome oxidase were confirmed and extended. Our investigations identified, however, conditions where no significant proton pumping is exhibited by cytochrome oxidase either in the mitochondrial membrane (34-36) or in the oxidase reconstituted in liposomes (37-38). Furthermore observations were obtained (see also 39) indicating that in certain cases vectorial and/or scalar processes other than proton pumping by the oxidases can, at least in part, if not entirely,account for the observed proton ejection accompanying electron flow in cytochrome c oxidase(13,34). This led us to think that the observed redox-linked proton ejection did not, in fact, represent physiological proton pumping activity of cytochrome oxidase. Although the implications of negative observations (13,39,40) may have been overemphasized, the fact remains that redox-linked proton translocation in cytochrome oxidase results experimentally to be widely variable.

Determination of the H^+/e^- stoicheiometry based on accurate spectrophotometric measurement of the rate of oxygen consumption (with hemoglobin) and proton release have produced with succinate pulses of aerobic mitochondria H^+/O ratios of 4 (35,36). The same $H^+/2e^-$ ratio is obtained when electron flow is limited from succinate (or quinol) to cytochrome c (13,20,36). Pulses of aerobic mitochondria with artificial reductants of cytochrome c give proton ejection with apparent $H^+/2e^-$ ratios as high as 1.6, 1.8(1, 34,36). Evidence was, however, produced that this proton ejection derives,at least in part, from residual re-reduction by hydrogenated donors of the oxidized forms of the artificial reductants used (35,36; see also 39,40). More recent experiments on oxygen pulses of anaerobic mitochondria have produced $H^+/2e^-$ ratios around 4.6 with succinate and around 1.4 with TMPD plus ascorbate (41,42). In the latter case it was, further, observed that the $H^+/2e^-$ ratio went down when the rate of electron flow was limited by TMPD concentration (41,42).

Investigations on isolated bovine cytochrome oxidase incorporated in liposomes have shown that the H^+/e^- stoicheiometry for redox-linked proton ejection varies considerably under the influence of modalities of activation of electron flow, pH of the medium, presence of divalent cations (Mg^{2+} or Ca^{2+}) (37,38).

All the above shows that the protonmotive activity of the oxidase can be modulated by a variety of factors which include: (i) the rate at which electrons are delivered to the oxidase by natural and artificial reductants (see also 43); (ii) the mechanism by which cytochrome c interacts with the oxidase; (iii) the actual $\Delta\mu H^+$ established across the membrane (see also 44); (iv) the functional state of the enzyme (monomer-dimer equilibrium) (1,47,48).

An important contribution towards elucidation of the mechanism of a protonmotive redox system is represented by identification of the individual redox steps which are under influence of the $\Delta\psi$ and ΔpH components of the protonmotive force. We have extended this exploration, already performed for cytochrome c reductase (19), to cytochrome oxidase (see also 49). In these experiments aerobic cytochrome oxidase vesicles were supplemented with cytochrome c, TMPD and ascorbate so that a respiring steady-state was established. Under these conditions in a few seconds the oxidase had gone through many turnovers and is conceivably all in the functional pulsed state (45). The steady-state redox levels of cytochrome c at 550-540 nm and that of cytochrome a + a_3 at 605-630 and 443-470 nm were continuously monitored with a dual wavelength spectrophotometer.

From the reported relative contributions of hemes a and a_3 to the overall absorbance changes at two wavelength couples (50), the specific redox changes of the two hemes throughout the observation time was estimated (see 50)(Fig.1). The addition of the reductants to the oxidized enzyme resulted in 60% reduction of cytochrome c. Heme a was rapidly reduced up to 50% whilst heme a_3 was reduced to around 10%. $\Delta\psi$ collapse by valinomycin caused substantial oxidation of cytochrome c. This was accompanied, during the interval in which $\Delta\psi$ was expected to be replaced by extra ΔpH, by reduction of heme a to around 70% and some oxidation of heme a_3. Further ΔpH collapse by nigericin caused definite oxidation of cytochrome c and even larger oxidation of heme a.

When the order of the addition of the two ionophores was reversed, nigericin, added in the absence of valinomycin, caused oxidation of heme a with practically no change of cytochrome c and heme a_3. Collapse of $\Delta\psi$ by further addition of valinomycin resulted in large oxidation of cytochrome c but small, if any, oxidation of heme a (there was no detectable change of heme a_3).

In Fig.2 the dependence on the pH of the suspending medium of the crossover effects exerted by valinomycin and nigericin on the steady-state redox levels of cytochromes in oxidase vesicles is shown. There are a number of points which emerge from these experiments. (i) The extra-reduction of heme a induced by the internal extra alkalinization produced by collapse of $\Delta\psi$ by valinomycin, which was accompanied by some oxidation of heme a_3 (it should always be kept in mind that the redox changes expected for a_3 are very small since this center is always almost completely oxidized in the presence of oxygen), increased markedly with pH. The same increase with pH was observed for the extent of oxidation induced by the subsequent addition of nigericin in the presence of valinomycin. No significant pH dependence

726

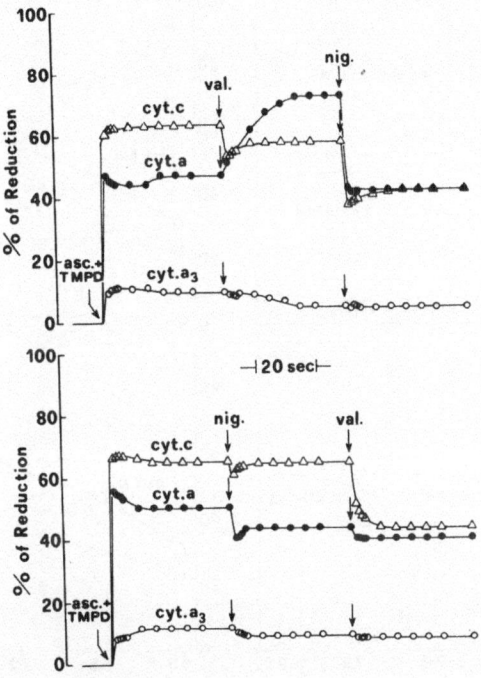

Fig.1. Redox transitions of cytochromes c , a and a_3 caused by
ionophores in steady-state respiring cytochrome c oxidase
vesicles. 1 μM cytochrome oxidase vesicles were suspended
in   180 mM sucrose, 20 mM KCl, 20 mM K-Hepes, pH 7.5 in
the presence of 1 μM cytochrome c. Where indicated 10 mM
ascorbate plus 0.2 mM TMPD, 2 μg/ml valinomycin, 2 μg/ml
nigericin were added. Specific redox levels of hemes a
and a_3 were calculated from the spectrophotometric traces.
For the estimation of the relative reduction levels of
hemes a and a_3 (51) a relative contribution of heme a of
72.5% and 35% at 605-630 and 443-470 respectively was
taken (see ref.50).

was, on the other hand, observed in the redox changes of cytochromes observed when nigericin was added before valinomycin. In other words the presence of Δψ obscured a pH dependence which seems to apply to the crossover effect exerted by internal alkalinization on electron flow from heme a to a_3.
As far as cytochrome c is concerned its steady-state reduction level which

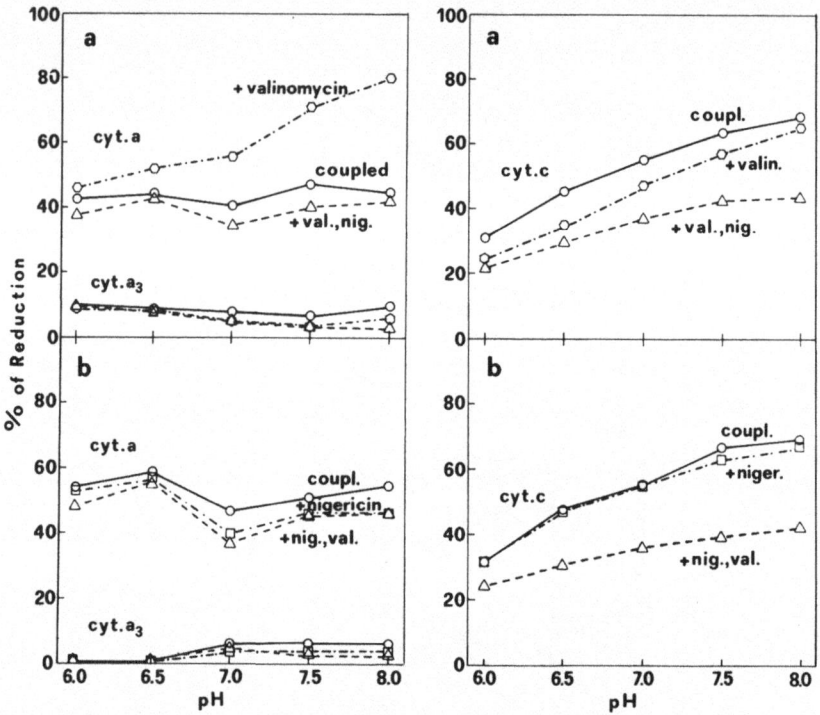

Fig.2. pH-Dependence of the steady-state redox levels of cytochromes c,a,a₃ in respiring cytochrome oxidase vesicles.
The experimental conditions were the same of Fig.1 with
the only exception of Hepes substitution with MES in the
suspending medium at pH.s 6.0 and 6.5. The values reported in panels a and b are means of two different sets
of experiments.

was primarily under the control of $\Delta\psi$ increased with pH in all the conditions examined.

It seems possible to conclude from these experiments that transmembrane
$\Delta\psi$ exerts a prominent crossover effect on electron flow from cytochrome c
to heme a. There is, on the other hand, very little if any control by $\Delta\psi$
on internal electron flow from heme a to heme a_3. These observations seem
among other things, to agree with the reported topology of cytochrome c
and hemes a and a_3 in the mitochondrial membrane (1,52). The internal alkalinization generated by respiration and magnified by $\Delta\psi$ collapse with valinomycin, clearly exerts a dramatic crossover effect between heme a and a_3.
Proton availability in the N phase doesn't, on the other hand, seem to be
rate limiting for the reaction of reduced a_3 center with O_2.

In respiring soluble cytochrome oxidase (Fig.3) the reduction level
of heme a was higher than that of cytochrome c and much higher than that of
heme a_3. The reduction levels of heme a and cytochrome c both increased
with pH. These observations together with those obtained in the reconstituted oxidase show that the rate of internal electron flow in the oxidase
from heme a to heme a_3 is a rate limiting step. It seems that, more than

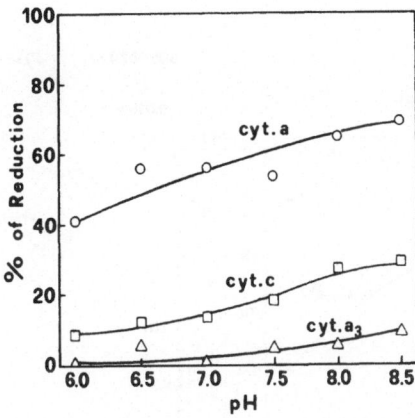

Fig.3. pH-Dependence of steady-state redox levels of cytochromes
c,a,a₃ in respiring soluble cytochrome oxidase.
1 µM soluble cytochrome oxidase was suspended in the same
media used for the vesicles experiments, supplemented with
0.5% TWEEN 80.

transmembrane ΔpH, it is the actual pH seen by sites in the oxidase, exposed
to protonic equilibration with the N side, to control the rate of electron
flow from heme a to heme a_3 center.

The data collected in Fig.4 compare the pH dependence of the crossover
effect exerted on heme a by specific collapse of ΔpH, with that of the
steady-state III respiration and the H^+/e^- stoicheiometry of proton ejection
elicited by reductant pulses in cytochrome oxidase vesicles. The extent of
oxidation of heme a induced by nigericin and the H^+/e^- stoicheiometry both
increased with pH from 6.0 to 7.7. State III respiration, on the contrary,
declined sharply in the same pH range. Fig.4 shows also the pH dependence
of redox Bohr effects of heme a (i.e. the equivalents of H^+ released <u>per</u>
heme a oxidized) (53). The H^+/e^- coupling number varied with pH (as, in
fact, expected from the observed pH dependence of E_m of heme a) (54,55)
reaching a maximum value of about 0.6 at pH around 7.7. The pH dependence
of the H^+/e^- coupling number of heme a resembled that of other functions
of the oxidase (see Fig.4 panel a). Comparison of the experimental curve
for the pH dependence of Bohr effects of heme a with theoretical curves indicated that the observed pH-dependence could be attributed to two acidic
groups with $pK_{1_{ox}}$=6.3, $pK_{2_{ox}}$=7.3, $pK_{1_{red}}$=7, $pK_{2_{red}}$=8.3

CONCLUSIONS

The present observations show that pH, apparently that of the aqueous
N phase (in protonic contact with the site of dioxygen reduction to water)
(6), effects a rate limiting step in intramolecular electron flow from heme
a to heme a_3 center (cf. 56). This pH effect may involve redox Bohr effects
of heme a, which appear also to exchange protons in the N phase (54). It is
possible that, in addition to the effect exerted by the actual pH in the N
phase, also the osmotic force represented by transmembrane ΔpH may exert

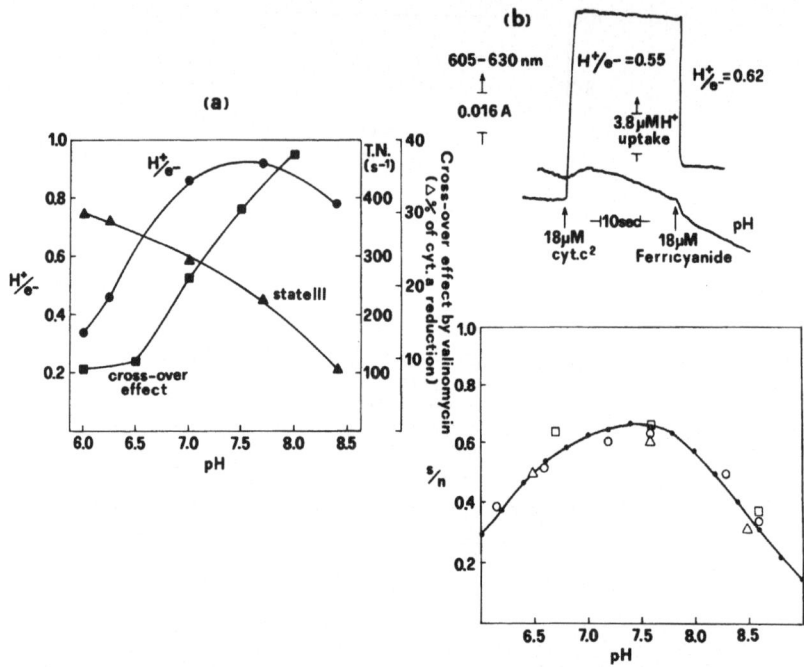

Fig.4. pH-Dependence of redox and protonmotive functions of bovine
cytochrome oxidase. a)pH-dependence in cytochrome oxidase
vesicles of H^+/e^- stoicheiometry of redox-linked proton
ejection (elicited by ferrocytochrome c pulse),steady-state
III respiration given as T.N.(s^{-1}) (for experimental conditions see 38) and crossover effect exerted on heme a by vali
nomycin in respiring oxidase vesicles (for details see also
Fig.1); b)pH-dependence of redox Bohr effects of heme a (H^+/
e^-, s/n coupling number). 10 µM soluble cytochrome oxidase
was suspended in 150 mM KCl and incubated overnight with 2
mM KCN; cycles of reduction and oxidation of heme a were
effected in the same medium by successive additions of ferro
cytochrome c and ferricyanide, see upper part of panel; pH
changes were followed electrometrically on the same sample.
The lower part of the panel shows the results of three different experiments.

control on electron flow from heme a to heme a_3. With these characteristics
the electron transfer steps between heme a ($+Cu_A$) to heme a_3 ($+Cu_B$) would
qualify as a site for redox-linked proton pumping in the oxidase (1,8-10).
Since this step seems to be scarcely affected if at all by transmembrane
$\Delta\psi$,electron and proton transfer may be merged closely together.
    It is conceivable that further experiments along these lines would
help to better understand the role of thermodynamic coupling in heme a (redox Bohr effects) in control of electron flow and protonmotive activity.
The observed variability in the H^+/e^- ratio reveals an interesting characteristic to be explored in attempting to define the molecular mechanism and
physiological relevance on the protonmotive activity of cytochrome c oxidase.

REFERENCES

1. M.Wikström, K.Krab and M.Saraste in:"Cytochrome oxidase, a Synthesis"
    pp.142-173, Academic Press, New York (1981)
2. P.Mitchell,"Chemiosmotic coupling in oxidative and photosynthetic phos-
    phorylation" Glynn Research Bodmin, (1966)
3. P.Mitchell, J.Theor.Biol.62:327 (1976)
4. P.Mitchell, R.Mitchell, J.Moody, I.West, H.Baum and J.Wrigglesworth
    FEBS Lett.188:1-7 (1985)
5. S.Papa, F.Guerrieri, M.Lorusso and S.Simone, Biochimie 55:703 (1973)
6. S.Papa, Biochim.Biophys.Acta, 456:39 (1976)
7. P.Pietrobon, M.Zoratti and G.F.Azzone, Biochim.Biophys.Acta 723:317 (1983)
8. D.F.Blair, J.Gelles and S.I.Chan, Biophys.J. 50:713-733 (1986)
9. B.G.Malmström, Biochim.Biophys.Acta 811:1-12 (1985)
10. B.G.Malmström, This Volume (1987)
11. S.Papa, in "Membranes and Transport", A.N.Martonosi, ed.,Vol.1, pp.363-
    368, Plenum, N.Y. (1982)
12. S.Papa, J.Bioenerg.Biomembr.14:69, (1982)
13. S.Papa and M.Lorusso,in: "Biomembranes", R.M.Burton et al.eds.,pp.257-
    290, Plenum Publ.Co. N.Y., (1984)
14. P.Mitchell, Nature 191:144-147 (1961)
15. S.Papa, M.Lorusso and F.Guerrieri, Biohcim.Biophys.Acta 387:425 (1975)
16. H.G.Lawford and P.B.Garland, Biochem.J. 136:711 (1973)
17. M.Wikström and K.Krab, Curr.Top.Bioenerg.10:51 (1980)
18. G.Von Jagow and W.D.Engel, FEBS Lett.111:1-5 (1979)
19. S.Papa, M.Lorusso, D.Boffoli and E.Bellomo,Eur.J.Biochem.137:405-412(1983)
20. M.Wikström and M.Saraste, in:"Bioenergetics", L.Ernster, ed.,pp.49-94,
    Elsevier, Sc.Publ.Amsterdam (1984)
21. P.R.Rich, J.Bioenerg.Biomembr.18:145-156 (1986)
22. G.Von Jagow, I.A.Link and T.Ohnishi, J.Bioenerg.Biomembr.18:157-180 (1986)
23. S.De Vries, J.Bioenerg.Biomembr.18:195-224 (1986)
24. J.S.Rieske, J.Bioenerg.Biomembr.18:235-257 (1986)
25. S. De Vries, A.N.Van Hoek, A.L.Bookum and J.A.Berden, this Volume (1987)
26. A.A.Konstantinov and E.Popova, this Volume (1987)
27. J.A.Berden, A.N.Van Hoek, S.De Vries and P.J.Shoppink, this Volume(1987)
28. P.R.Rich, this Volume (1987)
29. M.Lorusso, D.Boffoli, T.Cocco, D.Gatti and S.Papa, this Volume (1987)
30. T.Cocco, S.Meinhardt, D.Gatti, M.Lorusso, T.Ohnishi and S.Papa, this
    Volume (1987)
31. D.Boffoli, M.Lorusso, and S.Papa, this Volume (1987)
32. P.R.Casey and A.Azzi, FEBS Lett.154:237-242 (1983)
33. E.Sigel and E.Carafoli, Eur.J.Biochem.111:299-306 (1980)
34. M.Lorusso, F.Capuano, D.Boffoli, R.Stefanelli and S.Papa, Biochem.J.
    182:133-147 (1979)
35. S.Papa, F.Capuano, M.Markert and N.Altamura,FEBS Lett.111:243 (1980)
36. S.Papa, F.Guerrieri, M.Lorusso, G.Izzo, D.Boffoli, F.Capuano, N.Capi-
    tanio and N.Altamura, Biochem.J. 192:203 (1980)
37. S.Papa, M.Lorusso, N.Capitanio and E.De Nitto, FEBS Lett.157:7 (1983)
38. S.Papa, N.Capitanio and E.De Nitto, Eur.J.Biochem.164:507-516 (1987)
39. J.Moyle and P.Mitchell, FEBS Lett.88:268 (1978)
40. P.Mitchell, Ann.N.Y.Acad.Sci.341:564-584 (1980)
41. S.Papa,N.Capitanio,G.Izzo and E.De Nitto in "Advances in Membrane Bio-

energetics" C.H.Kim ed., Plenum Press, N.Y., in press.

42. N.Capitanio, E.De Nitto and S.Papa, this Volume (1987)

43. G.Proteau, J.M.Wrigglesworth and P.Nicholls, Biochem.J. 210:199-205 (1983)

44. M.Brunori, P.Sarti, A.Colosimo, G.Antonini, F.Malatesta, M.G.Jones and M.T.Wilson, EMBO J. Vol.4 n.9:2365-2368 (1985)

45. M.Brunori, A.Colosimo, G.Rainoni, T.Wilson and E.Antonini, J.Biol.Chem. Vol.254, 21:10769-10775 (1979)

46. M.T.Wilson, J.Peterson, E.Antonini, M.Brunori, A.Colosimo and J.Wyman Proc.Natl.Acad.Sci.USA vol.78, 11:7115-7118 (1981)

47. Finel, M. and M.Wikström, Biochim.Biophys.Acta 851:99-108 (1986)

48. D. Richard, A.Lehninger, M.Brunori, J.Bonaventura, and C.Bonaventura J. of Inorg.Biochem.23:365-372 (1985)

49. P.Moroney, T.A.Scholes and P.C.Hinckle, Biochemistry 23:4991-4997 (1984)

50. F.D.Blair, R.W.Ellis, H.Wang, H.B.Gray and S.I.Chan, J.Biol.Chem.261: 11524-11537 (1986)

51. S.Papa, M.Lorusso, G.Izzo, and F.Capuano, Biochm.J. 194:395-406 (1981)

52. T.Ohnishi, R.Lo Brutto, J.C.Salerno, R.C.Bruckner and I.G.Frey, J.Biol. Chem.257:1481-14825 (1982)

53. S.Papa, F.Guerrieri and G.Izzo, Method.Enzymol.Vol.126:331-343 (1986)

54. A.A.Konstantinov, T.Vygodina and I.M.Andreev, FEBS Lett.202:229-234 (1986)

55. T.Penttila and M.Wikström, in:"Vectorial Reactions in Electron and Ion Transport in Mitochondria and Bacteria" F.Palmieri er al.eds.,Elsevier/North Holland Biomedical Press. (1981)

56. P.E.Thörnström, B.Soussi, L.Arvidsson and B.G.Malmström, Chem.Scripta 24:230-235 (1984).

THE MECHANISM OF ELECTRON GATING IN CYTOCHROME c OXIDASE

Bo G. Malmström

Department of Biochemistry and Biophysics
University of Göteborg and Chalmers University of Technology
S-412 96 Göteborg (Sweden)

INTRODUCTION

Cytochrome c oxidase is an electron-transport-driven proton pump.[1,2] The operation of such a pump requires transitions between two different conformational states, which provide an alternating access of the proton-translocating group to the two sides of the membrane. In order to couple the electron-transfer reaction to the proton translocation, it is also necessary that the reduction and subsequent reoxidation of a redox center in the pump take place in different conformations. Such electron gating must be based on a structural control of the rate of electron transfer into and out of the pump redox site.[3]

The mechanism of electron gating must be approached within the framework of electron-transfer theory.[4] The rate of an electron-transfer reaction is strongly dependent on the driving force, i.e. the difference in the reduction potentials between the electron donor and acceptor. The reduction potential of cytochrome a is 0.285 V in the fully oxidized enzyme but drops to 0.220 V when cytochrome a_3 is reduced.[5] As the distance between these two redox centers is at least 12 Å,[6,7] this suggests a conformational control of the driving force for electron-transfer between them.

Another important factor controlling the electron-transfer rate is the reorganizational barrier associated with differences in structure between the oxidized and reduced states of the redox sites. On this basis, Blair

733

et al.[3,8] have argued for a mechanism of electron gating involving protonation-linked changes in the coordination of Cu_A. In this communica-cation I will review recent results from my own laboratory which provide strong evidence against such a mechanism. Instead they favor a more indirect control in which reduction of cytochrome a and Cu_A, followed by protonation, leads to a conformational transition that changes the structure of the electron acceptor, the cytochrome a_3-Cu_B pair.

THE CATALYTIC REACTION

In any ion pump, the energy necessary for ion translocation is provided by a catalytic reaction associated with considerable exergonicity.[2,9] In the case of cytochrome oxidase, this is the electron transfer from ferrocytochrome c to dioxygen, **via** the oxidase redox centers, cytochrome a, Cu_A and the cytochrome a_3-Cu_B unit.

The Electron-Transfer Sequence

A variety of observed kinetic properties of cytochrome oxidase can be described on the basis of a simple catalytic cycle.[10,11] In formulating this kinetic model, I use E(0000) to designate the fully oxidized enzyme, the zeros representing oxidized cytochrome a, Cu_A, Cu_B and cytochrome a_3 in that order. Reduction of a given redox center is shown by a change to the digit 1; E(0100), for example, represents a molecule with Cu_A reduced and all other centers oxidized. In these terms, the reaction cycle can be written:

$$E(0000) + c^{2+} \rightleftharpoons E(1000)\text{-}c^{3+} \rightleftharpoons E(1000) + c^{3+} \qquad (1)$$

$$E(1000) \rightleftharpoons E(0100) \qquad (2)$$

$$E(0100) + c^{2+} \rightleftharpoons E(1100)\text{-}c^{3+} \rightleftharpoons E(1100) + c^{3+} \qquad (3)$$

$$E(1100) \rightleftharpoons E(0011) \qquad (4)$$

$$E(0011) \xrightarrow{O_2} E(0000) \qquad (5)$$

To obtain the complete catalytic cycle, this reaction sequence is repeated with the difference that oxygen intermediates are bound at the cytochrome a_3-Cu_B site.

It has been shown[11] that this cycle can be used to simulate the time course of the redox changes in cytochrome c and cytochrome a in transient kinetics experiments with ferrocytochrome c as the only reducing substrate. Almost identical cycles have also been used[12,13] to describe the approach to the steady state and the steady-state reduction levels of cytochrome c and a in experiments with ascorbate and a redox mediator.

Essential features of the kinetic model are: 1. all electrons from ferrocytochrome c are donated to cytochrome a, which is in redox equilibrium with Cu_A; 2. internal electron transfer to the cytochrome a_3-Cu_B unit is possible in E(1100) only and not in E(1000) or E(0100), i.e. both cytochrome a and Cu_A must be reduced for this reaction to occur. Both features are required to account for the overshoot observed[12] in the approach to the steady-state reduction level of cytochrome a. The second feature is also supported by experiments[14,15] demonstrating that cytochrome a in E(1000) cannot be oxidized by O_2.

The Rate-Limiting Step

It might be expected that the redox change involved in electron gating limits the rate of the overall reaction, as this step should have a considerable reorganizational barrier. Consequently, it becomes important to identify the rate-limiting step in the reaction cycle.

Claims[16,17] that the dissociation of ferricytochrome c from the enzyme-product complex is rate-limiting can be disproved by a variety of experimental observations. First, this would have the result that the oxidation of cytochrome c at high concentrations would be zero order,[18] but it has long been known that it is first order at all concentrations of cytochrome c.[19,20] Second, it is not consistent with the fact that the primary electron acceptor, cytochrome a, is partially reduced during turnover. Instead the simulations of kinetic results already quoted[11-13] provide strong evidence for the internal electron transfer in step 4 as the rate-limiting reaction. Thus, the proton pump may be associated with both cytochrome a and Cu_A.

The reaction cycle described by equations 1-5 is obviously incomplete in at least two regards. First, it does not include two conformational states, E_1 and E_2, as required in the reaction sequence of any enzyme which is an ion pump and as also indicated by the nonhyperbolic nature of the steady-state rate equation.[21] Second, it lacks protonation-deprotonation steps, which are necessary not only for proton pumping but also to account for the strong dependence of $\underline{k}_{cat}$ on pH, as observed in steady-state experiments.[22,23] On the basis of recent unpublished experiments carried out by P. Brzezinski and P.-E. Thörnström in my laboratory, I would like to suggest that step 4 in the cycle represents a sum of the following sequence of reactions:

$$E_1(1100) + 2H^+ \rightleftharpoons E_1(H^+)_2(1100) \tag{6}$$

$$E_1(H^+)_2(1100) \rightleftharpoons E_2(H^+)_2(1100) \tag{7}$$

$$E_2(H^+)_2(1100) \rightleftharpoons E_2(1100) + 2H^+ \tag{8}$$

$$E_2(1100) \rightleftharpoons E_2(0011) \tag{9}$$

In this sequence it is the conformational change in step 7 rather than the electron transfer **per se** (step 9) which limits the rate of the overall reaction. Step 9 should more correctly be written as two consecutive one-electron transfers, but as both are rapid compared to step 7, they have been combined.

Evidence for this model has been derived from flash photolysis experiments with the mixed valence oxidase,[24] which can be written $E_2(0011)$-CO. Photodissociation of the bound CO initiates the following reaction sequence:

$$E_2(0011) \rightleftharpoons E_2(01[01,10]) \tag{10}$$

$$E_2(01[01,10]) \rightleftharpoons E_2(1100) \tag{11}$$

The designation [01,10] is used because there is a rapid redox equilibrium between cytochrome $\underline{a}_3$ and Cu_B in the one-electron reduced site, so that it is not possible to specify which center donates the electron in reactions 10 and 11.

Reaction 10 has earlier been observed by Boelens et al.,[25] but we have shown in addition that its equilibrium and rate constants are independent of pH, which is consistent with the suggestion that the deprotonation step (reaction 8) precedes the electron transfer. From the equilibrium constants for reactions 10 and 11 it can be estimated that the difference in reduction potentials between cytochrome $\underline{a}_3$ and cytochrome $\underline{a}$ is 0.12 V. This provides evidence for the claim that the enzyme is in the E_2 conformation, as the two cytochromes have the same potential in the E_1 state.[5,21]

The equilibrium and rate constants for reaction 10 is essentially independent of temperature. Electron-transfer theory[4] suggests that a temperature-independent rate may be obtained if the enthalpy change associated with electron transfer is close to zero and there is no reorganizational barrier. Thus, I would like to suggest that the transition $E_1 \longrightarrow E_2$ involves a structural change which removes the reorganizational barrier for the internal electron transfer (reaction 9). This is consistent with the high rate constant $(1.4 \times 10^4 \text{ s}^{-1})$ found for the back reaction in equilibrium 10, which corresponds to the oxidation of Cu_A in the normal catalytic cycle.

The high rate for the internal electron transfer in the mixed-valence enzyme excludes electron gating by a change in the coordination of Cu_A,[3,8] as Cu_A has the same EPR spectrum in this state as in the fully oxidized enzyme.[24,26] Instead I would like to propose that the reorganizational barrier is located in the cytochrome $\underline{a}_3$-Cu_B site. In the oxidized enzyme the Cu-Fe distance in this site is 3.0-3.5 Å,[27,28] but this must increase to about 5 Å on reduction[29] to be able to accomodate dioxygen as a μ-oxo bridge. As our results show that the barrier is absent in the E_2 state, it appears that reduction of both cytochrome $\underline{a}$ and Cu_A leads to a structural change which, in an allosteric fashion, is transmitted to the cytochrome $\underline{a}_3$-Cu_B site, changing the metal-metal distance. As this site in the oxidized state now has the same structure as it should have in the reduced state, there is no barrier for the electron transfer.

The mechanism for electron gating just described is supported by studies of the transition between a closed and an open form, observed in the

reactions with cyanide.[30,31] The closed form, which binds cyanide very
slowly, is converted to the rapidly reacting, open form on reduction of
cytochrome $\underline{a}$ and Cu_A. Just as in the case of electron transfer, **both** of
these redox centers must be reduced to trigger the transition to the open
form.[32] Since cyanide binds to oxidized cytochrome $\underline{a}_3$, it is obvious that
reduction of cytochrome $\underline{a}$ and Cu_A leads to a structural change in the
oxidized cytochrome $\underline{a}_3$-Cu_B site, as in the proposed electron-gating
mechanism.

It is often assumed that the mechanism of a proton pump involves a
thermodynamic linkage between oxidoreduction and protolysis,[2] i.e. the $p\underline{K}_a$
of the acid-base group of the pump is higher in the E_1 than in the E_2 conformation. It can be shown,[2,3] however, that this is not an obligatory
requirement. In the transition-state mechanism formulated by me,[2] the acid-
base group has a low $p\underline{K}_a$ in both the E_1 and the E_2 state. If the transition
between these states is rapid only when the acid-base group is protonated
(reaction 7), this will lead to proton pumping provided that there is enough
driving force for the overall reaction. It can be shown[33] that such a
mechanism, but not a $p\underline{K}_a$-controlled one, is consistant with the observa-
tion[23] that $\underline{k}_{cat}$ increases with decreasing pH whereas $\underline{k}_{cat}/\underline{K}_m$ is independent
of pH.

CONCLUDING REMARKS

The usual view[1] that cytochrome $\underline{a}$ constitutes the pump element in cytochrome oxidase has recently been questioned by Blair et al.,[3,8] who instead
favor that Cu_A plays this role. The results summarized in this paper
suggest that, in fact, both these redox center function in the pump
mechanism in a cooperative fashion, in the sense that both must be reduced
to effect the transition from the E_1 to the E_2 conformation.

The reason that Blair et al.[3,8] propose that Cu_A is the pump element is
the contention that it, but not cytochrome $\underline{a}$, is likely to undergo a
structural change on reduction. They assume a direct coupling in which the
redox center is also the proton-binding group. Thus, they postulate that a
ligand on Cu_A dissociates on reduction and binds a proton. They furthermore
suggest that only in this state can there be a rapid electron transfer to
the cytochrome $\underline{a}_3$-Cu_B site. Such a mechanism of electron gating is, however, made unlikely by our demonstration that there is a very rapid redox

equilibrium between cytochrome a_3 and Cu_A in a state in which oxidized Cu_A has a normal EPR signal. In my opinion the gating mechanism is more indirect in that the cytochrome a_3-Cu_B unit has different structures in the E_1 and E_2 states. Only in the E_2 state is rapid electron transfer possible, but the transition from E_1 to this state requires reduction of both cytochrome a and Cu_A as well as protonation of the proton-translocating group.

ACKNOWLEDGEMENTS

This investigation has been supported by the Swedish Natural Science Research Council. I wish to acknowledge very helpful discussions with Professors H.B. Gray and R.A. Marcus.

REFERENCES

1. M. Wikström, K. Krab, and M. Saraste, "Cytochrome Oxidase: A Synthesis", Academic Press, London (1981).

2. B. G. Malmström, Cytochrome c Oxidase as a Proton Pump. A Transition-State Mechanism, Biochim. Biophys. Acta 811:1 (1985).

3. D. F. Blair, J. Gelles, and S. I. Chan, Redox-Linked Proton Translocation in Cytochrome Oxidase: The Importance of Gating Electron Flow, Biophys. J. 50:713 (1986).

4. R. A. Marcus and N. Sutin, Electron Transfer in Chemistry and Biology, Biochim. Biophys. Acta 811:265 (1985).

5. L. C. Petersen and L.-E. Andréasson, The Reaction between Oxidized Cytochrome c and Reduced Cytochrome c Oxidase, FEBS Lett. 66:52 (1976).

6. T. Ohnishi, R. LoBrutto, J. C. Salterno, R. C. Bruckner, and T. C. Frey, Spatial Relationships between Cytochrome a and a_3, J. Biol. Chem. 257:14821 (1982).

7. G. W. Brudvig, D. F. Blair, and S. I. Chan, Electron Spin Relaxation of Cu_A and Cytochrome a in Cytochrome c Oxidase, J. Biol. Chem. 259:11001 (1984).

8. D. F. Blair, J. Gelles, and S. I. Chan, Proton Pumping by Cytochrome c Oxidase: The Importance and Mechanisms of Electron Gating, Rev. Port. Quim. 27:235 (1985).

9. C. Tanford, Mechanism of Free Energy Coupling in Active Transport, Annu. Rev. Biochem. 52:379 (1983).

10. B. G. Malmström and L.-E. Andréasson, The Steady-State Rate Equation for Cytochrome c Oxidase Based on a Minimal Kinetic Scheme, J. Inorg. Biochem. 23:233 (1985).

11. P. Brzezinski, P.-E. Thörnström, and B. G. Malmström, The Rate-Limiting Step and Nonhyperbolic Kinetics in the Oxidation of Ferrocytochrome c Catalyzed by Cytochrome c Oxidase, FEBS Lett. 194:1 (1986).

12. M. Brunori, A. Colosimo, and M. T. Wilson, Kinetic Studies of Cytochrome c Oxidase: Significance of Different Functional States of the Enzyme, in "Structure and Function Relationships in Biochemical Systems", F. Bossa, E. Chiancone, A. Finazzi-Agrò, and R. Strom, eds., Plenum Press, New York (1982).

13. D. Bickar, J. F. Turrens, and A. L. Lehninger, The Mechanism by Which Oxygen and Cytochrome c Increase the Rate of Electron Transfer from Cytochrome a to Cytochrome a_3 of Cytochrome c Oxidase, J. Biol. Chem. 261:14461 (1986).

14. E. Antonini, M. Brunori, C. Greenwood, and B. G. Malmström, Catalytic Mechanism of Cytochrome Oxidase, Nature 228:936 (1970).

15. M. Fabian, P.-E. Thörnström, P. Brzezinski, and B. G. Malmström, Two-Electron-Reduction Is Required for Rapid Internal Electron Transfer in Resting, Pulsed and Oxygenated Cytochrome c Oxidase, FEBS Lett., in press (1987).

16. S. H. Speck, D. Dye, and E. Margoliash, Single Catalytic Site Model for the Oxidation of Ferrocytochrome c Oxidase by Mitochondrial Cytochrome c Oxidase, Proc. Natl. Acad. Sci. USA 81:347 (1984).

17. K. M. C. Sinjorgo, J. H. Meijling, and A. Muijsers, The Concept of High- and Low-Affinity Reactions in Bovine Cytochrome c Oxidase Steady-State Kinetics, Biochim. Biophys. Acta 767:48 (1984).

18. N. C. Robinson, J. Neumann, and D. Wigintin, Influence of Detergent Polar and Apolar Structure upon the Temperature Dependence of Beef Heart Cytochrome c Oxidase Activity, Biochemistry 24:6298 (1985).

19. L. Smith and H. Conrad, A Study of the Kinetics of the Oxidation of Cytochrome c by Cytochrome c Oxidase, Arch. Biochem. Biophys. 63:403 (1956).

20. K. Minnaert, The Kinetics of Cytochrome c Oxidase I. The System: Cytochrome c-Cytochrome Oxidase-Oxygen, Biochim. Biophys. Acta 50:23 (1961).

21. P. Brzezinski and B. G. Malmström, Electron-Transport-Driven Proton Pumps Display Nonhyperbolic Kinetics: Simulation of the Steady-State Kinetics of Cytochrome c Oxidase, Proc. Natl. Acad. Sci. USA 83:4282 (1986).

22. J. Wilms, J. L. M. L. van Rijn, and B. F. van Gelder, The Effect of pH and Ionic Strength on the Steady-State Activity of Isolated Cytochrome c Oxidase, Biochim. Biophys. Acta 593:17 (1980).

23. P.-E. Thörnström, B. Soussi, L. Arvidsson, and B. G. Malmström, Effect of pH, Ionic Strength and D_2O on the Steady-State Kinetics of Cytochrome c Oxidase in Phospholipid Vesicles, Chemica Scripta 24:230 (1984).

24. C. Greenwood, M. T. Wilson, and M. Brunori, Studies on Partially Reduced Mammalian Cytochrome Oxidase. Reactions with Carbon Monoxide and Oxygen, Biochem. J. 137:205 (1974).

25. R. Boelens, R. Wever, and B. F. van Gelder, Electron Transfer after Flash Photolysis of Mixed-Valence Carboxycytochrome c Oxidase, Biochim. Biophys. Acta 682:264 (1982).

26. G. M. Clore, L.-E. Andréasson, B. Karlsson, R. Aasa, and B. G. Malmström, Characterization of the Intermediates in the Reaction of Mixed-Valence-State Soluble Cytochrome Oxidase with Oxygen at Low Temperatures by Optical and Electron-Paramagnetic-Resonance Spectroscopy, Biochem. J. 185:155 (1980).

27. B. Chance and L. Powers, Structure of Cytochrome Oxidase Redox Center in Native and Modified Forms: An EXAFS Study, Curr. Top. Bioenerg. 14:1 (1985).

28. R. A. Scott, J. R. Schwartz, and S. P. Cramer, Structural Aspects of the Copper Sites in Cytochrome c Oxidase. An X-ray Absorption Spectroscopic Investigation of the Resting-State Enzyme, Biochemistry 25:5546 (1986).

29. G. W. Brudvig, T. H. Stevens, and S. I. Chan, Reactions of Nitric Oxide with Cytochrome c Oxidase, Biochemistry 19:5275 (1980).

30. M. G. Jones, D. Bickar, M. T. Wilson, M. Brunori, A. Colosimo, and P. Sarti, A Re-Examination of the Reactions of Cyanide with Cytochrome c Oxidase, Biochem. J. 220:57 (1984).

31. P. Jensen, M. T. Wilson, R. Aasa, and B. G. Malmström, Cyanide Inhibition of Cytochrome c Oxidase. A Rapid-Freeze E.P.R. Investigation, Biochem. J. 224:829 (1984).

32. C. P. Scholes and B. G. Malmström, Two-Electron Reduction of Cytochrome c Oxidase Triggers a Conformational Transition, FEBS Lett. 198:125 (1986).

33. B. G. Malmström, Coupling between Electron Transfer and Proton Translocation in Cytochrome c Oxidase, Chemica Scripta, in press.

PROTON PUMP ACTIVITY IN

BACTERIAL CYTOCHROME OXIDASES

Nobuhito Sone

Department of Biochemistry
Jichi Medical School
Tochigi-ken, Japan

INTRODUCTION

Many aerobic bacteria contain cytochrome aa_3 as a terminal oxidase
as in the mitochondrial respiratory chain.   This enzyme, cytochrome
oxidase, is the coupling site (Site 3) where an electrochemical proton
gradient $(\Delta\tilde{\mu}H^+)$ is formed upon oxidation.   Since 1979 these bacterial
cytochrome oxidases have been highly purified from various bacteria (3-
12). These enzymes are characterized by their simple subunit structure
and similarity of prosthetic groups which consist of two a-hemes and two
Cu atoms.   For example cytochrome oxidase from the thermophilic
bacterium PS3 which is a Gram-positive spore-forming thermophilic
Bacillus,   contains one copy of these subunits and 2 a-hemes and Cu atoms
and shows very similar enzymic properties to the mitochondrial enzyme,
including possessing H^+ pump activity.   In the following, several topics
concerning with bacterial cytochrome oxidases will be described in
connection to proton pumping activity.

BACTERIAL $\underline{aa}_3$-TYPE CYTOCHROME OXIDASES

As summarized in Table 1, these bacterial cytochrome oxidases are
composed of 2 or 3 subunits and thus has a much simpler structure than
the mitochondrial enzyme.   These bacterial enzymes oxidize cytochrome c
with dioxygen and form $\Delta\tilde{\mu}H^+$ concomitantly. At least these enzymes
catalyze electron transfer across the membrane, since proteoliposomes
containing any of these enzymes showed "respiratory control",
acceleration of oxidation rate by the addition of an uncoupler, when it
is properly reconstituted.   Some of these enzymes such as those from
two types of thermophilic bacteria PS3 (13,14) and T. thermophilus
(15,16), are known to pump H^+ in addition to transferring electrons
across the membrane.   Among the enzymes from mesophilic bacteria, only
the P. denitrificans enzyme was reported to pump H^+ (17,18), after
several failures (19).

Table 1. Subunit Structure and Proton Pump Activity of
aa$_3$-type Bacterial Cytochrome Oxidases

Organism	Subunit Mr (kDa)			H$^+$ pump activity	Ref
	I	II	III		
Thermophilic bacterium PS3	56[a]	38(c)	22	+	7
Bacillus subtilis	57	37	21		9
Thermus thermophilus	55 71[a]	33(c) 34(c)		+	3 10
Paracoccus denitrificans	45 55[b]	28		+	4 15
Nitrobacter agilis	51[a]	31		–	6
Rhodobacter sphaeroides	45	37(35)		–	8
Pseudomonas AM1	50	32		–	11

[a]Obtained from Ferguson plot.

[b]Suggested by the data of DNA code.

SUBUNIT STRUCTURE

The PS3 enzyme is known to be composed of three subunits. These three subunits seem to correspond to the three largest subunits of mitochondrial cytochrome oxidase : PS3 subunit I showed a very similar amino acid composition to mitochondrial subunit I and exhibited abnormal behaviors in SDS-PAGE (7). As shown in Fig 1, the mobility of subunit I was highly dependent on the polyacrylamide concentration; its Rf value was 0.84, while those of subunits II, III and the standard proteins were 0.68. Subunit I forms a non-precipitating aggregate upon incubation at a temperature above 70°C in the presence of dodecyl sulfate. PS3 subunit II, to which cytochrome c binds covalently, crossreacted immunologically with subunit II from the yeast enzyme (19). The PS3 subunit III also bound DCCD with a concomitant loss of H$^+$ pumping activity, as was observed with the subunit III of the bovine enzyme (13). In contrast, purified enzymes from mesophilic Gram-negative bacteria are composed of two subunits, except for the enzyme of R. sphaeroides, for which a third band observed in SDS-PAGE may be a proteolytic product of subunit II (8). Saraste et al. have found a DNA sequence for subunit III (corresponding to the mitochondrial subunit III) in the cytochrome oxidase gene of P. denitrificons (20). Loss of subunit III during purification procedure may be responsible for the low or negligible H$^+$ pumping activity.

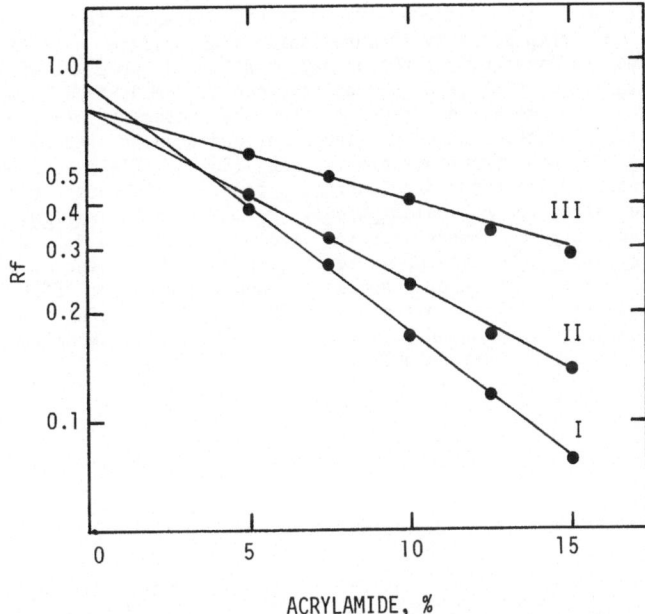

Fig. 1. Ferguson plot of each of the subunits of PS3 cytochrome oxidase.

CHROMOPHORES AND REACTION INTERMEDIATES

Spectra of the oxidized and reduced forms of the PS3 enzyme are very similar to that of the 1:1 cytochrome c-cytochrome aa_3 complex of the mammalian enzyme, except that a small peak of the oxidized form at 840 nm known to be due to one of the Cu atoms was replaced by a smaller peak at around 780 nm.   The spectrum of the CO-reduced form was also simiar to that of the mitochondrial enzyme (7,21).   Ligands such as NaN_3 and HCN inhibit the PS3 enzyme with concomitant spectral shifts with slightly lower affinities (22). Analysis with flash photolysis of the CO-reduced form of the PS3 enzyme at low temperatures (triple trap experiment of Chance et al.) showed a compound A-like spectrum at -113°C (23). The PS3 enzyme also exhibited resting-pulsed conversion (24).   These characteristics suggest that the intermediate reactions and catalytic mechanisms of the PS3 enzyme are the same as those of the mitochondrial enzyme.

PROTON PUMPING ACTIVITY

The PS3 enzyme was reconstituted into vesicles with soybean phospholipids by the freeze-thaw-sonication method (7,13).   When ferrocytochrome c was added, H^+ ejection coupling with oxidation took place in the presence of K^+ plus valinomycin (13).   The H^+/e ratio obtained (maximal amount of ejected H^+/ferrocytochrome c added) was close to 1, but simultaneous measurement of H^+ ejection and cytochrome c oxidation with a relatively small amount of the enzyme gave an H^+/e ratio of 1.2-1.4 at the beginning (14).   The enzyme from T. thermophilus did pump H^+ (15,16), while the N. agilis and Ps. AM1 enzymes did not (15,25). Gennis et al. reported that the purified R. sphaeroides enzyme did not pump H^+ in spite of a high respiratory control ratio when it was reconstituted into vesicles (8). As will be shown in the succeeding section, H$^+$ pump activity is more labile than oxidase activity. Some cytochrome oxidases of mesophiles may thus lose H$^+$ pump activity during purification. To test this possibility, one of the devised methods is to solubilize the membrane fraction from the bacterium of interest with heptyl thioglucoside (or octyl glucoside) and then to reconstitute the resulting soluble fraction into vesicles (26). Fig. 2 shows the pH meter traces upon a reduced cytochrome $\underline{c}$ pulse to liposomes recontituted from the extract of B. caldolyticus, Ps. AM1 or N. agilis. No H$^+$ pumping activity was observed in the case of Ps. AM1 and N. agilis, while the B. caldolyticus enzyme appeared to pump H$^+$. These vesicles showed a 3-4 times acceleration of respiration upon addition of FCCP. These results indicate that the enzymes of N. agilis and Ps. AM1 lose H$^+$ pumping activity even upon solubilization with heptyl thioglucoside, or they do not pump H$^+$ intrinsically.

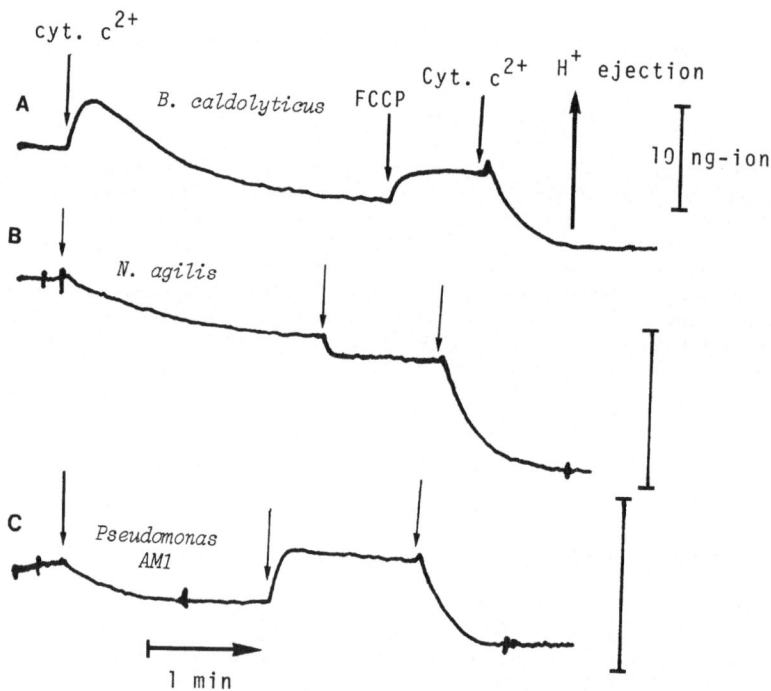

Fig. 2. Measurement of H$^+$ pumping activity with liposomes reconstituted from the heptyl thioglucoside-soluble fraction of bacterial membranes. Traces of the external pH upon a reduced cytochrome $\underline{c}$ pulse in the presence of K$^+$ and valinomycin are shown. The methods, for solubilization, reconstitsution and measurement were the same as in (26).
A: B. caldolyticus, B: Ps. AM1, C: N. agilis.

DO ALL BACTERIAL CYTOCHROME OXIDASES PUMP PROTONS INTRINSICALLY ?

In spite of the similarity of the chromophore, there is an indication that some bacterial cytochrome oxidases may not pump H^+. Jones et al. showed that the H^+/O ratios of B. subtilis and B. megaterium with endogeous substrate were as low as 4 (27), while B. stearothermophilus (28) and T. thermophilus (29) showed H^+/O ratios as high as 7-8, suggesting that cytochrome oxidases in the former bacteria do not pump H^+. A similar difference is also found in cytochrome aa_3-containing Gram-negative bacteria. The H^+/O ratio was 5-6 in Methylophilus methylotrophus (30) and Ps. AM1 (31), while P. denitrificans, at least in cells cultured with methanol as the C-source, showed an H^+/O ratio as high as 8 and sometimes 10 (32) with endogenous substrate. The respiration with ascorbate plus TMPD or ferrocyanide was reported to couple with proton translocation of $2H^+/O$ (33). The H^+ pumping activity at site 3 was examined, using Ps. AM1, which is closely related to R. sphaeroides, although it does not grow photosynthetically.

As shown in Fig. 3, Ps. AM1 cells translocate H^+, showing an H^+/O ratio of 5.9 with glycerol as the substrate, and 2.1 with ascorbate plus TMPD as substrates. Ascorbate oxidation via TMPD in the presence of FCCP showed neither H^+ ejection nor H^+ uptake, indicating that the apparent H^+ release was not due to H^+ translocation from the cytosol. It is likely that Ps. AM1 translocates $2H^+$ at site 1, $4H^+$ ($2e^-$) at site 2 and no H^+ but only $2e^-$ at site 3. These data suggest that some bacterial cytochrome oxidases such as of Ps. AM1 do not pump H^+ intrinsically.

IS A DIMERIC STRUCTURE NECESSARY FOR PROTON PUMPING ?

Cytochrome oxidases from PS3 and bovine heart were irradiated with a high-energy electronbeam. Both the oxidase and H^+ pumping activities by the two enzymes decreased as exponential functions of the radiation dosage. Applying the target theory, the following functional molecular

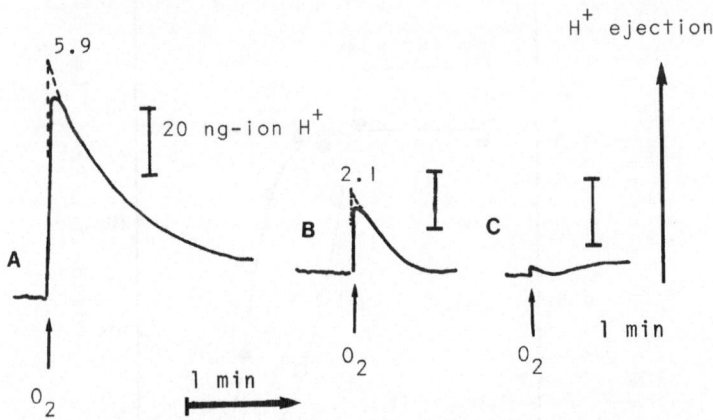

Fig.3. Traces of the external pH upon O_2 pulse. A suspension of starved cells of Pseudomonas AM1 was incubated in the reaction medium containing KSCN (90 mM) and valinomycin. As indicated by the arrow, an aliquot (30 ul) of air-saturated 150 mM KCl was added. The number in the figure shows the H^+/O ratio. A: with glycerol as a substrate, B: with ascorbate in the presence of N,N,N',N'-tetramethyl pphenylenediamine, C: as B except FCCP was added.

weights were obtained for oxidation and H^+ pumping: 63-73 kDa and 160-220 kDa, respectively, for the bovine enzyme and 80-100 kDa and 190-230 kDa, respectively, for the PS3 enzyme (34). These results suggest that a dimer structure is necessary for the H^+ pumping activity of the PS3 enzyme, while cytochrome c oxidation can be catalyzed by the monomer form. Since the chromophores of the PS3 enzyme and its reaction to oxygen are very similar to those of the bovine enzyme (23,24), it is likely that the dimer structure composed of the core subunits is necessary for the H^+ pump in the mitochondrial enzyme. In this respect the PS3 enzyme apparently exists as a dimer in several detergents (7), while the enzyme from P. denitrificans (8) and N. agilis (6) were each reported to be a monomer. The beef heart enzyme, not the PS3 enzyme, becomes a monmer (35) upon alkaline treatment (pH 9.5-10) and loses H^+ pumping activity (36); the oxidase activity was stimulated about 1.5 times by these treatment (35,36). Wikström et al. proposed a reciprocating hypothesis in which H^+-pumping cytochrome oxidase functions as a dimer (37,38).

WHAT HAPPENS IN UNCOUPLED CYTOCHROME OXIDASES ?

Several methods are known besides alkaline treatment which destroy the H^+ pumping activity without much change in the the oxidase activity. Treatment with DCCD (dicyclohexyl carbodiimide) is known to produce such a change (13,39). Fig. 4 shows the effect of heat treatment on the oxidase (●) and H^+-pumping activity (○). The PS3 enzyme pre-incubated at 55-60 C did not pump H^+ when reconstituted into vesicles, while oxidation occurred. Almost in parallel with the inactivation of the H^+ pumping activity, the Raman line at 214 cm^{-1} of the reduced form became weak, indicating that the Fe (cyt. a_3)-His stretching bond may confer the H^+ pumping activity (40). In the case of the bovine enzyme, inactivation of the H^+ pumping activity occurred at 45-50°C (40). However, the corelation between the H^+ pumping activity and the intensity of the Raman line at

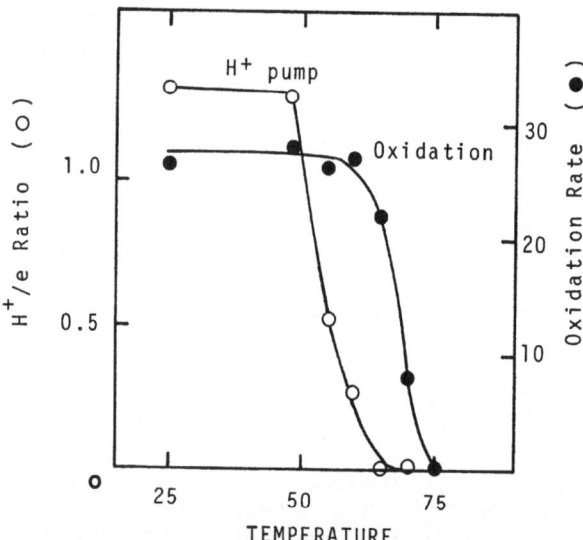

Fig. 4. Effects of the incubation temperature on the cytochrome c oxidase and H+ pumping activities.

214 cm^{-1} was obscure (36). Recently, Nilsson et al. reported that the ESR signal from Cu_A of the bovine enzyme changed dramatically upon the selective heat treatment (42). The ESR band at g=1.96 became shallow, when the heat treated (58 C for 30 min) PS3 enzyme was measured. Accordingly, the possibility that of Cu_A participates in the H^+ pump mechanism will be investigated further.

CONCLUSIONS

1. Bacterial cytochrome oxidases are composed of only two or three subunits, and yet have chromophores such as cytochrome aa_3 and two Cu atoms, the same as the mitochondrial enzyme. The two or three subunits corespond to the two (subunits I and II) or three (subunits I, II and III) largest subunits of the mitochondrial enzyme, which is encoded on the mitochondrial DNA.

2. The enzymes from the thermophilic bacterium PS3, T. thermophilus and P. denitrificans have been reported to have proton pumping activity. It is, however, not known whether other bacterial cytochrome oxidases lose their H^+ pumping activity during their purification or do not have H^+ pumping activity intrinsically, although they have trans-membrane electron transferring activity. In the case of Ps. AM1, the enzyme may lack intrinsic H^+ pump activity.

3. Proton pumping activity of the purified enzymes may be co-related to the presence of subunit III, which may be an DCCD-sensitive proton channel. As an alternative possibility, this subunit may be necessary for the formation of a dimer. Necessity of the dimeric structure for H^+ pumping activity has been shown by radiation-inactivation experiments. Both in the cases of the PS3 and the bovine enzymes, functional molecular weights of about 200 kDa are in accord with two times the sum of subunits I, II and III.

4. Heat inactivation of the H^+ pumping activity without much change in the oxidase activity is one of the clues for elucidating the H^+ pumping mechanism. It is likely that the H^+ pumping is not the direct result of oxidation, but probably mediated by conformational change of the protein which is sensitive to heat.

5. Bacterial cytochrome oxidases are similar to the mitochondrial enzyme as a whole, but still they show several variations in subunit numbers, their molecular weights and H^+ pumping activities. It will be of great interest to compare the amino acid and gene sequences of these enzymes.

ACKNOWLEDGMENTS
The author wishes to express his cordial thanks to Drs. B. Chance, T. Hamamoto, P.C. Hinkle, Y. Kagawa, T. Kitagawa, A. Naqui, P. Nicholls, T. Ohnishi, T. Ogura, Y. Orii, M. Saraste, M. Wikström, T. Yamanaka, Y. Yanagita and T.Yonetani, for their cooperations and valuable discussions.

REFERENCES
1. Yamanaka, T., Fujii, K. and Kamita, Y. (1979) J. Biochem. 86, 821-824
2. Sone, N., Ohyama, T. and Kagawa, Y. (1979) FEBS Lett. 106, 36-42
3. Fee, J. A., Choc, M. G., Findling, K. L., Lorence, R. and Yoshida, T. (1980) Proc. Natl. Acad. Sci. USA 77, 147-151

4. Ludwig, B. & Schatz, G. (1980) Proc. Natl. Acad. Sci. USA 77, 196-200
5. Yamanaka, T. and Fujii, K. (1980) Biochim. Biophys. Acta 591, 53-62.
6. Yamanaka, T., Kamita, Y. & Fukumori, Y. (1981) J. Biochem. 89, 265-273
7. Sone, N., and Yanagita, Y. (1982) Biochim. Biophys. Acta 682, 216-226
8. Gennis, R. B., Casey, R. P., Azzi, A., and Ludwig, B. (1982) Eur. J. Biochem. 125, 189-195
9. De Vrij, W., Azzi, A., and Konings, W. N. (1983) Eur. J. Biochem. 131, 97-103
10. Hon-nami, K. and Oshima, T. (1984) Biochemistry 23, 454-460
11. Fukumori, Y., Nakayama, K. and Yamanaka, T. (1985) J. Biochem. 98, 493-499
12. Yamazaki, T., Fukumori, Y. and Yamanaka, T. (1985) Biochim. Biophys. Acta 810, 174-183
13. Sone, N. and Hinkle, P. C. (1982) J. Biol. Chem. 257, 12600-12604
14. Sone, N. and Yanagita, Y. (1984) J. Biol. Chem. 259, 1405-1408
15. Sone, N., Yanagita, Y., Hon-nami, K., Fukumori, Y. and Yamanaka, T. (1983) FEBS Lett. 155, 150-154
16. Yoshida, T. and Fee, J. A. (1984) J. Biol. Chem. 259, 1031-1036
17. Solioz, M., Carafoli, E. and Ludwig, B. (1983) J. Biol. Chem. 257, 1579-1582
18. Püttner, I., Solioz, M., Carafoli, E. and Ludwig, B. (1983) Eur. J. Biochem. 134, 33-37
19. Ludwig, B. (1984) Biochim. Biophys. Acta 594, 177-189
20. Saraste, M., Raitio, M., Jalli, T. and Peramaa, A. (1986) FEBS Lett. 206, 154-156
21. Sone, N., Kagawa, Y. and Orii, Y. (1983) J. Biochem. 93, 1329-1336
22. Sone, N.,and Nicholls, P. (1985) Can. J. Biochem. 63, 153-161
23. Sone., Naqui, A., Kumar, C. and Chance, B. (1984) Biochem. J. 221, 529-533
24. Sone, N., Naqui, A., Kumar, C. and Chance, B. (1984) Biochem. J. 223, 809-813
25. Sone, N., Sekimachi, M., Fukumori, Y. and Yamanaka, T. (1987) submitted for publication
26. Sone, N. (1986) J. Biochem. 100, 1465-1470
27. Jones, C. W., Brice, M., Downs, A. and Drozd, J, W. (1975) Eur. J. Biochem. 52, 265-271
28. Chicken, E., Spode, J. and Jones, C.W. (1981) FEBS Lett. 111, 181-185
29. McKay, A., Quilter, J. & Jones, C.W. (1982) Arch. Microbiol. 131, 43-50
30. Dawson, M. J. and Jones, C. W. (1981) Biochem. J. 194, 915-924
31. Keevil, C. W. and Anthony, C. (1979) Biochem. J. 182, 71-79
32. Stouthamer, A. H. (1980) Trends Biochem. Sci. 5, 164-166
33. van Verseveld, H. W., Krab, K. and Stouthamer, A. H. (1981) Biochim. Biophys. Acta 635, 525-534
34. Sone, N. Kosako, T. (1986) EMBO J. 5, 1515-1519
35. Orii, Y. and Miki, T. (1983) in Frontiers in Biochemical and Biophysical Studies of Proteins and Membranes (Liu, T. Y., Sakakibara, S., Schechter, A.N., Yagi, K., Yajima, H. and Yasunobu, K.T., eds.) pp. 279-287. Elsevier, Amsterdam
36. Sone, N., Ogura, T. and Kitagawa, T. (1986) Biochim. Biophys. Acta 850, 139-145
37. Wikström, M., Krab, K. and Saraste, M. (1981) Cytochrome Oxidase-A Synthesis, Academic Press, London
38. Finel, M.,and Wikström, M. (1986) 851, 99-108
39. Casey, R. P., Chappll, J. B. and Azzi, A. (1979) Biochem. J. 182, 146-156
40. Ogura, T., Sone, N., Tagawa, K. and Kitagawa, T. (1984) Biochemistry 23, 2826-2831
41. Sone, N. and Nicholls, P. (1984) Biochemistry 23, 6550-6554
42. Nilsson, T., Li, P.M., Gells, J. & Chan, S. (1987) Biophys. J. 51, 2412.

750

TOPOGRAPHY AND PROTONMOTIVE MECHANISM OF

MITOCHONDRIAL COUPLING SITE 2

Alexander A. Konstantinov and Eugeniya Popova

A.N.Belozersky Laboratory of Molecular Biology and Bioorganic

Chemistry, Moscow State University, Moscow, 119899 USSR

INTRODUCTION

Since the general scheme of electron transfer in mitochondrial QH_2: cytochrome c reductase had been established (the Q-cycle) the mechanism of energy-transduction became the central problem in the site 2 mechanism studies.

According to the early chemiosmotic schemes of site 2 (1,2) including the original Q-cycle (3) it was vectorial transmembrane e^- transfer from cytochrome b_{566} to cytochrome b_{562} which gave rise to $\Delta\psi$ in the $b-c_1$ complex. However, later studies in three laboratories showed that electron transfer from b_{566} to b_{562} could account for only ~40% of $\Delta\psi$ generated in site 2 (4-6; see also 7,8). This conclusion has been corroborated recently by the cytochrome b gene sequence analysis which predicts the two hemes to be localized within 20 Å (Fe-to-Fe) from each other along the axis normal to the membrane plane (9,10).

Therefore a problem arises where the rest 60% of $\Delta\psi$ is generated (Fig.1). According to a version advocated in (5,6) heme b_{566} is located electrically at the C- (or P-)side of the membrane and heme b_{562} in the middle of the dielectric barrier (Fig.1C,D); consequently, the major electrogenic step complementary to $b_{566} \longrightarrow b_{562}$ electron transfer would be associated with either (i)vectorial e^- transfer from b_{562} to ubiquinone in centre $\underline{i}$, the latter located at the M-side (Fig.1C), or (ii)vectorial H^+ uptake by Q_i reduced by b_{562} in centre $\underline{i}$ in the middle of the membrane (Fig.1D).

An alternative model assumed in (4,7,11-13) suggests that heme b_{562} is near the M-side of the membrane electrically and heme b_{566} in the middle of it (Fig.1A,B). In this case the major additional electrogenic reaction (phase $\underline{a}$) would be located on the reducing side of cytochrome b and once

Abbreviations: SMP, submitochondrial particles; SDH, succinate dehydrogenase; $RuAM_6$; hexaammineruthenium chloride; FeCy, ferricyanide; Q_1H_2, ubiquinol-1; Q_1, ubiquinone-1.

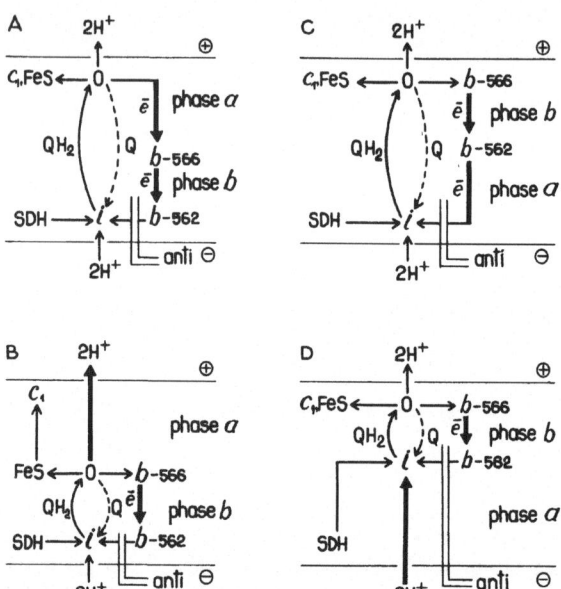

Fig.1. Electrogenic reactions in the Q cycle.

$\Delta\psi$-generation in complex b-c_1 is assumed to be comprised
of (I) a vectorial electron transfer from b_{566} to b_{562}
(phase b) contributing about 40% (4-6) and (II) an antimycin-sensitive phase (phase a) contributing the rest ~60%.
Two alternative models are considered according to which
phase $\underline{a}$ is located on the reducing (A,B) (4,7) or oxidizing (C,D) (5,6) side of cytochrome b.Within each of the
2 models, phase $\underline{a}$ can be visualized as vectorial electron
(A,C) or proton transfer (B,D). In (C,D) antimycin inhibits
phase merely by blocking the centre i-catalized Q reduction by b_{562}. In schemes (A,B) an additional inhibitory
effect of antimycin on the centre o-associated electrogenesis has to be postulated (4) in order to account for
the antimycin-sensitivity of phase $\underline{a}$ and for the apparent
electrical localization of heme b_{566} at the C-side of the
membrane as observed in the presence of antimycin (4-6)
whereas in the absence of antimycin b_{566} locates electrically within ~60-80 mv from phase M (4,7). This secondary
effect of antimycin is difficult to rationalize within
model (A). However as suggested in (4) (and see Fig.9 of
this paper)antimycin can abolish electrogenic proton release from centre $\underline{o}$ in scheme (B) as it transforms heme
b_{566} from an e$^-$ into an H-acceptor for QH_o, rendering
heme b_{566} reduction via centre $\underline{o}$ non electrogenic (see
the final section of this paper).

again can be visualized as vectorial e^- transfer from $\dot{Q}-$ to heme b_{566} (Fig. 1A, e.g.see 7) or as electrogenic proton extrusion from centre <u>o</u> to the C-phase (Fig.1B) (4,7,11-13). Earlier we reported evidence for heme b_{562} elec<u>t</u>rical localization at or near the M-side of the mitochondrial membrane (4) (see also 7). Here we would review the results of our spatial topography studies which corroborate heme b_{562} localization close to the M-aqueous phase. In addition evidence for antimycin-sensitive protonation of b_{562} from the M-phase is presented.

On the basis of these and earlier data from our studies, a protonmotive mechanism of $b-c_1$ site is formulated within the framework of the Q-cycle scheme. This mechanism is similar to one of the models considered by Mitchell in (7) but is further developed so as to accomodate site 2 energy-linked reactions in the antimycin-inhibited state.

CYTOCHROME b TOPOGRAPHY, REVIEW OF THE RESULTS

According to a widely quoted work by Case and Leigh (14) both b_{566} and b_{562} hemes are located within 10 Å from the C-phase. It was also shown that diazobenzene sulfonate treatment of mitochondria (but not of SMP) (15) inhibits electron transfer through centre <u>o</u> (16) and modifies heme b_{566} absor<u>p</u>tion spectrum (17), which would be consistent with those functional centres being localized somewhat nearer to the C-side of the membrane. Recently we have carried experiments using membrane-impermeable electron donors and acceptors with a view to elucidate heme b topography in the coupling membrane.

Heme b_{562} Reduction by Hexaammineruthenium

It was reported in (19) that a membrane-impermeable inorganic complex $Ru(NH_3)^{2+/3+}$ mediates heme b_{562} reduction by ascorbate in SMP but not in mitochondria. These results pointing to heme b_{562} accessibility from the M-side of the membrane are further substantiated by experiments with isola<u>t</u>ed complex $b-c_1$ and $b-c_1$ proteoliposomes (12,13) some of which are described below. As illustrated by Fig.2 (and see 12 for more details) about 90% of complex $b-c_1$ is oriented in proteoliposomes as in mitocondria with heme c_1 facing outwards. This unidirectional incorporation of the enzyme makes the proteoliposomes a good model for $b-c_1$ topography studies.

Fig.3 shows that b_{562} reduction by RuAm6 in beef-heart SMP occurs as rapidly as in the isolated complex $b-c_1$. At the same time in liposomes reduction by ascorbate + RuAm6 becomes very slow (Fig.4), the reaction may take an hour or more for completion, which probably corresponds to penetra<u>t</u>tion of the proteoliposome membrane by donors (12).

The reduction of b_{562} by RuAm6 in complex $b-c_1$ or SMP is not inhibited significantly by centre <u>i</u> or centre <u>o</u> inhibitors or by their combined presence (12,19); therefore, it is likely that RuAM6 reacts with b_{562} directly rather than via endogenous ubiquinone. These data show that ferric heme b_{562} is localized at or near the M-side of the mitochondrial membrane, rather than near its C-side as reported in 18 (14).

Cytochrome b Oxidation by Ferricyanide

Ferricyanide (FeCy) has been long used as a membrane-impermeable elec-

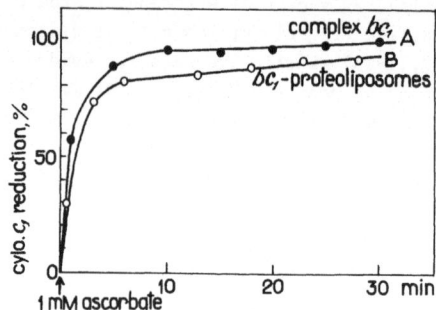

Fig.2. Cytochrome c_1 reducibility by ascorbate in the solubilized and liposome reconstituted complex b-c_1.
The sample and reference spectrophotometric cells contained complex b-c_1 proteoliposomes (0.1 mg protein/ml) in
0.2 M sucrose, 50 mM HEPES pH 7.0, 5 mM $MgSO_4$, 0.2 mM EDTA
and 2 mM KCN; the reference was supplemented with 50μM ferri
cyanide, 1 mM ascorbate was added to the sample as the zero
time and difference spectra of the sample vs the oxidized
reference were scanned in the 540-580 nm range to measure
cytochrome c_1 reduction at various time intervals. In case
of proteoliposomes, 100% reduction was achieved by adding
10 μM phenazine methosulfate or small amount od dithionite.
Bovine b-c_1 complex was prepared as in (18) and incorporated
in liposomes as in (12).The respiratory control in b-c_1 vesicles was higher than 20.

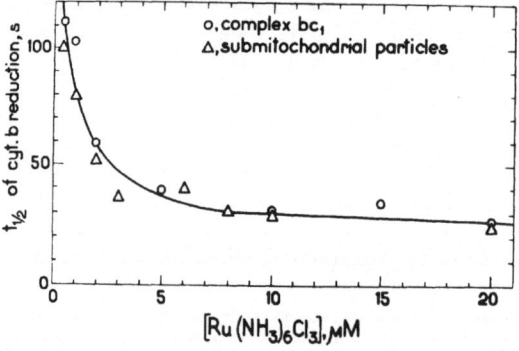

Fig.3. The rate of heme b_{562} reduction by ascorbate + hexaammineruthenium in submitochondrial particles and isolated complex
b-c_1. Spectrometric cell contained complex b-c_1 (0.1 mg prot/
ml) or SMP (1 mg prot/ml) in the basic medium (see Fig.2). 1
mM ascorbate together with indicated concentrations of RuAm6
was added and the kinetics of cytochrome b reduction was monitored at 562 minus 575 nm. Bovine subumitochondrial particles were prepared as in (20).

754

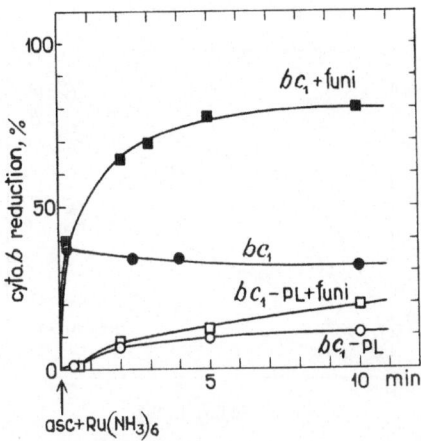

Fig.4. Kinetics of cytochrome b reduction by ascorbate plus
hexaammineruthenium in complex b-c_1 proteoliposomes.
Basic conditions as in Fig.2. Where indicated, 1.2
µg/ml of funiculosin was also present.At the zero
time 1 mM ascorbate + 20 µM RuAm6 was added to the
sample. Cytochrome b reduction has been determined
from the difference spectra as ΔA at 562 nm (vs the
baseline connecting the near-to-isobestic points at
540 and 575 nm) with an appropriate correction for
c_1 contribution; the dithionite induced reduction
level was taken as 100%. For more details see 12.

tron acceptor to probe redox chain topography in various biological membra
nes. It is well established that on the C-side of mitochondria FeCy accepts
electrons from cytochrome c (21) and to a lesser extent from cytochrome c_1
(22). FeS Rieske is likely to be oxidized by FeCy via c_1 (23) and none
of the respiratory carriers on the reducing side of the antimycin block is
accesible to FeCy in intact animal mitochondria (21) although there may be
some slow interaction in ubiquinone-depleted samples.

At the M-side of the mitochondrial membrane, e.g. in experiments with
the inside-out submitochondrial particles, FeCy can accept electrons from
succinate and NADH dehydrogenase (21). Whether there are additional interaction sites was not certain (see ref.s in 11).

FeCy-Induced Release on the Antimycin Block

Following original observations of Libermans' group (24), we established that FeCy addition to antimycin-inhibited SMP restores energy-coupled
succinate oxidase activity of the particles the effect being suppressed by
myxothiazol (11). This effect of FeCy can be nicely explained (11) in terms
of the Q-cycle by antimycin-insensitive oxidation of heme b_{562}(or/and centre
o generated ubisemiquinone) by FeCy at the M-side of the membrane. Further

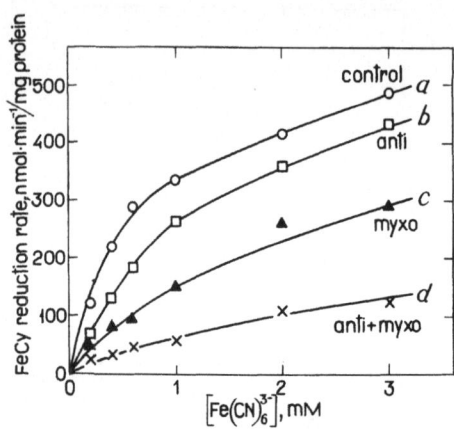

Fig.5. Effect of b-c$_1$ inhibitors on the succinate,ferricyanide
reductase activity of submitochondrial particles.
The rate of FeCy reduction was measured at 420 minus 460
nm at indicated concentrations of the acceptor. The
reaction mixture contained beef-heart SMP in the basic
medium (See Fig.2).Supplemented with 3 µM rotenone and,
where indicated, antimycin (0.5 µg/ml), myxothiazol
(0.5 µg/ml) or both these inhibitors. The reaction was
started with 10 mM succinate. Addition of α-thenoyltri
fluoroacetone did not further diminish the antimycin +
myxothiazol-inhibited ferricyanide-reductase activity
(27); hence the latter may be ascribed to FeCy reaction
with succinate dehydrogenase.

evidence for cytochrome c accessibility to FeCy is given below.

The Antimycin-Insensitive Succinate: FeCy-Reductase Activity of SMP Mediated by Complex b-c$_1$

As shown in Fig.5 at high FeCy concentration the succinate: $Fe(CN)_6^{3-}$
reductase activity of SMP becomes almost insensitive to antimycin (curve a).
This well known fact might be thought to be accounted for by FeCy interaction with SDH or ubiquinol with high K_m (25,26). However, the significant
sensitivity of the antimycin-resistant reaction to myxothiazol(curve d)
shows that the FeCy reduction in the presence of antimycin occurs largely
through b-c$_1$ complex, the SDH- and QH$_2$-mediated reactions contributing less
than 30% even at 3 mM FeCy (cf.curves b and d). Since both antimycin and
myxothiazol are required for complete inhibition of the b-c$_1$ catalyzed FeCy
reduction, cytochrome b is the likely candidate for the ferricyanide-reduc
tion site at the M-side of the SMP membrane.

Oxidation of b$_{562}$ by FeCy and Co(phen)$_3^{3+}$ in isolated complex b-c$_1$

We have shown recently that tris-phenanthroline complex of Co(III), an

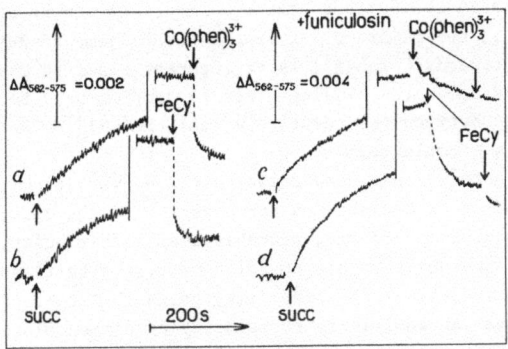

Fig.6. Heme b_{562} oxidation in complex $b-c_1$ by ferricyanide and
$Co(phen)_3^{3+}$. Spectrophotometric cell contained 0.55 μM
complex $b-c_1$ in the basic medium (Fig.2) with pH 7.3
in which KCN was replaced by 4 mM NaN_3 to avoid $Co(phen)_3^{3+}$
decomposition (27). Where indicated (c,d) 3 μM funiculosin
was also present which stimulated cytochrome b reduction
by succinate ∿2-3 fold. Additions: succinate 10 mM,FeCy
and $Co(phen)_3^{3+}$, 25 μM. Before the addition of the oxidants
heme b_{562} was reduced by 60% in the presence of funiculosin and by ∿ 25% in the absence of the inhibitor. The
breaks in the kinetic traces correspond to 10-15 min incubation.

inorganic complex with E_m similar to that of FeCy, serves as efficient electron acceptor for complex $b-c_1$ reacting specifically with heme c_1 (27). At
high concentrations $Co(phen)_3^{3+}$ can also accept electron from SDH with a
slightly higher efficiency than FeCy (27). At the same time $Co(phen)_3^{3+}$, in
contrast to FeCy (11), does not release the antimycin-inhibited electron
transfer through $b-c_1$ site in SMP (27); accordingly, the $b-c_1$ mediated part
of the succinate $Co(phen)_3^{3+}$-reductase activity of SMP (70% at 2 mM of the
acceptor) is completely inhibited by antimycin (as well as by myxothiazol)
(27). These observations allowed to suggest that $Co(phen)_3^{3+}$, in contrast to
FeCy, does not react at a significant rate with heme b_{562} in SMP (2).

Fig.6 compares the effects of $Co(phen)_3^{3+}$ and $Fe(CN)_6^{3-}$ on the redox
state of cytochrome b in complex $b-c_1$ pre-reduced with succinate via the
trace amounts of SDH in the preparation (cf.23). In the absence of $b-c_1$
site inhibitors both FeCy and $Co(phen)_3^{3+}$ bring about rapid oxidation of b_{562}
(traces, a,b). In case of $Co(phen)_3^{3+}$ the oxidation is largely blocked by
funiculosin (or other $b-c_1$ inhibitors, not shown) which indicates the reaction to occur via cytochrome c_1. At the same time, funiculosin does not
prevent heme b_{562} oxidation by FeCy (Fig.6,d) although there occurs some
deceleration of the reaction (cf.23); complete oxidation can be achieved
with ∿200 μM FeCy (not shown). Accordingly, FeCy but not $Co(phen)_3^{3+}$ brings
about oxidation of cytochrome b_{562} when added to succinate-reduced SMP inhibited with antimycin or myxothiazol (data not shown).

In conclusion the ferrous heme b_{562} is likely to be accessible to FeCy at the M-side of the membrane, as is the ferric heme to $Ru(NH_3)_6^{2+}$. The lack of reactivity towards $Co(phen)_3^{3+}$ is of interest since it may indicate the entrance to the heme b_{562} binding cleft in complex b-c$_1$ being tight enough to discriminate between the relatively small $Fe(CN)_6^{3-}$ or $Ru(NH_3)_6^{2+}$ and the bulky $Co(phen)_3^{3+}$ complexes.

We would note in this connection that the dysprosium complexes used in the recent studies of Ohnishi and co-workers to probe cytochrome b heme topography (as quoted in 28) are, probably also rather bulky, which might account for the apparently remote position of b_{562} with respect to the M-phase as found in that work. At the same time, accessibility to $Fe(CN)_6^{3-}$ and $Ru(NH_3)_6^{2+}$ implies accessibility to majority of common electrolyte ions like $H_3O^+, K^+, Na^+, Cl^-, OH^-$, etc., which would mean heme b_{562} being isoelectric with the M-phase.

Sidedness of Heme b_{562} Redox-Linked Protonation

It is well known that E_m values of mitochondrial cytochrome b hemes are pH-dependent. The form of protonic function (E_m/pH-dependence) shows that reduction of b_{566} as well as of b_{562} is associated with an uptake of proton by a heme-linked ionizable group with $pK_{ox} \sim 7$ and $pK_{red} > 8.5$ (29-33). It has been believed, although perhaps never tested, that E_m of b_{566} depends on pH of the C-phase and E_m of b_{562} on pH of the M-phase (7,8,28). Incidentally, this point of view means implicity that b_{566} oxidation by b_{562} at pH > pK_{ox} + 1 will give rise to full transmembrane charge separation (28,33), which is not likely to be the case (4-7). Here we have attempted to look whether it is pH of the M-phase that effects E_m of b_{562}. Proteoliposomes with mitochondrially oriented complex b-c$_1$ were equilibrated with the Q_1H_2/Q_1 redox buffer at ca. half-reduction of heme b_{562}. Subsequently pH inside the proteoliposomes was changed (at a constant pH of the buffered external aqueous phase) by virtue of Na^+/H^+ (or K^+/H^+) exchange catalyzed by monensin (or nigericin) as described (34). The effect of internal acidification or alkalinization on the reduction level of b_{562} was followed spectrophotometrically. Appropriate controls with pH indicators were carried out to verify development of pH-changes inside the b-c$_1$ proteoliposomes following monensin addition in the presence of Na^+-concentration gradient. The experiments were carried out in the presence of myxothiazol (centre i-catalized equilibration of b_{562} with Q) or in the presence of antimycin (centre o-catalyzed equilibration) as well as in the absence of inhibitors.

Experiments in the Presence of Myxothiazol - When Na^+-loaded b-c$_1$ proteoliposomes are poised with the Q_1H_2/Q_1 redox buffer in a Na^+, K^+-free medium the monensin-catalyzed acidification of the vesicle interior brings about oxidation of b_{562} (Fig.7, a,b).

Conversely, internal alkalinization induced by monensin addition to Na^+-free proteoliposomes suspended in 50 mM Na_2SO_4-containing medium resulted in increased reduction of b_{562} (data not included). The effects of monensin are abolished by ammonium salts (e.g.Fig.7,c) and are not observed in the absence of sufficient Na^+-gradient (data not shown). The same results were obtained in the absence of myxothiazol with KCN-supplemented b-c$_1$ proteoliposomes (not shown).

758

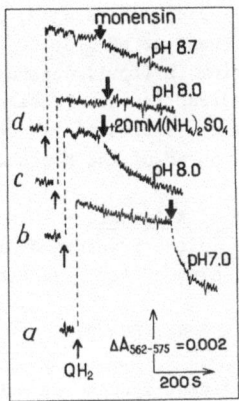

Fig.7. Heme b_{562} oxidation in QH_2/Q-equilibrated b-c_1 proteoliposomes induced by acidification of the vesicle interior.
Na^+ loaded b-c_1 proteoliposomes (0.35 μM in c_1) were suspended in a Na^+, K^+-free medium containing 75 mM choline
chloride and 20 mM HEPES-Tris buffer with indicated pH.
The suspension was supplemented with 0.5 μg/ml of myxothiazol and with Q_1. Q_1H_2 was added to bring about ca.
50% reduction of heme b_{562}. The Q_1H_2/Q_1 concentration was
40(a) or 0.8(b-d) at Q-1 concentrations of 4, 50, 50 and
20 μM for (a,b,c) and (d), respectively. Monensin was
added (thick arrows) to a final concentration of 10 μg/ml.
The difference spectra of the monensin induced absorbance
decrease in (a,b,d) showed oxidation of heme b_{562} (not shown).

It is important that the shift of redox equilibrium between ubiquinone
and b_{562} induced by the vesicle interior acidification attenuates at pH
above pK_{ox} of b_{562} (cf.traces a,b and d in Fig.7). These data can be rationalized as follows. Ubiquinone and heme b_{562} have different protonic functions (E_m/pH-dependencies). The former is a pure hydrogen carrier throughout the pH-range studied (29) whereas b_{562} would behave formally as a hydrogen carrier above pH~8 but as an electron carrier below pH~6 (29-32).
Consequently, the redox equilibration between ubiquinone and b_{562} can be
described

(1) $\frac{1}{2} QH_2 + X \cdot b_{ox} H^+ + (1-X) \cdot b_{ox} \rightleftharpoons \frac{1}{2}Q + b_{red} H + X \cdot H^+$

where X denotes the mole fraction of b_{562} operating as electron carrier at
given pH and, hence, the amount of protons released in the reaction (Eq.1)
per mole of b_{562} reduced by QH_2. Since

(1a) $X = 1 - 10 \exp (pK_{ox}- pH) \approx 1 - 10 \exp (7- pH)$

the proton release in (Eq.1) and, accordingly, pH-dependence of the reaction equilibrium constant would cease at pH $\gtrsim$ 8.

The fact that equilibrium in (Ep.1) depends on pH inside the liposomes shows that the $X \cdot H^+$ in this reaction are released inside the vesicles or, in other words, that during equilibration via cenre $\underline{i}$, E_ms of both QH_2/Q couple and heme b_{562} depend on pH of the M-aqueous phase.

Experiments in the Presence of Antimycin - In complex $b-c_1$ poised with the QH_2 couple via centre $\underline{o}$ in the presence of antimycin, E_h of cytochrome b hemes is related to E_h of heme c_1 (or Fe-S Rieske) by an equation:

$$(2) \qquad E_h \ (b) + E_h \ (c_1) = 2 \ E_h \ (QH_2/Q)$$

a phenomena known as "the oxidant-induced recuction of cytochrome b" (2,35) or the "redox see-saw mechanism" (7). As a consequence, at a given QH_2/Q ratio a stable equilibrium reduction level of cytochrome b can only be obtained if the redox level of cytochrome c_1 is maintained constant. To this end we carried out experiments with the antimycin-inhibited $b-c_1$ proteoliposomes in the presence of catalytic amounts ($\sim 10^{-8}$M) of cytochrome c. The latter was probably reoxidized by the traces of cytochrome c oxidase present in the preparation of complex $b-c_1$ since KCN abolished the "extra-reduction" of cytochrome b induced by the cytochrome c additions (not shown). Anyhow, under these conditions, cytochrome b could be titrated more or less reversibly with the Q_1H_2/Q_1 couple in agreement with the data of other workers (see 2,35).

It is important to remind that in the antimycin-inhibited state, E_m of b_{562} becomes pH-dependent throughout the pH range 5-9 as measured both under the conditions of equilibrium anaerobic redox titrations (31,32) and in the aerobic titrations of extra-reduced cytochrome b with the succinate/fumarate couple (5,31). Therefore electron transfer to b_{562} via centre $\underline{o}$ in the presence of antimycin has to be accompanied by protonation of this redox centre. Were this proton taken up from the M-phase, as found above (Fig.7), one would expect heme b_{562} to undergo oxidation or reduction in response to proteoliposome interior alkalinization or acidification, respectively, since redox potential of ubiquinone in centre $\underline{o}$ should not be dependent on pH of the M-phase.

However we found that in contrast to the above-described results with the myxothiazol-inhibited or with the uninhibited, $b-c_1$ proteoliposomes (Fig.7), intravesicular acidification or alkalinization exerts no effect on the reduction level of heme b_{562} poised with the Q_1H_2/Q_1 - couple in the presence of antimycin (e.g. Fig.8, a-c). The experiments were repeated with imposed gradients of K^+ and Na^+ of either sign at a wide range of pH and E_h. In no case did we observe oxidation or reduction of heme b_{562} in response to monensin or nigericin addition. Under the same conditions $\Delta\psi$-induced oxidation of b_{562} could be seen in K^+-loaded proteoliposomes upon addition of valinomycin (e.g. Fig.8,d), which shows that the lack of response to nigericin (Fig.8,c) is not due to the vesicles being "uncoupled".

These results allow to suggest that the proton bound by b_{562} upon reduction via centre $\underline{o}$ in the antimycin-inhibited $b-c_1$ proteoliposomes is not picked up by the protein from the M-phase, or in other words that E_m of b_{562} does not depend on pH inside the vesicles under these conditions.

Two thermodynamically equivalent but mechanistically different possi-

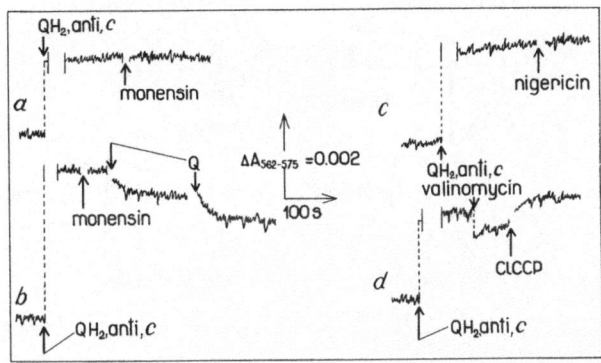

Fig.8. The absence of intravesicular pH effect on the redox state
of QH_2/Q-poised heme b_{562} in the antimycin-inhibited b-c_1
proteoliposomes.

To proteoliposomes in the appropriate medium supplemented
with Q_1, Q_1H_2 was added so as to bring about 40-70% reduction of heme b_{562} which was to followed by (i.e.30-55% of
the dithionite-induced slow oxidation of cytochrome b;
subsequently, cytochrome c was added to activate centre
o-catalyzed reaction at concentration which restored
(and stabilized) the initial reduction level observed
before the antimycin. This standard sequence of additions
is denoted in the Figure as QH_2, anti, c.
(a) Na^+-loaded proteoliposomes (0.26 µM of b-c_1 in the
Na^+, K^+-free medium (75mM choline chloride, 25 mM Tris-
HCl pH 7.6) supplemented with 50 µM Q_1. Additions: Q_1H_2,
40 µM; cytochrome c, 10 nM; monensin 10 ng/ml.
(b) Na^+,K^+-free proteoliposomes (0.26 µM of b-c_1) in the
medium (a) supplemented with 50 mM Na_2SO_4; initial Q_1
concentrations 20 µM. Additions: Q_1H_2, 80 µM; cytochrome
c, 10 nM; monensin, 10 ng/ml; Q_1 40 and 80 µM. (c,d) K^+-
loaded proteoliposomes (0.22 µM of b-c_1) in the Na^+, K^+-
free medium pH=8.5 supplemented with 50 µM Q_1. Additions:
Q_1H_2 , 40 µM; cytochrome c, 5 nM; nigericin, 0.7 µg/ml;
valinomycin, 0.4 µM; carbonyl-cyanide m-chlorophenyl hydrazone (ClCCP) 1 µM.

Monensin (or nigericin) brings about acidification (a,c) or alkalinization
(b) of the proteoliposome interior, which would induce reduction or oxidation of b_{562}, respectively bc E_m of this redox centre dependent on pH of
the M-aqueous phase. Additions of Q after monensin are shown in (b) to demonstrate that the redox response of b_{562} in these conditions does not limit the potential oxidizing effect of monensin.

bilities may be considered. First, in the antimycin-inhibited state all the
participants of the centre o-catalyzed reaction (i.e.ubiquinone, b_{566},b_{562})
may exchange redox-dependent protons with the C-phase independently of each

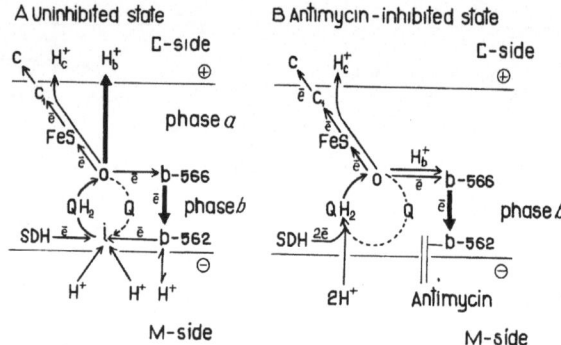

Fig.9. Effect of antimycin on electrogenic reactions in the mitochondrial complex b-c_1. See the text for discussion.

other. Second, one can visualize that (I) it is H-atom that is transferred
by ubiquinone to cytochrome b upon b_{566} reduction via centre o in the presence of antimycin (Fig.9,b) and (II) the proton remains bound to the cytochrome b protein during subsequent intramolecular vectorial transfer of the
electron from b_{566} to b_{562}, i.e.

$$(3) \quad (I) \quad \dot{Q}H_o + b_{566\ ox} \cdots^X\cdots b_{562\ ox} \longrightarrow Q + b_{566\ red}^{\qquad XH^+\cdots} b_{562\ ox}$$

$$(4) \quad (II) \quad b_{566\ red}^{\qquad XH^+\cdots} b_{562\ ox} \longrightarrow b_{566\ ox}^{\qquad XH^+} b_{562\ red}$$

where X denotes one of the two heme-linked ionizable groups of the two-heme
cytochrome b. It is then tempting to speculate that these two redox-linked
groups of mitochondrial cytochrome b with $pK_{ox} \sim 7$ previously thought to be
associated specifically one with b_{562} and another with b_{566} (7,28,30-33)
actually may not discriminate between e^- localization on the two heme groups
but rather respond to addition of the first and the second electron to the
cytochrome.

DISCUSSION

The results described in this paper and in (11,13,19,27) give strong
support to heme b_{562} localization at or near the M-side of the membrane.
This is in agreement with the electrical localization of b_{562} near the M-
side of the membrane as observed in the absence of antimycin (4,7,8). Altogether, these data favour the model of energy coupling in site 2 given by
schemes A,B in Fig.1. However it remains to be explained in terms of these
schemes why in the antimycin-inhibited state hemes b_{566} and b_{562} behave as
if located electrically at the C-side of the membrane and in the middle
of it, respectively (i.e., as in Fig.1,c,d) (4-6). As discusse earlier (4,
31, 12,13), this long-standing controversy between the results obtained in
the absence of antimycin (4,7,8) and in the presence of the inhibitor (4-6)

can be explained by antimycin-imposed arrest of electrogenic proton release from centre o. A proposed mechanism of the inhibitory effect of antimycin on the centre o-linked energy-transducing reaction is shown in Fig.9. Of the two protons released by QH_2 in centre o only one (associated with b_{566} reduction, H_b^+) is electrogenic as shown by the thick arrow whereas the other (H_c^+) can be viewed as going to the C-phase together with an electron, i.e. as electroneutral H-atom. The "electrogenic" proton will or will not be released to the C-phase at the stage of b_{566} reduction depending on whether the latter operates as an acceptor of electrons or hydrogen, respectively. In the uninhibited non-energized complex b-c_1, hemes b_{566} and b_{562} are known to switch from H to e^- transfer upon acidification with pK_{ox} ~7 (29-32).

However upon energization of the membrane, at $\Delta\psi$ of ~0.2V, pH in centre o may fall ~2 units below pH of the C-phase (7), i.e. well below pK_{ox} of b_{566} at any reasonable ambient pH. Accordingly, heme b_{566} is expected to operate in the energized membrane as electron acceptor (e.g., see ref.37) and the electrogenic proton release from centre o should occur at the stage of cytochrome b reduction (Fig.9,A).

An important finding was made in (31,32) that antimycin modifies drastically E_m/pH-dependence of both b_{566} and b_{562}, transforming the hemes into virtually pure hydrogen carriers throughout the entire pH range studied (5-9). Therefore b_{566} would accept both e^- and H^+ from ubiquinone in centre o in the antimycin-inhibited state and no electrogenic phase coupled to b_{566} reduction may be envisaged in this case (Fig.9,B), in agreement with (4,5). As discussed above (Fig.8), the proton bound by b_{566} during the reduction via centre o is likely to be retained by cytochrome b upon b_{566} oxidation by b_{562}. In principle, one could expect this redox-linked proton (H_b^+) to be released finally to the C-phase upon b_{562} reoxidation via centre i, but conceivably, this reaction does not take place in the presence of antimycin. As a consequence, antimycin not only inhibits electron transfer through centre i but also abolishes electrogenic proton release from centre o coupled to cytochrome b-reduction, as proposed earlier (4). Finally we would note that the suggested mechanism of membrane energization in mitochondrial site 2 may be fully applicable to b-c_1 complex of photosynthetic bacteria like Rhodobacter spaeroides. In these bacteria, the major electrogenic phase (antimycin-sensitive) in b-c_1 site complementary to $b_{566} \longrightarrow b_{562}$ vectorial electron transfer is known to be coupled to cytochrome b_{562} oxidation rather than to b_{566} reduction (6,37). This fact has been thought to favour schemes C,D, in Fig.1 and to be incompatible with the model in Fig.1,B and Fig.9 (6,37). In our opinion this is not necessarily so. The clue point may be that E_m/pH-dependence of cytochrome b in Rh.spaeroides is quite different from that of the mitochondrial cytochrome and approaches -60 mV/pH unit below, rather than above, pH 7, with pK_{red} ~7.5 (38). Thereafter in the energized chromatophore membrane, heme b_{566} (b-90) would serve as hydrogen acceptor in centre o at pH $\lesssim$ 9.5, i.e. the situation resembles that emerging in mitochondria for the antimycin-inhibited state (Fig.9,B).

It can be suggested that in chromatophores the proton accepted by b_{566} upon reduction via centre o is retained by cytochrome b protein during b_{566} oxidation by b_{562}, as discussed for the antimycin-blocked mitochondrial complex b-c_1, and is finally released to the C-phase upon reoxidation of cytochrome b via centre i. Thus the same antimycin-sensitive electrogenic step of proton release from centre o to the C-phase may appear as being coupled to cytochrome b reduction in mitochondria but to cytochrome b oxidation in chromatophores of photocynthetic bacteria, as regulated by E_m/pH dependence of cytochrome b in these objects.

Similar dislocation of the energy-coupled step from the reducing to the oxidizing side of cytochrome b and _vice versa_ can possibly occur under certain conditions in the membrane of the same organelle in response to changes in $\Delta\psi$ or in pH of the C-phase, which would allow for fine kinetic regulation of the energy-controlled electron flow through site 2 (cf. pH dependent shifts of crossover point in b-c_1 site described by Papa and co-workers, 39-41). The kinetic rather than thermodynamic role of cytochrome b redox-linked protonation in the protonmotive function of site 2 was suggested recently also in(28) and by Wikström (personal communication).

ACKNOWLEDGEMENTS

Thanks are due to Dr.W.Trowitzsch and Dr.P.Bollinger for the samples of myxothiazol and funicolosin and to Dr.E.V.Fok for Co(phen)$_3$Cl$_3$. We would also acknowledge helpful discussions with V.P.Skulachev, M.Wikström, W.S. Kunz, Yu.Kamensky and A.Yu.Mulkidjanyan. We are greatly indebted to Mr.S. Bogolowsky for drawing the figures.

REFERENCES

1. P. Mitchell, FEBS Symp.28: 353-370 (1972)
2. M.K.F.Wikström,Biochim.Biophys.Acta 301: 155-193 (1973)
3. P.Mitchell, FEBS Lett.56: 1-6 (1975).
4. A.A.Honstantinov, W.S.Kunz, and Yu.A.Kamensky, in:"Chemioosmotic Proton circuits in Biological Membranes" V.P.Skulachev and P.C.Hinkle eds., Addison-Wesley, Reading (Ms) pp.123-146 (1981).
5. A.Gopher and M.Gutman, J.Bioenerg.Biomembr.12: 349-367 (1980)
6. E.G.Glaser and A.R.Crofts, Biochim.Biophys.Acta 766: 322-333 (1984)
7. P.Mitchell, J.Theor.Biol.62, 327:367 (1976)
8. D.F.Wilson and M.Erecinska, Arch.Biochem.Biophys.167: 116-128 (1975)
9. M.Saraste, FEBS Lett.166: 367-372 (1983)
10. W.R.Widger, W.A.Cramer, R.Herrmann and A.Trebst, Proc.Natl.Acad.Sci.USA 81: 674-678 (1984)
11. W.S.Kunz, A.A.Konstantinov, L.M.Tsofina and E.A.Liberman, FEBS Lett.172: 261-266 (1984)
12. E.Yu.Popova and A.A.Konstantinov, Biological Membranes (U.S.S.R.) 3: 489-497 (1986)
13. A.A.Konstantinov, E.Yu.Popova and W.S.Kunz, EBEC Reports (Congress Ed.) Vol.4, pp.47 (1986).
14. G.D.Case and J.S.Leigh, Biochem.J. 160: 769-783 (1976)
15. I.V.Grigolava, Ph.Thesis, Moscow State University (1980)
16. I.V.Grigolava, A.A.Konstantinov, FEBS Lett.78: 36-70 (1977)
17. I.V.Grigolava, A.A.Konstantinov, Biokhimiya 44, 1329:
18. J.S.Rieske, Meth.Enzymol.10:239-245 (1967)
19. W.S.Kunz and A.A.Konstantinov, FEBS Lett.175:100-104 (1984)
20. R.E.Beyer, Meth.Enzymol.10: 186-194 (1967)
21. H.J.Harmon, J.D.Hall and F.L.Crane, Biochim.Biophys.Acta 344: 119-155 (1974)
22. A.V.Kiselev and A.A.Konstantinov, Bioorg.Chem.(U.S.S.R.) 2: 253-258 (1976)
23. M.Degli Esposti, A.L.Tsai, G.Palmer and G.Lenaz, Eur.J.Biochem.160:547-555 (1986)

24. E.A.Liberman, M.A.Vladimirova and L.M.Tsofina, Biofizika 22:255-259 (1977)

25. T.E.King, Advan.Enzymol.28:155-236 (1966).

26. A.D.Vinogradov, E.V.Gavrikova and V.G.Goloveshkina, Biophys.Res.Comm. 65:1264-1269 (1975)

27. E.V.Fok, E.Yu Popova, N.H.Subbotina, L.I.Zhyrov and A.A.Konstantinov Biological Membranes (U.S.S.R.) in press (1987).

28. G.Von Jagow, T.A.Link and T.Ohnishi, J.Bioenerg.Biomembr.18: 157-179 (1986)

29. F.Urban, and M.Klingenberg, Eur.J.Biochem.9: 519-525 (1969)

30. D.F.Wilson, M.Erecinska, J.S.Leigh, and M.Koppelma, Arch.Biochem.Bio-phys. 151: 112-121 (1972)

31. Yu.A.Kamensky, V.Yu.Artzatbanov, D.V.Shevchenko, A.A.Konstantinov, Dokl.Akad.Nauk.(U.S.S.R.) 249:994-997 (1979)

32. V.Yu.Artzatbanov and A.A.Konstantinov, EBEC Reports Vol.1,pp.73-74, P-tron Editrice, Bologna, (1980)

33. G.Von Jagow and W.D.Engel, FEBS Lett.111:1-5 (1980)

34. A.Konstantinov, T.Vygodina and I.U.Andreev, FEBS Lett.202:229-234 (1986).

35. J.S.Rieske, J.Bioener.Biomembr.18:235-257 (1986)

36. M.Hervas, F.F.De La Rosa, M.A.De La Rosa and M.Losada, Biochim.Biophys. Res.Comm.124: 807-814 (1984)

37. A.R.Crofts, in:"The enzymes of Biological Membranes" 2nd Edition, Marto-nosi, ed., pp.347-382, Plenum Press, N.Y. (1985)

38. K.M.Petty and P.L.Dutton, Arch.Biochem.Biophys.172: 346-353 (1976)

39. S.Papa, M.Lorusso, F.Guerrieri and G.Izzo, in: "Electron Transfer Chains and Oxidative Phosphorylation" E.Quagliariello et al.eds.,North-Holland Publ.Co., Amsterdam, pp.317-327 (1975)

40. S.Papa, M.Lorusso, G.Izzo and F.Capuano, Biochm.J. 194: 395-406 (1981)

41. S.Papa, M.Lorusso, D.Boffoli, and E.Bellomo, Eur.J.Biochm.137: 405-412 (1983)

THE Q-GATED PROTON PUMP MODEL OF UBIQUINOL CYTOCHROME c REDUCTASE:

ELECTRON AND PROTON TRANSFER PATHWAYS AND ROLE OF POLYPEPTIDES

Michele Lorusso, Domenico Boffoli, Tiziana Cocco,
Domenico Gatti and Sergio Papa

Institute of Medical Biochemistry and Chemistry, and Centre
for the Study of Mitochondria and Energy Metabolism, C.N.R.
University of Bari, Bari, Italy

INTRODUCTION

The finding that the H^+/e^- ratio for electron flow in the ubiquinol-
cytochrome c reductase is 4 (1,2) instead of 2 as predicted by the redox
loop mechanism (3) led Mitchell to revise his model and to develop the
Q-cycle (4). This mechanism, which also offers explanation for the peculiar features of electron transfer in the b-c$_1$ complexes of redox chains,
has met with general favour (5-9). At the same time that the Q-cycle was
proposed other groups developed indirect models for the protonmotive activity of the b-c$_1$ complex, based on co-operative interaction between the
redox reactions at the catalytic centers and proton transfer in proteins
(vectorial Bohr mechanism (10,11), b cycle (12); see also (13)). Further
refinement and/or revision of these models led to the proposal by Papa et
al.(14-17) of the Q-gated proton pump model and of the semiquinone-cycle
by Wikström and Krab (18).

The semiquinone-cycle, which is a direct type of mechanism, involves,
like the Q-cycle, cyclic electron flow effected by rapid exchange, at the
steady-state, of quinone molecules of the pool (Qp) with protein-bound
quinones. It departs from the Q-cycle in that it involves electrogenic migration of a special semiquinone, segregated in a quinone pocket, from the
quinol oxidation site at the P side of the membrane (proton output site,
center o) to a reduction site at the N side of the membrane (proton input
site, center i) (18). The semiquinone-cycle can explain observed electrogenicity of e$^-$-transfer between cytochrome b$_{562}$ and c$_1$ (8,18) and apparent
absence of lag (18,19) in the first turnover oxidation of fully reduced b
cytochromes (see however (20)).

The Q-gated proton pump model (Fig.1) (16,17,21) is essentially based
on the concept that the protonmotive stoicheiometry of b-c$_1$ complex results
from the protolytic properties of the semiquinone/quinone couple, which,
since of large difference in the pK's of $\dot{Q}H$ and QH_2 (22), can transfer
$2H^+$ per e$^-$. It is assumed that there is in the b-c$_1$ complex a $\dot{Q}H/QH_2$ couple (Qc) (23) which is tightly bound to protein(s) without significant exchange, at the steady-state, with Qp. Qc accepts both the first electron

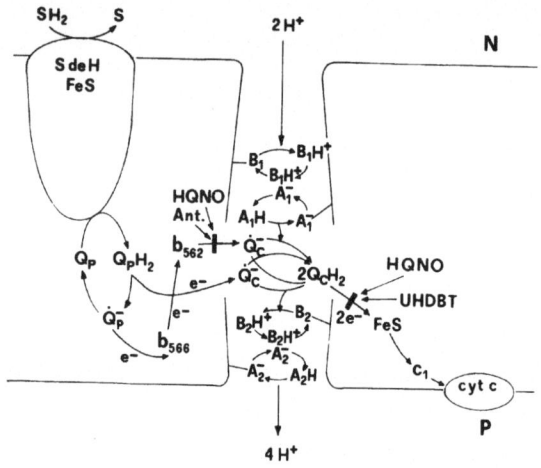

Fig.1. Q-gated proton pump model for electron transfer and
proton translocation in the b-c$_1$ complex.

of QpH$_2$ directly and the second electron via the b cytochromes in an antimycin-sensitive fashion. With these implementations a split pathway for
e$^-$ transfer in the b-c$_1$ complex (24,25) can apparently account (26,17) for
the various features of e$^-$ transfer and sensitivity to inhibitors without
the necessity of cyclic electron transfer. The third basic feature of the
Q-gated proton pump model is that the necessary anisotropy of protonation-
deprotonation of the quinone system, rather than deriving from specific
diffusion mobilities of Q, QH$_2$ and $\dot{Q}$ across the osmotic barrier of the
membrane (4,18) is instead imposed on the catalytic process of the system
by proteins which provide a co-operative protonation site from the N side
of the membrane and a deprotonation site to the external P side.

Here below some of the experimental work promoted by the Q-gated
proton pump model and the resulting supporting evidence are reported.

Electrogenic steps for internal electron flow in the cyt. c reductase

Work from our group (27,28,11,29) and others (25,7,4) has provided
evidence that electron transfer from b$_{566}$, on the substrate side, and b$_{562}$
on the oxygen side of the b-c$_1$ complex is electrogenic in that electrons
move across the membrane from b$_{566}$ closer to the P side to b$_{562}$ closer to
the N side. This results in a $\Delta\psi$-dependent crossover effects between the
two b hemes (4,11,25,29). Due to the pH dependence of the redox potential
of the two b hemes, the crossover effect results to be pH dependent and to
provide kinetics regulation of electron flow in the complex (29).These func-

768

tional studies have been substantiated by direct inspection of the membrane location of the hemes (30) and by genetic analysis of the structure of the apoprotein which has led to identify and locate in the membrane the two heme binding sites (31,32).

In the experiments illustrated in Table I the control site(s) and the relative influence of the ΔpH and $\Delta\psi$ components of $\Delta\mu H^+$ on internal electron transfer within the b-c$_1$ complex reconstituted into liposomes were characterized by testing the effect of valinomycin (which specifically collapses $\Delta\psi$) and nigericin (specific for ΔpH) on the steady-state redox levels of b and c$_1$ cytochromes.

Valinomycin addition to the b-c$_1$ vesicles under turning over conditions gave a substantial change towards oxidation of the steady-state redox level of cytochrome b$_{566}$, comparable reduction of cytochrome c$_1$ and little oxidation of b$_{562}$. The valinomycin induced redox transitions were not changed by the presence of nigericin, this showing that its effects did not depend on enhancement of intravesicular alkalinization. These observations, which are consistent with the sequence

$$\text{cyt.b}_{566} \xrightarrow{\text{e}^-} \text{cyt.b}_{562} \xrightarrow{\text{e}^-} \text{cyt.c}_1$$

indicate that $\Delta\psi$ controls electron flow both from b$_{566}$ to b$_{562}$ and from the latter to c$_1$. This, while inconsistent with the Q-cycle model, where transmembrane hydrogen conductions by QH$_2$ from b$_{562}$ at center i to the Fe-S protein and cytochrome c$_1$ at center o should rather be specifically depressed by the rise of transmembrane ΔpH induced by valinomycin, can be explained by electrogenic proton translocation associated to electron flow from b$_{562}$ to cyt.c$_1$ (as envisaged in the Q-gated proton pump, Fig.1) and vecto-

Table I. Redox transitions of b and c$_1$ cytochromes caused by addition of ionophores to turning-over b-c$_1$ vesicles.

Additions	Cyt.b$_{566}$		Cyt.b$_{562}$		Cyt.c$_1$	
	% red	ΔE_h (mV)	% red	ΔE_h (mV)	% red	ΔE_h (mV)
DQH$_2$	73		79		28	
DQH$_2$ + Val.	38	37	77	2	58	−32
DQH$_2$ + Val. + Nig.	8	50	61	20	70	−13
DQH$_2$	73		81		29	
DQH$_2$ + Nig.	68	7	75	10	35	− 7
DQH$_2$ + Nig. + Val.	12	69	63	14	74	−43

b-c$_1$ vesicles were supplemented with traces of purified cytochrome c and cytochrome oxidase so to establish a steady-state quinol oxidase activity. The steady-state reduction levels of cytochromes are expressed as percentage of the total dithionite reducible amounts. ΔE_h values refer to the difference in the redox level of cytochromes measured after and before addition of ionophores. The values represent the mean of three experiments. For experimental conditions and calculations see ref.s 16 and 29.

rial electron flow from b_{566} to b_{562}. It can be noted that the electron transfer step between cytochrome b_{562} and cytochrome c_1 was also under the control of the ΔpH component of the proton-motive force, as revealed by the effect of nigericin.

Characteristics of proton translocation in b-c_1 vesicles

Proton translocation in the b-c_1 complex in mitochondria (1,33) or in the isolated enzyme reconstituted in liposomes (16,34) has been followed either by reductant pulses of the oxidized enzyme or by oxidant pulses of the reduced system. In both cases the same $H^+/2e^-$ stoicheiometry for H^+ release of 4 was observed, this showing that the initial redox state of the enzyme and the modalities of activation of electron flow had no influence on the H^+/e^- stoicheiometry. Other experiments also showed that depression of the rate of electron flow in the complex, effected either by the use of low affinity quinols (16) or by chemical modification of proteins of the complex (35), did not lower the H^+/e^- stoicheiometry. Thus the pump of the b-c_1 complex doesn't exhibit molecular slipping at low rates (cf. 36).

The H^+/e^- stoicheiometry for the cytochrome c reductase in mitochondria or in the reconstituted system was found to be pH independent in the range from 5.5 to 7.5 (37,16), as expected from the large difference between the pKa's of $\dot{Q}H$ and QH_2. A small drop at pH's 8-8.5 was observed, which can be ascribed to negative contribution of Bohr effects in b cytochromes (37).

Kinetics of oxidation of exogenous quinols

Rapid flow analysis of kinetics of reduction of endogenous c cytochromes with different quinols added at concentrations close to their Km values, showed this to be much faster when the quinol were offered to "inside-out" submitochondrial particles than to intact mitochondria (38). These finding indicate a better accessibility of the ubiquinol oxidation site from the N side of the mitochondrial membrane, whereas according to the Q-cycle the oxidation site for ubiquinol should be located at or near the P side of the membrane (4).

Pre-steady state kinetics of b and c_1 cytochrome reduction: effect of antimycin

Addition of DQH_2 to fully oxidized b-c_1 complex resulted in multiphasic reduction of b cytochromes (5,39,40). A rapid phase amounting to about 35% of the total substrate reducible amount, followed by a steady phase and finally a second reduction phase were observed (Fig.2, Table II). The reduction of cytochrome c_1 showed a biphasic kinetics which could be resolved in two first order phases contributing by about 70% and 30% to the overall process and with kinetic constants differing by one order of magnitude (39,40). The first rapid process correlates kinetically with the rapid phase of cytochrome b reduction (Fig.2, Table II).

Antimycin lowered markedly the apparent initial rate of cytochrome c_1 reduction. The process was still biphasic, but the fast phase, whose kinetic constant remained unchanged, contributed now only by 30% to the overall process. The reduction of cytochrome b, in the presence of antimycin, was also biphasic and the rapid phase correlated with that of cytochrome c_1 reduction (40).

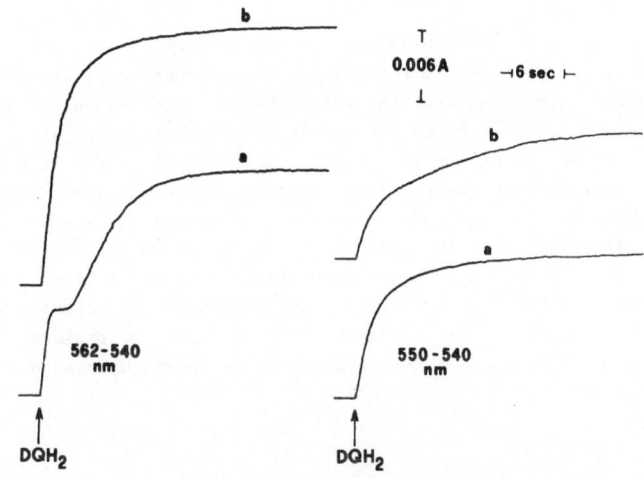

Fig.2. Pre-steady-state reduction kinetics of b and c_1 cytochromes in the b-c_1 complex. Effect of antimycin.
b-c_1 complex (1 μM cyt.c_1) was suspended in the reaction mixture containing 100 mM KCl, 20 mM Hepes, 0.1
mM EDTA, 1 mM KCN and, where indicated (trace b), 4
μM antimycin. Temperature, 1°C; pH, 7.2. Redox transitions of cytochromes were followed with a three channel air turbine spectrophotometer (Dept.of Biochemistry & Biophysics,Philadelphia). The reaction was started by the addition of 20 μM DQH$_2$. a, control; b, in
the presence of antimycin.

These antimycin effects which are apparently incompatible with the
Q-cycle (41), have yet been interpreted in terms of this mechanism by
assuming that in the initial reduction of b-c_1 complex by added quinols
after an initial rapid antimycin-insensitive reduction of half the amount
of Fe-S+c_1 and cyt.s b_{566} + b_{562}, a second slower phase sets in which is
considered to be inibited by antimycin on the basis of thermodynamic considerations (42-44).

Table II. Kinetic parameters for pre-steady-state reduction of
b and c_1 cytochromes in the b-c_1 complex.

	Control		+ Antimycin	
	$E_1(\%)$	$k_1(s^{-1})$	$E_1(\%)$	$k_1(s^{-1})$
Cyt.c_1	66	0.66	32	0.63
Cyt.b_{562}	38	0.55	62	0.70

The data presented were obtained by mathematical analysis of
traces shown in Fig.2. E_1 and k_1 represent respectively the relative contributions of the more rapidly reduced component and
the pseudo-first order reduction kinetic constant.

It seems to us that these observations can be, on the other hand, easily explained in terms of the Q-gated proton pump model (Fig.1). It is suggested, in this case, that the rapid phase of cytochrome c_1 reduction by duroquinol is mediated by Qc. Antimycin depresses this process by displacing $\dot{Q}c$ from its binding sites in the reaction pocket (23). The residual $\dot{Q}c$ is rapidly oxidized by the Fe-S protein and can mediate oxidation of QpH_2 to $\dot{Q}p$ which is the reductant for b cytochromes. This pathway may, indeed, rapidly proceed as long as oxidized b cytochromes are available to accept electrons from $\dot{Q}p$. At the steady-state since of the block of cytochrome b oxidation by antimycin, electron transfer through the complex will be practically suppressed. It should be recalled that the residual $\dot{Q}c$ acting in the rapid redox transitions, appears to be fully suppressed by antimycin under equilibrium conditions since of rapid dismutation (23).

Role of polypeptides

Role of polypeptides in the redox and proton motive activity of the $b-c_1$ complex was explored by means of chemical modification of specific aminoacid residues and selective proteolytic digestion of the enzyme.

These treatments produced, depending on the reagent and the conditions used, two types of effects: decoupling of proton pumping from electron flow or inhibition of electron flow without change in the H^+/e^- stoicheiometry.

Treatment of bovine $b-c_1$ complex in the soluble or reconstituted form with dicyclohexylcarbodiimide (DCCD, a specific modifier of acidic residues) under mild conditions leading to selective modification of the 8 kDa subunit resulted in decoupling of the proton pumping activity of the complex reconstituted into liposomes: vectorial proton translocation was suppressed, state 4 respiration was stimulated and the crossover effect exerted by $\Delta\mu H^+$ between cytochrome b_{562} and c_1 was partly abolished (35,45; cf. 46,47). More extensive reaction of DCCD with $b-c_1$ complex resulted in crosslinking of the 8 and 12 kDa subunits with the Rieske Fe-S protein (35,47), some modification of b cytochromes (46,47) and consequent inhibition of electron transfer.

Decoupling of proton pumping in reconstituted bovine $b-c_1$ complex was also brought about by digestion with papain of the oxidized soluble enzyme under conditions which resulted in the removal of a 3 kDa segment from core protein II and 1 kDa segment from the 15 kDa subunit (48).

These effects of papain resulted also in an apparent modification of the environment of the Rieske 2Fe-2S cluster as revealed by broadening of the EPR spectrum, particularly evident for the g_x signal, without any decrease of the total concentration of the cluster (49). It may be mentioned that similar modification of the environment of the 2Fe-2S cluster are caused by full reduction of the complex with dithionite (50) or by modification of core protein II by ethoxyformic anhydride (EFA) (51).

Evidence is available showing that the 15 kDa proteins is involved in the binding of $\dot{Q}c$ (52). Papain digestion of the partially reduced soluble $b-c_1$ complex resulted in a digestion of the Fe-S protein which was accompanied by disappearance of $\dot{Q}c$ and inhibition of electron transfer (49).

Fig.3 shows the effect of papain treatment on the pre-steady-state reduction of b and c_1 cytochromes in the $b-c_1$ complex supplemented with antimycin. Papain digestion of the oxidized complex had a further inhibitory effect on the apparent initial rate of c_1 reduction already depressed by antimycin (see Fig.2), without any effect on the rate of b cytochrome reduction

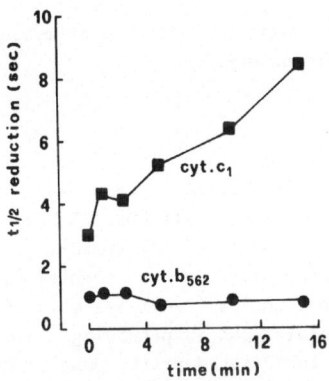

Fig.3. Effect of papain-digestion on the pre-steady-state
reduction of b and c_1 cytochromes in the b-c_1 complex inhibited by antimycin.

b-c_1 complex (120 µM cyt.c_1) in 100 mM KCl, 20 mM
Hepes (pH 6.8), 0.05 mM EDTA, was incubated with
papain at a concentration of 1 mg/20 mg complex protein, at 18°C. At the times indicated in the abscissa aliquots of the enzyme suspension were diluted (final concentration of 1.5 µM cyt.c_1) in the same reaction medium described in the legend to Fig.2, also
containing 5 µM antimycin and reduction of cytochromes monitored as in Fig.1. Temperature, 11°C; pH,
7.2. $t\frac{1}{2}$ is the time for 50% reduction of the total
substrate-reducible cytochromes (for experimental
conditions see 48).

(antimycin present). Kinetic analysis of cytochrome c reduction showed
that papain treatment caused the contribution of the fast phase of cytochrome c_1 reduction (see Fig.2 and Table II) to be lowered from 30% to
about 10%. Thus it seems that papain causes further displacement of $\dot{Q}c$ in
addition to that affected by antimycin.

Evidence has been reported that antimycin binds to the 12 kDa subunit (53). This subunit is, however, untouched by papain under conditions
where the Fe-S protein, Core protein II and the 15 kDa subunit were digested and $\dot{Q}c$ largely suppressed (49). It has been found that papain treatment did not affect the antimycin induced red-shift of cytochrome b_{562}.

It is conceivable that binding of antimycin to the 12 kDa subunit induces a large conformational change extending towards the $\dot{Q}c$ binding domains in other subunits (15 kDa and Fe-S protein) as well as to the heme
b_{562} site as indicated by its red-shift.

It was also found (51) that EFA modification of histidine residue(s)
in Core protein II caused inhibition of electron flow which had the same

characteristics of the inhibition affected by myxothiazol (center o, according to the Q-cycle terminology).

CONCLUSIONS

The work reviewed or presented in this paper identifies specific roles of oloproteins of the b-c$_1$ complex (8 kDa, 15 kDa, Core protein II) in the redox and proton-motive activity of the system. It should be recalled that the three models being used for the b-c$_1$ complex (Q-cycle, semiquinone-cycle and Q-gated proton pump) all envisage role of proteins in the binding of special quinone molecules and in providing proton conducting pathways. Of these three models, the Q-gated proton pump is the one which places particular emphasis on the role of proteins and co-operative events.

Evidence is presented for the existence in the b-c$_1$ complex of a quinone pocket where the antimycin-sensitive Q̇c species is located. This ubiquinone pocket with Qc appears to represent the critical center for both the redox and proton-motive activity of the b-c$_1$ complex. It seems that the quinone pocket is contributed by more proteins (15 kDa protein and the Rieske-iron sulfur protein). Oloproteins of the complex, 8 kDa, Co II and 15 kDa proteins, appear to be involved in the proton- motive activity of the complex. Ordered arrangement of these proteins appears to be critical. Chemical modification of 8 kDa or partial digestion of Co II and 15 kDa result in decoupling of proton pumping. The decoupling conditions exerted by controlled papain digestion causes also subtle changes in the environment of the Fe-S center. This may indicate critical role of this sites in the coupling activity.

The protolytic properties of the $\dot{Q}^-$/QH$_2$ system, combined with anisotropic protonation-deprotonation of these species provided by (co-operative) proton donating and proton withdrawing domains in the proteins, seems to offer a satisfactory working model for analyzing the redox-linked proton-motive activity of the system, without need of cyclic electron pathways as envisaged in the Q-cycle, double Q-cycle and semiquinone cycle.

REFERENCES

1. S. Papa, M. Lorusso and F. Guerrieri, _Biochim. Biophys. Acta_ 387: 425 (1975).
2. H.G. Lawford and P.B. Garland, _Biochem. J._ 136:711 (1973).
3. P. Mitchell, "Chemiosmotic Coupling in Oxidative and Photosynthetic Phosphorylation," Glynn Research, Bodmin (1966).
4. P. Mitchell, _J. Theor. Biol._ 62:327 (1976).
5. S. de Vries, _J. Bioenerg. Biomembr._ 18:195 (1986).
6. A. Konstantinov, S.W. Kunz and Y.A. Kamensky, _in_: "Chemiosmotic Proton Circuits in Biological Membranes," V.P. Skulachev and P.C. Hinkle, eds., Addison-Wesley Co., p. 123.
7. A.A. Konstantinov and E. Popova, this volume.
8. P.R. Rich, _J. Bioenerg. Biomembr._ 18:145 (1986).
9. P. Linke, G. Nechmann, A. Gothe and H. Weiss, Eur. J. Biochem. 158: 615 (1973).
10. S. Papa, F. Guerrieri, M. Lorusso and S. Simone, Biochimie 55:703 (1973).

11. S. Papa, Biochim. Biophys. Acta 456:39 (1976).
12. M.K.F. Wikström and K. Krab, Curr. Top. Bioenerg. 10:51 (1980).
13. G. von Jagow and W.D. Engel, FEBS Lett. 111:1 (1980)
14. S. Papa, in: "Membranes and Transport," A.N. Martonosi, ed., Plenum Publishing Co., New York, p. 363 (1982).
15. S. Papa, J. Bioenerg. Biomembr. 14:69 (1982).
16. S. Papa, M. Lorusso, D. Boffoli and E. Bellomo, Eur. J. Biochem. 137: 405 (1983).
17. S. Papa and M. Lorusso, in: "Biomembranes," R.M. Burton and F. Carvalho Guerra, eds., Plenum Publishing Co., New York, p. 257 (1984).
18. M. Wikström and K. Krab, J. Bioenerg. Biomembr. 18:181 (1986).
19. P.R. Rich and M.K.F. Wikström, FEBS Lett. 194:176 (1986).
20. S. De Vries, A.N. van Hoek, A. Ten Bokum and J.A. Berden, this volume.
21. S. Papa, M. Lorusso, D. Gatti and T. Cocco, in: "Structure and Function of Energy Transducing Systems," T. Ozawa and S. Papa, eds., Japan Sci. Soc. Press, Tokio, in press.
22. A.J. Swallow, in: "Function of Quinones in Energy Conserving Systems," B.L. Trumpower, ed., Academic Press, New York, p. 59 (1982).
23. T. Ohnishi and B.L. Trumpower, J. Biol. Chem. 255:3278 (1980)
24. M. Wikström and J.A. Berden, Biochim. Biophys. Acta 283:403 (1972).
25. M.K.F. Wikström, Biochim. Biophys. Acta 301:195 (1973).
26. S. Papa, F. Guerrieri, M. Lorusso, G. Izzo, D. Boffoli and I. Maida, in: "Vectorial Reaction in Electron and Ion Transport in Mitochondria and Bacteria," F. Palmieri et al., eds., Elsevier Biomedical Press, p.57, (1981).
27. S. Papa, A. Scarpa, C.P. Lee and B. Chance, Biochemistry 11:3091 (1972).
28. S. Papa, M. Lorusso, F. Guerrieri and G. Izzo, in: "Electron Transfer Chains and Oxidative Phosphorylation," E. Quagliariello et al., eds., North Holland, Amsterdam, p. 317 (1975).
29. S. Papa, M. Lorusso, G. Izzo and F. Capuano, Biochem. J. 194:395 (1981).
30. T. Ohnishi, H.J. Harmon and A.J. Waring, Biochem. Soc. Trans. 13:607, (1985).
31. M. Saraste, FEBS Lett., 166:367 (1984).
32. W.R. Widger, W.A. Cramer, R. Herman and A. Trebst, Proc.Natl.Acad.Sci. USA 81:674 (1984).
33. S. Papa, F. Guerrieri, M. Lorusso, G. Izzo, D. Boffoli, F. Capuano, N. Capitanio and N. Altamura, Biochem. J. 192:203 (1980).
34. K.H. Leung and P. Hinkle, J. Biol. Chem. 250:8467 (1975).
35. M. Lorusso, D. Gatti, D. Boffoli, E. Bellomo and S. Papa, Eur.J.Biochem. 137:413 (1983).
36. G. Proteau, J.M. Wrigglesworth and P. Nicholls, Biochem. J. 210:199, (1983).
37. S. Papa, F. Guerrieri, M. Lorusso, G. Izzo and F. Capuano, in: "Function of Quinones in Energy Conserving Systems," B.L. Trumpower, ed., Academic Press, New York, p. 527 (1982).
38. M. Degli Esposti, G. Lenaz, G. Izzo and S. Papa, FEBS Lett. 146:101, (1982).
39. S. De Vries, S.P.J. Albracht, J.A. Berden and E.C. Slater, Biochim. Biophys. Acta 681:41 (1982).
40. D. Boffoli, M. Lorusso and S. Papa, this volume.
41. M. Degli Esposti and G. Lenaz, FEBS Lett. 142:49 (1982).
42. P.R. Rich, Biochim. Biophys. Acta 722:271 (1983).

43. P.R. Rich, Biochim. Biophys. Acta 768:53 (1984).

44. A.R. Crofts, S.W. Meinhardt, K.R. Jones and M. Snozzi, Biochim. Biophys. Acta 723:202 (1983).

45. M. Degli Esposti, J.B. Saus, J. Timoneda, A. Bertoli and G. Lenaz, FEBS Lett. 147:101 (1982).

46. D.S. Beattie and L. Clejan, FEBS Lett. 149:245 (1982).

47. M.J. Nalecz, R.P. Casey and A. Azzi, Biochim.Biochim.Acta 724:75 (1983).

48. M. Lorusso, D. Gatti, M. Marzo and S. Papa, FEBS Lett. 182:370 (1985).

49. T. Cocco, S. Meinhardt, D. Gatti, M. Lorusso, T. Ohnishi and S. Papa, this volume.

50. S. De Vries, S.P.J. Albracht and F.Y. Leeuwerik, Biochim. Biophys. Acta 546:316 (1979).

51. M. Lorusso, D. Gatti, M. Marzo, D. Boffoli, T. Cocco and S. Papa, Eur. J. Biochem. 162:231 (1987).

52. T. Wang and T.E. King, Biochem. Biophys. Res. Commun. 104:591 (1982).

53. M.A. van Keulen and J.A. Berden, Biochim. Biophys. Acta 808:32 (1985).

PHOTOSYNTHETIC CONTROL AND ATP/ELECTRON RATIO IN BACTERIAL

PHOTOPHOSPHORYLATION

Veronique Adam, Marco Virgili, Giovanni Venturoli, Daniela
Pietrobon* and B.Andrea Melandri

Department of Biology, University of Bologna and
*CNR Center for the Study of the Physiology of
Mitochondria, University of Padua, Italy

INTRODUCTION

The quantitative validity of the delocalized chemiosmotic model for
energy transduction in photophosphorylation by bacterial membranes has
been extensively investigated. Conflicting results have been obtained,
some in apparent agreement with the model[1,2], and others documenting
serious discrepancies with the theoretical expectations (for a recent
review see Ref.3). As a possible interpretation, alternative to a fully
delocalized mechanism, a model for partial localization of the coupling
proton currents has been presented[4].

These quantitative tests rest generally on the reliability of the
techniques used for the evaluation of the electrochemical potential
difference of protons across the coupling membrane. Methods based on the
analysis of single and double inhibitor titrations have been proposed as
independent tests for localized coupling. This approach consists in the
evaluation of the response of coupled processes to inhibitors of the
primary or secondary pumps and in the independent evaluation of the
fraction of pumps inactivated by a given titer of inhibitor[5]. A
thorough analysis of this approach, based on linear and non linear non
equilibrium thermodynamics, has been also published[6,7].

In this paper we present some preliminary data on single inhibitor
titrations of bacterial photophosphorylation. The data are completed by
simultaneous measurements of the membrane potential (coincident under our
experimental conditions with $\Delta\mu_H^+$). The results, while indicating
that the mechanism of coupling can be delocalized, confirm the occurrence
of serious discrepancies in the flow-force relations of phosphorylation,
when the effects of inhibitors and of ionophore uncouplers are compared.

MATERIALS AND METHODS

Chromatophores from a green strain of <u>Rhodobacter</u> <u>capsulatus</u>, grown
photoheterotrophically on a malate synthetic medium, were prepared and
stored as previously described[8].

Photophosphorylation was measured as detailed in Ref.8, except
that 0.5 mM Na ascorbate plus 10 μM diaminodurne were added as redox
buffer in place of Na succinate. Also the assay for the ATPase activity
and the protocol for all kinetic measurements are described in Ref.8.

Inhibition by dicyclohexylcarbodiimide (DCCD) was obtained by

pretreating an aliquot of chromatophores with the inhibitor for 1 hour on
ice, as specified in Ref.9. The pretreated samples were stored at
16 °C in a glycerol containing buffer: under these conditions the degree
of inhibition was constant for at least 48 hours.

RESULTS AND DISCUSSION

The Correlation of the Rate of ATP Synthesis with the Fraction of Active Primary and Secondary Pumps

The rate of secondary electron transfer, and the rate of
photophosphorilation as well, is in chromatophores very sensitive
to the ambient redox potential[10,11,12]. This effect is specifically due
to the degree of reduction of ubiquinone pool and to its effect on the
kinetics of electron exchange with the bc complex[13,14]. In the
experimental conditions usually employed in our laboratory,and in many
others as well, the redox poise of the UQ pool was controlled by the
addition of 0.2 mM Na succinate, interacting with the UQ pool through the
respiratory succinate dehydrogenase; anaerobic conditions were simulated
by the inhibition of both terminal oxidases with 1 mM KCN. A more
effective redox control was obtained with the addition of 0.5 mM Na
ascorbate, interacting with the UQ pool via the artificial redox mediator
diamino durene (10 μM, a concentration not interfering significantly with
the kinetics of secondary electron transfer). The effects of these two
experimental conditions are compared in Table 1. The addition of
ascorbate results in a threefold stimulation of the rate of ATP synthesis
(J_p) , as compared to succinate; phosphorylation is however still fully
sensitive to inhibitors of the electron flow, confirming the absence of
any artificial electron transfer pathway catalyzed by 10 μM DAD.

The rate of phosphorylation as a function of the degree of
inhibition of ATP synthetases by DCCD, previously studied in the presence
of succinate[8], has been studied also under these new redox conditions
(compare Fig.3a, solid line). The absolute value of J_p in the control was
1040 umoles ATP synthetized per h per umole of Bacteriochlorophyll. For
these experiments the value of f_p was estimated from the rate of ATP
hydrolysis in the presence of 1 μM nigericin, 0.1 μM valinomycin and 50 mM
K^+, i.e. under partially uncoupled conditions in which the maximal rate
of ATPase can be measured. Evidence for the consistency of this approach
has been presented elsewhere[8]. The data confirm that the relative
inhibition of J_p is always markedly lower than the inhibition of ATPase.

Table 1. Effect of redox buffers on photophosphorylation.

Redox buffer	Rate of phosphorylation (μmoles ATP·h^{-1}· μmoles^{-1} BChl)			
	Control	Myxothiazol	Valinomycin	Oligomycin
succinate	290 (100)	68 (23)	28 (9.6)	48 (16)
ascorbate + DAD	840 (100)	40 (5)	175 (20)	50 (6)

The concentrations of redox carriers and inhibitors were: succinate,
0.2 mM; ascorbate 0.5 mM; DAD, 10 μM; myxothiazol, 1.5 μM; valinomycin,
7μM; oligomycin, 20 μg ml^{-1}.

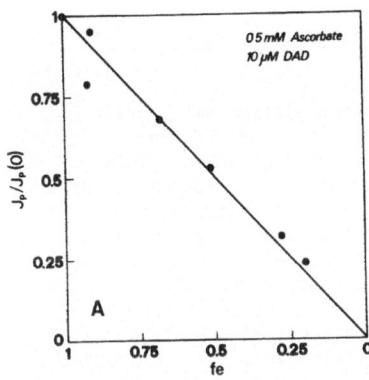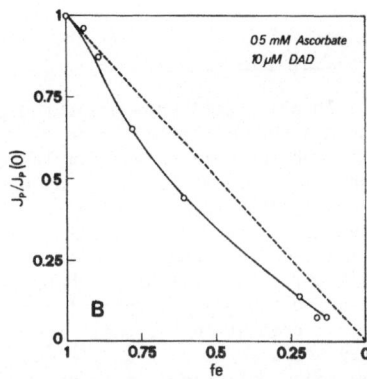

Fig.1. Relative inhibition of photophosphorylation as a function of fe
in a titration with antimycin (A) and myxothiazol (B). The control
value for Jp (Jp(0)) was 708 umoles ATP per hour per µmole BChl.

These results can be interpreted as unequivocal evidence for a strong
cooperative interaction in energy coupling among ATP synthetases.
These conclusions are further strengthened by the high absolute rates of
ATP synthesis obtained in the presence of ascorbate-DAD. Additional
information on the turnover of the ATP synthetase can be obtained from
this experiment. If J_p is normalized for the fraction af active ATP
synthetases, when photophosphorylation is progressively inhibited by
DCCD, rates as high as 5000 µmoles h^{-1}µmole ^{1}BChl. can be evaluated. This
value would correspond to a turnover number of about 200 s^{-1} ,if one
ATPase complex per Reaction Center is assumed to exist. This fast
turnover of the ATP synthetase is in good agreement with the estimation
by Schlodder et al.[15] for the CF_0 -CF_1 complex. Although this
evaluation is quite uncertain, being based on an assumption of the
ATPase/RC ratio, it certainly indicates that under our experimental
conditions the ATP synthetase is not limiting kinetically, when fully
activated by a fast electron transfer and/or by a large protonic
gradient.

The correlation of J_p with the fraction of active photosynthetic
chains, or, more strictly speaking, of the active bc_1 complexes, is
presented in Figure 1A for antimycin inhibition, and Figure 1B for
myxothiazol inhibition. In this case the fraction of active redox chains
was evaluated from the amplitude of the fast phase of the kinetics of
reduction of flash-oxidized reaction centers, as explained in details
elsewhere[8,9]. For both inhibitors the relative inhibition of
J_p is proportional, or even higher than the relative inhibition of
electron transfer. This indicates clearly that electron transfer is
generally limiting J_p , even when very large absolute rate of ATP
synthesis are achieved. This behaviour is obviously complementary to the
response to the inhibition by DCCD, and strongly support our earlier
conclusions that, in chromatophores, the rate of ATP synthesis is
strictly controlled by the rate of the redox reaction of the
photosynthetic chains.

The Lack of Correlation of J_p with the Amplitude of the Carotenoid Electrochromic Signal

In all experiments presented photophosphorylation was carried out in a spectrophotometer cuvette while the amplitude of the electrochromic signal was simultaneously recorded at 505 nm. This signal is usually utilized, and was used by us, for an estimation of the membrane potential, following a calibration with K^+ diffusion potentials. Transients of this signal have also been interpreted as measurements of ionic currents across the membrane; in this case the calibration in terms of elementary electric charges was obtained measuring the charge separation promoted by the photosynthetic reaction centers present in the same sample. The electrochromic shift has been amply utilized by us and by Jackson and collaborators[16,17] to study the flow-force relation of photophosphorylation.

In Figure 2 (curve a) the correlation of J_p with the amplitude of the carotenoid signal ($\Delta A\overline{5_{05}}$) is presented for the case of inhibition with myxothiazol. The curve includes data in which the redox poise was controlled either by succinate or by ascorbate-DAD. J_p depends very steeply from $\Delta\Psi$, but only above a certain threshold level (~230 mV). This behaviour is in good agreement with recent kinetic models of activation of the ATP synthetase by Δu_{H+} in chloroplasts.
The data of curve a agree also with recently presented results of Jackson et al.[1,2]. A steep dependence of J_p from $\Delta\Psi$, i.e. a large conductance of the secondary pump, is indeed the condition required for obtaining large cooperative effects of ATP synthetase during titrations with DCCD, according to the kinetic models of single and double inhibitor titrations recently developped[6,7].

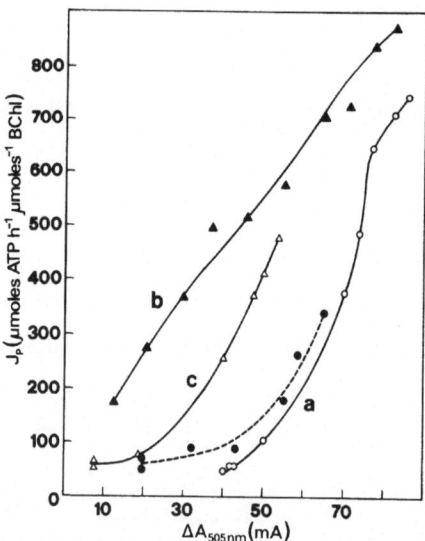

Fig.2. Rate of phosphorylation as a function of the steady state amplitude of the carotenoid signal during inhibition by myxothiazol (a) or uncoupling with valinomycin (b). Curve c refers to the response to myxothiazol of partially uncoupled membranes. Nigericin (1 μM) was present in all the assays.

An implicit assumption of these models is that energy coupling occurs uniquely through a delocalized protonic flow, and that, therefore, J_p vs. $\Delta\Psi$ curves (such as curve $\underline{a}$ of Figure 2) represent true flow-force relationships of the ATP synthetase.This simplifying interpretation conflicts, however, with the results obtained in Figure 2, curves $\underline{b}$ and $\underline{c}$. In these experiments the steady state value of $\Delta\Psi$ was decreased by progressively higher concentrations of valinomycin, being 1 μM nigericin always present in the assay (curve $\underline{b}$). A new and completely unrelated pattern in the J_p vs. ΔA_{505} plot was obtained, in which the dependence of J_p from $\Delta\Psi$ was much less steep than in curve $\underline{a}$. The flow-force relation for photophosphorylation is therefore not univocal, at least when it is evaluated from the carotenoid shift. Data similar to those presented here have been presented previously: the novel feature of this experiment is the high absolute rate of ATP synthesis obtained with the addition of ascorbate. Under these conditions J appears to be much more resistant to uncoupling by ionophores than in the presence of succinate; a substantial value of J_p (175 μmoles $\cdot$ h^{-1} μmoles^{-1} BChl), equal to 20 per cent of the control is observed with 1 μM nigericin, 7 μM valinomycin and 50 mM K$^+$, when practically the steady state amplitude of ΔA_{505} is reduced to less than 16 per cent. This observation is to be compared with previous data in the presence of succinate in which no phosphorylation was measured below an apparent threshold of 100-120 mV[1,18].

An intermediate situation is presented in Figure 2, curve $\underline{c}$. In this case chromatophores were partially uncoupled by 6 nM valinomycin, and a titration with myxothiazol was performed. The apparent flow-force relation obtained in this situation is not coincident with either of the two curves already described. It is clear therefore that, under our experimental conditions (i.e. pH 8.5, 50 mM KCl, continuous illumination for 30 s) any relation can be obtained between J_p and the steady state amplitude of the electrochromic carotenoid signal. These results, therefore, differ markedly from those obtained by Jackson and coll.[1,2], that show a univocal correlation between J_p and ΔA_{505} under different conditions of limiting light intensities or inhibition by myxothiazole or antimycin. The different experimental conditions used in these two sets of experiments should be however considered (pH = 8.5 vs. pH = 7.6, 30 s vs. 600 ms of illumination), which could affect the ionic distribution on both faces of the membrane. More importantly perhaps is the lack of utilization by the Birmingham group of any ionophore uncoupling in their experiments. It is, therefore, possible that the multiple relation of J_p vs. ΔA_{505} observed by us could be related to perturbation induced within the membrane dielectric by the ionic valinomycin-K$^+$ complexes, causing a distorsion of the effective electric potential profiles active in the coupling mechanism[19]. It is alternatively possible that ionophore perturb the natural protonic pathways in energy coupling[4], inducing thereby an alteration of the J_p vs. ΔA_{505} observed experimentally. In both cases the value of ΔA_{505} would not be directly related to the effective electrical forces acting in the mechanism of energy coupling in the local environment of the ATP synthetases.

The ATP/e ratio and the Control of Electron Transfer in DCCD Inhibited Chromatophores

The measure of the rate of electron transfer in bacterial photosynthesis is intrinsically difficult, due to the cyclic nature of the redox chain. When these measurements have to be performed in coupled chromatophores, moreover, the experimental difficulty is enhanced by the overlapping of the electrochromic response of the photosynthetic pigments over the redox signals of the electron carriers. We have recently developped a numerical method for resolving the redox and electrochromic

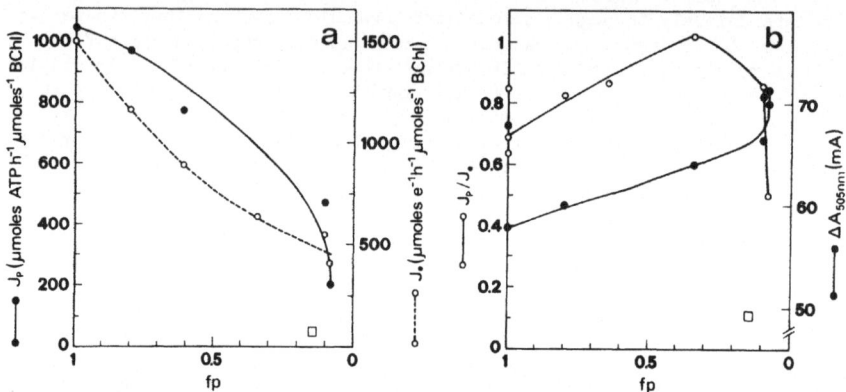

Fig.3. Effects of the inhibition of the ATP synthetase by DCCD on the
rate of phosphorylation (J_p) and of electron transfer (J_e)
(Fig.3a). Fig.3b shows the corresponding ATP/electron ratio
(J_p/J_e) and steady state amplitude of the electrochromic
carotenoid signal.

contributions in a complex kinetic trace[20]. This method has been
employed in this case to examine the effects of the block of the ATP
synthetases by DCCD on the rate of the redox reactions (J_e) and its
relation with the amplitude of $\Delta A505$ and to the rate of phosphorylation.
The rate of electron transfer has been evaluated by the rate of reduction
of cytochrome (c_1 + c_2)(measured at 551 - 542 nm and corrected for
electrochromic artifacts) after irradiation with continuous light for 600
milliseconds; this electron carrier(s) has been chosen since its reduction
is controlled by the rate of electron transfer within the bc_1 complex,
i.e. by the kinetic limiting step in the operation of the cyclic chain.
The results are presented in Figure 3a and 3b as a function of the
fraction of active ATP synthetases.

Progressive inhibition of the ATP synthetases results in a steady
decrease of J_e , that is eventually reduced to about 30 per cent of the
control value. These results agree, also quantitatively with those
presented by Myatt et al.[2], who observed an approximate threefold
stimulation in the reduction rate of reaction centers following
progressive uncoupling by FCCP in non-phosphorylating conditions. These
measurements were, however, performed without any correction for
overlapping electrochromic signals. The relative decrease in J_e following
ATP synthetase inhibition by DCCD, is constantly more pronounced than that
on photophosphorylation. Consequently the J_p /J_e ratio, i.e. the ATP/e
ratio is stimulated by DCCD (Figure 3b). This observation is consistent
with previous data on oxidative phosphorylation by Rb. capsulatus grown
aerobically[21], and indicates that a considerable part of the proton leak
causing a decrease of the photophosphorylation efficiency may occur
through "slipping" or damaged ATP synthetases. The experimental ATP/e

ratio goes through a maximum and eventually drops very steeply to zero, when nearly all ATP synthetases are blocked by the inhibitor. The maximum value of J_p / J_e , reached for $f_p = 0.4$ (corresponding to an incubation with 280 nmoles DCCD per μmoles BChl during the pretreatment with the inhibitor), approaches the value of 1. This is the maximum theoretical stoichiometry for a chemiosmotic model in which two protons per electrons are translocated by the photosynthetic chain, and two protons per ATP are utilized by the ATP synthetase. Under these conditions the dissipative proton currents through the membrane and the ATPases should have become negligible as compared to the phosphorylating H^+ flux. This point is still under investigation. Parallel to the decrease in J_e and inhibition of J_p , and consistent with a chemiosmotic model, DCCD causes a stimulation of the amplitude of the electrochromic signal (Figure 3b). The maximal stimulation observed is very limited, about 24 per cent of the amplitude in phosphorylating controls; also in this case, analogously to J_p , this would correspond to a very steep dependence of J_e from $\Delta\Psi$ in the flow-force relationship for photosynthetic control.

ACKNOWLEDGEMENTS

This research was partially supported by Consiglio Nazionale delle Ricerche and by Ministero della Pubblica Istruzione of Italy. V.A. was supported by a fellowship of Ministero degli Affari Esteri of Italy.

REFERENCES

1. A.J.Clark, N.P.J.Cotton and J.B.Jackson, The relation between membrane ionic current and ATP synthesis in chromatophores from Rhodopseudomonas capsulata, Biochim. Biophys. Acta, 723:440 (1983).
2. J.F.Myatt, N.P.J.Cotton and J.B.Jackson, Protonmotive activity of the cytochrome b/c1 complex in chromatophores of Rhodobacter capsulatus in the presence of myxothiazol and antimycin A, Biochim. Biophys. Acta, 890:251 (1987).
3. B.A.Melandri and G.Venturoli, Local and delocalized interactions in energy coupling, in "Encyclopedia of Plant Physiology,vol.19. Photosynthesis III. Photosynthetic Membranes and Light Harvesting Systems" L.A.Staehelin and C.J.Arntzen, eds., Springer-Verlag, Berlin (1986).
4. H.V.Westerhoff, B.A.Melandri, G.Venturoli, G.F.Azzone and D.B.Kell, A minimal hypothesis for membrane-linked free-energy transduction, Biochim. Biophys. Acta 768:257 (1984).
5. G.D.Hitchens and D.B.Kell, On the extent of localization of the energized membrane state in chromatophores from Rhodopseudomonas capsulata N22, Biochem. J. 206:351 (1982).
6. D.Pietrobon and S.R.Caplan, Double-inhibitor and uncoupler-inhibitor titrations. 1.Analysis with a linear model of chemiosmotic energy coupling, Biochemistry 25:7682 (1986).
7. D.Pietrobon and S.R.Caplan, Double-inhibitor and uncoupler-inhibitor titrations. 2.Analysis with a nonlinear model of chemiosmotic energy coupling, Biochemistry 25:7690 (1986).
8. M.Virgili, D.Pietrobon, G.Venturoli and B.A.Melandri, Single and double inhibitor titrations of bacterial photophosphorylation, in "Progress in Photosynthesis Research, vol.3" J.Biggins, ed., Martinus Nijhoff Publishers, Dordrecht (1987).
9. G.Venturoli and B.A.Melandri, The localized coupling of bacterial photophosphorylation, Biochim. Biophys. Acta, 680:8 (1982).
10. A.R.Crofts and C.A.Wraight, The electrochemical domain of photosynthesis, Biochim. Biophys. Acta 726:149 (1983).

11. A.Baccarini Melandri, B.A.Melandri and G.Hauska, The stimulation of photophosphorylation and ATPase by artificial redox mediators in chromatophores of Rhodopseudomonas capsulata at different redox potentials, J. Bioenerg. Biomembr. 11:1 (1979).

12. W.H.van den Berg, W.D.Bonner and P.L.Dutton, Redox potential dependence of photophosphorylation and electron transfer in continuous illumination of Rhodopseudomonas sphaeroides chromatophores, Archiv. Biochem. Biophys. 222:299 (1983).

13. A.R.Crofts, S.W.Meinhardt, K.R.Jones and M.Snozzi, The role of the quinone pool in the cyclic electron transfer chain of Rps. sphaeroides: a modified Q-cycle mechanism, Biochim. Biophys. Acta,723:208 (1983).

14. G.Venturoli, J.G.Fernandez-Velasco, A.R.Crofts and B.A.Melandri, Demonstration of a collisional interaction of ubiquinol with the ubiquinol-cytochrome c oxidoreductase complex in chromatophores from Rhodobacter sphaeroides, Biochim. Biophys. Acta, 851:340 (1986).

15. E.Schlodder, P.Graber and H.T.Witt, Mechanism of Photophosphorylation in Chloroplasts, in "Electron Transport and Photophosphorylation" J. Barber, ed., Elsevier Biomedical Press, Amsterdam (1982).

16. A.Baccarini Melandri, R,Casadio and B.A.Melandri, Electron transfer, proton translocation and ATP synthesis in bacterial chromatophores, in "Current Topics in Bioenergetics, vol.12" D.Rao Sanadi, ed., Academic Press, New York (1981).

17. W.Junge and J.B.Jackson, The development of electrochemical potential gradient across photosynthetic membranes, in "Photosynthesis. Energy Conversion by Plants and Bacteria" Govindjee, ed., Academic Press. New York (1982).

18. B.A.Melandri, G.Venturoli, A.De Santis and A.Baccarini Melandri, The induction kinetics of bacterial photophosphorylation, Biochim. Biophys. Acta 592:38 (1980).

19. V.P.Skulachev, The localized $\Delta\bar{\mu}H^+$ problem. The possible role of the local electric field in ATP synthesis, FEBS Lett. 146:1 (1982)

20. G.Venturoli, M.Virgili, B.A.Melandri and A.R.Crofts, Kinetic measurements of electron transfer in coupled chromatophores from photosynthetic bacteria: a method of correction for the electrochromic effects, FEBS Lett., in press (1987).

21. A.Baccarini Melandri and B.A.Melandri, Coincidence of the coupling factor of photosynthesis and respiration in Rps. capsulata, FEBS Lett. 21:131 (1972).

IX. PROTON MOTIVE ACTIVITY: Short Report

PROTONMOTIVE ACTIVITY OF MITOCHONDRIAL CYTOCHROME c OXIDASE

N. Capitanio, E. De Nitto, and S. Papa

Institute of Medical Biochemistry and Chemistry
University of Bari
Bari, Italy

Electron transfer catalyzed by cytochrome c oxidase, from cytochrome c to dioxygen, results in the generation of transmembrane electrochemical gradient ($\Delta\tilde{\mu}H^+$) provided firstly by the topological asymmetry of the reduction of dioxygen to water (1, 2). In addition, mitochondrial and some bacterial cytochrome c oxidases exhibit a redox-linked proton ejection generally considered as evidence for an electrogenic proton pumping activity from the matrix to the external space (3-5).

This paper reports on a systematic study of the characteristics of the redox-linked proton ejection by cytochrome oxidase both in intact mitochondria and in reconstituted vesicles. The main results can be summarized as follows:

1) <u>Proton translocation in rat-liver mitochondria</u>: When an anaerobic suspension of mitochondria, incubated with succinate plus rotenone is pulsed with O_2, the H^+/e^- ratio for proton output was around 2.3 independent of the amount of O_2 added (2→ 4 equivalents e^-/mg protein) and of

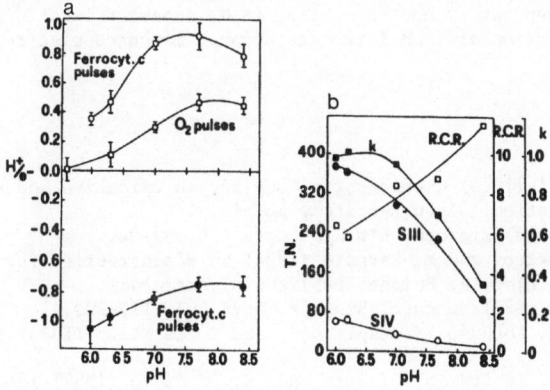

Fig. 1. Effect of pH on proton translocation elicited by ferrocytochrome
c and oxygen pulse, respiratory activity and rate constant of
cytochrome c oxidation in cytochrome oxidase vesicles.

the rate of electron flow (adjusted by malonate). With ascorbate plus TMPD, in the presence of antimycin plus myxothiazol, the H^+/e^- ratio, corrected for the H^+ release in the oxidation of ascorbate to dehydroascorbate, was around 0.7. The ratio decreased when the rate of electron flow was lowered by decreasing TMPD concentration (6).

2) Proton translocation in cytochrome oxidase vesicles.
    a) Ferrocytochrome c pulses of aerobic suspension of oxidase vesicles give, at pH 7.5, H^+/e^- ratios around 1. Oxygen pulses of anaerobic ferrocytochrome c-supplemented oxidase vesicles give, under the same conditions, an H^+/e^- ratio around 0.3 (5)..
    b) The redox linked proton ejection in cytochrome oxidase vesicles exhibits a marked pH dependence. As shown in Fig. 1 at pH below 6.0 negligible proton ejection occurs in the oxidant pulse; rising the pH the H^+/e^- ratio increases reaching a maximal value of 0.45 at pH 7.7.

In the reductant pulse the same pH dependence is observed but in all the pH range examined the H^+/e^- ratio was always two-four times larger than that measured in the oxidant pulse.

The respiratory activity measured, in the same pH range, both polarographically, at the steady-state, and spectrophotometrically, as rate of ferrocytochrome c oxidation, shows an opposite trend decreasing with enhancing pH (7).
    c) Millimolar concentrations of divalent cations (Mg^{2+}, Ca^{2+}) depress the rate of cytochrome c oxidation and in addition depress the H^+/e^- ratio to 0.5 with the ferrocytochrome c pulses and around 0.1 with the oxygen pulses (7).

In conclusion the H^+/e^- stoicheiometry of cytochrome c oxidase appears to vary significantly with the state of the enzyme, the rate of electron flow through the oxidase, the actual pH and the presence of divalent cations.

The mechanistic implications of those characteristics and their possible physiological significance is under investigation.

a) (o–o) Pulses of 4 µM ferrocytochrome c (cytochrome oxidase vesicles 0.5 µM); (□–□) pulses of 1 µM O_2; (●–●) pulses of 4 µM ferrocytochrome c in the presence of 3 µM CCP. (b) Polarographic assay of respiratory activity in the absence (o–o) and in the presence (●–●) of valinomycin plus CCP; (□–□) respiratory control ratio; (■–■) apparent first order constant k of the oxidation of 5 µM ferrocytochrome c measured spectrophotometrically at 4°C.

REFERENCES

1. P. Mitchell (1966) Chemiosmotic Coupling in Oxidative and Photosynthetic Phosphorylation, Glynn Research, Bodmin.
2. S. Papa (1976) Biochem. Biophys. Acta 456, 39–84.
3. M.K.F. Wikström and M. Saraste (1984) in Bioenergetics (L. Ernster, ed.) pp. 49–94, Elsevier Science Publishers, Amsterdam.
4. B. Ludwig (1980) Biochem. Biophys. Acta 594, 177–200.
5. S. Papa, M. Lorusso, N. Capitanio, and E. De Nitto (1983) FEBS Lett. 157, 7–14.
6. S. Papa, N. Capitanio, G. Izzo, and E. De Nitto (1987) in Advances in Membrane Biochemistry and Bioenergetics (C.H. Kim ed.), Plenum Press, in press.
7. S. Papa, N. Capitanio, and E. De Nitto (1987) Eur. J. Biochem., in press.

APPENDIX

PROPOSAL FOR A NOVEL NOMENCLATURE FOR THE SUBUNITS OF CYTOCHROME C OXIDASE

G. Buse, G.C.M. Steffens, R. Biewald, B. Bruch and
S. Hensel

RWTH Aachen
Abteilung Physiologische Chemie
Fachgebiet Molekulare Biologie der Proteine
Klinikum, Pauwelsstraße
5100 Aachen

Cytochrome c oxidase (E.C.1.9.3.1), has been isolated from a variety of eucaryotic and procaryotic organisms as oligomeric enzyme complexes with 2 to 13 subunits. We define a subunit as a protein, which can be obtained as a stoichiometric component of the oligomeric complex. The investigations on the subunit composition have been carried out by a number of groups and have lead to different nomenclatures. The most adopted nomenclatures for the subunits of the beef heart enzyme are listed in the table. From this table it is clear, that this development has lead to a rather confusing situation.
The authors therefore suggest to introduce a new nomenclature. This nomenclature is based on the available proteinchemical evidence for the so far most complex enzyme isolated from bovine heart. The subunits of this enzyme are basically listed according to their molecular masses and designated with Roman numerals I - XIII. On historical grounds an exception is made for the subunits II and III, they will keep their original nomenclature. In this and other cases this nomenclature does not necessarily correspond to the electrophoretic migration order (apparent Mr) in PAGE experiments. This can be seen from the comparison of the proposed nomenclature and the assignment of these components in the electrophoretic pattern (Swank-Munkres gel with 15% acrylamide).

Subunits of cytochrome c oxidases from other tissues and organisms might be represented by a nomenclature based on the same principle or on a nomenclature being used until exact protein Mr data are available. Homology to a specified subunit from the bovine heart cytochrome oxidase complex may then be indicated by the addition of a Roman numeral in parenthesis. Thus subunit VIII(XII) of yeast cytochrome c oxidase represents the second smallest subunit among the nine proteins of the yeast enzyme, and indicates its homology to subunit XII of the bovine heart enzyme.

BOVINE HEART CYTOCHROME C OXIDASE

YEAST OXIDASE

Nomenclature	Mr	N-terminal Sequences	Buse et al.	Capaldi et al.	Kadenbach et al.	YEAST OXIDASE
I	56993	Formyl-Met-Phe-Ile-Asn-	I	I	I	I
II	26049	Formyl-Met-Ala-Tyr-Pro-	II	II	II	II
III	29918	(Met→)Thr-His-Gln-	III	III	III	III
IV	17153	Ala-His-Gly-Ser-	IV	IV	IV	V(IV)
V	12436	Ser-His-Gly-Ser-	V	V	Va	VI(V)
VI	10668	Ala-Ser-Gly-Gly-	VIa	a	Vb	IV(VI)
VII	10063	Acetyl-Ala-Glu-Asp-Ile-	VII	c	VIb	–
VIII	9419	Ala-Ser-Ala-Ala-	VIb	b	VIa	–
IX	8480	Ser-Thr-Ala-Leu-	VIc	VI	VIc	–
X	6243	Phe-Glu-Asn-Arg-	VIIIc		VIIa	VII(X?)
XI	∼6000	Ile-His-Gln-Lys-	–	VII's	VIIb	–
XII	5441	Ser-His-Tyr-Glu-	VIIIa		VIIc	VIII(XII)
XIII	4962	Ile-Thr-Ala-Lys-	VIIIb		VIII	VIIa(XIII?)

Besides being based on exact data, this nomenclature is open for future developments and leads to some immediately understandable features:
a) Subunits I, II, III are those coded for in mitochondria or bacteria.
b) Subunits V, VI, VII are those without a membrane spanning sequence.
c) Subunits VII, VIII, IX, XI? do not have homologous counterparts in the yeast enzyme.
d) Subunits X, XI, XII, XIII are the smallest components.

AUTHOR INDEX

Friden H. <u>641</u>
Furushima R. 683

Gabellini N.A. <u>35</u>
Gadaleta M.N. 153
Gadsby P.M.A. 349
Gallerani R. 103, 133, 139
Gampel A. 67
Gatti D. 559, 767
Gennis R.B. <u>15</u>
Gilbert K. 79
Glaser E. <u>625</u>
Görrisen H. 215
Gorren A.C.F. 385
Gounaris K. 657
Grahn M.F. <u>341</u>, 697
Greenwood C. 349
Grivell L.A. 97
Guiard B. 189, 235

Hagen W.R. <u>459</u>
Hakvoort T. 141, <u>343</u>
Haltia T. 247, <u>335</u>
Harnisch U. 303
Haris P. 341
Hartl F.U. <u>189</u>, 235
Haser R. <u>423</u>
Hatfield J.S. 407
Hawkesford M.J. <u>87</u>
Hederstedt L. 641
Hensel S. 261, 791
Ho S.H. 309
Holm L. 247
Howel N. 79
Hüther F.J. 399

Jalli T. 247
Johnson M.K. <u>473</u>
Jordi W. 215
Joste V. <u>225</u>

Kadenbach B. 57, <u>399</u>
Kälin J. 585
Kanbay F. 119
Kearney E.B. 473
Kim C.H. <u>415</u>
King T.E. <u>309</u>, 415, <u>503</u>, 509
Kita K. <u>683</u>
Konstantinov A.A. 609, <u>751</u>
Kreike J. <u>111</u>
Krummeck G. 111
Kurowski B. 41

Kwakman J.H.J.M. 97

Labonia N. 239
Lanave C. 103
Leaver C.J. 87
Lee C.P. 407
Lenaz G. 337, 549, 561
Lezza A.M.S. 153
Link T.A. <u>289</u>
Lorusso M. 559, 669, <u>767</u>
Lottspeich B. 325
Ludwig B. <u>41</u>
Lunts T.L. <u>271</u>

Ma Y. 683
Macino G. <u>161</u>
Maguire J. 485
Maison-Peteri B. 439
Malatesta F. 433, 435, 689
Malmström B.G. 437, 439, 705, <u>733</u>
Margoliash E. 271
Marsh D. 215
Martens M.E. 407
Matsushita K. 443
Meinhardt S.W. 443, <u>533</u>, 559
Melandri B.A. 777
Mengel T. 57
Merlos-Lange A.M. 119
Metso T. 247
Meunier B. 135
Meunier-Lemesle D. 131, <u>673</u>
Michel H. 325
Morningstar J.E. 473
Mossé J. 423
Muijsers A.O. 141, 343
Müller M. <u>239</u>
Muroff I. 67

Nelson B.D. 225
Nelson M.A. 161
Neupert W. 189, 197, 235
Nicholls P. <u>391</u>
Nicholson D.W. <u>197</u>
Nishikimi M. 315

Ohnishi T. <u>443</u>, 533, 559
Oraler G. 119
Ostermann J. 189, 197, <u>235</u>
Oya H. 683
Ozawa T. <u>315</u>

Pacoda D. <u>133</u>

800

Cytochrome b (continued)
  redox reaction with SQ/QH_2 couple
  (continued)
    593
  reduction kinetics, 669, 770
  resistance to inhibitors, 80, 622
Cytochrome b_2
  import into yeast mitochondria,
    189, 195
Cytochrome b_{560} (mitochondrial SDH)
    649 ff.
Cytochrome b_{566}
  E. Coli deficient mutant, 566
  Cyb A gene, 566
Cytochrome b_{558}, 641 ff.
  chemical modification by diazoben-
    zen sulfonate, 644
  properties in Ascaris muscle mito-
    chondria, 683
Cytochromes b_{558}-b_{595}-d complex
  aminoacid sequence, 19
  chromosomal mutants, 19
  cyd c gene, 18
  cyd mutants, 18
  cyd operon, 18-19
  electron transport in, 570-571
  enzymatic properties, 569
  ESR spectra, 570
  molecular properties, 568
Cytochrome b_{559}
  location and function, 657
Cytochrome b_{561} (E.Coli)
  cyb B gene, 15, 566
Cytochrome b_{561} (R.Spheroides)
  electrogenicity of the reduction,
    625
Cytochrome b_{562}-o complex, 17, 565-
    574
Cytochrome c
  binding site to cytochrome oxidase
    241, 249, 274
  distance to redox centers of cyto-
    chrome oxidase, 249, 718
  kinetic interactions with cytochro-
    me oxidase, 272, 386
  redox titration of
    in Rdp.viridis, 603
  role in non sulfur bacteria, 579
Cytochrome c_1
  c DNA cloning, 318
  cristallisation, 304
  fbc C gene for, 36

Cytochrome c_1 (continued)
  gene for
    in P. Denitrificans, 44
  import, 235
  induction of
    by thyroid hormones, 227
  ligand of the heme, 38
  pet C gene for, 27
  primary structure, 304, 321
  reduction kinetics, 669, 770
Cytochrome c_2, 24-31
Cytochrome c_1 - c
  electron transfer between, 416-420
  kinetics of reduction, 528
Cytochromes c_3, 423
Cytochrome oxidase$_{260}$ (in Rhodobac-
    ter), 26
Cytochrome oxidase b_{410}, 24-26
Cytochrome c oxidases
  cristallisation, 320
  and cytoplasmic male sterility, 87
  electron transfer, 385, 425, 429
  expression of mt mRNAs for, 146,
    157
  genes expression
    in P. Denitrificans, 41
    in rat liver mitochondria, 57
    in Tripanosome, 141
  homologies of yeast and bovine
    subunits of, 256-258
  isologs of subunit V, 53
  mitochondrial genes for, 20,88,103
    120, 146, 154
  nuclear genes for, 49, 57, 137,
    253
  pet mutants defective in, 182
  synthesis and assembly in yeast,
    184
Cytochrome c peroxidase, 372
Cytoplasmic male sterility (CMS)
    87-93

DCCD
  reaction with sub.III of cytochro-
    me c oxidase, 243, 248, 391
D component in PSII, 541
Desulfovibrio desulfuricans
  cytochrome c_3, 423
Deutero-hemin, 202
D. discoideum cytochrome oxidase,
    282
Diffusion of quinones, 550, 561

Quinol oxidases
  in E.Coli (see terminal oxidases)
  mutants defective in, 26, 633
Quinone reaction domains, 495 ff.,
      518, 526, 533, 617, 762 ff.
QP-C (see ubiquinone binding proteins)
QP-S (see ubiquinone binding proteins)

Random collisional model, 9, 549
Rapid freeze/quench technique in study
      of bc_1 complex, 527
Reaction center
  cytochrome c complex, 589
  incorporation into SMP, 589
  in monolayer films, 601
  in Photosystem II, 657
  in Rhodobacter capsulata, 23,35,633
  in Rhodobacter sphaeroides, 593,633
  in Rhodopseudomonas viridis, 609
Red shift
  of cytochrome b, 496
Redox Bohr effect
  in cytochrome a, 727
Redox centers of cytochrome oxidase
  anticooperative redox coupling bet-
      ween cytochrome a and Cu_A,705
  location (see subunits of cytochro
      me oxidase)
  relative distance among, 250
  steady-state reductional levels
      pH-dependence, 439, 729
Redox components
  in Chloroflexus, 581
Respiratory control in cytochrome
      oxidase vesicles
  effect of ΔpH and $\Delta \psi$ on, 391
Rho° genome, 184
Rho⁻ genome, 70
Rhodobacter
  Capsulata
    bc_1 complex, 633
    photosynthetic control, ATP/e⁻
      ratio, 777
    properties of mutant strains,577
  Sphaeroides
    bc_1 complex, 585, 593
    reaction center, 586
      incorporation in SMP, 589
    reduction of cytochrome b_{561} in,
      625
Rhodopseudomonas sphaeroides
  (see Rhodobacter sphaeroides)

Rhodopseudomonas Viridis
  reaction center, 325, 609-610
Rhodospirillum rubrum
  isolation of UQ-cytochrome c_2
      reductase, 589
Rieske Fe-S protein
  aminoacid sequence, 297, 304
  effect of proteolytic digestion
      and chemical modification,
      559
  folding pattern, 299
  hydropathy pattern, 298
  inhibitor-resistant mutants,637
  ligands for the cluster, 299
RNA
  expression
    in human mitochondria,146, 153
    in yeast mitochondria,71
  processing
    consensus sequences for, 161
    site for
      in N.Crassa mitochondrial
        genes, 166

Saccaromyces Cerevisiae
  kinetics of cytochromes b and c
      oxidation in mitoplasts,518
SDS-page
  of subunit of bc_1 complex, 291
  of subunits of cytochrome oxidase
      283
Slip (molecular)
  mechanism of
    in bc_1 complex, 498
Spin coupling
  in succinate Q reductase, 467
Stigmatellin
  red shift of cytochrome b, 496
  resistance to, 30, 80
Subunits of cytochrome oxidase
  alignment of interspecies sequen-
      ces, 262-263
  aminoacid sequences of, 265, 275
  bacterial enzymes, 744
  binding of ATP to, 400, 285
  hydrophobic sequences of, 265
  interactions with phospholipid
      membranes, 241
  invariant residues, 248-250
  location of active centers, 240,
      248-250
  nomenclature of, 792

804